Cases in

Strategic Management

Cases in Strategic Management

EIGHTH EDITION

Charles W. L. Hill
UNIVERSITY OF WASHINGTON

Gareth R. Jones
TEXAS A&M UNIVERSITY

Houghton Mifflin Company   Boston   New York

For my children, Elizabeth, Charlotte, and Michelle
Charles W. L. Hill

For Nicholas and Julia and Morgan and Nia
Gareth R. Jones

Executive Publisher: George Hoffman
Executive Editor: Lisé Johnson
Senior Marketing Manager: Nicole Hamm
Development Editor: Suzanna Smith
Senior Project Editor: Carol Merrigan
Art and Design Manager: Jill Haber
Cover Design Director: Tony Saizon
Senior Photo Editor: Jennifer Meyer Dare
Senior Composition Buyer: Chuck Dutton
New Title Project Manager: James Lonergan
Editorial Assistant: Kathryn White
Marketing Assistant: Tom DiGiano

Cover image: Jason Hawkes, www.jasonhawkes.com

Printed in the U.S.A.

Library of Congress Control Number: 2007934814

Instructor's examination copy:
ISBN-10: 0-547-00483-4
ISBN-13: 978-0-547-00483-9

For orders, use student text ISBNs:
ISBN-10: 0-618-89471-3
ISBN-13: 978-0-618-89471-0

1 2 3 4 5 6 7 8 9–DOW–11 10 09 08 07

Contents

Introduction: Analyzing a Case Study and Writing a Case Study Analysis   C1

Cases

SECTION A: Business Level Cases: Domestic and Global

v

Section B: Corporate Level Cases: Domestic and Global

Preface

Since the seventh edition was published, this book has strengthened its position as the most widely used strategic management textbook on the market. This tells us that we continue to meet the expectations of existing users and attract many new users to our book. It is clear that most strategy instructors share with us a concern for currency in the text and its examples to ensure that cutting-edge issues and new developments in strategic management are continually addressed.

Just as in the last edition, our objective in writing the eighth edition has been to maintain all that was good about prior editions, while refining our approach to discussing established strategic management issues and adding new material to the text to present a more complete, clear, and current account of strategic management as we move steadily into the twenty-first century. We believe that the result is a book that is more closely aligned with the needs of today's professors and students and with the realities of competition in the new global environment.

Comprehensive and Up-to-Date Coverage

It is important to emphasize that we have overhauled the case selection. Twenty-nine of the thirty-four end-of-text cases are completely new, with the remaining five cases being heavily revised based on new data. As always, we have used a tight screen to filter out irrelevant cases, and we believe that the selection we offer is the best on the market.

The thirty four cases that we have selected for this edition will appeal, we are certain, to students and professors alike, both because these cases are intrinsically interesting and because of the number of strategic management issues they illuminate. The organizations discussed in the cases range from large, well-known ones, for which students can do research in order to update the information, to small, entrepreneurial businesses that illustrate the uncertainty and challenge of the strategic management process. In addition, the selections include many international cases, and most of the other cases contain some element of global strategy. Refer to the table of contents for a complete listing of the cases with brief descriptions.

To help students learn how to effectively analyze and write a case study, we continue to include a special section on this subject. It has a checklist and explanation of areas to consider, suggested research tools, and tips on financial analysis.

We feel that our entire selection of cases is unrivaled in breadth and depth, and we are grateful to the other case authors who have contributed to this edition:

Isaac Cohen, *San Jose State University*
William P. Barnett, *Stanford Graduate School of Business*
Mike Harkey, *Stanford Graduate School of Business*
Robert A. Burgelman, *Stanford Graduate School of Business*
Aneesha Capur, *Stanford Graduate School of Business*

David B. Yoffie, *Harvard Business School*
Michael Slind, *Harvard Business School*
Patricia Harasta, *Bentley College*
Alan N. Hoffman, *Bentley College*
Vivek Gupta, *ICFAI Center for Management Research*
Vinay Kumar, *ICFAI Center for Management Research*
Shengjun Liu, *University of Western Ontario*
Darryl Davis, *New York University*
Tom Davis, *New York University*
Sara Moodie, *New York University*
Melissa A. Schilling, *New York University*
Suresh Kotha, *University of Washington*
Sandip Basu, *University of Washington*
Robert J. Mockler, *St. John's University*
Christopher A. Bartlett, *Harvard Business School*
Anne T. Lawrence, *San Jose State University*

Teaching and Learning Aids

Taken together, the teaching and learning features of Strategic Management provide a package that is unsurpassed in its coverage and that supports the integrated approach that we have taken throughout the book

For the Instructor

- The **Instructor's Resource Manual: Cases** includes a complete list of case discussion questions as well as a comprehensive teaching note for each case, which gives a complete analysis of case issues. It is written in a user-friendly question-and-answer format.

- The **HMTesting CD** has been revised and offers a set of comprehensive true/false and multiple-choice questions, and new essay questions for each chapter in the book. The mix of questions has been adjusted to provide fewer fact-based or simple memorization items and to provide more items that rely on synthesis or application. Also, more items now reflect real or hypothetical situations in organizations. Every question is keyed to the teaching objectives in the *Instructor's Resource Manual* and includes an answer and page reference to the textbook.

- The **video program** highlights many issues of interest and can be used to spark class discussion. It offers a compilation of footage from the Videos for Humanities series.

- An extensive **website** contains many features to aid instructors, including downloadable files for the text and case materials from the *Instructor's Resource Manuals*, the downloadable Premium and Basic PowerPoint slides, the Video Guide, and sample syllabi. Additional materials on the student website may also be of use to instructors.

- **Eduspace®,** powered by Blackboard®, is a course management tool that includes chapter outlines, chapter summaries, audio chapter summaries and quizzes, all questions from the textbook with suggested answers, Debate Issues, ACE self-test questions, auto-graded quizzes, Premium and Basic PowerPoint slides, Classroom Response System content, links to content on the websites, video activities, and test pools. A Course Materials Guide is available to help instructor organization.

- **Blackboard®/Web CT®** includes course material, chapter outlines, chapter summaries, audio chapter summaries and quizzes, all questions from the textbook with suggested answers, Premium and Basic PowerPoint slides, Classroom Response System content, links to content on the websites, video activities, and Test Bank content.

For the Student

- The student **website** includes chapter overviews, Internet exercises, ACE self-tests, audio summaries and quizzes, case discussion questions to help guide student case analysis, glossaries, flashcards for studying the key terms, a section with guidelines on how to do case study analysis, and much more.

Acknowledgments

This book is the product of far more than two authors. We are grateful to Lisé Johnson, our sponsor; Suzanna Smith, our editor; and Nicole Hamm, our marketing manager, for their help in promoting and developing the book and for providing us with timely feedback and information from professors and reviewers, which allowed us to shape the book to meet the needs of its intended market. We are also grateful to Carol Merrigan and Kristen Truncellito, project editors, for their adept handling of production. We are also grateful to the case authors for allowing us to use their materials. We also want to thank the departments of management at the University of Washington and Texas A&M University for providing the setting and atmosphere in which the book could be written, and the students of these universities who reacted to and provided input for many of our ideas. In addition, the following reviewers of this and earlier editions gave us valuable suggestions for improving the manuscript from its original version to its current form:

Ken Armstrong, *Anderson University*
Richard Babcock, *University of San Francisco*
Kunal Banerji, *West Virginia University*
Kevin Banning, *Auburn University – Montgomery*
Glenn Bassett, *University of Bridgeport*
Thomas H. Berliner, *The University of Texas at Dallas*
Bonnie Bollinger, *Ivy Technical Community College*
Richard G. Brandenburg, *University of Vermont*
Steven Braund, *University of Hull*
Philip Bromiley, *University of Minnesota*
Geoffrey Brooks, *Western Oregon State College*
Amanda Budde, *University of Hawaii*
Lowell Busenitz, *University of Houston*
Charles J. Capps III, *Sam Houston State University*
Don Caruth, *Texas A&M Commerce*
Gene R. Conaster, *Golden State University*
Steven W. Congden, *University of Hartford*
Catherine M. Daily, *Ohio State University*
Robert DeFillippi, *Suffolk University Sawyer School of Management*
Helen Deresky, *SUNY – Plattsburgh*
Gerald E. Evans, *The University of Montana*
John Fahy, *Trinity College, Dublin*
Patricia Feltes, *Southwest Missouri State University*
Bruce Fern, *New York University*

Mark Fiegener, *Oregon State University*
Chuck Foley, *Columbus State Community College*
Isaac Fox, *Washington State University*
Craig Galbraith, *University of North Carolina at Wilmington*
Scott R. Gallagher, *Rutgers University*
Eliezer Geisler, *Northeastern Illinois University*
Gretchen Gemeinhardt, *University of Houston*
Lynn Godkin, *Lamar University*
Sanjay Goel, *University of Minnesota – Duluth*
Robert L. Goldberg, *Northeastern University*
James Grinnell, *Merrimack College*
Russ Hagberg, *Northern Illinois University*
Allen Harmon, *University of Minnesota – Duluth*
David Hoopes, *California State University – Dominguez Hills*
Todd Hostager, *University of Wisconsin – Eau Claire*
Graham L. Hubbard, *University of Minnesota*
Tammy G. Hunt, *University of North Carolina at Wilmington*
James Gaius Ibe, *Morris College*
W. Grahm Irwin, *Miami University*
Homer Johnson, *Loyola University – Chicago*
Jonathan L. Johnson, *University of Arkansas – Walton College of Business
    Administration*
Marios Katsioloudes, *St. Joseph's University*
Robert Keating, *University of North Carolina at Wilmington*
Geoffrey King, *California State University – Fullerton*
John Kraft, *University of Florida*
Rico Lam, *University of Oregon*
Robert J. Litschert, *Virginia Polytechnic Institute and State University*
Franz T. Lohrke, *Louisiana State University*
Paul Mallette, *Colorado State University*
Daniel Marrone, *SUNY Farmingdale*
Lance A. Masters, *California State University – San Bernardino*
Robert N. McGrath, *Embry-Riddle Aeronautical University*
Charles Mercer, *Drury College*
Van Miller, *University of Dayton*
Tom Morris, *University of San Diego*
Joanna Mulholland, *West Chester University of Pennsylvania*
John Nebeck, *Viterbo University*
Richard Neubert, *University of Tennessee – Knoxville*
Francine Newth, *Providence College*
Don Okhomina, *Fayetteville State University*
Phaedon P. Papadopoulos, *Houston Baptist University*
John Pappalardo, *Keene State College*
Paul R. Reed, *Sam Houston State University*
Rhonda K. Reger, *Arizona State University*
Malika Richards, *Indiana University*
Simon Rodan, *San Jose State*
Stuart Rosenberg, *Dowling College*
Douglas Ross, *Towson University*
Ronald Sanchez, *University of Illinois*

Joseph A. Schenk, *University of Dayton*
Brian Shaffer, *University of Kentucky*
Leonard Sholtis, *Eastern Michigan University*
Pradip K. Shukla, *Chapman University*
Mel Sillmon, *University of Michigan – Dearborn*
Dennis L. Smart, *University of Nebraska at Omaha*
Barbara Spencer, *Clemson University*
Lawrence Steenberg, *University of Evansville*
Kim A. Stewart, *University of Denver*
Ted Takamura, *Warner Pacific College*
Scott Taylor, *Florida Metropolitan University*
Bobby Vaught, *Southwest Missouri State*
Robert P. Vichas, *Florida Atlantic University*
Edward Ward, *St. Cloud State University*
Kenneth Wendeln, *Indiana University*
Daniel L. White, *Drexel University*
Edgar L. Williams, Jr., *Norfolk State University*
Jun Zhao, *Governors State University*

Charles W. L. Hill
Gareth R. Jones

Cases in Strategic Management

Introduction: Analyzing a Case Study and Writing a Case Study Analysis

What Is Case Study Analysis?

Case study analysis is an integral part of a course in strategic management. The purpose of a case study is to provide students with experience of the strategic management problems that actual organizations face. A case study presents an account of what happened to a business or industry over a number of years. It chronicles the events that managers had to deal with, such as changes in the competitive environment, and charts the managers' response, which usually involved changing the business- or corporate-level strategy. The cases in this book cover a wide range of issues and problems that managers have had to confront. Some cases are about finding the right business-level strategy to compete in changing conditions. Some are about companies that grew by acquisition, with little concern for the rationale behind their growth, and how growth by acquisition affected their future profitability. Each case is different because each organization is different. The underlying thread in all cases, however, is the use of strategic management techniques to solve business problems.

Cases prove valuable in a strategic management course for several reasons. First, cases provide you, the student, with experience of organizational problems that you probably have not had the opportunity to experience firsthand. In a relatively short period of time, you will have the chance to appreciate and analyze the problems faced by many different companies and to understand how managers tried to deal with them.

Second, cases illustrate the theory and content of strategic management. The meaning and implications of this information are made clearer when they are applied to case studies. The theory and concepts help reveal what is going on in the companies studied and allow you to evaluate the solutions that specific companies adopted to deal with their problems. Consequently, when you analyze cases, you will be like a detective who, with a set of conceptual tools, probes what happened and what or who was responsible and then marshals the evidence that provides the solution. Top managers enjoy the thrill of testing their problem-solving abilities in the real world. It is important to remember that no one knows what the right answer is. All that managers can do is to make the best guess. In fact, managers say repeatedly that they are happy if they are right only half the time in solving strategic problems. Strategic management is an uncertain game, and using cases to see how theory can be put into practice is one way of improving your skills of diagnostic investigation.

Third, case studies provide you with the opportunity to participate in class and to gain experience in presenting your ideas to others. Instructors may sometimes call on students as a group to identify what is going on in a case, and through classroom discussion the issues in and solutions to the case problem will reveal themselves. In such a situation, you will have to organize your views and conclusions so that you can present them to the class. Your classmates may have analyzed the issues differently from you, and they will want you to argue your points before they will accept your conclusions, so be prepared for debate. This mode of discussion is an example of the dialectical approach to decision making. This is how decisions are made in the actual business world.

Instructors also may assign an individual, but more commonly a group, to analyze the case before the whole class. The individual or group probably will be responsible for a thirty- to forty-minute presentation of the case to the class. That presentation must cover the issues posed, the problems facing the company, and a series of recommendations for resolving the problems. The discussion then will be thrown open to the class, and you will have to defend your ideas. Through such discussions and presentations, you will experience how to convey your ideas effectively to others. Remember that a great deal of managers' time is spent in these kinds of situations: presenting their ideas and engaging in discussion with other managers who have their own views about what is going on. Thus, you will experience in the classroom the actual process of strategic management, and this will serve you well in your future career.

If you work in groups to analyze case studies, you also will learn about the group process involved in working as a team. When people work in groups, it is often difficult to schedule time and allocate responsibility for the case analysis. There are always group members who shirk their responsibilities and group members who are so sure of their own ideas that they try to dominate the group's analysis. Most of the strategic management takes place in groups, however, and it is best if you learn about these problems now.

Analyzing a Case Study

The purpose of the case study is to let you apply the concepts of strategic management when you analyze the issues facing a specific company. To analyze a case study, therefore, you must examine closely the issues confronting the company. Most often you will need to read the case several times—once to grasp the overall picture of what is happening to the company and then several times more to discover and grasp the specific problems.

Generally, detailed analysis of a case study should include eight areas:

1. The history, development, and growth of the company over time
2. The identification of the company's internal strengths and weaknesses
3. The nature of the external environment surrounding the company
4. A SWOT analysis
5. The kind of corporate-level strategy that the company is pursuing
6. The nature of the company's business-level strategy
7. The company's structure and control systems and how they match its strategy
8. Recommendations

To analyze a case, you need to apply the concepts taught in this course to each of these areas. To help you further, we next offer a summary of the steps you can take to analyze the case material for each of the eight points we just noted:

1. *Analyze the company's history, development, and growth.* A convenient way to investigate how a company's past strategy and structure affect it in the present

is to chart the critical incidents in its history—that is, the events that were the most unusual or the most essential for its development into the company it is today. Some of the events have to do with its founding, its initial products, how it makes new-product market decisions, and how it developed and chose functional competencies to pursue. Its entry into new businesses and shifts in its main lines of business are also important milestones to consider.

2. *Identify the company's internal strengths and weaknesses.* Once the historical profile is completed, you can begin the SWOT analysis. Use all the incidents you have charted to develop an account of the company's strengths and weaknesses as they have emerged historically. Examine each of the value creation functions of the company, and identify the functions in which the company is currently strong and currently weak. Some companies might be weak in marketing; some might be strong in research and development. Make lists of these strengths and weaknesses. The SWOT Checklist (Table 1) gives examples of what might go in these lists.

3. *Analyze the external environment.* To identify environmental opportunities and threats, apply all the concepts on industry and macroenvironments to analyze the environment the company is confronting. Of particular importance at the industry level are Porter's five forces model and the stage of the life cycle model. Which factors in the macroenvironment will appear salient depends on the specific company being analyzed. Use each factor in turn (for instance, demographic factors) to see whether it is relevant for the company in question.

    Having done this analysis, you will have generated both an analysis of the company's environment and a list of opportunities and threats. The SWOT Checklist table also lists some common environmental opportunities and threats that you may look for, but the list you generate will be specific to your company.

4. *Evaluate the SWOT analysis.* Having identified the company's external opportunities and threats as well as its internal strengths and weaknesses, consider what your findings mean. You need to balance strengths and weaknesses against opportunities and threats. Is the company in an overall strong competitive position? Can it continue to pursue its current business- or corporate-level strategy profitably? What can the company do to turn weaknesses into strengths and threats into opportunities? Can it develop new functional, business, or corporate strategies to accomplish this change? *Never merely generate the SWOT analysis and then put it aside.* Because it provides a succinct summary of the company's condition, a good SWOT analysis is the key to all the analyses that follow.

5. *Analyze corporate-level strategy.* To analyze corporate-level strategy, you first need to define the company's mission and goals. Sometimes the mission and goals are stated explicitly in the case; at other times, you will have to infer them from available information. The information you need to collect to find out the company's corporate strategy includes such factors as its lines of business and the nature of its subsidiaries and acquisitions. It is important to analyze the relationship among the company's businesses. Do they trade or exchange resources? Are there gains to be achieved from synergy? Alternatively, is the company just running a portfolio of investments? This analy is should enable you to define the corporate strategy that the company is pursu

TABLE 1

A SWOT Checklist

Potential internal strengths	Potential internal weaknesses
Many product lines?	Obsolete, narrow product lines?
Broad market coverage?	Rising manufacturing costs?
Manufacturing competence?	Decline in R&D innovations?
Good marketing skills?	Poor marketing plan?
Good materials management systems?	Poor material management systems?
R&D skills and leadership?	Loss of customer good will?
Information system competencies?	Inadequate human resources?
Human resource competencies?	Inadequate information systems?
Brand name reputation?	Loss of brand name capital?
Portfolio management skills?	Growth without direction?
Cost of differentiation advantage?	Bad portfolio management?
New-venture management expertise?	Loss of corporate direction?
Appropriate management style?	Infighting among divisions?
Appropriate organizational structure?	Loss of corporate control?
Appropriate control systems?	Inappropriate organizational structure and control systems?
Ability to manage strategic change?	High conflict and politics?
Well-developed corporate strategy?	Poor financial management?
Good financial management?	Others?
Others?	

Potential environmental opportunities	Potential environmental threats
Expand core business(es)?	Attacks on core business(es)?
Exploit new market segments?	Increases in domestic competition?
Widen product range?	Increase in foreign competition?
Extend cost or differentiation advantage?	Change in consumer tastes?
Diversify into new growth businesses?	Fall in barriers to entry?
Expand into foreign markets?	Rise in new or substitute products?
Apply R&D skills in new areas?	Increase in industry rivalry?
Enter new related businesses?	New forms of industry competition?
Vertically integrate forward?	Potential for takeover?
Vertically integrate backward?	Existence of corporate raiders?
Enlarge corporate portfolio?	Increase in regional competition?
Overcome barriers to entry?	Changes in demographic factors?
Reduce rivalry among competitors?	Changes in economic factors?
Make profitable new acquisitions?	Downturn in economy?
Apply brand name capital in new areas?	Rising labor costs?
Seek fast market growth?	Slower market growth?
Others?	Others?

(for example, related or unrelated diversification, or a combination of both) and to conclude whether the company operates in just one core business. Then, using your SWOT analysis, debate the merits of this strategy. Is it appropriate given the environment the company is in? Could a change in corporate strategy provide the company with new opportunities or transform a weakness into a strength? For example, should the company diversify from its core business into new businesses?

Other issues should be considered as well. How and why has the company's strategy changed over time? What is the claimed rationale for any changes? Often, it is a good idea to analyze the company's businesses or products to assess its situation and identify which divisions contribute the most to or detract from its competitive advantage. It is also useful to explore how the company has built its portfolio over time. Did it acquire new businesses, or did it internally venture its own? All of these factors provide clues about the company and indicate ways of improving its future performance.

6. *Analyze business-level strategy.* Once you know the company's corporate-level strategy and have done the SWOT analysis, the next step is to identify the company's business-level strategy. If the company is a single-business company, its business-level strategy is identical to its corporate-level strategy. If the company is in many businesses, each business will have its own business-level strategy. You will need to identify the company's generic competitive strategy—differentiation, low-cost, or focus—and its investment strategy, given its relative competitive position and the stage of the life cycle. The company also may market different products using different business-level strategies. For example, it may offer a low-cost product range and a line of differentiated products. Be sure to give a full account of a company's business-level strategy to show how it competes.

Identifying the functional strategies that a company pursues to build competitive advantage through superior efficiency, quality, innovation, and customer responsiveness and to achieve its business-level strategy is very important. The SWOT analysis will have provided you with information on the company's functional competencies. You should investigate its production, marketing, or research and development strategy further to gain a picture of where the company is going. For example, pursuing a low-cost or a differentiation strategy successfully requires very different sets of competencies. Has the company developed the right ones? If it has, how can it exploit them further? Can it pursue both a low-cost and a differentiation strategy simultaneously?

The SWOT analysis is especially important at this point if the industry analysis, particularly Porter's model, has revealed threats to the company from the environment. Can the company deal with these threats? How should it change its business-level strategy to counter them? To evaluate the potential of a company's business-level strategy, you must first perform a thorough SWOT analysis that captures the essence of its problems.

Once you complete this analysis, you will have a full picture of the way the company is operating and be in a position to evaluate the potential of its strategy. Thus, you will be able to make recommendations concerning the pattern of its future actions. However, first you need to consider strategy implementation, or the way the company tries to achieve its strategy.

7. *Analyze structure and control systems.* The aim of this analysis is to identify what structure and control systems the company is using to implement its strategy and to evaluate whether that structure is the appropriate one for the company. Different corporate and business strategies require different structures. You need to determine the *degree of fit between the company's strategy and structure.* For example, does the company have the right level of vertical differentiation (e.g., does it have the appropriate number of levels in the hierarchy or decentralized control?) or horizontal differentiation (does it use a functional structure when it should be using a product structure?)? Similarly, is the company using the right integration or control systems to manage its operations? Are managers being appropriately rewarded? Are the right rewards in

place for encouraging cooperation among divisions? These are all issues to consider.

In some cases, there will be little information on these issues, whereas in others there will be a lot. In analyzing each case, you should gear the analysis toward its most salient issues. For example, organizational conflict, power, and politics will be important issues for some companies. Try to analyze why problems in these areas are occurring. Do they occur because of bad strategy formulation or because of bad strategy implementation?

Organizational change is an issue in many cases because the companies are attempting to alter their strategies or structures to solve strategic problems. Thus, as part of the analysis, you might suggest an action plan that the company in question could use to achieve its goals. For example, you might list in a logical sequence the steps the company would need to follow to alter its business-level strategy from differentiation to focus.

8. *Make recommendations.* The quality of your recommendations is a direct result of the thoroughness with which you prepared the case analysis. Recommendations are directed at solving whatever strategic problem the company is facing and increasing its future profitability. Your recommendations should be in line with your analysis; that is, they should follow logically from the previous discussion. For example, your recommendation generally will center on the specific ways of changing functional, business, and corporate strategies and organizational structure and control to improve business performance. The set of recommendations will be specific to each case, and so it is difficult to discuss these recommendations here. Such recommendations might include an increase in spending on specific research and development projects, the divesting of certain businesses, a change from a strategy of unrelated to related diversification, an increase in the level of integration among divisions by using task forces and teams, or a move to a different kind of structure to implement a new business-level strategy. Make sure your recommendations are mutually consistent and written in the form of an action plan. The plan might contain a timetable that sequences the actions for changing the company's strategy and a description of how changes at the corporate level will necessitate changes at the business level and subsequently at the functional level.

After following all these stages, you will have performed a thorough analysis of the case and will be in a position to join in class discussion or present your ideas to the class, depending on the format used by your professor. Remember that you must tailor your analysis to suit the specific issue discussed in your case. In some cases, you might completely omit one of the steps in the analysis because it is not relevant to the situation you are considering. You must be sensitive to the needs of the case and not apply the framework we have discussed in this section blindly. The framework is meant only as a guide, not as an outline.

Writing a Case Study Analysis

Often, as part of your course requirements, you will need to present a written case analysis. This may be an individual or a group report. Whatever the situation, there are certain guidelines to follow in writing a case analysis that will improve the evaluation your work will receive from your instructor. Before we discuss these guidelines and before you use them, make sure that they do not conflict with any directions your instructor has given you.

The structure of your written report is critical. Generally, if you follow the steps for analysis discussed in the previous section, *you already will have a good structure for your written discussion.* All reports begin with an *introduction* to the case. In it, outline briefly what the company does, how it developed historically, what problems it is experiencing, and how you are going to approach the issues in the case write-up. Do this sequentially by writing, for example, "First, we discuss the environment of Company X. . . . Third, we discuss Company X's business-level strategy. . . . Last, we provide recommendations for turning around Company X's business."

In the second part of the case write-up, the *strategic analysis* section, do the SWOT analysis, analyze and discuss the nature and problems of the company's business-level and corporate strategies, and then analyze its structure and control systems. Make sure you use plenty of headings and subheadings to structure your analysis. For example, have separate sections on any important conceptual tool you use. Thus, you might have a section on Porter's five forces model as part of your analysis of the environment. You might offer a separate section on portfolio techniques when analyzing a company's corporate strategy. Tailor the sections and subsections to the specific issues of importance in the case.

In the third part of the case write-up, present your *solutions and recommendations.* Be comprehensive, and make sure they are in line with the previous analysis so that the recommendations fit together and move logically from one to the next. The recommendations section is very revealing because your instructor will have a good idea of how much work you put into the case from the quality of your recommendations.

Following this framework will provide a good structure for most written reports, though it must be shaped to fit the individual case being considered. Some cases are about excellent companies experiencing no problems. In such instances, it is hard to write recommendations. Instead, you can focus on analyzing why the company is doing so well, using that analysis to structure the discussion. Following are some minor suggestions that can help make a good analysis even better:

1. Do not repeat in summary form large pieces of factual information from the case. The instructor has read the case and knows what is going on. Rather, use the information in the case to illustrate your statements, defend your arguments, or make salient points. Beyond the brief introduction to the company, you must avoid being *descriptive*; instead, you must be *analytical.*

2. Make sure the sections and subsections of your discussion flow logically and smoothly from one to the next. That is, try to build on what has gone before so that the analysis of the case study moves toward a climax. This is particularly important for group analysis, because there is a tendency for people in a group to split up the work and say, "I'll do the beginning, you take the middle, and I'll do the end." The result is a choppy, stilted analysis; the parts do not flow from one to the next, and it is obvious to the instructor that no real group work has been done.

3. Avoid grammatical and spelling errors. They make your work look sloppy.

4. In some instances, cases dealing with well-known companies end in 1998 or 1999 because no later information was available when the case was written. If possible, do a search for more information on what has happened to the company in subsequent years.

Many libraries now have comprehensive web-based electronic data search facilities that offer such sources as *ABI/Inform, The Wall Street Journal Index,* the *F&S Index,* and the *Nexis-Lexis* databases. These enable you to identify any article that has been written in the business press on the company of your choice within the past few years. A number of nonelectronic data sources are also useful. For example, *F&S Predicasts* publishes an annual list of articles relating to major companies that appeared in the national and international business press. *S&P Industry Surveys* is a great source for basic industry data, and *Value Line Ratings and Reports* can contain good summaries of a firm's financial position and future prospects. You will also want to collect full financial information on the company. Again, this can be accessed from web-based electronic databases such as the *Edgar* database, which archives all forms that publicly quoted companies have to file with the Securities and Exchange Commission (SEC; e.g., 10-K filings can be accessed from the SEC's *Edgar* database). Most SEC forms for public companies can now be accessed from Internet-based financial sites, such as Yahoo's finance site (http://finance.yahoo.com/).

5. Sometimes instructors hand out questions for each case to help you in your analysis. Use these as a guide for writing the case analysis. They often illuminate the important issues that have to be covered in the discussion.

If you follow the guidelines in this section, you should be able to write a thorough and effective evaluation.

The Role of Financial Analysis in Case Study Analysis

An important aspect of analyzing a case study and writing a case study analysis is the role and use of financial information. A careful analysis of the company's financial condition immensely improves a case write-up. After all, financial data represent the concrete results of the company's strategy and structure. Although analyzing financial statements can be quite complex, a general idea of a company's financial position can be determined through the use of ratio analysis. Financial performance ratios can be calculated from the balance sheet and income statement. These ratios can be classified into five subgroups: profit ratios, liquidity ratios, activity ratios, leverage ratios, and shareholder-return ratios. These ratios should be compared with the industry average or the company's prior years of performance. It should be noted, however, that deviation from the average is not necessarily bad; it simply warrants further investigation. For example, young companies will have purchased assets at a different price and will likely have a different capital structure than older companies do. In addition to ratio analysis, a company's cash flow position is of critical importance and should be assessed. Cash flow shows how much actual cash a company possesses.

● **Profit Ratios**　Profit ratios measure the efficiency with which the company uses its resources. The more efficient the company, the greater is its profitability. It is useful to compare a company's profitability against that of its major competitors in its industry to determine whether the company is operating more or less efficiently than its rivals. In addition, the change in a company's profit ratios over time tells whether its performance is improving or declining.

A number of different profit ratios can be used, and each of them measures a different aspect of a company's performance. Here, we look at the most commonly used profit ratios.

● **Return on Invested Capital**   This ratio measures the profit earned on the capital invested in the company. It is defined as follows:

$$\text{Return on invested capital (ROIC)} = \frac{\text{Net profit}}{\text{Invested capital}}$$

Net profit is calculated by subtracting the total costs of operating the company away from its total revenues (total revenues – total costs). Total costs are the (1) costs of goods sold, (2) sales, general, and administrative expenses, (3) R&D expenses, and (4) other expenses. Net profit can be calculated before or after taxes, although many financial analysts prefer the before-tax figure. Invested capital is the amount that is invested in the operations of a company—that is, in property, plant, equipment, inventories, and other assets. Invested capital comes from two main sources: interest-bearing debt and shareholders' equity. Interest-bearing debt is money the company borrows from banks and from those who purchase its bonds. Shareholders' equity is the money raised from selling shares to the public, *plus* earnings that have been retained by the company in prior years and are available to fund current investments. ROIC measures the effectiveness with which a company is using the capital funds that it has available for investment. As such, it is recognized to be an excellent measure of the value a company is creating.[1] Remember that a company's ROIC can be decomposed into its constituent parts.

● **Return on Total Assets (ROA)**   This ratio measures the profit earned on the employment of assets. It is defined as follows:

$$\text{Return on total assests} = \frac{\text{Net profit}}{\text{Total assets}}$$

● **Return on Stockholders' Equity (ROE)**   This ratio measures the percentage of profit earned on common stockholders' investment in the company. It is defined as follows:

$$\text{Return on stockholders' equity} = \frac{\text{Net profit}}{\text{Stockholders' equity}}$$

If a company has no debt, this will be the same as ROIC.

● **Liquidity Ratios**   A company's liquidity is a measure of its ability to meet short-term obligations. An asset is deemed liquid if it can be readily converted into cash. Liquid assets are current assets such as cash, marketable securities, accounts receivable, and so on. Two liquidity ratios are commonly used.

● **Current Ratio**   The current ratio measures the extent to which the claims of short-term creditors are covered by assets that can be quickly converted into cash. Most companies should have a ratio of at least 1, because failure to meet these commitments can lead to bankruptcy. The ratio is defined as follows:

$$\text{Current ratio} = \frac{\text{Current assets}}{\text{Current liabilities}}$$

● **Quick Ratio**   The quick ratio measures a company's ability to pay off the claims of short-term creditors without relying on selling its inventories. This is a valuable

[1] Tom Copeland, Tim Koller, and Jack Murrin, *Valuation: Measuring and Managing the Value of Companies* (New York: Wiley, 1996).

measure since in practice the sale of inventories is often difficult. It is defined as follows:

$$\text{Quick ratio} = \frac{\text{Current assets} - \text{inventory}}{\text{Current liabilities}}$$

● **Activity Ratios**   Activity ratios indicate how effectively a company is managing its assets. Two ratios are particularly useful.

● **Inventory Turnover**   This measures the number of times inventory is turned over. It is useful in determining whether a firm is carrying excess stock in inventory. It is defined as follows:

$$\text{Inventory turnover} = \frac{\text{Cost of goods sold}}{\text{Inventory}}$$

Cost of goods sold is a better measure of turnover than sales because it is the cost of the inventory items. Inventory is taken at the balance sheet date. Some companies choose to compute an average inventory, beginning inventory, and ending inventory, but for simplicity, use the inventory at the balance sheet date.

● **Days Sales Outstanding (DSO) or Average Collection Period**   This ratio is the average time a company has to wait to receive its cash after making a sale. It measures how effective the company's credit, billing, and collection procedures are. It is defined as follows:

$$\text{DSO} = \frac{\text{Accounts receivable}}{\text{Total sales}/360}$$

Accounts receivable is divided by average daily sales. The use of 360 is the standard number of days for most financial analysis.

● **Leverage Ratios**   A company is said to be highly leveraged if it uses more debt than equity, including stock and retained earnings. The balance between debt and equity is called the *capital structure*. The optimal capital structure is determined by the individual company. Debt has a lower cost because creditors take less risk; they know they will get their interest and principal. However, debt can be risky to the firm because if enough profit is not made to cover the interest and principal payments, bankruptcy can result. Three leverage ratios are commonly used.

● **Debt-to-Assets Ratio**   The debt-to-assets ratio is the most direct measure of the extent to which borrowed funds have been used to finance a company's investments. It is defined as follows:

$$\text{Debt-to-assets ratio} = \frac{\text{Total debt}}{\text{Total assets}}$$

Total debt is the sum of a company's current liabilities and its long-term debt, and total assets are the sum of fixed assets and current assets.

● **Debt-to-Equity Ratio**   The debt-to-equity ratio indicates the balance between debt and equity in a company's capital structure. This is perhaps the most widely used measure of a company's leverage. It is defined as follows:

$$\text{Debt-to-equity ratio} = \frac{\text{Total debt}}{\text{Total equity}}$$

● **Times-Covered Ratio**   The times-covered ratio measures the extent to which a company's gross profit covers its annual interest payments. If this ratio declines to less than 1, the company is unable to meet its interest costs and is technically insolvent. The ratio is defined as follows:

$$\text{Times-covered ratio} = \frac{\text{Profit before interest and tax}}{\text{Total interest charges}}$$

● **Shareholder-Return Ratios**   Shareholder-return ratios measure the return that shareholders earn from holding stock in the company. Given the goal of maximizing stockholders' wealth, providing shareholders with an adequate rate of return is a primary objective of most companies. As with profit ratios, it can be helpful to compare a company's shareholder returns against those of similar companies as a yardstick for determining how well the company is satisfying the demands of this particularly important group of organizational constituents. Four ratios are commonly used.

● **Total Shareholder Returns**   Total shareholder returns measure the returns earned by time $t + 1$ on an investment in a company's stock made at time t. (Time t is the time at which the initial investment is made.) Total shareholder returns include both dividend payments and appreciation in the value of the stock (adjusted for stock splits) and are defined as follows:

$$\text{Total shareholder returns} = \frac{\text{Stock price } (t+1) - \text{ stock price } (t) + \text{ sum of annual dividends per share}}{\text{Stock price } (t)}$$

If a shareholder invests $2 at time t and at time $t + 1$ the share is worth $3, while the sum of annual dividends for the period t to $t + 1$ has amounted to $0.20, total shareholder returns are equal to $(3 - 2 + 0.2)/2 = 0.6$, which is a 60 percent return on an initial investment of $2 made at time t.

● **Price-Earnings Ratio**   The price-earnings ratio measures the amount investors are willing to pay per dollar of profit. It is defined as follows:

$$\text{Price-earnings ratio} = \frac{\text{Market price per share}}{\text{Earnings per share}}$$

● **Market-to-Book Value**   Market-to-book value measures a company's expected future growth prospects. It is defined as follows:

$$\text{Market-to-book value} = \frac{\text{Market price per share}}{\text{Earnings per share}}$$

● **Dividend Yield**   The dividend yield measures the return to shareholders received in the form of dividends. It is defined as follows:

$$\text{Dividend yield} = \frac{\text{Dividend per share}}{\text{Market price per share}}$$

Market price per share can be calculated for the first of the year, in which case the dividend yield refers to the return on an investment made at the beginning of the year. Alternatively, the average share price over the year may be used. A company must decide how much of its profits to pay to stockholders and how much to reinvest in the company. Companies with strong growth prospects should have a lower dividend payout ratio than mature companies. The rationale is that shareholders can invest the money elsewhere if the company is not growing. The optimal ratio depends on the individual firm, but the key decider is whether the company can produce better returns than the investor can earn elsewhere.

● **Cash Flow**   Cash flow position is cash received minus cash distributed. The net cash flow can be taken from a company's statement of cash flows. Cash flow is important for what it reveals about a company's financing needs. A strong positive cash flow enables a company to fund future investments without having to borrow money from bankers or investors. This is desirable because the company avoids paying out interest or dividends. A weak or negative cash flow means that a company has to turn to external sources to fund future investments. Generally, companies in strong-growth industries often find themselves in a poor cash flow position (because their investment needs are substantial), whereas successful companies based in mature industries generally find themselves in a strong cash flow position.

A company's internally generated cash flow is calculated by adding back its depreciation provision to profits after interest, taxes, and dividend payments. If this figure is insufficient to cover proposed new investments, the company has little choice but to borrow funds to make up the shortfall or to curtail investments. If this figure exceeds proposed new investments, the company can use the excess to build up its liquidity (that is, through investments in financial assets) or repay existing loans ahead of schedule.

Conclusion

When evaluating a case, it is important to be *systematic*. Analyze the case in a logical fashion, beginning with the identification of operating and financial strengths and weaknesses and environmental opportunities and threats. Move on to assess the value of a company's current strategies only when you are fully conversant with the SWOT analysis of the company. Ask yourself whether the company's current strategies make sense given its SWOT analysis. If they do not, what changes need to be made? What are your recommendations? Above all, link any strategic recommendations you may make to the SWOT analysis. State explicitly how the strategies you identify take advantage of the company's strengths to exploit environmental opportunities, how they rectify the company's weaknesses, and how they counter environmental threats. Also, do not forget to outline what needs to be done to implement your recommendations.

The Apollo Group: University of Phoenix

This case was prepared by Charles W. L. Hill, the University of Washington.

Which is the largest university system in the United States? After some thought, you might be tempted to answer that it is the giant University of California system with its eleven campuses and 208,000 students. You would be wrong. The largest provider of high education in America is the University of Phoenix, which has 293,000 students and operates around 180 campuses and learning centers in thirty-four states. The University of Phoenix is the flagship subsidiary of the Apollo Group, which also runs Western International University, the Institute for Professional Development and the College for Financial Planning. In total, the Apollo Group serves some 330,000 students in thirty-nine states.

The Apollo Group has been a very successful enterprise. Between 1996 and 2006 its revenues expanded from $214 million to $2.48 billion, and net profits increased from $21.4 million to $438 million. The University of Phoenix accounts for about 90% of the revenues of the Apollo Group. Apollo's return on invested capital, a key measure of profitability, averaged around 25% over this period, well above its cost of capital, which has been calculated to be around 10%.[1]

The Apollo Group is also a controversial enterprise. Founded by John Sperling, a former economic history professor and one-time union organizer at San Jose State University, the University of Phoenix

has been depicted by defenders of the educational establishment as a low-quality "diploma mill" that has commoditized education and is all too willing to sacrifice educational standards for the opportunity to make profits. Scott Rice, a San Jose State University English professor who has become a vocal critic of for-profit education, summarizes this view when he states that "John Sperling's vision of education is entirely mercenary. It's merely one more opportunity to turn a buck. When education becomes one more product, we obey the unspoken rule of business: to give consumers as little as they will accept in exchange for as much as they will pay. Sperling is a terrible influence on American education."[2]

Sperling, who is still chairman at eighty-five, certainly does not see things this way. In his view, the University of Phoenix serves a niche that the educational establishment long ignored: working adults who need a practical education to further their careers and who cannot afford the commitment associated with full-time education. Some high-powered academics agree. The Nobel Prize–winning economist Milton Friedman regards the triumph of the for-profit sector as inevitable because traditional universities are run "by faculty, and the faculty is interested in its own welfare."[3]

Some analysts suggest that the for-profit sector still has significant growth opportunities ahead of it. The postsecondary education market in the United States is estimated to be worth almost $300 billion, with only $17 to $18 billion of that currently captured by for-profit enterprises. Looking forward, analysts expect enrollment at for-profit schools to grow 5 to 6% per annum as they gain share from traditional higher educational institutions. Supporting this thesis are estimates that 37% of all students (more than 6 million) are older than twenty-four. A large portion of these students are likely to be working and to be attracted to the flexibility that the for-profit sector provides.[4]

On the other hand, the educational establishment is not blind to this opportunity. Many long-established public and private not-for-profit universities are now offering part-time degree programs aimed at working adults. Some believe that this emerging threat, coupled with the brand advantage enjoyed by big name universities, will limit enrollment growth going forward at the University of Phoenix.

John Sperling and the Birth of the University of Phoenix

University of Phoenix founder John Sperling was born in rural Missouri in 1921 in a cabin that already housed a family of six.[5] His mother was overbearing; his father habitually beat him. When his farther died, Sperling recalled that he could hardly contain his joy. Sperling barely graduated from high school and went off to join the merchant marine—as far away from Missouri as he could get. There he started his real education, reading through the books of his shipmates, many of whom were socialists. Sperling emerged from this experience an unabashed liberal with a penchant for challenging the status quo, something that he still delights in. (Among other things, Sperling is a regular financial contributor to ballot initiatives aimed at legalizing marijuana.)

After two years in the merchant marine, Sperling went to Reed College in Oregon. This was followed by a master's at Berkeley and a PhD in economic history at the University of Cambridge. A conventional academic career seemed the logical next step for Sperling. By the 1960s, he was a tenured professor of economic history at San Jose State University. Always the activist, he joined the American Federation of Teachers (AFT) and rose to state and national positions in the union. In his leadership role at the AFT, he persuaded professors at San Jose State to mount a walkout to support striking professors at San Francisco State University. The strike was a failure and almost resulted in the mass firing of one hundred professors. Sperling lost his credibility on campus. He was widely reviled and lost his position as head of the United Professors of California, a union that he had built almost single-handedly. But Sperling claims that the humiliating defeat taught him an important

lesson: "It didn't make a goddamn bit of difference what people thought of me. Without that psychological immunity, it would have been impossible to create and protect the University of Phoenix from hostility, legal assaults, and attempts to legislate us out of existence."[6]

By the early 1970s, Sperling's academic career was going nowhere—but that was all about to change. As part of a federal project to fight juvenile delinquency, San Jose State University arranged a series of courses for the police and schoolteachers who had to deal with the youngsters. Sperling, who had been experimenting with novel approaches to delivering education, was to run the workshops. He devised a curriculum, divided the classes into small groups, and brought in as group leaders teachers who were expert practitioners in their fields but who were not professors. He then challenged each group to complete a project that addressed the problem of juvenile delinquency.

The student feedback was very favorable. More than that, the enthusiastic participants lobbied him to create a degree program. So Sperling sketched out a curriculum for working adults in the criminal justice area and pitched the idea to the academic vice president at San Jose State. In Sperling's words, the VP was impressed and sympathetic, but utterly discouraging. He told Sperling that the university had all it could do to educate regular students and had no need to create part-time programs for working adults. Moreover, to gain approval, such a program would have to navigate its way through the academic bureaucracy at San Jose, a process that could take several years, and at the end of the day what emerged might differ significantly from Sperling's original proposal due to the input of other faculty members.

Unperturbed by the rejection, Sperling started to cast around for other schools that might want to run the program. He contacted the vice president of development at Stanford University, Frank Newman, who told Sperling that educational bureaucracies were inherently inert and innovated only when they were in financial trouble. Newman advised Sperling to find a school in financial trouble and persuade it that his program would make a profit.

The former union organizer immediately saw the value in Newman's suggestion. Left wing he might have been, but Sperling was eager to try out his ideas in the marketplace. He formed a private organization, the Institute for Professional Development (IPD), with the mission of making higher education available to the working community. Sperling approached the University of San Francisco (USF), a financially troubled Jesuit school. USF agreed to sponsor the IPD program, using its accreditation to validate the degree. The program was an immediate financial success. Before long, Sperling was contracting with other schools for similar programs. The educational establishment, however, reacted with open hostility to Sperling's for-profit venture. For the first time, but not the last, Sperling was accused of devaluing education and producing a diploma mill. Sperling's sin, in his view, was that his model cut the professors out of the educational equation, and they were not about to let that happen.

Although he had been an academic for years, Sperling had up to this point paid little attention to the process of accrediting institutions and degree programs. What he quickly discovered was legitimacy required that the sponsoring institution for a degree program be accredited by recognized accreditation agencies. In the case of USF, this was the Western Association of Schools and Colleges (WASC), which, along with the California State Department of Education, had jurisdiction over public and private schools, colleges, and universities in California. For the first time, but not for the last, Sperling discovered that these regulatory agencies had enormous power and could destroy the legitimacy of his programs by refusing to grant accreditation to the sponsoring institutions. In Sperling's own words:

> We had no idea the extent to which education is a high politicized and regulated activity, not the extent to which innovators were to be searched out and destroyed as quickly as possible by the academics who controlled the institutions and by their allies in regulatory agencies.[7]

What followed was a bitter five-year battle between Sperling, who tried to get and maintain accreditation for his programs in California, and politicians, professors, and accreditation agencies, which blocked him every step of the way. Ultimately, Sperling decided that it would be impossible to fully develop his concepts of education for working adults within the confines of an existing institution. He decided to establish a university of his own. Sperling moved to Phoenix, Arizona, where he thought regulators would be more open to his ideas. They weren't. The established state institutions were openly hostile to Sperling's venture. It took more campaigning, which

included an all-out media campaign's intensive lobbying of the state's legislature, and vitriolic debates in the committee rooms of higher education regulators, before Arizona accredited Sperling's venture in 1978, which was now named the University of Phoenix. Sperling learned the lesson well—today the Apollo Group maintains a staff of forty or so political lobbyists whose job it is to get and maintain accreditation.

University of Phoenix Business Model[8]

The University of Phoenix (UOP) is designed to cater to the needs of working adults, who make up 95% of its students. The average age is thirty-six and, until recently, the minimum age was twenty-three. The emphasis is on practical subjects such as business, information technology, teaching, criminal justice, and nursing. In addition to undergraduate degrees, UOP offers several graduate degrees, including a master's degree in business (MBA), counseling, and nursing. Today, some 51% of students at the Apollo Group are enrolled in undergraduate courses, 22% are in masters' programs, 26% are earning two-year associates' degrees, and 1.4% are doctoral students.[9]

UOP views the student as the customer, and the customer is king. Classes are offered at times that fit the busy schedules of the fully employed—often in the evening. The schedule is year round; there are no extended breaks for summer vacation. Steps are taken to make sure that it is as easy as possible for students to get to classes. One of the golden rules is that there should be plenty of parking and that students should be able to get from their cars to their classrooms in five minutes.

UOP campuses lack many of the facilities found in traditional universities, such as dormitories, student unions, athletic facilities, research laboratories, extensive networks of libraries, and the support staff required for all of these facilities. Instead, the typical campus comprises a handful of utilitarian buildings sited close to major roads.

In designing a university for working adults, Sperling introduced several key innovations. The classes are small—ten to fifteen students each—and are run as seminars. Students usually take just one class at a time. Classes generally meet once or twice a week for five to nine weeks. Faculty members act as discussion leaders and facilitators rather than lecturers. They are there to guide students through the curriculum and to provide feedback and grading. In addition to their whole-class groups, students belong to "learning teams" of three to five students, which work together on group projects and studying.

Since the mid 1990s, UOP has relied heavily on online resources to deliver much of the course content. A typical five-week undergraduate course goes something like this: Students attend class on campus for four hours the first week, giving them a chance to meet the instructor and be introduced to their learning teams and coursework. Weeks two through four are completed over the Internet, with homework assignments and participation requirements fulfilled online. Students return to campus in week five for presentations.[10]

Sperling hired as teachers working professionals who were looking for part-time employment. In 2005, only 400 of the 21,000 faculty at UOP were full time. Part-time faculty must have a master's degree or higher and five years of professional experience in an area related to the subject they teach. New faculty are subject to peer review by other faculty members, are given training in grading and instructing students, and benefit from a teaching mentorship with more experienced faculty members. There is no such thing as academic tenure at UOP or research requirements for faculty, full or part time.

UOP established "ownership" over the curriculum taught in classrooms. In traditional universities, individual faculty members develop and "own" the curriculum. This can lead to significant variation in the content offered for the same class when taught by different professors in the same university. The decentralized nature of curriculum development in traditional universities makes it very difficult for the central administration to mandate changes to the curriculum. Moreover, in traditional universities, significant curriculum change can take a large amount of time and energy, involving faculty committees and, in the case of new programs, approval from central administration. In contrast, at UOP content experts, typically the small number of full-time faculty, develop the curriculum. Part-time teachers are then expected to deliver this standardized curriculum. This centralization allows UOP to have a uniform curriculum and to rapidly include new material in a curriculum and roll it out systemwide if the need arises. When designing the curriculum, UOP solicits input from students two years after graduation and from employers who hire UOP graduates.

The centralization of curriculum has also enabled UOP to challenge the publishers of traditional textbooks. UOP contacts authors directly and contracts with them to develop course materials exactly to their specifications, cutting textbook publishers out of the loop. The goal is for all UOP programs to use customized materials that exist entirely in digital form. Today, nearly all UOP students get course materials and resources digitally through the Apollo Group's rEsource Internet portal. This eliminates the need for textbooks and is a source of added profit for UOP. The cost to undergraduate students is roughly $60 a course, while the cost to UOP is about $20.[11]

The contrast between UOP and traditional not-for-profit universities is stark. At the undergraduate level, traditional universities focus on eighteen- to twenty-five-year-olds who attend school full time. Labor costs are high due to the employment of full-time faculty, the majority of whom have doctoral degrees. Newly minted professors straight out of doctoral programs often command high starting salaries—as much as $120,000 a year plus benefits in disciplines such as business. Faculty are given low teaching loads to allow them to focus on research, which is the currency of the realm in academia. Research output is required for tenure in the "publish or perish" model of academia adopted by traditional universities.

Although the knowledge produced by research faculty can be and often is socially and economically valuable, the research culture of these knowledge factories translates into a high cost of instruction. At the University of Washington, for example, one of the nation's premier research institutions, in 2005, 3,900 full-time faculty educated 40,000 students. The average faculty salary was $76,951 for the nine months of the academic year, which translated into an instructional cost of around $300 million. In contrast, the part-time faculty at UOP are inexpensive. In 2005, the 21,000 faculty at the Apollo Group were paid $195 million, or roughly $9,200 each—and this to instruct 307,400 students. In addition, student, faculty, and research facilities dramatically increase the capital intensity of traditional universities, while their attendant staff increases the labor costs.

As a consequence of these factors, the total cost of running a traditional university are much higher than at UOP. At the University of Washington, for example, total operating expenses in 2004–2005 were $2.7 billion, compared to $1.53 billion at the Apollo Group.[12]

According to one estimate, the average *cost to the institution* of educating an undergraduate student for two semesters at a public university is around two and a half times greater than that at a for-profit institution such as UOP. At a private institution, it is more than three times greater.[13] It is the inherently low cost structure of UOP that allows the Apollo Group to make its high profits. (For financial statements, go to http://finance.yahoo.com/q?s=apol).

Naturally, such comparisons ignore the fact that the mission of many traditional universities such as the University of Washington is fundamentally different from that of the University of Phoenix. UOP produces zero new knowledge, whereas the nation's research universities have been and will continue to be major producers of the knowledge that underlies technological progress and economic growth.

On the revenue side, estimates suggest that in 2005 it cost around $22,500 to earn an associate's degree at UOP, $51,000 to earn a bachelor's degree, and $22,932 to earn a master's degree (costs vary by program).[14] Students attending UOP rely heavily on federal assistance programs to help pay for their college educations. Some 63% of undergraduate students at UOP received financial aid under Title IV programs from the U.S. Department of Education (DOE); 72% at UOP's Axia College, which awards associates' degrees, received aid. To be eligible for Title IV funding, a student has to be registered at an institution that is accredited by an agency recognized by the DOE and enrolled in a program with at least thirty weeks of instructional time and twenty-four credit hours.

In addition to Title IV financial aid programs, some 45% of UOP students received some form of tuition assistance from their employers in 2005. The Internal Revenue Code allows an employee to exclude some $5,250 a year in tuition assistance from taxable income.

Accreditation

Accreditation by a respected agency is critical for any university. Accreditation verifies that a proper college education, consistent with the institution's mission, and meeting or exceeding thresholds of approved standards of education quality, is attainable at an institution.[15] Accreditation is an important element of the brand equity of an institution, is valued by employers, allows students to transfer credits to another institution, and is a prerequisite for Title IV financial aid. In addition, most employers offer tuition assistance only for courses from an accredited institution.

UOP is accredited by the Higher Learning Commission. Accreditation was first granted in 1978 and reaffirmed five times since. The next comprehensive review will take place in 2012. The Higher Learning Commission is one of six regional institutional accreditation agencies in the United States and is recognized by the Department of Higher Education. Regional accreditation is recognized nationally. In some states, it is sufficient authorization to operate a degree-granting institution, but in most, UOP must also get authorization from state authorities.

In addition to the Higher Learning Commission, the bachelor and master of science programs in nursing are accredited by the Commission on Collegiate Nursing Education, and the master's program in community counseling is accredited by the Council for Accreditation of Counseling and Related Educational Programs. However, the bachelor's and master's degree programs in business at UOP are not accredited by the Association to Advance Collegiate Schools of Business (AACSB). The AACSB is the largest and most influential accrediting organization for undergraduate, master's, and doctoral degree programs in business schools around the world, having granted international accreditation to more than five hundred business schools in thirty countries.

Throughout its history, UOP has found gaining accreditation an uphill battle. For example, UOP reentered California in 1980. After initially receiving a license to operate based on its accreditation by North Central, a regional accreditation agency recognized by the DOE, UOP was informed in 1981 that due to a change in California law, North Central accreditation was not sufficient to operate in California. Instead, accreditation was required from the Western Association of Schools and Colleges (WASC). The WASC was run by an old critic of Sperling, and there was zero chance that it would accredit UOP, leaving the institution with a stranded investment in California. It took another three years for UOP to resolve the issue, which it did by extensive political lobbying, ultimately getting a political ally to sponsor a bill in the California legislature that resulted in a change in the law, making WASC accreditation unnecessary for out-of-state institutions.

The hostility UOP encountered in California was repeated in many other states, and UOP was not always successful at countering it. Illinois, for example, refused to grant a license to UOP after existing institutions argued that there were already too many colleges in the state and that UOP was unnecessary since other institutions already offered similar programs.

In Sperling's view, the persistent hostility to his company reflects the cultural biases of higher education against the idea of for-profit universities. "The whole regulatory structure of higher education is designed to favor nonprofit and public colleges and universities, which it does by placing added regulatory burdens on those institutions organized for profit."[16] One of these burdens is that regulations grant Title IV eligibility to nonprofit and public institutions that have achieved candidacy for accreditation status, but grant Title IV eligibility only after the schools have achieved full accreditation.

Apollo's Growth Strategy

The company's strategy has been to grow by opening more campuses and learning centers in new states, by increasing enrollment at existing campuses and learning centers, and by offering product extensions, including online course offerings and expanded associate's degree offerings through Axia College.

UOP Expansion

The basic UOP business model has proved to be very scalable. In addition to centrally developed curriculum, UOP has developed customized computer programs that are used for student tracking, marketing, faculty recruitment and training, and academic quality management. These computer programs are intended to provide uniformity among UOP's campuses and learning centers. In turn, this enhances UOP's ability to expand rapidly into new markets.

To attract more students, UOP invests heavily in marketing and sales. In 2005, selling and promotional costs accounted for 21.5% of total revenues, much higher than at traditional universities. Of the $484 million spent on sales and promotions in 2005, $224 million went into advertising, $59 million into other promotions, and another $202 million into salaries for enrollment advisors. By way of comparison, few traditional universities spend more than $10 million on marketing.

UOP's aggressive marketing has got it into trouble with the DOE. In 2004 the department issued a report that was highly critical of how UOP compensated its enrollment advisors. According to the department, enrollment advisors at UOP soon found out that UOP based their salaries solely on the number of students they recruited, a practice that is prohibited by federal law. One recruiter who started out at $28,000 was bumped up to $85,000 after recruiting 151 students in six months. Another who started out at the same level got just a $4,000 raise after signing up 79 students. This report ultimately could have led to UOP being barred from federal loan programs, which would have been very damaging. Although an Apollo spokesperson called the report "very misleading and full of inaccuracies," the company agreed to change its compensation practices and paid a $9.8 million fine without admitting guilt.[17]

Online Education

One of the big engines of growth at UOP has been online education. UOP was an early mover in this area. In 1989, Sperling purchased a defunct distance learning company and instructed a team of technicians to come up with a viable portable electronic education system. By the time traditional universities started to discuss the idea of web-based distance education, they found that UOP was already there. Today, Apollo has more than 160,000 students enrolled in online programs and is the global leader in online education.[18]

Online classes are conducted in groups of ten to twelve students. Prior to the beginning of each class, students pay a fee to access eResource, the online delivery method for course materials. Online there is a series of eight newsgroups. The main newsgroup is designated for class discussion. There is an assignments newsgroup to which students submit their assignments, a chat newsgroup for students to discuss noncontent-related topics, a course materials newsgroup that houses the syllabus and lectures for the class, and four newsgroups that function as forums for the learning team assignments. Each week, the instructor posts a lecture to the classroom course materials newsgroup. Students log on and read the lecture or print the lecture to read at their convenience. Throughout the week, students participate in class discussions, based on the class content for that week, which is actively facilitated by the instructor. Both the instructor and students are expected to engage in content discussions five out of seven days each class week. In addition to the class participation requirement, students are also expected to complete individual assignments and to work within a small group of three to five students on a specific learning team assignment.

The online approach appeals to students who work irregular hours or who struggle to balance the demands of work, family, and school. Flexibility, not cost, is the prime selling point. The cost of an online MBA program at UOP is about $30,000, similar to online education program fees at traditional universities that are moving into this space. The cost of a getting a bachelor's degree online at UOP is about $475 per semester credit hour, which compares to an average of $398 for an online degree at a selection of state institutions, and $446 at private schools.[19]

Axia College

Another major thrust by the Apollo Group has been to expand its two-year associate's degree offerings. In the last few years, this has been done through Axia College, which initially was part of Apollo's Western International University. Today, Axia is part of UOP. The demographic strategy at Axia is very different from that at UOP. Axia targets eighteen- to twenty-four-year-old students with little or no college education. The revenue per student is lower, but this is balanced by larger class sizes (between thirty and forty), fewer dropouts, and lower student acquisition costs, which translates into slightly higher profit margins. The goal is for Axia to become a feeder for UOP, with students who gain an associate's degree at Axia transferring to UOP to gain a bachelor's, either immediately upon graduation or at some time in the future. Due to the rapid growth of Axia, most of which is online, associates' degrees have grown from about 3.9% of Apollo's student base in 2004 to about 23% in 2006. The growth of Axia has hurt Apollo's revenue per student numbers and the stock price, although many analysts see this as a good long-term strategy.[20]

The Competitive Landscape

The postsecondary education industry in the United States is estimated to be worth around $300 billion, with the for-profit sector capturing about $18 billion of that total in 2005. The industry will continue to grow, fueled by favorable demographics and tuition hikes, which historically have outpaced inflation by a wide margin. The DOE expects postsecondary enrollment to grow at 2% per annum. Analysts estimate that the for-profit sector could grow enrollments by 5 to 6% per annum as it gains share, and increase tuition at 4 to 5% per annum.[21] To back up these forecasts, analysts point to DOE figures that suggest that only 26% of Americans twenty-five and older have a bachelor's degree or higher.

Although UOP pioneered the for-profit university model and remains by far the largest institution, it is not alone in the space. Competition has increased and may continue to do so. Today, there are around 850 for-profit institutions offering degrees in the United States, up from around 600 in 1996. Most of these institutions, however, are quite small. The largest competitors to UOP are Corinthian College, with 66,000 students in 2005; ITT Educational Services, with 43,000 students; and Career Education.

Corinthian College focuses primarily on diploma or certificate courses designed for students with little or no college experience who are looking for entry-level jobs. As such, it is not a strong direct competitor to UOP. Florida Metropolitan University, the largest school operated by Corinthian College, is currently being investigated for marketing and advertising practices by the Florida attorney general. ITT Educational Services has traditionally focused on associates' degrees, but has been expanding its offerings of bachelors' degrees. ITT's niche is technical degrees, although like UOP it also offers business degrees. Career Education is the holding company for a number of for-profit establishments, including Colorado Technical University and American InterContinental University. Currently Career Education is mired in legal and accreditation issues that have constrained its ability to expand.

Analysts' estimates suggest that among for-profit universities, UOP has the premium brand but prices its offerings competitively, which constitutes a compelling value proposition for students (see Exhibit 1).

In addition to other nonprofits, UOP faces increased competition from traditional not-for-profit universities. In recent years, both private and public institutions have expanded their part-time and online offerings to adults, particularly in areas like business administration. Executive MBA programs have become major revenue generators at many state and private universities. To take one example, at the University of Washington business school, the number of students enrolled in part-time evening or executive MBA programs has expanded from around forty students ten years ago to over three hundred today. These students pay "market-based" fees, and the programs

EXHIBIT 1
Graduate Salary and Tuition for Bachelor's Degrees

School	Mean Graduate Salary	Mean Total Tuition
University of Phoenix	$52,597	$51,000
American InterContinental University	$44,363	$43,863
Florida Metropolitan University	$35,019	$50,400
ITT Technical Institute	$39,726	$69,480

Source: Data taken from Paul Bealand, "What's a Degree Worth?" *Citigroup Equity Research,* February 17, 2006.

are run as profit centers that contribute earnings to support the operations of the business school. The programs are structured to minimize the demands on working adults (classes are held in the evening or on weekends) and make heavy use of learning teams to facilitate the educational process.

Some traditional universities are also getting into the business of online education, although their success has been decidedly mixed so far. One of the leaders, the University of Massachusetts, had 9,200 students taking online courses in 2006. Most were working adults ages twenty-five to fifty, and 30% were from out of state. At UMass, online applicants undergo the same admission process as candidates for campus slots. Tuition is slightly higher than that for on-campus students since web-based courses are not subsidized by the state. At another state institution, Pennsylvania State University, there are some 6,000 students taking online courses, and demand is growing rapidly. The University of Maryland University College, the open enrollment arm of the state university, had 51,405 online students in 2005, up from 9,696 in 1998. Nearly 40% of these were U.S. military personnel around the world—a market that UOP also targets.[22]

On the other hand, many top schools have been reluctant to offer online courses, believing that doing so might compromise quality. Underlying this view is a belief that much of the value in education comes from face-to-face interactions with professors and other students in a classroom setting. This perspective is backed up by empirical and anecdotal evidence. In one recent survey, employers overwhelmingly preferred traditional bachelors' degrees when hiring over credentials even partially completed online. Two professors asked managers from 270 small and medium-sized companies in eight cities about their attitudes toward online credentials. The managers sought entry-level employees or managers in engineering, business, and information technology. Ninety-six percent said they would choose traditional candidates over those with online degrees.[23]

In response to a journalist's question about the value of online degrees, a spokesperson at Texas Instruments stated: "We do not hire people with online degrees. We primarily hire engineers, and we target very well established engineering degree programs. The chance for someone with an online degree program to get in is not very likely."[24] On the other hand, several employers told the same journalist that an online degree did not limit options so long as it was from an accredited institution. These organizations included Northrop Grumman, United Parcel Service, Boeing, and Discovery Communications.

October 2006

On October 18, 2006, Apollo issued its results for its financial fourth quarter and the 2006 financial year. The results were not as strong as had been forecasted. Beginning in 2005, enrollment growth rates had started to decline. This trend worsened in mid 2006, when UOP had a decline in enrollment of 15,000, which caused a drop in profits to $93.5 million, down from $106 million in the same period of 2005. Making matters worse, Apollo had spent more on marketing and sales than in the equivalent period a year earlier as it tried to attract more students. The bright spot in the results was continued rapid enrollment growth at Axia College. However, this growth came at a cost since the revenue per student was lower at Axia than at UOP. These events had analysts wondering whether Apollo's years of rapid growth had come to an end, and if so, what the corporation's strategy should be going forward.

ENDNOTES

1. Standard & Poor's Stock Report, Apollo Group Inc, October 14, 2006.
2. Quoted in B. Breen, "The Hard Life and Restless Mind of America's Educational Billionaire," *Fast Company*, March 2003, pages 80–86.
3. Quoted in Anonymous, "Survey: Higher Ed Inc," *The Economist*, September 10, 2005, pages 19–21.
4. Paul Bealand, "What's a Degree Worth?" *Citigroup Equity Research*, February 17, 2006.
5. Sperling describes his life in his autobiography, *Rebel with a Cause*, New York: John Wiley, 2006.
6. Quoted in B. Breen, "The Hard Life and Restless Mind of America's Educational Billionaire," *Fast Company*, March 2003, pages 80–86.
7. John Sperling, *Rebel with a Cause*, New York: John Wiley, 2006, page 78.
8. Much of the material in this section is drawn from the 10K Reports of the Apollo Group filed with the Securities and Exchange Commission.
9. Apollo Group Press Release, "Apollo Group Inc Reports Fiscal 2006 Fourth Quarter and Year End Results," October 18, 2006; Paul Bealand, "What's a Degree Worth?" *Citigroup Equity Research*, February 17, 2006.
10. S. Baltes, "Phoenix Builds Presence Amid Turmoil," *Des Moines Business Record*, September 20, 2004, page 14.
11. Paul Bealand, "What's a Degree Worth?" *Citigroup Equity Research*, February 17, 2006.
12. University of Washington data is taken from the UW Fact Book, which can be accessed online at http://www.washington.edu/admin/factbook/.
13. R. S. Ruch, *Higher Ed Inc: The Rise of the For Profit University*, Baltimore, John Hopkins University Press, 2001.
14. Paul Bealand, "What's a Degree Worth?" *Citigroup Equity Research*, February 17, 2006.
15. R. S. Ruch, *Higher Ed Inc: The Rise of the For Profit University*, Baltimore, John Hopkins University Press, 2001.
16. John Sperling, *Rebel with a Cause*, New York: John Wiley, 2006, page 105.
17. W. C. Symonds, "Back to Earth for Apollo Group?" *Business Week*, January 31, 2005, page 50.
18. D. Golden, "Degrees@StateU.edu," *Wall Street Journal*, May 9, 2006, page B1.
19. Paul Bealand, "What's a Degree Worth?" *Citigroup Equity Research*, February 17, 2006.
20. K. Rowland, "Apollo Group A," *Morning Star Research Report*, October 19, 2006.
21. Paul Bealand, "What's a Degree Worth?" *Citigroup Equity Research*, February 17, 2006.
22. D. Golden, "Degrees@StateU.edu," *Wall Street Journal*, May 9, 2006, page B1.
23. A. Wellen, "Degrees of Acceptance," *Wall Street Journal*, July 30, 2006, page A26.
24. A. Wellen, "Degrees of Acceptance," *Wall Street Journal*, July 30, 2006, page A26.

This case was prepared by Charles W. L. Hill, the University of Washington.

It looked as if 2006 would be the year that Boeing could boast of a comeback in its three-decades-long duel with Airbus Industries. Long the dominant player in the commercial aerospace industry, Boeing has been steadily losing market share to Airbus from the mid-1990s onwards (represented in Exhibit 1). In 1999, for the first time in its history, Airbus garnered more orders for new commercial jet aircraft than Boeing. The European upstart repeated this achievement regularly between 2001 and 2005.

By mid-2006, however, the tide seemed to be shifting in Boeing's favor. Underlying this were strong sales of Boeing's newest jet, the super-efficient wide-bodied 787, along with surging sales of its well-established 737 and 777 jets. For the first six months of 2006, Boeing took orders for 487 aircraft; Airbus took just 117. While Boeing seemed to be leaving a decade of production problems and ethics scandals behind it, Airbus was mired in problems of its own. Its largest jet to date, the A380 super jumbo, had been delayed from entering service while the company struggled with production problems. Orders for the A380 had stalled at 159 for almost a year, and analysts were beginning to question whether the aircraft would be a commercial success. Moreover, Airbus's contender to the Boeing 787, the A350, had to be scrapped before it even left the drawing board due to negative customer feedback. The challenge facing

Boeing's management was to translate this revival in fortunes for the company into a sustainable competitive advantage. It was off to a good start, but what else needed to be done?

The Competitive Environment

By the 2000s, the market for large commercial jet aircraft was dominated by just two companies, Boeing and Airbus. A third player in the industry, McDonnell Douglas, had been significant historically but had lost share during the 1980s and 1990s. In 1997, Boeing acquired McDonnell Douglas, primarily for its strong military business. Since the mid-1990s, Airbus had been gaining orders at Boeing's expense. By the mid-2000s, the two companies were splitting the market.

Both Boeing and Airbus now have a full range of aircraft. Boeing offers five aircraft "families" that range in size from 100 to over 500 seats. They are the narrow-bodied 737 and the wide-bodied 747, 767, 777, and 787 families. Each family comes in various forms. For example, there are currently four main variants of the 737 aircraft. They vary in size from 110 to 215 seats, and in range from 2,000 to over 5,000 miles. List prices vary from $47 million for the smallest member of the 737 family, the 737-600, to $282 million for the largest Boeing aircraft, the 747-8. The newest member of the Boeing family, the 787, lists for between $138 million and $188 million, depending on the model.[1]

Similarly, Airbus offers four families: the narrow-bodied A320 family and the wide-bodied A300/310, A330/340, and A380 families. These aircraft vary in size from 100 to 550 seats. The range of list prices is similar to Boeing's. The A380 super jumbo lists for between $282 million and $302 million, while the smaller A320 lists for between $62 million and $66.5 million.[2] Both companies also offer freighter versions of their wide-bodied aircraft.

Airbus was a relatively recent entrant into the market. Airbus began its life as a consortium between a French and a Germany company in 1970. Later, a British and a Spanish company joined the consortium. Initially few people gave Airbus much chance for success, but the consortium gained ground by innovating. It was the first aircraft maker to build planes that "flew by wire," made extensive use of composites, flew with only two flight crew members (most flew with three), and used a common cockpit layout across models. It also gained sales by being the first company to offer a wide-bodied twin engine jet, the A300, that was positioned between smaller single-aisle planes like the 737 and large aircraft such as the Boeing 747.

In 2001, Airbus became a fully integrated company. The European Defense and Space Company (EADS), formed by a merger between French, German, and Spanish interests, acquired 80% of the shares in EADS, and BAE Systems, a British company, took a 20% stake.

Development and Production

The economics of development and production in the industry are characterized by a number of facts. First, the R&D and tooling costs associated with developing a new airliner are very high. Boeing spent some $5 billion to develop the 777. Its latest aircraft, the 787, is expected to cost $8 billion to develop. Development costs for Airbus's latest aircraft, the A380 super jumbo, could run as high as $15 billion.

Second, given the high upfront costs, to break even a company has to capture a significant share of projected world demand. The breakeven point for the Airbus super jumbo, for example, is estimated to be between 250 and 270 aircraft. Estimates of the total potential market for this aircraft vary widely. Boeing suggests that the total world market will be no more than 320 aircraft over the next twenty years. Airbus believes that demand for this size aircraft will be more like 1,250 jets. In any event, it may take five to ten years of production before Airbus breaks even on the A380—and that's on top of years of negative cash flow during development.[3]

Third, there are significant learning effects in aircraft production.[4] On average, unit costs fall by about 20% each time *cumulative* output of a specific model is doubled. The phenomenon occurs because managers and shop floor workers learn over time how to assemble a particular model of plane more efficiently, reducing assembly time, boosting productivity, and lowering the marginal costs of producing subsequent aircraft.

Fourth, the assembly of aircraft is an enormously complex process. Modern planes have over 1 million component parts that have to be designed to fit with each other, and then produced and brought together at the right time to assemble the engine. At several times in the history of the industry, problems with the supply of critical components have held up production schedules and resulted in losses. In 1997, Boeing took a charge of $1.6 billion against earnings when it had to halt the production of its 737 and 747 models due to a lack of component parts.

Historically, airline manufacturers tried to manage the supply process through vertical integration, making many of the component parts that went into an aircraft (engines were long the exception to this). Over the last two decades, however, there has been a trend to contract out production of components and even entire subassemblies to independent suppliers. On the 777, for example, Boeing outsourced about 65 percent of the aircraft production, by value, excluding the engines.[5] While helping to reduce costs, contracting out has placed an enormous onus on airline manufacturers to work closely with their suppliers to coordinate the entire production process.

Finally, all new aircraft are now designed digitally and assembled virtually before a single component is produced. Boeing was the first to do this with its 777 in the early 1990s and its new version of the 737 in the late 1990s.

Customers

Demand for commercial jet aircraft is very volatile and tends to reflect the financial health of the commercial airline industry, which is prone to boom and bust cycles (see Exhibits 1 and 2). After a moderate boom during the 1990s, the airline industry went through a particularly nasty downturn during 2001–2005. The downturn started in early 2001 due to a slowdown in business travel after the boom of the 1990s. It was compounded by a dramatic slump in airline travel after the terrorist attacks on the United States on September 11, 2001. Between 2001

EXHIBIT 1

Commercial Aircraft Orders, 1990–2005

Sources: http://www.boeing.com/ (accessed September 2006) and http://www.airbus.com/en/ (accessed September 2006).

and 2005, the entire global airline industry lost some $40 billion, more money than it had made since its inception.[6]

For 2006, the industry is forecasted to lose $1.7 billion, which represents an incremental improvement over the $3.2 billion lost in 2005. The industry would have been profitable in both 2005 and 2006 were it not for surging jet fuel prices after January 2004 (prices for jet fuel more than doubled between 2004 and 2006—see Exhibit 3). The International Air Travel Association estimates that the fuel bill for all airlines in 2006 was around $115 billion. The bill for jet fuel represented over 25% of the industry's total operating costs in 2006, compared to less than 10% in 2001.[7]

EXHIBIT 2

World Airline Industry Revenues

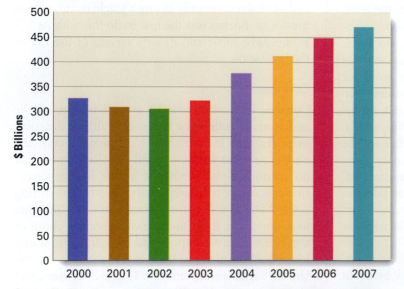

Source: IATA Data. Figures for 2006 and 2007 are forecasts. http://www.iata.org/whatwedo/economics/fuel_monitor/price_development.htm (accessed February 12, 2007).

EXHIBIT 3

Jet Fuel and Crude Oil Prices

Source: IATA Data. http://www.iata.org/whatwedo/economics/fuelmonitor/
price_development.htm (accessed February 12, 2007).

Losses were particularly severe among the big six airlines in the world's largest market, the United States (American Airlines, United, Delta, Continental, US Airways, and Northwest). Three of these airlines (United, Delta, and Northwest) were forced to seek chapter 11 bankruptcy protections. Even though demand and profits plummeted at the big six airlines, some carriers continued to make profits during 2001–2005, most notably the budget airline Southwest. In addition, other newer budget airlines, including AirTran and Jet Blue (which was started in 2000), gained market share during this period. Indeed, between 2000 and 2003, the budget airlines in the United States expanded capacity by 44%, even as the majors slashed their carrying capacities and parked unused planes in the desert. In 1998, the budget airlines held a 16% share of the U.S. market; by mid-2004, their share had risen to 29%.[8]

The key to the success of the budget airlines is a strategy that gives them a 30 to 50% cost advantage over traditional airlines. The budget airlines all follow the same basic script: They purchase just one type of aircraft (some standardize on Boeing 737s, others on Airbus 320s). They hire nonunion labor and cross-train employees to perform multiple jobs (to help meet turnaround times, for example, pilots might help check tickets at the gate). As a result of flexible work rules, Southwest needs only 80 employees to support and fly an aircraft, compared to 115 at the big six airlines. The budget airlines also favor flying "point to point" rather than through hubs, and often use less costly secondary airports rather than major ones. They focus on large markets with lots of traffic (up and down the East Coast, for example). There are no frills on the flights (passengers receive no in-flight food or complementary drinks, for example). And prices are set low to fill up the seats.

In contrast, major airlines base their operations on the network, or "hub and spoke," system. Network airlines route their flights through major hubs; one airline often dominates a single hub (United dominates Chicago's O'Hare airport, for example). This system was developed for good reason: It efficiently uses airline capacity when there isn't enough demand to fill a plane flying point to point. By using a hub and spoke system, major network airlines are able to serve some 38,000 city pairs, some of which generate fewer than fifty passengers per day. By focusing on a few hundred city pairs where there is sufficient demand to fill their planes, and flying directly between them (point to point), the budget airlines seem to have found a way around this constraint. The network carriers also suffer from a higher cost structure due to their legacy of a unionized workforce. In addition, their costs are pushed higher by their superior in-flight service. In good times, the network carriers can recoup their costs by charging higher prices than the discount airlines, particularly for business travelers, who pay more to book late and to fly business or first class. In the competitive environment of the early 2000s, however, this was no longer the case.

Due to the effect of increased competition, the real yield that U.S. airlines get from passengers has fallen from 8.70 cents per mile in 1980 to 6.37 cents per mile in 1990, 5.12 cents per mile in 2000, and 4.00 cents per mile in 2005 (these figures are expressed in constant 1978 cents).[9] Real yields are also declining elsewhere. With real yields declining, the only way that airlines can become profitable is to reduce their operating costs.

Outside of the United States, competition has intensified as deregulation has allowed low-cost airlines to enter local markets and capture share from long-established national airlines that have used the hub and spoke model. In Europe, for example, Ryanair and Easy Jet have adopted the business model of Southwest and used it to grow aggressively.

By the mid-2000s, large airlines in the United States were starting to improve their operating efficiency, helped by growing traffic volumes, higher load factors, and reductions in operating costs, particularly labor costs. Load factor refers to the percentage of a plane that is full on average, which hit a record 86% in 2006 in the United States, and 81% in international markets. Total losses for the U.S. industry were projected to be $4.5 billion in 2006, primarily due to one-time accounting charges. European airlines were projected to make profits of $1.8 billion in 2006, and Asian airlines profits of $1.7 billion. For 2007, the U.S.

airlines were projected to break even, and the global industry was projected to earn around $2 billion.[10]

Demand Projections

Both Boeing and Airbus issue annual projects of likely future demand for commercial jet aircraft. These projections are based on assumptions about future global economic growth, the resulting growth in demand for air travel, and the financial health of the world's airlines.

In its 2006 report, Boeing assumed that the world economy would grow by 3.1% per annum over the next twenty years, which should generate growth in passenger traffic of 4.8% per annum and growth in cargo traffic of 6.1% per year. On this basis, Boeing forecast demand for some 27,210 new aircraft valued at $2.6 trillion over the next twenty years (1,360 deliveries per year). Of this, some 9,580 aircraft will be replacements for aircraft retired from service, with the balance being aircraft to satisfy an expanded market. In 2025, Boeing estimates that the total global fleet of aircraft will be 35,970, up from 17,330 in 2005. Boeing believes that North America will account for 28% of all new orders, Asia Pacific for 36%, and Europe for 24%. Passenger traffic is projected to grow at 6.4% per annum in Asia versus 3.6% in North America and 3.4% in Europe.[11]

Regarding the mix of orders, Boeing believes that the majority will be for aircraft between regional jets (which have fewer than 100 seats) and the Boeing 747 (see Exhibit 4). Aircraft in the 747 range (including

EXHIBIT 4

Projected New Airplane Deliveries, 2006–2025

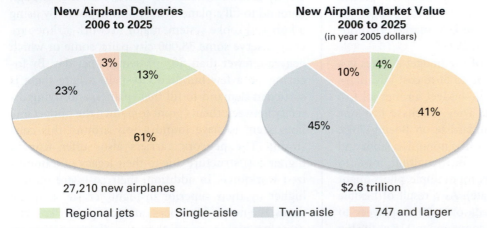

Source: Boeing, http://www.boeing.com/commercial/cmo/new.html (accessed 2007).

the Airbus A380) will account for some 3% of deliveries and 10% of value between 2006 and 2025, according to Boeing.

The latest Airbus forecast covers 2004–2023. Over that period, Airbus forecasts world passenger traffic to grow by 5.3% per annum and predicts demand for 17,328 new aircraft worth $1.9 trillion. (Note that Airbus excludes regional jets from its forecast; Boeing's forecasts include some 3,450 regional jet deliveries). Airbus believes that demand for very large aircraft will be robust, amounting to 1,648 large passenger aircraft and freighters in the 747 range and above, or 22% of the total value of aircraft delivered.[12]

The difference in the mix of orders projected by Boeing and Airbus reflect different views of how future demand will evolve. Airbus believes that hubs will continue to play an important role in airline travel, particularly international travel, and that very large jets will be required to transport people between hubs. Airbus bases this assumption partly on an analysis of data over the last twenty years, which shows that traffic between major airline hubs has grown faster than traffic between other city pairs. Airbus also assumes that urban concentrations will continue to grow, with fifteen cities having populations of more than 20 million by 2023, up from five in 2004. Airbus states that demand is simply a function of where people want to go, and most people want to travel between major urban centers. The company notes, for example, that 90% of travelers from the United States to China go to three major cities. Fifty other cities make up the remaining 10%, and Airbus believes that very few of these cities will have demand large enough to justify a nonstop service from North America or Europe. Based on this assumption, Airbus sees robust demand for very large aircraft, particularly its A380 offering.

Boeing has a different view of the future. The company theorizes that hubs will become increasingly congested and that many travelers will seek to avoid them. Boeing thinks that passengers prefer frequent nonstop service between the cities they wish to visit. Boeing also sees growth in travel between city pairs as being large enough to support an increasing number of direct long-haul flights. The company notes that continued liberalization of regulations governing airline routes around the world will allow for the establishment of more direct flights between city pairs. As in the United States, the company believes that long-haul, low-cost airlines will emerge that serve city pairs and avoid hubs.

In sum, Boeing believes that airline travelers will demand more frequent nonstop flights, not larger aircraft.[13] To support this, the company has data showing that all of the growth in airline travel since 1995 has been met by the introduction of new nonstop flights between city pairs and by an increased frequency of flights between city pairs, not by an increase in airplane size. For example, Boeing notes that following the introduction of the 767, airlines introduced more flights between city pairs in North America and Europe and more frequent departures. In 1984, 63% of all flights across the North Atlantic were in the 747. By 2004, the figure had declined to 13%, with smaller wide-bodied aircraft such as the 767 and 777 dominating traffic. Following the introduction of the 777, which can fly nonstop across the Pacific and is smaller than the 747, the same process occurred in the North Pacific. In 2006 there were seventy-two daily flights serving twenty-six city pairs in North America and Asia.

Boeing's History[14]

William Boeing established the Boeing Company in 1916 in Seattle. In the early 1950s, Boeing took an enormous gamble when it decided to build a large jet aircraft that could be sold both to the military as a tanker and to commercial airlines as a passenger plane. Known as the Dash 80, the plane had swept-back wings and four jet engines. Boeing invested $16 million to develop the Dash 80, two-thirds of the company's entire profits during the postwar years. The Dash 80 was the basis for two aircraft, the KC-135 Air Force tanker and the Boeing 707. Introduced into service in 1957, the 707 was the world's first commercially successful passenger jet aircraft. Boeing went on to sell some 856 Boeing 707s along with 820 KC-135s. The final 707, a freighter, rolled off the production line in 1994 (production of passenger planes ended in 1978). The closest rival to the 707 was the Douglas DC 8, of which some 556 were ultimately sold.

The 707 was followed by a number of other successful jet liners including the 727 (entered service in 1962), the 737 (entered service in 1967), and the 747 (entered service in 1970). The single aisle 737 went on to become the workhorse of many airlines. In the 2000s, a completely redesigned version of the 737 that could seat between 110 and 180 passengers was still selling strong. Cumulative sales of the 737 totaled 6,500 by mid-2006, making it by far the most popular commercial jet aircraft ever sold.

It was the 747 "jumbo jet," however, that probably best defined Boeing. In 1966, when Boeing's board decided to develop the 747, they were widely viewed as betting the company on the jet. The 747 was born out of the desire of Pan Am, then America's largest airline, for a 400-seat passenger aircraft that could fly 5,000 miles. Pan Am believed that the aircraft would be ideal for the growing volume of transcontinental traffic. However, beyond Pan Am, which committed to purchasing 25 aircraft, demand was very uncertain. Moreover, the estimated $400 million in development and tooling costs placed a heavy burden on Boeing's financial resources. To make a return on its investment, the company estimated it would have to sell close to 400 aircraft. To complicate matters further, Boeing's principal competitors, Lockheed and McDonnell Douglas, were each developing 250-seat jumbo jets.

Boeing's big bet turned out to be auspicious. Pan Am's competitors feared being left behind, and by the end of 1970, almost 200 orders for the aircraft had been placed. Successive models of the 747 extended the range of the aircraft. The 747-400, introduced in 1989, had a range of 8,000 miles and a maximum seating capacity of 550 (although most configurations seated around 400 passengers). By this time, both Douglas and Lockheed had exited the market, giving Boeing a lucrative monopoly in the very large commercial jet category. By 2005, the company had sold some 1,430 747s and was actively selling its latest version of the 747 family, the 747-8, which was scheduled to enter service in 2008.

By the mid-1970s, Boeing was past the breakeven point on all of its models (707, 727, 737, and 747). The positive cash flow helped to fund investment in two new aircraft, the narrow-bodied 757 and the wide-bodied 767. The 757 was designed as a replacement to the aging 727, while the 767 was a response to a similar aircraft from Airbus. These were the first Boeing aircraft to be designed with two-person cockpits, rather than three. Indeed, the cockpit layout was identical, allowing the crew to shift from one aircraft to the other. The 767 was also the first aircraft for which Boeing subcontracted a significant amount of work to a trio of Japanese manufacturers—Mitsubishi, Kawasaki, and Fuji—which supplied about 15% of the airframe. Introduced in 1981, both aircraft were successful. Some 1,049 757s were sold

during the life of the program, which ended in 2003. Over 950 767s had been sold by 2006, and the program is still going.

The next Boeing plane was the 777. A two-engine, wide-bodied aircraft with seating capacity of up to 400 and a range of almost 8,000 miles, the 777 program was initiated in 1990. The 777 was seen as a response to Airbus's successful A330 and A340 wide-bodied aircraft. Development costs were estimated at some $5 billion. The 777 was the first wide-bodied, long-haul jet to have only two engines. It was also the first to be designed entirely on computer. To develop the 777, for the first time Boeing used cross-functional teams composed of engineering and production employees. It also bought major suppliers and customers into the development process. As with the 767, a significant amount of work was outsourced to foreign manufacturers, including the Japanese trio of Mitsubishi, Kawasaki, and Fuji, which supplied 20% of the 777 airframe. In total, some 60% of parts for the 777 were outsourced. The 777 proved to be another successful venture. By mid-2006, 850 777s had been ordered, far greater than the 200 or so required to break even.

In December 1996, Boeing stunned the aerospace industry by announcing it would merge with long-time rival McDonnell Douglas in a deal estimated to be worth $13.3 billion. The merger was driven by Boeing's desire to strengthen its presence in the defense and space side of the aerospace business, where McDonnell Douglas was traditionally strong. On the commercial side of the aerospace business, Douglas had been losing market share since the 1970s. By 1996, Douglas accounted for less than 10% of production in the large commercial jet aircraft market and only 3% of new orders placed that year. The dearth of new orders meant the long-term outlook for Douglas's commercial business was increasingly murky. With or without the merger, many analysts felt that it was only a matter of time before McDonnell Douglas would be forced to exit from the commercial jet aircraft business. In their view, the merger with Boeing merely accelerated that process.

The merger transformed Boeing into a broad-based aerospace business within which commercial aerospace accounted for 40 to 60% of total revenue, depending on the stage of the commercial production cycle. In 2001, for example, the commercial aircraft group accounted for $35 billion in revenues out of a corporate total of $58 billion, or 60%. In 2005, with the delivery cycle at a low point (but the order cycle rebounding), the commercial airplane group accounted for $22.7 billion out of a total of $54.8 billion, or 41%. The balance of revenue was made up by a wide range of military aircraft, weapons and defense systems, and space systems.

In the early 2000s, in a highly symbolic act, Boeing moved its corporate headquarters from Seattle to Chicago. The move was an attempt to put some distance between top corporate officers and the commercial aerospace business, the headquarters of which remained in Seattle. The move was also intended to signal to the investment community that Boeing was far more than its commercial businesses.

To some extent, the move to Chicago may have been driven by a number of production missteps in the late 1990s that hit the company at a time when it should have been enjoying financial success. During the mid-1990s, orders had boomed as Boeing cut prices in an aggressive move to gain share from Airbus. However, delivering these aircraft meant that Boeing had to more than double its production schedule between 1996 and 1997. As it attempted to do this, the company ran into some severe production bottlenecks.[15] The company scrambled to hire and train some 41,000 workers, recruiting many from suppliers, a move it came to regret when many of the suppliers could not meet Boeing's demands and shipments of parts were delayed. In the fall of 1997, things got so bad that Boeing shut down its 747 and 737 production lines so that workers could catch up with out-of-sequence work and wait for back-ordered parts to arrive. Ultimately, the company had to take a $1.6 billion charge against earnings to account for higher costs and penalties paid to airlines for the late delivery of jets. As a result, Boeing made very little money out of its mid-1990s order boom. The head of Boeing's commercial aerospace business was fired, and the company committed itself to a major acceleration of its attempt to overhaul its production system, elements of which dated back half a century.

Boeing in the 2000s

In the 2000s, three things dominated the development of Boeing Commercial Aerospace. First, the company accelerated a decade-long project aimed at improving the company's production methods by adopting the lean production systems initially developed by Toyota and applying them to the manufacture of large jet aircraft. Second, the company considered and then rejected the idea of building a successor to the 747. Third, Boeing decided to develop a new wide-bodied, long-haul jetliner, the 787.

Lean Production at Boeing

Boeing's attempt to revolutionize the way planes are built dates back to the early 1990s. Beginning in 1990, the company started to send teams of executives to Japan to study the production systems of Japan's leading manufacturers, particularly Toyota. Toyota had pioneered a new way of assembling automobiles known as *lean production* (in contrast to conventional *mass production*).

Toyota's lean production system was developed by one of the company's engineers, Ohno Taiichi.[16] After working at Toyota for five years and visiting Ford's U.S. plants, Ohno became convinced that the mass-production philosophy for making cars was flawed. He saw numerous problems, including three major drawbacks. First, long production runs created massive inventories, which had to be stored in large warehouses. This was expensive because of the cost of warehousing and because inventories tied up capital in unproductive uses. Second, if the initial machine settings were wrong, long production runs resulted in the production of a large number of defects (that is, waste). And third, the mass-production system was unable to accommodate consumer preferences for product diversity.

In looking for ways to make shorter production runs economical, Ohno developed a number of techniques designed to reduce setup times for production equipment, a major source of fixed costs. By using a system of levers and pulleys, he was able to reduce the time required to change dies on stamping equipment from a full day in 1950 to three minutes by 1971. This advance made small production runs economical, which allowed Toyota to respond more efficiently to consumer demands for product diversity. Small production runs also eliminated the need to hold large inventories, thereby reducing warehousing costs. Furthermore, small production runs and the lack of inventory meant that defective parts were produced only in small numbers and entered the assembly process immediately. This reduced waste made it easier to trace defects to their source and fix the problem. In sum, Ohno's innovations enabled Toyota to produce a more diverse product range at a lower unit cost than was possible with conventional mass production.

Impressed with what Toyota had done, in the mid-1990s, Boeing started to experiment with applying Toyota-like lean production methods to the production of aircraft. Production at Boeing used to be all about producing parts in high volumes and then storing them in warehouses until they were ready to be used in the assembly process. After visiting Toyota, engineers realize that Boeing was drowning in inventory. A huge amount of space and capital was tied up in things that didn't add value. Moreover, expensive specialized machines often took up a lot of space and were frequently idle for long stretches of time.

Like Ohno at Toyota, company engineers started to think about how they could modify equipment and processes at Boeing to reduce waste. Boeing set aside space and time for teams of creative plant employees—design engineers, maintenance technicians, electricians, machinists, and operators—to start experimenting with machinery. They called these teams moonshiners. The term *moonshine* was coined by Japanese executives who visited the United States after World War II. They were impressed by two things in the United States—supermarkets and the stills built by people in the Appalachian hills. They noticed that people built these stills with no money. They would use salvaged parts to make small stills that produced alcohol that they sold for money. The Japanese took this philosophy back home with them and applied it to industrial machinery, which is where Boeing executives saw the concept in operation in the 1990s. With the help of Japanese consultants, they decided to apply the moonshine creative philosophy at Boeing to produce new low-cost, "right-sized" machines that could be used to increase profits.

The moonshine teams were trained in lean production techniques, given a small budget, and then set loose. Initially many of the moonshine teams focused on redesigning equipment to produce parts. Underlying this choice was a Boeing study that showed that more than 80% of the parts manufactured for aircraft were less than 12 inches long, and yet the metalworking machinery was huge, inflexible, and could economically produce parts only in large lots.[17]

Soon, empowered moonshine teams were designing their own equipment—small-scale machines that took up little space and used wheels to allow the machines to move around the plant. One team, for example, replaced a large stamping machine that cost six figures and was used to produce L-shaped metal parts in batches of 1,000 with a miniature stamping machine powered by a small hydraulic motor that could be wheeled around the plant. With the small machine, which cost a couple of thousand dollars, parts could be produced very quickly in small lots, eliminating the need for inventory. They also made a sanding machine and a parts cleaner of equal size. Now the entire process—from stamping the raw material to the finished part—was completed in minutes (instead of hours or days) just by configuring these machines into a small cell and having them serviced by a single person. The small scale and quick turnaround now made it possible to produce these parts just in time, eliminating the need to produce and store inventory.[18]

Another example of a moonshine innovation concerned the process for loading seats onto a plane during assembly. Historically, this was a cumbersome process. After the seats would arrive at Boeing from a supplier, wheels were attached to each seat, and then the seats were delivered to the factory floor in a large container. An overhead crane lifted the container up to the level of the aircraft door. Then the seats were unloaded and rolled into the aircraft, before being installed. The process was repeated until all of the seats had been loaded. For a single-aisle plane, this could take twelve hours. For a wide-bodied jet, it would take much longer. A moonshine team adapted a hay loader to perform the same job (see Exhibit 5). It cost a lot less, delivered seats quickly through the passenger door, and took just two hours, while eliminating the need for cranes.[19]

Multiply the examples given here, and soon you have a very significant impact on production costs: A drill machine was built for 5% of the cost of a full-scale machine from Ingersoll-Rand. Portable routers were built for 0.2% of the cost of a large fixed router. One process that took 2,000 minutes for a 100-part order (20 minutes per part because of setup, machining, and transit) now takes 100 minutes (1 minute per part). Employees building 737 floor beams reduced labor hours by 74%, increased inventory turns from 2 to 18 per year, and reduced manufacturing space by 50%. Employees building the 777 tail cut lead time by 70% and reduced space and work in progress by 50%. Production of parts for landing gear support used to take 32 moves from machine to machine and required 10 months; production now takes 3 moves and 25 days.[20]

In general, Boeing found that it was able to produce smaller lots of parts economically, often from machines that it built itself, which were smaller and cost less than the machines available from outside

EXHIBIT 5

The Converted Hay Loader at Work

vendors. In turn, these innovations enabled Boeing to switch to just-in-time inventory systems and reduce waste. Boeing was also able to save on space. By eliminating large production machinery at its Auburn facility, replacing much of it with smaller, more flexible machines, Boeing was able to free up 1.3 million square feet of space, and sold seven buildings.[21]

In addition to moonshine teams, Boeing adopted other process improvement methodologies, using them when deemed appropriate. Six Sigma quality improvement processes are widely used within Boeing. The most wide-reaching process change, however, was the decision to switch from a static assembly line to a moving line. In traditional aircraft manufacture, planes are docked in angled stalls. Ramps surround each plane, and workers go in and out to find parts and install them. Moving a plane to the next workstation was a complex process. The aircraft had to be down-jacked from its workstation, a powered cart was bought in, the aircraft was towed to the next station, and then it was jacked up. This could take two shifts. A lot of time was wasted bringing parts to a stall and moving a plane from one stall to the next.

In 2001, Boeing introduced a moving assembly line into its Renton plant near Seattle, which manu-

factures the 737 (see Exhibit 6). With a moving line, each aircraft is attached to a "sled" that rides a magnetic strip embedded in the factory floor, pulling the aircraft at a rate of 2 inches per minute, moving past a series of stations where tools and parts arrive at the moment needed, allowing workers to install the proper assemblies. The setup eliminates wandering for tools and parts, as well as expensive tug pulls or crane lifts (just having tools delivered to workstations, rather than having workers fetch them, was found to save twenty to forty-five minutes on every shift). Preassembly tasks are performed on feeder lines. For example, inboard and outboard flaps are assembled on the wing before it arrives for joining to the fuselage.[22]

Like a Toyota assembly line, the moving line can be stopped if a problem arises. Lights are used to indicate the state of the line. A green light indicates a normal work flow; the first sign of a stoppage brings a yellow warning light; and, if the problem isn't solved within fifteen minutes, a purple light indicates that the line has stopped. Each work area and feeder line has its own lights, so there is no doubt where the problem is.[23]

The cumulative effects of these process innovations have been significant. By 2005, assembly time for the 737 had been cut from twenty-two days to just

EXHIBIT 6

The Moving Line

eleven days. In addition, work-in-progress inventory had been reduced by 55 percent and stored inventory by 59 percent.[24] By 2006, all of Boeing's production lines except that for the 747 had shifted from static bays to moving lines. The 747 was expected to shift to moving line when Boeing starts production of the 747-8.

The Super-Jumbo Decisions

In the early 1990s Boeing and Airbus started to contemplate new aircraft to replace Boeing's aging 747. The success of the 747 had given Boeing a monopoly in the market for very large jet aircraft, making the plane one of the most profitable in the jet age. But the basic design dated back to the 1960s, and some believed there might be sufficient demand for a super-jumbo aircraft with as many as 900 seats.

Initially the two companies considered establishing a joint venture to share the costs and risks associated with a developing a super-jumbo aircraft, but Boeing withdrew in 1995, citing costs and uncertain demand prospects. Airbus subsequently concluded that Boeing was never serious about the joint venture, and the discussions were nothing more than a ploy to keep Airbus from developing its own plane.[25]

After Boeing withdrew, Airbus started to talk about offering a competitor to the 747 in 1995. The plane, then dubbed the A3XX, was to be a super jumbo with capacity for over 500 passengers. Indeed, Airbus stated that some versions of the plane might carry as many as 900 passengers. Airbus initially estimated that there would be demand for some 1,400 planes of this size over twenty years, and that development costs would total around $9 billion (estimates ultimately increased to some $15 billion). Boeing's latest 747 offering—the 747-400—could carry around 416 passengers in three classes.

Boeing responded by drafting plans to develop new versions of the 747 family—the 747-500X and the 747-600X. The 747-600X was to have a new (larger) wing, a fuselage almost 50 feet longer than the 747-400, would carry 550 passengers in three classes and have a range of 7,700 miles. The smaller 747-500X would have carried 460 passengers in three classes and had a range of 8,700 miles.

After taking a close look at the market for a super-jumbo replacement to the 747, in early 1997 Boeing announced that it would not proceed with the program. The reasons given for this decision included the limited market and high development costs, which at the time were estimated to be $7 billion. There were also fears that the wider wing span of the new planes would mean that airports would have to redesign some of their gates to take the aircraft. Boeing, McDonnell Douglas (prior to the merger with Boeing), and the major manufacturers of jet engines all forecast demand for about 500 to 750 such aircraft over the next twenty years. Airbus alone forecast demand as high as 1,400 aircraft. Boeing stated that the fragmentation of the market due to the rise of "point-to-point" flights across oceans would limit demand for a super jumbo. Instead of focusing on the super-jumbo category, Boeing stated that it would develop new versions of the 767 and 777 aircraft that could fly up to 9,000 miles and carry as many as 400 passengers.

Airbus, however, continued to push forward with planes to develop the A3XX. In December 2000, with more than fifty orders in hand, the board of EADS, Airbus's parent company, approved development of the plane, which was now dubbed the A380. Development costs at this point were pegged at $12 billion, and the plane was forecast to enter service in 2006 with Singapore Airlines. The A380 was to have two passenger decks, more space per seat, and wider aisles. It would carry 555 passengers in great comfort, something that passengers would appreciate on long transoceanic flights. According to Airbus, the plane would carry up to 35% more passengers than the most popular 747-400 configuration, yet cost per seat would be 15 to 20% lower due to operating efficiencies. Concerns were raised about turnaround time at airport gates for such a large plane, but Airbus stated that dual-boarding bridges and wider aisles meant that turnaround times would be no more than those for the 747-400.

Airbus also stated that the A380 was designed to operate on existing runways and within existing gates. However, London's Heathrow airport found that it had to spend some $450 million to accommodate the A380, widening taxiways and building a baggage reclaim area for the plane. Similarly, eighteen U.S. airports had reportedly spent some $1 billion just to accommodate the A380.[26]

The 787

While Airbus pushed forward with the A380, in March 2001 Boeing announced the development of a radically new aircraft. Dubbed the *sonic cruiser*, the plane would carry 250 passengers 9,000 miles and fly just below the speed of sound, cutting one hour off

transatlantic flights and three hours off transpacific flights. To keep down operating costs, the sonic cruiser would be built out of low-weight carbon fiber "composites." Although the announcement created considerable interest in the aviation community, in the wake of the recession that hit the airline industry after September 11, 2001, both Boeing and the airlines became considerably less enthusiastic. In March 2002, the program was cancelled. Instead, Boeing said that it would develop a more conventional aircraft using composite technology. The plane was initially known as the 7E7, with the *E* standing for *efficient* (the plane was renamed the 787 in early 2005).

In April 2004, the 7E7 program was formally launched with an order for fifty aircraft worth $6 billion from All Nippon Airlines of Japan. It was the largest launch order in Boeing's history. The 7E7 was a twin-aisle, wide-bodied, two-engine plane designed to carry 200 to 300 passengers up to 8,500 miles, making the 7E7 well suited for long-haul, point-to-point flights. The range exceeded all but the longest range plane in the 777 family, and the 7E7 could fly 750 miles more than Airbus's closest competitor, the mid-sized A330-200. With a fuselage built entirely out of composites, the aircraft was lighter and would use 20% less fuel than existing aircraft of comparable size.

The plane was also designed with passenger comfort in mind. The seats would be wider, as would the aisles, and the windows were larger than in existing aircraft. The plane would be pressurized at 6,000 feet altitude, as opposed to 8,000 feet, which is standard industry practice. Airline cabin humidity was typically kept at 10% to avoid moisture buildup and corrosion, but composites don't corrode, so humidity would be closer to 20 to 30%.[27]

Initial estimates suggested that the jet would cost some $7 to $8 billion to develop and enter service in 2008. Boeing decided to outsource more work for the 787 than on any other aircraft to date. Some 35% of the plane's fuselage and wing structure would be built by Boeing. The trio of Japanese companies that worked on the 767 and 777—Mitsubishi Heavy Industries, Kawasaki Heavy Industries, and Fuji Heavy Industries—would build another 35%, and some 26% would be built by Italian companies, particularly Alenia.[28] For the first time, Boeing asked its major suppliers to bear some of the development costs for the aircraft.

The plane was to be assembled at Boeing's wide-bodied plant in Everett, Washington. Large subassemblies were to be built by major suppliers and then shipped to Everett for final assembly. The idea was to "snap together" the parts in Everett in three days, cutting down on total assembly time. To speed up transportation, Boeing would adopt air freight as its major transportation method for many components.

Airbus's initial response was to dismiss Boeing's claims of cost savings as inconsequential. They pointed out that even if the 787 used less fuel than the A330, that was equivalent to just 4% of total operating costs.[29] However, even by Airbus's calculations, as fuel prices starting to accelerate, the magnitude of the savings rose. Moreover, Boeing quickly started to snag some significant orders for the 787. In 2004, Boeing booked 56 orders for the 787, and in 2005, some 232 orders. Another 85 orders were booked in the first nine months of 2006 for a running total of 373—well beyond breakeven point.

In December 2004, Airbus announced that it would develop a new model, the A350, to compete directly with the 787. The planes were to be long-haul, twin-aisle jets, seating 200 to 300 passengers, and constructed of composites. The order flow, however, was slow, with airlines complaining that the A350 did not match the Boeing 787 on operating efficiency, range, or passenger comfort. Airbus went back to the drawing board and, in mid-2006, announced a new version of the A350, the A350 XWB (for "extra wide body"). Airbus estimates that the A350 XWB will cost $10 billion to develop and enter service in 2012, several years behind the 787. The two-engine A350 XWB will carry between 250 and 375 passengers and fly up to 8,500 miles. The largest versions of the A350 XWB will be competing directly with the Boeing 777, not the 787. Like the 787, the A350 XWB will be built primarily of composite materials. The extra wide body is designed to enhance passenger comfort. To finance the A350 XWB, Airbus stated that it would probably seek launch aid from Germany, France, Spain, and the UK, all countries where major parts of Airbus are based.[30]

Trade Tensions

It is impossible to discuss the global aerospace industry without touching on trade issues. Over the last three decades, both Boeing and Airbus have charged that their competitor benefited unfairly from government subsidies. Until 2001 Airbus functioned as a consortium of four European aircraft manufacturers: one British (20.0% ownership stake), one French (37.9% ownership), one German (37.9% ownership), and

one Spanish (4.2% ownership). In the 1980s and early 1990s Boeing maintained that subsidies from these nations allow Airbus to set unrealistically low prices, to offer concessions and attractive financing terms to airlines, to write off development costs, and to use state-owned airlines to obtain orders. According to a study by the U.S. Department of Commerce, Airbus received more than $13.5 billion in government subsidies between 1970 and 1990 ($25.9 billion if commercial interest rates are applied). Most of these subsidies were in the form of loans at below-market interest rates and tax breaks. The subsidies financed research and development and provided attractive financing terms for Airbus's customers. Airbus responded by pointing out that Boeing had benefited for years from hidden U.S. government subsidies, particularly Pentagon R&D grants.

In 1992, the two sides appeared to reach an agreement that put to rest their long-standing trade dispute. The 1992 pact, which was negotiated by the EU on behalf of the four member states, limited direct government subsidies to 33% of the total costs of developing a new aircraft and specified that such subsidies had to be repaid with interest within seventeen years. The agreement also limited indirect subsidies, such as government-supported military research that has applications to commercial aircraft, to 3% of a country's annual total commercial aerospace revenues or 4% of commercial aircraft revenues of any single company in that country. Although Airbus officials stated that the controversy had now been resolved, Boeing officials argued that they would still be competing for years against subsidized products.

The trade dispute heated up again in 2004 when Airbus announced the first version of the A350 to compete against Boeing's 787. What raised a red flag for the U.S. government was a sign from Airbus that it would apply for $1.7 billion in launch aid to help fund the development of the A350. As far as the United States was concerned, this was too much. In late 2004, U.S. Trade Representative Robert Zoellick issued a statement formally renouncing the 1992 agreement and calling for an end to launch subsidies. According to Zoellick, "since its creation 35 years ago, some Europeans have justified subsidies to Airbus as necessary to support an infant industry. If that rationalization were ever valid, its time has long passed. Airbus now sells more large civil aircraft than Boeing." Zoellick went on to claim that Airbus has received some $3.7 billion in launch aid for the A380 plus another $2.8 billion in indirect subsidies including $1.7 billion in taxpayer-funded infrastructure improvements for a total of $6.5 billion.

Airbus shot back that Boeing too continued to enjoy lavish subsidies and that the company had received some $12 billion from NASA to develop technology, much of which had found its way into commercial jet aircraft. The Europeans also contended that Boeing would receive as much as $3.2 billion in tax breaks from Washington State, where the 787 is to be assembled, and more than $1 billion in loans from the Japanese government to three Japanese suppliers, who will build over one-third of the 787. Moreover, Airbus was quick to point out that a trade war would not benefit either side and that Airbus purchased some $6 billion a year in supplies from companies in the United States.

In January 2005, both the United States and the EU agreed to freeze direct subsidies to the two aircraft makers while talks continued. However, in May 2005 news reports suggested, and Airbus confirmed, that the jet maker had applied to four EU governments for launch aid for the A350, and that the British government would announce some $700 million in aid at the Paris Air Show in mid-2005. Simultaneously, the EU offered to cut launch aid for the A350 by 30%. Dissatisfied, the U.S. side decided that the talks were going nowhere, and on May 31 the United States formally filed a request with the World Trade Organization (WTO) for the establishment of a dispute resolution panel to resolve the issues. The EU quickly responded, filing a countersuit with the WTO claiming that U.S. aid to Boeing exceeded the terms set out in the 1992 agreement. The dispute is currently before the WTO.[31]

Although the decision to scrap the original design of the A350 took some of the heat out of the dispute, Airbus is expected to ask for launch aid for the redesigned A350 XWB.

The Next Chapter

Huge financial bets have been placed on very different visions of the future of airline travel: Airbus with the A380 and Boeing with the 787. Airbus has hedged its bets by announcing the A350 XWB, but will this be too little too late? Moreover, there are signs of production turmoil at Airbus. Orders for the A380 have stalled. In mid-2006, the company announced that deliveries for the aircraft would be delayed by six months while the company dealt with "production issues" arising from problems installing the wiring bundles in the A380. Estimates suggest that the delay would cost Airbus some $2.6 billion over the next four years.[32] Within months, Airbus had revised the expected delay to eighteen months and stated that the number of A380s it now needed to sell to break even had increased from 250 to 420 aircraft. The company also stated that due to production problems, it would be able to deliver only 84 A380 planes by 2010, compared to an original estimate of 420.[33] In responses, several significant launch customers for the A380 were said to be reconsidering their purchase decisions. United Parcel Service, which has 10 A380 cargo planes on order, was reportedly considering switching to the Boeing 747-8, Boeing's latest offering in the venerable 747 family.

Boeing quietly launched the 747-8 program in November 2005. This plane will be a completely redesigned version of the 747 and will incorporate many of the technological advances developed for the 787, including significant use of composites. It will be offered in both a freighter and intercontinental passenger configuration that will carry 467 passengers in a three-seat configuration and have a range of 8,000 miles (the 747-400 can carry 416 passengers). The 747-8 will also use the fuel-efficient engines developed for the 787 and will have the same cockpit configuration as the 737, 777, and 787. Development costs are estimated to be around $4 billion. By October 2006, Boeing had orders for 44 787-8 freighters, but none for the passenger planes. However, some analysts speculated that with the A380 mired in delays, the 747-8 passenger configuration might begin to garner more orders.

Not all is smooth sailing at Boeing. The company experienced some problems with suppliers for the 787, who have fallen behind schedule designing some components for the project. As of late 2006, Boeing was insisting that the 787 was still on schedule. Some analysts, however, are concerned that this might be a sign of things to come and that the complexity associated with coordinating a diverse base of suppliers might lead to delays in the 787.

Complicating issues, both Airbus and Boeing have been through some changes in key management over the last few years. At Boeing, CEO Phil Condit resigned in late 2003 after it was revealed that the company's CFO, Mike Sears, had hired a key department of defense procurement officer in return for her backing of a huge order for air force tankers based on the 767. Sears was subsequently prosecuted and sent to jail. The Sears scandal was only the latest in a number that Boeing executives had become embroiled in during the early 2000s. Condit's resignation was widely taken to indicate that the board felt that a new CEO was needed to clean house. Condit was replaced by Harry Stonecipher, who was CEO of McDonnell Douglas when it was acquired by Boeing and later president of Boeing. Stonecipher resigned fifteen months later when it was revealed that he had an affair with a subordinate and communicated with her using the company's email service. Stonecipher was replaced by Jim McNerney, who moved to Boeing from the CEO position at 3M. Prior to joining 3M, McNerney had run the aircraft engine business at General Electric. McNerney was widely viewed as a skilled manager who had brought the operating discipline that GE is famous for to 3M. He was expected to do the same at Boeing, pushing the company to continue to pursue various productivity initiatives, such as lean production, Six Sigma, and global sourcing.

At Airbus, following the announcement of the delay in A380 production, there was pressure on Noel Forgeard, the CEO of EADS, Airbus's parent company, to resign. Forgeard refused, although Gustav Humbert, the CEO of Airbus, did offer to step down. After a three-week crisis, the board of EADS took matters into its own hands and fired both Forgeard and Humbert. They were replaced by Louis Gallois, a Frenchman who once ran an aerospace company that was acquired by EADS, and Christian Streiff, the former number 2 at Saint Gobain, the French glassmaker.

With new management in place at both companies, the focus is on the unfolding competitive battle. Can Airbus make money on the A380, and if it does, will it gain a monopoly that rivals Boeing's 747 dynasty? Will the 787 live up to its promise and become the right plane for a new era of global travel? Can Airbus come back at Boeing with its new version of the A350, the A350 XWB? And what of the ongoing trade dispute? How will this impact on the long-running dog fight between the two companies?

ENDNOTES

1. http://www.boeing.com/ (accessed September 2006).
2. http://www.airbus.com/en/ (accessed September 2006).
3. J. Palmer, "Big Bird," *Barron's*, December 19, 2005, pages 25–29; http://www.yeald.com/Yeald/a/33941/both_a380_and_787_have_bright_futures.html.
4. G. J. Steven, "The Learning Curve; From Aircraft to Space Craft," *Management Accounting*, May 1999, pages 64–66.
5. D. Gates, "Boeing 7E7 Watch: Familiar Suppliers Make Short List," *Seattle Times*.
6. The figures are from the International Airline Travelers Association (IATA).
7. IATA, "2006 Loss Forecast Drops to US $1.7 Billion," Press Release, August 31, 2006.
8. "Turbulent Skies: Low Cost Airlines," *The Economist*, July 10, 2004, pages 68–72; "Silver Linings, Darkening Clouds," *The Economist*, March 27, 2004, pages 90–92.
9. Data from the Air Transport Association at www.airlines.org.
10. IATA, "2006 Loss Forecast Drops to US $1.7 Billion," Press Release, August 31, 2006.
11. Boeing, Current Market Outlook, 2006. Archived on Boeing's website.
12. Airbus, http://www.airbus.com/en/myairbus/global_market_forcast.html.
13. Presentation by Randy Baseler, vice president of Boeing Commercial Airplanes, given at the Farnborough Air Show, July 2006. Archived at http://www.boeing.com/nosearch/exec_pres/CMO.pdf.
14. This material is drawn from an earlier version of the Boeing case written by Charles W. L. Hill. See C. W. L. Hill, "The Boeing Corporation: Commercial Aircraft Operations," in C. W. L. Hill and G. R. Jones, *Strategic Management*, third edition (Boston: Houghton Mifflin, 1995). Much of Boeing's history is described in R. J. Sterling, *Legend and Legacy* (St. Martin's Press, New York, 1992).
15. S. Browder, "A Fierce Downdraft at Boeing," *Business Week*, January 26, 1988, page 34.
16. M. A. Cusumano, *The Japanese Automobile Industry* (Cambridge, Mass.: Harvard University Press, 1989); Ohno Taiichi, *Toyota Production System* (Cambridge, Mass.: Productivity Press, 1990); J. P. Womack, D. T. Jones, and D. Roos, *The Machine That Changed the World* (New York: Rawson Associates, 1990).
17. J. Gillie, "Lean Manufacturing Could Save Boeing's Auburn Washington Plant," *Knight Ridder Tribune Business News*, May 6, 2002, page 1.
18. P. V. Arnold, "Boeing Knows Lean," *MRO Today*, February 2002.
19. Boeing Press Release, "Converted Farm Machine Improves Production Process," July 1, 2003.
20. P. V. Arnold, "Boeing Knows Lean," *MRO Today*, February 2002. Also "Build in Lean: Manufacturing for the Future," Boeing, http://www.boeing.com/aboutus/environment/create_build.htm; J. Gillie, "Lean Manufacturing Could Save Boeing's Auburn Washington Plant," *Knight Ridder Tribune Business News*, May 6, 2002, page 1.
21. J. Gillie, "Lean Manufacturing Could Save Boeing's Auburn Washington Plant," *Knight Ridder Tribune Business News*, May 6, 2002, page 1.
22. P. V. Arnold, "Boeing Knows Lean," *MRO Today*, February 2002.
23. M. Mecham, "The Lean, Green Line," *Aviation Week*, July 19, 2004, pages 144–148.
24. Boeing Press Release, "Boeing Reduces 737 Airplane's Final Assembly Time by 50 Percent," January 27, 2005.
25. "A Phony War," *The Economist*, May 5, 2001, pages 56–57.
26. J. D. Boyd, "Building Room for Growth," *Traffic World*, August 7, 2006, page 1.
27. W. Sweetman, "Boeing, Boeing, Gone," *Popular Science*, June 2004, page 97.
28. Anonymous, "Who Will Supply the Parts?" *Seattle Times*, June 15, 2003.
29. W. Sweetman, "Boeing, Boeing, Gone," *Popular Science*, June 2004, page 97.
30. D. Michaels and J. L. Lunsford, "Airbus Chief Reveals Plans for New Family of Jetliners," *Wall Street Journal*, July 18, 2006, page A3.
31. J. Reppert-Bismarck and W. Echikson, "EU Countersues Over U.S. Aid to Boeing," *Wall Street Journal*, June 1, 2005, page A2; United States Trade Representative Press Release, "United States Takes Next Steps in Airbus WTO litigation," May 30, 2005.
32. Anonymous, "Airbus Agonistes," *Wall Street Journal*, September 6, 2006, page A20.
33. Anonymous, "Forecast Dimmer for Profit on Airbus' A380," *Seattle Times*, October 20, 2006, Web Edition.

The Rise of Airbus, 1970–2005

This case was prepared by Dr. Isaac Cohen, San Jose State University.

For 16 consecutive months Airbus did not sell a single aircraft. As sales came to a halt in 1976, the number of "whitetails"—unsold aircraft sitting on the factory runway (their tails painted white with no airline insignia)—exceeded the consortium's total sales. Airbus was losing so much money at the time that the consortium's German partner urged Airbus management to stop production altogether. The consortium's French partner disagreed, and persuaded the German partner to keep the production line moving.

Keeping the production line moving saved the Airbus program. As sales rebounded in 1977, production shot up, the consortium gained new customers, and Airbus emerged as a global aircraft manufacturer. Over a period of 30 years and throughout the tenure of three CEOs—Bernard Lathiere (1975–1985), Jean Pierson (1985–1998), and Noel Forgeard (1998–2005)—Airbus has transformed itself from a distant competitor with an uncertain future to a leading commercial aircraft maker ahead of Boeing.

Bernard Lathiere put in place the three pillars that together made up Airbus's winning strategy. He developed families of planes with common design features—or commonalties—that ran across several related models; he introduced innovations in aircraft electronics, materials, and design which turned Airbus into a technological leader; and he devised a global sales strategy that singled out Asia as the world's fastest growing and most promising aircraft market. Jean Pierson implemented cost-cutting

This case was presented in the October 2005 meeting of the North American Case Research Association at North Falmouth, Cape Cod, Massachusetts. Dr. Cohen is grateful to the San Jose State University for its support.

measures that lowered Airbus's dependency on government subsidies, diversified Airbus's product line, and signed a landmark bilateral agreement that limited both Airbus's dependency on European governments' subsidies, and Boeing/McDonnell Douglas's dependency on indirect U.S. government funds.

As Jean Pierson retired in 1998, Noel Forgeard was selected CEO. Forgeard's most challenging task was reorganizing Airbus structurally, transforming the consortium into a stand-alone limited-liability company. Incorporated in 2001 in France, Airbus had become profitable under Forgeard, generating rates of return on sales of 7% in 2003, and nearly 10% in 2004. Under Forgeard's leadership, Airbus's total revenues jumped from $13 billion to $25 billion between 1998 and 2004. In 2003, for the first time ever, Airbus beat Boeing on total deliveries, and for the fourth time in five years, Airbus booked a larger number of aircraft orders than Boeing.[1]

Despite Airbus's remarkable achievements, Forgeard could not count on the continual prosperity of the company because Airbus faced several new challenges. Partly as a result of a steep rise in fuel prices that lowered airline profitability, and partly as a consequence of repeated threats of terrorist attacks in the skies, the worldwide demand for large commercial jets declined, and a number of major air carriers (customers of both Airbus and Boeing) cancelled previous orders. On the one side, Airbus experienced growing difficulties in selling its new 600-seat A380 "Superjumbo." On the other, Airbus faced a new threat: Boeing had just launched a brand new fuel-efficient aircraft, the 250-seat 787, in an attempt to leapfrog Airbus, yet again.

What should Forgeard do? Should Forgeard follow the strategies implemented by his predecessors in order to consolidate Airbus's competitive position relative to its arch-rival Boeing? Should he, instead, revise some of these policies? Or should he uncover whole new strategies in an attempt to weather the downturn and stay ahead of Boeing?

To assess Forgeard's strategic choices, the case looks back at Airbus's 35-year history.

The Commercial Aircraft Industry

Commercial aircraft manufacturing was an industry of enormous risks where failure was the norm, not the exception. The number of large commercial jet makers had been reduced from four in the early 1980s—Boeing, McDonnell Douglas, Airbus, and Lockheed—to two in late 1990s, turning the industry into a duopoly and pitting the two survivors—Boeing and Airbus—one against the other. One reason why aircraft manufacturers so often failed was the huge cost of product development.

Developing a new jetliner required an upfront investment of several billions of dollars, a lead time of five to six years from launch to first delivery, and the ability to sustain a negative cash flow throughout the development phase. The Boeing 747, for example, cost $1 billion to develop, the Boeing 767 cost $1.5 billion, the Airbus A320 cost $2.5 billion, the Airbus A330/A340 $3.5 billion, the Boeing 777 $5.5 billion, and the total cost of developing the Airbus A380 in the 2000s was estimated at about $15 billion.[2] Typically, to break even on an entirely new jetliner, aircraft manufacturers needed to sell a minimum of 400 planes and at least 50 planes per year.[3] Only a few commercial airplane programs had ever made money.

The price of an aircraft reflected its high development costs. New model prices were based on the average cost of producing 300 to 400 planes, not a single plane. Aircraft pricing embodied the principle of learning by doing, the so-called "learning curve":[4] workers steadily improved their skills during the assembly process, and as a result, labor cost fell as the number of planes produced rose.

The high and increasing cost of product development prompted aircraft manufacturers to utilize subcontracting as a risk-sharing strategy. For the 747, the 767, and the 777, the Boeing Company required subcontractors to share a substantial part of the airplane's development costs. Airbus did the same with its own later models, the A320, A330, A340, and A380. Risk sharing subcontractors performed detailed design

work, manufactured parts and components, and assembled subsections of the new plane, while airframe integrators (i.e., aircraft manufacturers) designed the aircraft, integrated its systems and equipment, assembled the entire plane, marketed it, and provided customer support for 20 to 30 years.[5]

Neither Airbus nor Boeing nor any other postwar commercial aircraft manufacturer produced jet engines. A risky and costly venture, engine building had become a highly specialized business. Aircraft manufacturers worked closely with engine makers—General Electric, Pratt and Whitney, and Rolls Royce—to set engine performance standards. In most cases, new airplanes were offered with a choice of engines. Over time, the technology of engine building had become so complex and demanding that it took longer to develop an engine than an aircraft. During the life of a jetliner, the price of the engines and their replacement parts was equal to the entire price of the airplane.[6]

A new model aircraft was normally designed around an engine, not the other way around. As engine performance improved, airframes were redesigned to exploit the engine's new capabilities. The most practical way to do so was to stretch the fuselage and add more seats in the cabin. Aircraft manufacturers deliberately designed flexibility into the airplane so that future engine improvements could facilitate later stretching. Hence the importance of the "family concept" in aircraft design, and hence the reason why Boeing as well as Airbus introduced families of planes made up of derivative jetliners built around a basic model, not single, standardized models.[7]

The commercial aircraft industry, additionally, gained from technological innovations in two other industries. More than any other manufacturing industry, aircraft construction benefited from advances in material applications and electronics. The development of metallic and non-metallic composite materials played a key role in improving airframe and engine performance. On the one hand, composite materials that combined light weight and great strength were utilized by aircraft manufacturers; on the other, heat-resisting alloys that could tolerate temperatures of up to 3,000 degrees were used by engine makers. Similarly, advances in electronics revolutionized avionics. The increasing use of semiconductors by aircraft manufacturers facilitated the miniaturization of cockpit instruments, and more importantly, it enhanced the use of computers for aircraft communication, navigation, instrumentation, and testing.[8] The use of computers contributed, in addition, to the design, manufacture, and assembly of new model aircraft.

Given the high cost of introducing technological innovations, commercial aircraft makers were unable to survive without government support. In the United States in the past, military contracts were extremely beneficial to commercial aircraft makers, most notably Boeing and McDonnell Douglas, especially insofar as expensive technologies like jet propulsion and swept wings were concerned. Since the mid-1960s, however, U.S. government support to commercial aircraft projects had declined, yet the Department of Defense continued funding research with potential military applications. Similarly, NASA had provided some direct funding to commercial jet makers like Boeing in recent years, but again, only for technology development, not product development. In Europe, the governments of France, Germany, Britain, and Spain furnished most of the working capital required for the development and production of Airbus's early models in the form of low-interest loans the consortium was expected to repay from future sales. Since the early 1990s, nonetheless, European governments' assistance to Airbus had declined.[9]

A final factor that influenced the dynamics of the aircraft industry was airline deregulation. Deregulation of the U.S. airlines in 1978 resulted in a substantial domestic increase in air travel, intense air-fare competition among carriers, the entry of new low-cost, low-capacity airlines into the industry, and the growing utilization of the hub-and-spoke system by the major carriers. The explosion in air travel led to a steep growth in demand for new aircraft of all kinds, yet the proliferation of low-cost, short-haul airline companies (i.e., Southwest Airlines, American West, Jet Blue), combined with the extensive use of hubs by the large carriers, brought about an increased demand for short-range, single-aisle airplanes like the Boeing 737 and the Airbus A320. Additionally, the deregulatory environment shifted the focus of airline competition from performance to cost and from service to price, as Frank Shrontz, Boeing CEO between 1988 and 1996, observed: "In the old days airlines were infatuated with technology for its own sake. Today the rationale for purchasing a new plane is cost savings and profitability."[10]

Outside the United States, international air travel experienced progressive deregulation during the 1980s and 1990s. By the early 2000s, the nations of Western Europe, Australia, and Japan had removed restrictive air travel regulations from their domestic as well as international markets. In 2001, about one-half of all worldwide air travel took place within a competitive deregulated environment, and by 2010 two-thirds of all air travel was expected to take place within a free market environment.[11] Such a trend was likely to encourage foreign (i.e., non-U.S.) air carriers to become more cost-conscious and more profit-oriented in the future. In all travel markets, in short—the U.S. domestic, international, and foreign markets—the economic deregulation of airline travel increased competition among aircraft manufacturers.

The Early History of Airbus

Airbus's early history dates back to the 1960s. Unable to develop a commercially viable passenger jet during the post-war years, French aircraft manufacturers arrived at the conclusion that the only way they could compete effectively against American jet makers was by forming an alliance with other aircraft manufacturers and their governments. Accordingly, during the Paris Air Show of June 1965, French aircraft executives initiated a series of informal meetings between representatives of the major European airline carriers and aircraft makers to discuss the possibilities of building a European short- to medium-range 250- to 300-seat wide-body jet called "airbus." Such a plane, the French officials believed, would meet the particular needs of the expanding European air travel market, and challenge America's global domination in the skies. At the time, American aircraft makers were busy launching three entirely new families of wide-body jets, the Boeing 747, the McDonnell Douglas DC-10, and the Lockheed L1011, and therefore European aircraft makers, led by the French, sought to act quickly to revive Europe's declining commercial aircraft industry before it was too late.[12]

During the next two years, representatives of the major French, British, and German aircraft companies lobbied their governments for financial assistance in support of the Airbus project. In 1967, government officials representing the three European nations signed an agreement approving "[t]he joint development and production of an airbus . . . [f]or the purpose of strengthening European cooperation in the field of aviation technology, and . . . promoting economic and technological progress in Europe." The approved Airbus model was the A300. The project was launched shortly thereafter, but not a single A300 was ordered by any air carrier during 1967, 1968, and 1969. With no orders in sight, the British government was reluctant to keep on investing in the risky venture, and in 1969 announced its decision to withdraw from the project (it rejoined ten years later). The French and German governments went ahead and formalized their partnership in 1970, creating Airbus Industrie—a cooperative partnership (or consortium) registered under French law as a "Grouping of Economic Interests" (GEI). A year later, in 1971, Spanish aircraft manufacturers associated with Construcciones Aeronauticas SA (CASA) joined Airbus Industries as a junior partner. The consortium's ownership shares were now as follows: France's aircraft maker Aerospatiale 47.9%, Germany's aircraft manufacturer Deutsche Airbus 47.9%, and Spain's CASA 4.2%.[13]

Throughout its first five years of operation, Airbus Industrie struggled as total orders fell well below the minimum number set by the partners as a precondition for launching the project. Initially, Air France, Lufthansa, and Iberia—the three national airlines representing the sponsoring governments—were reluctant to purchase the A300, yet, in the end, sustained government pressure persuaded these carriers to place orders (Iberia management, it should be noted, cancelled its early orders a few months later).[14] At the time Bernard Lathiere took the helms of Airbus—February 1975—total orders of the A300 numbered 20 units,[15] total deliveries averaged four aircraft a year,[16] and one contemporary writer concluded: "Airbus appeared to be a typical European airliner—well designed, well built, and a commercial flop."[17]

Infancy: Bernard Lathiere's Airbus, 1975–1985

Lathiere's tenure as Airbus's chief executive began with the crisis of 1975–1977. In 1975—the year referred to by Airbus executives as the consortium's "black year"—Airbus sold just one A300 aircraft while Boeing recorded a total sale of over 100 aircraft. As Airbus's sales came to a standstill, a growing criticism of the high cost of the program in the German Parliament prompted the German government to

intervene directly with Airbus management, and press Lathiere to halt production altogether. Backed by the French government and other French aircraft executives, Lathiere rejected the pressure to stop the line and decided, instead, to cut production from one aircraft to half an aircraft per month, keep the line moving, and wait a little longer for market conditions to improve.[18]

Lathiere's critical decision set Airbus on the road to recovery and success. During the three-year period, 1977–1979, Airbus sales exploded. By the end of 1979, Airbus sold over 250 planes to 32 different airlines, and held a 26% share in the global market for commercial aircraft. In 1981, as in 1979, Airbus sold a larger number of wide-body commercial planes than either Boeing or the McDonnell Douglas Corporation.[19] Airbus's sudden success prompted the British to join the consortium as full members in 1979. Under the new partnership agreement, the recently formed British Aerospace Corporation owned 20% of Airbus, Aerospatiale 37.9%, Deutsche Airbus 37.9%, and CASA 4.2%.[20]

Bringing the British back in, Lathiere moved on to consolidate the foundations under which Airbus would grow and prosper. Working closely with other Airbus executives, Lathiere devised and implemented a series of strategies that touched upon every important function of the company, including manufacturing, marketing, sales, product development, and R&D.

Technological Leadership

"You cannot compete with the dominant player if you don't offer something different," Roger Beteille, one of Airbus's co-founders, had famously said. To persuade the major airlines to switch to a new supplier, Airbus had to differentiate itself from Boeing and other aircraft manufacturers by incorporating the most advanced technologies into its planes. Airbus's technological innovations focused on three areas: materials applications, flight control systems, and aerodynamics. Under Lathiere's direction, Airbus produced the A300 model, developed and produced the A310, and designed the A320 model. On the A310, Airbus introduced a high-performance, aerodynamically efficient wing with a distinct twist at the root. To reduce total aircraft weight, Airbus increased the use of composite materials (particularly carbon fiber) in making the A310 tail surfaces and vertical fins. On the A320, Airbus introduced a computerized system of flight controls. The world's first fly-by-wire commercial aircraft, the A320 was controlled by a pilot transmitting commands to the rudder and flaps electronically, not mechanically. The fly-by-wire technology replaced pulleys, cables, and pedals with electronic signals transmitted by wire, and as such, reduced the A320's empty weight, and at the same time, improved its efficiency in cruise.[21]

Families of Planes

Boeing was the first company to use the family concept in aircraft design. Airbus took the Boeing approach several steps forward and made the concept the foundations of its manufacturing and marketing strategy.

A family of planes was made up of derivative jetliners built around a basic model. Since all derivatives of a given model shared maintenance, training, and operation procedures, as well as replacement parts and components, the use of such derivative airplanes to serve different markets enabled airline carriers to cut costs. Airbus used the family concept in two ways. First, it produced and marketed derivative jetliners with varying seat capacities and travel ranges, all belonging to a single family. Second, Airbus introduced substantial design commonalities across the entire range of its models, not just members of a single family, thus providing airline customers with additional sources of savings. Airbus's aggressive application of the family concept in aircraft design dates back to the 1970s and 1980s. Under the direction of Bernard Lathiere, Airbus introduced shared design commonalities among the A300 and A310 models, on the one hand, and among the A300/A310 and A320 families, on the other.[22]

Decentralized Production

Boeing relied heavily on subcontracting as a risk sharing strategy since at least the early 1950s. Airbus took subcontracting several steps further and made it a cornerstone of its manufacturing strategy.

Boeing built some parts of its own aircraft in the company's assembly plants and subcontracted other parts to outside suppliers. On the 747, for instance, Boeing built the wings and flight deck—as well as sections of the fuselage—and subcontracted the remaining 70% of the assembly work.[23] Airbus Industrie, by contrast, neither owned assembly plants, nor did the consortium produce any aircraft parts at all. On the contrary, the consortium subcontracted the entire assembly of any given model to its four shareholding companies, Aerospatiale, Deutsche Airbus, British Aerospace, and CASA.

During the aircraft's design and development phase, the four Airbus partner companies competed over particular work, and during the production phase, each partner performed its own share of work. Different parts of the aircraft were thus manufactured quite independently of each other, and were brought together for final assembly in Toulouse, France. Typically, on the A300, the British built the wings; the German assembled the front, rear, and (in part) center section of the fuselage; the Spanish produced the tail; and the French constructed the nose, flight deck, and control systems. The French additionally were responsible for the final assembly of the aircraft, a work performed at Aerospatiale's assembly plant in Toulouse. Stationed at Airbus headquarters in Toulouse, and spending much of his time traveling, Bernard Lathiere coordinated the entire program.[24]

Centralized Marketing

Lathiere's most important responsibility, however, was marketing and sales, not production. A former government official turned salesman, and a determined manager who often negotiated aircraft deals personally, Lathiere devised two distinctly different strategies that helped Airbus compete successfully with American aircraft manufacturers. He first targeted large segments of the emerging global markets where airline customers were willing to experiment with Airbus models. He next focused on the mature American market and offered U.S. airline customers exceedingly attractive financial incentives.

To begin with, Lathiere sought to penetrate those markets whose customers showed little loyalty to American aircraft manufacturers. Located in Asia and the Middle East, along the so-called "trans-Asian Silk Route" that ran westward from the Philippines to Europe, these markets were made up of small nationally owned airline carriers whose fleets were fast expanding. The strategic importance of dominating the Asian-Middle Eastern markets was underscored by two widely accepted industry estimates: first, a single aircraft sale was expected to generate further revenues in the form of product support for 18 to 20 years, and second, an initial aircraft sale amounted to only one-fourth to one-third of the value of the follow up orders.[25]

To persuade small neighboring airlines to purchase Airbus planes, Lathiere pointed out that the commonalities shared by Airbus models—the A300 and A310—reduced their operating cost. Such commonalities [Lathiere noted] could help Airbus's customers gain access to each other's spare parts, maintenance services, and crew training programs, and thereby benefit from substantial cost savings. Since no airline wished to become an "orphan" in its region (a carrier flying a particular type of jet not used by other carriers in the region), and since neighboring airlines often influenced each other's aircraft choice, Airbus's early success in the Far East led to subsequent successes all along the Euro-Asian Silk Road.[26]

During the three-year period 1977–1979, Airbus sold the A300/A310 to the national airlines of India, Korea, Malaysia, Indonesia, the Philippines, Singapore, Thailand, Pakistan, and Iran. Airbus sold its models both as replacements to older Boeing jets and as additional planes, practically shutting Boeing out of these markets. Following its successes in the Far East, Airbus moved on to supply the fleets of three Middle Eastern (Kuwait, Lebanon, Saudi Arabia) carriers, but this time Boeing fought back, offering these Middle Eastern airlines its newest aircraft—the wide-body B-767—as an alternative to the A300 and A310 models. "The[re] were three big battles and we won them all," Lathiere recalled.[27] By the early 1980s, the Silk Road network of Airbus customers was completed.

Airbus's successful breakthrough into the American market occurred in 1978. Eastern Airlines, a major U.S. air carrier experiencing financial difficulties, announced that it would buy 23 A300s with an option for 9 more in a deal valued a total of $778 million. Lathiere offered Eastern an unusually attractive financial deal. One element of Lathiere's offer was Airbus's "fly and try" proposal whereby Eastern could fly the aircraft for six months before buying it. Another element pertained to the deal's financial risk. To help Eastern pay for the aircraft, Airbus obtained low-interest loans from private banks and persuaded the French and German governments to guarantee these loans. As it happened, the performance of the A300/A310 in the U.S. skies—the world's busiest travel market—exceeded expectations, and Airbus had gained worldwide recognition.[28]

But Lathiere's breakthrough into the American market led to his eventual downfall. An industry downturn during 1984 left 14 "whitetail" aircraft on Airbus's tarmac at Toulouse, and Lathiere was desperate to sell them. Again, he targeted a struggling carrier—the Pan American World Airways—sending a team of 40 Airbus salespeople to negotiate the deal. Pan Am was already talking to Boeing at the time, but in the end, Airbus won the order. Although the full details of the Airbus-Pan Am $2.5 billion deal were not disclosed, one thing had become clear early on: rather than selling the planes, Airbus leased them to Pan Am, thereby undertaking the main financial risk itself. Pan Am, in turn, kept the entire transaction off the balance sheet, taking hardly any risk at all.[29]

The Pan Am deal evoked a great deal of opposition among Airbus's partner companies to Lathiere's sales strategy. When the German, British, and French partners became aware of the terms of the deal, they demanded Lathiere's resignation. Building planes without receiving orders, and selling planes with no regard to costs, let alone profits, was no longer acceptable to the consortium's partners.[30] Lathiere, consequently, stepped down in April 1985.

Growth: Jean Pierson's Airbus, 1985–1998

Replacing Lathiere in 1985, Jean Pierson led the consortium for 13 years. Pierson paved the way for the future transformation of Airbus from a government-supported partnership to a publicly owned company. An engineer by training and a gifted salesman, Pierson focused on improving Airbus's financial results, cutting costs, increasing sales, phasing out subsidies, and developing new planes. A ruthless executive with a blunt management style, Pierson turned Airbus profitable for the first time in 1995, following two decades of losses that amounted to $8 billion.[31]

Product Development

Under the leadership of Jean Pierson, Airbus embarked on two aircraft programs. First, it planned, designed, produced, and sold the A330/A340 family of planes. Second, it planned the development of the A380 program.

The Airbus A330 was designed to be powered by two engines, carry about 300 passengers in two-aisle configurations, and fly over medium- to long-range routes. A replacement for the aging A300, the A330 competed with the McDonnell Douglas's wide-body three-engine DC-10, and the Boeing's B-767. The A340 was designed to be powered by four engines and fly over "long thin" routes of up to 15,000 kilometers. Airbus's first four-engine aircraft, the A340, was intended to compete with the Boeing 747 over long-range routes where the demand for air travel was not sufficiently heavy to require the seating capacity of the B747.[32]

The design of the A330 and A340 embodied a remarkable degree of commonalities shared by other Airbus models. The A330/A340 fuselage was almost identical to that of the original A300, and the design of the A330/A340 cockpits and interiors followed closely the basic cockpit interior design of all former Airbus wide-body planes. Comparing Boeing's and Airbus's product lines in 1992, one design specialist commented: "Design development at Airbus ha[d] been more linear than at Boeing."[33]

To fill the last remaining gap in the Airbus product line, Pierson sought next to develop a model that could compete with the 747 in the lucrative market for planes carrying 400 or more passengers. Initially, in the early 1990s, Airbus collaborated with Boeing on the production of a "Very Large Commercial Transport," but in 1995, after three years of drawn out talks, the joint project collapsed and Airbus decided to go ahead with its own project. The distinctive characteristic of the A380 was its twin deck configuration, which provided for the accommodation of 600–800 passengers. Such a large aircraft was expected to compete with the 747 "from above," just as the A340 competed with the 747 "from below," squeezing the 747 from both directions in what one writer called a "pincer movement."[34]

Still, the A380 project was exceedingly risky as Hartmut Mehdorn, head of Deutsche Airbus, explained: the A380 "is outside the normal Airbus family. With the traditional step-by-step Airbus approach you have a commonality of anything between 60 to 80% between one plane and the next. But with the Superjumbo you have a commonality close to zero. Airbus has to be very careful."[35]

Sales

In his attempt to increase Airbus's sales, Pierson first focused on the North American market. Under Lathiere's leadership, Airbus's U.S. operations were tightly controlled from Toulouse, Airbus's sales force was made up of Europeans who spoke little English, and Airbus pricing decisions needed to be cleared in writing with the consortium's four partner companies before sales teams were authorized to sign deals. Under Pierson, by contrast, Airbus moved quickly to replace the Europeans with native-born Americans

and to streamline all pricing decisions. The result was a rapid increase in sales. In 1985, Airbus achieved its first sale to American Airlines, following a protracted battle with Boeing that ended up in a split order divided between the two arch rivals. A year later, Airbus sold 100 A320 to Northwest Airlines in a $3.2 billion transaction that pitted the A320 against the B-737. In both cases, Airbus charged competitive prices, selling its planes on the basis of their merit rather than giving them away in extraordinarily attractive financial deals, as had been the case formerly.[36]

Airbus's success in the U.S. was echoed elsewhere. During Pierson's first two years in office, Airbus sold more planes than it had done during Lathiere's entire ten year tenure. The A320 turned out to be Airbus's greatest sales success. In 1986, before the plane had ever gone into service, Airbus recorded nearly 250 orders, and by 1992, 35 airline carriers had ordered the plane, including two of Boeing's most loyal customers, United Airlines and All Nippon Airways. In 1992, after four years in service, the A320 achieved 700 sales, and by the late 1990s, the A320 was outselling its rival, the Boeing 737.[37] By the time Pierson entered his last year in office—Fall 1997—Airbus delivered 725 A320s, recorded a backlog of 750 additional orders,[38] and managed to capture a 33% share in the worldwide market for large commercial jets, as shown in Exhibit 1.

Subsidies

Airbus's growing success in challenging Boeing's dominant position precipitated a long-standing trade dispute between the United States and Europe. The dispute dates back to Airbus's 1978 breakthrough into the American market. The unusual financial agreement signed by Airbus and Eastern Airlines in 1978 prompted Boeing executives to seek Congressional action against Airbus, accusing the consortium of engaging in "predatory financing."[39] In subsequent years, as Pierson succeeded Lathiere, the dispute deepened. During the 1986 multilateral negotiations over the General Agreement of Tariffs and Trades (GATT), the U.S. government filed a complaint against Airbus stating that the consortium's failure to repay its government loans was in violation of the GATT accord.[40] Three years later, the U.S. Department of Commerce commissioned a consulting firm—Gellman Research Associates—to conduct an in-depth study of Airbus's financial history. Delivered to the Commerce Department in

EXHIBIT 1

Jean Pierson's Airbus: Worldwide Market Share of Shipments of Large Commercial Aircraft by Airbus, Boeing, McDonnell Douglas, and Lockheed, 1985–1997

	Airbus	Boeing	McDonnell Douglas	Lockheed
1985	13%	63%	22%	2%
1986*	8%	66%	25%	
1987*	8%	66%	25%	1%
1988	13%	60%	27%	1%
1989	21%	55%	24%	
1990	15%	62%	23%	
1991	22%	56%	2%	
1992	22%	61%	17%	
1993*	25%	60%	14%	
1994	28%	63%	9%	
1995	33%	54%	13%	
1996	32%	55%	13%	
1997	33%	67%		

* Percentages do not add up to 100 because of rounding.

Source: For Boeing, McDonnell Douglas, and Lockheed: *Aerospace Fact and Figures, 1989/1990*, p. 34, *1992/1993*, p. 34, *1997/1998*, p. 34, and the *Boeing Company 1997 Annual Report*, p. 19. For Airbus: "Airbus Orders and Deliveries 1984–2003," a document supplied by Mark Luginbill, Airbus Communication Director, January 13, 2005.

1990, the Gellman Report found that between 1970 and 1989, France, Germany, and Britain had granted Airbus loans totaling $13.5 billion, only $500 million of which had been paid back, and concluded: "No Airbus aircraft program is likely to be commercially viable."[41] Airbus, in response, rebutted the American allegations and issued its own report on federal subsidies paid to Boeing and the McDonnell Douglas Corporation. During the ten year period, 1978–1988 (the Airbus report estimated), the U.S. government granted the two American aircraft makers a total of $23 billion in subsidies, mostly in the form of indirect support delivered through defense contracts.[42]

Notwithstanding these charges and counter-charges, Airbus management eventually decided to reverse course and look for ways to diffuse the conflict. To do so, Pierson invited Boeing Chairman Frank Shrontz to Toulouse to discuss the subsidies issue. As Shrontz arrived in France in September 1990, Pierson offered him a deal: Airbus was willing to accept limits on government subsidies if the U.S.

government would agree to limit its indirect subsidies to American aircraft makers. Realizing that Boeing could no longer stop Airbus, only slow it down, Shrontz accepted the blue-prints of Pierson's offer, and went ahead to lobby the U.S. government to settle the dispute. The result was the 1992 "Airbus Accord"—a bilateral agreement signed by representatives of the European Commission and the U.S. government. The accord limited all direct subsidies to 33% of the developing costs of a given aircraft model, and all indirect subsidies to 4% of the total sales of a given aircraft manufacturing company.[43]

The historic accord helped Pierson achieve two goals. First, Airbus's right to receive direct subsidies for its aircraft programs—albeit limited—was now legitimized and recognized by the U.S. government, the Boeing Company, and the McDonnell Douglas Corporation. Second, Airbus's American rivals, as well as the U.S. government, had now acknowledged that the American aircraft industry benefited from indirect subsidies and were willing to subject such subsidies to restrictions imposed by an international treaty.

Cost Cutting

The signing of the bilateral agreement of 1992 co-incided with both the recession of the early 1990s and the decline in the value of the dollar (relative to European currencies and the yen). Partly as a result of the recession which intensified competition among aircraft makers, partly as a result of the weakening of the dollar which made European exports (shipped by Airbus) more expensive on the global markets, and also as a consequence of the bilateral agreement which limited the consortium's dependency on direct government subsidies, Airbus sought to reduce costs through deep cuts in jobs, the streamlining of the production process, and the speed up of deliveries. To achieve these goals, each of the consortium's partner companies implemented cost-cutting programs. In Britain, some 150 British Aerospace executives met in a conference in Spring 1993 to seek ways to gain substantial increases in productivity. Subsequent to the conference, British Aerospace cut its wing production time by 50% in two years while trimming its workforce from 15,000 to 7,000 in five years. In Germany, Daimler-Benz Airbus (formerly Deutsche Airbus, later Daimler Aerospace) reduced its fuselage production cost by 33%, fuselage production time by 50%, and workforce from 22,000 to 14,000 in six years (1992–1998). And in France, state-owned Aerospatiale (which produced cockpits and assembled aircraft models) cut its workforce by 17% between 1993 and 1996. Together, these efforts enabled Airbus to reduce its "lead time" between order and delivery from 15 to 9 months for single-aisle planes, and from 18 to 12 months for wide-body jets. Speeding up its deliveries, Airbus managed to slash costly inventories by 30%.[44]

Airbus's cost-cutting measures under Pierson stand in a stark contrast to Boeing's growing inefficiencies under Shrontz and his successor, Philip Condit. Nowhere was the contrast between the two manufacturing systems more conspicuous than on the shop floor. At Boeing's assembly plants in Seattle, a large number of workers with hand tools moved in and around the aircraft as they assembled them, one unit at a time. At Airbus's Toulouse plants, by contrast, a small number of employees worked simultaneously on four or five planes operating giant machines that fitted together cockpits, fuselages, and wings.[45] "The factory doesn't look or feel like an engineering plant," Stephen Aris, Airbus's historian

observed. "There is little noise, no waste, and what few people there are on the factory floor are working mainly as machine tenders and supervisors rather than as operatives. The atmosphere is purposeful, yet surprisingly relaxed."[46]

Comparative figures bear out these differences. In 1998, Boeing used 20-30 percent more labor hours to produce a jetliner that it had done in 1994.[47] One source of Boeing's troubles was its 1997 acquisition of the McDonnell Douglas Corporation. While Airbus had already adopted a flexible, lean-production manufacturing system by the mid-1990s, the combined Boeing-McDonnell Douglas Corporation was still utilizing a standardized, mass production system that had barely changed since WWII. Hence the gap in productivity between the "new" Boeing and Airbus. In 1998, the year Pierson stepped down, Airbus employed 143 workers for every commercial aircraft produced (230 jets made by 33,000 workers), and Boeing 211 workers (560 jets manufactured by 119,000 employees)—a productivity gap of 48% in favor of Airbus.[48]

Maturity: Noel Forgeard's Airbus, 1998–2005

Despite Pierson's impressive achievements, the transformation of Airbus was far from over. In 1998, Airbus Industrie still functioned as a GEI (groupement d'interet economique), a cooperative partnership organized for the purpose of pooling resources together for a common goal. Airbus Industrie was essentially a marketing and sales organization with a few other product-related functions such as coordinating aircraft design and development, conducting test flights, obtaining aircraft certification, and advertising. All other functions, especially those related to the financing and manufacturing of the aircraft, were the responsibility of the partner companies. Registered under French law as a GEI, Airbus neither paid taxes, nor published financial accounts, nor owned any assets (apart from an office building in Toulouse). On the other hand, Airbus's partner companies were each responsible for their own cost and profit accounting. Each partner, however, did not always distinguish in its balance sheet between Airbus and non-Airbus operations, and therefore it had become exceedingly difficult to obtain an accurate picture of Airbus's overall financial results.[49]

Airbus partner companies had planned all along to turn the consortium into a "single corporate entity," but not until 1997 did the partners begin conducting serious discussions on the issue. To carry out the reorganization, Airbus's Board of Directors selected Noel Forgeard to succeed Pierson.

Replacing Pierson in early 1998, Forgeard had a clear view of his central mission: "I joined Airbus to turn it into a company." "Otherwise, I would [have] never" taken the job. "The top priority of the GEI was . . . sales and I am . . . not a salesman. I am a manager."[50]

Forgeard's leadership style stood in a marked contrast to Pierson's. An imposing man known among Airbus's employees as the "Pyrenees Bear," Pierson was a hard-line executive, combative, abrasive, and explosive. Forgeard was a consensus builder. A soft spoken executive, Forgeard worked for the French defense conglomerates the Lagardere Group for 11 years before joining Airbus in 1998. Famous for his managerial, political, as well as diplomatic skills, Forgeard specialized in building and running joint ventures between European and American defense companies. "He appears low-key, but he can be very tough, and when he has set a goal, nothing can distract him from it," a Lagardere colleague described Forgeard, adding, "He has an impressive ability to set priorities, to focus on his goals, and [to] set up a very strong team to achieve these goals."[51]

Restructuring Airbus Ownership

The key to turning Airbus Industrie into a stand-alone corporation was a cross-border merger between three of the consortium's four partner companies. In the past, the consortium partners refused to share information about their Airbus business, let alone engage in merger discussions. Using his keen political sensibilities to allocate Airbus projects, Forgeard was careful to treat all partner companies equally, diffuse nationally-based rivalries, and encourage the partners to hold serious merger talks.[52] The initial move towards merger was undertaken by Airbus's two large partners, state-owned Aerospatiale and Daimler Aerospace. To begin with, the French government privatized Aerospatiale in 1998, selling the company's largest block of private shares to the Lagardere Group. Next, Daimler Aerospace merged with Aerospatiale in July 1999 to form the European Aerospace Defense and Space Company (EADS), Europe's largest defense and space firm. Six months later, Airbus's Spanish partner, CASA, was acquired by EADS. In the meantime, British Aerospace (BAE) sought to negotiate a partnership agreement with EADS, after it had rejected an EADS' invitation to begin merger talks (wishing to maintain its ties to the American defense establishment, BAE was reluctant to jeopardize its independent status). Following another six months of difficult negotiations, in June 2000, BAE and EADS finally reached an agreement: the two companies would own together all the stocks issued by the newly formed "Airbus Integrated Company" (AIC). Under the new partnership agreement, EADS owned 80% of Airbus Integrated Company and BAE owned 20%, an arrangement which mirrored BAE's 20% share in Airbus Industrie. Following the birth of AIC, Forgeard continued running Airbus, and in addition, served as a director on EADS's board.[53]

Airbus's reorganization into a limited liability company benefited the new company in several ways. The first and most obvious advantage of reorganization was cost savings, and such savings were achieved, above all, in materials' purchasing. Consider the following example. Formerly, each of the consortium's partners—the French, German, British, and Spanish—bought its own supply of aluminum separately, and together, the four partners spent about 12 billion Euros a year on purchasing aluminum. Following reorganization, Airbus's central office bought the entire aluminum supply consumed by the firm annually at a 10% discount, saving the European aircraft maker 1.2 billion Euros a year, according to Forgeard's estimate.[54]

Another benefit of Airbus's reorganization was the speed up of the decision making process. In the past, the consortium's four partner companies needed to reach a consensus on all major decisions. Once Airbus had become an integrated company, such a consensus was no longer needed, and as a result, disagreements were settled much faster. A disagreement over the construction of the A380's wing box is a case in point. Under the GEI structure, Airbus's partners spent months discussing the question of whether the Superjumbo's wing box should be made of metal or carbon fiber. Under the AIC structure, the issue was settled in weeks.[55]

Lastly, the restructuring of Airbus as an integrated company resulted in a leaner, more flexible organization where the lines of communication were shortened, functional units were consolidated, and redundant positions were eliminated. Airbus Industrie, for example, employed four technical directors on an on-going basis. Airbus Integrated Company, by contrast, employed only one.[56]

Diversification into Defense Products

The restructuring of Airbus offered Forgeard an opportunity. Because the commercial aircraft industry was subject to deep cyclical movements of booms and busts, and because the demand for defense products was relatively stable, military sales were likely to soften the impact of periodic slumps in commercial revenues and thus benefit Airbus and its parent company EADS. Under Forgeard's leadership, accordingly, Airbus diversified its product line to manufacture military jetliners. In May 2003, Airbus won a $23 billion contract to build military transport aircraft for the armed forces of seven European nations. The European governments considered bids from both Boeing and Airbus, and selected the Airbus A400M (a modified commercial jet) over the Boeing C-17, the standard transport jetliner used by the U.S. military. In 2004, Airbus beat Boeing again, winning a $24 billion 27-year contract to supply Britain's Royal Air Force (RAF) with fueling services, including a "filling station in the sky" anywhere in the world. The British government selected a tanker modeled on the Airbus A330 over a modified version of the Boeing B-767 because the A330 was newer than the B-767, had a larger payload, and flew over a longer range.[57]

More lucrative than these two deals was a pending contract offered by the U.S. Department of Defense. The U.S. Air Force planned to replace its giant fleet of aging tanker planes (some of which were 40 years old) beginning in 2010, and Forgeard was taking all necessary steps to prepare an Airbus bid acceptable to the Pentagon. To start, Airbus invested $90 million in redesigning its A330 passenger model according to the Pentagon's specification for tanker planes. Next, Airbus planned to use American-made parts and components for at least 50% of the content of the tanker. Additionally, Forgeard made plans to open an Airbus assembly plan in the United States either to build new A330 tanker planes or to convert old passenger aircraft to military tankers. And lastly, to improve its prospects of winning the Pentagon contract, Airbus sought a partnership agreement with a major American defense company. Under a typical agreement, Airbus would supply the aircraft, and the American partner would provide equipment such as electronics, and structural components such

as landing gears. To do so, Airbus held talks with both Lockheed and Northrop Grumman, two of the U.S.'s largest defense contractors.[58]

Airbus was likely to be awarded a share in the Pentagon contract because the U.S. Air Force could not afford relying on a single aircraft type manufactured by a single company. Such a choice was far too risky: technical problems associated with a single model could lead to the grounding of the entire fleet. Instead, to spread the risk among several different models, the U.S. government needed to divide the contract among competing manufacturers, as it had done in the past. The fleet currently in service (2005) was made up of about 500 Boeing, McDonnell Douglas, and Lockheed civilian planes. Since neither Lockheed nor McDonnell manufactured civilian planes any longer, the sole alternative to a Boeing tanker plane was an Airbus one.[59]

Furthermore, Airbus prospects of competing with Boeing improved as a result of a recent delay in the Pentagon plan to open the tanker contract to competition. Boeing planned to use the B-767 model as its proposed tanker plane, but the 767's production costs were rising. By summer 2005, commercial orders of the B-767 fell to such a low point that keeping the B-767 assembly line open was no longer economical, and Boeing needed to consider shutting down the line altogether. Announced in February 2005, the Pentagon's delay in holding competition over the contract—which could have lasted several years—thus placed Boeing in a competitive disadvantage: re-starting the assembly line in the future was bound to be expensive and add to the cost of manufacturing the B-767 tanker. Airbus, in contrast, had a substantial backlog of A330 commercial orders, and therefore did not anticipate any disruptions in the future production of the A330.[60]

Finally, EADS, Airbus's parent company, benefited from combining commercial and military sales as well. Following Airbus reorganization, EADS's revenue structure had changed to resemble that of Boeing. Just as Boeing's 1997 acquisition of the McDonnell Douglas Corporation—a major defense contractor— helped the Seattle company improve its performance during slumps in the commercial aircraft market, so did Airbus's 2001 incorporation as a subsidiary of EADS help EADS take advantage of the swings in the commercial aerospace business cycle. And just as Boeing derived 60% of its 2001 revenues from commercial aircraft sales, and 40% from the sale of defense, space and communication systems, so did EADS generate 65% of its 2002 revenues from commercial airplanes sales and 35% from the sale of defense, space, and aeronautics products and services.[61]

Globalization

The commercial [aircraft] industry "is now totally subject to the forces of globalization," an EADS executive said in 2004,[62] and indeed, by the mid-2000s, both Airbus and Boeing had become highly dependent on the global supply chain. Both aircraft makers sought to outsource the manufacture of aircraft parts, components, and subassemblies to risk sharing partners in strategic markets, a practice aimed at reducing production costs and increasing aircraft sales. Using global outsourcing as a marketing tool, Airbus focused on three strategic markets: the U.S., Japan, and China.

Under Forgeard's leadership, Airbus signed large outsourcing contracts with major U.S. suppliers, sold hundreds of jets to U.S. airline carriers, and won political friends in Washington, both among members of Congress and government officials. Between 1994 and 2004, Airbus's spending in the United States nearly doubled from $2.6 to $5 billion, as major suppliers performed extensive work on Airbus's late models. On the A380, for example, Airbus purchased engines from the General Electric Corporation, hydraulic systems from the Eaton Corporation, avionics from Honeywell, navigation equipment from Northrop Grumman, and landing gears as well as evacuation systems from the Goodrich Corporation. Altogether, the value of American-made products used in each A380 jetliner approached 45% of the plane's total cost. Airbus's heavy reliance on U.S. suppliers, Forgeard believed, was likely to help the company sell its Superjumbo in the United States as a future replacement for the Boeing 747.[63]

Similarly, Airbus signed outsourcing contracts with large Japanese suppliers in an attempt to increase its share in Japan's market for new commercial jets. In 2002, Japan's top carriers—Japan Airlines (JAL) and All Nippon Airways (ANA)—flew mostly Boeing-made jets, and Boeing held an 80% share in the market for Japanese commercial jets. Because JAL was the world's largest operator of the Boeing 747, Forgeard expected the A380 to sell well in Japan, hoping to increase Airbus's share in Japan's aircraft market from 20% to 50% in 20 years (2002–2022). To encourage JAL and ANA to purchase the Superjumbo,

Airbus contracted seven Japanese large firms—Mitsubishi Heavy Industries, Fuji Heavy Industries, Sumitomo Metal Industries, Japan Aircraft Manufacturing Corporation, and others—to supply the A380 in a deal valued at $1.5 billion in 2002.[64]

Airbus, in addition, explored outsourcing opportunities in China. In 2004, Airbus held a 25% share in the market for Chinese commercial jets—against Boeing's 72%—and in subsequent years, the European aircraft maker planned to increase its market share to 50%. Seeking to lower its labor cost as well as increase its share in China's market for commercial jets, Airbus invited two Chinese state-owned aerospace companies to participate in building its newest aircraft—the midsized long-range A350 model—awarding them in 2005 a 5% risk-sharing role in producing the new plane.[65]

Marketing and Sales

During Forgeard's seven-year tenure, Boeing continued losing ground to its European rival. While the Airbus A330/A340 series competed favorably with both the Boeing 777 and the Boeing 747, strong sales of the A320 (Exhibit 2) helped Airbus capture the industry's top spot and achieve a 53% share in the global market for large commercial jets, as shown in Exhibit 3.

Airbus's success in selling the A320 was evident among the major air carriers as well as the new discount airlines. Initially, the low-cost carriers had all followed Southwest Airlines's practice of operating an all Boeing 737 fleet, but in 2000, New York-based Jet Blue Airways had become the first budget carrier to

---

EXHIBIT 2

Total Number of Commercial Aircraft Ordered and Delivered by Airbus, 1970–Dec. 31, 2004

	Orders	Deliveries
A300/A310	851	792
A320	3,371	2,342
A330/A340	891	618
A380	139	
Total	**5,252**	**3,752**

Source: "Orders and Deliveries," Airbus.com, retrieved from Web February 1, 2005.

EXHIBIT 3

Noel Forgeard's Airbus (1998–2004): Worldwide Market Share of Shipments of Large Commercial Aircraft

	1998	1999	2000	2001	2002	2003	2004
Boeing	71%	68%	61%	62%	56%	48%	47%
Airbus	29%	32%	39%	38%	44%	52%	53%

Sources: "Commercial Airplanes: Orders and Deliveries," Boeing.com, retrieved from Web February 2, 2001, and January 15, 2005; "Airbus Orders and Deliveries 1984–December 30, 2003," a document supplied by Mark Luginbill, Airbus Communication Director, January 2005, in conjunction with Kevin Done, "The Big Gamble: Airbus Rolls Out Its New Weapon," *Financial Times*, January 17, 2005.

fly an all A320 fleet, selecting the Airbus model as its standard transport. Next, in 2002, Airbus scored a victory over Boeing when it sold 120 planes to Britain's Easy Jet, a discount carrier flying B-737s only, and in 2004, Airbus managed to persuade two other low-cost air carriers—Air Berlin, Germany's second largest airline, and AirAsia, Malaysia's principal discount carrier—to switch from the B-737 to the A320 in deals valued at $7 and $5 billion respectively.[66]

Airbus's success with a growing number of Boeing customers was rooted in its decentralized sales strategy. The European aircraft maker empowered its sales team to make pricing decisions on the spot and sign deals without having to seek approval from its corporate office at Toulouse. As such, Airbus's sales team developed, in turn, close relationships with its customer airlines. At Boeing, by contrast, the final pricing decisions were all made by a committee at the headquarters and therefore the sales process was slow and deals were more difficult to negotiate. As a result, the Chicago aircraft maker lost many of its loyal customers. The Air Berlin and AirAsia sales are two instructive examples. In each case, Boeing sales representatives on the ground had no real authority to match Airbus's lower prices, conclude the deal, and sign the contract. Speaking of the Air Berlin sale of 2004, one insider recalled: "The general sentiment [at] the [Boeing] committee was: 'They'll never switch to Airbus, so why go so far'" and accept the lower prices proposed by the sales team?[67]

Financial Performance

Airbus's sales success contributed favorably to its financial performance. As a consortium, Airbus had published no financial reports, and as a company that owned 80% of Airbus, EADS had published financial data pertaining to Airbus's operating income (earnings before taxes and interests) only, not net income. Using several reliable sources, in conjunction with EADS's financial reports, it is nevertheless possible to arrive at a close estimate of Airbus's rates of return on sales (operating income as percentage of revenues) during the seven-year period ending December 31, 2004.

Throughout Forgeard's tenure, Airbus rate of return on sales exceeded that of Boeing for every year except 1998. "From the first day I put my foot in Airbus, I was obsessed with preparing for a downturn,"[68] Forgeard said in 2002, and as shown in Exhibit 4, nowhere was Airbus's performance more impressive than during the recession that followed the terrorist attack of September 11, 2001. Between 2001 and 2004, Airbus revenues *grew* by 37% and its annual rate of return on sales averaged nearly 8%. During the same period, Boeing's revenues (Exhibit 4) declined by 10% and its rate of return on sales averaged 4.4%. Airbus's growth in sales and profits was the result of two developments: rigorous cost-cutting measures undertaken by Forgeard, and substantial cost savings generated by Airbus's transformation from a consortium to an integrated company. Hence the contrast between Airbus's and Boeing's performance: in 2004, Boeing continued to underperform and to remain narrowly profitable while Airbus came close to achieving Forgeard's target of a 10% operating margin, as shown in Exhibit 4.[69]

Future Prospects

Forgeard was expected to leave Airbus in the summer of 2005 and assume the leadership of its parent company, the European Aerospace Defense and Space Company. As Forgeard was preparing to take charge of EADS, Airbus faced two serious challenges that

EXHIBIT 4

Noel Forgeard's Airbus (1998–2004): Highlight of Financial Data,
Airbus versus Boeing

	Airbus		Boeing	
	Sales (bil.)	Operating Income as % of Sales	Sales (bil.)	Operating Income as % of sales
1998	$13.3	—	$56.2	2.8%
1999	$16.8	5.8%	$58.0	5.5%
2000	$17.2	7.3%	$51.3	6.0%
2001	$18.2	8.1%	$58.0	6.2%
2002	$20.3	7.0%	$53.8	6.4%
2003	$23.8	7.1%	$50.3	0.8%
2004	$25.0	9.5%	$52.5	3.8%

Sources: Airbus's revenues 1998–2002 in "Airbus S.A.S.," *Hoover Handbook of World Business*, 2004, p. 30. Airbus's revenues and operating profits 2003–2004 in EADS N.V. "Year 2003 Report," p. 7, and "Year 2004 Report," p. 7 , online, EADS.com, and in Daniel Michaels "Airbus Could Top Boeing in Sales," *Wall Street Journal*, January 13, 2005. Airbus's operating profits for 2002 in EADS "Year 2003 Report," p. 7; for 2001, in "EADS Delivers Solid Performance," *Business Wire*, March 10, 2003; for 2000, in Kevin Done, "EADS Forecasts 15% Rise in Profits," *Financial Times*, March 20, 2001; for 1999, in Stephen Dunphy, "The Seattle Times Business Newsletter Column," *Seattle Times*, June 28, 2000; and for 1998 in "Price War with Boeing Pushed Airbus into Red Ink Last Year," *Seattle Times*, February 29, 1999. For Boeing: *The Boeing Company 2001 Annual Report*, p. 1, and *The Boeing Company 2004 Annual Report*, p. 1.

could have severely undermined its position in the industry: first, the future prospects of the A380 gamble were uncertain, and second, a new model aircraft introduced by Boeing, the B-787 "Dreamliner," threatened Airbus's competitiveness in the market for midsized jets. Related to the introduction of both the A380 and the B-787 was the U.S. government's resolve to nullify the 1992 "Airbus Accord," and launch, once again, a trade war against the European aircraft maker.

In its 2004 Global Market Forecast, Airbus predicted sales of 1,650 A380 jets over a 20-year period. Boeing disputed this forecast and predicted that over the next two decades the market for very large commercial aircraft (larger than the 747) would not exceed 400 units.[70]

Boeing's analysis was based on the changing structure of the airline industry during the last two decades of the 20th century. Deregulation fragmented the domestic (U.S.) as well as the global air travel markets [Boeing's analysis pointed out], and thereby encouraged air carriers to replace large aircraft with smaller ones. "We believe more passengers are going to fly on direct routes on mid-size airplanes instead of to hubs on giant size airplanes," Boeing CEO Philip Condit said in 2003, and in fact, during the ten-year period 1990–2000, the number of transatlantic flights aboard Boeing 747 aircraft slightly declined while transatlantic flights aboard smaller wide-body jets like the A340 and B-777 almost tripled.[71]

A related source of concern was the plane's travel range. In the 1970s, the key to the 747's success was its giant wings and fuel tanks that gave the 747 the capability to fly farther than any commercial jet. The A380, in contrast, was not expected to fly farther than most wide-body models in service, and as a result, was likely to face stiff competition in the longhaul travel market from the B-777, B-787, A340, and A350 aircraft.[72]

Another potential risk for Airbus was the A380's cost overrun. By January 2005, the A380's development costs exceeded its projected costs by more than $4 billion, pushing the A380's breakeven point farther into the future. Initially, Airbus expected to recover the A380's development costs after selling 250 planes, but as the plane's costs climbed, the European aircraft maker acknowledged that at least 270 sales were now needed to recover its initial investment and break even. One reason why the A380 costs climbed so steeply was the decline in the value of the dollar against the Euro. In the five-year period ending January 2005, the dollar lost about 30% of its value relative to the Euro, a development that turned the A380 project far more expensive in dollar terms ($15 billion) than in Euro terms (12 billion).[73]

Still another obstacle facing Airbus was the growing difficulties the company experienced in selling the A380. By January 1, 2005, the European aircraft maker booked 139 A380 orders, yet the number of new orders recorded during the first six months of 2005—a total of 15—remained well below Airbus's expectations.[74] Moreover, neither Japan's air carriers—the world's leading users of large jets—nor any of the U.S. based airline carriers had yet ordered a single A380.

Regardless of the prospects of the A380, Boeing's introduction of the B-787 jetliner placed Airbus under increased competitive pressures. Scheduled to enter service in 2008, the Boeing 787 was a midsized 200-300 seat aircraft designed to fly over long distances of up to 9,200 nautical miles. Based on its travel market fragmentation theory, the Boeing Company expected the B-787 to compete successfully against both the A330/A340 and A380 jetliners. The first commercial aircraft built primarily of carbon fiber (composite materials that are lighter and more flexible than aluminum), the B-787 was expected to cut the costs of fuel consumption by 20%, and the costs of maintenance by up to 33%, compared to similar size jets.[75]

Boeing's decision to develop the "Dreamliner," however, was soon challenged by Airbus. Less than a year after Boeing announced the introduction of the B-787, in the summer of 2004, Airbus announced its own plans to develop a new midsized jet, the A350. Intended to compete against the B-787, the A350 was a modified version of the A330 aircraft, not a newly designed aircraft.

The B-787 had several advantages over the A350. The B-787 was more fuel efficient than the A350, was equipped with a more comfortable cabin, and flew over a longer range. The A350's basic design was 15 years old. Moreover, the new Airbus plane was not expected to enter service until 2010, two years after the introduction of the B-787. Furthermore, the A330 was still very popular among the airline carriers, and as such, was likely be "cannibalized" by the A350. Lastly, Airbus was unable to finance the A350 from its own

cash flow and needed to obtain European Government loans to support the project, as had been the case formerly with its A380 project.[76]

But the Boeing Company now vehemently opposed any government loans to Airbus. Because Airbus had already received billions of dollars in loans under the provisions of the 1992 bilateral agreement, Boeing executives contended, Airbus no longer needed any financial help, especially since it had captured the industry's top spot, passing Boeing in total deliveries in 2003, 2004, and 2005 (projected). Accordingly, the Boeing Company lobbied the U.S. government to reject the Airbus Accord of 1992 and bring charges against Airbus before the World Trade Organization.[77]

By June 2005, it had become clear that Airbus was losing its competitive edge. Sales of the A380 came to a halt with only 154 orders received, sales of the A350 did not move at all with just one customer placing ten orders, and the trade dispute with Boeing was hurting Airbus's sales, as Airbus chief commercial officer acknowledged. At Boeing, by contrast, sales of the B-787 were booming with a total number of 237 orders received from several large carriers including Northwest Airlines (Airbus's largest American customer), Korea Airlines (a major Airbus customer), Air India, and Air Canada.[78]

Suddenly, as Noel Forgeard was preparing to step up and assume EADS's leadership, Airbus faced tough strategic choices.

ENDNOTES

1. See Exhibits 3 and 4, and "The Boeing Beater," *The Economist,* January 17, 2004.
2. David C. Mowery and Nathan Rosenberg, *Technology and the Pursuit of Economic Growth* (New York: Cambridge University Press, 1989), pp. 172–173. For the A320, see Eric Vayle, "Collision Course in Commercial Aircraft: Boeing—Airbus—McDonnell Douglas, 1991 (A)," Harvard Business School, Case No. 9-391-106, October 1993, p. 3; for the A330/A340: Stanley Holmes, "Airbus Constructing Profitable Planes," *Europe,* March 1999 (online, ABI data base, Start Page 19); for the Boeing 777: Eugene Rodgers, *Flying High: The Story of Boeing* (New York: Atlantic Monthly Press, 1996), p. 431; and for the A380: J. Lynn Lunsford and Daniel Michaels, "New Friction Puts Airbus, Boeing, On Course for Fresh Trade Battle," *Wall Street Journal,* June 1, 2004, and "Taking Off In Toulouse" *The Economist,* April 30, 2005, p. 58.
3. Michael Dertouzos, Richard Lester, and Robert Solow, *Made in America: Regaining the Productive Edge* (New York: Harper Perennial, 1990), p. 203.
4. John Newhouse, *The Sporty Game* (New York: Alfred Knopf, 1982), p. 21, but see also pp. 10–20.
5. David C. Mowery and Nathan Rosenberg, "The Commercial Aircraft Industry," in Richard R. Nelson, ed., *Government and Technological Progress: A Cross Industry Analysis* (New York: Pergamon

Press, 1982), p. 116; Dertouzos et al., *Made in America*, p. 200; Paul Turk, "Aerospace: The Subsidy Question," *Europe*, May 1993 (online ABI data base, Start Page 6), and *Wall Street Journal*, June 1, 2004.

6. Dertouzos, et al., *Made in America*, p. 203.

7. Newhouse, *Sporty Game*, p. 188. Mowery and Rosenberg, "The Commercial Aircraft Industry," pp. 124–125.

8. Mowery and Rosenberg, "The Commercial Aircraft Industry," pp. 102–103, 126–128.

9. Dertouzos, et al., *Made in America*, pp. 206, 214.

10. Quoted in Janet Simpson, Lee Field, and David Garvin, "The Boeing 767: From Concept to Production," Harvard Business School, Case No. 9-688-040, April 1991, p. 6.

11. *The Boeing Company 2001 Annual Report*, p. 53.

12. "Airbus Industrie: 25 Flying Years," a *Flight International* Supplement (reprinted by Airbus Industrie, 1997, p. 7).

13. "Airbus Industrie: 25 Flying Years," pp. 8–9.

14. "Airbus 25 Years Old," *Le Figaro* magazine, October 1997 (reprinted in English translation by Airbus Industrie), p. 3; "Airbus Industrie: 25 Flying Years," p. 8.

15. Stephens Aris, *Close to the Sun: How Airbus Challenged America's Domination of the Skies* (London: Aurum Press, 2002), p. 81.

16. "Airbus 25 Years Old," p. 3.

17. Newhouse, *Sporty Game*, p. 28.

18. Ian McIntyre, *Dogfight: The Transatlantic Battle over Airbus* (Westport, Conn.: Praeger, 1992), p. 42; Aris, *Close to the Sun*, pp. 84–86.

19. Matthew Lynn, *Birds of Prey: Boeing vs. Airbus* (New York: Four Walls Eight Windows, 1995), p. 154; Newhouse, *Sporty Game*, p. 30.

20. "Airbus Industrie: 25 Flying Years," p. 11. The British decision, it should be noted, was an outcome of a protracted battle between Boeing and Airbus. While Airbus made concerted efforts to persuade British Aerospace to join the consortium, Boeing sought to establish a close alliance with British Aerospace in opposition to Airbus. Significantly, British Aerospace's decision to become a shareholder in Airbus was heavily influenced by the willingness of the British government to help subsidize the Airbus program. Aris, *Close to the Sun*, pp. 104–105.

21. "Airbus Industrie: 25 Flying Years," pp. 13, 14, 17. The quotation is on page 13. Dertouzos, et al., *Made in America*, pp. 212–213; Aris, *Close to the Sun*, p. 129; Lynn, *Birds of Prey*, p. 63.

22. Dertouzos, et al., *Made in America*, p. 212.

23. Mowery and Rosenberg, "The Commercial Aircraft Industry," p. 116; Aris, *Close to the Sun*, p. 57.

24. Aris, *Close to the Sun*, pp. 56–57.

25. Steve McGuire, *Airbus Industrie: Conflict and Cooperation in US-EC Trade Relations* (London: MacMillan, 1997), pp. 44–45; Newhouse, *Sporty Games*, p. 42.

26. Newhouse, *Sporty Games*, p. 38; McIntyre, *Dogfight*, p. 83; Lynn, *Birds of Prey*, p. 155.

27. Newhouse, *Sporty Games*, pp. 30–31, 38; but see also Lynn, *Birds of Prey*, pp. 155–156.

28. McGuire, *Airbus Industrie*, pp. 52–53; Lynn, *Birds of Prey*, pp. 120–121; Aris, *Close to the Sun*, pp. 100–102.

29. Lynn, *Birds of Prey*, pp. 165–166; Aris, *Close to the Sun*, pp. 134–135; Rodgers, *Flying High*, pp. 345, 351.

30. Aris, *Close to the Sun*, p. 136; Aris, *Close to the Sun*, p. 166.

31. According to a Lehman Brothers report cited in Gail Endmondson, "A Wake Up Call on the Continent," *Business Week*, December 30, 1996, p. 40.

32. McIntyre, *Dogfight*, p. xxi; Frank Spadars, "A Transatlantic Perspective," *Design Quarterly*, Winter 1992, pp. 22–23; McGuire, *Airbus Industrie*, pp. 115–116.

33. McGuire, *Airbus Industrie*, pp. 22–23.

34. Lynn, *Birds of Prey*, chapter 9; Aris, *Close to the Sun*, pp. 173–182.

35. Quoted in Aris, *Close to the Sun*, p. 182.

36. Lynn, *Birds of Prey*, pp. 169–170; see also Aris, *Close to the Sun*, pp. 139–140.

37. Northwest Airlines discovered early on that the A320's operating costs were lower than the B-737's, while United Airlines conducted a survey among its passengers and found that the travelling public preferred the A320 family over the B-737 family. McGuire, *Airbus Industrie*, pp. 99–100; Lynn, *Birds of Prey*, pp. 168–169; Frederic Biddle and John Helyar, "Flying Low: Behind Boeing Woes," *Wall Street Journal*, April 24, 1998.

38. *Hoover's Handbook of American Business, 1998* (Austin: Hoover's Business Press, 1998), p. 67.

39. Subsequently, a U.S. House of Representatives committee called for a subcommittee hearing on what one committee member described as "unfair trade practices" committed by Airbus, and "excessive export subsidies" received by the consortium. Airbus executives, in turn, defended the Eastern deal, pointing out that nearly a quarter of the value of the A300 was made up of parts and components manufactured in the United States. Aris, *Close to the Sun*, p. 103; McGuire, *Airbus Industrie*, p. 53.

40. Speaking for Airbus, Pierson countered that the American aircraft industry had been a long-standing recipient of indirect federal aid, and that Boeing in particular benefited from both U.S. military contracts and National Aeronautics Space Administration's R&D funding. Pierson estimated that federal spending on aerospace products and services in the Untied States exceeded $4 billion in 1984 alone. McGuire, *Airbus Industrie*, pp. 118–124.

41. Cited in Lynn, *Birds of Prey*, pp. 189–190; but see also Turk, "Aerospace: The Subsidy Question," Start Page 6.

42. Lynn, *Birds of Prey*, p. 191.

43. Aris, *Close to the Sun*, pp. 169–170; McGuire, *Airbus Industrie*, chapter 7; Lynn, *Birds of Prey*, pp. 200–201; Turk, "Aerospace: The Subsidy Question," Start Page 6.

44. Charles Goldsmith, "Re-Engineering: After Trailing Boeing for Years Airbus Aims for 50% of the Market," *Wall Street Journal*, March 16, 1998.

45. "Hubris at Airbus, Boeing Rebuilds," *The Economist*, November 28, 1998, p. 65.

46. Cited in Aris, *Close to the Sun*, p. 179.

47. According to Harry Stonecipher, Boeing President, cited in the *New York Times*, December 3, 1998.

48. *The Economist*, November 28, 1998, p. 65. My figures are slightly different than those given by the *The Economist* because I used the actual number of jets produced and the *The Economist* used projected figures.

49. McIntyre, *Dogfight*, pp. 70–71; Lynn, *Birds of Prey*, pp. 113–114; Aris, *Close to the Sun*, pp. 54–59.

50. Cited in Aris, *Close to the Sun*, pp. 196–197.

51. Cited in "Noel Forgeard, Airbus," *Business Week*, January 8, 2001, p. 76, but see also Aris, *Close to the Sun*, p. 197.

52. *Business Week*, January 8, 2001, p. 76.

53. Daniel Michaels, "Europe's Airbus Ready to Spread Wings," *Wall Street Journal*, June 23, 2000; Aris, *Close to the Sun*, chapter 13.

54. Aris, *Close to the Sun*, p. 213.

55. Aris, *Close to the Sun*, p. 213.

56. Aris, *Close to the Sun*, p. 222.

57. "Military Aircraft: Boeing Down Again," *The Economist*, January 24, 2004.

58. Leslie Wayne, "Boeing Pressed by Questions on Tunker Proposal," *New York Times*, May 8, 2004; Daniel Michaels, "Airbus Sees Military Sales Opening," *Wall Street Journal*, September 15, 2003; "Europe's Defense Industry: The Chinese Syndrome," *The Economist*, February 5, 2005, p. 59.

59. *The Economist*, February 5, 2005, p. 59.

60. Jonathan Karp, Andy Pasztor, and J. Lynn Lunsford, "Boeing Is Put at Disadvantage by Timing of U.S. Aircraft Order," *Wall Street Journal*, February 10, 2005.

61. For Boeing, see *The Boeing Company 2001 Annual Report*, p. 85; for Airbus: "EADS N.V. Year 2003 Report," p. 7, online, EADS.com. By 2004, Boeing had become far more dependent on defense sales with a 44% commercial – 54% defense breakdown of total sales. "Europe Defense Industry," *The Economist*, March 5, 2005, p. 59.

62. Cited in Daniel Michaels and J. Lynn Lunsford, "Globalization Blunts Air Trade Rivalry," *Wall Street Journal*, July 19, 2004.

63. *Wall Street Journal*, July 19, 2004; J. Lynn Lunsford and David Michaels, "New Friction Puts Airbus, Boeing on Course for Fresh Trade Battle," *Wall Street Journal*, June 1, 2004.

64. *Economist*, January 17, 2004; Todd Zaun, "Airbus Picks Japanese Parts Makers," *Wall Street Journal*, June 26, 2002.

65. Kevin Done, "The Big Gamble: Airbus Rolls Out Its New Weapon," *Financial Times*, January 17, 2005; Nisha Gopalan, "Airbus China Seeks to Challenge Boeing's Mainland Dominance," *Wall Street Journal*, October 27, 2004.

66. Pierre Sparaco, "Airbus Scores Low-Cost Market Coup," *Aviation Week and Space Technology*, October 21, 2002, pp. 50–51; Daniel Michael; J. Lynn Lunsford and Keith Johnson, "Airbus to Beat Boeing Once Again," *Wall Street Journal*, November 8, 2004.

67. Quoted in J. Lynn Lunsford, "Behind Slide in Boeing Orders," *Wall Street Journal*, December 23, 2004.

68. Quoted in Daniel Michaels, "Airbus Chief Says Company Won't Cut Jobs," *Wall Street Journal*, January 18, 2002.

69. Pierre Sparaco, "European Bounce Back: Airbus Lofty Prediction Seems to be Taking Steps," *Aviation Week and Space Technology*, June 14, 2004, pp. 34–35; Daniel Michaels, "Airbus Could Top Boeing in Sales," *Wall Street Journal*, January 13, 2005; Kevin Done, "EADS Forecasts 15% Rise in Profits," *Financial Times*, March 20, 2001.

70. Airbus, "Global Market Outlook for 2004–2023," Airbus.com; "The Super Jumbo of All Gambles," *The Economist*, January 22, 2005, pp. 55–56.

71. Carol Matlack and Stanley Holmes, "Mega Plane: Airbus Is Building the Biggest Jetliner Ever," *Business Week*, November 10, 2003, p. 55.

72. *The Economist*, January 22, 2005, p. 56.

73. Carol Matlack, "Is Airbus Caught in a Downdraft?" *Business Week*, December 27, 2004, p. 64; *The Economist*, January 22, 2005, p. 55; Robert Wall and Pierre Sparaco, "Financial Targets," *Aviation Week and Space Technology*, February 28, 2005, p 39.

74. "Taking Off in Toulouse," *The Economist*, April 30, 2005, p. 58.

75. J. Lynn Lunsford and David Michaels, "Airbus May Modify Its A330 Plane," *Wall Street Journal*, July 23, 2004; and "Northwest Nears Order of Boeing Jets," *Wall Street Journal*, April 12, 2005.

76. Mark Landler, "Airbus's Midsize Challenge to Boeing," *New York Times*, November 30, 2004; and "A Dogfight Between Jetliners," *New York Times*, April 13, 2005. See also *Wall Street Journal*, July 23, 2005.

77. *Business Week*, December 27, 2004, p. 64.

78. *The Economist*, April 30, 2005, p. 58; *New York Times*, April 13, 2005; and Bruce Stanley and John Larkin, "Boeing Wins 35-Jet Air India Order," *Wall Street Journal*, April 27, 2005.

Apple Computer

This case was prepared by Charles W. L. Hill, the University of Washington.

Back in 1997 Apple Computer was in deep trouble. The company that had pioneered the personal computer market with its easy-to-use Apple II in 1978, and had introduced the first graphical user interface with the Macintosh in 1984, was bleeding red ink. Apple's worldwide market share, which had been fluctuating between 7 and 9% since 1984, had sunk to 4%. Sales were declining. Apple was on track to lose $378 million on revenues of $7 billion, and that on top of a $740 million loss in 1996. In July 1997, the co-founder of the company, Steve Jobs, who had been fired from Apple back in 1985, returned as CEO. At an investor conference, Michael Dell, CEO of Dell Computer, was asked what Jobs should do as head of Apple. Dell quipped, "I'd shut it down and give the money back to shareholders."[1]

By 2006 the situation looked very different. Apple was on track to book record sales of over $19 billion and net profits of close to $1.9 billion. The stock price, which had traded as low as $6 a share in 2003, was in the mid-70s, and the market capitalization, at $63 billion, surpassed that of Dell Computer, which was around $48 billion. Driving the transformation were strong sales of Apple's iPod music player and music downloads from the iTunes store. In addition, strong sales of Apple's MacBook laptop computers had lifted Apple's market share in the U.S. PC business to 4.8%, up from a low of under 3% in 2004.[2]

Moreover, analysts were predicting that the halo effect of the iPod, together with Apple's recent adoption of Intel's microprocessor architecture, would drive strong sales going forward.

For the first time in twenty years, it looked as if Apple, the perennial also-ran, might be seizing the initiative. But serious questions remained. Could the company continue to build on its momentum? Would sales of Apple's computers really benefit from the iPod? Could the company break out of its niche and become a mainstream player? And how sustainable was the iPod driven sales boom? With new competitors coming along, could Apple hold onto its market leading position in the market for digital music players?

Apple 1976–1997

The Early Years

Apple's genesis is the stuff of computer industry legend.[3] On April Fools Day, 1976, two young electronics enthusiasts, Steve Jobs and Steve Wozniak, started a company to sell a primitive PC that Wozniak had designed. Steve Jobs was just twenty; Wozniak, or Woz as he was commonly called, was five years older. They had known each other for several years, having been introduced by a mutual friend who realized that they shared an interest in consumer electronics. Woz had designed the computer just for the fun of it. That's what people did in 1976. The idea that somebody would actually want to purchase his machine had not occurred to Woz, but it did to Jobs. Jobs persuaded a reluctant Woz to form a company and sell the machine. The location of the company was Steve Jobs's garage. Jobs suggested they call the company Apple and their first machine the Apple I.

EXHIBIT 1

The Apple II Computer

Source: Courtesy of Apple Inc.

They sold around two hundred of them at $666 each. The price point was picked as something of a prank.

The Apple I had several limitations—no case, keyboard, or power supply being obvious ones. It also required several hours of laborious assembly by hand. By late 1976, Woz was working on a replacement to the Apple I, the Apple II.[4] In October 1976, with the Apple II under development, Jobs and Woz were introduced to Mike Markkula. Only thirty-four, Markkula was already a retired millionaire, having made a small fortune at Fairchild and Intel. Markkula had no plans to get back into business anytime soon, but a visit to Jobs's garage changed all that. He committed to investing $92,000 for one-third of the company and promised that his ultimate investment would be $250,000. Stunned, Jobs and Woz agreed to let him join as a partner. It was a fateful decision. The combination of Woz's technical skills, Jobs's entrepreneurial zeal and vision, and Markkula's business savvy and connections was a powerful one. Markkula told Jobs and Woz that neither of them had the experience to run a company and persuaded them to hire a president, Michael Scott, who had worked for Markkula at Fairchild.

The Apple II was introduced in 1977 at a price of $1,200. The first version was an integrated computer with a Motorola microprocessor and included a keyboard, power supply, monitor, and the BASIC programming software. It was Jobs who pushed Woz to design an integrated machine—he wanted something that was easy to use and not just a toy for geeks. Jobs also insisted that the Apple II look good. It had an attractive case and no visible screws or bolts. This differentiated it from most PCs at the time, which looked as if they had been assembled by hobbyists at home (as many had).

In 1978, Apple started to sell a version of the Apple II that incorporated something new—a disk drive. The disk drive turned out to be a critical innovation, for it enabled third-party developers to write software programs for the Apple II that could be loaded via floppy disks. Soon programs started to appear, among them EasyWriter, a basic word processing program, and VisiCalc, a spreadsheet. VisiCalc was an instant hit and pulled in a new customer set, business types who could use VisiCalc for financial planning and accounting. Since VisiCalc was available only for the Apple II, it helped to drive demand for the machine.

By the end of 1980, Apple had sold over 100,000 Apple IIs, making the company the leader in the embryonic PC industry. The company had successfully executed an IPO, was generating over $200 million in annual sales, and was profitable. With the Apple II series selling well, particularly in the education market, Apple introduced its next product, the Apple III, in the fall of 1980. It was a failure. The computer was filled with bugs and crashed constantly. The Apple III had been rushed to market too quickly. Apple reintroduced a reengineered Apple III in 1981, but it continued to be outsold by Apple II. Indeed, successive versions of the Apple II family, each an improvement on the proceeding version, continued to be produced by the company until 1993. In total, over 2 million Apple II computers were sold. The series became a standard in American classrooms where it was valued for its intuitive ease-of-use. Moreover, the Apple II was the mainstay of the company until the late 1980s, when an improved version of the Macintosh started to garner significant sales.

The IBM PC and Its Aftermath

Apple's success galvanized the world's largest computer company, IBM, to speed up development of its entry into the PC market. IBM had a huge and very profitable mainframe computer business, but it had so far failed to develop a PC, despite two attempts. To get to market quickly with this, its third PC project, IBM broke with its established practice of using its own proprietary technology to build the PC. Instead, IBM adopted an "open architecture," purchasing the components required to make the IBM PC from other manufacturers. These components included a 16-bit microprocessor from Intel and an operating system, MS-DOS, which was licensed from a small Washington State company, Microsoft.

Microsoft had been in the industry from its inception, writing a version of the BASIC software programming language for the MITS Atari in 1977,

the first PC ever produced. IBM's desire to license BASIC brought them to Redmond to talk with the company's CEO, Bill Gates. Gates, still in his early twenties, persuaded IBM to adopt a 16-bit processor (originally IBM had been considering a less powerful 8-bit processor). He was also instrumental is pushing IBM to adopt an open architecture, arguing that IBM would benefit from the software and peripherals that other companies could then make.

Initially IBM was intent on licensing the CP/M operating system, produced by Digital Research, for the IBM PC. However, the current version of CP/M was designed to work on an 8-bit processor, and Gates had persuaded IBM that it needed a 16-bit processor. In a series of quick moves, Gates purchased a 16-bit operating system from a local company, Seattle Computer, for $50,000. Gates then hired the designer of the operating system, Tim Paterson, renamed the system MS-DOS, and offered to license it to IBM. In what turned out to be a master stroke, Gates persuaded IBM to accept a nonexclusive license for MS-DOS (which IBM called PC-DOS).

To stoke sales, IBM offered a number of applications for the IBM PC that were sold separately, including a version of VisiCalc, a word processor called EasyWriter, and a well-known series of business programs from Peachtree Software.

Introduced in 1981, the IBM PC was an instant success. Over the next two years, IBM would sell more than 500,000 PCs, seizing market leadership from Apple. IBM had what Apple lacked, an ability to sell into corporate America. As sales of the IBM PC mounted, two things happened. First, independent software developers started to write programs to run on the IBM PC. These included two applications that drove adoptions of the IBM PC; word processing programs (Word Perfect) and a spreadsheet (Lotus 1-2-3). Second, the success of IBM gave birth to clone manufacturers who made IBM-compatible PCs that also utilized an Intel microprocessor and Microsoft's MS-DOS operating system. The first and most successful of the clone makers was Compaq, which in 1983 introduced its first PC, a 28-pound "portable" PC. In its first year, Compaq booked $111 million in sales, which at the time was a record for first-year sales of a company. Before long, a profusion of IBM clone makers entered the market, including Tandy, Zenith, Leading Edge, and Dell. The last was established in 1984 by Michael Dell, then a student at the

University of Texas, who initially ran the company out of his dorm room.

The Birth of the Macintosh

By 1980 two other important projects were underway at Apple: Lisa and the Macintosh. Lisa was originally conceived as a high-end business machine, and the Macintosh as a low-end portable machine.

The development of the Lisa and ultimately the Macintosh were influenced by two visits Steve Jobs paid to Xerox's fabled Palo Alto Research Center (PARC) in November and December 1979. Funded out of Xerox's successful copier business, PARC had been set up to do advanced research on office technology. Engineers at PARC had developed a number of technologies that were later to become central to PCs, including a graphical user interface (GUI), software programs that were made tangible through on-screen icons, a computer mouse that let a user click on and drag screen objects, and a laser printer. Jobs was astounded by what he saw at PARC and decided on the spot that these innovations had to be incorporated into Apple's machines.

Jobs initially pushed the Lisa team to implement PARC's innovations, but he was reportedly driving people on the project nuts with his demands, so President Mike Scott pulled him of the project. Jobs reacted by essentially hijacking the Macintosh project and transforming it into a skunk works that would put his vision into effect. By one account:

> He hounded the people on the Macintosh project to do their best work. He sang their praises, bullied them unmercifully, and told them "they weren't making a computer, they were making history." He promoted the Mac passionately, making people believe that he was talking about much more than a piece of office equipment.[5]

It was during this period that Bud Tribble, a software engineer on the Mac project, quipped that Jobs could create a "reality distortion field." Jobs insisted that the Mac would ship by early 1982. Tribble knew that the schedule was unattainable, and when asked why he didn't point this out to Jobs, he replied: "Steve insists that we're shipping in early 1982, and won't accept answers to the contrary. The best way to describe the situation is a term from Star Trek. Steve has a reality distortion field. . . . In his presence, reality is malleable. He can convince anyone of practically anything. It wears off when he's not around, but it makes it hard to have realistic schedules."[6]

Andy Hertzfeld, another engineer on the Macintosh project, thought Tribble was exaggerating, "until I observed Steve in action over the next few weeks. The reality distortion field was a confounding mélange of a

---

The Macintosh

Source: Courtesy of Apple Inc.

charismatic rhetorical style, an indomitable will, and an eagerness to bend any fact to fit the purpose at hand. If one line of argument failed to persuade, he would deftly switch to another. Sometimes, he would throw you off balance by suddenly adopting your position as his own, without acknowledging that he ever thought differently."[7]

Back at Apple, things were changing too. Mike Scott had left the company after clashes with other executives, including Markkula, who had become chairman. Jobs persuaded John Sculley to join Apple as CEO. Sculley was the former vice president of marketing at Pepsi, where he had become famous for launching the Pepsi Challenge. Jobs had reportedly asked Sculley, "Do you want to sell sugar water for the rest of your life, or do you want to change the world?" Sculley opted for changing the world. A Wharton MBA, Sculley had been hired for his marketing savvy, not his technical skills.

While the Lisa project suffered several delays, Jobs pushed the Macintosh team to finish the project and beat the Lisa team to market with a better product. Introduced in 1984, the Macintosh certainly captured attention for its stylish design and its use of a GUI, icons, and a mouse, all of which made the machine easy to use and which were not found on any other PC at the time. Jobs, ever the perfectionist, again insisted that not a single screw should be visible on the case. He reportedly fired a designer who presented a mockup that had a screw that could be seen by lifting a handle.

Early sales were strong; then they faltered. For all of its appeal, the Macintosh lacked some important features—it had no hard disk drive, only one floppy drive, and insufficient computer memory. Moreover, there were few applications available to run on the machine, and the Mac proved to be a more difficult machine to develop applications for than the IBM PC and its clones. Jobs, however, seemed oblivious to the problems and continued to talk about outsized sales projections, even when it was obvious to all around him that they were unattainable.

In early 1985, Apple posted its first loss. Aware that the drastic action necessary could not be taken while Jobs was running the Macintosh division, Sculley got backing from the board of directors to strip Jobs of his management role and oversight of the Macintosh division. In late 1985, an embittered Jobs resigned from Apple, sold all of his stock, and left to start another computer company, aptly named NeXT.

The Golden Years

With Jobs gone, Sculley shut down the Lisa line, which had done poorly in the market due to a very high price point of $10,000, and pushed developers to fix the problems with the Macintosh. In January 1986, a new version of the Macintosh, the Mac Plus, was introduced. This machine fixed the shortcomings of the original Mac, and sales started to grow again.

What also drove sales higher was Apple's domination of the desktop publishing market. Several events came together to make this happen. Researchers from Xerox PARC formed a company, Adobe, to develop and commercialize the PostScript page description language. PostScript enabled the visual display and printing of high-quality page layouts loaded with graphics such as colored charts, line drawings, and photos. Apple licensed PostScript and used it as the output for its Apple LaserWriter, which was introduced in 1985. Shortly afterwards, a Seattle company, Aldus, introduced a program called PageMaker for the Mac. PageMaker used Adobe's PostScript page description language for output. Although Aldus introduced a version of PageMaker for MS-DOS in 1986, Apple already had a lead, and with the Mac's GUI appealing to graphic artists, Apple tightened its hold on the desktop publishing segment. Apple's position in desktop publishing was further strengthened by the release of Adobe Illustrator in 1987 (a freehand drawing program) and Adobe Photoshop in 1990.

The years between 1986 and 1991 were in many ways golden ones for Apple. Since it made both hardware and software, Apple was able to control all aspects of its computers, offering a complete desktop solution that allowed customers to "plug and play." With the Apple II series still selling well in the education market, and the Mac dominating desktop publishing, Apple was able to charge a premium price for its products. Gross margins on the Mac line got as high as 55%. In 1990, Apple sales reached $5.6 billion; its global market share, which had fallen rapidly as the IBM-compatible PC market had grown, stabilized at 8%; the company had a strong balance sheet; and Apple was the most profitable PC manufacturer in the world.

During this period, executives at Apple actively debated the merits of licensing the Mac operating system to other computer manufacturers, allowing them to make Mac clones. Sculley was in favor of this move. So was Microsoft's Bill Gates, who wrote two memos to Sculley laying out the argument for licensing the Mac OS. Gates argued that the closed architecture of the Macintosh prevented independent investment in the standard by third parties and put Apple at a disadvantage next to the IBM PC standard. However, some senior executives at Apple were against the licensing strategy, arguing that once Apple licensed its intellectual property, it would be difficult to protect it. In one version of events, senior executives debated the decision at a meeting and took a vote on whether to license. Given the controversial nature of the decision, it was decided that the vote in favor had to be unanimous. It wasn't—a single executive voted against the licensing decision, and it was never pursued.[8] In another version of events, Jean-Louis Gassée, head of R&D at Apple, vigorously opposed Sculley's plans to clone, and Sculley backed down.[9] Gassée was deeply distrustful of Microsoft and Bill Gates, and believed that Gates probably had an ulterior motive given how the company benefited from the IBM standard.

Ironically, in 1985 Apple had licensed its "visual displays" to Microsoft. Reportedly Gates had strong-armed Sculley, threatening that Microsoft would stop developing crucial applications for the Mac unless Apple granted Microsoft the license. At the time, Microsoft had launched development of its own GUI. Called Windows, it mimicked the look and feel of the Mac operating system, and Microsoft didn't want to be stopped by a lawsuit from Apple. Several years later, when Apple did file a lawsuit against Microsoft, arguing that Windows 3.1 imitated the "look and feel" of the Mac, Microsoft was able to point to the 1985 license agreement to defend its right to develop Windows—a position that the judge in the case agreed with.

1990–1997

By the early 1990s, the prices of IBM-compatible PCs were declining rapidly. So long as Apple was the only company to sell machines that used a GUI, its differential appeal gave it an advantage over MS-DOS-based PCs with their clunky text-based interfaces, and the premium price could be justified. However, in 1990 Microsoft introduced Windows 3.1, its own GUI that sat on top of MS-DOS, and Apple's differential appeal began to erode. Moreover, the dramatic growth of the PC market had turned Apple into a niche player. Faced with the choice of writing software to work with an MS-DOS/Windows operating system and an Intel microprocessor, now the dominant standard found on 90% of all PCs, or the Mac OS and a Motorola processor, developers logically opted for the dominant standard (desktop publishing remained an exception to this rule). Reflecting on this logic, Dan Eilers, then vice president of strategic planning at Apple, reportedly stated that "the company was on a glide path to history."[10]

Sculley, too, thought that the company was in trouble. Apple seemed boxed into its niche. Apple had a high cost structure. It spent significantly more on R&D as a percentage of sales than its rivals (in 1990, Apple spent 8% of sales on R&D, Compaq around 4%). Its microprocessor supplier, Motorola, lacked the scale of Intel, which translated into higher costs for Apple. Moreover, Apple's small market share made it difficult to recoup the spiraling cost of developing a new operating system, which by 1990 amounted to at least $500 million.

Sculley's game plan to deal with these problems involved a number of steps.[11] First, he appointed himself chief technology officer in addition to CEO, a move that raised some eyebrows given Sculley's marketing background. Second, he committed the company to bring out a low-cost version of the Macintosh to compete with IBM clones. The result was the Mac Classic, introduced in October 1990 and priced at $999. He also cut prices for the Macs and Apple IIs by 30%. The reward was a 60% increase in sales volume, but lower gross margins. So third, he cut costs. The workforce at Apple was reduced by 10%, the salaries of top managers (including Sculley's) were cut by as much as 15%, and Apple shifted much of its manufacturing to subcontractors (for example, the Power-Book was built in Japan, a first for Apple). Fourth, he called for the company to maintain its technological lead by bringing out hit products every six to twelve months. The results included the first Apple portable, the PowerBook notebook, which was shipped in late 1991 and garnered very favorable reviews, and the Apple Newton hand-held computer, which bombed. Fifth, Apple entered into an alliance with IBM, which realized that it had lost its hold on the PC market to companies like Intel, Microsoft, and Compaq.

The IBM alliance had several elements. One was the decision to adopt IBM's Power PC microprocessor architecture, which IBM would also use in its offerings. A second was the establishment of two joint ventures—Taligent, which had the goal of creating a new operating system, and Kaleida to develop multimedia applications. A third was a project to help IBM and Apple machines work better together.

While Sculley's game plan helped to boost the top line, the bottom line shrunk in 1993 due to a combination of low gross margins and continuing high costs. In 1994, Sculley left Apple. He was replaced by Michael Spindler, a German engineer who had gained prominence as head of Apple Europe.

It was Spindler who in 1994 finally took the step that had been long debated in the company—he decided to license the Mac OS to a handful of companies, allowing them to make Mac clones. The Mac OS would be licensed for $40 a copy. It was too little too late—the industry was now waiting for the introduction of Microsoft's Windows 95. When it came, it was clear that Apple was in serious trouble. Windows 95 was a big improvement over Windows 3.1, and it closed the gap between Windows and the Mac. While many commentators criticized Apple for not licensing the Mac OS in the 1980s, when it still had a big lead over Microsoft, ironically Bill Gates disagreed. In a 1996 interview with *Fortune*, Gates noted:

> As Apple has declined, the basic criticism seems to be that Apple's strategy of doing a unique hardware/software combination was doomed to fail. I disagree. Like all strategies, this one fails if you execute poorly. But the strategy can work, if Apple picks its markets and renews the innovation in the Macintosh.[12]

Spindler responded to Windows 95 by committing Apple to develop a next generation operating system for the Macintosh, something that raised questions about the Taligent alliance with IBM. At the end of 1995, IBM and Apple parted ways, ending Taligent, which after $500 million in investments had produced little.

By then, Spindler had other issues on his mind. The latter half of 1995 proved to be a disaster for Apple. The company seemed unable to predict demand for its products. It overestimated demand for its low-end Macintosh Performa computers and was left with excess inventory, while underestimating demand for its high-end machines. To compound matters, its new PowerBooks had to be recalled after batteries started to catch fire, and a price war in Japan

cut margins in one of its best markets. As a consequence, in the last quarter of 1995, gross margins slumped to 15%, down from 29% in 1994, and Apple lost $68 million. Spindler responded in January 1996 by announcing 1,300 layoffs. He suggested that up to 4,000 might ultimately go—some 23% of the workforce.[13] That was his last significant act. He was replaced in February by Gilbert Amelio.

Amelio, who joined Apple from National Semiconductor where he had gained a reputation for his turnaround skills, lasted just seventeen months. He followed through on Spindler's plans to cut headcount and stated that Apple would return to its differentiation strategy. His hope was that the new Mac operating system would help, but work on that was in total disarray. He took the decision to scrap the project after an investment of over $500 million. Instead, Apple purchased NeXT, the computer company founded by none other than Steve Jobs, for $425 million. The NeXT machines had received strong reviews, but had gained no market traction due to a lack of supporting applications. Amelio felt that the NeXT OS could be adapted to run on the Mac. He also hired Steve Jobs as a consultant, but Jobs was rarely seen at Apple; he was too busy running Pixar, his computer animation company that was riding a wave of success after a huge hit with the animated movie *Toy Story*.[14]

Amelio's moves did nothing to stop the slide in Apple's fortunes. By mid-1997, market share had slumped to 3%, from 9% when Amelio took the helm. The company booked a loss of $742 million in 1996 and was on track to lose another $400 million in 1997. It was too much for the board. In July 1997, Amelio was fired. With market share falling, third-party developers and distributors were rethinking their commitments to Apple. Without them, the company would be dead.

The Return of Steve Jobs

Following Amelio's departure, Steve Jobs was appointed interim CEO. In April 1998, he took the position on a permanent basis, while staying on at Pixar as CEO. Jobs moved quickly to fix the bleeding. His first act was to visit Bill Gates and strike a deal with Microsoft. Microsoft agreed to invest $150 million in Apple and to continue producing Office for the Mac through until at least 2002. Then Jobs ended the licensing deals with the clone makers, spending over $100 million to acquire the assets of the leading Mac clone maker, Power Computing, including its license.

Jobs killed slow-selling products, most notably the Apple Newton hand-held computer, and reduced the number of product lines from sixty to just four. He also pushed the company into online distribution, imitating Dell Computer's direct selling model. While these fixes bought the company time and caused a favorable reaction from the stock market, they were not recipes for growth.

New Computer Offerings

Almost immediately Jobs started to think about a new product that would embody the spirit of Apple. What emerged in May 1998 was the iMac. The differentiator for the iMac was not its software, or its power, or its monitor—it was the design of the machine itself. A self-contained unit that combined the monitor and central processing unit in translucent teal and with curved lines, the iMac was a bold departure in a world dominated by putty-colored PC boxes.

To develop the iMac, Jobs gave a team of designers, headed by Jonathan Ive, an unprecedented say in the development project. Ive's team worked closely with engineers, manufacturers, marketers, and Jobs himself. To understand how to make a plastic shell look exciting rather than cheap, the designers visited a candy factory to study the finer points of making jelly beans. They spent months working with Asian partners designing a sophisticated process capable of

producing millions of iMacs a year. The designers also pushed for the internal electronics to be redesigned, to make sure that they looked good through the thick shell. Apple may have spent as much as $65 a machine on the casing, compared with perhaps $20 for the average PC.[15]

Priced at $1,299, iMac sales were strong with orders placed for 100,000 units even before the machine was available. Moreover, one-third of iMac purchases were by first-time buyers, according to Apple's own research.[16] The iMac line was continually updated, with faster processors, more memory, and bigger hard drives being added. The product was also soon available in many different colors. In 1999, Apple followed up the iMac with introduction of the iBook portable. Aimed at consumers and students, the iBook had the same design theme as the iMac and was priced aggressively at $1,599.

Sales of the iMac and iBook helped push Apple back into profitability. In 1999, the company earned $420 million on sales of $6.1 billion. In 2000, it made $611 million on sales of almost $8 billion.

To keep sales growing, Apple continued to invest in development of a new operating system, based on the technology acquired from NeXT. After three years of work by nearly one thousand software engineers, and a cost of around $1 billion, the first version of Apple's new operating system was introduced in

EXHIBIT 3

(a) The iMac

(b) The iBook

Source: Courtesy of Apple Inc.

2001. Known as OS X, it garnered rave reviews from analysts who saw the UNIX-based program as offering superior stability and faster speed than the old Mac OS. OS X also had an enhanced ability to run multiple programs at once to support multiple users, connected easily to other devices such as digital camcorders, and was easier for developers to write applications for. In typical Apple fashion, OS X also sported a well-designed and intuitively appealing interface. Since 2001, new versions of OS X have been introduced almost once a year. The most recent version, OS X Tiger, was introduced in 2005 and retailed for $129.

To get the installed base of Mac users, who at the time numbered 25 million, to upgrade to OS X, Apple had to offer applications. The deal with Microsoft ensured that its popular Office program would be available for the OS X. Steve Jobs had assumed that the vote of confidence by Microsoft would encourage other third-party developers to write programs for OS X, but it didn't always happen. Most significantly, in 1998 Adobe Systems refused to develop a Mac version of their consumer video editing program, which was already available for Windows PCs.

Shocked, Jobs directed Apple to start working on its own applications. The first fruits of this effort were two video editing programs, Final Cut Pro for professionals, and iMovie for consumers. Next was iLife, a bundle of multimedia programs now preinstalled on every Mac, which includes iMovie, iDVD, iPhoto, Garage Band, and the iTunes digital jukebox. Apple also developed its own web browser, Safari.

Meanwhile, Apple continued to update its computer lines with eye-catching offerings. In 2001, Apple introduced its Titanium PowerBook G4 notebooks. Cased in Titanium, these ultralight and fast notebooks featured a clean postindustrial look that marked a distinct shift from the whimsical look of the iMac and iBook. As with the iMac, Jonathan Ive's design team played a central part in the product's development. A core team of designers set up a design studio in a San Francisco warehouse, far away from Apple's main campus. They worked for six weeks on the basic design and then headed to Asia to negotiate for widescreen flat-panel displays and to work with tool makers.[17]

The Titanium notebooks were followed by a redesigned desktop line that appealed to the company's graphic design customers, including the offering of elegantly designed very widescreen cinema displays. In 2004, Ive's design team came out with yet another elegant offering, the iMac G5 computer, which *PC Magazine* described as a "simple, stunning all-in-one design."[18]

EXHIBIT 4

The iMac G5

Source: Courtesy of Apple Inc.

EXHIBIT 5

World Wide Market Share and Units Sold, 2005

Company	Market Share (%)	Units Sold (millions)
Dell Computer	18.1%	37.76
Hewlett-Packard	15.6%	32.54
Lenovo	6.2%	12.93
Acer	4.7%	9.80
Fujistu-Siemens	4.1%	8.55
Apple	2.2%	4.59
Other	49.1%	102.42
Total	**100.0%**	**208.60**

Sources: Standard & Poor's Industry Surveys, Computers: Hardware, December 8, 2005.

For all of Apple's undisputed design excellence and the loyalty of its core user base—graphic artists and students—Apple's market share remained anemic, trailing far behind industry leaders Dell, Hewlett-Packard, and IBM/Lenovo (see Exhibit 5). Weak demand, combined with its low market share, translated into another loss for Apple in 2001, leading some to question the permanence of Steve Jobs's turnaround. While Apple's worldwide market share fell to as low as 1.9% in 2004, it started to pick up again in 2005 and throughout 2006. Momentum was particularly strong in the United States, where Apple shipped 1.3 million computers in the year through to July 2006, giving it a 12% year-over-year growth rate and a 4.8% share of the U.S. market. Driving growth, according to many analysts, was the surging popularity of Apple's iPod music player, which had raised Apple's profile among younger consumers and was having a spillover effect on Mac sales.[19]

Intel Inside, Windows on the Desktop

Since the company's inception, Apple had not used Intel microprocessors, which had become the industry standard for microprocessors since the introduction of the IBM PC in 1981. In June 2005, Apple announced that it would start to do so. Driving the transition was growing frustration with the performance of the PowerPC chip line made by IBM that Apple had been using for over a decade. The PowerPC had failed to keep up with the Intel chips, which were both faster and had lower power consumption—something that was very important in the portable computer market, where Apple had a respectable market share.

The transition created significant risks for Apple. Old applications and OS X had to be rewritten to run on Intel processors. By the spring of 2006 Apple had produced Intel-compatible versions of OS X and its own applications, but many other applications had not been rewritten for Intel chips. To make transition easier, Apple provided a free software program, known as Rosetta, that enabled users to run older applications on Intel-based Macs. Moreover, Apple went a step further by issuing a utility program, known as Boot Camp, which enabled Mac owners to run Windows XP on their machines. Boot Camp will be included as a part of the next version of OS X, OS X Leopard, which is due out in 2007.

Reviews of Apple's Intel-based machines were generally favorable, with many reviewers noting the speed improvement over the older PowerPC Macs—although the speed improvement tended to evaporate if the Rosetta program had to be used to run an application.[20]

In the fall of 2006, Apple reported that its transition to an Intel-based architecture was complete, some six months ahead of schedule. Although sales of Macs had been slow during late 2005 and early 2006, this seems to have been due to consumers putting off purchases while waiting for the new machines. The company's sales of the new Macs exhibited healthy growth in the second and third quarters of the year. Sales of portable MacBooks were particularly strong.

The move to Intel architecture may have helped Apple to close the price differential that had long existed between Windows-based PCs and Apple's offerings. According to one analysis, by September 2006 Apple's products were selling at a *discount* to comparable product offerings from Dell and Hewlett-Packard.[21]

Moving into Retail

In 2001 Apple made another important strategic shift—the company opened its first retail store. In an industry that had long relied on third-party retailers, or direct sales as in the case of Dell, this shift seemed risky. One concern was that Apple might encounter a backlash from Apple's long-standing retail partners. Another was that Apple would never be able to generate the sales volume required to justify expensive retail space; the product line seemed too thin. However, Apple clearly believed that it was hurt by a lack of retail presence. Many computer retailers didn't carry Apple machines, and some of those that did often buried Mac displays deep in the store.

From the start, Apple's stores exhibited the same stylish design that characterized its products with clean lines, attractive displays, and a postindustrial feel (see Exhibit 6). Steve Jobs himself was intimately involved in the design process. Indeed, he is one of the named inventors on a patent Apple secured for the design of the signature glass staircase found in many stores, and he was apparently personally involved in the design of a glass cube atop a store on New York's Fifth Avenue that opened in 2006. In an interview, Jobs noted that "we spent a lot of time designing the store, and it deserves to be built perfectly."[22]

Customers and analysts were immediately impressed by the product fluency that the employees in Apple stores exhibited. They also liked the highlight of many stores, a "genius bar" where technical experts helped customers fix problems with their Apple products. The wide-open interior space, however, did nothing to allay the fears of critics that Apple's product portfolio was just too narrow to generate the traffic required to support premium space. The critics couldn't have been more wrong. Spurred on by booming sales of the iPod, Apple's stores did exceptionally well. By 2005, Apple had 137 stores in upscale locations that generated $2.3 billion in sales and $140 million in profits. Sales per square foot during 2005 were an almost unprecedented $4,000, making Apple the envy of other retailers.[23]

The iPod Revolution

In the late 1990s and early 2000s the music industry was grappling with the implications of two new technologies. The first was the development of inexpensive portable MP3 players that could store and play digital music files such as Diamond Media's Rio, which was introduced in 1997 and could hold two hours of music. The second was the rise of peer-to-peer computer networks such as Napster, Kazaa, Grokster, and Morpheus that enabled individuals to efficiently swap digital files over the Internet. By the early 2000s, millions of individuals were downloading music files over the Internet without the permission of the copyright holders, the music publishing companies. For the music industry, this development had been devastating. After years of steady growth, global sales of music peaked in 1999 at $38.5 billion, falling to $32 billion in 2003. Despite the fall in sales, the International Federation of the Phonographic Industry (IFPI) claimed that demand for

EXHIBIT 6

An Apple Store

Source: Courtesy of Apple Inc.

music was higher than ever, but that the decline in sales reflected the fact that "the commercial value of music is being widely devalued by mass copying and piracy."[24]

The music industry had tried to counter piracy over the Internet by taking legal action to shut down the peer-to-peer networks, such as Napster, and filing lawsuits against individuals who made large numbers of music files available over the Internet. Its success had been limited, in part because peer-to-peer networks offered tremendous utility to consumers. They were fast and immediate, and enabled consumers to unbundle albums, downloading just the tracks they wanted while ignoring junk filler tracks. And of course, they were free.

The music industry was desperate for a legal alternative to illegal downloading. Its own initiatives, introduced in 2002, had gained little traction. MusicNet, which offered songs from Warner Music, BMG, and EMI, had a single subscription plan—$9.85 a month for one hundred streams and one hundred downloads. After thirty days, downloads expired and couldn't be played. Pressplay, which offered music from Sony, Universal, and EMI, had four subscription plans, from $9.95 to $24.95 a month, for up to one thousand streams and one hundred downloads. The higher subscription fee service from Pressplay let users burn up to twenty songs a month onto CDs that would not expire, but no more than two songs could be burned from any one artist.[25]

Then along came the iPod and iTunes. These products were born out of an oversight—in the late 1990s when consumers were starting to burn their favorite CDs, Macs did not have CD burners or software to manage users' digital music collections. Realizing the mistake, CEO Steven Jobs ordered Apple's software developers to create the iTunes program to help Mac users manage their growing digital music collections. The first iTunes program led to the concept of the iPod. If people were going to maintain the bulk of their music collection on a computer, they needed a portable MP3 player to take music with them—a Sony Walkman for the digital age. While there were such devices on the market already, they could hold only a few dozen songs each.

To run the iPod, Apple licensed software from PortalPlayer. Apple also learned that Toshiba was building a tiny 1.8 inch hard drive that could hold over one thousand songs. Apple quickly cut a deal with Toshiba, giving it exclusive rights to the drive for

eighteen months. Meanwhile, Apple focused on designing the user interface, the exterior styling, and the synchronization software to make it work with the Mac. As with so many product offerings unveiled since Jobs returned to the helm, the design team led by Jonathan Ive played a pivotal role in giving birth to the iPod. Ive's team worked in secrecy in San Francisco. The members, all paid extremely well by industry standards, worked together in a large open studio with little personal space. The team was able to figure out how to put a layer of clear plastic over the white and black core of an iPod, giving it tremendous depth of texture. The finish was superior to other MP3 players, with no visible screws or obvious joints between parts. The serial number of the iPod was not on a sticker, as with most products; it was elegantly etched onto the back of the device. This attention to detail and design elegance, although not without cost implications, was to turn the iPod into a fashion accessory.[26]

The iPod was unveiled in October 2001 to mixed reviews. The price of $399 was significantly above that of competing devices, and since the iPod worked only with Apple computers, it seemed destined to be a niche product. However, initial sales were strong. It turned out that consumers were willing to pay a premium price for the iPod's huge storage capacity. Moreover, Jobs made the call to develop a version of the iPod that would be compatible with Windows. After it was introduced in mid-2002, sales took off.

By this time, Jobs was dealing with a bigger strategic issue—how to persuade the music companies to make their music available for legal downloads. It was here that Steve Jobs's legendary selling ability came into play. With a prototype for an online iTunes store in hand, Jobs met with executives from the major labels. He persuaded them that it was in their best interest to support a legal music download business as an alternative to widespread illegal downloading of music over peer-to-peer networks, which despite its best efforts, the music industry had not been able to shut down. People would pay to download music over the Internet, he argued. Although all of the labels were setting up their own online businesses, Jobs felt that since they were limited to selling music owned by the parent companies, demand would be limited too. What was needed was a reputable independent online music retailer, and Apple fit the bill. If it was going to work, however, all of the labels needed to get on board. Under Jobs's scheme, iTunes files would be downloaded for 99 cents each. The only portable digital player that the files could be stored and played on was an iPod. Jobs's argument was that this closed world made it easier to protect copyrighted material from unauthorized distribution.

Jobs also meet with twenty of the world's top recording artists, including U2's Bono, Sheryl Crow, and Mick Jagger. His pitch to them was this—digital distribution is going to happen, and the best way to protect your interests is to support a legal online music distribution business. Wooed by Jobs, these powerful stakeholders encouraged the music recording companies to take Apple's proposal seriously.[27]

By early 2003 Jobs had all of the major labels on board. Launched in April 2003, within days it was clear that Apple had a major hit on its hands. A million songs were sold in the first week. In mid-2004, iTunes passed the 100 million download mark, and sales kept accelerating, hitting the 150 million download mark in October 2004. At that point, customers were downloading over 4 million songs per week, which represented a run rate of more than 200 million a year. While Steve Jobs admitted that Apple does not make much money from iTunes downloads—probably only 10 cents a song—it does make good margins of sales of the iPod, and sales of the iPod ballooned in 2005 (see Exhibit 7).

Helped by new models, which as always were elegantly designed, iPod sales continued to boom in the first half of Apple's fiscal 2006 (the last three months of 2005 and the first three months of 2006). In this six-month period, Apple sold 22.5 million iPods and generated $4.26 billion in sales, surpassing computer

EXHIBIT 7

Sales of Apple's Main Product Lines (millions)

	2003	2004	2005
Computers	$4,491	$4,923	$6,275
iPod	$345	$1,306	$4,540
iTunes	$36	$278	$899
Software	$644	$821	$1,091
Peripherals	$691	$951	$1,126

Source: Apple Computer 10K Reports, 2006.

sales for the first time, which stood at $3.29 billion for the six-month period. iTunes kicked in another $976 million.

As the installed base of iPods expanded, an ecosystem of companies selling iPod accessories started to emerge. The accessories include speakers, head phones, and add-on peripherals that allow iPod users to record their voices, charge their iPods on the go, play their tunes over the radio, or use their iPods wirelessly with a remote. There are also cases, neck straps, belt clips, and so on. By 2006 it was estimated that there were over one hundred companies in this system. Collectively they may have sold as much as $1 billion of merchandise during the last three months of 2005. Apple collects an unspecified royalty from companies whose products access the iPod's ports and thus benefits indirectly from the preference of buyers for the iPod over competing products that lack the same accessories.[28]

Success such as this attracts competitors, and soon there were plenty. RealNetworks, Yahoo, and Napster all set up legal downloading services to compete with iTunes. Even Wal-Mart got into the act, offering music downloads for 89 cents a track. However, iTunes continued to outsell its rivals by a wide margin. In mid-2006, iTunes was accounting for about 80% of all legal music downloads.[29] iTunes was also the fourth largest music retailer in the United States; the other three all had physical stores.

The iPod also had plenty of competition. Many of the competing devices were priced aggressively and had as much storage capacity as the iPod. Few, however, managed to gain share against the iPod, which by mid-2006 still accounted for 77% of annual sales in the U.S. market. The most successful rival to date has been SanDisk, which captured almost 10% of the market with its family of music players.

One reason for the failure of competitors to garner more market share has been hardware and software problems that arise when consumers try to download songs sold by one company onto a machine made by another. In contrast, iTunes and iPod have always worked seamlessly together.

In an effort to counter this, Microsoft announced the release of its own digital music player in 2006, Zune. Zune is designed to work with Microsoft's own online music store. Similarly, RealNetworks has announced a deal with SanDisk to make a digital music device that's specifically designed to work with RealNetworks' online music store, Rhapsody.[30] Both products are expected to debut in late 2007.

However, Apple was not standing still. New, even smaller versions of the iPod, such as the iPod Shuffle and iPod Nano, were keeping sales strong. The latest iPods, introduced in September 2006, had longer battery lives, bigger hard drives (enabling some models to store up to 15,000 songs or 150 hours of video), and brighter displays. They were priced aggressively, while still maintaining the thin, elegant look that characterized the line.

At the same time, Apple announced that the iTunes store would start to sell movie downloads. Initially, the movies were limited to offerings from Disney (where Steve Jobs had become the largest shareholder after Disney had acquired Pixar in 2005), but Apple expected to add other studios in the near future. Downloaded movies would have near DVD quality and could be played on TVs, computers, or iPods. In addition, Apple announced that it would be introducing a small "box," which would connect to a TV, cable set top box, or stereo, that would pull digital files (videos, music, and photos) wirelessly from any iTunes-enabled PC (Windows or Mac).

The Personal Computer Industry in the 2000s

While Apple dominated the music downloading and portable music player businesses with iTunes and iPod, it remained a niche player in the computer industry. After years of growth, sales of PCs had fallen for the first time ever in 2001, but the growth path had soon been resumed. According to IDC, a market research firm, total PC shipments were expected to hit 287 million units in 2008, up from 179 million units in 2004 (see Exhibit 8). The U.S. market would remain the world's largest, with 82 million units being sold in 2008, up from 58 million in 2004, representing a growth rate in the high single digits. Sales to consumers accounted for about 88.5 million of the 230 million PCs sold in 2006.[31]

The industry is characterized by a handful of players who collectively account for about half the market, and a long tail of small enterprises that produce unbranded or locally branded "white box" computers, often selling their machines at a significant discount to globally branded products (see Exhibit 5).

Among the larger players, consolidation has been a theme for several years. In 2002, Hewlett-Packard acquired Compaq Computer; Gateway and eMachines merged in 2004; and in 2005, the Chinese firm Lenovo acquired the PC business of IBM. The large PC firms compete aggressively by offering ever more powerful machines, producing them as efficiently as possible and lowering prices to sell more volume. The average selling price of a PC has fallen from around $1,700 in 1999 to under $1,000 in 2006, and projections are that it may continued to fall, fueled in part by aggressive competition between Dell Computer and Hewlett-Packard.[32]

All of these players focus on the design, assembly, and sales of PCs, while purchasing the vast majority of component parts from independent companies. In recent years, the top PC companies have reduced their R&D spending as a percentage of sales, as the industry has transitioned toward a commodity business.

The existence of the long tail of white box makers is made possible by the open architecture of the dominant PC standard, based on Intel-compatible microprocessors and a Microsoft operating system, and the low-tech nature of the assembly process. The components for these boxes, which are themselves commodities, can be purchased cheaply off the shelf. White box makers have strong positions in many developing nations. In Mexico, for example, domestic brands accounted for 60% of all sales in 2005, up from 44% in 2000. In Latin America as a whole, 70% of personal computers are produced locally. White box makers have much weaker positions in the United States, western Europe, and Japan, where consumers display a stronger preference for branded products that incorporate leading-edge technology. In contrast, in the developing world, consumers are willing to accept older components if it saves a few hundred dollars.[33]

During the 1990s and early 2000s, Dell grew rapidly to capture the market lead. Dell's success was based on the inventory management efficiencies associated with its direct selling model (Dell could build machines to order, which reduced its need to hold inventory). Dell was also helped by the problems Hewlett-Packard faced when it merged with Compaq Computer. By 2005, however, a resurgent Hewlett-Packard had lowered its costs, could price more aggressively, and was starting to gain ground against Dell. Apple Computer continued to be the odd man out in this industry and was the only major manufacturer that did not adhere to the Windows architecture.

EXHIBIT 8

Unit Shipments in the PC Industry

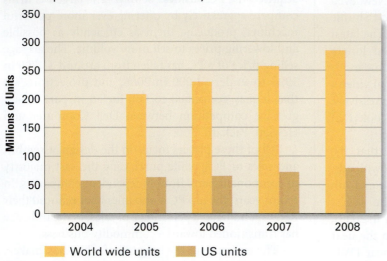

Source: Data from IDC. 2007 and 2008 are forecasts.

Strategic Issues

As 2006 drew to a close, Apple was in an enviable position. The iPod business was continuing to exhibit rapid growth, and sales of Apple computers, particularly portables, were strong. Still, there were questions surrounding the company. Apple had always been good at innovating, but never good at profiting from innovation. Would it be different this time? Forecasts called for 2006 and 2007 to be strong years for Apple, with record sales and profits, but much of this was due to the iPod boom, and there were questions about how sustainable that might be. In the PC business, Apple was still a niche player, albeit one with renewed growth prospects. The company had very limited presence in the large business market. Could this be changed? Would Apple be able to capitalize on the strong iPod business to expand its share of computer sales? And what were the implications for Apple's long-term competitive position?

ENDNOTES

1. Quoted in Pete Burrows, "Steve Jobs' Magic Kingdom," *Business Week*, February 6, 2006, pages 62–68.
2. N. Wingfield, "Apple Unveils New Computers," *Wall Street Journal*, August 8, 2006, page B3.
3. Much of this section is drawn from P. Freiberger and M. Swaine, *Fire in the Valley*, New York: McGraw-Hill, 2000.
4. For a detailed history of the development of the Apple II see Steve Weyhrich, "Apple II History," http://apple2history.org/history/ah01.html.
5. P. Freiberger and M. Swaine, *Fire in the Valley*, New York: McGraw-Hill, 2000, page 357.
6. Andy Hertzfeld, "Reality Distortion Field," http://www.folklore.org/ProjectView.py?project=Macintosh.
7. Andy Hertzfeld, "Reality Distortion Field," http://www.folklore.org/ProjectView.py?project=Macintosh.
8. This version of events was told to the author by a senior executive who was present in the room at the time.
9. Jim Carlton, "Playing Catch Up—Apple Finally Gives in and Attempts Cloning," *Wall Street Journal*, October 17, 1994, page A1.
10. D. B. Yoffie, "Apple Computer 1992," Harvard Business School Case, 792-081.
11. Andrew Kupfer, "Apple's Plan to Survive and Grow," *Fortune*, May 4, 1992, pages 68–71; B. R. Schlender, "Yet Another Strategy for Apple," *Fortune*, October 22, 1990, pages 81–85.
12. B. Schlender, "Paradise Lost: Apple's Quest for Life After Death," *Fortune*, February 1996, pp. 64–72.
13. Jim Carlton, "Apple's Losses to Stretch into 2nd Period," *Wall Street Journal*, January 18, 1996, page B7.
14. Peter Burrows, "Dangerous Limbo," *Business Week*, July 21, 1997, page 32.
15. Peter Burrows, "The Man Behind Apple's Design Magic," *Business Week*, September 2005, pages 27–34.
16. A. Reinhardt, "Can Steve Jobs Keep His Mojo Working?" *Business Week*, August 2, 1999, page 32.
17. Peter Burrows, "The Man Behind Apple's Design Magic," *Business Week*, September 2005, pages 27–34.
18. "Apple iMac G5 Review," *PC Magazine*, online at http://www.pcmag.com/article2/0,1759,1648796,00.asp.
19. Standard & Poor's Industry Surveys, Computers: Hardware, "Global Demand for PCs Accelerates," December 8, 2005; Mark Veverka, "Barron's Insight: Apple's Horizon Brightens," *Wall Street Journal*, July 23, 2006, page A4.
20. Peter Lewis, "Apple's New Core," *Fortune*, March 29, 2006, pages 182–184.
21. Citigroup Global Markets, "Apple Computer: New Products Position Apple Well for Holidays," September 13, 2006.
22. N. Wingfield, "How Apple's Store Strategy Beat the Odds," *Wall Street Journal*, May 17, 2006, page B1.

23. M. Frazier, "The Bigger Apple," *Advertising Age*, February 13, 2006, pages 4–6.
24. IFPI News Release, "Global Music Sales Down 5% in 2001," http://www.ifpi.org.
25. W. S. Mossberg, "Record Labels Launch Two Feeble Services to Replace Napster," *Wall Street Journal*, February 7, 2002, page B1.
26. Peter Burrows, "The Man Behind Apple's Design Magic," *Business Week*, September 2005, pages 27–34.
27. N. Wingfield and E. Smith. "U2's Gig: Help Apple Sell iPods," *Wall Street Journal*, October 20, 2004, page D5; Apple Computer Press Release, "iTunes Music Store Downloads Top 150 Million Songs," October 14, 2004.
28. Paul Taylor, "iPod Ecosystem Offers Rich Pickings," FT.com, January 24, 2006, page 1.
29. T. Braithwaite and K. Allison, "Crunch Time for Apple's Music Icon," *Financial Times*, June 14, 2006, page 27.
30. N. Wingfield and R. A. Guth, "iPod, They Pod: Rivals Imitate Apple's Success," *Wall Street Journal*, September 18, 2006, page B1.
31. IDC Press Release, "Long-term PC Outlook Improves," September 14, 2006.
32. Standard & Poor's Industry Surveys, Computers: Hardware, "Global Demand for PCs Accelerates," December 8, 2005.
33. M. Dickerson, "Plain PCs Sitting Pretty," *Los Angeles Times*, December 11, 2005, page C1.

This case was prepared by Charles W. L. Hill, the University of Washington.

An Industry is Born

In 1968, Nolan Bushnell, the twenty-four-year-old son of a Utah cement contractor, graduated from the University of Utah with a degree in engineering.[1] Bushnell then moved to California, where he worked briefly in the computer graphics division of Ampex. At home, Bushnell turned his daughter's bedroom into a laboratory. There, he created a simpler version of Space War, a computer game that had been invented in 1962 by an MIT graduate student, Steve Russell. Bushnell's version of Russell's game, which he called Computer Space, was made of integrated circuits connected to a nineteen-inch black-and-white television screen. Unlike a computer, Bushnell's invention could do nothing but play the game, which meant that, unlike a computer, it could be produced cheaply.

Bushnell envisioned videogames like his standing next to pinball machines in arcades. With hopes of having his invention put into production, Bushnell left Ampex to work for a small pinball company that manufactured 1,500 copies of his videogame. The game never sold, primarily because the player had to read a full page of directions before he or she could play the game—way too complex for an arcade game. Bushnell left the pinball company and with a friend, Ted Dabney, put up $500 to start a company that would develop a simpler videogame. They wanted to call the company Syzygy, but the name was already

taken, so they settled on *Atari*, a Japanese word that was the equivalent of "*check* in the *go*."

In his home laboratory, Bushnell built the simplest game he could think of. People knew the rules immediately, and it could be played with one hand. The game was modeled on table tennis, and players batted a ball back and forth with paddles that could be moved up and down sides of a court by twisting knobs. He named the game "Pong" after the sonar-like sound that was emitted every time the ball connected with a paddle.

In the fall of 1972, Bushnell installed his prototype for Pong in Andy Capp's tavern in Sunnyvale, California. The only instructions were "avoid missing the ball for a high score." In the first week, 1,200 quarters were deposited in the casserole dish that served for a coin box in Bushnell's prototype. Bushnell was ecstatic; his simple game had brought in $300 in a week. The pinball machine that stood next to it averaged $35 a week.

Lacking the capital to mass-produce the game, Bushnell approached established amusement game companies, only to be repeatedly shown the door. Down but hardly out, Bushnell cut his hair, put on a suit, and talked his way into a $50,000 line of credit from a local bank. He set up a production line in an abandoned roller skating rink and hired people to assemble machines while Led Zeppelin and the Rolling Stones were played at full volume over the speaker system of the rink. Among his first batch of employees was a skinny seventeen-year-old named Steve Jobs, who would later found a few companies of his own, including Apple Computer, NeXT, and Pixar. Like others, Jobs had been attracted by a classified ad that read "Have Fun and Make Money."

In no time at all, Bushnell was selling all the machines that his small staff could make—about ten per day—but to grow, he needed additional capital. While the ambience at the rink, with its mix of rock music and marijuana fumes, put off most potential investors, Don Valentine, one of the country's most astute and credible venture capitalists, was impressed with the growth story. Armed with Valentine's money, Atari began to increase production and expand their range of games. New games included Tank and Breakout; the latter was designed by Jobs and a friend of his, Steve Wozniak, who had left Hewlett-Packard to work at Atari.

By 1974, 100,000 Pong-like games were sold worldwide. Although Atari manufactured only 10% of the games, the company still made $3.2 million that year. With the Pong clones coming on strong, Bushnell decided to make a Pong system for the home. In fact, Magnavox had been marketing a similar game for the home since 1972, although sales had been modest.[2] Bushnell's team managed to compress Atari's coin-operated Pong game down to a few inexpensive circuits that were contained in the game console. Atari's Pong had a sharper picture and more sensitive controllers than Magnavox's machine. It also cost less. Bushnell then went on a road show, demonstrating Pong to toy buyers, but he received an indifferent response and no sales. A dejected Bushnell returned to Atari with no idea of what to do next. Then the buyer for the sporting goods department at Sears came to see Bushnell, reviewed the machine, and offered to buy every home Pong game Atari could make. With Sears's backing, Bushnell boosted production. Sears ran a major television ad campaign to sell home Pong, and Atari's sales soared, hitting $450 million in 1975. The home videogame had arrived.

Boom and Bust

Nothing attracts competitors like success, and by 1976 about twenty different companies were crowding into the home videogame market, including National Semiconductor, RCA, Coleco, and Fairchild. Recognizing the limitations of existing home videogame designs, Fairchild came out in 1976 with a home videogame system capable of playing multiple games. The Fairchild system consisted of three components—a console, controllers, and cartridges. The console was a small computer optimized for graphics processing capabilities. It was designed to receive information

from the controllers, process it, and send signals to a television monitor. The controllers were hand-held devices used to direct on-screen action. The cartridges contained chips encoding the instructions for a game. The cartridges were designed to be inserted into the console.

In 1976, Bushnell sold Atari to Warner Communications for $28 million. Bushnell stayed on to run Atari. Backed by Warner's capital, in 1977 Atari developed and brought out its own cartridge-based system, the Atari 2600. The 2600 system was sold for $200, and associated cartridges retailed for $25–$30. Sales surged during the 1977 Christmas season. However, a lack of manufacturing capacity on the part of market leader Atari and a very cautious approach to inventory by Fairchild led to shortages and kept sales significantly below what they could have been. Fairchild's cautious approach was the result of prior experience in consumer electronics. A year earlier it had increased demand for its digital watches, only to accumulate a buildup of excess inventory that had caused the company to take a $24.5 million write-off.[3]

After the 1977 Christmas season, Atari claimed to have sold about 400,000 units of the 2600 VCA, about 50% of all cartridge-based systems in American homes. Atari had also earned more than $100 million in sales of game cartridges. By this point, second-place Fairchild sold around 250,000 units of its system. Cartridge sales for the year totaled about 1.2 million units, with an average selling price of around $20. Fresh from this success and fortified by market forecasts predicting sales of 33 million cartridges and an installed base of 16 million machines by 1980, Bushnell committed Atari to manufacturing 1 million units of the 2600 for the 1978 Christmas season. Atari estimated that total demand would reach 2 million units. Bushnell was also encouraged by signals from Fairchild that it would again be limiting production to around 200,000 units. At this point, Atari had a library of nine games. Fairchild had seventeen.[4]

Atari was not the only company to be excited by the growth forecasts. In 1978, a host of other companies, including Coleco, National Semiconductor, Magnavox, General Instrument, and a dozen other companies, entered the market with incompatible cartridge-based home systems. The multitude of choices did not seem to entice consumers, however, and the 1978 Christmas season brought unexpectedly low sales. Only Atari and Coleco survived an industry shakeout. Atari lost Bushnell, who was ousted by Warner executives. (Bushnell went on to start Chuck E. Cheese Pizza Time Theater, a restaurant chain that had 278 outlets by 1981.) Bushnell later stated that part of the problem was a disagreement over strategy. Bushnell wanted Atari to price the 2600 at cost and make money on sales of software; Warner wanted to continue making profits on hardware sales.[5]

Several important developments occurred in 1979. First, several game producers and programmers defected from Atari to set up their own firm, Activision, and to make games compatible with the Atari 2600. Their success encouraged others to follow suit. Second, Coleco developed an expansion module that allowed its machine to play Atari games. Atari and Mattel (which entered the market in 1979) did likewise. Third, the year 1979 saw the introduction of three new games to the home market—Space Invaders, Asteroids, and Pac Man. All three were adapted from popular arcade games and all three helped drive demand for players.

Demand recovered strongly in late 1979 and kept growing for the next three years. In 1981, U.S. sales of home videogames and cartridges hit $1 billion. In 1982, they surged to $3 billion, with Atari accounting for half of this amount. It seemed as if Atari could do no wrong; the 2600 was everywhere. About 20 million units were sold, and by late 1982, a large number of independent companies, including Activision, Imagic, and Epyx, were now producing hundreds of games for the 2600. Second-place Coleco was also doing well, partly because of a popular arcade game, Donkey Kong, which it had licensed from a Japanese company called Nintendo.

Atari was also in contact with Nintendo. In 1982, the company very nearly licensed the rights to Nintendo's Famicom, a cartridge-based videogame system machine that was a big hit in Japan. Atari's successor to the 2600, the 5200, was not selling well and the Famicom seemed like a good substitute. The negotiations broke down, however, when Atari discovered that Nintendo had extended its Donkey Kong license to Coleco. This allowed Coleco to port a version of the game to its home computer, which was a direct competitor to Atari's 800 home computer.[6]

After a strong 1982 season, the industry hoped for continued growth in 1983. Then the bottom dropped out of the market. Sales of home videogames

plunged to $100 million. Atari lost $500 million in the first nine months of the year, causing the stock of parent company Warner Communications to drop by half. Part of the blame for the collapse was laid at the feet of an enormous inventory overhang of unsold games. About 15 to 20 million surplus game cartridges were left over from the 1982 Christmas season (in 1981, there were none). On top of this, around 500 new games hit the market in 1993. The average price of a cartridge plunged from $30 in 1979 to $16 in 1982, and then to $4 in 1983. As sales slowed, retailers cut back on the shelf space allocated to videogames. It proved difficult for new games to make a splash in a crowded market. Atari had to dispose of 6 million ET: The Extraterrestrial games. Meanwhile, big hits from previous years, such as Pac Man, were bundled with game players and given away free to try to encourage system sales.[7]

Surveying the rubble, commentators claimed that the videogame industry was dead. The era of dedicated game machines was over, they claimed. Personal computers were taking their place.[8] It seemed to be true. Mattel sold off its game business, Fairchild moved on to other things, Coleco folded, and Warner decided to break up Atari and sell its constituent pieces—at least, those pieces for which it could find a buyer. No one in America seemed to want to have anything to do with the home videogame business; no one, that is, except for Minoru Arakawa, the head of Nintendo's U.S. subsidiary, Nintendo of America (NOA). Picking through the rubble of the industry, Arakawa noticed that there were people who still packed video arcades, bringing in $7 billion a year, more money than the entire movie industry. Perhaps it was not a lack of interest in home videogames that had killed the industry. Perhaps it was bad business practice.

The Nintendo Monopoly

Nintendo was a century-old Japanese company that had built up a profitable business making playing cards before diversifying into the videogame business. Based in Kyoto and still run by the founding Yamauchi family, the company started to diversify into the videogame business in the late 1970s. The first step was to license videogame technology from Magnavox. In 1977, Nintendo introduced a home videogame system in Japan based on this technology that played a variation of Pong. In 1978, the company began to sell coin-operated videogames. It had its first hit with Donkey Kong, designed by Sigeru Miyamoto.

The Famicom

In the early 1980s, the company's boss, Hiroshi Yamauchi, decided that Nintendo had to develop its own videogame machine. He pushed the company's engineers to develop a machine that combined superior graphics processing capabilities and low cost. Yamauchi wanted a machine that could sell for $75, less than half the price of competing machines at the time. He dubbed the machine the Family Computer, or Famicom. The machine that his engineers designed was based on the controller, console, and plug-in cartridge format pioneered by Fairchild. It contained two custom chips—an 8-bit central processing unit and a graphics processing unit. Both chips had been scaled down to perform only essential functions. A 16-bit processor was available at the time, but to keep costs down, Yamauchi refused to use it.

Nintendo approached Ricoh, the electronics giant, which had spare semiconductor capacity. Employees at Ricoh said that the chips had to cost no more that 2,000 yen. Ricoh thought that the 2,000-yen price point was absurd. Yamauchi's response was to guarantee Ricoh a 3-million-chip order within two years. Since the leading companies in Japan were selling, at most, 30,000 videogames per year at the time, many within the company viewed this as an outrageous commitment, but Ricoh went for it.[9]

Another feature of the machine was its memory—2,000 bytes of random access memory (RAM), compared to the 256 bytes of RAM in the Atari machine. The result was a machine with superior graphics processing capabilities and faster action that could handle far more complex games than Atari games. Nintendo's engineers also built a new set of chips into the game cartridges. In addition to chips that held the game program, Nintendo developed memory map controller (MMC) chips that took over some of the graphics processing work from the chips in the console and enabled the system to handle more complex games. With the addition of the MMC chips, the potential for more sophisticated and more complex games had arrived. Over time, Nintendo's engineers developed more powerful MMC chips, enabling the basic 8-bit system to do things that originally seemed out of reach. The engineers also figured out a way to include a battery backup system in cartridges that allowed some games to store information independently—to keep track of where a player had left off or to track high scores.

The Games

Yamauchi recognized that great hardware that would not sell itself. The key to the market, he reasoned, was great games. Yamauchi had instructed the engineers, when they were developing the hardware, to make sure that "it was appreciated by software engineers." Nintendo decided that it would become a haven for game designers. "An ordinary man," Yamauchi said, "cannot develop good games no matter how hard he tries. A handful of people in this world can develop games that everyone wants. Those are the people we want at Nintendo."[10]

Yamauchi had an advantage in the person of Sigeru Miyamoto. Miyamoto had joined Nintendo at the age of twenty-four. Yamauchi had hired Miyamoto, a graduate of Kanazawa Munici College of Industrial Arts, as a favor to his father and an old friend, although he had little idea what he would do with an artist. For three years, Miyamoto worked as Nintendo's staff artist. Then in 1980, Yamauchi called Miyamoto into his office. Nintendo had started selling coin-operated videogames, but one of the new games, Radarscope, was a disaster. Could Miyamoto come up with a new game? Miyamoto was delighted. He had always spent a lot of time drawing cartoons, and as a student, he had played videogames constantly. Miyamoto believed that videogames could be used to bring cartoons to life.[11]

The game Miyamoto developed was nothing short of a revelation. At a time when most coin-operated videogames lacked characters or depth, Miyamoto created a game around a story that had both. Most games involved battles with space invaders or heroes shooting lasers at aliens; Miyamoto's game did neither. Based loosely on *Beauty and the Beast* and *King Kong*, Miyamoto's game involved a pet ape who runs off with his master's beautiful girlfriend. His master is an ordinary carpenter called Mario, who has a bulbous nose, a bushy mustache, a pair of large pathetic eyes, and a red cap (which Miyamoto added because he was not good at hairstyles). He does not carry a laser gun. The ape runs off with the girlfriend to get back at his master, who was not especially nice to the beast. The man, of course, has to get his girlfriend back by running up ramps, climbing ladders, jumping off elevators, and the like, while the ape throws objects at the hapless carpenter. Since the main character is an ape, Miyamoto called him Kong; because the main character is as stubborn as a donkey, he called the game Donkey Kong.

Released in 1981, Donkey Kong was a sensation in the world of coin-operated video arcades and a smash hit for Nintendo. In 1984, Yamauchi again summoned Miyamoto to his office. He needed more games, this time for Famicom. Miyamoto was made the head of a new research and development (R&D) group and told to come up with the most imaginative videogames ever.

Miyamoto began with Mario from Donkey Kong. A colleague had told him that Mario looked more like a plumber than a carpenter, so a plumber he became. Miyamoto gave Mario a brother, Luigi, who was as tall and thin as Mario was short and fat. They became the Super Mario Brothers. Since plumbers spend their time working on pipes, large green sewer pipes became obstacles and doorways into secret worlds. Mario and Luigi's task was to search for the captive Princess Toadstool. Mario and Luigi are endearing bumblers, unequal to their tasks yet surviving. They shoot, squash, or evade their enemies—a potpourri of inventions that include flying turtles and stinging fish, man-eating flowers and fire-breathing dragons—while they collect gold coins, blow air bubbles, and climb vines into smiling clouds.[12]

Super Mario Brothers was introduced in 1985. For Miyamoto, this was just the beginning. Between 1985 and 1991, Miyamoto produced eight Mario games. About 60 to 70 million were sold worldwide, making Miyamoto the most successful game designer in the world. After adapting Donkey Kong for Famicom, he also went on to create other top-selling games, including another classic, The Legend of Zelda. While Miyamoto drew freely from folklore, literature, and pop culture, the main source for his ideas was his own experience. The memory of being lost among a maze of sliding doors in his family's home was recreated in the labyrinths of the Zelda games. The dog that attacked him when he was a child attacks Mario in Super Mario. As a child, Miyamoto had once climbed a tree to catch a view of far-off mountains and had become stuck. Mario gets himself in a similar fix. Once Miyamoto went hiking without a map and was surprised to stumble across a lake. In the Legend of Zelda, part of the adventure is in walking into new places without a map and being confronted by surprises.

Nintendo in Japan

Nintendo introduced Famicom into the Japanese market in May 1983. Famicom was priced at $100, more than Yamauchi wanted, but significantly less than the products of competitors. When he introduced the machine, Yamauchi urged retailers to forgo profits on the hardware because it was just a tool to sell software, and that is where they would make their money. Backed by an extensive advertising campaign, 500,000 units of Famicom were sold in the first two months. Within a year, the figure stood at 1 million, and sales were still expanding rapidly. With the hardware quickly finding its way into Japanese homes, Nintendo was besieged with calls from desperate retailers frantically demanding more games.

At this point Yamauchi told Miyamoto to come up with the most imaginative games ever. However, Yamauchi also realized that Nintendo alone could not satisfy the growing thirst for new games, so he initiated a licensing program. To become a Nintendo licensee, companies had to agree to an unprecedented series of restrictions. Licensees could issue only five Nintendo games per year, and they could not write those titles for other platforms. The licensing fee was set at 20% of the wholesale price of each cartridge sold (game cartridges wholesaled for around $30). It typically cost $500,000 to develop a game and took around six months. Nintendo insisted that games not contain any excessively violent or sexually suggestive material and that they review every game before allowing it to be produced.[13]

Despite these restrictions, six companies (Bandai, Capcom, Konami, Namco, Taito, and Hudson) agreed to become Nintendo licensees, not least because millions of customers were now clamoring for games. Bandai was Japan's largest toy company. The others already made either coin-operated videogames or computer software games. Because of these licensing agreements, they saw their sales and earnings surge. For example, Konami's earnings went from $10 million in 1987 to $300 million in 1991.

After the six licensees began selling games, reports of defective games began to reach Yamauchi. The original six licensees were allowed to manufacture their own game cartridges. Realizing that he had given away the ability to control the quality of the cartridges, Yamauchi decided to change the contract for future licensees. Future licensees were required to submit all manufacturing orders for cartridges to Nintendo. Nintendo charged licensees $14 per cartridge, required that they place a minimum order for 10,000 units, (later the minimum order was raised to 30,000), and insisted on cash payment in full when the order was placed. Nintendo outsourced all manufacturing to other companies, using the volume of its orders to get rock bottom prices. The cartridges were estimated to cost Nintendo between $6 and $8 each. The licensees then picked up the cartridges from Nintendo's loading dock and were responsible for distribution. In 1985, there were seventeen licensees. By 1987, there were fifty. By this point, 90% of the home videogame systems sold in Japan were Nintendo systems.

Nintendo in America

In 1980, Nintendo established a subsidiary in America to sell its coin-operated videogames. Yamauchi's American-educated son-in-law, Minoru Arakawa, headed the subsidiary. All of the other essential employees were Americans, including Ron Judy and Al Stone. For its first two years, Nintendo of America (NOA), based originally in Seattle, struggled to sell second-rate games such as Radarscope. The subsidiary seemed on the brink of closing. NOA could not even make the rent payment on the warehouse. Then they received a large shipment from Japan: 2,000 units of a new coin-operated videogame. Opening the box, they discovered Donkey Kong. After playing the game briefly, Judy proclaimed it a disaster. Stone walked out of the building, declaring that "it's over."[14] The managers were appalled. They could not imagine a game less likely to sell in video arcades. The only promising sign was that a twenty-year employee, Howard Philips, rapidly became enthralled with the machine.

Arakawa, however, knew he had little choice but to try to sell the machine. Judy persuaded the owner of the Spot Tavern near Nintendo's office to take one of the machines on a trial basis. After one night, Judy discovered $30 in the coin box, a phenomenal amount. The next night there was $35, and $36 the night after that. NOA had a hit on its hands.

By the end of 1982, NOA had sold over 60,000 copies of Donkey Kong and had booked sales in excess of $100 million. The subsidiary had outgrown its Seattle location. They moved to a new site in Redmond, a Seattle suburb, where they located next to a small but fast-growing software company run by an old school acquaintance of Howard Philips, Bill Gates.

By 1984, NOA was riding a wave of success in the coin-operated videogame market. Arakawa, however, was interested in the possibilities of selling Nintendo's new Famicom system in the United States. Throughout 1984, Arakawa, Judy, and Stone met with numerous toy and department store representatives to discuss the possibilities, only to be repeatedly rebuffed. Still smarting from the 1983 debacle, the representatives wanted nothing to do with the home videogame business. They also met with former managers from Atari and Caloco to gain their insights. The most common response they received was that the market collapsed because the last generation of games was awful.

Arakawa and his team decided that if they were going to sell Famicom in the United States, they would have to find a new distribution channel. The obvious choice was consumer electronics stores. Thus, Arakawa asked the R&D team in Kyoto to redesign Famicom for the U.S. market so that it looked less like a toy (Famicom was encased in red and white plastic) and more like a consumer electronics device. The redesigned machine was renamed the Nintendo Entertainment System (NES).

Arakawa's big fear was that illegal, low-quality Taiwanese games would flood the U.S. market if NES was successful. To stop counterfeit games being played on NES, Arakawa asked Nintendo's Japanese engineers to design a security system into the U.S. version of Famicom so that only Nintendo-approved games could be played on NES. The Japanese engineers responded by designing a security chip to be embedded in the game cartridges. NES would not work unless the security chips in the cartridges unlocked, or "shook hands with," a chip in NES. Since the code embedded in the security chip was proprietary, the implication of this system was that no one could manufacture games for NES without Nintendo's specific approval.

To overcome the skepticism and reluctance of retailers to stock a home videogame system, Arakawa decided in late 1985 to make an extraordinary commitment. Nintendo would stock stores and set up displays and windows. Retailers would not have to pay for anything they stocked for ninety days. After that, retailers could pay Nintendo for what they sold and return the rest. NES was bundled with Nintendo's best-selling game in Japan, Super Mario Brothers. It was essentially a risk-free proposition for retailers, but even with this, most were skeptical. Ultimately, thirty

Nintendo personnel descended on the New York area. Referred to as the Nintendo SWAT team, they persuaded some stores to stock NES after an extraordinary blitz that involved eighteen-hour days. To support the New York product launch, Nintendo also committed itself to a $5 million advertising campaign aimed at the seven- to fourteen-year-old boys who seemed to be Nintendo's likely core audience.

By December 1985, between 500 and 600 stores in the New York area were stocking Nintendo systems. Sales were moderate, about half of the 100,000 NES machines shipped from Japan were sold, but it was enough to justify going forward. The SWAT team then moved first to Los Angeles, then to Chicago, then to Dallas. As in New York, sales started at a moderate pace, but by late 1986 they started to accelerate rapidly, and Nintendo went national with NES.

In 1986, around 1 million NES units were sold in the United States. In 1987, the figure increased to 3 million. In 1988, it jumped to over 7 million. In the same year, 33 million game cartridges were sold. Nintendo mania had arrived in the United States. To expand the supply of games, Nintendo licensed the rights to produce up to five games per year to thirty-one American software companies. Nintendo continued to use a restrictive licensing agreement that gave it exclusive rights to any games, required licensees to place their orders through Nintendo, and insisted on a 30,000-unit minimum order.[15]

By 1990, the home videogame market was worth $5 billion worldwide. Nintendo dominated the industry, with a 90% share of the market for game equipment. The parent company was, by some measures, now the most profitable company in Japan. By 1992, it was netting over $1 billion in gross profit annually, or more than $1.5 million for each employee in Japan. The company's stock market value exceeded that of Sony, Japan's premier consumer electronics firm. Indeed, the company's net profit exceeded that of all the American movie studios combined. Nintendo games, it seemed, were bigger than the movies.

As of 1991, there were over 100 licensees for Nintendo, and over 450 titles were available for NES. In the United States, Nintendo products were distributed through toy stores (30% of volume), mass merchandisers (40% of volume), and department stores (10% of volume). Nintendo tightly controlled the number of game titles and games that could be sold, quickly withdrawing titles as soon as interest appeared to decline. In 1988, retailers requested 110 million cartridges from Nintendo. Market surveys suggested that perhaps 45 million could have been sold, but Nintendo allowed only 33 million to be shipped.[16] Nintendo claimed that the shortage of games was in part due to a worldwide shortage of semiconductor chips.

Several companies had tried to reverse-engineer the code embedded in Nintendo's security chip, which competitors characterized as a lockout chip. Nintendo successfully sued them. The most notable was Atari Games, one of the successors of the original Atari, which in 1987 sued NOA for anticompetitive behavior. Atari claimed that the purpose of the security chip was to monopolize the market. At the same time, Atari announced that it had found a way around Nintendo's security chip and would begin to sell unlicensed games.[17] NOA responded with a countersuit. In a March 1991 ruling, Atari was found to have obtained Nintendo's security code illegally and was ordered to stop selling NES-compatible games. However, Nintendo did not always have it all its own way. In 1990, under pressure from Congress, the Department of Justice, and several lawsuits, Nintendo rescinded its exclusivity requirements, freeing up developers to write games for other platforms. However, developers faced a real problem: what platform could they write for?

Sega's Sonic Boom

Back in 1954, David Rosen, a twenty-year-old American, left the U.S. Air Force after a tour of duty in Tokyo.[18] Rosen had noticed that Japanese people needed lots of photographs for ID cards, but that local photo studios were slow and expensive. He formed a company, Rosen Enterprises, and went into the photo-booth business, which was a big success. By 1957, Rosen had established a successful nationwide chain. At this point, the Japanese economy was booming, so Rosen decided it was time to get into another business—entertainment. As his vehicle, he chose arcade games, which were unknown in Japan at the time. He picked up used games on the cheap from America and set up arcades in the same Japanese department stores and theaters that typically housed his photo booths. Within a few years, Rosen had two hundred arcades nationwide. His only competition came from another American-owned firm, Service Games (SeGa), whose original business was jukeboxes and fruit machines.

By the early 1960s, the Japanese arcade market had caught up with the U.S. market. The problem was that game makers had run out of exciting new games to offer. Rosen decided that he would have to get into the business of designing and manufacturing games, but to do that he needed manufacturing facilities. SeGa manufactured its own games, so in 1965 Rosen approached the company and suggested a merger. The result was Sega Enterprise, a Japanese company with Rosen as its CEO.

Rosen himself designed Sega's first game, Periscope, in which the objective was to sink chain-mounted cardboard ships by firing torpedoes, represented by lines of colored lights. Periscope was a big success not only in Japan, but also in the United States and Europe, and it allowed Sega to build up a respectable export business. Over the years, the company continued to invest heavily in game development, always using the latest electronic technology.

Gulf and Western (G&W), a U.S. conglomerate, acquired Sega in 1969, with Rosen running the subsidiary. In 1975, G&W took Sega public in the United States, but left Sega Japan as a G&W subsidiary. Hayao Nakayama, a former Sega distributor, was drafted as president. In the early 1980s, Nakayama pushed G&W to invest more in Sega Japan so that the company could enter the then-booming home videogame market. When G&W refused, Nakayama suggested a management buyout. G&W agreed, and in 1984, for the price of just $38 million, Sega became a Japanese company once more. (Sega's Japanese revenues were around $700 million, but by now the company was barely profitable.)

Sega was caught off guard by the huge success of Nintendo's Famicom. Although it released its own 8-bit system in 1986, the machine never commanded more than 5% of the Japanese market. Nakayama, however, was not about to give up. From years in the arcade business, he understood that great games drove sales. Nevertheless, he also understood that more powerful technology gave game developers the tools to develop more appealing games. This philosophy underlay Nakayama's decision to develop a 16-bit game system, Genesis.

Sega took the design of its 16-bit arcade machine and adapted it for Genesis. Compared to Nintendo's 8-bit machine, the 16-bit machine featured an array of superior technological features, including high-definition graphics and animation, a full spectrum of colors, two independent scrolling backgrounds that created an impressive depth of field, and near CD quality sound. The design strategy also made it easy to port Sega's catalog of arcade hits to Genesis.

Genesis was launched in Japan in 1989 and in the United States in 1990. In the United States, the machine was priced at $199. The company hoped that sales would be boosted by the popularity of its arcade games, such as the graphically violent Altered Beast. Sega also licensed other companies to develop games for the Genesis platform. In an effort to recruit licensees, Sega asked for lower royalty rates than Nintendo, and it gave licensees the right to manufacture their own cartridges. Independent game developers were slow to climb on board, however, and the $200 price tag for the player held back sales.

One of the first independent game developers to sign up with Sega was Electronic Arts. Established by Trip Hawkins, Electronic Arts had focused on designing games for personal computers and consequently had missed the Nintendo 8-bit era. Now Hawkins was determined to get a presence in the home videogame market, and aligning his company's wagon with Sega seemed to be the best option. The Nintendo playing field was already crowded, and Sega offered a far less restrictive licensing deal than Nintendo. Electronic Arts subsequently wrote several popular games for Genesis, including John Madden football and several gory combat games.[19]

Nintendo had not been ignoring the potential of the 16-bit system. Nintendo's own 16-bit system, Super NES, was ready for market introduction in 1989—at the same time as Sega's Genesis. Nintendo introduced Super NES in Japan in 1990, where it quickly established a strong market presence and beat Sega's Genesis. In the United States, however, the company decided to hold back longer to reap the full benefits of the dominance it enjoyed with the 8-bit NES system. Yamauchi was also worried about the lack of backward compatibility between Nintendo's 8-bit and 16-bit systems. (The company had tried to make the 16-bit system so that it could play 8-bit games but concluded that the cost of doing so was prohibitive.) These concerns may have led the company to delay market introduction until the 8-bit market was saturated.

Meanwhile, in the United States, the Sega bandwagon was beginning to gain momentum. One development that gave Genesis a push was the introduction of a new Sega game, Sonic the Hedgehog. Developed by an independent team that was contracted to Sega, the game featured a cute hedgehog that impatiently tapped his paw when the player took too long to act. Impatience was Sonic's central feature—he had places to go, and quickly. He zipped along, collecting brass rings when he could find them, before rolling into a ball and flying down slides with loops and underground tunnels. Sonic was Sega's Mario.

In mid-1991, in an attempt to jump-start slow sales, Tom Kalinske, head of Sega's American subsidiary, decided to bundle Sonic the Hedgehog with the game player. He also reduced the price for the bundled unit to $150, and he relaunched the system with an aggressive advertising campaign aimed at teenagers. The campaign was built around the slogan "Genesis does what Nintendon't." The shift in strategy worked, and sales accelerated sharply.

Sega's success prompted Nintendo to launch its own 16-bit system. Nintendo's Super NES was introduced at $200. However, Sega now had a two-year head start in games. By the end of 1991, about 125 game titles were available for Genesis, compared to twenty-five for Super NES. In May 1992, Nintendo reduced the price of Super NES to $150. At this time Sega was claiming a 63% share of the 16-bit market in the United States, and Nintendo claimed a 60% share. By now, Sega was cool. It began to take more chances with mass media–defined morality. When Acclaim Entertainment released its bloody Mortal Kombat game in September 1992, the Sega version let players rip off heads and tear out hearts. Reflecting Nintendo's image of their core market, its version was sanitized. The Sega version outsold Nintendo's two to one.[20] Therefore, the momentum continued to run in Sega's favor. By January 1993, there were 320 titles available for Sega Genesis, and 130 for Super NES. In early 1994, independent estimates suggested that Sega had 60% of the U.S. market and Nintendo had 40%, figures Nintendo disputed.

3DO

Trip Hawkins, whose first big success was Electronic Arts, founded 3DO in 1991.[21] Hawkins's vision for 3DO was to shift the home videogame business away from the existing cartridge-based format and toward a CD-ROM-based platform. The original partners in 3DO were Electronic Arts, Matsushita, Time Warner, AT&T, and the venture capital firm Kleiner Perkins. Collectively they invested over $17 million in 3DO, making it the richest start-up in the history of the home videogame industry. 3DO went public in May 1993 at $15 per share. By October of that year, the stock had risen to $48 per share, making 3DO worth $1 billion—not bad for a company that had yet to generate a single dollar in revenues.

The basis for 3DO's $1 billion market cap was patented computer system architecture and a copyrighted operating system that allowed for much richer graphics and audio capabilities. The system was built around a 32-bit RISC microprocessor and proprietary graphics processor chips. Instead of a cartridge, the 3DO system stored games on a CD-ROM that was capable of holding up to 600 megabytes of content, sharply up from the 10 megabytes of content found in the typical game cartridge of the time. The slower access time of a CD-ROM compared to a cartridge was alleviated somewhat by the use of a double-speed CD-ROM drive.[22]

The belief at 3DO—a belief apparently shared by many investors—was that the superior storage and graphics processing capabilities of the 3DO system would prove very attractive to game developers, allowing them to be far more creative. In turn, better games would attract customers away from Nintendo and Sega. Developing games that used the capabilities of a CD-ROM system altered the economics of game development. Estimates suggested that it would cost approximately $2 million to produce a game for the 3DO system and could take as long as twenty-four months to develop. However, at $2 per disc, a CD-ROM cost substantially less to produce than a cartridge.

The centerpiece of 3DO's strategy was to license its hardware technology for free. Game developers paid a royalty of $3 per disc for access to the 3DO operating code. Discs typically retailed for $40 each.

Matsushita introduced the first 3DO machine into the U.S. market in October 1993. Priced at $700, the machine was sold through electronic retailers that carried Panasonic high-end electronics products. Sega's Tom Kalinsky noted, "It's a noble effort. Some people will buy 3DO, and they'll have a wonderful experience. It's impressive, but it's a niche. We've done the research. It does not become a large market until you go below $500. At $300, it starts to get interesting. We make no money on hardware. It's a cutthroat business. I hope Matsushita understands that."[23] CD-ROM disks for the 3DO machine retailed for around $75. The machine came bundled with Crash 'n Burn, a high-speed combat racing game.

However, only 18 3DO titles were available by the crucial Christmas period, although reports suggested that 150 titles were under development. [24]

Sales of the hardware were slow, reaching only 30,000 by January 1994.[25] In the same month, AT&T and Sanyo both announced that they would begin to manufacture the 3DO machine. In March, faced with continuing sluggish sales, 3DO announced that it would give hardware manufacturers two shares of 3DO stock for every unit sold at or below a certain retail price. Matsushita dropped the price of its machine to $500. About the same time, Toshiba, LG, and Samsung all announced that they would start to produce 3DO machines.

By June 1994, cumulative sales of 3DO machines in the United States stood at 40,000 units. Matsushita announced plans to expand distribution beyond the current 3,500 outlets to include the toy and mass merchandise channels. Hawkins and his partners announced that they would invest another $37 million in 3DO. By July, there were 750 3DO software licensees, but only forty titles were available for the format. Despite these moves, sales continued at a very sluggish pace and the supply of new software titles started to dry up.[26]

In September 1996, 3DO announced that it would either sell its hardware system business or move it into a joint venture.[27] The company announced that about 150 people, one-third of the workforce, would probably lose their jobs in the restructuring. According to Trip Hawkins, 3DO would now focus on developing software for online gaming. Hawkins stated that the Internet and Internet entertainment constituted a huge opportunity for 3DO. The stock dropped $1.375 to $6.75.

Sega's Saturn

3DO was not alone in moving to a CD-ROM-based format. Both Sega and Sony also introduced CD-ROM-based systems in the mid-1990s. Sega, in fact, had beaten 3DO to the market with its November 1992 introduction of the Sega CD, a $300 CD-ROM add-on for the 16-bit Genesis. Sega sold 100,000 units in its first month alone. Sales then slowed down, however, and by December 1993 were standing at just 250,000 units. One reason for the slowdown, according to critics, was a lack of strong games. Sega was also working on a 32-bit CD-ROM system, Saturn, which was targeted for a mid-1995 introduction in the United States. In January 1994, Sega announced that Microsoft would supply the operating system for Saturn.[28]

In March 1994, Sega announced the Genesis Super 32X, a $150 add-on cartridge designed to increase the performance of Genesis cartridge and CD-ROM games. The 32X contained the 32-bit Hitachi microprocessor that was to be used in Saturn. Sega called the 32X "the poor man's 32-bit machine" because it sold for a mere $149. Introduced in the fall of 1994, the 32X never lived up to its expectations. Most users appeared willing to wait for the real thing, Sega Saturn, promised for release the following year.

In early 1995, Sega informed the press and retailers that it would release Saturn on "Sega Saturn Saturday, Sept. 2nd," but Sega released the 32-bit Saturn in May 1995. It was priced at $400 per unit and accompanied by the introduction of just ten games. Sega apparently believed that the world would be delighted by the May release of the Saturn. However, Saturn was released without the industry fanfare that normally greets a new game machine. Only four retail chains received the Saturn in May, while the rest were told they would have to wait until September. This move alienated retailers, who responded by dropping Sega products from their stores.[29] Sega appeared to have made a marketing blunder.[30]

Sony's Playstation

In the fall of 1995, Sony entered the fray with the introduction of the Sony PlayStation.[31] PlayStation used a 32-bit RISC microprocessor running at 33 MHz and using a double-speed CD-ROM drive. PlayStation cost an estimated $500 million to develop. The machine had actually been under development since 1991, when Sony decided that the home videogame industry was getting too big to ignore. Initially, Sony was in an alliance with Nintendo to develop the machine. Nintendo walked away from the alliance in 1992, however, after a disagreement over who owned the rights to any future CD-ROM games. Sony went alone.[32]

From the start, Sony felt that it could leverage its presence in the film and music business to build a strong position in the home videogame industry. A consumer electronics giant with a position in the Hollywood movie business and the music industry (Sony owned Columbia Pictures and the Columbia record label), Sony believed that it had access to significant intellectual property that could form the basis of many popular games.

In 1991, Sony established a division in New York: Sony Electronic Publishing. The division was to serve as an umbrella organization for Sony's multimedia offerings. Headed by Iceland native Olaf Olafsson, then just twenty-eight years old, this organization ultimately took the lead role in both the market launch of PlayStation and in developing game titles.[33] In 1993, as part of this effort, Sony purchased a well-respected British game developer, Psygnosis. By the fall of 1995, this unit had twenty games ready to complement PlayStation: The Haldeman Diaries, Mickey Mania (developed in collaboration with Disney), and Johnny Mnemonic, based on the William Gibson short story. To entice independent game developers such as Electronic Arts, Namco, and Acclaim Entertainment, Olafsson used the promise of low royalty rates. The standard royalty rate was set at $9 per disc, although developers that signed on early enough were given a lower royalty rate. Sony also provided approximately four thousand game development tools to licensees in an effort to help them speed games to market.[34]

To distribute PlayStation, Sony set up a retail channel separate from Sony's consumer electronics sales force. It marketed the PlayStation as a hip and powerful alternative to the outdated Nintendo and Sega cartridge-based systems. Sony worked closely with retailers before the launch to find out how it could help them sell the PlayStation. To jump-start demand, Sony set up in-store displays to allow potential consumers to try the equipment. Just before the launch, Sony had lined up an impressive 12,000 retail outlets in the United States.[35]

Sony targeted its advertising for PlayStation at males in the eighteen- to thirty-five-year-old age range. The targeting was evident in the content of many of the games. One of the big hits for PlayStation was Tomb Raider, whose central character, Lara Croft, combined sex appeal with savviness and helped to recruit an older generation to PlayStation.[36] PlayStation was initially priced at $299, and games retailed for as much as $60. Sony's Tokyo-based executives had reportedly been insisting on a $350–$400 price for PlayStation, but Olafsson pushed hard for the lower price. Because of the fallout from this internal battle, in January 1996, Olafsson resigned from Sony. By then, however, Sony was following Olafsson's script.[37]

Sony's prelaunch work was rewarded with strong early sales. By January 1996, more than 800,000 PlayStations had been sold in the United States, plus another 4 million games. In May 1996, with 1.2 million PlayStations shipped, Sony reduced the price of PlayStation to $199. Sega responded with a similar price cut for its Saturn. The prices on some of Sony's initial games were also reduced to $29.99. The weekend after the price cuts, retailers reported that PlayStation sales were up by between 350 and 1,000% over the prior week. [38] The sales surge continued through 1996. By the end of the year, sales of PlayStation and associated software amounted to $1.3 billion, out of a total for U.S. sales at $2.2 billion for all videogame hardware and software. In March 1997, Sony cut the price of PlayStation again, this time to $149. It also reduced its suggested retail price for games by $10 to $49.99. By this point, Sony had sold 3.4 million units of PlayStation in the United States, compared to Saturn's 1.6 million units.[39] Worldwide, PlayStation had outsold Saturn by 13 million to 7.8 million units, and Saturn sales were slowing.[40] The momentum was clearly running in Sony's favor, but the company now had a new challenge to deal with: Nintendo's latest generation game machine, the N64.

Nintendo Strikes Back

In July 1996, Nintendo launched Nintendo 64 (N64) in the Japanese market. This release was followed by a late fall introduction in the United States. N64 is a 64-bit machine developed in conjunction with Silicon Graphics. Originally targeted for introduction a year earlier, N64 had been under development since 1993. The machine used a plug-in cartridge format rather than a CD-ROM drive. According to Nintendo, cartridges allow for faster access time and are far more durable than CD-ROMs (an important consideration with children).[41]

The most-striking feature of the N64 machine, however, was its 3D graphics capability. N64 provides fully rounded figures that can turn on their heels and rotate through 180 degrees. Advanced ray tracing techniques borrowed from military simulators and engineering workstations added to the sense of realism by providing proper highlighting, reflections, and shadows.

N64 was targeted at children and young teenagers. It was priced at $200 and launched with just four games. Despite the lack of games, initial sales were very strong. Indeed, 1997 turned out to be a banner year for both Sony and Nintendo. The overall U.S. market was strong, with sales of hardware and software combined reaching a record $5.5 billion. Estimates suggest that PlayStation accounted for 49% of machines and games by value. N64 captured a 41% share, leaving Sega trailing badly with less than 10% of the market. During the year, the average price for game machines had fallen to $150. By year-end there were three hundred titles available for PlayStation, compared to forty for N64. Games for PlayStation retailed for $40, on average, compared to over $60 for N64. [42]

By late 1998, PlayStation was widening its lead over N64. In the crucial North American market, PlayStation was reported to be outselling N64 by a two-to-one margin, although Nintendo retained a lead in the under-twelve category. At this point, there were 115 games available for N64 versus 431 for PlayStation.[43] Worldwide, Sony had now sold close to 55 million PlayStations. The success of PlayStation had a major impact on Sony's bottom line. In fiscal 1998, PlayStation business generated revenues of $5.5 billion for Sony, 10% of its worldwide revenues, but accounted for $886 million, or 22.5%, of the company's operating income.[44]

The 128-Bit Era

When Nintendo launched its 64-bit machine in 1996, Sony and Sega didn't follow, preferring instead to focus on the development of even more powerful 128-bit machines.

Sega was the first to market a 128-bit videogame console, which it launched in Japan in late 1998 and in the United States in late 1999. The Dreamcast came equipped with a 56-kilobit modem to allow for online gaming over the Internet. By late 2000, Sega had sold around 6 million Dreamcasts worldwide, accounting for about 15% of console sales since its launch. Sega nurtured Dreamcast sales by courting outside software developers who helped develop new games, including Crazy Taxi, Resident Evil, and Quake III Arena. The company had a goal of shipping 10 million units by March 2001, a goal it never reached.[45]

Despite its position as first mover with a 128-bit machine, and despite solid technical reviews, by late 2000 the company was struggling. Sega was handicapped first by product shortages due to constraints on the supply of component parts and then by a lack of demand as consumers waited to see whether Sony's 128-bit offering, the much anticipated PlayStation 2 (PS2), would be a more attractive machine. In September 2000, Sega responded to the impending U.S. launch of Sony's PS2 by cutting the price for its console from $199 to $149. Then in late October, Sega announced that, due to this price cut, it would probably lose over $200 million for the fiscal year ending March 2001.[46]

Sony's PlayStation 2

PlayStation 2 was launched in Japan in mid-2000 and in the United States at the end of October 2000. Initially priced at $299, PS2 is a powerful machine. At its core was a 300-megahertz graphics processing chip that was jointly developed with Toshiba and consumed about $1.3 billion in R&D. Referred to as the Emotion Engine processor, the chip allows the machine to display stunning graphic images previously found only on supercomputers. The chip made the PS2 the most powerful videogame machine yet.

The machine was set up to play different CD and DVD formats, as well as proprietary game titles. As is true with the original PlayStation, PS2 could play audio CDs. The system was also compatible with the original PlayStation: any PlayStation title could be played on the PS2. To help justify the initial price tag, the unit doubled as a DVD player with picture quality as good as current players. The PS2 did not come equipped with a modem, but it did have networking capabilities and a modem could be attached using one of two USB ports.[47]

Nintendo GameCube

Nintendo had garnered a solid position in the industry with its N64 machine by focusing on its core demographic, seven- to twelve-year-olds. In 1999, Nintendo took 33% of the hardware market and 28% of the game market. Nintendo's next-generation videogame machine, GameCube, packed a modem and a powerful 400-megahertz, 128-bit processor made by IBM into a compact cube. GameCube marked a shift away from Nintendo's traditional approach of using proprietary cartridges to hold game software. Instead, software for the new player came on 8-centimeter compact disks, which are smaller than music compact disks. The disks held 1.5 gigabytes of data each, far greater storage capacity than the old game cartridges. Players could control Game-Cube using wireless controllers.[48]

Nintendo tried to make the GameCube easy for developers to work with rather than focusing on raw peak performance. While developers no doubt appreciated this, by the time GameCube hit store shelves in late 2001, PS2 had been on the market for eighteen months and boasted a solid library of games. Despite its strong brand and instantly recognized intellectual property, which included Donkey Kong, Super Mario Brothers, and the Pokemon characters, Nintendo was playing catch-up to Sony. Moreover, another new entrant into the industry launched its 128-bit offering at around the same time: Microsoft.

Microsoft's Xbox

Microsoft was first rumored to be developing a videogame console in late 1999. In March 2000, Bill Gates made it official when he announced that Microsoft would enter the home videogame market in fall 2001 with a console code named Xbox. In terms of sheer computing power, the 128-bit Xbox had the edge over competitors. Xbox had a 733-megahertz Pentium III processor, a high-powered graphics chip from Nvidia Corp, a built-in broadband cable modem to allow for online game playing and high-speed Internet browsing, 64 megabytes of memory, CD and DVD drives, and an internal hard disk drive. The operating system was a stripped-down version of its popular Windows system optimized for graphics processing capabilities. Microsoft claimed that because the Xbox was based on familiar PC technology, it would be much easier for software developers to write games for, and it would be relatively easy to convert games from the PC to run on the Xbox.[49]

Although Microsoft was a new entrant to the videogame industry, it was no stranger to games. Microsoft had long participated in the PC gaming industry and was one of the largest publishers of PC games, with hits such as Microsoft Flight Simulator and Age of Empires I and II to its credit. Sales of Microsoft's PC games have increased 50% annually between 1998 and 2001, and the company controlled about 10% of the PC game market in 2001. Microsoft had also offered online gaming for some time, including its popular MSN Gaming Zone site. Started in 1996, by 2001 the website had become the largest online PC gaming hub on the Internet with nearly 12 million subscribers paying $9.95 a month to play premium games such as Asheron's Call or Fighter Ace.

Nor is Microsoft new to hardware; its joysticks and game pads outsell all other brands, and it has an important mouse business.

To build the Xbox, Microsoft chose Flextronics, a contract manufacturer that already made computer mice for Microsoft. Realizing that it would probably have to cut Xbox prices over time, Microsoft guaranteed Flextronics a profit margin, effectively agreeing to subsidize Flextronics if selling prices fell below a specified amount. By 2003, Microsoft was thought to be losing $100 on every Xbox sold. To make that back and turn a profit, Microsoft reportedly had to sell between six and nine videogames per Xbox.[50]

Analysts speculated that Microsoft's entry into the home videogame market was a response to a potential threat from Sony. Microsoft was worried that Internet-ready consoles like PS2 might take over many web-browsing functions from the personal computer. Some in the company described Internet-enabled videogame terminals as Trojan horses in the living room. In Microsoft's calculation, it made sense to get in the market to try and keep Sony and others in check. With annual revenues in excess of $20 billion worldwide, the home videogame market is huge and an important source of potential growth for Microsoft. Still, by moving away from its core market, Microsoft was taking a big risk, particularly given the scale of investments required to develop the Xbox, reported to run as high as $1.5 billion.

Mortal Combat: Microsoft versus Sony

The launch of Xbox and GameCube helped propel sales of videogame hardware and software to a record $9.4 billion in 2001, up from $6.58 billion in 2000. Although both Xbox and Nintendo initially racked up strong sales, the momentum started to slow significantly in 2002. Microsoft, in particular, found it very difficult to penetrate the Japanese market. By September 2002, Sony had sold 11.2 million units of PS2 in the United States, versus 2.2 million units of Xbox and 2.7 million units of Nintendo's GameCube. Unable to hold onto market share in the wake of the new competition, Sega withdrew from the console market, announcing that henceforth it would focus on developing games for other platforms.

In June 2002, Sony responded to the new entry by cutting the price for PS2 from $299 to $199. Microsoft quickly followed, cutting the price for Xbox from $299 to $199, while Nintendo cut its price from $299 to $149.[51] A year later, Sony cut prices again, this time to $179 a console. Again, Microsoft followed with a similar price cut, and in March 2004 it took the lead, cutting Xbox prices to $149. Sony followed suit two months later.[52]

Microsoft's strategy, however, involved far more than cutting prices. In November 2002 Microsoft announced that it would introduce a new service for gamers, Xbox Live. For $50 a year, Xbox Live subscribers with broadband connections would be able to play online-enabled versions of Xbox games with other online subscribers. To support Xbox Live, Microsoft invested some $500 million in its own data centers to host online game playing.

Online game playing was clearly a strategic priority from the outset. Unlike the PS2 and GameCube, Xbox came with a built-in broadband capability. The decision to make the Xbox broadband-capable was made back in 1999 when less than 5% of U.S. homes were linked to the Internet with a broadband connection. Explaining the decision to build broadband capabilities into the Xbox at a time when rivals lacked them, the head of Xbox, Jay Allard, noted that "my attitude has always been to bet on the future, not against it."[53] While Sony's PS2 can be hooked up to the Internet via a broadband connection, doing so requires purchase of a special network adapter for $40.

By mid-2003, Xbox Live had some 500,000 subscribers, versus 80,000 who had registered to play PS2 games online. By this point, there were twenty-eight online games for Xbox and eighteen for PlayStation 2. By January 2004, the comparative figures stood at fifty for Microsoft and thirty-two for Sony. By mid-2004, Xbox Live reportedly had over 1 million subscribers, with Sony claiming a similar number of online players.[54] In May 2004, Microsoft struck a deal with Electronic Arts, the world's largest videogame publisher, to bring EA games, including its best-selling Madden Football, to the Xbox Live platform. Until this point, EA had produced live games only for Sony's platform.

In spite of all these strategic moves, by late 2004 Xbox was still a distant second of PlayStation 2 in the videogame market having sold 14 million consoles against Sony's 70 million (Nintendo had sold 13 million GameCube consoles by this point). While Sony was making good money from the business, Microsoft was registering significant losses. In fiscal 2004, Microsoft's home and entertainment division, of which Xbox is the major component, registered $2.45 billion in revenues, but lost $1.135 billion. By

way of contrast, Sony's game division had $7.5 billion of sales in fiscal 2004 and generated operating profits of $640 million.

Microsoft, however, indicated that it was in the business for the long term. In late 2004, the company got a boost from the release of Halo 2, the sequel to Halo, one of its best-selling games. As first-day sales for Halo 2 were totaled up, executives at Sony had to be worried. Microsoft announced that Halo 2 had sales of $125 million in its first twenty-four hours on the market in the United States and Canada, an industry record. These figures represented sales of 2.38 million units, and put Halo 2 firmly on track to be one of the biggest videogames ever with a shot at surpassing Nintendo's Super Mario 64, which had sold $308 million in the United States since its September 1996 debut. Moreover, the company was rumored to be ahead of Sony by as much as a year to bring the next-generation videogame console to market. In late 2004, reports suggested that Xbox 2 would be on the market in time for the 2005 Christmas season, probably a full year ahead of Sony's PlayStation 3. Sony was rumored to be running into technical problems as it tried to develop PlayStation 3.[55]

Microsoft Versus Sony: Round Two

As the battle between PS2 and Xbox drew to a close, it was clear that Sony was the big winner. From 2001 through to the fall of 2006, when PlayStation 3 (PS3) hit the market, Sony had sold around 110 million PS2 consoles, versus 25 million for Microsoft's Xbox and 21 million for Nintendo's GameCube.[56] Sony's advantage of an installed base translated into a huge lead in number of games sold—some 1.08 billion for PS2 by mid-2006, versus 200 million for the Xbox.[57] With the console companies reportedly making an average royalty on third-party software of $8 per game sold, the financial implications of Sony's lead with PS2 are obvious.[58] Indeed, in 2005 Sony's games division contributed to 6.24% of the company's total revenue but 38% of operating profit. In contrast, Microsoft's home and entertainment division lost $4 billion between the launch of Xbox and mid-2006.

However, by 2006, this was all history. In November 2005, Microsoft introduced its next-generation machine, Xbox 360, beating Sony and Nintendo to the market by a solid year. The Xbox 360 represented a big technological advance over the original Xbox. To deliver improved picture quality, the Xbox 360 could execute 500 million polygons/sec—a fourfold increase over the Xbox. The main microprocessor was a 3.2 gigahertz chip, thirteen times faster than the chip in the Xbox. Xbox 360 had 512 megabytes of memory, an eightfold increase, and a 20-gigabyte hard drive, two and one-half times bigger than that found on the Xbox. Xbox 360 is, of course, enabled for a broadband connection to the Internet.

The machine itself was made by Flextronics and Wistron, two contract manufactures (a third started production after launch). Priced at $299, Xbox 360 was sold at a loss. The cost for making Xbox 360 was estimated to be as high as $500 at launch, falling to $350 by late 2006. Microsoft's goal was to ultimately break even on sales of the hardware as manufacturing efficiencies drove down unit costs.

To seed the market with games, Microsoft had taken a number of steps. Taking a page out of its Windows business, Microsoft provided game developers with tools designed to automate many of the key software programming tasks and reduce development time and costs. The company had also expanded its own in-house game studios, in part by purchasing several independent game developers including Bungie Studios, makers of Halo. This strategy enabled Microsoft to offer exclusive content for the Xbox 360, something that third-party developers were reluctant to do.

With the costs of game development increasing to over $10 million for more complex games, and development time stretching out to between twenty-four and thirty-six months, Microsoft also had to provide an inducement to get third-party developers on board. Although details of royalty terms are kept private, it is believed that Microsoft offered very low royalty rates, and perhaps even zero royalties, for a specified period of times to game developers who committed early to Xbox 360. One of those to commit early was Electronic Arts, the leading independent game development company, which reportedly budgeted as much as $200 million to develop some twenty-five versions of its best-selling games, such as its sports games, for Xbox 360. Microsoft itself budgeted a similar amount to develop its own games.[59]

In the event, some 18 games were available for the November 2005 launch of Xbox 360, and by the end of 2006, this figure had increased to around 160. Halo 3, which is expected to be one of the biggest games for Xbox 360, is scheduled to be released in 2007. As a Microsoft game, this will be exclusive to the Xbox 360. Grand Theft Auto 4, the most popular franchise on PS2, will also be launched simultaneously for both Xbox 360 and PS3 in 2007—a major coup for Microsoft.

The initial launch of Xbox 360 was marred by shortages of key components, which limited the number of machines that Microsoft could bring to market. Had Sony been on time with its launch of PS3, this could have been a serious error, but Sony delayed its launch of PS3, first until spring of 2006, and then November 2006. By the time Sony launched PS3 in November 2006, some 6 million Xbox 360 consoles had been sold, and Microsoft was predicting sales of 10 million by the end of 2006.

As with Xbox, Microsoft is pushing Xbox Live with Xbox 360. The company invested as much as $1 billion in Live from its inception. By late 2006, Microsoft was claiming that some 60% of Xbox 360 customers had also signed on for Xbox Live and that the service now had 4 million subscribers. Xbox Live allows gamers to play against each other online and to download digital content from Xbox Live Marketplace, which registered some 10 million downloads of digital content in its first five months of operation. Looking forward, there is little doubt that Microsoft sees Xbox Live as a critical element of its strategy, enabling Xbox owners to download any digital content—games, film, music—onto their consoles, which could become the hub of a home digital entertainment system.

The business model for Xbox 360 depends on the number of games sold per console, the percentage of console owners who sign up for Xbox Live, sales of hardware accessories (for example, controllers, an HD-DVD drive, wireless networking adapter), and the console itself achieving breakeven production costs. Reports suggest that Microsoft will break even if each console owner buys six to seven games and two to three accessories, and if some 10 million sign on to Xbox Live (Microsoft splits Xbox Live revenues with game developers). By the end of 2006, it was estimated that some 33 million games had been sold for Xbox 360.[60]

Sony finally introduced PS3 in November 11 in Japan, and November 17 in the United States. The delay in the launch of PS3 was due to Sony's decision to bundle a Blu-ray drive with PS3 and problems developing the "cell" processor that sits at the core of the PS3. Blu-ray is Sony's proprietary high-definition DVD format. The company is currently locked in a format war with Toshiba, which is pushing its rival HD-DVD format (which can be purchased as an accessory for the Xbox 360). Sony has argued that the combination of its cell processor and Blu-ray DVD drive will give PS3 a substantial performance edge over Xbox 360. While this is true in a technical sense (the Blu-ray discs have five times the storage capacity of the DVD discs for Xbox 360), few reviewers have noticed much in the way of difference from a game-playing perspective—perhaps because few games were initially available that showed the true power of the PS3.

What is certain is that incorporating Blu-ray drives in the PS3 has significantly raised the costs of the PS3. Sony is selling its stand-alone Blu-ray drives for $999, which suggests that the PS3, initially priced at between $500 and $600 depending on configuration, is in a sense a subsidized Blu-ray player. Shortages of blue diodes, a critical component in high-definition DVD drives, also limited supply of the PS3 after its launch. Only 93,000 PS3 players were available for the Japanese launch. Sony estimates that it will ship 2 million PS3s by the end of 2006, and 6 million by March 2007. Analysts are skeptical of these targets, however, given continuing component shortages.

At launch, there were some twenty games available for the PS3. Sony also announced its own Live offering to compete with Xbox Live, and stated that it would be free to PS3 users.

Nintendo is also back in the fray. In November 2006, it launched its own next-generation offering, Wii. The Wii is a much more modest offering than the PS3 or Xbox 360, from a technical standpoint at least, but it has the virtue of being priced much lower—at just $250. Moreover, the Wii has an interesting feature—a wireless controller that can detect arm and hand motions and transfer them to the screen. This enables the development of interactive games, with players physically controlling the action on screen by moving their arms, whether by swinging an imaginary bat or slashing a sword through the air. Like the PS3, Wii was also launched with some twenty games. Early sales were apparently good, and Nintendo was forecasting sales of 1.5 million units by the year's end.

ENDNOTES

1. A good account of the early history of Bushnell and Atari can be found in S. Cohen, *Zap! The Rise and Fall of Atari*, New York: McGraw-Hill, 1984.
2. R. Isaacs, "Videogames Race to Catch a Changing Market," *Business Week*, December 26, 1977, p. 44B.
3. P. Pagnano, "Atari's Game Plan to Overwhelm Its Competitors," *Business Week*, May 8, 1978, p. 50F.
4. R. Isaacs, "Videogames Race to Catch a Changing Market," *Business Week*, December 26, 1977, p. 44B.
5. P. Pagnano, "Atari's Game Plan to Overwhelm Its Competitors," *Business Week*, May 8, 1978, p. 50F; and D. Sheff, *Game Over*, New York: Random House, 1993.
6. S. Cohen, *Zap! The Rise and Fall of Atari*, New York: McGraw-Hill, 1984.
7. L. Kehoe, "Atari Seeks Way out of Videogame Woes," *Financial Times*, December 14, 1983, p. 23.
8. M. Schrage, "The High Tech Dinosaurs: Videogames, Once Ascendant, Are Making Way," *Washington Post*, July 31, 1983, p. F1.
9. D. Sheff, *Game Over*, New York: Random House, 1993.
10. Quoted in D. Sheff, *Game Over*, New York: Random House, 1993, p. 38.
11. D. Sheff, *Game Over*, New York: Random House, 1993.
12. D. Golden, "In Search of Princess Toadstool," *Boston Globe*, November 20, 1988, p. 18.
13. N. Gross and G. Lewis, "Here Come the Super Mario Bros.," *Business Week*, November 9, 1987, p. 138.
14. D. Sheff, *Game Over*, New York: Random House, 1993.
15. D. Golden, "In Search of Princess Toadstool," *Boston Globe*, November 20, 1988, p. 18.
16. Staff Reporter, "Marketer of the Year," *Adweek*, November 27, 1989, p. 15.
17. C. Lazzareschi, "No Mere Child's Play," *Los Angeles Times*, December 16, 1988, p. 1.
18. For a good summary of the early history of Sega, see J. Battle and B. Johnstone, "The Next Level: Sega's Plans for World Domination," *Wired*, release 1.06, December 1993.
19. D. Sheff, *Game Over*, New York: Random House, 1993.
20. J. Battle and B. Johnstone, "The Next Level: Sega's Plans for World Domination," *Wired*, release 1.06, December 1993.
21. For background details, see J. Flower, "3DO: Hip or Hype?" *Wired*, release 1.02, May/June 1993.
22. R. Brandt, "3DO's New Game Player: Awesome or Another Betamax?" *Business Week*, January 11, 1993, p. 38.
23. J. Flower, "3DO: Hip or Hype?" *Wired*, release 1.02, May/June 1993.
24. S. Jacobs, "Third Time's a Charm (They Hope)," *Wired*, release 2.01, January 1994.
25. A. Dunkin, "Videogames: The Next Generation," *Business Week*, January 31, 1994, p. 80.
26. J. Greenstein, "No Clear Winners, Though Some Losers; the Videogame Industry in 1995," *Business Week*, December 22, 1995, p. 42.
27. Staff Reporter, "3DO Says 'I Do' on Major Shift of Its Game Strategy," *Los Angeles Times*, September 17, 1996, p. 2.
28. J. Battle and B. Johnstone, "The Next Level: Sega's Plans for World Domination," *Wired*, release 1.06, December 1993.
29. J. Greenstein, "No Clear Winners, Though Some Losers: The Videogame Industry in 1995," *Business Week*, December 22, 1995, p. 42.
30. D. P. Hamilton, "Sega Suddenly Finds Itself Embattled," *Wall Street Journal*, March 31, 1997, p. A10.
31. S. Taves, "Meet Your New Playmate," *Wired*, release 3.09, September 1995.

32. I. Kunni, "The Games Sony Plays," *Business Week,* June 15, 1998, p. 128.
33. C. Platt, "WordNerd," *Wired,* release 3.10, October 1995.
34. I. Kunni, "The Games Sony Plays," *Business Week,* June 15, 1998, p. 128.
35. J. A. Trachtenberg, "Race Quits Sony Just Before U.S. Rollout of Its PlayStation Video-Game System," *Wall Street Journal,* August 8, 1995, p. B3.
36. S. Beenstock, "Market Raider: How Sony Won the Console Game," *Marketing,* September 10, 1998, p. 26.
37. J. A. Trachtenberg, "Olafsson Calls It Quits as Chairman of Sony's Technology Strategy Group," *Wall Street Journal,* January 23, 1996, p. B6.
38. J. Greenstein, "Price Cuts Boost Saturn, PlayStation Hardware Sales," *Video Business,* May 31, 1996, p. 1.
39. J. Greenstein, "Sony Cuts Prices of PlayStation Hardware," *Video Business,* March 10, 1997, p. 1.
40. D. Hamilton, "Sega Suddenly Finds Itself Embattled," *Wall Street Journal,* March 31, 1997, p. A10.
41. Staff Reporter, "Nintendo Wakes Up," *The Economist,* August 3, 1996, pp. 55–56.
42. D. Takahashi, "Game Plan: Videogame Makers See Soaring Sales Now—And Lots of Trouble Ahead," *Wall Street Journal,* June 15, 1998, p. R10.
43. D. Takahashi, "Sony and Nintendo Battle for Kids Under 13," *Wall Street Journal,* September 24, 1998, p. B4.
44. I. Kunni, "The Games Sony Plays," *Business Week,* June 15, 1998, p. 128.
45. R. A. Guth, "Sega Cites Dreamcast Price Cuts for Loss Amid Crucial Time for Survival of Firm," *Wall Street Journal,* October 30, 2000, p. A22.
46. R. A. Guth, "Sega Cites Dreamcast Price Cuts for Loss Amid Crucial Time for Survival of Firm," *Wall Street Journal,* October 30, 2000, p. A22.
47. T. Oxford and S. Steinberg, "Ultimate Game Machine Sony's PlayStation 2 Is Due on Shelves Oct. 26. It Brims with Potential—But at This Point Sega's Dreamcast Appears a Tough Competitor," *Atlanta Journal/Atlanta Constitution,* October 1, 2000, p. P1.
48. R. A. Guth, "New Players from Nintendo Will Link to Web," *Wall Street Journal,* August 25, 2000, p. B1.
49. D. Takahashi, "Microsoft's X-Box Impresses Game Developers," *Wall Street Journal,* March 13, 2000, p. B12.
50. K. Powers, "Showdown," *Forbes,* August 11, 2003, pp. 86–87.
51. "Console Wars," *The Economist,* June 22, 2002, p. 71.
52. R. A. Guth, "Game Gambit: Microsoft to Cut Xbox Price," *Wall Street Journal,* March 19, 2004, p. B1.
53. K. Powers, "Showdown," *Forbes,* August 11, 2003, pp. 86–87.
54. E. Taub, "No Longer a Solitary Pursuit: Videogames Move Online," *New York Times,* July 5, 2004, p. C4.
55. J. Greene and C. Edwards, "Microsoft Plays Video Leapfrog," *Business Week,* May 10, 2004, pp. 44–45.
56. "Playing a Long Game," *The Economist,* November 18, 2006, pp. 63–65.
57. B. Thill, "Microsoft: Got Game? Update on Vista, Xbox and the Tender," *Citigroup Capital Markets,* August 30, 2006.
58. B. Thill, "Microsoft: Got Game? Update on Vista, Xbox and the Tender," *Citigroup Capital Markets,* August 30, 2006.
59. D. Takahashi, *The Xbox 360 Uncloaked,* Los Angeles: Spider Works, 2006.
60. B. Thill, "Microsoft: Got Game? Update on Vista, Xbox and the Tender," *Citigroup Capital Markets,* August 30, 2006.

Internet Search and the Rise of Google

This case was prepared by Charles W. L. Hill, the University of Washington.

The Google Juggernaut

In the early 2000s, many Internet users started to gravitate toward a new search engine. It was called Google, and it delivered remarkable results. Put in a keyword, and in a blink of an eye the search engine would return a list of links, with the most relevant links appearing at the top of the page. People quickly realized that Google was an amazing tool, enabling users to quickly find almost anything they wanted on the Web and to effortlessly sort through the vast sea of information contained in billions of webpages and retrieve the precise information they desired. It seemed like magic. Before long, "to Google" became a verb (in June 2006, the verb *Google* was added to the *Oxford English Dictionary*). To find out more about a person, you would "Google them." To find out more about a subject, you would "Google it." If you wanted to find a good or service, enter a keyword in Google, and a list of relevant links would be returned in an instant. For many users, Google quickly became the "go to" page every time they wanted information about anything. As a result, by mid-2006 some 45% of all U.S. Internet searches were conducted through Google, far ahead of Yahoo's search engine, which had a 28.5% share, and Microsoft's MSN network, which accounted for 12.8% of searches.[1]

What captured the attention of the business community, however, was the ability of Google to monetize its search engine. Google's core business model was the essence of simplicity. The company auctioned off the keywords used in searches to advertisers. The highest bidders would have links to their sites placed on the right-hand side of a page returning search results. The advertisers would then pay Google every time someone clicked on a link and was directed to their sites. Thus, when bidding for a keyword, advertisers would bid for the price per click. Interestingly, Google did not necessarily place the advertiser who bid the highest amount per click at the top of the page. Rather, the top spot was determined by the amount per click multiplied by Google's statistical estimate of the likelihood that someone would actually click on the advertisement. This refinement maximized the revenue that Google got from its valuable real estate.

As more users gravitated to Google's site, so more advertisers were attracted to it, and Google's revenues and profits took off. From a standing start in 2001, by 2005 revenues had grown to $6.14 billion and net income to $1.47 billion. Google had become the gorilla in the online advertising space. In 2001, Google garnered 18.4% of total U.S. search ad spending. By 2005, its share had increased to 48.5%, and, according to the research firm eMarketer, 57% of all search advertising dollars will go to Google in 2006.[2] Moreover, the future looked bright. Estimates suggest that Internet advertising spending could become a $40 billion worldwide market in 2008, up from $20.5 billion in 2005.[3] Forecasts called for Google's revenues to exceed the $12 billion range by 2008 as ever more advertisers moved from traditional media to the Web.[4]

Flushed with this success, Google introduced a wave of new products, including mapping services

(Google Maps and Google Earth), a free email service (Gmail), Google Desktop (which enables users to search files on their own computers), and free online word-processing and spreadsheet programs that had much of the look, feel, and functionality of Microsoft's Word and Excel offerings. These products fueled speculation that Google's ambitions extended outside search, and that the company was trying to position itself as a platform company that supported an ecosystem that would rival that fostered by Microsoft, long the software industry's dominate player. Google's competitors, however, had no intention of being steamrollered. Both Yahoo and Microsoft were investing significant amounts in search in an attempt to grow their shares. A number of smaller search companies, including Ask and snap.com, were looking to increase their share too. Moreover, few of Google's new products had gained share against entrenched competitors, suggesting to some that the company might be overreaching itself.

Search Engines[5]

A search engine connects the keywords that users enter (queries) to a database it has created of webpages (an index). It then produces a list of links to pages (and summaries of content) that it believes are most relevant to a query.

Search engines consist of four main components: a web crawler, an index, a runtime index, and a query processor (the interface that connects users to the index). The web crawler is a piece of software that goes from link to link on the Web, collecting the pages it finds and sending them back to the index. Once in the index, webpages are analyzed by sophisticated algorithms that look for statistical patterns. Google's page rank algorithm, for example, looks at the links on a page, the text around those links, and the popularity of the pages that link to that page to determine how relevant a page is to a particular query (in fact, Google's algorithm looks at more than one hundred factors to determine a page's relevance to a query term).

Once analyzed, pages are tagged. The tag contains information about the pages, for example, whether it is porn, or spam, written in a certain language, or updated infrequently. Tagged pages are then dumped into a runtime index, which is a database that is ready to serve users. The runtime index forms a bridge between the back end of an engine, the web crawler and index, and the front end, the query processor and user interface. The query processor takes a keyword inputted by a user, transports it to the runtime index, where an algorithm matches the keyword to pages, ranking them by relevance, and then transports the results back to the user, where they are displayed on the user interface.

The computing and data storage infrastructure required to support a search engine is significant. It must scale with the continued growth of the Web and with demands on the search engine. In 2005, Google had $949 million in information technology assets on its balance sheet, had close to 200,000 computers dedicated to the job of running its search engine, and spent around $400 million on maintaining its system.[6]

The Early Days of Search

Search did not begin with Google. The first Internet search engine was Archie. Created in 1990, before the World Wide Web had burst onto the scene, Archie connected users through queries to the machines on which documents they wanted were stored. The users then had to dig through the public files on those machines to find what they wanted. The next search engine, Veronica, improved on Archie insofar as it allowed searchers to connect directly to the document they had queried.

The Web started to take off after 1993, with the number of websites expanding from 130 to more than 600,000 by 1996. As this expansion occurred, the problem of finding the information you wanted on the Web became more difficult. The first web-based search engine was the WWW Wanderer, developed by Matthew Gray at MIT. This was soon surpassed, however, by Web Crawler, a search engine developed by Brian Pinkerton of the University of Washington. Web Crawler was the first search engine to index the full text of webpages, as opposed to just the title. Web Crawler was sold to AOL for $1 million in 1995. This marked the first time anyone had ascribed an economic value to a search engine.

In December 1995 the next search engine, AltaVista, appeared on the scene. Developed by Louis Monier, an employee at Digital Equipment (DEC), AltaVista, like Web Crawler, indexed the entire text of a webpage. Unlike Web Crawler, however, AltaVista sent out thousands of web crawlers, which enabled it to build the most complete index of the Web to date.

Avid web users soon came to value the service, but the search engine was handicapped by two things. First, it was very much a stepchild within DEC, which saw itself as a hardware-driven business and didn't really know what to do with AltaVista. Second, there was no obvious way for AltaVista to make much money, which meant that it was difficult for Monier to get the resources required for AltaVista to keep up with the rapid growth of the Web. Ultimately DEC was acquired by Compaq Computer. Compaq then sold AltaVista and related Internet properties to a high-flying Internet firm, CMGI, at the height of the Internet boom in 1999 for $2.3 billion in CMGI stock. CMGI did have plans to spin off AltaVista in an initial public offering, but it never happened. The NASDAQ stock market collapsed in 2000, taking CMGI's stock down with it, and the market had no appetite for another dot-com IPO.

Around the same time that AltaVista was gaining traffic, two other companies introduced search engines, Lycos and Excite. Both search engines represented further incremental improvement. Lycos was the first search engine to use algorithms to try and determine the relevance of a webpage for a search query. Excite utilized similar algorithms. However, neither company developed a way of making money directly from search. Instead they saw themselves as portal companies, like Yahoo, AOL, and MSN. Search was just a tool to increase the value of their portal as a destination site, enabling them to capture revenues from banner ads, e-commerce transactions, and the like. Both Lycos and Excite went public and then squandered much of the capital raised on acquiring other Internet properties, before seeing their value implode as the Internet bubble burst in 2000–2001.

Another company that tried to make sense out of the Web for users was Yahoo, but Yahoo did not use a search engine. Instead it created a hierarchical directory of webpages. This helped drive traffic to its site. Other content kept users coming back, enabling Yahoo to emerge as one of the most popular portals on the Web. In contrast to many of its smaller competitors, Yahoo's industry leading scale allowed it to make good money from advertising on its site. The company added a search engine to its offering, but until 2003 it always did so through a partner. At one time, AltaVista powered Yahoo's search function, then Inktomi, and ultimately Google. Yahoo's managers did consider developing their own search engine, but

they saw it as too capital intensive—search required a lot of computing power, storage, and bandwidth. Besides, there was no business model for monetizing search. That, however, was all about to change, and it wasn't Google that pioneered the way, it was a serial entrepreneur called Bill Gross.

GoTo.com: A Business Model Emerges[7]

Bill Gross made his first million with Knowledge Adventure, which developed software to help kids learn. After he sold Knowledge Adventure to Cendant for $100 million, Gross created IdeaLab, a business incubator that subsequently generated a number of Internet start-ups, including GoTo.com.

GoTo.com was born of Gross's concern that a growing wave of spam was detracting from the value of search engines such as AltaVista. Spam arose because publishers of websites realized that they could drive traffic to their sites by including commonly used search keywords such as "used cars" or "airfares" on their sites. Often the words were in the same color as the background of the website (for example, black words on a black background), so that they could not be seen by web users, who would suddenly wonder why their search for used cars had directed them to a porn site.

Gross also wanted a tool that would help drive good traffic to the websites of a number of Internet businesses being developed by IdeaLab. In Gross's view, much of the traffic arriving at websites was undifferentiated—people who had come to a site because of spam, bad portal real estate deals, or poor search engine results. Gross established GoTo.com to build a better search engine, one that would defeat spam, produce highly relevant results, and eliminate bad traffic.

Gross concluded that a way to limit spam was to charge for search. He realized that it was unworkable to charge the Internet user, so why not charge the advertiser? This led to his key insight—the keywords that Internet users typed into a search engine were inherently valuable to the owners of websites. They drove traffic to their sites, and many sites made money from that traffic, so why not charge for the keywords? Moreover, Gross realized that if a search engine directed higher quality traffic to a site, it would be possible to charge more for relevant keywords.

By this time, GoTo.com had decided to license search engine technology from Inktomi and focus its efforts on developing the paid search model. However, GoTo.com faced a classic chicken and egg problem—to launch a service, the company needed both audience and advertisers, but it had neither.

To attract advertisers, GoTo.com adopted two strategies.[8] First, GoTo.com would charge an advertiser only when somebody clicked on a link and was directed to its website. To Gross's way thinking, for merchants this pay-per-click model would be more efficient than advertising through traditional media or through banner ads on webpages. Second, GoTo.com initially priced keywords low—as low as 1 cent a click (although, of course, they could be bid above that).

To capture an audience, a website alone would not be enough. GoTo.com needed to tap into the traffic already visiting established websites. One approach was to pay the owners of high-traffic websites to place banner ads that would direct traffic to GoTo.com's website. A second approach, which ultimately became the core of GoTo.com's business, was to syndicate its service, allowing affiliates to place a cobranded GoTo.com search box on their sites, or to use GoTo.com's search engine and identify the results as "partner results." GoTo.com would then split the revenues from search with them. GoTo.com had to pay an upfront fee to significant affiliates, who viewed their websites as valuable real estate. For example, in late 2000 GoTo.com paid AOL $50 million to syndicate GoTo.com's listings on its sites, which included AOL, Compuserve, and Netscape.

To finance its expansion, GoTo.com raised some $53 million in venture capital funding—a relatively easy proposition in the heady days of the dot-com boom. In June 1999, GoTo.com raised another $90 million through an IPO.[9]

GoTo.com launched its service in June 1998 with just fifteen advertisers. Initially GoTo.com was paying more to acquire traffic than it was earning from click-through ad revenue. According to its initial IPO filing, in its first year of operation, GoTo.com was paying 5.5 cents a click to acquire traffic from Microsoft's MSN sites, and around 4 cents a click to acquire traffic from Netscape. The average yield from this traffic, however, was still less than the cost of acquisition, resulting in red ink, not an unusual situation for a dot-com in the 1990s.

However, the momentum was beginning to shift toward the company. As traffic volumes grew, and as advertisers began to understand the value of keywords, yields improved. By early 1999 the price of popular keywords was starting to rise. The highest bidder for the keyword "software" was 59 cents a click, "books" was 38 cents a click, "vacations" 36 cents a click, and "porn," the source of so much spam, 28 cents a click.[10]

The turning point was the AOL syndication deal signed in September 2000. Prior to signing with AOL, GoTo.com was reaching 24 million users through its affiliates. After the deal, it was reaching 60 million unique users, or some 75% of the U.S. Internet audience (AOL itself had 23 million subscribers, CompuServe 3 million, and Netscape—which was owned by AOL—another 31 million registered users).[11] With over 50,000 advertisers now in its network and a large audience pool, both keyword prices and click-through rates increased. GoTo.com turned profitable shortly after the AOL deal was put into effect. In 2001, the company earned net profits $20.2 million on revenues of $288 million. In 2002 it earned $73.1 million on revenues of $667.7 million, making it one of the few dot-com companies to break into profitability.

In 2001, GoTo.com changed its name to Overture Services. The name change reflected the results of a strategic shift. By 2001, the bulk of revenues were coming from affiliate sites, with the GoTo.com website garnering only 5% of the company's total traffic.[12] Still, the fact that GoTo.com had its own website that was in effect competing with traffic going to affiliates created potential channel conflict. Many in the company feared that channel conflict might induce key affiliates, such as AOL, to switch their allegiance. After much internal debate, the company decided to phase out the GoTo.com website, focusing all of its attention on the syndication network.

Around the same time, Bill Gross apparently talked to the founders of another fast-growing search engine, Google, about whether they would be interested in merging the two companies. At the time Google had no business model. Gross was paying attention to the fast growth of traffic going to Google's website. He saw a merger as an opportunity to join a superior search engine with Overture's advertising and syndication network (the company was still using Inktomi's search engine). The talks stalled, however, reportedly because Google's founders stated that they would never be associated with a company that mixed paid advertising with organic results.[13]

Within months, however, Google had introduced its own advertising service using a pay-for-click model that looked very similar in conception to Overture's. Overture promptly sued Google for patent infringement. To make matters worse, in 2002 AOL declined to renew its deal with Overture and instead switched to Google for search services.

By 2003 it was clear that although still growing and profitable, Overture was losing traction to Google (Overture's revenues were on track to hit $1 billion in 2003, and the company had 80,000 advertisers in its network).[14] Moreover, Overture was invisible to many of its users, who saw the service as a part of the offering of affiliates, many of whom were powerful brands in their own right, including Yahoo and MSN. Yahoo and Microsoft were also waking up to the threat posed by Google. Realizing that paid search was becoming a highly profitable market, both began to eye Overture to jump-start their own paid search services. While Microsoft apparently decided to build its own search engine and ad service from scratch, Yahoo decided to bid for Overture. In June 2003, a deal was announced, with Overture being sold to Yahoo for $1.63 billion in cash. The payday was a bitter sweet one for Bill Gross. IdeaLab had done very well out of Overture, but Gross couldn't help but feel that a bigger opportunity had slipped through his fingers and into the palms of Google's founders.

As for the patent case, this settled in 2004 when Google agreed to hand over 2.7 million shares to Yahoo. This represented about 1% of the outstanding stock, which at the time was valued at $330. Today the value of those shares is closer to $1 billion.[15]

Google Rising

Google started as a research project undertaken by Larry Page while he was a computer science PhD student at Stanford in 1996. Called BackRub, the goal of the project was to document the link structure of the Web. Page had observed that while it was easy to follow links from one page to another, it was much more difficult to discover links *back*. Put differently, just by looking at a page, it was impossible to know who was linking to that page. Page reasoned that this might be very important information. Specifically, one might be able to rank the value of a webpage by discovering which pages were linking to it, and if those pages were themselves linked to by many other pages.

To rank pages, Page knew that he would have to send out a web crawler to index pages and archive links. At this point, another PhD student, Sergey Brin, became involved in the project. Brin, a gifted mathematician, was able to develop an algorithm that ranked webpages according not only to the number of links into that site, but also the number of links into each of the linking sites. This methodology had the virtue of discounting links from pages that themselves had few, if any, links into them.

Brin and Page noticed that the search results generated by this algorithm were superior to those returned by AltaVista and Excite, both of which often returned irrelevant results, including a fair share of spam. They had stumbled onto the key ingredient for a better search engine—rank search results according to their relevance using a back-link methodology. Moreover, they realized that the bigger the Web got, the better the results would be.

With the basic details of what was now a search engine worked out, Brin and Page released it on the Stanford website in August 1996. They christened their new search engine Google after *googol*, the term for the number 1 followed by 100 zeros. Early on, Brin and Page talked to several companies about the possibility of licensing Google. Executives at Excite took a look but passed, as did executives at Infoseek and Yahoo. Many of these companies were embroiled in the portal wars—and portals were all about acquiring traffic, not about sending it away via search. Search just didn't seem central to their mission.

By late 1998, Google was serving some 10,000 queries a day and was rapidly outgrowing the computing resources available at Stanford. Brin and Page realized that to get the resources required to keep scaling Google, they needed capital, and that meant starting a company. Here Stanford's deep links into Silicon Valley came in useful. Before long they found themselves sitting together with Andy Bechtolsheim, one of the founders of another Stanford start-up, Sun Microsystems. Bechtolsheim watched a demo of Google and wrote a check on the spot for $100,000.

Google was formally incorporated on September 7, 1998, with Page as CEO and Brin as president. From this point on, things began to accelerate rapidly. Traffic was growing by nearly 50% a month, enough to attract the attention of several angle investors (including Amazon founder Jeff Bezos), who collectively put in another million.

That was not enough; search engines have a voracious appetite for computing resources. To run its search engine, Brin and Page had custom-designed a low-cost, Linux-based server architecture that was modular and could be scaled rapidly. But to keep up with the growth of the Web and return answers to search queries in a fraction of second, they needed ever more machines (by late 2005, the company was reportedly using over 250,000 Linux servers to handle more than 3,000 searches a second).[16]

To finance growth of their search engine, in early 1999 Brin and Page started to look for venture capital funding. It was the height of the dot-com boom and money was cheap. Never mind that there was no business model; Google's growth was enough to attract considerable interest. By June 1999, the company had closed its first round of venture capital financing, raising $25 million from two of the premier firms in Silicon Valley, Sequoia Capital and Kleiner Perkins Caufield & Byers. Just as importantly perhaps, the legendary John Doerr, one of Silicon Valley's most successful investors and a Kleiner Perkins partner, took a seat on Google's board.

By late 1999, Google had grown to around forty employees and was serving some 3.5 million searches a day. However, the company was burning through $500,000 a month and still had no business model. It had some licensing deals with companies that used Google as their search technology, but it was not bringing in enough money to stem the flow of red ink. At this point, Google started to experiment with ads, but they were not yet pay-per-click ads. Rather, Google began selling text-based ads to clients that were interested in certain keywords. The ads would then appear on the page returning search results, but not in the list of relevant sites. For example, if someone typed in "Toyota Corolla," an ad would appear at the top of the page, above the list of links for Toyota Corolla cars. These ads were sold on a "cost per thousand impressions" basis. In other words, the cost of an ad was determined by how many people were estimated to have viewed it, not by how many clicked on it. It didn't work very well.

The management team also started to ponder placing banner ads on Google's website as a way of generating additional revenue, but before it made that decision the dot-com boom imploded, the NASDAQ crashed, and the volume of online advertising dropped precipitously. Google clearly needed to figure out a different way to make money.

Google Gets a Business Model

Brin and Page now looked closely at the one search company that seemed to be making good money, GoTo.com. They could see the value of the pay-per-click model and of auctioning off keywords, but there were things about GoTo.com that they did not like. GoTo.com would give guarantees that websites would be included more frequently in web crawls, making sure they were updated, provided that the owners were prepared to pay more. Moreover, the purity of GoTo.com's search results was biased by the desire to make money from advertisers, with those who paid the most being ranked highest. Brin and Page were ideologically attached to the idea of serving up the best possible search results to users, uncorrupted by commercial considerations. At the same time, they needed to make money.

Although Bill Gross pitched the idea of GoTo.com teaming up with Google, Brin and Page decided to go it alone. They believed they could do as good a job as GoTo.com, so why share revenues with the company?[17]

The approach that Google ultimately settled on combined the innovations of GotTo.com with Google's superior relevance-based search engine. Brin and Page had always believed that Google's webpage should be kept as clean and elegant as possible—something that seemed to appeal to users. Moreover, they knew that users valued the fact that Google served up relevant search results that were unbiased by commercial considerations. The last thing they wanted to do was alienate their rapidly growing user base. So they decided to place text-based ads on the right-hand side of a page, clearly separated from search results by a thin line.

Like GoTo.com, they decided to adopt a pay-per-click model. Unlike GoTo.com, Brin and Page decided that in addition to the price an advertiser had paid for a keyword, ads should also be ranked according to relevance. Relevance was measured by how frequently users clicked on ads. More popular ads rose to the top of the list, less popular ones fell. In other words, Google allowed their users to rank ads. This had a nice economic advantage for Google, since an ad that is generating $1.00 a click but is being clicked on three times as much as an ad generating $1.50 a click would make significantly more money for Google. It also motivated advertisers to make sure that their ads were appealing. *Motivate others*

The system that Google used to auction off keywords was also different in detail from that used by GoTo.com. Google used a *Vickery second price auction* methodology. Under this system, the winner pays only 1 cent more than the bidder below it. Thus if there are bids of $1, 50 cents, and 25 cents for a keyword, the winner of the top place pays just 51 cents, not $1, the winner of the second place 26 cents, and so on. The auction is nonstop, with the price for a keyword rising or falling depending on bids at each moment in time. Although the minimum bid for a keyword was set at 5 cents, most were above that, and the range was wide. One of the most expensive search terms was reputed to be "mesothelioma," a type of cancer caused by exposure to asbestos. Bids were around $30 per click! They came from lawyers vying for a chance to earn lucrative fees by representing clients in suits against asbestos producers.[18]

While developing this service, Google continued to grow like wildfire. In mid-2000, the service was dealing with 18 million search queries a day and the index surpassed 1 billion documents, making it by far the largest search engine on the Web. By late 2000, when Google introduced the first version of its new service, which it called AdWords, the company was serving up 60 million search queries a day—giving it a scale that GoTo.com never came close to achieving. In February 2002, Google introduced a new version of AdWords that included for the first time the full set of pay-per-click advertising, keyword auctions, and advertising links ranked by relevance. Sales immediately started to accelerate. Google had hit on the business model that would propel the company into the big league.

In 2003, Google introduced a second product, AdSense. AdSense allows third-party publishers large and small to access Google's massive network of advertisers on a self-service basis. Publishers can sign up for AdSense in a matter of minutes. AdSense then scans the publisher's site for content and places contextually relevant ads next to that content. As with AdWords, this is a pay-per-click service, but with AdSense Google splits the revenues with the publishers. In addition to large publishers, such as online news sites, AdSense has been particularly appealing to many small publishers, such as webloggers. Small publishers find that by adding a few lines of code to their sites, they can suddenly monetize their content.

However, many advertisers feel that AdSense is not as effective as AdWords in driving traffic to their sites. Google allowed advertisers to opt out of AdSense in 2004. Despite this, AdSense has also grown into a respectable business, accounting for 15% of Google's revenues in 2005, or close to $1 billion.

Google Grows Up

Between 2001 and 2006 Google changed in a number of ways. First, in mid-2001 the company hired a new CEO, Eric Schmidt, to replace Larry Page. Schmidt had been the chief technology officer of Sun Microsystems and then CEO of Novell. Schmidt was brought on to help manage the company's growth with the explicit blessing of Brin and Page. Both Brin and Page were still in their twenties, and the board felt it needed a "grownup" who had run a large company to help Google transition to the next stage (Google turned a profit the month after Schmidt joined). Brin and Page became the presidents of technology and products, respectively. When Schmidt was hired, Google had over two hundred employees and was handling over 100 million searches a day.

According to knowledgeable observers, Schmidt, Brin, and Page act as a triumvirate, with Brin and Page continuing to exercise a very strong influence over strategies and policies at Google. Schmidt may be CEO, but Google is still very much Brin and Page's company.[19] Working closely together, the three drive the development of a set of values and an organization that have come to define the uniquely Google way of doing things.

Vision and Values

As Google's growth started to accelerate, there was concern that rapid hiring would quickly dilute the vision, values, and principles of the founders. In mid-2001, Brin and Page gathered a core group of early employees and asked them to come up with a policy for ensuring that the company's culture did not fracture as the company added employees. From this group, and subsequent discussions, emerged a vision and list of values that have continued to shape the evolution of the company. These were not new; rather, they represented the formalization of principles that Brin and Page felt they had always adhered to.

The central vision of Google is to *organize the world's information and make it universally acceptable* and useful.[20] The team also articulated a set of ten core philosophies (values), which are now listed on its website.[21] Perhaps the most significant, and certainly the most discussed of these values, is captured by the phrase "don't be evil." The central message underlying this phrase was that Google should never compromise the integrity of its search results. Google would never let commercial considerations bias its rankings. "Don't be evil," however, has become more than that at Google; it has become a central organizing principle of the company, albeit one that is far from easy to implement. Google got positive press from libertarians when it refused to share its search data with the U.S. government, which wanted the data to help fight child porn. However, the same constituency reacted with dismay when the company caved into the Chinese government and removed from its Chinese service offending results for search terms such as "human rights" and "democracy"! Brin justified the Chinese decision by saying that "it will be better for Chinese web users, because ultimately they will get more information, though not quite all of it."[22]

Another core value at Google is "focus on the user, and all else will follow." In many ways, this value captures what Brin and Page initially did. They focused on giving the user the best possible search experience—highly relevant results, delivered with lightening speed to an uncultured and elegant interface. The value also reflects a belief at Google that it is okay to deliver value to users first, and then figure out the business model for monetizing that value. This belief seems to reflect Google's own early experience.

Yet another key principle, although it is not one that is written down anywhere, is captured by the phrase "launch early and often." This seems to underpin Google's approach to product development. Google has introduced a rash of new products over the last few years, not all of which were initially all that compelling, but through rapid upgrades, it has subsequently improved the efficacy of those products.

Google also prides itself on being a company where decisions are data driven. Opinions are said to count for nothing unless they are backed up by hard data. It is not the loudest voice that wins the day in arguments over strategy, it is the data. In some meetings, people are not allowed to say "I think . . . ," but instead must say, "The data suggests . . ."[23]

Finally, Google devotes considerable resources to making sure that its employees are working in a supportive and stimulating environment. To quote from the company's website:

> Google Inc. puts employees first when it comes to daily life in our Googleplex headquarters. There is an emphasis on team achievements and pride in individual accomplishments that contribute to the company's overall success. Ideas are traded, tested and put into practice with an alacrity that can be dizzying. Meetings that would take hours elsewhere are frequently little more than a conversation in line for lunch and few walls separate those who write the code from those who write the checks. This highly communicative environment fosters a productivity and camaraderie fueled by the realization that millions of people rely on Google results. Give the proper tools to a group of people who like to make a difference, and they will.[24]

Organization

By all accounts, Google has a flat organization. In November 2005, Google had one manager for every 20 line employees. At times, the ratio has been as high as 1:40. For a while, one manager had 180 direct reports.[25] The structure is reportedly based on teams. Big projects are broken down and allocated to small tightly focused teams. Hundreds of projects may be going on at the same time. Teams often throw out new software in six weeks or less and look at how users respond hours later. Google can try a new user interface, or some other tweak, with just 0.1% of its users and get massive feedback very quickly, letting it decide a project's fate in weeks.[26]

One aspect of Google's organization that has garnered considerable attention is the company's approach toward product development. Software engineers are expected to spend 20% of their time on something that interests them, away from their main jobs. Seemingly based on 3M's famous 15% rule, Google's 20% rule is designed to encourage creativity. The company has set up forums on its internal network where anyone can post ideas and discuss them. Like 3M, Google has set up a process by which projects coming out of 20% time can be evaluated, receive feedback from peers, and ultimately garner funding. Marissa Myer, one of Google's early employees, acts as a gatekeeper, helping to decide when projects are ready to be pitched to senior management (and that typically means Brin and Page). Once in front of the founders, advocates have twenty minutes, and no more, to make their pitch.[27]

One of the early products to come out 20% time was Google News, which returns news articles ranked by relevance in response to a keyword query. Put the term "oil prices" into Google News, for example, and the search will return news dealing with changes in oil prices, with the most relevant at the top of the list. A sophisticated algorithm determines relevance on a real-time basis by looking at the quality of the news source (the *New York Times*, for instance, rates higher than local news papers), publishing date, the number of other people who click on that source, and numerous other factors. The project was initiated by Krishna Bharat, a software engineer from India, who in response to the events of September 11, 2001, had a desire to learn what was being written and said around the world. Two other employees worked with Bharat to construct a demo that was released within Google. Positive reaction soon got Bharat in front on Brin and Page, who, impressed, gave the project a green light, and Bharat started to work on it full time.[28]

Another feature of Google's organization is its hiring strategy. Like Microsoft, Google has made a virtue out of hiring people with high IQs. The hiring process is very rigorous. Each prospect has to take an "exam" to test his or her conceptual abilities. This is followed by interviews with eight or more people, each of whom rates the applicant on a 1-to-4 scale (4 being "I would hire this person"). Applicants also undergo detailed background checks to find out what they are like to work with. Reportedly, some brilliant prospects don't get hired when background checks find out that they are difficult to work with. In essence, all hiring at Google is by committee, and while this can take considerable time, the company insists that the effort yields dividends.

While accounts of Google's organization and culture tend to emphasize their positive aspects, not everyone has such a sanguine view. Brain Reid, who was recruited into senior management at Google in 2002 and fired two years later, told author John Battelle, "Google is a monarchy with two kings, Larry and Sergey. Eric is a puppet. Larry and Sergey are arbitrary, whimsical people. . . . [T]hey run the company with an iron hand. . . . Nobody at Google from what I could tell had any authority to do anything of consequence except Larry and Sergey."[29] According

Everyone aint happy

to Battelle, several other former employees made similar statements to him.

The IPO

As Google's growth started to accelerate, the question of if and when to undertake an IPO became more pressing. There were two obvious reasons for doing an IPO: gaining access to capital and providing liquidity for early backers and the large number of employees who had equity positions. On the other hand, from 2001 onwards the company was profitable, generating significant cash flows, and could fund its expansion internally. Moreover, management felt that the longer it could keep the details of what was turning out to be an extraordinarily successful business model private, the better. In the end, the company's hand was forced by an obscure SEC regulation that required companies that give stock options to employees to report as if they were a public company by as early as April 2004. Realizing that the cat would be out of the bag anyway, Google told its employees in early 2004 that it would go public.

True to form, Google flouted Wall Street tradition in the way it structured its IPO. The company decided to auction off shares directly to the public using an untested and modified version of a Dutch auction, which starts by asking for a high price and then lowers it until someone accepts. Two classes of shares were created, Class A and B, with Class B shares having ten times the votes of Class A shares. Only Class A shares were auctioned off. Brin, Page, and Schmidt were holders of Class B shares. Consequently, although they would own one-third of the company after the IPO, they would control 80% of the votes. Google also announced that it would not provide regular financial guidance to Wall Street financial analysts. In effect, Google had thumbed its nose at Wall Street.

The controversial nature of the IPO, however, was overshadowed by the first public glimpse of Google's financials, which were contained in the offering document. They were jaw-dropping. The company had generated revenues of $1.47 billion in 2003, an increase of 230% over 2002. Google earned net profits of $106 million in 2003, but accountants soon figured out that the number was depressed by certain one-time accounting items, and that cash flow in 2003 had been over $500 million!

Google went public on August 19, 2004, at $85 a share. The company's first quarterly report showed sales doubling over the prior year, and by November the price was $200.

In September 2005, with the stock close to $300 a share, Google undertook a secondary offering, selling 14 million shares to raise $4.18 billion. With positive cash flow adding to this, by June 2006 Google was sitting on almost $10 billion in cash and short-term investments, prompting speculation as to the company's strategic intentions.

Strategy

Since 2001, Google has endeavored to keep enhancing the efficacy of its search engine, improving the search algorithms, and investing heavily in computing resources. The company has branched out from being a text-based search engine. One strategic thrust has been to extend search to as many digital devices as possible. Google started out on personal computers, but can now be accessed through PDAs and cell phones. A second strategy has been to widen the scope of search to include different sorts of information. Google has pushed beyond text into indexing and now offers searches of images, news reports, books, maps, scholarly papers, blogs, a shopping network (Froogle), and, in 2006, videos. Google Desktop, which searches files on a user's PC, also fits in with this schema. However, not all of these new search formats have advertising attached to them (for example, images and scholarly papers do not include sponsored links, while maps and book searches do).

Not all of this has gone smoothly. Book publishers have been angered by Google's book project, which seeks to create the world's largest searchable digital library of books by systematically scanning books from the libraries of major universities (for example, Stanford). The publishers have argued that Google has no right to do this without first getting permission from the publishers, and is violating copyright by doing so. Several publishers have filed a complaint with the U.S. District Court in New York. Google has responded that users will not be able to download entire books and that, in any event, creating an easy-to-use index of books is fair use under copyright law and will increase the awareness and sales of books, directly benefiting copyright holders. On another front, the World Association of Newspaper Publishers has formed a task force to examine the exploitation of content by search engines.[30]

Over the last four years, Google has introduced a rash of product offerings that do not have a strong affinity with the company's search mission. Many of these products grew out of the company's new product development process. They include free email (Gmail) and online chat programs; a calendar; a blog site (Blogger); a social networking site (Orkut); finance site (Google Money); a service for finding, editing, and sharing photos (Picasa); and plans to offer citywide free WiFi networks.

Google has also introduced two new web-based products that seem aimed squarely at Microsoft's Office franchise. In March 2006, the company acquired a word-processing program, Writely. This was quickly followed by the introduction of a spreadsheet program, Google Spreadsheets. These products have the look and feel of Microsoft Word and Excel, respectively. Both products are designed for online collaboration. They can save files in formats used by Microsoft products, although they lack the full feature set of Microsoft's offerings.

In July 2006, Google introduced a product to compete with PayPal, a web-based payment system owned by the online auction giant, eBay. Google's product, known as Checkout, offers secure online payment functionality for both merchants and consumers. For merchants, the fee for using Checkout is being priced below PayPal's. Moreover, Checkout is being integrated into Google's AdWords product, so merchants who participate will be highlighted in Google's search results. In addition, merchants who purchase Google's search advertising will get a discount on processing fees. According to one analysis, a merchant with monthly sales of $100,000 that uses Checkout and AdWords stands to reduce its transaction costs by 28%, or $8,400 a year. If it uses just Checkout, it will reduce its transaction costs by 4%, or $1,200 a year.[31] However, with 105 million accounts in mid-2006, PayPal will be difficult to challenge.

Google's track record with new product offerings has been mixed. In mid-2006, two years after its introduction, Gmail generated 25% of the traffic of email on Yahoo and MSN. Also in mid-2006, Froogle was ranked number 8 among shopping networks; Google Talk was ranked 10 in the world, with 2% of the users of market leader MSN. After two years, Orkut had just 1% of the visitors of market leader MySpace. Google Maps and Google News, both seen as successful, were the number 2 offerings in their competitive space behind Map Quest and Yahoo

News, respectively. Google Finance had a tiny market share, way behind market leader Yahoo, although it was only three months old in mid-2006.[32]

Some analysts have questioned the logic behind Google's new product efforts. One noted that "Google has product ADD. They don't know why they are getting into all of these products. They have fantastic cash flow, but terrible discipline on products."[33] Another has accused Google of having an insular culture and argued that "neither Froogle [nor] Google's travel efforts has gained any traction, at least partly because of Google's tendency to provide insufficient support to its ecosystem partners and its habit of acting in an independent, secretive manner."[34] However, others argue that Google has been successful in upgrading the quality of its new offerings, and that several products that were once laggards, such as Google News, are now the best in breed.[35]

Google has also entered into several partnership agreements. In late 2005, Google renewed its three-year-old pact to provide search engine services to AOL. In addition, however, AOL agreed to make more AOL content available to Google users. To support the partnership, Google invested $1 billion in AOL for a 5% stake in the company. At the time, it was reported that Microsoft was also negotiating with AOL on a similar deal, but Google's offer was apparently more compelling to Time Warner management.

In mid-2006, Google inked a deal with Fox Interactive under which Google will provide advertising across Fox's online network, including Fox's market-leading social networking service, MySpace (social networking sites let users post diaries, pictures, videos, and music to share with friends online). MySpace is the dominant enterprise in the social networking field with some 100 million registered users and continues to grow rapidly. Google will be the exclusive provider of search service to Fox Interactive and will have the right of first refusal on display advertising. To get access to MySpace, Google committed itself to making minimum payments of $900 million by 2010.[36]

In another mid-2006 partnership agreement, Google announced that it had reached a deal with Dell Computer under which Dell would preload Google software onto all of its systems, including Google's desktop search product and toolbar, along with a cobranded Internet homepage. Google's search would also be set as the default on Dell machines.

On the acquisition front, until recently Google stuck to purchasing small technology firms. This changed in October 2006 when Google announced that it would purchase YouTube for $1.64 billion in stock. YouTube is a simple, fun website to which anybody can upload video clips in order to share them. By October 2006, some 65,000 video clips were being uploaded every day and 100 million were being watched. Like Google in its early days, YouTube has no business model. The thinking is that Google will find ways to sell advertising that is linked to video clips on YouTube. Google's financial resources will also help YouTube to grow, and the company's legal strengths will aid YouTube in a looming battle with copyright holders, many of whom object, not surprisingly, to their material being uploaded onto YouTube without their permission.[37]

The Search Economy in 2006

There is an old adage in advertising that half of all the money spent on advertising is wasted—advertisers just don't know which half. Estimates suggest that out of worldwide advertising spending of some $428 billion in 2006, a staggering $220 billion will be wasted ($112 billion in the United States) because the wrong message is sent to the wrong audience.[38] The problem is that traditional media advertising is indiscriminate. Consider a thirty-second ad spot on broadcast TV. Advertisers pay a rate for such a spot called CPM (costs per thousand, the M being the Roman numeral for thousand). The CPM is based on estimates of how many people are watching a show. There are numerous problems with this system. The estimates of audience numbers are only approximations at best. The owners of the TV may have left the room while the commercials are airing. They may be channel surfing during the commercial break, napping, or talking on the telephone. The viewer may not be among the intended audience—a Viagra commercial might be wasted on a teenage girl, for example. Or the household might be using a TiVo or a similar digital video recorder that skips commercials.

By contrast, new advertising models based on pay-for-click are more discriminating. Rather than sending out ads to a large audience, only a few of whom will be interested in the products being advertised, consumers select search-based ads. They do this twice—first, by entering a keyword in a search engine, and second, by scanning the search results as well as the sponsored links and clicking on a link. In effect, potential purchasers pull the ads toward them through the search process. Advertisers pay only when someone clicks on their ad. Consequently, the conversion rate for search-based ads is far higher than the conversion rate for traditional media advertising.

Moreover, traditional advertising is so wasteful that most firms only advertise 5 to 10% of their products in the mass media, hoping that other products will benefit from a halo effect. In contrast, the targeted nature of search-based advertising makes it cost effective to advertise products that sell only in small quantities. In effect, search-based Internet advertising allows producers to exploit the economics of the long tail. Pay-for-click models also make it economical for small merchants to advertise their wares on the Web.

The Growth Story

Powered by the rapid growth of search-based pay-for-click advertising, total global advertising spending on the World Wide Web was predicted to total $26.5 billion in 2006, up from $15.5 billion in 2004. By 2008, total World Wide Web ad spending could hit $40.6 billion (see Exhibit 1). In 2004, some 62% of this spending was in the United States. By 2008, the figure in the United States is still expected to account for 58% of the total.[39]

Some view the growth figures as conservative given that web advertising is still underrepresented. Estimates suggest that all web advertising in the United States accounted for about 6% of total advertising

EXHIBIT 2

Share of All U.S. Searches, June 2006

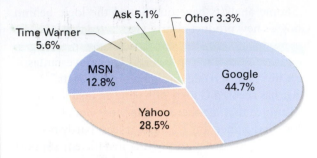

spending in 2005, even though consumers spent some 23% of their media time online.[40] Moreover, search is still growing at a rapid rate. In the second quarter of 2006, search engines dealt with 19.89 billion queries, up 30% from the same period a year earlier.[41]

Google has been the main beneficiary of this trend. In June 2006, Google was the dominant search engine in the United States with a 44.7% share of all searches. Yahoo was second with a 28.5% share, and Microsoft's MSN third with 12.8% share (see Exhibit 2).[42] Google's share of total U.S. paid search advertising was even larger, and was forecasted to hit 57.2% in 2006, up from 18.4% in 2001 (see Exhibit 3).[43] Google's lead also seemed to be accelerating. The company handled 8.75 billion queries in the second quarter of 2006, up 55% from a

EXHIBIT 1

WWW Internet Ad Spending ($ billions)

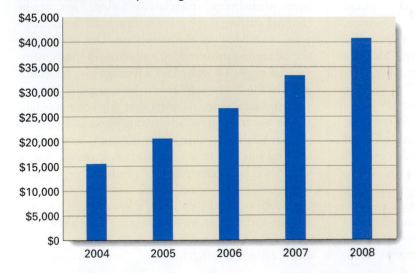

EXHIBIT 3

Google's Share of U.S. Paid Search Ad Spending Minus Traffic Acquisition Costs, 2001–2006

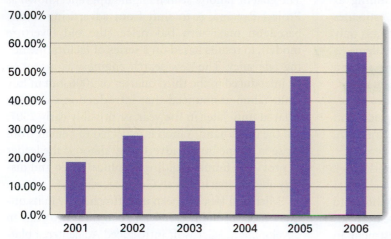

year earlier. Yahoo's search queries were up 21% over the same period, and MSN's just 8%.[44]

While search traffic volumes and online advertising revenues are growing, there are signs that the average bid price for keywords is declining, reflecting increased competition. On June 30, 2006, the average bid price was $1.27 per keyword, down from $1.43 at the end of 2005 and a high of $1.93 a word in April 2005.[45]

Google's rise is reflected in its significant share of all Internet traffic. By mid-2006, Google's websites had the fourth largest unique audience on the Web,

close behind the longer established portal sites maintained by Microsoft (MSN), Yahoo, and Time Warner (AOL), respectively (see Exhibit 4).[46]

One blemish in the growth story has been concern over click fraud. Click fraud occurs whenever a person or computer program clicks on an ad to generate a fake or improper charge per click. Perpetrators of click fraud set up bogus websites and contract with a search company like Google to place search ads on them. Then they use computer programs and anonymous proxy servers to create the illusion that visitors are clicking on the ads, resulting in charges to

EXHIBIT 4

Top 10 Websites by Parent Company, May 2006

Parent Company	Unique Audience	Time per person (hh:mm:ss)
Microsoft	114,330,000	2:06:28
Yahoo	105,504,000	3:26:55
Time Warner	102,247,000	4:40:22
Google	97,207,000	0:55:17
eBay	61,757,000	1:37:48
News Corp Online	58,423,000	1:29:12
InterActive Corp	57,717,000	0:27:51
Amazon	46,188,000	0:21:07
Walt Disney	39,406,000	0:31:41
New York Times	39,279,000	0:14:52

the advertiser, which as an affiliate site they then split with Google. The fraud perpetrators and search engine gain from this action; the advertisers lose. Early estimates suggest that click fraud was running as high as 20% of all clicks, but more recent estimates suggest that the figures are much lower, perhaps only 5%. Nevertheless, click fraud remains a problem. To deal with this, some search engines are mulling over a "cost-per-action" business model, in which an advertiser pays only when a potential customer does something that signals genuine interest, such as placing an item into an online shopping cart, filling out a form, or making a purchase.[47]

Google's Competitors

Google's most significant competitors are Yahoo and Microsoft's MSN, respectively. As paid search has grown, all three have increased their investment in search (see Exhibit 5).[48] Both Yahoo and Microsoft are playing catch-up, trying to improve their search engine technology and gain market share at the expense of Google.

Until 2004, when Yahoo purchased Overture, the company used Google's search technology. In 2005, Yahoo announced that it was making a major investment in its search engine technology to increase it monetization of search. Driving this investment were estimates that Google generated between 30% and 50% more revenue per search than Yahoo. About one-third of the higher search revenue was due to a

higher price per click on Google, and two-thirds was due to higher click-through rates, as consequence of Google's superior search engine ranking model.[49] The goal of Yahoo's search engine upgrade, known as Project Panama, is to shift from advertising results based on maximum bid price (the old Overture model), to results based on a series of factors, including relevancy. The new search engine was meant to be introduced in the third quarter of 2006, but in July 2006 Yahoo announced that introduction would be delayed until later in the year, or possibly early 2007. On the other hand, Yahoo is expected to benefit from a rise in online brand advertising. Yahoo is the leader in providing brand-building graphical video and display ads, an area in which Google is weak.

Microsoft too, has been investing heavily in its online search capabilities. In May 2006, after two years in development, Microsoft introduced AdCenter, a platform that will ultimately enable advertisers to place ads everywhere, from search results and webpages to videos games, cell phones, and Internet-connected TV. Prior to AdCenter, Microsoft had been buying ad services from Yahoo. With AdCenter, Microsoft will attempt to leverage its array of platform assets, including Xbox Live, MSN, Windows Mobile, Microsoft TV, MediaCenter, Windows Live, and Microsoft Office Live. Microsoft's goal is to link users and advertisers together across all these platforms. In the middle will sit AdCenter, which is intended to work as the advertising engine. The first version of AdCenter, however, is limited to placing text ads on search result pages. Microsoft is attempting to differentiate AdCenter by providing advertisers with demographic and behavioral data that should help them to place their ads and result in a higher click-through rate.[50]

In addition to AdCenter, Microsoft is working on upgrading its own search engine capabilities. Known as Windows Live Search, which went into testing in late 2006 and will allow users to search the Web, their own desktops, and corporate databases from one interface. A goal of the service is to help users to find intelligent answers to their questions.

However, for all of its capabilities and investments, Microsoft has significant ground to make up in the search economy. Not only is it trailing Google and Yahoo by a wide margin, but recent data suggest that MSN has the lowest conversion rate of homepage use to primary searching—less than one-third of MSN homepage users also use MSN for their search needs, compared to over 40% at Yahoo and 60% at Google.[51]

EXHIBIT 5

Search Engine Research and Development Spending by Company ($ millions)

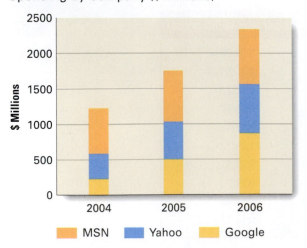

MSN   Yahoo   Google

Looking Forward

With online advertising predicted to grow strongly, Google seems to be in the driver's seat. It has the largest market share in search, enjoys the greatest name recognition, and is capturing a proportionately greater share of search-based advertising than its rivals.

However, Microsoft and Yahoo cannot be dismissed. Will they be able to leverage their substantial assets and capabilities to gain ground on Google? As for Google, what is its long-term game plan? Recent strategic moves suggest that it is attempting to expand beyond search, but where will this take the company, and what does that mean for other Internet companies?

ENDNOTES

1. Nielsen/Net Ratings, "Google Accounts for Half of All U.S. Searches," May 25, 2006.
2. David Hallerman, "Search Marketing: Players and Problems," eMarketer, April 2006.
3. Citigroup Global Markets, Internet Industry Note, "Key Take-Aways from Conference Call on MSFT/GOOG Search Competition," June 4, 2006.
4. eMarketer, "Google Revenues to Exceed $10 Billion in 2007," March 20, 2006.
5. This section draws heavily on the excellent description of search given by John Battelle. See John Battelle, The Search (Penguin Portfolio, New York, 2005).
6. Google 10K report for 2005.
7. The basic story of GoTo.com is related in John Battelle, The Search (Penguin Portfolio, New York, 2005).
8. Karl Greenberg, "Pay-for-placement Search Services Offer Ad Alternatives," Adweek, September 25, 2000, page 60.
9. M. Gannon, "GoTo.com Inc," Venture Capital Journal, August 1, 1999, page 1.
10. Tim Jackson, "Cash is the Key to a True Portal," Financial Times, February 2, 1999, page 16.
11. Karl Greenberg, "Pay-for-placement Search Services Offer Ad Alternatives," Adweek, September 25, 2000, page 60.
12. Sarah Heim, "GoTo.com Changes to Overture Services, Launches Campaign," Adweek, September 10, 2001, page 7.
13. This little gem comes from John Battelle, The Search (Penguin Portfolio, New York, 2005). There is no independent confirmation of the story.
14. Anonymous, "Yahoo to Acquire Overture Services for 2.44 Times Revenues," Weekly Corporate Growth Service, July 21, 2003, page 8.
15. Richard Waters, "Google Settles Yahoo Case with Shares," Financial Times, August 19, 2004, page 29.
16. Fred Vogelstein, "Gates vs Google: Search and Destroy," Fortune, May 2, 2005, pages 72–82.
17. This is according to David A. Vise, The Google Story (Random House, New York, 2004).
18. David A. Vise, The Google Story (Random House, New York, 2004).
19. John Battelle, The Search (Penguin Portfolio, New York, 2005). There is no independent confirmation of the story.
20. http://www.google.com/corporate/index.html.
21. http://www.google.com/corporate/tenthings.html.
22. Andy Kessler, "Sellout.com," Wall Street Journal, January 31, 2006, page A14.
23. Quentin Hardy, "Google Thinks Small," Fortune, November 14, 2005, pages 198–199.
24. http://www.google.com/corporate/tenthings.html.
25. Quentin Hardy, "Google Thinks Small," Fortune, November 14, 2005, pages 198–199.
26. Quentin Hardy, "Google Thinks Small," Fortune, November 14, 2005, pages 198–199.
27. Ben Elgin, "Managing Google's Idea Factory," Business Week, October 3, 2005, pages 88–90.
28. David A. Vise, The Google Story (Random House, New York, 2004).
29. John Battelle, The Search (Penguin Portfolio, New York, 2005), page 233.
30. Jacqueline Doherty, "In the Drink," Barron's, February 13, 2006, pages 31–36.
31. Mark Mahany, "Building Out the Option Value of Google," Citigroup Portfolio Strategist, July 13, 2006.
32. Ben Elgin, "So Much Fanfare, So Few Hits," Business Week, July 10, 2006, pages 26–30.
33. Ben Elgin, "So Much Fanfare, So Few Hits," Business Week, July 10, 2006, page 27.
34. David Card, "Understanding Google," Jupiter Research, March 10, 2006.
35. Mark Mahany, "Building Out the Option Value of Google," Citigroup Portfolio Strategist, July 13, 2006.
36. Aline Duyn and Richard Waters, "MySpace Teams Up with Google," Financial Times, August 8, 2006, page 15.
37. The Economist "Two Kings Get Together; Google and YouTube," October 14, 2006, pages 82–83.
38. The Economist, "The Ultimate Marketing Machine," July 8, 2006, pages 61–64.
39. Mark Mahaney, "Key Takeaways from Conference Call on MSFT/GOOG Search Competition," Citigroup Global Markets, June 4, 2006.
40. The Economist, "The Ultimate Marketing Machine," July 8, 2006, pages 61–64.
41. comScore Press Release, "Google's U.S. Search Market Share Continues to Rise," July 18, 2006.
42. The Economist, "The Alliance Against Google," August 12, 2006, pages 49–50.
43. David Hallerman, "Search Marketing: Players and Problems," eMarketer, April 2006.
44. comScore Press Release, "Google's U.S. Search Market Share Continues to Rise," July 18, 2006.
45. Fathom Online Press Release, "Fathom Online Reports Q2 Decrease in Average Bid for Search Marketing Keywords," July 18, 2006.
46. Nielsen/Net Ratings Press Release, "U.S. Broadband Composition Reaches 72 Percent at Home," June 21, 2006.
47. Chris Nuttall, "Google Moves to Tackle Click Fraud," Financial Times, July 27, 2006, page 22.
48. David Hallerman "Search Marketing: Players and Problems," eMarketer, April 2006.
49. Mark Mahaney, "YHOO: Revisiting the Long Thesis," Citigroup Global Market, August 17, 2006.
50. Brian Morrissey, "Microsoft Takes Giant Steps in Advertising," Adweek, May 8, 2006, pages 6–8.
51. Brian Haven, "Search Loyalty is Hard to Find," Forrester Research, December 19, 2005.

This case was prepared by Gareth R. Jones, Texas A&M University.

Yahoo is the world's best-known interactive web portal or entryway onto the World Wide Web (WWW). It averaged over 144 million page views per day in 2006, when it earned $2 billion on revenues of $6.4 billion. Today, Yahoo employs over 11,000 people, but the portal has its origins in the website directory created as a hobby by its two founders, David Filo and Jerry Yang. Filo and Yang, who were two PhD candidates in electrical engineering at Stanford University, wanted a quick and easy way to remember and revisit the websites they had identified as the best and most useful from the hundreds of thousands of sites that were quickly appearing on the WWW in the early 1990s. They soon realized that as the list of their favorite websites grew longer and longer, the list began to lose its usefulness since they had to look through a longer and longer list of URLs, or website addresses, to find the specific site they wanted. So to reduce their search time, Filo and Yang decided to break up their list of websites into smaller and more manageable categories according to their specific content or subject matter, such as sports, business, or culture. In April 1994, they published their website directory, "Jerry's Guide to the WWW," for their friends to use. Soon hundreds, then thousands, of people were clicking on their site because it saved them time and effort to identify the most useful sites.

As they continued to develop their directory, Filo and Yang found that each of the directory's subject categories also became large and unwieldy to search, so they further divided the categories into subcategories. Now, their directory organized websites into a hierarchy, rather than a searchable index of pages, so they renamed their directory "Yahoo," supposedly short for "Yet Another Hierarchical Officious Oracle," and Yahoo's hierarchical search directory was born. However, Filo and Yang insist they selected the name because they liked the word's general meaning as originated by Jonathan Swift in *Gulliver's Travels* as someone or something that is "rude, unsophisticated, and uncouth." As their directory grew, they realized they could not possibly identify all the best sites that were appearing in the WWW, so they recruited human volunteers to help them improve, expand, and refine their directory and make it a more useful, labor-saving search device.

By 1994, hundreds of thousands of users were visiting the site every day, and it had quickly become the primary search portal of choice for people using the Internet to find the websites that provided the most useful, interesting, and entertaining content. By the fall of 1994, the website recorded its first million "hits," or Internet-user visits, per day as word of mouth spread about the utility of the Yahoo search directory. Filo and Yang's increasingly comprehensive directory had outgrown the limited hosting capacity of their Stanford University site, and they arranged to borrow server space from nearby Netscape. Yang and Filo decided to put their graduate studies on hold while they turned their attention to building Yahoo into a business.

When they first created their directory, Filo and Yang had no idea they had a potential moneymaking business on their hands. They enjoyed surfing the Internet and just wanted to make it easier for others to do so, but by 1994 it became clear that they could make money from their directory if they allowed companies to advertise their products on the site. Because the Internet was rapidly expanding, Filo and Yang realized they had to move quickly to capitalize on Yahoo's popularity. Although their directory was the first of its kind to be up and running, they knew it could be imitated by other entrepreneurs. Indeed, competitive web-crawling search sites or "search engine" companies like AltaVista that used nonhuman mathematical algorithms had already emerged to help Internet users. The virtue of Yahoo, however, was that its human-powered search engine had already done the legwork for ordinary Internet users; it listed sites handpicked for their usefulness, and at this time, these web crawlers could not match its relevant results to user queries.

As Yahoo's hits continued to increase, so did requests by companies to advertise on its web portal; and as Yahoo's advertising revenues increased, which paid for the costs of hosting their online directory, Filo and Yang realized they had a potentially hot new business on their hands. Filo and Yang's business model was based on generating revenues by renting advertising space on the pages of their fast-growing web directory. When a user clicked on an ad, this "impression," as it is known, became a charge to the advertiser's account; in general, the more impressions, the more the advertising fees. As their fledgling company grew and the number of user visits increased, Filo and Yang realized they had to find the money to pay for a sophisticated IT infrastructure to support their portal's growth. They searched for backing from venture capitalists and soon struck a deal with Sequoia Capital, a Silicon Valley firm that had supported Apple Computer and Oracle, among others. Using the $2 million seed capital to build their company's IT infrastructure, Filo and Yang's portal continued to soar in popularity. In 1996, Yahoo had its initial public offering in April when it raised $338 million by selling 2.6 million shares at $13 each.

Sequoia Capital, with its experience helping start-ups and new entrepreneurs, insisted that Filo and Yang, who had no business background, should hire experienced executives to take control of developing Yahoo's business model. Sequoia's partners had learned that entrepreneurs often do not make good managers when they become responsible for running a company. The skills needed to be a successful manager often diverge from those necessary to notice opportunities and start new businesses, especially if entrepreneurs have technical or scientific backgrounds and no exposure to how businesses operate. Filo and Yang hired Tim Koogle, an experienced ex-Motorola executive with an engineering background, to be their chief executive officer (CEO). Jeffrey Mallett, an ex-Novell software manager with a marketing background, was hired as chief operating officer (COO). Filo and Yang became joint co-chairmen of Yahoo and both adopted the title of "Chief Yahoo."

Developing Yahoo's Business Model

Under the control of Koogle and Mallett, who both received a significant share of the company's stock, the four executives went about building Yahoo's business model. Their first step was to strengthen Yahoo's core competences in marketing and advertising to increase revenues and fund the company's further growth. So Mallett focused on recruiting marketing experts and building the company's advertising function. At the same time, revenue growth would be driven by increasing the number of Internet users, so continuous improvement of Yahoo's web directory was vital. Filo and Yang took overall responsibility here but hired experts such as Srinija Srinivasan, or "Ontological Yahoo" as she became known in the company because of her crucial role in refining and developing the classification system that is the hallmark of Yahoo's web directory. She helped hire hundreds more IT software engineers to broaden and increase the reach and usefulness of Yahoo's directory and to manage its burgeoning IT infrastructure that was being continuously installed and upgraded to handle the millions of requests the company was receiving each day. By 1996, Yahoo listed over 200,000 individual websites in over 20,000 different categories, and hundreds of companies had signed up to advertise their products on its portal to its millions of users. This, however, was just the beginning of their efforts.

Another first step Koogle took was to take Yahoo's business model and replicate it around the world. By the end of 1996, there were eighteen Yahoo portals operating outside the United States, and Yahoo could be accessed by users in twelve languages. In each country, Yahoo's portal and web directory were customized to the tastes and needs of local users. Because there was considerable overlap between countries in terms of global news and global websites, this also allowed Yahoo to enrich its U.S. directory and help create new products to appeal to its users.

Yahoo's success with its global operations convinced Koogle to craft a new vision of Yahoo, not as an Internet website directory but as a global communication, media, and retail company whose portal could be used to enable anyone to connect with anything or anybody on the Internet. Koogle's ambition was to transform Yahoo's directory service into an intermediary that could be used not only to link people to information, but also as a retail conduit to bring together buyers and sellers, thereby facilitating e-commerce transactions over the WWW. In the vision its top executives crafted, Yahoo would not only continue to generate increasing revenues from the sale of advertising space on its web directory pages, but it would also earn significant revenues from managing e-commerce transactions by taking a small percentage of the value of each transaction executed, using its portal as its fee. In 1998, Yahoo acquired the Internet shopping portal Viaweb and the direct marketing company Yoyodyne Entertainment to create its new retail shopping platform, Yahoo Stores. This service enabled businesses to quickly create, publish, and manage secure online stores to market and sell goods and services. After launching their stores, merchants were included in searches on Yahoo Shopping, which provided customers with price comparisons of the products they were interested in.

To build brand awareness and make Yahoo the portal of choice, the company spent heavily on advertising, using radio and television ads targeted at mainstream America. To make the company's portal more useful to users, Koogle pioneered Yahoo's strategy of expanding the range of content and services it provided. Over the next decade, Yahoo continuously developed technology and made acquisitions that allowed users to access an increasing number of services such as email, instant messaging, news, stock alerts, personals, and job placement services using digital devices from conventional PCs to wireless laptops to eventually to hand-held smart phones. Yahoo also began to work with content providers and merchants to help them build and improve their online content, which in turn increased the value of Yahoo's portal to users who could access the content

and merchants through Yahoo. Yahoo also increased its value to advertisers by enabling them to better target their advertising message to specific demographic groups, for example, sports fans, teens, or investors. For example, the online broker E*Trade heavily advertised its shopping and news services on Yahoo's financial pages, in sports magazines, eBay, and Blockbuster. Such targeted advertising increased the rates at which users clicked on online ads, which translated into more online transactions and increased yields or returns of online advertising to merchants.

The results of these strategies were spectacular. By the end of 1998, the company had 50 million unique users, up from 26 million in the prior year, and 35 million of these were now registered Yahoo users; 3,800 companies were advertising on Yahoo's pages, up from 2,600 in 1997 and 700 in 1996. By 1999, 5,000 merchants were selling products on the Yahoo Shopping channel, up from 3,500 in 1998, and the company's revenues had grown from $21.5 million in 1996 to $203 million in 1998. As a result, Yahoo's stock price soared from $5 a share in 1996 to a high of $244 a share in early 1999 near the height of the dot-com boom. This valued Yahoo at an incredible $45 billion, making Yang and Filo billionaires.

More Content and More Presence

To keep Yahoo's profits growing, it was necessary to drive more and more users to its site. For this reason, Koogle's new strategies revolved around making Yahoo a "megabrand" by becoming the most useful and well-known web portal on the Internet. Not only was Yahoo focused on improving its web directory, but it also wanted to create compelling news and entertainment content by adding more and more new services and features to increase its value and appeal to web users and so encourage them to register on its website. Its goal was to lock in users and increase their switching costs of turning to a new portal. So it began to increase the degree to which users could customize Yahoo's pages and services to better meet their specific needs. For example, Yahoo's registered users could customize its popular news service to show the specific news sections or pages in which they were the most interested, such as technology, entertainment, or financial news sections. In some areas, they could do more customization; to give one example, in Yahoo Finance they could also input and track the value of their personal stock portfolio. The financial page section also provides links to message boards where individual investors could join to discuss a company's prospects. Other links connect investors to valuable content about the companies in their personal stock portfolio, including news reports and commentary, research reports, and detailed financial data. Once again, this high level of customization creates major switching costs, for having created their portfolios, personal pages, shopping lists, and so on, users are less likely to want to repeat this process at another web portal—unless it offers some other "killer application," or compelling content.

Yahoo worked hard to remain the web portal of choice by introducing new kinds of online services soon after other kinds of Internet companies showed they were popular among Internet customers. It often acquired well-known Internet companies to increase the value of its portal to users; in 1999, for example, it made three important acquisitions: First, it bought Rocketmail, an email service provider that became the basis for Yahoo email. Second was GeoCities, which provided a free web hosting service to registered users that allowed them to publish their own personal homepages containing material of their choice that they could share with friends and any other interested parties. Third, it bought Broadcast.com, an early leader in broadcasting streaming audio and video programming on the WWW. This acquisition allowed Yahoo to broadcast audio and video content on all its channels to users, in addition to ordinary text, and so made Yahoo's services even more valuable to users—and thus to advertisers as well. Then, in 2000, Yahoo acquired eGroups, a free social group/mailing list hosting service that allowed registered users to set up any kind of online group of their choosing and use it as a forum to attract any other Internet users of their choice, from school groups to national hobby societies. eGroups was used to develop and strengthen its successful Yahoo Groups service, which today has millions of registered groups of users and is a very popular mailing list service for all kinds of social networking purposes.

As Koogle had hoped, as the range of services Yahoo offered expanded, its popularity increased and it worked toward its goal of becoming a "one-stop shop" that could cater to almost every kind of service that Internet users needed—information, entertainment, and retail. Beyond the services just mentioned, Yahoo also now provided Yahoo Messenger, an instant messaging client; online chat; a successful game-playing service, Yahoo Games; and various specialized kinds of information portals including online shopping but also an online auction service it had started up to compete with eBay's successful online auction site. Its original directory now became just one, although an important one, of the services it provided.

Most of these services were provided free to Yahoo users because the advertising revenues earned from the ads on the millions of webpages on its portal were the main source of its highly profitable business model. In addition, it earned some revenues from the fees it earned from joining sellers and buyers on its shopping and specialized retail sites. However, Yahoo also searched for opportunities to increase revenues by providing specialized, customized services to users for a monthly fee; for example, it established a personals dating service, a streaming stocks quotes service, job hunting service, and various premium email and web storage options that provided users with more kinds of value-added solutions. All this helped to increase revenues and earnings.

Indeed, the success of its strategy of bundling online services to attract ever-greater numbers of users became clear with Yahoo's explosive growth. By the end of the 1990s, 15 million people a day were visiting Yahoo; it had become the most visited portal on the WWW. Its business model—based on the idea that the more services it offered, the greater the number of Internet users it would attract, and so the greater would be the advertising fees it could charge—seemed to be working well. In 2000, Yahoo's stock price reached an astronomical height of $237.50 per share, giving the company a value of $220 billion.

Big Problems Face Yahoo

Just two years later, however, Yahoo's stock had plummeted to just $9 a share, which valued the company at less than $10 billion. Why? Because of the dot-com bust, which sent thousands of Internet companies into bankruptcy and caused the stock price of them all to fall. However, Yahoo was a dot-com powerhouse, and many analysts put some of the blame for the fall in its stock price (eBay's did not fall greatly) on managerial mistakes at the top of the company—in particular, on Yahoo's business model.

CEO Tim Koogle had staked Yahoo's continuing success on its ability to develop an increasing range of compelling web content and services to increase visits to its portal and so increase its advertising and e-commerce revenues. The problem with this business model was that it made Yahoo's profitability (and so its stock price) totally dependent on how fast advertising revenues increased—and of course how fast they fell. And the dot-com bust and the economic recession that followed in the early 2000s led to a huge decrease in the amount of money large and small companies were willing to spend on Internet advertising. As its advertising revenues plunged, Yahoo's stock price plummeted because its high stock price was based on investors' hopes of ever-increasing future growth.

Moreover, it turned out that Koogle had spent far too much money—billions too much—to pay for many of Yahoo's acquisitions such as GeoCities and eGroups, especially given that these companies' profits were also highly dependent on Internet advertising! At the same time, general advances in Internet technology lowered the value of the acquired companies' distinctive competencies and their competitive advantage in providing a specific online service—the main reason why Yahoo acquired them. Technological advances were making it easier for new upstart dot-coms to provide similar kinds of specialized Internet services as Yahoo offered, but with new twists or killer applications. Thus, in the 2000s competitors like Monster.com, MySpace, and YouTube emerged and in a few years became dominant portals in providing a particular kind of online application. These portals were major threats to Yahoo because they siphoned off its users and so reduced advertising revenues—which were based on the number of users visiting a website.

On the search engine front, too, a new threat was emerging for Yahoo—the growing popularity of Google, a small, relatively unknown search engine company in 2000. In the early 2000s, it became obvious to web watchers that Google was pioneering advances in WWW search technology that was making Yahoo's hierarchical directory classification obsolete. Yahoo, like other major web portals such as Microsoft and AOL, had not realized how the search function would increase so much in importance as the breadth and depth of the WWW increased and made it increasingly difficult for users to locate the specific information they needed. The search engine that found the information users wanted with the least number of clicks would be the one that won the search engine war, and Google's proprietary technology was attracting more and

more users by word of mouth—just as Yahoo's directory had grown in popularity. Yahoo had been providing more and more kinds of online services, but in the process had forgotten, or lost, the reason for its original success. Perhaps a professional manager at the helm was not such a good idea in the first place?

The Web Portal Industry

To appreciate the problems Yahoo is facing today, it is necessary to understand how the incredible growth in the 1990s of the Internet and WWW and quickly advancing Internet hardware and software changed the function of web portals dramatically.

Internet Service Provider Portals

The first commercial portals were entry or access portals called Internet Service Providers (ISPs) that provided people with a way to log onto the Internet; for example, companies such as CompuServe, MSN, and AOL offered customers email service and access to the WWW for time-related fees. Slow dial-up connections meant high monthly fees, and early on, ISPs charged for each email sent! Moreover, once on the WWW, users were hampered by the fact that there was no Internet web browser available to help them easily find and navigate to the thousands and then millions of webpages and websites that were emerging.

Yahoo's directory and then Netscape's Internet browser, introduced in 1994, changed all this, as did the growth in the number of search engines available to help surf the Web, including early leaders AltaVista, Inktomi, and Infoseek. Typically, a user would connect to the Web through an access portal and then go to a search engine to identify websites of interest, which could then be bookmarked as favorites using Netscape's web browser.

Product Bundling Portals Yahoo stole the lead from AltaVista with its advanced search directory, and this began the second phase of portal development, the product bundling or aggregation phase, as companies like Yahoo, AOL, MSN, and many other now defunct web portals began to compete to attract Internet users and become the portal of choice—to obtain advertising revenues. Major differences in the business models of different portals could be clearly discerned; for example, portals like Yahoo focused on offering users a wide range of free Internet services. Others, like AOL and MSN, adopted the fee-paying model in which users paid to access the Web through a dial-up connection the portal provided; then they could use the range of services they offered free or for a charge for a premium service, like personals.

Competition between these combined access/aggregation portals increased as they strived to attract the millions of new Internet users who were coming online at this time. The bigger their user base, the higher the potential fees and advertising revenues they could collect, so the price of Internet service quickly fell. By the middle 1990s, AOL made a major decision to offer its users unlimited Internet connection time for $19.95 a month. This attracted millions of new users, and AOL became the leading access and aggregation portal with over 30 million users at its height, followed by MSN, and many other smaller ISPs.

The competitive problem ISP/aggregated portals like AOL faced from the beginning was that once their users were online, they would search out the "best of breed" web portal that could provide them with the particular kinds of services they most wanted. So, millions of AOL subscribers, for example, left its entry portal and then used the myriad of services offered on Yahoo's portal—first, because they were familiar with and attracted to its search engine, and then subsequently, because they liked to use its innovative new services such as financial news, game playing, shopping site, and so on. The problem facing AOL, MSN, and others was how to improve their content to keep subscribers on their portals and so obtain the important advertising and e-commerce revenues that Yahoo was enjoying.

Also, an increasing number of new ISPs began to offer lower price Internet access service, and broadband technology started to grow in popularity by the end of the 1990s. This also worked in favor of free portals like Yahoo because fee-based portals like AOL and MSN had to find new ways to keep their revenues growing as the number of new Internet users first slowed and then dropped as they lost customers to other ISPs while their subscribers continued to desert to portals like Yahoo, eBay, and Amazon.com.

Customized Portals The next major development in web portals were those that increasingly allowed for some kind of user-customized online experience. Internet bookselling pioneer Amazon.com was one of the first portals to pioneer the development of the personalized or customized shopping experience.

Amazon.com's software focused on providing more information to users by, for example, allowing people who had bought books to provide detailed feedback to users about a particular book and, subsequently, about all kinds of products that it sold. Similarly, Amazon could track users around its site, helping them to find other similar products to the one they were interested in, and recording the products they had already considered to help users make a better buying decision. In addition, Amazon.com pioneered the 1-Click personalized checkout system that made the purchasing decision quick and easy once a buyer had registered on its site. Just as Yahoo began to provide a range of different services, so over time Amazon decided to sell an increasing range of products, but its personalized approach was the way it differentiated itself from other e-commerce portals. This became an important new development in competition between web portals of all kinds.

All the major portals began to realize the importance of offering users a customized online experience to increase their switching costs and keep them loyal and repeat users. They all began to make the "My" personal preferences choices on their portals—"MyAOL" or "MyYahoo," for instance—more important parts of their services. By offering easy online payment service, portals became more interactive with their users. This benefited Yahoo because with its wide range of offerings it was in a strong position to offer users a personalized service that locked them in to its website.

However, it was also increasingly clear that the best-of-breed web portals had developed a first-mover advantage in terms of the loyalty of their users. Amazon.com had developed a strong first place in Internet retailing. It was able to withstand the challenge from the thousands of other shopping portals that had sprung up, most of which went out of business during the dot-com bust. However, Amazon.com also beat out the shopping channels of portals such as Yahoo and AOL, which increasingly put their focus on providing a shopping advisory/comparison service that listed the prices of products of the major Internet retailers and received a fee from transactions that were completed. Similarly, Yahoo's online auction service, even though it was *free* to its registered users, could not compete with online auction leader eBay because eBay offered buyers and sellers a much larger market and therefore more selection and fairer prices.

By the early 2000s, it was clear that the two biggest sources of profit for web portals that could be gained from e-commerce would come from online advertising revenues and from the profits from retail and auction sales. So, in the early 2000s, it was rumored that Yahoo would use its strong stock price to buy eBay and that the companies would merge to capture all these sources of revenue. However, the two companies' top management could not agree on the terms of a merger, and each portal sought ways to improve its own specific competitive position—eBay by strengthening its presence in different kinds of retailing formats, including fixed price selling, for example, and Yahoo by increasing the range of its online service offerings.

The business models of these companies fared differently during the dot-com bust. While most of the dot-coms went out of business, major portals like Yahoo and Amazon survived because of their leading competitive positions. Some, like AOL and MSN, survived because of the resources of their parent organizations—Time Warner (which almost collapsed because of its mistaken acquisition of AOL) and Microsoft (which has never made a profit operating its MSN web portal). eBay was the least affected portal because its robust business model was based on the profits earned from the fees it obtained from auction sales, not the fickle revenues generated by online advertising. Indeed, eBay's stock has historically been the most resilient of any leading dot-com company.

Since the dot-com bust, some of the leading forces in the environment that have affected competition in the web portal industry have been the arrival of Google, with its unique advertising business model, and the emergence of social networking web portals that have taken personalization and customization of users' online experiences to new levels. Google, of course, not only developed advanced search capabilities that outperformed search engine competitors, including Yahoo, but it also realized that it could develop search technology that could better connect individual users to specific websites and then tailor the advertising on those sites to the specific interests of users. Thus Google invented the *website-customized advertising approach* that allowed it to offer any potential advertiser the ability to appear on a website currently being viewed by a user who is interested in the same kind of products that the potential advertiser has to offer. For example, if I

am looking for a landscaper, when I visit various landscaping websites, Google's advertising presents me with more related choices of landscaping sites to visit; the ones featured first are those who have bid more money (for example, 15 versus 10 cents a click). In addition, increasingly Google was able to personalize advertising and deliver better value to advertisers by charging them only for "impressions"—clicks on websites that actually resulted in sales—as opposed to charging advertisers for all clicks on an advertising button. This, in turn, has allowed advertisers to make better use of their advertising dollars. Also, when a particular website chose to host other Google-sponsored advertisers that offered related products, even if it did not secure a sale from a particular user, it enjoyed a small fee from being the site that provided the link that resulted in a sale. In sum, Google pioneered the concept of cross-website-tailored advertising, a huge market compared to the advertising possible on just one website such as Yahoo's. This allowed it to generate the ever-increasing advertising revenues that have led its stock price to soar.

Social Networking Portals The fourth major development in Internet portals over time has been the quick growth of social networking websites, such as MySpace and YouTube. These sites offer their registered users (1) many additional ways to personalize their personal webpages by uploading more and different kinds of content, and (2) additional avenues to find other users that share similar kinds of interests. Thus on a networking portal, users become interconnected and can often form online groups that are able to share content such as information, music, photographs, and videos, and chat with each other using webcams and so on. Although Yahoo had its Geocities service that allowed users to create personal webpages, specialist social networking websites were able to tweak and develop software that made creating personalized webpages a more exciting and enriching experience. Geocities quickly became "old hat" technology by the standards of MySpace users, especially as these networking websites were specifically targeted at young "hip" Internet users. Yahoo's expensive purchase of Geocities was increasingly looking like a major error as rapidly advancing Internet technology made newer sites more fashionable. It began to seem that fashions in the Internet industry, with the rapid growth of MySpace and

Apple's iTune, could change as quickly as fashions in the clothing industry.

A Changeover at the Top in 2001

As mentioned earlier, at the pinnacle of the Internet boom in the year 2000, it was reported that Yahoo and eBay were discussing a 50/50 merger. On January 3, 2000, Yahoo stock closed at an all-time high of $475 a share, and the company had billions of dollars it could have used to make a major acquisition such as eBay. Many analysts argued that when Yahoo's stock price was high, it should have purchased a company that was generating revenue by some other means than advertising so that it could broaden the source of its revenues. It was so heavily dependent on advertising revenues, that if they were to fall, Yahoo's profitability would also plunge and so would its stock price, but infighting among Yahoo's top managers who could not agree on the right course of action prevented the merger from occurring. And, in the next twelve months, Yahoo's stock price did plummet as the dot-com bust, coupled with a huge fall in advertising revenues caused by the economic recession that followed, showed investors how fragile the profitability of its business model was.

In fact, Yahoo's disastrous performance convinced its board of directors that new leadership was needed at the top, and both Tim Koogle and Jeff Mallett stepped down in March 2001. In April 2001, Terry Semel, an experienced Hollywood media executive who had once controlled Warner Brothers, took control as its new CEO, but Yahoo's stock was still in freefall, and in September 2001 it closed at an all-time low of $8.11! To resolve Yahoo's problems, especially as it could no longer afford to make an expensive acquisition, Semel had to redefine its business model and adopt strategies to find new ways to generate online revenues, especially as the economy recovered. Three interrelated strategies were at the center of his new business model for Yahoo.

First, there was a need to quickly develop new content and services to attract more users and so more advertising revenues. Second, Yahoo had to improve its search engine technology, a major portal attraction, to generate more users and advertising revenues. Third, as time went on and the success of Google's business model became evident, Yahoo needed to imitate Google and offer a high-quality customized advertising service (1) to companies that already had websites on Yahoo's portal, and (2) to any company that wanted to benefit from increased online sales. The result would be increased advertising revenues from Internet-wide advertising programs.

To pursue its new content-driven strategy, Yahoo both internally developed new kinds of services and acquired specialist Internet companies that could provide it with the competency it needed in an emerging new content area. In late 2001, for example, Yahoo acquired HotJobs, a leading Internet job hunting and placement company. Also starting in 2001, it began expanding its news and media services operations and started to hire experienced executives from major television networks and newspapers to build its competencies in news services. In 2002, SBC and Yahoo launched its national co-branded dial service to help build a presence in the growing broadband entry portal business, and in 2004 Yahoo made several acquisitions, such as email provider Oddpost.com, to improve its existing services.

In 2004, recognizing the growing importance of communications media for generating advertising revenues, Yahoo established a new Media Group to develop not only written but also video news content to take advantage of broadband Internet to transmit content to users as a shift away from TV took place. In 2004, Yahoo launched its video search engine, and in 2005 it launched a revamped Yahoo Music download service. In 2005 Yahoo also acquired Flickr, a leading photograph hosting and sharing site, and announced Flickr and its other social sites would become major parts of its new social networking strategy. This purchase was prompted by increasing concerns that advertising revenues were bypassing Yahoo in favor of social networking sites like MySpace and YouTube. Yahoo lost the battle to acquire YouTube to Google, which bought the company in 2006, and it was rumored to be looking at Facebook.com as a possible alternative.

Yahoo used new acquisitions and internally developed skills to give each of its hundreds of services a more customized, social network-like appeal to users. For example, it made more use of message boards and wikis to enhance the value of its travel and financial services. In 2005 Yahoo launched a personalized blogging and social networking service Yahoo 360°, revamped its MyWeb personal web hosting service, created a new PhotoMail service, and purchased online social event calendar company Upcoming.org to compete with Google's online calendar service. Continuing its push to strengthen customized and social networking services in 2005, Yahoo acquired blo.gs, a service based on RSS feed aggregation, primarily from weblogs (hence the name), which produces a simple list (and also an RSS feed) of freshly updated weblogs based on a user's specific interests. Yahoo also acquired del.icio.us, which allows registered users to create a scrapbook or notebook of information they wish to keep from the websites they visit, similar to Google's notebook service. More rumors continue to surface about Yahoo's possible acquisition intentions that may allow users to share common interests and trade information.

Thus under Semel, Yahoo has continually developed the competencies to engage its users in multiple online services, from email to financial services to job hunting. It is a leader in content categories such as finance, autos, and real estate. It can now use the thousands and millions of different web content pages it has created on its portal to sell more ads and generate more advertising revenues, and its user base has increased. Semel's other content-driven strategy has been to make Yahoo's content and services so useful and attractive to online customers that they are willing to pay for them—in the form of once-and-for-all or monthly fees for services. For example, Yahoo generates monthly fees for personal ads in its dating site or from ads to sell or rent merchandise like cars or homes; it receives fees from premium services in areas including email and storage, photo sharing, e-commerce services, message boards, and special interest topics. Yahoo also generates fees from small businesses that wish to link to its web portal and use Yahoo's specialist services to create, host, and manage their retail stores.

This user-fee strategy has worked well for Yahoo, and now over 40% of its total revenues come from the fees individuals and small business customers pay for its services. At the same time, the advertising revenues its webpages generate have also soared as the economy recovered and Yahoo kept its position as the most popular portal; its revenue more than tripled from 2003 to 2006 to over $6 billion.

Problems with a Content-Driven Strategy

In the summer of 2006, however, major questions came to be asked about how much Yahoo's content-driven strategy would continue to drive its revenues as competition, particularly from Google and social networking portals, increased dramatically. Yahoo's stock fell 25% in 2006 as analysts became worried that these other popular websites were taking away its users and so would reduce advertising revenues and user fees in the future. Yahoo might be in trouble as Google and other specialist portals were now offering free an increasing number of the services Yahoo provided; Google had started Gmail, for example, as well as chat, storage, and word-processing services. Fewer users would also mean lower advertising revenues.

In an internal memo leaked to the media, one of Yahoo's senior managers expressed concerns that many of its new investments in content and services were too expensive, were unlikely to generate much profit, and would not allow it to keep up with agile new competitors like social networking websites. In the "peanut butter" memo, senior executive Brad Garlinghouse described Yahoo as a company in search of a successful business model and strategies: "I've heard our strategy described as spreading peanut butter across the myriad opportunities that continue to evolve in the online world. The result: a thin layer of investment spread across everything we do and thus we focus on nothing in particular. I hate peanut butter. We all should." Reasons for his concern include the fact that MySpace, YouTube, and other social networking websites had beaten Yahoo's own sites such as Yahoo360° and MySpace. And Google's new instant messaging and email service were attracting away users from Yahoo's, which had been an early leader in this area. Similarly, Yahoo had been late into Internet VOIP telephone calling, and although it had purchased Dialpad in 2005 to gain a competency in this area, eBay's Skype was the current leader in this area. Similarly, in the increasingly important online imaging and video services area, Google, MSN, and AOL had all developed imaging and video channels that offered content similar to Yahoo's, and Google drew further ahead of Yahoo after its purchase of YouTube in 2006.

Nevertheless, Yahoo still had impressive content covering sports, entertainment, and finance, in particular, and had made major advances in the mobile delivery of its services to smartphones and other hand-held devices and embarked on a major program to enhance the wireless features of all its services to better meet the needs of people on the go. By 2008, for example, mobile video is expected to be a killer application and to compete with Google. Yahoo has recently invested heavily to upgrade this service.

The Search Engine Dilemma

One of the most important factors that generates return user visits and stimulates advertising revenues is the quality of a portal's search engine service. Semel recognized that for Yahoo to achieve significant revenue and earnings growth, it also had to maximize the value of its search services to Internet users to generate the high volume of web traffic that leads to significant revenues from online advertising and facilitating e-commerce transactions. As mentioned earlier, Yahoo's original search directory was developed by its own human editors or "surfers," who identified the best websites and organized them into categories by their content. However, as the WWW grew enormously, its human surfers could not keep up, and from the early 1990s Yahoo partnered with independent "crawler-based" search engine companies to provide answers to user queries when there were no matches within its own human-powered listings directory. The independent search providers were paid by Yahoo according to the volume of queries their engines handled, and since Yahoo was the most popular search site on the Web, being Yahoo's provider could earn the search engine company significant revenues. Each year Yahoo searched for the best search engine, the one with the best search technology, and offered the company a short-term contract. OpenText was the company's first search engine partner; then AltaVista won the contract in 1996, but was dumped for Inktomi in mid-1998. This happened because Yahoo thought that AltaVista was attempting to become a competing portal while Inktomi's business model was focused on developing state-of-the-art search technology and it made no attempt to compete with access portals like Yahoo.

In 2000, however, Inktomi lost the contract to Google, which had developed a growing reputation for its high-quality search results and which, at that time, was not a competitor to Yahoo. In 2001, Yahoo paid Google $7.1 million for the volume of search queries it handled, and in 2002 it renewed Google's contract to use its search results as part of its search listings. It even introduced a new Yahoo search results page that no longer separated Yahoo's own human-powered listings from Google's crawler-based results; rather, the two were blended together. Even in 2002, some top managers at Yahoo thought that this new contract

might be a mistake because as Yahoo users became increasingly aware that Google was powering their search results, they might began to move directly to Google's own website—still very "empty" of content at this time, however. Although Google handled a search volume more than double that of Yahoo's, as measured by "search hours," and had a 30% share of the U.S. search audience—very similar to Yahoo's—it was not perceived as a direct competitor because it had not developed its current content/services portal business model. In addition, Yahoo had initially partnered with Google, so its users would feel they were getting both the quality of Google and the unique view that Yahoo's human-powered results brought to the Web. Dropping Google might cause Yahoo problems if its users decided to leave for Google, even though other engines like Inktomi also provided high-quality search results.

By 2003, Google's growing popularity as the search portal of choice and its fast-developing customized advertising strategy showed Yahoo's managers they had made a major error. Recognizing the increasing threat posed by Google's customized search and advertising strategy, Semel began to look for acquisitions to strengthen and improve Yahoo's search engine. Its past relationship with search engine leader Inktomi made that company an obvious acquisition target. After buying Inktomi in 2002, Yahoo bought Overture Services in 2003, a company that specialized in identifying and ranking the popularity of websites and in helping advertisers find the best sites to advertise on; it also obtained Overture's search engine subsidiaries AltaVista and AlltheWeb. Then, in early 2004, Yahoo dropped Google's search engine service and rolled out its own, powered by Inktomi; its directory is now found in a separate category/tab on its search toolbar. Today, Yahoo and Google compete head-to-head with search engines that offer remarkably similar sets of features and services; however, Google's share of the search engine market is still growing, and it now has almost double Yahoo's share of search engine users—49% compared to Yahoo's 24% in 2006. This is one more factor that led Yahoo's stock price to fall by 25% in 2006 while Google's soared.

A Push for Customized Online Search/Advertising

The third, and related part of Semel's ongoing strategy to protect and increase Yahoo's revenues has evolved over the past few years in response to the growing success of Google's customized advertising model. All the other major portals—Amazon.com, AOL, MSN, and eBay—were slow to recognize that the better able a search engine is to match ads to search queries, the more likely a user is to click through to an advertiser's website and complete an online transaction, which generates the high advertising revenues Google enjoys. In addition, the real breakthrough in Google's strategy was that it was not advertising on a particular portal that was the main source of revenue; it was the ability to create the advertising that was most closely linked to any specific webpage—the advertising that comes up when a user clicks on the search results from a particular query. Google's advertising model is to help every potential website or advertiser host customized ads that drive online transactions so that everyone would benefit—website, advertiser, and, of course, Google, which collects a small fee for each click.

Consequently, these portals have come to realize the potential threat posed by Google's Internet-wide customized advertising strategy: It has the potential to generate an enormous amount of revenue, which Google can then use to enter their businesses if it chooses and compete head to head with them. When users return to portals like Google's that offer them the quickest and most relevant search results, they are barraged by relevant ads, many useful online services, and who knows what other services they may encounter in the future as Google expands its offerings?

To meet Google's challenge, Semel combined the distinctive competencies of Inktomi and Overture with the in-house technology developed by Yahoo's search engine and advertising software engineers to develop an improved search engine that would lead to a much improved customized online advertising program, one that could compete with Google's. Yahoo began a major technology upgrade, Project Panama, to improve its search-based advertising technology with a goal of bringing the new system online in 2006. But this massive project soon fell behind schedule, and the company could not meet its revised goal of launching it in the summer of 2006, which is one more reason for the company's 38% slide in third-quarter revenues and its fourth-quarter profit warning. Nevertheless, to fight back Google's challenge, Yahoo and eBay formed a marketing/advertising alliance in 2006 that gave Yahoo the contract for creating customized advertising on eBay's webpages;

however, later in the year, eBay, which is also a major partner of Google, gave that company the contract for creating the customized advertising on all its other global websites.

Google has also improved its advertising system and seems able to maintain its first-mover advantage in customized advertising on other websites as well as improved search engine technology—hence the jump to $500 a share it reached in November 2006. Yahoo is also struggling to catch up with Google's AdSense service, which sells search-based and banner advertisements to other people's websites and blogs. Google is entering new advertising areas, offering package deals for its customers that take in radio and newspaper advertising as well as online ads. Its goal seems to be to become the leading advertiser in every communications media.

Yahoo is fighting back. In the fall of 2006, it announced a deal with seven major U.S. newspapers that allows their local papers to post jobs on Yahoo's HotJobs recruitment website in return for a revenue sharing deal, and there will be more collaborations over time in other areas of local classified and display advertising. Yahoo is the only company that could have offered the newspapers cooperation spanning online job listings, technology, content, search, and online traffic. This deal attests to the unique breadth of Yahoo's offerings and services and the many benefits it can also offer advertisers if it can get its cross-channel advertising program up to speed.

In 2005, Yahoo and Google were neck and neck with roughly 18% of Internet advertising revenues of all kinds each. However, by the start of 2006, Google's portion had grown to 23% compared to 19% for Yahoo, and Google's grew to 25% by the end of 2006. The stakes are high since Internet advertising is soaring and the $16.7 billion spent on it in 2006 is expected to grow to $29.4 billion by 2010. In November 2006, Semel told analysts he was aware of the stakes involved; moreover he said most web portals had underestimated the growth potential of Internet advertising because predictions did not include the advertising possibilities on video, social media, or mobile devices that had become so apparent in 2006. Semel believes that video will also become a major factor on the Internet and more innovative and clever ways to integrate advertising with video online will all develop quickly. To meet this challenge, Yahoo purchased Ad-Interax, a company that specializes in the creation and management of video and animated online ads, such as animations, dynamically expandable banners, and streaming video ads; Rich Media; and Today, an online advertising company that specializes in designing and implementing customized advertising programs. Both acquisitions are intended to enhance Yahoo's new customized search advertising system by providing better support for video and rich media ads and to generate more ad volume—and compete with Google.

In December 2006, Semel decided to shake up the management structure of the company to allow it to better implement its business model and compete with its rivals, a shakeup sparked by the peanut butter memo. Yahoo's chief financial officer, Susan Decker, will replace Dan Rosensweig as the company's chief operating officer to rein in its expenditures. Yahoo announced it would focus on building its most successful online services, stop product development just to increase its breath, and considered pruning its weakest services. The new streamline organizational structure will group Yahoo's services into three core product groups, one focused on its website's audience, one on its advertising network, and one on developing new technology. A new executive will be hired to run the group focused on satisfying Yahoo's 418 million registered users. Like Decker and Farzad Nazem, Yahoo's chief technology officer, the new executive will report to Semel, who will remain CEO.

However, Garlinghouse had proposed a more radical reorganization involving the layoff of 15 to 20% of Yahoo's 11,000 employees to reduce its cost structure. This was something that Semel had done when he took over the company in 2001; he grouped the dozens of individual Yahoo service units into larger product-focused groups. Semel hopes the reorganization will make Yahoo more proficient at delivering online services and ads that capture the attention of online users.

Yahoo's Future

Some analysts wonder if Yahoo's problem today is that it has lost sight of its original business model and mission and that it is spreading itself too thin. It is no longer clear what the company is today and what kind of portal it aspires to be since it functions as an entry portal, a web search engine company, a retail portal, a media content and communications company, and a social networking platform service; it also provides companies with a range of online commercial

services and customized advertising programs. On top of all this, the push to generate advertising revenues across its entire website is paramount. Others argue that it is Yahoo's unique strength that it operates in all these areas and that as long as it can catch up with Google and other specialized dot-coms, it will perform well in the future. But can it catch up with rivals that offer Internet users a different and sometimes superior value proposition online?

The problem facing Yahoo is to transition so that it retains its status as the number 1 overall web portal of choice. It has to invest its resources to continually improve its wide range of content and services to meet the challenge of upstart new Internet companies that are constantly appearing to offer users something new. The Internet, by its very nature, makes entry into the WWW easy, and a company survives or fails by its continuing ability to improve and refine its products to better meet the needs of Internet users. In addition, Yahoo has to meet the advertising challenge of Google, which is continually expanding its own content and services, and growing its customized advertising so that over time it will become a direct threat to Yahoo.

In January 2007, Yahoo announced it would begin rolling out its new customized advertising system to advertisers in the spring. The company is hoping to see major improvements in advertising revenues by the summer. Revenue per search query may grow by 10% or more in the second half of the year, the company forecast, and Semel said: "We believe this will deliver more relevant text ads to users, which in turn should create more high-quality leads. By the time we get to 2008 and beyond, this is a very, very, significant amount of additional profit and I'm pleased with the tangible progress we have made. I'm convinced we're on the right path." Yahoo's stock soared by over 10% as investors bet that this would be a turnaround moment in Yahoo's battle with Google. However, in February 2007, Google once again announced record advertising revenues, so the battle is ongoing.

Some analysts believe the Internet will receive a greater share of global advertising spending by 2008 than outdoor outlets, such as billboards, and will overtake radio in the near future. Yahoo claims that about half a billion people around the world still regularly use its portal in some way, and so it is positioned to obtain a large share of these revenues. Yahoo's front page, which for so long has been the gateway of millions to the Internet, may be going out of fashion, however. Google is still winning Yahoo users over to use its web search and other services, and social networking websites siphon off millions of other users. Nevertheless, Yahoo has a lot more services to offer its users than Google or other specialized sites, and it is here particularly that Yahoo's business model under Semel has shined. Only time will tell in the fast-changing Internet world if Yahoo can maintain its premier status as the portal of choice.

SOURCES

http://www.yahoo.com, 1990–2007

Yahoo 10K reports, 1990–2007

Ask Yahoo—a question and answer column, http://ask.yahoo.com/

Blo.gs—a directory of recently updated blogs, http://blo.gs/

del.icio.us—popular social bookmarking site, http://del.icio.us/

Dialpad—a phone company, http://www.dialpad.com/

Flickr—popular photo sharing site, http://flickr.com/

GeoCities—free web hosting service, http://geocities.yahoo.com/

Kelkoo—price comparison service for ten European countries, http://www.kelkoo.co.uk/

My Yahoo—customizable portal, http://my.yahoo.com

Upcoming.org—Social event calendar driven by people, http://upcoming.org

Webjay—playlist sharing community, http://www.webjay.org/

Yahoo 360°—free blogging and social networking service, http://360.yahoo.com

Yodel Anecdotal—Yahoo's corporate blog, http://yodel.yahoo.com/

Yahoo Answers—a place where you can get your questions answered by real people in real time, http://answers.yahoo.com

Yahoo Avatars—http://avatars.yahoo.com/

Yahoo Auctions—an online auction site, http://auctions.yahoo.com/

Yahoo Autos—http://autos.yahoo.com/

Yahoo Assistant—a browser helper object for Internet Explorer

Yahoo Briefcase—free file hosting service, http://briefcase.yahoo.com/

Yahoo Broadway—http://broadway.yahoo.com/

Yahoo Buzz Log—a column that talks about what people are searching Yahoo for, http://buzz.yahoo.com/

Yahoo Developer Network—resources for software developers using Yahoo technologies and web services, http://developer.yahoo.com/

Yahoo Directory—hierarchical web directory, http://dir.yahoo.com/

Yahoo Finance—stock exchange rates and other financial information, http://finance.yahoo.com/

Yahoo Food—http://food.yahoo.com/

Yahoo Gallery—directory of applications built by third-party developers using Yahoo technology, http://gallery.yahoo.com/

Yahoo Games—playing games (online against other users), http://games.yahoo.com/

Yahoo Greetings—an e-card service with partners American Greetings, http://www.yahoo.americangreetings.com/

Yahoo Groups—electronic mailing list and Internet forum, http://groups.yahoo.com/

Yahoo HotJobs—job search engine, http://hotjobs.yahoo.com/

Yahoo Local—customized local information, http://local.yahoo.com/

Yahoo Mail—web-based email, http://mail.yahoo.com/

Yahoo Maps—mapping portal, http://maps.yahoo.com/

Yahoo Messenger—instant messaging client, http://messenger.yahoo.com/

Yahoo Mobile—Yahoo for mobile phones, http://mobile.yahoo.com/

Yahoo Movies—show times, movie trailers, movie information, gossip, http://movies.yahoo.com/

Yahoo Music—music videos and Internet radio (LAUNCHcast) plus pay service

Yahoo Music Unlimited, http://music.yahoo.com/ and Yahoo Music Engine.

Yahoo News—news updates and top stories at Yahoo News, including world, national, business, entertainment, sports, weather, technology, and weird news, http://news.yahoo.com/

Yahoo Personals—http://personals.yahoo.com/

Yahoo Photos—http://photos.yahoo.com/

Yahoo Podcasts (beta)—http://podcasts.yahoo.com/

Yahoo Publisher Network—advertising network, http://publisher.yahoo.com/

Yahoo Real Estate—http://realestate.yahoo.com/

Yahoo Research—http://research.yahoo.com/

Yahoo Search—web search engine, http://search.yahoo.com/

Yahoo Search Marketing—pay per click search engine, http://searchmarketing.yahoo.com/

Yahoo Shopping—shopping search and compare, http://shopping.yahoo.com/

Yahoo Small Business—domains, web hosting, and e-commerce services, http://smallbusiness.yahoo.com/

Yahoo Soccer Manager—online soccer game, http://uk.soccermanager.yahoo.net/

Yahoo Sports—scores, stats, and fantasy sports, http://sports.yahoo.com/

Yahoo Tech—product information and advice, http://tech.yahoo.com/

Yahoo Travel—travel guides, booking and reservation, http://travel.yahoo.com/

Yahoo TV—TV listings, scheduling recordings on TiVo box remotely, http://tv.yahoo.com/

Yahoo Video—video sharing site, http://video.yahoo.com/

Yahoo Widgets—a cross-platform desktop widget runtime environment, formerly called Konfabulator, http://widgets.yahoo.com

Yahooligans!—children's version of the web portal, http://yahooligans.yahoo.com

This case was prepared by Gareth R. Jones, Texas A&M University.

In just over a decade, Amazon.com (Amazon) has grown from an online bookseller to a virtual retail supercenter selling products as diverse as books, toys, food, and electronics. Today, its mission is to be "Earth's most customer-centric company, where customers can find and discover virtually anything they might want to buy online." In many ways, the last decade has been a wild ride for Amazon as its revenues, profits, and stock price have soared and plunged as a result of the dot-com boom and then bust of the early 2000s. It has also been a wild ride for Amazon's founder, Jeff Bezos, who through it all has consistently championed his company and claimed investors have to look long term to measure the success of Amazon's business model. Indeed, he originally said he did not expect his company to become profitable for several years, and his forecast turned out to be correct.

By the early 2000s, however, Amazon had become profitable, and its business model seemed to be working. But then, around the mid-2000s, its future prospects started to look bleak again as its revenue growth seemed to stall when its new retail ventures seemed not be succeeding. In 2007, the problem facing Amazon is to find new strategies to keep its revenues growing at a fast pace and to keep its costs under control, not easy when competition is increasing in Internet commerce.

Amazon's Beginnings: The Online Bookstore Business

In 1994, Jeffrey Bezos, a computer science and electrical engineering graduate from Princeton University, was growing weary of working for a Wall Street investment bank. Seeking to take advantage of his computer science background, he saw an entrepreneurial opportunity in the fact that usage of the Internet was growing enormously as every year tens of millions of new users were becoming aware of its potential uses. Bezos decided the bookselling market offered an excellent opportunity for him to take advantage of his IT skills in the new electronic, virtual marketplace. His vision was an online bookstore that could offer millions more books to millions more customers than a typical bricks-and-mortar (B&M) bookstore. To act on his vision, he packed up his belongings and headed for the West Coast to found his new dot-com start-up. On route, he had a hunch that Seattle, the hometown of Microsoft and Starbucks, was a place where first-rate software developers could be easily found. His trip ended there, and he began to flesh out the business model for his new venture.

What was his vision for his new venture? To build an online bookstore that would be customer-friendly, be easy to navigate, provide buying advice, and offer the broadest possible selection of books at low prices. Bezos's original mission was to use the Internet to offer books "that would educate, inform and inspire." And from the beginning, Bezos realized that compared to a physical B&M bookstore, an online bookstore could offer customers a much larger and more diverse selection of books. Indeed, there are about 1.5 million books in print, but most B&M bookstores stock only around 10,000 books; the largest stores in major cities might stock 40,000 to 60,000. Moreover, online customers would be able to search easily for any book in print using computerized catalogs. There was also scope for an online company to find ways to tempt customers to browse books in different subject areas, read reviews of books, and even ask other shoppers for online recommendations—all of which would encourage people to buy more books. A popular feature of Amazon is the ability of users to submit product reviews on its website. As part of their reviews, users rate the products on a scale from one to five stars and then provide detailed information that helps other users decide whether to purchase the products. In turn, the users of these ratings can then rate the usefulness of the reviews so the best reviews are those that rise to the top and are read first in the future!

Operating from his garage in Seattle with a handful of employees, Bezos launched his online venture in 1995 with $7 million in borrowed capital. Because Amazon was one of the first major Internet or dot-com retailers, it received a huge amount of free national publicity, and the new venture quickly attracted more and more book buyers. Book sales quickly picked up as satisfied Internet customers spread the good word and Amazon became a model for other dot-com retailers to follow. Within weeks Bezos was forced to relocate to larger premises, a 2,000-square-foot warehouse, and hire new employees to receive books from book publishers and fill and mail customer orders as book sales soared. Within six months he was once again searching for additional capital to fund his growing venture; he raised another $7 million from venture capitalists, which he used to move to a 17,000-square-foot warehouse that was now required to handle increasing book sales. As book sales continued to soar month by month over the next two years, Bezos decided that the best way to raise more capital would be to take his company public and issue stock. This, of course, would reward him as the founder and the venture capitalists who had funded Amazon because they would all receive significant percentages of the company's stock. On May 1997 Amazon.com's stock began trading on the NASDAQ stock exchange.

Building Up Amazon's Value Chain

Amazon's rapid growth continued to put enormous pressure on the company's physical warehousing and distribution capabilities. The costs of operating an online website, for example, continuously developing the website's software, and maintaining and hosting the computer hardware and Internet bandwidth connections necessary to serve customers are relatively low given the hundreds of millions of visits to its website and the millions of sales that are completed. However, Bezos soon found out that the costs of developing and maintaining the physical infrastructure necessary to obtain supplies of books from book publishers and then to stock, package, and ship the books to customers were much higher than he had anticipated, as was the cost of the employees required to perform these activities.

Developing and maintaining the physical side of Amazon's value chain is the source of the greatest proportion of its operating costs, and these high costs were draining its profitability, given the low prices at which it was selling its books. And price competition was also heating up because of new competition from B&M booksellers such as Barnes & Noble and Borders that had also opened online bookstores to compete in this market segment. In fact, in 1997, as it passed the 1-million-different-customers-served point, Amazon was forced to open up a new 200,000-square-foot warehouse and distribution center and expand its old one to keep pace with demand.

On the employee front, Bezos sought ways to increase the motivation of his employees across all the company. Working to fill customer orders quickly is vital to an online company; minimizing the wait time for a product like a book to arrive is a key success factor in building customer loyalty. On the other hand, motivating Amazon's rapidly expanding army of software engineers to develop innovative software, such as its patented 1-Click (SM) Internet ordering and payment software, was also a vital issue. To ensure good responsiveness to customers, Bezos implemented a policy of decentralizing significant decision-making authority to employees and empowered them to find ways of meeting customers needs quickly. Because Amazon.com employed a relatively small number of people—about 2,500 worldwide in 2000—Bezos also empowered employees to recruit and train new employees so that they quickly get up to speed in their new jobs. And to motivate employees, Bezos decided to give all employees stock in the company. Amazon employees own over 10% of their company, a factor behind Amazon.com's rapid growth.

In fact, Jeff Bezos is a firm believer in the power of using teams of employees to spur innovation. At

Amazon, teams are given considerable autonomy to develop their ideas and experiment without interference from managers. Teams are kept deliberately small, and, according to Bezos, no team should need more than "two pizzas to feed its members"; if more pizza is needed, the team is too large. Amazon's "pizza teams," which usually have no more than about five to seven members, have come up with many innovations that have made its site so user-friendly. For example, one team developed the "Gold Box" icon that customers can click on to receive special offers that expire within an hour of opening the treasure chest; another developed "Bottom of the Page Deals," low-priced offers for products such as batteries and power bars, and one more team developed the "Search Inside the Book" feature discussed later. These teams have helped Amazon expand into many different retail storefronts and provide the wide range of IT services it does today. Indeed, Bezos and his top managers believe that Amazon is a *technology company* first and foremost, and its mission is to use and develop its technological expertise to sell more and more goods and services in ways that satisfy customers and so keep its profit growing.

Since the beginning, Bezos has personally played a very important part in energizing his employees and representing his company to customers. He is a hands-on, articulate, forward-looking executive who puts in long hours and works closely with employees to find innovative and cost-saving solutions to problems. Moreover, Bezos has consistently acted as a figurehead for his company and become well recognized in the national media as he works to further Amazon's visibility with customers. He spends a great deal of time flying around the world to publicize his company and its activities, and he has succeeded because Amazon has one of the best recognized names of any dot-com company.

An important strategy that Amazon created in 1996 to attract new customers to its website and grow sales is its Amazon Associates program. Any person or small business that operates a website can become affiliated to Amazon by putting an official Amazon hyperlink to Amazon's website on its own website. If a referral results in a sale, the Associate receives a commission from Amazon. Today about 40% of Amazon's sales come from referrals from its Associates who have received over $1 billion in sales commissions. By 2004 Amazon had signed up over 1 million Associates, and its Associates program has been copied by many other Internet companies.

By 1998 Amazon could claim that 45% of its business was repeat business, which translated into lower marketing and sales expenses and higher profit margins. By using all his energies to act on the online bookselling opportunity, Bezos gave his company a first-mover advantage over rivals, and this has been an important contributor to its strong position in the marketplace. Nevertheless, Amazon still had to make a profit, just as Bezos had predicted.

The Bookselling Industry Environment

The book distribution and bookselling industry was changed forever in July 1995 when Jeff Bezos brought virtual bookseller Amazon.com online. His new company changed the whole nature of the environment. Previously, book publishers had sold their books indirectly to book wholesalers that supplied small bookstores, directly to large book chains like Barnes & Noble or Borders, or to book-of-the month clubs. There were so many book publishers and so many individual booksellers that the industry was relatively stable, with both large and small bookstores enjoying a comfortable, nonprice competitive niche in the market. In this stable environment, competition was relatively low, and all companies enjoyed good revenues and profits.

Amazon.com's electronic approach both to buying and selling books changed all this. First, since it was able to offer customers quick access to all of the over 1.5 million books in print and it discounted the prices of its books, a higher level of industry competition developed. Second, since it also negotiated directly with the large book publishers over price and supply because it wanted to get books quickly to its customers, the industry value chain changed: All players—book publishers, wholesalers, stores, and customers—became more closely linked. Third, as a result of these factors and continuing changes in information technology, the bookselling business began to change rapidly as the sources of competitive advantage changed, and price and service became important.

By being first into the online bookselling business, Amazon was able to capture customers' attention and establish a first-mover advantage. Its entry into the bookselling industry using its new IT posed a major threat for B&M bookstores, and Barnes &

Noble, the largest U.S. bookseller, and Borders, the second, realized that with its competitive prices, Amazon would be able to siphon off a significant percentage of industry revenues. So these B&M bookstores decided to launch their own online ventures to meet Amazon's challenge and to convince book buyers that they, not Amazon, were still the best places to shop for books. However, being first to market with a new way to deliver books to customers resulted in satisfied customers who become loyal customers. And once a customer had signed up as an Amazon customer, it was often difficult to get that person to register again at a competing website.

Amazon's early success also made it difficult for new "unknown" competitors to enter the industry because they faced the major hurdle of attracting customers to their websites rather than to Amazon.com's. Even well-known competitors such as Barnes & Noble and Borders, which imitated Amazon's online business model, faced major problems in attracting away Amazon's customer base and securing their positions. If large B&M bookstores had problems attracting customers, small specialized B&M bookstores were in desperate trouble. Their competitive advantage has been based on providing customers with hard-to-find books, a convenient location, and good customer service. Now they were faced with competition from an online bookstore that could offer customers all 1.5 million books in print at 10% lower prices, with delivery to anywhere in a few days.

Thousands of small specialized B&M bookstores closed their doors nationwide, and even the large B&M bookstores struggled to compete. Its strong competitive position, combined with Internet investors' "irrational exuberance," led Amazon's stock price to soar in the dot-com bubble of the late 1990s. By 1998, its market capitalization was $6.8 billion, almost twice that of its two biggest rivals, Barnes & Noble and Borders, whose combined sales at this time were many times that of Amazon's!

Competition increased in 1999 as large B&M bookstores began a price war with Amazon that resulted in falling book prices; this squeezed Amazon's profit margins and put more pressure on it to contain its increasing operating costs. In the spring of 1999, for example, Amazon and its largest competitors, Barnes & Noble and Borders, announced a 50% discount off the price of new best-selling books to defend their market shares; they were locked in a fierce battle to see which company would dominate the bookselling industry in the new millennium.

From Online Bookstore to Internet Retailer

While Bezos initially chose to focus on selling books, he soon realized that Amazon's IT could be used to sell other kinds of products, but he was cautious because he also now understood how high the value chain costs involved in delivering a wide range of products to customers were. However, Amazon's slow growth in the late 1990s led many of its stockholders to complain that the company was not on track to becoming profitable fast enough, so Bezos began to search for other products that could be sold profitably over the Internet. One growing online business was music CDs, and he realized CDs were a good fit with books, so in 1999 Amazon announced its intention to become the "earth's biggest book and music store." The company used its IT competences to widen its product line by selling music CDs on its retail website. The strategy of selling CDs also seemed like a good move because the leading Internet music retailers at this time, such as CD Now, were struggling because they too had discovered the high physical costs associated with delivering products bought online to customers. Amazon now had built up its skills in this area, and its online retail competencies were working to its advantage; for example, its IT now allowed it to constantly alter the mix of products it offered in its virtual store to keep up-to-date with changing customer needs.

Amazon also took many more steps to increase the usefulness of its retail sites to attract more customers and get its established customers to spend more. For example, to entice customers to send books and CDs as presents at important celebration and holiday shopping times such as birthdays, Christmas, and New Year's, Amazon opened a holiday gift store. Customers could take advantage of a gift-wrapping service as well as using a free greeting card email service to announce the arrival of the Amazon gift. Amazon began to explore other kinds of online retail ventures; for example, recognizing the growing popularity of online auctions pioneered by eBay, Bezos moved into this market by purchasing Livebid.com, the Internet's only provider of live online auctions at that time. Also in 1999, it entered into an agreement with Sotheby's, the famous auction house, to enter the high end of the online auction business.

Nevertheless, starting in 2000, Amazon's stock price fell sharply as investors came to believe that intense competition from Barnes & Noble and other retailers might keep its operating margins low into the foreseeable future. Despite his company's moves into CDs and the auction business, Bezos was being increasing criticized for being much too slow to take advantage of Amazon's brand name and core skills and to use them to sell other kinds of products online—much like a general B&M retailer sells many different kinds of products. Bezos responded that he had to make sure his company's business model would work successfully in book retailing before he could commit his company to a widespread expansion into new kinds of retail ventures. However, Amazon's plunging stock price forced him into action, and from 2000 on, it expanded its storefronts and began to sell a wider and wider range of electronic and digital products, such as cameras, DVD players, and MP3 players. To achieve a competitive advantage in these new product categories, Amazon used its IT to provide customers with more in-depth information about the nature of the products they were buying and to offer users better ways to review, rank, and comment on the products they bought on its website. Customers were increasingly seeing the utility of Amazon's service.

Bezos had pushed Amazon and its "pizza teams" to find new ways to use its core skills to expand into different kinds of retail segments, and by 2003, it had developed twenty-three different storefronts. By 2006, Amazon had thirty-five storefronts selling products as varied as books, CDs, DVDs, software, consumer electronics, kitchen items, tools, lawn and garden items, toys and games, baby products, apparel, sporting goods, gourmet food, jewelry, watches, health and personal-care items, beauty products, musical instruments, and industrial and scientific supplies. Increasingly consumers came to see Amazon as the low-price retailer for many products. Customers began to visit B&M retail stores to view the physical product, but then they would go online to buy from Amazon. One advantage Amazon has is that customers avoid paying state sales tax when they buy online, and for high-ticket items, this is an important savings, even though shipping costs must be paid for.

New Problems

As time went on, however, customers increasingly began to compare the prices charged by different online retail websites to locate the lowest priced product,

and many dot-coms, desperate to survive in a highly competitive online retail environment, undercut Amazon's prices and so put more pressure on its profit margins. To strengthen Amazon's competitive position and make it the preferred online retailer, Bezos moved aggressively to find ways to attract customers, such as by offering them free shipping or "deals of the day." To make its service more convenient, Amazon also began to forge alliances with B&M companies like Toys "R" Us, Office Depot, Circuit City, Target, and many others. Now, customers could buy products online at Amazon's website, but if they wanted their purchases immediately, they could pick them up from these retailers' local B&M stores. Amazon had to share its profits with these retailers, but it also avoided high product stocking and distribution costs. These alliances also helped Bezos quickly transform his company from "online bookseller" to "leading Internet product provider." His goal was for Amazon to become the leading online retailer across many market segments and drive out the weaker online competitors in those segments and so consolidate many segments of the online retail industry.

Bezos was helped because the online retailers quickly discovered the high costs of operating the value chain functions necessary to deliver products to customers. In the bookselling market, for example, with the exception of Barnes & Noble, which still has an Internet business unit, other booksellers, such as Borders.com, Borders.co.uk, and Waldenbooks.com, could not compete with Amazon. They closed down their online operations and became Amazon Associates, directing Internet traffic from their websites to Amazon's in return for sales commissions. Amazon's competitive advantage also strengthened in 2001 when the Internet bubble burst, the stock price of dot-com companies plunged, and thousands of cut-price online retailers went out of business. Even though its own stock price plunged too, Amazon was now the strongest dot-com in the most important retail segments, and losers like CD Now, Virginmega.com, and online toy and electronics retailers also redirected traffic to Amazon's website for a fee as they shut down their operations.

Many B&M retailers that had also established virtual storefronts found they could not make their online storefronts profitable in the 2000s because of high operating costs. The ones that did succeed were those like Lands' End that already had well-developed catalog sales operations. Their failure was another opportunity for Amazon; for example, when Toys "R" Us found its virtual site too expensive to operate, it also reached an agreement to redirect customers to Amazon's Toys and Games storefront, although at first customers could still pick up their toys from Toys "R" Us's stores if they chose. Many other established B&M companies that found online retailing too complex and expensive also formed agreements with Amazon to operate their online stores. Indeed, Amazon seized this opportunity to get into the new business of using its proprietary IT to design, operate, and host other companies' online storefronts for them for a fee. It had become an IT services company as well, and this helped its revenues grow. Amazon formed agreements to operate retail websites for Target, the NBA, Sears Canada, and Bombay Company, for example.

Branching off into all these new retail market segments also allowed Amazon to more fully utilize its expensive warehouse and distribution system; faster sales across product categories increased inventory turnover and reduced costs. Moreover, its alliances with retailers allowed it to reduce the quantity of expensive merchandise it had to purchase and warehouse until sold, which helped its profit margins. In addition, by offering many different kinds of products for sale, customers could now "mix" purchases and add a book or CD to their electronic product order, and so on, which led to economies of scale for Amazon. By giving customers more and more reasons to visit its site, Amazon hoped to drive business and sales across all its product categories, using its 1-Click system to make the transactions as easy as possible for consumers. However, to keep its operating costs low from the beginning, Amazon adopted a low-key approach to providing customer service; it did not reveal a customer service telephone number anywhere on its U.S. website. However, as the complexity of its business has grown, it recognized the need to provide some level of service, and in 2006 Amazon added to its website an email link. Using this link, customers provide their phone numbers, which Amazon customer service reps then call to provide whatever help is needed, for example, with parcel tracking information. Customer service for North American customers is now handled by centers in Washington State, North Dakota, and West Virginia, as well as a number of outsourced centers.

After its failure in the online auction market, in 2001, Amazon added a new retail service that turned out to be highly profitable and important to maintaining its online leadership position in retailing. Amazon launched zShops, a fixed-price retail marketplace that became the foundation of the current and very successful Amazon Marketplace Service. This retail service allows customers to sell their used books, CDs, DVDs, and other products alongside the identical brand-new products that Amazon offers on the product pages of its retail website. This significantly added to its sales revenues. eBay bought a company called half.com to compete with Amazon Marketplace and is Amazon's main rival today as both companies compete to provide a profitable fee-based service to sellers of used products.

In the 2000s, as Amazon became the acknowledged leader in Internet retailing, it decided to offer a consulting service to other virtual retailers (it already provided this service to B&M retailers) to create for them a unique, customer-friendly storefront using Amazon's proprietary IT. Moreover, to protect the competitive advantage its proprietary IT gives it, Amazon also started lawsuits against other virtual or B&M companies that it claimed implemented checkout systems similar to 1-Click by imitating and infringing on its proprietary software that is protected by patents. This consulting service has proved to be a very profitable activity business activity, and in the process of designing storefronts for other companies, Amazon has also found opportunities to improve its own IT systems by learning from its "leading customers."

Global Expansion

Since IT is not specialized to any one country or world region, a virtual company can use the Internet and World Wide Web to sell to customers around the world—providing, of course, that the products it sells can be customized to meet the needs of overseas consumers. Bezos was quick to realize that Amazon's IT could be profitably transferred to other countries to sell books. However, the ability to enter new overseas markets was limited by one major factor: Amazon.com offered its customers the biggest selection of books written in the *English* language, so overseas customers had to be able to read English. Where to locate them?

An obvious first choice would be the United Kingdom (UK), followed by other English-speaking nations such as Australia, New Zealand, India, and

Germany (of any nation in the world, Germany has one of the highest proportion of English-as-a-second-language speakers because English is taught in all its schools). To speed entry into overseas markets, Amazon searched for overseas Internet companies that had gained a strong foothold in its local domestic market and then acquired them. In the UK, Amazon bought Bookpages.com in 1996, installed its proprietary IT, replicated its value creation functions, and renamed it Amazon.co.uk. In Germany, it acquired a new online venture, ABC Bücherdienst/Telebuch.de, and created Amazon.de in 1998. Amazon continued its path of global expansion, and by 2006, it also operated retail websites in Canada, France, China, and Japan, and shipped its English language books to customers anywhere in the world.

To facilitate the growth of its global IT and distribution systems, Amazon also has product development centers in England, Scotland, India, Germany, and France. Just as Amazon expanded the range of products it sold on its U.S. website, it also increased the range of products it sold abroad as its warehouse and distribution systems became strong enough to sustain its expansion and its local managers decided on the mix of products best suited to the needs of local customers.

New Developments

After Amazon's stock price reached a low of around $6 a share in late 2001 after the Internet bubble burst and many dot-coms went out of business, Amazon continued to persevere. When it finally turned its first profit in the fourth quarter of 2002—a meager $5 million, just 1 cent per share on revenues of over $1 billion—this was an important signal to investors. It seemed to confirm that Amazon's business model was working, it would survive, and its stock price would increase. In fact, Amazon's stock price began to soar in the early 2000s as investors now believed it would become a highly profitable online retail leader; its stock price increased to $20 by the end of 2002 and to almost $60 by the end of 2003. Amazon's net profits also increased to $35 million in 2003 and to $588 million in 2004. Revenue kept growing because of its entry into many different retail segments and global markets, from $3.9 billion in 2002, to $5.3 billion in 2003, and $6.9 billion in 2004. Amazon's future looked bright indeed as it became the largest Internet retailer and achieved a dominant position in many market segments.

New Acquisitions and Business Opportunities

To make better use of its resources and capabilities and to maintain its profit growth, Amazon began to acquire many small companies in the late 1990s. One of its goals was to acquire small IT companies that would allow it to strengthen its distinctive competencies in IT and to develop more kinds of web-based IT commercial services that it could sell to both B&M and online companies. Bezos has always preached that Amazon is first and foremost a *technology company* and that its core skills drive its retail mission. Another goal in buying small companies was to find new opportunities to increase sales of its existing retail storefronts and to allow it to establish new storefronts in new segments of the retail market. Some acquisitions have been successful and some have not.

In 1998, for example, Amazon bought Internet Movie Database (www.IMDb.com), a company that hosted a comprehensive listing of all movies in existence. Formerly a free service, Amazon transformed it into a commercial venture whose function is to help customers easily find and identify DVDs to purchase and to make related suggestions to encourage additional purchases. As with Amazon's regular site, IMDb users are allowed to review and make detailed comments on movies including starting message boards. In 1999, Amazon acquired Exchange.com, which specializes in hard-to-find book titles at its Bibliofind.com website and hard-to-find music titles and memorabilia at MusicFile.com. The acquisition also helped Amazon develop user-friendly search engines to help customers identify and buy its products, once again using its 1-Click system.

In 1998, Amazon bought PlanetAll.com, which operated a web-based address book, calendar, and reminder service that had over 1 million registered users, and Junglee.com, an XML-based data-mining start-up that had technology for searching for and tracking Internet users' website visits based on their personal interests. In 2000, after Amazon had absorbed these companies' technology, it shut them down, making their employees Amazon employees and relocating to Amazon's Seattle headquarters. For example, PlanetAll's "relationship-building" software applications were folded into Amazon's Friends and Favorites area. Within Friends and Favorites, Amazon customers were now able to set up wish lists and view those of friends, view product critiques from specific reviewers, and create and view home pages from Amazon's website. Amazon's new employees also went on to build community-focused features for Amazon's website including the unsuccessful Amazon.com Auctions, and successful Amazon.com Marketplace and Amazon.com Purchase Circles. Amazon became driven by the need to find and use the most successful new web-based techniques for attracting and keeping Internet customers as rivalry with companies like Yahoo, eBay, and then Google started to increase as these companies increasingly started to enter each other's businesses.

In pursuit of this goal, in 1999 Amazon bought Alexa Internet, which had developed software that works in conjunction with Internet Explorer to track and monitor the way people search the Internet. Amazon hoped to use this technology to help it improve its ability to track its customers as they moved around the Internet and so provide them with a personalized browsing experience, which, for example, would allow it to make product suggestions based on the specific nature of their site visits—similar to Google offering customized advertising specific to the webpage a user was visiting. In 2003, Amazon launched a separately controlled subsidiary called A9.com, Inc. to take control of all its search engine research and build innovative technologies to improve users' search experiences and so increase the utility of its e-commerce applications.

A9.com's search engine, which searches both Amazon.com and other websites, used to be powered by Google's search engine. Today it is powered by Microsoft's Live Search technology because Google emerged as the leader in this area. The differentiating feature of Amazon's A9.com search technology was meant to be that users would log into the service, and then A9 would continually record every page they searched for. By creating a personalized memory of users' visits, A9 could provide them with a highly customized search service that could take them quickly to already visited sites but that would also be able to suggest relevant new sites based on all the personal data collected by the engine. In this way, Amazon hoped it could drive more traffic to its constantly increasing storefronts.

The search engine did not prove popular with Internet users, however, because many believed the engine was highly invasive of their privacy, creating as it does a permanent record of their website visits.

Instead, in the 2000s, Google's search engine has become the search engine of choice, both because it is the technologically most advanced and because users can opt out of creating a personalized search history if they choose to disable its advanced features. Thus Google struck the right balance between usefulness and privacy and thwarted Amazon's attempts to become the leader in the crucial search engine market. In 2006, Amazon announced its A9 site would no longer ask users to log in or accumulate such personal data. Instead, it would focus on improving the usefulness of the search results users obtained on Amazon's own storefronts. For example, one of the technologies A9.com had developed was a "mini" search engine feature called "Search Inside the Book," mentioned earlier, that allows users to search within the text of books as well as searching for text on the Web. "Search Inside the Book" is a feature that makes it possible for customers to search for keywords in the full text of many of the books in its catalog to identify books that may be of interest to them. There are currently about 250,000 books in the program, and Amazon has cooperated with around 130 publishers to allow users to perform these searches. To avoid copyright violations, Amazon.com does not return computer-readable text of the book but rather a picture of the page containing the relevant text, disables printing of the pages, and puts limits on the number of pages in a book a single user can access. In 2005, A9 also developed an interactive wiki feature that allows any Amazon customer who has purchased at least one product from the company to add to or edit the relevant product descriptions or wikis, such as for books.

Thus although Amazon has used these acquisitions to steadily improve its customers' ability to search and use its own storefronts, its attempt to gain a leading position in providing generalized web-based search services to Internet users failed. Today, its A9.com generates only 0.1% of all searches compared to the leader Google, which claims over 60%. Amazon also has failed in other areas; another search technology A9.com developed was the "Find It on the Block" feature that allowed users to find not just the phone number, address, map, and directions for a business, but also to see a picture of it as well as all the businesses and shops on that same street. However, in 2006, Amazon announced it was ending this service because most users preferred the mapping services offered by Google and Yahoo. Many of Amazon's failures can be explained by the fact that established Internet companies already had a first-mover advantage in specific industries in the Internet sector. For example, Amazon.com's Auctions could not compete successfully against eBay, which with its 30 million registered sellers and buyers dominated the online auction industry; and Google's quick growth in the search engine market has prevented Amazon, and many other leading portals, from succeeding in this area.

In an effort to keep its customers loyal, Amazon began providing a range of new customer services. In January 2006, it launched Amazon Prime, a $79 per year service that allows users to get unlimited free two-day shipping and upgraded overnight shipping for $3.99 on eligible items bought from its storefronts. Also in January, Amazon established a partnership with travel meta-search company SideStep and used its service to power searches in Amazon's travel store. In March, it launched an online storage service called Amazon S3 that allows users to store an unlimited number of data objects ranging in size from 1 byte to 5 gigabytes for a storage service charge of 15 cents per gigabyte per month and data transfer fees of 20 cents per gigabyte each when users distribute their data (for example, advertisements or catalog mailing lists) using HTTP or Bit Torrent services provided by Amazon.

In July 2006, Amazon entered the grocery delivery business when its website officially launched Amazon Grocery, a new storefront that sells a wide variety of nonperishable food and household items that, once ordered, can be reordered or modified easily using Amazon's shopping-list software. To ensure competitive pricing with B&M grocery stores, customers receive free shipping on purchases of canned and packed food products over $25.

In September 2006, Amazon Business Solutions group, which serves the needs of business customers, also extended the range of its services by launching Fulfillment by Amazon and WebStore by Amazon. These services give small and medium-sized businesses access to Amazon's order fulfillment, customer service, customer shipping offers, and underlying website technology to improve the retail experience they can offer customers on their own websites. For example, Fulfillment by Amazon allows small businesses to use Amazon's own order fulfillment and after-order customer services, and gives their customers the right to receive the benefit of Amazon.com shipping offers.

Fulfillment by Amazon performs the value chain activities that free online small businesses from the time and costs required to store, pick, pack, ship, and provide customer service for the products they sell online. After paying Amazon's service fee, small businesses ship their products to an Amazon fulfillment center, which stores and sends those products to customers who order them on the small business's or Amazon's storefront. Amazon will also manage post-order customer service such as customer returns and refunds for businesses that use Fulfillment by Amazon. Amazon.com customers can also use services such as Amazon Prime and Free Super Saver Shipping when buying products that have the Fulfilled by Amazon icon. Small businesses benefit from the cost savings that result when Amazon's service fees are lower than the costs of performing the value chain service themselves.

WebStore by Amazon allows businesses to create their own privately branded e-commerce websites using Amazon technology. Businesses can choose from a variety of website layout options and can customize their sites using their own photos and branding. For example, Seattle Gift Shop now has its own WebStore at http://www.seattlesgifts.com. WebStore by Amazon users pay a commission of 7% (price includes credit card processing fees and fraud protection) for each product purchased through their site and a monthly fee of $59.95. As one business owner commented, "Not only has WebStore increased my sales dramatically, but also its easy-to-use tools give me complete control of the look and feel of my site." WebStore allows small businesses to build their brand name while using Amazon's easy-to-use flexible "back-end" technology—including Amazon's 1-Click checkout system—and allows them to refer customers through the Amazon Associates program if they choose.

Jeff Bezos and his top management team seem committed to leveraging Amazon's core competencies in whatever ways they can to find ways to realize the value of the company's assets. The range of possible services Amazon can offer seems endless. For example, Amazon established a wholly owned subsidiary, CustomFlix, Inc., to provide first a DVD and then a CD on Demand Service. The DVD and CD on Demand Services allow independent musicians, artists, labels, and other video and music content owners an inventory-free way to reach a worldwide audience and make their videos and audio CDs available to

Amazon's customers. Customers can preview a DVD or CD on the CustomFlix website and then decide whether to make a purchase, much like in the past when customers in record stores could listen to tracks before making a purchase decision. Once again, because CustomFlix can burn the DVD/CD on demand, there are no inventory costs for musicians to bear, so the service offers an easy, attractive, and low-cost way for musicians, artists, and labels to profitably connect to customers. It also expands Amazon's content offerings, making its even more unique compared to other DVD/CD retailers. If they attract a following, successful musicians and artists can then also set up their own customizable Custom-Flix E-Store so that they can personalize the products they offer to customers. CustomFlix on Demand provides high-quality DVD and CD media with full-color hub-printed faces; full-color, double-sided tray cards; and four-page, full-color inserts in over-wrapped clear jewel cases.

In another bold venture, in September 2006, Amazon launched an eagerly awaited digital down-load video service. Called Amazon Unbox, the new download service offered customers thousands of television shows, movies, and other video content from more than thirty studio and network partners from Hollywood and around the world. Unbox claimed to be the only video download service to offer DVD-quality picture that could be downloaded from one PC (such as an office computer) and then transferred to another PC (such as a home computer). At no additional charge, Unbox automatically included a second file optimized for playback on any Windows Media-compatible portable device. Also, Unbox used progressive download, which eliminated the need to wait for the entire video to download before watching. A broadband customer could start watching a downloaded Unbox video or movie within five minutes of ordering.

However, within weeks, this important new download service—one that Amazon investors had eagerly awaited—generated many negative comments from users. The number of movies downloaded was disappointingly few because the service's poor software caused many glitches and very slow—hours—download time. Quickly Amazon updated the movie player to fix the bugs, but many complaints remained: long download time, poor resolution, and restrictions on when and where movies could be played. Amazon continues to improve this service and in January 2007 announced an agreement with TiVo, the set-box DVD recording company, to develop a joint program to allow TiVo's millions of customers easy access to Amazon's download service. Amazon is currently searching for more partners, but one development that may seriously impair its progress in this area is Wal-Mart's February 2007 agreement with the six major movie studios to offer movie downloads through its online store. Wal-Mart is the leading seller of DVDs with over 40% of the market, and its ability to negotiate this deal, rather than Amazon, might be a major setback.

Amazon's Future Prospects

Today, Amazon is the leading Internet retailer. It has over 12,000 employees and in 2006 earned $700 million on $10.7 billion revenues. This was a significant increase in profit from the year before, and its stock price rose significantly as investors became more optimistic about its future prospects. Nevertheless, its stock price is still lower than it was in 2004 because investors have realized many of its new ventures, such as its attempt to dominate the search engine segment, have not worked out, and because the future success of ventures such as movie downloads is not clear. Moreover, all its expenditures on developing the new IT platforms necessary to launch complex digital storefronts have been increasing its operating costs, which rose from 6.1% of revenue in 2005 to 7.8% in the second quarter of 2006. These increased operating costs have reduced its profit margins. Once again, Amazon's operating costs are rising, now not because of developing the physical infrastructure necessary to support its retail sales, but because of the investment in the IT infrastructure necessary to launch new digital products. So some analysts are concerned that in its attempts to grow profits, Amazon is losing its knack of creating the customer-friendly retail customer service technology that made it a leading dot-com company. And they are watching the growing success of Google as it enters new businesses, including retail Internet segments with its Froogle product-search service and its new online payment system that is a challenge to Amazon's 1-Click system. So investors are watching to see how operating costs will affect operating margins and net profits in the next few years and how Amazon will fend off increasing competition from companies like Wal-Mart that are building up their own online presence and are willing to charge low prices to build their market share. What new strategies can Bezos pursue to take Amazon to the next level, analysts wonder? Are any new mergers and acquisitions on the horizon?

SOURCES

Amazon.com, Annual and 10K Reports, 1997–2007. http://www.Amazon .com, 2007.

Mike Daisey. (2002). 21 Dog Years. New York: The Free Press.

A. Deutschman, "Inside the Mind of Jeff Bezos," *Fast Company*, August 2004, 50–58.

Robert Spector. (2001). Amazon.com—Get Big Fast: Inside the Revolutionary Business Model That Changed the World. New York: Harper Collins Publishers.

This case was prepared by Gareth R. Jones, Texas A&M University.

With 11,600 employees, eBay, headquartered in San Jose, California, manages and hosts an online auction and shopping website that people all around the world visit to buy and sell goods and services. eBay generated revenues of almost $6 billion in 2006, up from $4.55 billion in 2005, and generated $2 billion in earnings—an impressive figure that explains the company's stock market valuation of $46 billion in February 2007. eBay has been a stellar performer on the stock exchange under the guidance of Meg Whitman, its CEO. Its investors were extremely happy—until the last few years when its stock price fell sharply. Investors became worried its business model would not be so profitable in the future because the online auction market was becoming mature and opportunities for growth were declining. In 2006, its stock plunged in value, and it seemed like eBay's business model had run out of steam. But to understand the sources of eBay's success and the current challenges it faces, it is necessary to explore the way eBay's business model and strategies have changed over time.

eBay's Beginnings

Until the 1990s, the auction business was largely fragmented; thousands of small city-based auction houses offered a wide range of merchandise to local buyers. And a few famous global ones, such as

Sotheby's and Christie's, offered carefully chosen selections of high-priced antiques and collectibles to limited numbers of dealers and wealthy collectors. However, the auction market was not very efficient, for there was often a shortage of sellers and buyers, and so it was difficult to determine the fair price of a product. Dealers were often able to influence auction prices and so obtain bargains at the expense of sellers. Typically, dealers were able to buy at low prices and then charge buyers high prices in the bricks-and-mortar (B&M) antique stores that are found in every town and city around the world, so they reaped high profits. The auction business was changed forever in 1995 when Pierre Omidyar developed innovative software that allowed buyers around the world to bid online against each other to determine the fair price for a seller's product.

Omidyar founded his online auction site in San Jose on September 4, 1995, under the name Auction-Web. A computer programmer, Omidyar had previously worked for Microsoft, but he left that company when he realized the potential opportunity to develop new software that provided an online platform to connect Internet buyers and sellers. The entrepreneurial Omidyar changed his company's name to eBay in September 1997, and the first item sold on eBay was Omidyar's broken laser pointer for $13.83. A frequently repeated story that eBay was founded to help Omidyar's fiancée trade PEZ Candy dispensers was fabricated by an eBay public relations manager in 1997 to interest the media. Apparently the story worked, for eBay's popularity grew quickly by word of mouth, and the company did not need to advertise until the early 2000s. Omidyar had tapped into a huge unmet buyer need, and people flocked to use his software.

Another major reason eBay did not advertise in its early years was that its growing global popularity had put major pressure on its internal computer information systems, both its hardware and software. In particular, the technology behind its search engine—which was not developed by Omidyar but furnished by independent specialist software companies–could not keep pace with the hundreds of millions of search requests that eBay's users generated each day. eBay was also installing powerful servers as quickly as it could to manage its fast-growing database, and it was recruiting computer programmers and IT managers to run its systems at a rapid rate.

To finance eBay's rapid growth, Omidyar turned to venture capitalists to supply the hundreds of millions of dollars his company required to build its online IT infrastructure. Seeing the success of his business model, he was quickly able to find willing investors; as part of the loan agreement, however, the venture capitalists insisted that Omidyar give control of the running of his company to an experienced top manager. They were very aware that entrepreneurs often have problems in building and implementing a successful business model over time. They recommended that Meg Whitman, an executive who had had great success as a manager of several software start-up companies, be recruited to become eBay's CEO, while Omidyar would assume the role of chairman of the company.

eBay's Evolving Business Model

From the beginning, eBay's business model and strategies were based on developing and refining Omidyar's auction software to create an easy-to-use online market platform that would allow buyers and sellers to meet and transact easily and inexpensively. eBay's software was created to make it easy for sellers to list and describe their products, and easy for buyers to search for, compare, and bid on the products they wanted to purchase. The magic of eBay's software is that the company simply provides the electronic conduit between buyers and sellers; it never takes physical possession of the products that are listed, and their shipping is the responsibility of sellers and payment the responsibility of buyers. Thus, eBay does not need to develop all the high-cost functional activities like inventory, shipping, and purchasing to deliver products to customers, unlike

Amazon.com, for example, and so it operates with an extremely low cost structure given the huge volume of products it sells and sales revenues it generates—hence the $2 billion profits on $7 billion of revenues in 2007 mentioned earlier. Also, word of mouth enables eBay to avoid paying the high advertising costs, an especially important consideration early on since these are a major expense for many start-ups. And, as far as buyers are concerned, eBay is also low cost, for under current U.S. law, sellers located outside a buyer's state do not have to collect sales tax on a purchase. This allows buyers to avoid paying state taxes on expensive items such as jewelry and computers, which can save them tens or even hundreds of dollars and makes purchasing on eBay more attractive.

To make transactions between anonymous Internet buyers and sellers possible, however, Omidyar's software had to reduce the risks facing buyers and sellers. In particular, it had to convince buyers that they would receive what they paid for and that sellers would accurately describe their products online. Also, sellers had to be convinced that buyers would pay for the products they committed to purchase on eBay, although of course they were able to wait for the money to arrive in the mail, so their risk was lower; however, many buyers do not pay or pay extremely late. To minimize the ever-present possibility of fraud from sellers misrepresenting their products or from buyers unethically bidding for pleasure and then not paying, eBay's software contains a method for building and establishing trust between buyers and sellers—building a reputation over time.

After every transaction, buyers and sellers can leave online feedback about their view of the other's behavior and the value of the transaction they have completed. They can fill in an online comment form, which is then published on the Web for each seller and buyer. When sellers and buyers consistently act in an honest way in more and more transactions over time, they are able to build a stronger and stronger positive feedback score that provides them with a good reputation for honesty. More buyers are attracted to a reputable seller, so the seller obtains higher prices for their products, and sellers can also decide if they are dealing with a reputable buyer, one who pays quickly, for example. This may be more difficult because new "unknown" buyers come into the market continuously, but a seller can refuse to deal with any new or existing buyer if they wish and can remove that buyer's bid from an auction.

eBay generates the revenues that allow it to operate and profit from its electronic auction platform by charging a number of fees to sellers (buyers pay no specific fees). In the original eBay model, sellers paid a fee to list a product on eBay's site and paid a fee if the product was sold by the end of the auction. As its platform's popularity increased and the number of buyers grew, eBay has increased the fees it charges sellers. The eBay fee system is quite complex, but in the United States in 2006, eBay took between 20 cents and $80 per listing and between 2 and 8% of the final price, depending on the particular product being sold and the format in which it is sold. In addition, eBay now owns the PayPal payment system, which has fees of its own; this is discussed in detail below.

This core auction business model worked well for the first years of eBay's existence. Using this basic software platform, every day tens of millions of products such as antiques and collectibles, cars, computers, furniture, clothing, books, DVDs and a myriad of other items are listed by sellers all around the world on eBay and bought by the highest bidders. The incredible variety of items sold on eBay suggests why eBay's business model has been so successful—the same set of auction platform programs, constantly improved and refined over time from Omidyar's original programs, can be used to sell almost every kind of product, from low-priced books and magazines costing only cents, to cars and antiques costing tens or hundreds of thousands of dollars. Some of the most expensive items sold include a Frank Mulder 4Yacht Gigayacht ($85 million), a Grumman Gulfstream II jet ($4.9 million), and a 1993 San Lorenzo 80 Motoryacht (just under $2 million). One of the largest items ever sold was a World War II submarine that had been auctioned off by a small town in New England that decided it did not need the historical relic anymore.

Indeed, Meg Whitman's biggest problem was to find search engine software that could keep pace with the increasing volume of buyers' inquiries. Initially small independent suppliers provided this software; then IBM provided this service. But as search technology has advanced in the 2000s, eBay now has its own in-house search technology teams continually refining and improving its own search software. With the most pressing concerns of keeping the eBay website up and running twenty-four hours a day and meeting the needs of its growing number of buyers and sellers, CEO Whitman looked for new ways to improve eBay's business model.

First, to take advantage of the capabilities of eBay's software, the company began to expand the range and categories of the products it offered for sale to increase revenue. Second, it increased the number of retail or "selling" formats used to bring sellers and buyers together. For example, its original retail format was the seven-day auction format, where the last bidder within this time period "won" the auction, provided the bid met the seller's reserve or minimum price. Then, it introduced the "buy-it-now" format where a buyer could make an instant purchase at the seller's specified price, and later a real-time auction format in which online bidders, and bidders at a B&M auction site, compete against each other in real time to purchase the product up for bid. In this format, a live auctioneer, not the eBay auction clock, decides when to close an auction.

Beyond introducing new kinds of retail formats, over time eBay has continuously strived to improve the range and sophistication of the information services it provides its users—to make it easier for sellers to list, describe, present, and ship their products, and for buyers to make better purchasing decisions. For example, software was developed to make it easier for sellers to list their products for sale and upload photographs and add or change information to the listing. Buyers were able to take advantage of the services that are now offered in what is called My EBay; buyers can now keep a list of "watched" items so that over the life of a particular auction they can see how the price of a product has changed and how many bidders are interested in it. This is a useful service for buyers because frequently bidders for many items enter in the last few minutes to try to "snipe" an item or obtain it at the lowest possible cost. As the price of an item becomes higher, this often encourages more buyers to bid on it, so there is value to buyers (although not sellers, who want the highest prices possible) to wait or just bid a minimal amount so they can easily track the item.

By creating and then continually improving its easy-to-use retail platform for sellers and buyers, eBay revolutionized the auction market, bringing together buyers and sellers internationally in a huge, never-ending yard sale. eBay became the means of cleaning out the "closets of the world" with its user-friendly platform.

New Types of Sellers

Over time, eBay also encouraged the entry of new kinds of sellers into its electronic auction platform. Initially, it focused on individual, small-scale sellers; however, it then sought to attract larger-scale sellers using its eBay Stores selling platform, which allows sellers to list not only products up for auction but also all the items they have available for sale, perhaps in a B&M antique store or warehouse. Store sellers then pay eBay a fee for these "buy it now" sales. Hundreds of thousands of eBay stores became established in the 2000s, greatly adding to eBay's revenues.

Also by the early 2000s, not just small specialized stores but large international manufacturers and retailers such as Sears, IBM, and Dell began to open their own stores on eBay to sell their products using competitive auctions for "clearance goods" and fixed-priced buy-it-now storefronts to sell their latest products. By using eBay, these companies established a new delivery channel for their products, and they were able to bypass wholesalers such as discount stores or warehouses that take a much larger share of the profit than eBay does through its selling fees.

Software advances came faster and faster in the 2000s, in part due to eBay's new Developers Program that allows independent software developers to create new specialized applications that integrate seamlessly with eBay's electronic platform. By 2005, there were over 15,000 members in the eBay Developers Program, comprising a broad range of companies creating software applications to support specialized eBay sellers and buyers, as well as eBay Affiliates. All this progress helped speed and smooth transactions between buyers and sellers and drove up eBay's revenues and profits, something that resulted in a huge increase in the value of its stock.

Competition in the Retail Auction Industry

eBay's growing popularity and growing user or customer base made it increasingly difficult for the hundreds of other online auction houses that had also come online to compete effectively against it. Indeed, its competitive advantage was increasing because both sellers and buyers discovered they were more likely to find what they wanted and get the best prices from a bigger auction website's user base or market.

And from the beginning, eBay controlled the biggest market of buyers and sellers, and new users became increasingly loyal over time. So even when large, well-known online companies such as Yahoo and AOL attempted to enter the online auction business, and even when they offered buyers and sellers *no-fee* auction transactions, they found it was impossible to grow their user bases and establish themselves in the market. From network effects, eBay had obtained a first-mover advantage and was benefiting from this.

The first-mover advantage eBay gained from Pierre Omidyar's auction software created an unassailable business model that gave eBay effectively a monopoly position in the global online auction market. There are few online or B&M substitutes for the service that eBay provides. For example, sellers can list their items for sale on any kind of website or bulletin board, and specialist kinds of websites exist to sell highly specialized kinds of products like heavy machinery or large sailboats, but for most products, the sheer reach of eBay guarantees it a dominant position in the marketplace. There has been little new entry into the online auction business, and the fees eBay charges to sellers have steadily increased as it has grown, and so it skims off ever more of the profit in the auction value chain. Also, eBay does not have to worry about the ability of any particular buyer or seller to dictate terms to it, for it has access to millions of individual buyers and sellers. Only if sellers could band together and demand reductions in eBay's fees and charges would they be a threat to eBay.

This happened briefly in the early 2000s. Meg Whitman, desperate to keep eBay's revenues growing to protect its stock price, began to continually increase the fees charged to eBay stores to list their items on eBay. Store sellers rebelled and used the eBay community bulletin boards and chat rooms to register their complaints. eBay realized there was a limit to how much it could charge sellers. It would have to find new ways to attract more buyers to the sellers' products, and so get them better prices, if was going to be able to increase the fees it charged sellers. Or it would have to find new ways to extract profit from the auction value chain.

New Ways to Grow eBay's Value Chain

Meg Whitman has always preached to eBay's employees that to maintain and increase the value of its stock (and many employees own stock options in the company), eBay must (1) continually attract more buyers and sellers to its auction site, and (2) search for ways to generate more revenue from these buyers and sellers. To create more value from its auction business model, eBay has adopted many other kinds of strategies to grow profitability over time.

International Expansion

In the online world, buyers from any country in the world can bid on an auction, and so it became clear early on that one way to grow eBay's business would be to replicate its business model in different countries around the world. Accordingly eBay moved quickly to establish storefronts around the world customized to the needs and language of a particular country's citizens. Globally, eBay established its own online presence in countries like the United Kingdom and Australia, but in other countries, particularly non-English-speaking countries, it often acquired the national start-up online auction company that had stolen the first-mover advantage in a particular country. In 1999, for example, eBay acquired the German auction house Alando for $43 million and changed it into eBay Germany. In 2001, eBay acquired Mercado Libre, Lokau, and iBazar, Latin American auction sites, and established eBay Latin America. In 2003, eBay acquired EachNet, a leading e-commerce company in China, for $150 million to enter the Chinese market. And, in 2004, it bought Baazee.com, an Indian auction site, for $50 million and took a large stake in Korean rival Internet Auction Co. In 2006, eBay acquired Tradera.com, Sweden's leading online auction-style marketplace, for $48 million. All these global acquisitions have allowed eBay to retain firm control of the global online auction business to facilitate transactions both inside countries and between countries to build up revenue. Once eBay was up and running in a particular country, network dynamics took effect, and so it became difficult for a new auction start-up to establish a strong foothold in its domestic online auction market. Indeed, the only countries in which eBay has faced serious competition are Japan and Hong Kong, where Yahoo gained a head start over eBay and thus gained the first-mover advantage in these countries.

eBay Drop-Off Stores

A second way in which eBay has grown the revenues from its auction model is by providing more kinds of value-chain services. One service created in the early 2000s for individual sellers is eBay Drop Off. eBay licenses reputable eBay sellers who have consistently sold hundreds of items using its platform to open B&M consignment stores where any seller can "drop off" the products they want to sell. The owner of the Drop-Off Store describes, photographs, and lists the item on eBay and then handles all the payment and shipping activities involved in the auction process. The store owner receives a commission, often 15% or more of the final selling price (not including eBay's commission) for providing this service. These stores have proved highly profitable for their owners, and thousands have sprung up across the United States and the world (a search request on eBay's site allows buyers to identify the closest eBay Drop-Off Store). The advantage for eBay is that this drop-off service gives it access to the millions of people who have no experience in posting photographs online, organizing payment, or even opening an eBay account and learning how to list an item and so eBay gains from increased listing fees.

Increased Advertising

Another strategy eBay increasingly adopted in the 2000s to expand its user base was to increase its use of advertising—on television, newspapers, and on popular websites—to promote the millions of products it has for sale on its site. Its goal was to make eBay *the* preferred place to shop by demonstrating two things: first, the incredible diversity of products available for purchase on its site, and second, the frequency with which its products cost less than what buyers would pay in B&M stores or even on specialist online stores. New and used DVDs, CDs, books, designer clothing, electronic products, and computers are some of the multitude of products that can be obtained at a steep discount on eBay. Thus, while the range of the products eBay sells provides it with a differentiation advantage, the low prices that buyers can often obtain gives it a low-price advantage too—provided buyers are prepared to wait a few days to receive their newly purchased products.

PayPal Payment Service

Meg Whitman was also working to find ways to make transactions easier for eBay buyers and sellers, and one way to do this was to get involved in the other kinds of value chain activities required to complete online transactions. One of the most important functional activities is the payment system, for this poses the greatest risks to buyers that they may be taken advantage of by unscrupulous or fraudulent sellers who take their money and then fail to deliver the expected product. When eBay first started, sellers usually demanded money orders or bank cashiers' checks that are secure forms of payment from buyers, or insisted that ordinary checks had cleared through their accounts before mailing the product to customers. This increased the length of time and effort involved in a transaction for sellers and buyers and led to lost sales.

By the late 1990s, online companies like PayPal and Billpoint had emerged that offered secure online electronic payment services that greatly facilitated online commerce. To work efficiently, these services require sellers and buyers to register and enter a valid bank account number, and usually a credit card number, to authenticate the sellers' and buyers' identities and their ability to pay for the items purchased. Now payment became instantaneous; the money was taken directly from the buyer's bank account or paid for by credit card. Buyers could now purchase on credit, while sellers could immediately send off the product to the buyer. When buyers paid sellers, the online payment company collected a 3% commission, which was taken from the seller's proceeds.

Obviously, this is a very lucrative activity, and eBay realized it could increase its share of the fees involved in eBay transactions by becoming involved in online payment services. However, it was late entering this business, and it would take a long time to develop its own payment service from scratch. So, in 1999 eBay acquired the online payment service Billpoint and worked to get all eBay buyers and sellers registered with Billpoint. However, eBay found itself running up against a brick wall; just as eBay had gained the first-mover advantage in the auction business, so had PayPal gained it in the online payment business. Millions of eBay users were already signed up with PayPal. So, after failing to make Billpoint the market leader, in 2002 eBay acquired PayPal for $1.5 billion in stock—a great return for PayPal's stockholders. Then, to reduce costs, eBay switched all Billpoint customers to PayPal and shut down Billpoint. This purchase has been very profitable for eBay, for it now owns the world's leading online payment system. The PayPal acquisition has paid for itself many times over.

Indeed, eBay has since worked to make PayPal a financial powerhouse, making it a conduit through which buyers and sellers can transact internationally, something that often involves high fees for buyers and sellers. It also issues eBay credit cards. Finally, it has used PayPal as another way to reassure buyers that sellers are honest and reputable; eBay offers buyers who use PayPal free product insurance protection in the event that their purchases are either fraudulent or misrepresented. It also reassures sellers that they can trust buyers; through PayPal, eBay can police buyers and suspend their accounts if necessary.

More Retail Formats

eBay also began to make many acquisitions to facilitate its entry into new kinds of specialized retail and auction formats to increase its market reach. In 1999, it acquired the well-known auction house Butterfield & Butterfield to facilitate its entry into the auctioning of high-priced antiques and collectibles and so compete with upper-end auction houses such as Sotheby's and Christie's. However, eBay's managers discovered that a lot more involvement was needed to correctly identify, price, list, and then auction rare, high-priced antiques, and it exited the upper-end auction niche in 2002 when it sold Butterfield & Butterfield to Bonhams, an upscale auction house that wanted to develop a much bigger online presence.

To further its expansion into the highly profitable motor vehicle segment of the market, in 2003 eBay acquired CARad.com, an auction management service for car dealers, to strengthen eBay Motors. Now eBay controls the auctions in which vehicle dealers bid on cars that they then resell to individual buyers, often on eBay Motors. In another move to enter a new retail market in 2004, eBay acquired Rent.com for $415 million. This online site offers a completely free rental and roommate search service; indeed, it offers to pay users who have signed a new lease at a property found on its website $100 when they inform Rent.com. Once again, the "sellers" of the rentals on its websites are charged the fees; the online roommate search is free. Rent.com has millions of up-to-date rental listings, with thousands added every day; listings include a property's address and phone number, a detailed description, photos, floor plans, and so on, which makes it easier for prospective renters to research and select a rental.

In 2000, eBay acquired Half.com for $318 million. Half.com is an online retail platform that specializes in the sale of new and used fixed-price consumer products such as books, movies, video games, DVDs, and so on that are offered at a fixed price and sold on a first-come-first-served basis, not by auction. eBay's Buy It Now feature is similar, although sellers are allowed to set a lower start price than the buy-it-now price, and the selling process can develop into an auction if bidders start to compete for the product. In the 2000s, the popularity of fixed-price online retailing led to a significant expansion in eBay's activities in this segment of the retail market. In 2006, eBay opened its new eBay Express site, which was designed to work like a standard Internet shopping site to consumers with U.S. addresses. Select eBay items are mirrored on eBay Express, where buyers use a shopping cart to purchase products from multiple sellers. A UK version of eBay Express is also in development. The discussion of eBay Express is continued below in more detail.

In 2005, eBay acquired Shopping.com, an online price-comparison shopping site, for $635 million. With millions of products, thousands of merchants, and millions of reviews from the Epinions community, Shopping.com empowers consumers to make informed choices and, as a result, encourages more buyers to purchase products. Information provided by Shopping.com also facilitates eBay sellers' pricing knowledge about their online competitors and so helps them price their products competitively so that they can sell them more quickly. The site also allows customers to purchase products from various eBay retail formats.

In the 2000s, online local classifieds have become an increasingly popular way for people to sell their unwanted products, especially because there are usually no fees associated with them. Local classifieds are very popular for bulky products like furniture, appliances, exercise equipment, and so on, where high transportation costs represent a significant percentage of the purchase price. In 2004, to ensure its foothold in this online retail segment, eBay bought a 25% stake in the popular free online classifieds website Craigslist by buying the stock of one of Craigslist's founders.

These free local classified services have been hurting newspapers whose classified sales have decreased sharply. It remains to be seen in the future whether these classified services will remain free or whether they will also be charging fees. Clearly, eBay would like to charge a fee if it owned a controlling stake in Craigslist. Perhaps preparing for the future when money will be made from online classifieds, in 2004, eBay acquired Marktplaats, a Dutch competitor that had achieved an 80% market share in the Netherlands by focusing on small fixed-price ads, not auctions. Then, in 2005, eBay acquired Gumtree, a network of UK local city classifieds sites; the Spanish classifieds site, Loquo; and the German language classifieds site, Opus Forum.

The Skype Acquisition

Perhaps going furthest away from its core business, in 2005, eBay acquired Skype, a Voice-Over-Internet-Provider (VOIP) telephone company, for $2.6 billion. eBay's rationale for the purchase was that Skype would provide it with the ability to perform an important service for its users, specifically, to give them a quick, inexpensive way to communicate and exchange the information required to complete online transactions. Skype's software allows users to use their computers to make free calls over the Internet to anyone, anywhere in the world. Skype boasts superior call quality and the ability to allow users not just to make phone calls but also to send instant messages, transfer big files, chat with up to one hundred people at the same time, and make video conference calls. Skype also allows users to send SMS, or text, messages and to easily sort their contacts into groups like colleagues, friends, and family. It is a full-scale online communications company.

According to eBay, Skype helps eBay sellers build their online businesses. Using Skype, buyers can contact sellers anytime on their Skype phone number. Sellers can also call regular phone numbers anywhere in the world using SkypeOut at very low rates, and with a SkypeIn phone number, buyers can call a regular telephone number wherever the seller is in the world. Also, in the case of large sellers, Skype allows continuous contact between all the members of the store with SkypeIn numbers and Skype Voicemail. For buyers, Skype allows them to get all the product information they need to buy with confidence and to get answers immediately, without waiting for email. According to some analysts, it is questionable whether eBay needed to buy a VOIP company given that so many alternative methods of instant communication are now available and offered by so many online companies. However, eBay quickly started to create strategies to get sellers to integrate Skype into their storefronts and to find new ways to include it in the regular transaction process.

eBay ProStores

Another strategy eBay has used to grow its revenues is to create a new online retail consulting service called ProStores, which allows any potential seller to utilize eBay's functional competencies in online retailing to create its own online storefront using eBay's software. ProStores offers sellers a fully featured web store that can be customized specifically for each online seller and that will then be maintained and hosted by eBay. Sellers using the ProStores service might be B&M stores searching for a quick and easy way to establish an online presence, or any entrepreneur who wishes to start an online store The difference between eBay ProStores and regular eBay Stores is that ProStores sites are accessed through a URL unique to each seller and are not required to carry eBay branding. ProStores sellers are responsible for driving their own store traffic. While items on ProStores sites sell at fixed prices only, they can be simultaneously listed on the eBay marketplace in either the auction or fixed-price formats.

ProStores provides all software needed to build a storefront and then create the listing, promotion, and payment systems needed to make it work. ProStores uses templates and wizards that allow users to quickly and easily build an attractive, feature-rich store with no technical or design skills whatsoever. In return, eBay charges two basic fees to all sellers who purchase a ProStores web store: (1) a monthly subscription fee and (2) a monthly successful transaction fee calculated as a percentage of the sales price of items sold in the store. The subscription fee ranges from $6.95 to $249.95, depending on the size of the store. The successful transaction fee varies between 1.5 and 2.5%.

eBay Express

Finally, reacting to growing buyer demand for a discount, fixed-price retail format, in 2006, eBay established eBay Express, where a vast inventory of brand-new, brand-name, and hard-to-find products are offered at fixed prices by top eBay sellers. Buyers are able to obtain the products they want with no bidding and no waiting; they can fill their shopping carts from multiple eBay merchants and pay for everything, including shipping, in a single, secure payment using PayPal. eBay is touting the fact that every transaction is safe, secure, and fully covered by free buyer protection from PayPal.

New Problems for eBay

Despite all these new strategies to strengthen its business model, in the twelve months ending August 2006, eBay's stock declined 30% from its lofty height, while the stock market had risen about 8%. The problem facing eBay was that while the number of its users was increasing, it was increasing at a decreasing rate—even after all its promotional and advertising efforts and its emphasis on introducing new site features, functionality, retail formats and international expansion. Similarly, although the number of items listed on eBay's retail platforms was increasing (by 33% in 2005 and 45% in 2004), growth was also slowing. In fact, in eBay's U.S. retail segment, net transaction revenues increased only 31% in 2005 and 30% in 2004 compared to 43% in 2003, while gross merchandise volume increased 19% in 2005 and 27% in 2004 compared to 41% in 2003. eBay's revenue growth was slowing, and it seemed clear to investors that even all its new strategies and entry into online payment and communications activities would not be able to sustain its future growth—and so justify its lofty stock price.

Meg Whitman had to find new ways to increase eBay's revenues, especially since by 2006 it was clear to leading Internet companies like Yahoo, AOL, Microsoft, and eBay that they were all facing a major threat from Google, which was perfecting its incredibly lucrative online search and advertising model. Google was now the new eBay in terms of stock appreciation because of the way it was able to implant its advertising search software into its own and any other Internet website willing to share advertising revenues with Google. In fact, because eBay is one of the world's biggest buyers of web search terms, it is one of Google's largest customers. eBay manages a portfolio of 15 million keywords on different search sites, such as Google, Yahoo, and AOL. These searches are aimed at attracting bidders to one of eBay's retail formats, which is why eBay, or one of its subsidiaries, often comes up first on a search inquiry. All the large Internet companies realized they had underestimated the potential revenues to be earned from Internet advertising and were anxious to get a bigger share of the pie and copy Google's approach. eBay, which had not placed ads on its pages in the past to allow its users to focus on the products for sale, now began to have banner adds, pop-ups, and the other obtrusive and annoying ways of advertising developed by software advertising engineers. By 2007, it had placed several ads on each page in its desperate hurry to increase revenues.

In another controversial move, in the spring of 2006, eBay decided to sharply increase the fees it charged its fixed-cost storefronts to advertise on its site. By 2006, sales of fixed-price products, which carried smaller margins than auction products, had grown to over 80% of total retail sales. In charging higher fees, eBay risked alienating large fixed-cost sellers, which would be forced to pass on these increases to customers, and of alienating customers who now could choose a popular shopping comparison tool like eBay's Shopping.com or Google's Froogle to locate a lower-priced product. Analysts questioned if this strategy would backfire.

Moreover, eBay faced another threat from Google as rumors started that Google would be starting its own free online Internet auction site that would compete directly with eBay's. Since Google also had hundreds of millions of loyal users as the number 1 search engine, this could become a real threat to eBay. Also, Google had already established its own fixed-price shopping site, Froogle, that it was continually improving, so it was clearly interested in exploring the revenues that could be earned in the retail segment of the Internet. And, in 2006, Google made great progress in promoting its own online payment system that analysts thought would become a major competitor to eBay's PayPal; this was also a major threat. eBay became concerned Google would start to drain away even more of its revenues and customers, and it searched for ways to counter Google's threat. However, analysts noted that eBay could not abandon its "friendly" relationship with Google because Google is the most popular search engine on which eBay promotes its retail storefronts.

Google had also emerged as the biggest competitor to Yahoo in the growing search-based advertising market. In the spring of 2006, it was rumored that eBay and Yahoo, which was also suffering declining advertising revenues because of the popularity of Google's search engine, might form an important strategic alliance, or even merge to counter possible future threats from Google. (It was rumored these companies would merge in the 1990s, but this had

not happened.) Google was the most popular search engine and held a 43% share in the online search market in the United States compared to Yahoo's market share of 28% in early 2006.

Finally, in May 2006, Yahoo and eBay did announce a strategic alliance designed to boost their position against Google and also against Microsoft, which was also trying to increase revenues from online advertising. The alliance allowed eBay to use Yahoo search to drive buyers to eBay auctions. In return, Yahoo would be the exclusive third-party provider of all graphic ads throughout eBay's auction site. Also Yahoo agreed to promote PayPal, eBay's online payment service, as a preferred payment provider for purchases made online on the Yahoo website. PayPal would provide an array of payment options to Yahoo's users navigating the Web for shopping, auctions, and subscription services. Yahoo would also use eBay's PayPal to allow its own customers to pay for Yahoo web services.

In addition, Yahoo and eBay planned to form a cobranded toolbar that could be downloaded onto the user's web browser, which in turn would direct the users to eBay's auction site and Yahoo's search engine. On eBay's site, the toolbar would provide links to the Yahoo homepage, Yahoo Mail, and My Yahoo options on the Yahoo website. Yahoo and eBay further planned to collaborate on click-to-call functionality. Click-to-call provides a link inside an advertisement that allows buyers to directly call a seller or store to pursue a transaction. Buyers could use either eBay's Skype VOIP telephone service or Yahoo's email and messaging service. The alliance also gives Yahoo access to eBay's vast base of online shoppers, so it can hope to attract many more of them to use its services. Shares of eBay rose 8% and Yahoo's shares climbed 4% in premarket trade following the announcement.

The companies began to roll out their joint initiatives in 2007; however, talk of a merger between the two is still continuing because of slowing growth and increased competition in the Internet sector. The merged company would have the leading position in auctions, communications, payments, graphical advertising, audience reach, and geographic breadth. And the strengths of Yahoo and eBay are seen as complementary, with Yahoo in media and eBay in e-commerce. Also, Yahoo is a global leader in Asia while eBay is the leader in Europe. As Yahoo's CEO, Terry Semel, said, "The deal offers great opportunities for both companies to share great assets with each other. It's all about creating more value and a better experience for users as well as for advertisers."

A 2007 Turnaround

In February 2007, a merger seemed less likely after eBay announced some impressive financial results that provided a lift to its stock price and that once again seemed to suggest its competitive advantage was secure, even in the face of Google's challenge. Shares of eBay jumped by 8% in February 2007 when eBay reported a fourth-quarter profit that climbed 24% as sales rose more than expected, helped by a surge in its PayPal electronic payments business and higher prices for the items eBay sells online. Net income for the fourth quarter rose to $346 million, or 25 cents a share, from $279 million, or 20 cents, a year earlier. Revenue from eBay's PayPal payments business rose 37% to $417 million, or a quarter of the company's total, while sales in its online marketplace business rose 24%. These results suggested that eBay's decision to raise its charges to list items in eBay stores to some of its highest-volume sellers had paid off, the quality of the listing had improved, and more of these sellers had been encouraged to use the higher fee-paying auction method.

eBay also saw healthy revenues in its Skype Internet phone division; 170 million people were now using the service, and it had become the de facto standard for VOIP transmission. According to some estimates, about 25% of businesses are using it to phone internationally. Skype continues to expand its range of services, with such concepts as group email and instant messaging, to make it even more attractive to business users. It seems Skype may have the potential to create a great deal more new efficiencies in both the business and personal realms, and so may be a good revenue generator in the years ahead.

Finally, it was announced in February 2007 that eBay was participating in talks to supply electronic payments and auction features to the popular MySpace social network and other News Corp. online properties. Obviously, providing Skype service would be a potentially lucrative way of introducing it to a younger audience. It seems clear that eBay is now viewing Skype as a business in its own right and not just as an appendage to its auction business. Analysts started to wonder if new kinds of acquisitions were being planned and how the Internet powerhouse would morph in the future, especially if its battle with Google continues.

SOURCES

http://www.ebay.com, 1997–2007.

eBay Annual and 10K Reports, 1997–2007.

Belbin, David. (2004). *The eBay Book: Essential tips for buying and selling on eBay.co.uk.* London: Harriman House Publishing.

Cihlar, Christopher. (2006). *The Grilled Cheese Madonna and 99 Other of the Weirdest, Wackiest, Most Famous eBay Auctions Ever.* New York: Random House.

Cohen, Adam. (2002). *The Perfect Store: Inside eBay.* Boston: Little, Brown & Company.

Collier, Marsha. (2004) *eBay for Dummies*, 4th ed. New Jersey: John Wiley.

Jackson, Eric M. (2004). *The PayPal Wars: Battles with eBay, the Media, the Mafia, and the Rest of Planet Earth.* Los Angeles: World Ahead Publishing.

Nissanoff, Daniel. (2006). *FutureShop: How the New Auction Culture Will Revolutionize the Way We Buy, Sell and Get the Things We Really Want.* London: The Penguin Press.

Spencer, Christopher Matthew. (2006) *The eBay Entrepreneur.* New York: Kaplan Publishing.

SAP and the Evolving Enterprise Resource Planning Software Industry

This case was prepared by Gareth R. Jones, Texas A&M University.

In 1972, after the project they were working on for IBM's German subsidiary was abandoned, five German IBM computer analysts left the company and founded Systems Applications and Products in Data Processing, known today as SAP. These analysts had been involved in the provisional design of a software program that would allow information about cross-functional and cross-divisional financial transactions in a company's value chain to be coordinated and processed centrally—resulting in enormous savings in time and expense. They observed that other software companies were also developing software designed to integrate across value chain activities and subunits. Using borrowed money and equipment, the five analysts worked day and night to create an accounting software platform that could integrate across all the parts of an entire corporation. In 1973, SAP unveiled an instantaneous accounting transaction processing program called R/1, one of the earliest examples of what is now called an enterprise resource planning (ERP) system.

Today, ERP is an industry term for the multi-module applications software that allows a company to manage the set of activities and transactions necessary to manage the business processes for moving a product from the input stage, along the value chain, to the final customer. As such, ERP systems can recognize, monitor, measure, and evaluate all the transactions involved in business processes such as product planning, the purchasing of inputs from suppliers, the manufacturing process, inventory and order processing, and customer service itself. Essentially, a fully developed ERP system provides a company with a standardized information technology (IT) platform that gives complete information about all aspects of its business processes and cost structure across functions and divisions. This allows the business to (1) constantly search for ways to perform these processes more efficiently and lower its cost structure, and (2) improve and service its products and raise their value to customers. For example, ERP systems provide information that allows for the design of products that match customer needs and lead to superior responsiveness to customers.

To give one example, Nestlé installed SAP's newest ERP software across its more than 150 U.S. food divisions in the early 2000s. It thus discovered that each division was paying a different price for the same flavoring, vanilla. The same small set of vanilla suppliers was charging each division as much as they could get, so all divisions paid widely different prices depending on their bargaining power with the supplier. Before the SAP system was installed, managers had no idea this was happening because their IT system could not compare and measure the same transaction—purchasing vanilla—across divisions. SAP's standardized cross-company software platform revealed this problem, and hundreds of thousands of dollars in cost savings were achieved by solving this one transaction difficulty alone.

SAP focused its R/1 software on the largest multinational companies with revenues of at least $2.5 billion. Although relatively few in number, these companies, most of which were large manufacturers, stood to gain the most benefit from ERP, and they were willing to pay SAP a premium price for its product. Its focus on this influential niche of companies helped SAP develop a global base of leading companies. Its goal, as it had been from the beginning, was to create the global industry standard for ERP by providing the best business applications software infrastructure.

In its first years, SAP not only developed ERP software, but it also used its own internal consultants to install it physically on-site at its customers' corporate IT centers, manufacturing operations, and so on. Determined to increase its customer base quickly, however, SAP switched strategies in the 1980s. It decided to focus primarily on the development of its ERP software and to outsource, to external consultants, more and more of the implementation services needed to install and service its software on-site in a particular company. It formed a series of strategic alliances with major global consulting companies such as IBM, Accenture, and Cap Gemini to install its R/1 system in its growing base of global customers.

ERP installation is a long and complicated process. A company cannot simply adapt its information systems to fit SAP's software; it must use consultants to rework the way it performs its value chain activities so that its business processes, and the information systems that measure these business processes, became compatible with SAP's software. SAP's ERP system provides a company with the information needed to achieve best industry practices across its operations. The more a particular company wishes to customize the SAP platform to its particular business processes, the more difficult and expensive the implementation process and the harder it becomes to realize the potential gains from cost savings and value added to the product.

SAP's outsourcing consulting strategy allowed it to penetrate global markets quickly and eliminated the huge capital investment needed to provide this service on a global basis. For consulting companies, however, the installation of SAP's software became a major money-spinner, and SAP did not enjoy as much of the huge revenue streams associated with providing computer services, such as the design, installation, and maintenance of an ERP platform on an ongoing basis. It did earn some revenue by training consultants in the intricacies of installing and maintaining SAP's ERP system.

By focusing on ERP software development, SAP did not receive any profits from this highly profitable revenue stream and made itself dependent on consulting companies that now became the experts in the installation/customization arena. This decision had unfortunate long-term consequences because SAP began to lose firsthand knowledge of its customers' problems and an understanding of the changing needs of its customers, especially when the Internet and cross-company integration became a major competitive factor in the ERP industry. For a company whose goal was to provide a standardized platform across functions and divisions, this outsourcing strategy seemed like a strange choice to many analysts. Perhaps SAP should have expanded its own consulting operations to run parallel with those of external consultants, rather than providing a training service to these consultants to keep them informed about its constantly changing ERP software.

To some degree, its decision to focus on software development and outsource at least 80% of installation was a consequence of its German founders' "engineering" mindset. Founded by computer program engineers, SAP's culture was built on values and norms that emphasized technical innovation, and the development of leading-edge ERP software was the key success factor in the industry. SAP poured most of its money into research and development (R&D) to fund projects that would add to its platform's capabilities; consequently, it had much less desire and money to spend on consulting. Essentially, SAP was a product-focused company and believed R&D would produce the technical advances that would be the source of its competitive advantage and allow it to charge its customers a premium price for its ERP platform. By 1988, SAP was spending more than 27% of gross sales on R&D.

As SAP's top managers focused on developing its technical competency, however, its marketing and sales competency was ignored because managers believed the ERP platform would sell itself. Many of its internal consultants and training experts began to feel they were second-class citizens, despite the fact that they brought in the business and were responsible for the vital role of maintaining good relationships with SAP's growing customer base. It seemed that the classic problem of managing a growing business from the entrepreneurial to the professional management phase was emerging. SAP's top managers were not experienced business managers who understood the problems of implementing a rapidly growing company's strategy on a global basis; the need to develop a sound corporate infrastructure was being shoved aside.

In 1981, SAP introduced its second-generation ERP software, R/2. Not only did it contain many more value chain/business process software modules, but it also linked its ERP software to the databases and communication systems used on mainframe computers, thus permitting greater connectivity and ease of use of ERP throughout a company. The R/1 platform had been largely a cross-organizational accounting/financial software module; the new software modules could handle procurement, product development, and inventory and order tracking. Of course, these additional components had to be compatible with each other so that they could be seamlessly integrated together on-site, at a customer's operations. SAP did not develop its own database management software package; its system was designed to be compatible with Oracle's database management software, the global leader in this segment of the software industry. Once again, this was to have repercussions later, when Oracle began to develop its own ERP software, essentially moving from database software into ERP development.

As part of its push to make its R/2 software the industry standard, SAP had also been in the process of customizing its basic ERP platform to accommodate the needs of companies in different kinds of industries. The way value chain activities and business processes are performed differs from industry to industry because of differences in the manufacturing processes and other factors. ERP software solutions must be customized by industry to perform most effectively. Its push to become the ERP leader across industries, across all large global companies, and across all value chain business processes required a huge R&D investment. In 1988, the company went public on the Frankfurt stock exchange to raise the necessary cash. By 1990, with its well-received multilingual software, SAP had emerged as one of the leading providers of business applications software, and its market capitalization was soaring. SAP began to dominate ERP software sales in the high-tech and electronics, engineering and construction, consumer products, chemical, and retail industries. Its product was increasingly being recognized as superior to the other ERP software being developed by companies such as PeopleSoft, S. D. Edwards, and Oracle. One reason for SAP's increasing competitive advantage was that it could offer a broad, standardized, state-of-the-art solution to many companies' business process problems, one that spanned a wide variety of value chain activities spread around the globe. By contrast, its competitors, like PeopleSoft, offered more focused solutions aimed at one business process, such as human resources management.

SAP Introduces the R/3 Solution

SAP's continuing massive investment in developing new ERP software resulted in the introduction of its R/3, or third-generation, ERP solution in 1992. Essentially, the R/3 platform expanded on its previous solutions; it offered seamless, real-time integration for over 80% of a company's business processes. It had also embedded in the platform hundreds and then thousands of industry best practice solutions, or templates, that customers could use to improve their operations and processes. The R/3 system was initially composed of seven different modules corresponding to the most common business processes. Those modules are production planning, materials management, financial accounting, asset management, human resources management, project systems, and sales and distribution.

R/3 was designed to meet the diverse demands of its previous global clients. It could operate in multiple languages and convert exchange rates, and so on, on a real-time basis. SAP, recognizing the huge potential revenues to be earned from smaller business customers, ensured that R/3 could now also be configured for smaller customers and be customized to suit the needs of a broader range of industries. Furthermore, SAP designed R/3 to be "open architecturally," meaning that it could operate with whatever kind of computer hardware or software (the legacy system) that a particular company was presently using. Finally, in response to customer concerns that SAP's standardized system meant huge implementation problems in changing their business processes to match SAP's standardized solution, SAP introduced some limited customization opportunity into its software. Using specialized software from other companies, SAP claimed that up to 20% of R/3 could now be customized to work with the company's existing operating methods and thus would reduce the problems of learning and implementing the new system. However, the costs of doing this were extremely high and became a huge generator of fees for consulting companies. SAP used a variable-fee licensing system for its R/3 system; the cost to the customer was based on the number of users within a company, on the number of different R/3 modules that were installed, and on the degree to which users utilized these modules in the business planning process.

SAP's R/3 far outperformed its competitors' products in a technical sense and once again allowed it to charge a premium price for its new software. Believing that competitors would take at least two years to catch up, SAP's goal was to get its current customers to switch to its new product and then rapidly build its customer base to penetrate the growing ERP market. In doing so, it was also seeking to establish R/3 as the new ERP market standard and lock in customers before competitors could offer viable alternatives. This strategy was vital to its future success because, given the way an ERP system changes the nature of a customer's business processes once it is installed and running, there are high switching costs involved in moving to another ERP product, costs that customers want to avoid.

R/3's growing popularity led SAP to decentralize more and more control of the marketing, sale, and installation of its software on a global basis to its foreign subsidiaries. While its R&D and software development remained centralized in Germany, it began to open wholly owned subsidiaries in most major country's markets. By 1995, it had eighteen national subsidiaries; today, it has over fifty. In 1995, SAP established a U.S. subsidiary to drive sales in the huge U.S. market. Its German top managers set the subsidiary a goal of achieving $1 billion in revenues within five years. To implement this aggressive growth strategy, and given that R/3 software needs to be installed and customized to suit the needs of particular companies and industries, several different regional SAP divisions were created to manage the needs of companies and industries in different U.S. regions. Also, the regional divisions were responsible for training an army of both internal and external consultants, from companies such as Accenture, on how to install and customize the R/3 software. For every internal lead SAP consultant, there were soon about nine to ten external consultants working with SAP's customers to install and modify the software.

The problems with a policy of decentralization soon caught up with SAP, however. Because SAP was growing so fast and there was so much demand for its product, it was hard to provide the thorough training consultants needed to perform the installation of its software. Once SAP had trained an internal consultant, that consultant would sometimes leave to join the company for which he or she was performing the work or even to start an industry-specific SAP consulting practice, with the result that SAP's customers' needs were being poorly served. Since the large external consulting companies made their money based on the time it took their consultants to install a particular SAP system, some customers were complaining that consultants were deliberately taking too long to implement the new software to maximize their earnings, and were even pushing inappropriate or unnecessary R/3 modules.

The word started to circulate that SAP's software was both difficult and expensive to implement, which hurt its reputation and sales. Some companies had problems implementing the R/3 software; for example, Chevron spent over $100 million and two years installing and getting its R/3 system operating effectively. In one well-publicized case, Foxmeyer Drug blamed SAP software for the supply chain problems that led to its bankruptcy. The firm's major creditors sued SAP in court, alleging that the company had promised R/3 would do more than it could. SAP responded that the problem was not the software but the way the company had tried to implement it, but SAP's reputation was harmed nevertheless.

SAP's policy of decentralization was also somewhat paradoxical because the company's mission was to supply software that linked functions and divisions rather than separated them, and the characteristic problems of too much decentralization of authority soon became evident throughout SAP. In its U.S. subsidiary, each regional SAP division started developing its own procedures for pricing SAP software, offering discounts, dealing with customer complaints, and even rewarding its employees and consultants. There was a total lack of standardization and integration inside SAP America and indeed between SAP's many foreign subsidiaries and their headquarters in Germany. This meant that little learning was taking place between divisions or consultants, there was no monitoring or coordination mechanism in place to share SAP's *own* best practices between its consultants and divisions, and organizing by region in the United States was doing little to build core competences. For example, analysts were asking, "If R/3 has to be customized to suit the needs of a particular industry, why didn't SAP use a market structure and divide its activities by the needs of customers based in different industries?" These problems slowed down the process of implementing SAP software and prevented quick and effective responses to the needs of potential customers.

SAP's R/3 was also criticized as being too standardized because it forced all companies to adapt to what SAP had decided were best industry practices. When consultants reconfigured the software to suit a particular company's needs, this process often took a long time and sometimes the system did not perform as well as had been expected. Many companies felt that the software should be configured to suit their business processes and not the other way around, but again SAP argued that such a setup would not lead to an optimal outcome. For example, SAP's retail R/3 system could not handle Home Depot's policy of allowing each of its stores to order directly from suppliers, based upon centrally negotiated contracts between Home Depot and those suppliers. SAP's customers also found that supporting their new ERP platform was expensive and that ongoing support cost three to five times as much as the actual purchase of the software, although the benefits they received from its R/3 system usually exceeded these costs substantially.

The Changing Industry Environment

Although the United States had become SAP's biggest market, the explosive growth in demand for SAP's software had begun to slacken by 1995. Competitors such as Oracle, Baan, PeopleSoft, and Marcum were catching up technically, often because they were focusing their resources on the needs of one or a few industries or on a particular kind of ERP module (for example, PeopleSoft's focus on the human resources management module). Indeed SAP had to play catch-up in the HRM area and develop its own to offer a full suite of integrated business solutions. Oracle, the second largest software maker after Microsoft, was becoming a particular threat as it expanded its ERP offerings outward from its leading database knowledge systems and began to offer more and more of an Internet-based ERP platform. As new aggressive competitors emerged and changed the environment, SAP found it needed to change as well.

Competitors were increasing their market share by exploiting weaknesses in SAP's software. They began to offer SAP's existing and potential customers ERP systems that could be customized more easily to their situation; systems that were less expensive than SAP's, which still were charged at a premium price; or systems that offered less expensive module options. SAP's managers were forced to reevaluate their business model, and their strategies and the ways in which they implemented them.

New Implementation Problems

To a large degree, SAP's decision to decentralize control of its marketing, sales, and installation to its subsidiaries was due to the way the company had operated from its beginnings. Its German founders had emphasized the importance of excellence in innovation as the root value of its culture, and SAP's culture was often described as "organized chaos." Its top managers had operated from the beginning by creating as flat a hierarchy as possible to create an internal environment where people could take risks and try new ideas of their own choosing. If mistakes occurred or projects didn't work out, employees were given the freedom to try a different approach. Hard work, teamwork, openness, and speed were the norms of their culture. Required meetings were rare and offices were frequently empty because most of the employees were concentrating on research and development. The pressure was on software developers to create superior products. In fact, the company was proud of the fact that it was product driven, not service oriented. It wanted to be the world's leading innovator of software, not a service company that installed it.

Increasing competition led SAP's managers to realize that they were not capitalizing on its main strength—its human resources. In 1997, it established a human resources management (HRM) department and gave it the responsibility to build a more formal organizational structure. Previously it had outsourced its own HRM. HRM managers started to develop job descriptions and job titles, and put in place a career structure that would motivate employees and keep them loyal to the company. They also put in place a reward system, which included stock options, to increase the loyalty of their technicians, who were being attracted away by competitors or were starting their own businesses because SAP did not then offer a future: a career path. For example, SAP sued Siebel Systems, a niche rival in the customer relationship software business, in 2000 for enticing twelve of its senior employees, who it said took trade secrets with them. SAP's top managers realized that they had to plan long term, and that innovation by itself was not enough to make SAP a dominant global company with a sustainable competitive advantage.

At the same time that it started to operate more formally, it also became more centralized to encourage organizational learning and to promote the sharing of its own best implementation practices across divisions and subsidiaries. Its goal was to standardize the way each subsidiary or division operated across the company, thus making it easier to transfer people and knowledge where they were needed most. Not only would this facilitate cooperation, it would also reduce overhead costs, which were spiraling because of the need to recruit trained personnel as the company grew quickly and the need to alter and adapt its software to suit changing industry conditions. For example, increasing customer demands for additional customization of its software made it imperative that different teams of engineers pool their knowledge to reduce development costs, and that consultants should not only share their best practices but also cooperate with engineers so that the latter could understand the problems facing customers in the field.

The need to adopt a more standardized and hierarchical approach was also being driven by SAP's growing recognition that it needed more of the stream of income it could get from both the training and installation sector of the software business. It began to increase the number of its consultants. By having them work with its software developers, they became the acknowledged experts and leaders when it came to specific software installations and could command a high price. SAP also developed a large global training function to provide the extensive ERP training that consultants needed and charged both individuals and consulting companies high fees for attending these courses so that they would be able to work with the SAP platform. SAP's U.S. subsidiary also moved from a regional to a more market-based focus by re-aligning its divisions, not by geography, but by their focus on a particular sector or industry, for example, chemicals, electronics, pharmaceuticals, consumer products, and engineering.

Once again, however, the lines of authority between the new industry divisions and the software development, sales, installation, and training functions were not worked out well enough and the hoped-for gains from increased coordination and cooperation were slow to be realized. Globally, too, SAP was still highly decentralized and remained a product-focused company, thus allowing its subsidiaries to form their own sales, training, and installation policies. Its subsidiaries continued to form strategic alliances with global consulting companies, allowing them to obtain the majority of revenues from servicing SAP's growing base of R/3 installations. SAP's top managers, with their engineering mindset, did not appreciate the difficulties involved in changing a company's structure and culture, either at the subsidiary or the global level. They were disappointed in the slow pace of change because their cost structure remained high, although their revenues were increasing.

New Strategic Problems

By the mid-1990s, despite its problems in implementing its strategy, SAP was the clear market leader in the ERP software industry and the fourth largest global software company because of its recognized competencies in the production of state-of-the-art ERP software. Several emerging problems posed major threats to its business model, however. First, it was becoming increasingly obvious that the development of the Internet and broadband technology would become important forces in shaping a company's business model and processes in the future. SAP's R/3 systems were specifically designed to integrate information about all of a company's value chain activities, across its functions and divisions, and to provide real-time feedback on its ongoing performance. However, ERP systems focused principally on a company's internal business processes; they were not designed to focus and provide feedback on cross-company and industry-level transactions and processes on a real-time basis. The Internet was changing the way in which companies viewed their boundaries; the emergence of global e-commerce and online cross-company transactions was changing the nature of a company's business processes both at the input and output sides.

At the input side, the Internet was changing the way a company managed its relationships with its parts and raw materials suppliers. Internet-based commerce offered the opportunity of locating new, low-cost suppliers. Developing web software was also making it much easier for a company to cooperate and work with suppliers and manufacturing companies and to outsource activities to specialists who could perform the activities at lower cost. A company that previously made its own inputs or manufactured its own products could now outsource these value chain activities, which changed the nature of the ERP systems it needed to manage such transactions. In general, the changing nature of transactions across the company's boundaries could affect its ERP system in thousands of ways. Companies like Commerce One and Ariba, which offered this supply-chain management (SCM) software, were growing rapidly and posing a major threat to SAP's "closed" ERP software.

At the output side, the emergence of the Internet also radically altered the relationship between a company and its customers. Not only did the Internet make possible new ways to sell to wholesalers, its largest customers, or directly to individual customers, it also changed the whole nature of the company–customer interface. For example, using new customer relationship management (CRM) software from software developers like Siebel Systems, a company could offer its customers access to much more information about its products so that customers could make more informed purchase decisions. A company could also understand customers' changing needs so it could develop improved or advanced products to meet those needs; and a company could offer a whole new way to manage after-sales service and help solve customers' problems with learning about, operating, and even repairing their new purchases. The CRM market was starting to boom.

In essence the Internet was changing both industry- and company-level business processes and providing companies and whole industries with many more avenues for altering their business processes at a company or industry level, so that they could lower their cost structure or increasingly differentiate their products. Clearly, the hundreds of industry best practices that SAP had embedded in its R/3 software would become outdated and redundant as e-commerce increased in scope and depth and offered improved industry solutions. SAP's R/3 system would become a dinosaur within a decade unless it could move quickly to develop or obtain competencies in the software skills needed to develop web-based software.

These developments posed a severe shock to SAP's management, who had been proud of the fact that, until now, SAP had developed all its software internally. They were not alone in their predicament. The largest software companies, Microsoft and Oracle, had been caught unaware by the quickly growing implications of web-based computing. The introduction of Netscape's web browser had led to a collapse in Microsoft's stock price because investors saw web-based computing, not PC-based computing, as the choice of the future. SAP's stock price also began to reflect the beliefs of many people that expensive, rigid, standardized ERP systems would not become the software choice as the Web developed. One source of SAP's competitive advantage was based on the high switching costs of moving from one ERP platform to another. However, if new web-based platforms allowed both internal and external integration of a company's business processes, and new platforms could be customized more easily to answer a particular company's needs, these switching costs might disappear. SAP was at a critical point in its development.

The other side of the equation was that the emergence of new web-based software technology allowed hundreds of new software industry start-ups, founded by technical experts equally as qualified as those at SAP and Microsoft, to enter the industry and compete for the wide-open web computing market. The race was on to determine which standards would apply in the new web computing arena and who would control them. The large software makers like Microsoft, Oracle, IBM, SAP, Netscape, Sun Microsystems, and Computer Associates had to decide how to compete in this totally changed industry environment. Most of their customers, companies large and small, were still watching developments before deciding how and where to commit their IT budgets. Hundreds of billions of dollars in future software sales were at stake, and it was not clear which company had the competitive advantage in this changing environment.

Rivalry among major software makers in the new web-based software market became intense. Rivalry between the major players and new players, like Netscape, Siebel Systems, Marcum, I2 Technology, and SSA, also intensified. The major software makers, each of which was a market leader in one or more segments of the software industry, such as SAP in ERP, Microsoft in PC software, and Oracle in database management software, sought to showcase their strengths to make their software compatible with web-based technology. Thus, Microsoft strove to develop its Windows NT network-based platform and its Internet Explorer web browser to compete with Netscape's Internet browser and Sun Microsystems's open-standard Java web software programming language, which was compatible with any company's proprietary software, unlike Microsoft's NT.

SAP also had to deal with competition from large and small software companies that were breaking into the new web-based ERP environment. In 1995, SAP teamed with Microsoft, Netscape, and Sun Microsystems to make its R/3 software Internet-compatible with any of their competing systems. Within one year, it introduced its R/3 Release 3.1 Internet-compatible system, which was most easily configured, however, when using Sun's Java web-programming language. SAP raised new funds on the stock market to undertake new rounds of the huge investment necessary to keep its web-based R/3 system up to date with the dramatic innovations in web software development and to broaden its product range to offer new, continually emerging web-based applications, for example, applications such as the corporate intranets, business-to-business (B2B) and business-to customer (B2C) networks, web site development and hosting, security and systems management, and streaming audio and video teleconferencing.

Because SAP had no developed competency in web software development, its competitors started to catch up. Oracle emerged as its major competitor; it had taken its core database management software used by thousands of large companies and overlaid it with web-based operating and applications software. Oracle could now offer its huge customer base a growing suite of web software, all seamlessly integrated. The suite of software also allowed them to perform Internet-based ERP value chain business processes. While Oracle's system was nowhere near as comprehensive as SAP's R/3 system, it allowed for cross-industry networking at both the input and output sides, it was cheaper and easier to implement quickly, and it was easier to customize to the needs of a particular customer. Oracle began to take market share away from SAP.

New companies like Siebel Systems, Commerce One, Ariba, and Marcum, which began as niche players in some software applications such as SCM,

CRM, intranet, or website development and hosting, also began to build and expand their product offerings so that they now possessed ERP modules that competed with some of SAP's most lucrative R/3 modules. Commerce One and Ariba, for example, emerged as the main players in the rapidly expanding B2B industry SCM market. B2B is an industry-level ERP solution that creates an organized market and thus brings together industry buyers and suppliers electronically and provides the software to write and enforce contracts for the future development and supply of an industry's inputs. Although these niche players could not provide the full range of services that SAP could provide, they became increasingly able to offer attractive alternatives to customers seeking specific aspects of an ERP system. Also, companies like Siebel, Marcum, and I2 claimed that they had the ability to customize their low-price systems, and prices for ERP systems began to fall.

In the new software environment, SAP's large customers started to purchase software on a "best of breed" basis, meaning that customers purchased the best software applications for their specific needs from different, leading-edge companies rather than purchasing all of their software products from one company as a package—such as SAP offered. Sun began to promote a free Java computer language as the industry "open architecture" standard, which meant that as long as each company used Java to craft their specific web-based software programs, they would all work seamlessly together and there would no longer be an advantage to using a single dominant platform like Microsoft's Windows or SAP's R/3. Sun was and is trying to break Microsoft's hold over the operating system industry standard, Windows. Sun wanted each company's software to succeed because it was "best of breed," not because it locked customers in and created enormous switching costs for them should they contemplate a move to a competitor's product.

All these different factors caused enormous problems for SAP's top managers. What strategies should they use to protect their competitive position? Should they forge ahead with offering their customers a broad, proprietary, web-based ERP solution and try to lock them in and continue to charge a premium price? Should they move to an open standard and make their R/3 ERP Internet-enabled modules compatible with solutions from other companies, and indeed forge alliances with those companies to ensure that their software operated seamlessly together? Since SAP's managers still believed they had the best ERP software and the capabilities to lead in the web software arena, was this the best long-run competitive solution? Should SAP focus on making its ERP software more customizable to its customers' needs and make it easier for them to buy selected modules to reduce the cost of SAP software? This alternative might also make it easier for them to develop ERP modules that could be scaled back to suit the needs of medium and small firms, which increasingly were becoming the targets of its new software competitors. Once these new firms got toeholds in the market, it would then be a matter of time before they improved their products and began to compete for SAP's installed customer base. SAP realized that it had to refocus its business model, especially because rivals were rapidly buying niche players and, at the same time, filling gaps in their product lines to be able to compete with SAP.

The mySAP.com Initiative

In 1997, SAP sought a quick fix to its problems by releasing new R/3 solutions for ERP Internet-enabled SCM and CRM solutions, which converted its internal ERP system into an externally based network platform. SCM, now know as the "back end" of the business, integrates the business processes necessary to manage the flow of goods, from the raw material stage to the finished product. SCM programs forecast future needs, and plan and manage a company's operations, especially its manufacturing operations. CRM, known as the "front-end" of the business, provides companies with solutions and support for business processes directed at improving sales, marketing, customer service, and field service operations. CRM programs are rapidly growing in popularity because they lead to better customer retention and satisfaction and higher revenues. In 1998, SAP followed with industry solution maps, business technology maps, and service maps, all of which were aimed at making its R/3 system dynamic and responsive to changes in industry conditions. In 1998, recognizing that its future rested on its ability to protect its share of the U.S. market, it listed itself on the New York Stock Exchange and began to expand the scope of its U.S. operations.

In 1999, however, the full extent of the change in SAP's business model and strategies became clear

when it introduced its mySAP.com (mySAP) initiative to gain control of the web-based ERP, SCM, and CRM markets, and to extend its reach into any e-commerce or Internet-based software applications. The mySAP initiative was a comprehensive ebusiness platform designed to help companies collaborate and succeed, regardless of their industry or network environments. It demonstrated several elements of SAP's changing strategic thinking for how to succeed in the 2000s.

First, to meet its customers' needs in a new electronic environment, SAP used the mySAP platform to change itself from a vendor of ERP components to a provider of ebusiness solutions. The platform was to be the online portal through which customers could view and understand the way its Internet-enabled R/3 modules could match their evolving needs. SAP recognized that its customers were increasingly demanding access to networked environments with global connectivity, where decisions could be executed in real time through the Internet. Customers wanted to be able to leverage new ebusiness technologies to improve basic business goals like increasing profitability, improving customer satisfaction, and lowering overhead costs. In addition, customers wanted total solutions that could help them manage their relationships and supply chains.

MySAP was to offer a total solutions ERP package, including SCM and CRM applications, which would be fundamentally different from the company's traditional business application software. SAP's software would no longer force the customer to adapt to SAP's standardized architecture; mySAP software could be adapted to facilitate a company's transition into an ebusiness. In addition, the solution would create value for a company by building on its already developed core competencies; mySAP would help to leverage those core competencies, thus building a company's competitive advantage from within, rather than by creating it solely through the installation of SAP's industry best practices. SAP created a full range of front- and back-end products such as SCM and CRM software, available through its mySAP.com portal, that are specific to different industries and manufacturing technologies. These changes meant that it could compete in niche markets and make it easier to customize a particular application to an individual company's needs.

Second, mySAP provided the platform that would allow SAP's product offerings to expand and broaden over time, an especially important feature because web-based software was evolving into ever more varied applications. SAP was essentially copying other software makers, who were branching out into more segments of the software industry to capitalize on higher growth software segments and to prevent obsolescence should demand for their core software erode because of technological developments. Henceforth, SAP was not offering product-based solutions but customer-based solutions. Its mySAP ebusiness platform solutions are designed to be a scalable and flexible architecture that supports databases, applications, operating systems, and hardware platforms from almost every major vendor.

Third, SAP realized that cost was becoming a more important issue because competition from low-cost rivals demonstrated that customers could be persuaded to shift vendors if they were offered good deals. Indeed, major companies like Oracle often offered their software at discount prices or even gave it away free to well-known companies to generate interest and demand for their product. SAP focused on making mySAP more affordable by breaking up its modules and business solutions into smaller, separate products. Customers could now choose which particular solutions best met their specific needs; they no longer had to buy the whole package. At the same time, all mySAP offerings were fully compatible with the total R/3 system so that customers could easily expand their use of SAP's products. SAP was working across its whole product range to make its system easier and cheaper to use. SAP realized that repeat business is much more important than a one-time transaction, so they began to focus on seeking out and developing new, related solutions for their customers to keep them coming back and purchasing more products and upgrades.

Fourth, mySAP was aimed at a wider range of potential customers. By providing a simpler and cheaper version of its application software coupled with the introduction of the many mySAP ebusiness solution packages, SAP broadened its offerings targeted not only to large corporations but also small and medium-sized companies. MySAP allowed SAP to provide a low-cost ERP system that could be scaled down for smaller firms. For example, for small to mid-sized companies that lack the internal resources to maintain their own business applications on-site, mySAP offered hosting for data centers, networks, and applications. Small businesses could benefit greatly from the increased speed of installation

and reduced cost possible through outsourcing and by paying a fee to use mySAP in lieu of having to purchase SAP's expensive software modules. SAP also focused on making its R/3 mySAP offerings easier to install and use, and reduced implementation times and consulting costs in turn reduced the costs of supporting the SAP platform for both small and large organizations.

To support its mySAP initiative, SAP had continued to build in-house training and consulting capabilities to increase its share of revenues from the services side of its business. SAP's increasing web software services efforts paid off because the company was now better able to recognize the problems experienced by customers. This result led SAP to recognize both the needs for greater responsiveness to customers and customization of its products to make their installation easier. Its growing customer awareness had also led it to redefine its mission as a developer of business solutions, the approach embedded in mySAP, rather than as a provider of software products.

To improve the cost effectiveness of mySAP installations, SAP sought a better way to manage its relationships with consulting companies. It moved to a parallel sourcing policy, in which several consulting firms competed for a customer's business, and it made sure a SAP consultant was always involved in the installation and service effort to monitor external consultants' performance. This helped keep service costs under control for its customers. Because customer needs changed so quickly in this fast-paced market and SAP continually improved its products with incremental innovations and additional capabilities, it also insisted that consultants undertake continual training to update their skills, training for which it charged high fees. In 2000, SAP adopted a stock option program to retain valuable employees after losing many key employees—programmers and consultants—to competitors.

Fifth, SAP increasingly embraced the concept of open architecture, and its mySAP offerings are compatible with the products of most other software makers. It had already ensured that its mySAP platform worked with operating systems such as Microsoft NT, Sun's Java, and UNIX, for example. Now it focused on ensuring that its products were compatible with emerging web applications software from any major software maker—by 2001 SAP claimed to have over 1,000 partners.

Indeed, strategic alliances and acquisitions became increasingly important parts of its strategy to reduce its cost structure, enhance the functionality of its products, and build its customer base. Because of the sheer size and expense of many web-based software endeavors, intense competition, and the fast-paced dynamics of this industry, SAP's top managers began to realize they could not go it alone and produce everything in-house. SAP's overhead costs had rocketed in the 1990s as it pumped money into building its mySAP initiative. Intense competition seemed to indicate that continuing massive expenditures would be necessary. SAP's stock price had decreased because higher overhead costs meant falling profits despite increasing revenues. SAP had never seemed to be able to enjoy sustained high profitability because changing technology and competition had not allowed it to capitalize on its acknowledged position as the ERP industry leader.

Given existing resource constraints and time pressures and the need to create a more profitable business model, in the 2000s SAP's managers realized that they needed to partner with companies that now dominated in various niches of the software market. By utilizing already developed best of breed software, SAP would not have to deploy the capital necessary if it were to go it alone. In addition, synergies across partner companies might allow future development to be accomplished more efficiently and enable it to bring new mySAP products to the market more quickly.

Not only did SAP form alliances with other companies, but it also used acquisitions to drive its entry into new segments of the web software market. For example, SAP acquired Top Tier Software Inc. in 2001 to gain access to its iView technology. This technology allows seamless integration between the web software of different companies and is critical for SAP because it lets customers drag-and-drop and mix information and applications from both SAP and non-SAP platform-based systems, and thus enables the open systems architecture SAP has increasingly supported. Top Tier was also an enterprise portal software maker, and in 2001 SAP teamed up with Yahoo to use these competencies to create a new U.S. subsidiary called SAP Portals, which would deliver state-of-the-art enterprise portal products that would enable people and companies to collaborate effectively and at any time. It also opened SAP hosting to provide hosting and web maintenance services.

By 2002, SAP believed that its partnerships and alliances had maneuvered it into a position of continued market dominance for the twenty-first century. Many of the major vendors of the databases, applications, operating systems, and hardware platforms that mySAP supports were once considered the competition, but the companies were now working together to create value by maximizing the range of web-based products that could be offered to customers through a common interface. MySAP adds value to its competitors' products by decreasing the exclusivity between the applications of different companies. In essence, SAP was treating these other products as complementary products, which added to the value of its own, promoted mySAP as the industry standard, and increased its dominance of the ERP web software market.

SAP's managers were shocked when it became clear that Microsoft, also recognizing the enormous potential of web software ERP sales, particularly in the small and medium business segment of the market, might be planning to compete in this market segment in 2002. Microsoft had bought two companies that competed in this segment to bolster its own web software offerings. Also, when Microsoft introduced its new XP operating system in 2001, it had not included a Java applications package to allow web software developers to write ebusiness software that would be compatible with XP, undercutting its rival Sun's attempts to bypass the Window's platform using its Java language. However, this also undercut SAP's open architecture initiatives because many of its mySAP installations were based on Java, not Microsoft's NT platform. SAP's managers saw this move as an attempt by Microsoft to wipe out the competitive advantage SAP had been gaining since the introduction of mySAP in 1999. SAP challenged Microsoft to indicate its support for the Java language. Already under scrutiny and attack by Sun and other software companies for its anticompetitive trade practices, Microsoft seemed to step back when it announced in June 2002 that its next version of XP would contain support for Java-based programming. Clearly, however, an open architecture and industry standard for web-based software are not in Microsoft's interests, especially if word processing and other important office applications become available as part of any e-commerce platform such as mySAP.

Microsoft's goal was clearly to become a formidable competitor for SAP, and with its competencies in a wide area of software products and huge resources, it could quickly and easily develop an ERP system with web-based solutions. In the past, SAP had tried to avoid this competition problem by partnering with Microsoft in a wide variety of endeavors and making sure its products were compatible with Microsoft's, thus making their interests mutual rather than divisive. In the future, however, if Microsoft believed its Windows platform was coming under increasing threat from SAP, it could now quickly move to attack SAP's and Oracle's market. The competitive battle over industry standards was far from over.

The recession that started in 2000 also increased competition in the ERP industry. SAP and Oracle, in particular, battled to protect and increase their market share. The huge drop in spending on IT by major companies and the decrease in the number of new customers hit the industry hard. The stock prices of all these companies fell dramatically, with some, like I2 Systems, also a provider of SCM solutions, fighting to survive. Competition among software companies became intense, and customers took advantage of this rivalry to demand price discounts from SAP as well as the other companies, which hurts revenues and profits. Smaller competitors like I2 and Siebel were forced to lower their prices to the point where they took a loss on a particular sale to gain market share. The weakest companies were forced to fall back on their main strengths and reduce their range of product offerings, but SAP had the resources to withstand the downturn.

SAP's number of software installations and customers increased steadily between 1998 and 2002. The number of software installations grew at a faster pace than the number of customers, a characteristic of the lock-in feature of investment in one ERP platform. In 2002, SAP was still the number 1 vendor of standard business applications software, with a worldwide market share of over 30%. Oracle was next with a 16% share of the market. SAP claimed that it had 10 million users and 50,000 SAP installations in 18,000 companies in 120 countries in 2002, and that half of the world's top 500 companies used its software.

Implementing mySAP

SAP's problems were not just in the strategy area, however. Its mySAP initiative had increased its overhead costs, and it still could not find the appropriate organizational structure to make the best use of its resources and competencies. It continued to search for the right structure for servicing the growing range of its products and the increasing breadth of the companies, in terms of size, industry, and global location, it was now serving.

Recall that in the mid-1990s, SAP had began to centralize authority and control to standardize its own business processes and manage knowledge effectively across organizational subunits. While this reorganization resulted in some benefits, it had the unfortunate result of lengthening the time it took SAP to respond to the fast-changing web software ERP environment. To respond to changing customer needs and the needs for product customization, SAP now moved to decentralize control to programmers and its sales force to manage problems where and when they arose. SAP's managers felt that in an environment where markets are saturated with ERP vendors and where customers want service and systems that are easier to use, it was important to get close to the customer. SAP had now put in place its own applications software for integrating across its operating divisions and subsidiaries, allowing them to share best practices and new developments and thus avoid problems that come with too much decentralization of authority.

To speed the software development process, SAP divided its central German software development group into three teams in 2000. One team works on the development of new products and features, the second refines and updates functions in its existing products, and the third works on making SAP products easier to install. Also, to educate its customers and speed customer acceptance and demand for mySAP, SAP changed its global marketing operations in late 2000. Following its decentralized style, each product group once had its own marketing department that operated separately to market and sell its products. This decentralization had caused major problems because customers didn't understand how the various parts of mySAP fit together. It also wasted resources and slowed the sales effort. Announcing that "SAP had to develop a laser like focus on marketing," a far cry from its previous focus on its engineering competency, SAP's top managers centralized control of marketing at its U.S. subsidiary and put control of all global marketing into the hands of one executive, who was now responsible for coordinating market efforts across all mySAP product groups and all world regions.

EXHIBIT 1

mySAP.com Product Groups

mySAP.com Solutions	mySAP.com Industry Solutions
• Industry solutions	• mySAP aerospace and defense
• Solutions for small and mid-sized businesses	• mySAP automotive
• mySAP enterprise portals	• mySAP banking
• mySAP supply chain management	• mySAP chemicals
• mySAP customer relationship management	• mySAP consumer products
• mySAP supplier relationship management	• mySAP engineering and construction
• mySAP product life cycle management	• mySAP financial service provider
• mySAP exchanges	• mySAP health care
• mySAP business intelligence	• mySAP higher education and research
• mySAP financials	• mySAP high tech
• mySAP human resources	• mySAP insurance
• mySAP mobile business	• mySAP media
• mySAP hosted solutions	• mySAP mill products
	• mySAP mining
	• mySAP oil and gas
	• mySAP pharmaceuticals
	• mySAP public sector
	• mySAP retail
	• mySAP service providers
	• mySAP telecommunications

Soon after, in 2001, once again to speed up the implementation of the mySAP initiative, SAP folded the SAPMarkets and SAP Portals subsidiaries into SAP's other operations and split the SAP product line into distinct but related mySAP product groups, each of which was to be treated as an independent profit center, with the head of each product group reporting directly to SAP's chairperson. The type of web software application or ERP industry solution being offered to the customer differentiates each product group (see Exhibit 1).

SAP also changed the way its three German engineering groups worked with the different mySAP products groups. Henceforth, a significant part of the engineering development effort would take place inside each mySAP product group so that program engineers, who write and improve the specific new mySAP software applications, were joined with the sales force for that group. Now they could integrate their activities and provide better customized solutions. The software engineers at its German headquarters, besides conducting basic R&D, would be responsible for coordinating the efforts of the different mySAP engineering groups, sharing new software developments among groups, providing expert solutions, and ensuring all the different mySAP applications worked together seamlessly.

Each mySAP product group is now composed of a collection of cross-functional product development teams focused on their target markets. Teams are given incentives to meet their specific sales growth targets and to increase operating effectiveness, including reducing the length of installation time. The purposes of the new product group/team approach was to decentralize control, make SAP more responsive to the needs of customers and to changing technical developments, and still give SAP centralized control of development efforts. To ensure that its broadening range of software was customizable to the needs of different kinds of companies and industries,

SAP enlisted some of its key customers as "development partners" and as members of these teams. Customers from large, mid-sized, and small companies were used to test new concepts and ideas. Within every mySAP product group, cross-functional teams focused on customizing its products for specific customers or industries. SAP opened the development process to its competitors and allowed them to work with SAP teams to make their products compatible with SAP's products and with the computer platforms or legacy systems already installed in their customers' operations. Through this implementation approach, SAP was striving to pull its actual and potential customers and competitors toward the single, open standard of SAP. The company also instituted stricter training and certification methods for consultants to improve the level of quality control and protect its reputation.

At the global level, SAP grouped is national subsidiaries into three main world regions: Europe, the Americas, and Asia/Pacific. This grouping made it easier to transfer knowledge and information between countries and serve the specific demands of national markets inside each region. Also, this global structure made it easier to manage relationships with consulting companies and to coordinate regional marketing and training efforts, both under the jurisdiction of the centralized marketing and training operations.

Thus, in the 2000s SAP began to operate with a loose form of matrix structure. To increase internal flexibility and responsiveness to customers while at the same time boosting efficiency and market penetration, the world regions, the national subsidiaries, and the salespeople and consultants within them constitute one side of the matrix. The centralized engineering, marketing, and training functions and the twenty or so different mySAP product groups compose the other side. The problem facing SAP is to coordinate all these distinct subunits so they will lead to rapid acceptance of SAP's new mySAP platform across all the national markets in which it operates.

In practice, a salesperson in any particular country works directly with a client to determine what type of ERP system he or she needs. Once this system is determined, a project manager from the regional subsidiary or from one of the mySAP groups is appointed to assemble an installation team from members of the different product groups whose expertise is required to implement the new client's system.

Given SAP's broad range of evolving products, the matrix structure allows SAP to provide those products that fit the customer's needs in a fast, coordinated way. SAP's policy of decentralizing authority and placing it in the hands of its employees enables the matrix system to work. SAP prides itself on its talented and professional staff that can learn and adapt to many different situations and networks across the globe.

Developments in the 2000s

In April 2002, SAP announced that its revenues had climbed 9.2%, but its first-quarter profit fell 40% because of a larger-than-expected drop in license revenue from the sale of new software. Many customers had been reluctant to invest in the huge cost of moving to the mySAP system given the recession and continuing market uncertainty. Its rivals fared worse, however, and SAP announced it had several orders for mySAP in the works, and that the 18,000 companies around the world using its flagship R/3 software would soon move to its new software once their own customers had started to spend more money. In the meantime, SAP announced it would introduce a product called R/3 Enterprise, which would be targeted at customers not yet ready to make the leap to mySAP. R/3 Enterprise is a collection of web software that can be added easily to the R/3 platform to provide a company with the ability to network with other companies and perform many e-commerce operations. SAP hopes this new software will show its R/3 customers what mySAP can accomplish for them once it is running in their companies. SAP's managers believed these initiatives would allow the company to jump from being the third largest global software company to being the second, ahead of main competitor Oracle. They also wondered if they could use its mySAP open system architecture to overcome Microsoft's stranglehold on the software market and bypass the powerful Windows standard.

Pursuing this idea, SAP put considerable resources into developing a new business computing solution called SAP NetWeaver that is a web-based, open integration and application platform that serves as the foundation for enterprise service-oriented architecture (enterprise SOA) and allows the integration and alignment of people, information, and business processes across business and technology boundaries. Enterprise SOA utilizes open standards to enable integration with information and applications from almost any source or technology and is the technology of the future. SAP NetWeaver is now the foundation for all Enterprise SOA SAP applications and mySAP Business Suite solutions; it also powers SAP's partner solutions and a customer custom-built applications. Also NetWeaver integrates business processes across various systems, databases, and sources—from any business software supplier—and is marketed to large companies as a service-oriented application and integration platform. NetWeaver's development was a major strategic move by SAP for driving enterprises to run their business software on a single SAP platform.

Although SAP was developing and upgrading its products at a fast pace, throughout 2002 and 2003 companies worldwide continued to limit or reduce their IT expenditures, and SAP, like all other computer hardware and software companies, suffered as their revenues fell. In fact SAP's stock price plunged in 2002 from $40 to almost $10 as the stock market crashed. However, while SAP's revenues fell by 5% in 2003 because of lower ERP and consulting sales, its net income almost doubled because it had finally brought its global cost structure under control and was making better use of its resources. Strict new controls on expenses had been implemented, a hiring freeze imposed, and the company was focusing its German programmers to work on urgent problems. Consequently, its stock was back up to $35 by the end of 2003 as its future growth prospects looked good.

Outsourcing

As a part of its major push to reduce costs, SAP began to outsource its routine future programming development work overseas to low-cost countries such as India. By 2003, SAP employed 750 software programmers in India and had doubled that number by 2004. To help boost global revenues, SAP also began to use its expanding Indian research center to develop new ERP modules to serve new customers in more and more industries or vertical markets, and by 2003, it had mySAP systems designed for about twenty industry markets. At the same time, SAP used its growing army of low-cost Indian programmers to work the bugs out of its SAP modules and to increase their reliability when they were installed in a new company. This prevented embarrassing blows-ups that sometimes arose when a company implemented

SAP's ERP for the first time. Fewer bugs also made it easier to install its modules in a new company, which reduced the need for consulting and lowered costs, leading to more satisfied customers. By 2006, SAP had doubled its Indian work force again, and its Indian group was now bigger than its research group in Waldorf, Germany. Outsourcing has saved the company billions of Euros a year and has been a continuing contributor to its rising profitability in the 2000s.

The Small and Medium Enterprise Market

In 2003, SAP changed the name of its software from mySAP.com to mySAP Business Suite because more and more customers were now using a suite licensing arrangement to obtain its software rather than buying it outright. Part of the change in purchasing was because of the constant upgrades SAP was rolling out; in a licensing arrangement, its clients could expect to be continually upgraded as it improved its ERP modules. This also had the effect of locking its customers into its software platform for its raised switching costs. However, while SAP continued to attract new large business customers, the market was becoming increasingly saturated as its market share continued to grow—it already had around 50% of the global large business market by 2003. So, to promote growth and increase sales revenues, SAP began a major push to increase its share of the small and medium business enterprise (SME) market segment of the ERP industry.

The small size of these companies, and so the limited amount of money they had to spend on business software, was a major challenge for SAP, which was used to dealing with multinational companies that had huge IT budgets. Also, there were major competitors in this market segment that had specialized in meeting the needs of SMEs to avoid direct competition with SAP, and they had locked up a significant share of business in this ERP segment. By focusing primarily on large companies, SAP had left a gap in the market that large software companies like Oracle, Microsoft, and IBM took advantage of to developed their own SME ERP products and services to compete for customers and revenues in this market segment—one also worth billions of dollars in the years ahead and the main growth segment in the future ERP market. So, to reach this growing market segment as quickly as possible, SAP decided to develop two main product offerings for SMEs: SAP All-in-One and SAP Business One.

SAP All-in-One is a streamlined version of its R/3 mySAP Business Suite; it is much easier to install and maintain and much more affordable for SMEs. To develop All-in-One, SAP's software engineers took its mySAP Business Suite modules designed for large companies and scaled them down for users of small companies. All-in-One is a cut-down version of SAP's total range of products like SAP Customer Relationship Management, SAP ERP modules, SAP Product Lifecycle Management, SAP Supply Chain Management, and SAP Supplier Relationship Management. Despite its reduced size, it is still a complex business solution and one that requires a major commitment of IT resources for a SME.

So, recognizing the need to provide a much simpler and more limited and affordable ERP solution for smaller companies, SAP decided to also pursue a second SME ERP solution. To speed the development of a new suite of programs, SAP decided not to develop a new software package from scratch based on its leading R/3 product, as it did with its All-in-One solution. Rather, it took a new path and bought an Israeli software company called TopManage Financial Solutions in 2002 and rebranded its system as SAP Business One. SAP Business One is a much more limited ERP software package that integrates CRM with financial and logistic modules to meet a specific customer's basic needs. However, it still provides a powerful, flexible solution and is designed to be easy to work and affordable for SMEs. Business One software works in real time; no longer does an SME need to wait until the end of the month to do the accounts. The system manages and records the ongoing transactions involved in a business such as cost of goods received, through inventory, processing and sale, and delivery to customers, and automatically records transactions in a debit and credit account. Despite its streamlined nature, Business One contains fourteen important core modules:

- Administration Module that configures and links the activities involved in a business's value creation system
- Financials Module that controls accounting and financial activities
- Sales Opportunities Module that maintains contact with existing customers and tracks potential customers
- Sales Module that tracks when orders are entered, shipped, and invoiced

- Purchasing Module that issues purchase orders and records goods received into inventory
- Business Partners Module that maintains record and contact with customers and sellers
- Banking Module that tracks and records where cash is received and paid out
- Inventory Module that records and values inventory
- Production Module that tracks cost of materials and manufacturing
- MRP Module that increases the efficiency of input purchase and production planning
- Service Module that manages after-sales service activities and records
- Human Resources Module that records all employee information
- Reports Module that generates user-defined reports (as printouts or Excel files)
- E-commerce that allows customers to buy and sell online to consumers or other businesses

To speed the development of its new Business One solution, SAP chose its management team from engineers outside the company. Many of these managers came from TopManage, and one of these, Shai Agassi, has since risen in SAP to become its chief technology officer for all of its products and technologies. One reason is because of the growing importance of the SME segment, which became clear in 2005 when SAP began reporting revenues from the SME market segment separately from revenues for its larger customers, one way of showing its commitment to SME customers.

The Changing Competitive Environment

As mentioned above, one of the major reasons for SAP to enter and compete in the SME segment was that the large company segment was becoming increasing mature and saturated. By 2004, achieving rapid growth by increasing the number of new large business customers was becoming more and more difficult, simply because SAP's share of the global ERP market had now grown to 58%. As a result, SAP reported that it expected single digit growth in the future—growth worth billions in revenues but still growth that would not fuel a rapid rise in its stock price.

However, competition in the SME market was also increasing as its business software rivals watched

SAP develop and introduce its All-in-One and Business One solutions to dominate this segment. Now SAP's rapid growth in this segment led to increasing competition and to a wave of consolidation in the ERP industry. In 2003, PeopleSoft, the leader in the HRM software module segment, bought J. D. Edwards & Son, a leader in SCM, to enlarge its product offerings and strengthen its market share against growing competition from SAP and Oracle. However, Oracle, the dominant business software database management company, and its chairman, Larry Ellison, also realized the stakes ahead in the consolidating business software market. While SAP had never made large acquisitions to acquire new products and customers, preferring "organic growth" from the inside or small acquisitions, this was not true of Oracle. Ellison saw major acquisitions as the best way to expand Oracle's range of business modules to complement the suite of ERP modules it had been developing internally and so gain market share in the SME market segment. Through acquisitions it could quickly develop an ERP suite with the breadth of SAP's to meet the needs of SMEs. Also, it could use its new competencies and customers to attack SAP in the large company segment, which Oracle now regarded as a major growth opportunity.

So Oracle began a hostile takeover of PeopleSoft. PeopleSoft's managers battled to prevent the takeover, but Oracle offered PeopleSoft's customers special low-cost licensing deals on Oracle software and guaranteed them the changeover to its software would be smooth. It finally acquired PeopleSoft—and the resources and customers necessary to gain a large market share in the SME segment at the expense of SAP and Microsoft—in 2005. Oracle has kept up the pressure. Since January 2005, it acquired twenty-five more business software companies in a huge acquisition drive to build its distinctive competencies and market share in ERP software. PeopleSoft brought Oracle expertise in HRM, and J. D. Edwards, expertise in SCM; and, in a major acquisition of Siebel Systems, Oracle bought a leading CRM software developer. These acquisitions have allowed Oracle to dramatically increase its market share, particularly with small and medium-sized businesses. Before purchasing Seibel, for example, Oracle had a 6.8% share of this market; now it could add Seibel's 11% market share to become one of the top three CRM suppliers.

One of the latest additions to Oracle's new E-Business suite is Oracle Fusion middleware, which allows companies to leverage their existing investments in the software applications of other companies, including SAP, so that they work seamlessly with Oracle's new ERP modules. Fusion is Oracle's answer to SAP NetWeaver and is seen as a major threat to SAP, for it gives customers no incentive to move to SAP's All-in-One or Business One suite. Oracle hopes that because some of its modules, like PeopleSoft's HRM software module, have been regarded as stronger offerings than SAP's, many companies will be inclined to keep their existing PeopleSoft installations and then choose more offerings from Oracle's growing business applications suite. Also, Oracle hopes that SAP customers will now be able to keep any existing SAP application but still add on Oracle modules.

The third leading SME ERP supplier, Microsoft, is also keeping up the pressure. Using the competencies from its acquisition of Great Plains and Navision, it subsequently released a new business package called Microsoft Dynamics NAV, which is ERP software that can be fully customized to the needs of SME users, to their industries and scaled to their size. Microsoft's advantage lies in the compatibility of its ERP offerings with the Windows platform, which is still used by more than 85% of SMEs, especially as it can offer a discount when customers choose both types of software and upgrade to its new Windows Vista software in 2007 and beyond. Its offerings also work seamlessly with its Windows applications such as Word, PowerPoint, and Outlook, and with its Net framework, which is important in B2B transactions.

In 2006, many analysts were betting Oracle would emerge as the leader in the SME segment because they pointed out that SAP's reputation at the SME level was not good, and that it was perceived as a "big, scary, expensive option." SAP's managers realized the need to work hard to carefully position its All-in-One, but especially Business One, software to suit the needs of a company that might have only 30 or 300 employees rather than the 30,000 found at a large company. For example, in the U.S. and Canadian markets, it has been estimated that 90% of companies fall into the SME category, and while SAP might have the greatest product in the world, if it could not customize and market the product to suit these customers' needs, they will not adopt it. In 2004, Shai Agassi, SAP's CTO and expert in the SME software area, announced that as the $40 billion dollar a year business software industry headed for a shakeout,

SAP had to change its strategy to protect its global market share: "Training people on computer systems is stupid. We need to train the systems to work with people." SAP was finally facing up to the need to make its products easy to install, maintain, and especially use as a hoard of other competitors were now snapping at its heels.

In 2005, SAP established five new broad corporate goals: agility, high performance, simplicity, talent development, and co-innovation. Agility was becoming vital as new technological developments, particularly due to the Internet, were rapidly changing the value of its software to customers. For example, a new approach to delivering business software to customers by direct download from the Internet, along with constant upgrading from the Internet, was being pioneered by Internet start-ups such as sales-force.com, which offered its customers CRM software online at prices that undercut SAP and its competitors. High-performance meant ensuring that SAP's software worked seamlessly with its customers, was bug free, and that all the complex parts of its business suite worked totally in tandem. Simplicity meant that its software engineers should continuously work to make its modules easier to install and use by its clients.

Co-innovation was an affirmation of SAP's push through the mid-2000s to work with other software companies, including competitors, to offer products that better met the needs of some types of ERP customers. SAP had avoided making large acquisitions to grow its competencies and customer base; it relied on organic growth, that is, developing new solutions internally, from the ground up, as its growth model. Also, it sought to form strategic alliances with other software vendors to further the utility of its software and to increase the number of customers it could reach. Compare this to Oracle's aggressive and sometimes hostile acquisition strategy to grow its resources.

Co-innovation means cooperating with partners and customers to improve products and solutions, a strategy SAP had always pursued. However, SAP seemed not to realize that its rapid growth might be perceived by other large software companies as a major threat. It had used Oracle's database software for SAP applications, for example, and worked to make its modules compatible with Microsoft's software to make implementation of its own software easier for customers. It had also worked with companies like IBM to train their consultants to install its software. But Oracle and Microsoft were now major competitors and were taking advantage of their compatibility with SAP's software to lure away its customers.

Cooperation and Competition

By the mid-2000s, industry consolidation was leading to increased competition in all aspects of its business, and SAP faced the problem of having to cooperate with companies in some areas and yet be competitors in others. Indeed, after it became clear Oracle and PeopleSoft would merge, Microsoft and SAP began to talk about a possible merger. Their top managers met to discuss the issues involved and there seemed to be a natural fit, for each company would obtain access to all the customers of the other and their software was complementary. However, talks ended both because of antitrust issues and the fear that U.S. or European Union regulators would stop the merger. Talks also failed because there seemed to be major problems of merging the two different cultures: SAP's more bureaucratic German-based culture with Microsoft's more freewheeling culture. Nevertheless, the two companies realized they would gain more through cooperation than competition and formed an alliance to ensure interoperability between Microsoft's Net.platform and SAP's NetWeaver platform and create a new suite of software that will leverage each others' business applications. So they are working to cooperate, not compete, as business partners, which gives them leverage over customers and stops a movement to Oracle's suite. It also seems that Microsoft has abandoned its attempt to become the dominant player in the ERP market, sensing that it might obtain greater returns from ensuring its Windows standard remains dominant for all kinds of computing—including the increasingly important mobile computing. And, by 2006, its mobile platform, Microsoft CE, was winning the battle against other systems championed by Nokia and Sony, and SAP was working to make its software work seamlessly with Microsoft CE so, for example, managers would receive instant alerts from SAP's module when action was needed to correct some operational issue. Also, SAP seems to have reduced its support for the LINUX platform, which is a direct threat to Microsoft.

SAP also worked hard to develop strategic alliances with all kinds of software companies, and by

2007, it had formed contracts with over 1,000 independent software vendors (ISVs), who have helped it expand its offerings, and it has jointly developed 300 new ERP solutions for the 25 industries it now serves, and these applications are all powered by SAP NetWeaver3. An important alliance was announced in August 2006 when IBM announced it would invest $40 million over the next five years to develop the capabilities necessary to install SAP's new software. Also SAP will integrate NetWeaver with IBM's Blade Center and IBM Total Storage Systems, IBM's data storage solution for large companies. These moves will help boost sales, strengthen links with large companies, and offer SAP the chance to co-develop new software with IBM, which is the world's third largest global software seller. SAP and Siemens are collaborating on an IT solution to improve patient care and increase safety and efficiency and lower operating costs. In 2006, SAP and Cisco Systems entered into an agreement to jointly market governance, risk, and compliance business processes and IT control system offerings.

SAP has been making many small acquisitions to improve its position in various industries and to develop products to help companies meet the major changes in U.S. regulatory reporting requirements. For example, in the retail software industry, it acquired companies like Triversity and Khimetrics. Triversity provides point of sales, store inventory, customer relations and service solutions for retail companies, and Khimetrics helps retailers price and position products to manage demand, improve margins, and predict sales and income. It also acquired TomorrowNow, which specializes in providing maintenance and support services for PeopleSoft and J. D. Edwards & Company customers. SAP then created "safe passage programs" that are designed to help companies switch to SAP solutions, even though they now use software applications provided by Oracle. SAP plans to develop a variety of new-generation products by 2008, including new SAP industry solutions, and more applications for SMEs—so this is a direct challenge to Oracle's Fusion software.

To help companies manage complex regulations, SAP also made small acquisitions like Virsa Systems that have expertise in U.S. accounting laws and standards. Its software was then incorporated into SAP products to provide a complete approach to allowing compliance with the Sarbanes-Oxley Act, which mandates openness and conformity to strict accounting reporting requirements through their governance, Risk and Compliance (GRC) solutions. Also, SAP's modules now contain customized software that allows companies to manage trade compliance according to the regulations of different countries, for example, environmental, pharmaceutical, and banking requirements. Finally, the new Radio Frequency identification (RFID) that uses wireless ID tags to improve SCM and the tracking of shipments and inventory has required SAP incorporate software to manage this into its business applications. As all aspects of the environment change, so must SAP's software.

The Future

In 2006, software sales made up 33% of SAP's revenues, consulting 25%, maintenance 37%, and training 4%. (Maintenance provides continuous improvement, quality management, and problem solutions so clients stay up to date with the best business practices that SAP embeds into its software.) The company boasted over 2 million individual users working with SAP solutions in over 100,000 installations of SAP services in more than 36,000 companies in 25 industries ranging from aerospace and defense to wholesale distribution in 120 countries. SAP employed 38,500 people, had hired 3,500 in 2006, and was planning to hire 3,500 more in 2007. It had local offices in more than 50 countries and ran 77 training centers worldwide where people could come to learn how to install and operate its software packages.

However, major questions remain. Does SAP need to search out new ways to increase growth and generate revenues because the market is getting saturated now that most large companies have adopted best practices ERP software? Some analysts say SAP needs to generate increased revenues by increasing its involvement in service and training activities, but this would put it in direct competition with IT consulting companies such as IBM and Cap Gemini that are its allies. Or, it must continue to broaden the range of products it offers to the SME business segment, which would increase competition with Oracle, Microsoft, and new Internet companies such as salesforce.com, which are increasingly offering direct low-cost Internet download ERP services, so far mainly in CRM.

Another main issue is how big a threat is Oracle to SAP in the future? Some analysts say Oracle is not a major threat since Oracle's acquisitions in the B2B sector will not give it a permanent competitive advantage over SAP in SMEs or with large companies. What Oracle has gained is a short-term boost in market share brought about by obtaining the customers of the companies it acquired, but this will not lead to future gains. Others say Oracle is the major competitor, however, with the size, resources, and customer base to compete successfully against SAP. They point out that while over the past five years SAP's stock shot up 80%, Oracle's increased by only 25%. But also that in the last year Oracle's stock has doubled in price and increased much faster than SAP's because investors believe in the future growth potential of its acquisitions and business model.

SAP believes in its "organic growth" from the inside, however, and considers itself an innovator compared to Oracle. In a 2006 press release, SAP spokesperson Bill Wohl was quoted as saying that SAP offers a next-generation platform in business software today, while Oracle's next-generation applications exist only in "PowerPoint form" and won't be delivered until 2008 or beyond. Also that SAP had set aside $125 million to implement next-generation solutions in its current platform—so this is no idle boast. Also in 2006, SAP articulated four major priorities for the rest of the 2000s—to increase market share, especially in SME; to increase profitability by improving productivity; to better serve SAP users with new products and expand to new industries; and to help customers transition to and gain benefits from Enterprise SOA, which, using NetWeaver, allows customers to seamlessly integrate the software of different vendors into a whole and links it to the Internet, making possible real-time upgrades and improvements.

For all companies, future market growth may be limited as large companies expect to continue their efforts to tighten their IT spending budgets so the software market may grow only at a single digit rates in the next few years. However, the growth of the European Union offers SAP, much more than Oracle, many opportunities to build a worldwide ERP market as the number of countries expands and companies move their operations to low-cost locations within the EU. According to some estimates, the growth of the EU will increase the ERP market to around $13 billion by 2008, which is a 6% annual growth rate. Also, SAP is actively targeting the booming Asian, South American, and African markets.

A 2007 Surprise

SAP announced in January 2007 that its net income rose 29% in the fourth quarter from the year-earlier period to 799 million euros ($1 billion), on revenue of 3 billion euros ($3.9 billion). This was an excellent result, but its U.S. shares fell over 10% from $50 to $46, down from its December high of $56. Why the problem? SAP announced it would spend an additional 300 to 400 million euros over the next two years to attract new SME customers, and this investment will cut its operating margins by 1 to 2% and so its future profits.

The implication for investors is clear; by the end of 2006, SAP was meeting serious resistance from Oracle, it was having to work hard to build up its SME customer base, and the two companies were locked in what is likely to become a vicious battle—one that will reduce profit margins. This was a signal that profit margins were going to be lower than SAP had previously expected and that it needed to further develop tailored products, including hosted software and on-demand software delivered over the Internet, for the SME segment. SAP is facing competition in the SME market from CRM companies such as salesforce.com that specializes in on-demand software downloaded directly from the Internet. Complementing SAP's existing portfolio for midsized companies, a new solution will be introduced to leverage an "enterprise service-oriented architecture (enterprise SOA) by design" platform that will be available to customers through on-demand and hosted delivery at a significantly lower cost and that will allow them to "try-run-adapt" the software to meet their needs. This solution began initial market validation in early 2007. SAP's new CEO, Henning Kagermann, said: "We are combining the power of the new platform that SAP has developed over the last three years with a new approach in the way software is delivered and consumed to reach a broad segment of midsize companies with requirements not addressed by either traditional or on-demand solutions available today. This game-changing, 'enterprise SOA by design' addition to our product portfolio will open up an additional business that will deliver steady, continuous growth and, together with the ongoing advancement of our established business, accelerate SAP's long-term industry leadership." Also, it seems SAP may be signaling it is going to treat medium-sized customers differently from small customers. Clearly, many challenges lie ahead.

REFERENCES

Boudette, N. E., "E-Business: SAP Boosts Commerce One Stake," *Wall Street Journal,* July 2, 2001, p. B8.

Boudette, N. E., "Germany's SAP Reorganizes Its Marketing, Focuses on Web," *Wall Street Journal,* August 7, 2000, p. A8.

Boudette, N. E., "Results Show SAP Is Waiting to Benefit from Recovery," *Wall Street Journal,* April 19, 2002, p. A16.

"Burger King Corporation Selects SAP to Enable Information Technology Strategy," retrieved from http://mySAP.com (June 25, 2002).

Collett, S., "SAP: Whirlpool's Rush to Go Live Led to Shipping Snafus," Computerworld.com, November 4, 1999.

Conlin, R., "SAP Teams with Yahoo! On Portal Venture," CRMDaily.com, April 4, 2001.

Conlin, R., "SAP Upgrades CRM App, Unveils New Strategy," CRMDaily.com, April 23, 2001.

Edmondson, G., and Baker, S., "Silicon Valley on the Rhine," *Business Week,* November 7, 1997.

Hill, S., "SAP 'Opens Up,'" *Msi,* Oak Brook, August 2001.

Jacobs, F., and Whybark, D, *Why ERP? A Primer on SAP Implementation.* New York: McGraw-Hill, 2000.

Kersteller, J., "Software," *Business Week,* January 8, 2001.

Key, P. "SAP Strategy: Displace All Competing Gateways," *Philadelphia Business Journal,* September 27, 1999.

King, J., "Commerce One Deal Reflects SAP Strategy Shift," Computerworld. com, June 15, 2000.

King, S., and Ohlson, K., "Update: Commerce One Deal Reflects SAP Strategy Shift," Computerworld.com (2000).

Konicki, S., "Overwhelmed—SAP Regroups Software Business," *Information Week,* June 6, 2000.

Konicki, S., and Maselli, J., "SAP Touts Customers' Experiences," *Information Week,* June 3, 2002.

Krill, P., "SAP Takes on Its CRM Rivals," *Infoworld,* September 10, 2001.

Maselli, J., "Analysts Steer Customers Away from SAP CRM Upgrade," *Information Week,* September 10, 2001.

Meissner, G., *Inside the Secret Software Power.* New York: McGraw-Hill, 2000.

O'Brien, K., "Many Blows to SAP Strength," retrieved from http://www.it.mycareer.com.au/software/20000125/A39678-2000Jan21.html (January 25, 2000).

Pender, L., "SAP CEO: Don't Blame Us for Snafus," Zdnet.com, November 10, 1999.

SAP AG, "SAP Transforms E-Business with New mySAP Technology for Open Integration," *Business Wire,* November 6, 2001.

SAP, http://www.sap.com, 1995–2007.

SAP Annual Reports and 10K Reports, 1998–2002.

SAP 10K Reports, 2001–2007.

Scannell, E., "Accenture, SAP Jump into Bed," *Infoworld,* July 9, 2001.

Standard and Poor's Industry Overview—Software, *Industry Survey,* April 26, 2001.

Weston, R., "SAP Strategy Extends Scope," CNETNews.com, September 15, 1998.

Volantis

This case was prepared by Mike Harkey under the supervision of Professor
William P. Barnett, Stanford Graduate School of Business.

Life is about timing.

—*Carl Lewis, U.S. Olympian*

Introduction

Matt Harris, President and CEO of the telecommunications software provider Volantis Systems, knew plenty about the importance of timing. His company's investors and founders had mis-timed its market opportunity and, by March 2006, had spent more than five years waiting for mass adoption of mobile data services.

Volantis' customers were primarily *mobile phone carriers* (e.g., 3 and Cingular) and *content providers* (e.g., eBay and lastminute.com) that needed tools to help them most efficiently deliver a wide-range of mobile phone-related services to a huge and complex market.[1] In 2005, almost two billion mobile phone subscribers worldwide were using thousands of different mobile phone handset models. Further complicating matters, mobile phone manufacturers were introducing new devices and technologies every day. Accordingly, no single operating system for mobile phones prevailed, and standards were a mess (i.e., wireless network standards differed and multimedia/audio/video standards differed).

The pace of innovation in mobile phone technology had disastrous implications for any business that wanted its mobile offering to appear as compelling to users on all phones, on all networks, in all geographies. For example, a newspaper publisher like *Financial Times* that wanted its global readership to be able enjoy its publication on any device would be hard-pressed to keep up with the ever-changing technologies. Analogously, imagine if it had to retool its printing presses every day for dozens of layouts, while preparing for an increasing number of new layouts to come.

Enter Volantis: it had built a software solution—a so-called intelligent content adapter—that could remove the complexities for any company that wanted to deliver its content to mobile devices. In fact, the process by which Volantis built its technology was yielding huge scalability benefits, so much so that the company's flexible solution was adopted by the largest list of wireless carrier customers in its market.

Indeed, with mobile data services usage increasing rapidly in many markets worldwide, Volantis was poised to fulfill its long-awaited potential. However, the company was losing over $400,000 per month, and it needed to act quickly with an updated organization plan to capitalize on its new business opportunities. One opportunity would leverage the company's core infrastructure, but would require considerable investment and resources. A second opportunity risked threatening its current operating model. In either case, Volantis was fortunate to have the luxury of such compelling prospects, after so many other wireless solutions companies had long since disappeared. As luck would have it, Volantis' timing was not ideal once again; only this time around, Harris and his team could not afford to be wrong.

Mobile Industry Landscape

Mobile Phone Use Worldwide

By the end of 2005, there were over 1.85 billion mobile phone subscribers worldwide.[2] China was by far the world's largest market, with an estimated 400 million subscribers at the end of 2005. India, with 65 million wireless subscribers, on the other hand, was one of the world's fastest growing markets. In the second half of 2005, almost 2.5 million new subscribers were signing up for cellular service every month in India, and wireless penetration remained less than seven percent. The rest of Asia—that is, Asia less China and India—accounted for 186 million subscribers in 2005.[3]

In 2005, there were 195 million wireless subscribers in the U.S., an increase of 6.9 percent over 2004. As of December 2004, Latin America had 167.2 million wireless subscribers, 41.8 percent more than in 2003. Argentina had the strongest growth rate (107.9 percent growth), more than doubling the number of its subscribers to 13.5 million.[4] The Middle East and Africa were estimated to have almost 200 million subscribers in 2005.

Europe was the world's most mature wireless market. The number of subscribers grew only two percent in 2005 to 325 million subscribers, and penetration rates were averaging over 80 percent. Germany, Italy, and the U.K. led the way in Europe, with 71.3 million, 62.8 million, and 61.1 million wireless subscribers, respectively, in 2004.

Mobile Phone Vendors

In 2005, worldwide mobile phone shipments totaled 825.5 million units, a 16.7 percent increase over the 707.3 million shipments in 2004. Asia was the world's largest market for handsets. In 2005, 197.1 million handsets were sold in Asia excluding Japan. Shipments in Japan totaled 45.4 million. One hundred sixty million mobile phones were sold in Western Europe, and 147 million were sold in the U.S.[5]

Additionally, thousands of new mobile phone handset models were flooding the market every year by hundreds of manufacturers worldwide. Finnish manufacturer Nokia held the industry's largest market share with 34.1 percent of the market in Q4 2005. (See Exhibit 1 for statistics on leading mobile phone vendors.) In early 2006, Nokia was distributing over 60 phone models in the U.S., from the 8801 model sold at an MSRP of $799 (key features included a half-megapixel camera and a 208 x 208 pixel, 256K-color screen) to the N90 model sold at an MSRP of $399 (key features included a 2 megapixel camera and personal video capabilities) to the basic 2126i model offered at an MSRP of $29.99.

Motorola, on the other hand, earned 18.2 percent share of the mobile phone market in 2005. It expanded its market share over the previous year on the success of its wildly popular Razr series phones which had an ultra-thin design and a variety of advanced features. Motorola also offered a SLVR series phone that was compatible with Apple's iTunes digital music service.

Mobile Phone Innovation

Indeed, with so many new mobile phones coming to market every year, handset vendors were forced to compete on a number of dimensions. Of course, price was important to consumers, and handset

---

EXHIBIT 1

Leading Mobile Phone Vendors, Worldwide Shipments and Market Share (Unit shipments are in millions.)

Rank	Vendor	4Q 2005 Shipments	4Q 2005 Market Share	4Q 2004 Shipments	4Q 2004 Market Share	Growth
1	Nokia	83.7	34.1%	66.1	32.2%	26.6%
2	Motorola	44.7	18.2%	31.8	15.5%	40.6%
3	Samsung	27.2	11.1%	21.1	10.3%	28.9%
4	LG Electronics	16.2	6.6%	13.9	6.8%	16.5%
5	Sony Ericsson	16.1	6.6%	12.6	6.1%	27.8%
	Others	57.3	23.4%	60.2	29.2%	−4.8%
	Total	**245.2**	**100.0%**	**205.7**	**100.0%**	**19.3%**

Source: Brad Smith, "Revenues Ride Growth Curve," *Wireless Week*, February 15, 2006.

vendors offered models across a wide spectrum of MSRPs, ranging from the exorbitant (e.g., Symbol Technologies MC70 Enterprise Digital Assistant with an MSRP over $2,000) to the bargain basement sub-$50 models offered by a large number of vendors. In many cases, wireless carriers subsidized the price of handsets to win subscriber business. Watson said:

> Consumers buying mobile devices are making distinctions in terms of the camera, the screen, the usability of the keyboard, the form factor (whether it's a flip or slide or whatever), what features it has, whether it interacts with a Windows machine, and so on. All of those consumer-oriented features (and there are probably around ten or fifteen attributes that matter to consumers) create an enormous number of niches in the market for phones.

Indeed, handset vendors were competing on design, form factor, and physical appearance attributes, offering phones in all sorts of colors, shapes, sizes, and ergonomic conventions. The pace of innovation in handset technology was rapid, as vendors sought to tap into the market of almost two billion mobile phone subscribers worldwide. As a result, an inventory of all of the industry's handset features would compare favorably to almost any consumer technology. By early 2006, manufacturers were turning the mobile phone into the next generation's personal computer, a catch-all for any kind of application or technology.

With screen quality greatly improving on mobile phones, vendors were merging digital imaging and video capabilities into handsets. Some phones offered multimedia options, including streaming video, digital music, FM radio, and ring tones. Even so, most phones were engineered around communications and messaging, including text messaging, instant messaging, picture messaging, conference calling, video-conferencing, paging, information alerts, fax, and email. Bluetooth and infrared features allowed some mobile users to wirelessly connect with external devices like PDAs and PCs. Additionally, many phones offered a micro-browser to allow users to surf the Internet.

Notwithstanding all of the innovation occurring in the wireless industry in early 2006, mobile phones were only as useful as the user's subscriber plan would allow. Each mobile operator was bound by the constraints of its network. As a result, service offerings varied widely from carrier to carrier, many of which operated on different technology platforms, or network standards.

Wireless Network Standards

Even though many countries had adopted a single network standard for nationwide use, the U.S. market employed several standards in early 2006. Most U.S. carriers employed so-called second-generation network platforms, including global system for mobile communications (GSM) or code division multiple access (CDMA). (See Exhibit 2 for platforms used by major U.S. carriers.)

First-generation wireless networks Introduced in the late 1970s and early 1980s, the first generation wireless systems were analog.

Second-generation (2G) 2G wireless networks supported voice and certain data services. Data transmission speeds of 14.4 kilobits per second (kbps) were common on 2G networks. CMDA was a 2G digital wireless technology that was used primarily in China, India, Japan, South Korea, and North America. (See Exhibit 3 for global CDMA subscriber statistics.) GSM was a 2G digital technology that was mostly used for voice transmissions. It had been adopted by the European Union and was the most widely used digital cellular standard worldwide. According to the trade

---

EXHIBIT 2

Technology Platforms/Standards Used by Major U.S. Carriers, 2005

Code division multiple access (CDMA)
- Alltel
- Sprint Nextel
- Verizon Wireless
- United States Cellular

Integrated dispatch enhanced network (iDEN)
- Sprint Nextel
- Nextel Partners

Global system for mobile communications (GSM)
- Cingular Wireless
- T-Mobile

Time division multiple access (TDMA)
- Cingular Wireless

Source: Kenneth Leon and Nelson Wang, "Industry Surveys, Telecommunications: Wireless," *Standard & Poor's,* November 3, 2005.

EXHIBIT 3

Global CDMA Subscriber Statistics

	Total Subscribers in September 2005 (in millions)	Percent Growth in 2004
Asia-Pacific	124.9	30%
North America	102.6	17%
Caribbean and Latin America	53.4	37%
Europe, Middle East, and Africa	4.8	34%
Total	**285.7**	**26%**

Source: CDMA Development Group.

group GSM World Association, there were 1.2 billion GSM subscribers in more than 200 countries as of mid-September 2005.[6] (See Exhibit 4 for global GSM subscriber statistics.)

Second and a half generation (2.5G) 2.5G wireless networks were a stepping stone to 3G networks because they used some of the existing 2G infrastructure in GSM and CDMA networks.

Third-generation (3G) 3G networks integrated mobile technology with high-data transmission capacity. With transmission speeds exceeding 2.0 megabits per second (Mbps) on certain 3G networks, these platforms enabled the delivery of the widest array of applications to mobile handsets. By the end of 2005,

EXHIBIT 4

Global GSM Subscriber Statistics

	Total Subscribers in September 2005 (in millions)	Percent Growth in 2004
Asia	470.8	24%
Africa	68.9	62%
Americas	53.1	121%
Eastern Europe	150.3	57%
Western Europe	352.6	7%
Middle East	63.5	34%
USA/Canada	48.0	5%
Total	**1207.2**	**29%**

Source: GSM Association.

there were three main 3G platforms: CDMA2000, wideband CDMA (WCDMA), and universal mobile telecommunications (UMTS). In 2001, Japanese carrier NTT DoCoMo began operating on the WCDMA standard. Conversely, by the end of 2005, most U.S. carriers had yet to fully upgrade to a 3G standard. ABI Research estimated that there were 42.0 million 3G subscribers worldwide, a 142 percent increase over 2004, most of which were in Japan.[7] Even though fewer than 2.3 percent of worldwide subscribers were on a 3G network, many believed that the long-anticipated platform shift was finally set to take off in 2006.

Wireless Carriers

Worldwide carrier revenues reached almost $480 billion in 2005, split between Europe/Middle East/Africa ($180 billion), Asia-Pacific ($158 billion), and the Americas ($143 billion).[8] At least eight carriers had over 50 million wireless subscriber customers. (See Exhibit 5 for leading carriers by region.) For example, China's largest carrier, China Mobile, had over 230 million subscribers and over $21 billion in wireless services revenues in 2005. In early 2006, there were hundreds of carriers worldwide, and many new entrants were coming to the market employing a different model than traditional carriers.

Mobile virtual network operators (MVNOs) did not have networks of their own, but rather resold capacity from established carriers. In 1999, Virgin Mobile launched the first MVNO in the U.K. using T-Mobile's network capacity; but by early 2006, almost 200 MVNOs were operational or had announced plans to launch. MVNOs were taking advantage of the market opportunity by employing a few different

EXHIBIT 5

Leading Carriers, by Region

		United States		
Rank	Carrier	Number of Subscribers (millions)	Market Share (%)	Service Revenues (billions)
1	Cingular Wireless	51.4	28.4%	7.7
2	Verizon Wireless	47.4	26.1%	6.9
3	Sprint PCS	26.6	14.6%	3.4
4	T-Mobile	19.2	10.6%	3.6
5	Nextel	17.8	9.8%	3.4
6	Alltel	9.1	5.0%	1.4
7	US Cellular	5.2	2.9%	0.7
8	Nextel Partners	1.8	1.0%	0.4
9	Dobson Communications	1.6	0.9%	0.2
10	Western Wireless	1.5	0.8%	0.3
	Total	**181.7**	**100.0%**	**28.0**

Source: Kenneth Leon and Nelson Wang,"Industry Surveys, Telecommunications: Wireless," *Standard & Poor's*, November 3, 2005.

Europe		
Carrier	Number of Subscribers (millions)	Service Revenues (billions)
Vodaphone	171.0	42.1
T-Mobile	83.1	17.8
Orange	70.0	14.0
Telefonica Moviles	89.0	10.1
Telecom Italia Mobile	45.6	8.0
O2	25.7	6.3

Source: Nelson Wang, "Industry Surveys, Telecommunications: Wireless Europe," *Standard & Poor's*, January 2006.

Asia		
Carrier	Number of Subscribers (millions)	Service Revenues (billions)
China Mobile	234.9	21.5
China United	124.1	8.0
NTT DoCoMo	50.1	21.6
KDDI Corp	20.9	13.3
SK Telecom	19.3	2.5
Vodaphone KK	15.0	6.7
Bharti Tele-Ventures	14.1	N/A

Source: Nelson Wang, "Industry Surveys, Telecommunications: Wireless Asia," *Standard & Poor's*, January 2006.

Latin America	
Carrier	Number of Subscribers (millions)
America Movil SA de CV	73.8
Telefonica Moviles SA	63.7
Telcel	32.3
Vivo	28.5
Telecom Italia Mobile SpA	18.3
TIM Brasil	18.0

Source: Nelson Wang, "Industry Surveys, Telecommunications: Wireless Latin America," *Standard & Poor's*, November 2005.

strategies. Well known brands like ESPN and Disney launched MVNOs with premium content and communication services to extend their brands into new areas. Targeted niche players like Boost Mobile and Amp'd Mobile were competing for the under-30 demographic with low-cost services and trendy content. Additionally, cost leaders like EasyMobile and Tesco were targeting low budget users with basic voice and data offerings. In 2005, there were 13 million MVNO subscribers in Europe (out of 325 million total wireless subscribers).

Carriers were benefiting from selling excess network capacity to MVNOs, and consumers were enjoying the incremental service offerings in the market. Naturally, the carriers were monitoring any potential cannibalization of their own business, fearful of a price war with the MVNOs. Nevertheless, prices had already begun to fall.

Most carriers charged for voice and data services either by bundling for a flat rate or priced based on usage. In 2004, the average price per minute of mobile telephone usage fell 12 percent in the U.S., following a drop of 13 percent between 2002 and 2003, continuing a downward trend. In the Scandinavian countries and the Netherlands, low-cost MVNOs had driven down the average price per minute for voice calls from $0.20 to $0.11 over a three-year period.

As of early 2006, the financial health of carriers worldwide rested on their ability to move beyond the voice-only business. Metrics like customer acquisition, customer churn rate, average minutes of use (AMOU), and average revenue per user (ARPU) would continue to be important benchmarks for any carrier. Nevertheless, one measure that would become increasingly important would be revenues from data services (e.g., music and video downloads). Data services could be highly profitable for carriers, creating higher return than the typical carriers' primary revenue generators: device sales, sale and resale of voice minutes, and extended value-added services (e.g., warranties). In addition, the mobile data services market was predicted to reach over $100 billion by 2007.

At the end of June 2005, ARPU in Asia was $18.90, compared to $13.10 in Eastern Europe, $37.40 in Western Europe, and $49.60 in the U.S. and Canada. In 2005, data services revenues accounted for 20 percent of Japan's wireless services revenues, 17 percent of those of Europe, and 10 percent of those of the U.S. As of November 2005, worldwide data services leader DoCoMo had 18.6 million subscribers to its 3G services and was earning a $63 ARPU, 25 percent of which came from data services. Data services provided carriers with not only a new potential revenue stream, but also a key vehicle for achieving differentiation in the increasingly crowded marketplace.

Challenges for Carriers

In early 2006, MVNOs and traditional carriers alike were directing resources towards the mobile content, data services opportunity. However, there was a great deal of operational complexity in creating the new business opportunity, and carriers needed to overcome a number of hurdles to get into the data services market. Specifically, they needed to consider:

- *Deployment models*: How to choose and implement a content delivery model to meet the market opportunity.

- *Technology*: How to acquire high quality solutions and efficiently integrate them, particularly when no standards existed: 1) There was no single prevailing operating system for mobile devices; 2) Network standards ranged from first generation TDMA networks to 3G networks like WCDMA; 3) There was no standard for multimedia, audio, or video files, and 4) There was no standard system for billing and user management.

- *Device management/Device diversity*: How to support the thousands of different existing and next generation handset models, each characterized by a set of different attributes.

- *Content delivery*: How to manage a catalog of content.

- *Marketing & merchandising*: How to promote services and drive revenues with cross-selling and sales promotions.

- *Charging, billing, and settlement*: How to integrate proprietary or 3rd party billing systems.

Volantis Company History (1999–2005)

Founders

The four founders of Volantis—Jennifer Bursack, Martin Gaffney, Brett Nulf, and Mark Watson—met while they were working in the U.K. for Tivoli, a subsidiary of IBM. Each came from different backgrounds—Bursack, engineering and product management; Gaffney, sales; Nulf, consulting and business development; and Watson, development, sales, and management. (See Exhibit 6 for more information about the founders' backgrounds.) But each shared a passion for start-ups.

Tivoli had a very strong entrepreneurial culture and had launched a number of spin-outs and new ventures. Indeed, Tivoli itself was founded by two former IBM employees not far from IBM's offices in Austin, TX. The company developed system management software for enterprises including performance analysis, software distribution, and workload monitoring for Unix- and Windows-based systems from multiple

EXHIBIT 6

Background Information of Selected Executives

Founders

Jennifer Bursack: co-founder and Vice President, Product Management

Prior to Volantis, Jennifer joined a pre-IPO Tivoli in the Bay Area (CA) as an early member of the Professional Services Group. She moved from the U.S. to become one of Tivoli's first employees in Europe and was initially responsible for planning and implementing projects across various industry verticals.

Jennifer moved on to join the European Product Management group responsible for Tivoli's e-commerce products. Prior to Tivoli, Jennifer was a Lead Engineer in several Bay Area start-ups focusing on CAD (computer aided design) and publishing systems. Jennifer holds a Bachelor of Science in Computer Science from Syracuse University.

Martin Gaffney: co-founder and Vice President, Strategic Sales

Prior to Volantis, Martin was the second salesman in Europe to join Tivoli. He was responsible for securing GBP30M in business over 3.5 years across a variety of retail and financial enterprises.

Previously, Martin was the longest serving worldwide Sales Executive with 100 percent record of quota achievement at Sequent Computer Systems Limited where he was also the second UK salesman. Prior to that, Martin spent 7 years at Comshare where he undertook a variety of technical and sales roles.

Brett Nulf: co-founder and Vice President, Business Development

Prior to founding Volantis, Brett managed a European Business Consultancy team at Tivoli Systems. His team was responsible for developing financial business cases and implementation planning for strategic customers.

Previously, Brett was a Strategic Sales Consultant for the telecommunications industry leading substantial sales across the European Telecommunications sector. Before Tivoli, Brett was a Lead Engineer in EDS tasked with selling, qualifying, and executing client/server, middleware, and Internet consultancy projects for Global 1000 enterprises. Brett holds a Business degree from the University of Michigan School of Business Administration.

Mark Watson: co-founder and CTO

Mark Watson co-founded Volantis Systems and is responsible for developing and implementing the company's product direction. Prior to Volantis, Mark spent 15 years at IBM in a variety of positions, including development, sales and management roles in IBM Research, IBM's Development Laboratory at Hursley in the UK, IBM Global Network Services, IBM's AIX business and finally IBM's Tivoli subsidiary. Mark's focus was on advanced networking and open systems, including a spell working on behalf of IBM as part of an open systems development consortium at the British government's National Physical Laboratory in Teddington, UK.

Mark has been Volantis' CTO since the company's inception and in that role has led Volantis' product development, definition and architecture. As a member of Volantis' board, he has also been instrumental in fundraising and wider aspects of the company's development. Mark holds an Honours degree in Politics from the University of Nottingham, England.

Additional Management Team

Matt Harris: President and Chief Executive Officer

Prior to taking the CEO position at Volantis, Matt was President and CEO of Metrowerks Corporation, a 600+ person Austin-based provider of embedded software and related tools. Matt's prior experience includes roles as President, Metrowerks EMEA, President and CEO of Lineo, Inc., various other senior management positions, and five years as a systems engineer with EDS. Matt also practiced technology law for ten years, representing a variety of clients in matters ranging from securities litigation to licensing disputes and antitrust litigation.

Matt holds a BA in Finance from the University of Washington and a JD, magna cum laude, from the University of Michigan.

John Beale: VP Marketing

John has spent nearly twenty years developing marketing programs to support business development, product marketing and corporate communications strategies. In the past ten years, he has focused on the wireless industry, initially as a consultant based in Asia, and for the past five years as head of marketing for QUALCOMM's semiconductor division.

John has a BA in Economics from the University of Victoria, British Columbia.

(continued)

EXHIBIT 6   (*continued*)

Background Information of Selected Executives

Gareth Anderson: VP Finance

As Vice President Finance, Gareth has responsibility for all aspects of Finance, HR, Legal and Facilities. Prior to Volantis, Gareth served as VP International Business Planning at Gartner, where he implemented financial processes across EMEA and AP in coordination with American business units. Previously, Gareth spent several years at Sequent in a number of financial roles, culminating in the management of Finance and Operations for EMEA. Prior to this, he held various Commercial and Finance roles in the brewing operations of Grand Met and Courage.

Gareth holds a BA in Management Science from Trinity College Dublin. Member C.I.M.A.

Chris Smith: VP Telco

Chris is responsible for the Telco line of business at Volantis, including fixed line operators, mobile operators, MVNOs, MVNEs, ASPs and ISPs. He oversees Telco product strategy, partnerships strategy, market development, business development and the Telco PnL.

Prior to joining Volantis, Chris served as Senior Vice President of Operations at iXL (UK) Ltd. where he was responsible for delivery of eBusiness consulting solutions to a number of Fortune 500 clients. Prior to iXL, Chris performed the role of Vice President and Chief Technology Officer of Indus International, an Enterprise Asset Management solutions company headquartered in San Francisco, California. Prior to Indus, Chris was a Development Director at Oracle.

Chris holds an Honours degree in Mathematics from the University of Bristol.

Vivian Vendeirinho: VP Alliances & Business Development

Vivian Vendeirinho joined Volantis Systems from Metrowerks Inc. (Austin, TX) where he was responsible for Global Software and DevTool Sales. During his four years with Metrowerks, revenue increased nearly three-fold. Prior to Metrowerks, Vivian led Freescale Semiconductor's European 8/16-bit Embedded Microcontroller marketing team.

Vivian relocated from South Africa where he completed a Bachelor of Science Engineering degree at the University of Pretoria.

John Koyle: Director of Information Services

Before John joined Volantis, he served as the IT Director for RFP Depot where he was responsible for migrating their production systems from in-house to an off-site collocation. Before working at RFP Depot, John was the IS Manager at Lineo, Inc., where he set up and managed the company's IT infrastructure worldwide.

John has over ten years of experience in the IT systems industry, including Big Planet/Nuskin Enterprises, and Caldera, Inc. John holds a BS degree in Networking and Data Communications from Utah Valley State College, USA.

Phillip Swan: VP Worldwide Sales and Services

Phillip is responsible for Sales and Professional Services, overseeing the globally deployed sales force and the international customer deployments. He joins us from Dexterra—a technology company working on Java and Windows to deliver existing IT applications to a distributed workforce—where he was COO. His responsibilities included global Sales, Marketing, Professional Services and Business Development.

Before that he was Microsoft's VP of Device Solution Sales managing the OEM relationships for Windows Mobile, Windows Embedded and dedicated Server solutions. He has also held executive sales positions with Telogy Networks (now a Texas Instrument company) and Wind River Systems, starting his career as a software engineer.

Phillip graduated with a BSc in Mathematics and Computer Sciences from the University of Glasgow in 1984.

Source: Volantis.

vendors. Tivoli went public in 1995 and was acquired by IBM a year later for $743 million.[9]

While still working for Tivoli in late 1999, Bursack, Gaffney, Nulf, and Watson began meeting to discuss new venture concepts. They settled upon the idea of developing a yellow pages-like directory service for mobile phones for which they could sell placements to local businesses. InfoSpace, a U.S.-based company, had already been operating a similar business, but had not yet entered the U.K. market. Watson said:

> Brett had done sales in the telecommunications sector and was the one who got us thinking about mobile devices and technologies. During one of our brainstorming sessions, he put his

mobile phone in the middle of the table and said, "This is our future. This is what we should build this company around."

We all agreed with him and decided to move forward with the Infospace-like model, even if no one was particularly blown away by our copycat idea. Simply put, we believed in ourselves and thought we could make a go of it. In Europe, there is a pattern that if you ride a certain technology wave you can get away with being a few months or even a few years behind the Americans. Oftentimes you will see that when American-based start-ups become successful, they will buy into European-based start-ups for market entry. Consequently, even though a U.K. start-up may appear a little behind on an emerging trend, they may still have a shot at a decent exit opportunity, particularly in technology businesses.

Fundraising

In March 2000, the group resigned from Tivoli, drafted a business plan, and began pitching their ideas to investors. The team also came up with a name, Volantis, which comes from the Latin root *volant*, meaning quick, nimble, or capable of flying. Watson said:

The first group of investors we met with were angel investors. Even though we had an idea for a technology that to a certain extent we thought was going to be successful in the marketplace, we were mostly pitching ourselves and our desire to start a company.

On the one hand, investors seemed eager to fund Volantis' team. In fact, the group raised a small seed round from angels and friends and family to finance the company's early days. (See Exhibit 7 for a fundraising history of the company.) On the other hand, the founders and investors alike summarily rejected Volantis' initial founding concept in short order. Watson said:

I'm not quite sure why we killed the original idea. Perhaps, it was because the market was moving and because everybody hated it. The good news was that we had struck upon a new idea: we were going to create technologies to enable companies to build web sites for all sorts of devices—smart phones, kiosks, digital televisions, gaming consoles, and, of course, mobile phones.

The technology we had in mind would have to be flexible: we wanted to be able take any company's web presence and adapt it for any device. For example, we wanted to make nike.com accessible and user-friendly for mobile phone users. In total, we believed strongly in our value proposition: our customers would be able to develop one website which could then be accessed from any device anywhere.

Investors were more enthusiastic about Volantis' *enterprise* software idea because, for one, the founders had all come from an *enterprise* software company, Tivoli. In September 2000, Volantis closed a $3.2 million series A round of financing led by Kennet Venture Partners, a venture capital firm based in London. Shortly thereafter, the team began developing its product and even assembled a small salesforce. Watson said:

In 2000, we hired four salespeople, and we put them all out in the field. All of them were experienced enterprise sales veterans from Sequent

EXHIBIT 7

Fundraising History

Series	Common	A	B	C	D	TOTAL
Date of Closing		Sep - 2000	May - 2001	Jul -2002	Jul - 2005	
Lead		Kennet	Softbank	Accel	Accel, Kennet	
Other			Kennet	Kennet		
Funds Raised	$306,000	$3,213,000	$9,493,933	$11,107,326	$7,527,834	$31,648,092
Pre-Money Valuation		$6,747,297	$22,743,242	$28,000,183	$35,000,000	
Post-Money Valuation		$9,960,297	$32,237,175	$39,107,509	$42,527,834	

Note: All rounds of financing except Series D are converted from United Kingdom pounds (£1.00:$1.53).
Source: Volantis.

Computer Systems. I would argue that it was a relatively large sales team for what we had—which was not a lot—given that we didn't have a product yet. Nevertheless, we directed them to pitch prospective clients; and in return, we got a lot of customer feedback, if very little in sales volume.

In May 2001, Volantis raised an additional $9.5 million in venture capital, led by Softbank UK Ventures and including a follow-on investment from Kennet. Even though the organization had grown to over 50 employees, including a 10-person sales team, the company had yet to generate substantial revenues. Watson said:

> We had salespeople running off in a number of directions trying to find a market for our products. One of our first customers, Boots, was an online pharmacist that wanted to integrate a website into a television network it had recently acquired. Another early customer was iMPOWER, with whom we were working to make government services accessible through a wide variety of devices such as digital television, mobile phones, PCs, and kiosks at government offices. We had also engineered a prototype for Ford Motor Company and a satellite company. You might say we had cobbled together a small and fairly disparate customer base with a scattered collection of implementations. Nevertheless, revenues were weak and we were losing money.

By July 2001, the company employed over 80 people, including a sales office based in the U.S. Then, after the collapse of the Internet bubble and the tragic events of September 11th, the overall market for technology start-ups appeared bleak. As a result, Volantis was forced to re-evaluate its sales outreach and, in the end, decided to scale back the size of its organization in two rounds of layoffs. By October 2001, the company employed 49 people and had closed down its U.S.-based sales office.

However, during the first half of 2002, Volantis began to recover from the market slowdown and found some success closing sales leads again. Only this time around, revenues appeared to be flowing in from a single industry, telecommunications. Volantis landed two large accounts, Telefonica (a global mobile operator) and 3 (formerly known as Hutchinson 3G, 3 was the U.K.'s leading 3G carrier). In March 2002, Volantis was chosen as the delivery platform for Telefonica's mobile portal, which was being developed to include the mobile operator's messaging and mobile internet services (e.g., magazine, alerts, email, chat, commerce, downloads, games, and third-party applications and content). In May 2002, 3 enlisted Volantis to enable the delivery of data—including digital content from 3's information and entertainment content partners—to its mobile phone service subscribers in a deal worth $3 million to Volantis.

Volantis' success closing deals with mobile carriers represented a somewhat unexpected shift in focus for the company from a multi-device service to a single device service. Watson said:

> We were still pitching Volantis as middleware. However, we were no longer saying that we were middleware for enterprises to project their Internet presence to a variety of devices. We were saying that we were middleware as an enabler for mobile phone carriers. In particular, we were riding the momentum of 3G, which everyone thought was going to be wildly successful. Indeed, not long after the 3 and Telefonica transactions, we became pretty narrowly focused on landing more and more carrier accounts.

Additional Financing

In July 2002, Volantis raised an additional $11.1 million of venture capital in a series C financing led by Accel Partners Europe. The $28.0 million pre-money valuation Volantis received reflected the enthusiasm and excitement in the venture community around the anticipated platform shift in the mobile landscape from a voice-only industry to one where high speed data transmissions were possible. As with any major structural change in an industry, the mobile industry's shift to 3G was thought to create opportunities for all types of innovators, including Volantis, which seemed poised to be a technology leader for the next generation of mobile companies.

By 2003, however, it was clear that Volantis' founders and investors had mis-timed the market, and revenues for the year-ended 2003 fell below those generated in 2002. (See Exhibit 8 for company income statement.) But they were not alone. Some 200 venture funded companies that were launched to address market opportunities related to 3G had gone out of business, and Volantis was one of only a handful that endured. In 2004, business picked up again, and in 2005, revenues reached $14.4 million.

Matt Harris

In April 2005, Matt Harris was named CEO of Volantis. His experience included leadership roles in

EXHIBIT 8

Volantis Income Statement, 2001–2005

	2005	2004	2003	2002	2001
Revenues	14,397,768	6,891,337	2,924,500	6,225,856	411,440
Cost of sales	(5,791,202)	(3,264,136)	(1,710,806)	(1,700,639)	(952,587)
Gross profit	8,606,566	3,627,201	1,213,693	4,525,217	(541,147)
Selling & administrative expenses	(13,635,903)	(8,880,793)	(8,817,900)	(7,633,190)	(7,917,039)
Operating loss	(5,029,337)	(5,253,592)	(7,604,207)	(3,107,973)	(8,458,186)
Other interest receivable and similar income	57,904	76,229	297,089	189,044	264,690
Interest payable and similar charges	(6,010)	(4,759)	(2,682)	(1,308)	(378)
Loss on ordinary activities before taxation	(4,977,443)	(5,182,122)	(7,309,800)	(2,920,238)	(8,193,874)
Taxation	547,089	464,635	1,085,130		
Loss on ordinary activities after taxation	(4,430,354)	(4,717,488)	(6,224,670)	(2,920,238)	(8,193,874)
Preferred share appropriation	(1,322,675)	(1,220,340)	(1,125,922)	(450,380)	
Retained loss for the year	(5,753,029)	(5,937,828)	(7,350,592)	(3,370,618)	
Exchange Rate (converted from U.K. pounds)	1.80	1.80	1.80	1.53	1.53

All figures in U.S. $ converted from U.K. pounds.

business and law. (See Exhibit 6 for his executive biography.) He had been President and CEO of two software companies and also had been a practicing attorney and founding partner of the Summit Law Group.

In July 2005, Volantis raised an additional $7.5 million, for a total of $31.6 million venture capital raised. Early or not, Volantis had its financing in place and was ready for mass adoption of mobile data services. Watson said:

> We learned that the infrastructure we had built initially for websites to be accessed by all types of devices was actually very useful for the mobile device environment where standards were scarce. Our business—which we call "intelligent content adaptation"—thrives in mobile because of its device diversity, network diversity, and general lack of standards.
>
> Our platform turned out to be flexible and very capable. We have five generations of phones in our database today. Apart from getting a sense of vindication, we actually were able to adapt to the market as it moved because it was catching up with us rather than vice versa.

Volantis Company Overview (2006)

Products

In 2006, Volantis' products consisted of two principal components: its mobile content framework and its suite of mobile content applications. (See Exhibit 9 for a diagram of Volantis' products.) The mobile content framework provided the back-end (i.e., infrastructure) technology that drove the front-end (i.e., customer-facing) applications, which included (among others):

- **Volantis Mobile Content Storefront™:** an application that enabled wireless carriers and content providers to have a mobile storefront or commerce engine.

EXHIBIT 9

Diagram of Volantis' Products

- **Volantis Mobile Content Transcoder™:** an application that converted PC websites in real-time into mobile format.
- **Volantis Mobile Content Player™:** an on-device application that provided playback of downloaded content.

Customers

In 2006, Volantis reached over 100 million consumers on over 2,100 different mobile devices, serving primarily two types of customers: wireless carriers and content providers. In 2005, its roster of 21 wireless carrier customers—which included major players like Vodaphone and T-Mobile—had accounted

for over 90 percent of its revenues. (See Exhibit 10 for a list of carrier customers.) Volantis' collection of over a dozen content provider customers—which included Yahoo!, ebay.co.uk, lastminute.com, and Reuters—accounted for most of the remainder of the company's sales.

Organization Overview

In March 2006, Volantis employed over 130 people in five offices around the world. The company's corporate headquarters and U.S. regional sales office were in Seattle, WA; its European regional sales office and engineering staff were located in London; it also ran a development office in Krakow, Poland, and Asia Pacific regional sales offices in India and Hong Kong.

EXHIBIT 10

Volantis Wireless Carrier Customer List (as of March 2006)

Operator	% of Company Revenues	Revenue/Subscriber
Customer #1	24.7%	$ 0.37
Customer #2	21.6%	$ 0.06
Customer #3	8.2%	$ 0.03
Customer #4	8.0%	$ 0.06
Customer #5	5.9%	$ 0.04
Customer #6	5.5%	$ 0.02
Customer #7	5.0%	$ 0.01
Customer #8	3.8%	$ 0.02
Customer #9	3.4%	$ 0.20
Customer #10	3.3%	$ 0.37
Customer #11	3.2%	$ 0.06
Customer #12	2.9%	$ 0.08
Customer #13	1.9%	$ 0.01
Customer #14	1.2%	$ 0.06
Customer #15	0.7%	$ 0.08
Customer #16	0.7%	$ 0.13
Customer #17	0.1%	$ 0.00
Customer #18	0.0%	$ –
Customer #19	0.0%	$ –
Customer #20	0.0%	$ –
Customer #21	0.0%	$ –
Total	**100.0%**	**$ 0.04**

Volantis was organized in a matrix structure. (See Exhibit 11 for an organization chart.) Three of the four founders (Bursack, Gaffney, and Nulf) had settled into senior operating positions, and Watson had become CTO and a board member. Additionally, the company had hired (or was hiring) a number of other senior executives to cover each of the key functional areas (marketing, finance, alliances, and worldwide sales) and business units (telecommunications, content providers (open), and new markets (open)). In total, there were nine members on the company's internal executive board.

Technology Development

Watson managed the product development, product management, engineering, research and development, and managed services functions for Volantis, supporting all of the business units (carriers, content providers, and new markets). With 82 employees, the technology organization was by far the largest in the company. With the exception of the group of engineers based in Poland (a cost-saving measure), most technology employees were based in London. Watson said:

> We have a layered architecture, whereby each layer has its own set of characteristics and is developed separately. Therefore, our development teams are organized by layer, one group per layer, where each one knows the principles along which that layer must work. By working in accordance with those principles, our developers know that their layer will work with the other layers in a well organized way.
>
> Our philosophy of development builds a lot of automation into the system, where one dial controls

EXHIBIT 11

Organization Chart (as of March 2006)

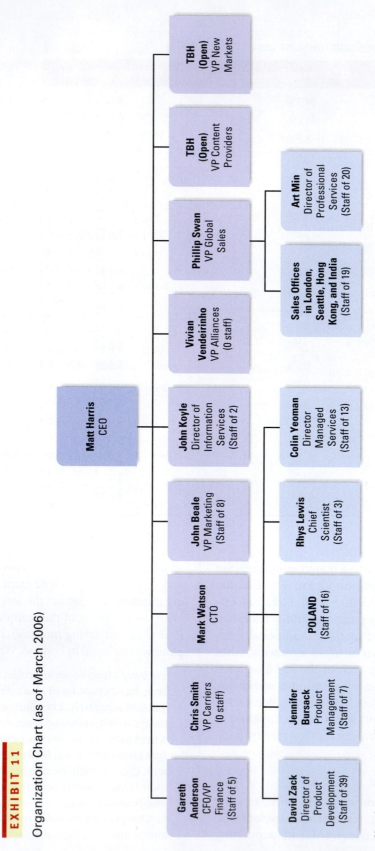

Note: In some cases, staff totals include personnel to be hired.

a bunch of other dials that controls a bunch of other dials. In other words, fine-tuning on one dial can cause a lot of different things to happen. Consequently, we have an extremely powerful system in which one person can build a site that will automatically adapt to the thousands of mobile devices and still adhere to site's design intention.

The database stored over 500 attributes on over 2,500 devices, and more were added each week. Bursack said:

We're adding at least 30 devices a week. We do that via a combination of testing the physical devices if we have them and then researching on the Internet for additional information. If we don't have the physical device, we try to find a device that we've already tested and make a best guess decision on which attributes apply. We've got three people working full-time to add new devices to our database, and we're looking to extend that by at least two more people as soon as we can find them. As we extend our business into more service offerings and as we extend into more regions, we end up having to play catch-up to keep pace with the new device launches.

We collect over 500 attributes per device and that number will grow because we are increasingly getting our information from our customers. As a result, it's actually a lot easier for us to add data than it used to be. All in all, I'd say we're fairly efficient doing our device research.

Carriers Business Unit

Chris Smith was VP/GM of carriers business unit, and he had no direct reports. He set the strategic direction for the business and was supported by each of the key functions (e.g., sales, marketing, and technology). Smith maintained an especially close relationship with the sales organization because it was responsible for sourcing and closing deals with the carriers.

In early 2006, Volantis' sales organization was run by Phillip Swan, VP of global sales, and included 39 additional personnel (when fully staffed). The company's U.S. and Latin America regional sales office based in Seattle, WA included five sales personnel and five technical support staff when fully staffed; its European regional sales office based in London included five sales personnel and six technical support staff when fully staffed; its Asia Pacific regional sales office in India included one sales account executive, and its Hong Kong office included one sales account executive and two technical support staff.

Volantis employed a traditional software sales model with most of its carrier customers like Huntington 3G: it sold licenses for the Volantis software, plus professional services for integration, plus support. In 2005, revenues were distributed as follows: 60 percent for software license fees, 25 percent for professional services, and 15 percent for support. Swan said:

Our ability to grow as a business relies on a couple of key factors. First, we must have every sales person, every region operating efficiently, which is a function of hiring the right people. Second, we must ensure that we have a core discipline, not processes for the sake of bureaucracy. We need discipline in how we forecast our business and in how we qualify opportunities. But make no mistake, this is all about execution. The mode We're in right now is execute, execute, execute, and if we don't execute, we will fail, and somebody else will come and take the place.

Indeed, the carrier business was the revenue engine for the company, and Volantis needed to rapidly accelerate its top-line growth to achieve profitability. The biggest opportunity, and the biggest challenge, facing both Smith and Swan was the Asia Pacific market, in China, Korea, India, and Japan more specifically. Even though Volantis had two small sales offices in Asia Pacific, it had yet to secure a meaningful revenue stream out of the region.

There were several challenges Volantis would have to overcome to penetrate the Asia Pacific market. First, sales cycles with the carriers were always long, and even more so in Asia where Volantis would be a newcomer. Swan said:

The trouble with middleware is that it is middleware. Your sales process and time to revenue is elongated by the fact that, by the time that your customers deploy your product, you're part of a larger system or implementation. For the most part, your opportunity to generate revenue is rarely in the near term. Sales cycles with telcos can be as short as like six to nine months or as long as 36 months. There's no such thing as turning a telco in 30 or 60 days to make a decision. These are large bureaucracies that are very cognizant of their brand, and with middleware, especially, they want to be able to control their brand.

Second, insofar as Volantis had been ahead of the market elsewhere, it was a laggard in Asia and had formidable competition. In addition, the infrastructure it had built out in Europe (including relationships with systems integrators and consultants) would take time to establish in Asia. Third, the size of the carrier customer had not historically correlated with the size of the revenue return to Volantis. (See Exhibit 10 for revenue per subscriber statistics.) Finally, entering the market required some additional fixed and variable investments beyond that of simply adding sales personnel on the ground. The Volantis solution would have to be modified to accommodate local requirements. Nevertheless, it was an enticing opportunity, and Smith and Swan would have to develop a market entry strategy.

Content Provider Business Unit

In early 2006, content providers of all kinds—media and entertainment companies, government and financial services companies, and online businesses—were developing strategies for adapting their content for mobile platforms. Companies were looking for solutions to ensure that their mobile experience approached the quality of their PC-based offering. In fact, Volantis had a deep backlog of leads from companies that had inquired about its services. Harris said:

> We heard from a number of content providers that they needed to get into the mobile space because they had learned from the Internet boom that everyone else was going do it eventually. Most of them told us that they didn't want to be left behind because with close to two billion people on mobile phones, everyone knows there will be opportunities in wireless.

For such customers, Volantis provided a suite of tools that enabled existing content sources such as websites, content management systems, and internal XML formats to be repurposed and optimized for delivery to mobile handsets. One such tool, the Volantis Mobile Content Transcoder, converted PC webpages into mobile format, with presentation optimized for each device. The tool was used to convert over 85 percent of Yahoo's 3,000 most commonly searched websites. In addition, Volantis' service had converted cnn.com and discoverychannel.com for easy access by mobile devices.

On the one hand, these accounts brought credibility and marketing value to Volantis. On the other hand, the larger the brand, the more competition

there was for the business and the higher the cost of customer acquisition. Further, these accounts were not generating a ton of revenue because, for one, Volantis was struggling to craft a compelling business model for that segment. Harris said:

> Clearly, there is value to a start-up in doing business with some of the most well-known brands in the world that goes beyond the revenues they generate. Sure it's been a low margin business for us and there's lots of competition. But eBay, Disney, and Discovery Channel are accounts that have an emotional attachment to them. If this were a pure economic discussion, it would be a lot easier to figure out.

Volantis employed a three-part sales model with most of its content provider clients. Harris said:

> Trying to find the right business model in a concept market has probably been more painful than trying to find the right technology solution. Our fees to our content provider customers consist of three parts: 1) a managed service fee, 2) a software rental fee, and 3) a revenue share. Our model is still evolving, but at scale, it can be very profitable for us.

Meanwhile, Volantis had uncovered a new potential business opportunity.

Self-Provisioned Internet Service

As early as 2003, when content providers had begun to come out of the recession and were investigating the mobile opportunity, Volantis executives were discussing the idea of a self-provisioned Internet service. The central premise was that the company's technology for adapting websites to mobile could be directed at the billions of websites that needed a mobile presence through a self-serve model. Small businesses, content owners, and web developers could come to Volantis' website and download its application to adapt their offering for mobile. Watson said:

> We have a product that we sold to Yahoo! which is a "transcoding" product, and it basically goes to PC sites and converts them through our rendering system to work on phones, taking full advantage of our underlying technology engines. We think we have the basis of a tool that would allow any mom and pop Internet site, any blogger, any type of content owner, and—with our storefront tool—any e-commerce site, to get up and running as a mobile site within 15 minutes.

The business model for such a product is a little less clear. There is a general view that if you can kick-start the mobile Internet with sufficient content then it will become compelling, and it will start to generate its own monetization models in the same way that the Internet has. Accordingly, the default business models we're looking at are: free entry for any company to create a site and then an Internet Service Provider-type business model for additional features. For example, we might charge for additional bandwidth.

Naturally, Volantis' management was attracted to the scale of the opportunity. However, without a clear business model, Harris was concerned that Volantis would repeat its past mistakes and get trapped selling the wrong package of services. On the one hand, Volantis' investors had proven that they were patient: Kennet, for example, had invested in the series A, B, C, and D rounds. On the other hand, the company was burning cash at a rate of over $400,000 every month. Harris said:

> There is no question that the self-provisioned Internet service is a huge opportunity. I just don't know how we can support both the new business and our traditional software licensing model in the same company, or even if we should do it at all? Perhaps, we should sell the opportunity to another company? If we do build it in-house, however, I am not sure how we should organize the company because the traditional side of the business—in development and in sales—won't adapt to the self-provisioned Internet model.

Watson added:

> Once again, we have found ourselves at the immature end of an immature market. To a certain extent, we would like to be able to build a detailed go-to-market strategy, set a budget, hire the appropriate resources, and get off to the races. On the other hand, it has been my experience that you can't over-plan these things. You have to basically address it with a degree of Internet instinct. The main thing you have to plan, I think, is agility.

Allocating Resources

The widespread adoption of mobile data services would certainly be a catalyst for Volantis' business, and there was no shortage of opportunities for the company to explore. The challenge for Harris was to select which markets to pursue and how to appropriately allocate and organize his resources. In a perfect world, he would love to invest in each of Volantis' compelling business opportunities. However, the board was eager to see Harris make inroads towards profitability in 2006. Consequently, he had a number of key decisions to make.

First, he needed to decide whether or not to fill two senior management positions. His 2006 organization plan had openings for VPs to run his new markets and content provider business units. The new markets VP would be enlisted to assess the market potential of: 1) selling to enterprises (i.e., would, say, McKinsey be interested in adapting its internal web content for its consultants to access from a mobile device?); 2) adapting video content for mobile, and 3) selling to new geographies. The content provider VP would be enlisted to: 1) refine the company's business model to ensure Volantis could extract enough financial value out of its roster of big brand name accounts; 2) determine how to proceed with its backlog of leads, and 3) craft a target list of strategic leads to Swan.

Second, he needed to decide whether or not to enter the Asia Pacific market. If so, he needed to determine how he and Swan should work to reallocate resources to capitalize on the opportunity. Finally, he needed to give Watson a go or no-go decision on the self-provisioned Internet business. If his decision was "go," then Watson would need to develop a new organization plan for his technology division and a new product roadmap to support the new service offering. All in all, for Volantis and its intelligent content adaptation service, widespread adoption of mobile data services could not happen fast enough.

ENDNOTES

1. The terms "mobile" and "wireless" are used interchangeably herein and mean the same thing. Similarly, the terms "operator," "carrier," and "telco" are also used interchangeably.
2. "The 2006 Telecommunications Industry Review," *Insight Research Corporation*, January 2006.
3. Nelson Wang, "Industry Surveys, Telecommunications: Wireless Asia," *Standard & Poor's*, January 2006.
4. Nelson Wang, "Industry Surveys, Telecommunications: Wireless Latin America," *Standard & Poor's*, November 2005.
5. Nelson Wang, "Industry Surveys, Telecommunications: Wireless Asia," *Standard & Poor's*, January 2006.
6. Kenneth Leon and Nelson Wang, "Industry Surveys, Telecommunications: Wireless," *Standard & Poor's*, November 3, 2005.
7. "3G Worldwide Subscribers," *eMarketer*, February 2006.
8. Nelson Wang, "Industry Surveys, Telecommunications: Wireless Europe," *Standard & Poor's*, January 2006.
9. Jim Duffy and Michael Cooney, "IBM Drops $743M on Management Makeover," *Network World*, February 5, 1996.

Infosys Consulting in 2006: Leading the Next Generation of Business and Information Technology Consulting

This case was prepared by Aneesha Capur under the supervision of Professor Robert A. Burgelman, Stanford Graduate School of Business.

There is no doubt in my mind that five years from now, the Infosys Consulting model will be the standard way of doing things where technology development is done off-site. We are one of the fastest growing IT consulting firms in the world. Our major bottlenecks right now are convincing clients to break with old habits and take a chance on a new, better model and recruiting the right people—top tier talent who understand our innovative approach and fit into our unique culture.

—*Steve Pratt, CEO, Infosys Consulting*

In January 2006, the five managing partners of Infosys Consulting (ICI), also known to the leadership of ICI's parent company Infosys Technologies as "the dream team," congregated at the St. Regis resort in Orange County, California for their first team meeting of the year. CEO and managing director Steve Pratt, COO and managing director Paul Cole, managing director Romil Bahl, managing director and founder Raj Joshi, and managing director Ming Tsai (see Exhibit 1 for management bios) were all proud of how much the company had achieved since its inception in April 2004 as a wholly owned U.S. subsidiary of Infosys Technologies. The firm had more than 100 consulting engagements and had grown from its inception in April 2004 to over 200 employees in January 2006, achieving its two year recruiting target. It was also on plan for both its own revenue target and its target contribution to Infosys Technologies' revenue through the third quarter of its second year of existence. Moreover, ICI's managing partners were confident that the subsidiary had contributed to Infosys Technologies' ranking in *Wired* magazine's Top Ten Company list in May 2005

and high ratings from analysts in 2004 and 2005 (see Exhibit 2).

However, the five managing partners saw several challenges ahead for ICI. Driven by Infosys Technologies' COO Kris Gopalakrishnan's edict to "compete with the best," the team aspired to be ranked alongside IBM and Accenture, leaders in the business and information technology consulting industry (see Exhibit 3 for company rankings). They also faced internal challenges of leveraging Infosys Technologies, interfacing productively with the parent company and managing growth as they built the organization. In addition, each managing partner was committed to "changing the rules of the game within the consulting industry" in the founding partner Raj Joshi's words. By applying Infosys Technologies' approach to global delivery, the leadership team at ICI believed the firm had created a unique model in business and information technology consulting that shortened the lifecycle from business consulting to technology implementation, reduced the costs of a typical client engagement and delivered measurable benefits to clients.

Flashback to April 2004: The Inception of Infosys Consulting

The evolution of global Information Technology (IT) service companies in India began in the 1990s with the procurement of application development

EXHIBIT 1

Executive Bios of ICI Managing Partners

Steve Pratt, Chief Executive Officer and Managing Director

With over 20 years of experience in business consulting, Pratt had an established track record of growing innovative consulting practices that excelled at client service. Prior to joining Infosys Consulting, Pratt was a partner with Deloitte Consulting and co-founder of the Deloitte CRM practice.

As a founder, CEO and managing director of Infosys Consulting, Pratt fundamentally transformed the consulting industry. He created a new brand of consulting firm—one that takes innovative approaches to delivering more competitive operations, with less risk, at an overall lower cost for its clients.

Pratt was nominated as one of the Top 25 Consultants in the World in 2003 and 2005 in *Consulting Magazine* and has helped several Fortune 500 companies.

His primary areas of expertise included helping clients improve the value of their relationships with customers, and helping them become more competitive. In a survey of Siebel systems customers, clients consistently rated Pratt as #1 in Customer Satisfaction.

As co-founder (with Bo Manning, now CEO of Pivotal Software) of the Deloitte CRM practice, from 1995 to 2002, Pratt grew the practice to over 3,000 people and over $750M in revenue.

Pratt was frequently published on the topics of Customer Strategy, CRM and Web-based Sales and Service. He received Bachelors and Masters Degrees in Electrical Engineering.

Paul Cole, Chief Operating Officer and Managing Director

As a founder and managing director of Infosys Consulting, Cole was responsible for all sales and operations. With over 25 years of experience in consulting and Information Technology, Cole provided IT consulting services to some of the world's largest companies.

Cole had extensive experience in customer relationship management and was the global leader for the DRM service line at Cap Gemini Ernst & Young. He was responsible for a $1B CRM practice at Cap Gemini and is a noted industry expert in the field. He also managed the mobilization and implementation of a three year company-wide transformation effort, which accomplished significant operating performance improvements. He was also a vice president with Mercer Management Consulting.

Throughout his career in IT consulting, Cole served global Fortune 500 clients across several industries. He has managed major consulting engagements for clients such as Lloyds TSB, Hewlett-Packard, Scottish Enterprises, SBC Communications, Walt Disney World, IBM, Texas Instruments, and GTE.

Cole received a Bachelor of Science in Marketing-Management from Bentley College

Romil Bahl, Managing Director

With more than 15 years experience helping clients with business/e-business strategies, strategic technology direction and large-scale technology-enabled transformations, Bahl led the Industry Practices and Service Offering portfolio for the firm. Specifically, Bahl led the firm's Business/IT Strategy areas including Business Alignment, Next Generation IT and Portfolio Assessment using the firm's Competitive Advantage framework.

Bahl spent over eight years at A.T.Kearney/EDS, with his last role as the leader of EDS' 6,000 person Consulting Services unit. He specialized in strategic planning, new business incubation and launch.

In addition to his EDS Consulting Services experience, Bahl's previous roles included leader of A.T. Kearney's European Strategic Technology and Transformation Practice, based in London. Prior to that he worked with Deloitte Consulting and led the Southwest region's Strategic Information Systems Planning team.

Bahl received an MBA with a specialization in Information Systems Management from the University of Texas at Austin and a Bachelor of Engineering from DMET, India.

Raj Joshi, Managing Director

As a founder and managing director of Infosys Consulting, Joshi had responsibility for developing and building the Enterprise Solutions and IT Strategy practices of the company. He was also architect of the firm's Value Realization Model—a new approach that guides technology-enabled business transformation engagements while delivering measurable business value.

(*continued*)

EXHIBIT 1   (continued)

Executive Bios of ICI Managing Partners

Joshi had extensive experience in Information Technology consulting services and has delivered client engagements that have spanned the entire systems development life cycle. Joshi managed projects in IT strategy, business transformation, ERP implementations, custom applications development, ADM outsourcing and offshore development and maintenance.

Joshi also delivered projects that included aspects of business strategy, business process reengineering, change management and organizational design along-with IT elements.

Prior to joining Infosys Consulting, Joshi was a partner with the U.S. practice of Deloitte Consulting where he held a number of leadership positions. He founded Deloitte Offshore in India and was the CEO of this entity for more than three years. He played a key role in structuring and managing client relationships that leveraged the offshore delivery model. Some of his other roles included managing global alliances and leading the IT practice for one of Deloitte's geographical regions.

Throughout his career in IT consulting, Joshi served global Fortune 500 clients across several industries. He managed major consulting engagements for clients such as AT&T, Agilent, Alcatel, BP, DHL, Fujitsu, General Motors, Hewlett-Packard, Honeywell, NEC, Nokia, Sun, Texas Instruments and Toshiba.

Joshi received an MBA from the University of Texas at Arlington and also received Masters and Bachelors degrees in Chemical Engineering.

Ming Tsai, Managing Director

With more than 21 years of management consulting experience, Tsai had overall responsibility for a number of industry groups at Infosys, including Retail and Consumer Products, High Technology and Discrete Manufacturing and Aerospace and Automotive. He also had overall responsibility for the professional development of employees.

Tsai focused on business strategy development, business transformation and process re-engineering, customer relationship and loyalty management, and e-commerce. His clients included Wal-Mart, Target, CVS, Royal Ahold, Walgreens, Sears, Boots, Metro, PepsiCo, Kraft Foods, Miller Brewing, Coca-Cola, P&G, American Express, AT&T, McGraw-Hill, Microsoft and Xerox.

Prior to Infosys, Tsai was with IBM Business Consulting Services where he held several leadership positions, including the Global Leader of the Retail Industry, where he had overall responsibility for driving IBM's retail business. Prior to that role, Tsai was the strategy consulting leader for the Distribution Sector (CPG, Retail and Travel & Transportation), where he had cross-industry responsibility for IBM's strategy consulting practice. Tsai joined IBM when it acquired Mainspring, an e-business strategy consulting firm in June of 2001.

Prior to joining Mainspring, Tsai was a partner at Ernst & Young where he was a co-leader of the eCommerce Strategy practice in North America. Earlier, Tsai was a senior manager with The Boston Consulting Group and a senior consultant with Arthur Andersen & Co.'s Management Information Consulting Division (which later became Accenture).

Tsai received an MBA with honors from Columbia Business School where he was elected to the Beta Gamma Sigma National Honor Society and awarded the Benjamin E. Hermann prize for Marketing Excellence. He also received a Bachelor of Science in Mechanical Engineering from Yale University.

Source: Infosys Consulting.

and maintenance services by American companies. Business Process Outsourcing (BPO) work in India was largely conducted by captive units, for example, companies like General Electric would perform BPO through subsidiaries in India rather than work with third party companies like Infosys Technologies. From 1993 through 1999, as U.S. firms gained confidence in working with Indian companies and wanted to leverage the benefits of offshoring services by taking advantage of high quality services at lower price points, Indian companies like Infosys Technologies started expanding their footprint by adding service lines.

One of Infosys Technologies' main objectives was to increase revenue through repeat business with the company's client base. To that end, Infosys Technologies offered clients new opportunities to work with the company. Infosys Technologies expanded its service offering to include package implementation (e.g., SAP's enterprise resource planning software), R&D,

EXHIBIT 2

Company Ranking and Analyst Commentary

The Wired 40—

"They're masters of technology and innovation. They're global thinkers driven by strategic vision. They're nimbler than Martha Stewart's PR team. They're The Wired 40."

Wired magazine, May 2005

1. Apple Computer
2. Google
3. Samsung Electronics
4. Amazon.com
5. Yahoo!
6. Electronic Arts
7. Genentech
8. Toyota
9. **Infosys Technologies**
10. eBay

"Infosys Leads the Pack"

Forrester Research, December 2005

● Infosys is most able to compete with both the former Big Five firms for business process consulting work and the tier-one Indian vendors for follow-on technical work. Prior to the formation of Infosys Consulting, Infosys, like other tier-one vendors, had strong technical consulting capabilities managed through horizontal or vertical groups. . . . Infosys Consulting represents Infosys' renewed commitment to business process consulting capability in its effort to be taken seriously as a global consulting and IT services firm.

"India Shows the Way to Next-Generation Consulting"

AMR—Lance Travis & Dana Stiffler, April 8, 2004

● The traditional consulting model is dead. The next-generation consulting model combines global delivery that capitalizes on low-cost resources with high-quality strategic consulting.
● Business consulting linked to Infosys' existing low-cost, process-centric delivery expertise offers companies a new, high-value type of strategic consulting partner.

"Infosys Looks to Local Talent for U.S. Consulting Business"

Gartner—Fran Karamouzis, April 13, 2004

● First Take: The creation of a U.S.-based consulting company is a major step forward in Infosys' long-term strategy of presenting itself as a global service provider. Infosys' $20 million investment in this subsidiary is designed to send a clear signal to the marketplace that Infosys is differentiating itself from its Indian competitors, and intends to compete for business consulting services with the traditional consultancies.
● Gartner believes many more offshore IT service providers will follow Infosys' lead. By the end of 2004, a number of offshore firms will seek to emulate the strategy of delivering a domestic consulting offering within the U.S. enterprise market (0.7 probability).

Source: Information compiled from Infosys Consulting.

infrastructure management, system integration, testing as a service, and BPO. As the company's menu of services expanded, its client relationships became more complex. Infosys Technologies started working with the business side of client organizations as well as the IT side in order to manage these complex organizations. Infosys Technologies saw the opportunity to enter a client relationship earlier in the lifecycle to define problems, identify solutions and then implement a solution as a natural evolution of their service offering. In 1999, Infosys Technologies, which then had approximately 3,700 employees and annual revenue of approximately $120 million, decided to initiate an in-house consulting business unit. However, the company's success in consulting was constrained due to its limited brand equity, investment allocation and recruiting abilities.

Raj Joshi, who drove Deloitte Consulting's recruiting in India in the late 1990s and then became the founder and CEO of Deloitte's Offshore Technology

EXHIBIT 3

Largest Computer and Internet Consulting Companies (rank based on sales; in thousands of U.S. dollars)

Rank	Company	2005 Sales (000s)	2004 Sales (000s)
1	INTERNATIONAL BUSINESS MACHINES (IBM)	$91,134,000[1]	$96,503,000
2	ELECTRONIC DATA SYSTEMS CORP (EDS)	$19,757,000[2]	$19,863,000
3	ACCENTURE	$17,094,400	$15,113,582
4	COMPUTER SCIENCES CORPORATION (CSC)	$14,058,600[3]	$14,767,600
5	CAPGEMINI	$8,305,300	$8,128,161
6	SCIENCE APPLICATIONS INTERNATIONAL CORP (SAIC)	$7,187,000	$6,720,000
7	ATOS ORIGIN SA	$6,519,790	$6,332,280
8	UNISYS CORP	$5,758,700	$5,820,700
9	AFFILIATED COMPUTER SERVICES INC	$4,351,159	$4,106,393
10	CGI GROUP INC	$3,173,600	$2,574,500
11	WIPRO LTD	$1,863,000	$1,349,800
13	**INFOSYS TECHNOLOGIES LTD**	**$1,592,000**	**$1,062,600**
NA	TATA CONSULTANCY SERVICES	NA	$1,614,000

[1] 2005 Sales from IBM's Global Services business segment were $47.4 billion.

[2] 2005 Sales from EDS' BPO services were $2.8 billion. During 2005, EDS approved a plan to sell 100 percent of its ownership interest in its A.T. Kearney management consulting business. That subsidiary, the sale of which was completed on January 20, 2006, is classified as "held for sale" in December 2005 and 2004 and its results for the years ended December 31, 2005, 2004 and 2003 are included in income (loss) from discontinued operations.

[3] 2005 Sales from CSC's IT & Professional Services business segment were $7.0 billion.

Note: Per the footnotes referenced above, with the exception of IBM and Accenture, the highest ranked companies derive sales from IT implementation services rather than Business and Information Technology consulting.

Source: Total Sales data from Plunkett Research Ltd. www.plunkettresearch.com; Segment Sales data from company annual reports.

Group in India in 2001, approached Kris Gopalakrishnan, the COO of Infosys Technologies, a few times (from 1997 to 2001) to initiate an alliance between the two firms. As Gopalakrishnan explained, a long-term partnership was not something Infosys Technologies was willing to consider:

> Our belief was that if we subcontracted to somebody else then the Infosys brand would get diluted. Consulting drives downstream work and our objective was to have control of the client account, and so a partnership was really not something we were looking for. We have always believed that joint ventures have very limited life or limited validity when you start competing with one of the partners, as there is an overlap of business with one of the partners, or the long-term objectives of either one of those partners is in conflict with objectives of the joint venture. So, there could have been opportunities for partnering on a project-by-project basis, but there was no way we could see a long-term partnership opportunity with any company because Infosys wanted to be in that space ultimately, and so it would have been in conflict with the long-term objectives of the company.

Raj Joshi started working with Steve Pratt, who had grown Deloitte's Customer Relationship Management practice from scratch to $750 million, to leverage the offshore model at Deloitte Consulting in 2003. The two had often discussed the concept of a new consulting model and considered Infosys Technologies a great potential partner.

By 2004, Infosys Technologies was a billion dollar company with an employee base of 25,000 and had established stronger brand equity. The firm decided to further develop its consulting practice. As the CEO of Infosys Technologies, Nandan Nilekani, explained:

> We believed that the IT services space was going through disruptive change and saw a new way of delivery by applying our Global Delivery Model into this space. We had a vision to create the next generation IT services company by combining our great reputation for business execution with consulting services.

Infosys Technologies' options for investing in its consulting offering included making an acquisition and organically growing the business. Since Infosys Technologies wanted to establish a new model in the consulting space, the firm decided against an acquisition. The company also realized from past experience that organically growing the business would limit its ability to attract the right kind of talent for consulting. Infosys Technologies decided to create a hybrid model by setting up a U.S.-based, wholly owned subsidiary.

Both Joshi and Pratt were interested in Infosys Technologies' idea to start a U.S.-based subsidiary, and recruited a team to lead the consulting subsidiary. With the leadership team in place in April 2004,[1] the firm set out to build the consulting organization. The five partners had not been given a business plan; they were only asked what they could achieve with a new consulting business. They set themselves aggressive targets. One was to reach 500 consultants in three years. Infosys Technologies invested $20 million in the consulting subsidiary.

2006: Overview of the Information Technology (IT) Services Industry

The market for IT services was large and growing. IDC, a provider of market intelligence for the IT industry, anticipated that overall spending on worldwide IT services would grow at a 7 percent compound annual rate through 2009, reaching $803.9 billion, from $524 billion in 2003. Forrester Research Inc., a technology research firm, projected IT consulting growing 5 percent compounded annually over the next five years. Apart from the two largest players—IBM and Accenture—who still had a relatively small share of the industry, the market for business and IT consulting was fragmented.

As the concept of global delivery achieved success, firms looked to third-party vendors to provide end-to-end services from business consulting to applications development and implementation, infrastructure management and BPO, using this model. Two different approaches to leveraging global delivery emerged in the marketplace: onshore U.S.-based firms such as IBM and Accenture leveraged offshore centers for development and implementation aspects of the value chain while offshore firms in India including Tata Consultancy Services (TCS) and Wipro Technologies (Wipro)—in addition to Infosys Technologies—started offering higher-end consulting services.

TCS, Infosys Technologies and Wipro generated combined service revenues of $4.5 billion in 2004, up 47 percent from 2003.[2] Their market share, however, remained small: a combined 0.8 percent of the total worldwide services market. If growth for these players continued at 20 percent to 30 percent annually, their combined market share could increase to 1.7 percent in five years.[3]

Competition from Indian companies caused Accenture to increase the size of its work force in India from less than 5,000 in 2003 to more than 11,000 in 2004. In 2006, Accenture had 18,000 workers in India and planned to reach 34,000 in a few years. IBM also added 6,000 employees to its Indian workforce through its April 2004 acquisition of Daksh eServices, a BPO firm and call center vendor, and launched a new Global Business Solution Center in Bangalore, India, in 2006 which expanded its presence there to over 38,500 employees.

As more global IT services companies built up a presence in India, prices and wages increased. At the end of 2004, Infosys Technologies and Wipro raised the wages of their midlevel workers between 15 percent and 20 percent to combat the threat of attrition (which remained between 10 percent and 15 percent). Indian firms also introduced stock-based compensation to boost productivity in the face of increased competition.[4]

Both Indian and U.S. IT companies also focused on building a presence throughout emerging markets such as China, Malaysia, Brazil and Eastern Europe, in addition to India.

Onshore (U.S.-Based) Leading Players

IBM Business Consulting Services IBM, one of the largest and most well established IT companies, had a large global presence with significant depth and breadth of skills and services. The company's major operations comprised a Global Services segment (which included Business Consulting Services), a Systems and Technology Group, a Personal Systems Group, a Software segment, a Global Financing segment, and an Enterprises Investments segment. IBM leveraged global delivery through hub-based strategic centers: the firm had three primary offshore hubs in India, Brazil and China that offered significant scale in application services and channeled offshore work to secondary locations in Mexico, Belarus, the Philippines, Romania and Argentina that offered smaller-scale operations with critical skill sets.

IBM had a very strong global brand, a large global client base, and global presence in client and offshore markets. The firm had established a successful record of offshoring application maintenance services through its presence in China for more than 15 years. Ming Tsai, who was an early leader of Mainspring and then became a global leader in IBM's Business Consulting Services after the company acquired Mainspring, pointed to the strengths and challenges associated with a company the size of IBM:

Along with IBM's great support network came a lot of baggage, as you can imagine. Because IBM's business was hardware, software and services, IBM had literally armies of people inside the big accounts. So you had to tread very carefully if you were trying to introduce a piece of services work because it could, in theory, put at risk the very lucrative software deal license or a perpetual hardware deal. But IBM's support network was, fortunately, everywhere also. If you had a point of view or a message or a product or an offering that you wanted to get out to lots of companies, you could do so very quickly. The marketing, the PR and the apparatus that IBM had were pervasive.

Given the scale of its global operations, IBM faced challenges with integrating its global delivery approach across all its practices and complexity in using appropriate sales channels to drive work to its global delivery in some markets. Ming Tsai believed that IBM operated more like a multinational company rather than a global company[5] and pointed to hurdles and inefficiencies he faced as a global leader at IBM when he tried to move a partner from Australia to London—a process which ended up taking over a year.

The firm also had potential conflicts with its business consulting services and custom application product offerings, especially when competing against "pure play" business consulting competitors. Ming Tsai described IBM's challenge with regard to delivering objective advice:

At Infosys, we provide services and we don't take over and run people's data centers and we don't sell various pieces of software—in that respect it actually makes it easier to coordinate and to deliver a message that's pure. It's easier both to claim and certainly deliver an objective perspective because we're never accused of recommending something just to sell additional software or hardware. At IBM you got questioned about that all the time: were we simply telling a client to do something because it would tee up a big software sell? So I think that's a real challenge, although I think the services part of IBM is so distinct from hardware and software that the issue didn't really materialize in all practical purposes. But it exists in the client's mind. So we had to carefully manage the perception at times.

For the fiscal year ended December 31, 2005, IBM's revenues decreased 5 percent to $91.13 billion and net income from continued operations increased 7 percent to $7.99 billion. Revenues reflected the impact of the firm's divestment of its PC business. For this period, net income was impacted by an increase in gross profit margins, a decrease in research and development expense and significant increases in other income.

IBM's Business Consulting Services had 60,000 business consultants worldwide. In addition, IBM had approximately 50,000 people located in its offshore centers. The offshore resources were shared across its business units; however, the firm had started to build industry expertise in some of its offshore locations.

Accenture Accenture, a management consulting, technology services and outsourcing organization headquartered in New York, had more than 110 offices in 48 countries including service operations in India, the Philippines, Spain, China, the Czech Republic, Slovakia, Brazil and Australia. The company's business was structured around five operating groups which comprised 17 industry groups serving clients across the world. The company's offerings included discrete project services and long-term outsourcing work for ongoing maintenance and management. Accenture's business consulting services included strategy and business architecture, customer relationship management, finance and performance management, human performance, learning, procurement and supply chain management. Accenture's services spanned all phases of application services including the design, development, implementation and ongoing support of custom or packaged, new and established applications.

Accenture demonstrated world–class industry and process depth on front-end projects while maintaining low-cost destinations globally, beyond India.[6] The firm had longstanding client relationships, a strong brand, depth and breadth of expertise and capital resources. However, although Accenture achieved relative parity on offshore price points, the firm had yet to fully leverage global delivery in terms of process, methods and tools, as well as cost.[7]

For the three months ended November 30, 2005, Accenture's revenues increased 12 percent to $4.54 billion and net income rose 10 percent to $214.9 million. Revenues reflected increased income from Communications and High Tech divisions, growth in the Insurance and Banking industry groups globally and increasing outsourcing revenues in the United States. For this period, net income was affected by increased cost of services and higher sales and marketing expenses. For the fiscal year ending August 31, 2005, sales were $17.09 billion and net income was $940 million.

Accenture had more than 126,000 employees worldwide. The firm had approximately 17,000 people in its global delivery center network which was comprised of more than 40 global delivery centers worldwide that provided technology and outsourcing services.

Offshore (Indian) Leading Players

Indian IT service providers offered two distinct types of consulting services: technical consulting and business consulting. While most Indian firms extended their strong technical capabilities to offering strong technical consulting services, their business consulting strategy and capabilities varied as the skills required for this offering—identification and assessment of strategic issues, an onsite presence, an understanding of the client's local culture and market, domain expertise—were different from their core capabilities.

Unlike Infosys Technologies' approach to creating a wholly owned U.S.-based consulting subsidiary, other Indian IT service providers' consulting operations were managed through their technology businesses.

Tata Consultancy Services (TCS) TCS, headquartered in Mumbai, India and a subsidiary of the Tata Group, was the largest offshore IT service provider in India. TCS commenced operations in 1968 and had leveraged the offshore model for more than 30 years. TCS had global service delivery locations in Hungary, Brazil, Uruguay and China. TCS offered consulting services, IT services, asset-based solutions (e.g., proprietary FIG and Quartz^{TM} software for the banking and financial services industry), IT infrastructure (e.g., complete outsourcing of IT networks), engineering and industrial services and BPO. TCS went public in 2004.

TCS had performed consulting work on an adhoc, opportunistic basis for many years, but only recently established a consulting strategy and created a Global Consulting business unit in 2004. In 2005, TCS brought in Per Bragee, former Skandia CIO and Ernst & Young CEO for Sweden to develop and manage a TCS Global Consulting practice.

Tata Group, made up of 90 companies ranging from steel and automobiles to IT services, had worldwide revenues of $17.8 billion for the 2005 fiscal year. The company accounted for three percent of India's GDP.

TCS had 34,000 employees and a presence in 34 countries across six continents.

Wipro Technologies (Wipro) Wipro, the third largest Indian application services provider, had a range of IT services, software solutions, IT consulting, BPO, and research and development services in the areas of hardware and software design. Wipro was part of Wipro Limited, which had three business segments: Wipro Technologies, the Global IT Services and Products business segment, which provided IT services to customers in the Americas, Europe and Japan; India and AsiaPac IT Services and Products which focused on meeting the IT products and service requirements of companies in India, Asia-Pacific and the Middle East region; and Customer Care and Lighting which offered soaps, toiletries and lighting products for the market in India. Wipro had a strong market presence in the United States and significant European representation. In addition to organic growth, Wipro made a series of strategic acquisitions such as SpectraMind in BPO, and American Management Systems' (AMS) utility practice and NerveWire in business consulting, to develop emerging market opportunities. Wipro, based in Bangalore, India, had a global service delivery operation in China.

At 225 consultants in 2005, Wipro's high-end business consulting arm, WCS, was comprised of the assets from two acquisitions: NerveWire and AMS' utility practice. Its technical consulting staff, an additional 1,000 resources, was spread throughout Wipro in different horizontal and vertical practices. The firm hired an ex-McKinsey Partner to lead the business consulting unit. Wipro's approach to consulting did not entail giving control of its consulting operations to outside experts, creating a separate sales team or investing money above and beyond what the consulting resources were able to generate.

For the fiscal year ended March 31 2005, Wipro Limited had annual sales of U.S.$1.9 billion. Wipro Technologies accounted for 75 percent of the company's revenue and 89 percent of its operating income.

Wipro had a total of 5,000 consultants spread across North America, Europe and Japan and over 10,000 itinerant employees. Wipro had a presence in 35 countries including 10 nearshore development centers.

ICI Strategy and Organization

The leadership team at ICI had a mission to lead a new generation of business consulting to help clients become more competitive and help develop their employees into great leaders. The strategy involved the delivery of high quality business consulting and disciplined technology implementation at an extremely competitive price. As explained further below, ICI could perform engagements at a blended rate of approximately $100 per hour while the rates of leading players like IBM and Accenture ranged from $175 to $225 per hour. The firm planned to extend Infosys Technologies' Global Delivery Model (GDM) to the business consulting arena and create a company structure for a unique culture which would differentiate ICI from other business consulting firms, enable the recruitment of top tier talent and deliver measurable value to clients.

Global Delivery Model (GDM)

Infosys Technologies developed a unique approach to global delivery more than 20 years ago and was considered a leader in the delivery of IT implementation projects using globally distributed teams. Projects were broken down into logical components and distributed to different locations (onsite, nearshore, or offshore) where they could then be delivered at maximum value in the most cost efficient manner (see Exhibit 4 for an application of the

EXHIBIT 4

Infosys Technologies' Global Delivery Model

GLOBAL DELIVERY MODEL	Client Location/PDC*	Offshore Development Centers	
	Discovery Project	**Project**	Intelligent project breakdown
	Analysis and planning	Project management	
	High level design	Detailed design	
	User interface design	Coding	
	Project coordination	Testing	
	Onsite testing	Documentation	Leverage extended workday
	Implementation		
	Post Implementation Support	**Post Implementation Support**	
	Rapid reaction support	Bug fixes	Leverage cost efficiencies
		Warranty support	
		Maintenance	

*PDC = Proximity development centers

Source: Data from Infosys Consulting.

EXHIBIT 5

Value Chain of Consulting and Implementation Services ICI Extending Infosys Technologies' Global Delivery Model

Source: Infosys Consulting company website.

global delivery value chain for Infosys Technologies). Infosys Technologies claimed that the GDM cut project costs by 30 percent and reduced time to market since the combined work of teams distributed around the world made a 24-hour project workday a reality. ICI applied this model to integrate the business consulting and technology implementation lifecycle (see Exhibit 5 for the GDM value chain including consulting services). This approach, called the "1-1-3 model," gave the client one ICI resource onsite, one Infosys Technologies resource onsite and three Infosys Technologies resources offshore (in India or other Infosys offshore centers in China, Australia, Mauritius, Czech Republic—see Appendix on Infosys, p. C193).

Ming Tsai pointed to the training and knowledge of global delivery of Infosys Technologies' onsite resources as a differentiating factor from competitors' approaches to global delivery:

Infosys Technologies' onsite resources are more trained in, comfortable with and knowledgeable about global delivery. So it's not just that we have lots of people that are in India. It's a question of the one onsite consultant being able to understand what are the limitations of global delivery and how and when to take advantage of global delivery. Frankly, there are situations where you don't want to be offshore. You cannot send somebody offshore if you need to do an executive workshop that has to be done in New York because that is where all the bankers are. The ability to recognize what can and can't be done to the clients' benefit offshore and onshore and how to structure a piece of work around that is, I would say, countercultural for the average IBM or Accenture consulting teams who are motivated to drive utilization up for their onshore teams.

Shortening the Lifecycle of Solution Design to Implementation

The firm had a different approach to implementing technology to enable operational improvements. For example, if a client wanted to implement SAP to improve its operations, the traditional approach to the engagement would be to analyze the firm's processes and then redesign them. The traditional approach entailed a design phase that was distinct from a development phase. Specifications would be written following the new processes or process requirements. The processes tended to be grouped by vertical functions such as sales, marketing, manufacturing, etc. SAP would then be implemented to deliver the specifications and client employees would be trained to use the technology. In the traditional cycle, the design and configuration of the specifications would be completed onsite. The data conversion and report building may have been completed offshore.

ICI's approach entailed looking at process requirements rather than functional requirements. The firm believed that inefficiencies could be identified better if horizontal processes, for example the product development process, were considered rather than vertical functional silos, such as sales and marketing. The firm also looked at process metrics. The rationale used was that every change ICI recommended needed to impact the client's performance and ultimately increase its shareholder value.

ICI applied the GDM to deploy a team onsite to work with a client and look at how the company was organized by process. There existed multiple levels of processes. Level 0 was the highest aggregation of business processes. Most companies had between five to 10 level 0 processes, for example the product development process—to develop a product from the inception of an idea—was a Level 0 process. ICI organized the project team against each identified Level 0 process. The onsite team contained process experts and SAP development experts. This team worked with the client during the day to capture the design of the process object. At night, the offshore team converted the design templates into a software configuration. The next day, the onsite team would test the software configuration with the client and undergo a second iteration of the design. At night, the offshore team would develop the second iteration.

Typically, there existed four or five iterations for each process object. Each sub-team organized against each process would take a week to design and develop the process. If there were six sub-teams, six process objects were created in one week. If a company had 200 process objects, the design and software configuration for all of them would be completed in six months, whereas using the traditional approach would take 10 to 12 months. Moreover, as the configuration was being performed on a real-time basis, the end result was intended to be exactly what the client wanted as each iteration could be tested for user acceptance during the design and configuration process.

Cost Reduction Steve Pratt pointed to several aspects of cost reduction as he described the 1-1-3 model:

This is a killer business model because it gives, on average, a lower cost to clients and much higher margins for us to use to pay our people well, to make investors happy and to invest in our business. The main benefit to our clients is that they can take these cost savings and reinvest them into their business, and become more competitive. We've been the pioneers in creating the model of

the future. Everyone is scrambling to get to our model, so the race is whether we can scale our model fast enough. Having been on both sides of the equation, this is a lot more fun: the building and growing quickly is a lot more fun than tearing down an old model which is an expensive, risky and demoralizing undertaking.

The value proposition of the 1-1-3 model was to offer business consulting resources onsite at the market rate for premium business consulting services ($150 to $400 per hour), an onsite IT implementation resource at a rate that was lower than the average onsite developer ($100 to $150 per hour) and three developers offshore at lower than market rates ($105 combined per hour). Using this model, ICI could perform major engagements for a blended rate of approximately $100 dollars an hour.

Steve Pratt also considered the timeframe and challenges involved in replicating the cost structure of ICI's 1-1-3 model:

Realistically, testing the replicability of our model will play out over the next three to five years, because it's at least that big of a problem for the legacy consulting firms such as IBM and Accenture to get to our model. The problem is not about scaling up offshore, but de-scaling here. If your core financial model is built on engaging your onshore employees and if the rates start collapsing, your cost structure is not sustainable. The model is not difficult to learn, but there's a structural challenge involved in replicating it. Another complicating factor for our U.S. competitors is that once we get sufficient scale, we will tip the market and collapse the price point in the consulting industry. This will hurt them in the capital markets because their margins will be squeezed. Then their utilization of people has to go up, and their ability to invest will go down.

Delivering Measurable Benefits ICI followed Infosys Technologies' philosophy of measuring everything. The parent company had raised awareness of quality standards in the software and services arena by marketing the quality of work it delivered using the Software Engineering Institute's Capability Maturity Model (CMM). CMM judged the maturity of an organization's software processes and identified key practices required to increase the maturity of these processes. Infosys Technologies was awarded a Level 5 rating, the highest quality of software development delivery, though in reality, the company exceeded the highest quality level by a factor of 20 (while the maximum allowed defects for Level 5 was 0.5, Infosys Technologies was rated at 0.026—approximately 20 times better).

ICI's focus from a broad services standpoint was to assist clients in dealing with business and technology related challenges/problems in customer operations, product operations and corporate operations. ICI determined that one clear way to deliver value was to achieve measurable improvement in business process metrics within the client's business operations as a result of its consulting engagement (see Exhibit 6 for sample metrics). Therefore, on every business transformation and operations consulting engagement, the firm made a concerted and structured effort to deliver measurable improvement in process metrics as a proxy to making a positive impact on shareholder value. For these engagements, ICI would first analyze the current operations of the client to establish a baseline of business process performance. The company would next assess process metrics that reflected the efficiency and effectiveness of each key business process and then design changes in business process structure and enable technology to deliver defined improvement in process metrics.

As an example, for a manufacturing client's order management process (quote-to-cash), process metrics such as the ones outlined below would be addressed to drive measurable improvement in process performance:

- Elapsed time between quote submission and receipt of cash from the client
- Capacity for processing orders within a specific timeframe
- Percent of orders configured with zero errors
- Percent of orders shipped on requested-ship-date
- Number of quotes with readjusted prices
- Number of days' sales outstanding per customer segment

Another example included the time-to-market metric that was critical for the high-tech industry. This metric was a key measure of success in the high-tech industry and companies recognized that the cost of coming in second with new products could be severe. So, in this case, the consulting engagement would focus on analyzing the new product introduction process with the intent of using process and technology enablers to reduce time-to-market, thereby influencing the client's success in the market by enhancing its revenue and hence impacting shareholder value.

ICI also structured engagements with clients where the fees owed to the company were contingent on project outcomes. One of ICI's clients, George Stelling, the CIO and global services leader of NVIDIA Corporation (a multi-billion leader in the graphics processor market), worked with ICI to create a "value based" case structure, where case fees were based on the success of a spend management engagement:

> We had ICI put some of their fees at risk, based on the identification of cost savings in targeted spend categories. We set clear metrics at the beginning of the engagement so there was a high degree of transparency for us and ICI. At the end of the engagement, ICI was paid their full fee. For us, we got value in terms of focusing on "quick hit" cost savings opportunities as well as long-term spend management strategies. Since the original case, we've engaged ICI in the implementation phase of our long-term strategy. These "value based" deals are great, if you can structure them. These kinds of "win-win" relationships work when you can align incentives on both sides.

George Stelling added that ICI's measurements-driven approach was the most important factor in his decision to hire the consulting firm.

ICI also developed its own set of metrics to track the quality of the work the firm performed by asking clients to rate each engagement (see Exhibit 7). The firm would elicit feedback from clients to see whether they had met the client's expectations, or even exceeded them. ICI created a rating scale of zero to 200 where 100 indicated that the firm had met client expectations. As of 2006, ICI maintained an average rating of over 130 based on more than 100 client engagements.

Company Organization

Although Infosys Technologies went to market as one company, in order to establish a successful consulting business, ICI was given the autonomy to create its

EXHIBIT 6

ICI Sample Core Process Metrics—Designed for an ERP Implementation Project for the Software Industry Sub-Vertical Within the High Tech Discrete Manufacturing Practice

High Tech Software Industry Segment Process Structure				
Level	Level No.	Level (Process) Name	Objective	Metric
0	1.0	Solution Development to Sunset	Develop and manage solutions that are valued by customers and maximize profitability for the business	● Product revenues ● Market share ● Cost of sale
0	2.0	Channel Development to Agreement	Identify channels and customer segments to maximize penetration in existing markets, increase customer base and drive growth in emerging markets.	● Market share by geography ● Market share by channel ● Market share by product category ● Pipeline conversion rates ● Account growth ● Account penetration ● Customer/channel acquisition cost
0	3.0	High Tech Channel Management	Manage channel customers effectively to drive customer satisfaction, strengthen relationships and increase revenues	● Length of accounts ● Profitability of accounts ● Revenue growth of channels ● Number of new product agreements with channels ● Channel feedback scores
0	4.0	Supply Chain Management	Effectively manage the supply chain process to manage partner/vendor resources to minimize inventory and optimize fulfillment needs that usher operational transparency	● Inventory age ● Inventory turns ● Obsolete/excess inventory per month ● Ratio of company and vendor managed inventory ● Variance of estimated & actual delivery dates ● Percent available to promise satisfied
0	5.0	Quote to Cash	Provide accurate and prompt billing for all products/services to ensure revenues are fully captured	● Percentage of shipments billed ● Days sales outstanding
0	7.0	Human Resources	Hire talent to fit role definitions, devise training to motivate employees and manage PR to enhance corporate image	● Staff turnover ● Training feedback score
0	8.0	Information Technology	Maintain and manage IT infrastructure; plan & execute IT requirement to support business strategy	● System down-time ● Return on investment of IT initiatives
0	9.0	Facilities	Manage company assets that maximize return on investment, support operations and minimize risk	● Maintenance costs ● Return on investment on real estate assets

Source: Data from Infosys Consulting.

own culture, recruitment strategy, organizational structure and compensation packages.

Building a Unique Culture The leadership team of ICI decided that they needed to create a unique culture to differentiate them from other business consulting firms while maintaining the attributes required for successful consultants and adopting the essential values of the parent company. Steve Pratt described this challenge:

> What we need to do is build a company that successfully straddles the personality of a confident, assertive business advice consultant while ensuring that we have integration with the Infosys culture. Creating the culture that fits in that square is very important because if we go too far to the extreme and become an arrogant consulting firm, that will be in direct conflict with the Infosys culture and will fail. Likewise, if we go too far to the side of being too deferential, we won't be able to give good advice to our clients. A big challenge internally is to build the right culture. A related challenge is how do we take a group of people from different consulting firms and build a unique culture. We're also facing the same issue we've always had in our careers, which is how do we take people that have no consulting experience and integrate them into our culture.

The leadership team set out to build a culture based on Infosys Technologies' values of delivering high quality work, measuring every aspect of performance and maintaining a sense of humility. The team wanted to apply the rigorous analytical process of providing advice within an open and transparent culture.

Recruiting the Right People ICI management decided to follow the chairman of the parent company, Narayana Murthy's philosophy: hire first-rate employees only. In addition to MBA recruiting, the firm used a referral-based system to target the top 10 percent of talent from other consulting companies. Steve Pratt explained:

> We hired an executive search firm and it didn't work. For whatever reason, people have to emotionally buy-in to our approach. That's a different kind of recruiting—more of a "Do you want to be a pioneer?" kind of recruiting. And we've done a good job convincing the people we

want—people that have come to us through referrals—to join us.

ICI also interviewed and retained approximately half of the employees from Infosys Technologies' original consulting business unit. ICI found that most of these employees were better aligned with the sales and delivery model of the parent organization and did not have relevant business development and client relationship experience for the consulting organization.

Although ICI had reached its recruiting target of 200 employees by the end of December 2005, Steve Pratt pointed to challenges that lay ahead for the firm to meet its recruitment goals:

> We're trying to hire more women. We're making good progress, but I'd like to do better there. One of the things we're doing strategically for Infosys Technologies is creating local presences. More than 80 percent of our consultants are citizens of the local country. We've started operations in the U.K. and Germany, so we want to establish a local presence in all of the markets in which we operate. It's very important for Infosys to continue to emerge as a global company. Right now, the vast majority of Infosys Technologies employees are Indian. The goal is to have more representation in local communities.

Creating a Differentiated Approach ICI decided to build an organizational structure based on meritocracy and transparency. Paul Cole, the COO, commented:

> What keeps me up at night is "Are we doing things differently?" If you take five guys from four different companies, each with 20 years of experience, God help us if we do the same old stuff we did with our predecessor companies. The big question is: how can we do things differently and better?

An example of ICI's approach to doing things differently was their staffing model where the responsibility for contributing to the firm was given to individual employees. Paul Cole explained how the model was different from the traditional consulting staffing model:

> Consulting firms use the terms *beach* and *bench* for unutilized staff. We don't have such things. Nobody's on the beach, nobody's sitting on the bench. They're learning, teaching, billing, contributing—so they're always adding useful value to the firm and we want them to take control of their careers.

EXHIBIT 7

ICI Client Feedback Form

Infosys® CONSULTING

CLIENT FEEDBACK FORM

Infosys Consulting would like to thank you for taking the time to provide feedback on the effort we have recently completed for your organization. This feedback is critical not only in improving the quality of service we will provide you and other clients in the future, but also in determining a portion of our consultants' compensation. The survey should only take about 15–30 minutes and can be kept anonymous if you prefer.

Would you like anonymity as the responder to this feedback form?

Yes _____   No _____

Client Name

Client Company

Address

Engagement Name
Project Code (if any)
Milestone
Period

I. Overall Satisfaction

Overall, we would like to understand how satisfied you were with the work delivered by Infosys Consulting on *(engagement)*, using a scale of 1–7 (where 7 is extremely satisfied, 6 is very satisfied, 5 is satisfied, 4 is neither satisfied/dissatisfied, 3 is dissatisfied, 2 is very dissatisfied, and 1 is extremely dissatisfied).

If your rating above was a 3 or lower, please share with us your key areas where we may improve. May we follow-up with you?   **Rating:** _____

For Sections 2–4, please rate each "attribute" on a scale from 1 to 7 in terms of its *importance to you* in selecting Infosys Consulting and *how well the team performed.*

II. Quality

Starting with the *quality* of what was delivered, how important was it that Infosys Consulting *(insert attribute)*? And how well did Infosys Consulting perform on *(same attribute)*?

Importance
(1 = not at all important
7 = extremely important)

Performance
(1 = poor performance
7 = excellent performance)

a. deliver significant business insights
b. deliver practical recommendations
c. demonstrate quantified financial benefits
d. provide the proper blend of fact-based and creative analysis
e. help your company to become more competitive

III. Project Management

Now, in terms of overall *project management*, how important was *(insert attribute)*? And how well did Infosys Consulting perform on *(same attribute)*?

Importance
(1 = not at all important
7 = extremely important)

Performance
(1 = poor performance
7 = excellent performance)

a. adherence to schedule
b. being on budget
c. handling ambiguity and ad hoc requirements
d. proactively identifying and managing of risks
e. timely closure of issues
f. making critical project resources available
g. transfer of knowledge to your organization
h. providing the appropriate level of change management

IV. Teamwork/Collaboration

Finally, in terms of how well Infosys Consulting collaborated with your organization, how important was *(insert attribute)*? And how well did Infosys Consulting perform *(same attribute)*?

Importance
(1 = not at all important
7 = extremely important
"N/A" = not applicable)

Performance
(1 = not at all important
7 = extremely important
"N/A" = not applicable)

a. oral communication skills
b. written communication skills
c. demonstrated industry knowledge
d. demonstrated functional knowledge
e. analytical skills
f. being confident but not arrogant
g. interacting effectively within your organization
h. being proactive
i. effectively using global resources
j. adapting to your culture

V. Infosys Consulting Core Values

One of the areas that Infosys Consulting takes very seriously in evaluating its people is living the Company's values. Please read these value statements and respond with whether our behavior lived up to each value.

a. Client Delight (Did we meet or exceed the results you expected?)   Yes   No
b. Leadership by Example (Did our project leaders lead by example?)   Yes   No
c. Integrity and Transparency (Were we truthful and open?)   Yes   No
d. Fairness (Were we fair?)   Yes   No
e. Pursuit of Excellence (Did we put in the effort to achieve excellent results?)   Yes   No

VI. Client Feedback

a. In general, what did you like best about working with Infosys Consulting?

b. In what ways could Infosys Consulting better serve your needs in the future? Are there services/capabilities/approaches we could add or strengthen?

c. In comparing your overall experience with Infosys Consulting vs. our competitors, how would you rate our performance?

   Infosys Consulting was better than other firms
   Infosys Consulting was equivalent to other firms
   Infosys Consulting was worse than other firms
   No experience with a competitor to make this judgement

d. Going forward, how likely would you be to recommend Infosys Consulting to someone else within your organization?

   Very likely
   Somewhat likely
   Not at all likely

e. Are there any other comments/feedback that you would like to provide?

VII. Business Value – Summary Rating

Infosys Consulting strives to maximize the business value we deliver to our clients. We would therefore like to understand the degree to which this project's expectations were met. Please rate us on a % basis of the anticipated *business value* that the engagement delivered, where:

200% = "Infosys Consulting greatly exceeded expectations"
100% = "Infosys Consulting met expectations"
0% = "Infosys Consulting drastically under-met expectations"

Rating: _____ %

IMPORTANT NOTE: This answer will be used as a quantitative input to our consultants' compensation.

Infosys Consulting would like to thank you for your candid and constructive feedback!

Source: Infosys Consulting.

ICI implemented a staffing system where employees could input their skills into a database. A project manager could then search the database, match results against a calendar and see which employees with the requisite skills were available for an engagement. Employees could request engagements they were interested in, and had the option to opt out of being selected for certain engagements. The firm purchased an auctioning module for its staffing system so that employees could bid on projects in a reverse auction.[8] ICI also created the Personal Margin Contribution where each employee could see his or her individual margin contribution or revenue allocation on each project.

Another example of ICI's efforts to create a meritocratic and transparent organization included incorporating staff nominations for promotion. Under this system, the firm's senior employees who were being considered for promotion published the criteria on which their promotions should be based and all the employees could nominate and score each leader.

The firm recognized that by leveraging the GDM, they had created a 24-hour work cycle, given the time differential of the various teams that were deployed on a specific engagement. Although this seemed to be the next wave of productivity in a global work environment, in order to prevent employees from burning out through overextending their hours (as there was the potential to work during every hour of the day), they asked employees to block out certain times in their calendars when they would not be available to work. Mark Holmstrom, a practice leader who was the seventh employee to join ICI, described the challenge of working in a global delivery environment:

> One of the challenges for this global delivery model is that it requires a different way of thinking about work that's not the traditional eight to five, eight to six model. A lot of what we do becomes much more asynchronous. What I mean by that is it's much more email based. There are traditional times when meetings take place that are during the week. I actually block my calendar at certain times that most people wouldn't think of in a traditional company. One of the things I really enjoy doing is putting my little daughters to bed. So I block out time to say, "I'm not going to work during these hours." Everyone has got to figure out their own rhythm, their own pace and figure out what success looks like within the global delivery model.

Rewarding Employees ICI generally compensated employees at the higher end of market rates; for example, the base compensation for MBA campus hires for 2005 was between $110,000 and $125,000. ICI's bonus structure linked back to the value ICI had created for its clients and overall client value. Steve Pratt explained: "We're the only consulting firm that actually pays people based on delivered client value. It always used to bug us that people got paid based on consulting revenue only, as we considered that to be a downstream metric while we wanted an upstream metric."

At the end of every engagement, ICI asked its clients what percentage of the business value that they had anticipated ICI would provide was actually realized. That percentage translated into a direct multiplier of employee bonuses. The firm also created a client mutual fund where the firm took the total amount of fees each client paid them and translated that amount into a purchase of each client's equity. ICI then monitored how their client fund performed against the S&P 500. That percentage differential was translated into a multiplier of employee bonuses as well.

Managing the Relationship with Infosys Technologies

The management of both Infosys Technologies and ICI recognized that building a seamless interface between the parent company and the subsidiary was essential for success. ICI was organized to mirror the parent company (both companies were organized by industry) and metrics were established in order to measure how well the two companies worked together. Steve Pratt described this process:

> First of all, getting the interface with Infosys Technologies right is very important. Get the right metrics, get the right business planning in place. Each of the Infosys Technologies business units has a specific goal related to consulting, and we have specific goals related to revenue for Infosys Technologies. So the goals are understood, and the metrics are largely correct to drive the behavior to work together. We're always redefining. There's a constant education. The more engagements we do with clients, the more we understand what Infosys Technologies really does, and they understand more what we really do.

Leveraging the Parent Company

ICI leveraged the relationships that already existed with Infosys Technologies to get client engagements.

The firm actively sought opportunities where there was a targeted need to offer existing Infosys Technologies' clients business consulting services. Ming Tsai provided a rationale for this approach:

> Out of the approximately 450 existing Infosys Technologies accounts, we have targeted ones that are the most strategic, most receptive or the most in need of skills that we provide and combined that with the account teams that are the most open minded and willing to work with us within the Infosys account teams. So they tend to be good clients of Infosys, having seen and worked with Infosys for multiple years. They tend to be clients that have particular pain points around business transformation—something in a particular business process or business area that is in need of change, or has a technical or technology aspect to it. Approximately 70 percent of our business comes from existing Infosys clients.

George Stelling explained that the rationale to hire ICI for a strategy engagement rather than first hold a competitive bidding process open to other consulting firms was because of the client relationship that Infosys Technologies had established with NVIDIA:

> In the past, we used Infosys Technologies in the IT area successfully on projects, but we had never used Infosys Consulting. There was a dialog going on with our CEO, CFO, and Infosys when I joined. It was clear that Infosys Consulting and NVIDIA shared common values around value creation. The chemistry was a key consideration. It's very important to pick consultants that you feel comfortable with and those that reflect your corporate style.

Infosys Technologies adapted its sales process to include ICI in its service offerings. The firm changed its incentive structure for its sales force to ensure that engagements awarded to ICI were rewarded as much as the engagements where the parent company had exclusive ownership. The parent company developed an internal program called "One Infy" to structure incentives and set goals to enhance collaboration among employees across the firm. The overall objectives of the initiative were to create and reinforce One Infy thinking through training programs; include One Infy behavior in the measurement systems across the organization; reward examples of collaborative business planning and create role models for the rest of the organization; and create cultural integration mechanisms such as forums for people to meet and learn from each other across the business units.

As Infosys Technologies grew in size and expanded its footprint of services, it became increasingly important that all the capabilities of the firm were in alignment with the goal of serving clients and winning in the marketplace. The program involved improving internal collaborative mechanisms so that clients saw Infosys Technologies as one company and not a collection of parts. One Infy focused on improving the training programs for employees—to improve understanding of service offerings across the organization, build collaborative skills and ensure that new employees went through cross-business training. The One Infy initiative served to focus the overall organization on the value of leveraging the broad and deep capabilities of the company across business units and subsidiaries. The initiative also focused on joint account planning and pursuit management. The intent was to create joint planning teams at the account level, with participation from the relevant business units. The account leader position was viewed as integrating efforts across different units and ensuring consistency in the value delivery processes. The firm planned to create forums where account leaders could strategize, develop opportunities and resolve delivery issues on an ongoing rather than opportunistic basis. The objective was to make the initiative self-sustaining. Infosys Technologies planned to structure goals and incentives of the individuals in line with the overall account strategies.

Initially, there were tensions in the company over which entity would lead the client relationship and pursuit of engagements. For example, the sales force was faced with client situations where an overlap between business transformational work and enterprise solutions offerings caused uncertainty whether the client pursuit and relationship would go to ICI or Infosys Technologies' Enterprise Solutions business unit. Both the parent company and ICI worked together to create a methodology, known as "The Fork in the Road," where the pursuit of the client relationship would be allocated to the area of the company that best served the client's situation. Raj Joshi and C. Kakal, the head of the Enterprise Solutions practice within Infosys Technologies, formalized an approach that had the two groups working together to collaboratively decide which opportunities were transformational in nature and better suited for ICI, versus more technology-related work which was better aligned with the Enterprise Solutions practice. This decision, representing the fork in the road, drove better collaboration and established clear ownership of the sales pursuit strategy and tactics. By clearly formulating accountability of tasks and decision-making, it enhanced the overall process of working together to pursue large complex client opportunities.

Romil Bahl described a practical approach that the company employed when dealing with client engagements that provided an overlap between Infosys Technologies' and ICI's services:

> It gets real muddy where there's a business process opportunity. Frankly, Infosys Technologies has phenomenal domain industry expertise and they have very smart people. They all want to do more anyway, so it gets real interesting in these situations and I find that often you can't talk about it and you can't conceptualize it, you have to go do engagements together. Infosys sees a better end product when a true cross-functional team of people comes together on it. There's no magical way for somebody to say, you guys will draw a line here in the middle. It just doesn't happen.

ICI also brought in new client relationships for Infosys Technologies. Ming Tsai described this second channel for ICI: "We also target old clients of ours that we've known personally in our past lives, whether at Capgemini, IBM, BCG, etc. We've brought in over a dozen marquee clients—Fortune 500 clients that Infosys had never done any work for before."

Interface Challenges

Infosys Technologies recognized that all pieces of the company needed to work together in a manner that optimized performance. A challenge facing Infosys Technologies was to ensure that ICI received enough airtime from the parent company given its relatively small size (ICI had 200 employees versus Infosys' 50,000 employees). Senior management realized that active intervention was required in order to ensure that the subsidiary received the attention it needed to be successful. Infosys Technologies set up a board led by Kris Gopalakrishnan to review the subsidiary's performance. Quarterly meetings were held where ICI's performance was monitored and issues were discussed.

Infosys Technologies also viewed their relationship with ICI as an opportunity to transform the company's culture and build the brand into a global transformation enabler. Senior management viewed the quarterly meetings as an opportunity to learn about a new space and evolve the company. The leadership of both Infosys Technologies and ICI agreed that interacting with each other regularly provided a constant education for everyone. Paul Cole described the attention to detail given by the leadership of Infosys Technologies to the operations of ICI, citing that the chairman, Narayana Murthy, regularly reviewed weekly status reports from the subsidiary. Steve Pratt described ICI's approach to interfacing with the parent company: "We're guests here and we have to be respectful of that. We're here to learn and listen more than we speak. We want to demonstrate over time, which we have already, that we're a good thing for the clients of Infosys."

In order to be viewed as a global company, Infosys Technologies recognized that it needed to incorporate different global perspectives by bringing in managers from the United States and Europe. The leadership of Infosys Technologies hoped to see migration of management from ICI to the parent company over time.

Conclusion

Steve Pratt was convinced that ICI had enabled disruptive change in the business and information technology industry through its unique approach and organization. However, in considering the firm's strategy in the future, he evaluated the ways in which the firm could "stay ahead of the game." In addition to the internal challenges of building the business, managing growth and interfacing productively with the parent company, plus the external challenge of capturing and maintaining market share in the consulting industry, CEO Steve Pratt's key concern was "to get the right people to do the right things":

> We need to make sure that we stay focused on the high priority things. Are we spending the right amount of time building the connection to Infosys Technologies? Are we spending the right amount of time selling? Are we spending the right amount of time developing our people, and who is doing what and where are they spending their time doing that? Are the MDs working together? Are we working optimally with clients, and when there are really important events with clients, where can I be helpful? I need to make sure that the right people are in the right roles.

Appendix: Infosys Technologies

Infosys Technologies Limited (NASDAQ: INFY), a global technology services company, was incorporated in 1981. The company provided end-to-end business solutions which leveraged technology for its clients, including consulting, design, development, software re-engineering, maintenance, systems integration, package evaluation and implementation, and infrastructure management services. Infosys Technologies' wholly owned subsidiaries included Infosys Technologies (Australia) Pty. Limited (Infosys Australia), Infosys Technologies (Shanghai) Co. Limited (Infosys China) and Infosys Consulting Inc. (Infosys Consulting). Through Progeon Limited (Progeon), a majority-owned subsidiary, Infosys Technologies provided business process management services, such as offsite customer relationship management, finance and accounting, and administration and sales order processing. Infosys Technologies marketed in North America, Europe and the Asia-Pacific region. The company served clients in financial services, manufacturing, telecommunications, retail, utilities, logistics and other industries. In 2006, the company had over 52,700 employees worldwide and planned to hire another 25,000 employees over the next year.

Through its Global Delivery Model, Infosys Technologies divided projects into components which were executed simultaneously at client sites and at its development centers in India and around the world. It had 25 global development centers, of which nine were located in India; 29 sales offices; one disaster recovery center and four subsidiary offices. Infosys Technologies' service offerings included custom application development, maintenance and production support, software re-engineering, package evaluation and implementation, information technology (IT) consulting and other solutions, including testing services, operations and business process consulting, engineering services, business process management, systems integration and infrastructure management services.

Infosys Technologies competitors included Accenture, BearingPoint, Capgemini, Deloitte Consulting, HP, IBM, Computer Sciences Corporation, EDS, Keane, Logica CMG, Perot Systems, Cognizant Technologies, Satyam Computer Services, Tata Consultancy Services, Wipro, Oracle and SAP.

For the three months ended March 31, 2006, Infosys Technologies' revenues increased 30.3 percent to $593 million and net income increased 19.6 percent to $152 million from the previous year. The profit margins for the company fell in the quarter ended in March, the fourth quarter of its fiscal year, to 26.3 percent from 29.4 percent in the previous quarter. The company cited a stronger rupee, higher depreciation on buildings and equipment, and accelerated hiring for the falloff. Yet, despite 15 percent wage increases in the spring, Infosys Technologies said that it expected its profit margins for the fiscal 2007 year to be about 28 percent, unchanged from the previous year. Infosys Technologies expected revenues to increase 28 percent to 30 percent in the fiscal 2007 year.

Custom Application Development

Infosys Technologies provided customized software solutions for its clients. The company created new applications and enhanced the functionality of its clients' existing software applications. Its projects involved all aspects of the software development process, including defining requirements, designing, prototyping, programming, module integration and installation of the custom application. Infosys Technologies performed system design and software coding, and ran pilots primarily at its global development centers, while transition planning, user training and deployment activities were performed at the client's site. The company's application development services spanned the entire range of mainframe, client server and Internet technologies. Infosys Technologies' application development engagements were related to emerging platforms, such as Microsoft's .NET, or open platforms, such as Java 2 enterprise edition (J2EE) and Linux.

Maintenance and Production Support

Infosys Technologies provided maintenance services for its clients' software systems that covered a range of technologies and businesses, and were typically critical to a client's business. The company focused on long-term functionality, stability and preventive maintenance to avoid problems that typically arise from incomplete or short-term solutions. While Infosys Technologies performed the maintenance work at its global development centers using secure and redundant communication links to client's systems, the company also maintained a team at the client's facility to coordinate key interface and support functions.

Software Re-engineering

The company's software re-engineering services assisted its clients in converting their existing IT systems to newer technologies and platforms developed by third-party vendors. Its re-engineering services included

Web-enabling its clients' existing legacy systems, database migration, implementing product upgrades and platform migrations, such as mainframe to client server and client server to Internet platforms. Infosys Technologies' solution provided an enterprise-wide platform for over 50 applications for 10,000 users spread across North America, Europe and Asia.

Package Evaluation and Implementation

Infosys Technologies assisted its clients in the evaluation and implementation of software packages, which were developed by third-party vendors, and provided training and support services in the course of their implementation. The company specialized in enterprise resource planning packages developed by vendors, including Oracle, PeopleSoft, Retek and SAP; supply chain management packages developed by vendors, including i2, Manugistics and Oracle; customer relationship management packages developed by vendors, including PeopleSoft (Vantive) and Siebel; business intelligence packages developed by vendors, such as Business Objects and Cognos, and enterprise application integration packages developed by vendors like IBM and TIBCO. It provided its services in a range of industries, such as automotive, beverages, financial services, food, healthcare, manufacturing, pharmaceuticals, retail, technology and telecommunications.

IT Consulting

The company provided technical advice in developing and recommending appropriate IT architecture, hardware and software specifications to deliver IT solutions designed to meet specific business and computing objectives. It offered IT consulting in migration planning, institution-wide implementation and overall project management involving multiple vendors under a common architecture. Infosys technologies also conducted IT infrastructure assessment, which included assessing its clients' IT capabilities against existing and future business requirements and appropriate technology infrastructure, and technology roadmap development, which allowed clients to evaluate emerging technologies and develop the standards and methodologies for applying those emerging technologies.

Other Solutions

Infosys Technologies offered testing services, engineering services, business process management, systems integration, infrastructure management, and operational and business process consulting. Testing services offered end-to-end validation solutions and services, including enterprise test management, performance benchmarking, test automation and product certification. Its consulting services included strategic and competitive analysis to help the clients improve their business operations. It also assisted clients in implementing operational changes to their businesses. The company offered engineering services which primarily assisted its clients in the manufacturing sector, in their new product development process and in managing the life cycles of their existing product lines.

The company's business process management offered services to banking industry, insurance and healthcare industries, and securities and brokerage industry. Systems integration developed and delivered solutions that enhanced the compatibility between various components of its clients' IT infrastructure. Infrastructure management services included data center management, technical support services, application management services and process implementation/enhancement services. Banking software products included Finacle Core Banking, Finacle eChannels, Finacle eCorporate, Finacle CRM and Finacle Treasury. The Finacle suite, a flexible, scalable and Web-enabled solution, addressed banks' core banking, treasury, wealth management, consumer and corporate e-banking, mobile banking and Web-based cash management requirements.

Source: Infosys Technologies company Web site and Reuters, Inc.

ENDNOTES

1. Ming Tsai joined formally in May but was involved from the start.
2. Standard & Poor's Industry Survey, "Computers: Commercial Services," *Standard & Poor's*, August 18, 2005, p. 5.
3. Ibid.
4. Infosys Technologies started offering ESOPs in 1994 and discontinued them in 2003.
5. "The multinational and the global corporation are not the same thing. The multinational corporation operates in a number of countries, and adjusts its products and practices in each—at high relative costs. The global corporation operates with resolute constancy—at low relative cost—as if the entire world (or major regions of it) were a single entity; it sells the same things in the same way everywhere." Theodore Leavitt, "The Globalization of Markets," *Harvard Business Review* (May-June 1983), pp. 92–93.
6. Gartner Research, "Magic Quadrant for Offshore Application Services, 2006," *Gartner, Inc.*, 16 February 2006, p. 9.
7. Ibid.
8. A reverse auction (also called "online reverse auction," "e-sourcing," "sourcing event," or "tender") is a type of auction in which the role of the buyer and seller are reversed. Unlike an ordinary auction, where buyers compete for the right to obtain a good, in a reverse auction, sellers compete for the right to provide a good. (Wikipedia, The Free Encyclopedia, http://en.wikipedia.org/wiki/Reverse_auction.)

Blockbuster's Challenges in the Video Rental Industry

This case was prepared by Gareth R. Jones, Texas A&M University.

In January 2007, John Antioco, Blockbuster Inc.'s CEO, was reflecting on the challenges facing the company in the year ahead. The pace of change was quickening as Netflix's online video rental business model was proving very robust. And there was a growing movement to directly download or stream videos using the Internet, which would bypass Blockbuster's store. With its nearly 9,000 global stores, 6,000 in the United States alone, Blockbuster had an enviable brand name and enormous marketing clout, but how could it best use its resources to keep its number 1 place in the movie-rental market and keep its revenues and profits growing? What strategies needed to be developed to strengthen Blockbuster's business model?

Blockbuster's History

David Cook, the founder of Blockbuster, formed David P. Cook & Associates, Inc., in 1978 to offer consulting and computer services to the petroleum and real estate industries. He created programs to analyze and evaluate oil and gas properties and to compute oil and gas reserves. When oil prices began to decline in 1983 due to the breakdown of the OPEC cartel, his business started to decline, and Cook began evaluating alternative businesses in which he could apply his skills. He decided to exit

his current business by selling his company and to enter the video-rental business based on a concept for a "video superstore." He opened his first superstore, called "Blockbuster Video," in October 1985 in Dallas.

Cook developed his idea for a video superstore by analyzing the trends in the video industry that were occurring at that time. During the 1980s, the number of households that owned VCRs was increasing rapidly and, consequently, so were the number of video-rental stores set up to serve their needs. In 1983, 7,000 video-rental stores were in operation, by 1985 there were 19,000, and by 1986 there were over 25,000, of which 13,000 were individually owned. These "mom-and-pop" video stores generally operated for only a limited number of hours, offered customers only a limited selection of videos, and were often located in out-of-the-way strip shopping centers. These small stores often charged a membership fee in addition to the tape rental charge, and generally, customers brought an empty box to the video-store clerk who would exchange it for a tape if it was available—a procedure that was often time-consuming, particularly at peak times such as evenings and weekends.

Cook realized that as VCRs became more widespread and the number of film titles available steadily increased, customers would begin to demand a larger and more varied selection of titles from video stores. Moreover, they would demand more convenient store locations and quicker in-store service than mom-and-pop stores could offer. He realized that the time was right for the development of the next generation of video stores, and he used this opportunity to implement his video superstore concept, which is still the center of Blockbuster's strategy.

The Video Superstore Concept

Cook's superstore concept was based on several components. First, Cook decided that in order to give his video superstores a unique identity that would appeal to customers, the stores should be highly visible stand-alone structures, rather than part of a shopping center. In addition, his superstores were to be large—between 3,800 and 10,000 square feet—well lit, and brightly colored (for example, each store has a bright blue sign with "Blockbuster Video" displayed in huge yellow letters). Each store would have ample parking and would be located in the vicinity of a large urban population to maximize potential exposure to customers.

Second, each superstore was to offer a wide variety of tapes, such as adventure, children's, instructional, and videogame titles. Believing that movie preferences differ in different locations, Cook decided to have each store offer a different selection of between 7,000 and 13,000 film titles organized alphabetically in over thirty categories. New releases were arranged alphabetically against the back wall of each store to make it easier for customers to make their selections.

Third, believing that many customers, particularly those with children, wanted to keep tapes for longer than a one-day period, he created the concept of a three-day rental period for $3. (In 1991, a two-evening rental program was implemented, making new releases only $2.50 for two evenings during the first three weeks after release; after this period, the usual $3 for three evenings would apply.) If the tape was available, it was behind the cover box. The customer would take the tape to the checkout line and hand the cassette and his or her membership card to the clerk, who would scan the bar codes on both the tape and the card. The customer was then handed the tape and told that it was due back by midnight two days later. For example, if the tape were rented Thursday afternoon, it would be due back Saturday at midnight.

Fourth, Cook's superstores targeted the largest market segments, adults in the eighteen- to forty-nine-year-old group, and children in the six- to twelve-year-old group. Cook believed that if his stores could attract children, then the rest of the family probably would follow. Blockbuster carried no X-rated movies, and its goal was to be "America's Family Video Store." New releases were carefully chosen based on reviews and box-office success to maximize their appeal to families.

Finally, believing that customers wanted to choose a movie and get out of the store quickly, Cook decided that his superstores would offer customers the convenience of long operating hours and quick service, generally from 10:00 A.M. to midnight seven days a week. Members received a plastic identification card that was read by the point-of-sale equipment that was developed by the company. This system used a laser bar-code scanner to read important information from both the rental cassette and the ID card. The rental amount was computed by the system and due at the time of rental. Movie returns were scanned by laser, and any late or rewind fees were recorded on the account and automatically recalled the next time the member rented a tape. This system reduced customer checkout time and increased convenience. In addition, it provided Blockbuster with data on customer demographics, cassette rental patterns, and the number of times each cassette has been rented, all of which resulted in a database that increased in value over time as it grew bigger.

These five elements of Blockbuster's approach were successful, and customers responded well. Wherever Blockbuster opened, the local mom-and-pop stores usually closed down, unable to compete with the number of titles and the quality of service that a Blockbuster store could provide. By 1986, Blockbuster owned eight stores and had franchised eleven more to interested investors who could see the potential of this new approach to video rental. Initially, the company opened stores in markets with a minimum population of 100,000; franchises were located in Atlanta, Chicago, Detroit, Houston, San Antonio, and Phoenix. New stores, which cost about $500,000 to $700,000 to equip, grossed an average of $70,000 to $80,000 a month.

Early Growth and Expansion

John Melk, an executive at Waste Management Corp. who had invested in a Blockbuster franchise in Chicago, was to change the history of the company. In February 1987, he contacted H. "Wayne" Huizinga, a former Waste Management colleague, to tell him of the enormous revenue and profits his franchise was making. Huizinga had experience in growing small companies in fragmented industries. In 1955, he had quit college to manage a three-truck trash-hauling operation; in 1962 he bought his own operation, Southern Sanitation. In 1968, Southern Sanitation merged with Ace Partnership, Acme Disposal, and Atlas Refuse Service to form Waste Management. In succeeding years, Huizinga borrowed against Waste Management stock to buy over 100 small companies that provided such services as auto-parts cleaning, dry cleaning, lawn care, and portable-toilet rentals. He used their cash flows to purchase yet more firms. By the time Huizinga, the vice chairman, resigned in 1984, Waste Management was a $6 billion *Fortune 500* company and Huizinga was a wealthy man.

Although Huizinga had a low opinion of video retailers, he agreed to visit a Blockbuster store. Expecting a dingy store renting X-rated films, he was pleasantly surprised to find a brightly lit family video supermarket. Detecting the opportunity to take Cook's superstore concept national, Huizinga, Melk, and Donald Flynn (another Waste Management executive) agreed to purchase 33% of Blockbuster from Cook for $18.6 million in 1986; they became directors at this time. In 1987, CEO David Cook decided to take his money and leave Blockbuster to pursue another venture at Amtech Corp. With the departure of the founder, Huizinga took over as CEO in April 1987 with the goal of making Blockbuster a national company and the industry leader in the video-rental market.

Blockbuster's Explosive Growth

Huizinga and his new top management team mapped out Blockbuster's growth strategy, the elements of which follow.

Location

Store location is a critical issue to a video-rental store, and Huizinga moved quickly with Luigi Salvaneschi, a marketing guru renowned for selecting retail locations for maximum profits, to obtain the best store locations in each geographic area that Blockbuster expanded into. They developed a "cluster strategy" whereby they targeted a particular geographic market, such as Dallas, Boston, or Los Angeles, and then opened up new stores one at a time until they had saturated the market. Thus, within a few years, the local mom-and-pop stores found themselves surrounded, and many, unable to compete with Blockbuster, closed down. Video superstores were always located near busy, well-traveled routes to establish a broad customer base. The cluster strategy eventually brought Blockbuster into 133 television markets (the geographic area that television reaches), where it reached 75 to 85% of the U.S. population.

Marketing

On the marketing side, Blockbuster's chief marketing officer, Tom Gruber, applied his knowledge of McDonald's family-oriented advertising strategy to strengthen Cook's original vision of the video retail business. In 1988, he introduced "Blockbuster Kids" to strengthen the company's position as a family video store. This promotion, aimed at the six- to twelve-year-old age group, introduced four characters and a dog to appeal to Blockbuster's young customers. To further demonstrate commitment to families, each store stocked forty titles recommended for children and a kids' clubhouse with televisions and toys so that children could amuse themselves while their parents browsed for videos. In addition, Blockbuster allowed its members to specify what rating category of tapes (such as PG or R) could be rented through their account. A policy called "Youth-Restricted Viewing" forbade R-rated tape rentals to children under seventeen. Blockbuster also implemented the free "Kidprint Program," through which a child's name, address, and height were recorded on a videotape that was given to parents and local police for identification purposes. In addition, Blockbuster started a program called "America's Most Important Videos Are Free," which offered free rental of public-service tapes about topics such as fire safety and parenting. Finally, to attract customers and to build brand recognition, Gruber initiated joint promotions between Blockbuster and companies like Domino's Pizza, McDonald's, and Pepsi-Cola, something it continues to do today.

Operations

Blockbuster also made great progress on the operations side of the business. As discussed earlier, the operation of a Blockbuster superstore is designed to provide fast checkout and effective inventory management. The company designed its point-of-sale computer system to make rental and return transactions easy; this system is available only to company-owned and franchised stores.

Rapid expansion strains a company's operating systems. To support its stores, Blockbuster opened a

25,000-square-foot distribution center in 1986 in Dallas. The distribution center had the capacity to store 200,000 cassettes tapes that were removed from the original containers and labeled with security devices affixed to the cassettes. Each videotape was then bar-coded and placed into a hard plastic rental case. The facility could process the initial inventory requirement of about 10,000 tapes for up to three superstores per day. In addition, Blockbuster supplied the equipment and fixtures needed to operate new stores, such as computer software and hardware, shelving, signs, and cash registers. In 1987, the physical facilities of the distribution center were expanded to double capacity to 400,000 videocassettes.

Blockbuster's growing buying power also gave it another operations advantage. As the then largest single purchaser of prerecorded videotapes in the U.S. market, it was able to negotiate discounts off retail price. Cassettes were bought at an average of $40 per tape and rented three nights for $3. Thus, the cash investment on "hit" videotapes was recovered in forty-five to sixty days, and the investment on non-hit titles was regained in two-and-a-half to three months. In its early days, Blockbuster was also able to use its efficient distribution system to distribute extra copies of films declining in popularity to new stores where demand was increasing. This ability to transfer tapes to where they were most demanded was very important because customers wanted new tapes on the shelves when they came out. It also allowed the company to use its inventory to the best advantage and to receive the maximum benefit from each videotape.

Management and Structure

For Blockbuster, as for any company, rapid growth posed the risk of losing control over daily operations and allowing costs to escalate. Recognizing this, Blockbuster established three operating divisions to manage the functional activities necessary to retain effective control over its operations as it grew. Blockbuster Distribution Corp. was created to handle the area licensing and franchising of new stores, and to service their start-up and operation—offering assistance with the selection, acquisition, assembling, packaging, inventorying, and distribution of videocassettes, supplies, and computer equipment. Blockbuster Management Corp. was established to assist with the training of new store management, facility location and acquisition, and

employee training. Finally, Blockbuster Computer Systems Inc. was formed to install, maintain, and support the software programs for the inventory and point-of-sale equipment. Together these three divisions provided all the support services necessary to manage store expansion.

Rapid growth also led Blockbuster to oversee store operations through a regional and district level organizational structure. In 1988, responsibility for store development and operations was decentralized to the regional level. However, corporate headquarters was kept fully informed of developments in each regional area, and even in each store, through its computerized inventory and sales system. For example, Blockbuster's corporate inventory and point-of-sale computer systems tracked sales and inventory in each store and each region. The role of regional management was to oversee the stores in their regions, providing advice and monitoring stores' performance to make sure that they kept up Blockbuster's high standards of operation as its chain of superstores grew.

New-Store Expansion

With Blockbuster's functional-level competencies in place, the next step for Huizinga was to begin a rapid program of growth and expansion. Huizinga believed that expanding rapidly to increase revenue and market share was crucial for success in the video-rental industry. Under his leadership, Blockbuster opened new stores quickly, developed a franchising program, and began to acquire competitors to increase the number of its stores.

To facilitate rapid expansion, Blockbuster began to use its skills in store location, distribution, and sales. At first Blockbuster focused on large markets, preferring to enter a market with a potential capacity for 500 stores—normally a large city. Later, Blockbuster decided to enter smaller market segments, like towns with a minimum of 20,000 people within driving distance. All stores were built and operated using the superstore concept described earlier. Using the services of its three divisions, Blockbuster steadily increased its number of new-store openings until by 1993 it owned over 2,500 video stores.

Blockbuster's rapid growth was also attributable to Huizinga's skills in making acquisitions. Beginning in 1986, the company began to acquire many smaller regional video chains to gain a significant market presence in a city or region. In 1987, for example, the twenty-nine video stores of Movies To Go were acquired to expand Blockbuster's presence in the Midwest. Blockbuster then used this acquisition as a jumping-off point for opening many more stores in the region. Similarly, in 1989, it acquired 175 video stores from Major Video Corp. and Video Library to develop a presence in southern California. In 1991, it took over 209 Erol's Inc. stores to obtain the stronghold that Erol's previously held in the Mid-Atlantic states. All acquired stores were made to conform to Blockbuster's standards, and any store that could not was closed down. Most acquisitions were financed by existing cash flow or by issuing new shares of stock rather than taking on new debt. These deals reflect Huizinga's reluctance to borrow money.

Licensing and Franchising

Recognizing the need to build market share rapidly and develop a national brand name, Huizinga also recruited top management to put in place his ambitious franchise program. Franchising, in which the franchisee is solely responsible for all financial commitments connected with opening a new store, allowed Blockbuster to expand rapidly without incurring debt. The downside of franchising was that Blockbuster had to share profits with the franchise owners. When franchising, it is important to maintain consistency in stores. Thus, the franchisees were required to operate their stores in the same way as company-owned stores and to follow the same store format for rental selection and the use of proprietary point-of-sale equipment.

Franchising facilitated the rapid expansion of Blockbuster Video. By 1992, the company had over 1,000 franchised stores as compared to 2,000 company-owned stores. However, recognizing the long-term profit advantages of owning its own stores, Blockbuster began to repurchase attractive territories from franchisees. In 1993, the company spent $248 million to buy the 400 stores of its two largest franchisees and, with a new store opening every day, by the end of 1993, it owned over 2,500 stores. However, by the end of 1992, despite its rapid growth, Blockbuster still controlled only about 15% of the market—its 27,000 smaller rivals shared the rest. Consequently, in 1993, Blockbuster announced plans for a new round of store openings and acquisitions that would give it a 25 to 30% market share within two or three years.

The Home-Video Industry

By 1990, revenues from video rentals exceeded the revenues obtained in movie theaters. For example, video-rental revenues rose to $11 billion in 1991 compared to movie theaters' $4.8 billion. The huge growth in industry revenues led to increased competition for customers, and, as noted above, 28,000 video stores operated in the United States in 1990.

Blockbuster's rapid growth had put it in a commanding position. In 1990, it had no national competitor and was the only company operating beyond a regional level. The next largest competitor, West Coast Video, had only $120 million in 1991 revenues while Blockbuster had revenues of $868 million. However, Blockbuster faced many competitors at the local and regional levels.

Mature Market

As the video-rental market matured, the level of competition in the industry changed. During the 1980s, video rentals grew rapidly due to the proliferation of VCRs. By 1990, however, 70% of households had VCRs, compared to 2% in 1980, and industry growth dropped from the previous double digits to 7%. The slow growth in VCR ownership and rentals made competition more severe. To a large degree, competition in the video-rental industry was fierce because new competitors could enter the market with relative ease; the only purchase necessary was videotapes. However, unlike small video-rental companies, Blockbuster was able to negotiate discounts with tape suppliers because it bought new releases in such huge volumes.

New Technology

One growing problem facing Blockbuster by the early 1990s was the variety of new ways in which customers could view movies and other kinds of entertainment. Blockbuster had always felt competition both from other sources of movies—such as cable TV and movie theaters—and from other forms of entertainment—such as bowling, baseball games, and outdoor activities. In the 1990s, technology began to give customers more ways to watch movies. New technological threats included pay-per-view (PPV) or video-on-demand (VOD) systems, digital compression, and direct broadcast satellites.

Pay-per-view movies became a major competitive threat to video-rental stores. With PPV systems, cable customers can call their local cable company and pay a fee to have a scheduled movie, concert, or sporting event aired on their television set. In the future, perhaps cable customers would be able to call up their local "video company" and choose any movie to be aired on their televisions for a fee; the cable company would make the movies available when customers wanted them. Increasingly, telephone companies were becoming interested in the potential for pay-for-view because the networks of fiber-optic cable they installed throughout the country in the 1990s can be used to transmit movies as well. Huizinga claimed Blockbuster was not overly concerned about PPV systems because only one-third of U.S. households have access to PPV, and fiber optics were expensive. Also, he claimed home-video rental was cheaper than PPV, and new releases are attained thirty to forty-five days before PPV.

VOD takes the PPV concept further. Bellcore, the research branch of the regional Bell companies, invented VOD. With this system (still in the development stage for many companies), a customer will use an interactive box to select a movie from a list of thousands and the choice will be transmitted to an "information warehouse" that stores thousands of tapes in digital formats. The selected video is then routed back to the customer's house through either fiber-optic cable or phone lines. This bypasses the local video-rental store because the movies are stored digitally on tape at the cable company's headquarters.

Movie companies or video stores like Blockbuster could function as the information warehouse from which the video selections are made; Blockbuster actively tried to canvass movie studios to become the warehouse so that it could control the VOD market. However, it could not put any deal together. The linking of phone companies with other entertainment companies could also become a direct threat, but Huizinga believed the local Blockbuster store would eventually become the hub of the VOD network. He felt that phone companies would prefer to deal with Blockbuster than with companies like Time Warner or Paramount, which lacked both Blockbuster's skills in video retailing and its established customer base— the 30 million customers who make 600 million trips per year to the local store.

Blockbuster's Emerging Strategies

In the 1990s, 70% of the world's VCRs were in countries outside the United States, and foreign countries accounted for half of total world video-rental revenues.

In 1991, the United States was the largest video market with revenues of $11 billion, Japan was second with $2.6 billion, followed by the UK with $1.4 billion and Canada with $1.2 billion. Blockbuster began to expand into international markets in 1989 when it saw the opportunity to exploit its marketing expertise, superstore concept, operating knowledge, financial strength, and ability to attract franchisees abroad.

Just as in the United States, Blockbuster started a program both to build new video superstores and to acquire foreign competitors abroad. Planning to be a leader in home entertainment around the world, Blockbuster's objective was to obtain a 25% share of international revenue by 1995 and to have 2,000 stores in international markets by 1996. In 1989, stores were opened in Canada and the UK. In 1990, Blockbuster opened its first store in Puerto Rico. It continued its expansion into the UK, Canada, the Virgin Islands, Venezuela, and Spain. Franchise agreements were also signed in Japan, Australia, and Mexico.

To expand in the UK in 1992, Blockbuster purchased Cityvision PLC, the UK's largest video retailer, for $81 million cash and 3.9 million shares of stock. At this time, Cityvision ran 875 stores in Britain and Austria under the name Ritz. Blockbuster transformed the Ritz outlets into Blockbuster stores and used the chain as a start for further expansion into Europe, just as it had taken over large video chains in the United States on its way to becoming the national leader. Joint ventures were also negotiated in France, Germany, and Italy. Blockbuster increased the number of franchise stores in Mexico, Chile, Venezuela, and Spain. By 1995, the company had over 2,000 stores in nine foreign countries.

Blockbuster created an international home-video division to oversee and manage its expansion into foreign markets. Besides having expertise in international operations, marketing, merchandising, product purchasing, distribution, franchising, real estate, and field support, this division is proficient at dealing with differences in entertainment, language, and business culture between different countries and is successfully implementing Blockbuster's domestic strategy in its foreign operations.

Blockbuster became a national video-rental chain because of the way it positioned itself in the market as a family-oriented store with a wide selection of videos, convenient hours and locations, and fast checkout. Blockbuster began to expand its entertainment concept into several new markets or industries such as film entertainment programming and music retailing. Also, to increase its revenue, Blockbuster made deals to broaden its range of product offerings.

To enter the entertainment programming, Blockbuster invested in Spelling Entertainment Group and Republic Pictures. Both of these companies have large film libraries—a source of inexpensive movies for Blockbuster's retail operations. Blockbuster also chose the music retail business as an area into which it could expand its entertainment concept. Blockbuster saw a fit between selling records, cassettes, and compact disks and renting or selling videos, so it decided to employ the same strategy it had used in the video-rental market: opening new stores and acquiring chains of music stores using the revenues from its video superstores. Blockbuster agreed to buy Sound Warehouse and Music Plus, two record-store chains, for $185 million. At the time, Sound Warehouse was the seventh largest music retailer and Music Plus was the twelfth largest. These two retail chains had a total of 236 stores in thirty-five states, primarily in California and the South. This acquisition made Blockbuster the seventh largest music chain.

Huizinga Sells Blockbuster to Viacom

Although Blockbuster, with its rapid growth and large positive cash flow, seemed poised to become an entertainment powerhouse, Huizinga knew there were clouds ahead. The rapid advance in digital technology including broadband Internet meant VOD was increasingly likely to become a reality. Some analysts were suggesting even that Blockbuster was a "dinosaur." At the same time, Huizinga soon found out the music retailing industry was highly competitive and had many more experienced competitors than the video-rental industry. Major competitors like Sam Goody's and Tower Records also had plans to accelerate the development of their own music megastores, and profit margins in music retailing were low. Moreover, Wal-Mart began a major push to lower the prices of CDs and then VHS tapes, and price wars were developing. Moreover, even in the video-rental business, entrepreneurs who had watched Blockbuster's rapid growth still believed there were opportunities for entry. Chains such as Hollywood Video began to expand rapidly, and increased competition seemed imminent here too.

Huizinga decided that the time was ripe to sell the Blockbuster chain, just as he had sold other chains before. His opportunity came when Sumner Redstone, chairman of Viacom, become involved in an aggressive bidding war to buy Paramount Studios, the movie company. Redstone recognized the value of Blockbuster's huge cash flow in helping to fund the debt needed to take over Paramount. Ignoring the risks involved in taking over Blockbuster, in 1994 Viacom acquired the company for $8.4 billion in stock (further details about the logic behind the acquisition are found in Case 30 on Viacom), and Huizinga cashed in his huge stockholdings.

Just the next year, in 1995, a tidal wave of problems hit the Blockbuster chain. First, a brutal price war hit the video-rental industry as new video chain start-ups fought to find a niche in major markets to get some of the lucrative industry revenues. Second, movie studios started to lower the price of tapes, realizing they could make more money by selling them directly to customers rather than letting companies like Blockbuster make the money through tape rentals. Third, as both Blockbuster's video and music operations expanded, it became obvious that the company did not have in hand the materials management and distribution systems needed to manage the complex flow of products to its stores. Overhead costs started to soar, so that together with declines in revenues, the company turned from making a profit to a loss. Blockbuster's cash flow was much less useful to Redstone now, burdened as he was by the huge debt for Paramount. Blockbuster's declining performance led to Viacom's stock price dropping sharply, and Redstone reacted by firing its top managers and searching for an experienced executive to turn the Blockbuster division around.

Blockbuster, 1996–1998

To control Blockbuster's soaring overhead costs, Redstone looked for an executive with experience in low-cost merchandising, and in 1996, he pulled off a coup by hiring William Fields, the heir apparent to David Glass, Wal-Mart's CEO, and an information systems and logistics expert. Fields began planning on a huge state-of-the-art distribution facility that would serve all Blockbuster's U.S. stores to replace its outdated facility. He also started the development of a new state-of-the-art point-of-sale merchandising information system that would give Blockbuster real-time feedback on which videos were generating the most money and when they should be transferred to stores in other regions to make the most use of Blockbuster's stock of videos—its most important physical resource. Third, Fields added more retail merchandise to Blockbuster's product mix, such as candy, comics, and audio books. The results of these efforts would take a couple of years to bear fruit, however.

Some analysts believed that by 1997, Redstone, recognizing the negative impact of Blockbuster's operations on Viacom's stock price, was trying to cut costs to boost short-term profits and "harvest" the company so that he could spin off Blockbuster—sensing that the troubled division was not going to be fixed quickly. Apparently, Fields and Redstone came into conflict over what was Blockbuster's future in the Viacom empire. And, with its performance continuing to decline in the first quarter of 1997 with a drop in profit of 20%, only thirteen months after taking over at Blockbuster, Fields resigned in April 1997. Viacom's stock fell to a three-year low. Redstone argued that this was absurd because Blockbuster generated $3 billion in revenue and $800 in cash flow for Viacom in 1996. However, the specter of video-on-demand and increased price competition in the music and video business made analysts wonder if Blockbuster was going to recover. Furthermore, Fields was the expert in distribution and logistics.

Once again, Redstone looked around for an executive who could help turn around Blockbuster, and in the news was John Antioco, the chief of PepsiCo's Taco Bell restaurants. In just eight months, Antioco, by introducing a new menu, new pricing, and new store setup, had engineered a 180-degree turnaround in Taco Bell's performance, turning a mounting loss into rising profit. Antioco seemed the perfect choice as Blockbuster's CEO.

After Antioco took the helm, he started to assess the situation. The video-rental market was still flat; sales of movie videos were soaring as their prices came down in outlets such as Wal-Mart. Fields's strategy of enlarging the entertainment product lines carried in Blockbuster stores, while it seemed like a logical move, had failed as costs continued to rise and products had short shelf lives because changing fads and fashions made the value of Blockbuster's inventory unpredictable. What should be Blockbuster's merchandising mix? And how should Antioco manage the purchase and distribution of Blockbuster's biggest ongoing expense, videotapes,

to create a value chain that would lead to increased profitability?

Antioco realized he needed to focus on how to reorganize Blockbuster's value chain to simultaneously reduce costs and generate more revenues. Blockbuster's biggest expense and asset was its inventory of videos, so this was the logical place to start. Antioco and Redstone examined the way Blockbuster obtained its movies. It was presently purchasing tapes from the big studios—MGM, Disney, and so on—at the high price of $65. Because it had to pay this high price, it could not purchase enough copies of a particular hit movie to satisfy customer demand when the movie was released. As a result, customers left unsatisfied and revenues were lost. Perhaps there was a better way of managing the process for both the movie studios and Blockbuster to raise revenues from movie tape rental.

Antioco and Redstone proposed that Blockbuster and the movie studios enter into a revenue sharing agreement, whereby the movie studios would supply Blockbuster with tapes at cost, around $8, which would allow it to purchase 800% more copies of a single title; Blockbuster would then split rental revenues with the studios 50/50. The result, they hoped, would be that they could "grow the market" for rental tapes by 20 to 30% a year; thus both Blockbuster's and the movie studios' revenues would grow. This would also counter the threat from satellite programming, which was taking away all their revenues; 6 million households were now subscribing to direct satellite services. While this deal was being negotiated in 1997, video rentals at Blockbuster dropped 4% more, and the studios that had been hesitating to enter into this radically different kind of sales agreement came on board. This came at a crucial point for Blockbuster, too, since its cash flow continued to drop as it faced higher write-off costs for outdated tapes. With the new revenue sharing agreement signed, however, the profitability of its new business model would increase dramatically. (Blockbuster's market share increased from something less than 30% to over 40% in the next five years, and after a few years, the division returned to profitability.) The move studios also benefited as their stream of income increased enormously.

Antioco's second major change in strategy was to abandon the attempt to transform Blockbuster's stores into more general entertainment outlets to refocus on its core movie-rental business. It abandoned its idea to expand its music chain, and, in October 1998, it sold its 378 Blockbuster music chains to Wherehouse Entertainment for $115 million.

Nevertheless, all these changes hurt Blockbuster's performance in the short term. In 1998, Viacom announced it would record a $437 million charge in the second quarter to write down the value of its Blockbuster tape inventory since it now had to revise the accounting method it adopted when it entered the new revenue sharing agreement for tapes from Hollywood studios. These charges wiped out Viacom's profits, and Redstone once again announced that a spinoff or initial public offering of Blockbuster was likely because the unit was punishing Viacom's stock price and threatening Viacom's future profitability.

On the plus side, however, significantly, the revenue sharing agreement resulted in a sharp increase in revenues; same-store video rentals increased by 13% in 1998. Since rental tapes would now be amortized over only a three-month period—the time of greatest rental sales—not the old six to twenty-six months, the new business model seemed poised to finally increase cash flows. One good year for Blockbuster would allow Redstone, who had been increasingly criticized for his purchase of Blockbuster, to go forward with his desire to pursue an "IPO carve out" whereby Viacom would sell between 10 and 20% of the Blockbuster stock to the public in an IPO to create a public market for the stock and make an eventual spinoff possible.

By the end of 1998, there were continuing signs of recovery. The move to a revenue sharing agreement had allowed Blockbuster's managers to develop strategies to increase responsiveness to customers that allowed them to pursue their business model in a profitable way. With the huge increase in the supply of new tapes made possible by the revenue sharing agreement, Blockbuster was now able to offer the Blockbuster Promise to its customers that their chosen title would be in stock or "next time, it's free." Also, lower prices could now be charged for older video titles to generate additional revenues without threatening profitability. It turned out that the real threat to Blockbuster in the 1990s was not from new technology like video-on-demand, but the lack of the right strategies to keep customers happy—like having the products in stock that they wanted—and a failure to understand the important dynamics behind the value chain, such as revenue sharing, that would grow the market.

Outside the United States, Blockbuster had been increasing the scope of its international operations. In 1994, it opened its first stores in Italy and New Zealand; in 1995, it entered Israel, Brazil, Peru, Colombia, and Thailand; in 1996, Ecuador, Portugal, El Salvador, Panama, and Scandinavia, where it purchased Christianshavn Video In Denmark. In 1996, in went into Taiwan and Uruguay; in 1998, it acquired Video Flick's stores in Australia; in 1999, it entered Hong Kong as a gateway to China and opened its two-hundredth store in Mexico; and in 2000, it expanded its operations in Central America to Costa Rica and Guatemala. By 2002, it operated almost 2,600 stores outside the United States. The main advantage of its global operations is that it can constantly distribute copies of tapes that are less in demand overseas to other countries where they will appear as new releases and customers will be willing to pay the highest rental prices for them. In turn, the tapes will trickle down to other countries so that even though revenues might be less, since the cost of the tape has already been amortized, operations will still be profitable. On the other hand, it can also identify foreign-made movies that might attract a large U.S. viewing audience as its customers search its shelves.

In 1998, Blockbuster finally opened its 820,000-square-foot distribution center in Kinney, Texas; now it was in a real position to reduce costs and speed delivery of tapes to locations where they were most in demand, and to move them when demand dropped. Also in 1998, Blockbuster began to offer "neighborhood favorites," a program in which each store stocked tapes customized to local tastes. In keeping with this differentiation approach, Blockbuster Rewards, its frequent renters program, was developed. It is a rewards program designed to keep its customers returning regularly to its stores and seeing the changes it has made, with a coupon for a free video every month.

Antioco Transforms Blockbuster, 1999–2002

A major turning point for Blockbuster occurred in 1999. After reestablishing Blockbuster's business model, Antioco orchestrated a successful initial public stock offering in August 1999. It turned out that 1999 was the first of four consecutive years of same-store sales increases as Antioco set about to change the entertainment mix in stores to increase revenues. Having gotten rid of music, candy, and comics, a new opportunity arose in 1999 with the introduction of DVDs, whose high quality suggested that they would soon become the next entertainment media of choice. DVDs were a natural product-line extension for Blockbuster. In 1999, Blockbuster introduced DVDs into 3,000 of its stores to assess their promise; customer reaction was favorable as sales of DVD players and other digital media were soaring.

It was here that Antioco apparently made a major error, for given the success of the video revenue sharing deal with movie studios, it seemed likely that the same kind of deal could be negotiated for DVDs. Reportedly Warner Brothers started the ball rolling by offering Blockbuster a DVD revenue sharing deal. Antioco turned down the offer, however; one reason seems to have been Antioco's belief that the high price of DVDs would deter rental customers from buying them. He believed that Blockbuster would reap more returns from buying the DVDs themselves and then renting them. Another reason was that Blockbuster was about to face a lawsuit from independent video retailers, who claimed that the company had gained an unfair competitive advantage from the sharing agreement; signing a new DVD revenue sharing agreement might therefore generate more potential lawsuits.

In any event, to test the popularity of DVD rentals, in 2000 Blockbuster increased the number of DVDs titles it carried because they had much higher profit margins than VHS tapes—DVDs rented for a couple of dollars more. The result was dramatic: revenues soared and the pace of change speeded up. In 2001, Blockbuster abandoned attempts to customize tape offerings to local markets and eliminated 25% of the company's less productive VHS tapes in order to focus on the booming market for DVD rentals. Once again, it took a charge to amortize these tapes, but then shipped them to its stores overseas to capitalize on growing global demand for its products. The result was that by the end of 2001 the company achieved record revenues, strong cash flow, and increased profitability while it lowered its debt by more then $430 million. Since 1997, Antioco had grown Blockbuster's revenues from $3.3 billion to over $5 billion and turned free cash flow from a negative position to over $250 million for 2001. Its stock rose as investors realized that the company now had a business model that generated cash.

By 2002, it became clear the future was in DVDs. Blockbuster announced it was switching even more quickly to high-margin DVDs and phasing out even more of its VHS and that DVDs would account for 40% of the chain's rental inventory. This percentage has increased sharply ever since. DVDs swept away VHS tapes much as CDs swept away vinyl records. DVD rentals increased 115%, and in the spring of 2002, Blockbuster made $66 million in net income.

Growing Videogame Market

Antioco searched for more ways to broaden Blockbuster's product line to keep revenues increasing and ward off possible future declines from rental revenues. One answer came at the end of 2001 when Microsoft introduced its Xbox videogame console to compete with the Sony PlayStation 2 and Nintendo GameCube and the robust nature of sales in the videogame market became clear—it was a $15 billion a year revenue market. Blockbuster decided to carry a full lineup of GameCube, Xbox, and PlayStation software and hardware for rental as well as deciding to rent and sell videogames in its stores. It also began to try to work exclusive deals with game makers for old gaming systems and software since there is a huge installed base of older-generation videogames. The attraction of this kind of products to customers is that they can try any game they want before they are forced to pay the high price of buying a game that they may not like. Videogames seemed to be a natural complementary product line, and in May 2002, Blockbuster announced that it wanted to become "gamers' most comprehensive rental and retail resource."

Blockbuster's new product line was a success, and it pushed to double its videogame rentals by 2003. To help achieve this goal, in the summer of 2002, Blockbuster began to offer $19.95 monthly rental service for unlimited videogame rentals. This fit well with Blockbuster's family profile since parents could come into a store to rent a DVD while their children picked up a videogame.

The company tested a new concept of a videogame store-in-store called Game Rush in 2003, and its success at attracting new customers, who also paid a monthly fee for unlimited videogame rental, led to its fast decision to roll the game program out to half its stores by 2004. However, all its new initiatives cost between $80 and $100 million marketing dollars, and this, together with the high capital costs of maintaining its stores, caused its net income to fall despite growing revenues.

A Blockbuster Performance?

In June 2003, Blockbuster went to court to confront independent video retailers who claimed that Blockbuster's VHS revenue sharing agreement that had saved the company in 1999 violated antitrust laws by discriminating against them since they did not obtain preferential price treatment. Independents argued that before the revenue sharing deals were negotiated, Blockbuster had only 24% of the market while they had 55%, but by 2003, Blockbuster's share had grown to 40%. The court ruled that the independents had had a similar opportunity to negotiate such revenue sharing agreements and dismissed the suit against Blockbuster, however. Now the case was over, and as DVD rentals soared, Antioco tried to establish a new revenue sharing agreement for DVDs with movie studios. Antioco argued that raising wholesale prices and developing a rental sharing agreement would generate the highest long-term returns for both movie studios and Blockbuster—but it was too late.

The main reason was that by 2002 the movie studios had began to sell DVDs directly to the general public, and they decided to set the wholesale price of DVDs relatively low to generate sales. However, sales took off, there was an unexpectedly strong customer demand to own DVDs and develop a home-movie library, and the movie studios were generating billions of dollars in DVD sales and they no longer saw the need for a middleman like Blockbuster to take a major share of DVD sales revenues.

This came as a major blow to Blockbuster, but Antioco tried to make the best of it by becoming a major player in the DVD retail market, hoping it could generate high DVD sales revenues, in addition to its increasing DVD rental revenues. However, he was in for a shock because the movie studios were obtaining such high revenues from DVD sales they were willing to reduce their wholesale prices for major low-cost retailers like Wal-Mart and Best Buy that could sell millions of copies in their stores. Wal-Mart, in particular, began to aggressively discount DVDs and sell at prices well below Blockbuster's; the result was that Blockbuster gained a much smaller share of the DVD retail market than expected. And, because customers were not going to its stores to buy

them, it also did not enjoy any spillover from increased DVD rentals.

In fact, the boom in DVD sales starting in 2002 caused a major shift as by 2003 customers spent significantly more on purchasing movies on DVDs and tapes than on movie rentals. Thus while Blockbuster's retail sales of movies rose 19% to $12.3 billion, movie rentals slipped 3% to $9.9 billion; the result was that same-store sales at Blockbuster stores opened for one year fell by 6%—a very disappointing result. Although Blockbuster could claim record revenues and profits because of its decision in 2002 and 2003 to switch to DVD rentals, revenues also had increased because it had opened over 550 new stores in 2003—so this was growth without profitability. Moreover, things were not so rosy as they might appear because a large part of these extra profits had come from aggressive cost-cutting efforts in its stores throughout this period and by a substantial reduction in local and national advertising to reduce operating costs—once and for all, gains that could not be repeated.

Blockbuster had to find new ways to increase rental revenues and do it quickly. To reduce customers' incentive to buy DVDs and build up their own movie libraries, Blockbuster tested a new marketing strategy, a monthly fee of $24.99 for unlimited DVD rentals in some of its stores. The program was successful, and Blockbuster began to roll it out nationally in 2004 and experiment with variations in pricing and number of rentals per visit. As mentioned earlier, it already had a similar program in videogame rentals that was performing well.

In another major move, it announced the end to late fees in 2004 as it became clear this was a major motivation of customers to buy DVDs and not to rent them; also, other forms of movie delivery such as pay-per-view were becoming more common, and these had no late fees. This was a significant decision because late fees were a significant contributor to Blockbuster's revenues and profits; indeed, it was estimated that late fees accounted for over 35% of Blockbuster's profit! It hoped no late fees would translate into more rentals, but this did not happen and put a damper on revenue growth in 2004 and 2005.

The Split from Viacom

Recall that Viacom had decided to take Blockbuster public once again in August 1999 at $15 a share, but it maintained an 82% stake in the company. Blockbuster stock traded as high as $30 a share in May 2000, and although Viacom originally planned to sell the rest of Blockbuster to the public soon after the 1999 stock offering, the company decided to retain its stake—in part because of the business's steady cash flow and because Viacom became distracted by integrating CBS, which it acquired in 2001, into its operations.

Through its aggressive cost cutting, particularly in marketing, Blockbuster continued to perform well financially into 2003 when Blockbuster generated 22.5% of Viacom's $19.1 billion in revenue and 12% of its $4.4 billion in cash flow. But Blockbuster's 8% revenue growth was anemic, and with most of the cost cuts already made and the continuing high fixed costs of running its stores, it was clear that future revenue growth and stock appreciation was going to be challenging. Also, the uncertainty concerning how quickly home-video and videogame rentals might fall in the future because of the growth in broadband technology once again began to worry Viacom. So throughout 2003, Redstone tried, but failed, to find a buyer for Viacom's Blockbuster shares while they were on the rise.

In January 2004 (well before it announced the end to late fees), Blockbuster's stock hit a high of $20. Believing that the two companies' business models were now diverging too fast, Viacom announced that it would totally spin off its Blockbuster unit by allowing holders of Viacom shares to swap them for shares in Blockbuster. To sweeten the deal, shareholders would also receive a substantial once-and-for all dividend for swapping their Viacom stock for Blockbuster stock. Enough shareholders took advantage of the offer for Viacom to unload its 82% stake, and Blockbuster was now spun off as a fully independent company. Antioco now had to find a way to increase Blockbuster's revenues and free cash flow, but there were still many challenges confronting the company.

The Growing Use of Broadband

Since the 1990s, the new technology of PPV or VOD, the direct download or streaming of movies to customers over cable, satellite, phone lines, or other forms of broadband connection, had been seen as a growing threat to Blockbuster's business model. Essentially, this technology would bypass the need for a bricks-and-mortar store, and the potential threat of this new technology had depressed Blockbuster's stock for years.

In 2000, recognizing the growing importance of satellite programming in PPV delivery, Blockbuster formed an alliance with DIRECTTV to provide a co-branded PPV service on DIRECTTV. Blockbuster also became a new distribution channel for DIRECTTV; under their deal, Blockbuster received a fee for each dish sold, a share of future monthly payments, and a share of revenues from DIRECTTV customers' future orders of PPV movies that would provide a higher net profit than Blockbuster made from each in-store rental and so lessen its dependence on video rentals. Antioco hoped this alliance would boost Blockbuster's ambition to be the major player in PPV, and at the very least, add 5% to Blockbuster's revenues, enough to make a substantial impact on its bottom line.

In an attempt to maintain its dominant position in the movie-rental marketplace and gain more control of the content or "entertainment software" end of the business, in 2000 Blockbuster announced an agreement with MGM to digitally stream and download recent theatrical releases, films, and television programming from the MGM library to Blockbuster's website for PPV consumption. It started to roll out its "Blockbuster on Demand" PPV, arguing that video rentals and PPV could exist side by side. Initial testing of the program started at the end of 2000, and Blockbuster announced it would try to form similar agreements with other movie studios. It even signed a deal with TiVo, a maker of set-top digital recorders, to offer a VOD service through broadband using TiVo's recorders. TiVo agreed to put demonstration kiosks in over 4,000 Blockbusters stores to its 65 million customers. However, all these moves failed to establish Blockbuster as a major player in the PPV delivery market.

The push toward VOD steadily increased in the mid 2000s as new technologies to ensure its fast delivery to customers over broadband connections improved. In August 2005, for example, five major movie studios—Sony, Time Warner, Universal, MGM, and Paramount—announced a plan to bypass powerful middlemen like Blockbuster and HBO and offer their own PPV service directly to customers, although this service was still not up and running by 2006. In addition, Disney and Twentieth-Century Fox also were planning their own PPV services, and in 2006, Disney announced its intention of being the hub of the future PPV service and make Blockbuster redundant with its new PPV technology that it reportedly is going to roll out in 2007. Also in 2006, Amazon.com launched a form of PPV service whereby its customers could download a wide range of movie content. Its PPV ran into technology glitches including long download times, which it has since improved, but it is not clear it has made much of an impression in the industry. Also in 2006, Apple made a big push into the VOD market with its new video iPods; by 2007, Apple had formed two major agreements with large media companies Disney and Paramount to allow its customers to download both TV shows and movies. Analysts believe Apple clearly intends to try to establish itself as the primary PPV video wholesaler, just as it has become the main wholesaler in the music download business.

PPV buy rates are still relatively low and below expectations, however, because cable TV companies and phone companies or satellite operators simply do not have the Internet bandwidth necessary for fast downloads, especially at peak periods such as in the evening or on weekends. Also, VOD was conceived as a more convenient way to watch movies at home; rather than fighting traffic and risking late fees, customers could watch new video releases without leaving their couches—and without waiting. But the process of selecting and downloading a movie is still not easy. Movie studios, too, have a policy of not releasing films for PPV/VOD for at least thirty days after they are first released to protect DVD rentals at video stores; this generates billions more in revenue than home PPV services.

Nevertheless, by 2007, the threat of new easy-to-use digital technology had become an emerging reality as movie studios and distributors like Amazon and Apple fought to become the hub of choice, and it was clear by now that although Antioco's goal, just as Huizinga before him, was that Blockbuster should provide this pivotal role, it obviously had no special technological competencies in the digital PPV media arena—no more than movie studios, cable operators, satellite providers, and so on. Moreover, in the future, all movies could be licensed to any VOD on a nonexclusive basis so each studio would control the pricing and availability of its films. Now, as PCs, TVs, and even MP3 players like iPod began to converge, the potentially huge VOD market would annihilate Blockbuster's niche. By 2006, Blockbuster's stock had dropped to a low of $5.

The Netflix Battle

Although the way future broadband PPV service will unfold will have major consequences for Blockbuster's business model, in the last few years, Blockbuster has also had to deal with the growing threat from online DVD rental services, such as that offered by Netflix, which has also cut into its rental business. The emergence of Netflix in 2003, with its business model of using the combination of the Internet and regular mail service to rent and deliver DVDs to customers, was revolutionary in the movie-rental industry. The big appeal of Netflix's new plan was the promise of multiple movie rentals for a single monthly price. With Netflix's most popular plan, subscribers can rent an unlimited number of movies for $17.99 a month, keeping as many as three DVDs at a time. Once they send the movies back, by popping them into a postage-paid envelope and dropping them in a mailbox, they can immediately get more. The services don't limit the number of DVDs that can be ordered in any one month.

Obviously, using the Internet to deliver DVDs to customers is a far less expensive way of renting DVDs than owning a chain of bricks-and-mortar video stores. Apparently Blockbuster was offered the chance to buy Netflix in the early 2000s for $100 million, but Antioco refused; he did not consider that this market segment was big enough to be profitable, given that most movie rentals tend to be spur of the moment decisions. He believed few customers would sit down and work out in advance which movies to watch. Netflix, however, went to work to attract customers, and through massive online advertising and mailing campaigns, it began to attract increasing numbers of customers and became a real threat. By 2004, Netflix claimed to have over 1.4 million customers, and the proven success of its business model showed Antioco he had made a mistake.

In 2004, Blockbuster announced it would also launch an online DVD rental service, although Antioco still commented that he thought this segment would only ever reach about 3 million customers. Blockbuster claimed its new program would be better than Netflix's because customers who ordered DVDs online could then return them to Blockbusters stores if they chose. Antioco argued Blockbuster's business model was the best because it was the only company able to provide a simultaneous online *and* bricks-and-mortar service that would give customers more options and better service. For example, if Blockbuster customers returned DVDs to their local store, as part of Blockbuster's "Total Service" plan, they would then receive a coupon for a free in-store rental.

The point, of course, is that by getting customers into its stores, Blockbuster could potentially generate more rental, sales, and other kinds of revenues. Also, Blockbuster's hybrid service overcame one of the big disadvantages of Netflix for rental customers—the inability to get a movie instantly if you suddenly decide Saturday night you want to rent something. Blockbuster's program allowed for advance planning *and* spontaneous rental.

Given that Blockbuster has 48 million members, an online DVD service may prove a useful way of increasing future revenues, but in the short run, the problem for Blockbuster was that the new service required a major financial investment to set up the online infrastructure and national marketing campaign. This helped drain Blockbuster's profits, and its stock price fell from $20 a share at the beginning of 2004 to just $10 share at the beginning of 2005 as investors became concerned it could not provide the online service in a cost-effective way. Analysts also wondered if Netflix had gained the first-mover advantage and so would be hard to compete with. To make things worse, Wal-Mart, which already sold low-priced DVDs to attract customers, started a similar online rental program.

However, in 2006, Antioco announced that the company, after a shaky start, had achieved its year-end goal of 2 million subscribers to Total Access. Moreover, significant subscriber growth was achieved without any broadcast media advertising, except in a handful of test markets; in-store and online marketing had been the key to Blockbuster's success. Nevertheless, Netflix and Blockbuster were now locked in a vicious battle for subscribers, and both companies were paying heavily for online ads on major websites such as eBay and Yahoo.

Once again, Antioco argued, because customers no longer have to choose between renting online or renting in-store, they never need to be without a movie, and this would make Blockbuster.com the fastest growing online DVD rental service in 2007.

And, of course, cable TV operators, and then movie studios, started PPV services that allowed consumers to order a movie over the TV or computer to watch immediately for $3 or $4. These offerings have all the convenience of a video because movies can be paused, rewound, or fast-forwarded for as long as twenty-four hours after the initial rental and they have no late fees.

Global Problems

Blockbuster has over 3,000 stores globally, but it has faced challenging problems in recent years in managing problems that have arisen in different countries. For example, in the UK it has maintained steady expansion both into DVDs and videogame rentals, and its video store chain is profitable. But in Germany it shut down its operations in 2006 because in the German rental market, there is no profit without sex and violence, which is not part of Blockbuster's policy of stocking only family entertainment and movie classics. Similarly, it closed all twenty-four of its Hong Kong stores in 2005 because of intense competition from pirated DVDs available for sale throughout China for a dollar each! Blockbuster had planned to use Hong Kong as a gateway to the huge market in mainland China, but the availability of pirated low-cost movies for sale in China made this impossible. Nevertheless, Blockbuster continues to operate in a number of markets where video piracy is a big problem, including Taiwan, Thailand, and Mexico.

The Future

Year 2007 may be a pivotal year in Blockbuster's history as the company tries to position itself for success in the quickly changing movie DVD sales and rental business. In January 2007, Blockbuster's stock rose when it announced that it would sell its Rhino videogame chain, which has ninety-four stores, and use the capital to pay down debt and fund its expansion into online movie rental. Its stock then rose sharply a few days later when Antioco announced that Blockbuster was contemplating reducing the size of its DVD inventory in its stores to focus more of its resources on its online business to attract more customers there.

However, a few days later, Netflix, responding to criticism that it was allowing Blockbuster to catch up and take its customers, announced a major new instant movie streaming service to its users' PCs over the Internet that is being offered at no additional charge. Netflix expects to introduce the instant viewing system to about 250,000 more subscribers each week through June 2007 to ensure its computers can cope with the increased demand. The allotted viewing time will be tied to how much customers already pay for their DVD rentals. Under Netflix's most popular $17.99 monthly package, subscribers will receive eighteen hours of Internet viewing time. A major drawback of the instant viewing system is that it works only on PCs and laptops equipped with a high-speed Internet connection and Windows; movies can't be watched on cell phones, TVs, or video iPods or on Apple Inc.'s operating system.

Also, new technology has emerged that allows for DVDs obtained through the mail or downloaded on-line to "self-destruct" within some defined time period, preventing the threat of video piracy. This technology is also available for physical DVDs, which also self-destruct when the rental time period has expired. This is likely to be important because of the growth in the number of DVD rental kiosks that have appeared in supermarkets and fast-food restaurants that allow users to quickly rent a just-released movie. Currently, these kiosks charge expensive late fees, but with self-destruct technology, they could be seen as a convenient way to rent new movies in the future.

So what future strategies Blockbuster will take was unclear in early 2007. Will Blockbuster contemplate closing more and more of its stores if its online business model proves more profitable? And if so, what will be its mix of mail versus Internet movie delivery, and what kind of PPV technology will it adopt? Certainly a virtual business would be a more appropriate hub for a complete VOD operation with a recognized brand name, but what then would happen to its physical stores? Is the combination of bricks-and-mortar and online retailing still the ideal mix in this market for movie and videogame rentals and sales? How quickly movie and video storefronts like Apple's, Amazon.com's, and Disney's become popular is likely to determine this. Is there a potential buyer for the company on the horizon? Could Blockbuster stores become Apple stores?

Finally, a new dilemma emerged for the company in 2007 when on January 25 Netflix announced it ended the fourth quarter with about 6.31 million subscribers, compared with a total of 4.18 million at the end of 2005. The total also represents 12% growth over the third-quarter total of 5.66 million, and its revenue climbed to $277.2 million from $193 million a year earlier. Now, its stock shot up and Blockbuster's plunged. Clearly, Netflix remains a major competitor, the fight to dominate the movie-rental market and movie and TV program instant streaming video service in the future is open, and who will win remains to be seen.

SOURCES

Bruce Apar, "Ruminations on Burstyn, Bezos & Blockbuster," *Video Store*, January 14–January 20, 2001, p. 6.

Thomas K. Arnold, "Broadbuster," *Video Store*, August 6–August 12, 2000, pp. 1, 38.

Blockbuster 10Ks and Annual Reports, 1988–2001, http://www.blockbuster.com.

"Citibank Reaches Pact To Install Its ATMs In Blockbuster Stores," *Wall Street Journal*, May 28, 1998, p. A11.

Greg Clarkin, "Fast Forward," *Marketing and Media Decisions*, March 1990, pp. 57–59.

Gail DeGeorge, *Business Week*, January 22, 1990, pp. 47–48.

Gail DeGeorge, Jonathan Levine, and Robert Neff, "They Don't Call It Blockbuster for Nothing," *Business Week*, October 19, 1992, pp. 113–114.

Doug Desjardins, "Blockbuster Scores With Games, DVDs," *DSN Retailing Today*, May 6, 2002, p. 5.

Geraldine Fabrikant, "Blockbuster President Resigns: Video Chain Revamps to Adapt to New Units," *New York Times*, January 5, 1993, p. D6.

Daniel Frankel, "Blockbuster Revamps Play Areas," *Video Business*, May 27, 2002, p. 38.

John Gaudiosi, "Blockbuster Pushes PS2," *Video Store*, December 2–December 8, 2001, pp. 1, 38.

"Global Notes: Focus 1-Blockbuster Entertainment Corp. (BV)," *Research Highlights*, October 26, 1990, p. 9.

Laurie Grossman and Gabriella Stern, "Blockbuster to Buy Controlling Stake in Spelling in Swap," *Wall Street Journal*, March 9, 1993, p. B9.

Laura Heller, "Radio Shack, Blockbuster Put Synergies to the Test," *DSN Retailing Today*, June 4, 2001, p. 5.

Scott Hume, "Blockbuster Means More than Video," *Advertising Age*, June 1, 1992, p. 4.

Daniel Kadlec, "How Blockbuster Changed the Rules," *New York Times*, August 3, 1998, pp. 48–49.

Kyra Kirkwood, "Blockbuster Moves Into Used DVDs," *Video Store*, March 25, 2000, p. 1.

M. McCarthy, *Wall Street Journal*, March 22, 1991, pp. A1, A6.

Bruce Orwall, "Five Studios Join Venture for Video on Demand," *Wall Street Journal*, August 17, 2001, p. A3.

QRP Merrill Lynch Extended Company Comment, November 16, 1990.

Johnnie Roberts, "Blockbuster Officials Envision Superstores for Music Business," *Wall Street Journal*, October 28, 1992, p. B10.

Trudi M. Rosenblum, "Blockbuster to Add Audiobooks," *Publishers Weekly*, June 19, 2000, p. 14.

S. Sandomir, *New York Times*, June 19, 1991, pp. S22–S25.

Eric Savitz, "An End to Fast Forward?" *Barron's*, December 11, 1989, pp. 13, 43–46.

Eben Shapiro, "Heard on the Street: Chief Redstone Tries to Convince Wall Street There's Life Beyond Blockbuster at Viacom," *Wall Street Journal*, April 24, 1997, p. C2.

Eben Shapiro, "Movies: Blockbuster Seeks a New Deal With Hollywood," *Wall Street Journal*, March 25, 1998, p. B1.

Eben Shapiro, "Viacom Net Drops 70% as Cash Flow Slips on Weakness at Blockbuster Unit," *Wall Street Journal*, October 30, 1997, p. B8.

Eben Shapiro, "Viacom Sets Major Charge Tied to Blockbuster," *Wall Street Journal*, July 23, 1998, p. A3.

Eben Shapiro, "Viacom Trims Blockbuster's Expansion, Igniting Speculation of Eventual Spinoff," *Wall Street Journal*, March 28, 1997, p. B5.

Eben Shapiro and Nikhil Deogun, "Antioco Takes Top Job at Troubled Blockbuster," *Wall Street Journal*, June 4, 1997, p. A3.

Eben Shapiro and Susan Pulliam, "Heard on the Street: Viacom to Name Wal-Mart's Heir Apparent, William Fields, to Head Blockbuster Video," *Wall Street Journal*, March 29, 1996, p. C2.

Paul Sweeting, "Big Blue Trimming Tapes," *Video Business*, September 17, 2001, p. 1.

Greg Tarr, "DirecTB Teams With Blockbuster," *Twice*, May 15, 2000, p. 1.

Richard Tedesco, "MGM, Blockbuster to Stream TV, Films," *Broadcasting & Cable*, January 24, 2000, p. 128.

"TiVo, Blockbuster Ink Cross-Promo Deal," *Twice*, January 17, 2000, p. 24.

"Video Stocks Stumbled," *Video Business*, September 3, 2001, p. 4.

Joan Villa, "Blockbuster Game Exclusive," *Video Store*, January 20–January 26, 2002, pp. 1, 40.

Audrey Warren and Martin Peers, "Video Retailers Have Day in Court—Plaintiffs Say Supply Deals Between Blockbuster Inc. and Studios Violate Laws," *Wall Street Journal*, June 13, 2002, p. B10.

The Evolution of the Small Package Express Delivery Industry, 1973–2006

This case was prepared by Charles W. L. Hill, the University of Washington.

The small package express delivery industry is that segment of the broader postal and cargo industries that specializes in rapid (normally one to three days) delivery of small packages. It is generally agreed that the modern express delivery industry in the United States began with Fred Smith's vision for Federal Express Company, which started operations in 1973. Federal Express transformed the structure of the existing air cargo industry and paved the way for rapid growth in the overnight package segment of that industry. A further impetus to the industry's development was the 1977 deregulation of the U.S. air cargo industry. This deregulation allowed Federal Express (and its emerging competitors) to buy large jets for the first time. The story of the industry during the 1980s was one of rapid growth and new entry. Between 1982 and 1989, small package express cargo shipments by air in the United States grew at an annual average rate of 31%. In contrast, shipments of air freight and air mail grew at an annual rate of only 2.7%.[1] This rapid growth attracted new entrants such as United Parcel Service (UPS) and Airborne Freight (which operated under the name Airborne Express). The entry of UPS triggered severe price cutting, which ultimately drove some of the weaker competitors out of the market and touched off a wave of consolidation in the industry.

By the mid-1990s, the industry structure had stabilized with four organizations—Federal Express, UPS, Airborne Express, and the U.S. Postal Service—accounting for the vast majority of U.S. express shipments. During the first half of the 1990s, the small package express industry continued to grow at a healthy rate, with shipments expanding by slightly more than 16% per annum.[2] Despite this growth, the industry was hit by repeated rounds of price cutting as the three big private firms battled to capture major accounts. In addition to price cutting, the big three also competed vigorously on the basis of technology, service offerings, and the global reach of their operations. By the late 1990s and early 2000s, however, the intensity of price competition in the industry had moderated, with a degree of pricing discipline being maintained, despite the fact that the growth rate for the industry slowed down. Between 1995 and 2000, the industry grew at 9.8% per year. In 2001, however, the volume of express parcels shipped by air fell by 5.9%, partly due to an economic slowdown and partly due to the aftereffects of the September 11 terrorist attack on the United States.[3] Growth picked up again in 2002, and estimates suggest that the global market for small package express delivery should continue to grow by a little over 6% per annum between 2005 and 2025. Most of that growth, however, is forecasted to take place outside of the now mature North American market, where the annual growth rate is predicted to be 3.8%.[4]

In North America, the biggest change to take place in the early 2000s was the 2003 entry of DHL into the North American market with the acquisition of Airborne Express for $1 billion. DHL is itself owned by Deutsche Post World Net, formally the German post office, which since privatization has been rapidly transforming itself into a global express mail and logistics operation. Prior to 2003 DHL lacked a strong presence in the all-important U.S. market. The acquisition of Airborne has given DHL a foothold in the United States. Still, DHL has a very long way to go before it can match the dominance of UPS and FedEx, particularly in the important air express market (see Exhibit 1), although the scale of its parent, which in 2005 had revenues of $60 billion, suggests that it could use its deep pockets to support aggressive expansion in North America.

The Industry Before FedEx

In 1973, roughly 1.5 billion tons of freight were shipped in the United States. Most of this freight was carried by surface transport, with air freight accounting for less than 2% of the total.[5] While shipment by air freight was often quicker than shipment by surface freight, the high cost of air freight had kept down demand. The typical users of air freight at this time were suppliers of time-sensitive, high-priced goods, such as computer parts and medical instruments, which were needed at dispersed locations but which were too expensive for their customers to hold as inventory.

The main cargo carriers in 1973 were major passenger airlines, which operated several all-cargo planes and carried additional cargo in their passenger planes, along with a handful of all-cargo airlines such as Flying Tiger. From 1973 onward, the passenger airlines moved steadily away from all-cargo planes and began to concentrate cargo freight in passenger planes. This change was a response to increases in fuel costs, which made the operation of many older cargo jets uneconomical.

With regard to distribution of cargo to and from airports, in 1973 about 20% of all air freight was delivered to airports by the shipper and/or picked up by the consignee. The bulk of the remaining 80% was accounted for by three major intermediaries: (1) Air Cargo Incorporated, (2) freight forwarders, and (3) the U.S. Postal Service. Air Cargo Incorporated was a trucking service, wholly owned by twenty-six airlines, which performed pickup and delivery service for the airlines' direct customers. Freight forwarders were trucking carriers who consolidated cargo going to the airlines. They purchased cargo space from the airlines and retailed this space in small amounts. They dealt primarily with small customers, providing pickup and delivery services in most cities, either in their own trucks or through contract agents. The U.S. Postal Service used air service for transportation of long-distance letter mail and air parcel post.[6]

The Federal Express Concept

Founded by Fred Smith Jr., Federal Express was incorporated in 1971 and began operations in 1973. At that time, a significant proportion of small package air freight flew on commercial passenger flights. Smith believed that there were major differences between packages and passengers, and he was convinced that the two had to be treated differently. Most passengers moved between major cities and wanted the convenience of daytime flights. Cargo shippers preferred nighttime service to coincide with late-afternoon pickups and next-day delivery. Because small package air freight was subservient to the requirements of passengers' flight schedules, it was often difficult for the major airlines to achieve next-day delivery of air freight.

Smith's aim was to build a system that could achieve next-day delivery of small package air freight (less than seventy pounds). He set up Federal Express with his $8 million family inheritance and $90 million in venture capital (the company's name was changed to FedEx in 1998). Federal Express established a hub-and-spoke route system, the first airline to do so. The hub of the system was Memphis, chosen for its good weather conditions, central location, and the fact that it was Smith's hometown. The spokes were regular routes between Memphis and shipping facilities at public airports in the cities serviced by Federal Express.

EXHIBIT 1

U.S. Market Share Estimates for Small Package Delivery Market, 2006

Organization	Ground Market Share	Air Express Market
UPS	63%	35%
FedEx	19%	45%
U.S. Postal Service	16%	6%
DHL	NA	10%
Other	3%	5%

Source: Raw data from John Kartsonas, "United Parcel Service," Citigroup Global Capital Markets, November 13, 2006, B. Barnard, "Logistics Spur Deutsche Post," Journal of Commerce, November 8, 2006, page 1.

Every weeknight, aircraft would leave their home cities with a load of packages and fly down the spokes to Memphis (often with one or two stops on the way). At Memphis, all packages were unloaded, sorted by destination, and reloaded. The aircraft then returned back to their home cities in the early hours of the morning. Packages were ferried to and from airports by Federal Express couriers driving the company's vans and working to a tight schedule. Thus, from door to door, the package was in Federal Express's hands. This system guaranteed that a package picked up from a customer in New York at 5 p.m. would reach its final destination in Los Angeles (or any other major city) by noon the following day. It enabled Federal Express to realize economies in sorting and to utilize its air cargo capacity efficiently. Federal Express also pioneered the use of standard packaging with an upper weight limit of seventy pounds and a maximum length plus girth of 108 inches. This standard helped Federal Express to gain further efficiencies from mechanized sorting at its Memphis hub. Later entrants into the industry copied Federal Express's package standards and hub-and-spoke operating system.

To accomplish overnight delivery, Federal Express had to operate its own planes. Restrictive regulations enforced by the Civil Aeronautics Board (CAB), however, prohibited the company from buying large jet aircraft. To get around this restriction, Federal Express bought a fleet of twin-engine executive jets, which it converted to minifreighters. These planes had a cargo capacity of 6,200 pounds, which enabled Federal Express to get a license as an air taxi operator.

After 1973, Federal Express quickly built up volume. By 1976, it had an average daily volume of 19,000 packages, a fleet of 32 aircraft, 500 delivery vans, and 2,000 employees, and it had initiated service in 75 cities. After three years of posting losses, the company turned in a profit of $3.7 million on revenues of $75 million.[7] However, volume had grown so much that Federal Express desperately needed to use larger planes to maintain operating efficiencies. As a result, Smith's voice was added to those calling for Congress to deregulate the airline industry and allow greater competition.

Deregulation and Its Aftermath

In November 1977, Congress relaxed regulations controlling competition in the air cargo industry, one year before passenger services were deregulated. This involved a drastic loosening of standards for entry into the industry. The old CAB authority of naming the carriers that could operate on the various routes was changed to the relatively simple authority of deciding which among candidate carriers was fit, willing, and able to operate an all-cargo route. In addition, CAB controls over pricing were significantly reduced. The immediate effect was an increase in rates for shipments, particularly minimum- and high-weight categories, suggesting that prices had been held artificially low by regulation. As a result, the average yield (revenue per ton mile) on domestic air freight increased 10.6% in 1978 and 11.3% in 1979.[8]

Freed from the constraints of regulation, Federal Express immediately began to purchase larger jets and quickly established itself as a major carrier of small package air freight. Despite the increase in yields, however, new entry into the air cargo industry was limited, at least initially. This was mainly due to the high capital requirements involved in establishing an all-cargo carrier. Indeed, by the end of 1978, there were only four major all-cargo carriers serving the domestic market: Airlift International, Federal Express, Flying Tiger, and Seaboard World Airlines. While all of these all-cargo carriers had increased their route structure following deregulation, only Federal Express specialized in next-day delivery for small packages. Demand for a next-day delivery service continued to boom. Industry estimates suggest that the small package priority market had grown to about 82 million pieces in 1979, up from 43 million in 1974.[9]

At the same time, in response to increasing competition from the all-cargo carriers, the passenger airlines continued their retreat from the all-cargo business (originally begun in 1973 as a response to high fuel prices). Between 1973 and 1978, there was a 45% decline in the mileage of all-cargo flights by the airlines. This decrease was followed by a 14% decline between 1978 and 1979. Instead of all-cargo flights, the airlines concentrated their attentions on carrying cargo in passenger flights. This practice hurt the freight forwarders badly. The freight forwarders had long relied on the all-cargo flights of major airlines to achieve next-day delivery. Now the freight forwarders were being squeezed out of this segment by a lack of available lift capacity at the time needed to ensure next-day delivery.

This problem led to one of the major post-deregulation developments in the industry: the acquisition and operation by freight forwarders of their own fleets of aircraft. Between 1979 and 1981, five of the six largest freight forwarders became involved in this activity. The two largest were Emery Air Freight and Airborne Express. Emery operated a fleet of sixty-six aircraft at the end of 1979, the majority of which were leased from other carriers. In mid-1980, this fleet was providing service to approximately 129 cities, carrying both large-volume shipments and small package express.

Airborne Express acquired its own fleet of aircraft in April 1980 with the purchase of Midwest Charter Express, an Ohio-based all-cargo airline. In 1981, Airborne opened a new hub in Ohio, which became the center of its small package express operation. This enabled Airborne to provide next-day delivery for small packages to 125 cities in the United States.[10] Other freight forwarders that moved into the overnight mail market included Purolator Courier and Gelco, both of which offered overnight delivery by air on a limited geographic scale.

Industry Evolution, 1980–1986

New Products and Industry Growth

In 1981, Federal Express expanded its role in the overnight market with the introduction of an overnight letter service, with a limit of two ounces. This guaranteed overnight delivery service was set up in direct competition with the U.S. Postal Service's Priority Mail. The demand for such a service was illustrated by its expansion to about 17,000 letters per day within its first three months of operation.

More generally, the focus of the air express industry was changing from being predominantly a conduit for goods to being a distributor of information—particularly company documents, letters, contracts, drawings, and the like. As a result of the growth in demand for information distribution, new product offerings such as the overnight letter, and Federal Express's own marketing efforts, the air express industry enjoyed high growth during the early 1980s, averaging more than 30% per year.[11] Indeed, many observers attribute most of the growth in the overnight delivery business at this time to Federal Express's marketing efforts. According to one industry participant, "Federal Express pulled off one of the greatest marketing scams in the industry by making people believe they absolutely, positively, had to have something right away."[12]

Increasing Price Competition

Despite rapid growth in demand, competitive intensity in the industry increased sharply in 1982 following the entry of UPS into the overnight-delivery market. UPS was already by far the largest private package transporter in the United States, with an enormous ground-oriented distribution network and revenues in excess of $4 billion per year. In addition, for a long time, UPS had offered a second-day air service for priority packages, primarily by using the planes of all-cargo and passenger airlines. In 1982, UPS acquired a fleet of twenty-four used Boeing 727-100s and added four DC-8 freighters from Flying Tiger. These purchases allowed UPS to introduce next-day air service in September 1982—at roughly half the price Federal Express was charging at the time.[13]

Federal Express countered almost immediately by announcing that it would institute 10:30 A.M. priority overnight delivery (at a cost to the company of $18 million). None of the other carriers followed suit, however, reasoning that most of their customers are usually busy or in meetings during the morning hours, so delivery before noon was not really that important. Instead, by March 1983, most of the major carriers in the market (including Federal Express) were offering their high-volume customers contract rates that matched the UPS price structure. Then three new services introduced by Purolator, Emery, and Gelco Courier pushed prices even lower. A competitive free-for-all followed, with constant price changes and volume discounts being offered by all industry participants. These developments hit the profit margins of the express carriers. Between 1983 and 1984, Federal Express saw its average revenue per package fall nearly 14%, while Emery saw a 15% decline in its yield on small shipments.[14]

Beginning around this time, customers began to group together and negotiate for lower prices. For example, Xerox set up accounts with Purolator and Emery that covered not only Xerox's express packages but also those of fifty other companies, including Mayflower Corp., the moving company, and the Chicago Board of Trade. By negotiating as a group, these companies could achieve prices as much as 60% lower than those they could get on their own.[15]

The main beneficiary of the price war was UPS, which by 1985 had gained the number 2 spot in the industry, with 15% of the market. Federal Express, meanwhile, had seen its market share slip to 37% from about 45% two years earlier. The other four major players in the industry at this time were Emery Air Freight (14% of market share), Purolator (10% of market share), Airborne Express (8% of market share), and the U.S. Postal Service (8% of market share).[16] The survival of all four of these carriers in the air express business was in question by 1986. Emery, Purolator, and the U.S. Postal Service were all reporting losses on their air express business, while Airborne had seen its profits slump 66% in the first quarter of 1986 and now had razor-thin margins.

Industry Evolution, 1987–1996

Industry Consolidation

A slowdown in the growth rate of the air express business due to increasing geographic saturation and inroads made by electronic transmission (primarily fax machines) stimulated further price discounting in 1987 and early 1988. Predictably, this discounting created problems for the weakest companies in the industry. The first to go was Purolator Courier, which had lost $65 million during 1985 and 1986. Purolator's problems stemmed from a failure to install an adequate computer system. The company was unable to track shipments, a crucial asset in this industry, and some of Purolator's best corporate customers were billed 120 days late.[17] In 1987, Purolator agreed to be acquired by Emery. Emery was unable to effect a satisfactory integration of Purolator, and it sustained large losses in 1988 and early 1989.

Consolidated Freightways was a major trucking company and parent of CF Air Freight, the third largest heavy shipment specialist in the United States. In April 1989, Consolidated Freightways acquired Emery for $478 million. However, its shipment specialist, CF Air Freight, soon found itself struggling to cope with Emery's problems. In its first eleven months with CF, Emery lost $100 million. One of the main problems was Emery's billing and tracking system, described as a "rat's nest" of conflicting tariff schedules, which caused overbilling of customers and made tracking packages en route a major chore. In addition, CF enraged corporate customers by trying to add a "fuel surcharge" of 4 to 7% to prices in early 1989. Competitors held the line on prices and picked up business from CF/Emery.[18]

As a result of the decline of the CF/Emery/Purolator combination, the other firms in the industry were able to pick up market share. By 1994, industry estimates suggested that Federal Express accounted for 35% of domestic air freight and air express industry revenues; UPS had 26%; Airborne Express was third with 9%; and Emery and the U.S. Postal Service each held onto 4% of the market. The remainder of the market was split among numerous small cargo carriers and several combination carriers, such as Evergreen International and Atlas Air. (Combination carriers specialize mostly in heavy freight but do carry some express mail.)[19]

The other major acquisition in the industry during this time was the purchase of Flying Tiger by Federal Express for $880 million in December 1988. Although Flying Tiger had some air express operations in the United States, its primary strength was as a heavy cargo carrier with a global route structure. The acquisition was part of Federal Express's goal of becoming a major player in the international air express market. However, the acquisition had its problems. Many of Flying Tiger's biggest customers, including UPS and Airborne Express, were Federal Express's competitors in the domestic market. These companies had long paid Tiger to carry packages to those countries where they had no landing rights. It seemed unlikely that these companies would continue to give international business to their biggest domestic competitor. Additional problems arose in the process of trying to integrate the two operations. These problems included the scheduling of aircraft and pilots, the servicing of Tiger's fleet, and the merging of Federal's nonunionized pilots with Tiger's unionized pilots.[20]

During the late 1980s and early 1990s, there were also hints of further consolidations. TNT Ltd., a large Australian-based air cargo operation with a global network, made an unsuccessful attempt to acquire Airborne Express in 1986. TNT's bid was frustrated by opposition from Airborne and by the difficulties inherent in getting around U.S. law, which currently limits foreign firms from having more than a 25-percent stake in U.S. airlines. In addition, DHL Airways, the U.S. subsidiary of DHL International, was reportedly attempting to enlarge its presence in the United States and was on the lookout for an acquisition.[21]

Pricing Trends

In October 1988, UPS offered new discounts to high-volume customers in domestic markets. For the first time since 1983, competitors declined to match the cuts.

Then in January 1989, UPS announced a price increase of 5% for next-day air service, its first price increase in nearly six years. Federal Express, Airborne, and Consolidated Freightways all followed suit with moderate increases. Additional rate increases of 5.9% on next-day air letters were announced by UPS in February 1990. Federal Express followed suit in April, and Airborne also implemented selective price hikes on noncontract business of 5%, or 50 cents, per package on packages up to twenty pounds.

Just as prices were stabilizing, however, the 1990–1991 recession came along. For the first time in the history of the U.S. air express industry, there was a decline in year-on-year shipments, with express freight falling from 4,455 million ton miles in 1989 to 4,403 million ton miles in 1990. This decline triggered off another round of competitive price cuts, and yields plummeted. Although demand rebounded strongly, repeated attempts to raise prices in 1992, 1993, and 1994 simply did not stick.[22]

Much of the price cutting was focused on large corporate accounts, which by this time accounted for 75% by volume of express mail shipments. For example, as a result of deep price discounting in 1994, UPS was able to lure home shopping programmer QVC and computer mail-order company Gateway 2000 away from Federal Express. At about the same time, however, Federal Express used discounting to capture retailer Williams-Sonoma away from UPS.[23] This prolonged period of price discounting depressed profit margins and contributed to losses at all three major carriers during the early 1990s. Bolstered by a strong economy, prices finally began to stabilize during late 1995, when price increases announced by UPS were followed by similar announcements at Federal Express and Airborne.[24]

Product Trends

Second-Day Delivery Having seen a slowdown in the growth rate of the next-day document delivery business during the early 1990s, the major operators in the air express business began to look for new product opportunities to sustain their growth and margins. One trend was a move into the second-day delivery market, or deferred services, as it is called in the industry. The move toward second-day delivery was started by Airborne Express in 1991, and it was soon imitated by its major competitors. Second-day delivery commands a substantially lower price point than next-

day delivery. In 1994, Federal Express made an average of $9.23 on second-day deliveries, compared to $16.37 on priority overnight service. The express mail operators see deferred services as a way to utilize excess capacity at the margin, thereby boosting revenues and profits. Since many second-day packages can be shipped on the ground, the cost of second-day delivery can more than compensate for the lower price.

In some ways, however, the service has been almost too successful. During the mid-1990s, the growth rate for deferred services was significantly higher than for priority overnight mail because many corporations came to the realization that they could live with a second-day service. At Airborne Express, for example, second-day delivery accounted for 42% of total volume in 1996, up from 37% in 1995.[25]

Premium Services Another development was a move toward a premium service. In 1994, UPS introduced its Early AM service, which guaranteed delivery of packages and letters by 8:30 a.m. in select cities. UPS tailored Early AM toward a range of businesses that needed documents or materials before the start of the business day, including hospitals, who were expected to use the service to ship critical drugs and medical devices; architects, who needed to have their blueprints sent to a construction site; and salespeople. Although demand for the service was predicted to be light, the premium price made for high profit margins. In 1994, UPS's price for a letter delivered at 10:30 a.m. was $10.75, while it charged $40 for an equivalent Early AM delivery. UPS believed that it could provide the service at little extra cost because most of its planes arrived in their destination cities by 7:30 a.m. Federal Express and Airborne initially declined to follow UPS's lead.[26]

Logistics Services Another development of some note was the move by all major operators into third-party logistics services. Since the latter half of the 1980s, more and more companies have been relying on air express operations as part of their just-in-time inventory control systems. As a result, the content of packages carried by air express operators has been moving away from letters and documents and toward high-value, low-weight products. By 1994, less than 20% of Federal Express's revenues came from documents.[27] To take advantage of this trend, all of the major operators have been moving into logistics services that are designed to assist business customers in their warehousing, distribution, and assembly operations. The emphasis of this business is on helping their customers reduce the time involved in their production cycles and gain distribution efficiencies.

In the late 1980s, Federal Express set up a Business Logistics Services (BLS) division. The new division evolved from Federal Express's Parts Bank. The Parts Bank stores critical inventory for clients, most of whom are based in the high-tech electronics and medical industries. On request, Federal Express ships this inventory to its client's customers. The service saves clients from having to invest in their own distribution systems. It also allows their clients to achieve economies of scale by making large production runs and then storing the inventory at the Parts Bank.

The BLS division has expanded this service to include some assembly operations and customs brokerage and to assist in achieving just-in-time manufacturing. Thus, for example, one U.S. computer company relies on BLS to deliver electronic subassemblies from the Far East as a key part of its just-in-time system. Federal Express brings the products to the United States on its aircraft, clears them through customs with the help of a broker, and manages truck transportation to the customer's dock.

UPS moved into the logistics business in 1993 when it established UPS Worldwide Logistics, which it positioned as a third-party provider of global supply-chain management solutions, including transportation management, warehouse operations, inventory management, documentation for import and export, network optimization, and reverse logistics. UPS's logistics business is based at its Louisville, Kentucky, hub. In 1995, the company announced that it would invest $75 million to expand the scope of this facility, bringing total employment in the facility to 2,200 by the end of 1998.[28]

Airborne Express also made a significant push into this business. Several of Airborne's corporate accounts utilize a warehousing service called Stock Exchange. As with Federal Express's Parts Bank, clients warehouse critical inventory at Airborne's hub in Wilmington, Ohio, and then ship those items on request to their customers. In addition, Airborne set up a commerce park on 1,000 acres around its Wilmington hub. The park was geared toward companies that wanted to outsource logistics to Airborne and could gain special advantages by locating at the company's hub. Not the least of these advantages is the ability to make shipping decisions as late as 2 a.m. Eastern time.

Information Systems

Since the late 1980s, the major U.S. air express carriers have devoted more and more attention to competing on the basis of information technology. The ability to track a package as it moves through an operator's delivery network has always been an important aspect of competition in an industry where reliability is so highly valued. Thus, all the major players in the industry have invested heavily in bar-code technology, scanners, and computerized tracking systems. UPS, Federal Express, and Airborne have also all invested in Internet-based technology that allows customers to schedule pickups, print shipping labels, and track deliveries online.

Globalization

Perhaps the most important development for the long-run future of the industry has been the increasing globalization of the airfreight industry. The combination of a healthy U.S. economy, strong and expanding East Asian economies, and the move toward closer economic integration in western Europe all offer opportunities for growth in the international air cargo business. The increasing globalization of companies in a whole range of industries from electronics to autos, and from fast food to clothing, is beginning to dictate that the air express operators follow suit.

Global manufacturers want to keep inventories at a minimum and deliver just in time as a way of keeping down costs and fine-tuning production, which requires speedy supply routes. Thus, some electronics companies will manufacture key components in one location, ship them by air to another for final assembly, and then deliver them by air to a third location for sale. This setup is particularly convenient for industries producing small high-value items (for example, electronics, medical equipment, and computer software) that can be economically transported by air and for whom just-in-time inventory systems are crucial for keeping down costs. It is also true in the fashion industry, where timing is crucial. For example, the clothing chain The Limited manufactures clothes in Hong Kong and then ships them by air to the United States to keep from missing out on fashion trends.[29] In addition, an increasing number of wholesalers are beginning to turn to international air express as a way of meeting delivery deadlines.

The emergence of integrated global corporations is also increasing the demand for the global shipment of contracts, confidential papers, computer printouts, and other documents that are too confidential for Internet transmission or that require real signatures. Major U.S. corporations are increasingly demanding the same kind of service that they receive from air express operators within the United States for their far-flung global operations.

As a consequence of these trends, rapid growth is predicted in the global arena. According to forecasts, the market for international air express is expected to grow at approximately 18% annually from 1996 to 2016.[30] Faced with an increasingly mature market at home, the race is on among the major air cargo operators to build global air and ground transportation networks that will enable them to deliver goods and documents between any two points on the globe within forty-eight hours.

The company with the most extensive international operations by the mid-1990s was DHL. In 1995, DHL enjoyed a 44% share of the worldwide market for international air express services (see Exhibit 2).[31] Started in California in 1969 and now based in Brussels, DHL is smaller than many of its rivals, but it has managed to capture as much as an 80% share in some markets, such as documents leaving Japan, by concentrating solely on international air express. The strength of DHL was enhanced in mid-1992 when Lufthansa, Japan Airlines, and the Japanese trading company Nisho Iwai announced that they intended to invest as much as $500 million for a 57.5% stake in DHL. Although Lufthansa and Japan Airlines are primarily known for their passenger flights, they are also among the top five airfreight haulers in the world, both because they carry cargo in the holds of their passenger flights and because they each have a fleet of all-cargo aircraft.[32]

EXHIBIT 2

International Air Express Market Shares, 1995

Company	Market Share
DHL International	44%
Federal Express	21%
UPS	12%
TNT	12%
Others	11%

Source: Standard & Poor's, "Aerospace and Air Transport," Industry Surveys, February 1996.

TNT Ltd., a $6 billion Australian conglomerate, is another big player in the international air express market, with courier services from 184 countries as well as package express and mail services. In 1995, its share of the international air express market was 12%, down from 18% in 1990.[33]

Among U.S. carriers, Federal Express was first in the race to build a global air express network. Between 1984 and 1989, Federal Express purchased seventeen other companies worldwide in an attempt to build its global distribution capabilities, culminating in the $880 million purchase of Flying Tiger. The main asset of Flying Tiger was not so much its aircraft but its landing rights overseas. The Flying Tiger acquisition gave Federal Express service to 103 countries, a combined fleet of 328 aircraft, and revenues of $5.2 billion in fiscal year 1989.[34]

However, Federal Express has had to suffer through years of losses in its international operations. Start-up costs were heavy, due in part to the enormous capital investments required to build an integrated air and ground network worldwide. Between 1985 and 1992, Federal Express spent $2.5 billion to build an international presence. Faced also with heavy competition, Federal Express found it difficult to generate the international volume required to fly its planes above the breakeven point on many international routes. Because the demand for outbound service from the United States is greater than the demand for inbound service, planes that left New York full often returned half empty.

Trade barriers have also proved very damaging to the bottom line. Customs regulations require a great deal of expensive and time-consuming labor, such as checking paperwork and rating package contents for duties. These regulations obviously inhibit the ability of international air cargo carriers to effect express delivery. Federal Express has been particularly irritated by Japanese requirements that each inbound envelope be opened and searched for pornography, a practice that seems designed to slow down the company's growth rate in the Japanese market.

Federal Express has also found it extremely difficult to get landing rights in many markets. For example, it took three years to get permission from Japan to make four flights per week from Memphis to Tokyo, a key link in the overseas system. Then, in 1988, just three days before the service was due to begin, the Japanese notified Federal Express that no packages weighing more than seventy pounds could pass through Tokyo. To make matters worse, until 1995 Japan limited Federal Express's ability to fly on from Tokyo and Osaka to other locations in Asia. The Japanese claimed, with some justification, that due to government regulations, the U.S. air traffic market is difficult for foreign carriers to enter, so they see no urgency to help Federal Express build a market presence in Japan and elsewhere in Asia.[35]

After heavy financial losses, Federal Express abruptly shifted its international strategy in 1992, selling off its expensive European ground network to local carriers to concentrate on intercontinental deliveries. Under the strategy, Federal Express relies on a network of local partners to deliver its packages. Also, Federal Express entered into an alliance with TNT to share space on Federal Express's daily trans-Atlantic flights. Under the agreement, TNT flies packages from its hub in Cologne, Germany, to Britain, where they are loaded onto Federal Express's daily New York flight.[36]

UPS has also built up an international presence. In 1988, UPS bought eight smaller European airfreight companies and Hong Kong's Asian Courier Service, and it announced air service and ground delivery in 175 countries and territories. However, it has not been all smooth sailing for UPS either. UPS had been using Flying Tiger for its Pacific shipments. The acquisition of Flying Tiger by Federal Express left UPS in the difficult situation of shipping its parcels on a competitor's plane. UPS was concerned that its shipments would be pushed to the back of the aircraft. Since there were few alternative carriers, UPS pushed for authority to run an all-cargo route to Tokyo, but approval was slow in coming. "Beyond rights" to carry cargo from Tokyo to further destinations (such as Singapore and Hong Kong) were also difficult to gain.

In March 1996, UPS sidestepped years of frustrations associated with building an Asian hub in Tokyo by announcing that it would invest $400 million in a Taiwan hub, which would henceforth be the central node in its Asian network. The decision to invest in an Asian hub followed closely on the heels of a 1995 decision by UPS to invest $1.1 billion to build a ground network in Europe. In September 1996, UPS went one step further toward building an international air express service when it announced that it would start a pan-European next-day delivery service for small packages. UPS hoped that these moves would push the international operations of the carrier into the black after eight years of losses.[37]

Industry Evolution, 1997–2006

Pricing Trends

The industry continued to grow at a solid rate through 2000, which helped to establish a stable pricing environment. In 2001, things took a turn for the worse, with recessionary conditions in the United States triggering a 7.6% decline in the number of domestic packages shipped by air. Even though the economy started to rebound in 2002, growth remained sluggish by historic comparison, averaging only 4% per annum.[38] Despite this, pricing discipline remained solid. Unlike the recession in 1990–1991, there was no price war in 2001–2002. Indeed, in early 2002, UPS pushed through a 3.5% increase in prices, which was quickly followed by the other carriers. The carriers were able to continue to raise prices, at least in line with inflation, through to 2006. They were also successful in tacking on a fuel surcharge to the cost of packages to make up for sharply higher fuel costs in 2001, and again during 2005 and 2006.[39] During 2002–2006, the average revenue per package at both UPS and FedEx increased as more customers opted for expedited shipments and as both carriers shipped high proportions of heavier packages.[40]

Continuing Growth of Logistics

During 1997–2006, all players continued to build their logistics services. During the 2000s, UPS was much more aggressive in this area than FedEx. By 2006, UPS's logistics business had revenues of over $6 billion. UPS was reportedly stealing share from FedEx in this area. FedEx reportedly decided to stay more focused on the small package delivery business (although it continues to have a logistics business). Most analysts expected logistics services to continue to be a growth area. Outside of the North American market, DHL emerged as the world's largest provider of logistics services, particularly following its 2006 acquisition of Britain's Exel, a large global logistics business.

Despite the push of DHL and UPS into the global logistics business, the market remains very fragmented. According to one estimate, DHL, now the world's largest logistics company, has a 5.5% share of the global market in contract logistics, UPS has a 3% share, and TNT has a 2.2% share.[41] The total global market for contract logistics was estimated to be worth over $200 billion in 2005. In 2006, TNT sold its logistics business to Apollo Management LP for $1.88 billion so that it could focus more on its small package delivery business.

Expanding Ground Network

In the late 1990s and early 2000s, all the main carriers began supplementing their air networks with extensive ground networks and ground hubs to ship packages overnight. With more customers moving from overnight mail to deferred services, such as second-day delivery, this shift in emphasis became a necessity. Demand for deferred services held up reasonably well during 2001, even as demand for overnight packages slumped. Prices for deferred and ground services were considerably lower than were prices for air services, but so were the costs.

UPS has been the most aggressive in building ground delivery capabilities (of course, it already had extensive ground capabilities before its move into the air). In 1999, UPS decided to integrate overnight delivery into its huge ground transportation network. The company spent about $700 million to strengthen its ground delivery network by setting up regional ground hubs. By doing so, it found it could ship packages overnight on the ground within a 500-mile radius. Because ground shipments are cheaper than air shipments, the result was a significant cost savings for UPS. The company also deferred delivery of about 123 aircraft that were on order, reasoning that they would not be needed as quickly because more of UPS's overnight business was moved to the ground.[42]

FedEx entered the ground transportation market in 1998 with its acquisition of Caliber Systems for $500 million. This was followed by further acquisitions in 2001 and 2006 of significant U.S. trucking companies, including the 2006 acquisition of Watkins Motor Lines, a provider of long-haul trucking services in the United States with sales of around $1 billion. Watkins was rebranded as FedEx National LTL. By 2002, FedEx was able to provide ground service to all U.S. homes, giving it a similar capability to UPS.

In addition, FedEx struck a deal in 2001 with the U.S. Postal Service (USPS), under which FedEx would provide airport-to-airport transportation for 250,000 pounds of USPS Express Mail packages nightly and about 3 million pounds of USPS Priority Mail packages. The Priority Mail would be moved on FedEx planes that normally sit idle during the day. The deal was reportedly worth $7 billion in additional revenues to FedEx over the seven-year term of the agreement. In addition, FedEx was expected to reap cost savings from the better utilization of its lift capacity.[43]

Bundling

Another industrywide trend has been a move toward selling various product offerings—including air delivery, ground package offerings, and logistics services—to business customers as a bundle. The basic idea behind bundling is to offer complementary products at a bundled price that is less than would have been the case if each item had been purchased separately. Yet again, UPS has been the most aggressive in offering bundled services to corporate clients. UPS is clearly aiming to set itself up as a one-stop shop offering a broad array of transportation solutions to customers. FedEx has also made moves in this area. Airborne Express started to bundle its product offerings in mid-2001.[44]

Retail Presence

In 2001, UPS purchased Mail Boxes Etc. for $185 million. Mail Boxes Etc. had 4,300 franchisees, most in the United States, who operated small retail packaging, printing, and copying stores. At the time, Mail Boxes Etc. was shipping some 40 million packages a year, around 12 million of which were via UPS. UPS stated that it would continue to allow the Mail Boxes stores to ship packages for other carriers. In 2003, the stores were rebranded as the UPS Store. While some franchisees objected to this move, the vast majority ultimately switched to the new brand.[45] In addition to the franchise stores, UPS has also begun to open wholly owned UPS stores, not just in the United States, but also internationally, and by 2006 had 5,600 outlets. In addition to the UPS Store, UPS put UPS Centers in office supplies stores, such as Office Depot, and by 2006 it had some 2,200 of these.

In 2004, FedEx followed UPS by purchasing Kinko's for $2.4 billion. Kinko's, which had 1,200 retail locations, 90% in the United States, focused on providing photocopying, printing, and other office services to individuals and small businesses. FedEx has plans to increase the network of Kinko's stores to 4,000. In addition to providing printing, photocopying, and package services, FedEx is also experimenting with using Kinko's stores as mini-warehouses to store high-value goods, such as medical equipment, for its supply-chain management division.[46]

Deutsche Post and the Entry of DHL

In the late 1990s, DHL was acquired by Deutsche Post. Deutsche Post also spent approximately $5 billion to acquire several companies in the logistics business between 1997 and 1999. In November 2000, Deutsche Post went private with an initial public offering that raised $5.5 billion and announced its intention to build an integrated global delivery and logistics network. Many believed it was only a matter of time before the company entered the United States. Thus, few were surprised when in 2003 DHL acquired Airborne. Under the terms of their agreement, Airborne Express sold its truck delivery system to DHL for $1.05 billion. Airborne's fleet of planes were spun off into an independent company called ABX Air, owned by Airborne's shareholders, and which continues to serve DHL Worldwide Express under a long-term contract. This arrangement overcame the U.S. law that prohibits foreign control of more than 25% of a domestic airline. In the meantime, DHL spun its own fleet of U.S.-based planes into a U.S.-owned company called Astar, also to escape the charge that its U.S. airline was foreign owned. Between 2003 and 2005, DHL reportedly invested some $1.2 billion to upgrade the capabilities of assets acquired from Airborne.[47]

The DHL acquisition created three major competitors in both the U.S. and global delivery markets (see Exhibit 3 for a comparison). By the fall of 2003, DHL had launched an ad campaign aimed at UPS and FedEx customers promoting the service and cost advantages that they would benefit from because of its merger with Airborne. DHL targeted specific zip code areas in its advertising promoting its claim to be the number 1 in international markets, something important to many companies given the increasing importance of global commerce. In its ads, DHL reported that "current Airborne customers will be connected to DHL's extensive international delivery system in more than 200 countries."[48]

DHL's stated goal is to become a powerhouse in the U.S. delivery market. While its share of the U.S. small package express market remains small at around 10%, DHL clearly stands to benefit from ownership by Deutsche Post and from its own extensive ex-U.S. operations. When it first acquired Airborne, Deutsche Post stated that the U.S. operation would be profitable by the end of 2006. However, the company ran into "integration problems" and suffered from reports of poor customer services and missed delivery deadlines. Now management does not see the unit turning profitable until 2009—although the express delivery service is profitable in the rest of the world. DHL lost some $500 million in the United States in 2006 and is forecasted to do the same in 2007.[49]

In 2005, Deutsche underlined its commitment to building a global logistics business when it purchased Exel of Britain for $7.2 billion. Exel was one of the

---

EXHIBIT 3

The Major Express Package Operators in 2005

	FedEx	UPS	DHL (Deutsche Post)	TNT
Revenues	$32,294 million	$42,581 million	$32,646 million[1]	$12,500 million[3]
Net Income	$1,806 million	$3,870 million	$405 million[2]	$951 million
Employees	221,000	407,000	280,000 (DHL only)	128,000
Countries Served	220	200+	220	200+
Aircraft	671	579	420	NA
Average Daily Shipment Volume	14.8 million	6 million	NA	NA

Sources: Company documents.

[1] Revenues and profits are for DHL only. DHL accounts for 57% of Deutsche Post revenues.

[2] Loss in United States reduced DHL's operating profits by $500 million in 2005.

[3] Figures for TNT include logistics business, which was sold off in 2006.

largest independent third-party logistics companies in the world with extensive operations in Europe, Asia, and North America. Combining Exel with Deutsche Post's existing businesses created a global logistics business with projected revenues of $25 billion, four times as large as the logistics business of UPS. Quickly on the heels of this acquisition, DHL won a contract worth $3 billion over ten years to manage the supply chain and deliver some 500,000 products to the 600 hospitals in Britain's National Health Service.[50]

Continued Globalization

Between 1997 and 2006, UPS and FedEx continued to build out their global infrastructure. By 2006, UPS delivered to more than 200 countries. Much of the within-country delivery is handled by local enterprises. The company has five main hubs. In addition to its main U.S. hub in Louisville, Kentucky, it has hubs in Cologne, Taipei, Miami (serving Latin American traffic), and the Philippines. In 2002, UPS launched an intra-Asian express delivery network from its Philippines hub. In 2004, it acquired Menlo World Wide Forwarding, a global freight forwarder, to boost its global logistics business. In the same year, it also acquired complete ownership of its Japanese delivery operation (which was formally a joint venture with Yamato Transport Company). In 2005, UPS acquired operators of local ground networks in the UK and

Poland, and it is pushing into mainland China, which it sees as a major growth opportunity.

Like UPS, FedEx serves more than 200 countries around the world, although also like UPS, most of the local ground delivery is in the hands of local partners. FedEx has recently been focusing on building a presence in both China and India. The company has announced the development of a new Asian Pacific hub in Guangzhou, China. This will be FedEx's fourth international hub. The others are in Paris (handling intra-European express), the Philippines (handling intra-Asian express), and Alaska (handling packages flowing between Asia, North America, and Europe). In 2006, FedEx signaled its commitment to the Chinese market by buying out its joint venture partner, Tianjin Datian W. Group, for $400 million. The acquisition will give FedEx control of 90 parcel handling facilities and a 3,000 strong work force in China.[51]

While UPS and FedEx dominate the U.S. market for small package express delivery services, in Europe DHL and TNT lead with 23% and 11% respectively (TNT, formally an Australian enterprise, was acquired by the Royal Netherlands Post Office in 1996). In the intercontinental market, DHL leads with a 36% share, while in intra-Asian traffic Asia Yamato of Japan is the leader with a 20% share, followed by Sagawa with 16% (see Exhibit 4). The fragmented nature of the European and intra-Asia Pacific markets suggest that much is still at stake in this increasingly global business.

EXHIBIT 4

Market Share (%) for Small Package Express, 2005

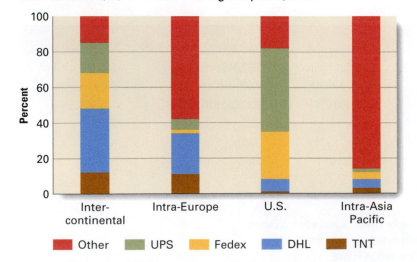

Source: Estimates from TNT posted on company website at www.tnt.com.

ENDNOTES

1. Standard & Poor's, "Aerospace and Air Transport," Industry Surveys, February 1996.
2. Ibid.
3. Standard & Poor's, "Airlines," Industry Surveys, March 2002.
4. John Kartsonas, "United Parcel Service," *Citigroup Global Capital Markets*, November 13, 2006.
5. Christopher H. Lovelock, "Federal Express (B)," Harvard Business School Case No. 579–040, 1978.
6. Standard & Poor's, "Aerospace and Air Transport," Industry Surveys, January 1981.
7. Lovelock, "Federal Express (B)."
8. Standard & Poor's, "Aerospace and Air Transport," Industry Surveys, January 1981.
9. Ibid.
10. Ibid.
11. Standard & Poor's, "Aerospace and Air Transport," Industry Surveys, January 1984.
12. Carol Hall, "High Fliers," *Marketing and Media Decisions*, August 1986, p. 138.
13. Standard & Poor's, "Aerospace and Air Transport," Industry Surveys, January 1984.
14. Standard & Poor's, "Aerospace and Air Transport," Industry Surveys, December 1984.
15. Brian Dumaine, "Turbulence Hits the Air Couriers," *Fortune*, July 21, 1986, pp. 101–106.
16. Ibid.
17. Chuck Hawkins, "Purolator: Still No Overnight Success," *Business Week*, June 16, 1986, pp. 76–78.
18. Joan O'C. Hamilton, "Emery Is One Heavy Load for Consolidated Freightways," *Business Week*, March 26, 1990, pp. 62–64.
19. Standard & Poor's, "Aerospace and Air Transport," Industry Surveys, February 1996.
20. "Hold That Tiger: FedEx Is Now World Heavyweight," *Purchasing*, September 14, 1989, pp. 41–42.
21. Standard & Poor's, "Aerospace and Air Transport," Industry Surveys, April 1988.
22. Standard & Poor's, "Aerospace and Air Transport," Industry Surveys, February 1996.
23. David Greising, "Watch Out for Flying Packages," *Business Week*, November 1994, p. 40.
24. "UPS to Raise Its Rates for Packages," *Wall Street Journal*, January 9, 1995, p. C22.
25. Marilyn Royce, "Airborne Freight," Value Line Investment Survey, September 20, 1996.
26. Robert Frank, "UPS Planning Earlier Delivery," *Wall Street Journal*, September 29, 1994, p. A4.
27. Frank, "Federal Express Grapples with Changes in U.S. Market." Wall Street Journal, March 24, 1995, p. A6.
28. Company press releases (http://www.ups.com/news/).
29. Joan M. Feldman, "The Coming of Age of International Air Freight," *Air Transport World*, June 1989, pp. 31–33.
30. Standard & Poor's, "Aerospace and Air Transport," Industry Surveys, February 1996.
31. Ibid.
32. Peter Greiff, "Lufthansa, JAL, and a Trading Firm Acquire a Majority Stake in DHL," *Wall Street Journal*, August 24, 1992, p. A5.
33. Standard & Poor's, "Aerospace and Air Transport," Industry Surveys, February 1996.
34. "Hold That Tiger: FedEx Is Now a World Heavyweight."
35. Douglas Blackmon, "FedEx Swings from Confidence Abroad to a Tightrope," *Wall Street Journal*, March 15, 1996, p. B4.
36. Daniel Pearl, "Federal Express Plans to Trim Assets in Europe," *Wall Street Journal*, March 17, 1992, p. A3.
37. Company press releases (http://www.ups.com/news/).
38. C. Haddad and M. Arndt, "Saying No Thanks to Overnight Air," *Business Week*, April 1, 2002, p. 74.
39. Salomon Smith Barney Research, "Wrap It Up—Bundling and the Air Express Sector," May 3, 2002; John Kartsonas, "United Parcel Service," *Citigroup Global Capital Markets*, November 13, 2006.
40. John Kartsonas, "FedEx Corp," *Citigroup Global Capital Markets*, November 13, 2006.
41. Data from Deutsche Post World Net, 2005 Annual Report.
42. C. Haddad and M. Arndt, "Saying No Thanks to Overnight Air," *Business Week*, April 1, 2002, p. 74.
43. E. Walsh, "Package Deal," *Logistics*, February 2001, pp. 19–20.
44. Salomon Smith Barney Research, "Wrap It Up—Bundling and the Air Express Sector," May 3, 2002.
45. R. Gibson, "Package Deal: UPS's purchase of Mail Boxes Etc. Looked Great on Paper," *Wall Street Journal*, May 8, 2006, p. R13.
46. Andrew Ward, "Kinko's Plans to Push the Envelope Further," *Financial Times*, August 7, 2006, p. 22.
47. J. D. Schultz, "DHL Crashes the Party," *Logistics*, August 2005, pp. 59–63.
48. P. Needham, "Coming to America," *Journal of Commerce*, April 22, 2002, p. 12.
49. B. Barnard, "Logistics Spurs Deutsche Post," *Journal of Commerce*, November 8, 2006, p. 1.
50. "DHL Gets $3 Billion UK Deal," *Journal of Commerce*, September 5, 2006, p. 1.
51. A. Ward, "A Dogfight for Courier Service Dominance," *Financial Times*, February 15, 2006, p. 10.

Airborne Express: The Underdog

This case was prepared by Charles W. L. Hill, the University of Washington.[1]

Airborne Inc., which operated under the name Airborne Express, was an air express transportation company providing express and second-day delivery of small packages (less than seventy pounds) and documents throughout the United States and to and from many foreign countries. The company owned and operated an airline and a fleet of ground-transportation vehicles to provide complete door-to-door service. It was also an airfreight forwarder, moving shipments of any size on a worldwide basis. In 2003, Airborne Express held third place in the U.S. air express industry, with 9% of the market for small package deliveries. Its main domestic competitors were Federal Express, which had 26% of the market, and United Parcel Service (UPS), which had 53% of the market. There were several smaller players in the market at the time, including DHL Airways, Consolidated Freightways (CF), and the U.S. Postal Service, each of which held under 5% of the market share.[2] In 2003, after years of struggling to survive in the fiercely competitive small package express delivery industry, Airborne was acquired by DHL, which was itself owned by Deutsche Post, the large German postal, express package, and logistics company.

The evolution of the air express industry and the current state of competition in the industry were discussed in a companion case to this one, "The Evolution of the Small Package Express Delivery Industry, 1973–2006." The current case focuses on the operating structure, competitive strategy, organizational structure, and cultures of Airborne Express from its inception until it was acquired by DHL in 2003.

History of Airborne Express

Airborne Express was originally known as Pacific Air Freight when it was founded in Seattle at the close of World War II by Holt W. Webster, a former Army Air Corps officer. (See Exhibit 1 for a listing of major milestones in the history of Airborne Express.) The company was merged with Airborne Freight Corp. of California in 1968, taking the name of the California company but retaining management direction by the former officers of Pacific Air Freight. Airborne was initially an exclusive airfreight forwarder. Freight forwarders such as Airborne arrange for the transportation of air cargo between any two destinations. They purchase cargo space from the airlines and retail this in small amounts. They deal primarily with small customers, providing pickup and delivery services in most cities, either in their own trucks or through contract agents.

Following the 1977 deregulation of the airline industry, Airborne entered the air express industry by leasing the airplanes and pilots of Midwest Charter, a small airline operating out of its own airport in Wilmington, Ohio. However, Airborne quickly became dissatisfied with the limited amount of control they were able to exercise over Midwest, which made it very difficult to achieve the kind of tight coordination and control of logistics that was necessary to become a successful air express operator. Instead of continuing to lease Midwest's planes and facility, in 1980 Airborne decided to buy "the entire bucket of slop; company, planes, pilots, airport and all."

EXHIBIT 1

Major Milestones at Airborne Express[3]

1946: Airborne Flower Traffic Association of California is founded to fly fresh flowers from Hawaii to the mainland.

1968: Airborne of California and Pacific Air Freight of Seattle merge to form Airborne Freight Corp. Headquarters are in Seattle, Washington.

1979–1981: Airborne Express is born. After purchasing Midwest Air Charter, Airborne buys Clinton County Air Force Base in Wilmington, Ohio, becoming the only carrier to own and operate an airport. The package sort center opens, creating the "hub" for the hub-and-spoke system.

1984–1986: Airborne is first carrier to establish a privately operated Foreign Trade Zone in an air industrial park.

1987: Airborne opens the Airborne Stock Exchange, a third-party inventory management and distribution service. In the same year, service begins to and from more than 8,000 Canadian locations.

1988: Airborne becomes the first air express carrier to provide same-day delivery, through its purchase of Sky Courier.

1990: The International Cargo Forum and Exposition names Airborne the carrier with the most outstanding integrated cargo system over the previous two years.

1991: A trio of accolades: Airborne is the first transportation company to receive Volvo-Flyg Motors' Excellent Performance Award. Computerworld ranks us the "most effective user of information systems in the U.S. transportation industry." In addition, we receive the "Spread the Word!" Electronic Data Interchange (EDI) award for having the largest number of EDI users worldwide in the air express and freight forwarding industry.

1992: Airborne introduces Flight-ReadySM, the first prepaid Express Letters and Packs.

1993: Airborne introduces Airborne Logistics Services (ALS), a new subsidiary providing outsourced warehousing and distribution services. IBM consolidates its international shipping operation with Airborne.

1994: Airborne opens its Ocean Service Division, becoming the first express carrier to introduce ocean shipping services. Airborne Logistics Services (ALS) establishes the first new film distribution program for the movie industry in 50 years. We also become the first company to provide online communication to Vietnam.

1995: Airborne Alliance Group, a consortium of transportation, logistics, third-party customer service operations and high-tech companies providing value-added services, is formed. Airborne opens a second runway at its hub, which is now the United States' largest privately owned airport. We also expand our fleet, acquiring Boeing 767-200 aircraft.

1996: Airborne Express celebrates 50 years of providing value-added distribution solutions to business.

1997: Airborne Express has its best year ever, with net earnings increasing three-and-a-half-fold over the previous year. Airborne's stock triples, leading to a two-for-one stock split in February, 1998.

1998: Airborne posts record profits and enters the Fortune 500. The first of 30 Boeing 767s is introduced to our fleet. The Business Consumer Guide rates Airborne as the Best Air Express Carrier for the 4th consecutive year.

1999: Airborne@home, a unique alliance with the United States Postal Service, is introduced. It enables e-tailers, catalog companies and similar businesses to ship quickly and economically to the residential marketplace. Optical Village is created. Part of Airborne Logistics Services, this new division brings together some of the biggest competitors in the optical industry to share many costs and a single location in their assembly, logistics, and delivery options.

2000: Airborne announces several changes in senior management, including a new President and Chief Operating Officer, Carl Donaway. Several new business initiatives are announced, most notably a ground service scheduled to begin April 1, 2001. Airborne also wins the Brand Keys Customer Loyalty Award, edging out our competition for the second consecutive year.

2001: Airborne launches Ground Delivery Service and 10:30 A.M. Service, giving Airborne a comprehensive, full-service industry competitive capability. Airborne.com launches its Small Business Center, as well as a variety of enhancements to help all business customers speed and simplify the shipping process. We also release the Corporate Exchange shipping application, simplifying desktop shipping for customers while giving them greater control. Advanced tracking features are added to airborne.com and Airborne eCourier is released, enabling customers to send confidential, signed documents electronically.

2003: Airborne's ground operations acquired by DHL for $1.1 billion.

Among other things, the Midwest acquisition put Airborne in the position of being the only industry participant to own an airport. Airborne immediately began the job of developing a hub-and-spoke system capable of supporting a nationwide distribution system. An efficient sorting facility was established at the Wilmington hub. Airborne upgraded Midwest's fleet of prop and propjet aircraft, building a modern fleet of DC-8s, DC-9s, and YS-11 aircraft. These planes left major cities every evening, flying down the spokes carrying letters and packages to the central sort facility in Wilmington, Ohio. There the letters and packages were unloaded, sorted according to their final destinations, and then reloaded and flown to their final destinations for delivery before noon the next day.

During the late 1970s and early 1980s, dramatic growth in the industry attracted many competitors. As a consequence, despite a high growth rate, price competition became intense, forcing a number of companies to the sidelines by the late 1980s. Between 1984 and 1990, average revenues per domestic shipment at Airborne fell from around $30 to under $15 (in 2003, they were just under $9). Airborne was able to survive this period by pursuing a number of strategies that increased productivity and drove costs down to the lowest levels in the industry. Airborne's operating costs per shipment fell from $28 in 1984 to around $14 by 1990, and to $9.79 by 2001. As a consequence, by the late 1980s Airborne had pulled away from a pack of struggling competitors to become one of the top three companies in the industry, a position it still held when acquired by DHL in 2003.

Air Express Operations

The Domestic Delivery Network

As of 2002, its last full year as an independent enterprise, Airborne Express had 305 ground stations within the United States. The stations were the ends of the spokes in Airborne's hub-and-spoke system, and the distribution of stations allowed Airborne to reach all major population centers in the country. In each station, there were about fifty to fifty-five or so drivers plus staff. About 80% of Airborne's 115,300 full-time and 7,200 part-time employees were found at this level. The stations were the basic units in Airborne's delivery organization. Their primary task was to ferry packages between clients and the local air terminal. Airborne utilized approximately

14,900 radio-dispatch delivery vans and trucks to transport packages, of which 6,000 were owned by the company. Independent drivers under contract with the company provided the balance of the company's pickup and delivery services.

Airborne's drivers made their last round of major clients at 5 P.M. The drivers either collected packages directly from clients or from one of the company's 15,300 plus drop boxes. The drop boxes were placed at strategic locations, such as in the lobbies of major commercial buildings. To give clients a little more time, in most major cities there were also a few central drop boxes that are not emptied until 6 P.M. If a client needed still more time, so long as the package could be delivered to the airport by 7 P.M., it would make the evening flight.

When a driver picked up a package, he or she read a bar code that is attached to the package with a hand-held scanner. This information was fed directly into Airborne's proprietary FOCUS (Freight, On-Line Control and Update System) computer system. The FOCUS system, which had global coverage, recorded shipment status at key points in the life cycle of a shipment. Thus, a customer could call Airborne on a twenty-four-hour basis to find out where in Airborne's system their package was. FOCUS also allowed a customer direct access to shipment information through the Internet. All a customer needed to do was access Airborne's website and key the code number assigned to a package, and the FOCUS system would tell the customer where in Airborne's system the package was.

When a driver completed a pickup route, she or he took the load to Airborne's loading docks at the local airport. (Airborne served all ninety-nine major metropolitan airports in the United States.) There the packages were loaded into C-containers (discussed later in this case study). C-containers were then towed by hand or by tractor to a waiting aircraft, where they were loaded onto a conveyor belt and in turn passed through the passenger door of the aircraft. Before long the aircraft was loaded and took off. It would either fly directly to the company's hub at Wilmington, or make one or two stops along the way to pick up more packages.

Sometime between midnight and 2 A.M., most of the aircraft would have landed at Wilmington. An old strategic air command base, Wilmington's location places it within a 600-mile radius (an overnight drive or one-hour flying time) of 60% of the U.S.

population. Wilmington has the advantage of a good-weather record. In all the years that Airborne operated at Wilmington, air operations were "fogged out" on only a handful of days. In 1995, Airborne opened a second runway at Wilmington. Developed at a cost of $60 million, the second runway made Wilmington the largest privately owned airport in the country. The runway expansion was part of a $120 million upgrade of the Wilmington sort facility.

After arrival at Wilmington, the plane taxied down the runway and parked alongside a group of aircraft that were already disgorging their load of C-containers. Within minutes the C-containers were unloaded from the plane down a conveyor belt and towed to the sort facility by a tractor. The sort facility had the capacity to handle 1.2 million packages per night. At the end of 2001, the facility handled an average of 1 million packages a night. The bar codes on the packages were read, and then the packages were directed through a labyrinth of conveyor belts and sorted according to final destination. The sorting was partly done by hand and partly automated. At the end of this process, packages were grouped together by final destination and loaded into a C-container. An aircraft bound for the final destination was then loaded with C-containers, and by 5 A.M. most aircraft had taken off.

Upon arrival at the final destination, the plane was unloaded and the packages sorted according to their delivery points within the surrounding area. Airborne couriers then took the packages on the final leg of their journey. Packages had a 75% probability of being delivered to clients by 10:30 A.M., and a 98% probability of being delivered by noon.

Regional Trucking Hubs

Although about 71% of packages were transported by air and passed through Wilmington, Airborne also established ten regional trucking hubs that dealt with the remaining 29% of the company's domestic volume. These hubs sorted shipments that originated and had destinations within approximately a 300-mile radius. The first one opened in Allentown, Pennsylvania, centrally located on the East Coast. This hub handled packages transported between points within the Washington, D.C., to Boston area. Instead of transporting packages by air, packages to be transported within this area were sorted by the drivers at pickup and delivered from the driver's home station by scheduled truck runs to the Allentown hub. There

they were sorted according to destination and taken to the appropriate station on another scheduled truck run for final delivery.

One advantage of ground-based transportation through trucking hubs was that operating costs were much lower than for air transportation. The average cost of a package transported by air was more than five times greater than the cost of a package transported on the ground. However, this cost differential was transparent to the customer, who assumed that all packages were flown. Thus, Airborne could charge the same price for ground-transported packages as for air-transported packages, but the former yielded a much higher return. The trucking hubs also had the advantage of taking some of the load of the Wilmington sorting facility, which was operating at about 90% capacity by 2003.

International Operations

In addition to its domestic express operations, Airborne was also an international company providing service to more than 200 countries worldwide. International operations accounted for about 11% of total revenues in 2002. Airborne offered two international products: freight products and express products. Freight products were commercial-sized, larger-unit shipments. This service provides door-to-airport service. Goods were picked up domestically from the customer and then shipped to the destination airport. A consignee or an agent of the consignee got the paperwork and cleared the shipment through customs. Express packages are small packages, documents, and letters. This was a door-to-door service, and all shipments were cleared through customs by Airborne. Most of Airborne's international revenues come from freight products.

Airborne did not fly any of its own aircraft overseas. Rather, it contracted for space on all-cargo airlines or in the cargo holds of passenger airlines. Airborne owned facilities overseas in Japan, Taiwan, Hong Kong, Singapore, Australia, New Zealand, and London. These functioned in a manner similar to Airborne's domestic stations. (That is, they had their own trucks and drivers and were hooked into the FOCUS tracking system.) The majority of foreign distribution, however, was carried out by foreign agents. Foreign agents were large, local, well-established surface delivery companies. Airborne entered into a number of exclusive strategic alliances with large foreign agents. It had alliances in Japan, Thailand, Malaysia, and South Africa. The rationale for entering strategic alliances, along with Airborne's approach to global expansion, is discussed in greater detail later in this case.

Another aspect of Airborne's international operations was the creation at its Wilmington hub of the only privately certified Foreign Trade Zone (FTZ) in the United States. While in an FTZ, merchandise is tax free and no customs duty is paid on it until it leaves. Thus, a foreign-based company could store critical inventory in the FTZ and have Airborne deliver it just in time to U.S. customers. This allowed the foreign company to hold inventory in the United States without having to pay customs duty on it until the need arose.

Aircraft Purchase and Maintenance

As of 2002, Airborne Express owned a fleet of 118 aircraft, including 24 DC-8s, 74 DC-9s, and 20 Boeing 767s. In addition, approximately 70 smaller aircraft were chartered nightly to connect smaller cities with company aircraft that then operated to and from the Wilmington hub. To keep down capital expenditures, Airborne preferred to purchase used planes. Airborne converted the planes to suit its specifications at a maintenance facility based at its Wilmington hub. Once it got a plane, Airborne typically gutted the interior and installed state-of-the-art electronics and avionics equipment. The company's philosophy was to get all of the upgrades that it could into an aircraft. Although this could cost a lot up front, there was a payback in terms of increased aircraft reliability and a reduction in service downtime. Airborne also standardized cockpits as much as possible. This made it easier for crews to switch from one aircraft to another if the need arose. According to the company, in the early 1990s, the total purchase and modification of a secondhand DC-9 cost about $10 million, compared with an equivalent new-plane cost of $40 million. An additional factor reducing operating costs was that Airborne's DC-9 aircraft required only two-person cockpit crews, as opposed to the three-person crews required in most Federal Express and UPS aircraft at the time.

After conversion, Airborne strove to keep aircraft maintenance costs down by carrying out virtually all of its own fleet repairs. (It was the only all-cargo carrier to do so.) The Wilmington maintenance facility could handle everything except major engine repairs and had the capability to machine critical aircraft parts if needed. The company saw this in-house facility as a major source of cost savings. It estimated that maintenance labor costs were 50 to 60% below the costs of having the same work performed outside.

In December 1995, Airborne announced a deal to purchase twelve used Boeing 767-200 aircraft between the years 1997 and 2000, and it announced plans to purchase an additional ten to fifteen used 767-200s between the years 2000 and 2004. These were the first wide-bodied aircraft in Airborne's fleet. The cost of introducing the first twelve aircraft was about $290 million, and the additional aircraft would cost $360 million. The shift to wide-bodied aircraft was promoted by an internal study, which concluded that with growing volume, wide-bodied aircraft would lead to greater operating efficiencies.

During 2001, Airborne was using about 66.6% of its lift capacity on a typical business day. This compared with 76.7% capacity utilization in 1997, and 70% utilization in 2000. In late 2001, Airborne reduced its total lift capacity by some 100,000 pounds to about 4 million pounds a day. It did this to try to reduce excess capacity of certain routes and better match supply with demand conditions.

C-Containers

C-containers are uniquely shaped 60-cubic-foot containers developed by Airborne Express in 1985 at a cost of $3.5 million. They are designed to fit through the passenger doors of DC-8 and DC-9 aircraft. They replaced the much larger A-containers widely used in the air cargo business. At six times the size of a C-container, A-containers can be loaded only through specially built cargo doors and require specialized loading equipment. The loading equipment required for C-containers is a modified belt loader, similar to that used for loading baggage onto a plane, and about 80% less expensive than the equipment needed to load A-containers. The use of C-containers meant that Airborne did not have to bear the $1 million per plane cost required to install cargo doors that would take A-containers. The C-containers are shaped to allow maximum utilization of the planes' interior loading space. Fifty of the containers fit into a converted DC-9, and about 83 fit into a DC-8-62. Moreover, a C-container filled with packages can be moved by a single person, making it easy to load and unload. Airborne Express took out a patent on the design of the C-containers.

Information Systems

Airborne utilized three information systems to help it boost productivity and improve customer service. The first of these systems was the LIBRA II system. LIBRA II equipment, which included a metering device and PC computer software, was installed in the mailroom of clients. With minimum data entry, the metering device weighed the package, calculated the shipping charges, generated the shipping labels, and provided a daily shipping report. By 2002, the system was in use at approximately 9,900 domestic customer locations. The use of LIBRA II not only benefited customers but also lowered Airborne's operating costs since LIBRA II shipment data were transferred into Airborne's FOCUS shipment tracking system automatically, thereby avoiding duplicate data entry.

FOCUS was the second of Airborne's three main information systems. As discussed earlier, the FOCUS system was a worldwide tracking system. The bar codes on each package were read at various points (for example, at pickup, at sorting in Wilmington, at arrival, and so forth) using hand-held scanners, and this information was fed into Airborne's computer system. Using FOCUS, Airborne could track the progress of a shipment through its national and international logistics system. The major benefit was in terms of customer service. Through an Internet link, Airborne's customers could track their own shipment through Airborne's system on a twenty-four-hour basis.

For its highest-volume corporate customers, Airborne developed Customer Linkage, an electronic data interchange (EDI) program and the third information system. The EDI system was designed to eliminate the flow of paperwork between Airborne and its major clients. The EDI system allowed customers to create shipping documentation at the same time they were entering orders for their goods. At the end of each day, shipping activities were transmitted electronically to Airborne's FOCUS system, where they were captured for shipment tracking and billing. Customer Linkage benefited the customer by eliminating repetitive data entry and paperwork. It also lowered the company's operating costs by eliminating manual data entry. (In essence, both LIBRA II and Customer Linkage pushed off a lot of the data-entry work into the hands of customers.) The EDI system also included electronic invoicing and payment remittance processing. Airborne also offered its customers a program known as Quicklink, which significantly reduced the programming time required by customers to take advantage of linkage benefits.

Strategy

Market Positioning

In the early 1980s, Airborne Express tried hard to compete head to head with Federal Express. This included an attempt to establish broad market coverage, including both frequent and infrequent users. Frequent users are those that generate more than $20,000 of business per month, or more than 1,000 shipments per month. Infrequent users generate less than $20,000 per month, or less than 1,000 shipments per month.

To build broad market coverage, Airborne followed Federal Express's lead of funding a television advertising campaign designed to build consumer awareness. However, by the mid-1980s, Airborne decided that this was an expensive way of building market share. The advertising campaign bought recognition but little penetration. One of the principal problems was that it was expensive to serve infrequent users. Infrequent users demanded the same level of service as frequent users, but Airborne would typically get only one shipment per pickup with an infrequent user, compared with ten or more shipments per pickup with a frequent user, so far more pickups were required to generate the same volume of business. Given the extremely competitive nature of the industry at this time, such an inefficient utilization of capacity was of great concern to Airborne.

Consequently, in the mid-1980s, Airborne decided to become a niche player in the industry and focused on serving the needs of high-volume corporate accounts. The company slashed its advertising expenditure, pulling the plug on its TV ad campaign, and invested more resources in building a direct sales force, which grew to be 460 strong. By focusing on high-volume corporate accounts, Airborne was able to establish scheduled pickup routes and use its ground capacity more efficiently. This enabled the company to achieve significant reductions in its unit cost structure. Partly due to this factor, Airborne executives reckoned that their cost structure was as much as $3 per shipment less than that of FedEx. Another estimate suggested that Airborne's strategy reduced labor costs by 20% per unit for pickup, and 10% for delivery.

Of course, there was a downside to this strategy. High-volume corporate customers have a great deal more bargaining power than infrequent users, so they can and do demand substantial discounts. For example, in March 1987, Airborne achieved a major coup when it won an exclusive three-year contract to handle all of IBM's express packages weighing less than 150 pounds. However, to win the IBM account, Airborne had to offer rates up to 84% below Federal Express's list prices! Nevertheless, the strategy does seem to have worked. As of 1995 approximately 80% of Airborne's revenues came from corporate accounts, most of them secured through competitive bidding. The concentrated volume that this business represents helped Airborne to drive down costs.

Delivery Time, Reliability, and Flexibility

Another feature of Airborne's strategy was the decision not to try to compete with Federal Express on delivery time. Federal Express and UPS have long guaranteed delivery by 10:30 A.M. Airborne guaranteed delivery by midday, although it offered a 10:30 guarantee to some very large corporate customers. Guaranteeing delivery by 10:30 A.M. would mean stretching Airborne's already tight scheduling system to the limit. To meet its 10:30 A.M. deadline, FedEx has to operate with a deadline for previous days' pickups of 6:30 P.M. Airborne could afford to be a little more flexible and can arrange pickups at 6:00 P.M. if that suited a corporate client's particular needs. Later pickups clearly benefit the shipper, who is, after all, the paying party.

In addition, Airborne executives felt that a guaranteed 10:30 A.M. delivery was unnecessary. They argued that the extra hour and a half does not make a great deal of difference to most clients, and they are willing to accept the extra time in exchange for lower prices. In addition, Airborne stressed the reliability of its delivery schedules. As one executive put it, "A package delivered consistently at 11:15 A.M. is as good as delivery at 10:30 A.M." This reliability was enhanced by Airborne's ability to provide shipment tracking through its FOCUS system.

Deferred Services

With a slowdown in the growth rate of the express mail market toward the end of the 1980s, in 1990 Airborne decided to enter the deferred-delivery business with its Select Delivery Service (SDS) product. The SDS service provides for next-afternoon or second-day delivery. Packages weighing five pounds or less are generally delivered on a next-afternoon basis, with packages of more than five pounds being delivered on a second-day basis. SDS shipment comprised approximately 42% of total domestic shipments in 1995. They were priced lower than overnight express products, reflecting the less time-sensitive nature of these deliveries. The company utilized any spare capacity on its express flights to carry SDS shipments. In addition, Airborne used other carriers, such as passenger carriers with spare cargo capacity in the bellies of their planes, to carry less urgent SDS shipments.

Early in 1996, Airborne began to phase in two new services to replace its SDS service. Next Afternoon Service was available for shipments weighing five pounds or less, and Second Day Service was offered for shipments of all weights. By 2001, deferred shipments accounted for 46% of total domestic shipments.

Ground Delivery Service

In April 2001, Airborne launched a Ground Delivery Service (GDS) in response to similar offerings from FedEx and UPS. Airborne came to the conclusion that it was very important to offer this service in order to retain parity with its principal competitors, and to be able to offer bundled services to its principal customers (that is, to offer them air, ground, and logistics services for a single bundled price). Airborne also believed that it could add the service with a relatively minor initial investment, $30 million, since it leveraged existing assets, including trucks, tracking systems, and regional ground hubs and sorting facilities.

The new service was initially introduced on a limited basis and targeted at large corporate customers. GDS was priced less than deferred services, reflecting the less time-sensitive nature of the GDS offering. GDS accounted for 1.5% of domestic shipments in 2001, and 4% in the fourth quarter of 2001.

Logistics Services

Although small package express mail remained Airborne's main business, through its Advanced Logistics Services Corp. (ALS) subsidiary the company increasingly promoted a range of third-party logistics services. These services provided customers with the ability to maintain inventories in a 1-million-square-foot "stock exchange" facility located at Airborne's Wilmington hub or at sixty smaller "stock exchange" facilities located around the country. The inventory could be managed either by the company or by the customer's personnel. Inventory stored at Wilmington could be delivered utilizing either Airborne's airline system or, if required, commercial airlines on a next-flight-out basis. ALS's central print computer program allowed information on inventories to be sent electronically to customers' computers located at Wilmington, where Airborne's personnel monitored printed output and shipped inventories according to customers' instructions.

For example, consider the case of Data Products Corp., a producer of computer printers. Data Products takes advantage of low labor costs to carry out significant assembly operations in Hong Kong. Many of the primary component parts for its printers, however, such as microprocessors, are manufactured in the United States and have to be shipped to Hong Kong. The finished product is then shipped back to the United States for sale. In setting up a global manufacturing system, Data Products had a decision to make: either consolidate the parts from its hundreds of suppliers in-house and then arrange for shipment to Hong Kong, or contract out to someone who could handle the whole logistics process. Data Products decided to contract out, picking Airborne Express to consolidate the component parts and arrange for shipments.

Airborne controlled the consolidation and movement of component parts from the component part suppliers through to the Hong Kong assembly operation in such a way as to minimize inventory-holding costs. The key feature of Airborne's service was that all of Data Products' materials were collected at Airborne's facility at Los Angeles International Airport. Data Products' Hong Kong assembly plants could then tell Airborne what parts to ship by air as they are needed. Airborne was thus able to provide inventory control for Data Products. In addition, by scheduling deliveries so that year-round traffic between Los Angeles and Hong Kong could be guaranteed, Airborne was able to negotiate a better air rate from Japan Air Lines for the transportation of component parts.

International Strategy

One of the major strategic challenges that Airborne faced (along with the other express mail carriers) was how best to establish an international service that is comparable to their domestic service. Many of Airborne's major corporate clients were becoming ever more global in their own strategic orientations. As this occurred, they were increasingly demanding a compatible express mail service. In addition, the rise of companies with globally dispersed manufacturing operations that relied on just-in-time delivery systems to keep inventory holding costs down created a demand for global air express services that could transport critical inventory between operations located in different areas of the globe (consider the example of Data Products discussed earlier in this case study).

The initial response of FedEx and UPS to this challenge was to undertake massive capital investments to establish international airlift capability and international ground operations based on the U.S. model. Their rationale was that a wholly owned global delivery network was necessary to establish the tight control, coordination, and scheduling required for a successful air express operation. In the 1990s, however, FedEx pulled out of its European ground operations, while continuing to fly its own aircraft overseas.

Airborne decided on a quite different strategy. In part born of financial necessity (Airborne lacks the capital necessary to imitate FedEx and UPS), Airborne decided to pursue what it referred to as a *variable cost strategy*. This involved two main elements: (1) the utilization of international airlift on existing air cargo operators and passenger aircraft to get packages overseas, and (2) entry into strategic alliances with foreign companies that already had established ground delivery networks. In these two ways, Airborne hoped to be able to establish global coverage without having to undertake the kind of capital investments that Federal Express and UPS have borne.

Airborne executives defend their decision to continue to purchase space on international flights rather than fly their own aircraft overseas by making a number of points. First, they pointed out that Airborne's international business was 70% outbound and 30% inbound. If Airborne were to fly its own aircraft overseas, this would mean flying them back half-empty. Second, on many routes Airborne simply didn't have the volume necessary to justify flying its own planes. Third, national air carriers were giving Airborne good prices. If Airborne began to fly directly overseas, the company would be seen as a competitor and might no longer be given price breaks. Fourth, getting international airlift space was not a problem. While space can be limited in the third and fourth quarters of the year, Airborne was such a big customer that it usually had few problems getting lift.

On the other hand, the long-term viability of this strategy was questionable given the rapid evolution in the international air express business. Flying Tiger was once one of Airborne's major providers of international lift. However, following the purchase of Flying Tiger by FedEx, Airborne has reduced its business with Flying Tiger. Airborne worried that its packages will be "pushed to the back of the plane" whenever Flying Tiger had problems of capacity overload.

With regard to strategic alliances, Airborne had joint venture operations is Japan, Thailand, Malaysia, and South Africa. The alliance with Mitsui was announced in December 1989. Mitsui is one of the world's leading trading companies. Together with Tonami Transportation Co., Mitsui owns Panther Express, one of the top five express carriers in Japan and a company with a substantial ground network. The deal called for the establishment of a joint venture between Airborne, Mitsui, and Tonami. To be known as Airborne Express Japan, the joint venture combined Airborne's existing Japanese operations with Panther Express. Airborne handled all of the shipments to and from Japan. The joint venture was 40% owned by Airborne, 40% by Mitsui, and 20% by Tonami. The agreement specified that board decisions had to be made by consensus among the three partners. A majority of two could not outvote the third. In addition, the deal called for Mitsui to invest $40 million in Airborne Express through the purchase of a new issue of nonvoting 6.9% cumulative convertible preferred stock and a commitment to Airborne from Mitsui of up to $100 million for aircraft financing. There is no doubt that Airborne executives saw the Mitsui deal as a major coup, both financially and in terms of market penetration into the Japanese market. The primary advantage claimed by Airborne executives for expanding via strategic alliances is that the company got an established ground-based delivery network overseas without having to make capital investments.

Organization

In 2001, Carl Donaway became CEO, replacing the long-time top management team of Robert Cline, the CEO, and Robert Brazier, the president and COO, both of whom had been with the company since the early 1960s. Prior to becoming CEO, Donaway was responsible for the airline operations, included managing the Wilmington hub, the package sorting facility, and all aircraft and flight maintenance operations. The philosophy at Airborne was to keep the organizational structure as flat as possible, to shorten lines of communication and allow for a free flow of ideas within the managerial hierarchy. The top managers generally felt that they were open to ideas suggested by lower-level managers. At the same time, the decision-making process was fairly centralized. The view was that interdependence between functions made centralized decision making necessary. To quote one executive, "Coordination is the essence of this business. We need centralized decision making in order to achieve this."

Control at Airborne Express was geared toward boosting productivity, lowering costs, and maintaining a reliable high-quality service. This was achieved through a combination of budgetary controls, pay-for-performance incentive systems, and a corporate culture that continually stressed key values.

For example, consider the procedure used to control stations (which contained about 80% of all employees). Station operations were reviewed on a quarterly basis using a budgetary process. Control and evaluation of station effectiveness stressed four categories. The first was service, measured by the time between pickup and delivery. The goal was to achieve 95 to 97% of all deliveries before noon. The second category was productivity, measured by total shipments per employee hour. The third category was controllable cost, and the fourth station profitability. Goals for each of these categories were determined each quarter in a bottom-up procedure that involved station managers in the goal-setting process. These goals were then linked to an incentive pay system whereby station managers could earn up to 10% of their quarterly salary just by meeting their goals with no maximum on the upside if they go over the goals.

The direct sales force also had an incentive pay system. The target pay structure for the sales organization was 70% base pay and a 30% commission. There was, however, no cap on the commissions for salespeople. So in theory, there was no limit to what a salesperson could earn. There were also contests that were designed to boost performance. For example, there was a so-called Top Gun competition for the sales force, in which the top salesperson for each quarter won a $20,000 prize.

Incentive pay systems apart, however, Airborne is not known as a high payer. The company's approach is not to be the compensation leader. Rather, the company tries to set its salary structure to position it in the middle of the labor market. Thus, according to a senior human resource executive, "We target our pay philosophy (total package—compensation plus benefits) to be right at the 50th percentile plus or minus 5 percent."

A degree of self-control was also achieved by trying to establish a corporate culture that focused employees' attention on the key values required to maintain a competitive edge in the air express industry. The values continually stressed by top managers at Airborne, and communicated throughout the organization by the company's newspaper and a quarterly video, emphasized serving customers' needs, maintaining quality, doing it right the first time around, and excellent service. There was also a companywide emphasis on productivity and cost control. One executive, when describing the company's attitude to expenditures, said, "We challenge everything. . . . We're the toughest sons of bitches on the block." Another noted that "among managers I feel that there is a universal agreement on the need to control costs. This is a very tough business, and our people are aware of that. Airborne has an underdog mentality—a desire to be a survivor."

Airborne in 2002

By 2002 Airborne Express faced a number of key strategic opportunities and threats. These included (1) the rapid globalization of the air express industry, (2) the development of logistics services based on rapid air transportation, (3) the growth potential for deferred services and ground-based delivery services, (4) lower margins associated with the new GDS offering, (5) the superior scale and scope of its two main competitors, FedEx and UPS, (6) an economic slowdown in the United States, and (7) persistently high fuel costs (oil prices rose from $18 a barrel in mid-1995 to $25 a barrel in 2002). The company's financial performance, which had always been volatile, was poor during 2001, when the company lost $12 million on revenues of $3.2 billion. In 2002, Airborne earned $58 million on revenues of $3.3 billion, even though average revenue per shipment declined to $8.46 from $8.79 a year earlier. Management attributed the improved performance to strong employee productivity, which improved 9.4% over the prior year. In their guidance for 2003, management stated that they would be able to further improve operating performance—then, in March 2003, DHL made its takeover bid for the company. Under the terms of the deal, which was finalized in 2003, DHL acquired the ground assets of Airborne Express, while the airline continued as an independent entity.

ENDNOTES

1. This case was made possible by the generous assistance of Airborne Express. The information given in this case was provided by Airborne Express. Unless otherwise indicated, Airborne Express and Securities and Exchange Commission's 10–K filings are the sources of all information contained within this case. The case is based on an earlier case, which was prepared with the assistance of Daniel Bodnar, Laurie Martinelli, Brian McMullen, Lisa Mutty, and Stephen Schmidt.
2. Standard & Poors Industry Survey, Airlines, March, 2002.
3. *Source:* http://www.airborne.com/Company/History.asp?nav= AboutAirborne/CompanyInfo/History.

American Airlines Since Deregulation: A Thirty-Year Experience, 1978–2007

This case was prepared by Dr. Isaac Cohen, San Jose State University.

Since the passage of the Airline Deregulation Act in 1978, eight major U.S. air carriers filed for bankruptcy. All were old, established carriers flying domestic as well as international routes. Three of the major carriers—Pan American Airways, Eastern Airlines, and Trans World Airways (TWA)—were eventually liquidated and their assets were sold to rival carriers. Two others—Continental Airlines and U.S. Air—filed for bankruptcy protection at least twice. And the remaining three—United, Delta, and Northwest Airlines—were operating in 2005–2006 under Chapter 11 of the Bankruptcy Code. Alone among all U.S. international majors, American Airlines (AA) had never filed for bankruptcy protection.

American's financial position was stronger than that of its competitors all through the era of deregulation. During the first two decades of the new era, Robert Crandall ran AA, first as President (1980–1985), and then as CEO (1985–1998). An executive widely regarded as the industry's most innovative strategist, Crandall introduced the frequent-flier program and the two-tier wage system, expanded American globally, formed alliances with other carriers, and established a successful regional airline affiliated with AA.

As Crandall retired in 1998, Donald Carty was selected CEO. An insider whose tenure was overshadowed by the terrorist attack of September 11, 2001, Carty was a lackluster leader, and his career ended in a public scandal that led to his replacement by Gerald Arpey in April 2003. Arpey needed to act quickly. Following the unprecedented losses incurred by American as a result of the September 11 attack—a loss of over $5 billion dollars during 2001 and 2002, and an additional loss of over $1 billion in the first quarter of 2003—American Airlines was on the brink of bankruptcy.

What should Arpey do?

Should Arpey follow the strategies undertaken by Crandall to cut operating costs, improve AA's financial position, and turn the carrier profitable? Should Arpey, rather, reject some of the policies introduced by his predecessor? Or should he, instead, introduce brand new innovative strategies applicable to the airline industry in the 21st century?

To assess Arpey's strategic choices, this case looks back at the experience of his legendary predecessor. How precisely did Robert Crandall manage to turn American around?

The Airline Industry

The airline industry dates back to the Air Mail Service of 1918–1925. Using its own planes and pilots, the Post Office Department directly operated scheduled flights to ship mail. With the passage of the Air Mail Act (Kelly Act) of 1925, the Post Office subcontracted air mail transport to private companies and thereby laid the foundation of a national air transport system. The Post Office paid contractors substantial sums and encouraged them to extend their routes, buy larger planes, and expand their services.

The formative period of the private airline industry was the Great Depression. The five or six years following Charles Lindbergh's 1927 flight across the Atlantic were years of mergers and acquisitions in which every major carrier came into existence, mostly through the acquisition of smaller lines. American,

This case was presented in the October 2006 meeting of the North American Case Research Association at San Diego, California. Copyright Isaac Cohen and NACRA. Dr. Cohen is grateful to the San Jose State University College of Business for its support.

United, Delta, Northwest, Continental and Eastern Airlines were all formed during this period. The increase in passenger transport during the 1930s led, in turn, to growing competition, price cutting, bankruptcies, and serious safety problems. It convinced the architects of the New Deal that the entire transport system—not just the air mail—required federal regulation. The outcome was the passage of the Civil Aeronautics Act (CAA) of 1938.[1]

The CAA had two major provisions. First, it prohibited price competition among carriers, and second, it effectively closed the industry to newcomers. The Civil Aeronautics Board (CAB) required that all air carriers flying certain routes charge the same fares for the same class of passengers. Similarly, the CAB required all applicants wishing to enter the industry to show that they were "fit, willing and able" to do so and that their service was "required by the public convenience and necessity." Typically, between 1950 and 1975 the board denied all 79 applications it had received from carriers asking to enter the domestic, scheduled airline industry.[2] The number of scheduled air carriers was reduced from 16 in 1938 to just 10 in the 1970s, following mergers, consolidations, and route transfers among carriers.[3]

By the mid-1970s, the airline industry had experienced serious financial troubles. Rising fuel prices, an economic recession, and the introduction of expensive wide-body aircraft (Boeing 747s, Lockheed L-1011s, and McDonnell Douglas DC-10s) led to climbing costs, higher fares, reduced traffic, falling revenues, and a growing public demand for opening up the airline industry to competition. As a result, in 1975, a Senate subcommittee chaired by Edward Kennedy held hearings on the airlines. Working closely with Kennedy was a Harvard law professor named Stephen Breyer, who later became a U.S. Supreme Court Justice. A specialist in regulation, the author of *Regulation and Reform*, and the Staff Director of the Kennedy hearings, Breyer helped Kennedy build up a strong case against airline regulation.

Together, Breyer and Kennedy contrasted intrastate air service—which had never been regulated by the CAB—with interstate service—which had been regulated since 1938. The figures were astounding. Air fares charged by an interstate carrier flying the New York-Boston route (191 miles) were almost double the fares charged by an intrastate carrier (Southwest Airlines) flying the Houston-San Antonio route (also 191 miles), and air fares charged by an interstate airline

servicing the Chicago-Minneapolis city pair market (339 miles) were more than double those charged by an intrastate airline (Pacific Southwest Airlines) serving the Los Angeles-San Francisco market (338 miles). The experience of Southwest Airlines in Texas—like that of Pacific Southwest Airlines in California—Breyer and Kennedy concluded, demonstrated the efficiency of the free market and the urgent need for deregulation.[4] Three years later, in 1978, Congress deregulated the airline industry.

Company Background

The early history of American Airlines dates back to 1929 when dozens of small airline companies merged together to form American Airways, a subsidiary of an aircraft manufacturing/airline service conglomerate called the Aviation Corporation (AVCO). From the outset, American Airlines shipped mail along the southern sub-continental route from Los Angeles to Atlanta via Dallas. With the passage of the Air Mail Act of 1934, Congress prohibited aircraft manufacturing firms from owning airline companies, and redistributed existing airmail contracts on a new, competitive bidding basis. To bid successfully on the new contracts, American Airways changed its name to American Airlines, and reorganized itself as a stand alone company, independent of AVCO. Winning back its original government contracts, AA resumed its air mail operations, and moved aggressively to expand its nascent passenger service.[5]

For the next 35 years, 1934–1968, a single CEO—Cyrus Rowlett Smith—ran American Airlines. A Texan, C. R. Smith managed to improve AA performance in the 1930s, and led the company to sustained growth during the following three decades. He paid particular attention to two critical aspects of airline management, namely, aircraft technology, and labor relations.

Smith played a key role in the introduction of the DC-3 aircraft in 1936, a well-designed, and efficient plane with two piston engines. The first commercially viable passenger aircraft ever produced, the DC-3 dominated the world's airways until after WWII. Because AA operated the largest fleet of DC-3s in the industry, it soon became the industry leader, carrying about 30% of the domestic passenger traffic in the late 1930s.[6]

Working together with Donald Douglas on the design and development of the DC-3, C. R. Smith laid the foundations for long lasting relations between AA and the Douglas (since 1967, McDonnell Douglas) Corporation. Not until 1955 did Smith select a Boeing model over a Douglas one (AA ordered its first jet—the B-707—from Boeing),[7] but soon thereafter American Airlines resumed its customer relations with Douglas. The two companies continued cooperating for decades. In 2005, long after C.R. Smith had retired, and nearly a decade after the Boeing Company bought the McDonnell Douglas Corporation, American Airlines' fleet was made up of 327 MD-80 McDonnell Douglas planes, and 320 Boeing planes (the B-737, 757, 767, and 777 models), a 46/45% mix which reflected AA's traditional ties with the McDonnell Douglas Corporation.[8]

C. R. Smith, in addition, played a central role in shaping AA's labor relations. AA employees, like the employees of virtually all other major airlines, had become highly unionized by the late 1940s, and subsequently, the company experienced growing labor troubles. Responding to two large-scale pilot strikes that shut down American airlines in 1954 and 1958, C. R. Smith proposed the establishment of a cooperative arrangement among air carriers known as the Mutual Aid Pact (MAP). Thinking in terms of the entire industry, Smith saw the pact as a self-protecting measure designed to check the rising power of unions. Originally established in 1958 by American and five other carriers (United, TWA, Pan American, Eastern, and Capital), the pact authorized airlines benefiting from a strike that shut down one or more carriers to transfer their strike-generated revenues to the struck carrier(s), an arrangement which reduced the financial losses of the struck carrier(s) and thereby increased management bargaining power across the industry. In several different forms, the MAP survived for twenty years, providing AA and its rival carriers with a measure of protection against lengthy strikes.[9]

Smith's last four years at American Airlines, 1964–1967, were AA's most profitable. In 1968, he retired, and was succeeded by George Spater, a corporate lawyer whose tenure at American was marred by recession and scandal. Spater not only failed to improve AA's performance during the recession of the early 1970s, but he also admitted making illegal corporate contributions to President Nixon's reelection campaign. As a result, the AA board forced Spater to resign in 1973, and invited C.R. Smith to rejoin American as a caretaker for a short transitional period. Smith served just seven months until the board recruited Albert Casey, a media executive, to head the company.[10]

Casey's early years at American coincided with the political debate over airline deregulation. On the one side, AA financial results during these years were impressive: Casey turned a loss of $34 million in 1975 to a record profit of $122 million in 1978, and raised AA's cash position from $115 million in 1974 to $537 million in 1978. But on the other, Casey opposed deregulation. Casey's management team believed that airline deregulation would promote competition with low-cost carriers and shift passenger traffic away from transcontinental and semi-transcontinental routes—AA's most profitable ones—to short and medium haul routes. "We opposed [deregulation] all the way," Casey recalled years later. "We had the wrong route structure. We had the wrong aircraft. . . . We weren't equipped right. [And w]e had very unfavorable union contracts."[11]

Notwithstanding his opposition to deregulation, Casey expected Congress to pass the deregulation act. To prepare for the passage of the act, Casey undertook two early initiatives which later contributed to AA's eventual success under deregulation. First, he established a major hub airport at Dallas/Fort Worth (D/FW) and moved the company's headquarters from New York to Dallas. Second, he promoted Robert Crandall to the presidency of American Airlines.

The Crandall Era, 1980–1998

Crandall's management style was distinctly different from that of Casey. Casey had a personable, relaxed, and jolly manner. Crandall was famous for his charismatic, intense, and combative style. Casey was diplomatic. Crandall was forthright, temperamental, and impatient. "The [airline] business is intensely, vigorously, bitterly, savagely competitive,"[12] Crandall once said, adding, "I want to crush all my competition. That is what competition is about."[13]

Crandall served as AA President for five years, and as CEO for 13 years. During the early period of 1980–1985, Casey turned over to Crandall the day-to-day operation of the company, and focused his attention on American's financial performance.[14] During the later period, Crandall assumed full responsibility for AA's financial performance, becoming one of the industry's longest serving chief executives. As both President and CEO, Crandall developed a large body of corporate level strategies which helped American gain a competitive advantage over its rivals.

Developing the Hub-and-Spoke System

The hub-and-spoke system was the product of airline deregulation. During the regulatory era, government rules restricted the entry of carriers into new travel markets. With the coming of deregulation, such restrictions were removed, and airlines were free to establish their own connecting hubs for the purpose of transferring passengers from incoming to outgoing flights. Utilizing the hub-and-spoke system, carriers were able to cut costs in at least two ways. First, centralizing aircraft maintenance in hubs reduced the fleet's maintenance costs, and second, increasing the carriers' load factor and bringing it close to capacity resulted in a more efficient operation. In addition, the hub-and-spoke system resulted in greater flight frequency for passengers—a service benefit valued especially by business travelers.[15]

Throughout the first two years of his presidency, 1981–1982, Crandall added 17 new domestic cities to AA's D/FW hub, and seven new international destinations (in Mexico as well as the Caribbean). The sheer number of daily flights AA operated in D/FW climbed from 100 to 300 in 1981 alone. Building its central hub in D/FW, American shifted passenger traffic away from other carriers serving Dallas's outlaying cities, subjecting these carriers to relentless competitive pressure. Braniff International Airways is a case in point. The leading carrier serving the D/FW airport in the 1970s, Braniff filed bankruptcy and suspended operation in 1982 largely as a result of the cutthroat competition it was subject to by American Airlines in the Dallas area.[16]

Under Crandall's direction, AA expanded its hub-and-spoke operations in the 1980s, establishing major hubs in Chicago, Miami, and San Juan, Puerto Rico, and focusing on long-haul fights, the most profitable segment of the industry. By the mid-1990s, these new hubs—together with the D/FW one—had all become major international airports serving passengers flying to destinations in Europe, South America, Central America, and the Caribbean.[17]

Introducing the Two-Tier Wage System

Dubbed "the father of the two-tier pay scale," Crandall had little to do with the origins of the two-tier plan. The idea grew out of management's endless discussions of the need to achieve low cost growth. Rejecting employee concessions as an insufficient means to attain a low cost operation, Crandall nurtured the two-tier idea and transformed it from an abstract notion into a concrete policy—practical, consistent, and effective.[18]

The two-tier wage system distinguished between two types of employees: current employees paid by an A-scale and newly-hired employees paid by a B-scale. Initially, under the system established by Crandall at American, the two scales were not intended to merge at all; in other words, the top pay received by B-scale employees was expected to be significantly lower than the top pay received by A-scale employees. To persuade AA's labor unions to accept the two-tier plan, Crandall offered employees job security, job expanding opportunities, higher wages and benefits, and profit sharing. He also threatened to shrink the carrier unless the unions accepted the two-tier deal. Believing that lay-offs were eminent, American unionized employees agreed to the new wage structure, and in 1983, AA signed the industry's first two-tier contracts with its principal unions, the Allied Pilots Association (APA, representing the pilots), the Transport Workers Union (TWU, representing the machinists and other ground workers), and the Association of Professional Flight Attendants (APFA, representing the flight attendants). AA's major competitors—United, Delta, U.S. Air, and others—negotiated similar labor agreements. Consequently, the number of two-tier union contracts signed in the airline industry jumped from 8 in 1983, to 35 in 1984, and 62 in 1985.[19]

AA's two-tier wage plan resulted in a significant pay gap between old and new employees. A newly-hired B-727 captain with a five year experience earned $68 an hour or less than half the $140 paid to his/her veteran counterpart. Such a wage gap led to substantial cost savings: between 1984 and 1989 American Airlines' labor cost fell from 37% to 34% of the carrier's total expenses.[20]

Creating a Holding Company

In 1982, Crandall oversaw the formation of the AMR Corporation—a holding company created "to provide [American] with access to sources of financing that otherwise might be unavailable."[21] AMR owned American Airlines together with several other non-airline subsidiaries, an arrangement which gave management greater flexibility in shifting assets among airline and non-airline subsidiaries, and in identifying new profit sources. Equally important was the protection AMR gave the airline from the swings of the business cycle: profits generated by AMR's non-airline units were expected to mitigate the impact of the industry's periodic downturns.

Consider the following example. During the downturn of 1990–1993, Crandall devised a "transition plan" that called for shifting assets from AMR's unprofitable airline operation to its profitable non-airline businesses. He even suggested leaving the airline business altogether. As AA's losses were mounting—and profits generated from AMR's non-airline units were increasing—Crandall threatened to sell AA and keep instead AMR's non-airline subsidiaries only.[22]

AMR's principal subsidiary—apart from AA—was the Sabre computer reservation system. Owned by AMR, Sabre (Semi Automatic Business Research Environment) had become AMR's most profitable unit during the 1990s, generating far higher returns on sales than the airline itself. In 1995, for instance, Sabre recorded total sales of $1.5 billion, or 9% of AMR revenues, and an operating profit of 19%.[23]

Building a Regional Airline

Another subsidiary of AMR was American Eagle. American Eagle was established in 1984 as AA's regional affiliate. Operating under the affiliate name, several small regional airlines were franchised by AA to supply connecting flights to American air services. From the start, American Eagle offered customers "seamless service," that is, assigned seats, boarding passes, and frequent flyer mileage. In 1987, AMR began acquiring American Eagle's franchised carriers, and in 1990, it consolidated these carriers into six airline systems that served the D/FW, Nashville, New York City, Chicago, Raleigh/Durham and San Juan regional markets. To better coordinate planning, operation, schedules, training, and marketing of commuter services, AMR sought further consolidation. Accordingly, in 1998, it merged the six regional airlines into a single entity carrier, the America Eagle Airlines, creating the world's largest regional airline system. Operating 1,450 daily flights to 125 destinations in the U.S., Canada, and the Caribbean; employing 10,000; and generating $1 billion in revenue; American Eagle was named "Airline of the Year" by *Commuter World* magazine in 1998.[24]

American Eagle's growth helped improve AMR's financial results. Originally, American Eagle operated as a regional carrier feeding passengers to American Airlines flights. But by the mid-1990s, Crandall had replaced a growing number of routes flown by AA pilots with routes flown by American Eagle pilots, a move which resulted in substantial labor cost savings, given the higher pay received by American than Eagle pilots (in 1997 AA pilots earned an average yearly pay of $120,000 and Eagle pilots $35,000).[25]

Upgrading the Computer Reservation System (CRS)

The Sabre computer reservation system was born in 1962, following a decade-long research effort carried out jointly by American Airlines engineers and IBM technicians. Initially, Sabre lagged behind comparable CRS systems used by its competitors, namely, United's Apollo, TWA's PARS, and Eastern Airlines' System One. But by the mid-1970s, with the appointment of Crandall to the position of AA's Vice President for Marketing, Sabre received a new lease of life. As marketing chief, Crandall controlled the company's budget for technology research and development. He recruited a strong team of Sabre computer engineers, and supplied the team with ample funding. At the same time, he launched a campaign to build an industry-wide CRS owned jointly by the major airlines, and used by travel agents. Confident that its own CRS was ahead of its competitors, United declined to join the industry-wide project, and instead, decided to sell its Apollo system's services directly to travel agents. Crandall reacted quickly. Implementing a carefully crafted back-up plan, he sent hundreds of sales people and technicians to travel agents all across the country, offering them a variety of Sabre services. Caught unprepared, United was unable to deliver its own computer reservation system's services until months later. The result was a swift victory of American over United in the race to wire travel agents.[26]

Sabre provided American Airlines with several information technology services. First, it calculated the yield of each American flight, setting and resetting the price of every seat sold. Second, it managed an inventory of close to one billion spare parts used by American's fleet in its maintenance facilities. Third, it directed the routing and tracking of all baggage and freight. And fourth, it supplied American with ongoing data on aircraft fuel requirements, take off weight, and flight plan.[27]

More important were Sabre's travel services. Sabre provided travel agents around the world with fares and schedules for flights offered by hundreds of carriers, not only American and American Eagle. In 1997, Sabre signed a comprehensive 25-year agreement to manage the information technology infrastructure of U.S. Air, and in addition, it renewed a five-year contract with Southwest Airlines to operate the carrier's reservation and inventory systems. Sabre and Canadian Airlines International signed a similar agreement in 1994.

Sabre's clients, it should be noted, were not limited to the airline industry. Both the London Underground and the French National Railway were Sabre's customers in the 1990s; the first contracted Sabre to manage its train and crew scheduling, the second, to design its computer reservation system. Under Crandall's leadership, furthermore, Sabre signed agreements with both Dollar Rent-a-Car and Thrifty Rent-a-Car to manage each company's reservation system.[28]

Under Crandall's leadership, Sabre had become the largest U.S. computer reservation system with a 40% share of all travel agent bookings in 1996. Nearly 30,000 travel agent offices in 70 countries subscribed to Sabre, and more than 2.5 million individual passengers subscribed to Travelocity, Sabre's Internet service. In 1995, the total value of travel-related products and services reserved through Sabre was estimated at $40 billion.[29]

Promoting Yield Management

Developing a revenue maximizing process called yield management was impossible without enhanced computer capabilities. To fill all empty seats on a given flight, American Airlines needed to obtain information pertaining to the desirable number of seats that could be sold at full versus discount fares, and the optimal mix of fares that could maximize the yield of a given flight. Obtaining such information required complex computer calculations based on the carrier's past performance. Hence the key role played by Sabre. Sabre could track any passenger on any seat traveling any distance at any time. It could find out how early business travelers booked their flights, how far in advance coach passengers did so, and how sensitive each of these two groups was to fare price changes. With Sabre's growing computer capabilities, American began offering a large variety of discounted fares, as Don

Reed, author of *Bob Crandall and American Airlines,* explained:

> Instead of offering first-class, coach, and one level of discount fares, American began offering several layers of discounts. The bigger the savings off full-fare prices, the more restrictions the tickets had. The more modest the savings, the fewer restrictions. So fourteen-day and seven-day advance purchase discount fares cost more than twenty-one-day fares, but they were less restricted. Because of this sliding scale of discounts, American could juggle the percentage of seats on any airplane allocated to one fare type or another. . . . By the late 1980s American would be able to, and often did, juggle the mix of fares right up until the moment of departure.[30]

Sabre's yield management system gave American a clear competitive advantage over its rivals. On any given flight, AA was able to offer a variety of discounted fares using projections based on past experience. Sabre's technology permitted Crandall to match or undercut the cheaper fares offered by competitors by simply lowering American's own discount prices for some seats and/or increase the number of seats available at the lowest price category. There was no need to reduce fares on all seats. While competitors lacking American's technology were unable to match AA's price flexibility, they soon introduced their own yield management systems; nevertheless, American Airlines managed to retain its leadership position in the field for decades.

Pioneering the Frequent-Flyer Program

Just as Sabre promoted the development of AA's yield management system, so did it facilitate the introduction of American's AAdvantage frequent flyer program, an innovation that allowed regular passengers to earn free tickets on miles traveled with American. And just as the hub-and spoke system was the outgrowth of deregulation, so was the frequent flyer program. While deregulation promoted competition, the frequent flyer program protected carriers from the competitive market forces by creating brand loyalty among travelers.

Crandall introduced the AAdvantage program—the first in the industry—in 1981, a year after he became president. Managed by Sabre, the frequent flyer innovation was an effective marketing program which lowered the advertising costs by targeting individual AAdvantage card-holders reachable through mailing and/or email distribution lists. Sabre had been gathering information on passengers early on. As Mike Gunn, AA's Vice President for Marketing under Crandall, noted: "One reason we were able to seize the competitive edge was that we already knew who many of our best customers were and how to reach them quickly. As other airlines struggled to match our initiative and identify their base of frequent-flyers, we were already placing AAdvantage cards and welcome letters in the hands of our best customers."[31]

More than one million passengers joined AAdvantage before the end of 1981, and another million joined the frequent flyer programs introduced by other airlines in 1981 in response to AAdvantage. Ten years later, 28 million travelers were card-carrying members of at least one frequent flyer program, and they held, on average, membership in 3.5 programs. American Airlines' program was the industry's largest. In 1991, American's frequent flier program had one million members more than that of its closest competitor, United, and four million more than Delta, the nation's third largest carrier.[32]

At the time Crandall left office in 1998, the frequent flyer program had become an airline industry standard feature. It impacted other industries as well, and generated both revenues and profits for the airlines. American sold miles to a variety of companies which awarded, in turn, AA miles to loyal customers as an incentive. In 1998, over 2,500 companies awarded miles to customers using the AAdvantage Incentive Miles program, most of which were retail stores and food serving establishments.[33]

Expanding Internationally

Before the passage of the airline regulation act in 1978, American Airlines had virtually no international presence. The dominant U.S. international carriers at the time were TWA and Pan America World Airways, and neither United nor Delta Airlines served any foreign destinations.[34] The Deregulation Act removed government restrictions on entry into new travel markets, promoted the development of hub-and-spoke systems, and as such, prompted the leading domestic airlines—United, American, and Delta—to begin serving a growing number of international destinations.

From the outset, AA's domestic hub system supported international expansion, helping the carrier fill empty seats on overseas flights. In the early 1980s, Crandall extended AA's route network to Mexico and the Caribbean, but not until 1990 did he launch a massive drive at global expansion, adding many more overseas destinations in Europe and Latin America.

Crandall's decision to extend AA's international route network was informed by air-traffic projections. Over the ten-year period 1990–2000, U.S. air traffic was expected to grow at a modest rate of 3%–4% a year while transatlantic air traffic, as well as traffic between the U.S. and Latin America's destinations, was projected to increase at an annual rate of 6%–7%. To take advantage of these projections, Crandall committed $11 billion, or half of AA's investment budget, to global expansion over the five-year period, 1990–1995. He also made two important acquisitions, both in 1989–1991. He first bought TWA's Chicago-London route in 1989, and six more TWA-London routes in 1991. He next acquired Eastern Airline's Latin America route system in 1990. In the Latin American market, AA used its strong Miami hub to handle traffic from 20 cities in 15 South and Central American countries. In the European market, Crandall embarked on what he called a "fragmentation strategy," namely, the break-up of the traditional route system linking one international city to another, for example, New York-London (and flying large commercial aircraft such as the 400-seat Boeing B-747), and replacing it with a route system that linked less congested cites like Chicago and Brussels or Chicago and Glasgow (and flying smaller 200-seat aircraft such as the Boeing B-767).[35]

Five years later, Crandall's plan achieved its main goals. By the mid-1990s, AA had become the dominant U.S. carrier serving Latin America, and the number two U.S. carrier serving Europe, closely behind Delta. In Latin America, AA carried 58% of all U.S. airline traffic to and from the region, served 27 nations, and opened two new U.S. gateway hubs, one in New York, the other in Dallas/Fort Worth, in addition to its principal one in Miami. In the transatlantic travel market, AA's share accounted for 23% of all airline traffic. In 1995, American derived 14%–15% of its airline revenues from the Latin America market, and 13% from the European market. As expected, both international markets were quite profitable: in 1996, AA generated an operating profit margin of 10% in Latin America, and 8% in Europe.[36]

Forming Alliances

Signing code-sharing agreements with foreign carriers was another growth strategy undertaken by Crandall.

Code-sharing allowed American to assign its two let-ter code—AA—to flights operated by another carrier, thereby offering passengers flights to destinations not served by American. Enhanced by shared computer reservation systems and joint frequent-flyer pro-grams, such agreements enabled American to increase its passenger traffic without extending its own route network, hence saving the carrier the expensive and risky cost of starting new international services.

American signed its first code-sharing agree-ment with Canadian Airlines International (CAI) in 1995. The agreement extended AA's route network to dozens of Canadian cities served by CAI and linked CAI route system to dozens of U.S. destina-tions served by AA. Seeking to extend AA's route structure to Asia, Crandall signed another code-sharing agreement with CAI in 1997. The 1997 agreement offered AA passengers trans-Pacific serv-ice on flights operated by CAI between Vancouver and Taipei. To further increase its Asia-bound traf-fic, American formed an alliance with China Eastern Airlines in 1998—the first code-sharing agreement between a U.S. carrier and an airline based in the People Republic of China. Under the agreement's provisions, American placed its code on flights oper-ated by China Eastern from Los Angeles and San Francisco to both Shanghai and Beijing, thereby of-fering passengers from destinations as distant as Latin America full service to Mainland China. Fi-nally, in September 1998, a few months after Cran-dall stepped down, American Airlines announced the formation of OneWorld Alliance, a code-sharing agreement signed by five international carriers: American Airlines, British Airways, Canadian Air-lines International, Qantas Airway (Australia), and Cathy Pacific Airlines (Hong Kong).[37]

Escalating the War with the Unions, 1990–1998

AA's labor relations under Crandall may be divided into two distinctly different periods: 1980–1989, and 1990–1998. In the 1980s, relations between labor and management at American were, for the most part, cooperative and peaceful. Crandall, as discussed, managed to convince the leadership of the pilots', flight attendants', and machinists' unions to negotiate and sign two-tier labor agreements which allowed management to place newly hired employees on a lower, B-type wage scale.

In the 1990s, by contrast, labor relations at American were stormy and contentious. Contract negotiations were long and difficult to conclude, and labor disputes triggered strikes, strike threats, and re-peated instances of federal intervention to avert strikes. As a consequence, labor disputes were costly, resulting in revenue and income losses.

One major cause of the 1990s labor troubles was the lingering dissatisfaction—expressed by AA employees—with the two-tier wage system. For any unionized job, B-scale employees were paid much lower wages than their veteran counterparts, and over the years, these lower paid employees had turned ex-tremely resentful towards management. As Crandall hired a growing number of B-scale recruits in the 1980s and 1990s, the "B-scalers" had eventually be-come the majority of all AA's unionized employees.

Two labor disputes at American during the 1990s stand out. The first involved a strike staged by the Professional Association of Flight Attendants. In 1993, 21,000 flight attendants struck American air-lines during Thanksgiving Day weekend, crippling the carrier and ruining whatever prospects manage-ment had of posting profits that year (AA ended the year with a small loss of $110 million on $15.8 billion in revenues). Union leaders pointed out that Cran-dall's unwillingness to bend during negotiations pre-cipitated the strike. Industry analysts agreed, noting Crandall's compulsion to keep labor cost low. As the strike entered its fifth day, President Clinton inter-vened and pressured both sides to accept binding ar-bitration. The dispute was later settled, but the flight attendants remained disgruntled.[38]

A pilots' strike-threat underlay the second labor dispute. In November 1996, the Allied Pilots Associa-tion's board of directors approved a tentative pilots' contract, and presented it to the union membership for ratification. Persuaded by a dissident group of grassroots union activists made largely of B-scale pi-lots, the membership rejected the contract by a mar-gin of almost two to one. The union leadership, in turn, hardened its position, and threatened to strike the carrier. As the strike deadline approached, President Clinton intervened, invoking a rarely used provision of the 1926 Railway Act which empowered him to appoint a three-member emergency board to help settle the dispute. In the meantime American's losses were mounting. By April 1997, AA lost at least $100 million in advanced bookings, as passengers avoided flying an airline facing impending walkout days. The contract was eventually ratified, but here again, the pilots remained embittered, and they

EXHIBIT 1

Robert Crandall's American Airlines Highlights of Financial Data, 1985–1998

	Revenues ($Mil.)	Net Income ($Mil.)	Income as % of Revenues
1985	6,131	346	5.6%
1986	6,018	279	4.6%
1987	7,198	198	2.8%
1988	8,824	477	5.4%
1989	10,480	455	4.3%
1990	11,120	(40)	—
1991	12,887	(240)	—
1992	14,396	(935)	—
1993	15,816	(110)	—
1994	16,137	228	—
1995	16,910	167	1.0%
1996	17,753	1,067	5.7%
1997	18,570	985	5.3%
1998	19,205	1,314	6.8%

Sources: "AMR Corporation," *Hoover's Handbook of American Business*, 1992, p. 110; 2002, p. 165.

continued resenting Crandall's heavy-handed management methods.[39]

Improving Financial Results, 1985–1997

AA's financial performance under Crandall needs to be analyzed in conjunction with Crandall's evolving strategy. Serving as CEO for 13 years, Crandall shaped and reshaped his strategy, paying close attention to changes in the business cycle. In the 1980s, Crandall undertook a growth strategy that resulted in a rapid expansion of American Airlines' fleet, as well as workforce. The larger AA grew, the lower were its costs, the higher its revenues, and the larger its profits. In the early 1990s, as the air travel market slid into a protracted recession, and AA experienced four years of losses, Crandall embarked on a retrenchment strategy, laying off employees, grounding old planes, exiting unprofitable markets, and outsourcing selected services. Following the recession of 1990–1993, the industry expanded once again, and Crandall introduced a second growth plan. His renewed efforts at increasing revenues and improving profits were sustained by AA's industry-leading yield management system, its formidable AAdvantage frequent flyer program, and its extensive global route network. Notwithstanding the

labor troubles of 1996–1997, the carrier had become profitable again, posting a net income of over $1 billion in 1996, close to $1 billion in 1997, and $1.3 billion in 1998, as Exhibit 1 shows, and reducing its debt as a percentage of capitalization from 83% in 1994 to 66% at the end of 1996.[40]

Donald Carty and the September 11, 2001 Terrorist Attack

Donald Carty served as American Airlines CEO for five years. An AA career executive, he was hand picked by Crandall to lead the carrier, first as President, and then, following Crandall's retirement in 1998, as CEO. Carty's five-year tenure was marred by labor troubles, recession, and terrorism, and ended in a public scandal: as a result of the September 11, 2001 attack, American Airlines was losing several million dollars a day, yet in Spring 2003, at the time the carrier was inching towards bankruptcy, AA's senior executives—including Carty—received undisclosed bonuses and pension guarantees worth millions of dollars.

Carty's labor problems began early on. In 1999, he convinced the AMR board to acquire a small low-cost commuter airline called Reno Air. The proposed acquisition evoked a staunch opposition on the part of American pilots. Believing that Carty planned to replace them with low-paid Reno pilots, members of the Allied Pilots Association staged an 11-day sickout which forced American to cancel 6,700 fights, left 600,000 passengers stranded, and cost the carrier $225 million in lost earnings. Also in 1999, AA flight attendants rejected a tentative contract offer and threatened to strike the carrier. In 2001, AA's flight attendants agreed to accept a contract agreement only after exhaustive negotiations that ended hours before a strike deadline.[41]

Notwithstanding these labor differences, Carty moved to expand the airline by merger, purchasing TWA—a trunk-line carrier experiencing serious financial problems. Approved in April 2001, AA's merger with TWA created the nation's largest airline, adding 188 commercial airplanes to American's fleet (TWA's 104 McDonnell Douglas MD-80 jets fit nicely into AA's fleet), and providing American with a central hub at St. Louis. The cost of the transaction was just $742 million—a modest sum by any industry standards—and more importantly, the merger was supported by all major unions. Backed by the unionized employees of both carriers, Carty managed to integrate the two companies smoothly, earning the praise of industry analysts.[42]

Yet the TWA acquisition was untimely. The merger was approved at the time the entire airline industry was moving rapidly into a recession. Following the merger's approval in Spring 2001, business travel dropped precipitously, leisure travel fell too, and fuel prices were rising. As a result, AA lost $550 million during the first half of 2001.[43] Less than three months later, the 9/11 terrorist attack erupted, destroying two AA passenger jets at midair, and shutting down all airline travel in the U.S. for two days.

The impact of the 9/11 attack on American's financial performance was long lasting. As shown in Exhibit 2, AA lost $1.8 billion in 2001, and a record $3.5 billion in 2002. In April 2003, following another loss of a billion dollars during the first quarter of the year, American Airlines was nearly bankrupt.

To avoid filing bankruptcy under Chapter 11, Carty asked the three unions representing the majority of AA employees to agree to major wage and benefit concessions. The leadership of each union accepted management's demand for a concessional contract and put the issue before the membership for a vote. Within two weeks, AA employees ratified a collective bargaining agreement that gave the carrier back a total of $1.8 billion, or 20% of the carrier's annual payroll.[44]

A day later the deal began to unravel. Following the contract ratification, union leaders, as well as members, learned from news reports that the AMR corporation awarded Carty and five other executives bonuses that equaled twice their annual salaries, and set aside a $41 million trust that was intended to protect the pensions of 45 executives in the event of bankruptcy. As it turned out, the carrier delayed filing a report detailing these executive compensation plans with the Security and Exchange Commission until after the contract vote was completed.[45]

The belated disclosure angered the employees and prompted two of the three unions to call for another contract vote. Carty, in turn, sent a letter to AA employees apologizing for his conduct, and announcing the cancellation of the proposed bonuses: "My mistake was failing to explicitly describe these

---

EXHIBIT 2

Donald Carty's American Airlines Highlights of Financial Data, 1998–2002

	Revenues ($Mil.)	Net Income ($Mil.)	Income as % of Revenues	Stock Prices FY Close
1998	19,205	1,314	6.8%	$26.54
1999	17,730	985	5.3%	29.95
2000	19,703	813	5.7%	39.19
2001	18,963	(1,762)	—	22.30
2002	17,299	(3,511)	—	6.60

Source: "AMR Corporation," Hoover's Handbook of American Business, 2005, p. 88.

retention benefits. . . . Please know that it was never my intention to mislead you."[46] The disclosure, in addition, surprised several members of the AMR board who felt misled by top management, believing that Carty had discussed the executive compensation package with the union leaderships prior to the contract vote. In response to the mounting public outcry over the disclosure, AMR board of directors sought Carty's resignation. Pressured by the board, Carty promptly stepped down, and the directors moved at once to elect a new CEO.[47]

The Future: Gerard Arpey's American Airlines, 2003–

A few board members suggested rehiring Robert Crandall. Others rejected Crandall's choice and sought instead a candidate who was likely to create a sense of management continuity in AA and act quickly to save the company from filing bankruptcy. Such a candidate, the majority of directors agreed, was American Airlines President Gerard Arpey. Elected by the board to replace Carty, Arpey had 24 hours to save the carrier. Crafting a revised labor management agreement that included the essential $1.8 billion cuts in wages and benefits, and offered the employees a number of additional non-monetary gains, Arpey managed to convince the union leaderships to approve the new labor agreement and thereby save the carrier from filing for bankruptcy protection. Passing his first test as a chief executive, Arpey outlined a key management objective he would strive to accomplish throughout his tenure as AA CEO: "There is a definite need to rebuild trust [between management and labor] within the company. I hear that loud and clear . . . and I commit myself to earning everybody's trust."[48]

Gerard Arpey spent his entire career at American Airlines, joining the company as a financial analyst in 1982. Before accepting the top job, the 46-year-old Arpey sought, and received, the approval of AA's union leaders: "He said he wouldn't take the position unless . . . he had our support," John Darrah, President of the Allied Pilots Association recalled, adding, "I have a great deal of respect for Mr. Arpey. . . . I can honestly [say] there's not a person I have more respect for or trust in."[49]

Arpey's turnaround plan was based on several elements. First, Arpey believed that in order to compete successfully in the post 9/11 world, American

Airlines needed to shift its strategic focus from revenue growth to cost reduction. To achieve this goal, he introduced a cooperative labor management scheme, a continuous improvement program, and other labor cost cutting measures. Second, Arpey realized that American could take advantage of its global positioning to expand profitable international operation and curtail unprofitable domestic services. To achieve this goal, he sought to form closer alliances with foreign carriers. Altogether, Arpey embarked on four distinct strategies in his efforts to turn American around.

International Expansion

Referring to his plan to expand AA's international operation, Arpey explained:

> One of the things that we can capitalize on is the depth and breadth of our network. It's one of the ways that we can compete more effectively with low-cost carriers that operate primarily in the domestic market. . . . We have very aggressive plans internationally. . . . Our strengths include a very broad network that spans the globe . . . the [industry's] largest frequent-flyer program, Admiral airport clubs, and a great first-class product. . . . [W]e get more revenue per passenger than the low cost carrier[s and] . . . we can sustain a revenue premium.[50]

Arpey expected AA's international service to grow from over 30% of capacity in 2005 to 40% by the end of the decade. He planned to expand, above all, trans-Pacific travel service. In 2005, American introduced two non-stop services to Japan, operating flights between Chicago and Nagoya, and between Dallas and Osaka. Similarly, in 2005, AA started a non-stop service to India, flying the 7,500-mile route between Chicago and New Delhi, American's longest, in 14–15 hours. American also competed aggressively over the contested rights to serve China, planning to introduce a Chicago-Shanghai non-stop service as early as approval by the Chinese government was granted. Additionally, AA formed alliances with Aloha Airlines and Mexicana Airlines, on the one side, and consolidated its code-sharing agreement with British Airways, on the other.[51]

Labor-Management Cooperation

To improve his relations with the unions, Arpey instituted an open door policy. During his first two years in office, Arpey spent more time meeting union leaders than the time spent for this purpose by any other chief executive in the company's 75-year history. "You demonstrate commitment by where you put your time," he told a *Financial Times* reporter in 2005. "We are trying to make our unions our business partners."[52] Unlike Crandall and Carty, Arpey constantly highlighted the importance of getting AA employees involved in the business of airline management. Once elected CEO, he traveled widely, visited AA operations in one city after another, conducted town-hall meetings with AA employees, and solicited employee suggestions. "I try to spend as much time as I can [with the employees] when I travel," Arpey explained in a 2004 interview, "going to break rooms, talking to agents at the gate, talking to flight attendants on board [of] the airplane, riding jump seats, and . . . answering all the email[s I] get."[53]

Still, Arpey was unable to change AA's climate of labor-relations single-handedly. He needed external help. To improve labor management relations at American, Arpey hired an employee-relations consultancy called the Overland Resource Group in Summer 2003. Instrumental in improving labor-relations at Boeing, Ford, and the Goodyear Corporation, the Overland group instructed AA managers to follow three fundamental principles, or maxims, in their relations with AA's employees: "Involve before Deciding," "Discuss before Implementing," and "Share before Announcing." More importantly, the Overland group created a Joint Leadership Team (JLT) chaired by Arpey and the national presidents of AA's three main unions (representing the pilots, flight attendants, and mechanics and ground workers), and attended by the company CFO as well as four vice presidents, on management side, and three representatives of each union, on labor side. The team met once a month to discuss issues ranging from AA's corporate-level strategies to union demands and grievances. The team also reviewed AA's financial data on a quarterly basis, an arrangement that helped senior union officials understand the airline business.[54] To help team members communicate, two Overland consultants attended all JLT meetings, acting as the dialogue facilitators. To ensure an honest, open, and free-flowing discussion with no fear of reprisal, each JLT participant signed a non-disclosure agreement.[55]

In addition to the team headed by Arpey and the union presidents, Overland facilitated the formation of seven regional JLTs located in different airports and maintenance bases throughout AA network. A local JLT met once a month to review the region's financial performance and to evaluate employee cost-saving ideas.[56]

Overland presence at AA enhanced employee motivation and morale. The higher level of employee motivation was reflected, first and foremost, in the growing number of cost savings suggestions initiated by employees. While AA management routinely ignored employee suggestions in the past [one union leader observed], Overland consultants now encouraged the adoption of such suggestions. And while Arpey's management team was actively soliciting employee ideas, no employee whose ideas were adopted received any compensation; on the contrary, helping the company was the employee's sole motivation.[57]

As a result of implementing employee-identified cost-saving ideas, AA saved about $100 million in 2004.[58] The overall decline in labor cost was larger. Partly as a consequence of introducing cost-saving ideas, and partly as a result of implementing the landmark concessional contract of April 2003, AA unit labor cost under Arpey declined by more than 20% in two years, as shown in Exhibit 3.

Continuous Improvement

The Continuous Improvement (CI) program was implemented across all AA's maintenance facilities. During 2001–2004, United Airlines, Northwest Airlines, and U.S. Airways closed several of their maintenance

EXHIBIT 3

Labor Cost of U.S. Network Carriers, 4th Quarter 2002 and 4th Quarter 2004, Cents per Available Seat Mile (CASM)

Network	4Q02 CASM	4Q04 CASM
American	3.93	3.12
Continental	3.10	30.2
Delta	4.01	3.67
Northwest	3.98	3.82
United	4.51	3.25
US Airways	4.15	3.11
Network	4.01	3.34

Sources: Eclat Consulting, *Aviation Daily*, May 4, 2004, p. 7, and May 26, 2005, p. 7.

bases, and sought instead to outsource heavy maintenance to outside contractors.[59] American Airlines, by contrast, kept maintenance work in house, and launched a massive drive at efficiency, seeking productivity gains in the shop floor.

The Continuous Improvement program had three main goals: the elimination of waste in any form, the standardization of maintenance work, and the optimal utilization of "human talent." The idea— and practice—of CI was based on the assumption that workers, not managers, were the real experts, and that employee empowerment was critical for building effective work teams. The CI program addressed a variety of issues ranging from shop floor reorganization to engine-overhaul turnover time reduction. To achieve these objectives, a "5S" technique ("sort, strengthen, standardize, shine, sustain") was introduced throughout AA's maintenance facilities. At American's largest maintenance base in Tulsa, Oklahoma, for example, Continuous Improvement teams in the avionic shop used the 5S technique to free nearly 12,000 sq. ft. of floor space and thereby save the company $1.5 million in inventory cost.[60]

Employee-identified CI ideas included new ways to reduce the cost of replacing aircraft parts and components. On the McDonnell Douglas MD-80 model, for instance, the cargo door torque (spring) tube needed to be replaced once a year. To do so, the company bought new tubes at a cost of $660 per tube. The CI team investigated the issue and ascertained that repairing broken tubes at a cost of only $134 per unit saved the company a total of $250,000 a year. On the Boeing 737, similarly, AA economized by replacing passenger light bulbs and cabin windows only when needed. In the past, AA replaced all light bulbs and cabin windows at the same time regardless of whether the bulbs were burned out or the windows worn out. The selective replacement of light bulbs and cabin windows saved AA $100,000 per year.[61]

American used CI teams to reduce engine overhaul times as well. One team of engine mechanics drafted a series of diagrams showing the most efficient way to disassemble a jet engine. Another devised a "point-of-use tool box" which contained all the tools necessary for an engine's assembly and disassembly. Together, the two teams helped AA cut an engine's overhaul turnaround time from 53 days in 2003 to 40 days in 2004, an improvement of 25% in a single year.[62]

Continuous Improvement teams helped AA cut costs in still other ways. To service American Airlines fleet, company mechanics used thousands of drill bits monthly at a cost of $20 to $200 a piece. Two AA mechanics invented a drill bit-sharpening tool which refurbished bits for reuse at a cost savings of $300,000–400,000 a year. And in 2004, a CI team came up with the idea of reusing parts of obsolete DC-10 coffee makers on other AA airplanes, generating a one-time savings of $675,000.[63]

Taken together, all these improvements helped AA reduce its maintenance cost by 34% in two years (2002–2004). A comparison between American's maintenance cost reduction and that of five other U.S.-based network carriers shows that AA led the way, exceeding the industry average by 13 percentage points, and well ahead of any of its competitors (Exhibit 4).

Other Cost Cutting Measures

"Simplification and standardization drives efficiency,"[64] Arpey said in 2004, and he moved quickly to both simplify and standardize AA's fleet of aircraft. To simplify the fleet, Arpey reduced the number of aircraft types flown by American from 14 to 6, retiring many old models. The move reduced American spending on spare parts as well as crew training, especially pilots and mechanics training. In addition, Arpey standardized aircraft seating, arranging all seats on a given aircraft type in a single configuration, as

EXHIBIT 4

Maintenance Cost of U.S. Network Carriers, 4th Quarter 2002 and 4th Quarter 2004, Cents per Available Seat Mile (CASM)

Network	4Q02 CASM	4Q04 CASM	% CASM
American	1.65	1.09	34%
Continental	0.96	0.93	3%
Delta	0.98	0.92	6%
Northwest	1.43	1.08	24%
United	1.41	1.24	12%
U.S. Airways	1.67	1.30	22%
Network	1.36	1.08	21%

Sources: Eclat Consulting, *Aviation Daily*, May 4, 2004, p. 7, and May 26, 2005, p. 7.

the two following examples suggest. Under Carty's leadership, the MD-80 fleet had two seating configurations, one designed to serve AA's business routes, the other to serve AA's low fare routes. Under Carty likewise, the B-777 had two seating configurations, one aimed at flights over the Pacific, the other at flights over the Atlantic. In an effort to simplify both aircraft maintenance and flight schedules, Arpey standardized all seating on the MD-80 and B-777 models in a single arrangement, a reconfiguration that resulted in substantial cost savings.[65]

Arpey reversed two other Carty initiatives, first, the creation of more legroom for passengers, and second, the transformation of TWA's St. Louis hub into a major AA hub. In 2000, Carty launched the "More Room in Coach" marketing campaign in an attempt to increase revenues. AA, accordingly, removed more than 7,000 economy seats from its fleet, reducing the fleet's seating capacity by 6.4%. Carty's initiative, however, failed to generate the expected revenues, and therefore Arpey decided to undo it. In 2004, AA added two rows of seats to its fleet of 140 B-757s and 34 A-300s, and used both models to serve low-fare leisure markets. In 2005, AA added six more seats to its B-737 fleet, seven more to its fleet of MD-80s and B-767s, and nine more seats to its fleet of B-777s. The change in seating capacity was projected to generate a revenue increase of over $100 million a year.[66]

Lastly, Arpey announced early on his decision to scale back significantly AA's St. Louis operation. Expecting TWA's central hub in St. Louis to fit nicely into American route system, Carty, as noted, purchased TWA in 2001. Arpey, however, did not share Carty's vision. To improve AA's financial performance, Arpey shifted flights from routes out of the St. Louis hub to more profitable routes out of AA's Chicago and Dallas hubs. As a result, AA laid off more than 2,000 employees at the St. Louis airport in 2003 alone.[67]

Future Prospects and Concerns

One result of the successful implementation of Arpey's turnaround strategy was the deep decline in AA's operating costs. As shown in Exhibit 5, by 2005, American operating costs were lower than those of any other network carriers save Continental. American's stock prices too performed well. Following a sharp drop in AMR stock price during the post 9/11 years, AMR's stock more than doubled in value in 2005, rising

EXHIBIT 5

Operating Cost of U.S. Network Carriers, 1st Quarter 2005, Cents per Available Seat Mile (CASM)

Network	1Q05 CASM
American	9.9
Continental	9.9
United	10.4
U.S. Air	10.7
Northwest	11.2
Delta	12.2

Source: Back-Aviation Solutions in Micheline Maynard and Jeremy Peters, "Circling a Decision," *New York Times,* August 18, 2005.

101% and outperforming the share prices of all major U.S. carriers, including Southwest Airlines. AA's cash position, furthermore, was stronger than that of other network carriers. AA managed to increase its cash surplus from $3 billion in 2004 to $4.3 billion in 2005, a margin sufficiently comfortable to give the carrier a greater staying power in the industry than its rivals.[68]

Nevertheless, American Airlines still faced a number of daunting challenges. First and most important was the need to achieve profitability. During Arpey's first three years in office, AMR continued to post large losses that amounted to $1.2 billion in 2003, $0.8 billion in 2004, and $0.9 billion in 2005. While analysts were impressed by AA's cost cutting measures (as well as its collaborative labor management relations, strong cash position, rising fares, and trimmed capacity), and while AA stock doubled in value in 2005 in anticipation of profits in 2006, the continual increase in fuel costs during 2006 clouded AA's recovery prospects.[69]

Another concern pertained to labor relations. AA employees resented a stock-related bonus paid to American managers in 2006. The payout was authorized by an 18-year-old "Long Term Incentive Program" which tied executive pay to AA's stock performance. Because AA's stock prices outperformed the stock prices of its five competitors (United, Delta, Continental, U.S. Air, Northwest) in 2005, American's top 1,000 mangers were eligible to share $80 million in cash. The payout, however, was viewed by American's unionized employees as extra compensation for managers not shared by other AA employees. A letter sent by top management to members of the Allied Pilots Association congratulating the pilots on saving $80 million in fuel cost in 2005—an amount equivalent to management's bonus—angered the pilots further, and threatened to undermine the cooperative labor relations at American.[70]

A final concern stemmed from AA's pension crisis. In 2005, American's pension plans were underfunded by about $2.7 billion. To be sure, AA's funding deficit was smaller than that of Delta ($5.3 billion) and Northwest ($3.8 billion), yet unlike Delta and Northwest, American's commitment to protecting its employees' pensions was embedded in a collective bargaining agreement: a key union demand incorporated into the 2003 labor agreement that saved AA from bankruptcy was the preservation of the carrier's pension plan intact. In 2006, Delta, Northwest, United, and other network carriers were all engaged in a process of converting their pension plans from defined benefit plans (plans that paid employees lifetime retirement pensions funded by the employer) to the less expensive defined contribution plans (plans that operated like retirement saving accounts funded by both the employee and the employer). American Airlines, accordingly, experienced a growing competitive pressure to convert its pension plans too, but such a move was likely to jeopardize the long-standing industrial peace at American which Arpey had worked so hard to craft and preserve.[71]

ENDNOTES

1. Henry Ladd Smith, *Airways: The History of Commercial Aviation in the United States* (1942, reprinted, New York: Russell and Russell, 1964).

2. Stephen Breyer, *Regulation and Its Reform* (Cambridge, Mass.: Harvard University Press, 1982), p. 205.

3. Thomas K. McCraw, *Prophets of Regulations* (Cambridge, Mass.: Harvard University Press, 1984), p. 3.

4. McCraw, *Prophets of Regulations*, pp. 266–67; Breyer, *Regulation and Its Reform*, pp. 204–205.

5. Smith, *Airways*, Chapters 12, 16, 22.

6. "AMR Corporation," *Hoover's Handbook of American Business 1992* (Austin: Hoovers Business Press, 1992), p. 110; "AMR Corporation," *International Directory of Company Histories* (Detroit: St. James Press, 1999), p. 23.

7. Robert Serling, *Eagle: The Story of American Airlines* (New York: St. Martin, 1985), p. 280.

8. "Carrier Profile," *Aviation Daily*, April 5, 2005.

9. Mark Kahn, "Airlines," in Gerald Somers, ed., *Collective Bargaining: Contemporary American Experience* (Bloomingdale, Illinois: Industrial Relations Research Association Series, 1980), pp. 354–58; Serling, *Eagle*, pp. 270–273, 304–306.

10. Dan Reed, *The American Eagle: The Ascent of Bob Crandall and American Airlines* (New York: St. Martin, 1993), Chapter 2.

11. Dan Reed, *American Eagle*, pp. 100–102. The quotation is on page 101.

12. Cited in Stewart Toy and Seth Payne, "The Airline Mess," *Business Week*, July 6, 1992, p. 50.

13. Cited in, "American Airlines Loses its Pilot," *Economist*, April 18, 1998, p. 58.

14. Reed, *American Eagle*, p. 207.

15. Steven Morrison and Clifford Winston, *The Evolution of the Airline Industry* (Washington D.C.: The Brooking Institution, 1995), pp. 44–45.

16. Reed, *American Eagle*, pp. 158–164, 174–175.

17. AA, in addition, established secondary hubs in Nashville, Tennessee, Raleigh/Durham, North Carolina, and San Jose, California, but following the recession of the early 1990s, American closed these three hubs, withdrawing from unprofitable short-hall travel markets. See Suzanne Loeffelholz, "Competitive Anger," *Financial World*, January 10, 1989, p. 31; and Perry Flint and Danna Henderson, "American at Bay," *Air Transport World*, March 1997. Online. ABI database, Start Page 28.

18. Dan Reed, *American Eagle*, pp. 204–205.

19. Seth Rosen, "A Union Perspective," in Jean McKelvey, ed., *Cleared for Takeoff: Airline Labor Relations Since Deregulation* (Ithaca, New York: ILR Press, 1988), p. 22; Robert Crandall, "The Airlines: On Track or Off Course," in McKelvey, ed., *Clear for Takeoff*, p. 352; Dan Reed, *American Eagle*, pp. 202–204.

20. *Financial World*, January 10, 1989, pp. 29–30.

21. According to the company's annual report cited in "AMR Corporation," *International Directory of Company Histories*, p. 24.

22. Don Bedwell, *Silverbird: The American Airlines Story* (Sandpoint, Idaho: Airway International Inc., 1999), pp. 137, 244.

23. Perry Flint, "Sabre Unlimited," *Air Transport World*, November 1996, p. 95.

24. Bedwell, *Silverbird*, p. 132, and Chapter 20.

25. Ronald Lieber, "Bob Crandall's BOO-BOOS," *Fortune*, April 28, 1997, p. 368; Don Lee and Jennifer Oldham, "American Woos Wary Travelers," *Los Angeles Times*, February 16, 1997.

26. Reed, *American Eagle*, Chapter 5; Bedwell, *Silverbird*, pp. 130–131, 250–251.

27. Kenneth Labich, "The Computer Network that Keeps American Flying," *Fortune*, September 24, 1990, p. 46.

28. Bedwell, *Silverbird*, p. 248.

29. *Air Transport World*, November 1996, p. 95.

30. Reed, *American Eagle*, p. 184.

31. Cited in Bedwell, *Silverbird*, p. 161.

32. Reed, *American Eagle*, pp. 176–177; Morrison and Winston, *The Evolution of the Airline Industry*, p. 59.

33. Bedwell, *Silverbird*, p. 161.

34. Seth Rosen, "Corporate Restructuring," in Peter Cappelli, ed., *Airline Labor Relations in the Global Era* (Ithaca, New York: ILR Press, 1995), p. 33.

35. Kenneth Labich, "American Takes on the World," *Fortune*, September 24, 1990, pp. 41–42; Read, *American Eagle*, pp. 249, 251, 269; and "AMR Corporation," *International Directory of Company Histories*, p. 24.

36. *Air Transport World*, March 1997. Online. ABI Data Base. Start page 28.

37. Bedwell, *Silverbird*, pp. 233–236; "AMR Corporation," *International Directory of Company Histories*, p. 25.

38. Jeri Clausing, "Crandall's Hard-Ball Style Legendary," *Seattle Times*, November 25, 1993; James Peltz, "A 'Mellower' AMR Chief?" *Los Angeles Times*, February 14, 1997.

39. *Fortune*, April 28, 1997, p. 368; *Los Angeles Times*, February 14, 1997; Scott McCartney, "The Deal Breakers," *Wall Street Journal*, February 11, 1997; "American Airlines Loses its Pilot," *Economist*, April 18, 1998, p. 58.

40. *Air Transport World*, March 1997. Online. ABI Data Base. Start page 28.

41. Peter Elkind, "Flying for Fun & Profits," *Fortune*, October 25, 1999, pp. 36–37; James Peltz, "Carty Has Been Forced to Guide AMR Through Turbulent Times," *Los Angeles Times*, November 14, 2001; John Helyar, "American Airlines: A Wing and a Prayer," *Fortune*, December 10, 2001, p. 182.

42. *Los Angeles Times*, November 14, 2001; "American, TWA Deal Approved," *Aviation Daily*, April 10, 2001; and U.S. Senate, *TWA/American Airlines Workforce Integration*, Hearing before the Committee on Health, Education, and Pensions, 108th Cong., 1st Sess., June 12, 2003, p. 24.

43. *Los Angeles Times*, November 14, 2001.

44. Scott McCarthney, "At American, 48 Hours of Drama Help Airline Avert Bankruptcy," *Wall Street Journal*, April 28, 2003.

45. Brad Foss, "How It All Went Wrong," *Chicago Sun Times*, April 27, 2003.

46. Cited in *Chicago Sun Times*, April 27, 2003.

47. *Wall Street Journal*, April 28, 2003; and Edward Wong and Micheline Maynard, "A Taut, Last-minute Stretch to Save an Airline," *New York Times*, April 27, 2003.

48. Cited in the *Wall Street Journal*, April 28, 2003; but see also *New York Times*, April 27, 2003.

49. Cited in Eve Tahmincioglu, "Back from the Brink," *Workforce Management*, December 2004. Online. ABI Data Base. Start page 32. See also Sara Goo, "Key Union Accepts Cuts at American," *Washington Post*, April 26, 2003.

50. Cited in Melanie Trottman, "Boss Talk," *Wall Street Journal*, December 30, 2004.

51. David Field, "The American Way," *Airline Business*, December 2004, p. 31; "American Enters India," *Aviation Daily*, July 13, 2005.

52. Cited in Caroline Daniel, "A Top Flight Employee Strategy," *Financial Times*, April 4, 2005.

53. Cited in the *Wall Street Journal*, December 30, 2004.

54. *Financial Times*, April 4, 2005; *Workforce Management*, December 2004. Online. ABI Data Base. Start page 32.

55. *Workforce Management*, December 2004. Online. ABI Data Base. Start page 32.

56. *Financial Times*, April 4, 2005.

57. *Workforce Management*, December 2004. Online. ABI Data Base. Start page 32.

58. *Workforce Management*, December 2004. Online. ABI Data Base. Start page 32.

59. Perry Flint, "Rewired for Success: American Embraces Continuous Improvement," *Air Transport World*, August 2004, p. 39.

60. *Air Transport World*, August 2004, p. 39.

61. *Air Transport World*, August 2004, p. 39.

62. *Air Transport World*, August 2004, p. 39.

63. *Workforce Management*, December 2004. Online. ABI Data Base. Start page 32.

64. Cited in *Airline Business*, December 2004, p. 31.

65. *Wall Street Journal*, December 30, 2004; Michael Maynard, "No Longer on the Brink, American Air is Still in Peril," *New York Times*, March 18, 2004; Scott McCartney, "Low Cost Rivals Prompt American Airlines to Try Flying Like One of Them," *Wall Street Journal*, June 8, 2004; *Airline Business*, December 2004, p. 31.

66. *Airline Business*, December 2004, p. 33; Edward Wong, "American Air is Adding Seats," *New York Times*, May 22, 2003; "American Looks to Counteract $1.4 Billion Fuel Cost Increase," *Aviation Daily*, March 13, 2005.

67. *Wall Street Journal*, June 8, 2004; Edward Wong, "In a Sign of Stronger Finances, American Reports a Profit," *New York Times*, October 23, 2003.

68. Melanie Trottman, "AMR Investors Bet on Clearer Skies Ahead," *Wall Street Journal*, February 16, 2006; Caroline Daniel, "In Hard Times, Saving Dollars Makes Sense," *Financial Times*, March 15, 2005.

69. "AMR Company Records, Financials," *Hoovers*. Online. ABI Data Base. *Wall Street Journal*, February 16, 2006.

70. Scott McCartney, "Airline Discord May Hurt Travelers," *Wall Street Journal*, February 7, 2006.

71. Brad Foss, American Path Less Traveled," *Seattle Times*, June 11, 2005.

Cola Wars Continue: Coke and Pepsi in 2006

This case was prepared by David B. Yoffie and Michael Slind, Harvard Business School.

For more than a century, Coca-Cola and Pepsi-Cola vied for "throat share" of the world's beverage market. The most intense battles in the so-called cola wars were fought over the $66 billion carbonated soft drink (CSD) industry in the United States.[1] In a "carefully waged competitive struggle" that lasted from 1975 through the mid-1990s, both Coke and Pepsi achieved average annual revenue growth of around 10%, as both U.S. and worldwide CSD consumption rose steadily year after year.[2] According to Roger Enrico, former CEO of Pepsi:

> The warfare must be perceived as a continuing battle without blood. Without Coke, Pepsi would have a tough time being an original and lively competitor. The more successful they are, the sharper we have to be. If the Coca-Cola company didn't exist, we'd pray for someone to invent them. And on the other side of the fence, I'm sure the folks at Coke would say that nothing contributes as much to the present-day success of the Coca-Cola company than . . . Pepsi.[3]

That cozy relationship began to fray in the late 1990s, however, as U.S. per-capita CSD consumption declined slightly before reaching what appeared to be a plateau. In 2004, the average American drank a little more than 52 gallons of CSDs per year. At the same time, the two companies experienced their own distinct ups and downs, as Coke suffered several operational setbacks and as Pepsi charted a new, aggressive course in alternative beverages. Although their paths diverged, however, both companies began to modify their bottling, pricing, and brand strategies.

As the cola wars continued into the 21st century, Coke and Pepsi faced new challenges: Could they boost flagging domestic CSD sales? Would newly popular beverages provide them with new (and profitable) revenue streams? Was their era of sustained growth and profitability coming to a close, or was this slowdown just another blip in the course of the cola giants' long, enviable history?

Economics of the U.S. CSD Industry

Americans consumed 23 gallons of CSDs annually in 1970, and consumption grew by an average of 3% per year over the next three decades. (See Exhibit 1—U.S. Beverage Industry Consumption Statistics.) Fueling this growth were the increasing availability of CSDs and the introduction of diet and flavored varieties. Declining real (inflation-adjusted) prices played a large role as well.[4] There were many alternatives to CSDs, including beer, milk, coffee, bottled water, juices, tea, powdered drinks, wine, sports drinks, distilled spirits, and tap water. Yet Americans drank more soda than any other beverage. Within the CSD category, the cola segment maintained its dominance, although its market share dropped from 71% in 1990 to 60% in 2004.[5] Non-cola CSDs included lemon/lime, citrus, pepper-type, orange, root beer, and other flavors. CSDs consisted of a flavor base (called "concentrate"), a sweetener, and carbonated

Professor David B. Yoffie and Research Associate Yusi Wang prepared the original version of this case "Cola Wars Continue: Coke and Pepsi in the Twenty-First Century," HBS Case No. 702-442 which derives from earlier cases by Professor David B. Yoffie and Professor Michael E. Porter (HBS Case No. 391-179). This version was prepared by Professor David B. Yoffie and Research Associate Michael Slind from published sources. HBS cases are developed solely as the basis for class discussion. Cases are not intended to serve as endorsements, sources of primary data, or illustrations of effective or ineffective management.

EXHIBIT 1

U.S. Beverage Industry Consumption Statistics

	1970	1975	1981	1985	1990	1994	1996	1998	2000	2002	2003	2004
Historical Carbonated Soft Drink Consumption												
Cases (millions)	3,090	3,780	5,180	6,500	7,780	8,710	9,290	9,880	9,950	10,087	10,140	10,240
Gallons/capita	22.7	26.3	34.2	40.3	46.9	50.0	52.0	54.0	53.0	52.5	52.3	52.3
As share of total beverage consumption	12.4%	14.4%	18.7%	22.1%	25.7%	27.4%	28.5%	29.6%	29.0%	28.8%	28.7%	28.7%
U.S. Liquid Consumption Trends (gallons/capita)												
Carbonated soft drinks	22.7	26.3	34.2	40.3	46.9	50.0	52.0	54.0	53.0	52.5	52.3	52.3
Beer	22.8	21.8	20.6	24.0	24.0	22.4	21.8	21.8	21.8	21.8	21.7	21.6
Milk	18.5	21.6	24.3	25.0	24.2	23.0	22.7	22.0	21.3	20.7	20.4	20.1
Bottled Water[b]	—	1.2	2.7	4.5	8.1	9.6	11.0	11.8	13.2	15.4	16.6	17.7
Coffee[a]	35.7	33	27.2	26.9	26.2	23.3	20.2	18.0	16.8	16.8	16.7	16.6
Juices[a]	6.5	6.8	6.9	8.1	8.5	9.0	9.0	9.5	9.5	8.9	8.5	8.6
Tea[a]	5.2	7.3	7.3	7.3	7.0	7.1	6.9	6.9	7.0	7.0	7.0	7.0
Sports Drinks[c]	—	—	—	—	—	1.2	1.5	1.9	2.2	2.6	3.0	3.5
Powdered drinks	—	4.8	6	6.2	5.4	4.8	4.8	3.7	3.0	2.4	2.5	2.6
Wine	1.3	1.7	2.1	2.4	2.0	1.7	1.8	1.9	1.9	2.0	2.1	2.1
Distilled spirits	1.8	2	2	1.8	1.5	1.3	1.2	1.2	1.2	1.3	1.3	1.3
Subtotal	114.5	126.5	133.3	146.5	153.8	153.3	152.2	152.7	150.9	151.4	152.1	153.4
Tap water/hybrids/all others	68.0	56.0	49.2	36.0	28.7	29.2	30.3	29.8	31.6	31.1	30.4	29.1
Total[d]	182.5	182.5	182.5	182.5	182.5	182.5	182.5	182.5	182.5	182.5	182.5	182.5

Sources: Compiled from *Beverage Digest Fact Book 2001, The Maxwell Consumer Report,* Feb. 3, 1994; *Adams Liquor Handbook,* casewriter estimates; and *Beverage Digest, Beverage Digest Fact Book 2005.* Data for 1990 and afterward comes from *Beverage Digest Fact Book 2005,* which reports that some of that data has been "restated compared to previous editions of the Fact Book."

[a] For 1985 and afterward, coffee, and tea data are based on a three-year moving average.
[b] Bottled water includes all packages, single-serve as well as bulk.
[c] For pre-1992 data, sports drinks are included in "Tap water/hybrids/all others."
[d] This analysis assumes that each person consumes, on average, one half-gallon of liquid per day.

water. The production and distribution of CSDs involved four major participants: concentrate producers, bottlers, retail channels, and suppliers.[6]

Concentrate Producers

The concentrate producer blended raw material ingredients, packaged the mixture in plastic canisters, and shipped those containers to the bottler. To make concentrate for diet CSDs, concentrate makers often added artificial sweetener; with regular CSDs, bottlers added sugar or high-fructose corn syrup themselves. The concentrate manufacturing process involved little capital investment in machinery, overhead, or labor. A typical concentrate manufacturing plant cost about $25 million to $50 million to build, and one plant could serve the entire United States.[7]

A concentrate producer's most significant costs were for advertising, promotion, market research, and bottler support. Using innovative and sophisticated campaigns, they invested heavily in their trademarks over time. While concentrate producers implemented and financed marketing programs jointly with bottlers, they usually took the lead in developing those programs, particularly when it came to product development, market research, and advertising. They also took charge of negotiating "customer development agreements" (CDAs) with

nationwide retailers such as Wal-Mart. Under a CDA, Coke or Pepsi offered funds for marketing and other purposes in exchange for shelf space. With smaller regional accounts, bottlers assumed a key role in developing such relationships, and paid an agreed-upon percentage—typically 50% or more—of promotional and advertising costs. Concentrate producers employed a large staff of people who worked with bottlers by supporting sales efforts, setting standards, and suggesting operational improvements. They also negotiated directly with their bottlers' major suppliers (especially sweetener and packaging makers) to achieve reliable supply, fast delivery, and low prices.[8]

Once a fragmented business that featured hundreds of local manufacturers, the U.S. soft drink industry had changed dramatically over time. Among national concentrate producers, Coca-Cola and Pepsi-Cola (the soft drink unit of PepsiCo) claimed a combined 74.8% of the U.S. CSD market in sales volume in 2004, followed by Cadbury Schweppes and Cott Corporation. (See Exhibit 2—U.S. Soft Drink Market Share by Case Volume. See also Exhibit 3—Financial Data for Coca-Cola, Pepsi-Cola, and Their Largest Bottlers.) In addition, there were private-label manufacturers and several dozen other national and regional producers.

EXHIBIT 2

U.S. Soft Drink Market Share by Case Volume (percent)

	1966	1970	1975	1980	1985	1990	1995	2000	2004E
Coca-Cola Company									
Coke Classic	—	—	—	—	5.2	20.1	20.8	20.4	17.9
Coca-Cola	27.7	28.4	26.2	25.3	16.5	0.6	0.1	—	—
Diet Coke	—	—	—	—	6.8	9.3	8.8	8.7	9.7
Sprite and Diet Sprite	1.5	1.8	2.6	3.0	4.7	4.5	5.7	7.2	6.3
Caffeine Free Coke, Diet Coke, Tab	—	—	—	—	1.8	2.9	2.6	2.2	2.0
Fanta[a]	—	—	—	—	0.9	0.7	0.7	0.2	1.3
Barq's and Diet Barq's	—	—	—	—	—	—	0.2	1.2	1.2
Minute Maid brands	—	—	—	—	—	0.7	0.7	1.5	0.4
Tab	1.4	1.3	2.6	3.3	1.1	0.2	0.1	—	—
Others	2.8	3.2	3.9	4.3	2.5	2.1	2.6	2.6	4.3
Total	**33.4**	**34.7**	**35.3**	**35.9**	**39.5**	**41.1**	**42.3**	**44.1**	**43.1**

(continued)

EXHIBIT 2   (*continued*)

U.S. Soft Drink Market Share by Case Volume (percent)

	1966	1970	1975	1980	1985	1990	1995	2000	2004E
PepsiCo, Inc.									
Pepsi-Cola	16.1	17.0	17.4	20.4	19.3	17.6	15.0	13.6	11.5
Mountain Dew	1.4	0.9	1.3	3.3	3.1	3.9	5.7	7.2	6.3
Diet Pepsi	1.9	1.1	1.7	3.0	3.9	6.3	5.8	5.3	6.1
Sierra Mist	—	—	—	—	—	—	—	0.1	1.4
Diet Mountain Dew	—	—	—	—	—	0.5	0.7	0.9	1.3
Caffeine Free Pepsi, and Diet Pepsi	—	—	—	—	2.5	2.3	2.0	1.7	1.4
Mug Root Beer	—	—	—	—	—	0.3	0.3	0.8	0.7
Wild Cherry Pepsi (reg and diet)	—	—	—	—	—	—	0.2	0.5	0.6
Mountain Dew Code Red	—	—	—	—	—	—	—	—	0.4
Slice and Diet Slice	—	—	—	—	0.7	1.0	1.0	0.5	0.3
Others	1.0	0.8	0.7	1.1	0.8	0.5	0.2	0.8	1.7
Total	**20.4**	**19.8**	**21.1**	**27.8**	**30.3**	**32.4**	**30.9**	**31.4**	**31.7**
Cadbury Schweppes[b]									
Dr Pepper (all brands)	—	—	—	—	—	—	6.8	7.5	7.2
7UP (all brands)	—	—	—	—	—	—	3.3	2.8	1.8
A&W brands	—	—	—	—	—	—	1.7	1.5	1.4
Royal Crown brands	—	—	—	—	—	—	—	—	1.1
Sunkist	—	—	—	—	1.2	0.7	0.7	0.8	1.0
Canada Dry	—	—	—	—	1.5	1.2	1.0	0.9	0.8
Schweppes	—	—	—	—	0.5	0.6	0.5	0.4	0.4
Others	—	—	—	—	1.5	0.7	1.1	0.8	0.8
Total					**4.7**	**3.2**	**15.1**	**14.7**	**14.5**
Dr Pepper/Seven-Up Cos.[c]									
Dr Pepper brands	2.6	3.8	5.5	6.0	4.5	5.2	—	—	—
7UP brands	6.9	7.2	7.6	6.3	5.8	3.9	—	—	—
Others	—	—	—	—	—	0.5	—	—	—
Total						**9.6**	—	—	—
Cott Corporation	—	—	—	—	—	—	**2.7**	**3.3**	**5.5**
Royal Crown Cos.	**6.9**	**6.0**	**5.4**	**4.7**	**3.1**	**2.6**	**2.0**	**1.1**	**—**
Other companies	**29.8**	**28.5**	**25.1**	**19.3**	**12.1**	**11.1**	**7.0**	**5.4**	**5.2**
Total (million cases)	**2,927**	**3,670**	**4,155**	**5,180**	**6,385**	**7,780**	**8,970**	**9,950**	**10,240**

Sources: Compiled from *Beverage Digest Fact Book 2001; The Maxwell Consumer Report*, February 3, 1994; the Beverage Marketing Corporation, cited in *Beverage World*, March 1996 and March 1999; and *Beverage Digest Fact Book 2005*.

[a] For the period before 1985, Fanta sales are included under "Others."

[b] Cadbury Schweppes acquired A&W brands in 1993, Dr Pepper/Seven-Up Cos. (DPSU) brands in 1995, and Royal Crown in October, 2000.

[c] Dr Pepper/Seven-Up Companies (DPSU) was formed in 1988. Prior to 1988, Dr Pepper and 7UP brand shares refer to the shares of the respective independent companies, the Dr Pepper Company and the Seven-Up Company. DPSU was acquired by Cadbury Schweppes in 1995.

EXHIBIT 3

Financial Data for Coca-Cola, Pepsi-Cola, and Their Largest Bottlers ($ millions)

	1975	1980	1985	1990	1995	2000	2001	2002	2003	2004
Coca-Cola Company[a]										
Beverages, North America										
Sales	—	1,486	1,865	2,461	5,513	7,870	7,526	6,264	6,344	6,643
Operating profits/sales	—	11.1%	11.6%	16.5%	15.5%	17.9%	19.7%	23.9%	18.9%	24.2%
Beverages, International										
Sales	—	2,349	2,677	6,125	12,559	12,588	12,386	13,089	14,477	15,076
Operating profit/sales	—	21.0%	22.9%	29.4%	29.1%	27.1%	37.1%	35.8%	33.3%	33.6%
Consolidated										
Sales	2,773	5,475	5,879	10,236	18,127	20,458	20,092	19,564	21,044	21,962
Net profit/sales	9.0%	7.7%	12.3%	13.5%	16.5%	10.6%	19.8%	15.6%	20.7%	22.1%
Net profit/equity	21.0%	20.0%	24.0%	36.0%	55.4%	23.4%	34.9%	25.8%	30.9%	30.4%
Long-term debt/assets	3.0%	10.0%	23.0%	8.0%	7.6%	4.0%	5.4%	11.0%	9.2%	3.7%
PepsiCo, Inc.[b]										
Beverages, North America										
Sales	1,065	2,368	2,725	5,035	7,427	6,171	6,888	7,200	7,733	8,313
Operating profit/sales	10.4%	10.3%	10.4%	13.4%	16.7%	22.3%	21.3%	21.9%	21.9%	23.0%
Beverages, International										
Sales	—	—	—	1,489	3,040	1,981	2,012	2,036	—	—
Operating profit/sales	—	—	—	6.3%	3.9%	8.0%	10.5%	12.8%	—	—
Consolidated										
Sales	2,709	5,975	7,585	17,515	19,067	20,438	26,935	25,112	26,971	29,261
Net profit/sales	4.6%	4.4%	5.6%	6.2%	7.5%	10.7%	9.9%	13.2%	13.2%	14.4%
Net profit/equity	18.0%	20.0%	30.0%	22.0%	19.4%	30.1%	30.8%	35.6%	30.0%	31.0%
Long-term debt/assets	35.0%	31.0%	36.0%	33.0%	35.9%	12.8%	12.2%	9.3%	6.7%	
Coca-Cola Enterprises (CCE)										
Sales	—	—	—	3,933	6,773	14,750	15,700	16,889	17,330	18,158
Operating profit/sales	—	—	—	8.3%	6.9%	7.6%	4.3%	8.0%	8.6%	7.9%
Net profit/sales	—	—	—	2.4%	1.2%	1.6%	−2.0%	2.9%	3.9%	3.3%
Net profit/equity	—	—	—	6.0%	5.7%	8.3%	−11.5%	14.9%	15.5%	11.1%
Long-term debt/assets	—	—	—	39.0%	46.3%	46.7%	43.7%	46.1%	41.1%	39.9%
Pepsi Bottling Group (PBG)[b]										
Sales	—	—	—	—	—	7,982	8,443	9,216	10,265	10,906
Operating profit/sales	—	—	—	—	—	7.4%	8.0%	9.7%	9.3%	9.0%
Net profit/sales	—	—	—	—	—	2.9%	3.6%	4.6%	4.1%	4.2%
Net profit/equity	—	—	—	—	—	13.9%	19.1%	23.5%	22.1%	23.4%
Long-term debt/assets	—	—	—	—	—	42.3%	41.8%	45.1%	38.9%	41.6%

Sources: Company annual reports.

[a] Coca-Cola's beverage sales consisted mainly of concentrate sales. Coke's stake in CCE was accounted for by the equity method of accounting, with its share of CCE's net earnings included in its consolidated net income figure. In 1994, Coke began reporting U.S. data as part of a North American category that included Canada and Mexico.

[b] PepsiCo's sales figures included sales by company-owned bottlers. In 1998, PepsiCo began reporting U.S. data as part of a North American category that included Canada. As of 2000, data for "Beverages, North America" combined sales for what had been the Pepsi-Cola and Gatorade/Tropicana divisions. In 2003, PepsiCo ceased reporting its international beverage business separately from its international food business. PBG financial data for the pre-1999 period refer to the PepsiCo bottling operations that were combined and spun off to form PBG in 1998. From 1999, PepsiCo's share of PBG's net earnings was included in PepsiCo's consolidated net income figure.

Bottlers

Bottlers purchased concentrate, added carbonated water and high-fructose corn syrup, bottled or canned the resulting CSD product, and delivered it to customer accounts. Coke and Pepsi bottlers offered "direct store door" (DSD) delivery, an arrangement whereby route delivery salespeople managed the CSD brand in stores by securing shelf space, stacking CSD products, positioning the brand's trademarked label, and setting up point-of-purchase or end-of-aisle displays. (Smaller national brands, such as Shasta and Faygo, distributed through food store warehouses.) Cooperative merchandising agreements, in which retailers agreed to specific promotional activity and discount levels in exchange for a payment from a bottler, were another key ingredient of soft drink sales.

The bottling process was capital-intensive and involved high-speed production lines that were interchangeable only for products of similar type and packages of similar size. Bottling and canning lines cost from $4 million to $10 million each, depending on volume and package type. In 2005, Cott completed construction of a 40-million-case bottling plant in Fort Worth, Texas, at an estimated cost of $40 million.[9] But the cost of a large plant with four lines, automated warehousing, and a capacity of 40 million cases, could range as high as $75 million.[10] While a handful of such plants could theoretically provide enough capacity to serve the entire United States, Coke and Pepsi each required close to 100 plants to provide effective nationwide distribution.[11] For bottlers, packaging accounted for 40% to 45% of sales, concentrate for roughly the same amount, and sweeteners for 5% to 10%. Labor and overhead made up the remaining variable costs.[12] Bottlers also invested capital in trucks and distribution networks. Bottlers' gross profits routinely exceeded 40%, but operating margins were usually in the 7% to 9% range. (See Exhibit 4—Comparative Costs of a Typical U.S. Concentrate Producer and Bottler, 2004.)

The number of U.S. soft drink bottlers had fallen steadily, from more than 2,000 in 1970 to fewer than 300 in 2004.[13] Coke was the first concentrate producer to build a nationwide franchised bottling network, and Pepsi and Cadbury Schweppes followed suit. The typical franchised bottler owned a manufacturing and sales operation in an exclusive geographic territory, with rights granted in perpetuity by the franchiser. In the case of Coke, territorial rights did not extend to national fountain accounts, which the company handled directly. The original Coca-Cola franchise agreement, written in 1899, was a fixed-price contract that did not provide for renegotiation, even if ingredient costs changed. After considerable negotiation, often accompanied by bitter legal disputes, Coca-Cola amended the contract in 1921, 1978, and 1987. By 2003, more than 88% of Coke's

EXHIBIT 4

Comparative Costs of a Typical U.S. Concentrate Producer and Bottler, 2004

	Concentrate Producer		Bottler	
	Dollars per Case[a]	Percent of Sales	Dollars per Case	Percent of Sales
Net sales	$0.97	100%	$4.70	100%
Cost of sales	$0.16	17%	$2.82	60%
Gross profit	$0.81	83%	$1.88	40%
Selling and delivery	$0.02	2%	$1.18	25%
Advertising and marketing	$0.42	43%	$0.09	2%
General and administration	$0.08	8%	$0.19	4%
Pretax profit	$0.29	30%	$0.42	9%

Sources: Industry analysts and casewriter estimates. Profit and loss percentage data are adapted from Andrew Conway, "Global Soft Drink Bottling Review and Outlook: Consolidating the Way to a Strong Bottling Network," Morgan Stanley Dean Witter, August 4, 1997, p. 2, and supplemented with 2004 data supplied by Corey Horsch, of Credit Suisse First Boston.

[a] One case is equivalent to 192 oz.

EXHIBIT 5

U.S. CSD Industry Pricing and Volume Statistics, 1998–2004

	1988	1990	1992	1994	1996	1998	2000	2002	2004
Retail price per case[a]	$8.78	$8.99	$8.87	$8.63	$8.70	$8.55	$9.08	$9.38	$9.68
Change in retail price[b]	—	1.2%	−0.7%	−1.4%	0.4%	−0.9%	3.1%	1.6%	1.6%
Total Change 1988–2004: 0.6%									
Concentrate price per case	$0.79	$0.86	$0.97	$1.00	$1.07	$1.14	$1.29	1.35	1.45[c]
Change in concentrate price	—	4.3%	6.2%	1.5%	3.4%	3.2%	6.4%	2.3%	3.6%
Total Change 1988–2004: 3.9%									
Volume (cases, in billions)	4.9	5.2	5.3	5.8	6.2	6.6	6.6	6.7	6.8
Change in volume	—	3.0%	1.0%	4.6%	3.4%	3.2%	0.0%	0.8%	0.7%
Total Change 1988–2004: 2.1%									
Consumption (gallons/capita)	40.3	46.9	47.2	50.0	52.0	54.0	53.0	52.5	52.3
Change in consumption	—	7.9%	0.3%	2.9%	2.0%	1.9%	−0.9%	−0.5%	−0.2%
Total Change 1988–2004: 1.6%									
Consumer Price Index[d]	100	110	119	125	133	138	146	152	160
Change in CPI	—	5.1%	3.6%	2.8%	2.9%	1.9%	2.8%	2.0%	2.6%
Total Change 1988–2004: 3.0%									

Sources: Compiled from *Beverage Digest Fact Book 2001* and *Beverage Digest Fact Book 2005*, and using the Inflation Calculator tool, U.S. Bureau of Labor Statistics website, http://data.bls.gov/cgi-bin/cpicalc.pl, accessed November 2005.

[a] "Case" refers to a 288-oz case.

[b] All change figures are calculated using Compounded Annual Growth Rate (CAGR).

[c] Concentrate price for 2004 is based on a weighted average of concentrate prices for the top 10 CSD brands. Concentrate price data for previous years appear in aggregated form in *Beverage Digest Fact Book 2003*, p. 64.

[d] CPI data use 1988 as the index year (1988 = 100).

U.S. volume was covered by its 1987 Master Bottler Contract, which granted Coke the right to determine concentrate price and other terms of sale.[14] Under this contract, Coke had no legal obligation to assist bottlers with advertising or marketing. Nonetheless, to ensure quality and to match Pepsi, Coke made huge investments to support its bottling network.[15] In 2002, for example, Coke contributed $600 million in marketing support payments to its top bottler alone.[16]

The 1987 contract did not give complete pricing control to Coke, but rather used a formula that established a maximum price and adjusted prices quarterly according to changes in sweetener pricing. This contract differed from Pepsi's Master Bottling Agreement with its top bottler. That agreement granted the bottler perpetual rights to distribute Pepsi's CSD products but required it to purchase raw materials from Pepsi at prices, and on terms and conditions, determined by Pepsi. Pepsi negotiated concentrate

prices with its bottling association, and normally based price increases on the consumer price index (CPI).[17] From the 1980s to the early 2000s, concentrate makers regularly raised concentrate prices, even as inflation-adjusted retail prices for CSD products trended downward. (See Exhibit 5—U.S. CSD Industry Pricing and Volume Statistics, 1998–2004.)

Franchise agreements with both Coke and Pepsi allowed bottlers to handle the non-cola brands of other concentrate producers. These agreements also allowed bottlers to choose whether to market new beverages introduced by a concentrate producer. Bottlers could not carry directly competing brands, however. For example, a Coke bottler could not sell Royal Crown Cola, yet it could distribute 7UP if it chose not to carry Sprite. Franchised bottlers could decide whether to participate in test marketing efforts, local advertising campaigns and promotions, and new package introductions (although they could only use packages authorized by their franchiser). Bottlers also had the final say in decisions about retail pricing.

In 1971, the Federal Trade Commission initiated action against eight major concentrate makers, charging that the granting of exclusive territories to bottlers prevented intrabrand competition (that is, two or more bottlers competing in the same area with the same beverage). The concentrate makers argued that interbrand competition was strong enough to warrant continuation of the existing territorial agreements. In 1980, after years of litigation, Congress enacted the Soft Drink Interbrand Competition Act, which preserved the right of concentrate makers to grant exclusive territories.

Retail Channels

In 2004, the distribution of CSDs in the United States took place through supermarkets (32.9%), fountain outlets (23.4%), vending machines (14.5%), mass merchandisers (11.8%), convenience stores and gas stations (7.9%), and other outlets (9.5%). Small grocery stores and drug chains made up most of the latter category.[18] Costs and profitability in each channel varied by delivery method and frequency, drop size, advertising, and marketing. (See Exhibit 6—U.S. Refreshment Beverages: Bottling Profitability Per Channel, 2005.)

The main distribution channel for soft drinks was the supermarket, where annual CSD sales reached $12.4 billion in 2004.[19] CSDs accounted for 5.5% of "the total edible grocery universe," and were also a big traffic draw for supermarkets.[20] Bottlers fought for shelf space to ensure visibility for their products, and they looked for new ways to drive impulse purchases, such as placing coolers at checkout counters. An ever-expanding array of products and packaging types created intense competition for shelf space.

The mass merchandiser category included warehouse clubs and discount retailers, such as Wal-Mart. These companies formed an increasingly important channel. Although they sold Coke and Pepsi products, they (along with some drug chains) often had their own private-label CSD, or they sold a generic label such as President's Choice. Private-label CSDs were usually delivered to a retailer's warehouse, while branded CSDs were delivered directly to stores. With the warehouse delivery method, the retailer was responsible for storage, transportation, merchandising, and stocking the shelves, thereby incurring additional costs.

Historically, Pepsi had focused on sales through retail outlets, while Coke had dominated fountain sales. (The term "fountain," which originally referred to drug store soda fountains, covered restaurants, cafeterias, and any other outlet that served soft drinks by the glass using fountain-type dispensers.) Competition for national fountain accounts was intense, and CSD companies frequently sacrificed profitability in order to land and keep those accounts. As of 1999, for example, Burger King franchises were believed to pay about $6.20 per gallon for Coke syrup, but they received a substantial rebate on each gallon; one large Midwestern franchise owner said that his annual rebate ran $1.45 per gallon, or about 23%.[21] Local fountain accounts, which bottlers handled in

---

EXHIBIT 6

U.S. Refreshment Beverages: Bottling Profitability per Channel, 2005

	Super-markets	Convenience and Gas	Super-centers[a]	Mass Retailers[a]	Club Stores[a]	Drug Stores	Fountain and Vending	Total
Share of industry volume[b]								
	31%	15%	9%	4%	4%	3%	34%	100%
Index of bottling profitability[c]								
Net Price	1.00	1.54	0.95	1.08	1.07	1.19	1.48	NA
Variable Profit	1.00	1.86	0.90	1.17	0.81	1.31	1.80	NA

Sources: Compiled from estimates provided by beverage industry source, April 2006.

[a] "Supercenters" include Wal-Mart Supercenter stores and similar outlets. "Mass Retailers" include standard Wal-Marts stores, Target stores, and the like. "Club Stores" include Sam's Club, Costco, and similar membership-based retailers.

[b] Figures here and below refer to the entire refreshment beverage industry, encompassing CSD and non-carb beverage volume.

[c] Using supermarket information as a baseline, these figures indicate variance by channel of both by-volume pricing and by-volume profit. The variable profit figures take into account cost of goods sold as well as delivery costs.

most cases, were considerably more profitable than national accounts. Overall, according to a prominent industry observer, operating margins were 10 percentage points lower in fountain sales than in bottle and can sales.[22] To support the fountain channel, Coke and Pepsi invested in the development of service dispensers and other equipment, and provided fountain customers with cups, point-of-sale advertising, and other in-store promotional material.

After Pepsi entered the fast-food restaurant business by acquiring Pizza Hut (1978), Taco Bell (1986), and Kentucky Fried Chicken (1986), Coca-Cola persuaded competing chains such as Wendy's and Burger King to switch to Coke. In 1997, PepsiCo spun off its restaurant business under the name Tricon, but fountain "pouring rights" remained split along largely pre-Tricon lines.[23] In 2005, Pepsi supplied all Taco Bell and KFC restaurants and the great majority of Pizza Hut restaurants, and Coke retained exclusivity deals with Burger King and McDonald's (the largest national account in terms of sales). Competition remained vigorous: In 2004, Coke won the Subway account away from Pepsi, while Pepsi grabbed the Quiznos account from Coke. (Subway was the largest account as measured by number of outlets.) And Coke continued to dominate the channel, with a 68% share of national pouring rights, against 22% for Pepsi and 10% for Cadbury Schweppes.[24]

Coke and Cadbury Schweppes had long retained control of national fountain accounts, negotiating pouring rights contracts that in some cases (as with big restaurant chains) covered the entire United States or even the world. Local bottlers or the franchisors' fountain divisions serviced these accounts. (In such cases, bottlers received a fee for delivering syrup and maintaining machines.) Historically, PepsiCo had ceded fountain rights to local Pepsi bottlers. In the late 1990s, however, Pepsi began a successful campaign to gain from its bottlers the right to sell fountain syrup via restaurant commissary companies.[25]

In the vending channel, bottlers took charge of buying, installing, and servicing machines, and for negotiating contracts with property owners, who typically received a sales commission in exchange for accommodating those machines. But concentrate makers offered bottlers financial incentives to encourage investment in machines, and also played a large role in the development of vending technology. Coke and Pepsi were by far the largest suppliers of CSDs to this channel.

Suppliers to Concentrate Producers and Bottlers

Concentrate producers required few inputs: the concentrate for most regular colas consisted of caramel coloring, phosphoric or citric acid, natural flavors, and caffeine.[26] Bottlers purchased two major inputs: packaging (including cans, plastic bottles, and glass bottles), and sweeteners (including high-fructose corn syrup and sugar, as well as artificial sweeteners such as aspartame). The majority of U.S. CSDs were packaged in metal cans (56%), with plastic bottles (42%) and glass bottles (2%) accounting for the remainder.[27] Cans were an attractive packaging material because they were easily handled and displayed, weighed little, and were durable and recyclable. Plastic packaging, introduced in 1978, allowed for larger and more varied bottle sizes. Single-serve 20-oz PET bottles, introduced in 1993, steadily gained popularity; in 2005, they represented 36.7% of CSD volume (and 56.7% of CSD revenues) in convenience stores.[28]

The concentrate producers' strategy toward can manufacturers was typical of their supplier relationships. Coke and Pepsi negotiated on behalf of their bottling networks, and were among the metal can industry's largest customers. In the 1960s and 1970s, both companies took control of a portion of their own can production, but by 1990 they had largely exited that business. Thereafter, they sought instead to establish stable long-term relationships with suppliers. In 2005, major can producers included Ball, Rexam (through its American National Can subsidiary), and Crown Cork & Seal.[29] Metal cans were essentially a commodity, and often two or three can manufacturers competed for a single contract.

The Evolution of the U.S. Soft Drink Industry[30]

Early History

Coca-Cola was formulated in 1886 by John Pemberton, a pharmacist in Atlanta, Georgia, who sold it at drug store soda fountains as a "potion for mental and physical disorders." In 1891, Asa Candler acquired the formula, established a sales force, and began brand advertising of Coca-Cola. The formula for Coca-Cola syrup, known as "Merchandise 7X," remained a well-protected secret that the company kept under guard in an Atlanta bank vault. Candler granted Coca-Cola's first bottling franchise in 1899 for a nominal one dollar, believing that the future of the drink rested with soda fountains. The company's bottling network grew quickly, however, reaching 370 franchisees by 1910.

In its early years, imitations and counterfeit versions of Coke plagued the company, which aggressively fought trademark infringements in court. In 1916 alone, courts barred 153 imitations of Coca-Cola, including the brands Coca-Kola, Koca-Nola, and Cold-Cola. Coke introduced and patented a 6.5-oz bottle whose unique "skirt" design subsequently became an American icon.

Candler sold the company to a group of investors in 1919, and it went public that year. Four years later, Robert Woodruff began his long tenure as leader of the company. Woodruff pushed franchise bottlers to place the beverage "in arm's reach of desire," by any and all means. During the 1920s and 1930s, Coke pioneered open-top coolers for use in grocery stores and other channels, developed automatic fountain dispensers, and introduced vending machines. Woodruff also initiated "lifestyle" advertising for Coca-Cola, emphasizing the role that Coke played in a consumer's life.

Woodruff developed Coke's international business as well. During World War II, at the request of General Eisenhower, he promised that "every man in uniform gets a bottle of Coca-Cola for five cents wherever he is and whatever it costs the company." Beginning in 1942, Coke won exemptions from wartime sugar rationing for production of beverages that it sold to the military or to retailers that served soldiers. Coca-Cola bottling plants followed the movement of American troops, and during the war the U.S. government set up 64 such plants overseas—a development that contributed to Coke's dominant postwar market shares in most European and Asian countries.

Pepsi-Cola was invented in 1893 in New Bern, North Carolina, by pharmacist Caleb Bradham. Like Coke, Pepsi adopted a franchise bottling system, and by 1910 it had built a network of 270 bottlers. Pepsi struggled, however; it declared bankruptcy in 1923 and again in 1932. But business began to pick up when, during the Great Depression, Pepsi lowered the price of its 12-oz bottle to a nickel—the same price that Coke charged for a 6.5-oz bottle. In the years that followed, Pepsi built a marketing strategy around the theme of its famous radio jingle: "Twice as much for a nickel, too."

In 1938, Coke filed suit against Pepsi, claiming that the Pepsi-Cola brand was an infringement on the Coca-Cola trademark. A 1941 court ruling in Pepsi's favor ended a series of suits and countersuits between the two companies. During this period, as Pepsi sought to expand its bottling network, it had to rely on small local bottlers that competed with wealthy, established Coke franchisees.[31] Still, the company began to gain market share, surpassing Royal Crown and Dr Pepper in the 1940s to become the second-largest-selling CSD brand. In 1950, Coke's share of the U.S. market was 47% and Pepsi's was 10%; hundreds of regional CSD companies, which offered a wide assortment of flavors, made up the rest of the market.[32]

The Cola Wars Begin

In 1950, Alfred Steele, a former Coke marketing executive, became CEO of Pepsi. Steele made "Beat Coke" his motto and encouraged bottlers to focus on take-home sales through supermarkets. To target family consumption, for example, the company introduced a 26-oz bottle. Pepsi's growth began to follow the postwar growth in the number of supermarkets and convenience stores in the United States: There were about 10,000 supermarkets in 1945; 15,000 in 1955; and 32,000 in 1962, at the peak of this growth curve.

Under the leadership of CEO Donald Kendall, Pepsi in 1963 launched its "Pepsi Generation" marketing campaign, which targeted the young and "young at heart." The campaign helped Pepsi narrow Coke's lead to a 2-to-1 margin. At the same time, Pepsi worked with its bottlers to modernize plants and to improve store delivery services. By 1970, Pepsi bottlers were generally larger than their Coke counterparts. Coke's network remained fragmented, with more than 800 independent franchised bottlers (most of which served U.S. cities of 50,000 or less).[33] Throughout this period, Pepsi sold concentrate to its bottlers at a price that was about 20% lower than what Coke charged. In the early 1970s, Pepsi increased its concentrate prices to equal those of Coke. To overcome bottler opposition, Pepsi promised to spend this extra income on advertising and promotion.

Coke and Pepsi began to experiment with new cola and non-cola flavors, and with new packaging options, in the 1960s. Previously, the two companies had sold only their flagship cola brands. Coke launched Fanta (1960), Sprite (1961), and the low-calorie cola Tab (1963). Pepsi countered with Teem (1960), Mountain Dew (1964), and Diet Pepsi (1964). Both companies introduced non-returnable glass bottles and 12-oz metal cans in various configurations. They also diversified into non-CSD industries. Coke purchased Minute Maid (fruit juice), Duncan Foods (coffee, tea, hot chocolate), and Belmont Springs Water. In 1965,

Pepsi merged with snack-food giant Frito-Lay to form PepsiCo, hoping to achieve synergies based on similar customer targets, delivery systems, and marketing orientations.

In the late 1950s, Coca-Cola began to use advertising messages that implicitly recognized the existence of competitors: "American's Preferred Taste" (1955), "No Wonder Coke Refreshes Best" (1960). In meetings with Coca-Cola bottlers, however, executives discussed only the growth of their own brand and never referred to its closest competitor by name. During the 1960s, Coke focused primarily on overseas markets, apparently basing its strategy on the assumption that domestic CSD consumption was approaching a saturation point. Pepsi, meanwhile, battled Coke aggressively in the United States, and doubled its U.S. share between 1950 and 1970.

The Pepsi Challenge

In 1974, Pepsi launched the "Pepsi Challenge" in Dallas, Texas. Coke was the dominant brand in that city, and Pepsi ran a distant third behind Dr Pepper. In blind taste tests conducted by Pepsi's small local bottler, the company tried to demonstrate that consumers actually preferred Pepsi to Coke. After its sales shot up in Dallas, Pepsi rolled out the campaign nationwide.

Coke countered with rebates, retail price cuts, and a series of advertisements that questioned the tests' validity. In particular, it employed retail price discounts in markets where a company-owned Coke bottler competed against an independent Pepsi bottler. Nonetheless, the Pepsi Challenge successfully eroded Coke's market share. In 1979, Pepsi passed Coke in food store sales for the first time, opening up a 1.4 share-point lead. In a sign of the times, Coca-Cola president Brian Dyson inadvertently uttered the name Pepsi at a 1979 bottlers' conference.

During this period, Coke renegotiated its franchise bottling contract to obtain greater flexibility in pricing concentrate and syrups. Its bottlers approved a new contract in 1978, but only after Coke agreed to link concentrate price changes to the CPI, to adjust the price to reflect any cost savings associated with ingredient changes, and to supply unsweetened concentrate to bottlers that preferred to buy their own sweetener on the open market.[34] This arrangement brought Coke in line with Pepsi, which traditionally had sold unsweetened concentrate to its bottlers. Immediately after securing approval of the new agreement, Coke announced a significant concentrate price increase. Pepsi followed with a 15% price increase of its own.

Cola Wars Heat Up

In 1980, Roberto Goizueta was named CEO of Coca-Cola, and Don Keough became its president. That year, Coke switched from using sugar to using high-fructose corn syrup, a lower-priced alternative. Pepsi emulated that move three years later. Coke also intensified its marketing effort, more than doubling its advertising spending between 1981 and 1984. In response, Pepsi doubled its advertising expenditures over the same period. Meanwhile, Goizueta sold off most of the non-CSD businesses that he had inherited, including wine, coffee, tea, and industrial water treatment, while retaining Minute Maid.

Diet Coke, introduced in 1982, was the first extension of the "Coke" brand name. Many Coke managers, deeming the "Mother Coke" brand sacred, had opposed the move. So had company lawyers, who worried about copyright issues. Nonetheless, Diet Coke was a huge success. Praised as the "most successful consumer product launch of the Eighties," it became within a few years not only the most popular diet soft drink in the United States, but also the nation's third-largest-selling CSD.

In April 1985, Coke announced that it had changed the 99-year-old Coca-Cola formula. Explaining this radical break with tradition, Goizueta cited a sharp depreciation in the value of the Coca-Cola trademark. "The product and the brand," he said, "had a declining share in a shrinking segment of the market."[35] On the day of Coke's announcement, Pepsi declared a holiday for its employees, claiming that the new Coke mimicked Pepsi in taste. The reformulation prompted an outcry from Coke's most loyal customers, and bottlers joined the clamor. Three months later, the company brought back the original formula under the name Coca-Cola Classic, while retaining the new formula as its flagship brand under the name New Coke. Six months later, Coke announced that it would henceforth treat Coca-Cola Classic (the original formula) as its flagship brand.

New CSD brands proliferated in the 1980s. Coke introduced 11 new products, including Caffeine-Free Coke (1983) and Cherry Coke (1985). Pepsi introduced 13 products, including Lemon-Lime Slice (1984) and Caffeine-Free Pepsi-Cola (1987). The number of packaging types and sizes also increased dramatically, and the battle for shelf space in supermarkets and other stores became fierce. By the late 1980s, Coke and Pepsi each offered more than 10 major brands and 17 or more container types.[36] The struggle for market share intensified, and retail price discounting became the norm. Consumers grew accustomed to such discounts.

Throughout the 1980s, the growth of Coke and Pepsi put a squeeze on smaller concentrate producers. As their shelf space declined, small brands were shuffled from one owner to another. Over a five-year span, Dr Pepper was sold (all or in part) several times, Canada Dry twice, Sunkist once, Shasta once, and A&W Brands once. Philip Morris acquired Seven-Up in 1978 for a big premium, racked up huge losses in the early 1980s, and then left the CSD business in 1985. In the 1990s, through a series of strategic acquisitions, Cadbury Schweppes emerged as the third-largest concentrate producer—the main (albeit distant) competitor of the two CSD giants. It bought the Dr Pepper/Seven-Up Companies in 1995, and continued to add such well-known brands as Orangina (2001) and Nantucket Nectars (2002) to its portfolio. (See Appendix A—Cadbury Schweppes: Operations and Financial Performance.)

Bottler Consolidation and Spin-Off

Relations between Coke and its franchised bottlers had been strained since the contract renegotiation of 1978. Coke struggled to persuade bottlers to cooperate in marketing and promotion programs, to upgrade plant and equipment, and to support new product launches.[37] The cola wars had particularly weakened small, independent bottlers. Pressures to spend more on advertising, product and packaging proliferation, widespread retail price discounting—together, these factors resulted in higher capital requirements and lower profit margins. Many family-owned bottlers no longer had the resources needed to remain competitive.

At a July 1980 dinner with Coke's 15 largest domestic bottlers, Goizueta announced a plan to refranchise bottling operations. Coke began buying up poorly managed bottlers, infusing them with capital, and quickly reselling them to better-performing bottlers. Refranchising allowed Coke's larger bottlers to expand outside their traditionally exclusive geographic territories. When two of its largest bottling companies came up for sale in 1985, Coke moved swiftly to buy them for $2.4 billion, preempting outside bidders. Together with other recently purchased bottlers, these acquisitions placed one-third of Coke's volume in company-owned operations. Meanwhile, Coke began to replace its 1978 franchise agreement with what became the 1987 Master Bottler Contract.

Coke's bottler acquisitions had increased its long-term debt to approximately $1 billion. In 1986, the company created an independent bottling subsidiary, Coca-Cola Enterprises (CCE), selling 51% of its shares to the public and retaining the rest. The minority equity position enabled Coke to separate its financial statements from those of CCE. As Coke's first "anchor bottler," CCE consolidated small territories into larger regions, renegotiated contracts with suppliers and retailers, merged redundant distribution and purchasing arrangements, and cut its work force by 20%. CCE also invested in building 50-million-case production lines that involved high levels of automation. Coke continued to acquire independent franchised bottlers and to sell them to CCE.[38] "We became an investment banking firm specializing in bottler deals," said Don Keough. In 1997 alone, Coke put together more than $7 billion in such deals.[39] By 2004, CCE was Coke's largest bottler. It handled about 80% of Coke's North American bottle and can volume, and logged annual sales of more than $18 billion. Some industry observers questioned Coke's accounting practice with respect to CCE, since Coke retained substantial managerial influence in the putatively independent anchor bottler.[40]

In the late 1980s, Pepsi acquired MEI Bottling for $591 million, Grand Metropolitan's bottling operations for $705 million, and General Cinema's bottling operations for $1.8 billion. After operating the bottlers for a decade, Pepsi shifted course and adopted Coke's anchor bottler model. In April 1999, the Pepsi Bottling Group (PBG) went public, with Pepsi retaining a 35% equity stake in it. By 2004, PBG produced 57% of PepsiCo beverages in North America and about 40% worldwide, while the total number of Pepsi bottlers had fallen from more than 400 in the mid-1980s to a mere 102.[41]

Bottler consolidation made smaller concentrate producers increasingly dependent on the Pepsi and Coke bottling networks for distribution of their products. In response, Cadbury Schweppes in 1998 bought and merged two large U.S. bottling companies to form its own bottler. In 2004, Coke had the most consolidated system, with its top 10 bottlers producing 94.7% of domestic volume. Pepsi's and Cadbury Schweppes' top 10 bottlers produced 87.2% and 72.9% of the domestic volume of their respective franchisors.[42]

Adapting to the Times

Starting in the late 1990s, the soft drink industry encountered new challenges that suggested a possible long-term shift in the marketplace. Most notably, demand for its core product seemed to have leveled off. Although Americans still drank more CSDs than any other beverage, U.S. sales volume grew at a rate of 1% or less in the years 1998 to 2004. Total U.S. volume topped 10 billion cases in 2001, but had risen to only 10.2 billion cases in 2004. (A case was equivalent to 24 eight-ounce containers, or 192 ounces.) That was in contrast to annual growth rates of 3% to 7% during the 1980s and early 1990s.[43] Globally, too, demand remained flat. Worldwide volume in 2003 was 31.26 billion cases, which marked only a slight increase over the 1999 total of 31 billion cases. During that period, worldwide annual per-capita consumption declined from 125 eight-ounce servings to 119 servings.[44]

In responding to changing times, Coca-Cola struggled more than PepsiCo, in part because of its own internal difficulties and execution failures, and in part because of its greater reliance on a traditional CSD-oriented model. But, in their different ways, both companies sought to retain or recapture their historically high growth and profitability within an apparently new environment. Toward that end, they focused on addressing challenges related to performance and execution, on providing alternative beverages to increasingly health-conscious consumers, on adjusting key strategic relationships, and on cultivating international markets.

Reversal of Fortune

When Coke CEO Robert Goizueta died unexpectedly in 1997, the company that he had led was at its zenith. During Goizueta's 16-year tenure, Coke's share price rose by 3,500%, and its brand was routinely deemed the most valuable in the world.[45] Pepsi, meanwhile, lagged behind its rival in most key measures of its beverage operations, including market share and sales growth.[46] By the middle of the following decade, however, Coke appeared to stumble from one embarrassment to another, while Pepsi was flying high.

Under the brief, rocky tenure of CEO Douglas Ivester (1997–1999), Coke lost a high-profile race-discrimination suit, underwent financial shocks caused by currency crises in Asia and Russia, and conducted the largest recall in its history after a contamination scare in Belgium. In the latter episode, there was no evidence of actual contamination; nonetheless, it was a public relations disaster.[47] Troubles continued under the next CEO, Douglas Daft (1999–2004). Layoffs of 7,000 employees from 2001 to 2004 cut Coke's work force by 20%—damaging morale and seriously weakening its executive ranks, many observers believed.[48] A contamination scare in India in 2003 hindered Coke's (as well as Pepsi's) push into a promising market, and a similar crisis in 2004 led the company to abort plans to roll out its Dasani water brand in Europe.[49] A series of legal problems burdened the company as well. In 2003, Coke agreed to pay Burger King $21 million following the revelation that it had rigged a marketing test involving the restaurant chain. That same year, the U.S. Justice Department and the Securities Exchange Commission (SEC) launched wide-ranging investigations of various Coke accounting practices, focusing on allegations of "channel stuffing." Under this practice, Coke pressured bottlers to buy excess concentrate in order to meet earnings targets. Coke in 2005 settled with the SEC on charges involving the Japanese market, but a shareholder suit alleging such practices in Europe, North America, and elsewhere remained in the courts.[50]

Coke also suffered from clumsy execution (or non-execution) of several initiatives. In 2001, it bailed out on a planned joint venture with Procter & Gamble. Around the same time, after two years of negotiation, it opted against buying the South Beach Beverage Co. (SoBe), only to watch Pepsi acquire that company. Similarly, in 2000 Coke allowed Pepsi to purchase Quaker Oats. Daft had agreed to buy Quaker for $15.75 billion, but several Coke directors halted the deal, arguing that the price was too high.[51] Coke installed a new CEO, E. Neville Isdell, in April 2004.[52] A 35-year Coke veteran, Isdell focused early in his tenure on regaining the company's lost luster as a high-performing soft drink maker. "We are not talking about radical change in strategy. We are talking about a dramatic change in execution," he said in November 2004.[53] Yet, at around the same time, he noted the need for Coke to take "corrective actions with a great urgency." During his first year as CEO, he committed to spending an additional $400 million per year on marketing and innovation, and on addressing Coke's "people deficit and skills deficit."[54]

While Coke struggled, Pepsi quietly flourished. In 2001, Steve Reinemund succeeded Roger Enrico as its CEO.[55] At a broad level, both men pursued the same simple strategy, which Reinemund couched in this way: "Grow the core and add some more."[56] Along with launching new CSDs, such as Sierra Mist (2000) and Mountain Dew Code Red (2001), Pepsi expanded into other beverage categories—an effort capped by its $14 billion acquisition of Quaker Oats, maker of Gatorade, in 2000.[57] Partly as a result, the company's North American beverage volume grew by 3% in 2004, compared with virtually flat volumes for Coke.[58] As the world's fourth-largest food and beverage company, meanwhile, Pepsi also benefited from having a more diversified portfolio of products.

Financial returns for the two companies told a stark tale. Between 1996 and 2004, Coca-Cola logged an average annual growth in net income of 4.2%—a huge drop from the 18% average growth of the years 1990–1997. PepsiCo, by contrast, saw its net income rise by an average of 17.6% per year over the 1996–2004 period.[59] In 2003, Pepsi recorded a return on invested capital of 29.3%, up from 9.5% in 1996; for the first time in decades, it surpassed Coke in that measure.[60] From 1997 to 2004, Pepsi shareholders enjoyed a return of 46%, while Coke shareholders suffered a return of -26%.[61] (Coke shares, which reached a peak price of $89 in 1998, traded at half that amount in 2005.[62])

The Quest for Alternatives

Early in 2005, Pepsi announced that it would no longer set its marketing course by its regular cola brand. "We are treating Diet Pepsi as the flagship brand," said Dave Burwick, chief marketing officer for Pepsi-Cola North America. Although the marketing budget for regular Pepsi still exceeded that of the diet brand, the balance of attention and resources would now shift within the company.[63] More importantly, the move was a bellwether of a larger shift throughout the beverage industry. After several years of little or no growth in CSD sales—especially sales of regular, sugared sodas—companies responded aggressively to consumers' increasing demand for alternative beverages.

New federal nutrition guidelines, issued in 2005, identified regular CSDs as the largest source of obesity-causing sugars in the American diet.[64] Schools in New York City, throughout California, and elsewhere banned the sale of soft drinks on their premises.[65] Late in 2005, using earlier actions against tobacco companies as a model, lawyers planned to file a suit against CSD makers for allegedly causing harm to children's health.[66] The American Beverage Association, an industry group, responded to such pressures by announcing

rules to limit CSD sales in some schools. (In another noteworthy development, the ABA had changed its name from the National Soft Drink Association in 2004.)[67] But the widespread linkage of CSDs with obesity and other health-related concerns was hard to dispel from people's minds. From 2003 to 2004, according to a Morgan Stanley survey, the proportion of Americans who said that cola was "too fattening" increased from 48% to 59%.[68]

In such a climate, diet sodas offered one path to reviving sales. In the U.S. market, their share of total CSD volume grew from 24.6% in 1997 to 29.1% in 2004, thus making up for a decline in regular-soda consumption.[69] New or renamed products, such as Coca-Cola Zero (2005) and Sierra Mist Free (2004), targeted consumers—especially younger men—who shunned the "diet" label. With products like Pepsi One (2005) and Diet Coke with Splenda (2005), CSD makers sought to expand the diet market still further.[70]

But the search for alternatives centered on non-carbonated beverages, or "non-carbs"—a category that included juices and juice drinks, sports drinks, energy drinks, and tea-based drinks—and also on bottled water. In 2004, CSD volume in the United States grew by just 1%, whereas non-carb volume increased by 7.6% and single-serve bottled-water volume leaped by 18.8%. That year, CSDs accounted for 73.1% of U.S. non-alcoholic refreshment beverage volume (down from 80.8% in 2000), with bottled water comprising 13.2% (up from 6.6% in 2000) and non-carbs comprising 13.7% (up from 12.6%) of the remainder.[71] In 2001, non-carbs and bottled water together contributed more than 100% of Coke's total volume growth and roughly three-fourths of Pepsi's volume growth.[72]

Pepsi was more aggressive than Coke in shifting to non-CSDs. "Politicians expect us to be on the defensive when we talk about health and wellness but we're not," said Pepsi CEO Reinemund. "It's a huge opportunity to build new brands and products."[73] His company launched a "Smart Spot" program that labeled all products (including diet sodas and non-carbs) that met certain "good for you" criteria; in 2004, such products reportedly grew at twice the rate of other Pepsi food and beverage items.[74] Declaring itself to be a "total beverage company," Pepsi developed a portfolio of non-CSD products that outsold Coke's rival product in each key category: In 2004 volume sales, Gatorade (80.4%) led PowerAde (18.1%) in the $5.4 billion sports drink segment, Lipton (35.2%) led

Nestea (23.9%) in the $3.2 billion tea-based drink segment, and Tropicana (26.8%) led Minute Maid (14.8%) in the $3.8 billion refrigerated juice segment. In the U.S. non-carb market overall (excluding bottled water), Pepsi had a market share of 47.3%, compared with Coke's share of 27.0%.[75]

Missed opportunities marked Coke's U.S. non-carb operations. In 2001, Coke acquired the Planet Java coffee-drink brand and the Mad River line of juices and teas; two years later, it folded both brands.[76] KMX, the company's entry in the fast-growing, $1.9 billion energy-drink segment, also foundered. Coke hoped for better luck with Full Throttle, introduced in 2005 to compete with segment leader Red Bull.[77] Observers noted Coke's continued

focus on its traditional source of strength. "Regardless of what the skeptics think, I know carbonated soft drinks can grow," said Coke CEO Isdell.[78] In 2005, CSDs still accounted for 80% of Coke's worldwide beverage volume, while making up just two-thirds of Pepsi's volume.[79]

Coke fared better in the $11.4 billion bottled-water category. Both Pepsi (with Aquafina, 1998) and Coke (with Dasani, 1999) had introduced purified-water products that had surged to become leading beverage brands. (See Exhibit 7—Non-Alcoholic Refreshment Beverge Megabrands, 2004 and 2000.) Using their distribution prowess, they had outstripped competing brands, many of which sold spring water. By 2004, Aquafina (13.6%) led the segment in market

EXHIBIT 7

Non-Alcoholic Refreshment Beverage Megabrands,[a] 2004 and 2000

Brand (Owner)	Category	2004 Cases (mil)	2004 Share	2000 Cases (mil)	2000 Share	Annual Volume Change[b] 2004–04	Annual Share Change[b] 2004–04
Coke (Coke)	CSD	3,272.3	23.4%	3,192.6	25.9%	0.6%	−2.5%
Pepsi (Pepsi)	CSD	2,098.4	15.0%	2,159.9	17.5%	−0.7%	−3.8%
Mountain Dew (Pepsi)	CSD	871.1	6.2%	809.8	6.6%	1.8%	−1.5%
Dr Pepper (Cadbury)	CSD	738.3	5.3%	747.5	6.1%	−0.3%	−3.5%
Sprite (Coke)	CSD	683.2	4.9%	713.0	5.8%	−1.1%	−4.1%
Gatorade (Pepsi)	Non-Carb	546.0	3.9%	325.0	2.6%	13.9%	10.7%
Aquafina (Pepsi)	Water	251.0	1.8%	100.7	0.8%	25.7%	22.5%
Dasani (Coke)	Water	223.0	1.6%	65.1	0.5%	36.0%	33.8%
Poland Spring (Nestlé Waters)	Water	217.0	1.5%	91.8	0.7%	24.0%	21.0%
7UP (Cadbury)	CSD	186.7	1.3%	276.1	2.2%	−9.3%	−12.3%
Minute Maid (Coke)	CSD/Non-Carb	176.4	1.3%	145.0	1.2%	5.0%	2.0%
Sierra Mist (Pepsi)	CSD	166.9	1.2%	—	—	—	—
Lipton (Pepsi/Unilever)	Non-Carb	164.0	1.2%	155.2	1.3%	1.4%	−2.0%
Crystal Geyser (CG Roxanne)	Water	135.5	1.0%	50.2	0.4%	28.2%	25.7%
Arrowhead (Nestlé Waters)	Water	127.0	0.9%	46.6	0.4%	28.5%	18.9%
PowerAde (Coke)	Non-Carb	122.7	0.9%	62.6	0.5%	18.3%	15.9%
Nestlé Pure Life (Nestlé Waters)	Water	113.2	0.8%	—	—	—	—
Barq's (Coke)	CSD	112.5	0.8%	121.2	1.0%	−1.8%	−5.4%
Sunkist (Cadbury)	CSD	105.2	0.8%	80.3	0.7%	7.0%	3.4%

Sources: Compiled from Beverage Digest Fact Book 2005; Beverage Digest Fact Book 2001; and casewriter estimates.

[a] Beverage Digest Fact Book defines a "megabrand" as a "brand or trademark with total volume of more than 100 million 192-oz cases." A megabrand encompasses all varieties (Coke Classic, Diet Coke, Cherry Coke, and so on) of a given trademark ("Coke"). Only single-serve products are included here.

[b] All changes calculated using Compounded Annual Growth Rate (CAGR).

share, with Dasani (12.1%) trailing close behind.[80] Moreover, by arrangement with Danone, Coke handled U.S. marketing and distribution of that company's water brands, including Dannon and Evian. In 2004, Coke/Danone had an overall market share of 21.9%, behind market leader Nestlé Waters (42.1%) and ahead of Pepsi (13.6%). Coke bought out Danone's share of the venture in 2005.[81]

Evolving Structures and Strategies

Early in the 21st century, both Coke and Pepsi worked to improve "system profitability"—the arrangement whereby concentrate makers and their bottlers created and then divided overall profits from beverage sales. Bottler consolidation continued apace, and the relationship between Coke or Pepsi (on the one hand) and bottlers like CCE or PBG (on the other) became a key element of the cola wars. In the 1990s, a price war in the supermarket channel had highlighted a divergence of interest between the two camps. To compete against bargain private-label brands, bottlers had pursued a low-price strategy. Through the decade, retail CSD prices decreased or remained flat, even as the CPI inched up and as concentrate prices rose; Coke, for instance, raised its concentrate prices by 7.6% in 2000. Bottlers, already burdened by huge debts from consolidation and infrastructure investments, saw profit margins dwindle. In 1999 and 2000, they shifted course, as CCE increased its retail pricing in the supermarket channel by 6% to 7% and as PBG followed suit. Consumers balked, sales volume dipped, and concentrate makers saw their profits drop as a result.[82]

In later years, Coke struggled to adjust its relations with CCE and other bottlers—relations that one writer in 2004 called "dysfunctional."[83] In 2001, the company made an arrangement with CCE to link concentrate prices more tightly to CCE's wholesale CSD prices.[84] Starting in 2003, the two companies began negotiating a deal that would move toward "incidence pricing," an approach that Coke often used with its overseas bottlers. Under that system, concentrate prices varied according to prices charged in different channels and for different packages. As a rule, bottlers favored such arrangements in a deflationary market (which the CSD market had become) but resisted them in an inflationary market.[85] Neville Isdell, Coke's new CEO in 2004 and a former bottler himself, emphasized the need to improve bottler relations. Yet late that year, he tabled the CCE pricing initiative.[86] He also oversaw a proposed rise in concentrate prices

that led Coca-Cola FEMSA, the Coke system's largest Mexican bottler, to threaten a cut in its marketing expenditure.[87]

Pepsi, observers noted, had less difficulty than Coke in aligning its strategy with that of its bottlers. "We believe PBG's relationship with PepsiCo is strong and has been critical to its success," one analysts' report asserted in 2003. During that period, PBG consistently posted net-revenue-per-case growth that exceeded CCE's growth by several percentage points. Supported by Pepsi, PBG excelled in higher-margin channels—especially the convenience-and-gas channel, in which the bottler actually led CCE. Bottlers profited immensely in such "immediate consumption" venues, where sales of the increasingly popular 20-oz PET bottle yielded margins as high as 35%, compared with the 5% to 7% margin on cans.[88]

All CSD companies faced the challenge of achieving pricing power in the take-home, or future-consumption, channels. Supermarket retail prices did rise, modestly but steadily, in the mid-2000s.[89] Yet retailers, accustomed to using CSD sales to drive in-store traffic, still resisted price increases.[90] Rapid growth of the mass-merchandiser channel, led by Wal-Mart and various club stores, posed a new threat to profitability for Coke, Pepsi, and their bottlers. By 2004, Wal-Mart was the largest U.S. food retailer; for PepsiCo, it represented 14% of the company's total (food and beverage) net revenue.[91] Such retailers not only used their size to exert pricing pressure; they also demanded that beverage companies alter long-standing business practices. Wal-Mart, for example, insisted on negotiating chain-wide marketing and shelving arrangements directly with concentrate makers. Although bottlers continued to handle deliveries to these accounts, relations between Coke or Pepsi and their bottlers underwent a great deal of stress because of this channel shift.[92]

To counter these pressures, CSD makers focused on enticing consumers through stepped-up marketing and innovation. In 2005, Coke combined authority for all of its marketing and product development in a new position that became the company's "de facto No. 2 spot."[93] It also launched a major advertising campaign, built around a new tag line: "The Coke Side of Life."[94] (See Exhibit 8—Advertisement Spending for Selected Refreshment Beverage Brands.) Packaging innovation received special emphasis. Coke in 2001 rolled out its Fridge Pack (later imitated by Pepsi, which introduced a Fridge Mate package), a reconfiguration of the

EXHIBIT 8

Advertisement Spending for Selected Refreshment Beverage Brands ($ thousands)

	Share of market[a]		Advertisement Spending[b]		
	2004	2003	2004	2003	per 2004 share point
Coca-Cola	23.4%	24.3%	246,243	167,675	10,523
Pepsi-Cola	15.0%	15.5%	211,654	236,396	14,110
Mountain Dew	6.2%	6.4%	57,803	60,555	9,323
Dr Pepper	5.3%	5.3%	104,762	96,387	19,766
Sprite	4.9%	5.3%	45,035	31,835	9,191
Gatorade	3.9%	3.5%	141,622	130,993	36,313
Aquafina	1.8%	1.7%	22,037	24,647	12,243
Dasani	1.6%	1.5%	17,633	18,833	11,021
7UP	1.3%	1.5%	34,608	25,071	26,206
Minute Maid	1.3%	1.5%	35,797	21,097	27,228
Sierra Mist	1.2%	1.2%	60,327	64,129	50,273
PowerAde	0.9%	0.8%	11,008	10,100	12,231

Sources: Compiled from "Special Report: 100 Leading National Advertisers," *Advertising Age,* June 27, 2005, and casewriter estimates.

[a] Share of the total single-serve non-alcoholic beverage market (about 14 billion cases in 2004).

[b] Spending as measured across 17 national media channels using data compiled by TNS Media Intelligence.

standard 12-pack of cans that seemed to improve CSD sales.[95] In 2004, the company introduced a 1.5-liter bottle in select markets, aiming to replace the 2-liter version and thus to boost per-ounce pricing. While the launching of new products and packages brought clear benefits, it also increased costs for bottlers, which had to produce and manage an ever-rising number of stock-keeping units (SKUs).[96] (See Exhibit 9—Retailers' Assessment of Brand Performance, 2004.) That problem was most salient in the area of non-CSD beverages. The proliferation of such products, many of them sold in relatively low volume, led to an increasing use of "split pallets." By loading more than one product type on a pallet (the hard, wooden bed used to organize and transport merchandise), bottlers incurred higher labor costs.

In general, alternative beverages complicated CSD makers' traditional production and distribution practices. CSD manufacturing was a cold-fill process. Some non-CSD beverages (such as Lipton Brisk) were also cold-fill products, and bottlers could adapt their infrastructure to those products with little difficulty. But other beverage types (such as Gatorade and Lipton Iced Tea) required costly new equipment and major process changes. More often than not, Coke and Pepsi took direct charge of manufacturing such beverages, which they then sold to their bottlers. The bottlers, in turn, distributed these finished goods alongside their own bottled products at a percentage markup. In others cases, especially that of bottled water, Coke and Pepsi paid for half or more of the cost of building bottling plants that allowed for filtration and other necessary processes. Bottlers then either purchased concentrate-like additives from the concentrate maker (as with Dasani's mineral packet) or compensated Coke or Pepsi via per-unit royalty fees (as with Aquafina). In addition, Coke and Pepsi distributed some non-carbs (such as Gatorade) through food brokers and wholesalers, rather than through DSD delivery.[97]

These arrangements affected profitability in ways that were complex and evolving. With many non-carb beverages, especially energy drinks and sports drinks, high retail pricing and consumers' preference for immediate, single-serve consumption meant that margins were actually higher than they were for CSDs. Yet

EXHIBIT 9

Retailers' Assessment of Brand Performance, 2004

	Top 6 Brands[a]					
	P&G	**Kraft**	**Gen'l Mills**	**Pepsi-Cola**	**Coca-Cola**	**Unilever**
Brands most important to retailers	57.1%	47.3%	19.8%	15.8%	13.7%	11.8%
	Kraft	**P&G**	**Gen'l Mills**	**Nestle**	**Con-Agra**	**Pepsi-Cola**
Best combination of growth, profitability	33.3%	27.6%	26.3%	13.6%	12.5%	11.2%
	Kraft	**P&G**	**Gen'l Mills**	**Pepsi-Cola**	**Nestle**	**Frito-Lay**
Best sales force/customer teams	32.7%	31.5%	26.4%	14.1%	13.9%	8.4%
	P&G	**Kraft**	**Gen'l Mills**	**Pepsi-Cola**	**Coca-Cola**	**Unilever**
Most innovative marketing programs	30.7%	29.6%	28.9%	14.7%	13.4 %	12.7%
	P&G	**Kraft**	**Gen'l Mills**	**Nestle**	**Pepsi-Cola**	**Coca-Cola**
Most helpful customer information	50.3%	27.2%	23.1%	13.1%	9.4%	9.1%
	P&G	**Kraft**	**Gen'l Mills**	**Nestle**	**Campbell's**	**Unilever**
Best supply chain management	55.0%	36.9%	25.9%	15.9%	10.2%	8.8%

Source: Cannondale Associates, PoweRanking Survey®, 2004.

[a] Each brand measured by percentage of respondents who rank the brand first, second, or third for each category.

volume for such products, while growing fast, remained very small in comparison with CSD volume.[98] With bottled water, a different set of dynamics was in play. Here, sales volume soared (bottled water, one observer noted, was "the most frequent next stop for lapsed soft-drink users"[99]), and the cost, production, and distribution structures closely matched those of the traditional CSD industry. In the early 2000s, bottler margins on water were high; one research report estimated that a bottle of Pepsi's Aquafina garnered a profit of 22.4%, compared with a 19.0% profit for a bottle of Pepsi-Cola.[100] But as consumption shifted from single-serve to multi-pack options, pricing shifted accordingly. At some locations, at one point in 2002, a 24-bottle case of Dasani or Aquafina sold for $3.99, which was less than the cost of bottling it.[101] By 2006, according to one estimate, multi-serve products accounted for about 70% of the bottled water market, up from about 30% a decade earlier. Rising plastic costs also cut sharply into margins in this category.[102] In addition, compared with the CSD market, the water market appeared to involve low brand loyalty and high price sensitivity. A 2002 survey found that while 37% of respondents said that they chose a CSD because "it's my favorite brand," only 10% of respondents said so about a bottled water choice.[103]

Internationalizing the Cola Wars

As U.S. demand for CSDs reached an apparent plateau, Coke and Pepsi increasingly looked abroad for new growth. In 2004, the United States remained by far the largest market, accounting for about one-third of worldwide CSD volume. The next largest markets were, in order, Mexico, Brazil, Germany, China, and the United Kingdom.[104] But improved access to markets in Asia and Eastern Europe stimulated a new, intense phase of the cola wars. In many such markets, per-capita consumption levels were a small fraction of the level seen in the United States. For example, while the average American drank 837 eight-ounce cans of CSDs in 2004, the average Chinese drank just 21. Among major world regions, Coke dominated in Western Europe and much of Latin America, while Pepsi had a marked presence in the Middle East and Southeast Asia.[105] (See Exhibit 10—CSD Industry: Selected International Consumption Rates and Market Shares, 2003 and 1999.) Although the growth potential of both established and emerging markets held great attraction, those markets also posed special challenges.

Coke flourished in international markets, and also relied upon them, far more than Pepsi. As far back as the end of World War II, the company had

EXHIBIT 10

CSD Industry: Selected International Consumption Rates and Market Shares, 2003 and 1999

	Population (thousands)	Consumption (8-oz servings per capita)		Annual Growth[a]	2003 Share[b]			1999 Share[b]		
		2003	1999	1999–2003	Coke	Pepsi	Cadbury	Coke	Pepsi	Cadbury
Europe (23.4%)										
Germany	82,476	340	344	−0.3%	51	5	1	56	8	1
United Kingdom	59,251	420	370	3.2%	47	11	0	43	12	0
Spain	41,060	425	386	2.4%	65	15	5	60	16	5
Italy	57,423	216	212	0.5%	44	6	1.5	45	8	1
France	60,144	180	158	3.3%	60	6	18.6	60	8	5
Russia	143,246	70	52	7.7%	21	18	0	26	12	0
Poland	38,587	167	155	1.9%	19	15	1	28	17	1
Netherlands	16,149	335	356	−1.5%	80	14	0	45	15	1
Hungary	9,877	279	273	0.5%	49	25	4	57	29	5
Romania	22,334	145	104	8.7%	46	8	0	44	9	0
Czech Republic	10,236	410	215	17.5%	13	7	1	36	13	2
Latin America (24.3%)										
Mexico	103,457	610	590	0.9%	73	20	5.1	70	19	3
Brazil	178,470	312	276	3.1%	46	7	0	51	7	0
Argentina	38,428	400	374	1.7%	50	19	0	59	24	0
Colombia	44,222	159	181	−3.2%	51	11	0	60	8	0
Venezuela	25,699	205	290	−8.3%	49	21	0	70	30	0
Chile	15,805	402	392	0.6%	73	5	0	81	4	0
Peru	27,167	166	108	11.4%	39	9	0	50	16	0
Asia Pacific (13.6%)										
China	1,304,196	21	22	−1.2%	51	24	0	34	16	0
Philippines	79,999	187	205	−2.3%	80	16	0	70	18	0
Japan	127,654	80	92	−3.4%	64	11	0	55	11	0
Australia	19,731	490	502	−0.6%	56	10	18.5	57	10	16
Thailand	62,833	95	114	−4.5%	56	43	0	52	45	0
India	1,065,462	8	6	7.5%	45	43	0	56	44	0
South Korea	47,700	118	108	2.2%	47	17	0	54	13	0
Indonesia	219,883	14	9	11.7%	75	5	0	94	6	0
Pakistan	153,578	24	14	14.4%	26	73	0	25	71	3
Vietnam	81,377	20	15	9.3%	39	34	0	63	36	0
Africa/Middle East (7.8%)										
South Africa	45,026	218	207	1.3%	94	0	0	97	0	0
Saudi Arabia	24,217	270	229	4.2%	15	82	0	24	76	0
Egypt	71,931	61	50	5.1%	48	42	0	60	40	0
Israel	6,433	452	400	3.1%	55	11	0	70	14	0
Morocco	30,566	56	63	−2.9%	87	3	8	96	4	0
North America										
United States	290,809	837	874	−1.1%	44	31	14	44	31	15
Canada	31,510	463	489	−1.4%	38	37	9	39	35	9
Total Worldwide	6,305,252	119	125	−1.2%	51	22	6	53	21	6

Sources: Compiled from *Beverage Digest Fact Book 2005* and *Beverage Digest Fact Book 2001.*

[a] Change calculated using Compounded Annual Growth Rate (CAGR).   [b] Share of worldwide market by volume.

secured a position as the largest international producer of soft drinks. Coke steadily expanded its overseas operations in the following decades, and the name Coca-Cola became synonymous with American culture. By the early 1990s, Coke CEO Roberto Goizueta would note, "Coca-Cola used to be an American company with a large international business. Now we are a large international company with a sizable American business."[106] Roughly 9 million outlets, located in more than 200 countries, sold Coke products in 2004.[107] About 70% of Coke's sales and about 80% of its profits came from outside the United States; only about one-third of Pepsi's beverage sales took place overseas.[108] Coke enjoyed a world market share of 51.4%, compared with 21.8% for Pepsi and 6% for Cadbury Schweppes.[109]

Pepsi entered Europe soon after World War II. Later, benefiting from Arab and Soviet exclusion of Coke, it moved into the Middle East and Soviet bloc. During the 1970s and 1980s, however, Pepsi put relatively little emphasis on its overseas operations. By the early 1990s, the company once again attacked Coke in the latter's core international markets—though with relatively little success, since Coke struck back aggressively. In one high-profile skirmish, Pepsi's longtime bottler in Venezuela defected to Coke in 1996, temporarily reducing Pepsi's 80% share of the cola market there to nearly nothing.[110] Pepsi had moved away from bruising head-to-head competition with Coke by the early 2000s. Instead, it focused on emerging markets that were still up for grabs.[111] In 2004, its international division (which also covered food offerings) grew faster than any other division, and that division's operating profit was up by 25%. Its international beverage volume was up by 12% overall for the year, driven by a strong performance in its Asia Pacific (up 15%) and Europe, Middle East, and Africa (up 14%) divisions. For both CSDs and non-carbs, the company logged double-digit growth overseas, and double-digit growth also marked volume sales in China, India, and Russia.[112]

Both beverage giants encountered obstacles in their international operations, including antitrust regulation, price controls, advertising restrictions, foreign exchange controls, lack of infrastructure, cultural differences, political instability, and local competition. When Coke acquired most of Cadbury Schweppes's international CSD business in 1999, regulators in Europe, Mexico, and Australia barred the transaction from occurring in those markets.[113] In Germany, a 2003 bottle return law (later rescinded) led many retailers to stop carrying Coke and Pepsi products; for Coke, that disruption resulted in a year-over-year sales drop of 11%.[114] In Colombia, Marxist rebels in 2003 killed a local Coke executive in a bombing, while union activists accused the company of collaborating with right-wing death squads.[115] In many Latin American countries, low-cost upstarts like Peru's Kola-Real dented market share or eroded pricing power for the larger companies. In 2003, for example, these "B-brands" claimed 30% of CSD share in Brazil, up from about 3% in the early 1990s.[116]

Waging the cola wars in non-U.S. markets enabled Coke and Pepsi not only to expand revenue, but also to broaden their base of innovation. To cope with immature distribution networks, for example, they created novel systems of their own, such as Coke's network of vending machines in Japan—a high-margin channel that at one point accounted for more than half of the company's Japanese sales.[117] Japan also proved to be an impressive laboratory for new products. Teas, coffees, juices, and flavored water made up the majority of that country's 200-plus Coke items, and Coke's largest-selling product there was not soda but canned coffee. "If you're looking for a total beverage business we've got one in Japan," said Coke CEO Isdell.[118] During the same period, Coke introduced 20 new products with a health or diet emphasis into the Mexico market. New approaches to packaging abounded as well.[119] In China and India, use of small returnable glass bottles allowed Coke to reach poor, rural consumers at a very low price point, while boosting revenue-per-ounce.[120]

The End of an Era?

In the early years of the 21st century, growth in soft drink sales for both Coke and Pepsi was falling short of precedent and of investors' expectations. Was the fundamental nature of the cola wars changing? Was a new form of rivalry emerging that would entail reduced profitability and stagnant growth—both inconceivable under the old form of rivalry? Or did the changes under way represent simply another step forward in the evolution of two of the world's most successful companies? In 2000, a Coke executive noted, "the cola wars are going to be played now across a lot of different battlefields."[121] What remained unclear in 2006 was whether those wars were still about "cola," and whether anyone knew for certain where those battlefields were located.

Appendix A—Cadbury Schweppes: Operations and Financial Performance

By the late 1990s, Cadbury Schweppes had emerged as the clear, albeit distant, third-largest player in the U.S. soft drink industry. Its products accounted for 14.5% of CSDs and 9.3% of non-carbs sold in 2004. Its brands include Dr Pepper, 7UP, RC Cola, Schweppes, Canada Dry, A&W, Squirt, Sundrop, Welch's, Country Time, Clamato, Hawaiian Punch, Snapple, Mistic, and Stewart's.

The U.K.-based firm was born of the 1969 merger between Jacob Schweppes' mineral water business (founded in 1783) and John Cadbury's cocoa and chocolate business (founded in 1842). In the mid-1980s, the group decided to focus on its core international confectionery and soft drink businesses. In 1989, its beverage headquarters relocated from London, England, to Stamford, Connecticut. During the 1980s and the early 1990s, its soft drink and confectionery brand portfolio was extended through the acquisition of a number of key brands, notably Mott's (1982), Canada Dry (1986), Trebor (1989), and Bassett's (1989). Its acquisition of Dr Pepper/Seven-Up Companies in 1995 boosted its U.S. CSD market share from 4.6% in 1994 to 15.1% in 1995, and its acquisition of Triarc's Mistic and Snapple brands in 2001 more than doubled its non-carb market from 6.0% in 1999. Further acquisitions included the Orangina and Yoo-Hoo brands (bought from Pernod Ricard in 2001), Squirt (a top-selling brand in Mexico, purchased in 2002), and Nantucket Nectars (bought in 2002 and folded into the Snapple brand). In 1999, Cadbury Schweppes disposed of its soft drink brands in around 160 countries, concentrating its beverages interests on North America, Europe, and Australia.

In 2004, Cadbury Schweppes operated primarily as a licensor, selling concentrate and syrup to independently owned bottling and canning operations (some of which were affiliated with competitors). It also provided marketing support and technical manufacturing oversight to these companies. In the United States, Cadbury Schweppes had a 40% interest in the Dr Pepper/Seven Up Bottling Group (DPSUBG), which accounted for 28.7% of its CSD volume. With its non-carb products and in certain markets (particularly Mexico), it manufactured and distributed its beverages directly or through third-party bottlers.

TABLE A

Cadbury Schweppes Financial Data ($ millions)

	2004	2003	2002	2001	2000
Americas Beverages					
Sales	$3,854	$3,239	$3,190	$2,770	$1,950
Operating profits/sales	25.2%	29.3%	29.5%	29.7%	32.7%
Europe Beverages[a]					
Sales	$1,253	$1,236	$882	$560	$477
Operating profit/sales	17.9%	17.3%	19.0%	18.2%	15.4%
Consolidated[b]					
Sales	$12,927	$11,500	$8,528	$7,220	$6,161
Operating margin	13.6%	11.6%	17.4%	17.9%	18.9%
Return on assets	5.2%	3.9%	7.0%	7.6%	8.4%

Sources: Company financial reports; OneSource, Global Business Browser, http://globalbb.onesource.com/web/Reports/cia.aspx?KeyID=L5018&Process=CP, accessed November 2005.

[a] Soft drink sales in Asia Pacific; Africa, India, and Middle East; and Central and Other divisions are not reported separately from confectionary sales in those regions.
[b] Consolidated figures include worldwide confectionary sales.

ENDNOTES

1. *Beverage Digest Fact Book 2005*, p. 14.
2. See Exhibit 1 and Exhibit 3 at the end of this case.
3. Roger Enrico, *The Other Guy Blinked and Other Dispatches from the Cola Wars* (Bantam Books, 1988).
4. Robert Tollison, et al., *Competition and Concentration* (Lexington Books, 1991), p. 11.
5. *Beverage Digest Fact Book 2005*, p. 45.
6. Unless otherwise noted, information on industry participants and structures comes from Michael E. Porter (with research associate Rebecca Wayland), "Coca-Cola versus Pepsi-Cola and the Soft Drink Industry," HBS Case No. 391-179 (Harvard Business School Publishing, 1994); Andrew J. Conway, et al., "Global Soft Drink Bottling Review and Outlook: Consolidating the Way to a Stronger Bottling Network" (analysts' report), Morgan Stanley Dean Witter, August 4, 1997; and from casewriter interviews with industry executives.
7. Casewriter conversation with industry insider, April 2006.
8. Ibid.
9. "Cott Begins Shipping from New Fort Worth, Texas Plant," Cott Corporation press release, July 13, 2005; casewriter conversation with industry analyst, November 2005.
10. "Louisiana Coca-Cola Reveals Crown Jewel," *Beverage Industry*, January 1999.
11. Casewriter conversation with industry insider, April 2006.
12. Bonnie Herzog and Daniel Bloomgarden, "Coca-Cola Enterprises" (analysts' report), Salomon Smith Barney, February 19, 2003, pp. 31–32; Bonnie Herzog and Daniel Bloomgarden, "Pepsi Bottling Group" (analysts' report), Salomon Smith Barney, February 24, 2003, pp. 26–27.
13. Timothy Muris, David Scheffman, and Pablo Spiller, *Strategy, Structure, and Antitrust in the Carbonated Soft Drink Industry* (Quorum Books, 1993), p. 63; *Beverage Digest Fact Book 2005*, p. 76.
14. Coca-Cola 2003 Annual Report.
15. Bonnie Herzog, "The Coca-Cola Company" (analyst's report), Credit Suisse First Boston, September 8, 2000, p. 16.
16. Dean Foust, with Geri Smith, "Coke: The Cost of Babying Bottlers," *BusinessWeek*, December 9, 2002, p. 93.
17. Herzog, "The Coca-Cola Company," p. 16.
18. *Beverage Digest Fact Book 2005*, p. 43.
19. Ibid, p. 20.
20. Ibid.
21. Nikhil Deogun and Richard Gibson, "Coke Beats Out Pepsi for Contracts with Burger King, Domino's," *The Wall Street Journal*, April 15, 1999.
22. Casewriter conversation with industry observer, December 2005.
23. "History" section of entry for PepsiCo, Hoover's Online, http://www.hoovers.com, accessed December 2005; *Beverage Digest Fact Book 2005*, p. 62.
24. *Beverage Digest Fact Book 2005*, pp. 62–63.
25. Ibid, p. 63.
26. Casewriter examination of ingredients lists for Coke Classic and Pepsi-Cola, November 2005.
27. Casewriter conversation with industry analyst, January 2006.
28. *Beverage Digest Fact Book 2005*, p. 71.
29. Ibid, p. 74.
30. Unless otherwise attributed, all historical information in this section comes from J.C. Louis and Harvey Yazijian, *The Cola Wars* (Everest House, 1980); Mark Pendergrast, *For God, Country, and Coca-Cola* (Charles Scribner's, 1993); and David Greising, *I'd Like the World to Buy a Coke* (John Wiley & Sons, 1997).
31. Louis and Yazijian, *The Cola Wars*, p. 23.
32. David B. Yoffie, *Judo Strategy* (Harvard Business School Press, 2001), Chapter 1.
33. Pendergrast, *For God, Country, and Coca-Cola*, p. 310.

34. Ibid, p. 323.
35. Timothy K. Smith and Laura Landro, "Coke's Future: Profoundly Changed, Coca-Cola Co. Strives to Keep on Bubbling," *The Wall Street Journal*, April 24, 1986.
36. Timothy Muris, et al., *Strategy, Structure, and Antitrust in the Carbonated Soft Drink Industry*, p. 73.
37. Greising, *I'd Like the World to Buy a Coke*, p. 88.
38. Ibid, p. 292.
39. *Beverage Industry*, January 1999, p. 17.
40. Albert Meyer and Dwight Owsen, "Coca-Cola's Accounting," *Accounting Today*, September 28, 1998; Herzog and Bloomgarden, "Coca-Cola Enterprises," p. 22; Dean Foust, with Nanette Byrnes, "Gone Flat," *BusinessWeek*, December 20, 2004, p. 76.
41. *Beverage Digest Fact Book 2005*, p. 77.
42. Ibid.
43. Ibid, p. 38.
44. Ibid, pp. 90, 93; *Beverage Digest Fact Book 2001*, pp. 77, 80.
45. Foust, with Byrnes, "Gone Flat." On Coca-Cola, see also Andrew Ward, "Coke Gets Real," *Financial Times*, September 25, 2005, p. 17; Michael Santoli, "A New Formula for Coke: How to Put the Fizz Back in the World's Most Famous Brand," *Barron's*, October 4, 2004, p. 21; Betsy Morris, "The Real Story: How Did Coca-Cola's Management Go from First-Rate to Farcical in Six Short Years?" *Fortune*, May 31, 2004, p. 84; Chad Terhune and Betsy McKay, "Bottled Up: Behind Coke's Travails," *The Wall Street Journal*, May 4, 2004, p. A1; Julie Creswell and Julie Schlosser, "Has Coke Lost Its Fizz?" *Fortune*, November 10, 2003, p. 215.
46. Jeremy Grant and Andrew Ward, "A Better Model? Diversified Pepsi Steals Some of Coke's Sparkle," *Financial Times*, February 28, 2005, p. 19. On PepsiCo, see also Patricia Sellers, "The Brand King's Challenge," *Fortune*, April 5, 2004, p. 192; Bethany McLean, "Guess Who's Winning the Cola Wars," *Fortune*, April 2, 2001, p. 164; John A. Byrne, "PepsiCo's New Formula," *BusinessWeek*, April 17, 2000, p. 172.
47. Luisa Dillner, "Mass Hysteria Blamed in Coke Safety Scare," *Chicago Sun-Times*, July 7, 1999, p. 42; Bert Roughton Jr., "Food Scare Put Belgium on Edge," *Atlanta Journal-Constitution*, July 17, 1999, p. D1; "Coca-Cola Recalls Bottles of Drink Sold in Belgium," *The Wall Street Journal*, May 21, 2001, p. B11.
48. Claudia H. Deutsch, "Coca-Cola Reaches into Past for New Chief," *The New York Times*, May 5, 2004, p. 1.
49. Amy Waldman, "India Tries to Contain Tempest over Soft Drink Safety," *The New York Times*, August 23, 2003, p. 3; Terhune and McKay, "Bottled Up: Behind Coke's Travails."
50. Creswell and Schlosser, "Has Coke Lost Its Fizz?"; Betsy McKay and Chad Terhune, "Coca-Cola Settles Regulatory Probe," *The Wall Street Journal*, April 19, 2005, p. A3.
51. Foust, with Byrnes, "Gone Flat"; Morris, "The Real Story."
52. Theresa Howard, "Coke CEO Takes Open Approach to Problems," *USA Today*, September 29, 2004, p. B3.
53. Foust, with Byrnes, "Gone Flat."
54. Chad Terhune, "CEO Says Things Aren't Going Better with Coke," *The Wall Street Journal*, September 16, 2004, p. A1; Renee Pas, "The Top 100 Beverage Companies," *Beverage Industry*, June 1, 2005, p. 38
55. Barbara Murray, "PepsiCo, Inc.," Hoover's Online, http://www.hoovers.com, accessed November 2005; Nanette Byrnes, "The Power of Two at Pepsi," *BusinessWeek*, January 29, 2001, p. 102.
56. Theresa Howard, "Deal Puts Reinemund on the Fast Track," *USA Today*, December 5, 2000, p. B3.
57. Betsy McKay, "Pucker Up! Pepsi's Latest Weapon Is Lemon-Lime," *The Wall Street Journal*, October 2000, p. B1; Greg Winter, "PepsiCo Looks to a New Drink to Jolt Soda Sales," *The New York Times*, May 1, 2001, p. C1; McLean, "Guess Who's Winning the Cola Wars."
58. Grant and Ward, "A Better Model?"

59. "Historical Financials" section of entries for both Coca-Cola and PepsiCo, Hoover's Online, http://www.hoovers.com, accessed December 2005; Foust, with Byrnes, "Gone Flat"; Grant and Ward, "A Better Model?"

60. Sellers, "The Brand King's Challenge."

61. Foust, with Byrnes, "Gone Flat."

62. Caroline Wilbert, "Coke CEO Neville Isdell: Boss Confident About Strategy," *The Atlanta Journal-Constitution*, November 13, 2005, p. D1.

63. Chad Terhune, "In Switch, Pepsi Makes Diet Cola Its New Flagship," *The Wall Street Journal*, March 16, 2005, p. B1.

64. Rosie Mestel, "Soft Drink, Soda, Pop: Whatever You Call Them, These Sugar Drinks Are Getting Nutritional Heat," *The Evansville Courier*, September 26, 2005, p. D1; Scott Leith, "Obesity Weighs Heavily on Colas," *The Atlanta Journal-Constitution*, February 6, 2005, p. C1; Raja Mishra, "In Battle of Bulge, Soda Firms Defend Against Warning," *The Boston Globe*, November 28, 2004, p. A1.

65. Jeff Cioletti, "Weathering the Perfect Storm," *Beverage Aisle*, April 15, 2004, p. 23.

66. Melanie Warner, "Lines Are Drawn for Big Suit Over Sodas," *The New York Times*, December 7, 2005, p. C1.

67. Betsy McKay, "Soda Marketers Will Cut Back Sales to US Schools," *The Wall Street Journal*, August 17, 2005, p. B1.

68. Ward, "Coke Gets Real."

69. *Beverage Digest Fact Book 2005*, p. 51.

70. Stuart Elliott, "What's in a Name? Higher Sales, or That's the Hope of Some Soft Drink Makers Excising the Word 'Diet,'" *The New York Times*, December 20, 2004, p. C9; Scott Leith, "Refining Diet Drinks: Fewer Men Equate 'Low-Cal' with 'Girly,'" *The Atlanta Journal-Constitution*, February 16, 2005, p. C1.

71. *Beverage Digest Fact Book 2005*, p. 11; *Beverage Digest Fact Book 2001*, p. 11.

72. Herzog and Bloomgarden, "Coca-Cola Enterprises," pp. 36–37.

73. Grant and Ward, "A Better Model?"

74. Joanna Cosgrove, "The 2005 Soft Drink Report," *Beverage Industry*, March 2005, p. 22; Melanie Wells, "Pepsi's New Challenge," *Forbes*, January 10, 2003, p. 68; Grant and Ward, "A Better Model?"

75. *Beverage Digest Fact Book 2005*, pp. 104, 109, 184–195.

76. Scott Leith, "Coke Just So-So in Small Brands: Record Less Than Stellar in Noncarbonated Category," *The Atlanta Journal-Constitution*, June 13, 2004, p. G1.

77. Terhune and McKay, "Bottled Up: Behind Coke's Travails"; Leith, "Coke Just So-So in Small Brands"; Alan R. Elliott, "Energy Drinks Fuel Soda Field," *Investor's Business Daily*, May 23, 2005, p. A11.

78. Terhune, "CEO Says Things Aren't Going Better with Coke."

79. Grant and Ward, "A Better Model?"

80. *Beverage Digest Fact Book 2005*, pp. 116–118.

81. Ibid, p. 118; Chad Terhune, "Coke to Buy Danone's Stake in Bottled-Water Joint Venture," *The Wall Street Journal*, April 25, 2005, p. B4; Barbara Murray, "The Coca-Cola Company," Hoover's Online, http://www.hoovers.com, accessed November 2005.

82. Foust, with Byrnes, "Gone Flat"; Bonnie Herzog and Bloomgarden, "Pepsi Bottling Group," p. 23.

83. Santoli, "A New Formula for Coke."

84. Herzog and Bloomgarden, "Coca-Cola Enterprises," p. 17.

85. Casewriter conversation with industry insider, April 2006.

86. Scott Leith, "Coke, Bottler Work on Plan to Align Goals," *The Atlanta Journal-Constitution*, December 5, 2003, p. C1; Chad Terhune and Betsy McKay, "Coke Shelves Initiative of Ex-Chief," *The Wall Street Journal*, September 28, 2004, p. A3.

87. Chad Terhune, "Coke Bottler in Mexico Threatens to Cut Marketing," *The Wall Street Journal*, November 1, 2005, p. B5.

88. Herzog and Bloomgarden, "Pepsi Bottling Group," pp. 18, 20, 26.

89. *Beverage Digest Fact Book 2005*, pp. 66–68.

90. Herzog and Bloomgarden, "Pepsi Bottling Group," pp. 23–25.

91. Herzog and Bloomgarden, "Coca-Cola Enterprises," pp. 33–34; Richard Joy, "Foods and Nonalcoholic Beverages" (industry survey), Standard & Poor's, June 9, 2005, pp. 11–12.

92. Casewriter conversation with industry insider, April 2006.

93. Melanie Warner, "Making Room on Coke's Shelf Space," *The New York Times*, April 5, 2005, p. C1.

94. Chad Terhune, "Coke Readies New Ads to Boost Its Soda Sales," *The Wall Street Journal*, December 8, 2005, p. A3.

95. Scott Leith, "Designing the Next Big (or Small) Thing," *The Atlanta Journal-Constitution*, September 27, 2003, p. B1; "Fridge Packs Appear to Be Plus for Coke System," *Beverage Digest*, March 28, 2003, http://www.beverage-digest.com/editorial/030328.php, accessed December 2005.

96. "CSDs Have Most—and Proliferating—SKU's, but Number Is Small Relative to Volume," *Beverage Digest*, November 22, 2002, http://www.beverage-digest.com/editorial/021122.php, accessed December 2005; casewriter communication with industry analyst, November 2005.

97. Casewriter conversation with industry insider, April 2006.

98. Ward, "Coke Gets Real"; casewriter communication with industry analyst, November 2005.

99. Ward, "Coke Gets Real."

100. Sherri Day, "Summer May Bring a Bottled Water Price War," *The New York Times*, May 10, 2003, p. C1.

101. Betsy McKay, "Liquid Assets: In a Water Fight, Coke and Pepsi Try Opposite Tacks," *The Wall Street Journal*, April 18, 2002, p. A1.

102. Casewriter conversation with industry insider, April 2006.

103. "Water: Supermarkets Account for 50+% of Volume, Morgan Stanley Study Finds Low Brand Loyalty," *Beverage Digest*, June 7, 2002, http://www.beverage-digest.com/editorial/020607.php, accessed December 2005.

104. *Beverage Digest Fact Book 2005*, pp. 90–91.

105. Ibid, pp. 92–93.

106. John Huey, "The World's Best Brand," *Fortune*, May 31, 1993.

107. Paul Klebnikov, "Coke's Sinful World," *Forbes*, December 22, 2003, p. 86.

108. Ward, "Coke Gets Real."

109. *Beverage Digest Fact Book 2005*, p. 90.

110. Nikhil Deogun, "Burst Bubbles: Aggressive Push Abroad Dilutes Coke's Strength As Big Markets Stumble," *The Wall Street Journal*, February 8, 1999, p. A1.

111. Grant and Ward, "A Better Model?"

112. PepsiCo 2004 Annual Report, p. 60.

113. *Beverage Digest Fact Book 2005*, p. 90.

114. James Kanter, "European Court Sides with Coke Against Germany," *The Wall Street Journal*, December 15, 2004, p. 18.

115. Klebnikov, "Coke's Sinful World."

116. David Luhnow and Chad Terhune, "Latin Pop: A Low-Budget Cola Shakes Up Markets South of the Border," *The Wall Street Journal*, October 27, 2003, p. A1.

117. June Preston, "Things May Go Better for Coke amid Asia Crisis, Singapore Bottler Says," *Journal of Commerce*, June 29, 1998, p. A3.

118. Creswell and Schlosser, "Has Coke Lost Its Fizz?"; Ward, "Coke Gets Real."

119. Caroline Wilbert and Shelley Emling, "Obesity Weighs on Coke," *Atlanta Journal-Constitution*, October 27, 2005, p. A1.

120. Leslie Chang, Chad Terhune, and Betsy McKay, "As Global Growth Ebbs, Coke Makes Rural Push into China and India," *The Asian Wall Street Journal*, August 11, 2004, p. A1.

121. Betsy McKay, "Juiced Up: Pepsi Edges Past Coke, and It Has Nothing to Do with Cola," *The Wall Street Journal*, November 6, 2000, p. A1.

Staples

This case was prepared by Charles W. L. Hill, the University of Washington

It was 1985, and a thirty-six-year-old retailer named Tom Stemberg was being interviewed by the CEO of the Dutch-based warehouse club, Makro, for the top job at Makro's nascent U.S. operation. Stemberg didn't think Makro's concept would work in the United States, but he was struck by one thing as he toured Makro's first U.S. store in Langhorne, Pennsylvania: Office supplies were flying off the shelves. "It was obvious that this merchandise was moving very fast," he later recalled, "That aisle (where the office supplies were located) was just devastated."[1] Stemberg began to wonder whether an office supplies supermarket would be a viable concept. He thought it might be possible that a supermarket selling just office supplies could do to the office supplies business what Toys "R" Us had done to the fragmented toy retailing industry: consolidate it and create enormous economic value in the process.

Within a year Stemberg had founded Staples, the first office supplies supermarket. Twenty years later, Staples was a leading retailer in the office supplies business with 1,800 stores in the United States and Canada, and another 250 in Europe. Its revenues for 2006 were forecast to exceeded $17.8 billion, net profit was over $950 million, the company had earned a return on invested capital of between 12.6% and 18.5% for the last six years (which is considered high for retailing), and the company generated $2 billion in free cash flow during the prior three years.[2]

The Founding of Staples

Tom Stemberg

Despite his young age, by 1985 Stemberg had assembled an impressive resume in retailing. Stemberg had been born in Los Angeles but spent much of his teens in Austria, where his parents were originally from. He moved back to the United States to enter Harvard University, ultimately graduating with an MBA from Harvard Business School in 1973. Stemberg was hired out of Harvard by the Jewel Corp., which put him to work at Star Market, the company's supermarket grocery division in the Boston area.

Henry Nasella, Stemberg's first boss at Jewel, who would later work for Stemberg at Staples, remembers meeting Stemberg on his first day at Jewel: "He came in 15 minutes late, his hair too long, his tie over his shoulder, his shirt hanging out over the back of his pants. I thought, what in the world do I have here?"[3] (Stemberg is still known for his disheveled appearance.) What he had was a man who started out on the store floor, bagging groceries, stocking the aisle, and ringing up sales at the checkout counter. Stemberg rose rapidly, however, and by the time he was twenty-eight he had been named vice president of sales and marketing at Star Market, the youngest VP in the history of the Jewel Corp.

At Jewel, Stemberg became known as an aggressive marketer, competing vigorously on price and introducing generic brands (Stemberg developed and launched the first line of "generic" foods sold in the country).[4] According to Stemberg, "It was a nutso thing we were trying to do, and the fact that it worked out well was a miracle. We opened all these big stores, and we were trying to take market share away from people who were much better financed than we were. They retaliated and lowered prices. . . . I learnt to experience the challenges of rapid growth. There was no better experience to have been through. It taught me the necessity of having infrastructure and putting it in place."[5]

One of the supermarkets that Stemberg found himself battling with was Heartland Food Warehouse, the first successful deep discount warehouse supermarket in the country. Heartland was run by Leo Kahn, one of the country's leading supermarket retailers. Kahn had started the Purity Supreme supermarket chain in the late 1940s, making him one of the founding fathers of the supermarket business. Stemberg and Kahn fought relentless marketing battles with each other. In a typical example of their tussles, at one point Kahn ran ads guaranteeing that his customers would get the best price on Thanksgiving turkeys. Stemberg responded with his own ads promising that Star would match the lowest advertised price on turkeys. Technically that made Kahn's claim incorrect, a point that Stemberg made to the Massachusetts attorney general's office, which told Kahn to pull his ad.

In 1982 Stemberg left Jewel to run the grocery division of another retailer, First National Supermarkets Inc. To build market share, he decided to take the company into the warehouse food business, imitating Leo Kahn's Heartland chain. Stemberg soon came into conflict with the CEO at First National. As he later admitted, "I probably didn't do a very good job, in a corporate political sense, of making sure he understood the risks in what we were trying to do. The situation was very stressful."[6] In January 1985, things came to a head and Stemberg was fired. It was probably the best thing that ever happened to him.

When Kahn heard that Stemberg had been fired, he quickly got in touch with him. Kahn had just sold his own business for $80 million, and he was looking for investment opportunities. He had developed a great respect for his old adversary, and wanted to back him in a new retailing venture. As Stemberg paraphrases it, Kahn said, "I want to back you in a business, kid, what have you got in mind?"[7] Kahn agreed to put up $500,000 in seed money to help Stemberg develop a new venture opportunity. He also took on the role of mentor, evaluating Stemberg's ideas.

Initially Kahn and Stemberg looked at the business they both knew best, supermarket grocery retailing. But they were put off by the intense competition now raging in the business, and the high price they would have to pay for properties. At this juncture, Bob Nakasone, then president of Toys "R" Us, stepped into the picture. Nakasone had worked at Jewel alongside Stemberg before moving to Toys "R" Us. It was Nakasone who urged Stemberg to "think outside of the food box." Nakasone told Stemberg that there were more similarities than differences across product categories, and that profit margins were much better outside of the grocery business.

While mulling over possible entrepreneurial opportunities, Stemberg continued to explore other options, including working for an established retailer. It was this parallel search that took him down to Makro for a job interview, and it was there that he suddenly realized there was a possible opportunity to be had in starting the Toys "R" Us of office supplies.

Stemberg's Insight

Hot on the heels of his trip to Makro, Stemberg started to think about his idea. The first thing was to get a handle on the nature of the market. Stemberg started by asking people if they knew how much they spent on office supplies. In his words: "There was this lawyer I knew in Hartford, which is where I lived then. If ever there was a cheap bastard in this world, he was a cheap bastard. And I said, 'Gee, how much do you spend on office supplies?' He said, "Oh, I don't know, I guess about a couple of hundred bucks a person, 40 people in the office, I bet you we spend ten grand.' I said, 'Do me a favor will you? You've got good records. Go through your records and tell me exactly how much you spend: he calls me up the next day.' 'Son of a bitch, I spend $1,000 apiece! But I'm getting a discount, I'm paying 10% of list.' I said, 'Toys "R" Us' is paying 60% of list.' He says, 'Are you kidding me? You mean I could save like half? I could save like twelve grand?' In his mind, this is the payment on his new Jaguar."[8]

Stemberg began to think that this idea had some potential. He reasoned that people want to save money, and in this case the money they could save might be substantial, but they didn't even know they were paying too much. Small businesses in particular, he thought, might be a viable target market. While working on the idea, the printer ribbon on Stemberg's printer ran out. It was a weekend. He drove down to the local office supply store in Hartford, and it was closed. He went to another, but that was also closed. He ended up going to BJ's Wholesale Club, a deep discount warehouse club. BJ's was open, they sold office supplies at low prices, but the selection was limited and they didn't carry the type of ribbon Stemberg wanted. Stemberg immediately saw the opportunity.

Around the same time, Stemberg went to see another mentor of his, Walter Salmon, who taught retailing at Harvard Business School. Over lunch they discussed the supermarket business and Stemberg's quest. Salmon asked Stemberg if he had thought of applying his retailing skills to a product category that was growing faster than the grocery business and was not well served by modern retailers. Stemberg replied that he had been thinking about office supplies. Salmon's response, "Gee, this is a really big idea."

Scoping Out the Opportunity

Stemberg ended up hiring a former teaching assistant of Salmon's for $20,000 to do some basic market research on the industry and validate the market. As he tells the story: "I never forget the night I went to her house and we went through the slide deck. I always want to jump ahead. And she puts her hand on my hand and says, 'Wait, we will walk though it.' She's teasing us! Finally she said it was a $45 billion market growing at 15% per year. And it turns out she was lying. That was actually at the manufacturer level. It was actually more than $100 billion already if you looked at retail. She confirmed that the pricing umbrellas were as big as we thought they were, and that small businesses were getting raped the way we had said they were. I was pretty damn excited during the long drive home."[9]

The market growth, it turned out, was being driven by some favorable demographic trends. The U.S. economy was recovering from the recessions of the late 1970s and early 1980s, and underlying economic growth was strong. A wave of new technology was finding its way into U.S. businesses, including personal computers, printers, faxes, and small copiers, and this was driving demand for office supplies including basic equipment along with consumables from paper and printer ink, to diskettes and copy toner.

The wave of downsizing that had swept corporate America in the early 1980s also had a beneficial side effect—unemployed people were starting their own businesses. The rate of new business formation was the highest in years. There were 11 million small businesses in the country, Stemberg's proposed target market, the vast majority of which had less than twenty employees. This sector was the engine of job growth in the economy—between 1980 and 1986 small enterprises had been responsible for a net increase of 10.5 million jobs. Many of these new jobs were in the service sector, which was a big consumer of office supplies. Each new white-collar job meant another $1,000 a year in office supplies.

Stemberg's research started to uncover an industry that was highly fragmented at the retail level, but had some huge participants. Upstream in the value chain were the manufacturers. This was a very diverse collection of companies that included paper manufacturers such as Boise Cascade; office furniture makers; manufacturers of pencils, pens, and markers such as the Bic Corp.; companies like 3M, which supplied Post-it Notes and a whole lot more besides; office equipment companies such as Xerox and Canon (manufacturers of copiers and consumables); and manufacturers of personal computers, printers, and faxes such as Apple, Compaq, and Hewlett-Packard.

Then there were the wholesalers, some of which were very large such as United Stationers and McKesson. The wholesalers bought in bulk and sold to business clients and smaller retail establishments, either directly or through a network of dealers. The dealers often visited businesses to collect orders and arranged for delivery. The dealers themselves ranged in scale from small one-person enterprises to large firms that sold through central warehouses. Some dealers also had a retail presence, while other did not. Manufacturers and wholesalers also sold directly to large business through catalogs or a direct sales presence.

The retailers fell into two main categories. There were the local office supply retailers, generally small business themselves, and there were the general merchandise discounters, such as BJ's Wholesale and Wal-Mart. The smaller retailers had an intrinsically high cost structure. They were full-service retailers who purchased in small lots and delivered in trucks or sold out of the store. The general merchandise discounters purchased from wholesalers or direct from manufacturers, and their prices were much lower, but they did not carry a wide range of product.

On the consumer side, most large businesses had dedicated personnel for purchasing office supplies. They either bought from dealers, who purchased directly from manufacturers or through wholesalers, or bought direct from the manufacturer themselves. Large firms were able to negotiate on price and received discounts that could be as large as 80% of the list price on some items. Businesses of fewer than one hundred people did not generally have someone dedicated to managing office supplies, and they tended to rely primarily on dealers. For these companies, product availability, not price, was viewed as key. In even smaller firms, it was the convenience of being able to get office supplies that seemed to matter more than anything else.

Consistent with his initial insight, Stemberg found that smaller firms were ignored by the big dealers. To verify this he called Boise Cascade, which operated as both a dealer and a manufacturer, to see what service they might offer. First he called on behalf of Ivy Satellite Network, a small company that Stemberg owned that broadcast events of Ivy League schools to alumni around the world. Boise couldn't even be bothered to send a catalog to this company. Then he called Boise back, this time representing the one-hundred-person office of a friend of his who was a food broker. This time Boise was happy to send a representative to the food broker. The representative offered the broker deep discounts. A Bic pen from Boise that cost Ivy $3.68 from the local stationary store was offered for just $0.85. More generally, Stemberg found that while an office manager in a company with more than one thousand employees could often obtain discounts averaging 50% from dealers, small businesses with fewer than twenty employees were lucky to get a 10% discount, and often had to pay full price.[10]

Stemberg also found a study produced by researchers at the Wharton School that seemed to confirm his suspicions. "Essentially they first asked dealers, 'What does the customer want?' Ninety percent of the dealers said, 'Better service' and 10% said, 'Other.' Then they asked customers, and 90% of the customers said what they really wanted was lower prices. Ha! The dealers were totally out of touch. They were making 40% to 50%, the wholesalers were making 30%, and the manufacturers were making huge margins. Everybody's rich, fat, and happy, and they're all going, 'What's wrong with this?'"[11]

Creating the Company

Stemberg know from experience that for Staples to succeed it would have to execute well, and do to that, it needed experienced management. Stemberg turned to people he knew, managers who, like him, had risen quickly through the ranks at the Jewel Corp. or other Boston area retailers. From Jewel came Myra Hart,

who was to become Staples's group vice president for growth and development; Todd Krasnow, who became vice president for marketing; Paul Korian, the Staples vice president of merchandising; and Henry Nasella, Stemberg's mentor at Star Market who subsequently became president of Staples. The CFO was Bob Leombruno, who had bought Mammoth Mart, a failed retail operation, out of bankruptcy for a group of investors. Stemberg took on the CEO role, while Kahn became chairman. Most of these people started working full time on January 1, 1986. They gave up secure jobs, high salaries, and annual bonuses for salary cuts, loss of bonuses, and fourteen-hour days.

According to Stemberg, the pitch to prospective managers was this: "I'm going to give you a big chunk of stock in this thing. This is your chance. We're all going to work our tails off. We're going to work crazy hours. But here you'll be part of a retailing revolution. If you own 2% of the company and it gets to be worth $100 million, you're going to make $2 million."[12] In the end, each member of the top management team got a 2.5% stake in the company.

By now Stemberg had a name for this nascent company, Staples. Reflecting on how it came about years later, he noted that "I'm driving between Hartford and Boston. I'm thinking about names. Pencils? Pens? 8½ by 11? Staples? Staples! Staples the Office Superstore. That was it. The bad thing about the name was that when we started out, we had to explain to everybody what it was. Office Depot basically copied Home Depot and put the 'office' in front. It was Home Depot for the office, and it lived off the Home Depot name. Office Club was a Price Club for the office. It lived off the Price Club name. In the early days ours was actually a problem. But those other names aren't a brand. Ours is a brand."[13]

With the management team in place, the next steps were to refine the concept and raise capital. The concept itself was relatively straightforward; implementing it would not be. The plan was to offer a wide selection of merchandise in a warehouse-type setting with prices deeply discounted from those found in mom-and-pop retailers. Because it was to be a supermarket, the idea was to move from full service to a self-service format. At the same time, the management team recognized the staff would need to be trained in office supplies so that they could provide advice when asked.

To make the concept viable, a number of issues had to be dealt with. They had to decide where to locate the stores. How big a population base would be needed to support a store? What kind of selection was required? How many Stock Keeping Units (SKUs) should the store offer? There was the problem of educating customers. If potential customers currently didn't know that they were paying excessive prices for office supplies and consistently underestimated how much they spent on the category, what could Staples do to change this?

To get low prices, Staples would need to cut costs to the bone and be managed very efficiently. They would have to get manufacturers or wholesalers to deliver directly to Staples. How could this be done? Wouldn't wholesalers and manufacturers create channel conflict with dealers and established retailers by delivering straight to Staples? How was this to be resolved? Staples also needed to minimize its inventory, thereby reducing its working capital needs. Management knew that if they could turn inventory over twelve times a year and delay payment to vendors for thirty days, then vendors would essentially finance Staples's inventory. Pulling that off would require state-of-the-art information systems, and the state of the art at the time in office supplies did not include bar coding on individual items. How was Staples to deal with this?

There was also the potential competition to worry about. Stemberg was sure that once Staples unveiled its concept, others would follow quickly. To preempt competitors, the plan called for rapid rollout of the concept, with sales ramping up from nothing to $42 million after three years. This would require a lot of capital. It also required that the concept be very easy to replicate so that once the first store was opened, others could be opened in quick succession. This meant that the systems that were put in place for the first store had to be the right ones and able to support rapid expansion. There wasn't much room for error here.

As the management team refined the concept, they came to the realization that the information systems were one of the keys to the entire venture. With the right information systems in place, Staples could track sales and inventory closely at the level of individual items, figure out its gross profit on each item sold, and adjust its merchandising mix accordingly. This would be a departure from existing retailers, the majority of whom lacked the ability to calculate profit on each item sold and could calculate only the average gross profit across a range of items. The right information systems could also be used to collect data on customers at the point of sales, and this would assist greatly in market research and direct marketing to customers.

On the other hand, raising capital proved to be easier than they thought. Stemberg valued Staples, which was still little more than a concept, a management team, and a business plan full of unanswered questions at $8 million. He went looking for $4 million, which he would exchange for 50% of the company. The venture capitalists were initially reluctant. They seemed to hold back, waiting to see who would commit first. They valued Staples at $6 million and wanted a 67% stake for the $4 million in first-round financing. Stemberg balked at that and instead focused his efforts on one firm that seemed more willing to break away from the pack. The firm was Bain Venture Capital, whose managing general partner, Mitt Romney, later observed that "a lot of retailing startups come by, but a lot of them are a twist on an old theme, or a better presentation. . . . Stemberg wasn't proposing just a chain of stores, but an entirely new retailing category. That really captures your attention. It slaps you in the face with the idea that this could be big."[14]

To validate the business concept, Romney's firm surveyed one hundred small businesses after being urged to do so by Stemberg. Auditing invoices from these companies for office supplies, Romney discovered what Stemberg already knew—the companies were spending about twice what they estimated. Romney then ran the numbers on his own company and found that his firm would save $117,000 a year by purchasing supplies at the discount that Stemberg promised. That was enough for Romney, and he committed to investing. Others followed, and Staples raised $4.5 million in its first round of financing, which closed on January 23, 1986. This gave the company enough capital to go ahead with the first store. In return for the financing, Staples had to give the VCs a 54% stake in the company. To get the money, however, Staples had to commit to opening its first store on May 1, 1986, and to meet a plan for rolling out additional stores as quickly as possible.

The First Store

With just four months to open their first store, the management team went into overdrive. They would meet every morning at about 7 A.M. in a session that could run from thirty minutes to two hours. Someone would rush out to get sandwiches for lunch, and they would keep working. The workday came to a close at 9:00 P.M. or 10:00 P.M. Not only was there no template for what they were doing, they knew they had to put a system in place that would allow them to quickly roll out additional stores.

One of the most difficult tasks fell on the shoulders of Leombruno, the CFO. In addition to setting up an accounting system, he was put in charge of installing the entire information system for Staples. The system had to be able to track customer purchases so that Staples could reorder products. The cash registers, which were to be connected individually to the system, had to be easy to operate so that there would be no congestion at the checkout stands. Stemberg himself was adamant that the register receipts indicate the list price of each item, as well as a much lower Staples price, and an even lower price for customers who became Staples members. He also wanted the system to collect detailed demographics on each customer.

Leombruno insisted that the system be able to do two things: first, calculate the gross profit margin Staples made on each item sold. Most retailers at the time could calculate only the average profit margin across the mix of inventory. Second, Leombruno wanted to make sure that inventory turned over at least twelve times a year, and good information systems were the key to that. With most vendors requiring payment in thirty days, an inventory turnover of greater than twelve would allow Staples to cut its working capital requirements.

As the wish list for the information systems grew, it soon became apparent that it would not be possible to do everything in the allotted time span. No existing software package did what the management team wanted, and they had to hire consultants to customize existing packages. In the end, several proposed features were dropped. However, at Stemberg's insistence, the three-way price requirements remained. To track sales and inventory levels, Staples assigned a six-digit look-up code for each item. While entering the codes was a slower process than scanning items, most manufacturers in the office supplies business were still not marking their products with bar codes, which meant scanning was not feasible.

Another problem was to get suppliers to ship products to the first Staples store. The company was asking suppliers to bypass the existing distribution system and risk alienating long-time customers in the established channel of distribution. To get suppliers on board, Staples used a number of tactics. One was a visionary pitch. The company told suppliers that it was out to revolutionize the retail end of the industry. Staples would be very big, they said, and it was in the best interests of the suppliers to back the start-up. Stemberg's punch line was simple: "I'm going to be very loyal to those who stick their necks out for us. But it's going to cost you a lot more to get in later."[15] Connections also helped to get suppliers to deliver to Staples. One of the VC backers of Staples, Bessemer Venture Partners, also owned a paper manufacturer, Ampad. Bessemer told Ampad to start selling to Staples, which it did, even though existing distributors complained bitterly about the arrangement.

Finding real estate also presented a problem. As an enterprise with no proven track record, Staples found it difficult to rent decent real estate large enough to stock and display the 5,000 SKUs that it was planning for its first store, and to do so at a decent price. Most landlords wanted sky-high rent from Staples. In the end, the best that Staples could do was a site in Brighton, Massachusetts, that was within site of a housing project and had failed as a site for several different retailers. The one redeeming feature of the site was that it was smack in the middle of a high concentration of small businesses.

Despite all of the problems, Staples was able to open its first store on May 1, 1986. The opening day was busy, but only because everybody who worked at Staples had invited everybody they knew. On the second day, just sixteen people came through the store. On the third day, it was the same number. A few weeks of this, and Staples would have to shut its doors. Desperate, Krasnow decided to bribe customers to get them into the store. The company sent $25 to each of thirty-five office managers, inviting them to shop in the store and pass along their reactions. According to Krasnow, "A week later we called them back. They had all taken the money, but none of them had come into the store. I was apoplectic."[16] In the end, nine of them finally came in, and they gave Staples rave reviews. Slowly the momentum started to build, and by August lines were starting to form at the cash registers at lunch time.

The 1990s: Growth, Competition, and Consolidation

Growth

Staples had set of target of $4 million in first year sales from its Brighton store, but within a few months the numbers were tracking up toward a $6 million annual run rate. The concept was starting to work. The number of customers coming through the door every month was growing, but it was not only customers who were coming. One day Joe Antonini, the CEO of Kmart, was spotted walking around the Staples store. Around the same time, Stemberg heard from contacts that Staples had been mentioned at a Wal-Mart board meeting. He realized that if other discount retailers were noticing Staples when it had just one store, competition could not be far behind.

Within five months of the opening of the first Staples store, a clone had appeared in the Southeast: Office Depot. Needing money fast to fund expansion and lock in Staples territory, Stemberg went back to the venture capitalists. While the initial backers were willing to value Staples at only $15 million, Stemberg held out for and got a valuation of $22 million, raising another $14 million. He pulled off this trick by finding institutional investors who were willing to invest on a valuation of $22 million. He then went back to the original VCs and told them that the deal was closing fast, which persuaded them to commit.

By May 1987, Staples had three stores open and planed to increase the number to twenty by the end of 1988 (it actually opened twenty-two). Sales were running at anywhere from $300 to $800 per square foot. In contrast, high-volume discount stores were lucky to get $300 per square foot. By mid-1989, three years after its first store opened, Staples had twenty-seven stores open in the Northeast and an annual sales run rate of $120 million, way above the original three-year target of $42 million. The stores now averaged 15,000 square feet and stocked 5,000 items.

Explaining the success, Stemberg noted: "From a value perspective, I think there is no question that we have been a friend to the entrepreneur. If you look at the average small town merchant, we've lowered the costs of his office products—where he was once paying say $4,000 to $5,000 a year, now he's paying $2,000 or $3,000. We've made him more efficient."[17]

Helping to drive sales growth was the development of a direct marketing pitch. Every time Staples opened a store, it purchased a list of small businesses within fifteen minutes' driving distance. Then a group of telemarketers would go to work, calling up the buyer of office supplies at the businesses. The telemarketers would tell them Staples was opening up a store like Toys "R" Us for office supplies, ask them how much they spent on office supplies every year (often they did not know), cite typical cost savings at small businesses, and send them a coupon for a free item such as copy paper. Slowly at first the customers would come in, but momentum would build up as customers realized the scale of the savings they were getting.

Every time a customer redeemed a coupon at a store, they were given a free Staples Card. This "membership" card entitled cardholders to even deeper discounts on select items. The card quickly became the lynchpin of Staples's direct marketing effort. From the card application, Staples gathered information about the customer—what type of business it was in, how many employees it had, where it was located. This information was entered into a customer database, and every time a card member used that card, the card number and purchases were logged into the database via the cash register. This gave Staples up-to-date information about what was being purchased and by whom. This information then allowed Staples to target promotions at certain customer groups—for example, card members who were not making purchases. The goal was to get existing customers to spend more at Staples, a goal that over time was attained.

Because Staples started to reach so many of its customers through direct marketing, (about 80% of its sales were made to cardholders) it was able to spend less on media ads—in some areas, it dropped media advertising altogether, saving on costs. This was an important source of cost savings in the Northeast where the media is expensive.

A problem that continued to bedevil Staples as it expanded was the shortage of good real estate locations that could be rented at a reasonable price, particularly in the Northeast. Finding a good site in the early days required flexibility; at various times Staples converted anything and everything, from restaurants to massage parlors, into Staples stores. As the company grew, its real estate strategy started to take a defensive aspect, with Staples bidding for prime sites in order to preempt competitors.

The high cost of real estate in the Northeast led Staples to establish its first distribution center in 1987 (today it has some thirty such centers in North America). This decision was hotly debated within the company and opposed by some of the investors who thought that the capital should be used to build more stores, but Stemberg prevailed. The distribution center was located off an interstate highway in an area of rural Connecticut where land was cheap. The facility cost $6 million to build and tied up a total of $10 million in working capital, almost $0.29 out of every dollar that the company had raised to that point. But Stemberg saw this as a necessary step. The inventory storage capacity at the distribution center enabled the company to operate with smaller stores than many of its rivals, but still offer the same variety of goods. By 1989 the average Staples store was 35% smaller than the Office Depot outlets that were then opening up all over the Southeast, saving on real estate costs. The distribution center also helped save labor costs since wages are lower in rural areas. Equally important, inventory storage at the distribution centers allowed the stores to remain fully stocked. As Stemberg noted: "In competition with the clones, it will come down to who has the lowest costs and the best in stock position."[18]

The expansion strategy at Staples was very methodical. Stores were clustered together in a region, even to the extent that they cannibalized each other on the margin, so that Staples could become the dominant supplier in that market. The early focus was on major metropolitan areas such as Boston, New York, Philadelphia, and Los Angeles. Although high real estate and labor costs in these areas were a disadvantage, strong demand from local businesses helped compensate, as did the distribution centers. In 1990, Staples opened its second distribution center in California to support expansion there.

The expansion at Staples was fueled by the proceeds from a 1989 initial public offering, which raised $61.7 million of capital—enough for Staples to accelerate its store openings. By mid-1991, Staples's store count passed over one hundred.

Competition

A rash of imitators to Staples soon appeared on the market. The first of these was Office Depot, focused on the Southeast. By the end of 1988, Office Depot had twenty-six stores, Office Club had opened fifteen, Biz Mart had established ten, and Office Max around a dozen. More than a dozen other office supplies superstores had sprung up. Some of these businesses were financed by venture capitalists looking to repeat the success with Staples; other were financed by established retailers, or even started by them. For example, Ben Franklin started Office Station in 1987, but shut it down in 1989 as it failed to gain traction.

Initially, most of the competitors focused in unique regions—Office Depot on the Southeast, Office Club on California, Office Max on the Midwest,

BizMart on the Southwest—but as the number of entrants increased, head-to-head competition started to become more frequent. Stemberg's belief had always been that competition was inevitable and that the winners in the competitive race would not necessarily be those that grew the fastest, but those that executed best. It was this philosophy that underpinned Stemberg's insistence that the company should grow by focusing on key urban areas and achieving a critical mass of stores served by a central distribution system.

Not everyone agreed with this recipe for success. Office Depot did the opposite—the company grew as fast as possible, entering towns quickly to preempt competitors. Office Depot lacked the centralized distribution systems, but made up for that by locating in less expensive areas than Staples, persuading suppliers to ship directly to stores and keeping more backup inventory on the premises. Although this meant larger stores, the lower rental costs in Office Depot's markets offset this.

What soon became apparent was that the rash of entrants included a number of companies that simply could not execute. Very quickly a handful of competitors emerged in the forefront of the industry—Staples, Office Depot, Office Max, and Office Club. As the market leaders grew, they increasingly came into contact with each other. The result was price wars. These first broke out in California. Staples entered the market in 1990 and initially focused on pricing not against Office Club, but against Price Club. Although Price Club was a warehouse store selling food and general merchandise, it still had the largest share of the office supplies market in California. Staples positioned itself as having the same low prices as Price Club, but a wider selection of office supplies and no membership fee.

Todd Krasnow, the executive VP of marketing at Staples, describes what happened next: "What we failed to realize was that Price Club was very worried about Office Club—and was pricing against Office Club. So when we went and matched Price Club, we were matching Office Club. And Office Club was saying: 'We are not going to let anybody have the same prices as us.'"[19] Office Club lowered its prices, causing Price Club to lower prices, and Staples followed. Not willing to be beat, Office Club cut prices again, and so they continued the spiral down. The price war drove profit margins down by as much as 8%.

Ultimately, Krasnow noted, "We realized that by engaging in this price war, we were focusing on our competitors, not our customers. Our customers weren't paying attention to this spat. So we raised our prices a little. You feel like you're just doing absolutely the wrong thing, because your whole position is: We have the lowest price."[20] Be that as it may, Office Club and Price Club followed suit, and prices started to rise again. Ultimately the three companies carved out different prices niches, each unwilling to be undercut on about twenty or so top-selling items, but in general, they were not the same items.

What happened in California also occurred elsewhere. When Office Max entered the Boston market in 1992, for example, a price war broke out again. There was an unanticipated effect this time, though— the price cuts apparently broadened the market by making buying from Staples attractive to customers with between twenty-five and one hundred employees, who previously bought directly from mail-order and retail stationers.[21]

Ultimately, Kransow noted, price wars such as those that started to break out in California and Boston started to moderate. "We finally realized that it's not in any company's self-interest to have a price war because you can get lots of market share without having a price war. And having a price war among low priced competitors doesn't get you more market share. It doesn't serve any purpose."[22] Other factors that may have contributed toward more rational pricing behavior in the market were the strong economy of the 1990s and industry consolidation.

Industry Consolidation

At its peak in 1991, there were twenty-five chains in the office supply industry.[23] Industry consolidation started when some of the clones began to fall by the wayside, filing for bankruptcy. U.S. Office Supply, itself the result of a merger between two office supplies chains, filed for bankruptcy in 1991, as did Office Stop. Consolidation was also hastened by acquisitions. In 1991, Office Depot acquired Office Club, giving the primary rival of Staples more than twice the number of stores. For its part, Staples acquired HQ Office Supplies Warehouse in 1991, and in 1992, it purchased another smaller chain, Workplace.[24]

As these trends continued, by the mid-1990s it was apparent that three players were rising to dominance in the industry: Office Depot, Staples, and Office Max. By mid-1996, Office Depot led the industry with 539 stores, followed by Staples with 517, and Office Max with around 500 stores. In terms of revenues, Office Depot had a clear lead with $5.3 billion in 1996, Staples was second with $3.07 billion, and Office Max third with $2.6 billion. Staples remained concentrated in the Northeast and California, with a large number of stores in dense urban areas. Office Depot's stores were concentrated in the South, and the company continued to stay clear of congested cities. Office Max was still strongest in the Midwest.[25]

The consolidation phase peaked in September 1996 when Staples announced an agreement to purchase its larger rival, Office Depot, for $3.36 billion. The executives of the two companies had apparently been talking about merger possibilities for years, while continuing to pursue their own independent growth strategies. If the merger went through, Tom Stemberg would step into the CEO role. The two companies sold the merger to the investment community of the basis of cost savings. The combined firm would have almost 1,100 stores and revenues of $8.5 billion. The combination, Stemberg argued, would attain terrific economies of scale that would allow it to significantly lower costs, saving an estimated $4.9 billion over five years, including $2.2 billion in product cost savings.

In a move to preempt a possible investigation by the Federal Trade Commission (FTC), the companies claimed that since their stores focused on different territories, the combination would not reduce competition. They also noted that Staples still faced intense competition not only from Office Max, but also from the likes of Wal-Mart, Circuit City, and mail-order outlets. Indeed, Stemberg claimed that the combined company would still account for only 5% of the total sales of office supplies in the United States.[26]

The FTC didn't buy the arguments, quickly started an investigation, and, in May 1997, sought an injunction to block the deal. The FTC claimed that the deal would stifle competition and raise prices for office supplies, especially in those markets where the two firms competed head to head. To buttress its case, the FTC released a report of pricing data that showed that nondurable office supplies such as paper were 10% to 15% higher in markets where Staples faced no direct rivals. Staples claimed that the FTC's pricing surveys were done selectively and were biased.

In July 1997, a federal judge granted the FTC's request for an injunction to halt the merger. Staples realized that it was in a losing fight and pulled its bid for Office Depot. But the failure had a silver lining— not anticipating much interference from the FTC,

Office Depot had put most of its expansion plans on hold, opening just two stores in eight months. In comparison, Staples opened forty-three, allowing the company to close the gap between itself and its larger rival.

Staples's Evolving Strategy

Moving into Small Towns

Stemberg has described Staples initial strategy to deal with the high costs of doing business in the Northeast as follows: "Establish superstores that were smaller than most, save on rent and operating costs, cluster them in densely populated areas to justify paying for expensive advertisements, and stock the stores from a distribution center."[27] The drawback with this strategy, in retrospect, was that Staples ignored a lot of potentially lucrative markets in smaller towns. While Office Depot was barnstorming into towns with populations of just 75,000, Staples could not see how they made it pay. Surely towns of that size were just too small to support an office supplies superstore?

As it turned out, they were not. The mistake Staples made was to assume that a store would serve customers within a ten- to fifteen-minute drive. But in smaller cities, customers would drive much further to get good prices. The revelation did not hit home until Staples opened its first store in Portland, Maine. With a population of 200,000, the town was smaller than most areas focused on by Staples, but within a few months the store was doing very well. To test the hypothesis, in 1992 and 1993 Staples opened stores in a number of smaller towns. The results were surprising. Many of the stores actually generated higher sales per square foot that those located in large cities. Sales were helped by the fact that in many of these small towns the only competitors were small mom-and-pop stationers, and that many small towns also lacked supermarket electronic retailers, such as Circuit City, selling low-priced office equipment, allowing Staples to pick up a much larger share of that business. Moreover, the lower rent, labor costs, advertising costs, and shrinkage made these stores significantly more profitable.

From that point on, Staples moved into small towns and suburban locations, where the same economics apply. Stemberg has described not moving into small towns earlier as "one of the dumbest mistakes I made." In 1994, some 10% of Staples stores were in small towns; by 1998, that figure had risen to 28%, and some of the most profitable stores in the Staples network were located in small towns.[28]

Selling Direct

Established as a retailer, Staples initially turned its back on customer requests for delivery and mail- or telephone-order service. The reason for doing this was simple; Staples saw itself as a low-cost retailer, and a delivery service would probably raise costs. However, Staples's competitors started to offer mail-order and delivery service, and customers continued to ask for the service, so in 1988 Staples began to experiment with this.

Initially the experimentation was halfhearted. Store managers were not enthusiastic about supporting a delivery service that they believed decreased store sales, and Staples discouraged delivery by tacking a 5% delivery charge onto the order price. Moreover, the company questioned whether it could generate the volume of business to cover the costs of a delivery service and make a decent return on capital.

What changed this was a study undertaken for Staples by a management consulting firm. The study found that the customers who purchased via a catalog and required delivery were not always the same ones who brought directly from the store. While there was a lot of cross shopping, the mail-order customers tended to be bigger and somewhat more interested in service, whereas those buying from the store were often buying for home offices. Staples also could not help but notice that its major rivals were offering a delivery service and that business seemed to be thriving.

In 1991, Staples set up an independent business unit within the company to handle the mail/telephone order and delivery service, known as Contract and Commercial. The guts of this business unit was a division know as Staples Direct (it is now called Staples Business Delivery). The man put in charge of this business, Ronald Sargent, would ultimately replace Stemberg as CEO of Staples in 2003.

One issue that had to be dealt with was the potential conflict between Staples Direct and the stores. The stores didn't want to push business the way of Staples Direct because they would not get credit for the sale. As Sargent commented later, "We were like the bad guys inside Staples, because the feeling was that if customers got products delivered they wouldn't shop inside our stores."[29] To align incentives, Staples changed the compensation systems so that (a) the store would get credit if a delivery order was placed through the store, and (b) the annual bonus of store employees was based partly on how well they met goals for generating delivery sales.

As Staples Direct started to grow, the company discovered that the delivery infrastructure it put in place could be used to serve clients in addition to the company's established small-business customers, which typically had less than fifty employees. Increasingly, medium-sized business (with fifty to one hundred employees), and larger businesses with more than one hundred employees started to utilize Staples Direct. To support this new business, Staples started to grow by acquisition, purchasing a number of regional stationary companies with established customers and delivery systems. Typically Staples kept the owners of these businesses on as Staples employees, often because they had long-established relationships with key accounts in large organizations such as Xerox, Ford, and PepsiCo. Staples, however, established a consistent product line, brand image, and computer and accounting systems across all of the acquisitions.

Between 1991 and 1996, Staples Direct grew from a $30 million business to an almost $1 billion one. As sales volume ramped up, so Staples was able to get greater efficiencies out of its distribution network, which helped to drive down the costs of doing business through this channel. Staples used a network of regional distribution centers to hold an inventory of some 15,000 SKUs for delivery, compared to 8,000 SKUs in a typical store. In 1998, a web-based element was added to Staples Direct, Staples.com. Through the Web or catalog, Staples customers could get access to some 130,000 SKUs, many of which were shipped directly from manufacturers with Staples acting as an intermediary and consolidator.

To continue building the direct business, in 1988, Staples acquired Quill Corp. for $685 million in Staples stock. Established in 1956, Quill is a direct mail catalog business with a targeted approach to servicing the business products needs of around a million small and medium-sized businesses in the United States. Quill differentiated itself through excellent customer service. Staples decided to let Quill keep its own organization, setting it up as a separate division within the Contract and Commercial business unit, but integrated Quill's purchasing with those of the rest of Staples to gain economies on the input side. Quill now operates under two brands—Staples National Advantage, which focuses on large multiregional businesses, and Staples Business advantage, which focuses on large and medium-sized regional companies and which has the flexibility to handle smaller accounts (although these are mostly handled via Staples Direct). In justifying the acquisition of Quill, Stemberg noted that the direct business amounted to a $60 billion a year industry, but it was highly fragmented with the top eight players accounting for less than 20% of the market.[30]

By 2005, the combined delivery business had grown to become a $4.95 billion enterprise in its own right.

Going International

Staples's first foray into international markets occurred in the early 1990s when the company was approached by a Canadian retailer, Jack Bingleman, who wanted to start a Staples-type chain north of the border. Bingleman also approached Office Depot and Office Max, but preferred Staples because of the close geographic proximity. Board members at Staples initially opposed any expansion into Canada, arguing that scarce resources should be dedicated toward growth in the much larger United States, but Stemberg liked Bingleman's vision and pushed the idea. Ultimately, in 1991, Staples agreed to invest $2 million in Bingleman's start-up for a 16% equity stake.

Known as Business Depot, the Canadian venture expanded rapidly, modeling itself after Staples. Between 1991 and 1994, the number of Canadian Business Depot stores expanded to 30, and the enterprise turned profitable in 1993. In 1994, Staples announced an agreement to purchase Business Depot outright for $32 million.[31] By 2006, there were more than 260 stores in Canada.

The Canadian venture was soon followed by investments in Europe. Staples entered the UK market in 1992, partnering with Kingfisher PLC, a large UK retailer that operated home improvement and consumer electronics stores among other things. The Canadian venture had taught Staples that a local partner was extremely valuable. As one Staples executive noted later: "You absolutely cannot do it yourself. There are too many cultural impediments for you to know where the booby traps lie. In a retail startup, the most important task is to generate locations. There's no way a U.S. national can go into any country and generate the real estate it needs. That person will be chasing his tail for a long time."[32]

On the heels of entry into the UK, Staples purchased MAXI-Papier, a German company that was attempting to copy what Staples had done in the United States. This was followed by entry into the Netherlands and Portugal. By 2006, Staples had 137 stores in the UK, 55 in Germany, 44 in the Netherlands, 19 in Portugal, and 3 in Belgium. By 2006, the European operations were generating close to $2 billion in revenues. In late 2002, Staples purchased the mail-order business of a French company, Guilbert, for nearly $800 million, which boosted delivery sales in Europe from $50 million a year to $450 million a year almost overnight.[33]

Changing the Shopping Experience

By the early 2000s, Staples started to realize that its stores looked very similar to those of its two main competitors, Office Depot and Office Max. As the number of markets where all three companies competed grew, head-to-head competition increased. Management then started to look for ways to differentiate their stores from those of competitors. What emerged was a new store design, known as "Dover." The core to "Dover" was a customer-centric philosophy known as "Easy." Rolled out across the company in 2005, "Easy" is all about making the shopping experience for customers as easy as possible— through store design and layout, through a merchandising strategy that aims to ensure that items are never out of stock, and through superior in-store customer service. The idea is to help to get the customer in and out of the store as expeditiously as possible.

To execute Easy, Staples has had to redesign its store layout, invest in upgrading the knowledge level of its sales associates, and improve its supply-chain management processes.[34] Staples started a big push to improve the efficiency of its supply-chain management

process in 2003, and that is still ongoing today. Elements of this push include better use of information systems to link Staples with its suppliers and extensive use of "cross-docking" techniques at distribution centers, so that merchandise spends less time in distribution centers. As a consequence of this strategy, Staples has increased inventory turnover, reduced inventory holdings, and improved its in-stock experience for customers.

Staples in 2006

In February 2002, Tom Stemberg announced that he was stepping down as CEO and passing the baton on to Ron Sargent. Stemberg would remain on as chairman. On taking over as CEO, Sargent put the brakes on store expansion, declaring that Staples would open no more than 75 new stores a year, down from over 130 in 2000. He used the slowdown to refocus attention on internal operating efficiencies. The product line within stores was rationalized, with Staples cutting back on the stocking of low-margin items such as personal computers. He also set up a task force to look for ways to take every excess cent out of the cost structure. As a result, operating margins at Staples stores came in at 5.9% of sales in 2002, the best in the industry, and up from 4.5% in 2000. (See Exhibit 1.)

By 2003, Sargent was refocusing on attaining profitable growth for the company. Although by this point Staples or one of its competitors operated in all major markets in North America, the company's management decided that Staples was in a strong enough position to go head-to-head with major competitors. In 2005, Staples pushed into Chicago, a market previously served by just Office Depot and

---

EXHIBIT 1

Leaders in Office Supplies

Company	2006 Revenues	Number of Stores in North America	% of Sales from Retail
Staples	$17.8 billion	1522	56%
Office Depot	$15.0 billion	1047	46%
Office Max	$9.2 billion	874	50%

Source: Company reports.

Office Max, where the company opened twenty-five stores. The Chicago experience proved to be a pivotal one for Staples. In the words of COO, Mike Miles, "What we found in Chicago was we can come into a two-player market and make it a three-player market successfully. There was a little trepidation about that because the model in the first 10 to 15 years was that office superstores were interchangeable."[35]

As of 2006, there were still a lot of major markets in North America where Staples lacked a presence, including Houston, Miami, Denver, Las Vegas, St. Louis, and Minneapolis. Reflecting on this, Sargent is on record as stating that Staples could more than double its North American network to some 4,000 stores. (See Exhibit 2 as evidence of the growth rate.) Commenting on this, he notes that "I don't think Wal-Mart spends a lot of time worrying if K-Mart is in the market when they decide to open new stores."[36]

Outside of the retail market, Sargent has turned his attention to the business where he made his name, the direct delivery business. He points out that although the number of independent office supplies dealers is down to 6,000 from 15,000 a decade ago, the delivery market is still highly fragmented and very large. Ultimately Sargent believes that direct delivery from warehouses can be as big a business as Staples office supplies stores. He also sees huge potential for growth in Europe, which is the second largest office supplies market in the world and still years behind the United States in terms of consolidation.

At the same time, Staples continues to face strategic challenges. Clearly additional expansion by Staples in North America is likely to bring it into head-to-head contact with Office Depot or Office Max. To compound matters, in mid-2003, Boise Cascade, the large wood and paper products company that has long had its own direct delivery business, purchased Office Max for $1.2 billion. Prior to the purchase, Office Max had 2002 sales of $4.8 billion against Staples's sales of $11.6 billion and Office Depot's sales of $11.4 billion. The merger boosted the combined office supplies sales of the new company to $8.3 billion. In 2006, Boise Cascade sold off its timber and paper assets to focus on the office supplies business. The company, which changed its corporate name back to Office Max, has 874 office superstores in North America and a large delivery business. Staples also faces continued competition from Sam's Club and Costco, both of which are focusing on small businesses and continue to sell office supplies. In addition, FedEx Kinko's, which has a nationwide network of 1,000 copying and printing stores, is contemplating offering more office supplies in a new store layout.

EXHIBIT 2

Staples Stores in North America, 1996–2006

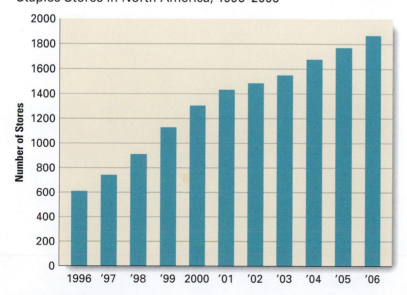

Source: Company reports.

ENDNOTES

1. Stephen D. Solomon. "Born to be Big," *Inc.,* June 1989, page 94.
2. Value Line. Value Line Investment Survey, Staples, October 13, 2006.
3. Stephen D. Solomon. "Born to be Big," *Inc.,* June 1989, page 96.
4. Tom Stemberg. *Staples for Success,* Knowledge Exchange, Santa Monica, California, 1996.
5. Michael Barrier, "Tom Stemberg Calls the Office," *Nation's Business,* July 1990, page 42.
6. Michael Barrier, "Tom Stemberg Calls the Office," *Nation's Business,* July 1990, page 44.
7. Michael Barrier, "Tom Stemberg Calls the Office," *Nation's Business,* July 1990, page 44.
8. Tom Stemberg and David Whiteford. "Putting a Stop to Mom and Pop," *Fortune Small Business,* October 2002, page 39.
9. Tom Stemberg and David Whiteford. "Putting a Stop to Mom and Pop," *Fortune Small Business,* October 2002, page 40.
10. Tom Stemberg. *Staples for Success,* Knowledge Exchange, Santa Monica, California, 1996.
11. Tom Stemberg and David Whiteford. "Putting a Stop to Mom and Pop," *Fortune Small Business,* October 2002, page 40.
12. Tom Stemberg. *Staples for Success,* Knowledge Exchange, Santa Monica, California, 1996, page 17.
13. Tom Stemberg and David Whiteford. "Putting a Stop to Mom and Pop," *Fortune Small Business,* October 2002, page 41.
14. Stephen D. Solomon. "Born to be Big," *Inc.,* June 1989, pages 94 and 95.
15. Tom Stemberg. *Staples for Success,* Knowledge Exchange, Santa Monica, California, 1996, page 24.
16. Tom Stemberg. *Staples for Success,* Knowledge Exchange, Santa Monica, California, 1996, page 27.
17. Tom Stemberg and David Whiteford. "Putting a Stop to Mom and Pop," *Fortune Small Business,* October 2002, page 40.
18. Stephen D. Solomon. "Born to be Big," *Inc.,* June 1989, page 100.
19. Tom Stemberg. *Staples for Success,* Knowledge Exchange, Santa Monica, California, 1996, page 97.
20. Tom Stemberg. *Staples for Success,* Knowledge Exchange, Santa Monica, California, 1996, page 97.
21. Norm Alster. "Penney Wise," *Forbes,* February 1, 1993, pages 48–51.
22. Tom Stemberg. *Staples for Success,* Knowledge Exchange, Santa Monica, California, 1996, page 97.
23. Renee Covion Rouland. "And Then There Were Three," *Discount Merchandiser,* December 1994, page 27.
24. Leland Montgomery. "Staples: Buy the Laggard," *Financial World,* November 9, 1993, page 22; Anonymous, "The New Plateau in Office Supplies," *Discount Merchandiser,* November 1991, pages 50–54.
25. James S. Hirsch and Eleena de Lisser. "Staples to Acquire Archrival Office Depot," *Wall Street Journal,* September 5, 1996, page A3.
26. Joseph Pereira and John Wilke. "Staples Faces FTC in Antitrust Showdown on Merger," *Wall Street Journal,* May 19, 1997, page B4.
27. Tom Stemberg. *Staples for Success,* Knowledge Exchange, Santa Monica, California, 1996, page 128.
28. William M. Bulkeley. "Office Supplies Superstores Find Bounty in the Boonies," *Wall Street Journal,* September 1, 1998, page B1.
29. William C. Symonds. "Thinking Outside the Big Box," *Business Week,* August 11, 2003, page 62.
30. William M. Bulkeley. "Staples, Moving Beyond Superstores, Will Buy Quill for $685 Million in Stock," *Wall Street Journal,* April 8, 1998, page A1.
31. Steff Gelston. "Staples Goes on Buying Spree to Acquire Business Depot, National Office Supply Company," *Boston Herald,* January 25, 1994, page 24.
32. Tom Stemberg. *Staples for Success,* Knowledge Exchange, Santa Monica, California, 1996, page 90.
33. William C. Symonds. "Thinking Outside the Big Box," *Business Week,* August 11, 2003, pages 62–64.
34. Mike Troy. "Office Supplies: Staples Positioned as the Architect of 'Easy,'" *Retailing Today,* August 7, 2006, page 30.
35. Anonymous. "Moving In on Major Markets," *DSN Retailing Today,* May 22, 2006, page 10.
36. Anonymous. "Moving In on Major Markets," *DSN Retailing Today,* May 22, 2006, page 10.

Whole Foods Market: Will There Be Enough Organic Food to Satisfy the Growing Demand?

This case was prepared by Patricia Harasta and Alan N. Hoffman, Bentley College.[a]

Reflecting back over his three decades of experience in the grocery business, John Mackey smiled to himself over his previous successes. His entrepreneurial history began with a single store which he has now grown to the nation's leading natural food chain. While proud of the past, John had concerns about the future direction the Whole Foods Market chain should head. Whole Foods Market was an early entrant into the organic food market and it has used its early mover advantage to solidify its position and continue its steady growth.

With the changing economy and a more competitive industry landscape, John Mackey is uncertain about how to meet the company's aggressive growth targets. Whole Foods Market's objective is to reach $10 billion in revenue with 300+ stores by 2010 without sacrificing quality and its current reputation. This is not an easy task and John is unsure of the best way to proceed.

Company Background

Whole Foods carries both natural and organic food offering customers a wide variety of products. "Natural" refers to food that is free of growth hormones or antibiotics, where "certificated organic" food conforms to

the standards, as defined by the U.S. Department of Agriculture in October 2002.[1] Whole Foods Market® is the world's leading retailer of natural and organic foods, with 172 stores in North America and the United Kingdom. John Mackey, current president and cofounder of Whole Foods, opened "Safer Way" natural grocery store in 1978. The store had limited success as it was a small location allowing only for a limited selection, focusing entirely on vegetarian foods.[2] John joined forces with Craig Weller and Mark Skiles, founders of "Clarsville Natural Grocery" (founded in 1979), to create Whole Foods Market.[3] This joint venture took place in Austin, Texas, in 1980, resulting in a new company, a single natural food market with a staff of nineteen.

In addition to the supermarkets, Whole Foods owns and operates several subsidiaries. Allegro Coffee Company was formed in 1977 and purchased by Whole Foods Market in 1997, now acting as its coffee roasting and distribution center. Pigeon Cove is Whole Foods' seafood processing facility, which was founded in 1985 and known as M & S Seafood until 1990. Whole Foods purchased Pigeon Cove in 1996, located in Gloucester, Massachusetts. The company is now the only supermarket to own and operate a waterfront seafood facility.[4] The last two subsidiaries are Produce Field Inspection Office and Select Fish, which is Whole Foods' West Coast seafood processing facility acquired in 2003.[5] In addition to the above, The company has eight distribution centers, seven regional bake houses and four commissaries.[6]

"Whole Foods Market remains uniquely mission driven: The company is highly selective about what they sell, dedicated to stringent quality standards, and committed to sustainable agriculture. They believe in a virtuous circle entwining the food chain, human

[a] The authors would like to thank Ann Lawrence, Christopher Ferrari, Robert Marshall, Julie Giles, Jennifer Powers and Gretchen Alper for their research and contributions to this case.

beings and Mother Earth: each is reliant upon the others through a beautiful and delicate symbiosis."[7] The message of preservation and sustainability are followed while providing high quality goods to customers and high profits to investors.

Whole Foods has grown over the years through mergers, acquisitions and several new store openings.[8] Today, Whole Foods Market is the largest natural food supermarket in the United States.[9] The company consists of 32,000 employees operating 172 stores in the United States, Canada, and the United Kingdom with an average store size of 32,000 square feet.[10] While the majority of Whole Foods locations are in the U.S., the company has made acquisitions expanding its presence in the UK. European expansion provides enormous potential growth due to the large population and it holds "a more sophisticated organic-foods market than the U.S. in terms of suppliers and acceptance by the public."[11] Whole Foods targets its locations specifically by an area's demographics. The company targets locations where 40% or more of the residents have a college degree as they are more likely to be aware of nutritional issues.[12]

Whole Foods Market's Philosophy

Its corporate website defines the company philosophy as follows, "Whole Foods Market's vision of a sustainable future means our children and grandchildren will be living in a world that values human creativity, diversity, and individual choice. Businesses will harness human and material resources without devaluing the integrity of the individual or the planet's ecosystems. Companies, governments, and institutions will be held accountable for their actions. People will better understand that all actions have repercussions and that planning and foresight coupled with hard work and flexibility can overcome almost any problem encountered. It will be a world that values education and a free exchange of ideas by an informed citizenry; where people are encouraged to discover, nurture, and share their life's passions."[13]

While Whole Foods recognizes it is only a supermarket, it is working toward fulfilling its vision within the context of its industry. In addition to leading by example, it strives to conduct business in a manner consistent with its mission and vision. By offering minimally processed, high quality food, engaging in ethical business practices and providing a motivational,

respectful work environment, the company believes it is on the path to a sustainable future.[14]

Whole Foods incorporates the best practices of each location back into the chain.[15] This can be seen in the company's store product expansion from dry goods to perishable produce, including meats, fish and prepared foods. The lessons learned at one location are absorbed by all, enabling the chain to maximize effectiveness and efficiency while offering a product line customers love. Whole Foods carries only natural and organic products. The best tasting and most nutritious food available is found in its purest state—unadulterated by artificial additives, sweeteners, colorings, and preservatives.[16]

Whole Foods continually improves customer offerings, catering to its specific locations. Unlike business models for traditional grocery stores, Whole Foods products differ by geographic regions and local farm specialties.

Employee and Customer Relations

Whole Foods encourages a team based environment allowing each store to make independent decisions regarding its operations. Teams consist of up to eleven employees and a team leader. The team leaders typically head up one department or another. Each store employs anywhere from 72 to 391 team members.[17] The manager is referred to as the "store team leader." The "store team leader" is compensated by an Economic Value Added (EVA) bonus and is also eligible to receive stock options.[18]

Whole Foods tries to instill a sense of purpose among its employees and has been named one of the "100 Best Companies to work for in America" by *Fortune* magazine for the past six years. In employee surveys, 90% of its team members stated that they always or frequently enjoy their job.[19]

The company strives to take care of its customers, realizing they are the "lifeblood of our business," and the two are "interdependent on each other."[20] Whole Foods' primary objective goes beyond 100% customer satisfaction with the goal to "delight" customers in every interaction.

Competitive Environment

American shoppers spent nearly $45.8 billion on natural and organic products in 2004, according to research published in the *24th Annual Market Overview* in the June issue of *The Natural Foods Merchandiser*. In 2004, natural products sales increased 6.9% across all sales channels, including supermarkets, mass marketers, direct marketers, and the Internet. Sales of organic products rose 14.6% in natural products stores. As interest in low-carb diets waned, sales of organic baked goods rose 35%. Other fast-growing organic categories included meat, poultry and seafood, up 120%; coffee and cocoa, up 64%; and cookies, up 63%.

At the time of Whole Foods' inception, there was almost no competition with less than six other natural food stores in the United States. Today, the organic foods industry is growing and Whole Foods finds itself competing hard to maintain its elite presence. As the population has become increasingly concerned about their eating habits, natural foods stores, such as Whole Foods, are flourishing. Other successful natural food grocery chains today include Trader Joe's Co. and Wild Oats Market[21] (see Exhibit 1).

Trader Joe's, originally known as Pronto Markets, was founded in 1958 in Los Angeles by Joe Coulombe. By expanding its presence and product offerings while maintaining high quality at low prices, the company has found its competitive niche.[22] The company has 215 stores, primarily on the west and east coasts of the United States. The company "offers upscale grocery fare such as health foods, prepared meals, organic produce and nutritional supplements."[23] A low cost structure allows Trader Joe's to offer competitive prices while still maintaining its margins. Trader Joe's stores have no service department and average just 10,000 square feet in store size. A privately held company, Trader Joe's enjoyed sales of $2.5 million in 2003, a 13.6% increase from 2002.[24]

Wild Oats was founded in 1987, in Boulder, Colorado. Its founders had no experience in the natural foods market, relying heavily on their employees to learn the industry. Acknowledging the increased competition within the industry, Wild Oats is committed to strengthening and streamlining its operations in an effort to continue to build the company.[25] Its product offerings range from organic foods to traditional grocery merchandise. Wild Oats, a publicly owned company on NASDAQ, is traded under the ticker symbol of OATS and "is the third largest natural foods supermarket chain in the United States in terms of sales." Although it falls behind Whole Foods and Trader Joe's, the company enjoyed $1,048,164 in sales in 2004, a 7.5% increase over 2003. Wild Oats operates 100 full service stores in 24 states and Canada.[26]

Additional competition has arisen from grocery stores, such as Stop 'N Shop and Shaw's, which now incorporate natural foods sections in their conventional stores, placing them in direct competition with Whole Foods. Because larger grocery chains have more flexibility in their product offerings, they are more likely to promote products through sales, a strategy Whole Foods rarely practices.

Despite being in a highly competitive industry, Whole Foods maintains its reputation as "the world's #1 natural foods chain."[27] As the demand for natural and organic food continues to grow, pressures on suppliers will rise. Only 3% of U.S. farmland is organic so there is limited output.[28] The increased demand for these products may further elevate prices or result in

EXHIBIT 1

Sales

Company	Sales (in millions)						
	2000	2001	% Growth	2002	% Growth	2003	% Growth
Whole Foods Market[1]	$1,838.60	$2,272.20	23.60%	$2,690.50	18.40%	$3,148.60	17.00%
Trader Joe's Company[2]	$1,670.00	$1,900.00	13.80%	$2,200.00	15.80%	$2,500.00	13.60%
Wild Oats Market[3]	$838.10	$893.20	6.60%	$919.10	2.90%	$969.20	5.50%

[1] Hoovers Online: http://www.hoovers.com/whole-foods/–ID_10952–/free-co-factsheet.xhtml: December 1, 2004.

[2] Hoovers Online: http://www.hoovers.com/trader-joe's-co/–ID_47619–/free-co-factsheet.xhtm: December 1, 2004.

[3] Hoovers Online: http://www.hoovers.com/wild-oats-markets/–ID_41717–/free-co-factsheet.xhtml: December 1, 2004.

goods being out of stock, with possible price wars looming.

The Changing Grocery Industry

Before the emergence of the supermarket, the public was largely dependent upon specialty shops or street vendors for dairy products, meats, produce, and other household items. In the 1920s, chain stores began to threaten independent retailers by offering convenience and lower prices by procuring larger quantities of products. Appel explains that the emergence of the supermarkets in the 1930s was a result of three major changes in society:

(1) The shift in population from rural to urban areas

(2) An increase in disposable income

(3) Increased mobility through ownership of automobiles.[29]

Perhaps the earliest example of the supermarket as we know it today is King Kullen, "America's first supermarket," which was founded by Michael Cullen in 1930. "The essential key to his plan was volume, and he attained this through heavy advertising of low prices on nationally advertised merchandise." As the success of Cullen's strategy became evident, others such as Safeway, A&P, and Kroger adopted it as well. By the time the United States entered World War II, 9,000 supermarkets accounted for 25% of industry sales.[30]

Low prices and convenience continue to be the dominant factors driving consumers to supermarkets today. The industry is characterized by low margins and continuous downward pressure on prices made evident by coupons, weekly specials, and rewards cards. Over the years firms have introduced subtle changes to the business model by providing additional conveniences, such as the inclusion of bakeries, banks, pharmacies, and even coffee houses co-located within the supermarket. Throughout their existence, supermarkets have also tried to cater to the changing tastes and preferences of society such as healthier diets, the Atkins diet, and low carbohydrate foods. The moderate changes to strategy within supermarkets have been imitated by competitors, which are returning the industry to a state of price competition. Supermarkets themselves now face additional competition from wholesalers such as Costco, BJ's and Sam's Club.

A Different Shopping Experience

The setup of the organic grocery store is a key component to Whole Foods' success. The store's setup and its products are carefully researched to ensure that they are meeting the demands of the local community. Locations are primarily in cities and are chosen for their large space and heavy foot traffic. According to Whole Foods' 10K, "approximately 88% of our existing stores are located in the top 50 statistical metropolitan areas."[31] The company uses a specific formula to choose its store sites that is based upon several metrics, which include but are not limited to income levels, education, and population density.

Upon entering a Whole Foods supermarket, it becomes clear that the company attempts to sell the consumer on the entire experience. Team members (employees) are well trained and the stores themselves are immaculate. There are in-store chefs to help with recipes, wine tasting and food sampling. There are "Take Action food centers"[32] where customers can access information on the issues that affect their food such as legislation and environmental factors. Some stores offer extra services such as home delivery, cooking classes, massages and valet parking.[33] Whole Foods goes out of its way to appeal to the above-average income earner.

Whole Foods uses price as a marketing tool in a few select areas, as demonstrated by the 365 Whole Foods brand name products, priced less than similar organic products that are carried within the store. However, the company does not use price to differentiate itself from competitors.[34] Rather, Whole Foods focuses on quality and service as a means of standing out from the competition.

Whole Foods only spent 0.5%[35] of its total sales from the fiscal year 2004 on advertising; it relies on other means to promote its stores. The company relies heavily on word-of-mouth advertising from its customers to help market itself in the local community. It is also promoted in several health conscious magazines, and each store budgets for in-store advertising each fiscal year.

Whole Foods also gains recognition via its charitable contributions and the awareness that its brings to the treatment of animals. The company donates 5% of its after tax profits to not-for-profit charities.[36] The company is also very active in establishing systems to make sure that the animals used in its products are treated humanely.

The Aging Baby Boomers

The aging of the Baby Boomer generation will expand the senior demographic over the next decade as their children grow up and leave the nest. Urban singles are another group that has extra disposable income due to their lack of dependents. These two groups present an opportunity for growth for Whole Foods. Americans spent 7.2% of their total expenditures on food in 2001, making it the seventh highest category on which consumers spend their money.[37] Additionally, U.S. households with income of more than $100,000 per annum represent 22% of aggregate income today compared with 18% a decade ago.[38]

This shift in demographics has created an expansion in the luxury store group, while slowing growth in the discount retail market.[39] To that end, there is a gap in supermarket retailing between consumers who can only afford to shop at low cost providers, like Wal-Mart, and the population of consumers who prefer gourmet food and are willing to pay a premium for perceived higher quality.[40] "'The Baby Boomers are driving demand for organic food in general because they're health-conscious and can afford to pay higher prices,' says Professor Steven G. Sapp, a sociologist at Iowa State University who studies consumer food behavior."[41]

The perception that imported, delicatessen, exotic and organic foods are of higher quality, therefore commanding higher prices, continues to bode well for Whole Foods Market. As John Mackey explains, "'We're changing the [grocery-shopping] experience so that people enjoy it.' . . . 'It's a richer, [more fun], more enjoyable experience. People don't shop our stores because we have low prices.'"[42] The consumer focus on a healthy diet is not limited to food. More new diet plans emerged in America in the last half of the 20th century than in any other country. This trend has also increased the demand for nutritional supplements and vitamins.[43]

In recent years, consumers have made a gradual move toward the use of fresher, healthier foods in their everyday diets. Consumption of fresh fruits and vegetables, pasta and other grain-based products has increased.[44] This is evidenced by the aggressive expansion by consumer products companies into healthy food and natural and organic products.[45] "Natural and organic products have crossed the chasm to mainstream America."[46] The growing market can be attributed to the acceptance and widespread expansion of organic product offerings, beyond milk and dairy.[47] Mainstream acceptance of the Whole Foods offering can be attributed to this shift in consumer food preferences as consumers continue to cite taste as the number one motivator for purchasing organic foods.[48]

With a growing percentage of women working out of the home, the traditional role of home cooked meals, prepared from scratch, has waned. As fewer women have the time to devote to cooking, consumers are giving way to the trend of convenience through prepared foods. Sales of ready-to-eat meals have grown significantly. "The result is that grocers are starting to specialize in quasi-restaurant food."[49] Just as women entering the work force has propelled the sale of prepared foods, it has also increased consumer awareness of the need for the one-stop shopping experience. Hypermarkets such as Wal-Mart, that offer non-food items and more mainstream product lines, allow consumers to conduct more shopping in one place rather than moving from store to store.

The growth in sales of natural foods is expected to continue at the rate of 8–10% annually, according to the National Nutritional Foods Association. The sale of organic food has largely outpaced traditional grocery products due to consumer perception that organic food is healthier.[50] The purchase of organic food is perceived to be beneficial to consumer health by 61% of consumers, according to a Food Marketing Institute (FMI)/*Prevention* magazine study. Americans believe organic food can help improve fitness and increase the longevity of life.[51] Much of this perception has grown out of fear of how non-organic foods are treated with pesticides for growth and then preserved for sale. Therefore, an opportunity exists for Whole Foods to contribute to consumer awareness by funding non-profit organizations that focus on educating the public on the benefits of organic lifestyles.

Operations

Whole Foods purchases most of its products from regional and national suppliers. This allows the company to leverage its size in order to receive deep discounts and favorable terms with its vendors. The company still permits stores to purchase from local producers to keep the stores aligned with local food trends and is seen as supporting the community. The company owns two procurement centers and handles the majority of procurement and distribution itself.

Whole Foods also owns several regional bake houses, which distribute products to its stores. The largest independent vendor is United Natural Foods which accounted for 20% of Whole Foods total purchases for fiscal year 2004.[52] Product categories at Whole Foods include, but are not limited to:

- Produce
- Seafood
- Grocery
- Meat and Poultry
- Bakery
- Prepared Foods and Catering
- Specialty (Beer, Wine and Cheese)
- Whole body (nutritional supplements, vitamins, body care and educational products such as books)
- Floral
- Pet Products
- Household Products[53]

While Whole Foods carries all the items that one would expect to find in a grocery store (and plenty that one would not), its "heavy emphasis on perishable foods is designed to appeal to both natural foods and gourmet shoppers."[54] Perishable foods accounted for 67% of its retail sales in 2004 and are the core of Whole Foods' success.[55] This is demonstrated by its own statement that, "We believe it is our strength of execution in perishables that has attracted many of our most loyal shoppers."[56]

Whole Foods also provides fully cooked frozen meal options through its private label Whole Kitchen, to satisfy the demands of working families. For example, the Whole Foods Market located in Woodland Hills, California has redesigned its prepared foods section more than three times[57] in response to a 40% growth in prepared foods sales.[58]

Whole Foods doesn't take just any product and put it on its shelves. In order to make it into the Whole Foods grocery store, products have to undergo a strict test to determine if they are "Whole Foods material." The quality standards that all potential Whole foods products must meet include:

- Food that is free of preservatives and other additives
- Food that is fresh, wholesome and safe to eat
- Promote organically grown foods
- Foods and products that promote a healthy life[59]

Meat and poultry products must adhere to a higher standard:

- No antibiotics or added growth hormones
- An affidavit from each producer that outlines the whole process of production and how the animals are treated
- An annual inspection of all producers by Whole Foods Market
- Successful completion of a third party audit to attest to these findings[60]

Also, due to the lack of available nutritional brands with a national identity, Whole Foods decided to enter into the private label product business. It currently has three private label products with a fourth program called Authentic Food Artisan, which promotes distinctive products that are certified organic. The three private label products: 1) 365 Everyday Value: A well recognized and trusted brand that meets the standards of Whole Foods and is less expensive then the regular product lines; 2) Whole Kids Organic: Healthy items that are directed at children; and 3) 365 Organic Everyday Value: All the benefits of organic food at reduced prices.[61]

When opening a new store, Whole Foods stocks it with almost $700,000 worth of initial inventory, which their vendors partially finance.[62] Like most conventional grocery stores, the majority of Whole Foods inventory is turned over fairly quickly; this is especially true of produce. Fresh organic produce is central to Whole Foods' existence and turns over on a faster basis than other products.

Financial Operations

Whole Foods Market focuses on earning a profit while providing job security to its workforce to lay the foundation for future growth. The company is determined not to let profits deter it from providing excellent service to its customers and a quality work environment for its staff. Its mission statement defines its recipe for financial success.

Our motto—Whole Foods, Whole People, Whole Planet—emphasizes that our vision reaches far beyond just being a food retailer. Our success in fulfilling our vision is measured by customer satisfaction, Team Member excellence and happiness, return on capital investment, improvement in the state of the environment, and local and larger community support.[63]

EXHIBIT 2

Whole Foods Annual Sales

	Annual Income (values in 000's)			
	2001	**2002**	**2003**	**2004**
Sales	2,272,231	2,690,475	3,148,593	3,864,950
%	23.58%	18.04%	17.03%	22.75%
Net Income	$67,880	$84,491	$103,687	$132,657
%		24.47%	22.72%	27.94%
Increase from 2000–2003 = 87%				

Whole Foods also caps the salary of its executives at no more than fourteen times that of the average annual salary of a Whole Foods worker; this includes wages and incentive bonuses as well. The company also donates 5% of its after tax profits to non-profit organizations.[64]

Over a five-year period from 2000 through 2004, the company experienced an 87% growth in sales, with sales reaching $3.86 billion in 2004. Annual sales increases during that period were equally dramatic: 24% in 2001, 18% in 2002, 17% in 2003 and 22% in 2004.[65] (See Exhibit 2.) This growth is perhaps more impressive, given the relatively negative economic environment and recession in the United States.

Whole Foods strategy of expansion and acquisition has fueled growth in net income since the company's inception. This is particularly evident when looking at the net income growth in 2002 (24.47%), 2003 (22.72%) and 2004 (27.94%).[66]

The Ticker for Whole Foods, Inc. is WFMI. In reviewing the performance history of Whole Foods stock since its IPO reveals a mostly upward trend. The 10-year price trend shows the company increasing from under $10 per share to a high of over $100 per share, reflecting an increase of over 1,000%.[67] For the past year, the stock has been somewhat volatile, but with a mostly upward trend. The current price of $136 with 65.3 million shares outstanding gives the company a market valuation of $8.8 billion (Aug. 2005).[68]

The Code of Conduct

From its inception, the company has sought to be different from conventional grocery stores, with a heavy focus on ethics. Besides an emphasis on organic foods, the company has also established a contract of animal rights, which states the company will only do business with companies that treat their animals humanely. While it realizes that animal products are vital to its business, it opposes animal cruelty.[69]

The company has a unique fourteen-page Code of Conduct document that addresses the expected and desired behavior for its employees. The code is broken down into the following four sections:

- Potential Conflicts of Interest,
- Transactions or situations that should never occur
- Situations where you may need the authorization of the Ethics committee before proceeding and finally
- Times when certain actions must be taken by executives of the company or team leaders of individual stores.[70]

This Code of Conduct covers, in detail, the most likely scenarios a manager of a store might encounter. It includes several checklists that are to be filled out on a regular, or at least an annual, basis by team leaders and store managers. After completion, the checklists must be signed and submitted to corporate headquarters and copies retained on file in the store.[71] They ensure that the ethics of Whole Foods are being followed by everyone. The ethical efforts of Whole Foods don't go unrecognized; they were ranked number 70 out of the "100 Best Corporate Citizens."[72]

Possible Scarce Resources: Prime Locations and the Supply of Organic Foods

Prime store locations and the supply of organic foods are potential scarce resources and could be problematic for Whole Foods Market in the future.

Whole Foods likes to establish a presence in highly affluent cities, where its target market resides. The majority of Whole Foods customers are well-educated, thereby yielding high salaries enabling them to afford the company's higher prices. Whole Foods is particular when deciding on new locations, as location is extremely important for top and bottom line growth. However, there are a limited number of communities where 40% of the residents have college degrees.

Organic food is another possible scarce resource. Organic crops yield a lower quantity of output and are rarer, accounting for only 3% of U.S. farmland usage.[73] Strict government requirements must be satisfied; these are incredibly time consuming, more effort intensive, and more costly to adhere to. With increased demands from mainstream supermarkets also carrying organics, the demand for such products could outreach the limited supply. The market for organic foods grew from $2.9 billion in 2001 to $5.3 billion in 2004, an 80.5% increase in the three-year period.[74]

Whole Foods recognizes that the increased demand for organic foods may adversely affect its earnings and informs its investors as such. "Changes in the availability of quality natural and organic products could impact our business. There is no assurance that quality natural and organic products will be available to meet our future needs. If conventional supermarkets increase their natural and organic product offerings or if new laws require the reformulation of certain products to meet tougher standards, the supply of these products may be constrained. Any significant disruption in the supply of quality natural and organic products could have a material impact on our overall sales and cost of goods."[75]

ENDNOTES

1. http://www.organicconsumers.org/organic/most071904.cfm.
2. *Fortune:* September 15, 2003, Volume 148, Issue 5, page 127. "No Preservatives, No Unions, Lots of Dough"; Julia Boorstin.
3. Whole Foods: http://www.wholefoods.com/company/timeline.html (November 4, 2004).
4. *Fortune:* September 15, 2003, Volume 148, Issue 5, page 127. "No Preservatives, No Unions, Lots of Dough"; Julia Boorstin.
5. Whole Foods: http://www.wholefoods.com/company/facts.html (November 5, 2004).
6. Whole Foods: http://www.wholefoods.com/issues/org_commentsstandards0498 .html (November 5, 2004).
7. Whole Foods: http://www.wholefoods.com/company/index.html (November 5, 2004).
8. Whole Foods: http://www.wholefoods.com/company/history.html (November 5, 2004).
9. "The Natural: Whole Foods Founder John Mackey Builds an Empire on Organic Eating" Time, Inc. 2002.
10. Whole Foods: http://www.wholefoods.com/company/facts.html (November 11, 2004).
11. "Whole Foods Buying Chain of Stores Based in London: $38 Million Deal Marks U.S. Health-food Retailer's Initial Thrust into Overseas Market," Robert Elder Jr., January 17, 2004.
12. *Puget Sound Business Journal:* Seattle August 13, 2004. Volume 25, issue 15, page 1. "Whole Foods is Bagging Locations"; Jeanne Lang Jones.
13. Whole Foods: http://www.wholefoodsmarket.com/company/sustainablefuture.html (November 5, 2004).
14. Whole Foods: http://www.wholefoodsmarket.com/company/sustainablefuture.html (November 5, 2004).
15. *Fortune:* September 15, 2003, Volume 148, Issue 5, page 127. "No Preservatives, No Unions, Lots of Dough"; Julia Boorstin.
16. http://www.wholefoodsmarket.com/products/index.html (July 25, 2005).
17. Whole Foods 10K-Q 2003 (page 7). November 11, 2004, http://www.wholefoodsmarket.com/investor/10K-Q/2003_10K.pdf.
18. Whole Foods10K-Q 2003 (page 7). November 11, 2004, http://www.wholefoodsmarket.com/investor/10K-Q/2003_10K.pdf.
19. Whole Foods 10K-Q 2004 (page 10). August 15, 2005, http://www.wholefoodsmarket.com/investor/10K-Q/2004_10KA.pdf.
20. http://www.wholefoodsmarket.com/company/declaration.html (July 29, 2005).
21. Hoovers Online: http://www.hoovers.com/whole-foods/–ID_10952-/free-co-factsheet.xhtml (November 8, 2004).
22. Trader Joe's Company: www.traderjoes.com (November 8, 2004).
23. Hoovers Online: http://www.hoovers.com/trader-joe's-co/–ID-47619-/free-co-factsheet.xhtm (November 8, 2004).
24. Hoovers Online: http://www.hoovers.com/trader-joe's-co/–ID-47619-/free-co-factsheet.xhtm (November 8, 2004).
25. Wild Oats Market: www.wildoats.com (November 8, 2004).
26. Hoovers Online: http://www.hoovers.com/wild-oats-markets/–ID_41717–/free-co-factsheet.xhtml (November 8, 2004).
27. Hoovers Online: http://www.hoovers.com/whole-foods/–ID_10952-/free-co-factsheet.xhtml (November 8, 2004).
28. *Knight Ridder Tribune Business News.* Washington: September 28, 2004. page 1. "Providence, RI, Grocery Targets New Approach to Pricing"; Paul Grimaldi.
29. Appel, David. "The Supermarket: Early Development of an Institutional Innovation." *Journal of Retailing.* Volume 48, Number 1, Spring 1972. (p. 40).
30. Appel, David. "The Supermarket: Early Development of an Institutional Innovation." *Journal of Retailing.* Volume 48, Number 1, Spring 1972. (p. 40). (Appel, 47).
31. Whole Foods 10K-Q for 2003 (page 8) November 11, 2004 http://www.wholefoodsmarket.com/investor/10K-Q/2003_10K.pdf.
32. Whole Foods 10K-Q for 2003 (page 8) November 11, 2004, http://www.wholefoodsmarket.com/investor/10K-Q/2003_10K.pdf.
33. Whole Foods 10K-Q for 2003 (page 8) November 11, 2004, http://www.wholefoodsmarket.com/investor/10K-Q/2003_10K.pdf.
34. Whole Foods http://www.wholefoodsmarket.com/investor/10K-Q/2003_10K.pdf (page 10) November 12, 2004.
35. Whole Foods 10K-Q 2004 (page 10) August 15, 2005. http://www.wholefoodsmarket.com/investor/10K-Q/2004_10KA.pdf.
36. Whole Foods 10K-Q 2003 (page 9) November 11, 2004, http://www.wholefoodsmarket.com/investor/10K-Q/2003_10K.pdf.
37. Consumer Lifestyles in the United States (May 2003) 12.2 Expenditure on Food. *Euromonitor.* Solomon Smith Baker Library, Bentley College, Waltham, MA. November 1, 2004.
38. Gapper, John. "Organic Food Stores are on a Natural High." *The Financial Times,* September 2004.
39. Gapper, John. "Organic Food Stores are on a Natural High." *The Financial Times,* September 2004.
40. Gapper, John. "Organic Food Stores are on a Natural High." *The Financial Times,* September 2004.
41. Murphy McGill, Richard, "Truth or Scare." *American Demographics.* March 2004, Ithaca. Vol. 26, Issue 2, page 26.

42. Sechler, Bob, "Whole Foods Picks Up the Pace of its Expansion." *Wall Street Journal* (Eastern edition), September 29, 2004. New York, NY. Page 1.

43. Consumer Lifestyles in the United States (May 2003) 12.7 What Americans Eat. *Euromonitor*. Solomon Smith Baker Library, Bentley College, Waltham, MA. November 1, 2004.

44. Consumer Lifestyles in the United States (May 2003) 12.4 Popular Foods. *Euromonitor*. Solomon Smith Baker Library, Bentley College, Waltham, MA. November 1, 2004.

45. "Profile in B2B Strategy: Supermarket News Sidles into Natural, Organic Trend with New Quarterly." *Business CustomerWire*. Regional Business News. October 25, 2004.

46. "Profile in B2B Strategy: Supermarket News Sidles into Natural, Organic Trend with New Quarterly." *Business CustomerWire*. Regional Business News. October 25, 2004.

47. The World Market for Dairy Products (January 2004). 4.5 Organic Foods. 4.5.1 Global Market Trends in Organic Foods. *Euromonitor*. Solomon Smith Baker Library, Bentley College, Waltham, MA. November 1, 2004.

48. The World Market for Dairy Products (January 2004). 4.5 Organic Foods. 4.5.1 Global Market Trends in Organic Foods. *Euromonitor*. Solomon Smith Baker Library, Bentley College, Waltham, MA. November 1, 2004.

49. "Supermarkets' Prepared Meals Save Families Time." *KRTBN Knight-Ridder Tribune Business*. Daily News, Los Angeles. September 13, 2004.

50. Packaged Food in the United States (January 2004) 3.4 Organic Food. *Euromonitor*. Solomon Smith Baker Library, Bentley College, Waltham, MA. November 1, 2004.

51. Packaged Food in the United States (January 2004) 3.4 Organic Food. *Euromonitor*. Solomon Smith Baker Library, Bentley College, Waltham, MA. November 1, 2004.

52. Found on 10K-Q for 2004 (page 10) August 15, 2005. http://www.wholefoodsmarket.com/investor/10K-Q/2004_10KA.pdf. Found on 10K-Q for 2003 (page 8) November 11, 2004.

53. Whole Foods 10K-Q for 2003 (page 6) November 13, 2004.

54. Whole Foods 10K-Q 2003 (page 5) Whole Foods http://www.wholefoodsmarket.com/investor/10K-Q/2003_10K.pdf, November 13, 2004.

55. Whole Foods 10K Q 2004 (page 14) August 15, 2005 http://www.wholefoodsmarket.com/investor/10K-Q/2004_10KA.pdf.

56. Whole Foods 10K-Q 2003 (page 6) http://www.wholefoodsmarket.com/investor/10K-Q/2003_10K.pdf, November 13, 2004.

57. "Supermarkets' Prepared Meals Save Families Time." *KRTBN Knight-Ridder Tribune Business*. Daily News, Los Angeles. September 13, 2004.

58. "Supermarkets' Prepared Meals Save Families Time." *KRTBN Knight-Ridder Tribune Business*. Daily News, Los Angeles. September 13, 2004.

59. Whole Foods 10K-Q 2003 (page 5) http://www.wholefoodsmarket.com/investor/10K-Q/2003_10K.pdf, November 13, 2004.

60. Whole Foods 10K-Q 2003 (page 6) http://www.wholefoodsmarket.com/investor/10K-Q/2003_10K.pdf, November 13, 2004.

61. http://www.wholefoodsmarket.com/investor/10K-Q/2003_10K.pdf Found on 10K-Q for 2003 (page 7) November 11, 2004.

62. Whole Foods 10K-Q for 2003 http://www.wholefoodsmarket.com/investor/10K-Q/2003_10K.pdf (Page 8) November 7, 2004.

63. Whole Foods www.WholeFoodsmarket.com/company/declaration.html, November7, 2004.

64. Whole Foods www.WholeFoodsmarket.com/company/declaration.html, November7, 2004.

65. Whole Foods 10K-Q for 2003 www.WholeFoodsmarket.com/investor/10k-Q/2003_10k.pdf, November 7, 2004.

66. Whole Foods 10K-Q for 2003 www.WholeFoodsmarket.com/investor/10k-Q/2003_10k.pdf, November 7, 2004.

67. Nasdaq.com Market Symbol for Whole Foods is WFMI http://quotes.nasdaq.com/quote.dll?page=charting&mode=basics&intraday=off&timeframe=10y&charttype=ohlc&splits=off&earnings=off&movingaverage=None&lowerstudy=volume&comparison=off&index=&drilldown=off&symbol=WFMI&selected=WFMI, November 11, 2004.

68. Nasdaq.com Market Symbol for Whole Foods is WFMI http://quotes.nasdaq.com/Quote.dll?mode=stock&symbol=wfmi&symbol=&symbol=&symbol=&symbol=&symbol=&symbol=&symbol=&symbol=&symbol=&multi.x=31&multi.y=6, November 11, 2004.

69. Whole Foods: http://www.wholefoodsmarket.com/investor/10K-Q/2003_10K.pdf (Page 6) November 11, 2004.

70. Whole Foods Code of Conduct found at company website http://www.wholefoodsmarket.com/investor/codeofconduct.pdf, November 11, 2004.

71. Whole Foods Code of Conduct found at company website http://www.wholefoodsmarket.com/investor/codeofconduct.pdf (page 11).

72. Business Ethics 100 Best companies to work for http://www.business-ethics.com/100best.htm, November 12, 2004.

73. *Knight Ridder Tribune Business News*. Washington: September 28, 2004. page 1. "Providence, RI, Grocery Targets New Approach to Pricing"; Paul Grimaldi.

74. http://www.preparedfoods.com/PF/FILES/HTML/Mintel_Reports/Mintel_PDF/Summaries/sum-OrganicFoodBeverages-Aug2004.pdf.

75. Whole Foods 10K (Page 14) http://www.wholefoodsmarket.com/investor/10K-Q/2004_10KA.pdf.

Organizational Transformation at the BBC

This case was prepared by Vinay Kumar, under the direction of Vivek Gupta, ICFAI Center for Management Research (ICMR).

"My main challenge in the BBC is taking a fantastic British institution and figuring out, with everyone in the BBC, how to get it ready for this completely different world. All of my energy is going into getting the organisation to think about quite radical change. So I see myself as a bit of a gadfly in a way, saying, 'don't assume that we can carry on as we always have.'"[1]

—Mark Thompson, Director General,
British Broadcasting Corporation, in 2006.

"The last 10 years at the BBC, we have seen terrible mismanagement. We had two director generals who really did not know how to run a large corporation."[2]

—Kate Adie, Former BBC Reporter,
on the leadership of John Birt and Greg Dyke, in 2004.

Thompson Makes His Mark

On May 21, 2004, Mark Thompson (Thompson) was appointed Director General of the British Broadcasting Corporation (BBC), the world's first public broadcasting corporation. The immediate task on his hands—to reform the 82-year-old BBC, which had been severely criticized in the Hutton Report.[3] The Hutton Report, which went into a BBC report on the British Government's claims about Iraq's weapons of mass destruction, described the BBC's editorial system as defective and said that the editors had not scrutinized the script before it was aired. It also found fault with the BBC's management for having failed to act on a complaint given by the Government saying that the report by BBC correspondent Andrew Gilligan (Gilligan) was false. On January 29, 2004, following the publication of the

Hutton Report, Greg Dyke (Dyke), Thompson's predecessor, who had stood by Gilligan's story, resigned.

Thompson took charge on June 21, 2004. He was quick to acknowledge the efforts of Dyke, but emphasized that the corporation would require some "real and radical changes" to sustain itself in the coming years. On his very first day, he announced the restructuring of the BBC's executive committee, the first of the many steps toward creating a simpler and more effective organization structure. The executive committee was divided into three boards—creative, journalism, and commercial—covering the principal activities of the BBC. Thompson himself headed the creative board (refer to Exhibit 1 for the Old and New Executive Committees).

Thompson also announced that the other businesses of the BBC such as production, commercial businesses, and commissioning would be reviewed with the sole aim of cutting costs and improving the efficiency of the organization as a whole. He said, "We're going to have to change the BBC more rapidly and radically over the next three to five years than at

---

This case was written by Vinay Kumar, under the direction of Vivek Gupta, ICFAI Center for Management Research (ICMR). It was complied from published sources, and is intended to be used as a basis for class discussion rather than to illustrate either effective or ineffective handling of a management situation.

EXHIBIT 1

BBC's Old and New Executive Committees

Previous Executive Committee

DG	Greg Dyke
Deputy DG and Dir. World Service & Global News	Mark Byford
Dir. Finance, Property & Business Affairs	John Smith
Dir. Strategy & Distribution	Carolyn Fairbairn
Dir. Policy & Legal	Caroline Thomson
Dir. BBC People	Stephen Dando
Dir. Marketing, Communications & Audiences (MC&A)	Andy Duncan
Dir. Television	Jana Bennett
Dir. Radio & Music	Jenny Abramsky
Dir. New Media & Technology	Ashley Highfield
Dir. News & Current Affairs	Richard Sambrook
Dir. Drama, Entertainment & CBBC (DEC)	Alan Yentob
Dir. Sport	Peter Salmon
Dir. Nations & Regions (N&R)	Pat Loughrey
Chief Executive, BBC Worldwide	Rupert Gavin

New Executive Board and Committees

DG	Mark Thompson
Deputy DG	Mark Byford
Chief Operating Officer	John Smith
Dir. Strategy & Distribution	Carolyn Fairbairn
Dir. BBC People	Stephen Dando
Dir. MC&A	Andy Duncan
Dir. Television	Jana Bennett
Dir. Radio & Music	Jenny Abramsky
Dir. New Media & Technology	Ashley Highfield

Creative Board

Chair	Mark Thompson
Deputy DG	Mark Byford
Creative Director and Dir. DEC	Alan Yentob
Dir. F&L	John Willis
Dir. Sport	Peter Salmon
The directors of TV, Radio, New Media, N&R, MC&A News divisional heads as appropriate	

Journalism Board

Chair	Mark Byford
Dir. News & Current Affairs	Richard Sambrook
Dir. N&R	Pat Loughrey
Dir. World Service & Global News	To be confirmed
Directors of TV, Radio, New Media, F&L as appropriate	

(continued)

EXHIBIT 1   (continued)

BBC's Old and New Executive Committees

Commercial Board	
Chair	John Smith
Chief Exec, BBC Worldwide	Rupert Gavin
Heads of BBC Broadcast, BBC Resources, BBC Vecta	
Dir. MC&A	Andy Duncan
Dir. Strategy & Distribution	Carolyn Fairbairn

Source: "Change and Reorganization—Signs of Things to Come as Thompson Becomes DG,"
www.bbc.co.uk, June 22, 2004.

any previous point in its history. It feels like the task of really changing the BBC has only begun."[4]

A number of people felt that Thompson had come in at a critical time when the BBC's integrity was under question, employee morale was down, and the impact of digital technology was looming large. They predicted that the journey further down the road would in no way be an easy one for him. However, analysts were confident about Thompson's capability to solve at least some of BBC's problems. Tessa Jowell (Jowell), Secretary of State for Culture, Media, and Sport, believed that Thompson was the right man for the post under such circumstances. Jane Root, Former Controller of the BBC-owned BBC2, said, "He thinks very strategically about the big issues in television, and that is more than anything what the BBC needs its new director general to do. There is going to be an incredible amount of turbulence in television in the next few years; Mark was always a big-range thinker who didn't just think about the here and now."[5]

Background Note

The BBC was created on October 18, 1922, as the British Broadcasting Company, by a group of wireless manufacturers including Guglielmo Marconi (Marconi), inventor of the radio. Regular broadcasting began from Marconi's London studio on November 14, 1922. The company's mission was "to inform, educate, and entertain."

In 1927, the company's name was changed to the British Broadcasting Corporation and it was granted a Royal Charter, which put it under the control of the UK government (refer to Exhibit 2 for details on Royal Charter). The Charter defined the BBC's objectives, powers, and obligations. The BBC was operated through a 12-member Board of Governors, who acted

EXHIBIT 2

BBC's Royal Charter

A Royal Charter was the only way to get incorporated in the early 20th century. A number of cities, theaters, and charity institutions were established under the Charter. For the BBC, the Charter along with an agreement gives it editorial independence (freedom to report) and sets out public obligations. It also gives the BBC the flexibility to adapt to changes. This makes the BBC answerable only to the public. The Charter is renewed every ten years and the review process takes around three years. For example, if the due date for renewing the Charter is January 2007, the review starts from January 2003 onward and ends in December 2006.

During the Charter review, the public is consulted and its opinion regarding the services rendered by the BBC is considered. The BBC, meanwhile, would have to justify the extension of the Charter and also the license fee. It has to give its own charter manifesto outlining what it wants to do during the next charter period. The government issues a Green Paper in response to the manifesto. The Green Paper outlines initial options for the BBC on how it should operate in the future, raises issues if any, and gives the BBC time to respond. After the BBC responds, the government issues a White Paper which firms up the options in the Green Paper. There will be further deliberations in Parliament before the government publishes the Royal Charter.

Adapted from various sources.

as trustees and ensured that the organization was accountable for its work to the public while maintaining its independence in reporting news. The day-to-day operations were managed by an Executive Board, which consisted of nine members and was led by a Director General. The BBC, which had no competitor at that time, gained revenues only through a license fee (10 shillings), set by the British parliament and paid for by radio owners. It was not allowed to indulge in commercial activities such as advertising. In 1932, the BBC began broadcasts (BBC Empire Service) outside Britain for the English-speaking people under the then British Empire.

After starting experimental broadcasts in 1932, the BBC officially started television services in November 1936, under the name BBC Television Service. It also issued 8.5 million radio licenses covering around 98% of Britain's population. However, during the Second World War, television broadcasts were suspended for security reasons and these recommenced only in 1946. Though television services were suspended during the War, the BBC continued with its radio broadcasts. The Corporation earned a reputation for honest and accurate news reporting and its 9 o'clock news became very popular. The BBC Empire Service, which was renamed BBC External Service in 1940, was broadcasting radio programs in 40 languages by the end of the War. The BBC acquired the reputation of being impartial and its news was regarded as authoritative. The Third Programme service, which it launched in 1946, triggered the expansion of radio services. The Third Programme broadcast cultural programs such as concerts, opera, drama, talks, and features. In the same year, the combined license fee of £2 for television and radio was introduced. The Wireless Telegraphy Act of 1949 required any person who possessed a television set to pay the license fee.

Till the early 1950s, radio dominated over television in Britain. There were around 12 million exclusive radio licenses while the combined licenses for radio and TV were only 350,000. The budget allocated for the television division was also negligible. However, this scenario changed with the coronation of Queen Elizabeth II in 1953. For the first time, television was allowed to cover a royal ceremony and it was estimated that around 20 million TV viewers worldwide watched the coronation ceremony.

In September 1955, the BBC's monopoly ended with the launch of ITV[6] (Independent Television), which was not funded through license fees and thus was the first commercial channel in the UK. ITV bought television programs from the US television channels and aired them along with its own programs. Its popularity rose very quickly and the BBC's market share fell to as low as 28% in 1957. By the end of the 1950s, innovative programs such as *Grandstand with David Coleman, Monitor with Huw Weldon, Benny Hill Show, Your Life in Their Hands,* and *Whicker's World* did help the BBC increase its viewership. However, it was never the same, post the ITV launch.

In 1964, BBC2 was launched to provide experimental and new kinds of programs to the audience. In the same year, the BBC Television Service was renamed BBC1. In 1967, BBC2 started color broadcasts and BBC1 joined in 1969. In 1971, the radio only licenses were abolished and the license fee was meant only for television. The BBC saw its popularity and income increase in the 1970s as more and more people bought televisions. It offered a variety of programs belonging to various genres such as drama and comedy, documentaries, etc.

Need for Restructuring

Until 1982, there were only four television channels in the UK—BBC1, BBC2, ITV, and Channel 4[7]—all of which used the terrestrial television broadcasting[8] method to air their programs. The early 1980s saw the rise of satellite television[9] in the UK. Launched in 1982, Satellite Television was the first of such channels. It was purchased by News Corporation[10] in 1984 and re-launched as Sky Channel, a pan European network. In February 1989, Sky Channel was again launched as a four-channel network for the UK—Sky Channel (later Sky One), Sky News, Sky Movies, and Eurosport. After a lot of delay, the British Satellite Broadcasting[11] (BSB) was launched in March 1990, to compete with Sky Channel. Both companies lost huge amounts and in December 1990, they merged to form BSkyB. BSkyB slowly rose to become a major competitor of BBC.

Meanwhile, in 1984, the UK government decided to introduce cable television, which had already gained huge popularity in the US, and it passed the Cable and Broadcasting Act the same year. Swindon Cable was given the first license in 1984. The Cable Authority was created with a view to further expanding the cable television business, and it awarded licenses to the cable operators. Aberdeen Cable (later known

EXHIBIT 3

Growth in Television Channels in the UK (1950–2002)

Source: www.ofcom.org.uk.

as Atlantic) was given the first license by the Cable Authority. By the end of 1990, the Cable Authority had issued about 124 licenses to independent cable operators (refer to Exhibit 3 for the growth of television channels in the UK between 1950 and 2002).

Apart from competition, the BBC also faced pressure to reduce its rising operating costs during the 1990s. In 1992, Sir John Birt (Birt) was appointed as BBC's Director General. Birt reduced the workforce by 4000, which resulted in a saving of US$ 465 million, and merged the news divisions of radio, television, and BBC World Service.[12] The BBC expanded overseas by forming a joint venture with the Public Broadcasting System in the US. In February 1997, Birt sold the home transmission division to Castle Transmission Services for £244 million. In November 1997, Birt started BBC News 24, a satellite channel that was offered without any subscription fee, and later launched four more subscription channels. It imported hit serials such as *ER*, *X-Files*, etc. from the US and sold its programs to television channels in other countries.

By the late 1990s, digital broadcast services began in the UK. The digital technology was superior to analog in terms of picture quality and the number of channels offered. Moreover, it provided other services such as accessing the Internet and other interactive services. In 1997, Birt launched BBC Online (www.bbc.co.uk), which went on to become one of the most popular websites in the UK. In the same

year, he started BBC Worldwide,[13] a commercial arm of the BBC, which was involved in global channels and television sales, content and production, etc. In September 1998,[14] BBC Choice, the first complete digital broadcast service in the UK, was started.

Some of Birt's decisions, however, came in for a lot of criticism from industry analysts and the media. In 1993, he introduced the internal market concept dubbed "Producer Choice" which gave producers the right to choose between the production resources (studios, cameras, crew, etc.) provided by the BBC and outsiders. The BBC's in-house production department had already been affected by the Broadcasting Act of 1990, which required all the television channels to source 25% of their television programs from independent producers—people who did not own more than 25% shareholding in a broadcaster or were not owned more than 25% by a broadcaster.

Under this concept, the producers favored outsiders as the BBC departments were charging high prices. Each individual item borrowed was charged and nearly 400,000 bills were issued to producers every year. In fact, the departments were asked to charge real prices for their services. For example, the BBC pronunciation department, which helped drama actors and news readers in the pronunciation of difficult words, charged £12 per word. Hence, the producers usually looked to outside people or managed themselves. Renting a CD from the BBC library was also costlier than buying a CD outside and charges were levied even if the producers wanted video and audio clips. The same was the case with the other departments such as costumes, scenic, and make-up. Ironically, the high costs charged left these resources idle most of the time. This resulted in a number of job losses with 5000 alone in very first year. "Producer Choice" was described as an "abysmal act of vandalism" by a number of media and industry observers.

In another major decision to restructure the BBC, Birt separated the production and broadcast divisions as he felt that the in-house production department was not considering the views of the audience while producing programs and the BBC was becoming a producer-controlled organization. However, this step boomeranged as the broadcast commissioners showed little faith in the in-house production department. The developers went through a long bureaucratic process to submit their programs only to find most of them being rejected. The production department, therefore, started producing programs that had been ordered by the commissioners. The commissioners, for their part, looked to market researchers and focus groups for advice on the type of programs to be made for gaining public attention. Thus, control over the nature of the program shifted to these groups which affected the quality of programs. Further, fewer dramas were produced as their cost of production was higher than that of fact-based programs and reality shows.

Birt also made the BBC bigger. The BBC internal market had 190 business units which looked after the trading between various BBC departments. He started a new department called Corporate Center to provide key strategic services to the BBC such as legal services, planning, personnel, etc. The Center employed hundreds of people and cost the BBC around £60 million pounds every year, which was more than the costs incurred in running BBC's Radio 1. He also used the services of around five management consultancies at a cost of about £22 million per year. Former BBC officials came down heavily on this step, but Birt convinced everyone of the increasing importance of management consultants.

There was no cooperation between the various departments. The Corporate Center and the drama division had differences over budget allocation. The drama department was forced to air programs on the lines of the popular programs on ITV. The radio division was left with the feeling that it was being sidelined by the television division. The BBC was not able to acquire broadcast rights for prestigious sporting events such as Formula One, the Ryder Cup, etc. and lost out to BSkyB, Channel 4, and ITV. Further, the competition from satellite and cable television affected the BBC and its audience share fell from 51% in 1981 to less than 38% in 2000. Above all, employee morale was at a real low.

A number of analysts expressed concern over the BBC's declining audience share as it directly affected the corporation's revenues. They wanted the license fee to be abandoned and advocated alternate methods such as commercial advertising, privatization through share holding, etc. to fund the BBC. Analysts said that the BBC should generate more revenues through advertising rather than through the license fee.

Greg Dyke Becomes Director General

In January 2000, Birt was replaced by Dyke, CEO of Pearson Television. Dyke, who took over as Director General on February 1, 2000, found the BBC's organizational structure extremely complex. There were far too many layers and the organization was much too bureaucratic. He immediately announced the creation of the "One BBC" program where various departments and their employees would cooperate with each other and work toward achieving common goals. Commenting on the program, Dyke said, "Our aim is to create One BBC, where people enjoy their job and are inspired and united behind the common purpose of making great programs and delivering outstanding services."[15]

Dyke announced a change in the organization structure aimed at giving the top management more power and reducing duplication. He abandoned the Corporate Center and replaced it with six Professional Service Divisions—Public Policy; Human Resources & Internal Communications; Distribution & Technology; Finance, Property & Business Affairs; Marketing & Communications; and Strategy—to support the BBC's operations. Though he retained "Producer Choice," the number of business units was reduced from 190 to 50. He removed the library charges and producers and researchers could access video clips and printed materials for free.

Dyke created a new Executive Committee with 17 directors who reported directly to him. Of the 17, nine were heads of programming and broadcasting. This move aimed at shifting the decision making on programming to the top management (refer to Exhibit 4 for BBC's Organizational Chart under Dyke). It brought

EXHIBIT 4

BBC's Organizational Chart under Dyke

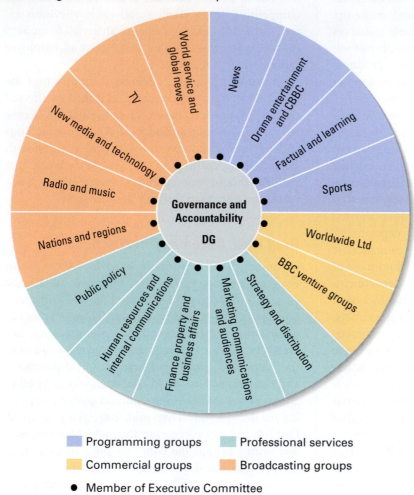

- ▮ Programming groups   ▮ Professional services
- ▮ Commercial groups   ▮ Broadcasting groups
- ● Member of Executive Committee

Source: www.bbc.co.uk.

Dyke closer to all the key operations of the BBC. The division heads were given full autonomy to run their own divisions, which was new to them. Dyke soon found that all the divisions were fighting for a bigger slice of the annual budget and so announced budgets for each of the divisions until the year 2006. He created a new Leadership Group by pooling 60 people from the organization. This group discussed the latest developments in the market and came up with new ideas for improving the BBC.

Dyke said that the BBC would reduce overhead costs from 24% of its total income to 15% by 2005. He laid off 900 employees and planned to reduce the amount spent on consultants. These savings were to be used for developing quality programs and another £200 million were to be spent on programming every

year. Dyke aimed to save a cumulative amount of about £1.2 billion by 2007.

Dyke invested money on developing dramas and increased the budget for this by £100 million every year. The BBC also started spending more on sports and other events such as the Queen's Jubilee celebrations, concerts in Buckingham Palace, etc. In November 2001, the BBC launched the BBC interactive television service (BBCi), which was made available on all digital television platforms—digital cable, digital satellite, and digital terrestrial television (refer to Exhibit 5 for the list of BBC's television and radio services in the UK).

In April 2002, ITV Digital[16] shut down its operations and its digital terrestrial TV (DTT) licenses went up for sale. The consortium led by the BBC and backed by Crown Castle and BSkyB won the DTT

EXHIBIT 5

BBC's Television and Radio Services in the UK

Television	Radio
BBC One	Radio 1
BBC Two	1Xtra
BBC Three	Radio 2
BBC Four	Radio 3
CBBC	Radio 4
CBeebies	Five Live
BBC News 24	Five Live Sports Extra
BBC Parliament	6 Music
Interactive TV	BBC 7
	Asian Network

Source: www.bbc.co.uk.

license in July 2002. BBC got one license while Crown Castle got two. The BBC announced that it would offer 24 free-to-air digital channels, some channels of BSkyB, and interactive and digital radio services. To receive all the channels, consumers would have to pay £99 for a set-top box. All the channels were available after the launch of Freeview in October 2002.

In its annual report for the financial year 2002–03, the BBC said it had reduced its overheads by 13%. This was 2% more than the announced target and the corporation also increased its net income by £54 million. BBC's digital services reached 35% of people who received digital television programs as against 23% during the year 2001–02. To gain popularity among the young audience, the BBC started BBC Three and IXtra, a radio channel. There was better understanding among the BBC staff and corporate level communication too improved. However, issues such as collaboration between various departments still remained a concern.

Just when things seemed to be finally going right for the BBC, the Dr. David Kelly episode happened and the Hutton report exposed BBC's vulnerable editorial process. According to the report:

- The editorial system at the BBC was defective as the editors did not see Gilligan's script before allowing it to be broadcast.

- The BBC management did not examine the notes of Gilligan's interview with Dr. Kelly.

- The BBC management had defects in the complaints investigation process.

- The BBC governors failed to order an enquiry into the truthfulness of the Gilligan report and to accept that his notes did not support his May 29 broadcast.

Dyke, who strongly defended the BBC during the row, apologized for the unfortunate incident. Accepting responsibility, he resigned twenty hours after the BBC's Chairman Gavyn Davies stepped down. At the time of his resignation, Dyke said, "I don't want to go. But if in the end you screw up you have to go. I do not necessarily accept the findings of Lord Hutton."[17]

Many analysts and the media criticized the BBC in light of the revelations in the Hutton report. The British newspapers carried articles on the front page—*The Times'* headline read "Blizzard of blame chills BBC" and *The Guardian's* said "Crisis cuts through the BBC." Gerald Kaufman, Labour Member of Parliament, said, "The BBC is no longer relied on in the way it was claimed. It's placed itself in a situation where its word isn't accepted automatically anymore. It's gone from being an institution to just another broadcaster, and a shoddy one at that."[18]

BBC radio saw a decrease in the number of listeners after the publication of the report though the BBC itself attributed the decline to factors such as the absence of Sarah Montague, presenter of the *Today* program, who was on maternity leave. Strong doubts were raised on the BBC's ability to regain the faith of the viewers. The worst was the timing of the incident, coming as it did before the renewal of the Charter, due in December 2006. This was described as "the worst crisis in the BBC's 80-year history."

On February 18, 2004, Mark Byford (Byford), acting Director General,[19] appointed a committee led by the BBC's former Director of News and Current Affairs Ronald Neil (Neil) to examine the issues raised in the Hutton Report, to identify the lesson to be learnt from the episode, and to make recommendations on improving the editorial and complaints handling mechanism at the BBC. Neil was supported by other former and working BBC executives.[20]

Thompson Takes Charge

The committee submitted its report on June 23, 2004, a day after Thompson took charge as the Director General of the BBC. The Neil Report called for a vast improvement in the training process of the journalists. It suggested establishment of a college of journalism and a greater role for editors and lawyers in the BBC's editorial process. The committee wanted the BBC to continue to broadcast reports based on a single source but only after proper examination. It emphasized that only the most accurate information should be given to the public (refer to Exhibit 6 for a summary of the Neil Report).

Neil said, "As the largest employer of journalists in the UK, the BBC has an obligation to take the lead in strengthening training in craft skills and promoting debate about journalistic standards and ethics in broadcasting. All programs operating under the BBC's journalistic banner must work to the same values, professional disciplines, and journalistic culture."[21]

Thompson asked Byford to implement the Neil Report recommendations as soon as possible. He announced new journalism guidelines under which the rules were tightened on the use of reports prepared from conversations, anonymous sources, and a single source. These could be used only after a thorough internal review. As the Neil Report wanted the program editors to take full responsibility for whatever content their team produced, the editors were given the right to know the identity of the source (single or anonymous) from the journalist before approving the story for broadcast. It was up to the editors to exercise this right after considering the experience and track record of the journalist. It was reported that the disclosure of an anonymous source was required only if the report contained any serious allegations.

During the Neil investigation, seniors in the BBC news division expressed the fear that journalists who were not qualified were aiming to climb up the corporate ladder and take on higher responsibilities. The BBC therefore planned to establish a training college led by an academic by mid-2005 to give the minimum level of training every year to its 7000 journalists.

EXHIBIT 6

Summary of the Neil Report

- Accuracy and precision in all BBC journalism is paramount. It must be based on robust and tested evidence and reinforced by accurate note-taking.

- Accurate and reliable note-taking is a prime journalistic skill and should be part of journalist training in the BBC.

- It is a guiding principle of BBC journalism that we are fair to all—fair to those against whom allegations are being made, fair to the audience, and to contributors. Fairness to people and organizations against whom allegations are going to be made by the BBC is of great importance.

- Serious and potentially defamatory allegations must always be put in time for a considered response before transmission other than in rare cases when there are compelling countervailing reasons not to do so.

- Because of the trusted place in which BBC's journalism is held, allegations made by a third party will often be regarded by many viewers and listeners as also being made by the BBC itself.

- The BBC should not normally break stories making serious allegations in live two-ways.

- Granting anonymity to a source should never be done casually or automatically. A named on the record source is always to be preferred. However, with an anonymous source, the audience must be told why the source is anonymous and, in the BBC's view, credible. Protection of confidential sources is a fundamental principle of journalism.

- The BBC transmits hundreds of hours of news and current affairs output every day. As the custodians of the BBC's editorial values, individual editors and executive producers must take the day-to-day responsibility for them.

- Presenters are answerable to their individual editors and in all of their journalistic work must embody the BBC's core editorial values.

- At the heart of the BBC's journalism is a well-trained journalistic workforce. In a fast-changing world, life-long training at every level is vital. Competence based training should be the key to competence based promotion. We recommend that the BBC establishes an industry-wide, residential college of journalism under the leadership of an academic principal.

- The handling of complaints needs reform. All complaints should be handled in the same way regardless of who is making them. The Director-General should not be directly involved in the normal process of responding to complaints. The Head of the Editorial Complaints Unit must be empowered to act independently of those responsible for output. When mistakes are made, the BBC must develop a system and a culture that encourages fast clarification and unambiguous correction.

Source: "BBC Journalism: The Neil Report," www.bbc.co.uk, June 2004.

Changes were also brought about in the complaints procedure. These included keeping the Director General out of the process of responding to the complaints. This change came in the wake of Dyke's strong resistance to accepting the BBC's fault involving Dr. Kelly. Lawyers were put in the main newsrooms to review the complaints. The BBC said that it would start to accept and apologize for its mistakes and try to learn from them. In this connection, it started a website, NewsWatch, which dealt with complaints and feedback from the audience. All serious mistakes and their corrections were to be published across all the BBC platforms along with explanations. The BBC also commenced a similar feedback program NewsWatch on the News 24 Channel.

A few analysts criticized the BBC's actions post the Hutton Report and, in particular, the recommendations of the Neil Report. They felt that the BBC had always set very high standards and the Neil Report was absolutely unnecessary. According to Julie Kirkbride, Secretary of Shadow Culture,[22] the establishment of a training college was an additional expenditure and would require the BBC to go beyond its core activities. According to Brian MacArthur, a columnist at *The Times*, the BBC had been better than most of the British newspapers which never apologized for their mistakes. He said, "The Neil Report does not expose a single real problem with the standards of BBC journalism, because there never was a problem in the first place. In my view, if you take away the lapse by Andrew Gilligan, newspapers could learn a lot from BBC journalism. It seems to me to be of a very high standard, and always has been."[23]

Charter Manifesto

Since the early 2000s, the license fee charged by the BBC had come under severe criticism. In August 2003, the Conservative Party, the second largest political party in the UK, charged that the viewers were paying for programs that had been copied from commercial channels and demanded that the fee be cut. It said that the BBC was getting an unfair advantage by receiving £2.7 billion[24] as annual fee (refer to Exhibit 7 for how the license fee is spent by the BBC).

On June 29, 2004, the BBC announced its Charter manifesto called "Building Public Value" aimed at providing value to its customers in the wake of changing customer preferences and the competition. The Charter manifesto, which consisted of BBC's proposals

EXHIBIT 7

How the Monthly License Fee Is Spent by BBC

	2006 (Monthly Cost in £)
BBC One	3.52
BBC Two	1.52
Transmission and collection costs	1.08
Nations and English Regions television	1.04
BBC Radio 1,2,3,4 and Five Live	1.02
Digital television channels	1.00
Local and Nations' radio	0.68
Bbc.co.uk	0.36
BBC Jam	0.14
Digital radio stations	0.10
Interactive TV (BBCi)	0.08
Total	**10.54**

Source: www.bbc.co.uk.

for the coming years, would be sent to the government to peruse while reviewing the Royal Charter. The manifesto justified the continuance of the license fee and the Charter for the next ten years. In the wake of criticism over the license fee, Thompson announced sweeping measures in the nine-point manifesto. The measures were:

- **Leading the digital transformation:** The BBC reiterated its commitment to leading the UK in the digital television segment by fully shifting to digital terrestrial broadcasting by 2012. It would launch a service that would allow all its television programs to be downloaded within seven days of broadcast.

- **Original programs:** The BBC would develop original content and try to refrain from being a "copycat," a criticism that it often faced. It would produce quality programs by understanding the customers' needs, producing better dramas on its television and radio, and investing more on current affairs and comedy shows.

- **Public value test:** To assess the quality of new programs and monitor the performance of current programs, the BBC governors would put all the BBC's programs to a public value test on four criteria—reach, quality, impact, and value for money—before they were launched. The BBC also established a framework of measuring the performance of the Corporation based on the same criteria (refer to Exhibit 8 for the framework for measuring BBC's performance).

- **Scale and scope of services:** The BBC would use public value to decide on the scale and scope of its services. This would be applicable to the breadth of the BBC (multimedia and a range of other services) and depth (BBC-owned commercial divisions, etc.).

- **Fostering partnerships:** The BBC planned to enter into joint ventures with outside partners to carry out educational, cultural, and other activities. It would publish a partnership contract by the end of 2004, which would set forth the principles and standards that the BBC would bring to any partnership. It would also publish a partner guide to attract potential partners.

- **Expanding out of London:** The BBC would shed its image of being "too London-centric" and move about half of its businesses out of the capital over the next ten years. It would spend more than £1 billion every year on programs made out of London.

- **A transparent BBC:** The BBC, which had always been more of a closed organization, planned to open up to suit the views of the modern day customers. More information would be provided about the organization on its website (www.bbc .co.uk/info). Its various media would feature comments and complaints about its programs. On the whole, the BBC would put the audience at the center of all its activities.

- **Reforming license fee payment:** In the opinion poll conducted by the Market and Opinion Research International[25] (MORI) in early 2004, two-thirds of the respondents did not support the license fee and

EXHIBIT 8

Framework for Measuring Performance of BBC

Source: www.bbc.co.uk.

suggested alternate methods such as advertising, sponsorship to programs, etc. to fund the BBC. However, the BBC believed that the license fee would enable it to perform better. To reduce the burden of license fee on the public the BBC would try to reduce its overhead costs by 10% of the expenditure. It said it would modernize the license fee payment by moving from a paper-based system to online payment and make the fee affordable to the poor.

- **Improving the BBC governance:** The role and responsibilities of the governors would be clearly outlined to make them more independent of the management. It would create a new 'governance unit' to help them regulate the BBC and to do tests of public value for the approval of programs. This was in response to the criticism in the Hutton Report that the BBC governors were being controlled by the management.

Implementing Change at BBC

In the first week of December 2004, Thompson began implementing the manifesto by announcing a new vision aimed at making the BBC a more creative and efficient digital broadcaster. He announced that his vision had three aspects—"a bold new program and content strategy based above all around the idea of excellence," "a transformation of the BBC into a state-of-the art digital broadcaster," and "an irreversible shift in the culture of the BBC toward simplicity, opportunity, and creativity."

Thompson announced that 2,900 of the BBC's employees (more than one-tenth of its total workforce) would be laid off to reduce costs. Of the total job cuts, 2,500 would be in finance, marketing, legal services, and other departments that were not involved in program making and the remaining in the educational departments. According to Thompson, the job cuts were aimed at reducing costs by up to £320 million per year within the next three years. This was £165 million more than the savings announced before Thompson's appointment. Further, Thompson asked the individual departments (radio, television, news, etc.) of the BBC to reduce their costs by 15% and hinted at outsourcing some of the other jobs.

Thompson also announced that BBC's main channel BBC1 would broadcast fewer reruns and would reduce the production of formula-based and copied shows (refer to Exhibit 9 for details of BBC's television channels). He said the BBC would try and differentiate its programs from the ones being aired by competing commercial channels by developing original content. According to Thompson, the change was necessitated by the emergence of digital technology, which had raised people's expectations of the BBC. He said that it would have to make investments in developing

---

EXHIBIT 9

Details of BBC's Television Channels

BBC One: It is the oldest channel in the BBC stable and broadcasts news, sports, drama, comedy shows, film premieres, and documentaries.

BBC Two: The second oldest among the BBC channels, it initially broadcast programs catering to a niche audience and programs related to educational and community functions. However, in the recent years it has moved away to become a mainstream channel.

BBC Three: Launched in 2003, the channel focuses on young adults with new comedy, drama, entertainment, current affairs, etc.

BBC Four: Launched in March 2002, the channel is available to the digital television audience. It focuses on arts, culture, and world cinema, dramas, documentaries, and debates.

CBBC: CBBC (Children's BBC) targets children between six and twelve years.

CBeebies: Launched in February 2002, CBeebies target children below six years.

NEWS24: Started in 1997, News24 is a 24-hour news channel.

BBC Parliament: Launched in 1998, BBC Parliament broadcasts live and recorded versions of the sessions of the British House of Commons, House of Lords, etc.

BBCi: Started in 1999 as BBC Text, BBCi stands for BBC interactive television. It offers up to date information on the weather, education, entertainment, etc. to all digital television audiences.

Compiled from various sources.

programs related to big-budget drama, factual event shows, music, comedy, reality shows, children's TV and radio, and others where the BBC was strong.

Thompson also addressed the contentious issue of the percentage of BBC programs that could be made by independent producers, which was at 25%. Though he retained the existing quota, he introduced a new concept called "window of creative competition" which allowed the independent companies to compete against the in-house production department of the BBC for another 25% of its programs. Thus, the BBC was guaranteed only 50% in-house production for its programs. According to Thompson, this kind of competition would provide the best of the programs to the BBC's viewers.

In order to make the BBC represent the whole of the UK, nearly 1,800 staff of various divisions—Children's TV and radio, BBC Sport, BBC Radio 5 Live, research and development, etc. were planned to be moved to the newly created state-of-the-art center in Manchester. It was also decided that the television drama production outside London would be increased from 30% to 50% from the next charter period between 2007 and 2016.

Regarding the commercial activities of the BBC, Thompson said such activities should "exploit and/or export BBC content and its brand," and hinted that the some of the activities would be carried out in collaboration with private parties. BBC's divisions such as BBC Broadcast and BBC Resources would enter into partnerships and joint ownerships for commercial purposes.

The job cuts proposed by Thompson were met with severe opposition from the employee union Broadcasting Entertainment Cinematograph and Theatre Union (BECTU)[26] and also from a number of analysts. BECTU members said that Thompson was trying to appease the British government in its efforts to retain the license fee. Analysts charged that the BBC had always promised something or the other before every Charter review but never really gone about achieving it. The "window of creative competition" was seen more as vindicating the fact that Thompson had no faith in the efficiency of the BBC's production department. Analysts felt that Thompson was taking too many measures at one time.

Thompson defended his decision and said, "Both I, Greg Dyke, and John Birt before him have all looked at the issue of the BBC's bureaucracy, our processes, our layers. Now is the moment where we really do have to grasp some nettles there and say is there a way

we can run this organization more simply, more directly, with fewer meetings and less complexity and therefore transfer many, many millions of pounds out of that part of the BBC and into programs."[27]

In March 2005, Thompson announced that another 1,500 jobs would be cut in the news and programs division over the next three years. He also increased the savings target from £320 million to £355 million. In the same month, the Department for Culture, Media, and Sport (on behalf of the government) published the Green Paper[28] based on the feedback given by Lord Burns, the Secretary of State's independent adviser on the Charter Review, and his team. The feedback was prepared based on the views of a number of viewers consulted by the team.

According to the Green Paper, the BBC was to be granted a new Charter for the next ten years starting from January 1, 2007, and ending December 31, 2016. It was felt that the ten years would enable the BBC, and the television industry, to stabilize during the switchover to digital television. The government also saw no viable alternative to the license fee and decided to continue with it, but said it would review it to find suitable alternatives after the digital transformation took place in 2012.[29] All the BBC governors would be removed and replaced by a new entity called the BBC Trust.

The Green Paper also raised some issues. About 33% of the respondents felt that the BBC was not providing value for money. One third of the viewers felt that the quality of programs was deteriorating. They expressed concern over the BBC's lack of accountability to the viewers. To address this concern, it was proposed that the BBC governors would be replaced by the BBC Trust, which would be accountable to the viewers. All BBC services should try to accomplish a set of five purposes during the next charter period (refer to Table 1 for the five purposes).

The issues raised would be considered by a parliamentary committee and an independent enquiry would be conducted by the House of Commons Select Committee on Culture, Media, and Sport. Further, parliamentary scrutiny and consultations would take place and these would form the basis for the Royal Charter.

In May 2005, the BBC responded to the Green Paper. It welcomed the decision to grant a new Charter and to continue the license fee funding. Thompson gave the assurance that the BBC would provide original and quality content to the viewers and try to explore opportunities to serve people better. However,

TABLE 1

BBC's Five Purposes

- Sustaining citizenship and civil society,
- Promoting education and learning,
- Stimulating creativity and cultural excellence,
- Representing the UK, its nations, regions and communities,
- Bringing the UK to the world and the world to the UK.

Another purpose was to be technically ahead in adopting technology and to play an active part during the transformation to digital television.

Source: "Review of the BBC's Royal Charter," www.bbc.co.uk, March 2005.

Michael Grade, Chairman of the BBC, said that the Paper had underrated the impact of digital technologies on the relationship between audience and media and expressed opposition to the review of the license fee after the digital transformation.

The BBC Journalism College

In the last week of June 2005, the BBC launched the BBC Journalism College at an investment of £5 million to train journalists working in various divisions of the BBC such as news, the World Service, etc. As opposed to the concept of classroom training, the instructions were imparted through interactive e-learning sessions, seminars, and workshops (conducted by Neil) at various locations across the globe. The training was aimed at supporting the five editorial principles mentioned in the Neil Report—truth and accuracy; serving the public interests; independence from any external influence; accountability to audience and; impartiality in reporting. The e-learning module would reduce costs for the BBC, which planned to increase the spending on journalism training to £10 million by 2008 to develop "interactive learning modules" which could be accessed by BBC journalists from any BBC office across the world. Every journalist was to be provided a minimum of 20 hours of training every year.

The staff was given "training passports" which were stamped after they completed the training sessions. Completion of training was made one of the requirements for promotion. Further, no journalist was allowed to apply for senior posts unless he/she

had completed training and acquired the necessary skills, even if he/she had the relevant work experience. For example, a senior broadcast journalist would have to finish some training sessions before becoming an editor. Training would also focus on the environment and issues in Europe, the Middle East etc. which were thought to be complicated.

Most of the courseware was developed in-house except for the material for the external training activities. The college concentrated not only on imparting core journalistic skills to the reporters, but also values and ethics at the editorial level. Commenting on this, Byford said, "This is an exciting and ambitious training initiative which will, we hope, set a gold standard for broadcast journalism training in the UK. We want to offer our staff career-long training and development to support them in their dealing with today's complex journalistic environment."[30]

Despite these efforts, the BBC believed that its training and editorial procedures did not face any major problem. It said that it produced 120 hours of news programming every day and due to the size of its operations, mistakes were bound to happen. Richard Sambrook, Director of the BBC's Global News division, said, "It's not that there was a big problem before but the environment has changed very rapidly. New technology such as digital cameras, laptops, and the Internet have brought about more 24-hour services. Competition and pressures on journalists in terms of decisions they have to take have vastly increased."[31]

In October 2005, the BBC submitted a proposal for an increase in the license fee by 2.3% above the inflation rate to meet its cumulative requirement of £5.5 billion in the next seven years in order to improve its programs and digital services. Of the total requirement, the BBC would get £3.9 billion through the ongoing cost cutting measures and the license fee increase would bridge the gap. This meant that the license fee, which was £126.50 per annum, would be increased by £3.14 every year until 2013.

In March 2006, the Department for Culture, Media, and Sport published a White Paper which outlined the way the BBC should be run. This paper was to be the basis for the renewal of BBC's Royal Charter. While the purpose set in the Green Paper and other proposals such as scrapping of the post of governors remained the same, the BBC was asked to give priority to entertainment and stop being "copycats" or "rating chasers." The Government retained its proposal to consider alternatives to the license fee such as subscriptions, etc. after 2012. Further, in April 2006, Jowell said that the license fee increase would be much lower than the BBC had proposed. There would be further deliberations in Parliament and the Royal Charter would be published during the last quarter of 2006.

In April 2006, Thompson announced "Creative Future"—a set of themes and ideas proposed to achieve the purposes laid out in the White Paper and prepare the BBC for the digital age. Thompson appointed two teams in April 2005 to study how the world might be in 2012, the tastes and preferences of the audiences and the steps the BBC should take to meet the requirements. The "Creative Future" strategy aimed at making the BBC content appealing and easily available to the young audience.

Recommendations were made on the "eight critical areas of output"—Journalism, Sport, Drama, Music, Comedy, Entertainment, Children & Teens, and Knowledge Building. According to Thompson, "Five Big Themes" emerged out of the study—Martini Media, Serious About Entertainment, The Young, Findability, and The Active Audience (refer to Exhibit 10 for details of BBC's Creative Future Strategy). Commenting

EXHIBIT 10

BBC—Details of the Creative Future Strategy

Recommendations on Eight Critical Areas of Output

Sport: Start a broadband portal that offers live video and audio, comments, and analysis from specialists, interactive comments on sporting events. Start an exclusive news program for sports on television, appoint a BBC Sports Editor, and phase out old programs.

Music: Have a single music strategy across all platforms along with regular cross-platform events and make them available for download through broadband, mobile, and podcasting.

Kids & Teens: Consolidate children's programs across all platforms under CBeebies and CBBC brands. Launch a broadband-based teen brand targeting 12–16-year-olds.

Comedy: Invest in developing more sitcoms and comedy shows across all television and radio networks. Foster talent, start a comedy website, and increase access to the shows through new media.

Drama: Make television dramas more energetic while retaining the hit shows. Create fewer long television dramas and support single and experimental dramas.

Entertainment: Improve Saturday night's content on BBC ONE and have an effective collaboration with other genres like leisure and factual to create innovative shows.

Knowledge Building: Make available all the BBC content to audience permanently after transmission on all platforms.

Five Themes

Martini Media: Martini Media is the media that allows the content to move from one media to another across various devices and is available everywhere and at any time. This means that the BBC would have to follow an entirely new process for developing, commissioning, and production of programs. The BBC has already started working on this project called BBC Web 2.0.

Serious About Entertainment: The new generation audience doesn't want just knowledge and information from the BBC. They want the BBC to provide thorough entertainment through drama, comedy, and factual programs.

The Young: The young audience has been moving away from the BBC since the beginning of the 2000s and this trend is rising. The BBC would aim to reach the younger audience by starting exclusive websites and television programs, etc. for them without neglecting the older sections.

Findability: The BBC plans to coordinate the whole content efficiently in order to make it easy for the viewers to search and find. Powerful search tools would be launched and the content would be branded to make the search more user-friendly in fields like Sport, Music, Natural History, Leisure, and Health.

The Active Audience: In future, the viewers are expected to take part in discussions and debates, and create, communicate, etc. apart from watching programs. The BBC would encourage the audience to add their content and ideas in areas like Natural History, Leisure, Health, etc.

Adapted from "BBC Creative Future: Mark Thompson's speech in full," www.media.guardian.co.uk, April 25, 2006 & "Creative Future—BBC Addresses Creative Challenges of On-Demand," www.bbc.co.uk, April 25, 2006.

EXHIBIT 11

BBC—Pictorial Representation of the Organizational Changes (July 2006)

Source: www.bbc.co.uk.

on the strategy, Thompson said, "The BBC should no longer think of itself as a broadcaster of TV and radio and some new media on the side. We should aim to deliver public service content to our audiences in whatever media and on whatever device makes sense for them, whether they are at home or on the move."[32]

The BBC also started exploring various opportunities to develop its international commercial activities through BBC Worldwide. It planned video-on-demand services and to start BBC.com, a commercial website for people outside the UK, by the end of 2006.

In July 2006, the BBC announced organizational changes to facilitate the implementation of Creative Future. Future media and technology formed the core of the new change and the BBC content was organized into journalism, BBC vision, and audio

and music (refer to Exhibit 11 for pictorial representation of the organizational changes under Thompson in July 2006). According to Thompson, the main aim of the reorganization, effective from April 2007, was to facilitate cross-platform commissioning and production and make the BBC a creative organization.

The Road Ahead

Though the BBC had been cutting costs, the compensation paid to the top executives remained the same, and for a few executives, it was actually rising every year. The bonuses paid to them were criticized severely by many industry analysts and BECTU as they came at a time when the television viewership was falling. For 2004-05, Thompson received a bonus of £64,000 on a £210,000 basic pay and Byford received £92,000 on his salary of £351,000. BBC's CEO John Smith (Smith) received £72,000 on £287,000 and BBC People director, Stephen Dando, received £65,000 bonus on £245,000. Byford's salary jumped 30% from the financial year 2003–04 and Smith's basic pay by 20%. However, they also assumed additional responsibilities in the BBC.

In July 2005, reacting to the criticism related to compensation, Thompson waived his performance-related incentives worth £135,000 for the year 2004–05. This cut, along with the reduction in the size of the executive board, reduced cumulative bonuses from £546,000 in 2003–04 to £320,000 in 2004–05. Similarly, the incentives for the BBC executive board members were also cut from about 30% of the basic salary to 10% starting from 2005–06 fiscal. Later, the salary of the members was increased after it was found that their compensation had fallen below the market average.

Many analysts, politicians, and competitors flayed the BBC's proposal to increase the license fee. They said that the BBC had overstated its costs while understating its savings. Charles Allen, CEO of ITV, said, "The BBC's back-of-a-fag-packet figures should come with their own health warning. They systematically underplay their estimates for savings and efficiencies and overplay their funding requirements. The government should reject the BBC's bid and send them back to the drawing board."[33]

Analysts also found fault with the newly formed BBC Trust.[34] They said that it was not too different from the earlier Board of Governors and would not last long. According to Dame Pauline Neville-Jones, Member of BBC's Board of Governors between 1997 and 2004, the governors were caught between their conflicting roles of governing and regulating. The Trust would be no different in dealing with such issues and this could affect the functioning of the whole organization. She said, "The new structures created to govern and regulate the corporation will be elaborate and complex and a great deal more expensive to run than the present set-up. Will they be more effective and will they result in better programs? This is a good deal less clear. The White Paper . . . creates in the trust, having both governance and regulatory duties, a body as likely to suffer from schizophrenia as the existing governors."[35]

The BBC faced ire of the public over its repeat telecasts. Though Thompson had promised to reduce the number of repeat telecasts, BBC1 aired 2,683 hours of

repeat telecasts in 2004-05 fiscal, 88 hours more than 2003–04. On the whole, 24,000 hours of repeat telecasts were aired across all the BBC channels. However, if the BBC had reduced its repeat telecasts and increased original content, it would have increased costs enormously. For example, a repeat telecast would cost between £15,000 and £30,000 every hour while an original comedy or drama would cost between £500,000 and £600,000. Further, as the government had not accepted the BBC's proposal to increase the license fee, analysts predicted that the BBC would have to again concentrate on cost cutting.

Another problem for the BBC was the poaching of its employees by independent production companies. In 2005, a number of channel controllers, producers, and directors from BBC1 and BBC3 were lured by private production companies who offered higher pay, a share in the profits, etc.

Thompson's much hyped Creative Future too came in for a lot of criticism from the UK media. The BBC planned to launch websites with high quality audio and video content in fields like sports, music, etc. aimed at attracting the youth. These websites were pitted directly against commercial websites such as MySpace.[36] The UK media complained that that the BBC was obsessed with the youth segment and questioned the rationale behind Thompson using public money to create competition to commercial websites. The rivals complained that the government was not putting any brakes on the BBC, whose steps, they said, could prove detrimental to the Corporation. The Guardian Media Group[37] said that the BBC's plan to launch a commercial website for overseas users would hit its online and regional newspaper business. It found fault with the BBC spending £69.2 million in 2004–05 for developing the bbc.co.uk website (into the most popular website in the UK), as the license fee money was originally intended to fund only television operations.

Despite the criticism, a number of analysts commended Thompson's leadership and his vision for the BBC. They said that the BBC had never targeted young audiences earlier as it had not been funded by the advertisers who craved young audiences. In this context, they appreciated Thompson's efforts to take the BBC to the new generation audience. According to John Naughton, columnist at *The Observer*,[38] "Most broadcasters seem to be unable to see what's coming—a world where all media products will be delivered and accessed via the Internet, with all that implies in terms of active, empowered, fickle, and knowledgeable audiences. Somehow, Mark Thompson and his team have shaken off that mindset and understood what's required if the BBC is to thrive in the new environment. So they clearly understand what needs to be done. The question is: can they do it?"[39]

ENDNOTES

1. "Mark Thompson Interview," www.libdems.org.uk, March 17, 2006.

2. Claire Cozens, "BBC Review 'Doesn't Go Far Enough'," www.mediaguardian.co.uk, December 7, 2004.

3. In September 2002, the UK government produced a dossier about the weapons of mass destruction allegedly possessed by Iraq. In that, it claimed that the weapons could be deployed within 45 minutes. On May 29, 2003, Andrew Gilligan in the *Today* program on BBC Radio 4 reported that the 45-minute claim had been intentionally and was not supported by the intelligence authorities. The UK government condemned the report while the BBC said that it had received the information from a reliable source. On July 9, 2003, the BBC revealed the name of Dr. David Kelly (a weapons expert) as the source. On July 17, 2003, Kelly was found dead. The government appointed Lord Hutton to probe into the "circumstances surrounding the death of Kelly." On January 28, 2004, the findings of Hutton were published. The report did not find the government guilty but found fault with the BBC's editorial system. It also said that Kelly had committed suicide.

4. "New BBC Boss Announces Shake-up," www.news.bbc.co.uk, June 22, 2004.

5. "Grade Gets His Man as BBC Ends Months of Turmoil," www.media.guardian.co.uk, May 22, 2004.

6. ITV was started by a network of commercial television broadcasters. For 2004, ITV's net operating revenues were £2,053 million with a net profit of £139 million.

7. Channel 4 was started in 1982 by an Act of Parliament. It was initally managed by the Independent Broadcasting Authority and the revenues were received from ITV franchises located across the UK. The advertising was taken care of by the franchises operating in a particular region and thus ITV had no direct relationship with advertisers.

8. Terrestrial broadcasting, also called over-the-air broadcasting, is a broadcasting method where television signals are sent over the air and are received using an antenna.

9. The satellite television service involves the use of satellite for broadcasting. Signals, sent from the earth using an uplink transmitter, are received by one of the transponders in the satellite which converts them to another frequency and sends them back to earth. These signals are received using a downlink antenna and a receiver.

10. News Corporation, controlled by Rupert Murdoch, is one of the largest media conglomerates in the world. Its businesses consist of production and distribution of films, television networks, newspapers and magazines, websites, book publishing, etc. For the year ended July 31, 2005, its total sales were US$ 24 billion and its net income was US$ 2 billion.

11. British Satellite Broadcasting was started in 1986 to provide direct to home satellite television service in the UK. However, due to technical problems, it started to broadcast services only in early 1990.

12. The External Service was renamed BBC World Service in 1988.

13. BBC Worldwide distributes and licenses the BBC TV programs across the world. It owns or has a stake in about 20 channels, owns nearly 40 magazines, sells books, videos, music, and DVDs. It also provides radio content, language teaching products, etc. For the year ended March 2005, its total sales were £706 million and net income was £28 million.

14. BBC Choice went off the air in February 2003 and was replaced by BBC Three.

15. "Dyke Unveils Moves to Build 'One BBC'," www.bbc.co.uk, April 3, 2000.

16. Started in 1998, ITV Digital was the first terrestrial digital broadcaster offering about 35 channels. In August 2001, it bought the broadcasting rights to the Football League for three years for £315 million and launched ITV Sport. This proved to be a costly step as sports failed to attract audience and advertisers. In October 2002, Freeview, a new digital terrestrial television service, was launched to replace ITV Digital.

17. "BBC Apologizes as Dyke Quits," www.news.bbc.co.uk, January 29, 2004.

18. Dame Anita Roddick, "Rupert vs. The BBC—The 'Foxification' of Britain," www.mediachannel.org, October 23, 2003.

19. Mark Byford was appointed as the Deputy Director General of the BBC in January 2004. After Dyke left, he became the acting Director General of the BBC until Mark Thompson was appointed. Thompson appointed Byford as the Head of Journalism in June 2004 in addition to his Deputy Director General post.

20. The other members of the group were Glenwyn Benson (Controller Factual Commissioning Television), Helen Boaden (Controller Radio 4 and BBC 7), Adrian Van Klaveren (Head of Newsgathering, BBC News), Richard Tait (Former Editor-in-Chief, ITN), and Stephen Whittle (Controller Editorial Policy, BBC).

21. "BBC Outlines Post-Hutton Reforms," www.news.bbc.co.uk, June 23, 2004.

22. A group of members from the opposition party (officially called Her Majesty's Loyal Opposition) in the House of Commons forms a cabinet called The Official Loyal Opposition Shadow Cabinet or simply The Shadow Cabinet. The Shadow Cabinet members scrutinize their counterparts in the government and suggest alternative policies.

23. "BBC Report: 'A Lot of Unnecessary Self-Laceration'," www.business.timesonline.co.uk, June 23, 2004.

24. For 2006–07, the license fee was £131.50 per year for a color television and £44 for a black and white television. The license was free if the person was more than 75 years old, and the fee was half in the case of persons registered as blind.

25. MORI combined with Ipsos UK in October 2005 to form the second largest research company in the UK. The company conducts research in five segments—Marketing, Advertising, Media, Loyalty, and Public Affairs.

26. Formed in 1991, BECTU is an independent union which comprises workers belonging to broadcasting, theater, film, leisure, entertainment, and related areas in the UK.

27. "Thompson Says BBC 'Must Keep Up'," www.news.bbc.co.uk, December 8, 2004.

28. A Green Paper contains government's policy proposals for stimulating debate and discussion, based on which a final decision can be taken.

29. The UK government planned to discontinue with analog transmissions completely and switch over to digital television by 2012. The process which would start in 2008 was expected to be completed by 2012. Shifting to digital television provides benefits such as extra channels as standard, better quality, new features, etc.

30. "BBC Journalism College Launched," www.news.bbc.co.uk, June 28, 2005.

31. "What You'll Need to Get a Passport to Promotion," www.pressgazette.co.uk, July 7, 2005.

32. "The Future Starts Here? BBC Strengthens Its Role in Digital World," www.iabuk.net, April 27, 2006.

33. "What the BBC's Critics Say," www.ft.com, May 30, 2006.

34. The BBC Trust which would replace the BBC Board of Governors would consist of twelve trustees headed by Michael Grade, Chairman of the BBC. As of May 2006, the government had announced the names of only four members.

35. Chris Tryhorn and Ben Dowell, "Dyke's 'Posh Lady' Attacks BBC Trust," www.media.guardian.co.uk, April 12, 2006.

36. MySpace, founded in 2003 and owned by News Corporation, is a US-based community website. It is one of the world's most popular community websites.

37. The Guardian Media Group (GMG) is UK-based multimedia organization whose core business is publishing and printing. Apart from publishing newspapers (regional and national), the group is also into regional radio stations, websites, television station and magazines.

38. The *Observer*, founded in 1791 and owned by Guardian Media Group, is a newspaper published on Sundays.

39. "The BBC's Digital Future—But Will It Work?" www.media.guardian.co.uk, April 30, 2006.

NBC in Trouble

This case was prepared by Vinay Kumar, under the direction of Vivek Gupta, ICFAI Center for Management Research (ICMR).

"I can tell you, it's like a weird monkey off the back in a way. Business is cyclical . . . nobody stays on top all the time."[1]

> —Kevin Reilly, President, NBC Entertainment, on the declining NBC Viewership, in 2005.

"We're not as strong as we've been, maybe, but we're only one breakout hit away from being there again. Of course, breakout hits are harder to come by these days."[2]

> —Jeff Zucker, then President of NBC Universal Television Group, on NBC's poor performance in 2004–05.

"NBC is still arguably the face of that division. Should NBC have another year like last year, there could be advertising fallout and the perception of NBC may change for investors"[3]

> —Robert Schenosky, Analyst at Boyd Jefferies & Company[4] in 2005.

Introduction

In the television rankings for the 2005–06 season,[5] NBC Television Network (NBC) was ranked fourth for the second consecutive year in the most popular broadcast network category. The rankings were released by Nielsen Media Research[6] in May 2006. NBC trailed behind rival networks CBS Television (CBS), FOX Broadcasting Company (FOX) and American Broadcasting Company (ABC) (refer to Exhibit 1 for details of NBC's competitors). CBS had been the top network since 2002–03 season during which it dethroned NBC from the top spot. In the 2005–06 season, NBC had lost 1% of its viewers as compared to 2004–05 season (refer to Table 1 for viewership details in 2005–06). FOX emerged as the most popular network among the

This case was written by Vinay Kumar, under the direction of Vivek Gupta, ICFAI Center for Management Research (ICMR). It was complied from published sources, and is intended to be used as a basis for class discussion rather than to illustrate either effective or ineffective handling of a management situation.

18–49 year-old segment (where advertisers paid premiums) for the second consecutive time, while NBC stood fourth here too. Moreover, the Thursday night primetime[7] slot, which had earlier been dominated by NBC, was now taken over almost completely by CBS (refer to Exhibit 2).

NBC, the television network division of NBC Universal, suffered as its own hit series like *Friends, ER,* etc. completed their run, while at the same time, rivals moved in (refer to Exhibit 3 for logo of NBC). FOX's *American Idol* was the "most popular television show" (second consecutive time) during the 2005–06 season. CBS had a great hit in *CSI: Crime Scene Investigation* and ABC had *Desperate Housewives.* But NBC had no new shows to boast of. Its biggest hit was the game show *Deal or No Deal,* but this came in 13th in terms of viewership in the year 2005–06 (refer to Exhibit 4 for primetime rankings for 2005–06). Even the telecast of Winter Olympics (held in Turin) in February 2006, which usually drew a big audience, could not help NBC. Bill

EXHIBIT 1

Profile of Major Competitors of NBC

CBS: In 1928, William S. Paley acquired United Independent Broadcasters Inc., a network of 16 independent radio stations, and renamed it Columbia Broadcast System. In July 1931, CBS began television broadcasting. By 1944, CBS Radio Network had 144 stations, making it the largest in the US. In 1960, CBS became the first network to broadcast the Olympics. From 1967 on, CBS started broadcasting all its programs in color. In April 1971, Columbia Broadcast System officially changed its name to CBS Inc. In mid-1980s, Laurence Tisch (Tisch) acquired 25% stake in CBS. CBS suffered under his leadership. Its financial performance weakened and its shows often appealed only to older people.

Under pressure from all quarters, Tisch sold CBS to Westinghouse Electric Corporation (WEC) for US$ 5.4 billion in 1995. In 1996, WEC acquired Infinity Broadcasting Corporation (IBC) and CBS Radio Network was put under Westwood One, a subsidiary of IBC. In December 1997, WEC changed its name to CBS Corporation. In May 2000, CBS was acquired by Viacom to form Viacom Inc. In December 2005, Viacom Inc. divided its businesses into two: i) CBS Corporation, which consisted of the CBS Television Network, UPN, CBS Stations Group, CBS Paramount Television, King World, Showtime, CBS Radio, CBS Outdoor, Simon & Schuster, Paramount Parks, CBS Digital Media, CSTV and CBS Consumer Products; and ii) Viacom Inc. which consisted of BET, Famous Music, MTV Networks (MTV, VH1, Nickelodeon, Nick at Nite, Comedy Central, etc.), Paramount Pictures and Paramount Home Entertainment.

ABC: ABC was formed in 1944 when NBC sold its NBC Blue Network to Edward J. Noble, owner of Lifesavers Candy. He renamed it American Broadcasting Company in 1945. In April 1948, ABC began its television broadcasting services. In February 1953, ABC merged with United Paramount Theatres Inc., a spin-off of Paramount Pictures Corporation and owned by Leonard Goldenson. In 1954, ABC entered into an alliance with Disney for a Walt Disney TV series called *Disneyland*. This was ABC's first series to be included in Nielsen Top Ten Hits. In 1955, ABC had another successful primetime series *Cheyenne*, produced by Warner Brothers. In mid-1960s, ABC started its own production division called ABC Films.

In 1984, ABC acquired 80% stake in ESPN (the other 20% was held by Hearst Corporation). By this time, ABC found itself in trouble due to lack of innovation, high expenses and declining ratings. In 1986, Capital Cities Communication, a U.S. media company, purchased ABC for US$ 3.5 billion and formed Capital Cities/ABC Inc. Under the new management, ABC again bounced back. In 1995, Walt Disney acquired Capital Cities/ABC for US$ 19 billion. In 1999, ABC started the blockbuster show *Who Wants To Be A Millionaire*? As the show was aired 5 or 6 days a week, its popularity faded. In 2004, ABC bounced back with its blockbuster series *Desperate Housewives*. As of 2006, ABC network consisted of ABC News, ABC Family, ABC Kids, ABC Sports and ABC Radio apart from its flagship ABC.

FOX: In March 1985, the Rupert Murdoch-owned News Corporation acquired Fox Studios[a] for US$ 575 million. He brought together Fox Studios and Metromedia's independent television stations, acquired in the same year, and formed Fox Broadcasting Company in 1986. FOX's first television program was launched in October 1986. Since its launch, FOX positioned itself as a vibrant and youthful channel attracting the 18–34 market. FOX was seen as a potential competitor to CBS, ABC and NBC. In 1993, NFL awarded FOX the rights to broadcast its league till 1997. In early 2000s, FOX lost its foothold due to heavy competition. However, it bounced back with *American Idol*, launched in June 2002. The show was rated number one even in 2006. As of 2006, Fox Broadcasting Company is the third largest broadcast television network in the U.S. after CBS and ABC, with about 200 affiliate stations and 35 own broadcast outlets.

[a] FOX Studios was involved in the development, production and worldwide distribution of feature films and television programs, television broadcasting and cable network programming.
Compiled from various sources.

Caroll, Vice president and Director of Programming at Katz Television Group, remarked, "If you were optimistic about the Olympics, you'd have to be somewhat disappointed with the numbers NBC delivered."[8]

To revive its sagging ratings, NBC acquired the rights to televise the prestigious National Football League[9] (NFL) games which were to start in September 2006. NBC acquired these rights after a gap of seven years. NBC was hopeful that the NFL games along with its new shows would boost its ratings in 2006. Walter Podrazik, Chicago-based writer and communications and logistics consultant said, "Getting NFL football onto the NBC primetime lineup is a major accomplishment. If they have that as an initial lure, it's not that they're one hit away from being the No. 1 network, because they're a little too far behind. But if they can start getting clusters of shows that spill over and get people interested in other shows, then they build in something that gives them, over two or three years, the potential for a comeback."[10]

Viewership of Television Networks (2005–2006)

Network	Viewer Average (in millions)	% Change from 2004–05
CBS	12.6	−2
ABC	10.8	+7
FOX	10.1	+1
NBC	**9.7**	**−1**
WB	3.1	−7
UPN	3.1	−7

Source: Andrew Wallenstein, "Primetime Wrap-up," www.hollywoodreporter.com, May 26, 2006.

Top Primetime Network (1994–2006)

Year	Overall	18–49 Age Group	Thursday (8:00–10:30 pm)
1994–95	ABC	ABC	**NBC**
1995–96	**NBC**	**NBC**	**NBC**
1996–97	**NBC**	**NBC**	**NBC**
1997–98	**NBC**	**NBC**	**NBC**
1998–99	CBS	**NBC**	**NBC**
1999–00	ABC	ABC	**NBC**
2000–01	ABC	**NBC**	**NBC**
2001–02	**NBC**	**NBC**	**NBC**
2002–03	CBS	**NBC**	CBS
2003–04	CBS	**NBC**	CBS
2004–05	CBS	FOX	CBS
2005–06	CBS	FOX	CBS

Adapted from various sources.

NBC Logo

Source: NBCU Photo Bank

Primetime Rankings (2005–2006)

S. No.	Series	Channel	Viewers (in millions)
1	American Idol (Tuesday)	FOX	31.2
2	American Idol (Wednesday)	FOX	30.2
3	CSI: Crime Scene Investigation	CBS	25.2
4	Desperate Housewives	ABC	22.2
5	Grey's Anatomy	ABC	19.9
6	Without a Trace	CBS	18.7
7	Dancing With the Stars (Thursday)	ABC	18.6
8	Survivor: Guatemala	CBS	18.3
9	CSI: Miami	CBS	18.1
10	House	FOX	17.3
11	Survivor: Panama-Exile Island	CBS	16.8
12	Monday Night Football	ABC	16.0
13	Deal or No Deal (Monday)	NBC	15.8
14	The Unit	CBS	15.5
15	Lost	ABC	15.5
16	NCIS	CBS	15.3

Source: Andrew Wallenstein, "Primetime Wrap-Up," www.hollywoodreporter.com, May 26, 2006.

Background Note

In 1919, Radio Corporation of America (RCA) was created to market radio receivers produced by GE, Westinghouse, AT&T and United Fruit Company. In 1926, RCA started the National Broadcasting Company (NBC) for radio broadcasting. In 1927, RCA divided NBC into NBC-Red for broadcasting entertainment and music programs, and NBC-Blue for cultural and news items. In the late 1920s, RCA also began working on television broadcasting and started putting its profits from radio into television R&D. In 1931, NBC began experimental television broadcasts from the Empire State Building in New York.

In 1932, differences among the four companies resulted in an independent RCA with NBC coming under its control. RCA continued funding NBC's television research and in 1939, NBC started regular television broadcasts. RCA slowly became a major producer and marketer of radio receivers and radio content. The NBC network also gained significant popularity and achieved a dominant position in the broadcasting business. This dominance received attention of the U.S. government which ordered the Federal Communications Commission (FCC)[11] to investigate into NBC's practices. FCC found that NBC's two stations dominated the broadcasting market and suggested the sale of one of the networks. RCA took the matter to the court but lost the case. In 1943, NBC-Blue was sold to Edward J. Noble and it was later renamed ABC Networks.

The early 1950s saw a rapid increase in the sales of television sets in the U.S. In 1952, NBC started early morning news. In 1953, it started color broadcasts. In 1964, NBC produced the first movie made for television. In the fifties and sixties, NBC started investing in other television stations, and by the mid-1960s, it owned 13 television stations and one television network in eight countries. During the same time, CBS had emerged as a strong competitor to NBC. With shows such as *The Ed Sullivan Show*, *Gunsmoke*, *The Beverly Hillbillies* and *Green Acres*, *All in the Family*, and *M*A*S*H*, CBS dominated over NBC between the mid-1950s and mid-1970s both in the primetime and daytime rankings.

The rapid boom in television sales affected NBC's radio business, and by 1975, it had nothing much to offer on radio except some hourly news. While NBC was battling with the strong CBS, ABC came up as another formidable television network and pushed NBC from second to third place in the ratings (refer to Exhibit 5 for a note on the U.S. television industry).

EXHIBIT 5

The U.S. Television Industry

The television industry picked up in the U.S. after World War II with radio companies CBS, NBC owned by RCA, and ABC starting their own television stations—CBS, NBC and ABC. DuMont Television Network, owned by DuMont Laboratories, was the fourth television network. They used, and still use, the terrestrial television broadcasting method to air their programs. The early 1950s saw a rapid increase in the sales of television sets and by 1955 nearly half of the U.S. households owned a television set, mostly black and white, though color transmissions had already started. In 1953, DuMont was in deep financial trouble and merged with ABC.

During the 1950s, television networks were allowed to only own up to five television stations across the U.S. Naturally, the networks opted for big cities[b] with huge populations and used affiliates—independent television stations with whom networks share a relationship—to reach smaller markets. Initially, the networks used to start the day with news in the morning while dramas filled the afternoon slot. In the evening, news was followed by shows. Most of the dramas and shows were modified versions of radio programs.

In the 1940s, advertising agencies conceived and produced programs on behalf of sponsors, and even decided the network and the slot to air the program. However, this model didn't work and by the 1950s, the networks controlled the scheduling and programming. The networks allotted a one-minute slot to each advertiser who communicated the uniqueness of the product. The shift to full color transmissions in the 1960s increased advertising revenues rapidly.

In late 1960s, to restrict the monopoly of the three networks, the Federal Communications Commission announced the Financial Interest and Syndication Rules (Fin-Syn) which did not permit networks to produce, distribute and syndicate (selling the program after the first broadcast to others) television programs. Instead, the rights were given to the independent production companies (Hollywood studios which were into television production). The production companies also had the right to own the profits that were generated through syndication.

THE DAWN OF CABLE TELEVISION

The three networks accounted for nearly 90% of the U.S. households during the primetime in the early 1970s. The U.S. had about 600 television stations by 1972, up from 104 stations in 1950. This was also the period that saw the rise of cable television or community antenna television—first used during 1950s to broadcast programs of networks to far-off places which couldn't catch the broadcast signal.

(continued)

EXHIBIT 5   (*continued*)

The U.S. Television Industry

In 1972, Time Life Inc. started the first cable television channel called Home Box Office (HBO), a movie channel for its local cable system in New York. By 1975, HBO became a national channel. In 1977, it started using satellite to distribute its signals to cable operators who received them using a dish. The operator was charged 10 cents a month per subscriber (basic service). This was a huge success as viewers were shown movies without commercials. Soon after this, Ted Turner (Turner), who owned WTBS station, put his station's signal on the same satellite as HBO and started broadcasting games. This meant that cable operators got WTBS programs with their existing dishes for free.

This attracted many other cable services which could be got only for money (paid service). In 1978, Viacom, which owned cable systems across the U.S., launched pay channels called Showtime which showed movies, and Spotlight, a sports channel. In 1979, Warner launched a paid movie channel—The Movie Channel. It also started Nickelodeon, a children's channel. Time started another network called Cinemax, a sibling to HBO. Other services to join the race included Bravo, Playboy and The Entertainment Channel.

During the same time, cable services that accepted advertisements were also started. ESPN was one such channel whose sports events became very popular. The others included MTV, USA, CBN, etc. In 1980, Turner started Cable News Network (CNN), which went on to become one of the most popular news channels in the world. These also came under basic service as they could be obtained for a low fee.

As the cable channels had specific target audiences such as sports fans, movie buffs, etc., much of the network audience became cable viewers. The growing popularity of cable television attracted CBS and ABC. In 1981, CBS launched CBS Cable, a cultural channel. However, it proved a disaster as the service evoked little response among subscribers and advertisers. In 1983, CBS shut down the service after losing US$ 50 million. During the same time, ABC started its own cultural channel called ARTS. It also launched Satellite News Channel (SNC), a 24-hour news channel in partnership with Westinghouse, to compete with CNN.

During the early and mid-1980s, a number of cable services were announced. However, most of them couldn't either materialize or sustain themselves. After the early 1980s, a number of changes took place in the cable television industry. Some of the paid services such as Bravo converted themselves to basic services. ARTS and The Entertainment Channel combined their programming to form Arts and Entertainment. ABC/Westinghouse's SNC was acquired by CNN. Playboy and its partner Escapade parted ways while MTV was acquired by Viacom. In 1984, ABC purchased ESPN from Texaco. Apart from these, a number of channels either changed their programming content or target audience.

THE MAKEOVER

Since mid-1980s, the US television industry has seen many changes. In March 1985, Rupert Murdoch-owned News Corporation acquired Fox Studios and formed the fourth broadcast network FOX Broadcasting Company (FOX) in 1986. In the process, he acquired 100 independent television stations (not affiliated to the big three networks) which became a part of FOX. The acquisition of FOX Studios facilitated the in-house production of its television shows.

In 1986, RCA sold NBC to GE and Capital Cities Communication, a US media company, purchased ABC and formed Capital Cities/ABC Inc. In 1986, Laurence Tisch, a businessman, bought 25% of CBS and assumed the posts of president and CEO. In 1990, Time and Warner Bros. combined to form Time Warner.

By the early 1990s, technology had improved which allowed delivery of up to 500 channels to homes. Channels that aired specific content such as news, cartoons, traveling, religion and science fiction increased. Though cable television reached 85% (according to some estimates) of the U.S. households, its average viewership was half of CBS, ABC, NBC and FOX in a given week. One of the reasons has been the increasing subscription costs for consumers.

In 1991, the networks challenged the Fin-Syn rule in the Los Angeles US Circuit Court. The court was convinced that the networks were no longer the dominant force in the television industry and ruled out the Fin-Syn rule. Judge Manuel Real wrote, "Certainly with the entry of the Fox network, the substantial rise in the number of program producers, the dramatic increase in cable television stations and the development in the sophistication of VCRs, the competitive climate today would unfairly penalize NBC, ABC and CBS in the financing and syndication of off-network programming."[c]

(*continued*)

EXHIBIT 5   *(continued)*

The U.S. Television Industry

This gave rise to a number of changes in the US media and entertainment industry. In 1995, the major studio Walt Disney acquired Capital Cities/ABC while Tisch sold CBS to Westinghouse Electric Corporation (WEC) in 1995 and the merged entity was later called CBS Corporation (CBSC). A few Hollywood studios entered the network race to create their own broadcast network or cable network. In 1995, Warner Brothers launched WB network (WB) and Paramount (owned by Viacom) launched UPN and thus increased the total number of broadcast networks to six. Warner Brothers partnered with Tribune Broadcasting while Paramount Pictures partnered with Chris-Craft's United Television. The two broadcast networks fought intense battles during their early days. In 1996, Time Warner acquired Turner Broadcasting System.

Further changes occurred with Viacom acquiring CBSC in 1999. The new entity, called Viacom, was the second largest media company (worth US$ 80 billion) behind Time Warner. Meanwhile, troubles started between Chris-Craft and Paramount. In 2000, the differences between the two UPN partners aggravated and Viacom acquired Chris-Craft's stake completely. In 2003, NBC acquired the U.S. entertainment assets of Vivendi Universal, a French media company, to form NBC Universal. The assets consisted of Universal Studios, Universal Parks, etc.

In December 2005, Viacom divided itself into Viacom Inc. and CBS (UPN was brought under CBS). In January 2006, Warner Bros. and CBS announced their intention to merge WB and UPN networks to form CW by September 2006. This was because UPN and CW failed to compete with the big four networks and usually commanded lower viewership. This resulted in five major broadcast networks which had studios—CBS (Paramount), NBC (Universal), ABC (Disney), FOX (FOX Studios), and CW (both Paramount and Warner Brothers).

[b] The networks opted for New York, Chicago, Philadelphia, Schenectady, Chicago, and Los Angeles.
[c] Cynthia Littleton, "A Tale of Two Networks," www.hollywoodreporter.com, January 11, 2005.
Compiled from various sources.

In 1981, Grant Tinker[12] (Tinker) was appointed as the Chairman and CEO of NBC. Together with the Chief Programmer Brandon Tartikoff (Tartikoff), Tinker initiated a program to revive NBC's fortunes. NBC started airing series like *St. Elsewhere*, *Family Ties* and *Cheers*—all of which received moderate ratings to begin with. Tinker and Tartikoff continued with these programs even though they were not immediate winners, as they felt that they had the potential to become hits. Meanwhile, the duo launched another series called *Hill Street Blues*.

Things changed dramatically for NBC in 1984 with its situational comedy *The Cosby Show*, which featured the popular comedian, Bill Cosby, who chose to work with NBC over CBS. The show was a blockbuster and enjoyed good viewership on Thursdays 8:00 pm until the year 1990 (refer to Exhibit 6 for top television programs between 1980 and 2005). Meanwhile, the other television series from NBC also started gaining popularity. *The Cosby Show*, *Family Ties*, *Cheers*, *Night Court* and *Hill Street Blues* established NBC as a dominant network on Thursday nights between 8 and 10 pm. The Thursday night lineup, called "Must See TV," continued its dominance until the early 2000s (refer to Exhibit 7 for programs

in Must See TV). In the year 1984–85, NBC's eight shows featured among the top 20 TV shows and the number increased to nine in the following season. Its profits jumped from US$ 48 million in 1984 to US$ 333 million in 1985.

GE Acquires NBC

In 1986, General Electric (GE) purchased RCA, mainly to acquire control of NBC, for US$ 6.3 billion. In 1986, Tinker announced his resignation. John F. Welch (Welch), then Chairman of GE, appointed Robert C. Wright, who had been serving as the President of GE Credit Corporation, as the President and CEO of NBC in August 1986.

Wright's Strategy

Wright, in a bid to focus solely on television, sold NBC's radio network operations to Westwood One[13] in 1988. In the same year, he sold RCA's music network RCA-Victor to Germany-based media company Bertelsmann AG. He felt that NBC was overstaffed and laid off 150 workers. In 1987, he sold RCA's consumer electronics operations to Thomson.

EXHIBIT 6

Top Television Programs (1980–2005)

Year	Program	Channel
1980–81	Dallas	CBS
1981–82	Dallas	CBS
1982–83	60 Minutes	CBS
1983–84	Dallas	CBS
1984–85	Dynasty	ABC
1985–86	**The Cosby Show**	**NBC**
1986–87	**The Cosby Show**	**NBC**
1987–88	**The Cosby Show**	**NBC**
1988–89	**The Cosby Show**	**NBC**
1989–1990	**The Cosby Show**	**NBC**
1990–91	**Cheers**	**NBC**
1991–92	60 Minutes	CBS
1992–93	60 Minutes	CBS
1993–94	60 Minutes	CBS
1994–95	**Seinfeld**	**NBC**
1995–96	**ER**	**NBC**
1996–97	**ER**	**NBC**
1997–98	**Seinfeld**	**NBC**
1998–99	**ER**	**NBC**
1999–2000	Who Wants To Be A Millionaire?	ABC
2000–01	Survivor	CBS
2001–02	**Friends**	**NBC**
2002–03	CSI: Crime Scene Investigation	CBS
2003–04	CSI: Crime Scene Investigation	CBS
2004–05	American Idol	FOX
2005–06	American Idol	FOX

Adapted from various sources.

During this period, the cable television market was growing rapidly. Since its introduction in the late 1970s, cable television had grown to reach 56% of U.S. homes in 1989. The cable channels were grabbing advertising revenues from television networks. Wright felt that a presence in the cable business was a must for NBC, and to this end, he launched a 24-hour financial news channel CNBC (Consumer News and Business Channel) in 1989. However, CNBC lost US$ 60 million in the first two years of its operation due to the slowdown in the U.S. stock market. In 1991, NBC bought CNBC's major rival, the Financial News Network, for more than US$ 100 million and merged it with CNBC.

In the early 1990s, the audience of NBC's TV programs was losing interest in shows like *The Golden Girls*, *The Cosby Show*, and *L.A. Law*. To regain viewership, NBC paid a whooping US$ 401 million to acquire the broadcasting rights for the 1992 Olympics in Barcelona. The next highest bid was US$ 300 million by CBS and ABC. NBC also spent about US$ 225 million for promoting and producing its Olympics coverage. To recoup the costs, NBC partnered with Cablevision to broadcast Olympics on a pay-per-view basis. For US$ 125, viewers would get commercial-free Olympics coverage on three channels (Triplecast) along with the normal over-the-air network. However, this venture proved a disaster as it could attract only 250,000 homes. NBC lost more than US$ 60 million and Cablevision lost US$ 50 million. NBC registered its first loss making year under GE in 1991. In 1992, though it reported a profit of US$ 204 million, it was far lower than US$ 603 million profit in 1989. For the 1992–93 season, NBC's only top-ten hit show was *Cheers* and all its episodes had been aired, so it would not be carrying on into the next year.

Welch had decided to sell any of GE's business divisions if they were not among top 1 or 2 worldwide, so he started looking out for potential buyers for NBC. In 1992, he came close to finalizing a deal with Paramount Communications Inc.'s Chairman Martin S. Davis, but the latter backed out at the last moment.

Between 1990 and 1993, NBC had lost nearly one-third of its viewers. A number of analysts suggested that Wright should be replaced. However, Welch persisted with him. In 1993, Wright appointed Don Ohlemeyer (Ohlemeyer), then executive producer of sports at NBC, as President of NBC West Coast. Ohlemeyer and Wright began taking steps to bring out NBC from the slump.

In February 1993, with *Cheers* (9:00 pm Thursday) nearing completion, NBC moved *Seinfeld* (a sitcom started in 1989) to Thursday nights (9:30 pm) after *Cheers*. This move clicked as *Seinfeld* quickly entered the top ten. After *Cheers* ended, *Seinfeld* was moved to 9:00 pm. By late 1993, *Seinfeld* became the most popular of all NBC's shows drawing viewers of all ages. In the same year, NBC launched another sitcom *Frasier*, touted as a spin-off of *Cheers*, and *Late Night with Conan O'Brien*, a talk show. In 1994, NBC started another sitcom, *Friends*. NBC also signed up

EXHIBIT 7

Must See Television

Season	Time	Series	Season	Time	Series
1984–85	8:00	The Cosby Show		9:30	Frasier
	8:30	Family Ties		10:00	L.A. Law
	9:00	Cheers	1994–95	8:00	Mad About You
	9:30	Night Court		8:30	Friends
	10:00	Hill Street Blues		9:00	Seinfeld
1985–86	8:00	The Cosby Show		9:30	Madman Of
	8:30	Family Ties			The People
	9:00	Cheers		10:00	ER
	9:30	Night Court	1995–96	8:00	Friends
	10:00	Hill Street Blues		8:30	The Single Guy
1986–87	8:00	The Cosby Show		9:00	Seinfeld
	8:30	Family Ties		9:30	Caroline In The City
	9:00	Cheers		10:00	ER
	9:30	Night Court	1996–97	8:00	Friends
	10:00	Hill Street Blues		8:30	The Single Guy
1987–88	8:00	The Cosby Show		9:00	Seinfeld
	8:30	A Different World		9:30	Suddenly Susan
	9:00	Cheers		10:00	ER
	9:30	Night Court	1997–98	8:00	Friends
	10:00	Hill Street Blues		8:30	Union Square
1988–89	8:00	The Cosby Show		9:00	Seinfeld
	8:30	A Different World		9:30	Veronica's Closet
	9:00	Cheers		10:00	ER
	9:30	Dear John. . .	1998–99	8:00	Friends
	10:00	L.A. Law		8:30	Jesse
1989–90	8:00	The Cosby Show		9:00	Frasier
	8:30	A Different World		9:30	Veronica's Closet
	9:00	Cheers		10:00	ER
	9:30	Dear John. . .	1999–00	8:00	Friends
	10:00	L.A. Law		8:30	Jesse
1990–91	8:00	The Cosby Show		9:00	Frasier
	8:30	A Different World		9:30	Stark Raving Mad
	9:00	Cheers		10:00	ER
	9:30	Grand	2000–01	8:00	Friends
	10:00	L.A. Law		8:30	Cursed
1991–92	8:00	The Cosby Show		9:00	Will & Grace
	8:30	A Different World		9:30	Just Shoot Me
	9:00	Cheers		10:00	ER
	9:30	Wings	2001–02	8:00	Friends
	10:00	L.A. Law		8:30	Inside Schwartz
1992–93	8:00	A Different World		9:00	Will & Grace
	8:30	Final Appeal		9:30	Just Shoot Me
	9:00	Cheers		10:00	ER
	9:30	Wings	2002–03	8:00	Friends
	10:00	L.A. Law		8:30	Scrubs
1993–94	8:00	Mad About You		9:00	Will & Grace
	8:30	Wings		9:30	Good Morning, Miami
	9:00	Seinfeld		10:00	ER

Source: "The Shows of NBC's 'Must See TV'," www.cse.psu.edu, 2003.

popular director Steven Spielberg as an executive producer of the medical drama *ER*.

All these series were primarily targeted at the youth. The tremendous success of *Seinfeld* helped in gaining a huge audience for the other primetime series like *Friends* and *ER*. *Seinfeld* led NBC's Thursday night primetime during most of its broadcasting period which ended in May 1998. *Friends* and *ER* were also popular, with *Friends* becoming one of the most popular sitcoms in the history of television in the U.S. This made NBC regain its popularity with the 18–49 year segment and it emerged as the top network in the U.S. in the early 1990s. In the meantime, the stock market picked up and CNBC gained popularity. It doubled its profits to US$ 50 million in 1995.

In October 1994, it was reported that Time Warner and GE were in talks, and there was speculation that GE was going to sell NBC to Time Warner. It was reported that Time Warner was ready to acquire a 49% stake in NBC for US$ 2.5 billion and would manage NBC's entertainment operations. Welch wanted Time Warner to take control of NBC's other operations such as news, sports, etc. also. But the deal never materialized.

In 1995, NBC launched CNBC Asia, a 24-hour business news channel for the Asian region. In the same year, NBC started NBC Digital Publishing for publishing CD-ROMs and other digital products and NBC Online Ventures to start websites for its news, sports and entertainment channels. In 1995, NBC became the first television network to launch a full-fledged website—NBC.com.

During the late 1980s and 1990s, when the media industry was witnessing consolidations, Wright too wanted to acquire other media companies. However, the finance department of GE stopped him, citing financial constraints. Wright remarked, "We would try to do things, but the financial guys would say, 'This is going to kill us'."[14] Welch also supported them saying that a big media company required huge investment which could hit GE's earnings per share. In the mid-1990s, Wright asked Welch why it was possible for News Corporation, which was smaller than GE, to create the first global entertainment and news network (by acquiring Fox Studios in 1985), while GE was unwilling to make NBC a global network (which would make and distribute programs globally).

Welch was convinced, and Wright and he started scouting around for possible acquisitions. However, acquisitions weren't easy to come by. NBC failed to persuade Ted Turner to merge his Turner Broadcasting System (TBS), which owned channels such as CNN and TNT, with NBC. If it had come through, this deal would have made NBC the largest cable network in the U.S. However, Turner differed with NBC on the issue of managing the merged entity and finally sold TBS and its assets to Time Warner in 1996. Commenting on this, John Malone, CEO of Tele-Communications Inc. said, "If NBC had joined with Ted (Turner), it would have caught Rupert Murdoch.[15] They would have married a domestic broadcast network to worldwide cable networks. It's all about trying to catch Rupert. He's the guy out in the lead. The broad strategy is to take the programming you create and to exploit it as a worldwide business by using facilities that you own. To become vertically integrated worldwide—that's the game."[16]

Welch wanted Wright to make NBC a prominent part of GE and to go global just like Fox which promoted and distributed its programs globally. His aim was to make NBC the top television network in the world. In July 1996, NBC entered into an alliance with Microsoft Corporation[17] (Microsoft) and started MSNBC, a 24-hour cable news channel, and a website, MSNBC.com. Microsoft agreed to invest US$ 220 million for a 50% share in the cable channel and to share half of the operating expenses for both television and website for an unspecified time. By the end of 1996, MSNBC had 22 million subscribers, the highest for any new cable channel. NBC also launched CNBC Europe in the same year.

Again in mid-1999, there were rumors that NBC would be sold to Time Warner. In December 1999, Welch announced publicly that NBC would not be put for sale again. This stance led some analysts to believe that Welch was aiming to take on Rupert Murdoch.

In 1999, NBC bought a 32% stake in Paxson Communications Corporation (Paxson) for US$ 415 million. Paxson owned PAX-TV which completely owned or had a financial stake in 72 television stations in the U.S., plus contracts with 52 affiliate stations.[18] Under this deal, Paxson aired NBC programs after they were aired on NBC. The deal, which was visualized as the first step towards acquiring Paxson, gave NBC the option to acquire a controlling stake in Paxson within ten years. However, this would be possible only if the FCC raised the rule which did not permit companies to own a broadcasting network that reached more than 35% of the U.S. households (refer to Table 2 for details of FCC rules).

TABLE 2

FCC Rules Before 2003

- The owners of a broadcast station were not allowed to own daily newspapers in the same market and vice versa.

- No company could own broadcast stations that reached more than 35% of US households.

- A company should not own more than eight radio stations in a single listening area. The number of stations varied depending on the population of the area.

- A company should not own more than two broadcast television stations in a particular market.

- The four major networks—NBC, CBS, FOX and ABC—were prevented from merging with each other.

Adapted from "Action Alert: FCC Ready to Roll Back Limits on Media Consolidation," www.fair.org, December 5, 2002.

In 1999, during the dot-com boom, NBC launched NBCi (NBC Internet), a publicly held Internet firm. NBCi tied up with Xoom.com, a San Francisco-based online community center and e-commerce website with 7.5 million viewers, and Snap.com, news and search website jointly owned by NBC (60%) and Cnet (40%). GE owned a 53% stake in NBCi while Xoom.com and Snap.com owned 34% and 13% respectively. NBCi was positioned as a general-interest website to attract a large audience and many advertisers by leveraging the rich content and e-commerce experience of the two sites. The site, which operated under Snap.com name, included a search facility, email, chat, NBC content, e-commerce, etc. and was seen as a competitor to Yahoo! Describing NBCi, Marty Yudkovitz, President of NBC Interactive, said, "To users, this means that they will only have to go to one place—Snap.com—on the Web to search, chat with users of like interest, email . . . and purchase products."[19]

NBC in the New Millennium

The year 2000 brought bad news for NBC. Due to the dot-com bubble bust,[20] Internet advertising fell drastically. The U.S. economy was experiencing a downturn, and a number of online companies were closed. NBCi, which had grown rapidly and employed about 800 employees, also ran into trouble. It lost US$ 662 million in 2000 and a number of employees were laid off. Apart from the fall in advertising revenues, there were other reasons for NBCi's problems. NBC did not have a clearly defined Internet strategy, according to some analysts, and it had not differentiated NBCi from other portals such as Yahoo! David Card, Analyst at Jupiter Research said, "There's nothing wrong with a general-purpose portal, especially for a media company that is already a network. But they executed horribly. They didn't take advantage of their TV network or the natural affinities of their programming. On top of that, they were late."[21]

In April 2001, NBC bought the remaining equity stake in NBCi from Xoom.com and Snap.com and integrated all its assets. Commenting on the acquisition, Wright said, "NBC has been a pioneer in new technologies, and the steps we took to create NBCi were in keeping with that tradition. However, recent changes in the portal space and the Internet advertising market have caused us to reexamine this initiative. This acquisition will enable us to build on our competitive advantage in the Internet arena while leveraging our core competencies as a network."[22]

On September 7, 2001, Jeffrey R. Immelt (Immelt), who was working as President and CEO of GE Medical Systems, replaced Welch as the Chairman and CEO of GE. Immelt was keener on media businesses than his predecessor and thus he complemented Wright's ambitions. In April 2002, NBC purchased the broadcast and cable business of Telemundo Communications Group (Telemundo), a Spanish television network, for US$ 1.98 billion in equity. The acquisition of Telemundo made NBC the only major television network to devote a full channel to the rapidly growing Spanish-speaking population in the U.S.

This deal resulted in a feud with Paxson. With the acquisition of Telemundo, NBC owned three stations each in four markets—New York, Dallas, Chicago and Miami; this could be considered a violation of the FCC rule.[23] However, since NBC had a 32% stake (less than the FCC threshold of 35%) in Paxson, the stations were not counted as "NBC-owned" by the FCC. According to Paxson, this was violating their contract, as NBC would not be able to purchase it in future. In December 2001, Paxson commenced a binding arbitration process against NBC. It also made a filing with the FCC requesting it to disallow

NBC from acquiring Telemundo. In April 2002, the FCC rejected the appeal stating that it was a private matter of NBC and Paxson.

In December 2002, NBC acquired Bravo cable network, managed by Rainbow Media Holdings LLC, a subsidiary of Cablevision Systems Corporation (Cablevision) for US$ 1.25 billion. Industry analysts felt the acquisition was a good bet as Bravo reached more than 68 million homes in the U.S. It generated close to US$ 100 million in cable licensing fees, and earned about US$ 60 million through advertising in 2002.

In June 2003, FCC revised the media rules and increased the national television ownership limit from 35% to 45%. However, this ruling was stayed by the U.S. Court of Appeals for the Third Circuit in Philadelphia, after some coalition groups such as the Media Alliance, Fairness and Accuracy in Reporting, the Center for Digital Democracy and the Consumer Federation of America appealed against the proposed changes. They alleged that the new rules would give a few media companies too much control over the industry which would nullify the public voice. This further aggravated the disagreement with Paxson.[24]

Forming NBC Universal

Wright had long been interested in acquiring companies that created content. This was something he couldn't do under Welch. However, in mid-2003 when Vivendi Universal Entertainment (Vivendi), the French media and telecommunications company, announced the sale of its U.S. entertainment business—Universal Pictures, Universal Parks, Universal Television and a number of cable channels, many U.S. media giants were interested. Metro Goldwyn Mayer (MGM), Viacom, Liberty Media and NBC competed with each other to acquire Universal's assets.

One of Vivendi's largest shareholders, Edgar Bronfman (Bronfman),[25] made an offer of €13 billion in cash to buy all of Vivendi's assets and promised to pay off some of the debts of the division. Wall Street analysts estimated that Vivendi was worth US$ 11 billion. Bronfman's high offer forced MGM and Liberty Media out of the bidding. There was speculation that Bronfman would be selected. However, Vivendi preferred NBC over Bronfman, and thus NBC had its first big acquisition under Wright. Vivendi's preference for GE (NBC) was surprising because GE wanted to be a majority stakeholder and was not interested in putting cash into

the deal. Vivendi may have not wanted to be fully taken over by Bronfman. NBC was keen to leverage on Universal's rich content in its film and television production divisions. It also intended to sell and distribute Universal's DVD titles, television programs and films in more than 200 countries.

In October 2003, Vivendi and GE signed agreements to combine Vivendi's U.S. entertainment assets with NBC. The new company was named NBC Universal and was expected to generate US$ 15 billion in revenues every year while its assets were worth around US$ 43 billion. As per the deal, GE paid US$ 3.8 billion in cash and assumed Vivendi's US$ 1.7 billion debt. GE also allowed Vivendi to acquire a 20% stake (worth US$ 8.6 billion) in NBC Universal. Wright was appointed as the CEO of the new entity. Commenting on the importance of the deal, Immelt said, "With this merger, NBC will stay in the forefront of the fundamental changes taking place in television and other media. The new NBC Universal will have the assets, the management team and the operating focus to prosper in a digital world and enhance value for GE and Vivendi Universal shareholders."[26] The merger was completed by May 2004 (refer to Exhibit 8 for businesses of NBCU).

NBC Slips in Ratings

The ratings woes for NBC started in February 2001, when CBS shifted its blockbuster reality series *Survivor* to Thursdays (between 8:00 and 9:00 pm) opposite *Friends* on NBC. To counter this, NBC increased the duration of *Friends* by 10 minutes (up to 8:40 pm) to affect the second half of *Survivor*. CBS also moved its crime series *CSI: Crime Scene Investigation* after *Survivor* to take on NBC's *Will & Grace*.

When the ratings for the first week were reported, *Survivor* beat *Friends* convincingly even in the 18–49 demographics. Though NBC was still the winner with four of its shows featuring in the Top 5, CBS exposed NBC's vulnerability on Thursday nights. *CSI* had lost to *Will & Grace*, but its popularity rose continuously. Even so, NBC had topped the overall ratings for the year 2001–02.

CBS tightened the screws starting from the 2002–03 season. Led by the increasingly popular *CSI*, CBS became the most watched network for the 2002–03 season. CSI, watched by 26.2 million viewers, comfortably overtook *Friends* which had 21.8 million viewers. Other shows of CBS's such as *Survivor* and

Everybody Loves Raymond also featured in the top ten. On the whole, CBS had four series in the top ten while NBC and Fox had three each. CBS's average viewership increased by 2% as compared to the previous season, while NBC's decreased by 2%. The CBS shows continued their dominance even during the 2003–04 season with *CSI* being the most watched show and CBS being the top network in terms of viewership.

The start of 2004 spelled more trouble for NBC. Its blockbuster sitcom *Friends* was due to end in May 2004 while *Scrubs* was receiving moderate ratings. *Friends* had been the linchpin for NBC's dominance on Thursday nights and the network had still to find another suitable show to match the blockbuster. *Frasier*, another sitcom aired on Tuesday nights, was also due to end in May.

Meanwhile, NBC started *The Apprentice* in January 2004 on Thursday at 8:30 pm. The popular one-hour show was shifted to Wednesday nights after the first two weeks. However, it could not match the popularity of FOX's *American Idol*. In the face-off, *American Idol* attracted 29 million viewers while *The Apprentice* managed only 12 million viewers. NBC shifted back the show to Thursday nights at 9:00 pm from the next week. This shuffle was also aimed at strengthening NBC's Thursday lineup after *Friends* was over. Commenting on the shuffling, Mitch Metcalf, Head of Scheduling at NBC said, "Two of the hottest shows on television right now are 'The Apprentice' and 'American Idol.' We think it's a disservice to viewers to have them squaring off against each other. We consider these moves a 'win-win' for NBC and the audience."[27]

In early 2004, NBC had about 14 new shows in development. At that time, it was reported that *Friends* would be replaced with *Father of the Pride*, which contained computer-generated animation by Dreamworks SKG.[28] However, later NBC announced that *Friends* would be replaced by another sitcom *Joey* with Matt LeBlanc (of *Friends* fame) in the lead role as an aspiring actor who wanted to make it big in Los Angeles.

There were very high expectations of *Joey* in the media and in the audience. NBC spared no efforts in promoting *Joey*. It advertised in more than 6,500 movie screens which were showing big films like *Spider-Man 2, I, Robot*, etc. Meanwhile, analysts felt that NBC would be much weaker after *Friends*. Gail Berman, President of FOX Entertainment said, "We believe that NBC will remain competitive on Thurs-

day night. But we also believe that they will be down significantly from where they were with *Friends*."[29]

Meanwhile, CBS announced that it would start the second spin-off of *CSI* called *CSI: New York* (*CSI: Miami* was the first spin-off announced in 2002). The new show was scheduled for October 2004 (Wednesday 10:00 pm) airing and would take on NBC's super hit show *Law & Order*.

The first episode of *Joey* was aired on September 9, 2004 and was watched by 18.5 million viewers. Contrary to NBC's expectations, most of them termed the show "average" and said it was no match for *Friends*. In September 2004, NBC as a whole lost 16% of its audience, with *Joey* losing 48%. Also, *CSI: New York* comfortably surpassed *Law & Order* to take the Wednesday night crown for the first time. About 18.51 million people watched the premier of *CSI: New York* which was 2 million more than *Law & Order*. This continued even after the first week. Also, NBC's Thursday night show *ER* was beaten by CBS's, *Without a Trace* (which showed an FBI's Missing Persons Squad searching for missing persons) for the first time. As a result, CBS now took over NBC's primetime viewership.

The decline of popularity for *Joey* continued as people thought it was awful and lacked humor. Other NBC shows such as *Father of the Pride, LAX* and *Hawaii* had also been disappointments. The failure of *Joey* resulted in NBC slipping to fourth position among the 18–49 year olds and brought down its advertising revenues significantly. The advertising commitments which were US$ 2.9 billion for 2004–05 season, slipped to US$ 1.9 billion for the 2005–06 season. Advertisers were not impressed by NBC's 2005–06 schedule and shows which included sitcom *My Name Is Earl*, drama *E-Ring*, and the reality series *Three Wishes*. On the other hand, ABC which climbed to third in rankings was expected to increase its advertising revenues by US$ 500 million.

Further, NBC's Sunday night successes like *Crossing Jordan* and *Law & Order: Criminal Intent* started facing stiff competition from ABC's *Desperate Housewives*. In fact, NBC's executives had rejected the script of *Desperate Housewives* when its writer Marc Cherry approached them before finalizing the deal with ABC. Series like *American Dreams* (aired during ABC's reality show *Extreme Makeover: Home Edition*) and *ER* (aired during CBS's *Without a Trace*) decreased viewership for NBC. On the other hand, CBS had a strong 2004–05 season with *Survivor, CSI: Miami* (Monday). NBC's management was very disappointed with the

EXHIBIT 8

NBCU

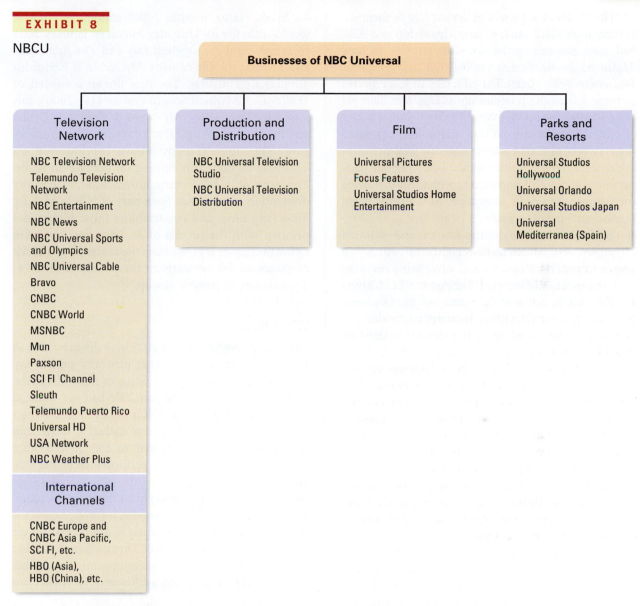

Businesses of NBC Universal

Television Network

NBC Television Network

Telemundo Television Network

NBC Entertainment

NBC News

NBC Universal Sports and Olympics

NBC Universal Cable

Bravo

CNBC

CNBC World

MSNBC

Mun

Paxson

SCI FI Channel

Sleuth

Telemundo Puerto Rico

Universal HD

USA Network

NBC Weather Plus

International Channels

CNBC Europe and CNBC Asia Pacific, SCI FI, etc.

HBO (Asia), HBO (China), etc.

Production and Distribution

NBC Universal Television Studio

NBC Universal Television Distribution

Film

Universal Pictures

Focus Features

Universal Studios Home Entertainment

Parks and Resorts

Universal Studios Hollywood

Universal Orlando

Universal Studios Japan

Universal Mediterranea (Spain)

Source: www.nbcuni.com.

decline in ratings and felt that it would take at least two years to turn things around. Commenting on this, Jeff Zucker (Zucker), President of NBC Universal said, "There's no question we're in a downturn right now, and it doesn't turn around overnight."[30]

The Turnaround Efforts

To revive its sagging fortunes, NBC turned its focus to sports. Zucker said, "Sports is going to play a critical role in the rebuilding of NBC prime time."[31] On April 18, 2005, NBC finalized an important six-year deal with the National Football League (NFL) to bring back the NFL telecasts to the channel after having lost the rights to CBS in 1998. The deal was the result of the ABC's, decision to not renew the contract with NFL for the NFL season starting in 2006. The deal, worth approximately US$ 3.6 billion, would give NBC the right to broadcast primetime American football[32] on Sunday nights (Sunday Night Football) and the highlights of the Sunday afternoon games on its pre-game show (scheduled before the start of the Sunday night game). NBC also bagged rights to broadcast two Super Bowls in 2009 and 2012.

The deal was expected to revive NBC's fortunes. Sunday nights had usually more viewership and ABC had been dominating the slot with hits like *Extreme Makeover: Home Edition* (8:00–9:00), and *Desperate Housewives* (9:00–10:00). The NFL telecast was expected to bring advertising revenues up to US$ 6 million per hour. Elaborating on this, Wright said, "Content is king at NBC Universal and NFL programming represents the very best in strong and consistently well-performing content. We are thrilled to be re-igniting our partnership with the NFL and joining with them in moving the 36-year American institution of Monday Night Football to Sunday Nights."[33]

NBC also banked on the winter and summer Olympics, for which it had rights till 2012.[34] It hoped to gain both viewers and advertising revenues with the most watched sporting event. NBC Universal planned to sell specific events of the Olympics through its cable television, Internet and video-on-demand format to cash in on the viewer's interest for real-time highlights.

NBC also had high hopes on *The Apprentice* show with Martha Stewart[35] (Stewart) on September 21, 2005. The series, in which 16 candidates competed for an opportunity to work with Stewart, was named *The Apprentice: Martha Stewart*. The show's original host Donald Trump made way for Stewart and acted as one of the executive producers. However, the show was unable to match the popularity of the original version and was thus limited to just one series. However, NBC claimed that it always wanted to telecast only one series with Stewart.

Commenting on NBC's futile efforts, Bill Carroll, Vice-president and Director of Programming at Katz Television Group, said, "NBC is struggling and executives have to be disappointed. The one bright spot is *My Name Is Earl* but there's not much other than that. Having the Winter Olympics on the near horizon and football for the Fall will help but ultimately, it is series programming that makes the difference and NBC hasn't been able to make a turnaround in that area yet."[36]

In December 2005, NBC inked a deal with Apple Computers Inc.[37] to sell its television shows through iTunes Music Store, from where people could download and play on an Apple video iPod. Under the deal, NBC offered about 300 specific episodes from its new shows such as *Law & Order*, and *The Office*, and old shows such as *Alfred Hitchcock Presents* etc., through the iTunes Music Store.

In the same month, NBC announced that it would reshuffle its Thursday lineup in January 2006 by removing the struggling *Joey* and *The Apprentice* and moving the hit comedy *My Name Is Earl* from Tuesday to Thursday. The new lineup consisted of *Will & Grace* (which was to end in May 2006), followed by *Four Kings*, *My Name Is Earl*, *The Office*, and the long standing *ER* at 10:00 pm. The shuffling gave NBC four comedy shows continuously on Thursday nights. Commenting on this, Kevin Reilly, President of NBC Entertainment, said, "Certainly destination comedy has been part of NBC's identity for a long time, and reassembling those blocks is a priority. With the success of *Earl* this year and with *Office* finding its legs, we have the makings of a block of shows we felt perfectly fit the profile of an NBC Thursday night comedy lineup."[38]

What Next?

NBC's revenues for the year 2005 were down by 23% to US$ 5.1 billion while all other networks gained revenues (refer to Table 3 for revenues of networks in the years 2004 and 2005). The year 2006 had not changed NBC's fortunes by much. NBC's hopes for the Winter Olympics in February 2006 were dashed as viewership was down 34% as compared to the 2002 Winter Olympics. Though the poor performance of the U.S. athletes was one of the reasons, the viewership loss was primarily due to competition from *American Idol*, *Desperate Housewives*, *Grey's Anatomy*, *Survivor*, etc. NBC's aggressive cross promotion of its Olympics coverage on USA Network, CNBC, and NBCOlympics.com couldn't increase its viewership. Commenting on this, Jordan Breslow, Director of Broadcast Research at MediaCom

TABLE 3

Revenues of Television Networks for the Years 2004 and 2005

Network	Revenues (in million US$)		
	2004	2005	Growth
CBS	4,449	4,671	5%
ABC	3,514	3,911	11%
NBC	5,062	3,900	−23%
FOX	2,405	2,624	9%

Source: John M. Higgins, "CBS: In the Money," January 9, 2006.

said, "The Olympics rarely go up against original programming, and the other networks decided to put their best products forward. It has never gone up against *American Idol*, and I don't think anyone should be surprised that the older-skewing Olympics should not have any impact on 'Idol.' I look at the Olympics as fallback programming. It's like, take your pick of first-run product and if there isn't anything there, then, great, tune into NBC."[39]

In March 2006, *Joey* returned on NBC and this time against *American Idol* on Tuesday. The serial attracted only 4 million viewers as against 7.28 million when it was aired on Thursdays, and was immediately pulled back. In April 2006, Katie Couric, the Co-host of the *Today* show, the most profitable news program on television generating close to US$ 500 million in advertising revenues annually for NBC, announced that she was moving to CBS, after being with NBC for 15 years. Some analysts said that it would have a major impact on NBC.

In May 2006, NBC announced its schedule for 2006–07, which included the important *Sunday Night Football* and six new dramas such as *Friday Night Lights, Studio 60 on the Sunset Strip, Kidnapped,* and four comedy series such as *Twenty Good Years and 30 Rock,* etc. Commenting on this, Reilly said, "The face of NBC is changing. We took the first step this season with Thursday hits *My Name Is Earl* and *The Office.* Next season we'll add momentum and excitement with the addition of 'Sunday Night Football' and establish a foundation of quality across the week by standing behind shows that each say something about who we are."[40]

However, NBC announced a revised lineup in the very next week, after ABC announced that it was moving its *Grey's Anatomy* to Thursday 9:00 pm slot during which NBC planned to air its big bet *Studio 60 on the Sunset Strip.* NBC also shuffled some of its other programs which were against its rival's big hits. Reilly said that NBC aimed to not to put its best bets against top programs of the rivals to allow them to gain popularity.

Analysts felt that NBC could not continue with such defensive strategies for long and advocated that it should take some measures to come back strongly. They found fault with NBC pushing *Studio 60 on the Sunset Strip* to Monday night at 10:00 pm. They felt it should have been shown early to gain a larger audience, and also to avoid clashing with ESPN's *Monday Night Football.*

Analysts felt that NBC was unable to leverage the brand image it had built through its hit shows like *Cheers, Friends,* and *Seinfeld.* It couldn't develop great new programs to fill the slots vacated by *Friends* and other hit shows. David Thomas, a Chicago-based writer and publisher of blogs—Miami Dolphins and OrangeAndTeal.com—said, "NBC could never fill that 8:30 p.m. slot between *Friends* and *Seinfeld* ever. It was poor development. That slot was like the sure sign of death for a new show. . . . If you couldn't get success there for all those years, the development everywhere else was probably not doing so well. . . . There was never an interesting drama or cult hit like *Alias.* So they had no credibility. And then they lost the folks like us who loved the network but went elsewhere like HBO for good content."[41]

Despite NBC's poor show, some analysts said that the network was finally making serious turnaround efforts. They supported NBC's rescheduling and felt that it was important for the network to shield its new big programs against the established mighty ones. As NBC acquired *Studio 60 on the Sunset* Strip by winning a bid against CBS and would pay around US$ 3 million per episode, it was important for it to be off the competition to gain advertising revenues and viewers. Analysts were optimistic about the advertising revenues that could be generated by the drama *Friday Night Lights,* and the NFL games. Satisfied with the efforts of NBC, John Rash of Campbell Mithun, a marketing communications agency, said, "I'm encouraged at the direction NBC is headed. They've definitely got some buzz going for a few new shows."[42]

ENDNOTES

1. David Bianculli, "We Got Clobbered, but We'll be Back," www.nydailynews.com, July 25, 2005.
2. "NBC: Now It's Wait-And-See TV," www.businessweek.com, May 9, 2005.
3. Paul R. La Monica, "Must-flee TV?" www.money.cnn.com, August 31, 2005.
4. Started in 1962 by Boyd Jefferies, Jefferies & Company is a global investment bank and institutional securities firm. Headquartered in New York, the company is into financial advisory services, institutional brokerage, securities research and asset management business.
5. A television season in the U.S. usually starts in mid-September and ends in May of the next year. Networks vie with each other to attract advertisers by showcasing their lineups for the Fall (September–December).
6. Headquartered in New York, Nielsen Media Research provides television audience measurement and advertising information services worldwide. It has offices around the world in more than 40 countries.
7. Thursday night primetime, between 8:00 pm and 10:00 pm, was made a most popular slot for TV viewers by NBC during the 1980s

and 1990s when it began showing blockbuster serials at this time. Since then, the television networks have been vying with each other to dominate this slot by airing their best shows and advertisers have been paying premiums to advertise during that time.

8. Paul R. La Monica, "Olympics Didn't Sweep Away ABC and FOX," www.money.cnn.com, March 2, 2006.

9. Started in 1920 as American Professional Football Association, National Football League is the largest professional American football league with thirty-two teams from all of America. The teams are divided into two groups—American Football Conference (AFC) and National Football Conference (NFC). Each Conference is further divided into East, West, North and South, each consisting of four teams. The NFL pre-season starts somewhere in August while the regular season starts on the first Sunday after the Labor Day (first Monday of September every year). Majority of the matches are played on Sundays and Mondays and a few on Thursdays. The winner is selected in the final Super Bowl, usually held in February. The season ends with a match between the stars of AFC and NFC groups called Pro Bowl.

10. David B. Wilkerson, "NBC's Bid To 'Heist' Ratings Gold," www.marketwatch.com, February 6, 2006.

11. Established in 1934, the FCC is an independent government agency which regulates interstate and international communications by radio, television, wire, satellite and cable (Source: www.fcc.gov).

12. Grant Tinker co-founded MTM Enterprises, a production company, along with his wife in 1970 to produce *The Mary Tyler Moore Show* for CBS. The show became highly popular. The company was sold to News Corporation in 1996.

13. Based in New York, Westwood One is one of the largest radio networks in the U.S. It produces and distributes radio programs in the U.S. and is managed by CBS Radio.

14. Devin Leonard, "The Unlikely Mogul Jack Welch was his Friend. But Jeff Immelt has Given NBC Chief Bob Wright What He's Always Wanted: An Empire," www.money.cnn.com, September 29, 2003.

15. Born in March 1931 in Melbourne, Australia, Rupert Murdoch is the chairman and managing director of News Corporation, one of the largest media conglomerates in the world which owns FOX Broadcasting Company.

16. "The Race for a Global Network," www.kenauletta.com, 1996.

17. Headquartered in Redmond, Washington, Microsoft Corporation is the world's largest software company. The company provides operating systems such as Windows XP, home entertainment products, owns an internet portal MSN and has presence in the television market. For the year ended June 2005, Microsoft's annual revenues were US$ 39.8 billion and profits were US$ 12.25 billion.

18. Affiliate stations are television stations owned by other companies which enter into a contractual agreement with the network stations to air programs of the network.

19. Deborah Solomon, "NBC Links up With Xoom, Snap to Form New Net Firm," www.sfgate.com, May 11, 1999.

20. Between 1995 and 2000, a number of firms that provided products and services related to or by using the Internet grew rapidly in number, as many individuals ambitiously started their own companies. The firms, known as dot-com companies, offered more or less similar products and services. The uncontrolled proliferation of such companies ended with the bubble bursting in March 2000 leading to the closure of many such companies.

21. Aparna Kumar, "Short Life, Long Death of NBCi," www.wired.com, April 12, 2001.

22. "NBC to Acquire NBC Internet Inc. (NBCi)," www.prnewswire.com, April 9, 2001.

23. In addition, the acquisition resulted in NBC owning three stations in Los Angeles–one already owned by NBC (KNBC-TV, Channel 4) and the other two (KWHY-TV Channel 22 and KVEA(TV) Channel 52) acquired from Telemundo. NBC requested FCC for one year time to divest KWHY-TV, Channel 22).

24. The dispute ended in November 2005, when NBC agreed to buy a controlling stake in Paxson. Under the deal, NBC got an 18-month's time to buy all of Bud Paxson's shares. If the federal rules didn't change within the next 18 months, NBC could transfer the right to a third party. In case the third party could not exercise the rights, NBC would have to pay US$ 105 million to Paxson's shareholders.

25. Bronfman was the biggest shareholder of VU. He was heading Seagram in 2000 when it merged with Vivendi to form Vivendi Universal.

26. Kenneth N. Gilpin, "GE and Vivendi Agree on Terms of NBC Universal Merger," www.nytimes.com, October 8, 2003.

27. "Idol Sends NBC, Apprentice Scrambling," www.zapt2it.com, January 23, 2004.

28. Dreamworks SKG was a studio started by noted film director Steven Spielberg, and David Geffen and Jeffrey Katzenberg in 1994. It was sold to Viacom in late 2005.

29. Ronald Grover, "Filling the Shoes of Missing Friends," www.businessweek.com, August 18, 2004.

30. Andrew Wallenstein, "NBC Doldrums Might Continue, Reilly Admits," www.mediaweek.com, July 25, 2005.

31. Paul J. Gough, "Zucker: NBC Expected Upfront Hit," www.mediaweek.com, June 22, 2005.

32. American football, called football in America and Canada, is different from the normal football and is played with an oval shaped ball. The game closely resembles rugby.

33. "NFL Returns to NBC," www.thefutoncritic.com, April 18, 2005.

34. NBC had acquired Olympic broadcasting rights for the U.S. for Athens (2004), Torino (2006), Beijing (2008), Vancouver (2010) and London (2012).

35. Martha Stewart, born in August 1941, is a multimedia and lifestyle entrepreneur. In October 2004, Stewart was jailed for five months at a federal prison for lying to federal investigators, in connection with her involvement in a dubious stock sale of ImClone Systems, a pharmaceutical company.

36. Paul R. La Monica, "ABC and CBS Clean House During Sweeps," www.money.cnn.com, November 30, 2005.

37. Based in Cupertino, California, Apple is considered the pioneer of the personal computer revolution in the late 1970s. Started by Steve Jobs and Steve Wozniack in 1976, Apple started manufacturing computers and later developed the powerful Macintosh range of computers. Apple now is more famous for its iPod, a hard-drive based music player. For the financial year ended September 2005, Apple's sales were US$ 13.93 billion and profits were US$ 1.335 billion.

38. Andrew Wallenstein, "NBC to Shuffle Primetime Lineup in January," www.hollywoodreporter.com, December 2, 2005.

39. Kevin Downey, "NBC's New Big Worry: Losing Sweeps," www.medialifemagazine.com, February 16, 2006.

40. "NBC Announces 2006–07 Primetime Schedule," www.comingsoon.net, May 15, 2006.

41. Diego Vasquez, "On Giving The Axe To NBC's Jeff Zucker," www.medialifemagazine.com, June 15, 2006.

42. Brooks Barnes, "Can 'Studio 60' Save NBC," www.online.wsj.com, May 15, 2006.

Tsingtao Brewery Co., Ltd. (A)

This case was prepared by Shengjun Liu, Richard Ivey School of Business, the University of Western Ontario.

IVEY

On July 31, 2001, Peng Zuoyi, the charismatic general manager of Tsingtao Brewery Co., Ltd. (Tsingtao Brewery), died of a sudden heart attack while swimming in the sea. This sudden event made the company, which had been running fast on the road of acquisition, lose its "driver." Since 1996, Peng had expanded Tsingtao Brewery to a giant, by merging dozens of beer enterprises. As a result, the company raised its market share from 2.2 per cent in 1998 to 11 per cent in 2001, and regained the leading position in China. Nonetheless, frequent acquisitions also led to some negative effects. Although as its major business revenue rose from RMB1.05 billion in 1993 to RMB5.28 billion in 2001, the net profit decreased from RMB225 million to RMB103 million.[1] By the end of April 2002, one-third of the company's 48 subsidiaries were making profits, another one-third were breaking even and the remaining subsidiaries were in deficit.[2] Investors doubted the value of company's acquisitions: the H-share price of Tsingtao Brewery decreased by 52.38 per cent while the Hang Seng Index increased by 45.30 per cent between 1995 and 2001.

On August 29, 2001, the board of Tsingtao Brewery appointed Jin Zhiguo, ex-president of the North China Region, as general manager.[3] Jin began his employment in the company in 1975, as a worker. Later, he worked as a workshop head, as an assistant to the factory manager and as the general manager of Xi'an subsidiary. Jin was recognized by his competitors as a person who was a tough rival and had a good knowledge of beer. In 1996, he was appointed as general manager of the Xi'an subsidiary. Within four years, he turned the company from a loss-maker into a profit-generator. The sales volume of Xi'an subsidiary rose from 30,000 tons to 180,000 tons, with the annual profit reaching more than RMB70 million, half of the total profit of all of Tsingtao Brewery's acquired subsidiaries. Although it was the third time for him to face a great challenge, Jin still felt nervous. The excessive expansion put extreme pressures on funds and personnel in the company. Approximately 50 subsidiaries needed to be restructured, and 100 brands needed to be refreshed. Jin remarked:

> In the past few years, Tsingtao Brewery was pursuing an expansion growth strategy, which was like driving a car on an expressway and even sometimes overtaking other cars. The situation is highly risky and there is danger of losing control in the integration of acquired companies.

After a careful investigation, Jin believed that the company should change its strategy from "growing large to become powerful" to "becoming powerful to grow large." The current challenge of the company was implementing the post-acquisition integration.

China's Beer Industry

General Situation

China's beer producing can be traced back to the beginning of the 20th century. By 1949, China's annual beer output was only 7,000 tons. In the period from 1980 to 2001, the output enjoyed an annual growth rate of six per cent, compared with America's one per cent. Until 2000, beer accounted for 78 per cent of the total output of alcoholic beverage drinks. In 2001, beer output reached 22.74 million tons (see Exhibit 1). After nine years of being the second largest beer market, China overtook the United States as the world's largest beer producer in 2002.

The beer brewing process consists of four basic but sophisticated procedures: making malt, boiling, fermentation and aging. The beer industry was considered both capital- and technology-intensive; therefore, entry barriers into the industry were quite high.[4] Moreover, brewing equipment needed to be in line with strict sanitation standards, and beer companies were difficult to transform into other businesses. As a result, many brewers had to struggle for survival despite continuous losses. Furthermore, more than 90 per cent of beer producers in China used glass bottles. Due to the drawbacks of glass

bottles, such as their friability and short shelf-life, producers had a small market coverage. Consequently, regional markets were largely dominated, usually with no more than three beer companies. Compared with multinational companies, whose normal production capacities were more than 10 million tons annually, most Chinese beer producers were on a smaller scale, with approximately 200,000 tons in annual output capacity.

Industry Competition Competition was extremely severe in the beer industry in China. Most companies sought to differentiate their products by packaging, because they all shared similar core technologies and techniques purchased from developed countries. Although there were more than 1,000 kinds of beers in the United States, almost all the beers in Chinese market were ales. Due to the similarities in taste, most beer brands competed by means of advertising, price-cutting and government protection. Management, marketing and production scales became key factors in determining competence.[5] Since the removal of investment constrictions in the beer industry in 1994, more than 700 beer companies had emerged. Most of them were small, poorly equipped

---

EXHIBIT 1

Beer Output and its Growth in China, 1980 to 2001 (in 000s tons)

Source: Shi Yanping, "Mergers, Acquisitions and Restructuring: An Intensified Integration in the Beer Industry," *CITIC Securities Research,* 2002, No. 9.

EXHIBIT 2

Financial Indices of the Beer Industry in China (RMB millions)

Indices	1996	1997	Y2Y Increase (%)	1998	Y2Y Increase (%)	2001
Production value	328.0	398.0	21.3	410.0	3.0	469.0
Output (10,000 tons)	1,681.9	1,888.5	12.3	1,987.7	5.3	2,274.0
Sales revenue	363.0	377.0	3.9	378.0	0.3	499.0
Earning before tax	80.0	85.3	6.6	92.8	8.8	104.8
Profit	22.0	14.3	(0.4)	16.7	16.8	18.9
Profit per ton	130.8	75.7	—	84.2	—	82.9

Source: Shi Yanping, "Mergers, Acquisitions and Restructuring: An Intensified Integration in the Beer Industry," *CITIC Securities Research,* 2002, No. 9.

and badly managed. They were owned by the state or a collective and tried to survive by means of local protection and price wars. By the end of 2001, there were more than 500 beer companies in China, an average of one beer company for every three counties. However, only 23 companies reached an output of more than 200,000 tons annually, accounting for 50.4 per cent of the total output. Seventy-nine companies had an output between 50,000 and 200,000 tons annually, accounting for 20.8 per cent of the total output. The lack of economies of scale resulted in the loss of 41.7 per cent of the companies in the industry. This industry situation encouraged Peng Zuoyi to implement his aggressive expansion plan. Peng said in a humorous tone: "In front of us are wolves, behind us are tigers and in the middle are mice. We will beat mice first and then tigers and wolves."[6]

After 1996, the beer market changed to a buyer's market, due to the slowdown of demand. The fiercer competition reduced the profitability of large companies, threw medium and small companies into corners and slackened the increase of profit and revenue in the beer industry (see Exhibit 2.[7]) The beer industry had become one of the most competitive and market-oriented industries in China. The industry's competition could be divided into three levels. The first level of competition was between domestic producers and foreign producers. In the early 1990s, more than 50 foreign brands rushed into China and seized the high-grade market. The second level was the competition among major domestic producers. Tsingtao Brewery, China Resources Beer (CR Beer)

and Yanjing Beer initiated the "big fish eating little fish" acquisitions by taking advantage of their strong brands and abundant capital. All three, who had a production capacity of more than two million tons, formed the first group. Harbin Beer, Chongqing Beer and Zhujiang Beer formed the second group of competitors with a production capacity of about one million tons each (see Exhibit 3). The third level of competitors was the alliance of middle- and small-sized enterprises. Due to their complementary brands, technology and management, they chose to respond to competition in a cooperative way, by sharing resources, markets and benefits.

EXHIBIT 3

China's Top 10 Brewers in 2001 (in 10,000 tons)

Ranking	Name	Output
1	Tsingtao Brewery	251.2
2	Yanjing Beer	170.0
3	Zhujiang Beer	75.1
4	Sichuan CR Lanjian Beer	68.4
5	Golden Star Beer	60.9
6	Harbin Beer	54.9
7	Chongqing Beer	53.2
8	Shenyang CR Snow Beer	41.3
9	Huiquan Beer	40.1
10	Jinlongquan Beer	39.8

Source: China Beer Association.

At present, global beer consumption amounted to 130 million tons. Despite having the largest population in the world, China had a per capita beer consumption of only 18 litres, much less than the global average level of 25 litres, and 83 litres, 55 litres and 30 litres in America, Japan and Hong Kong respectively. Hence, with improving living standards and growth in the rural markets, a steady growth was expected in China's beer consumption. In fact, the Chinese market could be described as a combination of regional markets, as very few companies were allowed to engage in nationwide marketing. There was a dominant beer producer in almost every major city—people from Beijing drank Yanjing beer; Tsingtao people preferred Tsingtao beer and Guangzhou people were loyal to Zhujiang beer.

The Three Beer Giants

In China, Tsingtao Brewery, Yanjing Beer and CR Beer accounted for 30 per cent of the national market, and were humorously referred to as the "Three Kingdoms."[8]

Tsingtao Brewery Tsingtao Brewery, the former Tsingtao Company Stock of the German Beer Corporation, established by British and German businessmen in 1903, was the first beer producer in China. In 1993, Tsingtao Brewery was transformed from a state-owned enterprise (SOE) to a joint stock company and issued H-shares in the Hong Kong Stock Exchange and A-shares in the Shanghai Stock Exchange.[9] By the end of 2001, Tsingtao Brewery had established manufacturing bases in 17 provinces, with a total annual capacity of more than three million tons. Tsingtao Brewery was the largest brewery with respect to output, sales, earnings before tax, market share and export. As the most famous Chinese beer brand, Tsingtao Brewery focused on high-grade beers and successfully sold its Tsingtao Beer, made from Laoshan spring water, to developed countries, accounting for half of China's total beer export.

In spite of its famous brand, Tsingtao Brewery market dominance was once surpassed by Yanjing Beer and CR Beer, in the mid-1990s. After 1996, Tsingtao Brewery switched from its focus on a high-grade market to a mass market, to implement its strategy of "reducing cost by low-end beer and making money by high-grade beer." Meanwhile, Tsingtao Brewery tried to raise its market share through a series of acquisitions, building its existence from South China to North China with an emphasis on the Yangtze Delta and Zhujiang Delta, the most developed areas in China. In the hinterlands, its North Department, Northeast Department and Luzhong Department constituted a powerful triangle (see Exhibit 4).

Yanjing Beer The Beijing-based Yanjing Beer (Yanjing) surprised Chinese by its quick growth. Established in 1980, Yanjing Beer's total assets amounted to RMB6.3 billion, and its output reached 1.7 million tons in 2001. Thanks to its 85 per cent market share in Beijing, Yanjing Beer was the number one producer in 1995. Yanjing also expanded by acquiring companies that had large market shares, abundant assets, sound management and mature corporate cultures. By the end of 2001, Yanjing Beer owned 14 subsidiaries. In 2000, Yanjing entered Shandong market as a counterattack to Tsingtao Brewery's acquisition of Beijing-based Five-Star Beer. Yanjing acquired Wuming Beer and Sankong Beer, which were respectively the third- and second-largest producers in Shandong, the hometown of Tsingtao Brewery, and which together accounted for 25 per cent of Shandong market.

CR Beer China Resources was one of China's "window companies" in Hong Kong. It successfully expanded its business from an agent to a well-diversified business in both Hong Kong and the Chinese mainland. Its principal activities covered retail, beverage, food processing and distribution, and textile and petroleum distribution. In 1993, China Resources set up CR Beer Co., Ltd. as a joint venture with South African Breweries (SAB). China Resources controlled a 51 per cent stake of CR Beer. China Resources also established Shenyang CR Snow Beer, Dalian CR Beer and Anshan CR Beer, thereby controlling the Northeast China market. In addition, CR Beer acquired Lanjian Beer, the second largest producer in Southwest China. Although most of CR Beer's management were not beer experts, SAB was one of the top four beer producers in the world,[10] and China Resources was also powerful in terms of capital availability.[11] By the end of 2001, CR Beer controlled 24 subsidiaries with a total annual capacity of more than three million tons.

Foreign Beer Producers

In the mid-1990s, nearly 60 foreign beer producers, including Budweiser, Heineken, San Miguel and Carlsberg, established joint ventures in China by focusing on high-grade markets. However, most were unsuccessful,

EXHIBIT 4

Tsingtao Brewery's Organization Chart

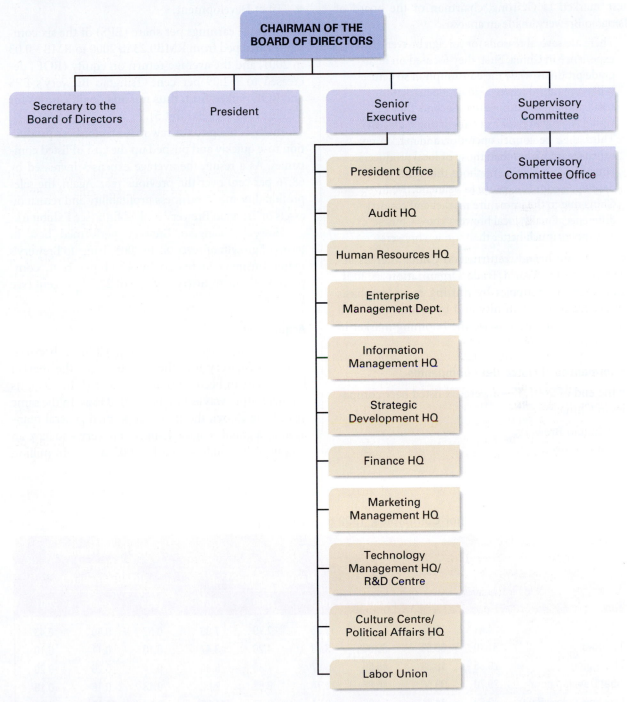

Source: www.tsingtaobeer.com.cn.

due to prices, tastes and positioning strategies incompatible with the Chinese market. Some chose to withdraw parts of their investment or retreat from the Chinese market. Li Guirong, chairman of the board of Tsingtao Brewery, made an analysis:

> There are several reasons for foreign brewers' bad experience in China. First, they focused on high-grade products while the consumption structure is like a pyramid where high-grade market is small and highly competitive. Second, they invested heavily in fixed asset, incurring high costs. Third, their personnel, operation and marketing expenses are higher than those of local producers. Fourth, the marketing methods that work well in developed countries prove to be ineffective in China due to the immature market and country difference. Finally, local brewers know Chinese consumers much better than foreign brewers.

Many foreign brands returned to China after its accession into the World Trade Organization in 2001. They changed strategies by putting more emphasis on localization and affinity and by teaming up with local brands, hoping to seize the booming market in an incremental way.

Performances of Listed Beer Companies

By the end of 2001, there were six listed beer companies in China:

- Tsingtao Brewery,
- Yanjing Beer,
- Lanzhou Yellow River Beer,
- Chongqing Beer,
- Honghe Guangming and
- Tibet Development.

The average earnings per share (EPS) of the six companies dropped from RMB0.23 in 2000 to RMB−0.03 in 2001, and the average return on equity (ROE) decreased to −2.09 per cent. Tsingtao Brewery's EPS and ROE ranked fifth, thus missing qualifications for a rights offer (see Exhibit 5).[12]

In 2001, the price of raw material for beer production rose quickly and pushed up the cost of listed companies. As a result, the average expenses increased by 68.76 per cent over the previous year. Again, the sales profitability, major business profitability and return on assets of Tsingtao Brewery ranked fifth (see Exhibit 6).

However, Tsingtao Brewery performed best in terms of growth of revenue. In 2001, Tsingtao Brewery's major business increased by 40.11 per cent, compared with the industry average of 22.57 per cent (see Exhibit 7).

Acquisitions

The Expansion Motivation Among Chinese brewers, Tsingtao Brewery was the first to enter the market but the last to become market-oriented. In 1996, its annual output was as low as 350,000 tons. In the same year, Peng Zuoyi, the newly appointed general manager, set a grand goal for Tsingtao Brewery—to have an output of five million tons by 2005, and eight million

EXHIBIT 5

Comparison Among Listed Beer Companies, 1999 to 2001

Companies	Debt/Asset (%)			Net Profit/Equity (%)			Net Profit/Number of Shares (RMB per share)		
	1999	2000	2001	1999	2000	2001	1999	2000	2001
Yanjing	4.41	10.85	12.70	12.25	7.79	7.96	0.53	0.40	0.43
Tsingtao	51.10	60.53	55.82	3.98	4.26	3.47	0.10	0.11	0.10
Chongqing	29.85	48.33	46.59	6.97	7.35	5.95	0.24	0.26	0.20
Tibet Development	39.70	33.56	40.62	20.74	8.53	9.02	0.43	0.16	0.18
Lanzhou Yellow River	49.53	44.61	54.96	6.21	0.67	(44.92)	0.33	0.03	(1.29)
Honghe Guangming	10.53	13.92	9.85	6.60	11.40	6.10	0.22	0.42	0.21
Average	30.85	35.30	36.76	9.45	6.67	(2.09)	0.31	0.23	(0.03)

Source: 2001 Annual Reports of relevant companies.

EXHIBIT 6

Comparison of Profitability of Listed Beer Companies, 1999 to 2001

Company	Gross Margins/Sales (%)			Net Profit/Major Business Revenue (%)			Net Profit/Asset (%)		
	1999	2000	2001	1999	2000	2001	1999	2000	2001
Yanjing	44.48	43.30	31.05	19.22	15.37	12.49	11.54	6.63	6.50
Tsingtao	40.14	40.38	28.74	3.66	2.53	1.95	1.73	1.36	1.25
Chongqing	49.14	46.71	35.85	13.68	13.25	6.33	4.64	3.57	1.67
Tibet Development	53.45	42.42	33.55	40.49	25.22	23.48	12.36	5.61	4.20
Lanzhou Yellow River	32.89	37.15	(33.55)	12.25	1.77	(98.52)	2.84	0.36	(19.34)
Honghe Guangming	46.89	54.37	45.74	27.75	37.33	29.10	8.29	9.81	5.44
Average	44.49	44.05	23.58	19.50	15.91	(4.20)	6.90	4.56	(0.05)

Source: 2001 Annual Reports of relevant companies.

tons by 2010. In 1993, Tsingtao Brewery got listed on the Hong Kong Stock Exchange and raised HK$890 million, and then raised HK$638 million in the Shanghai Stock Exchange in the same year. Sufficient capital reserves facilitated Tsingtao Brewery's acquisitions. Meanwhile, the resounding "CSH phenomenon" further encouraged Peng's aggressive plan.[13]

Since the 1990s, beer multinational companies (MNCs) expanded their business in China through establishing factories, acquiring factories or original equipment manufacturers (OEM), or entering such important markets as the Zhujiang River Delta and the Yangtze River Delta. Many gained exclusive sales in hotels, which seriously threatened the market for high-grade Tsingtao beers. By 1996, the consumption of high-grade beer was about one million tons, which was six per cent of total beer consumption. Foreign brands, Tsingtao Brewery and other brewers respectively accounted for 630,000, 300,000 and 100,000 tons in total volume of high-grade beer consumption. To respond to the foreign impact, Tsingtao Brewery put forward the strategy of "low-cost expansion, high jump-off point" to raise its market share.

In addition, the environment was favorable for expansion. Tsingtao Brewery was one of the 512 pillar SOEs listed by the State Council, one of the 10 beer enterprises supported by the Light Industry Institute and one of the eight key enterprises listed by Shandong municipal government. The strong position made the company qualified for many favorable policies concerning acquisitions.[14]

Expansion Strategy   Peng judged that Tsingtao Brewery was facing a historic opportunity for acquisition of other companies:

> First, the government encouraged large companies to take over medium- and small-sized enterprises by favorable policies; second, many foreign brewers wanted to retreat due to poor performance; third, many local government invited Tsingtao Brewery to acquire some unprofitable beer SOEs.

Thus, Tsingtao Brewery decided to realize an extraordinary growth, based on the concepts of a "big famous brand strategy," "pyramid ideology," "low-cost expansion, high jump-off point," "fresh rate management" and "regional department system." The "big famous brand strategy" was considered the core of its company strategy, implying that the Tsingtao brand facilitated growth and interactively enhanced the value of other companies that were associated with it. Before 1996, Tsingtao Brewery considered itself a "nobleman" and focused on high-grade products. Unfortunately, it was finally surpassed by Yanjing Beer, which focused on medium- and low-grade products. The "pyramid strategy" was intended to form a high-medium-low product structure for creating more market space (see Exhibit 8). The "fresh rate management" was a quality strategy to ensure that customers living in Tsingtao could drink fresh beer produced within one week, and customers in Shandong province could access the beer produced within one month.

EXHIBIT 7

Comparison of Growth Rate of Listed Beer Companies, 2000 to 2001 (RMB10,000)

Companies	Major Business Revenue				Operation Profit				Net Profit			
	2000	Growth Rate (%)	2001	Growth Rate (%)	2000	Growth Rate (%)	2001	Growth Rate (%)	2000	Growth Rate (%)	2001	Growth Rate (%)
Yanjing	174,587	15.14	228,788	29.00	28,668	(13.14)	27,092	(5.50)	26,828	(7.96)	28,569	6.49
Tsingtao	376,625	54.01	527,672	40.11	9,168	5.72	7,132	(22.21)	9,520	15.18	10,288	8.08
Chongqing	33,815	8.58	46,671	38.01	4,567	(6.22)	4,624	1.25	4,479	7.26	3,428	(23.44)
Tibet Development	11,010	(7.54)	13,452	22.17	2,276	(54.57)	3,227	41.78	2,776	(42.44)	3,158	13.75
Lanzhou Yellow River	18,591	(30.31)	15,451	(16.88)	107	(60.81)	(17,569)	—	329	(89.93)	(15,222)	—
Honghe Guangming	5,644	40.57	6,941	22.98	2,205	152.00	2,180	(1.13)	2,106	89.14	2,020	(4.13)
Average	103,379	13.41	139,829	22.57	7,831	3.83	4,448	2.84	7,673	(4.79)	5,374	0.15

Source: 2001 Annual Reports of relevant companies.

EXHIBIT 8

The Product Pyramid

Superior beer — Tsingtao beer

High-quality beer —

Average beer —

Tsingtao Brewery beer family

Preparation Tsingtao Brewery held that proposed acquisitions should be low cost and profit-oriented to avoid possible burdens. Tsingtao Brewery made detailed plans to guide acquisitions:

- The Development Department organized other related departments, including finance, production and quality control, to conduct a feasibility analysis. Final decisions would be made by the board.

- All acquisitions adhered to four principles: (1) reasonable market arrangement: a target should have a minimum market circle with a radius of 150 kilometres without overlap with other subsidiaries; (2) significant demand potential: the local population density, consumption level and consumption habit should be in line with beer sales; (3) qualified staff: teams were to be created with skillful workers and experienced managers and (4) a balance of short-term and long-term interests.

- Annual investment budget should be approved by the board, and each acquisition should be sanctioned by the general manager.

- Any investment of more than RMB10 million was to be evaluated by the board.

- Restrictions on the size of the deals: no more than RMB10 million for a capacity of 30,000 tons and corresponding production startup investment should be no more than RMB5 million;

no more than RMB30 million for a capacity of 50,000 to 60,000 tons and corresponding production startup investments should be no more than RMB15 million.

To facilitate the expansion plan, Tsingtao Brewery adjusted its organization structure accordingly. First, it switched to a regional department system, and set up South China Holdings, East China Holdings, North Department, Northeast Department, Huaihai Department, Luzhong Department and Southwest Department. In the new system, Tsingtao Brewery was the hub of the entire system, controlling strategic decisions, capital operations, and investment and corporate culture. Regional departments were responsible for making profits and regional management decisions, and all subsidiaries were in charge of quality control and cost control.

Tsingtao Brewery established the Development Department, which specialized in acquisition implementation, and the Investment Management Department, which specialized in after-acquisition integration.[15] The Investment Management Department generally entered the acquired subsidiary when negotiations ended. The five employees of this department were in charge of transplanting Tsingtao Brewery's management model, harmonizing the relationship between subsidiaries and headquarters, and monitoring production and operation. Upon receiving complaints from the subsidiary, the Investment Management Department made on-site investigations and handled possible problems. Each month, the department would submit two reports on the acquired subsidiaries to the board: one on production and operation and the other on sales performance. Both reports were the basis for the subsidiaries' performance appraisal.[16] The chief executives of all subsidiaries were called to headquarters to make reports every half year.

Integration Plan The transplant of the Tsingtao Brewery model was regarded as the core of integration. The so-called Tsingtao Brewery model consisted of one core, six systems and two supports. One core referred to a combination of scientific and strict management and harmonious interpersonal relationships. Six systems included quality assurance, production, human resource management, marketing, financial management, and development and innovation systems. Two supports were technologies and corporate culture. To implement the integration, Tsingtao Brewery established an integration team led by a vice general manager. The team would enter the acquired target when negotiations were completed and stayed only until the target passed its final examination. Duties of the team included the following:

1. *Inoculating Tsingtao Brewery culture*—The team focused on people, publicizing the history of Tsingtao Brewery and educating employees to share the honors and duties. Tsingtao Brewery tried to make employees more aggressive through post-competitions in acquired subsidiaries. Moreover, subsidiaries set positions paralleled to those of Tsingtao Brewery and introduced an interactive selection system in which employees elected their favorite managers, and managers selected employees. Staff training was another key element. Tsingtao assigned experienced workers to educate workers in newly acquired organizations and organized face-to-face training courses. Finally, Tsingtao Brewery emphasized internal promotion and annual salary bonuses. Managers were required to sign subcontracts with subordinates to spread out responsibilities.

2. *Building rules and systems to enforce the Tsingtao Brewery model*—Most of the targets set out by SOEs did not have effective regulations and management systems. The rules and systems of the team required that all new mergers were well-organized and systematic without repetition, and overlap was to be abided by all employees. After a thorough investigation, the team was expected to make suggestions for improvements in nine areas that included general management, material, production, statistics, equipment, computation, human resources, finance and marketing. Meanwhile, the subsidiaries were required to work out a detailed schedule and arrangement of duties under the supervision of the team. The team would re-examine and confirm the working schedule after one or two months and provide a formal appraisal and further suggestions about half a year later.

3. *Implementing the ISO 9000 system*—Tsingtao Brewery's ISO team consisted of members who were well-trained and had related certifications. When the acquired subsidiary reached basic qualifications, the ISO team would provide on-site guidance. Before formal authentication, the ISO team would conduct a pre-authentication.

4. *Sharing market networks*—Subsidiaries were expected to implement a marketing system characterized by fresh rate management, direct supply, intensive networks and market expansion. The implementation would be conducted by the marketing and sales department, as well as by the acquired subsidiary. The detailed measures of this system included segmenting the market according to the pyramid ideology, fully utilizing the Tsingtao brand, enhancing the value of local brands and carefully positioning products, strengthening market networks, implementing fresh rate management, enhancing market management and feedback, and establishing a common information and fund network to share resources.

5. *Establishing a financial management system focusing on complete budget management,*[17] *cost control and fund management*—The subsidiary needed to improve its financial structure and strengthen its financial analysis and cost control. In addition, Tsingtao Brewery sent a financial director to each subsidiary.

6. *Absorbing the Tsingtao Brewery techniques*—As soon as the acquisition was complete, a technique team would be sent to diagnose the production operation of the subsidiary, and recommend improvements to its product quality, technique design and production procedure. The headquarters would review the improvements, examine beer quality periodically and organize beer contests.

Acquisitions By April 2002, Tsingtao Brewery had acquired 47 beer companies in 17 provinces. The total output of the acquired companies reached 2.02 million tons in 2001, which was approximately 80 per cent of the total output of Tsingtao Brewery.

In 1994, Tsingtao Brewery took over Yangzhou Beer for RMB80 million, starting its expansion battle. It then acquired Xi'an Hans Beer in 1995. In 1997 and 1998, Tsingtao Brewery merged two and three small beer companies respectively in Shandong province. Most acquisitions happened in 1999 and 2000, when Tsingtao Brewery purchased a total of 30 companies. In 1999, Tsingtao Brewery took over 14 beer companies—half of them located out of Shandong province—with a total output of 1.5 million tons for a cost of more than RMB400 million. In 2000, Tsingtao Brewery acquired 16 companies with a total output of 1.2 million tons for about RMB600 million. It purchased controlling stakes of Shanghai Carlsberg, Beijing Five Star and Beijing Sanhuan Beer for RMB150 million, US$10 million and US$12.5 million respectively. In 2001, Tsingtao Brewery slowed down its expansion and acquired only nine companies with a total output of 600,000 tons for RMB260 million (see Exhibit 9). The frequent acquisitions resulted in a sharp increase in asset and production capacity (see Exhibits 10 to 13). As Peng commented, "We are in battle for 360 days a year."

In 2000, those subsidiaries that had joined Tsingtao before the end of 1999 achieved output of 927,500 tons (up 57.6 per cent year to year), revenue of RMB2.47 billion (up 123.8 per cent year to year) and profit of RMB63.4 million (up 580 per cent). Meanwhile, subsidiaries that had joined Tsingtao Brewery before the end of 1998 produced 551,600 tons in 2000 (up 60.11 per cent year to year), reaching a revenue of RMB1.74 billion (up 93.58 per cent year to year) and profit of RMB96.1 million (up 379 per cent year to year). The most significant example of growth was Xi'an subsidiary that raised its output from 25,000 tons in 1996 to 180,000 tons in 2000, turning a loss of RMB24.3 million into a profit of RMB75.4 million.

EXHIBIT 9

Geographic Distribution of Acquired Subsidiaries

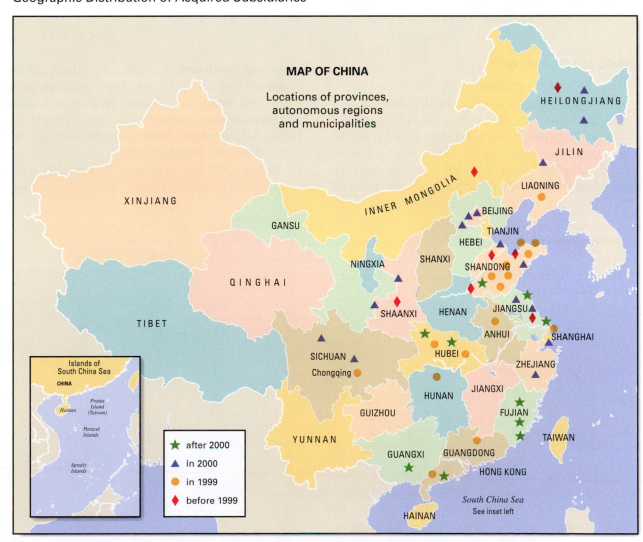

EXHIBIT 10

Asset Increase of Tsingtao Brewery, 1997 to 2001
(in RMB100 million)

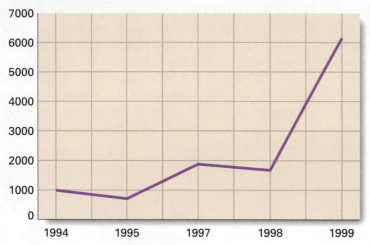

Source: Annual Reports of Tsingtao Brewery.

Risks and Challenges

Tsingtao Brewery adopted various acquiring means, including bankruptcy and bearing debt and mergers with the benefit of interest exemption.[18] Many acquired companies had a heavy debt burden, due to the high interest rate in the 1980s, when most of these companies were founded. Tsingtao Brewery promised to repay the principal when the acquired companies began making profit, under the condition of interest exemption. Tsingtao Brewery's integration effort won praises from some local governments: "Companies that foreigners and local people felt [were] helpless have been activated, showing the value of Tsingtao Brewery model."

However, the low acquisition cost may have implied a high integration cost.[19] One symptom was

EXHIBIT 11

Changes in Tsingtao Brewery Output, 1978 to 2002
(in 10,000 tons)

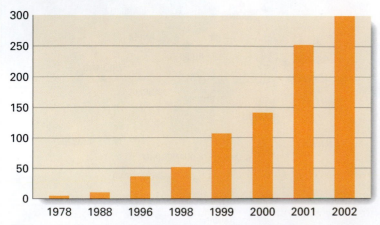

Source: "Tsingtao Brewery Strategic Expansion," www.holyhigh.com.

EXHIBIT 12

Acquired Assets and Liabilities by Year (RMB10,000)

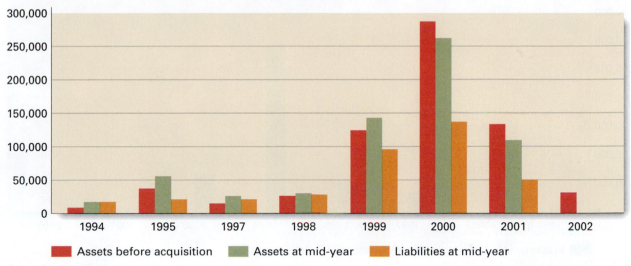

Source: Company files.

the high expenditure of technology improvement, which ranged from millions to tens of millions (see Exhibit 14). Wang Wei, a mergers and acquisitions (M&A) expert said:

> Tsingtao Brewery's acquisitions have obvious characteristics of a planned economy. Though many targets are problematic and should bankrupt,

Tsingtao Brewery spent much resources in saving them, which may negatively influence Tsingtao itself rather than achieving economies of scale.

A research fellow of an investment bank pointed out:

> Peng's aggressive plan has brought about huge fund pressure to Tsingtao Brewery. With the excuse of economies of scale, many useless companies joined

EXHIBIT 13

Change in Acquired Capacities by Year (in 10,000 tons)

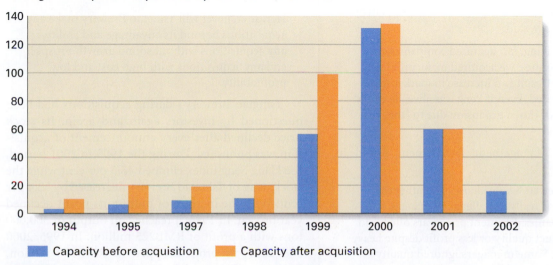

Source: Company files.

EXHIBIT 14

Investment In Technology Improvement and Policy Benefits by Year (RMB10,000)

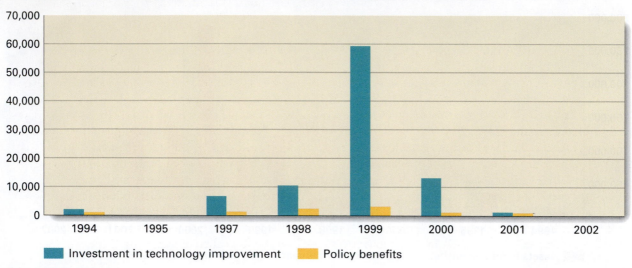

Source: Company files.

Tsingtao Brewery. Taking into consideration . . . possible government intervention behind the scene, these kinds of acquisitions will do harm to Tsingtao Brewery's profitability in the end.

Wu Feng of the Investment Management Department said:

> Seemingly, many acquired companies have many difficulties in product quality and market expansion. The fundamental reason for it is poor management. . . . Sometimes they prefer plots to strategies and prefer maneuvers to plots.

Zhang Ruixiang, the securities representative of Tsingtao Brewery, said:

> Frankly speaking, few acquired companies are profitable because we acquired many problem companies. Despite an increase in market share, profit decreased. Even if Peng was alive, he would have slow[ed] down expansion due to [the] current situation.

The Quality Management Department found in investigation:

> Tsingtao Brewery's subsidiaries are rather scattered and it is really a challenge to manage so many companies. Frequent price wars often lead to bad product quality or less profit despite heavy investment. Some managers ignored quality control and internal management.

In December 1994, Tsingtao Brewery took over Yangzhou Beer Factory in Jiangsu province at a cost of RMB80 million. Despite its estimated annual capacity of 50,000 tons, the factory only realized an output of 20,000 tons. After consuming a lot of money in technology improvements, the factory failed to increase its sales. As a result, it suffered a loss of RMB50 million despite doubling its output in three years. However, Tsingtao Brewery had forecasted optimistically that Jiangsu province was a high-potential beer market without any influential brewer. Peng concluded in an emotional tone:

> Hereafter, never will Tsingtao Brewery make any acquisitions beyond its advantage and ability, any acquisitions without sound growth prospect and any acquisitions with high cost and low profitability.

Tsingtao Brewery's daring acquisitions had been questioned by investors again and again. Its stock price declined after every announcement of acquisition was published. During the 1995 to 2001 period, the Hang Seng index climbed 45.3 per cent while the stock price of Tsingtao Brewery decreased by 52.4 per cent. With the increase of output, its profit declined year by year. In 1993, it reached an output of 300,000 tons with a profit of RMB225 million. In 1995, 2000 and 2001, its profit dropped to RMB170 million, RMB92 million and RMB103 million respectively.

In its 2001 annual report, Tsingtao Brewery attributed the poor performance to the heated competition, negative policy and management turnover:

> Initiated by our company, the beer industry is undergoing restructuring. Beer giants all choose [the] purchase of medium- and small-sized companies as their strategies, resulting in the changing of competition pattern. Beer giants have all penetrated some key regional markets, seizing market shares, and intensifying competition.[20] Since May 1, 2001, the consumption tax has been raised from 220 to 250 yuan per ton for beers with a price of more than 3,000 yuan per ton, reducing our profit by 10 million yuan. In the second half of 2001, beer consumption dropped greatly and the sales growth rate decreased from 4.6 per cent in the first half to −0.6 per cent in the second half. Sales decreased by 38.5 per cent in the fourth quarter over the third quarter in [the] medium and high-grade market. The sudden death of Peng Zuoyi, our former general manager, did influence the company's operation, sales, and staffs.

Nonetheless, its poor performance was considered the result of an unsuccessful integration by some analysts.[21] According to a report by Nomura International Hong Kong, half of the 46 acquired subsidiaries were running a deficit in 2001. Among 46 acquired subsidiaries, South China Department, Xi'an subsidiary and Tsingtao subsidiary made a profit of RMB150 million, RMB80 million and RMB170 million respectively. Comparatively, Tsingtao Brewery suffered a severe loss in the region of East China, North China and Northeast China, even in the two largest cities, Shanghai and Beijing (see Exhibit 15). Jin Zhiguo admitted that:[22]

> Among all the acquired subsidiaries, one-third are profitable, another one-third are losing money and the remaining subsidiaries narrowly make ends meet. Except for Tsingtao and Weifang, Tsingtao Brewery failed to gain a market share of more than 30 per cent in all neighboring markets. This high-investment-low-profit situation will definitely lead to an increase in sales expenses and consequently influence profitability.
>
> Losses may be attributed to several reasons. The first is the poor cost control, loose budget execution and high-cost marketing operation; the second is the unreasonable product structure, low price and low profitability; the third is the lack of modern marketing concepts and techniques and a scientific analysis of marketing plans.
>
> We have invested in 48 subsidiaries which requested a lot of capital and managers. We now feel that it is hard to meet these requirements. We have sent too many people from headquarters into the integration process. Some employees from headquarters considered themselves gods and looked down upon local managers, turning the integration into an individual show.

Sun Mingbo, the vice-general manager of Tsingtao Brewery and chief in M&A, said:

> Hubris did exist in the process of acquisition. Sometimes we underestimate competitors, and sometimes we are overconfident in our brand power. The lack of talented people is the primary bottleneck of integration. Tsingtao Brewery does

EXHIBIT 15

The Most Profitable and Unprofitable Subsidiaries in 2001 (RMB10,000)

Ranking	Subsidiaries	Assets	Major Business Revenue	Net Profits
1	Xi'an	50,179	66,792	6,483
2	Shenzhen Asahi	83,591	39,122	6,333
3	Shenzhen Sales	11,539	69,641	2,611
Last	Beijing Sanhuan	29,163	12,674	(3,590)
Second last	East China Sales	3,631	6,287	(3,573)
Third last	Xingkaihu	13,955	4,595	(1,716)

Source: 2001 Annual Report of Tsingtao Brewery.

EXHIBIT 16

Number of Acquired Employees by Year

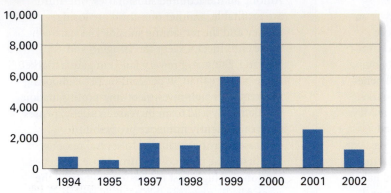

Source: Company files.

have a scientific integration method, but reality is always different from what you expected.

In China's SOEs, employment is the utmost issue and also a focus of local government. Thus it is difficult to shut down a factory without considering the local employment, so you have to act cautiously [see Exhibit 16]. Many employees had outdated concepts and reimbursed all their expenses including family expenses. It would take a long time to change their mindsets. It is a big challenge to prepare enough managers because internal training is time-consuming and external recruitment is often unsuccessful.

Zhang Ruixiang said:

What worries us most are Shandong province and Northeast China, where there is heated competition or low consumption ability. We try to minimize our losses. In South China and coastal regions, there is a huge growth potential. With the government's favorable policies, the demand in western regions will increase gradually.

Admittedly, some integration turned out to be very successful, such as the South China Department. Led by Yan Xu, a competent professional manager recruited by Peng Zuoyi, Tsingtao Brewery's market share increased 184 per cent in South China in one year. Some subsidiaries, including Sanshui, Zhujiang and Shenzhen Asahi, made considerable profits in the same year they were acquired. Yan Xu said:

The successful integration should be attributed to both sound conditions of these companies and strong integration ability. A favorable factor is that Southern people have a strong market

consciousness and make analysis from a pure business perspective, making it easy to establish a cooperative relationship.

According to Tsingtao Brewery's acquisition strategy, Tsingtao Brewery should send three managers—the general manager, chief engineer and financial director—to each subsidiary. It was hardly possible to prepare more than 100 managers for these subsidiaries in a short period. Jin Zhiguo admitted that what Tsingtao Brewery needed most was effective management. From the eyes of the media, Tsingtao Brewery was still in an SOE style. Executives at the general management level still had administrative titles equivalent to those of government officials, making turnover a difficult decision. In order to eliminate government intervention, Jin planned to recruit vice general managers publicly.

Brand integration was another challenge. Having acquired several companies in the same regions, Tsingtao Brewery found itself trapped in two conflicts—conflict between different local brands and conflict of local brands and the Tsingtao Beer brand. As an illustration, Tsingtao Brewery took over three factories in Weifang—Weicheng, Shouguang and Anqiu. Tsingtao Brewery made Weicheng produce Lanzai beer, a local brand owned by Shouguang. However, the two companies had been direct competitors for years and could not sit together to resolve discrepancies. As a result, Tsingtao Brewery still lost money despite its 80 per cent market share in Weifang. Although Tsingtao Brewery wanted to shut down some factories, it was committed to not reducing staff. Taking into consideration the probable resistance from local government, Tsingtao Brewery had to give up this idea.

As expressed by an expert, Tsingtao Brewery was very careful in using its core brand:

> Tsingtao Brewery didn't give everything to its subsidiaries. For example, beers with the brand "1903" could only be made [at Tsingtao headquarters]. As far as the use of brands is concerned, subsidiaries either adopted original brands plus "Produced by Tsingtao Brewery" or put "Tsingtao Brewery" before the original brand names. No acquired subsidiary could use the core brand name, avoiding the risk of destroying this valuable asset.

Tsingtao Brewery had more than 100 brands, and the output for its core brand had reached 600,000 to 700,000 tons in 2001, about one-fourth of total output. A consultant analysed:

> Tsingtao Brewery's core brand should realize an output of one million tons or one-third of the total. Moreover, it should develop several regional brands such as Hans and Five-Star as the second rundle. Other brands should go their own way to form the third rundle.

Though Tsingtao Brewery had regained the position of top seller, an article pointed out sharply:

> Companies acquired by Tsingtao Brewery each do things in their own way, continuing [the] original brand, original production line and sales region, and the only change is the beer itself. The output of 1.8 million tons in 2000 was nothing but a simple sum of all subsidiaries. The largest single-factory output of Tsingtao Brewery is 400,000 tons; much lower than the 800,000 tons of Yanjing Beer. Tsingtao Brewery is probably the only brewer that has so many small-sized subsidiaries with so many brands in the world. On average, the capacity of each subsidiary is as small as 45,000 tons.[23]

An investigation by the investment management department found:

> Since each subsidy has its own sales team, there are some overlap of sales networks and internal conflicts in the same market sometimes.

In addition, it was a real challenge to hold a meeting of chiefs of all subsidiaries due to the difficulty in time arrangements and the huge travel costs. Li Guirong was worried:

> The size expansion and increase in management levels have caused information delay and distortion and some wrong executions. If we do nothing with this, Tsingtao Brewery will definitely catch the so-called "big company disease."

Tsingtao Brewery's financial condition was not optimistic either. By mid-2001, its debt-asset ratio was 56 per cent, and its current ratio and quick ratio were on the low side. Meanwhile, its short-term loan and liquid liabilities reached RMB2.5 billion and RMB4.3 billion respectively. Without the financing cash flow, its net cash flow would have been negative for two consecutive years. After raising RMB787 million through seasoned offering in February 2001, its financial condition improved greatly, and the debt-asset ratio dropped to 40 per cent. However, Zhang Ruixiang said:

> In the beer industry, a debt-asset ratio of 60 per cent is reasonable due to the capital-intensive nature of beer industry. Since the production cycle of Tsingtao Brewery is relatively long, it should have a reasonable debt-asset ratio.

Frequent acquisitions also pushed up its operation and management expenses. In 1998, the operation and management expenses of Tsingtao Brewery were RMB402 million, about 76.3 per cent of major business profit. By 2001, the number rose to RMB1.380 million and 88.4 per cent respectively. Meanwhile, the corresponding expenses of all subsidiaries rose from the RMB85.4 million in 1998 to RMB929.4 million in 2001, increasing by 1,088 per cent. The corresponding profit increased from the RMB91.2 million in 1998 to RMB889.7 million in 2001, increasing 976 per cent.[24]

Facing the Crisis

Jin Zhiguo earned fame through the successful integration of Tsingtao Brewery Xi'an Company. After the acquisition of Xi'an Hans Beer in 1995, Jin was appointed as the new general manager in 1996. At that time, Tsingtao Brewery's market share in Xi'an was less than one per cent, and the output was as low as 20,000 tons, resulting in an annual loss of RMB24 million and a debt-asset ratio of 64 per cent. By counting beer bottles in the open market every night, Jin obtained first-hand sales information. Then he managed to smooth the sales network channel and stimulate dealers. Within four years, Tsingtao Brewery's market share jumped to more than 90 per cent with a profit of RMB70 million. A small change reflected Jin's management style: two-thirds of the general manager's office in the Tsingtao Beer Tower had been the manager's working area and one-third had been for meeting guests before Jin moved into office.

Now only one-third was used for working and two-thirds had been allocated to guests.

After taking the post, Jin suddenly stopped the unreasonable expansion of Tsingtao Brewery and conducted only two acquisitions in one year. Recognizing the importance of integration, Jin held that Tsingtao Brewery should change its strategy from "growing large to become powerful" to "growing powerful to become large." He said: "Acquisition is only a means while integration is essence!"

Jin had his own experience of integration:

> Integration teams should be concerned with the emotion of their staff. It needs to be borne in minds that you should not act as a god, and rather as a missionary assisting them in transforming concepts and improving management and technology.
>
> The after-acquisition integration is actually a Revolution, of which the most important part is concept transformation.

Jin also called on a slogan of "Speculating today on the prospect of the future":

> No company alone can monopolize the beer market in China. The future market would be dominated by five to 10 regional giants. There is no need for Tsingtao Brewery to exert its force in every corner and fight for every regional market. Thus the market competition will become more rational rather than destructive.

A focus on integration doesn't necessarily mean a slowdown of growth. Jin explained:

> Hereafter, Tsingtao Brewery should help each subsidiary to develop its full potential and strengthen market development. Meanwhile, Tsingtao Brewery will choose suitable targets in non-existence market or high-consumption market to perfect its market arrangement.

Jin Zhiguo, a practice-oriented person, investigated all the subsidiaries within two months after his inauguration. His final conclusion was that Tsingtao Brewery should make a strategic transformation, from "growing large to become powerful" to "growing powerful to become large," from external expansion to "system integration and mechanism innovation so as to enhance core competence." Jin said:

> Tsingtao Brewery has merged 47 beer companies and set up nine regional departments or holding companies with a sales team of more than 5,000 people. Cost is rising, hierarchy is becoming more and more bureaucratic, and power-control and self-interest is moving in the wrong direction. The "big company disease" is worsening due to the concentration of operation risk.
>
> Tsingtao Brewery is still a production and finance oriented company in that its complete budget management emphasizes control rather than market.

Jin Zhiguo had a strong sense of crisis:

> Guided by the Big Famous Brand Strategy, Tsingtao Brewery has made significant achievements. However, these achievements were a result of the maladjustment of foreign brewers, the poor management of most domestic companies, the lack of dominant players in the industry, the inertia of a long-history company and the grasp of opportunities. We are still young and immature and should be aware of continuity and cruelty of competition.
>
> God only blesses those who are well prepared. To face changes, Tsingtao Brewery should focus on developing its core resources from now on, which is beer itself including beer-related people, technology, networks, brand, and so on.
>
> What helped Tsingtao Brewery survive over the past 100 years were results of its brand, product as well as its culture—the most important factor. The culture management of Tsingtao Brewery still needed improvement. The highest destination of beer business is making it an art and taking into consideration the cultural characteristics of beer.
>
> If the size of a company doubled or tripled in a short time, former operation models must be updated and the company's environment, mission and core competence shall be adjusted accordingly.

A comment in *China Business* said:

> The major challenge of Tsingtao Brewery is to integrate the different cultures and values of more than 40 subsidiaries. Discrepancy of value is considered the primary reason for the failure of most acquisitions in the world. Though Tsingtao Brewery has a 100-year history and rich culture, it also has a malpractice of old SOEs including the obscure property rights, poor incentive systems, and a lack of professional managers. Moreover, it acquired various kinds of enterprises including SOEs, foreign invested companies, joint ventures and collectively owned enterprises, which have different cultures and values.[25]

Overlooking the beautiful beach of Tsingtao, Jin Zhiguo fell into deep thoughts. What should he do to reorganize the jumbled system, integrate various resources and enhance the performance so that Tsingtao Brewery could "grow powerful to become large"?

ENDNOTES

1. Yuan is the basic unit of the Chinese currency, Renminbi (RMB), which literally means "the people's currency." In 2003, US$1 was equivalent to 8.28 yuan.

2. Yuan Zhaohui, "Tsingtao Brewery in Strategic Restructuring," *Securities Market Weekly*, August 12, 2002.

3. According to the board's announcement, Jin Zhiguo possessed the capability and experience of whole programming and leadership, and had strategic vision, as well as a strong innovative consciousness. He would surely endure more risky and challenging tasks.

4. It takes about RMB500 million to build a well-equipped beer factory with a capacity of 100,000 tons.

5. In the first three quarters of 2001, 41 per cent of beer companies lost money. The 90 large beer companies accounted for 55.9 per cent of the total sales and 60.2 per cent of the total profit, the 144 middle-sized companies accounted for 23.9 per cent of the total sales and 24.96 per cent of the total profit.

6. The beer industry concentration in China was relatively low. By 1999, there were only 19 companies with an annual output of 200,000 tons, accounting for 35.3 per cent of the total output. In comparison, the top 10 manufacturers controlled 94 per cent of the market in the United States, and 48.2 per cent by A-B alone. In Japan, the top four manufacturers grabbed a 80 per cent market share.

7. In 1997 and 1998, the sales per ton decreased by 7.5 per cent and 4.99 per cent respectively on a year-to-year basis.

8. "The Romance of Three Kingdoms" was one of the most popular historical novels of China. The story tells of the epic battles among the three kingdoms for the dominance of all of China, from 184–286 AD, a total of 96 years.

9. A share referred to the stock issued by a mainland company in domestic stock exchanges, and denominated and traded in RMB. H share referred to the stock issued by a mainland company in the Hong Kong Stock Exchange, denominated and traded in Hong Kong dollars.

10. SAB was a public company listed in London and South Africa, and the second largest beer producer in the world in terms of sales.

11. By the end of 2002, China Resources' assets amounted to HK$56 billion with a revenue of HK$32.2 billion. The company had 80,000 employees and five listed companies, as the largest Chinese enterprises in Hong Kong.

12. According to rules of the China Securities Regulatory Commission, a listed company required a weighted average ROE of no less than six per cent in the most recent three years to apply for a rights offer.

13. Since 1992, China Strategic Holdings Ltd. (CSH), owned by a Singapore businessman, acquired many SOEs in China. By 1994, it had invested in more than 100 joint ventures in various industries, including beer, rubber and so on, with a total investment of RMB2.5 billion. It also reorganized Beijing Beer Factory, Hangzhou Beer Factory, Yantai Beer Factory, etc. to form the China Beer Holdings registered in Bermuda, and then made an initial public offering (IPO) in Toronto. More recently, CSH sold beer assets to Asahi, a Japanese brewer.

14. Such favorable policies included interest exemption, exemption of value-added tax (VAT), consumption tax, operation tax, city maintenance and construction tax, additional education expenses, land tax and other local taxes temporarily and exemption of Fixed Asset Investment Tax Suspended.

15. These two departments were later integrated into one department: the Strategic Development Department.

16. The centre for economic responsibility appraisal was a budget management system in which development plans were made on the basis of the economic objectives of Tsingtao Brewery. Performance appraisal was a quantitative description of profit, output, sales and asset objectives.

17. A complete budget was an integration of the operation budget, the capital expenditure budget and the financial budget. Sub-budgets were well connected and coherent. A complete budget started from operation objectives, analysed and forecasted market demand, focused on the sales budget and included aspects such as production, cost and cash income and expenditure. The complete budget also analysed the influence of operation activities on financial conditions and profits and ended with a foreseeing financial report.

18. In an acquisition by bearing debt, the acquirer gained all assets and debts of the target without any payment. Thus, the acquiring company could increase its capacity quickly if only liquid funds were available.

19. It would take RMB6 billion to invest in a new company with an output of two million tons, while an equivalent output could be achieved through acquisitions for only RMB1 billion.

20. Due to the fury fight between Tsingtao Brewery and Yanjing Beer in Shandong province, the 42 beer companies there reached an output of 2.8 million tons and raised their sales by 13.2 per cent, while profit declined by 21.2 per cent. Meanwhile, profit per ton dropped from RMB112 to RMB79, RMB0.01 for each bottle of beer.

21. CR Beer and Yanjing Beer also encountered a crisis in integration. According to the Shandong Beer Association, the three acquired subsidiaries of Yanjing were far from making ends meet. Despite years of fighting, CR Beer didn't make a profit until 2001.

22. Tan Yihua, "Is Tsingtao Brewery Changed?" CEO & CIO, *Tsingtao Beer Tides*, August 2002, all issues.

23. Guo Hong, "How Strong Is Tsingtao Brewery's Integration Ability?" *China Business*, December 12, 2000.

24. Liu Lijuan, "Tsingtao Brewery: The Large Integration After Acquisitions," *Business Weekly*, June 2002.

25. Guo Hong, "How Strong is Tsingtao Brewery's Integration Ability?" *China Business*, December 12, 2000.

This case was prepared by Shengjun Liu, Richard Ivey School of Business, the University of Western Ontario.

Overview

After several months of rumors about the incoming successor, the board of Tsingtao Brewery finally appointed Jin Zhiguo as the new president in August 2001. Despite his past achievements, most people continued to doubt whether he would succeed. Employees were in a state of anxiety; the company was striving hard to meet analysts' expectations, while implementing internal reform and fighting against its competitors. It was easy to change the slogan from "Getting Bigger to Be Stronger" to "Getting Stronger to Be Bigger," but turning it into reality was much more challenging. Jin was given little time to warm up for the new role. He said:

> Even I myself doubted my competence too at that time. After all, it will be unforgivable to ruin the company. Since I have worked in the company for about 27 years, people here know my merits and shortcomings well. Some of them have been my superordinates. My primary achievements were gained in Tsingtao Brewery

Xi'An, so no wonder people shed doubt on my new role, I had to demonstrate my ability through my performance.[1]

The first training organized by Jin was a mountain-climbing game. In the game, Jin acted as the guide, and other people, blindfolded, followed him hand-in-hand. After finally making it to the peak, everyone cried because of the tough journey. Jin Zhiguo understood his responsibility better through the game, and he said, "No matter how rugged the road will be, I am determined to lead them to the peak."[2]

After a long time of investigation in the company's subsidiaries, Jin had a clear picture in his mind and decided to implement an overall restructuring in organization structure, marketing, brands, capital structure, etc.

A Tough Situation

After three months of investigation, Jin was quite anxious about the situation:

> The quick expansion imposed high pressures on the company. Despite a quick increase in output, Tsingtao Brewery's profit decreased significantly. Many negative symptoms appeared. Some subsidiaries boosted their sales and profits, the headquarters had little information about subsidiaries, and debts rose to a dangerous level. Moreover, the huge difference in technology and management across subsidiaries may endanger product quality as well as the Tsingtao brand.

Jin was familiar with these challenges. In his tenure at Xi'An, he kept a close eye on the company's acquisitions and gave suggestions to top management from time to time. Jin only supported acquisitions that could bring about a synergy effect. Jin questioned the company's post-acquisition integration process:

> The previous integration model looks good but it was not effective. It lacks adaptation and functionality. In addition, introducing Tsingtao Brewery's management model without adaptation may result in "indigestion." We have to move step-by-step cautiously, and make specific solutions for each company acquired rather than a uniform plan. The integration should focus on brands, profitability and management.

Back to the Core

In order to stop the blind expansion, Jin put forward a slogan, which said "What we want is not factory but market." Accordingly, Tsingtao Brewery should put more resources into building strong marketing networks and increasing market share rather than making more acquisitions. Jin defined the core competence of the company as the following:

> Tsingtao Brewery must focus on its core resources— the beer. If we successfully build beer-related talents, technology, network and brand, then the company will have strong core competences.
>
> Core competence is more concerned with "soft" resources, such as values, management system, sales channel, upper and lower stream of the value chain, brand, network and responsiveness, than with "hard" resources, such as equipment and technologies. Especially, the company should strengthen abilities in four aspects: knowledge management, supply chain management, integration of external resources and process reengineering.
>
> Fast expansion urgently requires effective integration. A fighter cannot forget to defend while attacking. Therefore, post-acquisition integration is one of the most important tasks ahead. We will not slow down, but we will switch from expansion through acquisitions to efficient organic growth.[3]

Jin made a list of the pros and cons of the company. The positives were that the company would enhance its image, product, sales and market position; but on the other hand, it would reduce investments in or even divest non-core businesses. Jin said: "The number one challenge is to change one's mindset. It is a kind of a revolution to discard traditional ideas. This is a painful but necessary process."

An important step of divestment was to outsource logistics to a third-party logistics company. In the first season of outsourcing, its logistic costs decreased by 36 per cent. Jin said: "The outsourcing of logistics will enable Tsingtao Brewery to commit to high quality and low cost, and expand geographic coverage."

As a means to leverage its financial resources, Tsingtao Brewery only acquired 30 per cent, rather than a majority stake as it did before in its stake of Guangxi Nanning Wantai Brewery Co. According to Jin's strategy, Tsingtao Brewery should learn to cooperate with other companies to attain a win-win solution.

Personnel Reform

Jin made a radical personnel reform after taking the post. At the beginning of 2002, seven out of the eight business units and 20 out of the 46 subsidiaries changed leaders. The number of departments was reduced from more than 20 to nine, and management-level staff decreased from more than 300 to 82 people. Managers were forced to compete for each position and received two internal reviews each year. Some general managers of subsidiaries were removed from their positions and even became unemployed. In August 2002, around 80 middle-level managers lost their current positions. In addition, the company ordered some employees close to retirement age to retire ahead of time. According to Jin, the personnel reform would be a continuous process:

> For such a large company whose staff and sales increased several times in a short period, top management must review the management system, culture as well as adaptability to the new situation, and then make necessary adjustments.
>
> Actually, Tsingtao Brewery has no human resource management system. Therefore, it is an urgent task to establish this type of system.
>
> We have to break the so called "communal pot" and "iron rice bowl" through competition. Roughly speaking, about 20 per cent of the staff lost their jobs.

The new human resource management (HRM) system gave more weight to talents. According to Jin, everybody has talents, and innovative people were special resources and the source of core competences. Moreover, in the new system, compensation would be based on performance.

Process Reengineering Through ERP

In order to facilitate internal communication and ease the "big company disease," Jin Zhiguo accelerated the implementation of enterprise resource planning (ERP) introduced by his predecessor. Jin explained: "By investing in ERP, we are not chasing fashion but upgrading the inefficient management system."[4]

In order to minimize the risk of ERP implementation, Tsingtao Brewery first introduced the ERP system to its South China Business Unit and then to other business units step-by-step. After implementing ERP in all units, headquarters then merged the system at the company level.

The return of ERP investment was surprising and greatly enhanced management efficiency. In the past, all heads of the 48 subsidiaries had to fly to Tsingtao city for important meetings. Now, what they needed was just to push a button to enjoy the convenience of video conferencing. Most importantly, ERP made information sharing possible at all levels of the company with an average employee able to access all public information. Even during the nationwide Severe Acute Respiratory (SARS) Syndrome in 2003, Tsingtao Brewery still held more than 10 video conferences, thus ensuring unhindered communications. Jin said: "ERP makes it possible for headquarters to oversee and guide each subsidiary 24 hours a day."

The benefits went beyond that. Through this electronic platform, the company integrated all factories, hundreds of sales agents and thousands of retailing units, making all units market-driven and customer-oriented.

Redesigning the Incentive System

With assistance from Stern Stewart & Corporation, Tsingtao Brewery established a management-by-objective system which was based on the economic value-added (EVA) concept.[5] In the new system, performance measurements would be value added instead of profits. Wang Tianyu, the finance director, explained:

> For example, the profit of one subsidiary is RMB1.62 million, but actually it is making a loss of RMB420,000 according to the EVA method. EVA can accurately reflect the real cost of capital.[6]

Despite its famous brand, Tsingtao Brewery still had a state-owned enterprise-style incentive system, characterized by low compensation and egalitarianism. Though the company promised to give bonuses at the end of year, the promise seldom came to fruition, due to a high threshold. Now, Jin bravely threw away previous practices and significantly increased compensation for executives and managers.

Jin Zhiguo admitted that it was hardly possible for a president to take care of everything in such a large company. Therefore, he delegated each of the vice-presidents (VPs) to be in charge of a business region and receive performance-related pay. As a result, VPs had more autonomy and passion while taking more risks and duties at the same time. In the past, all top management of subsidiaries had been selected by headquarters, but now Jin only decided on the candidates for the general manager, finance director and chief engineer positions.

Organizational Restructure

Jin took measures to make the organization structure horizontal to cure the big company disease. After restructuring, headquarters was positioned as the center for investment decisions, resource allocation and strategic planning. Meanwhile, each business unit was positioned as the center for regional management as well as the profit center, and would take care of all tasks related to production, marketing, sales and finance in its own region. Zhang Ruixiang, the company's representative for securities affairs, said:

> Each business unit can control several subsidiaries, and each business unit reports to the headquarters. In this way, we reduced management levels and enhanced efficiency.[7]

With the re-positioning of headquarters, several new departments were established: the department of strategy, marketing, human resource management, management integration and information management. Meanwhile, the finance department expanded its functions to include investment and financing management, and the political department switched its focus to corporate culture.

Another problem is that most business divisions were primarily production-oriented instead of market-oriented. Therefore, Jin decided to restructure the divisions according to geographic coverage, factory distribution, production capacity, consumption demands, traffic conditions, the difficulty of management, and so on. Business divisions were cut down from 10 to seven. Moreover, all subsidiaries were reorganized into independent legal entities and the headquarters only assumed limited liabilities. After the reorganization, the number of subsidiaries was reduced from 49 to 17.

Strategic Alliances

According to Jin, Tsingtao Brewery should focus more on strategy than tactics. Jin emphasized the importance of external partners.

> We hired Johnson Stokes & Master as counselor, HSBC as financial counselor, PWC as taxation counselor, and Stern Stewart as strategy counselor. These world-class companies can provide independent opinions. . . . However, we regard their suggestions as a reference rather than ready-made plans.

On October 21, 2002, Tsingtao Brewery and Anheuser Busch (A-B) entered into a strategic partnership agreement.[8] According to the agreement, A-B would buy Tsingtao Brewery's convertible bonds of $182 million, and was entitled the rights to convert the bonds into shares within seven years. If all bonds were converted into shares, A-B's stake in Tsingtao Brewery would increase from 4.5 per cent to 27 per cent. From Tsingtao Brewery's perspective, this alliance provides a great opportunity to learn from A-B. Zhang Ruixiang said:

> A-B has developed an effective method of integration during its long history. Hopefully, Tsingtao Brewery can transplant these experiences to China and integrate its subsidiaries in a better way.[9]

As agreed by both sides, A-B will send expatriates to Tsingtao Brewery to help improve integration and management. A-B representatives would take seats in the boards of Tsingtao Brewery. Jin Zhiguo said:

> We initiated the communication of best practices immediately. The first phase includes best practices in finance, marketing, human resource management, quality management and strategy.
>
> Tsingtao Brewery will take advantage of this opportunity to improve corporate governance and form a health check and balance among the board, top management and supervisory board.[10]

According to the proposal of the A-B team, the first phase of communication would center on consistency of beer quality, standard operation procedures, beer techniques and so on. Tsingtao Brewery staff were surprised at A-B's management concept focusing on implementation, continuous improvement and details, rational decision based on data analysis, effective supervision over material quality, perfect quality control and generous investments in quality, environment protection and employee safety. After achieving quality consistency, Tsingtao Brewery would go on to improve production efficiency.

Integration of Culture and Values

Post-acquisition integration is one of the most challenging things in the business world. In the integration process, the change of mindset is especially difficult. According to Jin, the key to a successful change of mindset lay in instilling, integrating and innovating corporate culture. How does one make all the subsidiaries accept Tsingtao Brewery's culture of "strenuous enterprising and devotion to society"? To solve this problem, Tsingtao Brewery sent specialists to subsidiaries to give cultural training workshops. Meanwhile, the subsidiaries' representatives were invited to the headquarters in Tsingtao to understand the culture through first-hand experience. Some subsidiaries initiated programs that were modeled after the No. 1 and No. 2 factories of Tsingtao Brewery. In addition, the company promoted corporate values by means of newspaper articles, clubs, and so on, to stimulate the staff's interest in company culture. The company set up a beer museum to leverage its long history. In order to minimize the resistance from acquired companies, Tsingtao Brewery established a dining hall, shed and bathhouse for their employees.

Inspired by the successful experiences in the Shenzhen and Xi'An branches, Jin Zhiguo firmly believed in the value of corporate culture. Tsingtao Brewery Xi'An, located inland in Western China, was formerly a typical company with an outdated mindset and poor management. Jin was shocked to find that the salesmen only sat in their company offices comfortably waiting for orders. In order to change their mindset, Jin took the lead to visit restaurants to conduct market research. Jin explained to his underlings:

> We have to know, in a given restaurant, how much beer is consumed and what percentage our beer accounts for? Why do consumers disregard our beer? What is wrong with our product?[11]

Tsingtao Brewery also considered the integration process an opportunity for headquarters to learn from subsidiaries, as illustrated by "investment in product quality will lead to success in the market," a slogan used in Xi'An's Tsingtao Brewery. It was a quote that was put on the first page of *Quality First*, a book published inside the company and designed especially for building corporate culture.

In the process of integration, a key issue is how to balance consistency and localization. Some subsidiaries overemphasized the importance of localization, resulting in poor cultural integration. Therefore, Tsingtao Brewery required that the Tsingtao Brewery model should be implemented without any comprise, i.e., "to reform rather than to amend."

Building a Learning Organization

Jin considered that the improvement of a manager's competence was a necessary precondition for sustainable success. Thus, various workshops and programs were held to help the management team learn management skills and enhance their internal

---

Recent History of Tsingtao Brewery

2001	
August 29	The board appointed Jin Zhiguo as general manager.
November 14	Tsingtao Brewery acquired 30 per cent stake in Guangxi Nanning Wantai Brewery Co. Ltd. at the cost of RMB96 million.
December 31	Tsingtao Brewery invested RMB401 million to establish the Tsingtao Brewery Industrial Park with a capacity of 400,000 tons of beer.
2002	
April 15	Tsingtao Brewery and Merchants Logistics Co. signed a cooperation agreement.
May 31	Tsingtao Brewery and Tsingtao Beer Festival Office established Beer World, which is the largest recreation ground characterized by the city's beer culture in Tsingtao.
July 1	The Southeast Division of Tsingtao Brewery was founded.
July 10	Tsingtao Brewery established a joint venture in Taiwan with an investment of 1.5 billion Taiwan dollars.
July 21	The No. 1 Factory of Tsingtao Brewery initiated an advice-giving program and received 61 suggestions, thereby reducing the electricity cost by about 20 per cent.
July 30	Tsingtao Brewery and A-B signed an exclusive negotiation agreement.
August 22	Tsingtao Brewery's net profits, sales and export increased 73, 27 and 61 per cent respectively in the first half of 2002 over the same period of 2001. Meanwhile, its market share rose by two percentage points to 12.8 per cent.
September 18	In the first eight months, Tsingtao Brewery's export increased by 99 per cent. Its market share in Taiwan jumped to 7.5 per cent. Meanwhile, its share prices increased from HK$2.20 to HK$3.90.
October 21	Tsingtao Brewery signed a strategic investment agreement with A-B.
2003	
January 20	Tsingtao Brewery Xi'An announced that it would sell the assets of Baoji Brewery.
February 22	Tsingtao Brewery received 1,619 suggestions from employees and reduced cost by more than RMB3 million.
April 1	Tsingtao Brewery delivered convertible bonds of HK$116.4 million to A-B.
August 15	Tsingtao Brewery celebrated its 100th anniversary and established the first beer museum in China.
November 4	Tsingtao Brewery gained the first Hazard Analysis Critical Control Point (HACCP) certification in China's beer industry.
2004	
February 21	Guangxi Nanning Tsingtao Brewery Co., Ltd. was founded.

communications. As a good example of the so-called "study forever," Jin himself completed his EMBA studies in a business school in Shanghai. He was determined to build Tsingtao Brewery into a learning organization that could adapt to the rapidly changing business environment. Jin put an emphasis on team spirit:

> There is a perfect team but no perfect individual.
>
> We need a management team with strong learning abilities. Only passion and experience are not enough. Why a learning organization? For a long time, Tsingtao Brewery has been an arrogant company. We must have an open mind and learn from other companies. Only then can we achieve sustainable success. In the end, a strong learning ability will lead to powerful innovations.[12]

Look Into the Future

Led by Jin Zhiguo, a low-profile and practical person, Tsingtao Brewery put more emphasis on efficiency and effectiveness. As a result, its profits increased faster than revenues, and revenues increased faster than sales. Not surprisingly, its stock price had been gradually picking up (see Exhibit 1). Jin Zhiguo passionately longed for the future of Tsingtao Brewery:

> Tsingtao Brewery will transform from a production-oriented to a service-oriented company and establish strong connections between the company and the market.
>
> Looking into the future, we will spare no effort to build a "perfect team" and establish a management model characterized by modern management and harmonious interpersonal relationships.... Staff will develop with the growth of the company.
>
> I dream that the 100-year old Tsingtao Brewery has the soul of a small company, i.e., "the ability to

act quickly and having infinite vigor and innovation ability."

Having celebrated its 100th anniversary in August 2003, Tsingtao Brewery still had a long way to go.

ENDNOTES

1. Nan Yan, "Jin Zhiguo: Changing the Taste of Tsingtao Beer," (Jin Zhi Guo Gei Qing Pi Huan Ge Kou Wei) *China Entrepreneur* (Zhong Guo Qi Ye Jia), July 2002.
2. Tian Ge, "The New Smell of Tsingtao Beer," (Qing Dao Pi Jiu De Xin Wei Dao) *Financial Weekly* (Cai Jing Zhou Kan), August 18, 2004.
3. Lei Yongjun, "The First Year of Jin Zhiguo's New Role in Tsingtao Brewery," (Qing Dao Pi Jiu Jin Zhi Guo Yong Jie Shuai Yin, Lin Wei Shou Ming Di Yi Nian) *Tank* (Zhi Nang), October 14, 2002.
4. Li Yun, "Capital Remolds Tsingtao Brewery According to Global Standard," (Yi Quan Qiu Wei Zuo Biao, Zi Ben Chong Su Qing Pi) *Southern Metropolitan Newspaper* (Nan Fang Du Shi Bao), July 25, 2002.
5. EVA is the financial performance measure that comes closer than any other to capturing the true economic profit of an enterprise. EVA = Net Operating Profit after Taxes − Capital × Cost of Capital. See www.sternstewart.com.
6. CCTV, "Reborn with Enhanced Corporate Governance, Tsingtao Brewery Advanced into Top 10 Beer Makers in the World," (Zai Zhi Li Zhong Huan Fa Xin Sheng, Bai Nian Qing Pi Ji Shen Shi Jie Shi Qiang) www.cctv.com.
7. Yuan Chaohui, "Tsingtao Brewery with a New Strategy," (Zhan Lue Chong Gou Xia De Qing Pi) *Securities Market Weekly* (Zheng Quan Shi Chang Zhou Kan), August 12, 2002.
8. Anheuser-Busch is the largest beer maker in the world, accounting for around half of the U.S. market.
9. Wang Gongbin, "Selling State-owned Assets," (Mai Mai Guo Zi) *21st Century Business Herald* (21 Shi Ji Jing Ji Bao Dao), December 30, 2002.
10. Jiang Peiyu, "Compatible with Tsingtao Brewery: The Foreign Sands in the Beer," (Jian Rong Anheuser Busch, Qing Dao Pi Jiu Zhong De Yang Sha Zi) *21st Century Business Herald* (21 Shi Ji Jing Ji Bao Dao), January 27, 2005.
11. "M&A Is Nothing but Means, While Integration Is the Essence," (Gou Bing Shi Shou Duan, Zheng He Shi Ben Zhi) *World Manager's Digest* (Shi Jie Jing Li Ren Wen Zhai), June 10, 2002.
12. Tian Ge, "The New Smell of Tsingtao Beer," (Qing Dao Pi Jiu De Xin Wei Dao) *Financial Weekly* (Cai Jing Zhou Kan), August 18, 2004.

Honda Motor Company and Hybrid Electric Vehicles

This case was prepared by Darryl Davis, Tom Davis, Sara Moodie, and Melissa A. Schilling, New York University.[a]

In 1997, Honda Motor Company introduced a two-door gas/electric hybrid vehicle called the Insight to Japan. The Insight's fuel efficiency was rated at 61 miles per gallon in the city, and 68 miles per gallon on the highway, and its battery did not need to be plugged into an electrical outlet for recharging. By 1999, Honda was selling the Insight in the United States, and winning accolades from environmental groups. In 2000 the Sierra Club gave Honda its "Award for Excellence in Environmental Engineering," and in 2002 the Environmental Protection Agency rated the Insight the most fuel-efficient vehicle sold in the U.S. for the 2003 model year. By August, 2005, Honda had sold its 100,000th hybrid to retail customers.[1]

Developing environmentally friendly automobiles was not a new strategy for Honda. In fact, Honda's work on developing cleaner transportation alternatives had begun decades earlier. Honda had achieved remarkable technological successes in its development of solar cars and electric cars and was an acknowledged leader in the development of hybrid cars. Gaining mass-market acceptance of such alternatives, however, had proven more challenging. Despite apparent enthusiasm over environmentally-friendly technologies, market adoption of environmentally-friendly vehicles had been relatively slow, making it difficult for automakers to achieve the economies of scale and learning curve effects that would enable efficient mass production. Some industry participants felt that the hybrid market would never be large enough to make it worth the research and development expense; Honda and Toyota were betting otherwise, and hoping that their gamble would pay off in the form of leadership in the next generation of automobiles.

Honda's History

Honda was founded in Hamamatsu Japan by Soichiro Honda in 1946 as the Honda Technical Research Institute. The company began as a developer of engines for bicycles, but by 1949 it had produced its first motorcycle, called the "Dream." In 1959, Honda entered the U.S. automobile and motorcycle market by opening the American Honda Motor Company. A few years later, in 1963, Honda released its first sports car, the S500, in Japan. Honda Motor Co. Inc. grew rapidly to become one of the largest automobile companies in the world. Its "Glocalization" strategy of building factories around the world that would meet the needs of local customers had resulted in a total worldwide presence of more than 100 factories in 33 countries. Furthermore, while

[a] This case builds on an earlier case, "Honda Insight: Development and Launch of a Hybrid-Electric Vehicle." Special thanks go to James Johng, Yong-Joo Kang, Jane Sul, and Masayuki Takanashi who contributed to the earlier version of the case. For permission contact Melissa Schilling at mschilli@stern.nyu.edu.

other auto manufacturers engaged in a frenzy of merger and acquisition activities in the late 1990s, Honda steadfastly maintained its independence. Honda has grown into one of the world's largest automobile manufacturers and has also evolved into one of the most respected global brands.

For the year ended March 31, 2006, the company boasted operating profits of ¥464 billion ($5.1 billion). See Exhibits 1 and 2 for summary financials, Exhibit 3 for some key events in Honda's evolution, and Tables 1 and 2, which highlight Honda's sales by major business divisions and geographic mix.

EXHIBIT 1

Honda Income Statement (millions of $US)

	Mar 06	Mar 05	Mar 04
Revenue	84,218.0	80,446.0	75,912.2
Cost of Goods Sold	59,588.0	56,155.0	52,171.2
Gross Profit	24,629.9	24,291.0	23,741.0
Gross Profit Margin	29.2%	30.2%	31.3%
SG&A Expense	15,015.3	16,323.9	16,174.6
Depreciation & Amortization	2,228.9	2,099.5	1,985.0
Operating Income	7,385.7	5,867.6	5,581.3
Operating Margin	8.8%	7.3%	7.4%
Nonoperating Income	(360.3)	1,555.8	483.4
Nonoperating Expenses	101.2	421.8	94.8
Income Before Taxes	6,924.2	6,108.3	5,969.9
Income Taxes	2,696.1	2,480.0	2,350.5
Net Income After Taxes	4,228.1	3,628.3	3,619.4
Continuing Operations	5,074.8	4,521.6	4,318.3
Discontinued Operations	—	—	—
Total Operations	5,074.8	4,521.6	4,318.3
Total Net Income	5,074.8	4,521.6	4,318.3
Net Profit Margin	6.0%	5.6%	5.7%
Diluted EPS from Total Net Income ($)	—	4.84	—
Dividends per Share	0.39	0.28	0.18
Total Current Liabilities	33,910.0	34,861.6	31,013.8
Long-Term Debt	15,971.5	14,503.3	12,969.9
Other Noncurrent Liabilities	4,908.9	6,692.4	6,741.9
Total Liabilities	54,790.4	56,057.4	50,725.6
Shareholder's Equity			
Preferred Stock Equity	—	—	—
Common Stock Equity	35,068.9	30,590.4	26,731.9
Total Equity	35,068.9	30,590.4	26,731.9
Shares Outstanding (mil.)	36.5	36.5	1,948.8

Source: Retrieved from Hoovers, January 2007.

EXHIBIT 2

Honda Balance Sheet

	Mar 06	Mar 05	Mar 04
Assets			
Current Assets			
Cash	6,352.3	7,193.9	6,737.1
Net Receivables	20,334.3	18,845.2	17,300.0
Inventories	8,808.6	8,020.0	7,118.5
Other Current Assets	3,825.0	3,222.1	2,819.6
Total Current Assets	39,320.1	37,281.3	33,975.3
Net Fixed Assets	15,429.8	14,733.5	13,350.4
Other Noncurrent Assets	35,109.4	34,633.0	30,131.8
Total Assets	89,859.3	86,647.8	77,457.5
Liabilities and			
** Shareholder's Equity**			
Current Liabilities			
Accounts Payable	18,460.9	18,530.4	16,332.3
Short-Term Debt	11,485.2	12,131.1	11,359.0
Other Current Liabilities	3,963.8	4,200.1	3,322.5

Source: Retrieved from Hoovers, January 2007.

EXHIBIT 3

Selected Key Events in Honda's History

Date	Event
1946	Soichiro Honda establishes Honda Technical Research Institute
1948	Honda Motor Co., Ltd. incorporated
1959	American Honda established
1960	Motorcycle production begins
1963	Honda's first sports car and light truck launched
1982	Honda's first American plant begins production
1989	Second car production plant begins production
1995	Honda introduces first gasoline powered vehicle to meet ultra low emission standards
1996	Human robot prototype announced
1998	Honda's 50th anniversary
1999	Honda announces its FCX-V1 and FCX-V2 fuel cell vehicles
2000	FCX-V3 announced
2001	FCX-V4 announced, Alabama plant begins operations
2002	Honda FCX fuel cell vehicle delivered in Japan and the U.S.
2004	Honda's FC stack, next generation fuel cell, developed; launches first hybrid scooter
2005	Honda delivers FCX fuel cell vehicle to world's first individual consumer; 100,000th hybrid vehicle sold in U.S.

Source: Honda fiscal 2004 20-F Securities and Exchange Commission filing and authors' calculations.

TABLE 1
Honda Sales by Business Unit, 2006

Fiscal Period 2006	% of Total Revenue
Automobile Business	80.8%
Motorcycle Business	12.4%
Financial Services	3.0%
Other	3.7%

Source: Company annual report and case writers' calculations.

TABLE 2
Honda Geographic Sales Mix

	Net Sales (millions of Yen) 2006
Japan	1,693,994
North America	5,463,359
Europe	1,009,421
Asia	1,085,451
Other	655,721

Source: Company annual report and case writers' calculations.

Hybrid Electric Vehicles

The standard combustion engine has been a part of daily human life for well over a century now, first in factories and in large forms of transportation (locomotives, ships) and then as the power source for automobiles. Hybrid automobile engines—engines that utilize *both* petrochemicals and electricity for power—were developed well over 150 years ago, but until recently, technological limitations hindered the advancement of these innovations for practical use. Electric-powered vehicles were used in the late 1800s, but they required large, heavy batteries, which limited their adoption.

In the early 1900s, American auto buyers preferred electric cars to gasoline-powered cars almost 2:1, and American automakers responded by producing along that ratio.[2] However, in 1904 Henry Ford's quieter gas engines and production process innovations (the famed assembly-line methodology) allowed gas-powered engines to be made cheaply, reliably, and quickly. Consequently, hybrid and electric engine technology took a back seat for generations. While experimentation and innovation in the hybrid and electric engine arena never died, the research on these engines became more academic. It was not until the 1970s, when oil embargoes severely reduced U.S. access to oil and petrol products, that interest in hybrid engine technology was revived. The U.S. Congress passed the "Electric and Hybrid Vehicle Research, Development, and Demonstration Act" in 1976 to spur research related to the technologies, and some of the larger automakers also established hybrid and alternative fuel vehicle R&D efforts. General Motors (GM), for example, spent $20 million in 1977-9 years on electric car development.[3]

The 1990s economic boom and the Sport Utility Vehicle (SUV) trend stifled consumer interest, and thus industry interest, in smaller more fuel-efficient cars. Bigger gas-powered engines were popular and rising consumer incomes offset the declining mileage-per-gallon (mpg) ratings in each new model year.[4] Electric cars were marketed in the late 1990s (especially by GM, Honda, and Toyota), but they failed to catch on beyond a small segment of consumers and interest in purely electric vehicles withered.[5]

In 2004, however, the combination of concerns about global warming, high gasoline prices and the costs (direct and indirect) of U.S. dependence on foreign oil brought hybrid engines back in the news. Celebrity interest and industry timing all appeared to be aligning to make hybrid vehicles a market reality. In fact, in 2004 demand for hybrid cars far outpaced supply.[6] A 2006 survey by Advertising Age indicated that 45% of Americans expected to be driving an alternative-fuel vehicle such as a hybrid within ten years.

Hybrid electric vehicles (HEVs) have several advantages over gasoline vehicles such as regenerative braking capability, reduced engine weight, lowered overall vehicle weight, and increased fuel efficiency and decreased emissions. First, the regenerative braking capability of HEVs helps to minimize energy loss and recover the energy used to slow down or stop a vehicle. Given this fact, engines can also be sized to accommodate average loads instead of peak loads, significantly reducing the engine weight of HEVs. Additionally, the special lightweight materials that are used for the manufacture of HEVs further reduce the overall vehicle weight of the vehicle. Finally, both the lowered vehicle weight and the dual power system greatly increase the HEV's fuel efficiency and reduce its emissions.

Honda's Hybrid Engine

While Toyota was the first to market hybrid cars (Prius debuted in Japan in 1997), Honda was the first to market hybrids in the U.S. The Insight was released in 1999 and quickly won accolades.[7] Though both vehicles use a combination of electricity and gasoline for power, they do not use identical hybrid designs. Honda's hybrid models are designed for fuel-efficiency, in contrast to Toyota's hybrid vehicles, which are designed for reduced emissions. These differences in design goals translate into very different hybrid engine architectures.

The Honda Insight was designed as a "parallel" hybrid system, where the electrical power system and the gasoline power system run in parallel to simultaneously turn the transmission, and the transmission then turns the wheels (see Exhibit 4).[8] The electric motor in the Insight aided the gas engine by providing extra power while accelerating or climbing, and supplemented braking power. The electric motor could also start the engine, obviating the need for a traditional starter component. The Insight's electric engine was not powerful enough alone to propel the car; therefore, the gas engine had to be running simultaneously. The Insight mileage ratings were 61 mpg in cities and 70 mpg on highways, with 0-60 miles per hour acceleration in approximately 11 seconds. At lower speeds the electrical components provided the extra horsepower to propel the car, reducing the gas engine's effort and thus saving fuel. The batteries were regenerated by capturing energy during braking or slowing and through standard electricity-generation provided by the traditional generator component in a standard car engine. Therefore, one did not have to plug in the Insight, or any of Honda's hybrids, to recharge the batteries.

In contrast to the parallel system configuration, a "series" hybrid system is designed to have a gas-powered engine turn a generator, which in turn powers an electric motor that rotates the transmission or recharges the batteries. The gas-powered engine does not directly power the vehicle.[9] The Toyota Prius was designed to reduce emissions during urban driving, and its design incorporates both parallel and series system elements (see Exhibit 5). To reduce emissions, the Prius utilizes a power-train design, in which the car runs at its most efficient speed by virtue of a "power split device" that links the gas and electric engines through the generator with a parallel system design, but allows the car to run exclusively on electrical power at lower speeds similar to a "pure" series

EXHIBIT 4

Parallel Hybrid System (e.g., Honda Insight)

Source: Adapted from E. Kawahara & S. Ogawa, "Automobile Industry: Special Report—Hybrid Car Diffusion Offers New Players Expanding Business Opportunities," J. P. Morgan Asia Pacific Equity Research report, July 7, 2004.

EXHIBIT 5

Series-Parallel Hybrid System

Source: Adapted from E. Kawahara & S. Ogawa, "Automobile Industry: Special Report—Hybrid Car Diffusion Offers New Players Expanding Business Opportunities," J. P. Morgan Asia Pacific Equity Research report, July 7, 2004.

system design (see Exhibit 6). Consequently no gas is burned and emissions are negligible under these conditions.[10] Thus, for low speed urban traffic, the Prius meets its engine design goal of reduced emissions, with better mileage ratings than the heavier Honda Insight. In addition, unlike the Insight, the Prius was a four-door mid-sized sedan with back seats for extra passengers, something that the original two-door Honda Insight lacked, but was later offered on hybrid Civic and Accord models.

EXHIBIT 6

Toyota's Power Split Device

Planetary Gear Set

Ring Gear
Connects to motor and differential

Sun Gear
Connects to generator

Planetary Carrier
Connects to engine

Planetary Gears
Connect to planetary carrier

©2000 HowStuffWorks

Source: K. Nice, Howthingsworks.com, "How Hybrid Cars Work," Figure 9, (http://auto.howstuffworks.com/hybrid-car.html), accessed December 2, 2004.

TABLE 3

Total Hybrid Electric Passenger Vehicle Sales
in the U.S., 2000–2006

Year	Units Sold in U.S.
2000	9,367
2001	20,287
2002	35,961
2003	47,525
2004	83,153
2005	189,916[a]
2006	232,590[b]

[a] Does not include Ford Escape/Mercury Mariner Hybrid sales of 15K+.

[b] Does not include one month of Camry Hybrid sales, three months of GS450h sales, and eight months of Escape/Mariner Hybrid sales.

Source: Electric Drive Transportation Association, www.electricdrive.org, April 15, 2006.

Obstacles to the Adoption of Hybrids

The hybrid market had exhibited rapid growth (see Table 3). However, the numbers of hybrid vehicles sold were still very small compared to traditional automobiles. There was still considerable uncertainty about the direction engine design would go in the next few years. Would one hybrid design rise to dominate the others? By late 2006, hybrid customers were clamoring for versions of the cars that could be plugged in to increase their driving range on electric power alone. Adding to this uncertainty were questions about whether hybrids would be quickly displaced by other alternative fuel technologies such as new "green diesel" engines, fuel cells or hydrogen combustion.

Hybrid cars were also expensive to produce relative to traditional automobiles. While Honda charged a sales price for the Insight that was comparable to its non-hybrid counterparts—around $20,000 depending on options—it was estimated that Honda lost as much as $8,000 per car when the hybrids were originally launched due to insufficient volume to achieve economies of scale.[11]

Strategy at Honda

At Honda, being an environmental leader means never uttering the words, "It can't be done." That's why for more than two decades Honda has led the way in balancing what consumers want with what the

environment needs. Technologies change over time—but our commitment to the environment never will.

—Honda Corporate Website

Honda's strategy had consistently emphasized innovation, independence, and environmental friendliness. In 1972, Honda introduced the Civic, which became an immediate success, ranking first in U.S. fuel-economy tests for four consecutive years starting in 1974. Through the 1980s and 1990s, Honda made a number of advancements in environmentally-friendly transportation. In 1986, it developed the first mass-produced four-cylinder car that could break the 50 miles per gallon barrier, the Civic CRX-HF. In 1989, it became the first auto manufacturer in the U.S. to use solvent-free paint in its mass production facilities. In 1996, Honda introduced a record-breaking solar powered car (a prototype not designed for commercial production), and in 1998 it introduced a completely electric vehicle. Though the electric car was not a commercial success, developing the electric vehicle built a foundation of expertise that Honda would later employ in its development of fuel cell technology. Fuel cells were considered to offer great potential for the eventual replacement of combustion engines.

Manufacturing and Logistics

Like most of the large automakers, Honda utilizes a Japanese-style logistics and operations program for its production, both in the United States as well as abroad.[12] Just-in-time inventory ordering and storage, as well as "lean" manufacturing processes, keep production efficient, as costs remain low and productivity high. Honda's production processes are technology intensive using robots, automated manufacturing lines, and proprietary software to coordinate work. Honda's international presence and large U.S. domestic presence provide economies of scale and scope for its inbound logistics and production efforts. Outbound logistics are also aided by economies of scale, where Honda utilizes its extensive network to transport and distribute Honda products—including hybrids—to its dealers. Furthermore, by using franchised dealerships Honda avoids most direct retail-based costs for sales to end-users.

Research and Development

Honda places tremendous emphasis on research and development. Since its inception, Honda has supported and promoted a culture of innovation. This focus on innovation transcends all of Honda's businesses, from hand-pushed mowers to hybrid scooters. To achieve its leading position in hybrids, Honda spent billions of dollars and assigned a generation of engineers to research and develop the technology. Though Honda's size put it at a disadvantage in terms of R&D expenditures compared to larger automakers (Honda's R&D budget was roughly 35% smaller than most automaker R&D budgets), Honda's R&D program was highly efficient and its success at R&D was world-renowned.

Honda's management believed strongly that visionary research required independence from manufacturing operations. Honda thus created two autonomous firms called Honda R&D Co. Ltd. and Honda Engineering Co. Ltd., which operated without interference from the business units.[13] Honda R&D conducts product related research, while Honda Engineering focuses on manufacturing and process innovations. These organizations were complemented by additional research centers on each continent that could work on more market-specific projects. Each of the R&D centers were permitted great autonomy to encourage independence and long-term focus, as noted by Takeomi Mihyoshi, former executive chief engineer at Honda's Tochigi R&D center: "Our R&D operates as a separate entity that allows for creative freedom. We are isolated from outside voices. R&D is a long-term operation."[14]

Despite their independence, all of the research entities coordinated closely through significant and constant communication to promote cross fertilization of ideas. Honda, for example, has always moved its employees around the world to observe and learn from other internal groups. Honda employees and managers also conduct quasi-brainstorming sessions called "waigayas" to generate and parse new ideas. One previous chairman said, "Although [Mr. Honda] was a genius who served as an inspiration to others, he was a man who did things his own way. So a waigaya is an avenue through which a group of non-genius people can use their collective brainpower to express their dreams and desires to produce new ideas and concepts."[15]

Marketing

Honda advertised its hybrids through television and radio advertising campaigns, and select magazine advertisements. Honda also leveraged public exposure of its hybrids by placing them with urban area car

---

TABLE 4

Brand Ranking and Advertising Spending

Rank	Brand	Market Share 2005	Market Share 2004	Ad Spending in 18 Measured Media, 2005 (millions of $US)	Ad Spending in 18 Measured Media, 2004 (millions of $US)	Ad Spending in 18 Measured Media, per 2005 Unit Sold
1	Toyota Camry	5.4%	5.5%	$65.6	$118.6	$151.9
2	Honda Accord	4.6	5.0	114.3	156.0	309.4
3	Honda Civic	3.9	4.0	112.0	116.1	363.1
4	Nissan Altima	3.2	3.0	132.1	211.1	517.2
5	Chevrolet Impala	3.1	3.8	58.5	10.6	237.3
6	Toyota Corolla	2.9	2.8	47.7	65.9	205.8
7	Chevrolet Cobalt	2.7	0.1	116.8	48.0	549.3
8	Chevrolet Malibu	2.6	2.3	27.5	140.5	135.2
9	Ford Taurus	2.5	3.2	0.1	4.0	0.5
10	Ford Focus	2.3	2.7	50.5	82.9	273.1
	Total top 10	33.2	32.4			

Source: Halliday, J. "Amid Sea Change, Goal is to Stay Afloat." Advertising Age, June 26, 2006:S17.

TABLE 5

Honda and Toyota U.S. Hybrid Sales, 2006

Honda Hybrid Models		Toyota Hybrid Models	
Honda Accord	5,598	Toyota Prius	106,971
Honda Civic	31,253	Toyota Highlander	31,485
Honda Insight	722	Lexus RX 400h	20,161

Source: Electric Drive Transportation Association, www.electricdrive.org, April 15, 2006.

rental agencies such as ZipCar. The Insight also played a "starring role" in the John Travolta movie *Be Cool*, the sequel to *Get Shorty*.[16]

Despite its smaller size, Honda spent amounts on advertising its main models comparable to Toyota, Nissan, and Chevrolet. According to data from Advertising Age, the Honda Accord and Honda Civic were the number 2 and number 3 (respectively) auto brands in the U.S., behind the Toyota Camry (see Table 4).

Collaboration Strategies . . . or Rather Lack Thereof

In Honda's research and development of its hybrid engine system, management decided to keep collaboration to a minimum, essentially "going solo" with a risky—but potentially profitable—strategy to change basic automotive power design for the first time in a century. Honda's decision to not collaborate stood in stark contrast to the licensing and joint venture strategies pursued by Toyota. Toyota had aggressively pursued collaboration agreements for its hybrid technology and had accrued over 1,000 patents on hybrid-related technology as of 2006. Toyota also promoted its hybrid technology design by licensing the technology to Ford and Nissan.[17] While some industry observers were perplexed by Honda's decision to avoid collaboration, others pointed out that Honda's independence both gave it more control over its technological direction, and ensured that the accumulated learning remained in-house. Consistent with this, Honda's management insisted that keeping development exclusively in-house compelled Honda to understand all aspects of a technology, from its strengths to its weaknesses. This in-house know-how could lead to sources of competitive advantage that were difficult for competitors to imitate.

It's better for a person to decide about his own life rather than having it decided by others.

—Hiroyuki Yoshino, 2002

By the end of 2006, Toyota's hybrids were outselling Honda's hybrids by about four-to-one (see Table 5), causing many analysts to question Honda's staunch position on pursuing a different hybrid technology from Toyota and to not collaborate or license with other auto producers. Honda's Insight was faring so poorly, in fact, that Honda decided to cease production in September of 2006.[18]

The Future of Hybrids

By the end of 2006, hybrid electric vehicles were widely believed to have the potential to allow continued growth in the automotive sector, while also reducing critical resource consumption, dependence on foreign oil, air pollution, and traffic congestion. The success of hybrids, however, was far from assured. While the technology's capabilities held great promise, the widespread penetration of hybrids hinged on the economics of producing a complex hybrid power system. The hybrid's complexity, and the fact that some of the necessary complementary technologies (such as storage and conversion systems) still had room for improvement, caused opinions to be mixed on the hybrids' ultimate impact in the marketplace. Some industry analysts believed that the success of hybrids would require convergence on a single hybrid standard that could gain economies of scale through production by multiple producers. Some skeptics, however, still felt that automakers should not bother with hybrid technology at all—it was a diversion of R&D funds away from better long-term alternatives such as fuel cells or hydrogen combustion engines.

Hydrogen Combustion, Hydrogen Fuel Cells, Natural Gas and Diesel

Hydrogen is the most abundant resource on earth and its combustion produces only water vapor as an emission. Many environmentalists and industry participants thus believed that the auto industry should focus its investment on technologies that utilized hydrogen as the fuel source. The two primary technologies under consideration were direct hydrogen combustion and hydrogen fuel cells. Hydrogen combustion worked much like traditional engines except that hydrogen would be used instead of gasoline in an internal combustion engine. Fuel cells converted fuel to electricity that was stored in a large battery. By converting chemical energy directly into electrical energy, fuel cells had been known to achieve a conversion efficiency of better than 50%—twice the efficiency of internal combustion engines. Either method resulted in only water vapor being produced as an emission. However the development and commercialization of fuel-cell powered vehicles had been significantly hindered by the state of battery technology.[19] Furthermore, widespread adoption of either alternative would first require building an almost entirely new fuel infrastructure. There was also speculation that fuel cell or hydrogen combustion vehicles would be dangerous since the hydrogen fuel (a highly combustible substance) would have to be stored under great pressure.

Honda had developed fuel cell vehicles in parallel with its hybrid development. In July 2002, Honda succeeded in manufacturing the first fuel cell vehicle to receive certification by the U.S. Environment Agency (EPA) and the California Air Resources Board (CARB) by meeting all applicable standards. This new fuel cell vehicle, called the FCX, was certified as a Zero Emission Vehicle and by the EPA as a Tier-2 Bin 1 National Low Emission Vehicle (NLEV), the lowest national emission rating. In 2005, Honda's FCX became the very first fuel cell vehicle in the world to be sold to an individual consumer (a family in southern California).

Honda had also invested in developing vehicles that burned natural gas and developing "new age" diesel engines that would burn much cleaner than traditional diesel. Honda began selling the Civic GX natural gas vehicle in 2005, and planned to expand retail distribution in 2006. Honda hoped to introduce new vehicles with clean diesel technology by 2009.

While Honda claimed that its work in hybrids helped it create internal knowledge of component design and manufacture that improved its options with respect to fuel cell technologies, some questioned whether it made sense to invest simultaneously in multiple technologies. Was simultaneously pursuing multiple technology paths spreading Honda too thin? Would it make more sense for Honda to focus solely on a single technology? Or was it important for Honda to pursue synergies (and preserve its options) by developing and promoting multiple alternatives to traditional gasoline-combustion vehicles? Honda senior researcher Akira Fujimura noted, "The ultimate technology that solves both harmful emissions and depletion of oil reserves is fuel cell technology. But hybrid technologies will be around for a very long time."[20]

ENDNOTES

1. J. Johnson, "Production of Cleaner-burning Hybrids on the Rise for All," Waste News, 11(19):12, 2006.
2. Hybridcars.com (www.hybridcars.com/history), accessed September 26, 2004.
3. Ibid.
4. J. Voorheis, "Hybrid Gasoline-Electric Cars: Driving to a Brighter Future," webpage (www.unc.edu/~voorheis/research.html), September 26, 2004.
5. Hybridcars.com (www.hybridcars.com/history), September 26, 2004.
6. R. Rayasam, "Austin Faces 2-year Wait for Prius," Austin American Statesman, June 3, 2004; M. Garriga, "Gas Costs Keep Honda, Toyota Hybrids Hot Sellers in New Haven, Conn.-Area," New Haven Register, June 9, 2004; G. Chambers Williams III, "Hybrid Demand Outpaces Supply," San Gabriel Valley Tribune, May 28, 2004.
7. Hybridcars.com (www.hybridcars.com/history), accessed September 26, 2004.
8. K. Nice, Howthingswork.com, "How Hybrid Cars Work" (http://auto.howstuffworks.com/hybrid-car.htm), accessed September 26, 2004.
9. Ibid.
10. Ibid.
11. D. Welch, "Reinventing the Hybrid Wheel," BusinessWeek Online, October 6, 2003.
12. Honda website (www.hondacorporate.com/worldwide), accessed October 23, 2004.
13. Ibid.
14. Ibid.
15. R Shook, "Honda: An American Success Story," 1988, pp. 154–155.
16. Gregory Solman, "Honda Charts Fresh Hybrid Territory," BrandWeek, October 18, 2004.
17. Reuters, "Mercedes, Porsche Eye Hybrid Cars," October 25, 2004; "Porsche Seeks Toyota Hybrid Deal," November 23, 2004.
18. "Honda's Pioneer Bites the Dust," Automotive News, 80(6203):62, May 22, 2006.
19. M. Wald, "Cheaper Part for Fuel Cells to be Announced Today," New York Times, p. C4, October 5, 2004.
20. J.B. Treece, "Hybrid Who's Who," Automotive News, 80(6208):28f, June 12, 2006.

vCustomer: Shaping the Outsourcing Industry

This case was prepared by Sandip Basu under the guidance of Professor Suresh Kotha, the University of Washington.

Sanjay Kumar sat in the conference room at his office in Kirkland, a rapidly expanding suburb of Seattle, Washington. He was getting ready for a meeting that could decide the future strategic direction of vCustomer, the company he founded in October 1999. The room had two clocks, one displaying U.S. Pacific Time and the other, Indian Standard Time. It was a warm Seattle morning in the spring of 2005. As he glanced to see what time it was in India, he reflected on the disparities between the two countries, which extended well beyond the twelve-and-a-half hour time difference. Indeed leveraging these differences had been the primary value proposition of his foray into the IT Enabled Services (ITES) and Business Process Outsourcing (BPO) space with the formation of vCustomer.

Since its founding, vCustomer had a track record of coupling aggressive growth with 100% customer retention. *Inc.* magazine ranked it as the fastest growing private company in business services in 2004. Currently, vCustomer was one of the largest private companies involved in "consumer based technical support" in the world. Its 18 clients were some of the largest diversified global leaders in the computer/networking/peripherals manufacturing space. With a total capacity of around 3,300 workstations, the company handled 3 million calls a month.[1]

The Offshore Outsourcing Phenomenon

From Manufacturing to Services

Outsourcing is a generic business practice in which firms decide to buy inputs or services from external sources rather than make them in-house. While over 85% of outsourcing activity is domestic, the term has come to be associated with "offshore outsourcing" or simply "off-shoring," which involves sourcing from business organizations in foreign countries. The adoption of offshore outsourcing in manufacturing activity started taking off in the late 1980s and early 1990s. As transport and communications costs fell and logistics technology improved, American manufacturers of automobiles and consumer electronics began moving production to cheaper nearby countries like Mexico. By the late 1990s, China had emerged as a major destination for outsourcing of manufacturing.[2]

When telecommunications costs fell similarly, U.S. firms started moving their business services abroad too. Countries like India, where skilled labor could be accessed at relatively lower costs, became attractive destinations for this type of work. IT services were one of the primary activities to become outsourced. Indian IT companies got their first big boost with the "Y2K crisis" at the turn of the millennium as they still had programmers who could read old computer code such as COBOL. Meanwhile, internal IT departments of corporations were struggling to cope with the growing complexity of managing their own information systems. Since different sorts of computer systems had been bought at different times, these departments were spending most of their time maintaining the tangle of legacy systems and trying to adapt these systems to changing needs. These companies also looked to outsource their IT work offshore. Standardization of network protocols now allowed easy routing of voice and data traffic through global networks. To deal with new IT concerns, globally dispersed development teams could be quickly assembled based on expertise and cost considerations.

Business Process Outsourcing

After IT offshoring gained momentum, U.S. companies recognized that other IT-related service jobs not requiring highly qualified computer programmers and engineers could also be farmed out. They began digitalizing and telecommunicating paper-based back office functions around the world. Routine telephone inquiries were bundled together into call-centers in locations outside the United States. Such operations collectively called Business Process Outsourcing included sales and marketing, human resources, finance and administration, and logistics activities (see Exhibit 1).

India's BPO industry started with foreign "captives," or subsidiary organizations that handled the respective parents' in-house work. Pioneers in BPO operations like GE, American Express, and British Airways arrived in India in the late 1990s. For instance, GE's Indian subsidiary, GECIS, handled administrative processing work for the parent firm's financial businesses. These companies were joined by some domestic call-center operations such as 24 × 7, EXL, Spectramind, Daksh, and vCustomer.[3]

Indian BPO firms also faced competition from specialist American call-center companies, which like the IT firms earlier, had been adjusting to competition from Indian companies by locating their operations in India. Among the more successful of these firms were Convergys, the world's largest call-center operator with a staff of 60,000, and the Sutherland Group, a U.S.-based company with over 6,000 employees. See Exhibit 2 for a list of major players engaged in BPO in India. However, given that the global volume of BPO activity is estimated to grow from $125 billion in 2000 to around $175 billion by 2008 (Exhibit 3), many analysts believe that there is enough room for multiple players in this space.

EXHIBIT 1

Scope of BPO Services

Function	Human Resources	Payment Services	Manufacturing, Distribution, Logistics	Finance and Administration	Sales, Marketing, Customer Care
Activities	Payroll/Benefits Processing	Loan Administration	Inventory and Warehousing	Document Management	Customer Service
	Training and Development	Credit/Debit Card Services	Industry Management	Billings	Customer Analysis
				Claims Processing	
	Hiring/ Staffing	Check Processing	Order Fulfillment/ Procurement	Accounts Receivable	Call Centers
					Consumer Information Services
	Employee Benefits Management		Transportation and Distribution	Accounts Payable	
				General Ledger	
	401K				
				Accounting Services	
				Shareholder Services	
Share of Revenues	14%	9%	59%	11%	7%

Source: Gartner Dataquest.

EXHIBIT 2

Categories of Players in Indian BPO Market

Category	Geographic Presence	Process Competences	IT Competences	Major Players
Former captive operations	Limited but expanding	Built in captive context, limited consulting skills	Limited	Genpact, WNS Global
Major IT players	Moving aggressively	Learning as they go	Obvious strength	Cognizant, HCL, Infosys, TCS, Wipro
Voice-oriented players	Global players are well-established	Established but shallow	Limited	Indian: 24/7, ICICI OneSource, ITC Infotech, Transworks, vCustomer Global: Convergys, SITEL, Sykes, Sutherland
Niche players	Highly limited	Deep but narrow	Limited but focused	Datamatics, Outsource Partners International
Knowledge services specialists	Highly limited	Often not relevant since work undertaken is discrete	Limited	Office Tiger, EMR Technology Ventures, Evaluserve

Source: Forrester Research, March 2006.

Outsourcing's Impact on Firms and Societies

The advantages to corporations outsourcing business operations abroad were not limited to cost savings alone. First, outsourcing allowed companies to move from a fixed cost structure to a variable cost structure, resulting in greater financial and strategic agility. Second, work outsourced abroad could be carried out round-the-clock as data was ferried back and forth.

EXHIBIT 3

Global Spending on IT and BPO Offshoring

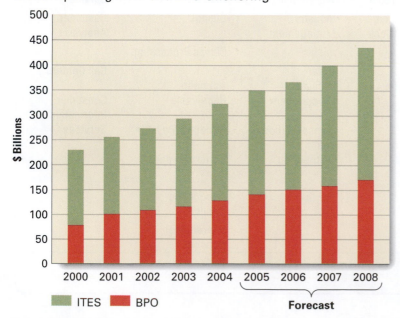

Source: Gartner, reproduced in *The Economist*, November 2004.

This enabled companies to leverage the time differences between the two nations to their advantage. Third, they could exploit local programming talent, which might have customization skills not found in the home country. Finally, by outsourcing non-critical operations, organizations could focus on core operations vital to their survival and prosperity.[4]

Outsourcing brought several benefits for destination countries, the primary one being employment. For example, forecasts indicate that more than 3.5 million people in India will be employed in the ITES and BPO industries by 2012.[5] Besides, firms in destination countries had the opportunity to develop cutting-edge capabilities in such services, which could then stimulate further innovation.

Contrary to the political rhetoric often heard in the U.S., there were also advantages for the home country that offshored work. For the U.S., the resultant savings in costs allowed businesses to stay competitive globally, thereby benefiting both shareholders and consumers. Besides, these increased earnings resulting from cost savings often made their way back into the U.S. economy. U.S. companies, in turn, often spent their increased profits on improving existing products and introducing new ones. Such investments also stimulated innovation and created new value-added jobs to replace those lost to other nations. Lastly, outsourcing firms in countries like India needing infrastructure and equipment usually bought these from large U.S. multinationals.[6] McKinsey & Co, the U.S. consulting firm, estimates that for every dollar that American firms spend on service work from India, the U.S. economy receives $1.14 in return, while India gains just $0.33 (see Exhibit 4).

EXHIBIT 4

Value Potential to the U.S. from $1 of Spending Offshored to India, 2002

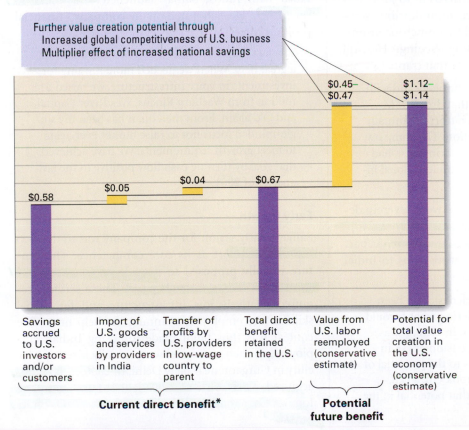

Further value creation potential through
Increased global competitiveness of U.S. business
Multiplier effect of increased national savings

$0.45– / $0.47

$1.12– / $1.14

$0.58

$0.05

$0.04

$0.67

| Savings accrued to U.S. investors and/or customers | Import of U.S. goods and services by providers in India | Transfer of profits by U.S. providers in low-wage country to parent | Total direct benefit retained in the U.S. | Value from U.S. labor reemployed (conservative estimate) | Potential for total value creation in the U.S. economy (conservative estimate) |

Current direct benefit*   **Potential future benefit**

* Estimated based on historical reemployment trends from job loss through trade in the U.S. economy

Source: McKinsey Global Institute.

The Genesis of vCustomer

The Entrepreneur and Opportunity Recognition

At the age of seventeen, Sanjay Kumar left India to study at Carnegie Mellon University in the United States. Upon finishing his studies there, he moved to the University of Pennsylvania to earn a doctorate in Computer Science, which he completed in 1991. Sanjay's first visit to Seattle was for an interview with the aerospace giant, Boeing Corporation. Based on conversations with friends, he instead ended up at Microsoft.

Microsoft's recognition of the potential of the Internet led to investments in networking, broadband and telephony using the Windows platform, all of which Sanjay was a part of because of his technical computing expertise. At Microsoft, Sanjay was soon promoted to lead a group of around 200 people. Most of his subordinates benefited from Microsoft's explosive growth during that period and were already millionaires.

In the late '90s, Sanjay left Microsoft to join Teledesic Corporation, a satellite communications services start-up, which was funded by numerous prominent Seattle investors including Boeing. He still vividly remembered why he made that transition:

> Working on the broadband technology and with the Winsock Forum, a group that drove ATM support to the Windows NT platform eventually took me to Teledesic Corporation. The company, in which Bill Gates himself was an investor, had launched an amazing project to build a global hi-speed services network.

Unfortunately, Teledesic's projects were severely delayed.[7] During his stint at Teledesic, Sanjay was toying with the idea of starting his own venture. As part of his work, he had made numerous trips to India. He particularly remembered one such visit:

> While my first transition to Teledesic had been very smooth, I was now wondering what I would do once I left this organization. In 1998, it was the visit to the facility of a big customer GE in Gurgaon[8] that opened my eyes to the potential of the BPO industry in India. It took GE, a U.S.-based company, to figure out that potential in the early days.

Sanjay considered riding this wave on his own. He was confident that he could do so effectively because of his expertise in communications technology, his experiences in dealing with the FCC and other regulatory bodies at Teledesic, and his tenure at Microsoft, a company that often outsourced. Although friends and colleagues were skeptical about outsourcing as a business opportunity, Sanjay felt that the venture he was proposing was more likely to secure funding. Sanjay went on to put together an impressive team of financial backers including Scott Oki, who had built up Microsoft's international division, and the noted venture capital firm Warburg Pincus. His early investors put in about $20 million, a level of venture funding rare for a start-up intending to enter the outsourcing business. Recalls Sanjay:

> In those days, people were willing to put a lot of money behind ideas, and this business had a ready clientele. There was an unfulfilled demand for critical support that already existed. We were not banking on some kind of futuristic technology, hoping and praying that it worked and someone bought it.

Flush with funds, Sanjay launched vCustomer in June 1999.[9] He elaborated on the company's financial position since:

> The fact that Scott agreed to sit on our board was a great help. When we needed more funding for investments in voice infrastructure, we raised $11 million from Warburg Pincus, WestRiver Capital, and Oki again. From then on, it has been my single-minded focus not to raise money ever again to meet growth requirements. We have achieved that goal by turning cash flow positive in the last quarter of 2001.

Early Growth

Sanjay's early vision for the company was to develop technical support as its core competence. The venture initially proposed to provide off-line technical support to clients through email. These services required relatively low infrastructure and few social skills of the employees manning the help lines. The context was thus tailor-made for using Indian employees, and ten personnel were initially hired at a facility in Gurgaon near New Delhi. In 2000, vCustomer acquired its first client, the data storage company Iomega Corp that needed support for the FAQs on its portal.

The year 2000 proved to be a remarkable one for the young firm in terms of increasing its scope of services. During that year, the company also moved to "real-time" technical support using instant messaging. Then, later that year, Sanjay spotted another emerging opportunity, this time in telephony services, as Voice-Over-Internet-Protocol (VoIP) technology became operational and scalable. He noted the significance of that decision:

> We made a bit of a technological gamble at that point, betting the company's voice services on the yet untested VoIP rather than the traditional Time Division Multiplexing (TDM) standard, which required a large amount of equipment to be installed at the delivery side. A key reason for choosing the VoIP network was the ease of integrating business applications resulting in significant cost savings. All applications today are based on IP and it becomes easy to offer customized solutions for our clients. Since vCustomer was an IP installation from the very beginning, we felt that we would reap maximum benefits from this technology without worrying about interoperability with classic TDM based systems.

Soon, vCustomer was using a combination of communication media (voice, chat, and email) to provide hardware and software product support for PCs, peripherals, networking and storage equipment, and enterprise applications for its clients.

vCustomer's initial growth came from a focus on customer satisfaction that was largely influenced by its founder's approach. Sanjay had a "hands-on" attitude towards attending to operational problems and decisions, which kept the company tuned to customer needs. He spent nearly five or six hours a day talking to customers, a practice which he retained even when the company grew bigger. In this he was aided by technology—he had one phone number that clients could contact him at, irrespective of whether he was at home, at his Seattle office, or anywhere in India. Hence, his primarily U.S.-based customers were assured that the vendor's senior personnel were relatively close by and therefore accessible. A large portion of his remaining time was spent talking to department heads in New Delhi and trying to solve their operational problems.

At the same time, Sanjay recognized that he would have to inculcate customer quality at vCustomer through more formal mechanisms. Moreover, the company needed to provide a greater breadth of services to a client, which would also help in building switching costs and thus enable the company to retain clients.

Assembling the Management Team

As the company's customer base grew, expanding the management team became imperative. The management team at Seattle kept expanding and by 2003, comprised 15 personnel at senior levels for important functions like sales and marketing, client services, finance, and human services. Many managers were recruited either through a formal hiring process that aimed to get the best available talent in this fledgling business, or were personally persuaded by Sanjay to join the firm.

A few senior-level managers were also hired in India so that Sanjay and the U.S. team could focus on broader strategic issues and cut down on travel between Seattle and India. Additionally, the number of operating employees increased exponentially when the company started two other centers in New Delhi by 2003. There were about 3,000 employees in December 2003. The company had plans to double this base in the next few years. More employees were hired as two new centers commenced operations in Pune, Maharashtra and New Delhi again, in mid-2004 and end-2004 respectively (see Exhibit 5 for milestones in the company's growth).[10]

vCustomer's Approach to Outsourcing

The Value Proposition

The primary value proposition that vCustomer offered its clients was significant cost savings. Moreover, these savings would accompany a quality of service that was comparable to, or even better than, what the client could accomplish in-house. Clients could also increase revenues significantly without corresponding expenditure on infrastructure and scale. Describes Sanjay:

> To achieve these objectives for every client, we put together dedicated teams trained extensively in the respective businesses. These teams acted like the de-facto employees of the client, except that they were operating out of our offices. Each associate went live only after rigorous training in computer skills, accent and modulation, language, culture, listening and comprehension, tele-etiquette, not to mention industry and process-specific issues.

To upgrade skills, vCustomer frequently brought in teachers from the U.S. to impart soft skills to the employees. These procedures and systems may have

EXHIBIT 5

Key Milestones

- June 1999: vCustomer incorporated with funding from founders
- October 1999: First India processing center set up
- January 2000: First client signed for email support—50 startup employees
- June 2000: Second round of funding in which Warburg Pincus invests
- December 2000: Voice support enabled from vCustomer India
- June 2001: First million dollar quarter
- March 2002: Second processing center goes live in New Delhi
- June 2002: First million dollar month
- September 2002: Touches the 1000 employee mark
- January 2003: Third round of funding from WestRiver Capital
- May 2003: Touches the 2000 employee mark
- October 2003: Third processing center goes live in New Delhi, total capacity reaches 2300 workstations
- November 2003: Touches the 3000 employee mark
- April 2004: Fourth processing center in Pune goes live
- September 2004: Fifth facility goes live in New Delhi

Source: vCustomer website, accessed in September 2005.

increased the costs of servicing a contract, but contributed substantially to building quality and trust, thereby helping retain existing customers and draw new ones.

Emphasizing Quality and Security

Sanjay's faith in the superior value provided by vCustomer stemmed from the confidence that it had developed certain technology-based distinctive capabilities derived from timely investments in advanced technology infrastructure. The venture capital funding obtained provided sufficient cash reserves to execute its plans. Sanjay recalled those plans as follows:

> Using the money raised, we equipped the delivery centers with cutting-edge hardware and software, self-generated power facilities, and secure back-up recovery capabilities. For communicating between the U.S. and India we used one of the world's largest Wide Area Networks that utilized four pathways between the two countries and spanned both oceans. We also formed a beneficial working relationship with Sprint in 2002 to acquire private line circuits exclusively for our client base. These investments gave us the reliability and scalability to provide real-time services.

Additionally, he also built more formal quality systems early on by instituting processes such as ISO 9001 and Six Sigma, groundbreaking steps for a company engaged in outsourcing at that time. Obtaining certification in these processes formed the foundation for creating the company's service delivery methodology. Besides, resources were invested at all levels to ensure that desired quality levels were sustained. For instance, the company had one quality supervisor for every 16 agents as compared to the industry norm of one supervisor for every 35 agents.

The company had launched new initiatives in physical and data security, believing that this would become a key issue for clients in the future. For example, vCustomer evolved into a paperless office. Agents were not allowed to carry pens and paper to work, and could not loiter around another area where the work of a different client was being handled.[11]

As the business grew, vCustomer could also afford to get selective about its future clients. The company's management was less inclined now to sign on clients like Wal-Mart or Dell who merely emphasized cost savings and negotiated deals accordingly. They believed that the "superior" value that vCustomer provided could not be offered at the prices that these firms demanded.

Creating Barriers

Through investments in technology and scale, the company was able to offer some distinctive benefits to clients vis-à-vis rivals. Sanjay described how this was possible:

> Early on, I noticed that many players in this business were building a similar set of competences. So I wanted to differentiate vCustomer from the competition. The idea was that even in an industry thought to have "zero" intellectual property, it would take a while for competitors to duplicate our approach if we focused on developing solutions through advanced technology and more rigorous process management.

His willingness to exploit emerging technologies earlier than anyone else also enabled development of important technological capabilities. This was best exemplified in the investment in yet uncertain VoIP technology, which transferred data through packets instead of circuits, leading to easy integration of the voice services with other existing services that were already using the IP network.[12] The company continued to invest heavily in R&D, especially for an IT-enabled services (ITES) company. In 2003, despite the growing need to support growth, the company committed itself to spending $2-3 million over the next 12 months toward building new solutions for its clients in ITES, workflow analyses, and other emerging applications discussed later.[13]

Sanjay's overall vision kept the company focused on its core competence of technology support even while branching out into other BPO activities. This focus paid off handsomely when billing rates charged for services plummeted due to intense competition and price wars in the BPO space. vCustomer, however, could still maintain billing rates of $10–$16 an hour for tech support.[14] At the same time, he differentiated vCustomer from Indian rivals by focusing exclusively on inbound call-center operations and shunning telemarketing altogether. Explains Sanjay:

> Typically, our contracts last between one to three years, whereas in telemarketing this can be just one to three months. There is no comparison between the two services, because if there has been no impact for a client from a telemarketing campaign, people will look back at the value of the contract and say it amounted to a zero benefit.

Exploiting the Context

Sanjay elaborated how some early decisions pertaining to location of the call-centers turned out to quite advantageous for the company in retrospect.

> vCustomer's initial call center was set up in New Delhi rather than in South India.[15] A significant reason for this decision was the lower wage levels in Northern India, which was relatively untouched by the IT boom happening in the South. There was an apparent negative aspect of this decision because English was more prevalent in the South than in the North. However, I did not view this necessarily as a deterrent to setting up the Delhi center. My thinking at that time was that it was probably easier to train people who weren't natural English speakers to listen carefully and develop a new accent, than those who already spoke English in a particular way.

Sanjay's experience in dealing with regulatory agencies allowed him to work effectively with relevant Indian governmental agencies too. For instance, to ensure uptime of the network that was critical to the voice and chat services that the company offered, he made intensive efforts early on to strike up cooperative relations with the Videsh Sanchar Nigam Ltd. (VSNL). VSNL was a government-controlled organization that regulated the direction of the country's telecommunications progress.[16] Sanjay got VSNL's managers to subscribe to his vision and subsequently make authorization decisions more quickly.

Willingness to Take Risks

The investments made in promoting quality and technology infrastructure represented Sanjay's differing approach to risk vis-à-vis his competitors. He was willing to invest up-front in building distinctive competences through process management techniques. As long as an initiative was consistent with the values of the company, it was not considered too risky (see Exhibit 6): Notes Sanjay:

> Of the 8 Indian start-up firms in 2000 with call-center operations, only two, 24 × 7 and EXL, remained owned by their original founders in 2004. Many of the others exited the market by selling out at good prices to larger corporations, probably because the founders lacked the appetite for greater risk and were quite happy with where they had gotten so far. My approach to bearing risk was to go ahead with a risky initiative

EXHIBIT 6

vCustomer Values

- **Partnership**
  Growth through shared goals
- **Quality**
  Continuous process improvement
- **Excellence**
  Recognizing and rewarding employee excellence
- **Integrity**
  Doing the right thing
- **Respect**
  Dignity at every level in the organization
- **Exceeding Customer Expectations**
  Consistently encouraging proactive behavior

Source: vCustomer website, accessed in September 2005.

provided the potential adverse impact to the core business was low and that the timeline one had for turning things around was long (say, by using equity/internal accruals for investments as against debt).

Moving Beyond IT Services

Although Sanjay initially focused his venture on IT services, he subsequently expanded into the emerging BPO business services segment. By 2002, vCustomer had signed up clients interested in back-office processing operations such as customer relationship management and business documentation management. Sanjay remembered the initial difficulties:

> The BPO end of the services, especially the more real-time ones, though requiring less technical skill from the associates, often required them to be trained extensively on cultural norms, etiquette and language idiosyncrasies of the stakeholders they would be interacting with.

The company also began to provide services to a wider range of sectors. Notes Sanjay:

> With the move to BPO came diversification into services to other sectors or "verticals" like retail, hospitality and utilities. Our moves were somewhat serendipitous as they resulted from positive reactions to casual enquiries made by prominent players in each of these sectors. The addition of a new sector required a dramatically non-linear effort from the company to execute

successfully since the complexities of the new business had to be effectively understood by the operating personnel.

Enhancing seat utilization, a key driver of business success in the industry, was the primary motivation towards moving into greater back-office work for existing and new clients. vCustomer's current seat utilization went up to around 1.2–1.3 (one workstation was being utilized for a little more than a shift of eight hours), but the objective was to push it up to 1.5 by 2005.

Challenges Confronting vCustomer

For the fiscal year 2003–04, the company recorded revenues of $33 million, nearly twice the levels of the previous year, and intended to maintain a similar growth rate in 2004.[17] Sanjay had accumulated a war chest of $25 million that could be used for acquisitions. He had built a talented pool of executives of whom nearly 50% were engineers. To strengthen his management team, he was recruiting MBAs from the top Indian business schools. vCustomer was now a mid-sized BPO company and faced a new set of challenges. Sanjay and his management team were concerned with increasing service and resource competition and possible imitation of vCustomer's competences. They also felt the need to scout for new low-cost destinations with complementary skill sets in other parts of the world.

Emerging Low-Cost Labor Destinations

The wage differential between the U.S. and India was gradually shrinking, further eroding the competitive advantage of firms operating in India. Sanjay estimated that the differential was about 5 times when he started out in 1999, but this was down to around 3 times in 2005. Increasing wage structures on account of the demand for skilled employees outstripping supply were partly responsible.[18] As wages in India grew, and as the outsourcing phenomenon spread beyond the IT industry, the Philippines was fast emerging as an alternative destination for outsourced work. It offered similar benefits in terms of workforce because basic education there was also primarily in English, and its citizens had always been customer-service oriented. Besides, it was probably culturally closer to the U.S., having been a U.S. territory for the first half of the 20th century. Additionally, China and Russia were also fast attracting a

EXHIBIT 7

Cross-Country Comparison

	U.S.A.	India	China	Philippines	Russia
Land Area (sq. km)	9,161,923	2,973,190	9,326,410	298,170	16,995,800
Population ('000)	295,734	1,080,264	1,306,314	87,857	143,420
Median age	36.27	24.66	32.26	22.27	38.15
Literacy	97%	59.5%	90.9%	92.6%	99.6%
GDP per capita	$40,100	$3,100	$5,600	$5,000	$9,800
GDP growth	4.4%	6.2%	9.1%	5.9%	6.7%
Unemployment rate	5.5%	9.2%	20%	11.7%	8.3%
Inflation rate	2.5%	4.2%	4.1%	5.5%	11.5%
Electricity consumption (billion kWh)	3,660	510.1	1,630	46.05	894.3
Oil consumption (million bbl/day)	19.65	2.13	4.956	0.338	2.31
Telephone lines in use (million)	181.599	48.917	263	3.311	35.5
Cellular phones in use ('000)	158,722	26,154.4	269,000	15,201	17,608.8
TV broadcast stations	>1,500	562	3,240	225	7,306
Internet users (million)	159	18.481	94	3.5	6
Airports	14,857	333	472	255	2,586
Highways (km)	6,393,603	2,525,989	1,765,222	202,124	537,289

Source: CIA —The World Factbook, accessed in December 2005.

healthy share of IT and R&D work. China in particular, had a large pool of employable engineering graduates, and infrastructure in that country was better than that available in India.[19] Exhibit 7 compares relevant data across these countries.

Sanjay believed that India was still very competitive geographically. Though wage levels in the bigger cities were rising rapidly, firms could move towards hiring employees from Tier II and Tier III cities where there was an abundant talent pool able and willing to work at lower wages. Additionally, vCustomer had already taken some effective steps in order to retain skilled employees by making employment

in this sector seem more socially acceptable.[20] Sanjay reflected:

> We see increased demand for skilled people but do not expect a shortfall in the supply. Recruiting people with the right mix of capabilities could become challenging, but Indian suppliers who possess highly evolved and targeted processes should not be impacted.[21]

Sanjay was bullish about the Philippines emerging as an alternative destination. Besides exploiting the larger wage differential, a base in this part of Asia might also be beneficial in enhancing revenues. Local companies with the U.S. as their key market would look to work with an outsourcing firm closer to home. Moreover, it would not be an alien context for the company as their present CFO was from the Philippines. However, the management team at vCustomer was concerned whether the company could maintain the quality of services it was proud of, from a new location. It would also take a while to understand and work within the regulatory context of a new country.

Growing Competitive Threats

The nature of the outsourcing industry was changing. Some large IT companies were entering this space and recognizing potential synergies that could be achieved with their existing businesses. In mid-2004 IBM acquired one of vCustomer's rivals, Daksh Services, in a deal worth about $170 million.[22] The acquisition sparked off speculation about similar deals in the offing from IBM's global IT competitors.[23] Besides, domestic IT firms such as Wipro and others were also consolidating to meet the challenge of multinationals entering their home turf.[24] How could vCustomer continue to hold onto its competitive advantage in the face of a direct challenge from IBM and other large rivals?

However, the BPO market in India was forecasted to grow at a compounded rate of 46% annually (see Exhibit 8). Potential new clients were looking for new services to outsource and for vendors who had a broad set of capabilities. Currently, a typical client maintained outsourcing relationships with several vendors for its diverse requirements. This pattern of behavior had emerged not only because outsourcing companies had built up core competencies in different areas over time, but also because clients sought to avoid excessive dependence on any one such vendor.[25] This was expected to change in the future.

Besides the larger incumbents and new entrants, there were nearly 4,000 firms involved in BPO in 2005, though quite a few of these were little more than fly-by-night operators. Margins were falling and contracts were becoming more short-term as clients were increasingly looking for new vendors to associate with. Therefore, it was becoming clear that the company could not maintain its rate of growth by remaining focused only on its current businesses.

Available Options

Entering the Healthcare Segment In the face of growing competition, one option that vCustomer had was to diversify into a business area that offered a great potential for growth. This move could increase vCustomer's scale of operations resulting in improved efficiencies and could potentially reduce the threat posed by new large entrants. Currently a typical business relationship fetched revenues of $50,000–$200,000 a month for vCustomer and was assigned 50–100 dedicated personnel (workstations). The managers that advocated further expansion in BPO activity recognized the importance of getting clients to sign up for transactions of higher value, say $200,000–$1,000,000 a

Growth of BPO Market in India

Source: vCustomer website, 2005.

month. Higher value transactions would make vCustomer more important to its clients and they would be more reluctant to switch to other vendors in the future. However, to make the transition to bigger deals, the company needed a broader base of delivery capabilities so that clients would consider it a "one-stop-shop" for all their outsourcing needs.

Specifically, Sanjay was considering the entry into the Healthcare vertical. Outsourcing of services in healthcare was slowly gaining traction as U.S. companies recognized that a variety of activities could potentially be outsourced (see Exhibit 9). Primary reasons why healthcare firms were looking to outsource, specifically to offshore destinations, included reducing operating costs, focusing on core business, avoiding necessary investments, overcoming inability to staff appropriately, and upgrading current service levels.[26]

Sanjay recognized the challenges inherent in entering this new vertical:

Moving into a new vertical such as healthcare is extremely challenging. It is almost like starting over. It is difficult to convince potential customers that they should be our first client in this new vertical. Healthcare has its own significant challenges in terms of core competencies and service platforms that we would have to create to show that we understand the business. Acquisition of capability in this vertical is probably an easier path for us to go down.

Despite these difficulties, he was of the opinion that vCustomer should try and provide greater value to their clients than basic call-center services in this new vertical. vCustomer's management had come to realize that the data generated through more basic operations

---

EXHIBIT 9

Outsourcing Trends in Healthcare Sector in 2005

Issues facing Healthcare players:
- Managing increasing medical costs and balancing customer satisfaction
- Reducing operating back-office costs
- Complying with the standards and requirements of the Health Insurance Portability and Accountability Act
- Upgrading IT infrastructure and moving to the web to provide real time connectivity
- Focusing on survival and developing strategies to differentiate products from competitors

Organizations most likely to pursue an offshore initiative:
- Health plans
- Healthcare payers
- Third party health benefit administrators
- Independent software vendors
- Application service and BPO service providers

Activities being outsourced offshore:
- Enrollment services (enrollment of new members, eligibility verification)
- Claims adjudication (claims data entry, reference to policy, managing billing and EOBs, claims re-pricing)
- Customer service (call-center handling, email/web support)
- Imaging and data digitization (mailroom services, scanning of documents, converting text into electronic data)
- Premium administration (application of money received to individual accounts, end of day balancing of suspense accounts)
- Policy administration (maturities, policy changes, beneficiaries)
- Underwriting (risk assessment, pre-existing condition evaluation)

Emerging models in Healthcare offshore BPO:
- Managed services outsourcing (outsourcing of low value and non-strategic activities that are transactional in nature, e.g., imaging and data digitization)
- Business function outsourcing (outsourcing of complete business functions and processes, e.g., claims adjudication, policy administration)
- Enterprise operations outsourcing (outsourcing of complete back-office operations in one package to specialized vendor)

Source: Report by NewHorizons Consulting, 2005.

was usually amenable to a greater degree of analysis, which made more value-add possible. However, personnel with suitable skills would have to be hired.

Acquisition of MCI's Assets vCustomer had come to learn that the telecommunications company MCI, Inc. was looking for a buyer for its call-center operations comprising eight call-centers in multiple locations across the U.S. and one call-center in the Philippines. MCI itself was on the verge of a mega-merger with its competitor Verizon, which also possessed similar call-center resources.

This acquisition could potentially be the answer to the challenges that vCustomer was confronted with. It would nearly double the company's size and bring its employee strength close to 6,000 (the Philippines center employed around 1,500 people alone). The company would acquire the capabilities to start onshore outsourcing, and even cater to regional requirements due to the diversity of locations of the U.S. call-centers. It could then better match its clients' diverse needs and provide a migration path over the lifecycle of the relationship with a specific client. It would provide a base in the Philippines, which was emerging as an attractive location. If vCustomer drove a hard bargain, they could consummate the acquisition for $45 million, a figure just around their budgeted levels.[27]

vCustomer would also diversify its businesses through the acquisition. Among the services that these call-centers were performing were Relay Service and Directory & Operator Assistance (DA). The Relay Service business had been born as a result of the U.S. government's ADA initiative to support equality of access to services for deaf and hard of hearing persons. It involved carrying out telephonic transactions on behalf of handicapped persons through dedicated call-centers. Billing was done on a per-call per-minute basis to State and Federal Governments, which fix the compensation level for these services. In contrast, DA involved services to provide round-the-clock directory information to callers with enquiries. These could range from mundane information on phone numbers or street addresses to more specific "enhanced" enquiries on weather forecasts, sports scores or stock prices. MCI was willing to let the acquirer perform these operations on its behalf for an initial 7-year period. Therefore, these new services could become a significant revenue stream for the company. The relay services could bring in

$70-90 million annually, whereas the DA services would be likely to generate $10-30 million annually. Though vCustomer had now reached a size of nearly $50 million through its existing ITES and BPO businesses, the acquisition could still more than double its size.

The acquisition would change the primary business of the company from a business-to-business (b-to-b) model to a business-to-customer (b-to-c) model. Doing business directly with the end-customer diversified the risks associated with relying upon sales to large enterprises, which were characterized by long cycle-times and high degrees of variability. Moreover, with MCI's U.S. assets vCustomer could begin meeting the growing demand for "onshore" outsourcing of operations. The domestic (U.S.) market had always been the largest market for outsourcing. Additionally, many corporations had realized by now that offshore outsourcing was not a panacea for all their troubles. If improperly managed, offshoring lead to a drop in the quality of the services outsourced or cost advantages initially conceived were significantly offset by higher monitoring requirements. These corporations were looking for some critical activities primarily involving voice communication, to be outsourced to firms with U.S. operations and were willing to pay a higher price for such services.

In spite of some clear benefits, Sanjay and his management team recognized that there were risks. First, MCI was a large and mature organization and their employees possessed a different mindset than their counterparts at vCustomer. The cultural differences might also make integration of these employees into vCustomer and retaining them a tougher task than imagined. Therefore, the proposed advantages due to the skills they possessed might not accrue. Second, vCustomer didn't have any brand equity as a b-to-c services provider. The capabilities required for these emerging services would have to be developed afresh, a difficult task in an uncertain environment. While this was still synergistic with its current b-to-b operations, it could divert attention away from its core ITES and BPO businesses at a time when these segments were still growing. Going ahead with this acquisition would probably force the company to postpone plans of entering the healthcare vertical. Third, although "onshore" outsourcing was an appealing prospect for vCustomer, the cost advantages in starting onshore outsourcing, especially through an acquisition, were unclear. Further, since vCustomer had never managed a U.S. operation or operated out of the Philippines, integrating these geographically dispersed assets might prove to be challenging for a small company with limited resources.

It Was Time to Make Some Decisions

As the members of his top management began entering the conference room, Sanjay glanced at the clock showing Indian Standard Time and began to call the Head of his Indian operations, who was probably ending his workday. Given the way the industry was evolving, it was clear that the current strategy of growing the company organically was not enough to meet expected growth rates in the future. Hence, would the MCI acquisition be the right approach to take the company in new directions? Alternatively, would the company be better off by focusing its efforts on entering the healthcare vertical?

Finally, Sanjay was also grappling with a personal dilemma that not all members of his team were aware of. IBM's acquisition of Daksh had opened the floodgates for similar acquisitions by other IT corporations. vCustomer had also been approached recently as an acquisition target, by a large IT firm wanting to enter the BPO business. With the "hot" market for acquisitions, a sale at this point could generate around 12 times earnings. This would definitely be a right time for vCustomer to exit the market. On a personal level, this decision would offer Sanjay a well-deserved break from his hectic lifestyle and true financial freedom. Sanjay had to decide how to proceed, and once he was clear, he had to inform his managers about his decision.

ENDNOTES

1. "vCustomer Upbeat, in Expansion Mode." *Financial Times*. November 27, 2003.
2. "Men and Machines." *The Economist*, November 11, 2004.
3. "The Place to Be." *The Economist*, November 11, 2004.
4. "Relocating the Back Office—Offshoring." *The Economist*, December 13, 2003.
5. "The Place to Be." *The Economist*, November 11, 2004.
6. "Relocating the Back Office—Offshoring." *The Economist*, December 13, 2003.
7. In 2002, Teledesic cut back on capital expenditures required to construct and launch satellites and significantly reduced its staff as well. The venture is still in existence but the commercial launch of its proposed services is yet to happen.
8. Gurgaon is a suburb of New Delhi, the capital city of India.
9. "Sleepless in Seattle." *The Economic Times*, October 2003.
10. "vCustomer—Emerging BPO Vendor." *ComputerWire*, April 16, 2004.
11. "vCustomer Set to Double Revenue." *Rediff.com*, June 16, 2004.
12. "Managing Calls with Voice Over IP." *Networking Computing Asia*, August 2, 2004.
13. "vCustomer to Invest $18 m in Ramp-up." *Indian Express*, October 13, 2003.
14. "vCustomer to Set Up More Facilities." *Financial Times*, August 16, 2003.
15. Cities like Bangalore and Hyderabad, located in South India, are the epicenter of India's IT activity.
16. VSNL was divested in part by the Indian government to a large corporate house in 2002.
17. "vCustomer Set to Double Revenue." *Rediff.com*, June 16, 2004.
18. Many also believed that Indian companies were overstaffed to ensure comparable quality to a similar U.S. operation and hence had lower productivity and growing operating costs. Moreover, because of the rapid turnover of personnel in this business, costs spent on training employees were never fully recovered.
19. "Ensuring India's Offshoring Future." *McKinsey Quarterly*, Special edition, 2005.
20. It was portraying employment here as a long-term career rather than a short-term arrangement. Employees were encouraged to travel across centers to understand the company's culture, values, and capabilities. In case employees of proven ability wanted to get further education in business administration, the company often paid 50% of the tuition fees at select business schools it had a tie-up with.
21. "India 2005: Facing the Challenges of Labor Shortage and Rising Costs." *Outsourcing Journal*, January 2005.
22. "Can Big Blue Succeed in BPO?" *Knowledge@Wharton*, November, 2004.
23. Also GE sold a major stake in its captive unit GECIS to two U.S. investment firms. GE was thereby asking its erstwhile subsidiary to survive as a stand-alone enterprise and seek orders externally.
24. Wipro had already acquired Spectramind, India's largest call-center firm, and NerveWire, a Massachusetts-based IT consultancy. Infosys had established a BPO subsidiary called Progeon, and acquired Expert, an Australian IT firm. TCS had purchased Phoenix, a Bangalore-based subsidiary of an American insurance and asset management firm.
25. Having ensured standardization of its processes through formal quality systems like ISO and Six Sigma, vCustomer was well poised to take advantage of this trend. The company was highlighting that clients didn't need to become tied down to its services since they were compatible with other services of the same standard.
26. Report by Ravi Shah of NewHorizons Consulting.
27. "vCustomer in Deal for Onshore Center in US." *Cyber Media*, April 21, 2005.

Verizon Communications Inc.: The Telecommunications Industry

This case was prepared by Dr. Robert J. Mockler.

Introduction

As of December 2005, Verizon Communications Inc. maintained the position as the largest U.S. fixed-line and wireless services provider and earned the number one ranking in *Fortune's* list of most admired telecommunications companies. Under the leadership of chairman and chief executive officer, Ivan Seidenberg, the company achieved the enviable position of having a reputation for operational excellence and the most satisfied customers in the wireless industry [Verizon Communications Inc., 2004]. In a dynamic industry, such as telecommunications, and faced with increasing deregulation in the wireless industry, new opportunities were created for competition. The overall task for Mr. Seidenberg was to develop an effective differentiating enterprise-wide strategy if Verizon Communications Inc. was to survive and prosper against aggressive competition over the intermediate and long-term future.

The telecommunications industry was once dominated by a single, regulated monopoly, AT&T, until 1984 when changes in government regulation, which resulted in its divestiture, led to the introduction of competition which consisted of seven regional Bell operating companies (Baby Bells), including Bell Atlantic. Bell Atlantic pursued unregulated businesses such as wireless, Internet, directory publishing, and catalog sales of computer parts and office supplies. In 1999, the FCC granted Bell Atlantic permission to sell long-distance phone services in New York, making the company the first of the seven Baby Bells to be allowed to offer long-distance in its home territory.

In 2000, Bell Atlantic and Vodofone combined their U.S. wireless operations to form Verizon Wireless. Verizon Communications, Inc. was formed later that year upon approval for acquisition of the non-Bell local phone company, GTE. In 2001, the Company received permission to offer long-distance in Massachusetts, Connecticut, and Pennsylvania; in 2002, it received permission for Delaware, New Hampshire, and Rhode Island, and in 2003, it received permission for Maryland, West Virginia, and Washington, D.C.

Apart from concerns of increasing competition brought about by the deregulation of the industry, Verizon Communications Inc. was faced with a number of critical long-term decisions. Some of these strategic decisions included: Should the company undergo a drastic upgrade of the equipment used in the transmission of an increasing variety of data? What services should the company offer that were better suited to the needs of its customers? How could the company retain the customers it had and increase market share? The main question to be resolved was how to differentiate Verizon Communications Inc. from its competition and so achieve a winning edge over competitors within intensely competitive, rapidly changing immediate, intermediate, and long-term time frames.

Industry and Competitive Market Analysis: the Telecommunications Industry

The telecommunications industry in 2005 was the most dynamic industry in the United States. During the 1990s, the growth of the Internet, advances in a range of technologies, the deregulation of the telecommunications industry, and rapid increases in the demand for telecommunications services helped fuel swift growth [Bureau of Labor Statistics, 2005]. The industry was based primarily on services provided for the transmission of a variety of information using fixed-line or wireless networks, or a combination of both. Each network was made by using specific equipment housed in the facilities described below. The main consumer product was telephone handsets while other products included accessories to telephone handsets and calling cards.

Transmission was defined as any method by which a variety of information including data, graphics and video was conveyed. The method of transmission could be one of three types: fixed-line, wireless, or fixed-wireless. Information conveyed over a fixed-line network used wire, cable or fiber optic links to connect devices while wireless networks used radio signals for mobile devices allowing for convenience and portability.

The industry consisted of two types of companies: companies that provided services and companies that provided accompanying products or electronic devices. Telephone companies were companies that provided primarily voice services and data services. Some telephone companies provided services using both fixed-line and wireless networks while other telephone companies focused on providing services specific to a particular network. Companies such as AT&T Inc. and Verizon Communications Inc. provided primarily local and international voice and data services, using both fixed-line and wireless networks. MCI Inc. provided long-distance voice and data communications using traditional and broadband fixed-line networks and Sprint Nextel Corporation provided mainly wireless voice and data services. Changes in technology and regulation allowed cable and satellite television providers to compete with telephone companies. Cable companies such as Time Warner Cable provided high-speed data and digital voice services that competed directly with the fixed-line broadband services offered in the industry. Direct TV was an example of a satellite television company that provided high-speed data and digital voice services over a wireless network and competed directly with the wireless broadband services offered in the industry. Other companies that participated in this industry were product manufacturers such as Nokia, Motorola and Siemens whose main consumer product was wireless telephone handsets.

Figure 1 outlines the main sections of the telecommunications industry, which were Transmission, Facilities and Equipment, Services/Products, Customers, Customer Service, Geographic Region, Distribution/Marketing, Mergers and Acquisitions, and Competition.

The Essence of the Telecommunications Business Model

Customers were either individuals requiring telecommunications services for personal use or businesses requiring telecommunications services for operational purposes. Customers wished to exchange data or non-voice information and to have conversations with other customers within the area (locally), in other areas within the same country (long-distance) or in other countries (internationally). They could talk to each other and send and receive information such as messages, documents, pictures or graphics and video, and they were also able to perform searches for any kind of information. Transmission occurred as signals across three types of networks: fixed-line along the cables that connected telecommunications facilities and equipment; wireless as radio waves or fixed wireless, which was a combination of fixed-line and wireless networks.

Customers purchased products (handsets, computers, laptops, personal digital assistants and other electronic devices) that had all the features they desired. They also had to purchase the accompanying services offered by telecommunications services providers that allowed the products to function as communication devices. These services gave customers access to a company's network over which they could send information. Examples of services were voice services (exchange of information through conversation), data services which could be short text or picture messages and email through the use of the Internet, and information/directory publishing services where customers could access contact information for businesses and individuals alike.

Advantages of immediate response and increasing instant gratification paved the way for modern day communications. Telephones, also known as handsets, allowed for direct conversation between any two entities. Data consisted of pictures, graphics, and text documents. Information was sent using facsimile devices over fixed-line networks. With the advent of the Internet, data could be sent to and from

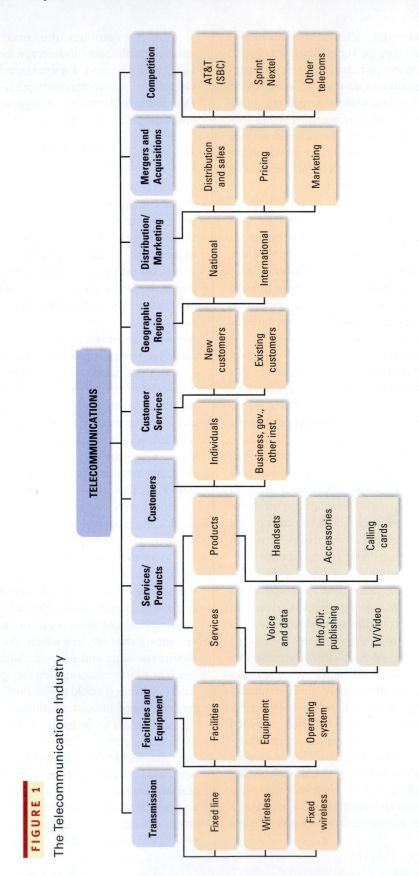

FIGURE 1

The Telecommunications Industry

virtually anywhere in the world. Electronic mail or email made it easier, faster and cheaper to correspond when compared to the use of Postal Services. The Internet provided the ability to send short messages through instant messaging applications and recently, voice as data packets over the Internet. An example of the use of digital signals in the transmission of conversations over the Internet was known as Voice over Internet Protocol (VoIP). The Internet could be accessed through the use of a desktop computer connected to a fixed-line or a laptop computer that used wireless transmission. The increasing popularity of the Internet has also caused product manufacturers to develop innovative wireless handsets through which customers could access the Internet. The growing popularity of wireless services promoted the development of devices that provided customers with continuous accessibility to information and the added advantage of mobility. Examples of these devices were Palm Pilot and RIM Blackberry. Many of these devices provided the ability to access web content remotely, over wireless networks.

Individuals selected telecommunications services providers based on affordability, reliability, customer service, look and features of the products, and the ability of the company to satisfy all of their needs such as conversation, exchange information, entertainment, and others. Business customers focused on reliability of the network, security, and the company's ability to provide all services needed by the particular business such as video conferencing, web access, information security, remote access and e-business applications. Customers chose companies based on the ability of the company to appeal to most or all of their needs, a "one stop and shop" deal where that one company would provide services for different networks.

Customers who wished to have telecommunications services solicited information from company-owned retail stores, independent retail stores, company websites, or advertisements. It was through these channels that a customer could also purchase such services on a subscription basis. Products such as phones and accessories of product manufacturers with whom agreements were made were also sold through these channels. Companies had to have the facilities and equipment needed to provide any kind of service; they either had their own or they leased it to other companies known as telecommunications resellers. To effectively provide services for customers they were expected to have top quality transmission

facilitating faster transmission rates and network reliability, and better coverage over a greater area. Customer Service played a key role in a company's performance as this would have a tremendous effect on customer retention rates, also known as churn rates in the telecommunications industry.

Given a competitive industry such as this, companies had to mass market their services through all forms of media in an effort to promote services and establish brand recognition. In addition to the services offered, it was the innovative, attractive products that gripped the customer's attention and therefore product design was important. A services provider was expected to obtain agreements with telecommunications product manufacturers gaining exclusive access to "hot" or impressive new products, particularly handsets, to maintain a competitive advantage.

Transmission

Original forms of communication included Morse code and telegrams, and mail sent through the use of postal services. In subsequent years, voice communication provided direct contact where two individuals anywhere in the world were able to converse or send information to each other. There was no longer an extended period of time lapse between correspondence and exchange. Since the 1990s, the Internet has played a major part in the ease of communication. The Internet, sometimes called simply "the Net," is a worldwide system of computer networks—a network of networks in which users can, if they have permission, send and get information. For many Internet users, electronic mail has practically replaced the Postal Service for short written transactions and was the most widely used application on the Internet. The Internet was an increasingly popular method of communication as it provided the transfer of large amounts of data which ranged from documents, pictures and graphics, video, music.

There were three types of networks used in transmission: fixed-line, wireless, and a combination of the two, known as fixed-wireless.

Fixed-Line   Fixed-line networks used coaxial and fiber optic cables to connect customers' premises to central offices. The rising popularity of the Internet led to an increase in customers' use of the fixed-line network to transmit data and other electronic materials.

Increasing demands for the transmission of a wider variety of information has led to the development of new technology known as broadband, which was a high-capacity, two-way link used to transmit information. Information was sent on many different channels within the band concurrently, allowing more information to be transmitted in a given amount of time (similar to having more lanes on a highway allowing for more cars to travel on it at the same time). Broadband gave users access to the Internet and Internet-related services at significantly higher speeds. It had the potential technical capability to meet consumers' broad communication, entertainment, information, and commercial needs and preferences [FCC, 2005]. Customers were also capable of transmitting voice over the Internet (VoIP) through the use of broadband networks.

Wireless Wireless communication involved transmitting signals through air and space using radio waves. A higher radio frequency required greater bandwidth to allow for a better data carrying capacity of the wireless system. Wireless networks communicated with each other and a variety of devices allowed subscribers to send and receive data and/or video messages by using satellites. Narrowband was broadly defined by the FCC to provide wireless telephony, data, advanced paging, and other services to individuals and businesses [FCC, 2005]. Narrowband was only that portion devoted to voice and limited data transmission. Wireless broadband referred to larger band of frequencies over which a variety of data could be transmitted such as pictures and video.

Fixed Wireless Fixed wireless was essentially a combination of fixed-line and wireless networks. It was a method for providing a network segment between two set locations using wireless devices or systems. Fixed wireless referred to the operation of wireless devices or systems such as laptops and wireless printers in set locations such as homes and offices. Fixed wireless devices normally derived their electrical power from electricity outlets, as opposed to portable wireless devices that normally derived their power from batteries. The fixed-line was connected to the antenna, which created a wireless environment by converting fixed-line signals into wireless signals enabling wireless transmission. With advancing technology and increasing consolidation in the industry, many companies began offering both fixed-line and wireless services. "The wireless communications industry has been experiencing consolidation and [analysts] expect that this trend will continue. This consolidation trend may enhance the ability of wireless service providers . . ." [Mergent Online, 2005]. It was those companies that operated multiple networks that were better able to provide any and all services that fit a wide variety of customers' needs and desires.

In addition to this, most companies were moving away from traditional fixed-line services to offering services using broadband, which offered greater bandwidth and faster transmission rates. "They seem to think that the way to expand and thrive in today's telecom world is by focusing on growth in the profitable wireless and broadband markets . . ." [Rosenbush, 2005]. The overall industry trend was to develop the wireless and the fixed-line broadband services. Companies had to have the necessary facilities and equipment to expand services. Changes in technology brought about by the introduction of broadband and wireless capability created new markets for telecommunications services providers. Online usage grew significantly in the last few years with 70% of U.S. households now having access to the Internet and over 1/3 of those homes using broadband connections [Verizon Communications Inc., 2004].

It was more important to provide a network that was reliable, fast and efficient and these qualities depended on the equipment used.

Facilities and Equipment

The facilities, equipment and operating systems used in the telecommunications industry are discussed in more detail below.

Facilities Facilities referred to the central offices maintained by telecommunications companies that contain switching equipment which route content to its final destination or to another switching center. This was typical of fixed-line networks.

Wireless equipment was used to create cell sites. A cell was the geographical area covered by a wireless transmitter. The transmitter facility itself was called the cell site. The cell provided by a cell site could be from one mile to twenty miles in diameter, depending on terrain and transmission power. Several coordinated cell sites were called a cell system. Wireless services providers generally gave customers access to their cell system, which was essentially local. When traveling out of the range of this cell system, the cell system enabled you to be transferred to a neighboring company's cell system without one being aware of it.

In order to increase coverage, network reliability and transmission rates of wireless networks, companies had to increase the number of cell sites. The cost to build new cell sites was estimated to be anywhere from $100,000 to $1 million per cell site, depending on the difficulty associated with building it [Rulison, 2005]. An increase in cell sites facilitated price competitiveness as companies used their own facilities to provide wireless transmission.

A company had to have significant capital resources to expand and build-out any of the above networks in order to introduce new services. Companies should upgrade their networks to provide faster transmission, more bandwidth for the increasing amount of information customers wished to exchange and remain competitive. These qualities were attributed to the equipment used for each network.

The following is a discussion of the equipment housed in these facilities.

Equipment The main equipment used in the fixed-line network included switches and routers, converters, remote access servers, IP telephony equipment used to transmit data and voice communications over the same network, optical networking components, and network service and security systems. These devices were connected by copper lines, coaxial cables or fiber optic links. The main equipment used in setting up wireless connectivity included transreceivers, bridges, signal amplifiers, modems and antennas. Fixed-wireless network equipment consisted of the equipment used in setting up a fixed-line network, except for the cables used to connect the devices, and equipment used to create the wireless connection for the operation of wireless devices. The companies that owned their own equipment were able to lease it to other companies called telecommunications resellers.

Switches channeled incoming data from any of multiple input ports to the specific output port that took the data toward its intended destination in a telecommunications network.

Routers determined the next system point to which a data packet should be forwarded enroute toward its destination. Each data packet sent contained a unique address that was stored in an address look-up table. The router was connected to at least two systems and determined which way to send each data packet based on the address look-up table.

Converters were used to transfer data across different media, that is, they were used to change data

signals to voice signals or vice versa. For phone conversations, fixed-line networks had to convert voice signals to data signals that were transferred across the coaxial cables or optical cables and these signals were reconverted to voice signals by other converters at the end of transmission.

A remote access server sometimes called a communications server was the computer and associated software that was set up to handle users seeking access to a network from an isolated location.

IP telephony equipment included all equipment used to exchange spoken or other telephone information over the Internet rather than through the use of traditional telephone service. A modem varied the frequency of outgoing data signals from electronic devices to voice signals for a conventional copper twisted pair telephone line and extracted information from the varied frequency of the incoming voice signal and converted it to a data signal for the electronic device.

Copper lines formed the traditional medium used to connect networks. These were either twisted or shielded twisted pair. Twisted pair was the ordinary copper wire that connected home and many business computers to the telephone company. It was made up of two insulated copper wires twisted around each other. Each connection on twisted pair required both wires. Since some telephone sets or desktop locations required multiple connections, twisted pair was sometimes installed in two or more pairs, all within a single cable. For some business locations, twisted pair was enclosed in a shield; this was known as shielded twisted pair.

Coaxial cable was the kind of copper cable used by cable TV companies between the community antenna and user homes and businesses. It was sometimes used by telephone companies from their central office to the telephone poles near users. It was also widely installed for use in business and corporation. Coaxial cables had more bandwidth than copper lines and faster transmission rates.

Fiber optic (or "optical fiber") referred to the medium and the technology associated with the transmission of information as light impulses along a glass or plastic wire or fiber. Fiber optic wire carried more information than any other type of connection and was far less subject to electromagnetic interference. It was also much cheaper to maintain.

Bandwidth referred to the transmission capacity of a telecommunications network and was a measurement of a network's transmission speed, that is, how much data a network could transfer in a given amount of time. Efficiency of the network was based on the speed of data transmission.

It was important to focus on the type of connections used create the networks. Different types of connections varied in the transmission capacity, bandwidth, and hence varied in speed. Increased bandwidth could have been used to deliver new services. Faster transmission rates led to improved customer perception of the services and increased competitiveness against cable providers.

Equipment used in setting up wireless connectivity included transreceivers, bridges, signal amplifiers, modems and antennas.

A station that transmitted and received data referred to as a transceiver was used to create an access point which connected users to other users within the network. It also served as the point of interconnection between the wireless and a fixed-line network. The number of access points a wireless network needed was determined by the number of users and the size of the network.

A wireless bridge was used to connect two or more system segments that were separated physically. A bridge worked at the data-link or physical level of a network, copying data from one network to the next network along the communications path. Signal amplifiers are electronic devices that increase the power of signals so that information carried as signals can be transmitted.

An antenna was a specialized transducer (an electronic device) that converted radio-frequency (RF) fields into alternating current (AC) or vice versa. There were two basic types: the receiving antenna, which intercepted RF energy and delivered AC to electronic equipment, and the transmitting antenna, which was fed with AC from electronic equipment and generated a RF field.

Operating Systems Operating systems were the software platforms telecommunications equipment and devices used to transmit voice and data. Operating systems were found as part of any electronic device, especially those used every day, from computers to cell phones to wireless access points. The purpose of an operating system was to organize and control hardware and software so that the device it "lived in" behaved in a flexible but predictable way. It manages the hardware and software resources of the system. The operating systems used for fixed-line networks managed hardware, which included

such things as the processor, memory, disk space and so forth. The most common operating systems were the Windows family of operating systems developed by Microsoft, the Macintosh operating systems developed by Apple and the UNIX family of operating systems [Coustan and Franklin, 2005]. With respect to functionality, operating systems were very similar for fixed-line networks and were comparable in their ability to transmit information efficiently.

For wireless networks, different operating systems had distinct functionality. An operating system provided electrical devices with the ability to operate as a functional unit. An example of this was the ability of the operating system to make the hardware of a wireless phone, which included the keypad, the screen, the address book, the phone dialer, the battery and the network connection work effectively to transmit information. It provided a stable, consistent way for applications to deal with the hardware without having to know all the details of the hardware. The Palm OS and Windows Mobile, CDMA (Code Division Multiple Access) and GSM (Global System for Mobile communication) for wireless devices were other examples of operating systems. CDMA was a better technology than GSM because GSM was not able to handle both voice and data effectively. It was also important to have an operating system that was equipped enough to handle the transmission of a variety of voice and data, like CDMA.

The key was to have an operating system that could effectively operate on any network, fixed-line, wireless, or fixed-wireless. The operating system determined what functions the devices could perform and how the different parts of devices would interact with each other to perform as a functional unit. It was important that the operating system allowed devices to work regardless of location. Although CDMA was a better technology, GSM was more widely used. It was the world's most popular wireless handset technology used by more than one billion people in more than 200 countries and offered customers unparalleled global roaming capabilities [U.S. Business Reporter, 2001]. It was also important for operating systems to have a high degree of commonality of design worldwide. Interoperability of operating systems led to advantages of compatibility of services and worldwide roaming capability.

Services/Products

Traditionally, the main services provided were voice and data messaging services but these services were expanded to include information/directory publishing services and TV/Video services. Products were mainly telephone handsets which the customers use to transmit data and other electronic materials. Other products included accessories and calling cards.

Services   There were three main areas of services offered in the telecommunications industry: voice and data services, information/directory publishing services, and TV/Video services.

Voice and Data Services. Fixed-line voice services were considered to be local, long-distance or international and different charges applied with international services being more expensive than local or long-distance. Customers were able to make calls to other customers in different locations. Local services involved the use of the local central offices where lines from homes and businesses terminated at a central office. These offices were connected to other central offices within a local access and transport area or to long-distance carriers. Long-distance carriers were telephone companies that provided connections between local central offices in different geographic areas. Customers with fixed-line voice calling services were able to make and receive calls from customers with wireless voice calling services and vice versa.

Other voice services provided for fixed-line, wireless and fixed-wireless networks included messaging, caller identification, call waiting, call-forwarding and three-way calling. Messaging such as voicemail allowed a caller to leave a brief message for a customer who was unable to answer the call. Customers were able to determine the name and/or number of an incoming call through caller identification devices. Call waiting, call forwarding and three-way calling were calling features that customers were able to use. Customers who were on the phone were alerted that another call was coming in by the call waiting feature. If a customer wished to have his or her calls transferred to another telephone number (fixed-line-or wireless), that customer was able to activate the call-forwarding feature. Similarly, a customer was able to speak to two other customers simultaneously by using the three-way calling feature. These services were interoperable for both fixed-line and wireless networks.

Data services provided customers with the ability to send information to each other. Through the use of facsimile devices, customers were able to transmit data using fixed-lines. The main data service used in transmission over any network was the Internet. The Internet was accessed over fixed-line networks through the use of desktop computers or over wireless networks through the use of wireless handsets and laptops. The Internet provided the ability to send short messages through instant messaging applications, unlike messaging services for fixed-line voice services; this was essentially a conversation over the Internet. Customers were able to send documents, pictures, graphics and other data to other customers through electronic mail or email. Recently, the Internet has been used to transmit voice conversations as data packets. An example of this transmission of conversations over the Internet was known as Voice over Internet Protocol (VoIP). The increasing popularity of the Internet has also caused product manufacturers to develop innovative wireless handsets through which customers could access the Internet. Manufacturers were producing handsets and other electronic devices built with advanced equipment that would facilitate the services a customer wished to have.

Information/Directory Publishing Services. These services included all search prints and directory services offered by companies. Traditionally, this consisted of print directories, which were hard copies of contact information for individuals or businesses who gave permission to have their information printed. Customers were able to search for the address or telephone number of any person or entity listed in alphabetical order in the directory. With advancing technologies, these services were extended to include fixed-line and wireless Internet searches used for shopping and information. Customers were able to perform searches for contact information for individuals and businesses that were usually listed in the print directories. They were also able to search for maps and directions, shopping centers, points of interest and many other things based on location, type of business, and several other categories.

TV/Video Services. TV/Video services included not only area TV stations, but dozens of other programming services which consisted of FM radio, movie and special interest channels on a subscription or fee basis. Many cable companies produced their own programs to serve local needs and interests. Cable companies used fixed-lines to transmit television and other programming services to customers. TV/Video was transmitted directly from the company to the customer's television set. Satellite companies used wireless transmission to deliver television and other programming services directly to the customer's television set. For cable companies, the fixed-lines ran directly into a customer's premises but for satellite companies, customers used specific equipment, satellite, provided by the company to receive the services. Deregulation in the industry and the ability of cable TV and satellite companies to offer telephone services began a trend of telephone companies entering the video-delivery technology and vice versa. "The new holy grail of the communications industry is the triple play: the ability to offer customers data, video, and voice" [Bensinger, 2005].

The keys to success were to offer services that were required by customers, those that were either not offered or least likely to be offered by competitors. Customers chose companies based on the ability of the company to appeal to most or all of their needs, a "one stop and shop" deal. "Nearly two thirds of all American homes now subscribe to both wireless and wireline [fixed-line] services, and wireless calls now outnumber calls from traditional wireline [fixed-line] telephones" [Verizon Communications Inc., 2004].

Services were designed to appeal to a customer's need to converse with anyone—locally, long-distance, or internationally; to be able to access information such as driving directions, to retrieve contact information for businesses or the meaning of a word; to be entertained by music, games, or video; to send pictures or short messages; to shop, e-commerce, conduct meetings through video-conferencing and other needs. Companies were also expected to provide additional wireless services to keep up with the industry trend, wireless services such as being able to perform banking transactions, or manage personal account information through the use of the wireless device, or even the ability to be entertained by music or video. It was important that companies provided such a wide variety of services to suite any type of customer. In addition to this, companies offered bundled services which could include local, long-distance, wireless, Internet, and cable TV and satellite services. According to a study done in 2001 by the U.S. Business Reporter, companies in this industry who were not full service providers were at a substantial disadvantage; therefore offering bundles services was a crucial key to success.

Products Products offered by the telecommunications product manufacturers were mainly telephone handsets, corded and cordless. Other products included calling cards and accessories.

Handsets. Handsets were mostly sold with accompanying services provided by telecommunications services providers. However, a customer could purchase only a handset but that customer would have to pay for the services needed to use the handset for telecommunication purposes. Handsets had to be attractive to entice the customers. Product design was especially important with regards to appearance, size and weight. For wireless handsets, smaller, lighter-weight handsets with better display capabilities and a wider range of functions were becoming more popular. It was important for telecommunications services providers to gain exclusive access to "hot" new products, particularly handsets as this gave them a competitive advantage. Products should be designed to perform all requirements needed by customers based on the services they desired; that is, if a customer wished to take pictures and send those pictures to another customer then products should be equipped with a camera and Internet access. "The high-end cellphone [handset] is rapidly gaining functionality formerly reserved for the laptop. [They] have full keyboards, and are getting better . . . at email, instant messaging, Web browsing, and even displaying and editing office documents. Other companies, like Motorola and Nokia, are racing to market with new entries in this category of do-it-all phones" [Mossberg, 2005].

Accessories. Accessories were other electronic or non-electronic devices that enhanced the use of communications systems. Accessories consisted of caller identification devices used to determine the origination of incoming calls; answering machines used to record voice messages; headsets, amplifiers, protective cases and many other devices that enhanced the use of handsets. Companies offered a wide variety of accessories that enhanced the use of telecommunications products.

Calling Cards. Calling cards were specific to each customer and had a unique identification number attached to them. Customers were capable of making calls from anywhere whether it was local, long-distance or international. The customer dialed a toll free number, entered the unique identification number from any phone and the calls were billed to the customer's account. Calling cards could have been customized or personalized to attract customer's attention. Calling cards had different prints based on the season or holiday and they could have been used as marketing tools to advertise the company; this provided companies with an effective way to promote brand recognition.

Customers

Anyone who wanted to be connected to the world was a potential customer. Customers were broken down into two groups: Individuals, and Business, Government, and Other Institutions. Individuals required telecommunications services based on personal use and interest. Business customers included small, medium, and large businesses or enterprises. These business customers along with government and other institutions obtained telecommunications services on the basis of having a secure, faster, reliable network with the services leading to increased productivity and efficiency of business operations among other things.

Individuals As of 2005, 95% of U.S. homes and businesses had a fixed-line telephone [The Insight Research Corporation, 2005]. As innovative technologies reshaped customer behavior around convenience, ease of use and instant gratification, there was a need for faster transmission, improved content and services that enticed individuals. Network speed and reliability were important factors as customers' expectations of the kind of information that could be transmitted increased. Companies with a wide variety of services that provided individuals with the ability to send and receive vast amounts of data at fast rates, be entertained, and be better able to manage all the telecommunications services and devices were in a better position to attract these customers. Companies needed to ensure strong market presence and brand recognition. While wireless services were not a replacement for fixed-line services, they provided customers with a good substitution. Customers favored wireless services mainly because of the mobility, convenience and comparative rates in calling patterns and pricing of local and long-distance calls. "Nearly 65% of Americans, or 195 million people, are expected to be mobile phone subscribers by the close of 2005" [The Insight Research Corporation, 2005]. Individuals increasingly utilized wireless services more than fixed-line services and this shift caused a reduction in the number of fixed-line subscribers. It was necessary that companies offered competitive pricing plans and packages.

Customers that favored wireless-only services were young, single people living in urban areas, typically college students. More mature customers were familiar with the traditional fixed-line services and were more reluctant to part with such services. A study performed by The Insight Research Corporation showed that 51.6% of households had both fixed-line and wireless telephone services, while only 6% of households had only wireless telephone services. In addition to this, wireless transmission was not as fast as fixed-line and many customers preferred both types of services to fit their needs. The Latino market has been a steadily growing market in the U.S. Two factors have driven Hispanic spending growth: higher population growth among Hispanics and the expected growth of Hispanic household incomes. Hispanic household incomes are expected to grow from 77% of the national average in 2000 to 82% by 2020. It was expected that Hispanic spending would grow way above the nation's average in most consumer sectors. Online Hispanic customers outpaced the general online population in several areas of Internet usage, particularly entertainment. In addition to this, about 61% of online Latinos were 34 or under, compared to 37% of Whites and 54% of African Americans [Jordan, 2004].

Business, Government, and Other Institutions Businesses, government and other institutions obtained telecommunications services on the basis of having a secure, faster, reliable network with services that led to increased productivity and efficiency of business operations. Business customers included small businesses (fewer than 20 employees), medium businesses (between 20 and 500 employees or 2 to 25 locations), large businesses and enterprises. Customers required networks that were fast and reliable to facilitate the efficiency of business operations. "They all realize that promotions, cool new handsets and promises of data services won't get them anywhere if users can't get a reliable, clear connection" [Marks, 2001]. It was those companies with a reputation for reliable networks offering fast transmission rates that attracted this market. These customers proved to be profitable because unlike individual customers who could frequently change providers, they could not easily switch to a new telecommunications services provider as they would be forced to buy and implement tons of new equipment, an expensive and time-consuming venture.

Telecommunications services providers offered business, government and other institutions a complete range of basic and advanced communications services and products to meet the voice, video, data and Internet related needs of the customers. It was important that companies provided a wide variety of services suited to the needs of these customers such as video-conferencing, on-hold services for their customers, automatic call back or response systems. Business, government and other institutions chose telecommunications services providers that provided seamless integration of all services needed by these customers. Services providers generally managed the design, operation and maintenance of end-to-end integrated network solutions for these customers. Network security was a paramount factor as many of these customers had e-commerce and dealt with private information. Their systems needed to be able to withstand hackers and prevent unwanted intrusions.

Customer Service

Customer service was an important aspect of the telecommunications industry as this played an essential part in customer retention. Customer service was based on new customers and existing customers.

New Customers Customer service played a major role in which company was chosen by a customer. It was important for a company to gain the confidence of new customers for them to purchase the services. To achieve this the company had to have transparency, which referred to the ability of a company to be open and honest about aspects of the company most important to the customer, things like privacy, speed of processing and quality of services so that customers would more likely trust the company. Strong brand recognition was important because if customers remembered the company's name and business, they were more likely to acquire the services of that particular company. To ensure that customers recognized and remembered a company's name and business, many companies used catchy slogans and logos, and some even had distinct affiliation with particular colors like AT&T whose thematic color was blue. It was important to have friendly and helpful staff that was better able to assist customers in making more informed decisions. The company website had to be user-friendly, that is, it should not be confusing or difficult to navigate as a customer would be unlikely to return to that website. Similarly, the website had to provide interesting and informative content to hold the customer's attention.

Existing Customers Customer service was measured by the churn rate, which is the turnover of existing customers, a closely watched metric measuring the average monthly percentage of customers who left a company in a given quarter. Changes in churn rate provided feedback for a company as it was a good measure for the average length of time an individual remained a customer based on reaction to services provided and pricing. Companies strove to achieve the lowest churn rates possible, which indicated that customers were satisfied with the services they were receiving.

Key factors that affected churn rate were usability of website, good web content, customer satisfaction, customer support, and operational excellence. The website was expected to be secure as many e-commerce activities were performed through the website. Customers were able to view and pay bills online and they could shop for new plans, handsets or packages. Customer satisfaction was determined by how well services and products provided by a company fit the needs of customers; customers demanded high quality of services provided. A company that provided good customer support through the website, 24-hour call support or other means attended to customers' concerns more efficiently and improved customer loyalty; these customers were more likely to stay with that company. It was also important to have a reputation for operational excellence, which could be reflected through simplified billing to customers.

Geographic Region

With national and international coverage it was important to understand what was roaming and the effect it had on coverage. Roaming is the ability to get access to another company's network when away from "home" access. Wireless services providers generally gave customers access to their cell system, which was essentially local. When traveling out of the range of this cell system, the cell system enabled you to be transferred to a neighboring company's cell system without you being aware of it. The use of a neighboring company's cell system caused a customer to be roaming. Geographic region referred to the coverage area of a particular company's wireless network. Networks provided national or international coverage.

National National coverage was the ability of a company to provide services across the United States. Due to Federal Communications Commission (FCC) regulation on fixed-lines, licenses had to be obtained before companies could utilize access lines to operate within a specific area. For companies to expand coverage nationally, they were expected to obtain licenses to operate in specific areas. Wireless coverage depended on several key factors: the number of cell sites, the amount of spectrum band covering an area and roaming agreements between neighboring companies for use of their cell systems. The more cell sites a company had, the larger the national network. Spectrum band referred to the range of frequencies that could be used to transmit wireless signals. The more spectrum band a company acquired, the greater its ability to cover a wider area. Companies were expected to obtain licenses for spectrum bands in different geographic areas. It was also necessary that companies obtained roaming agreements with neighboring companies to allow each other's customers to utilize the cell systems. For example, if a customer normally got access to the company's network from a provider such as Cingular in Brooklyn, New York, and was traveling to Miami, Florida, the customer would get wireless access through a designated provider in Florida such as Verizon, only if the customer's company (Cingular) did not have cell sites in that area.

International   International coverage was the ability of a company to provide services in different geographic areas. Customers were able to send and receive calls and data from others in different countries. Telecommunications services providers were expected to obtain necessary roaming agreements with other countries for wireless networks. Roaming was made possible through service providers who had cooperative agreements to grant each other's customers access to their network. For example, if a customer normally got access to the company's network from a provider in Brooklyn, New York, and was traveling to Hong Kong, the customer would get wireless access through a designated provider in Hong Kong. Instead of paying long-distance charges to the telecommunications services provider in Brooklyn, the customer would pay the local phone connection charge in Hong Kong and possibly a modest additional charge for the service. The access to designated providers was dependent on agreements made between the customer's services provider and the designated services provider.

Distribution/Marketing

Companies distributed services and products through various channels discussed below. These products and services were priced competitively and marketed through all forms of media. Each of the sections, distribution, pricing and marketing, is discussed in detail in the following sections.

Distribution and Sales   Companies in the telecommunications industry sold their products and services through sales distribution channels such as company-owned retail stores or through independent retail stores, which included agent resellers and electronic stores. Most companies also sold their products and services through their own websites. Company-owned retail stores catered primarily to individual customers seeking more information about services and products provided. Setting up their own distribution channels to sell services and products gave those direct sellers more exclusivity with the search-sale-service-support process to the customers. It was important for these stores to have knowledgeable, friendly and helpful staff that made customers feel welcomed, comfortable and better informed to make decisions. This enabled the development of good customer relationships with current and potential customers. It was also necessary to have a user-friendly, attractive and informative website. With growing e-commerce and the ability of customers to pay bills online, it was important to ensure a secure website. By utilizing all distribution channels companies were able to ensure brand recognition of their services. In addition to this, an increased number of distribution channels provided companies with mass market presence.

Pricing   The growing popularity of wireless services, which were far less regulated and hence less expensive, made it increasingly difficult for fixed-line services providers. For companies to survive such pricing competitiveness, pricing plans and packages were implemented. Companies that provided many different services offered bundled packages at more affordable prices to attract customers and thus obtain competitive advantage. Bundling generally referred to the inclusion of two or more services or products sold as a single package. The price of a bundled package was usually less than the cost of acquiring the bundled products or services separately. An example of such bundled packages was the ability of a customer to purchase a wireless handset, wireless services such as network connection, text messaging, voicemail and call forwarding and possibly accessories for a lower price than the combined cost of each individual item.

Bundled packages also consisted of family plans where services and products were offered to families at a discounted rate. As the dynamics of the industry changed it was important for the existing companies to revise packaged rates as new services were added and as packages offered may have also changed.

Apart from bundled packages, another method of pricing was to offer competitive plans to customers. Plans consisted of flat rates for services that may have included voice services with charges for local and long-distance calls on a monthly basis for a certain number of minutes, or voice and data services. With the introduction of new services such as TV/Video services, flat rate services would be revised to offer customers value-added services. Companies with different networks and thus a wider variety of services were better able to offer customers discount rates. An example of this would be to offer customers discount rates for calls made to one of the customer's designated fixed-line phones.

Marketing Companies used all media through which to market their services and products. They spent large sums of money per year on print media and television advertising. Many companies also advertised by sponsoring programs geared toward community involvement such as grants programs, nonprofit projects that used technology to build stronger communities, and sponsorship of sports events. Companies were also able to effectively advertise through the distribution channels by offering promotions such as introductory discounted packages for new customers. By having mass market presence companies strengthened brand recognition. As the Latino market continued to increase at a constant rate, it was important that companies focus on target marketing. About 45% of online Hispanic customers said they wished that more advertisements were in Spanish. One-third of that 45% said they would pay more attention to Spanish ads and 23% said that they would more likely buy a service or product that was advertised in Spanish [Jordan, 2004]. New York was one of the top ten states with the fourth largest Latino market (California, Texas and Florida being the top three) and ranked as the seventh state with the largest shares of total buying power that was Latino.

Mergers and Acquisitions

Changes in technology and the industry as a whole led to the consolidation of companies specialized in different networks transmissions and associated services.

Telecommunication giants got bigger by merging with one another, resulting in less and less competition. This made it harder for new entrants to gain a toehold in the market [Consumer Federation of America, 2005]. Deal making was seen as the best way to grow quickly. Through mergers and acquisitions, companies were able to offer a wider variety of services to a larger group of customers. Since there were significant barriers to entry for local fixed-line networks, consolidation gave companies an avenue to offer and bundle disparate services together. It was thought that this would be an effective way to gain market share and ". . . offer customers the industry's coveted "triple play"—voice, video and data [services] . . ." [Senia, 2004].

A company needed to merge or acquire companies that would provide the most benefits, benefits such as large customer base, new or different technological services, and licenses to operate in more regions. This was particularly important because of the high cost of establishing new territories. A good example of this was the recent acquisition of AT&T Corp. by SBC Communications, which increased its customer base with the addition of AT&T's 30 million customers, including its Fortune 1000 customers. It also gained AT&T's wireless services and strong name brand, one of the most recognized brand names worldwide [Hoovers, 2005]. This is the main reason that SBC Communications has changed its name to AT&T. Companies that were considered long-distance companies such as AT&T Corp. and MCI, Inc. consisted of nearly 100% fiber optic cables [U.S. Business Reporter, 2001]. This was an added advantage for telecommunications services provider as fiber optic connections meant more information could be transferred at faster rates. In addition to this, companies that wished to upgrade network connection to fiber optic cables gained the fiber optic networks of long-distance companies. The deals also expanded the national and international presence of companies that merged or acquired other companies. Mergers and acquisitions were also expected to provide more financial resources for innovation and investment in new technology.

Competition

Competition in this industry was quite intense. Competitors included companies that provided fixed-line and wireless voice and data services, companies that provided primarily wireless voice and data services, companies that provided fixed-line data and TV/Video services only and those that provided wireless data and TV/Video services. Companies such as AT&T Inc. and Verizon Communication Inc. provided voice and data services, using both fixed-line and wireless networks while companies such as Sprint Nextel Corporation provided primarily wireless voice and data services. Time Warner Cable was an example of a provider of fixed-line TV/Video services while Direct TV provided wireless TV/Video services.

TV/Video services providers such as Time Warner Cable and Direct TV offered high-speed data and digital voice services to compete directly with the broadband services offered in the telecommunications industry. While these companies increased competition in this industry, they posed no major threat to telecommunications services providers as TV/Video services providers lacked the necessary equipment (switching equipment) and were ". . . generally seen as not having much technological nor networking experience" when compared to the telecommunications services providers [Anonymous, 2005].

The main competitors discussed here were those who maintained the highest market share and were key players in the telecommunications industry. Wireless services constituted a significant source of competition to any company's fixed-line telecommunications services since more end users were substituting wireless services for basic fixed-line services. TV/Video services providers fell under the category of other services providers. The major competitors were fixed-line and wireless voice and data services providers such as AT&T Inc., mainly wireless voice and data services providers such as Sprint Nextel and other telecommunications services providers such as voice and data broadband services providers, fixed-line or wireless TV/Video services providers or any combination of the above. AT&T Inc., Sprint Nextel and other telecommunications services providers are discussed in detail in the following section.

AT&T Inc. (formerly SBC) SBC Communications was the number two provider of fixed-line voice and data services in the U.S., behind Verizon. It had 52 million local access lines and 22 million long distance customers. Its wireless division known as Cingular Wireless held the position as the number one wireless voice and data services provider with more than 50 million customers [Hoovers, 2005]. The company

operated fixed-line and wireless networks and maintained the facilities and equipment used to create these networks. It is also considered one of the major telecommunications resellers. In 2005 for $16 billion, SBC acquired AT&T Corp., a long-distance, fixed-line services provider and a provider of wireless voice and data services (AT&T Wireless) with valuable business customers who included all of the Fortune 1000, particularly those within its major markets (California, Illinois and Texas which account for 60% of its lines) [Hoovers, 2005]. AT&T was the long-distance voice services leader in the U.S. with more than 30 million customers and it boasted the largest and most advanced global network. SBC gained one of the world's most recognized brand names and it is because of this SBC has changed its name to AT&T Inc.

It planned to deploy fiber optic lines to customers' premises in an effort to improve network speed, a $6 billion in investment for the new network. The project, expected to be completed by the end of 2007, would allow the company to offer video over the Internet and voice and data services simultaneously over these new and improved methods of transmission. The company was the market leader in providing fixed-line broadband services transmitted over coaxial cables. The acquisition of AT&T and the fiber-optic network that came with it helped to improve transmission but this only affected a small number of the customers. The company planned to build 142 new cell sites at a cost of $130 million in an effort to expand network coverage and capacity. In an effort to improve capital spending the company was driven to cut expenses, including deep cuts in its workforce in 2002 and 2003 and it also sold off stakes it held in many other companies to raise money for the necessary upgrades. AT&T Inc. reported net revenues of $40.7 billion, which exhibited the financial resourcefulness of the company as a result of the acquisition. This provided the company sufficient resources necessary for upgrades.

The wireless division, Cingular, used the GSM operating system which provided customers with limited information transmission capacity; however, it was strong for operation in any location due to its popularity and strong roaming capabilities and also had a high degree of commonality. With respect to operating systems, the effectiveness of operation on different networks was comparable for all companies. AT&T offers fixed-line and wireless voice and data services and information/directory publishing services.

The company also made an agreement with EchoStar Communications, a satellite TV services provider, to market satellite TV services as part of its services bundle. It was strong at offering customers bundled services. It was strong at offering services not offered or least likely to be offered by competitors such as TV services and providing a wide variety of services. As the leader in wireless services, the company was strong at gaining exclusive access to "hot" new products. Also it provided a wide variety of accessories and customized calling cards.

AT&T was good at network reliability for individual customers; it provided a wide variety of services to attract customers and cater to their needs. The company had strong market presence and brand recognition. It had competitive pricing plans and packages offering customers unlimited calls to other customers and rollover minutes where unused minutes can be transferred to next month. As a provider of services for the Fortune 1000 companies, the company was strong in providing a fast and reliable network with a wide variety of services such as business solutions and network maintenance that were seamlessly integrated. Network security was a main concern for all telecommunications services providers and AT&T was as good as its competitors in providing such security.

AT&T had a user-friendly website that was easy to navigate; it provided information on its services and products for both individual and business customers. The company's website allowed customers to make purchases and pay bills online. Similar to other telecommunications services providers it maintained a secure website that was interesting and an informative way to alert customers to new products. Similar to other companies, it maintained a good degree of transparency through honesty with customers of business processes, services and ventures. The company was good with respect to having a knowledgeable, friendly and helpful staff to assist customers seeking to purchase services and those requesting support for services already purchased. The company was considered to be operating efficiently and had a churn rate of 2.2% in the first quarter of 2005.

AT&T, namely Cingular, was good at obtaining necessary licenses to operate fixed-line networks in other areas and those licenses required for spectrum band to operate wireless network in other areas. It was also good at obtaining roaming agreements with neighboring companies to utilize cell systems nationally and was strong on an international level. AT&T distributed and sold its products through company-owned retail stores, which gave them more exclusivity. The company used all distribution channels available such as independent retail stores and electronic stores and the company website to ensure brand recognition and had many distribution channels to provide mass market presence. AT&T was very strong at pricing by offering bundled packages such as fixed-line and wireless data services, and affordable pricing plans like flat rates for local, long-distance and international calls and offering discount rates to customers who require many services provided by the different networks. It was also strong at revising package rates and plans to reflect changes. With respect to marketing, AT&T used all forms of media to advertise including sponsorship programs and community involvement and they both offered promotions through the various distribution channels. The company marketed to college students and families as well as business individuals.

Sprint Nextel Corporation In 2005, Sprint Corp., the number three U.S wireless services provider and Nextel Corp., the number five U.S. wireless services provider, merged companies to form the overall third largest wireless services provider in the U.S., behind Cingular and Verizon. Sprint Nextel's main business operations were wireless voice and data services and fixed-line broadband data services using coaxial cables. It operated both wireless and fixed-line networks and it was a telecommunications reseller, which meant that it did not own the facilities and equipment used in transmission. In September 2005, Sprint and Nextel merged to form the third largest wireless services provider in the U.S. Its combined wireless operations served approximately 44 million customers and the fixed-line business served more than 750,000 customers with both fixed-line broadband services in the United States. Sprint Nextel reported net revenues of $27.4 billion and expressed no immediate plans to build new cell sites.

It used CDMA operating systems for wireless devices, which allowed a large number of users to utilize services on the same frequency and it planned to introduce new technology, EvDo (Evolution Data Optimized), which provided faster wireless data speeds. Sprint Nextel was the first in the telecommunications industry to offer wireless services that allowed customers to listen to live TV and download songs to their wireless devices. It was also excellent at providing a wide variety of wireless services that allowed customers to browse the Internet and check email, play games, utilize text messaging and instant messaging services and customize their wireless devices such as customers could choose from a variety of screen savers and they were also able to assign ring tones to specific telephone numbers of callers in their address book. These services were all seamlessly integrated.

It offered a wide range of fixed-line services for business, government and other institutions such as email protection and Centrex services that directed calls, managed voicemail and set up conference calls. In a joint venture with fixed-line broadband company, Sunflower Broadband, Sprint Nextel offered bundled fixed-line broadband voice and data services, wireless voice and data services and cable TV services. Sprint Nextel made agreements with the four largest cable TV companies in the U.S. to offer customers the convergence of video entertainment, fixed-line and wireless data and communications products and services beginning in 2006. The joint venture is believed ". . . to deliver to consumers a comprehensive portfolio of entertainment and communication services . . ." [RCR Wireless News, 2004].

Sprint Nextel had agreements with product manufacturers such as Samsung to gain access to advanced new products. The wireless devices allowed customers to receive the benefits of many of Sprint Nextel's services such as video mail, picture mail, games, ringers, Internet browsing and email access. It was comparable to its competitors in providing a wide variety of accessories but it did not provide calling cards. It was good at providing reliable networks for all customers. Like many of its competitors, the company placed great emphasis on network security. Like other competitors, the website was user-friendly, easy to navigate and listed newsworthy information and reviews of the company's services and product providing interesting content for customer's reading pleasure. Like many of its competitors, Sprint Nextel maintained a secure website through which customers performed e-commerce transactions.

Similar to other competitors it maintained a good degree of transparency through honesty with customers of the company's business processes, services and ventures and it was good with respect to having a knowledgeable, friendly and helpful staff to assist customers seeking to purchase services and those requesting support for services already purchased. It operated a nationwide wireless network and had roaming agreements with some international countries and most major Caribbean islands. Its ability to obtain necessary licenses for spectrum band was weak compared to other competitors as this would cause regulatory issues. As the third largest wireless services provider in the U.S., Sprint Nextel maintained strong brand recognition. It had a limited number of company-owned retail stores but it distributed and sold its services and products through many independent stores.

The company offered bundled packages that included fixed-line broadband voice and data and cable TV services. Customers purchased competitively priced plans similar to that of Cingular. Sprint was good at using all forms of media to advertise and offered customers promotions such as discounted prices for upgrades of handsets or get $25 if you refer a friend to use the company's services. The company is an active participant in sponsorships of program such as NASCAR racing and the Emmy Awards. It marketed to college students and families, as well as business customers who utilized the wireless "walkie-talkie" technology that allowed customers to communicate with the push of a button. It was used mainly for business purposes and was a cheap and easy form of communication.

Other Telecommunications Services Providers Other telecommunications services providers included Time Warner Cable and Direct TV, which were providers of TV/Video services and fell under the category of other services providers. Their services were primarily TV/Video services and fixed-line broadband voice and data services. Other telecommunications services providers operated fixed-line networks that used fiber-optic connections and had transmission rates that were very fast. Since they lacked telecommunications equipment, to build the facilities and acquire the necessary switching equipment would have been a very expensive venture. They formed joint ventures with many telecommunications services providers as a way to compete in the market without having to purchase telecommunications equipment. This meant that these companies did not have to worry about licenses and other factors that affected wireless business. These companies were weak in operating multiple networks as companies provided either fixed-line services only or wireless services only. The networks were fast and reliable and had good level of security.

With the introduction of VoIP, these companies were able to provide voice services using fixed-line broadband network. This development gave these companies the ability to offer a wider variety of services but they were still limited because of the lack of switching equipment. With a limited variety of services there was not much of a bundled service to offer customers. These bundled services often included data services which were mostly Internet-related, VoIP services and cable TV services. Since these services used the same network, they had to be seamlessly integrated for efficiency. These new competitors into the telecommunications industry had little bargaining power for exclusive products, limited accessories and offered no calling cards. The idea of TV/Video services providers being providers of voice and data services was a fairly new concept for customers and was not as easily accepted. These companies had to ensure a high quality of services provided to gain customers' business in such a competitive industry. The company websites were user-friendly, easy to navigate and provided necessary information for customers. The websites were also secure as many customers performed e-commerce transactions. Staff was friendly, knowledgeable and helpful; they provided good customer support.

Many of these companies utilized a limited number of independent retailers such as Best Buy and Circuit City since they did not have company-owned retail stores. Given limited services compared to services providers like AT&T, they offered limited bundled packages at competitive prices. It was difficult to have revised package rates and affordable pricing plans as TV/Video services were quite expensive. These companies were good at utilizing various forms of media through which to advertise to all customers but they were not known for partaking in sponsorships or community programs.

The Company

History

Verizon Communications Inc. was a telecommunications services provider of fixed-line and wireless services primarily in the Americas and Europe. It also provided Information/Directory Publishing, which consisted of yellow pages and search services in print, over the Internet and on cell phones. In 2000, Bell Atlantic and Vodofone combined their U.S. wireless operations to form Verizon Wireless. Verizon Communications Inc.

was formed later that year upon approval for acquisition of the non-Bell local phone company, GTE. In 2001, the Company received permission to offer long-distance in Massachusetts, Connecticut, and Pennsylvania; in 2002, it received permission for Delaware, New Hampshire, and Rhode Island; and in 2003, it received permission for Maryland, West Virginia, and Washington, D.C. The company, being based in New York City, felt severe effects from the terrorist attack on lower Manhattan in 2001. Verizon reported damage to its central office facility adjacent to the World Trade Center and the loss of eleven cell sites in the surrounding area of the destruction. The company also provides phone services to the Pentagon and suffered damage in that attack. As part of an effort to reduce debt, in 2002 Verizon divested many of its non-core assets, which included several wireless holdings, access lines and its European based directory businesses.

Led by Ivan Seidenburg, chairman and chief executive officer, Verizon achieved the 2005 top ranking position in *Fortune's* list of most admired telecommunications companies and had the enviable position of attaining a reputation for operational excellence and having the most satisfied customers in the wireless industry. As Mr. Seidenburg expressed, "Our commitment to network quality and customer service has made us the industry leader in customer growth, loyalty and profitability" [Verizon Communications Inc., 2005]. Verizon Communications Inc. was a provider of telecommunications services and operated fixed-line and wireless networks. The focus of the company was to transform the networks to provide additional fixed-line and wireless services. In 2004, Verizon experienced strong revenue growth with revenues up 5.7% from 2003. Fueling this growth was a 23% gain in revenues from the wireless division and growth in high-speed data services in fixed-line [Verizon Communications Inc., 2005]. Verizon's operations are shown in Figure 2.

Transmission

Verizon operated two types of networks: fixed-line and wireless networks.

Fixed-Line The fixed-line division accounted for 54% of total revenues. Verizon has nearly 145 million access line equivalents in 29 states and Washington, D.C. The company offered fixed-line broadband network, which provided customers with improved content and

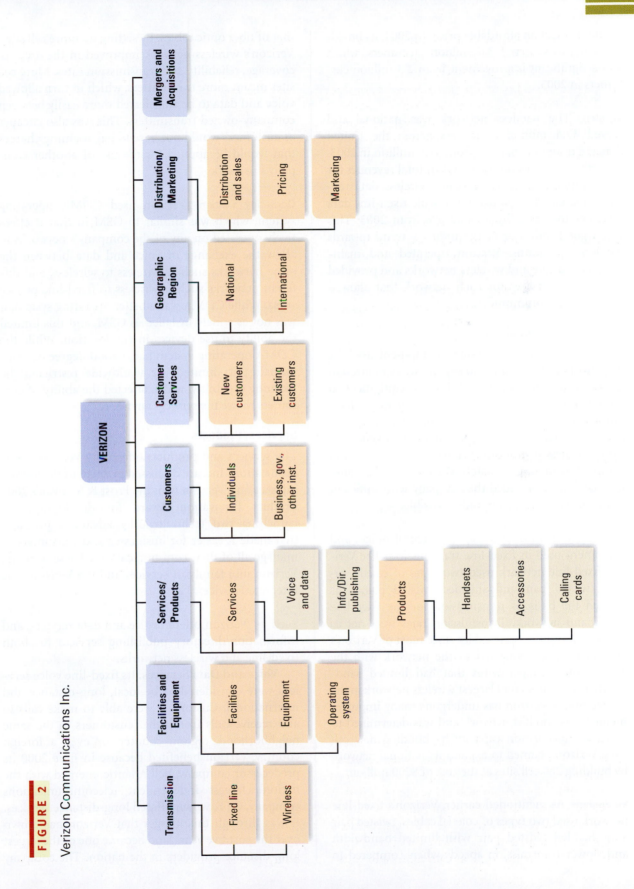

FIGURE 2
Verizon Communications Inc.

great service at an affordable price. In 2004, its broadband network served 3.6 million customers, which was a significant improvement from 2.3 million customers in 2003.

Wireless The wireless network was national and served 47.4 million customers across the United States, a dramatic increase from 37.5 million in 2003. This division accounted for 38% of total revenues for the company. In 2004, Verizon's wireless data revenues increased by almost 60% while fixed-line data revenues increased by a mere 6% from 2003. This was a good indicator of the industry trend towards wireless operations. Verizon operated and maintained fixed-line and wireless networks and provided any and all services for each network that allowed customers to communicate.

Facilities and Equipment

Verizon owned its facilities and equipment used for its networks and intended to expand services through its use. It also leased its facilities and equipment to other telecommunication resellers that generated additional revenues. With the revenues received from leasing its facilities and equipment and that generated from business operations, Verizon was a very sound company with approximately $71 billion in revenues in 2004, which provided the company with sufficient resources to make the upgrades possible.

Facilities Verizon owned most its central offices and equipment used in fixed-line transmission. The Verizon fixed-line network used two types of coaxial cables, twisted pair and shielded twisted pair. This formed the basis of transmission for the fixed-line broadband network. Transmission rates were not as fast as that of fiber optic cables since most of Verizon's customers were connected to the network with the much slower copper wires that had limited bandwidth. It was the second largest wireless network in the United States. Verizon has undergone many improvements to its wireless network and was determined to increase transmission capacity by building new cell sites. Verizon planned to expand its national network by building 280 cell sites at the cost of $200 million.

Equipment As mentioned earlier, Verizon's fixed-line network used two types of coaxial cables, twisted pair and shielded twisted pair with limited bandwidth and slower transmission speeds when compared to that of fiber optic cables. By setting up more cell sites, Verizon's wireless network improved in the areas of coverage, reliability and transmission rates. More cell sites meant more transmitters, which in turn allowed voice and data to be transferred more easily between company-owned transmitters. This was also cheaper as customers would not have to pay roaming charges that would be applied for the use of another company's network.

Operating Systems Verizon used CDMA operating system, which was similar to GSM in that it effectively operated on any of the company's networks to allow the exchange of voice and data between the same networks such as wireless to wireless, and different networks such as wireless to fixed-line or vice versa. While CDMA was a better operating system, it was not as widely installed as GSM, and this limited the ability to use devices in any location. While the CDMA operating system had a good degree of commonality, its limited use worldwide restricted the roaming capability, which affected the ability of customers to use the services anywhere.

Services/Products

The services and products offered by Verizon Communications Inc. are discussed in detail in the following sections. Verizon won the Frost & Sullivan's 2005 Product Innovation Award for developing and launching two technologically advanced products that made it easier for businesses and consumers to manage all of their communications. These were the Verizon iobi family of services and the Verizon One integrated device.

Services Verizon offered voice and data services, and information/directory publishing services for both fixed-line and wireless networks.

    Voice and Data Services. Its fixed-line voice services were considered to be local, long-distance and international. Customers were able to make calls to and receive calls from other customers in the same neighborhood, region, country, or even a foreign country. Verizon benefited because in June 2000 its predecessor company, Bell Atlantic, merged with the nation's largest independent telecommunications company, GTE, which offered long-distance services. It was through this merger that Verizon has grown over the past five years, and became one of the largest long-distance providers in the nation. The company offered all its customers a wide variety of other voice services for fixed-line and wireless networks. These services included voice, text and picture messaging, caller identification, call waiting, call forwarding and three-way calling. It also offered speed-dialing where customers could store the most frequently dialed numbers and use a one digit number to reference that number when dialing and it offered customers a "Gold Telephone Number," which was a customized telephone number using letters and digits that were meaningful and easy to remember. These features added value for customers and were often sold as part of bundled services.

Its data services consisted primarily of Internet services to customers in two-thirds of the top 100 U.S. markets. Customers accessed the Internet using fixed-line or wireless devices to exchange information. Customers sent short messages to each other through instant messaging applications and they sent documents, pictures, graphics and other data through email. It also offered "VoiceWing," which was VoIP, where customers were able to make calls over any broadband Internet connection. The Verizon iobi family of services allowed customers to email voicemail, have the computer hold calls or schedule call forwarding to any phone. It provided customers with an integrated service that made it easier to stay connected. Customers were not only capable of speaking to other customers but their wireless devices allowed them to be able to play games, download ring tones, and take, send and receive pictures as messages.

Information/Directory Publishing Services. Verizon provided its customers with yellow pages and search services in print, over the Internet and on wireless devices. It was the leading print and online directory publisher and content provider with revenues of $3.6 billion in 2004 with 134 million monthly searches on SuperPages.com. These information services were expanded in new electronic markets allowing customers the luxury of searching and retrieving information as well as shopping. It was good at developing and introducing innovative services to the market quickly. A good example of this was the development of the high-speed EvDO (Evolution Data Only) network which allowed Palm's Treo smartphones to access wireless services and the Internet, posing many advantages for corporate IT as a less costly alternative for mobile email. Another example was the development of the fixed-line product known as Verizon

One, which was the simplicity of a telephone combined with the richness of the Internet and this provided customers with an all-in-one information touch-point. It was also a major services provider offering a variety of services for both fixed-line and wireless networks.

Products Verizon sold accompanying products such as handsets, accessories and calling cards. These products were discussed in detail in the following sections.

Handsets. Verizon was not as good as its competitors in obtaining exclusive access to new, impressive and attractive products. The company found it difficult to work out cost and pricing issues with manufacturers and so has not made any agreements with any manufacturer [Business Week, 2005]. Its competitors were very good at obtaining exclusive access to such products.

Accessories. It provided accessories like caller id devices, answering machines, headsets, battery packs, amplifiers for wireless devices, protective cases, adaptors, car chargers and many other accessories that gave customers the convenience of utilizing communications services.

Calling Cards. Verizon offered calling cards that allowed customers to make calls from their fixed-line or wireless handsets that were conveniently billed to the customers' home phone bill. It allowed customers to use one number, 800-255-CALL, to make calls from any phone to anywhere in the world. The company also offered calling cards known as the Verizon Phone-In Card that permitted calls to be made to a customer's home phone from anywhere in the world. This was used by customers as an alternative to collect calls. These cards were usually customized with the company's logo and used as marketing tools to advertise the company and promote brand recognition.

Customers

Verizon provided network services and products for a variety of customers ranging from individuals, small and medium-sized businesses to large businesses, government, and other institutions.

Individuals It was voted as the number one provider of telecommunications services in the United States and had an excellent reputation for network speed and reliability. It was strong at providing a wide variety of fixed-line and wireless services and products that fit the needs of its customers. While the company maintained strong market presence and brand recognition through which it attracted most of its competitors, the services and products offered were quite costly.

Business, Government and Other Institutions Verizon provided a wide variety of services for all types of businesses, government and other institutions. These services included voice and data services, network security services, and wireless services, which included Global Phone where business customers could access to the Internet and voice services anywhere in the world through international roaming capabilities. It also offered business solutions services that managed the design, operation and maintenance of end-to-end integrated network services for large business, government, and other institutions such as educational institutions, across the U.S. Verizon was strong in providing services that appeared seamlessly integrated on and between networks. This promoted network reliability for which Verizon had an excellent reputation. Verizon believed that its strongest market segment was individual customers. There was tremendous competition for the business, government and other institutions market, in which AT&T was the dominant telecommunications services provider. In 2005, the business segment, though an $85 billion market, was fading fast and revenues were shrinking about 10% a year. It is because of this, Verizon was not convinced "... that the potential for such gains is worth the high price of buying into the [business] market" [Rosenbush, 2005]. This meant that the company would focus its energies on more profitable markets but it was not going to neglect the business segment. Verizon felt that it was necessary to have faster networks that allow for high-speed Internet connections and services to compete for the business market share.

Customer Service

In 2004, Verizon achieved a reputation for having the best customer service. Customer service was based on that for new customers and that for existing customers.

New Customers Verizon's goal was to operate with the highest level of integrity, responsibility and accountability that led to an increased level of trust the company has earned over the years. It maintained a good level of transparency. Verizon was excellent at making sure that customers recognized and remembered

its name. The company's logo was its name Verizon, with an emphatic red V and Z, symbolic of network speed and also echoed the origin of the company name: veritas, which was a Latin word for certainty, reliability, and horizon, signifying forward-looking and visionary. Its slogan was "We never stop working for you" and this was reflected in the quality of staff. Verizon was strong at having a knowledgeable, friendly and helpful staff. The company also maintained a user-friendly, easy-to-navigate website that contained information on all services and products offered by Verizon.

Existing Customers The company placed great emphasis on providing the best possible quality of service. In the first quarter of 2005, Verizon posted a churn rate of 1.33% compared to 1.5% at the end of 2004. This was a new low for the industry. Verizon maintained a reputation for having operational excellence by providing the highest quality of services to customers, offering a wide variety of services to fit customers' needs, maintaining a secure and interesting website for customers and by having excellent customer support staff. The company has a 24-hour customer support telephone number that customers could call and it also maintained a quick reference and easy to understand customer support section on the company website. According to Mr. Seidenberg, it provided the best customer service because of "... the commitment of our ... dedicated Verizon employees who constantly find new ways to serve customers ..." [Verizon Communications Inc., 2004].

Geographic Region

Verizon's wireless network provided national and limited international coverage.

National Verizon has national presence in fixed-line and wireless markets, with approximately 100 million Americans connecting to a Verizon network daily. It was good at obtaining necessary licenses to operate fixed-line networks in other areas and it was also good at obtaining wireless spectrum bands in different geographic areas. In 2005, Verizon acquired a significant portion of spectrum band covering central Arkansas from other companies within the area [RCR Wireless News, 2005]. It planned to increase the number of cell sites which would allow the company to provide better network coverage over a larger area. As mentioned earlier, the company had the resources necessary to do this. It was one of the largest wireless services providers that owned and operated its facilities and equipment. Verizon had more than 23,000 cell sites nationally, which made it less dependent on roaming agreements; however it also made it easier for the company to obtain roaming agreements with neighboring companies to utilize each others' cell systems.

International It also provided international services using both fixed-line and wireless networks primarily in the Americas and Europe. Verizon's international coverage was limited as it did not possess the necessary roaming agreements with many international telecommunications services providers to utilize their networks to facilitate transmission and a greater coverage area.

Distribution/Marketing

Verizon distributed through various channels and offered competitively priced services and products using all forms of media to market its services and products. Distribution and sales, pricing, and marketing were discussed in detail in the following sections.

Distribution and Sales The company's main distribution channel was its company-owned retail stores. This gave Verizon more exclusivity with the search-sale-service support process to customers. Verizon also sold its services and products through independent retail stores, which included agent resellers and other electronic stores such as RadioShack, Best Buy and Circuit City. It was necessary that staff was knowledgeable, friendly and helpful to make the customer feel welcomed, comfortable and better informed to make decisions. This allowed the customers and staff to develop trusting relationships. Verizon also used its website to sell its services and products. The company had a strong website with interesting and informative content for both potential and existing customers. Its website was also designed for e-commerce and provided customers with the convenience and ease of access to account information, hassle-free online billing and payment methods, shopping and informational resources. Many existing customers performed such activities through the company's very secure website. Verizon offered promotions such as free phones when customers signed up for particular pricing plans of services, or additional features supplied as part of a package, through

its distribution channels as a way to ensure brand recognition. All of its channels boasted the company's logo and slogan. Verizon sold its services and products through a limited number of distribution channels and only those channels that sold Verizon services and products exclusively; however, it still maintained good mass market presence because of the large number of company-owned retail stores.

Pricing It offered customers a wide variety of bundled packages such as wireless handset, a few pieces of accessories and wireless voice and data services, and plans such as flat monthly rates for the use of the services and products. Many of these packages and plans were varied combinations of services and products that gave customers the feeling of added value. The company was strong at revising package rates as packages changed and it was also strong at revising the plans as new services were added or as value was added to the services. However, Verizon's services and products were more expensive than most companies in the industry and discount rates to customers were minimal.

Marketing Verizon was extremely successful at mass marketing its services and products. It utilized all forms of media through which to advertise. It advertised using television advertisements, print, billboards, flyers and in-store promotions to effectively grab customers' attention. In 2005, Verizon won the "Stevies Award," presented by the American Business Awards, for its national literacy program, Verizon Reads, and also that year, the Verizon Foundation won a "Gold Award" from the Council on Foundations for its website, www.verizon.com/foundation, which was honored for excellence in communication. Verizon was instrumental in sponsorship programs and community involvement. The company had mass market presence and strong brand recognition. It used its distribution channels to offer customers promotions like special packages, an example of which included voice and data services, the handset, a headset, and the protective case at a combined discounted price. It marketed its products to all customers but was not as effective in target marketing to the Latino population.

Mergers and Acquisitions

In December 2005, Verizon acquired MCI Inc., one of its major competitors. The merger was expected "... to enhance the base of business customers ... and also expand their national and international presence" [Information Week, 2005]. Verizon saw the acquisition as an opportunity to expand its services to large corporate business. MCI, Inc. was a leading global communications provider, delivering innovative, cost-effective, advanced communications connectivity to businesses, governments and consumers. MCI also had similar business values to those of Verizon, "To serve customers with innovation, value and integrity" [MCI, 2005]. MCI offered an advanced VoIP service in the business VoIP market and was one of the nation's largest long-distance voice services providers. This meant that MCI owned and operated fiber optic networks and had the most robust set of converged communications services in the industry, including integrated voice, data, and Internet services. In addition to this, MCI was expected to provide Verizon with additional financial resources; it brought with it revenues of $20 billion to Verizon.

Finances

In response to the general industry decline in the early part of the decade, most other telecommunications companies sharply reduced capital spending on network infrastructure. During this time, Verizon emphasized overall expense control as newer technologies made networks and operations more efficient. Verizon also sold non-strategic assets, both domestically and internationally, and the company maintained strong, consistent cash flows from operating activities ($21.8 billion in 2004). This enabled the company, unlike its peers, to maintain a healthy level of network spending in growth areas—investing more in wireless and fixed-line broadband networks than anyone else in the industry. In 2004, Verizon experienced strong revenue growth with revenues up 5.7% from 2003. Fueling this growth was a 23% gain in revenues from the wireless division and growth in high-speed data services in fixed-line [Verizon Communications Inc., 2005]. Verizon reported consolidated revenues of $71.3 billion. In 2005, Verizon planned to sell or spin-off its information/directory publishing services in a deal valued at more than $17 billion. "Some analysts questioned the wisdom of giving up the strong, profitable cash flows from directories despite Verizon's need to bolster its finances . . ." [Los Angeles Times, 2005]. The company explored different means of acquiring additional financial resources to concentrate more on providing wireless, data and phone services.

Management and Strategy

With increasing competition in the telecommunications industry, Mr. Seidenberg, chairman and chief executive officer, was faced with the challenge of raising the standards for performance and redefining the growth possibilities for the telecommunications industry. Mr. Seidenberg aimed to transform Verizon into a full-service provider of video, Internet, wireless, and other services by improving the equipment used in transmission. He perceived that the best way to expand and thrive in the telecommunications world was by focusing on growth in the profitable wireless and broadband markets while building up in the business, government and other institutions market. He saw the acquisition of MCI Corp. as an opportunity to expand services and increase market share by acquiring MCI's customers. Under his leadership, Verizon maintained the position as the largest telecommunications provider; however, it ranked second to Cingular in providing wireless services. While the company maintained an advantageous position as the largest telecommunications provider, Mr. Seidenberg realized that in a dynamic industry such as this, standing still meant falling behind and it was therefore necessary to focus on the opportunities ahead.

Looking Towards the Future

Mr. Seidenberg was faced with many decisions that affected the future of Verizon. The major decisions included a drastic redesign of the equipment used in the transmission of an increasing variety of data, allowing for an array of services the company offered that were better suited to the needs of its customers, retention of the customers the company had and the ability to increase market share. Verizon believed that it was more important to be the best network operator than the biggest.

The decision revolved around two alternatives. The first was the drastic upgrade of the wireless network and the fixed-line broadband network providing services for business, government and other institutions only, while the second was the drastic upgrade of the wireless network and the fixed-line network providing services for all customers but target marketing to the Latino population.

The first alternative proposed that Verizon built new cell sites to increase the wireless network and that it would also improve the fixed-line broadband networks by drastically upgrading the coaxial cables to fiber optic cables. Verizon's upgrades to the networks were expected to attract the lucrative businesses, government and other institutions market.

The company was expected to expand its services to include necessary business services such as video conferencing, business network solutions, VoIP services and network equipment maintenance services and it would increase international coverage for business customers utilizing wireless services. Pricing strategies for these customers such as plans for long-distance calls or cheaper international calls were to be implemented to compete with other companies that dominated this market niche.

The implementation of fiber optic cables was expected to provide increased bandwidth, faster transmission and the ability to transmit additional information that was necessary for businesses, government and other institutions. By upgrading the networks and offering a wider variety of services tailored to these customers, Verizon would put itself in a more competitive position to gain market share and increase profitability in this $85 billion market.

This alternative was feasible because the company had more financial resources than its competitors. It also maintained a good reputation for network reliability and customer satisfaction. Verizon had a long history of providing services and products that enabled efficiency and productivity of businesses, which contributed to its reputation. Verizon was good at developing and introducing innovative services and products to the market quickly; a good example of this is the development of the high-speed EvDO (Evolution Data Only) network, which allowed Palm's Treo smartphones to access wireless services and the Internet, posing many advantages for corporate IT as a less costly alternative for mobile email. By building new cell sites, national coverage would be improved. The company had to obtain roaming agreements with other countries to improve international coverage; the benefit of this greater coverage was that the brand would become internationally recognized and that would provide great opportunity for international expansion.

Verizon was an industry leader and maintained notable positions for customer satisfaction and network reliability. Its merger with MCI placed it in a better position than its competitors with sufficient scale and presence to be a major supplier to national and global business entities, governments and other institutions. MCI was the industry leader and better

than AT&T in the VoIP market, which was an increasingly popular voice and data service business used. Verizon had more financial resources compared to its competitors and was capable of financing the drastic upgrade of both networks simultaneously; it could do this much more easily than its competitors. Verizon also had a stronger reputation for operational excellence and customer satisfaction. It was better than its competitors at providing the highest quality of services and having excellent customer support. Verizon had stronger brand recognition than most of its competitors and was the only company to offer services that were specifically for network security, its network security solutions.

A drawback to this alternative was that upgrading the fixed-line and wireless networks simultaneously, expanding services significantly and also expanding coverage internationally would place a tremendous strain on finances. One way around this drawback would be to merge with or acquire a company that offers either of these technological services and would provide additional licenses, therefore expanding the coverage area.

The second alternative proposed was that Verizon would focus on the drastic upgrade of fixed-line coaxial cables to fiber optic cables, and simultaneously build new cell sites to improve the wireless network. To facilitate this upgrade the company was expected to sell or spin-off its information/directory publishing services. Upgrades in fixed-line and wireless networks would allow the company to expand its services to include TV/Video services, enhanced data services, particularly Internet, and offer a wider variety of bundled services. Verizon was expected to target all customers with special focus on the potential Latino population. It was expected to improve national coverage but maintain a limited international coverage.

By replacing all copper lines with fiber optic links the amount of bandwidth would be dramatically increased. This would lead to best overall values in broadband, with improved content, faster speeds and allow for a host of next-generation services to be delivered, services such as fast Internet access and high definition and quality of video. The fiber infrastructure was expected to reduce operating costs and allow for new revenue streams from high-capacity applications like video and music. The sale or spin-off of the information/directory publishing services was expected to generate $17 billion which would be used towards the upgrade of the networks to offer a faster, more reliable network with greater information carrying capacity and hence position itself as a wireless and fixed-line broadband competitor. Focusing on the individual customers, specifically target marketing the Latino population, would give Verizon first mover advantage and secure its position within the Latino community. The U.S. market was also the company's strongest market and by improving national coverage, Verizon stands to gain significant market share.

This alterative was feasible because the company was financially strong and with the additional resources provided from the sale of the information/directory publishing services, it would be able to cover this massive investment. It also maintained a good reputation for network reliability and had excellent customer service. Verizon offered an already wide variety of services and had a long history of offering services and products that enabled efficiency and productivity for business customers and convenience for its individual customers. Verizon was good at developing and introducing innovative services and products to the market quickly.

Verizon had more financial resources than its competitors and it stood to gain considerable financial leverage from the sale of its information/directory publishing services to cover the cost of financing the drastic upgrade of both networks simultaneously. Its merger with MCI placed it in a better position than its competitors with sufficient scale and presence to be a major supplier to national and global business entities, governments and other institutions. MCI was the industry leader and better than AT&T in the VoIP market, which was an increasingly popular voice and data service business used. Verizon also had a stronger reputation for operational excellence and customer satisfaction. It was an industry leader and maintained notable positions for customer satisfaction and network reliability. It was better than its competitors at providing the highest quality of services and having excellent customer support. Verizon had stronger brand recognition than most of its competitors and was the only company to offer services that were specifically for network security, its network security solutions. To improve national coverage, Verizon was better than its competitors at obtaining roaming agreements with neighboring companies to use their cell systems and they had significant resources necessary to build more cell

sites that improved the wireless transmission and coverage; it had more cell sites than its competitors.

A drawback was that Verizon could potentially harm itself from the sale of its industry leading information/directory publishing services and end up spreading its financial resources too thinly by drastic upgrades in all networks. A way around this drawback would be to drastically upgrade the fixed-line network and gradually expand the wireless network. Another drawback was that Verizon would experience tremendous competition from other companies particularly in the wireless services area that offer cheaper services and products. A way around this drawback would be to promote brand recognition, network reliability, and revise pricing plans and packages bundling services and products that provide customers with value added services and products in contrast to its competitors.

Both alternatives seemed reasonable. Deciding among the two alternatives under consideration and other strategic decisions areas was now the problem Verizon Communications Inc. was faced with resolving.

REFERENCES

Anonymous (2005). "The Communications Industry: Past, Present and Future." [Online]. *http://www.sims.berkely.edu.* Accessed November 11, 2005.

Bensinger, A. (2005). "IPTV: Big Potential—but When?" [Online]. *http://www.businessweek.com.* Accessed October 11, 2005.

Bureau of Labor Statistics (2004). "Telecommunications." [Online]. *http://www.bls.gov/oco/cg/cgs020.htm.* Accessed October 18, 2005.

Business Week (2005). "Verizon Wireless' Wizard." *Business Week,* June 21, 2005, p.N1.

Consumer Federation of America (2005). "Review and Denial of the Plan for Merger." [Online]. *http://consumerfed.org.* Accessed October 24, 2005.

Coustan, D., and Franklin, C. (2005). "How Operating Systems Work." [Online]. *http://howstuffworks.com.* Accessed October 10, 2005.

Cybercollege (2004). "Mass Media Course: Cable and Satellite TV Services." [Online]. *http://www.cybercollege.com/frtv/frtv029.htm.* Accessed October 10, 2005.

FCC (2005). "Broadband." [Online]. *http://www.fcc.gov/cgb/ broadband. html#broadband.* Accessed October 15, 2005.

FCC (2005). "Statistical Trends in Telephony." [Online]. *http://www.fcc.gov/wcb/iatd/trends.html.* Accessed October 15, 2005.

FCC (2005). "Wireless Communication Service." [Online]. *http://wireless.fcc.gov/wcs/.* Accessed October 15, 2005.

Hoovers (2005). "AT&T Corp." [Online]. *http://premium.hoovers. com/subscribe/co/overview.xhtml?ID=10103.* Accessed October 24, 2005.

Hoovers (2005). "SBC Communications Inc." [Online]. *http://premium .hoovers.com/subscribe/co/overview.xhtml?ID=11379.* Accessed October 24, 2005.

Jordan, M. (2004). "Latinos Embrace Web Entertainment; Hispanics Are Outpacing General Online Population for Internet Music Usage." *Wall Street Journal,* April 14, 2004, p.B3.

Los Angeles Times (2005). "Verizon May Sell or Spin Off Directory Unit to Raise Cash." *Los Angeles Times,* December 6, 2005, p.C7.

Marks, A. (2001). "Local Carriers Bolster Service for Edge." *Crain's New York Business*, September 24, 2001, p.16.

MCI (2005). "About MCI." [Online]. *http://global.mci.com/about/company/facts.* Accessed November 24, 2005.

Mergent Online (2005). "Verizon Communications Inc. (United States)." [Online]. *http://www.mergentonline.com/compdetail.asp?company=-1&company_mer=36979&Page=business.* Accessed October 29, 2005.

Mossberg, W. (2005). "Imagine It: The Sun, Some Ancient Ruins, You With No Laptop." *Wall Street Journal*, November 10, 2005, p.B1.

RCR Wireless News (2004). "Broadband Company Offers Sprint PCS in Bundle." *RCR Wireless News*, March 22, 2004, p.1

RCR Wireless News (2005). "Verizon Plans Ark. Expansion in November." *RCR Wireless News*, August 15, 2005, p.9.

Rosenbush, S. (2005). "Telecom: To Buy or To Build." *Business Week*, February 21, 2005, p.38.

Rulison, L. (2005). "Verizon Adds Cell Sites to Increase Coverage." *Knight Ridder Tribune Business News*, September 13, 2005, p.1.

Senia, A. (2004). "Smart Spending Spells Transformation." *America's Network*, June 15, 2005, p.25.

The Insight Research Corporation (2005). "Fixed Mobile Convergence: Single Phone Solutions for Wireless, Wireline, and VoIP Convergence 2005-2010." [Online]. *http://www.insight-corp.com/reports/fixmobcon.asp.* Accessed November 2, 2005.

U.S. Business Reporter (2001). "Industry Trends." [Online]. *http://www.activemediagiude.com/smp_telecos.htm.* Accessed November 2, 2005.

Verizon Communications Inc. (2004). "Verizon Communications Annual Report 2004." [Online]. *http://www22.verizon.com.* Accessed October 10, 2005.

Wireless Review (2005). "Deals and Deployments." *Wireless Review*, August 2005, p.16.

This case was prepared by Dr. Robert J. Mockler.

Introduction

In 2005, A.G. Lafley, chairman, president, and chief executive of Procter & Gamble (P&G), told the shareholders that since 2000 sales had grown more than 40% to $57 billion and profit had more than doubled [P&G Annual Report, 2005]. P&G was a global manufacturing, distribution, and marketing company focusing on providing branded products with superior quality and value. Two billion times a day, P&G brand products touched the lives of people around the world. The company provided over 300 brands reaching consumers in about 140 countries.

P&G was formed in 1837 by William Procter and James Gamble. It all started by making and selling soaps and candles. On August 22, 1837, they formalized their business relationship by pledging $3,596.47 a piece; in early 2006, the company made approximately $68 billion annually in sales. In 1862, during the civil war, the company was awarded several contracts to supply soap and candles to the Union armies. These orders kept the factory busy day and night, building the company's reputation as soldiers returned home with their P&G products. Since then P&G had continued to grow in sales and in the introduction of new products [P&G Company Information, 2006].

Over the years P&G has acquired new product brands and companies such as Iams, Clairol, and Wella. The most recent one was on October 1, 2005, when P&G added Gillette to expand the Company's product mix to 22 brands. The Gillette Company was a manufacturer and distributor of various types of

consumer goods in the following five areas/brands: Blades and Razors, Duracell (batteries), Oral Care, Braun (small appliances), and Personal Care. The merger with Gillette made P&G a more balanced company in terms of brands, employees, and sales against its competitors over the intermediate and long-term future.

The consumer goods industry was changing drastically in the last few years leading up to 2006. Retail power was increasing and today's consumers were more confidently deciding when, where, and how to shop, and at what price to buy. There were various reasons for these changes, such as more variety of products in the market place. In addition, according to the Bureau of Economic Analysis (BEA), personal income increased to $41.1 billion and disposable personal income (DPI) increased to $35.5 billion, in December 2005 [BEA, 2006].

P&G, as illustrated in Figure 1, was structured into four organizational units: Market Development Organization (MDO), Global Business Services (GBS), Corporate Functions (CF), and Global Business Unit (GBU).

- **Market Development Organizations (MDO)** studied consumers to build local understanding which was used as a foundation for marketing campaigns. Interacting with consumers helped ensure that the company's marketing plans and campaigns were structured to change the game to favor P&G at the point of purchase.

- **Global Business Services (GBS)** provided business technology and services that drove business success and won customers and consumers. This unit provided services and solutions that enabled the company to operate efficiently around the world, collaborate effectively with business partners, and help employees to become more productive.

FIGURE 1

Procter & Gamble's Structure Division

- **Corporate Functions (CF)** worked to maintain P&G's place as the leader of the consumer good's industries. This unit ensured that the functional capability integrated into the rest of the company remained on the cutting edge of the industry.

- **Global Business Unit (GBU)** created strong brand equities, robust strategies, and ongoing innovation in products and marketing to build major global brands [P&G Corporate Information, 2006]. The main philosophy of the GBU was to think globally instead of locally. This case study will concentrate on this unit to get a better understanding of the global operations of P&G. In early 2006, P&G had 5 divisions in its GBU: Baby/Family care, Fabric/Home care, Snacks and Beverage, Health care, and Beauty/Feminine care.

With the acquisition of Gillette, P&G's product mix of billion-dollar brands was well-balanced. In early 2006, the company had 12 billion-dollar brands in Baby/Family care and Fabric/Home care, and 10 billion-dollar brands in Beauty/Feminine care and Health care [P&G Annual Report, 2005]. The effects on the Beauty/Feminine care segment due to the acquisition of Gillette and the natural fast growth nature of this segment will be further discussed in detail later in this case. It is also important to note that even though this division is named Beauty/Feminine care, most people would assume it focuses just on products for females, but in reality quite a few products in this division are geared towards men.

P&G was always creating and acquiring new products. To make the public aware of these products, the company had high advertising and marketing expenses. It also had a very good distribution channel that acted as a revenue source for the company, when it partnered with other companies to help distribute its products. Some of the threats facing P&G were the increase in commodity costs and competition in the consumer goods industry. There were a couple of strategic business decisions that P&G could focus on: it could produce more products with natural ingredients and more men's products because these were the growing trends in the industry; or it could focus on one of its product segments such as skin products for a while and then later introduce its other products. All these were possible alternatives, but the main question to be resolved was how to differentiate P&G from its competition, and so achieve a winning edge over competitors within intensely competitive, rapidly changing immediate, intermediate, and long-term time frames.

The Overall Industry and Competitive Market Analysis: The Consumer Goods Industry

Consumer goods companies were those that provided services primarily to consumers. The industry, as shown in Figure 2, was divided into durable goods and nondurable goods.

Durable Goods

Durable goods were items with a normal life expectancy of three years or more, such as furniture, household appliances, jewelry, and mobile homes. Due to the nature of these goods, the durable good industry was sensitive to business cycles. Business cycles were predictable long-term patterns of alternating periods of economic growth (recovery) and decline

FIGURE 2

The Consumer Goods Industry

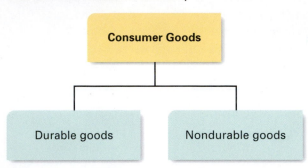

(recession), characterized by changing employment, industrial productivity, and interest rates [Webster's Dictionary, 2006].

Nondurable Goods

On the other hand, nondurable goods were items that generally lasted for only a short time (three years or less), such as petroleum, beverages, apparel, tobacco, pharmaceutical, and beauty/feminine care products. Nondurable goods were not responsive to any economic conditions such as interest rate, inflation, business cycle, and the like. They were not responsive, because some of these products met the needs of people. Consumers had to buy these products such as food, medicine, and apparel to survive. They also bought these goods when they needed them because of their short life span; they did not want to buy a lot in bulk and then would not be able to use them. In the United States, the Bureau of Economic Analysis (BEA) released reports stating that nondurable goods manufacturing turned up in 2004—increasing 2.7% after decreasing 1.2% in 2003 [BEA, 2006].

Industry and Market Segment: The Nondurable Goods Industry

As mentioned earlier, examples of nondurable goods were petroleum, beverages, apparel, tobacco, pharmaceutical, and beauty/feminine care products, as shown in Figure 3.

Petroleum

Petroleum products were divided into three major categories: fuels, finished nonfuel products, and feedstocks.

- **Fuels**—These are products such as motor gasoline and distillate fuel oil (diesel fuel).

- **Finished Nonfuel Products**—These are products such as solvents and lubricating oils.

- **Feedstocks**—These products were for the petrochemical industry such as naphtha and various refinery gases.

Petroleum products were used by everyone: from gasoline used to fuel cars to heating oil used to warm homes. The demands for these products varied dramatically, but the greatest demand was for products in the fuels category, especially motor gasoline [EIS, 2005]. In the United States (U.S.), petroleum products contributed about 40.2% of the energy used, more than that of natural gas, coal, nuclear, and hydroelectric. It was estimated that by 2025, the U.S. would increase its consumption of these products to 27.9 million barrels per day [EIS, 2005].

FIGURE 3

The Nondurable Goods Industry

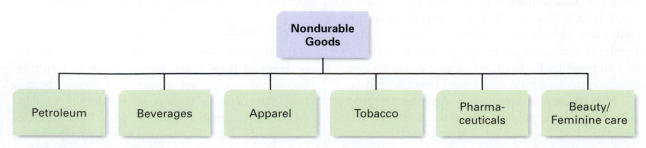

Beverages

This industry group included alcoholic beverage and non-alcoholic beverage products.

- **Alcoholic Beverage**—These were drinks that contained ethanol. There were two types, those that included low-alcohol-content, which were produced by the fermenting of sugar of starch-containing products, and high-alcohol-content beverages produced by distillation of the low-alcohol-content beverage [Wikipedia, 2006]. Examples of these products were beer, wine, ale, and cider.

- **Non-alcoholic Beverage**—These were drinks that did not contain ethanol, such as coffee, juice, tea, and soda water.

Apparel

This industry group included products for men, women, children, and infants. The products consisted of both inner and outerwear clothes.

Tobacco

This industry group included products that were made from tobacco, which was a plant that grew in a wide range of soil and climate conditions. Its nonedible leaf was dried and used to manufacture products such as cigarettes, pipe tobacco, cigars, chewing tobacco, and snuff. Companies who produced these products constantly had problems because of the health risk associated with using their products. According to the World Health Organization (WHO), tobacco killed more than two and a half million people prematurely every year.

Pharmaceuticals

This industry group included companies that researched, developed, produced, and sold chemical or biological substances for medical or veterinary use. These substances included prescription, generic, and OTC drugs; vitamins and nutritional supplements; drug delivery systems; and diagnostic substances [Hoovers, 2006].

The Beauty/Feminine care industry, the focus of this study, is discussed in detail in the following section.

Industry and Competitive Market: Beauty/Feminine Care Goods

The desire to be beautiful is as old as civilization. This desire created an industry which generates $160 billion a year. Americans spent more each year on beauty than they did on education [Economist, 2006]. The industry, as shown in Figure 4, encompassed some of the following products: hair products, skin products, feminine products, fine fragrances, cosmetics, and personal cleansing.

Companies that produced beauty/feminine care products were influenced by fashion, seasons, and culture. The latest trends to affect this market were the movement by consumers towards natural products and the increased interest by men to look clean and well groomed, creating a large emerging men's market. From 2003 to 2008, as shown in Figure 5, the sale of most beauty/feminine care products, such as hair products, cosmetics, and skin products increased. Each of these beauty/feminine care products are further described in the following section.

FIGURE 4

Beauty/Feminine Care Goods Segment

FIGURE 5

Projected U.S. Retail Dollar Sales of Ethnic Specific Cosmetics (in millions), 2003–2008

Year	Hair Care $	Hair Care % Change	Cosmetics $	Cosmetics % Change	Skin Care $	Skin Care % Change	Total $
2003	$1,030	−4.0%	$367	5.6%	$118	3.3%	$1,515
2004	$1,009	−2.0%	$387	5.5%	$121	2.5%	$1,517
2005	$1,019	1.0%	$410	6.0%	$124	2.5%	$1,553
2006	$1,035	1.5%	$437	6.5%	$129	4.0%	$1,601
2007	$1,055	2.0%	$463	6.0%	$132	2.3%	$1,650
2008	$1,030	2.5%	$493	6.5%	$137	3.6%	$1,712

Source: Packaged Facts (2005). "The U.S. Market for Ethnic HBC Products." [Online]. http://cpprod.stjohns.edu/cp/tag.b9b5fA3031868bbe.render. userLayoutRootNode.uP?uP_root=root&uP_sparam=activeTab&activeTab=U11l1S39&uP_tparam=frm&frm=fram. Accessed January 25, 2006.

How Industry Segment Works: The Business Process Model

The beauty/feminine care industry was comprised of various segments as shown in Figure 6. This industry included companies that manufactured goods that were used to fulfill the needs of consumers.

The products these companies produced included hair products, skin products, feminine products, fine fragrances, cosmetics, and personal cleansing products.

Consumers used each product for their own personal reasons, but the main purposes were to make people look beautiful and feel clean. The consumers for these products included both females and males from all age groups. Even though it was called beauty/feminine care, males were actually a large part of the consumer base because they used a lot of beauty products. Consumers also included people from different ethnic groups, marital status, and also low income consumers.

Consumers seemed to be more confident about what they wanted and this played a major role in determining what products were manufactured. In early 2006, a national survey of consumer goods executives showed that a majority of respondents believed that their organizations were well on the way to becoming demand-driven. Demand-driven enterprises were defined as those that not only identified real-time changes in demand, but were also organizationally prepared to profitably respond to these opportunities. The benefits of becoming more demand-driven were that the companies had 15% less inventory, a 17% better perfect-order performance,

and a 35% shorter cash-to-cash cycle time [Findarticles, 2006]. So as consumers changed, the companies also changed in order to remain in the competitions with their competitors.

These products were produced in factories all over the world with raw materials ranging from materials as simple as water to chemicals such as stearic acid and sodium hydroxide. These materials were mixed in unique ways to make each product. Regardless of the raw materials or procedures used to make them, each product had to meet regulatory standards. In the United States of America, an example of such a regulatory body was the U.S. Food and Drug Administration (FDA). These standards varied by country, and they helped to ensure that these products were safe enough to be used by the consumers.

After production, these products were packaged and distributed to consumers through various distribution channels such as distribution companies, individual stores, and chain store outlets. Packaging was another important factor in selling products, for example, male products had to be packaged in a different way to attract them. Most times, the packets for men's products were normally dark colored to make the products look more masculine. Distribution companies were companies that bought and sold large amounts of products to various retailers, which then sold to the consumers. Individual stores were stores that were owned by companies, and these companies sold their products directly to the consumers from these stores. While the chain store outlets included some multinational companies such as

FIGURE 6

FIGURE 6

Beauty/Feminine Care Goods Industry

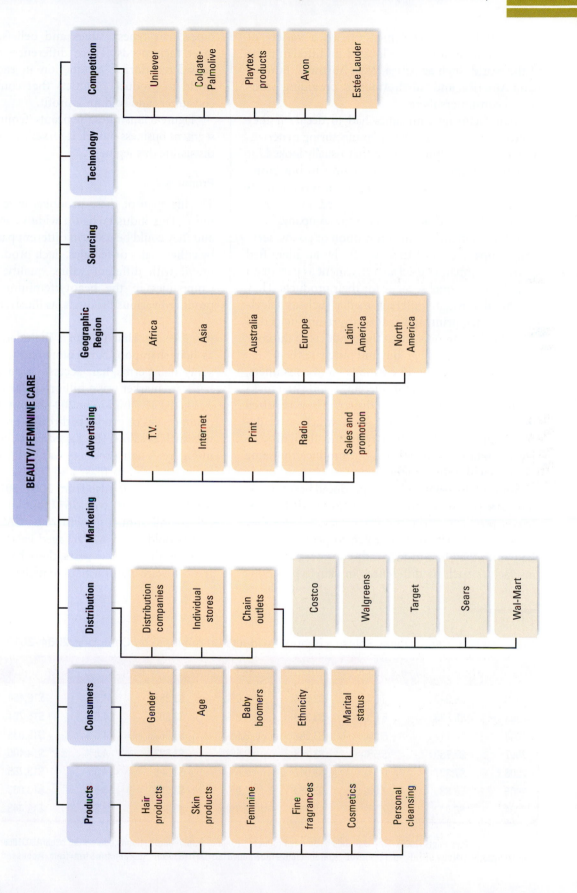

Costco and Wal-Mart, which carried a variety of products, these stores were located in different parts of the world, such as Africa, Asia, Australia, Europe, Latin America, and North America, providing products to consumers there.

Manufacturing companies had to decide if they wanted to make or buy their manufacturing materials. If they decided to buy any item they usually looked for the cheapest and most efficient source to buy from. This process was called Sourcing and it was a process that had to be continuously reviewed in order to maintain the best deals that suited the company.

Advertisement was the promotion of goods, services, companies and ideas, usually by an identified sponsor. Companies used advertisement as part of an overall promotional strategy for their products. They advertised through different media such as television, Internet, print, and radio. Advertising helped to bring some awareness about the products to the consumers, so they could go out and purchase them.

Due to the variety in customers and consumers, technology played a major role in this industry, making it a capital intensive industry. They required highly mechanized assembly lines which were designed for long production runs and flexibility, so that it could be easily changed to produce the same products with minor alterations.

Some of the companies that produced beauty/feminine care products were Unilever, Colgate-Palmolive, Playtex products, Avon, and Estée Lauder. Since they produced products that appealed to people all over the world, they had to take into consideration various factors such as differences in skin types, body types, hair types, values and beliefs, to efficiently meet their needs. These differences were seriously considered during production in each part of the world to produce products that could be used by consumers and sold for a profit.

Figure 6 illustrates the beauty/feminine care goods segment business model. It serves as the framework in discussing this segment.

Products

The life span of these products were three years or more. This industry had a wide variety of products and they could be used on different parts of the body, by either males or females. Each product had its own brand with different value, quality, and quantity. Companies in the beauty/feminine care segment produced various products, as illustrated in Figure 6.

Hair Products Hair products included products such as hair shampoo, hair color, hair conditioner, hair spray, hair perms, hair accessories, and the like. The hair care market was a billion dollar market, with an estimated $7.6 billion in 2004 from retail market, excluding sales of products through professional channels such as salons [Packaged Facts, 2005]. As shown in Figure 7, hair products was estimated to top $3.5 billion at retail in mass and prestige channels combined, as of 2010. Also from 2004–2010, the category would gain 22.9%, or $657 million. The resultant compound annual growth rate (CAGR) for the six years would be 3.5% [Packaged Facts, 2005].

Over the past few years, there has been a growing trend toward natural hair remedies and treatments.

FIGURE 7

Projected U.S. Retail Dollar Sales of Beauty Products (in millions) by Category, 2004–2010

Year	Skincare	% Change	Haircare	% Change	Make-up	% Change	Total	% Change
2010	$8,949	5.0%	$3,524	4.0%	$3,981	4.5%	$16,454	4.7%
2009	$8,523	5.0%	$3,389	4.0%	$3,809	4.0%	$15,721	4.5%
2008	$8,117	5.0%	$3,258	3.5%	$3,663	4.0%	$15,038	4.4%
2007	$7,730	5.5%	$3,148	3.5%	$3,522	4.0%	$14,400	4.7%
2006	$7,327	6.5%	$3,042	3.0%	$3,386	4.0%	$13,755	5.1%
2005	$6,880	7.0%	$2,953	3.0%	$3,256	3.5%	$13,089	5.2%
2004	$6,430	7.3%	$2,867	2.8%	$3,146	3.9%	$12,443	5.4%

Source: Packaged Facts (2005). "The U.S. Sale of Beauty Products." [Online]. http://cpprod.stjohns.edu/cp/tag.b9b8fA3031868bbe.render. userLayoutRootNode.uP?uP_root=root&uP_sparam=activeTab&activeTab=U11I1S39&uP_tparam=frm&frm=fram. Accessed January 25, 2006.

Consumers were more aware of, and growing wary of chemicals that could be in some mass market hair treatment products. The other trend mentioned above about men's interest was also obvious in the hair care industry, because there was an increased effort by men to keep their hair well groomed.

The keys to success included several factors. The hair products had to be competitively priced and affordable. There had to be a wide selection of these products available to the consumers. The quality of these products had to be considered during production to maintain the company's brand quality reputation. Brand recognition was also an important factor because consumers had to feel as if they could relate with the brand and its attributes. Location and distribution were also important to ensure that these products had a mass market presence. They also had to frequently introduce new products. The packaging for the products had to be designed to attract the right consumer.

Skin Products Skin products were further divided into two product classes: mass market products, which were generally lower priced and sold in such mass outlets as drugstores, discount stores, and food stores, and prestige products, which were higher priced, usually packed stylishly and contained special ingredients, and often sold in department and specialty stores. Skin products included moisturizers, cleansers, gels, conditioners, toners, and the like. Factors that affected this segment of this industry were the aging U.S. consumers and technological development; mass market went upscale, and new products were introduced into the market. As illustrated in Figure 7, it was estimated that the sale of skin care products would reach $8.9 billion in combined mass and prestige channels in 2010. This segment would grow a total of 39.2%, or $2.5 billion, during 2004–2010. That translated into a highly desirable 5.7% CAGR over the six years [Packaged Facts, 2005]

The way people looked after their skin was often dictated by the degree of affluence. In rural parts of Africa, men and women still made crude bars of soap using crude potassium hydroxide produced from burnt tree bark. Many used coconut oil as a moisturizer. In addition many people tried to lighten their skin by using skin creams containing certain drugs. Steroid creams were freely available for sale in some places, as were creams containing skin-lightening ingredients called hydroquinone. In the developed world, these ingredients could legally be incorporated in low concentrations in well-formulated cosmetic preparations [P&G Skin Care, 2003].

The keys to success included several factors. The skin products had to be competitively priced and affordable. There had to be a wide selection of these products available to the consumers. The quality of these products had to be considered during production to maintain the company's brand quality reputation. Brand recognition was also an important factor because consumers had to feel like they could relate with the brand and its attributes. Location and distribution were also important to ensure that these products had a mass market presence. They also had to develop these products according to fashion trends. The packaging for the products had to be designed to attract the right consumer.

Feminine Products Feminine products were the only products under the beauty/feminine care segment that were used only by females. They included products such as sanitary pads, tampons, heat patches, and disposable cups. In early 2006, the trends were that consumers wanted products that were more comfortable and easy to use. Some of these products affected the health of the consumers, so companies who produced them had to warn consumers about the possible side effects from using these products. An example of a product that came with such warnings was tampons. A possible side effect from using these products was Toxic Shock Syndrome, which was caused by a particularly virulent and penicillin resistant strain of bacterium.

The keys to success included several factors. There had to be a wide variety of these products available to the consumers. These products had to be competitively priced and affordable. The quality of these products had to be considered during production to maintain the company's brand quality reputation. Brand recognition was also an important factor. Location and distribution were also important to ensure these products had a mass market presence. The packaging for the products had to be designed to attract the right consumer.

Fine Fragrances The fragrance industry was a growing industry with companies like Estée Lauder, Calvin Klein, Tommy Hilfiger, and the like. It was a billion dollar industry and it was constantly changing due to the trends in fashion. In early 2006, many people enjoyed using these fragrances so they could smell clean and attractive.

The keys to success included several factors. Quality of these products had to be maintained to retain the company's brand quality reputation. These products had to be competitively priced. Brand recognition was also important. Location and distribution were also important to ensure these products had a mass market presence. They also had to develop these products according to fashion trends. The packaging for the products had to be designed to attract the right consumer.

Cosmetics The cosmetic industry was constantly changing according to its customer's need, but in early 2006, the growth in the industry was tremendous. Cosmetics have a temporary benefit and effect, so they have to be reapplied on a regular basis depending on the particular customer. This temporariness of the product made the market a continuous and strong one, because customers had to constantly go out and purchase new products. There were various products in this industry, which included concealers, powders, blushers, and the like, which were for the skin, and those for the lips, which included lip gloss, lip sticks, lip liner, and the like. It was estimated, as shown in Figure 7, that cosmetics (for face, lips, and eyes) should be worth just under $4 billion in 2010, in mass and prestige channels combined. From 2004–2010, this segment would expand by 26.5%, or $835 million. Cosmetic's CAGR for the same span was therefore calculated at 4% [Packaged Facts, 2005].

The cosmetic industry was also divided based on the customer's skin type. An example was the ethnic color-specific cosmetics, which were the best in this category and were predicted, as shown in Figure 5, to push to $493 million at retail by 2008.

The keys to success included several factors. The cosmetics products had to be competitively priced. Brand recognition was also an important factor because consumers needed to feel like they could relate with the brand and its attributes. Availability of a variety of these products was required to suit all consumers' needs. Location was also important, so that the companies manufacturing these products could maintain their brand quality reputation. New products had to be frequently developed according to fashion trends. Location and distribution were also important to ensure these products had a mass market

presence. The packaging for the products had to be designed to attract the right consumer.

Personal Cleansing The personal cleansing products included products such as soap bars, body wash, body scrubbers, and the like. This segment of the industry had witnessed tough times as it sales declined by 11.9% from 2000 to 2004. This decline was largely due to consumers substituting bath products with higher multi-benefit skin care products at comparatively lower prices. The sales of personal cleansing products were projected to continue to decline by $210.3 million, from an estimated $2.4 billion in 2005, to $2.2 billion in 2010 [Packaged Facts, 2005].

The keys to success included several factors. The personal cleansing products had to be competitively priced. Availability of a variety of these products was required to suit all consumers' need. Brand recognition was also an important factor. Location and distribution were also important to ensure these products had a mass market presence. The manufacturing companies had to maintain their brand quality reputations. They had to also frequently introduce new products. The packaging for the products had to be designed to attract the right consumer.

Consumers

Consumers were those that ultimately used the products. Consumers made better purchasing decisions when they were aware of the products in the market. When they knew about the products, such as their price and quality, they had the choice to make a better purchase. The common mistakes that some consumers made were instinctive purchases and ignorantly following trends that did not necessarily affect them. There was a wide variety of products in the market place so most consumers could easily get the products they wanted. Consumers for this industry's products could be segmented into gender, age, ethnicity, marital status, and low income consumers.

Gender While most people thought that beauty/feminine care products were just for females, this was not the case because most of the products in this division were also used by males. Both groups needed these products to meet their basic needs such as cleansing products to keep their bodies clean. For many years, women represented a larger part of the customer and consumer base because of several factors, such as women were usually the ones that bought products for their homes and families, and some segments of this industry, like the feminine care, manufactured products that could be used only by women. But in early 2005, there was a trend for men to beautify themselves. This trend made manufacturing companies increase their production of men's products.

The keys to success included several factors. The beauty/feminine care products had to be competitively priced and affordable. There had to be a wide selection of these products available to the consumers, distributed through various channels. The quality and value had to be high for each of the products. Brand loyalty was also an important factor because some consumers had always used these products and wanted to continue using them. Location and distribution of these products were also important because these products had to have mass market presence. The packaging for the products had to be designed to attract the right consumer. Consumers had to have promotions targeted at them. An example of a promotion that attracted male consumers was to get a popular male celebrity to promote products.

Age Age was another major factor that companies considered when analyzing the market. What was the age for their consumers? The answer was everyone, from infants to senior citizens. Everyone used beauty/feminine products. The manufacturing companies addressed each age group differently. For example, the baby boomers age group, which included consumers who were born during the period of an increased birth rate when economic prosperity arose in many countries following World War II. This term was commonly used to refer to the generation which demographic popularizers had identified as people who were born between 1946 and 1964 [Wikipedia, 2006].

In the United States the baby boomers made up the lion's share of the cultural, political, academic leadership and industrial class. They therefore were a group of people that had significant influence on the beauty/feminine care products. An example of their effect on a particular product can be seen using the hair care products. The number of men in the 55–64 age group, which represented half of the baby boomers, was expected to grow from 11.39 million in 1999 to 17.39 million in 2010, thus increasing

as percentage of the total male population from 8.3% to 11.5% [Packaged Facts, 2005]. As men grew older they were faced with issues like loss and dryness of hair. This forced them to spend more on hair care products. Companies were aware of this trend and were willing to produce these products because of the increase in that particular target age group.

The keys to success included several factors. The beauty/feminine care products had to be competitively priced and affordable. There also had to be a wide selection of these products available to the consumers. Brand recognition was also an important factor because consumers needed to feel like they could relate with the brand and its attributes. Location and distribution of these products were also important because these products had to have mass market presence. These products had to have a strong brand image. Brand loyalty was also an important factor because some consumers had always used their products.

Ethnicity An ethnic group was a human population whose members identified with each other, usually on the basis of a common genealogy or ancestry. Ethnic groups were also usually united by common cultural, linguistic, religious, and behavioral practices [Wikipedia, 2006].

Each ethnic group had distinct tastes looks, and needs. It was important that the companies manufactured products that were suitable for them to use. To meet these different ethnic needs, the manufacturers had to perform in-depth research into each group. For example, in the United States, the population of the African American and Hispanics, which were big buyers of the hair care products, was very high. The Hispanics were estimated to increase from 12.6% in 2000 to 15.5% in 2010, while the African Americans would increase from 12.7% in 1999 to 13.1% in 2010. On the other hand, non-Hispanic whites were estimated to decline from 69.4% to 50.1% of the total population during 2000–2050 [U.S. Census Bureau, 2004].

Although ethnicity was an issue for manufacturers in the United States, it was not necessarily an issue for manufacturers in countries with one main ethnic group like Ghana. Consumers in countries like Ghana generally had the same hair type, skin types, beliefs, and the like. These differences in countries were issues that manufacturing companies had to take into consideration before manufacturing and promoting any products.

The keys to success included several factors. The beauty/feminine care products had to be competitively priced and affordable. There also had to be a wide selection of these products, tailored to meet the needs of each ethnic group. The products had to be of high quality and value. Brand loyalty was also an important factor because some consumers had always used their products. Brand recognition was also an important factor because consumers needed to feel like they could relate with the brand and its attributes. They also always had to be the development of products according to fashion trends.

Marital Status In 1998, 110.6 million adults (56% of the adult population) were married and living with their spouses [USCB, 1998]. This meant that there was a bigger part of the adult population which was buying things in bulk because they had to buy for the family. If 56% of the adult population was married, it meant that the remaining 44% were single. Single consumers had more disposable income, because they had more to spend on themselves. These consumers also spent a lot on beauty care products, because they wanted to keep themselves looking good and probably attract people to them.

The keys to success included several factors. The beauty/feminine care products had to be competitively priced and affordable. There also had to be a wide selection of these products available to the consumers that were tailored to meet their needs. The products had to be of high quality and value. Brand recognition was also an important factor because consumers needed to feel like they could relate with the brand and its attributes. The products had to be distributed properly to ensure that there was mass market presence. Brand loyalty was also an important factor because some consumers had always used their products.

Low Income Consumers The indebtedness of American households grew substantially in the last decade. The outstanding balance of all consumer credit, excluding mortgage debt, was $800 billion at the end of 1990 [Wikipedia, 2006]. This group of consumers was a very large part of the beauty/feminine care industry. Companies in this industry had to manufacture products that would be affordable for them. Some of the methods used to reduce the costs of the

products were reducing the size of the package and reducing the quality of the packaging.

The keys to success included several factors. The beauty/feminine care products had to have a wide selection of these products available to the consumers that were tailored to meet their needs. Brand recognition was also an important factor because consumers needed to feel like they could relate with the brand and its attributes. Brand loyalty was also an important factor because some consumers had always used their products. There also had to be mass market presence. The packaging for the products had to be designed to attract the right consumer.

Distribution

Distribution was the act of dispersing products from the point of production to the final consumer. Most distribution channels had a designated sales force which was in charge of selling and promoting their products. The sales force included individuals who were recruited to move from place to place encouraging customers to purchase their products. These individuals were encouraged to do a better job by offering them incentives such as days off and monetary incentives. Companies had various channels of distributions, such as distribution companies, individual stores, and chain store outlets.

Distribution Companies These were the middlemen that purchased directly from the manufacturers and resold them to the retailers for a profit. They were experts at moving things into the market. To do this most of them generally had a good transportation system. These companies normally bought in bulk to control their inventory and increase their profits.

The keys to success included several factors. Distribution companies had to offer competitive pricing. Prices they set were not only competitive with that of their competitors but also that of the manufacturing companies, which sold directly to the outlet store chains. Distributors had to also establish good relationships with the store managers to get good product display and shelf space. Some companies also incorporated supply chain technology with their retailers to ensure proper distribution of their products. Distribution companies had to recruit good employees and offer incentives for them to work hard.

Individual Stores Individual stores were stores that were owned by companies, where consumers could walk into and purchase the product they wanted. An advantage of this kind of service provided by companies was that they were able to remove the extra price allocated by the middlemen. It also gave them a chance to relate with their consumers and learn what they liked and disliked about their products, especially the male consumers who were generally not thought to purchase beauty/feminine care products. They also learned trends amongst their consumers and were able to educate them on their products. Also the presence of these stores in different communities helped to build a household name amongst the consumers.

The keys to success included several factors. Individual stores had to competitively price their products. Employees in these stores had to be willing to interact with customers to get their opinion about the products. The companies had to offer incentives to their employees to do a good job. These stores had to have a variety of products. Brand recognition was also an important factor. These stores had to be located in prime locations to attract more consumers.

Chain Store Outlets All over the world, the numbers of chain outlets were growing. In Taiwan the total number of chain store outlets grew 11% to 62,637 in 2004, according to a survey released in late April by the Taiwan Chain Store and Franchise Association. These were stores that sold a variety of products. In the United States, a large percentage of the population purchased beauty/feminine products in these types of stores. There were different types of chain stores outlets; some were specialized chain stores, where they sold a wide variety of products and offered very good customer service. Another kind of store was the discount store that offered a limited variety of products and did not spend too much of its resources on customer services. These stores had to pay special attention to their customers, especially the male customers, by offering sales and promotions on products that they thought these customers might be interested in. Some of these chain store outlets were Costco, Walgreens, Target, Sears, and Wal-Mart.

Costco. Costco was the largest membership warehouse club chain in the world. It was a discount chain store with about 456 locations worldwide. In 2004, the company's store sales rose 13% to $47.1 billion and its main competitor was Wal-Mart-owned Sam's Club [Wikipedia, 2006]. Since it was a discount chain store, it sold very high volume products for low prices, by keeping overhead low and using idiosyncratic inventory practices. It also bulk-packaged its products and sold primarily to large families and small businesses [Costco Services, 2006].

Walgreens. Walgreens was the nation's leading drugstore chain. It was a specialized chain store with about 4,000 locations. In January of 2005, its sales increased by 11.8% [Walgreens Corporate News, 2006]. It provided a wide array of products and was totally geared to providing its customers with complete satisfaction.

Target. Target was an upscale discounter that provided high-quality, on-trend merchandise at attractive prices in clean, spacious and guest-friendly stores. In addition, Target operated an online business, Target.com [Target Corporate News, 2006]. It had 1397 locations and had revenue of $15.2 billion for the last quarter of 2005.

Sears. Sears was a specialty outlet stores that provided a wide variety of services to its customers. It had revenues in 2004 of $36.1 billion. It had more than 2,400 Sears-branded and affiliated stores in the U.S. and Canada, which included approximately 870 full-line and 1,100 specialty stores in the U.S. Sears also offered its services through sears.com, land-send.com, and specialty catalogs [Aboutsears, 2006]. It was also the only retailer where consumers could find each of the Kenmore, Craftsman, DieHard, and Lands' End brands together.

Wal-Mart. Wal-Mart was a discount store outlet that sold to more than 138 million customers worldwide each week, with more than 1,500 locations. The company was growing constantly and had over $56 billion in international sales in 2005. It operated like Costco, which is described above [Wikipedia, 2006].

The keys to success included several factors. Chain store outlets had to be competitively priced. The stores had a variety of products for each consumer. They offered sales and promotions that attracted more consumers. They also provided free samples and trials for their consumers. The companies also provided websites that made it more convenient for consumers to shop from home. These stores were located in prime locations to attract more consumers. These stores had to recruit and maintain quality employees. Also they had to offer incentives to their employees. Manufacturers had to build strong relationships with these retailers to get shelf space, store promotion, and product display area.

Advertising

Advertising was used in the beauty/feminine care product industry to make consumers aware of the products that were available. It was done through various forms, but companies had to be careful in choosing the form that would be suitable to convey their message to their target consumers. Advertising could be done through television, Internet, print, radio, and sales and promotions.

Television Television was a very good form for advertising products because it had a large audience. Companies advertised through different methods; some would produce commercials that focused on their products while some would introduced their products in shows that they thought their target audience regularly watched. An example of a show that companies spent a lot of money on advertising was the Super Bowl in 2006. Some companies paid $3.5 million for 30 seconds to advertise their products. They believed that advertising their product during the show would help create awareness of their product.

The keys to success included several factors. Television stations had to be competitively priced. Manufacturers had to choose the appropriate channels and shows to advertise on. To do this successfully, they had to choose the audience they wanted to target for each product. The rating of the shows was an important factor that most companies considered before advertising on them. Sales promotions, coupons, and free products were good ways to attract the consumers.

Internet Globally, the Internet was quickly becoming the most popular form of advertising because it was accessible to potential customers all over the world. The Internet affected many aspects of consumers' lives: the way they worked, played, and communicated, etc. The keys to success included several factors. Websites had to be competitively priced. Manufacturers had to choose the appropriate sites to advertise on. To do this successfully, they had to choose the audience they wanted to target for each product. Sales promotions, coupons, and free products were good ways to attract the consumers.

Print This advertisement included those in the newspapers, magazines, and the like. In early 2006, companies were gradually reducing the use of newspaper for advertising. They were moving to other forms of advertising, because in the United States, studies showed that people were reading less. These made some companies change from this form of advertising to others so that they were sure their products' information would reach their target audience. The keys to success included several factors. Printing media had to be competitively priced. Manufacturers had to choose the appropriate books, magazines, and newspapers to advertise in. To do this successfully, they had to choose the audience they wanted to target for each product. Sales promotions, coupons, and free products were good ways to attract the consumers.

Radio Radio was another effective form of advertising. There were no visuals in radio advertising, just vocal information of the products. It had a large audience, especially people listening at work or in their cars. In 2005, the XM satellite radio was launched, and it offered a variety of channels including commercial free music channels. These features would encourage more people to listen to radio, creating a better channel for advertisement. The keys to success included several factors. Radio stations had to be competitively priced. Manufacturers had to choose the appropriate channels and shows to advertise on. To do this successfully, they had to choose the audience they wanted to target for each product. The rating of the shows was an important factor that most companies considered before advertising on them. Sales promotions, coupons, and free products were good ways to attract the consumers.

Advertisement was important to this industry. It helped educate the consumers on their products. It made them aware of the products, informed them of the uses, and encouraged them to go out and purchase them.

Sales and Promotions Various sales and promotions such as free samples, coupons, and discounts were used by companies to attract more consumers. These methods were especially effective for new products. Sales and promotions for these products normally encouraged the consumers to take the risk and try the new product. Chain store outlets also used these methods to attract more customers. The keys to success included several factors. Customers and consumers had to be aware of the sales and promotions. They also had to be easy to use and be available to the consumers and customers.

Geographic Region

A geographic region was a term used to refer to a separated place on earth, such as Africa, Asia, Australia, Europe, Latin America, and North America.

- **Africa**—Africa was a continent with countries like Botswana, which had a population of 1,640,115 people, and Nigeria, which had a population of 128,771,988 as of January, 2006 [CIA, 2006].

- **Asia**—Asia was a continent with countries like China, which had a population of 1,306,313,812 people, and Taiwan, with a population of 22,894,384 people [CIA, 2006].

- **Australia**—Australia was the sixth largest country in the whole world with about 20,090,437 people [CIA, 2006]. It was known for its uniqueness.

- **Europe**—Europe was a continent with countries like the United Kingdom, which had a population of about 60,441,457 people, and Spain, with about 40,341,462 people [CIA, 2006].

- **South America**—South America included countries like Brazil, with about 186,112,794 people, and Colombia, with about 42,954,279 people [CIA, 2006].

- **North America**—This was a continent with countries like the United States of America, which had a population of about 295,734,134 people, and Canada, with about 32,805,041 people [CIA, 2006].

These geographical regions had people who consumed beauty/feminine care products. So they were important for the existence of this industry. The keys to success included several factors. They had to be tailored to meet the needs of the consumers; for example, in Asia, manufacturers had to produce hair products that were suitable for straight, not curly hair. Brand recognition was also an important factor because consumers needed to feel like they could relate with the brand and its attributes. Products had to be competitively priced, and companies had to have a mass market presence in these regions.

Sourcing

Sourcing was a systematic procurement process that continuously improved and re-evaluated the purchasing activities of a company. It was a form of supply chain management. It involved various processes, such as formally selecting a vendor to supply a particular product or service that was routinely purchased by the company. This process included the definition of product and service requirements, identification of qualified suppliers, negotiation of pricing, service, delivery and payment terms, and supplier selection. Most times, the end result of the sourcing process was a negotiated contract with a preferred supplier [ICG Commerce, 2006].

Some manufacturing companies chose to outsource some or all of their processes to other companies in the same country they operated in or in another country. There were various reasons why companies outsourced; some did it because it was cheaper, while others did it because they lacked the expertise required to make their products better.

The keys to success included several factors. Sources who wanted to sell to these manufacturing companies had to make their products competitively priced. They also had to be conveniently located to the manufacturing companies. Lastly they had to have a good transportation system to move these materials to and from the manufacturing company.

Technology

The beauty/feminine care industry was a capital intensive industry. The companies that manufactured these products required highly mechanized assembly lines which were designed for long production runs and flexibility. These companies constantly manufactured the same products over and over again, so they had to have machines that could run for long periods of time. Also, due to the differences in their consumers, products sometimes had to be manufactured with some differences. An example was in the production of moisturizers; some consumers had oily skin while some had dry skin. During production, the companies had to make slight changes in the ingredients for their products to suit these differences in their consumers. In order to achieve this, the machineries used had to be designed in a way that it allowed such changes and flexibility.

The Internet made business easier for some companies because it provided a fast and efficient way for them to communicate amongst themselves, with their customers, suppliers, and distributors. It also gave them the opportunity to research and get more information that helped to make their products better. With the introduction of the Internet, companies created and designed websites that helped their consumers and customers learn more about them; it gave them an opportunity to purchase things from the companies without leaving their homes.

The keys to success included several factors. The companies had to use high quality machines and technology systems, so they continuously had problems with them. These equipments also had to be flexible in their functions so they could be used to manufacture different products. They also had to be competitively priced so that it was affordable by these companies. The websites had to be designed properly so that they were easy to use.

Competition

Competition in the beauty/feminine product was based on price, brand quality reputation, mass market presence, variety of products, brand recognition, and introduction of new products. Some of the companies in the beauty/feminine care industry were Unilever, Colgate-Palmolive, Playtex products, Avon, and Estée Lauder.

Unilever Unilever was founded in 1930 in England; it was an international manufacturer of leading brands in foods, home care and personal care, such as Axe, Dove, Lux, Pond's, Rexona, Sunsilk, and Vaseline. Every day 150 million people in over 150 countries used one of its products. Unilever believed that most of its brands gave the benefits of feeling and looking good. The trends the company addressed in early 2006 were aging populations, urbanization, changing diets, and lifestyles [Unilever Annual Report, 2005].

In regard to hair products, Unilever was strong in brand quality reputation, price competition, mass market presence, variety of products, and brand recognition. It was moderately competitive in frequently introducing new products. In regard to skin product, Unilever was also strong in all keys to success except for development of products according to fashion trends, in which the company was only moderately competitive. Lastly, in regard to the company's cleansing product, it was strong in all keys to success except for frequent new product introduction, in which the company was only moderately competitive. In early 2006, Unilever did not manufacture feminine products, fine fragrances, and cosmetics.

In regard to gender and age, it was strong in all keys to success. In regard to ethnicity, Unilever was strong in all keys to success except for manufacturing products that were tailored to meet their needs and developing products according to trends, in which the company was a weak competitor. In regard to marital status, it was strong in all keys to success except for manufacturing products that were tailored to meet their needs, high quality and value, and mass market presence, in which the company was only moderately competitive. In regard to low income consumers, Unilever was strong in all keys to success except for manufacturing products that were tailored to meet their needs, in which it was only moderately competitive.

In regard to distribution companies, it was moderately competitive in all keys to success except for competitive price, in which the company was strongly competitive. In regard to chain store outlets, Unilever was strong in all keys to success except for recruiting quality employees, offering them incentives, and developing strong relationship with the store managers, in which it was only moderately competitive.

In regard to television advertising, the company was strong in all keys to success. The company was strong in all keys to success relating to Internet advertising. In regard to print advertising, the company was strong in all keys to success. The company was strong in all keys to success relating to radio advertising. In regard to geographic regions, it was strong in all keys to success except for mass market presence, in which it was moderately competitive. And in regard to sourcing, operations, and technology, Unilever was strong in all keys to success.

Colgate-Palmolive Colgate-Palmolive was a $10.6 billion global consumer goods company, operating in more than 200 countries, with approximately 70% of its sales coming from international operations. The Company focused on strong global brands in its core businesses—Oral Care, Personal Care, Home Care, and Pet Nutrition. Its worldwide sales were up 5.5% on unit volume growth of 4.5%, on top of 9.0% volume growth in the 2005 [Colgate Corporate News, 2006]. Worldwide it sold more than 40 different products and encouraged customers to try products by offering an array of sales promotions, such as coupons, free products, and discounts. Its beauty/feminine care products were Irish Spring, Palmolive, Softsoaps, Colgate, Protex, Speed Sticks, and Lady Sticks.

In regard to skin products, Colgate-Palmolive was strong in brand recognition, variety of products, brand quality reputation, price competition, and mass market presence. The company was moderately competitive in the development of products according to fashion trends. Also in regard to the company's cleansing products, Colgate-Palmolive was strong in all keys to success except for frequent new product introduction, in which the company was only moderately competitive. In early 2006, Colgate-Palmolive did not manufacture hair products, feminine products, fine fragrances, and cosmetics.

In regard to gender, age, and marital status, it was strong it all keys to success. In regard to ethnicity, the company was strong in all keys to success except for manufacturing products that were tailored to meet their needs and development of products according to fashion trends, in which it was a weak competitor. And in regard to low income consumers, it was moderately competitive in all keys to success.

In regard to distribution companies, it was strong in all keys to success. In regard to chain store outlets, Colgate-Palmolive was strong in all keys to success except for developing strong relationship with the store managers, in which it was only moderately competitive.

In regard to television advertising, the company was strong in all keys to success. The company was strong in all keys to success relating to Internet advertising. In regard to print advertising, the company was strong in all keys to success. The company was strong in all keys to success relating to radio advertising. In regard to geographic regions, it was strong in all keys to success except for mass market presence, in which it was moderately competitive. And in regard to sourcing, operations and technology, the company was strong in all keys to success.

Playtex Products Playtex Products was a leading manufacturer and distributor of personal care products. It was founded in 1932 as the "International Latex Corporation" in Rochester, New York, selling latex products under the "Playtex" name. In January 1994, the Company went public as Playtex Products, Inc. Since then, Playtex has acquired many leading consumer brands, including Banana Boat, Wet Ones, Mr. Bubble, Ogilvie, Binaca, Diaper Genie and Baby Magic. Approximately 98% of the Company's net sales were from products that were number one or two in their respective markets. Net sales for the company from October 1, 2004 to October 1, 2005 were $651 million, continuing the Company's upward trend in sales of non-divested brands [Playtex Products Corporate News, 2006].

The company's Feminine Care products were leading the plastic applicator and deodorant tampon categories with brands like Gentle Glide, Beyond, and Portables. Also its skin care segment included Banana Boat sun care, Wet Ones hand and face wipes and Playtex Gloves. The Banana Boat brand offered a full spectrum of sun block, tanning, sunless tanning, and after-sun products. Banana Boat was the number two brand overall and the number one brand in after-sun care. Wet Ones and Playtex Gloves were both leaders in their markets [Playtex Products Corporate News, 2006].

In regard to skin products, Playtex Products was strong in brand quality reputation and price competition. It was moderately competitive in its variety of products and mass market presence, and it was competitively weak in terms of brand recognition and development of products according to fashion trends. In regard to feminine products, the company was strong in all keys to success except for brand recognition and variety of products, in which the company was only moderately competitive. In early 2006, Playtex Products did not manufacture hair products, fine fragrances, cosmetics, and personal cleansing products.

In regard to gender, it was strong in all keys to success except for various distribution channels and mass market presence, in which the company was only moderately competitive. In regard to age, Playtex Products was moderately competitive in all keys to success except in competitive pricing, in which it was strongly competitive. In regard to marital status, it was moderately competitive in all keys to success. And in regard to low income consumers, it was moderately competitive in all keys to success except for brand recognition, in which it was a weak competitor.

In regard to distribution companies and chain stores outlets, it was moderately competitive in all keys to success. In regards to television advertising, the company was strong in all keys to success. The company was strong in all keys to success relating to Internet advertising. In regard to print advertising, the company was strong in all keys to success. The company was strong in all keys to success relating to radio advertising. In regard to geographic regions, it was moderately competitive in all keys to success, except for competitive pricing, in which it was strongly competitive. And in regard to sourcing, operations and technology, Playtex Products was strong in all keys to success.

Avon Avon was the world's largest direct seller with almost 5 million representatives. Its products were available to consumers in 100 countries, with its representatives earning about $3 billion annually. It all started in 1886 in the United States. In 2005, it became the world leader in anti-aging skin care products [Avon Annual Report, 2005].

The company's skin care brands included Anew—a ground-breaking line of anti-aging skincare products. This brand contained popular products like Anew Retroactive+ and Anew Ultimate. Other products were the new blockbuster, Anew Clinical brands, a brand of targeted skin treatments that offered at-home alternatives to professional cosmetic treatments, and also Avon solutions—which was a full line of products that simplified the process of buying skincare without compromising results. Its hair care brands included Advance Techniques—which offered high performance hair products for every hair type, age group, and ethnic background to accommodate a diverse worldwide consumer base, and all of the products were formulated with conditioning ingredients that prevented long-term damage to hair. Avon was also the world's largest sellers of perfumes, with brands like Treselle, Perceive, Today, Tomorrow, and Always Trilogy. In early 2006, Avon did not manufacture hair products and feminine products.

In regard to skin products, Avon was strong in brand quality reputation, price competition, and mass market presence. The company was moderately competitively in terms of brand recognition, variety of products, and development of products according to fashion trends. In regard to fine fragrances, the company was strong in brand quality reputation, price competition, and mass market presence. It was moderately competitive in brand recognition and development of products according to fashion trends. In the cosmetics segment of Avon, the company was strong in brand quality reputation, price competition, and mass market presence. It was moderately competitive in the variety of products, brand recognition, development of new products according to fashion trends. The cleansing products manufactured by Avon were strong in all keys to success except for brand recognition and frequent introduction of new products, in which it was moderately competitive.

In regard to gender, it was strong in all keys to success except for various distribution channels and mass market presence, in which the company was only moderately competitive. In regard to age, Avon was moderately competitive in all keys to success except in competitive pricing, in which it was strongly competitive. In regard to ethnicity, the company was strongly competitive in price competition and high quality and value; it was moderately competitive in tailoring products to meet their needs, brand recognition, and brand loyalty, and weakly competitive when it came to the development of products according to fashion trends. In regard to marital status, it was moderately competitive in all keys to success except for competitive pricing and high quality and value, in which it was strongly competitive. And in regard to low income consumers, it was moderately competitive in all keys to success.

In regard to distribution companies and chain stores outlets, it was moderately competitive in all keys to success, except for competitive pricing, in which it was strongly competitive. In regard to television advertising, the company was strong in all keys to success. The company was strong in all keys to success relating to Internet advertising. In regard to print advertising, the company was strong in all keys to success. The company was strong in all keys to success relating to radio advertising. In regard to geographic regions, it was moderately competitive in all keys to success, except for competitive pricing, in which it was strongly competitive. And in regard to sourcing, operations and technology, Avon was strong in all keys to success.

Estée Lauder Estée Lauder was founded in 1946; this technologically advanced, innovative company has gained a worldwide reputation for elegant, luxurious products in over 100 countries. The Company distributed its various products through department and specialty stores. The company was very involved in the breast cancer awareness program, being the largest corporate sponsor of The Breast Cancer Research Foundation, founded by Evelyn H. Lauder in 1993 [Estée Lauder Annual Report, 2005].

Its skin care segment included brands such as Re-Nutriv—which was an anti-aging cream for the eyes, Self-Tan—an air-brush self-tan spray for body, and Perfectionist—an anti-aging product for skin and lips. The cosmetics segments also included brands such as Pure Color Crystals, Graphic Color Eye

Shadow Quad, Double Wear, and Prime FX. Lastly its fragrance segment included brands like Beautiful, Pleasure, Intuitions, and Paradise. In early 2006, Estée Lauder did not manufacture hair products, feminine products, and personal cleansing products.

In regard to skin products, Estée Lauder was strong in brand quality reputation and price competition. It was moderately competitive in its variety of products and mass market presence, and it was competitively weak in terms of brand recognition and development of products according to fashion trends. In regard to fine fragrances, the company was strong in brand quality reputation, price competition, and mass market presence. It was moderately competitive in brand recognition and development of products according to fashion trends. In the cosmetics segment of Estée Lauder, the company was strong in brand quality reputation and price competition. It was moderately competitive in the variety of products and brand recognition. In terms of mass market presence and the frequent development of new products according to fashion trends, the company was competitively weak.

In regard to gender, it was moderately competitive in all keys to success except for high quality and value and promotion targeted to them, in which Estée Lauder was strongly competitive. In regard to age and marital status, it was moderately competitive in all keys to success. And in regard to low income consumers, it was a weak competitor in all keys to success, except for brand recognition, in which it was moderately competitive.

In regard to distribution companies and chain stores outlets, it was moderately competitive in all keys to success. In regard to television advertising, the company was strong in all keys to success. The company was strong in all keys to success relating to Internet advertising. In regard to print advertising, the company was strong in all keys to success. The company was strong in all keys to success relating to radio advertising. In regard to geographic regions, it was moderately competitive in all keys to success. And in regard to sourcing, operations, and technology, Estée Lauder was strong in all keys to success.

The Company

P&G was a company that manufactured, distributed and marketed consumer goods products. It was established in 1837 in the United States. It later started expanding to other countries, and in early 2006 it was one of the global leaders in the consumer goods industry. It acquired its first overseas subsidiary with the purchase of Thomas Hedley & Sons Company, UK, in 1930. Also in 1915, P&G built a manufacturing facility in Canada, its first outside the U.S. [Datamonitor, 2006].

In early 2006, the company had its headquarters in Cincinnati, Ohio. In the United States, the company owned and operated 35 manufacturing facilities, which were located in 21 different states. Worldwide, the company owned and operated 83 manufacturing facilities in 42 countries. P&G provided branded products and services of superior quality and value that improved the lives of consumers all over the world. And as a result, it believed that the consumers rewarded it with leadership sales, profit, and value creation. These results allowed its people, shareholders, and the communities in which they lived and worked to prosper [P&G Company Information, 2006].

P&G's top 10 customers were Ahold, Albertson's, Carrefour, Costco, Kmart, Kroger, Metro, Target, Tesco, and Wal-Mart. The company always acquired new brands and products, either by creating them or by merging with other companies. An example of these mergers was in 1985, P&G expanded its over-the-counter and personal health care business with the acquisition of Richardson-Vicks, owners of Vicks respiratory care and Oil of Olay product lines. Also in 1988, the company announced a joint venture to manufacture products in China. This marked the company's foray into the largest consumer market in the world [Datamonitor, 2006].

One of the threats that P&G faced was intense competition. It operated in an industry with rivals such as Unilever, Colgate-Palmolive, Playtex Products, Avon, and Estée Lauder. These companies operated and sold their products worldwide. Their presence in the same industry put pressure on P&G to competitively price its products and continually strive to develop innovative products. Another threat was the increase in prices of raw materials. These prices were subject to price volatility caused by weather, supply conditions, and other unpredictable factors.

Lastly, the risk associated with merger integration was another threat for this company. In September 2003, P&G acquired Wella, owning 79.2 percent of the company's total shares. This acquisition contributed about $3.3 billion in sales to P&G's overall beauty business—around $1.6 billion in the professional hair care segment, $1 billion in the retail hair care segment, and $800 million in fragrances. However, Wella's results (as of October 2003) were falling below P&G's stated long-term targets, giving an early indication of disruptions post its takeover [Datamonitor, 2006]. Other brands acquired by P&G were Clairol from Bristol-Myers Squibb in 2001 and Gillette in 2005.

In 2004, P&G did not manufacture products that were specifically for different ethnic groups, such as Hispanic and African American, and products that were made with natural ingredients. There was a high demand for these types of products because some consumers wanted to use products that were made from natural ingredients and some consumers wanted products that were made for their ethnic group.

In the United States it was virtually impossible to calculate the absolute number of companies that produced and marketed beauty/feminine care products. The field of competition was highly fragmented, for example, between those companies active in mass channels (supermarkets, chain drugstores, and mass merchandisers) and prestige channels, not to mention those active in the natural food and beauty care channel. The company size was another factor, between globally-oriented mega-corporations like P&G and kitchen table-based entrepreneurs limited to regional or even local distribution.

Although it was impossible to calculate the number of companies that produced and marketed beauty/feminine care products, it was obvious that P&G was one of the leaders in this industry because, as illustrated in Figure 8, P&G was well ahead of the industry.

P&G faced various challenges in 2006, such as consumers' interest in natural products. This trend was as a result of consumers questioning the ingredients used in making products and their effects. Some activists claimed that these products contained toxic chemicals known to cause cancer, fertility problems, and birth defects. Another challenge was the stagnant sales of some products due to low product development and innovation. Duane Reade Inc.'s Divisional Merchandise Manager, Mike Cirilli, said, "The market's poor sales will only turn around with the launch of dramatically different products. We need the leaders in these categories, such as P&G and L'Oreal, to come out with some revolutionary products, spend $100 million on them in advertising and get all the

FIGURE 8

Financial Information of P&G and the Industry

	P&G	Industry
Market Capital	202.67B	275.79M
Employees	110,000	2.81K
Quarterly Revenue Growth	26.90%	10.40%
Revenue	61.68B	1.74B
Gross Margin	51.05%	36.68%
EBITDA	14.42B	262.13M
Operating Margins	19.95%	7.40%
Net Income	7.77B	13.16M
EPS	2.733	1.23
P/E	22.55	22.50
PEG (5 yr expected)	2.02	2.02
P/S	3.28	2.05

Source: Yahoo Finance (2006). "Procter & Gamble 2006." [Online]. *http://finance.yahoo.com/q/co?s=PG.* Accessed March 17, 2006.

consumers excited again. We need excitement. Excitement and advertising spending will bring sales dollars to these categories" [Packaged Facts, 2005].

The emerging men's market was another trend that was affecting the industry. The number of men spending time in front of the mirror, grooming themselves had increased. The acquisition of Gillette helped P&G to start to address this trend with products like Gillette's complete skin care for men and Gillette's Fusion. This was some of the steps that P&G decided to take to remain at the top in the beauty/feminine care segment. Following were detailed analyses of P&G's business model, as illustrated on the next page in Figure 9. It serves as the framework in discussing the company's strategy on business development.

Products

When the company started in 1837, it was producing only two products, candles and soap. In early 2006, P&G was manufacturing, marketing, and distributing close to a hundred different brands. These brands and products were sold to consumers worldwide.

In 2005, the beauty/feminine care segment of P&G delivered its third consecutive year of double digit growth in volume, sales, and profit. Volume increased 12%, sales increased 14%, and net earnings

FIGURE 9

Procter & Gamble (P&G)

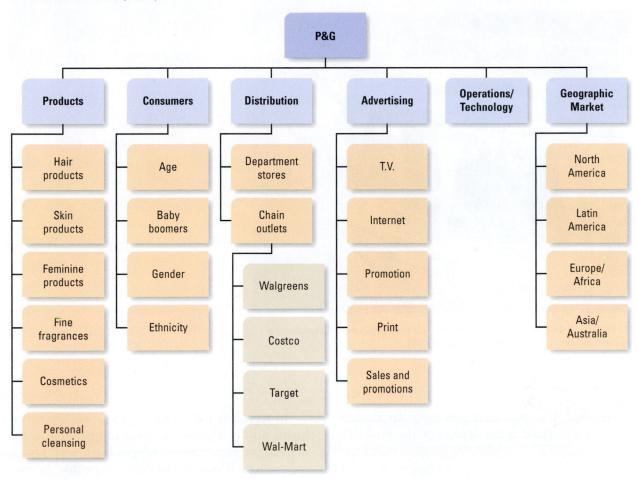

increased 22%. The industry leading performance was driven mainly by broad-based organic growth across geographies and brands. Each of its top 10 countries delivered higher sales than 2004, with solid gains in both developed and developing markets. Global market shares continued to grow, with most of its leading brands at record highs [P&G Annual Report, 2005].

P&G produced products that were used by male and females. With the growing trend for men to use beauty products, the company started manufacturing more products for them. They designed the products so that they would attract male consumers, by using dark colors for the packaging so that it looked more masculine. Some of P&G's products were hair products, skin products, feminine products, fine fragrances, cosmetics, and personal cleansing products.

Hair Products P&G offered a variety of hair products. These products passed through different processes before they reached the consumers. A major process was the testing phase. These products were developed for different types of hair—normal, dry, greasy, permed, bleached, and so on. So each product had to be tested, not only as a formulation that was to be stored for months in a bottle or tube and then sold, but also as a product that was to be used on human hair and scalp.

The process started in the laboratory; the experimental formulation was thoroughly tested on cut lengths of human hair, as shown in Figure 10, before production was considered.

The product under test was applied to the hair and rinsed off, and an experienced technician judged the amount of tangling, stretching, perming, and coloring

FIGURE 10

Cut Lengths of Human Hair

Source: Procter & Gamble (2006). "Hair product." [Online]. http://www.pg.com/science/ haircare/hair_twh_116.htm. Accessed March 17, 2006.

that resulted. After that, a complex computer-assisted technology assessed many aspects of the product's performance. If all went well, the products were evaluated in real life conditions, on the hair of clients in salons. This was an essential part of testing, because it was the only way to judge whether the new product was acceptable to consumers. Only when these tests were completed safely and satisfactorily did the products go on the open market for the consumers to try. This whole process might have involved thousands of tests and took up to a couple of months or even years to complete [P&G Hair Care, 2003].

Some of the hair products brands which were produced by P&G were: Herbal Essences—this brand offered a variety of shampoo, conditioners and styling aids; Infusium 23—this brand included shampoos, conditioners, specialty care products, leave-ins; Physique—these products included cutting-edge technology formulas; Pantene—these products included amino pro-v complex; Aussie—these products were produced using Australian ingredients; and Head and Shoulders—products used to eliminate dryness, irritation, and itchiness of the scalp.

In regard to hair products, P&G was strong in brand quality reputation, price competition, mass market presence, variety of products, and brand recognition. It was moderately competitive in frequently introducing new products.

Skin Products P&G tried to address the three main types of skin, which were oily, normal, and dry. Some of the skin care products brands it produced were: Noxzema—this included facial cleansers in the form of creams, pads, and astringents; Gillete—this included shave multigel, facial moisturizers, razors, shaving sticks, and skin soothing after shave; and Olay—this brand offered products that provided multiple benefits that were designed for women of all ages.

Each product was made for a different function. The skin cleanser was used to remove surface dirt, make-up, top layer of dead skin cells and potentially harmful micro-organisms (bacteria). Skin toner was used after cleansing to ensure complete removal from the skin of all cleansing preparations, and also after a face mask to remove all traces of the mask. These products were based on plant extracts and sometimes contained alcohol. Skin moisturizers hydrated the skin, and/or protected the skin from dehydration. That is, they were designed to improve water retention in the skin. They could be in the form of creams, lotions or serums [P&G Skin Care, 2003].

In regard to skin products, P&G was strong in brand recognition, variety of products, brand quality reputation, price competition, and mass market presence. It was moderately competitive in the development of products according to fashion trends.

Feminine Products   Some of the feminine products brands produced by P&G were: Tampax—this brand included different sizes of tampons. Another brand was Always, which included different styles and sizes of sanitary pads. Always was the world's leading feminine care brand; it grew in volume by 11% and reached record-high global market share of 22% [P&G Annual Report, 2005]. Feminine products were specifically for females to use during their menstrual cycles. The target consumers for these products were generally females from the ages of 12 to 50 years old.

In regard to feminine products, P&G was strong in brand quality reputation, price competition, mass market presence, variety of products, and brand recognition.

Fine Fragrances   P&G was a major distributor of fine fragrances brands such as: Giorgio Beverly Hills—this included products such as Giorgio, G and Red. Another brand was Hugo Boss—which included Hugo Deep Red, Hugo Woman and Hugo Energise, which were used by either men or women. Hugo Boss, along with Lacoste—which was now 10 times bigger than when P&G acquired the license in 2001—further strengthened its global leadership position in men's fine fragrances [P&G Annual Report, 2005].

In regard to fine fragrances, P&G was strong in brand quality reputation, price competition, brand recognition, and mass market presence. It was moderately competitive in the development of products according to fashion trends.

Cosmetics   P&G's target consumer for cosmetics were women of all ages. The cosmetics included those for lips, face, nails, eyes, etc. P&G had two major brands for cosmetics. First was CoverGirl, which was for women who wanted to have a clean, fresh, and natural look. It included foundation, loose powder, eye shadow, mascara, etc. The other brand was the Max Factor, which gave women a more edgy look, making them look more like celebrities. This brand also included various products, such as lip gloss, mascara, eye shadow, etc.

In regard to cosmetics, P&G was strong in variety of products, brand quality reputation, brand recognition, price competition, and mass market presence. It was moderately competitive in the development of products according to fashion trends and in frequently introducing new products.

Personal Cleansing   P&G had a couple of brands that included personal cleansing products. These products included bar soaps, body wash and cleansing bars that were used for cleaning the body. The target consumers for these products were everybody. People needed to stay clean to reduce infections, illness, and smell that were related to dirt. One of the brands that P&G provided was Zest. It believed that this product was refreshingly different from ordinary soap. It rejuvenated the consumer with a combination of great, refreshing scent and clean-rinsing lather that would not dry skin like soap [P&G Product Information, 2006]. Other products were Camay, which was a moisturizing bar soap enriched with perfumes of French inspiration that P&G believed would leave skin feeling fresh, soft and sensual, and Noxzema, which included creams, astringents, and pads used for deep cleaning.

In regard to personal cleansing products, P&G was strong in brand recognition, price competition, variety of products, brand quality reputation, and mass market presence. It was moderately competitive in frequently introducing new products.

Consumers

Consumer goods were used by everyone. Consumers for P&G's products could be segmented into age, gender, ethnicity, and low-income consumers.

Age   P&G addressed each age group differently and produced products that were suitable for them to use. An example was the group of people who were showing signs of aging. P&G understood that as people aged, their skin's vitality and radiance were reduced. So in the skin care segment, the company produced products that would address these issues. One of the products it produced was Olay's Total Effects, which it believed would fight seven signs of aging. These products diminished the appearance of fine lines and wrinkles, smoothed skin texture, evened skin tone, improved surface dullness, gave skin a radiant, healthy glow, minimized the appearance of pores, visibly reduced the appearance of blotches and age spots, and soothed dry skin [P&G Product Information, 2006].

When it came to the company's hair products, an example of the group of people it considered was the baby boomers and senior citizens. These people had similar issues such as loss and dryness of hair. P&G produced products like Head and Shoulders, which eliminated dryness, itchiness, and irritations. Another product which P&G produced that could be used by these age groups was the Pantene Sheer Volume, because it increased hair volume and made it look healthier.

In regard to age, P&G was strong in brand image, brand recognition, price competition, variety of products, brand loyalty, and mass market presence.

Gender P&G manufactured products that could be used by both men and women. Some products could be used by both groups, while others were specifically for either one of them.

In 2005, the men's beauty market was emerging and growing at a very fast rate. Men were more interested in grooming themselves and looking good. Some people called this group of men metrosexuals because they liked to groom and take care of themselves. P&G acknowledged this trend and in late 2005, the company acquired Gillette. This acquisition put P&G at the top of this market. It produced products like Gillette Fusion, Gillette Complete Skin Care, and Gillette MacH3, which were used by men to keep themselves looking good.

Women, on the other hand, have always been interested in looking beautiful. P&G had various products that satisfied their needs, from Olay's base moisturizers that smoothed and softened skin to CoverGirl cosmetics that were used to put on the most beautiful face possible [P&G Product Information, 2006]. The P&G Beauty segment was focused on delivering consumer understanding that reached beyond functional needs to connect at a deeper emotional level. It was a leader in innovation that went beyond science to include sophisticated design that created a total beauty experience and delight for consumers [P&G Annual Report, 2005]. These processes made the consumers connect with the company and its attributes, building consumer loyalty and brand recognition.

In regard to gender, P&G was strong in price competition, high quality and value, brand loyalty, promotion targeted to them, various distribution channels, and mass market presence.

Ethnicity P&G understood that its consumers belonged to different ethnic groups. It produced products that would suit their different needs. To be very effective in reaching these groups, P&G set up strategies to market these groups. In 2005, P&G was one of the leaders in multicultural marketing and was awarded for its jobs by agencies. An example of an agency that awarded the company was the Association of Hispanics Advertising Agencies.

Another ethnic group that P&G was actively involved with was the African Americans. In 2005, Anne Sempowski Ward, the Associate Marketing Director for the African American Marketing team of P&G, released the following statement:

> P&G's commitment to African-Americans is stronger today than ever before. It has spanned more than a century and is still growing—a collective accomplishment rooted in the vision and actions of our leadership, the involvement of our local plants, and the interest of individual employees. African-American ideas, experiences, customs and lifestyles are represented throughout our advertising and packaging and have inspired several product innovations. We look forward to the next 100 years, and thank you for your support as P&G continues to make journeys of hope, freedom and success possible. [P&G Ethnic Echoes, 2005]

An example of how P&G incorporated ethnicity into its products was in the hair care segment for ethnic groups such as Caucasians, which included people who had different colors of hair. The company produced Clairol's highlighting and blonding, which helped to color and maintain the color of hair.

In regard to ethnicity, P&G was strong in products tailored to meet their needs, brand recognition, developing products according to fashion trends, price competition, high quality and value, and brand loyalty.

Low Income Consumers P&G was constantly innovating ways to reach more consumers. The low income consumers were a group that the company really wanted to target. It understood that these people had low disposable income and decided to manufacture products that they could afford. Some ways it reduced the prices of its products were to reduce the sizes of these products. It also changed some of its packages, so that the product was cheaper and easier to store. An example was changing the package from boxes to bags.

In regard to low income consumers, P&G was strong in products tailored to meet their needs, brand recognition, mass market presence, and brand loyalty.

Distribution

P&G had a very effective distribution system. It was used to distribute its products to its consumers. This function was also a form of capital for the company, when it helped other companies distribute their products. P&G had various distribution centers all over the world. In June 2005, P&G built a new Canadian Distribution Center in Brantford, Ontario. This center was built to serve the company's $2 billion national business. The site employed more than 150 people and the total investment was estimated to be $70 million [P&G Annual Report, 2005].

In the United States, a major distribution center was the Brown Summit, which was located in Greensboro, North Carolina. The center held over 1,000 different products. Most of these products were from U.S. plants and were shipped when orders were made

by the customers. The distribution channels of P&G included department stores, such as Macy's and JCPenney, and discount stores, such as Wal-Mart and Costco. P&G's biggest customer is Wal-Mart. In the 1980s, the two giants built a software system that linked P&G up to Wal-Mart's distribution centers. This system was called the Supply Chain System (SCS). It was used to facilitate the coordination with outside business entities. In the case of P&G and Wal-Mart, whenever the inventory level of P&G's products at Wal-Mart's distribution centers reached re-order point, the system automatically alerted P&G to ship more products. This process helped to manage inventory and increase profit. P&G distributed its products through distribution companies and chain store outlets.

In regard to distribution, P&G was strong in all keys to success, such as price competition, variety of products, recruiting good employees, offering incentives to employees, strong relationship with store manager, and store sales and promotion.

Advertising

With over 300 brands to market, P&G was specialized in advertising its products. For the past 5 years, the company has constantly increased its advertising cost, as shown in Figure 11, to accommodate its growing brands. The company used various media to reach its consumers, such as the television, Internet, radio and print. It offered sale promotions, such as free trials, discounts and coupons. These advertisements

FIGURE 11

Advertising Expenses

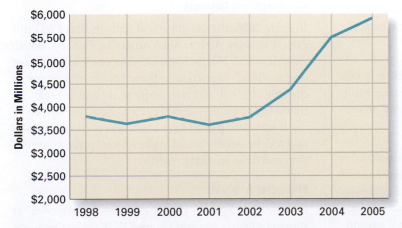

Source: P&G Annual Report (2005). [Online]. *http://www.pg.com/annualreport/2005/pdf/ pG2005annualreport.pdf.* Accessed March 17, 2006.

served different purposes for the company. First they made consumers aware of the products. These advertisements were sometimes made to be interactive, so that they held the consumer's attention. They also served to make the consumers aware of sale promotions that were going on at a particular time. And lastly they helped to convince consumers that they needed the products, so they actually went out and purchased them.

In each segment of the company, P&G hired employees who were responsible for marketing its products. These representatives would move from store to store, selling its products to the store managers. These interactions helped to build a better relationship with the store managers, because these managers helped increase and maximize shelf space and also provided better displays for P&G's products. P&G advertised on television, Internet, print, and radio.

Television P&G created commercials and it was careful to choose the right channels and shows that it hoped its target consumers viewed. Most of its commercials showed people using its products and their experiences after using them.

Internet P&G used the Internet to advertise because it could reach its consumers worldwide. It did this advertisement through various methods, such as posters on websites, emailing codes for samples and discounts, and the like.

Print In 2000, advertising in prints such as newspapers, magazines, and the like was declining. In early 2006, P&G still used this form of advertising to reach those consumers that read these prints. It advertised its products by showing pictures of people using its products or just by showing its products and explaining their uses.

Radio P&G also advertised on radio because it was effective in reaching some consumers. Since radio was audio, P&G did not have to spend money on creating and directing visual commercials.

Sales and Promotions P&G also used various sales and promotions such as free samples, coupons, and discounts. These methods were used by the company to attract more consumers. These methods were especially effective for new products. Sale and promotion for these products normally encouraged the

consumers to take the risk and try the new product. P&G's consumers had to be made aware of the sales and promotions so they could go out and use them to purchase the products.

In regard to advertising, P&G was strong in all keys to success, such as ratings, audience, price of advertisement, offering coupons and samples, availability, easy to use, and awareness.

Operations/Technology

P&G was a manufacturing company that prided itself on the quality of its products. To achieve such high quality, the company had to ensure it had the right machines and facilities required to manufacture its products. When the company could not effectively manufacture parts of its product, it outsourced that function to another company to help it do it better.

With the introduction of the Internet, P&G moved to greater heights. It created numerous ways for the company to do business in a faster and more efficient way. It was easier for it to communicate with its customers, suppliers, and distributors. It also gave P&G the opportunity to research and get more information that helped to make its products better. With the introduction of the Internet, P&G created and designed its website that helped its consumers and customers learn more about the company; it gave them an opportunity to purchase things from the company without leaving their homes.

In regard to operations/technology, P&G was strong in all keys to success, such as high quality machines and technology, flexibility, competitive price, affordability, and properly designed websites.

Geographical Regions

In early 2006, the geographical regions that P&G operated in were Africa, Asia, Australia, Europe, South America, and North America. The company did not operate in all countries in these continents. Some of the countries it did not operate in had a high demand for consumer goods such as Togo in Africa.

It was strong in all keys to success such as products tailored to needs, brand recognition, price competitive, and mass market presence.

Financial Analysis

For the past 5 years, P&G's net sales have grown, as shown in Figure 12a and Figure 12b. The company was a global leader with sales growth of more than 40%,

FIGURE 12

P&G's Financial Data—Net Sales

(a)

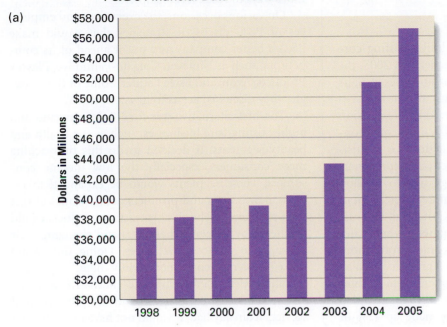

(b)

Amounts in millions except per share amounts	Years Ended June 30					
	2005	**2004**	**2003**	**2002**	**2001**	**2000**
Net sales	$56,741	$51,407	$43,377	$40,238	$39,244	$39,951
Operating income	10,927	9,827	7,853	6,678	4,736	5,954
Net earnings	7,257	6,481	5,186	4,352	2,922	3,542
Net earnings margin	12.8%	12.6%	12.0%	10.8%	7.4%	8.9%
Basic net earnings per common share	$2.83	$2.46	$1.95	$1.63	$1.08	$1.30
Diluted net earnings per common share	2.66	2.32	1.85	1.54	1.03	1.23
Dividends per common share	1.03	0.93	0.82	0.76	0.70	0.64

Source: P&G Annual Report (2005). [Online]. *http://www.pg.com/annualreports/2005/pdf/ pG2005annualreport.pdf.* Accessed March 17, 2006.

increasing to $57 billion. P&G's profit also more than doubled in 2005, and it generated more than $30 billion in free cash flow. Shareholders received $11 billion in cash through dividends, and this increased their value with another $60 billion by nearly doubling the price of P&G stock. The company has increased sales per employee nearly 40% over the past five years, and even though Research and Development (R&D) investment has increased over the past years, R&D as a percentage of sales has declined from 4.8% in 2000 to 3.4% in 2005. More than 80% of initiatives succeeded in creating shareholder value,

an improvement of 25% over the past three years. The productivity of P&G's product supply organization has increased at a high single-digit rate since 2000, and there had been a decrease in P&G's Global Business Services (GBS) costs by more than 15% on base business services since 2000.

Companies tried to increase profit by various methods. One of these methods was to reduce cost. P&G reduced capital spending as a percentage of sales since 2000 from nearly 8% to less than 4%, without forgoing any strategic investment in growth. They also added an incremental growth point to the company's top line over the past two years with marketing Return on Investment (ROI) initiatives [P&G Annual Report, 2005].

Management Strategy

One of P&G's strategies was to build existing core businesses into stronger global leaders. In 2005, the company grew market share, profit, and sales in all its core categories, such as its beauty and health segments. These increases were achieved by the decision to reach more consumers, especially low income consumers and the acquisition of Gillette. This acquisition increased the brands, products, and consumers of the company. Another strategy was to develop faster-growing, higher-margin, more asset efficient businesses with global leadership potential. In 2005, this was evident in the beauty segment, where sales nearly doubled to $19.5 billion and profit more than doubled to $2.9 billion. This growth was also noticed in the Health Care segment, where sales doubled to $7.8 billion and profit more than tripled to $1 billion. These two segments made up 47% of P&G's sales and 50% of the company's profit [P&G Annual Report, 2005].

Internationally, P&G tried to regain growth momentum and leadership in Western Europe, by introducing new products and increasing advertisements. In 2005, the Western Europe volume went up mid-single digit and on average it went up twice the rate of Western Europe Gross Domestic Profit (GDP) growth. At the end of the year, the company's brands growing share in categories accounted for more than half of Western Europe sales. Another major strategy for P&G was to increase growth among lower-income consumers in developing markets, such as Nigeria and Ghana. To attract these consumers, P&G changed the package, making it small and reducing the quality of the packaging, so it was more affordable for these consumers. This strategy has delivered mid-teens volume growth, on average, in these countries.

Looking Towards the Future

Since 2000, A.G. Lafley and his colleagues have been successful in trying to maximize the strengths of the company, while also reducing its weaknesses. They have worked to increase P&G's brands, net sales, and profit. In 2005, male consumers became more interested in beauty products, and to satisfy this need and other issues the company were facing, P&G acquired

Gillette. It also entered a major multimedia marketing partnership with Viacom Plus in 2001, to create more ways to reach its consumers.

On various occasions, the executives and employees of P&G discussed strategies that would make P&G a better company and put it ahead of its competitors, such as Unilever, Colgate-Palmolive, Playtex Products, Avon, and Estée Lauder. Some of the strategies they discussed are as follows:

The first alternative was for P&G to expand and build existing core businesses, such as the health and beauty segments. It decided to do this by reaching more consumers, especially the low income consumers. These segments would be expanded to include new brands and products which would attract such consumers. The already existing products would be altered by reducing their sizes and changing their packages to reduce their prices. Doing this would make it easier for consumers to buy them.

The benefit of this strategic alternative was that P&G would only have to expand on products and services it already had. It would not have to spend a lot of money on research and development, reducing the cost for the company. At the same time it would reach more customers just by altering some of its products.

This alternative was feasible because P&G had already built strong brand recognition and loyalty with its consumers. Consumers would need little conviction to buy another product from the same company. P&G had also already built a strong relationship with most of the large chain stores outlets, such as Wal-Mart. So the distribution process would remain effective for the new products that would be introduced into the market. The company already had the expertise within each of its segments required to support the introduction of new brands. From 2000 to 2005, P&G's net income increased, so the company had the financial resources to create or acquire new brands. It would also be able to afford the costs that would be attributed to these brands, and at the same time maintain its position as the global leader in the Consumer goods industry.

This alternative would win against the competition such as multinational firms like Unilever, Colgate-Palmolive, Playtex Products, Avon, and Estée Lauder, because P&G would increase its brands and products to reach more consumers. The company would do this by merging with other companies to create more products and specifically targeting the low income consumers. These consumers represented a large part of the consumer base, and changing its products by reducing the packaging size and quality would reduce the price of the products, making it more attractive and affordable for these consumers. These changes would increase its sales and make its products more price competitive.

The drawback of this alternative was the reduction in its expertise in one particular product. P&G had so many products that it was difficult to appropriately manage each and every one of them. Another drawback was the lack of enough prestigious products, such as very expensive fragrances. There was not enough attention given to high earning consumers who were able to afford such products. This alternative also did not address consumers who were interested in products that contained natural ingredients. The current trend was to use products with natural ingredients because of the uncertainty that came with using products manufactured with chemicals. People feared that using such products resulted in health problems, such as cancer and infertility. A way around this drawback was to get more qualified employees so P&G could continue to appropriately manage each product. The company also needed to manufacture products that incorporated the trends as mentioned above.

The second alternative was for P&G to focus and expand just on its skin care segment of the beauty/feminine care segment. The company would focus and specialize just on these products. It would produce different types of products for each ethnic group, products that had natural ingredients (such as herbs), and more skin products for men. It would have to sell all its other products, such as its hair products, cosmetics, feminine products and fine fragrances. The money from the sale of these products would be used to acquire more brands and products in the skin care segment.

The benefit of this alternative was that it would enable the company to focus just on one segment of the beauty/feminine care division and do it well. P&G would be able to apply all its resources and skills to this segment. Its employees would all be working in the same field, making it easier to share information between each other. The marketing team would only need to collect information from its consumers about skin products, making it easier to market and advertise these products.

This alternative was feasible because P&G already had a skin care segment. It just had to expand its

products to incorporate every trend. P&G was financially capable of doing this, especially after selling off its other segments. The company already had a strong relationship with most of the large chain stores outlet, such as Costco and Wal-Mart. So the distribution process would remain effective for the new products that would be introduced into the market. P&G's employees already had the expertise within this segment required to support the introduction of new brands.

This alternative would win against the competition because P&G would increase its products and expertise in the skin care segment. The company would offer a wider variety of skin care products that would satisfy more consumers' needs. Satisfying more consumers would increase the company's sale and number of consumers, allowing P&G to win against its competitors such as Unilever, Colgate-Palmolive, Playtex Products, Avon, and Estée Lauder. Concentrating on this segment would also create a better environment for P&G to create more innovative products according to trends and this would keep it ahead of its competitors.

The drawback of this alternative was the loss of its other segments. The company would lose those consumers who wanted other products, such as hair products, cosmetics, fine fragrances, and feminine products. P&G's employees would also lose the flexibility of moving from one segment to the other. This flexibility would have allowed them to learn about different segments in the consumer goods industry. A way around this drawback was to allow another company such as Unilever that sold products in these other segments to use P&G's name to sell its products. This would satisfy the needs of those consumers who would prefer to use products associated with P&G. And also those employees who wanted to get more experience and flexibility could go to this other company and work for a while.

Lafley and his colleagues had a tough choice to make. These and other alternatives needed to be considered very carefully before reaching a decision which will impact the Company's future substantially.

REFERENCES

Aboutsears (2006). [Online]. *http://www.aboutsears.com/*. Accessed February 15, 2006.

Avon Annual Report (2005). [Online]. *http://www.avoncompany.com/investor/annualreport/index.html*. Accessed February 15, 2006.

BEA (2006). "News release." [Online]. *http://www.bea.gov/bea/newsrel/pinewsrelease.htm*. Accessed January 25, 2006.

CIA (2006). "The World Fact Book." [Online]. *http://www.cia.gov/cia/publications/factbook/fields/2119.html*. Accessed March 21, 2006.

Colgate Corporate News (2006). [Online]. *http://www.colgate.com/app/Colgate/US/Corp/ChairmansMessage.cvsp*. Accessed February 15, 2006.

Costco Services (2006). [Online]. *http://www.costco.com/*. Accessed February 15, 2006.

Datamonitor (2006). "Procter and Gamble." [Online]. *http://cpprod.stjohns.edu/cp/tag.b9b8fA3031868bbe.render.userLayoutRootNode.uP?uP_root=root&uP_sparam=activeTab&activeTab=U1l1lS39&uP_tparam=frm&frm=frame*. Accessed March 17, 2006.

Economist (2006). "Pots of Promise." [Online]. *http://www.economist.com/printedition/displayStory.cfm?Story_ID=1795852*. Accessed January 25, 2006.

EIS (2005). [Online]. *http://www.eia.doe.gov/neic/infosheets/petroleumproducts.htm*. Accessed February 12, 2006.

Estée Lauder Annual Report (2005). [Online]. *http://www.esteelauder.com/home.html*. Accessed February 15, 2006.

Hoovers (2006). "Companies Information." [Online]. *http://www.hoovers.com/company-information/—HICID__1486—/free-ind-factsheet.xhtml*. Accessed February 12, 2006.

ICG Commerce (2006). "Strategic Sourcing." [Online]. *http://www.icgcommerce.com/corporate/doc/html/resource/procurement_terms.htm*. Accessed March 17, 2006.

Packaged Facts (2005). A division of marketresearch.com. "The U.S. Market for Hair Products." [Online]. *http://cpprod.stjohns.edu/misc/timedouT2.html*. Accessed January 25, 2006.

Playtex Products Corporate News (2006). [Online]. *http://www.playtexproductsinc.com/index.htm*. Accessed February 15, 2006.

Procter & Gamble 2005 Annual Report (2006). [Online]. *http://www.pg.com/annualreports/2005/pdf/pG2005annualreport.pdf*. Accessed January 22, 2006.

Procter & Gamble Company Information (2006). [Online]. *http://www.pg.com/company/index.jhtml*. Accessed February 22, 2006.

Procter & Gamble Corporate News (2006). [Online]. *http://pg.com/news/index.jhtml. http://ccbn.mobular.net/ccbn/7/1142/1201/*. Accessed January 22, 2006.

Procter & Gamble Product Information (2006). [Online]. *http://www.pg.com/product_card/brand_overview.jhtml*. Accessed February 27, 2006.

Procter & Gamble Ethnic Echoes (2005). [Online]. *http://www.pg.com/images/company/who_we_are/diversity/multi/echo_feb_april05.pdf*. Accessed March 5, 2006.

Procter & Gamble Hair Care (2003). [Online]. *http://www.pg.com/science/haircare/hair_twh_116.htm*. Accessed February 27, 2006.

Procter & Gamble Skin Care (2003). [Online]. *http://www.pg.com/science/skincare/Skin_tws_toc.htm*. Accessed February 27, 2006.

Target Corporate News (2006) [Online]. *http://sites.target.com/site/en/corporate/page.jsp?contentId=PRD03-000482*. Accessed February 15, 2006.

Unilever Annual Report (2005). [Online]. *http://www.unilever.com/ourcompany/investorcentre/*. Accessed February 22, 2006.

U. S. Census Bureau (2004). "U. S. Interim Projections by Age, Sex, Race and Hispanic Origin." [Online]. *http://www.census.gov/prod/99pubs/P20-514u.pdf*. Accessed February 12, 2006.

Walgreens Corporate News (2006). [Online]. *http://investor.walgreens.com/home.cfm*. Accessed February 15, 2006.

Wal-Mart Corporate News (2006). [Online]. *http://www.walmartstores.com/GlobalWMStoresWeb/navigate.do?catg=316*. Accessed February 15, 2006.

Webster's Dictionary (2006). [Online]. *http://www.webster.com/*. Accessed February 10, 2006.

Wikipedia (2006). [Online]. *http://en.wikipedia.org/wiki/Main_Page. http://en.wikipedia.org/wiki/Baby_boomer*. Accessed January 30, 2006.

This case was prepared by Charles W. L. Hill, the University of Washington.

Established in 1902, by 2006 3M was one of the largest technology driven enterprises in the United States with annual sales of $23 billion, 61% of which were outside the United States. Throughout its history, 3M's researchers had driven much of the company's growth. In 2006, the company sold some 50,000 products, including Post-it Notes, Flex Circuits, Scotch tape, abrasives, specialty chemicals, Thinsulate insulation products, Nexcare bandage, optical films, fiber-optic connectors, drug delivery systems, and much more. Around 6,500 of the company's 69,000 employees were technical employees. 3M's annual R&D budget exceeded $1.25 billion. The company had garnered over 7,000 patents since 1990, with 487 new patents awarded in 2005 alone. 3M was organized into thirty-five different business units in a wide range of sectors including consumer and office products; display and graphics; electronics and telecommunications; health care; industrial; safety, security, and protection services; and transportation (see Exhibit 1 for more details).

The company's one-hundred-year anniversary was a time for celebration, but also one for strategic reflection. During the prior decade, 3M had grown profits and sales by between 6 to 7% per annum, a respectable figure but one that lagged behind the growth rates achieved by some other technology-based enterprises and diversified industrial enterprises like General Electric. In 2001, 3M took a step away

from its past when the company hired the first outsider to become CEO, James McNerney Jr. McNerney, who joined 3M after heading up GE's fast-growing medical equipment business (and losing out in the race to replace legendary GE CEO, Jack Welch), was quick to signal that he wanted 3M to accelerate its growth rate. McNerney set an ambitious target for 3M—to grow sales by 11% per annum and profits by 12% per annum. Many wondered if McNerney could achieve this without damaging the innovation engine that had propelled 3M to its current stature. The question remained unanswered, as McNerney left to run the Boeing Co. in 2005. His successor, however, George Buckley, seemed committed to continuing on the course McNerney had set for the company.

The History of 3M: Building Innovative Capabilities

The story of 3M goes back to 1902 when five Minnesota businessmen established the Minnesota Mining and Manufacturing Co. to mine a mineral that they thought was corundum, which is ideal for making sandpaper. The mineral, however, turned out to be low-grade anorthosite, nowhere near as suitable for making sandpaper, and the company nearly failed. To try and salvage the business, 3M turned to making the sandpaper itself using materials purchased from another source.

In 1907, 3M hired a twenty-year-old business student, William McKnight, as assistant bookkeeper. This turned out to be a pivotal move in the history of the company. The hardworking McKnight soon made his mark. By 1929, he was CEO of the company, and in 1949, he became chairman of 3M's board of directors, a position that he held until 1966.

EXHIBIT 1

3M Financial Facts—Year-End 2005[a]

Sales	
Worldwide	$21.167 billion
International	$12.900 billion
	61% of company's total
Net Income	
Net Income	$3.199 billion
Percent to sales	15.1%
Earnings per share—diluted	$4.12
Taxes	
Income tax expense	$1.694 billion
Dividends (Paid every quarter since 1916)	
Cash dividends per share	$1.68
One original share, if held, is now . . .	3,072 shares
R&D and Related Expenditures	
For 2005	$1.242 billion
Total for last five years	$5.814 billion
Capital Spending	
For 2005	$943 million
Total for last five years	$4.3 billion
Employees	
Worldwide	69,315
United States	33,033
International	36,282

Organization

- More than 35 business units, organized into 6 businesses: Consumer and Office; Display and Graphics; Electro and Communications; Health Care; Industrial and Transportation; Safety, Security and Protection Services
- Operations in more than 60 countries—29 international companies with manufacturing operations, 35 with laboratories
- In the United States, operations in 22 states

Contributions

Cash and gifts-in-kind (3M and 3M Foundation)	Nearly $39 million

Patents

U.S. patents awarded	487

3M Values

- Provide investors an attractive return through sustained, quality growth.
- Satisfy customers with superior quality, value, and service.
- Respect our social and physical environment.
- Be a company employees are proud to be part of.

[a] 3M is one of 30 companies in the Dow Jones Industrial Average and also is a component of the Standard & Poor's 500 Index.

Source: 3M website, http://www.3m.com.

From Sandpaper to Post-it Notes

It was McKnight, then 3M's president, who hired the company's first scientist, Richard Carlton, in 1921. Around the same time, McKnight's interest had been peaked by an odd request from a Philadelphian printer by the name of Francis Okie for samples of every sandpaper grit size that 3M made. McKnight dispatched 3M's East Coast sales manager to find out what Okie was up to. The sales manager discovered that Okie had invented a new kind of sandpaper that he had patented. It was waterproof sandpaper that could be used with water or oil to reduce dust and decrease the friction that marred auto finishes. In addition, the lack of dust reduced the poisoning associated with inhaling the dust of paint that had a high lead content. Okie had a problem, though; he had no financial backers to commercialize the sandpaper. 3M quickly stepped into the breach, purchasing the rights to Okie's Wetordry waterproof sandpaper and hiring the young printer to come and join Richard Carlton in 3M's lab. Wet and dry sandpaper went on to revolutionize the sandpaper industry and was the driver of significant growth at 3M.

Another key player in the company's history, Richard Drew, also joined 3M in 1921. Hired straight out of the University of Minnesota, Drew would round out the trio of scientists, Carlton, Okie and Drew, who under McKnight's leadership would do much to shape 3M's innovative organization.

McKnight charged the newly hired Drew with developing a stronger adhesive to better bind the grit for sand paper to paper backing. While experimenting with adhesives, Drew accidentally developed a weak adhesive that had an interest quality—if placed on the back of a strip of paper and stuck to a surface, the strip of paper could be peeled off the surface it was adhered to without leaving any adhesive residue on that surface. This discovery gave Drew an epiphany. He had been visiting auto-body paint shops to see how 3M's wet and dry sandpaper was used, and he noticed that there was a problem with paint running. His epiphany was to cover the back of a strip of paper with his weak adhesive and use it as "masking tape" to cover parts of the auto body that were not to be painted. An excited Drew took his idea to McKnight and explained how masking tape might create an entirely new business for 3M. McKnight reminded Drew that he had been hired to fix a specific problem and pointedly suggested that he concentrate on doing just that.

Chastised, Drew went back to his lab, but he could not get the idea out of his mind, so he continued to work on it at night, long after everyone else had gone home. Drew succeeded in perfecting the masking tape product, and then went to visit several auto-body shops to show them his innovation. He quickly received several commitments for orders. Drew then went to see McKnight again. He told him that he had continued to work on the masking tape idea on his own time, had perfected the product, and got several customers interested in purchasing it. This time it was McKnight's turn to be chastised. Realizing that he had almost killed a good business idea, McKnight reversed his original position, and gave Drew the go-ahead to pursue the idea.[1]

Introduced into the market in 1925, Drew's invention of masking tape represented the first significant product diversification at 3M. Company legend has it that this incident was also the genesis for 3M's famous 15% rule. Reflecting on Drew's work, both McKnight and Carlton agreed that technical people could disagree with management and should be allowed to go and do some experimentation on their own. The company then established a norm that technical people could spend up to 15% of their own workweeks on projects that might benefit the consumer, without having to justify the project to their managers.

Drew himself was not finished. In the late 1920s, he was working with cellophane, a product that had been invented by DuPont, when lightening struck for a second time. Why, Drew wondered, couldn't cellophane be coated with an adhesive and used as a sealing tape? The result was Scotch Cellophane Tape. The first batch was delivered to a customer in September 1930, and Scotch Tape went on to become one of 3M's best-selling products. Years later, Drew noted: "Would there have been any masking or cellophane tape if it hadn't been for earlier 3M research on adhesive binders for 3M™ Wetordry™ Abrasive Paper? Probably not!"[2]

Over the years, other scientists followed Drew's footsteps at 3M, creating a wide range of innovative products by leveraging existing technology and applying it to new areas. Two famous examples illustrate how many of these innovations occurred—the invention of Scotch Guard and the development of the ubiquitous Post-it Notes.

The genesis of Scotch Guard was in 1953 when a 3M scientist named Patsy Sherman was working on a new kind of rubber for jet aircraft fuel lines. Some of the latex mixture splashed onto a pair of canvas tennis shoes. Over time, the spot stayed clean while the rest of the canvas soiled. Sherman enlisted the help of fellow chemist Sam Smith. Together they began to investigate polymers, and it didn't take long for them to realize that they were onto something. They discovered an oil and water repellant substance, based on the fluorocarbon fluid used in air conditioners, with enormous potential for protecting fabrics from stains. It took several years before the team perfected a means to apply the treatment using water as the carrier, thereby making it economically feasible for use as a finish in textile plants.

Three years after the accidental spill, the first rain and stain repellent for use on wool was announced. Experience and time revealed that one product could not, however, effectively protect all fabrics, so 3M continued working, producing a wide range of Scotch Guard products that could be used to protect all kinds of fabrics.[3]

The story of Post-it Notes began with Spencer Silver, a senior scientist studying adhesives.[4] In 1968, Silver had developed an adhesive with properties like no other; it was a pressure-sensitive adhesive that would adhere to a surface, but it was weak enough to easily peel off the surface and leave no residue. Silver spent several years shopping his adhesive around 3M, to no avail. It was a classic case of a technology in search of a product. Then one day in 1973, Art Fry, a new product development researcher who had attended one of Silver's seminars, was singing in his church choir. He was frustrated that his bookmarks kept falling out of his hymn book, when he had a Eureka moment. Fry realized that Silver's adhesive could be used to make a wonderfully reliable bookmark.

Fry went to work the next day and, using 15% time, started to develop the bookmark. When he started using samples to write notes to his boss, Fry suddenly realized that he had stumbled on a much bigger potential use for the product. Before the product could be commercialized, however, Fry had to solve a host of technical and manufacturing problems. With the support of his boss, Fry persisted, and after eighteen months, the product development effort moved from 15% time to a formal development effort funded by 3M's own seed capital.

The first Post-it Notes were test marketed in 1977 in four major cities, but customers were lukewarm at best. This did not gel with the experience within 3M, where people in Fry's division were using samples all the time to write messages to each other. Further

research revealed that the test-marketing effort, which focused on ads and brochures, didn't resonate well with consumers, who didn't seem to value Post-it Notes until they had the actual product in their hands. In 1978, 3M tried again, this time descending on Boise, Idaho, and handing out samples. Follow-up research revealed that 90% of consumers who tried the product said they would buy it. Armed with this knowledge, 3M rolled out the national launch of Post-it Notes in 1980. The product subsequently went on to become a bestseller.

Institutionalizing Innovation

Early on, McKnight set an ambitious target for 3M—a 10% annual increase in sales and 25% profit target. He also indicated how he thought that should be achieved with a commitment to plow 5% of sales back into R&D every year. The question, though, was how to ensure that 3M would continue to produce new products?

The answer was not apparent all at once, but rather evolved over the years from experience. A prime example was the 15% rule, which came out of McKnight's experience with Drew. In addition to the 15% rule and the continued commitment to push money back into R&D, a number of other mechanisms evolved at 3M to spur innovation.

Initially research took place in the business units that made and sold products, but by the 1930s, 3M had already diversified into several different fields, thanks in large part to the efforts of Drew and others. McKnight and Carlton realized that there was a need for a central research function. In 1937, they established a central research laboratory that was charged with supplementing the work of product divisions and undertaking long-run basic research. From the outset, the researchers at the lab were multidisciplinary, with people from different scientific disciplines often working next to each other on research benches.

As the company continued to grow, it became clear that there was a need for some mechanism to knit together the company's increasingly diverse business operations. This led to the establishment of the 3M Technical Forum in 1951. The goal of the Technical Forum was to foster idea sharing, discussion, and problem solving among technical employees located in different divisions and the central research laboratory. The Technical Forum sponsored "problem solving sessions" at which businesses would present their most recent technical nightmares in the hope that somebody might be able to suggest a solution—and that often was the case. The forum also established an annual event in which each division put up a booth to show off its latest technologies. Chapters were also created to focus on specific disciplines, such as polymer chemistry or coating processes.

During the 1970s the Technical Forum cloned itself, establishing forums in Australia and England. By 2001, the forum had grown to 9,500 members in eight U.S. locations and nineteen other countries, becoming an international network of researchers who could share ideas, solve problems, and leverage technology.

According to Marlyee Paulson, who coordinated the Technical Forum from 1979 to 1992, the great virtue of the Technical Forum is to cross-pollinate ideas:

> 3M has lots of polymer chemists. They may be in tape; they may be medical or several other divisions. The forum pulls them across 3M to share what they know. It's a simple but amazingly effective way to bring like minds together.[5]

In 1999, 3M created another unit within the company, 3M Innovative Properties (3M, IPC) to leverage technical know-how. 3M IPC is explicitly charged with protecting and leveraging 3M's intellectual property around the world. At 3M there has been a long tradition that while divisions "own" their products, the company as a whole "owns" the underlying technology, or intellectual property. One task of 3M IPC is to find ways in which 3M technology can be applied across business units to produce unique marketable products. Historically, the company has been remarkably successful at leveraging company technology to produce new product ideas (see Exhibit 2 for some recent examples).

Another key to institutionalizing innovation at 3M has been the principle of "patient money." The basic idea is that producing revolutionary new products requires substantial long-term investments, and often repeated failure, before a major payoff occurs. The principle can be traced back to 3M's early days.

EXHIBIT 2

Recent Examples of Leveraging Technology at 3M[6]

Richard Miller, a corporate scientist in 3M Pharmaceuticals, began experimental development of an antiherpes medicinal cream in 1982. After several years of development, his research team found that the interferon-based materials they were working with could be applied to any skin-based virus. The innovative chemistry they were working with was applied topically and was more effective than other compounds on the market. They found that the cream was particularly effective in interfering with the growth mechanism of genital warts. Competitive materials on the market at the time were caustic and tended to be painful. Miller's team obtained FDA approval for its Aldara (imiquimod) line of topical patient-applied creams in 1997.

Miller then applied the same Aldara-based chemical mechanism to basal cell carcinomas and found that, here too, it was particularly effective to restricting the growth of the skin cancer. "The patient benefit is quite remarkable," says Miller. New results in efficacy have been presented for treating skin cancers. His team recently completed phase III clinical testing and expects to apply later this year for FDA approval for this disease preventative. This material is already FDA-approved for use in the treatment of genital warts. Doctors are free to use it to treat those patients with skin cancers.

Andrew Ouderkirk is a corporate scientist in 3M's Film & Light Management Technology Center. 3M has been working in light management materials applied to polymer-based films since the 1930s, according to Ouderkirk. Every decade since then 3M has introduced some unique thin film structure for a specific customer application from high-performance safety reflectors for street signs to polarized lighting products. And every decade, 3M's technology base has become more specialized and more sophisticated. Their technology has now reached the point where they can produce multiple-layer interference films to 100-nm thicknesses each and hold the tolerances on each layer to within $+/-3$ nm. "Our laminated films are now starting to compete with vacuum-coated films in some applications," says Ouderkirk.

Rick Weiss is technical director of 3M's Microreplication Technology Center, one of 3M's twelve core technology centers. The basic microreplication technology was discovered in the early 1960s when 3M researchers were developing the fresnel lenses for overhead projectors. 3M scientists have expanded on this technology to a wide variety of applications including optical reflectors for solar collectors, and adhesive coatings with air bleed ribs that allow large area films to be applied without having the characteristic "bubbles" appear. Weiss is currently working on development of dimensionally precise barrier ribs that can be applied to separate the individual "gas" cells on the new high-resolution large screen commercial plasma displays. Other applications include fluid management where capillary action can be used in biological testing systems to split a drop of blood into a large number of parts.

It took the company twelve years before its initial sandpaper business started to show a profit, a fact that drove home the importance of taking the long view. Throughout the company's history, similar examples can be found. Scotchlite reflective sheeting, now widely used on road signs, didn't show much profit for ten years. The same was true of flurochemicals and duplicating products. Patient money doesn't mean substantial funding for long periods of time, however. Rather, it might imply that a small group of five researchers is supported for ten years while they work on a technology.

More generally, if a researcher creates a new technology or idea, he or she can begin working on it using 15% time. If the idea shows promise, the researcher may request seed capital from his or her business unit managers to develop it further. If that funding is denied, which can occur, the researcher is free to take the idea to any other 3M business unit. Unlike the case in many other companies, requests for seed capital do not require that researchers draft detailed business plans that are reviewed by top management. That comes later in the process. As one former senior technology manager has noted:

> In the early stages of a new product or technology, it shouldn't be overly managed. If we start asking for business plans too early and insist on tight financial evaluations, we'll kill an idea or surely slow it down.[7]

Explaining the patient money philosophy, Ron Baukol, a former executive vice president of 3M's international operations and a manager who started as a researcher, has noted:

> You just know that some things are going to be worth working on, and that requires technological patience. . . . [Y]ou don't put too much money into the investigation, but you keep one to five people working on it for twenty years if you have to. You do that because you know that, once you have cracked the code, it's going to be big.[8]

An internal review of 3M's innovation process in the early 1980s concluded that despite the liberal process for funding new product ideas, some promising ideas did not receive funding from business units or the central research budget. This led to the establishment in 1985 of Genesis Grants, which provide up to $100,000 in seed capital to fund projects that do not get funded through 3M's regular channels. About a dozen of these grants are given every year.

One of the recipients of these grants, a project that focused on creating a multilayered reflective film, has subsequently produced a breakthough reflective technology that may have applications in a wide range of businesses, from better reflective strips on road signs to computer displays and the reflective linings in light fixtures. Company estimates in 2002 suggested that the commercialization of this technology might ultimately generate $1 billion in sales for 3M.

Underlying the patient money philosophy is recognition that innovation is a very risky business. 3M has long acknowledged that failure is an accepted and essential part of the new product development process. As former 3M CEO Lew Lehr once noted:

> We estimate that 60% of our formal new product development programs never make it. When this happens, the important thing is to not punish the people involved.[9]

In an effort to reduce the probability of failure, in the 1960s, 3M started to establish a process for auditing the product development efforts ongoing in the company's business units. The idea has been to provide a peer review, or technical audit, of major development projects taking place in the company. A typical technical audit team is composed of ten to fifteen business and technical people, including technical directors and senior scientists from other divisions. The audit team looks at the strengths and weaknesses of a development program and its probability of success, both from a technical standpoint and a business standpoint. The team then makes nonbinding recommendations, but they are normally taken very seriously by the managers of a project. For example, if an audit team concludes that a project has enormous potential but is terribly underfunded, managers of the unit would often increase the funding level. Of course, the converse can also happen, and in many instances, the audit team can provide useful feedback and technical ideas that can help a development team to improve its project's chance of success.

By the 1990s, the continuing growth of 3M had produced a company that was simultaneously pursuing a vast array of new product ideas. This was a natural outcome of 3M's decentralized and bottom-up approach to innovation, but it was problematic in one crucial respect: The company's R&D resources were being spread too thinly over a wide range of opportunities, resulting in potentially major projects being underfunded. To try to channel R&D resources into projects that had blockbuster potential, in 1994, 3M introduced what was known as the Pacing Plus Program.

The program asked business to select a small number of programs that would receive priority funding, but 3M's senior executives made the final decision on which programs were to be selected for the Pacing Plus Program. An earlier attempt to do this in 1990 had met with limited success because each sector in 3M submitted as many as two hundred programs. The Pacing Plus Program narrowed the list down to twenty-five key programs that by 1996 were receiving some 20% of 3M's entire R&D funds (by the early 2000s, the number of projects funded under the Pacing Plus Program had grown to sixty). The focus was on "leapfrog technologies," revolutionary ideas that might change the basis of competition and lead to entirely new technology platforms that might, in typical 3M fashion, spawn an entire range of new products.

To further foster a culture of entrepreneurial innovation and risk taking, over the years 3M established a number of reward and recognition programs to honor employees who make significant contributions to the company. These include the Carton Society award, which honors employees for outstanding career scientific achievements, and the Circle of Technical Excellence and Innovation Award, which recognizes people who have made exceptional contributions to 3M's technical capabilities.

Another key component of 3M's innovative culture has been an emphasis on duel career tracks. Right from its early days, many of the key players in 3M's history, people like Richard Drew, chose to stay in research, turning down opportunities to go into the management side of the business. Over the years, this became formalized in a dual career path. Today, technical employees can choose to follow a technical career path or a management career path, with equal advancement opportunities. The idea is to let researchers develop their technical professional interests without being penalized financially for not going into management.

Although 3M's innovative culture emphasizes the role of technical employees in producing innovations, the company also has a strong tradition of emphasizing that new product ideas often come from watching customers at work. Richard Drew's original idea for masking tape, for example, came from watching workers use 3M wet and dry sandpaper in auto-body shops. As with much else at 3M, the tone was set by McKnight who insisted that salespeople needed to "get behind the smokestacks" of 3M customers, going onto the factory floor, talking to workers, and finding out what their problems were. Over the years this theme has become ingrained in 3M's culture, with salespeople often requesting time to watch customers work and then bringing their insights about customer problems back into their organization.

By the mid-1990s, McKnight's notion of getting behind the smokestacks had evolved into the idea that 3M could learn a tremendous amount from what were termed "lead users," who were customers working in very demanding conditions. Over the years, 3M had observed that in many cases, customer themselves can be innovators, developing new products to solve problems that they face in their work settings. This was most likely to occur for customers working in very demanding conditions. To take advantage of this process, 3M has instituted a lead user process in the company in which cross-functional teams from a business unit observe how customers work in demanding situations.

For example, 3M has a $100 million business selling surgical drapes, which are drapes backed with adhesives that are used to cover parts of a body during surgery and help prevent infection. As an aid to new product development, 3M's surgical drapes business formed a cross-functional team that went to observe surgeons at work in very demanding situations—including on the battlefield, hospitals in developing nations, and in vets' offices. The result was a new set of product ideas, including low-cost surgical drapes that were affordable in developing nations, and devices for coating a patient's skin and surgical instruments with antimicrobial substances that would reduce the chance of infection during surgery.[10]

Driving the entire innovation machine at 3M has been a series of stretch goals set by top managers. The goals date back to 3M's early days and McKnight's ambitious growth targets. In 1977, the company established "Challenge 81," which called for 25% of sales to come from products that had been on the market for less than five years by 1981. By the 1990s, the goal had been raised to the requirement that 30% of sales should come from products that had been on the market less than four years.

The flip side of these goals were that over the years, many products and businesses that had been 3M staples were phased out. More than twenty of the businesses that were 3M mainstays in 1980, for example, had been phased out by 2000. Analysts estimate that sales from mature products at 3M generally fall by 3 to 4% per annum. The company has a long history of inventing businesses, leading the market for long periods of time, and then shutting those businesses down or selling them off when they can no longer meet 3M's own demanding growth targets. Notable examples include the duplicating business, a business 3M invented with Thermo-Fax copiers (which were ultimately made obsolete by Xerox's patented technology) and the video and audio magnetic tape business. The former division was sold off in 1985, and the latter in 1995. In both cases, the company exited these areas because they had become low-growth commodity businesses that could not generate the kind of top-line growth that 3M was looking for.

Still, 3M was by no means invulnerable in the realm of innovation and on occasion squandered huge opportunities. A case in point was the document copying business. 3M invented this business in 1951 when it introduced the world's first commercially successful Thermo-Fax copier (which used specially coated 3M paper to copy original typed documents). 3M dominated the world copier business until 1970, when Xerox overtook the company with its revolutionary xerographic technology that used plain paper to make copies. 3M saw Xerox coming, but rather than try to develop its own plain paper copier, the company invested funds in trying to improve its (increasingly obsolete) copying technology. It wasn't until 1975 that 3M introduced its own plain paper copier, and by then it was too late. Ironically, 3M turned down the chance to acquire Xerox's technology twenty years earlier, when the company's founders had approached 3M.

Building the Organization

McKnight, a strong believer in decentralization, organized the company into product divisions in 1948, making 3M one of the early adopters of this organizational form. Each division was set up as an individual profit center that had the power, autonomy, and resources to run independently. At the same time, certain functions remained centralized, including significant R&D, human resources, and finance.

McKnight wanted to keep the divisions small enough that people had a chance to be entrepreneurial and retained their focus on the customer. A key philosophy of McKnight's was "divide and grow." Put simply, when a division became too big, some of its embryonic businesses were spun off into a new division. Not only did this new division then typically attain higher growth rates, but the original division had to find new drivers of growth to make up for the contribution of the businesses that had gained independence. This drove the search for further innovations.

At 3M, the process of organic diversification by splitting divisions became known as "renewal." The examples of renewal within 3M are legion. A copying machine project for Thermo-Fax copiers grew to become the Office Products Division. When Magnetic Recording Materials was spun off from the Electrical Products division, it grew to become its own division, and then in turn spawned a spate of divisions.

However, this organic process was not without its downside. By the early 1990s, some of 3M's key customers were frustrated that they had to do businesses with a large number of different 3M divisions. In some cases, there could be representatives from ten to twenty 3M divisions calling on the same customer. To cope with this problem, in 1992, 3M started to assign key account representatives to sell 3M products directly to major customers. These representatives typically worked across divisional lines. Implementing the strategy required many of 3M's general managers to give up some of their autonomy and power, but the solution seemed to work well, particularly for 3M's consumer and office divisions.

Underpinning the organization that McKnight put in place was his own management philosophy. As explained in a 1948 document, his basic management philosophy consisted of the following values:

> As our business grows, it becomes increasingly necessary to delegate responsibility and to encourage men and women to exercise their initiative. This requires considerable tolerance. Those men and women to whom we delegate authority and responsibility, if they are good people, are going to want to do their jobs in their own way.
>
> Mistakes will be made. But if a person is essentially right, the mistakes he or she makes are not as serious in the long run as the mistakes management will make if it undertakes to tell those in authority exactly how they must do their jobs.
>
> Management that is destructively critical when mistakes are made kills initiative. And it's essential that we have many people with initiative if we are to continue to grow.[11]

At just 3% per annum, employee turnover rate at 3M has long been among the lowest in corporate America, a fact that is often attributed to the tolerant, empowering, and family-like corporate culture that McKnight helped to establish. Reinforcing this culture has been a progressive approach toward employee compensation and retention. In the depths of the Great Depression, 3M was able to avoid laying off employees while many other employers did because the company's innovation engine was able to keep building new businesses even through the worst of times.

In many ways, 3M was ahead of its time in management philosophy and human resource practices. The company introduced its first profit sharing plan in 1916, and McKnight instituted a pension plan in 1930 and an employee stock purchase plan in 1950. McKnight himself was convinced that people would be much more likely to be loyal in a company if they had a stake in it. 3M also developed a policy of promoting from within and of giving its employees a plethora of career opportunities within the company.

Going International

The first steps abroad occurred in the 1920s. There were some limited sales of wet and dry sandpaper in Europe during the early 1920s. These increased after 1929 when 3M joined the Durex Corp., a joint venture for international abrasive product sales in which 3M was involved along with eight other U.S. companies. In 1950, however, the Department of Justice alleged that the Durex Corp. was a mechanism for achieving collusion among U.S. abrasive manufacturers, and a judge ordered that the corporation be broken up. After the Durex Corp. was dissolved in 1951, 3M was left with a sandpaper factory in Britain, a small plant in France, a sales office in Germany, and a tape factory in Brazil. International sales at this point amounted to no more than 5% of 3M's total revenues.

Although 3M opposed the dissolution of the Durex Corp., in retrospect it turned out to be one of the most important events in the company's history, for it forced the corporation to build its own international operations. By 2002, international sales amounted to 55% of total revenues.

In 1952, Clarence Sampair was put in charge of 3M's international operations and charged with getting them off the ground. He was given considerable strategic and operational independence. Sampair and his successor, Maynard Patterson, worked hard to protect the international operations from getting caught up in the red tape of a major corporation. For example, Patterson recounts:

> I asked Em Monteiro to start a small company in Colombia. I told him to pick a key person he wanted to take with him. "Go start a company," I said, "and no one from St. Paul is going to visit you unless you ask for them. We'll stay out of your way, and if someone sticks his nose in your business you call me."[12]

The international businesses were grouped into an International Division that Sampair headed. From the get go, the company insisted that foreign ventures pay their own way. In addition, 3M's international companies were expected to pay a 5 to 10% royalty to the corporate head office. Starved of working capital, 3M's International Division relied heavily on local borrowing to fund local operations, a fact that forced those operations to quickly pay their own way.

The international growth at 3M typically occurred in stages. The company would start by exporting to a country and working through sales subsidiaries. In that way, it began to understand the country, the local marketplace, and the local business environment. Next 3M established warehouses in each nation and stocked those with goods paid for in local currency. The next phase involved converting products to the sizes and packaging forms that the local market conditions, customs, and culture dictated. 3M would ship jumbo rolls of products from the United States, which were then broken up and repackaged for each country. The next stage was designing and building plants, buying machinery and getting them up and running. Over the years, R&D functions were often added, and by the 1980s, considerable R&D was being done outside of the United States.

Both Sampair and Patterson set an innovative, entrepreneurial framework that according to the company, still guides 3M's International Operations today. The philosophy can be reduced to several key and simple commitments: (1) Get in early (within the company, the strategy is known as FIDO—"First in Defeats Others"). (2) Hire talented and motivated local people. (3) Become a good corporate citizen of the country. (4) Grow with the local economy. (5) American products are not one-size-fits-all around the world; tailor products to fit local needs. (6) Enforce patents in local countries.

As 3M stepped into the international market vacuum, foreign sales surged from less than 5% in 1951 to 42% by 1979. By the end of the 1970s 3M was beginning to understand how important it was to integrate the international operations more closely with the U.S. operations and to build innovative capabilities overseas. It expanded the company's international R&D presence (there are now more than 2,200 technical employees outside the United States), built closer ties between the U.S. and foreign research organizations, and started to transfer more managerial and technical employees between businesses in different countries.

In 1978 the company started the Pathfinder Program to encourage new product and new business initiatives born outside the United States. By 1983, products developed under the initiative were generating sales of over $150 million a year. 3M Brazil invented a low-cost, hot-melt adhesive from local raw materials, 3M Germany teamed up with Sumitomo 3M of Japan (a joint venture with Sumitomo) to develop electronic connectors with new features for the worldwide electronics industry, 3M Philippines developed a Scotch-Brite cleaning pad shaped like a foot after learning that Filipinos polished floors with their feet, and so on. On the back of such developments, in 1992 international operations exceeded 50% for the first time in the company's history.

By the 1990s 3M started to shift away from a country-by-country management structure to more regional management. Drivers behind this development included the fall of trade barriers, the rise of trading blocks such as the European Union and NAFTA, and the need to drive down costs in the face of intense global competition. The first European Business Center (EBC) was created in 1991 to manage 3M's chemical business across Europe. The EBC was charged with product development, manufacturing, sales, and marketing for Europe, but also with paying attention to local country requirements. Other EBCs soon followed, such as EBCs for Disposable Products and Pharmaceuticals.

As the millennium ended, 3M seemed set on transforming the company into a transnational organization characterized by an integrated network of businesses that spanned the globe. The goal was to get the right mix of global scale to deal with competitive pressures, while at the same time maintaining 3M's traditional focus on local market differences and decentralized R&D capabilities.

The New Era

The DeSimone Years

In 1991, Desi DeSimone became CEO of 3M. A long-time 3M employee, the Canadian-born DeSimone was the epitome of a twenty-first-century manager—he had made his name by building 3M's Brazilian business and spoke five languages fluently. Unlike most prior 3M CEOs, DeSimone came from the manufacturing side of the business rather than the technical side. He soon received praise for managing 3M through the recession of the early 1990s. By the late 1990s, however, his leadership had come under fire from both inside and outside the company.

In 1998 and 1999, the company missed its earnings targets, and the stock price fell as disappointed investors sold. Sales were flat, profit margins fell, and earnings slumped by 50%. The stock had underperformed the widely tracked S&P 500 stock index for most of the 1980s and 1990s.

One cause of the earnings slump in the late 1990s was 3M's sluggish response to the 1997 Asian crisis. During the Asian crisis, the value of several Asian currencies fell by as much as 80% against the U.S. dollar in a matter of months. 3M generated a quarter of its sales from Asia, but it was slow to cut costs there in the face of slumping demand following the collapse of currency values. At the same time, a flood of cheap Asian products cut into 3M's market share in the United States and Europe as lower currency values made Asian products much cheaper.

Another problem was that for all of its vaunted innovative capabilities, 3M had not produced a new blockbuster product since Post-it Notes. Most of the new products produced during the 1990s were just improvements over existing products, not truly new products.

DeSimone was also blamed for not pushing 3M hard enough earlier in the decade to reduce costs. An example was the company's supply-chain excellence program. Back in 1995, 3M's inventory was turning over just 3.5 times a year, subpar for manufacturing. An internal study suggested that every half point increase in inventory turnover could reduce 3M's working capital needs by $700 million and boost its return on invested capital. But by 1998, 3M had made no progress on this front.[13]

By 1998, there was also evidence of internal concerns. Anonymous letters from 3M employees were sent to the board of directors, claiming that DeSimone was not committed to research as he should have been. Some letters complained that DeSimone was not funding important projects for future growth, others that he had not moved boldly enough to cut costs, and still others that the company's duel career track was not being implemented well, and that technical people were underpaid. Critics argued that he was a slow and cautious decision maker in a time that required decisive strategic decisions. For example, in August 1998, DeSimone announced a restructuring plan that included a commitment to cut 4,500 jobs, but reports suggest that other senior managers wanted 10,000 job cuts, and DeSimone had watered down the proposals.[14]

Despite the criticism, 3M's board, which included four previous 3M CEOs among its members, stood behind DeSimone until he retired in 2001. However, the board began a search for a new top executive in February 2000 and signaled that it was looking for an outsider. In December 2000, the company announced that it had found the person they wanted, Jim McNerney, a fifty-one-year-old General Electric veteran who ran GE's medical equipment businesses and, before that, GE's Asian operations. McNerney was one of the front runners in the race to succeed Jack Welsh as CEO of GE, but lost out to Jeffrey Immelt. One week after that announcement, 3M hired him.

McNerney's Plan for 3M

In his first public statement days after being appointed, McNerney said that his focus would be on getting to know 3M's people and culture and its diverse lines of business:

> I think getting to know some of those businesses and bringing some of GE here to overlay on top of 3M's strong culture of innovation will be particularly important.[15]

It soon became apparent that McNerney's game plan was exactly that: to bring the GE playbook to 3M and use it to try to boost 3M's results, while simultaneously not destroying the innovative culture that had produced the company's portfolio of 50,000 products.

The first move came in April 2001 when 3M announced that the company would cut 5,000 jobs, or about 7% of the work force, in a restructuring effort that would zero in on struggling businesses. To cover severance and other costs of restructuring, 3M announced that it would take a $600 million charge against earnings. The job cuts were expected to save $500 million a year. In another effort to save costs, the company streamlined its purchasing processes, for example, by reducing the number of packaging suppliers on a global basis from fifty to five, saving another $100 million a year in the process.

Next, McNerney introduced the Six Sigma process, a rigorous statistically based quality control process that was one of the drivers of process improvement and cost savings at GE. At heart, Six Sigma is a management philosophy, accompanied by a set of tools, that is rooted in identifying and prioritizing customers and their needs, reducing variation in all business processes, and selecting and grading all projects based on their impact on financial results. Six Sigma breaks every task (process) in an organization down into increments to be measured against a perfect model.

McNerney called for Six Sigma to be rolled out across 3M's global operations. He also introduced a 3M-like performance evaluation system at 3M under which managers were asked to rank every single employee who reported to them.

In addition to boosting performance from existing business, McNerney quickly signaled that he wanted to play a more active role in allocating resources between new business opportunities. At any given time, 3M has around 1,500 products in the development pipeline. McNerney believed that was too many and indicated that he wanted to funnel more cash to the most promising ideas, those with a potential market of $100 million a year or more, while cutting funding to weaker looking development projects.

In the same vein, he signaled that he wanted to play a more active role in resource allocation than had traditionally been the case for a 3M CEO, using cash from mature businesses to fund growth opportunities elsewhere. He scrapped the requirement that each division get 30% of its sales from products introduced in the past four years, noting that:

> To make that number, some managers were resorting to some rather dubious innovations, such as pink Post-it Notes. It became a game, what could you do to get a new SKU?[16]

Some long-time 3M watchers, however, worried that by changing resource allocation practices, McNerney might harm 3M's innovative culture. If the company's history proved anything, they said, it's that it is hard to tell which of today's tiny products will become tomorrow's home runs. No one predicted that Scotch Guard or Post-it Notes would earn millions. They began as little experiments that evolved without planning into big hits. McNerney's innovations all sound fine in theory, they said, but there is a risk that he will transform 3M into "3E" and lose what is valuable in 3M in the process.

In general, though, securities analysts greeted McNerney's moves favorably. One noted that "McNerney is all about speed" and that there will be "no more Tower of Babel—everyone speaks one language." This "one company" vision was meant to replace the program under which 3M systematically spun off successful new products into new business centers. The problem with this approach, according to the analyst, was that there was no leveraging of best practices across businesses.[17]

McNerney also signaled that he would reform 3M's regional management structure, replacing it with a global business unit structure that would be defined by either products or markets.

At a meeting for investment analysts, held on September 30, 2003, McNerney summarized a number of achievements.[18] At the time, the indications seemed to suggest that McNerney was helping to revitalize 3M. Profitability, measured by return on invested capital, had risen from 19.4% in 2001 and was projected to hit 25.5% in 2003. 3M's stock price had risen from $42 just before McNerney was hired to $73 in October 2003 (see Exhibit 3 for details).

Like his former boss, Jack Welsh at GE, McNerney seemed to place significant value on internal executive education programs as a way of shifting to a performance-oriented culture. McNerney noted that some 20,000 employees had been through Six Sigma

training by the third quarter of 2003. Almost 400 higher level managers had been through an Advanced Leadership Development Program set up by McNerney and offered by 3M's own internal executive education institute. Some 40% of participants had been promoted on graduating. All of the company's top managers had graduated from an Executive Leadership Program offered by 3M.

McNerney also emphasized the value of five initiatives that he had put in place at 3M: indirect cost control, global sourcing, e-productivity, Six Sigma, and the 3M Acceleration program. With regard to indirect cost control, some $800 million had been taken out of 3M's cost structure since 2001, primarily by reducing employee numbers, introducing more efficient processes that boost productivity, benchmarking operations internally, and leveraging best practices. According to McNerney, internal benchmarking highlighted another $200 to $400 million in potential cost savings over the next few years.

On global sourcing, McNerney noted that more than $500 million had been saved since 2000 by consolidating purchasing, reducing the number of suppliers, switching to lower cost suppliers in developing nations, and introducing duel sourcing policies to keep price increases under control.

The e-productivity program at 3M embraces the entire organization and all functions. It involves the digitalization of a wide range of processes, from customer ordering and payment, through supply-chain management and inventory control, to managing employee process. The central goal is to boost productivity by using information technology to more effectively manage information within the company and between the company and its customers and suppliers. McNerney cited some $100 million in annual cost savings from this process.

EXHIBIT 3

Selected Financial Data, 1996–2006

	1996	1997	1998	1999	2000	2001	2002	2003	2004	2005	2006
Sales (billion)	$14.2	$15.1	$15.0	$15.7	$16.7	$16.1	$16.3	$18.2	$20.0	$21.0	$22.9
Operating margin	23.7%	23.5%	22.6%	24.7%	23.3%	20.3%	24.5%	26.5%	30.6%	31.1%	31.0%
ROIC	21.7%	23.9%	20.7%	22.5%	25.2%	19.4%	25.1%	25.5%	27.3%	28.5%	28.0%
EPS	$1.82	$1.94	$1.87	$2.11	$2.32	$1.79	$2.50	$3.02	$3.75	$4.12	$4.55

Source: 3M Company, Value Line Investment Survey, November 17, 2006.

The Six Sigma program overlays the entire organization and focuses on improving processes to boost cash flow, lower costs (through productivity enhancements), and boost growth rates. By late 2003, there were some 7,000 Six Sigma projects in process at 3M. By using working capital more efficiently, Six Sigma programs had helped to generate some $800 million in cash, with the total expected to rise to $1.5 billion by the end of 2004. 3M has applied the Six Sigma process to the company's R&D process, enabling researchers to engage customer information in the initial stages of a design discussion. According to Jay Inlenfeld, the vice president of R&D, Six Sigma tools

> Allow us to be more closely connected to the market and give us a much higher probability of success in our new product designs.[19]

Finally, the 3M Acceleration program is aimed at boosting the growth rate from new products through better resource allocation, particularly by shifting resources from slower growing to faster growing markets. As McNerney noted:

> 3M has always had extremely strong competitive positions, but not in markets that are growing fast enough. The issue has been to shift emphasize into markets that are growing faster.[20]

Part of this program is a tool termed 2X/3X. 2X is an objective for two times the number of new products that were introduced in the past, and 3X is a business objective for three times as many winning products as there were in the past (see Exhibit 4). 2X focuses on generating more "major" product initiatives, and 3X on improving the commercialization of those initiatives. The process illustrated in Exhibit 4 is 3M's "stage gate" process, where each gate represents a major decision point in the development of a new product, from idea generation to post-launch.

Other initiates aimed at boosting 3M's organization growth rate through innovation include the Six Sigma process, leadership development programs, and technology leadership (see Exhibit 5). The purpose of these initiatives was to help implement the 2X/3X strategy.

As a further step in the Acceleration program, 3M decided to centralize its corporate R&D effort. Prior to the arrival of McNerney, there were twelve technology centers staffed by 900 scientists that focused on core technology development. The company is replacing these with one central research lab, staffed by 500 scientists, some 120 of whom will be located outside the United States. The remaining 400 scientists will be relocated to R&D centers in the business

---

EXHIBIT 4

The New Product Development Process at 3M

2X/3X Strategy: 2X Idea Velocity/3X Winning Products Out

Source: Adapted from a presentation by Jay Inlenfeld, 3M Investor Meeting, September 30, 2003, archived at http://www.corporate-ir.net/ireye/ir_site.zhtml?ticker=MMM&script=2100.

EXHIBIT 5

R&D's Role in Organic Growth

Source: Adapted from a presentation by Jay Inlenfeld, 3M Investor Meeting, September 30, 2003, archived at http://www.corporate-ir.net/ireye/ir_site.zhtml?ticker=MMM&script=2100.

units. The goal of this new corporate research lab is to focus on developing new technology that might fill high-growth "white spaces," which are areas where the company currently has no presence, but where the long-term market potential is great. An example is research on fuel cells, which is currently a big research project within 3M.

Responding to critics' charges that changes such as these might impact on 3M's innovative culture, vice president of R&D Inlenfeld noted:

> We are not going to change the basic culture of innovation at 3M. There is a lot of culture in 3M, but we are going to introduce more systematic, more productive tools that allow our researchers to be more successful.[21]

For example, Inlenfeld repeatedly emphasized that the company remains committed to basic 3M principles, such as the 15% rule and leveraging technology across businesses.

By late 2003, McNerney noted that some 600 new product ideas were under development and that collectively, they were expected to reach the market and generate some $5 billion in new revenues between 2003 and 2006, up from $3.5 billion eighteen months earlier. Some $1 billion of these gains were expected to come in 2003.

The Acceleration program was helping to increase 3M's organic growth rate in earnings per share, which hit an annual rate of 3.6% in the first half of 2003, up from 1% a year earlier and a decline in 2001. To complement internally generated growth, McNerney signaled that he would make selected acquisitions in business that 3M already had a presence in.

George Buckley Takes Over

In mid-2005, McNerney announced that he would leave 3M to become CEO and chairman of Boeing, a company on whose board he had served for some time. He was replaced in late 2005 by another outsider, George Buckley, the highly regarded CEO of Brunswick Industries. Over the next year in several presentations Buckley outlined his strategy for 3M, and it soon became apparent that he was essentially sticking to the general course laid out by McNerney, albeit with some minor corrections.[22]

Buckley does not see 3M as an enterprise that needs radical change. He sees 3M as a company with impressive internal strengths, but one that has been too cautious about pursuing growth opportunities.[23] Buckley's overall strategic vision for 3M is that the company must solve customer needs through the provision of innovative and differentiated products that increase the efficiency and competitiveness of customers. Consistent with long-term 3M strategy, he sees this as being achieved by taking 3M's multiple technology platforms and applying them to different market opportunities.

Controlling costs and boosting productivity through Six Sigma continue to be a major thrust under Buckley. This was hardly a surprise, since Buckley had pushed Six Sigma at Brunswick. By late 2006, some 55,000 3M employees had been trained in Six Sigma methodology, 20,000 projects had been completed, and some 15,000 were still under way. 3M was also adding techniques gleaned from Toyota's lean production methodology to its Six Sigma tool kit. As a result of Six Sigma and other cost control methods, between 2001 and 2005 productivity measured by sales per employee increased from $234 to $311, and some $750 million were taken out of overhead costs.

In addition to productivity initiatives, Buckley has stressed the need for 3M to more aggressively pursue growth opportunities. He wants the company to use its differentiated brands and technology to continue to develop core businesses and extend those core business into adjacent areas. In addition, like McNerney, Buckley wants the company to focus R&D resources on emerging business opportunities, and he too seems to be prepared to play a more proactive role in this process. Areas of focus include filtration systems, track and trace information technology, energy and mineral extraction, and food safety. 3M made a number of acquisitions during 2005 and 2006 to achieve scale and acquire technology and other assets in these areas. In addition, it increased its own investment in technologies related to these growth opportunities, particularly nanotechnology.

In addition to focusing on growth opportunities, 3M under Buckley has made selective divestures of businesses not seen as core. Most notably, in November 2006, 3M reached an agreement to sell its pharmaceutical business for $2.1 billion. 3M took this step after deciding that slow growth combined with high regulatory and technological risk made the sector an unattractive one that would dampen the company's growth rate.

Finally, Buckley is committed to continuing internationalization at 3M. The goal is to increase foreign sales to 70% of total revenues by 2011, up from 61% in 2006. 3M plans to double its capital investment in the fast-growing markets of China, India, Brazil, Russia, and Poland by 2009. All of these markets are seen as expanding two to three times as fast as the U.S. market.

Judged by the company's financial results between 2001 and 2006, the McNerney and Buckley eras do seem to have improved 3M's financial performance. Most notably, return on invested capital increased from 19.4% to 28%, earning per share from $1.79 to $4.55, operating margins from 20.3% to 31%, and sales from $16 billion to $23 billion. Despite this improvement, the company's stock price had remained mired in the $70 to $80 range since 2003, raising the question of what Buckley needs to do to deliver value to shareholders.

ENDNOTES

1. M. Dickson, "Back to the Future," *Financial Times*, 1994, May 30, page 7. http://www.3m.com/profile/looking/mcknight.jhtml.
2. http://www.3m.com/about3M/pioneers/drew2.jhtml.
3. http://www.3m.com/about3M/innovation/scotchgard50/index.jhtml.
4. 3M, "A Century of Innovation, the 3M Story." 3M, 2002. Available at http://www.3m.com/about3m/century/index.jhtml.
5. 3M, "A Century of Innovation, the 3M Story." 3M, 2002, page 33. Available at http://www.3m.com/about3m/century/index.jhtml.
6. Tim Studt, "3M—Where Innovation Rules," *R&D Magazine*, April 2003, Vol. 45, pages 20–24.
7. 3M, "A Century of Innovation, the 3M Story." 3M, 2002, page 78. Available at http://www.3m.com/about3m/century/index.jhtml.
8. 3M, "A Century of Innovation, the 3M Story." 3M, 2002, page 78. Available at http://www.3m.com/about3m/century/index.jhtml.
9. 3M, "A Century of Innovation, the 3M Story." 3M, 2002, page 42. Available at http://www.3m.com/about3m/century/index.jhtml.
10. Eric Von Hippel et al., "Creating Breakthroughs at 3M," *Harvard Business Review*, September–October 1999.
11. From 3M website at http://www.3m.com/about3M/history/mcknight.jhtml.
12. 3M, "A Century of Innovation, the 3M Story." 3M, 2002, pages 143–144. Available at http://www.3m.com/about3m/century/index.jhtml.
13. Michelle Conlin, "Too Much Doodle?" *Forbes*, October 19, 1998, pages 54–56.
14. De'Ann Weimer, "3M: The Heat Is on the Boss," *Business Week*, March 15, 1999, pages 82–83.

15. Joseph Hallinan, "3M's Next Chief Plans to Fortify Results with Discipline He Learned at GE Unit," *Wall Street Journal*, December 6, 2000, page B17.

16. Jerry Useem, "(Tape) + (Light bulb) = ?" *Fortune*, August 12, 2002, pages 127–131.

17. Rick Mullin, "Analysts Rate 3M's New Culture," *Chemical Week*," September 26, 2001, pages 39–40.

18. 3M Investor Meeting, September 30, 2003, archived at http://www.corporate-ir.net/ireye/ir_site.zhtml?ticker=MMM&script=2100.

19. Tim Studt, "3M—Where Innovation Rules," *R&D Magazine*, April 2003, page 22.

20. 3M Investor Meeting, September 30, 2003, archived at http://www.corporate-ir.net/ireye/ir_site.zhtml?ticker=MMM&script=2100.

21. Tim Studt, "3M—Where Innovation Rules," *R&D Magazine*, April 2003, page 21.

22. Material here drawn from George Buckley's presentation to Prudential's investor conference on "Inside Our Best Ideas," September 28, 2006. This and other relevant presentations are archived at http://investor.3m.com/ireye/ir_site.zhtml?ticker=MMM&script=1200.

23. Jeffery Sprague, "MMM: Searching for Growth with New CEO Leading," *Citigroup Global Markets*, May 2, 2006.

GE's Growth Strategy: The Immelt Initiative

This case was prepared by Christopher A. Bartlett, Harvard Business School.

In February 2006, after four and a half years in the CEO role, Jeff Immelt felt General Electric (GE) was finally poised for the double-digit growth for which he had been positioning it. Having just announced an 11% increase in revenues for 2005 (including 8% organic growth), he was now forecasting a further 10% revenue increase in 2006. And following 12% growth in earnings from continuing operations in 2005 (with all six businesses delivering double-digit increases), he committed to leveraging the 2006 revenues into an even greater 12% to 17% earnings increase. It was a bold pledge for a $150 billion global company. (See Exhibit 1 for GE financial data, 2001–2005.)

Yet, for the past year GE's share price had been stuck at around $35, implying a multiple of around 20 times earnings, only half its price-to-earnings (P/E) ratio in the heady days of 2000. (See Exhibit 2 for GE's 10-year share price history.) It frustrated Immelt that the market did not seem to share the belief that he and his management team had in his growth forecasts. "The stock is currently trading at one of the lowest earnings multiples in a decade," he said. "Investors decide the stock price, but we love the way GE is positioned. We have good results and good governance. . . . What will it take to move the stock?"[1]

Taking Charge: Setting the Agenda

On Friday, September 7, 2001, Immelt took over the reins of GE from Jack Welch, the near-legendary CEO who preceded him. Four days later, two planes crashed into the World Trade Center towers, and the world was thrown into turmoil. Not only did 9/11 destabilize an already fragile post-Internet-bubble stock market, but it also triggered a downturn in an overheated economy, leading to a fall in confidence that soon spread into other economies worldwide.

After the chaos of the first few post-9/11 days during which he checked on GE casualties, authorized a $10 million donation to the families of rescue workers, and dispatched mobile generators and medical equipment to the World Trade Center, on September 18 Immelt finally focused on reassuring the financial markets by purchasing 25,000 GE shares on his personal account. Three days later, he appeared before a group of financial analysts and promised that 2001 profits would grow by 11% and by double digits again in 2002. As impressive as such a performance might have appeared, it was less than Welch's expansive suggestion in the heady days of 2000 that GE's profits could grow at 18% per annum in the future.[2] The net result was that by the end of Immelt's first week as CEO, GE's shares had dropped 20%, taking almost $80 billion off the company's market capitalization.

To make matters worse, as the year wore on, a scandal that had been engulfing Enron finally led to that company's bankruptcy. Soon, other companies were caught up in accusations of financial manipulation, including Tyco, a company that had billed itself as a "mini GE." Again, the market punished GE stock, concerned that its large and complex operations were too difficult to understand.

EXHIBIT 1

GE's Performance, 2001–2005: Selected Financial Data

Selected Financial Data	General Electric Company and Consolidated Affiliates (in millions, per share amounts in dollars)				
	2005	2004	2003	2002	2001
Revenues	$149,702	$134,481	$112,886	$113,856	$107,558
Earnings from continuing operations before accounting changes	18,275	16,285	13,766	15,798	12,948
Earnings (loss) from discontinued operations, net of taxes	−1,922	534	2,057	−616	1,130
Earnings before accounting changes	16,353	16,819	15,823	15,182	14,078
Cumulative effect of accounting changes	—	—	−587	−1,015	−287
Net earnings	16,353	16,819	15,236	14,167	13,791
Dividends declared	9,647	8,594	7,759	7,266	6,555
Return on average shareowners' equity (a)	17.60%	17.60%	19.60%	27.20%	24.70%
Per share					
Earnings from continuing operations before accounting changes—diluted	$1.72	$1.56	$1.37	$1.58	$1.29
Earnings (loss) from discontinued operations—diluted	−0.18	0.05	0.2	−0.06	0.11
Earnings before accounting changes—diluted	1.54	1.61	1.57	1.51	1.4
Cumulative effect of accounting changes—diluted	—	—	−0.06	−0.1	−0.03
Net earnings—diluted	1.54	1.61	1.51	1.41	1.37
Earnings from continuing operations before accounting changes—basic	1.73	1.57	1.37	1.59	1.3
Earnings (loss) from discontinued operations—basic	−0.18	0.05	0.21	−0.06	0.11
Earnings before accounting changes—basic	1.55	1.62	1.58	1.52	1.42
Cumulative effect of accounting changes—basic	—	—	−0.06	−0.1	−0.03
Net earnings—basic	1.55	1.62	1.52	1.42	1.39
Dividends declared	0.91	0.82	0.77	0.73	0.66
Stock price range	37.34–32.67	37.75–28.88	32.42–21.30	41.84–21.40	52.90–28.25
Year-end closing stock price	35.05	36.5	30.98	24.35	40.08
Total assets of continuing operations	626,586	618,241	503,610	441,768	373,550
Total assets	673,342	750,507	647,828	575,236	495,012
Long-term borrowings	212,281	207,871	170,309	138,570	77,818
Shares outstanding—average (in thousands)	10,569,805	10,399,629	10,018,587	9,947,113	9,932,245
Shareowner accounts—average	634,000	658,000	670,000	655,000	625,000
Employees at year-end					
United States	161,000	165,000	155,000	161,000	158,000
Other Countries	155,000	142,000	150,000	154,000	152,000
Total Employees	316,000	307,000	305,000	315,000	310,000

Source: GE 2005 Annual Report.

EXHIBIT 2

GE Stock Price and P/E Multiple vs. S&P 500 Performance, 1995–2005

GE Price and P/E vs. S&P 500
1995–2006 (indexed 1/1995 = 100)

GE P/E   S&P 500   GE Price

Source: Thomson Datastream International.

Beyond all this immediate market pressure, Immelt was acutely aware that he stood in the very long shadow cast by his predecessor, Welch. During his 20 years as CEO, Welch had built GE into a highly disciplined, extremely efficient machine that delivered consistent growth in sales and earnings—not only through effective operations management that resulted in organic growth (much of it productivity-driven) of 5% annually, but also through a continuous stream of timely acquisitions and clever deal making. This two-pronged approach had resulted in double-digit profit increases through most of the 1990s.

The consistent reliability of GE's growth had created an image in shareholders' minds of a powerful machine that could not be stopped and earned the company a significant premium over price/earnings multiples in the broad stock market. As a result, over two decades, GE had generated a compound annual total return to shareholders of more than 23% per annum through the 1980s and 1990s. (See Exhibit 3 for summary GE financials, 1981–2000.) But Immelt was very conscious that he could not hope to replicate that performance by simply continuing the same strategy. "I looked at the world post-9/11 and realized that over the next 10 or 20 years, there was not going to be much tailwind," he said. "It would be more driven by innovation, and a premium would be placed on companies that could generate their own growth."[3]

Building on the Past, Imagining the Future

While recognizing the need for change, Immelt saw little need to challenge the basic business model on which GE had operated for decades. Like his predecessor, he bristled at the characterization of GE as a conglomerate, preferring to see it as a well-integrated, diversified company. On taking charge, he explained:

> Our businesses are closely integrated. They share leading edge business initiatives, excellent financial disciplines, a tradition of sharing talent and best practices, and a culture whose cornerstone is absolute unyielding integrity. Without these powerful ties, we could actually merit the label "conglomerate" that people often inaccurately apply to us. That word just does not apply to GE.... What we have is a company of diverse benefits whose sum is truly greater than the parts; a company executing with excellence despite a brutal global economy.... We believe GE is different, and one of the things that makes us different is that—in good times and in bad—we deliver. That is who we are.[4]

Immelt committed to building on what he saw as the core elements of the company's past success: a

EXHIBIT 3

GE and Consolidated Affiliates' Financial Performance: 1981–2000 ($ millions)

	2000	1999	1998	1997	1996	1991	1986	1981
Revenues	$129,853	$111,630	$100,469	$90,840	$79,179	$51,283	$36,725	$27,240
Earnings from continuing operations	12,735	10,717	9,296	8,203	7,280	3,943	3,689	N/A
Loss from discontinued operations	—	—	—	—	—	492	N/A	N/A
Net earnings	12,735	10,717	9,296	8,203	7,280	2,636	2,492	1,652
Dividends declared	5,647	4,786	4,081	3,535	3,138	1,808	1,081	715
Earned on average shareowners' equity	27.5%	26.8%	25.7%	25.0%	24.0%	12.2%	17.3%	19.1%
Per share:								
Net earnings	3.87	3.27	2.84	2.50	2.20	2.55	2.73	N/A
Net earnings—diluted	3.81	3.21	2.80	2.46	2.16	1.51	N/A	N/A
Dividends declared	1.71	1.47	1.25	1.08	0.95	1.04	1.18	N/A
Stock price range[a]	181.5–125.0	159.5–94.3	103.9–69.0	76.6–47.9	53.1–34.7	78.1–53.0	44.4–33.2	69.9–51.1
Total assets of continuing operations	437,006	405,200	355,935	304,012	272,402	166,508	84,818	20,942
Long-term borrowings	82,132	71,427	59,663	46,603	49,246	22,602	100,001	1,059
Shares outstanding—average (in thousands)	3,299,037	3,277,826	3,268,998	3,274,692	3,307,394	1,737,863	912,594	227,528
Employees at year-end:								
United States	168,000	167,000	163,000	165,000	155,000	173,000	302,000	N/A
Other countries	145,000	143,000	130,000	111,000	84,000	62,000	71,000	N/A
Discontinued operations (primarily U.S.)	—	—	—	—	—	49,000	N/A	N/A
Total employees	313,000	310,000	293,000	276,000	239,000	284,000	373,000	404,000

Source: GE Annual Reports, various years.

[a]Price unadjusted for four 2-for-1 stock splits during the period.

portfolio of strong businesses, bound through a set of companywide strategic initiatives and managed by great people in a culture that was performance driven and adaptive. It was a source of competitive advantage that Immelt felt was not easily imitated. "It requires financial and cultural commitments over decades," he said.

Having committed to GE's fundamental business model, Immelt wasted little time in articulating a new vision of growth based on using GE's size and diversity as strengths rather than weaknesses. He wanted to take the company into "big, fundamental high-technology infrastructure industries," places where he felt GE could have competitive advantage and where others could not easily follow. He elaborated this into a vision of a global, technology-based, service-intensive company by defining a growth strategy based on five key elements:

- **Technical leadership:** Believing that technology had been at GE's core since the day Thomas Edison founded the company, Immelt committed to technical leadership as a key driver of future growth.

- **Services acceleration:** By building service businesses on its massive installed base of aircraft engines, power turbines, locomotives, medical devices, and other hardware, Immelt believed GE could better serve customers while generating high margins and raising entry barriers.

- **Commercial excellence:** Reflecting his own sales and marketing background, Immelt committed to creating a world-class commercial culture to overlay the engineering bias and financial orientation of GE's dominant business approach under Welch.

- **Globalization:** Building on an old Welch initiative, Immelt committed to expanding GE's sourcing strategy and market access worldwide, in particular focusing on its underexploited opportunities in developing world countries such as China and India.

- **Growth platforms:** Finally, he recognized that significant resource reallocation would be necessary to build new business platforms capitalizing on "unstoppable trends" that would provide growth into the future.

Because plans at GE always came with measurable goals attached, Immelt committed to increasing the company's organic growth from its historical 5% annual rate to 8% and, beginning in 2005, to generating consistent double-digit earnings growth.

Investing through the Down Cycle

Perhaps predictably, the press was skeptical of the notion that a $130 billion company could grow at two to three times the global gross national product (GNP) rate. Still, there was no shortage of advice for the new CEO in his attempt to make the company do so. Some suggested he should sell off the mature lighting and appliances businesses.[5] Others proposed bold expansions—into the hospital business, for example.[6] And as always, there were calls for GE to break up the company and sell off its component businesses.[7] But Immelt insisted GE had great businesses that provided a strong foundation for the future. All he planned to do was rebalance and renew the portfolio, then drive growth from the revitalized base.

Within weeks of taking charge, he started making significant investments to align GE's businesses for growth. Seeing opportunities to expand its NBC broadcast business to capture the fast-growing Hispanic advertising market, for example, the company acquired the Telemundo and Bravo networks. And its power-generation business acquired Enron's wind energy business as a new platform that management felt was positioned for long-term growth and high returns in the future.

In addition to these and other natural business extensions, management identified whole new segments that provided a stronger foundation for innovation and where future market opportunities would drive rapid growth. For example, in security systems, GE acquired Interlogix, a medium-sized player with excellent technology, and in water services, it bought BetzDearborn, a leading company with 2,000 sales engineers on the ground.

Internally, Immelt also lost little time in making big financial commitments to the growth strategy. Within his first six months, he committed $100 million to upgrade GE's major research and development (R&D) facility at Nishayuna in upstate New York. In addition to building new laboratories, the investment provided for new meeting centers on Nishayuna's 525-acre campus, creating an environment where business managers and technologists could meet to discuss priorities. Scott Donnelly, a 40-year-old researcher who led GE's overall R&D activity, said, "GE is not the place for scientists who want to work on a concept for years without anybody bothering them. Here scientists can do long-term research, but they have to be willing to spar with the marketing guys. This is the best of both worlds."[8]

Although Immelt was willing to increase his commitment to R&D, he pushed to change the balance of work being done. In addition to developing technologically sophisticated new products, he wanted to commit more resources to longer-term research that might not pay off for a decade or more. In the past, limited commitment to such long-term research had frustrated many of the center's science and engineering Ph.Ds. ("Science was a dirty word for a while," said Anil Duggal, a project leader on the advanced lighting project. "Now it's not.")[9] In selecting the long-term projects for funding, Donnelly whittled down more than 2,000 proposals and then worked with researchers to come up with the technologies that could transform a business. From the 20 big ideas his staff proposed, Donnelly had them focus on a group of five, representing fields as diverse as nanotechnology, advanced propulsion, and biotechnology.

Beyond its historic Nishayuna R&D facility, in 2000 the company had established a center in Bangalore, India. To build on that global expansion, in 2002 Immelt authorized the construction of a new facility in Shanghai, China. And as the year wore on, he began talking about adding a fourth global facility, probably in Europe.[a] Despite the slowing economy, he upped the R&D budget from $286 million in 2000 to $327 million in 2002. When asked about this increase in spending during such a difficult time for the company, he said, "Organic growth is the driver. Acquisitions are secondary to that—I can't see us go out and pay a start-up $100 million for technology that, if we had just spent $2 million a year for 10 years, we could've done a better job at. I hate that, I just hate that."[10]

Reflecting on his extensive investments in 2002, a year in which the stock dropped a further 39% from its 2001 close, Immelt said:

> Financial strength gives us the ability to invest in growth and we have viewed this economic cycle as a time to invest. We've increased the number of engineers, salespeople, and service resources. We

will invest more than $3 billion in technology, including major investments in our global resource centers. We've strengthened our commitment to China, increasing resources there 25% in 2002, and we've increased our presence in Europe. Acquisitions are a key form of investment for us and we have invested nearly $35 billion in acquisitions over the past two years. They are a key way for us to redeploy cash flow for our future growth.[11]

Ongoing Operations: Rigor and Responsiveness

To fund his strategy, Immelt drew his first source of capital from the sale of underperforming businesses, and the company's struggling insurance business was his prime target for divesture. But in the depths of an economic downturn, getting good prices for any business was not easy. So the investments needed to drive the company's growth still relied primarily on funds generated by ongoing operations, and Immelt drove the organization to deliver on the market's expectations for current-year performance. Picking up on initiatives launched years earlier, he harnessed well-embedded capabilities such as Six Sigma and digitization to drive out costs, increase process efficiency, and manage resources more effectively.

In this tough environment, Immelt's primary operating focus was on cash flow, and he realigned all the powerful tools in GE's toolbox to meet that objective. For example, Six Sigma discipline was applied to reducing the cash tied up in inventory and receivables, while process digitization was focused on sourcing economies and infrastructure efficiencies. By 2002, digitization alone was generating savings of almost $2 billion of savings a year. As always at GE, initiatives were tied to metrics, with 60% of incentive compensation dependent on cash flow generation. So, despite a tough 2002 economy that held GE's revenue growth to 5%, its cash flow from operations was $15.2 billion, up 10% on the previous year.

Although this disciplined approach was reminiscent of GE in decades past, Immelt's management style contrasted with Welch's in many ways. First, he recognized that in a post-Enron world, corporate executives faced a more skeptical and often cynical group of critics. For example, an article in *BusinessWeek* suggested, "Increasingly, the Welch record of steady double digit growth is looking less like a miracle of brilliant management and more like clever accounting that kept investors fat and happy in boom

---

[a] In 2003, GE opened its Shanghai research center and broke ground for another center in Siemens's backyard in Munich, Germany. In 2004, its 2,500 researchers worldwide filed for more than 450 patents.

times."[12] And *The Economist* opined, "Immelt has had a torrid time since taking over from Jack Welch, GE's former boss, in 2001. Waking from the dreamy 1990s, investors discovered that GE was not, after all, a smooth earnings machine that pumped out profit growth of 16 to 18% a year."[13]

Immelt understood that in such a skeptical environment, there was a need for a CEO to establish much more openness and trust. Since his natural style tended to be open and communicative, he was perfectly comfortable with the idea of increasing the transparency of GE's often complex operations. In July 2002, to make the performance of GE's financial businesses easier to understand, he broke GE Capital into four separate businesses, each with its own balance sheet and explicit growth strategy. He also committed to communicating more frequently and in more detail with investors. "We have the goal of talking about GE externally the way we run it internally," he said. After his first analysts meeting, where everyone got an advance bound copy of the data and forecasts, *BusinessWeek* commented, "That's already a break with the Welch regime where, some say, you were scared to blink in case you missed a chart."[14]

The new CEO also wanted to create a more open and less hard-edged environment within the company. He asked the 2002 class of GE's Executive Development Course (EDC) to study where GE stood in its approach to corporate responsibility.[b] Historically, this was not an issue that had received much attention at GE. Although Welch had always emphasized the importance of integrity and compliance, he had shown little interest in reaching beyond that legal requirement. The several dozen participants in the 2002 EDC visited investors, regulators, activists, and 65 companies in the U.S. and Europe to understand how GE was performing in terms of corporate responsibility. They reported to top management that although the company was ranked in the top five for its financial performance, investment value, and management talent, it was number 72 for social responsibility.

One outcome of the EDC group's report was that Immelt appointed GE's first vice president for corporate citizenship. He tapped Bob Corcoran, a trusted colleague from his days running GE Medical Systems, to lead an effort to ensure that the company was more sensitive and responsive to its broader societal responsibilities. Ever the pragmatist, Immelt saw this as more than just an altruistic response. He believed it was important for the company to remain effective:

> To be a great company today, you also have to be a good company. The reason people come to work for GE is that they want to be involved in something bigger than themselves. They want to work hard, they want to get promoted, they want stock options. But they also want to work for a company that makes a difference, a company that's doing great things in the world. . . . It's up to us to use our platform to be a good citizen. Because not only is it a nice thing to do, it's a business imperative.[15]

Rebuilding the Foundation: Beginning a Marathon

As 2003 began, Immelt was not sorry to see the end of his first full year as CEO. Despite all his efforts, 2002 had been a terrible year for the company. Revenues were up only 5% after a 3% decline the prior year. And rather than the double-digit growth he had promised, 2002 earnings increased by only 7%. By year's end the stock was at $24, down 39% from the year before and 60% from its all-time high of $60 in August 2000. Having lived through a struggling economy, the post-9/11 chaos, new regulatory demands following the corporate scandals, and an unstable global political situation, Immelt commented, "This was a not a great year to be a rookie CEO."[16]

In the midst of the turmoil, however, he reminded himself of advice he received from his predecessor. "One of the things Jack said early on that I think is totally right is: It's a marathon, it's not a sprint," Immelt recalled. "You have to have a plan, and you have to stick with it. You have to modify it at times, but every day you've got to get out there and play it hard."[17] Entering 2003 with that thought in mind, Immelt continued to drive his growth-strategy agenda.

Rebalancing the Portfolio

The year turned out to be an important one in the new CEO's efforts to rebuild the business portfolio on which he would drive GE's growth. Even after

---

[b] EDC was the top-level course at GE's renowned Crotonville training center and was reserved for those destined for the most senior echelons of management at GE. As part of their studies, each EDC class was assigned a major corporate issue to study in teams and then report back to GE's Corporate Executive Council.

completing $35 billion worth of acquisitions in the previous two years, 2003 became the biggest acquisition year in GE's history with total commitments exceeding $30 billion. The first megadeal came when the company decided to bid for the Universal entertainment business of French conglomerate Vivendi. Defying those who suggested that GE should exit the volatile media business, Immelt pushed ahead with the acquisition, which included Universal's film library, film studio, cable services, and theme park. "This is about stuff we know how to do," he said. "We understand the nuances of this industry and where it's going."[18]

Immelt's vision was to create a media business that was better positioned for a digital future. The NBC franchise, although strong, was being buffeted by changes in media distribution that saw the share of broadcast television's market shrinking. Universal added content, production facilities, cable distribution, and a strong management team—all assets that Immelt felt could greatly strengthen GE's core business. On top of that, the $5.5 billion up-front purchase price for assets valued at $14 billion was seen as an excellent buy.

Two days after announcing final terms in its purchase of Vivendi-Universal Entertainment (VUE), GE announced an agreement to purchase Amersham, a British life sciences and medical diagnostic company that Immelt had been pursuing for many months. He believed that health care was moving into an era of biotechnology, advanced diagnostics, and targeted therapies, and combining GE's imaging technology with Amersham's pharmaceutical biomarkers, for example, could create whole new ways of diagnosing and treating diseases. At $10 billion, this was a more expensive acquisition but one that he believed could boost GE's $9 billion medical products business to a $15 billion business by 2005. More important, he saw it as an engine of growth that would continue for years and even decades into the future. In his mind, it was a classic "growth platform."

The real issue that many saw in the deal, however, was less about strategic fit than organizational compatibility. The concern was that the highly innovative, science-oriented talent that Amersham had developed in the U.K. would not thrive when swallowed up by GE. It was the same criticism that Immelt had heard when critics wondered whether the creative talent in Universal's film studios would tolerate the management discipline for which GE was so well-known. But the idea of bringing creative and innovative outsiders

into GE was part of the appeal to Immelt. He saw people like Sir William Castell, Amersham's CEO, as major assets who could help develop in GE the culture of innovation that he longed to build. To emphasize the point, he put U.K.-based Castell in charge of the combined $14 billion business renamed GE Health Care and made him a vice chairman of GE. For the first time, one of the company's major businesses would be headquartered outside of the United States, a move that Immelt felt fit well with his thrust of globalization.

The other great challenge in the ongoing task of portfolio rebalancing was that GE was finding it difficult to dispose of some of the assets it no longer regarded as vital. While the recession provided lots of buying opportunities if one was willing to step up and invest, it was hardly an ideal environment in which to be selling businesses. For GE, the biggest challenge was to find buyers for the struggling insurance businesses. Although its 2003 sale of three of its major insurance entities had freed up $4.5 billion in cash, the company was still trying to find a buyer for Employers Reinsurance Company (ERC), a business generating huge ongoing losses due to its poor underwriting in the late 1990s.[c] And several other GE businesses from motors to super adhesives remained on the blocks with no bidder offering a price the company was willing to accept. Part of the problem was that bidders felt that if GE had run the business for years, most of the potential savings had already been extracted, making the units being offered less attractive for a company that wanted to squeeze out costs.

To communicate the major portfolio transformation he had undertaken to date, in 2003 Immelt began describing GE's businesses as "growth engines" and "cash generators" (see Exhibit 4). He characterized the former, which accounted for 85% of earnings, as market leaders that could grow at 15% annually through the business cycles with high returns. The latter were acknowledged as being more cyclical in nature but with consistently strong cash flows.

Focusing on Customers, Emphasizing Services

In addition to his portfolio changes, the new CEO kept working on his internal growth initiatives. As an

---

[c] After taking a $1.4 billion write-off in 2004 due to claims relating to asbestos and September 11, the company finally sold ERC for $8.5 billion in 2005, but only after booking another $2.9 billion insurance loss.

EXHIBIT 4

GE Portfolio: Growth Engines and Cash Generators

GROWTH ENGINES

Commercial Finance
GE Commercial Finance offers businesses an array of financial services and products worldwide. With particular expertise in the mid-market segment, Commercial Finance also offers loans and financing leases for major capital assets, including aircraft fleets, industrial facilities and equipment, and energy-related facilities; real estate loans and investments; and loans to and investments in public and private entities in diverse industries.

Consumer Finance
GE Consumer Finance is a leading provider of credit services to consumers, retailers and auto dealers in over 38 countries around the world. The business offers a range of financial products, including private label credit cards, personal loans, bank cards, auto loans and leases, residential mortgages, corporate travel and purchasing cards, debt consolidation, home equity loans and credit insurance.

Energy
GE Energy is one of the world's leading suppliers of technology to the energy industry, providing a comprehensive range of solutions for oil and gas, traditional and renewable power generation and energy management.

Healthcare
GE Healthcare is a global leader in diagnostic and interventional medical imaging, information and services technology. The pending acquisition of Amersham plc, a world leader in diagnostic imaging agents and life sciences, will transform GE Healthcare into the world's most comprehensive medical diagnostics company.

Infrastructure
GE Infrastructure is a high-technology platform comprising some of GE's fastest-growing businesses. They offer a set of protection and productivity solutions to some of the most pressing issues that industries face: pure water, safe facilities, plant automation and sensing applications for operating environments.

NBC
America's first broadcast network, NBC is a diverse, international media company with the Number One-ranked U.S. television network, 29 owned and operated stations, cable channels CNBC, MSNBC, and Bravo, and Spanish-language broadcaster Telemundo. NBC and Vivendi Universal Entertainment have agreed to merge and form NBC Universal, creating one of the world's fastest-growing media companies.

Transportation
GE Transportation comprises Aircraft Engines and Rail, two industry-leading business units whose products and services span the aviation, rail, marine and off-highway industries with jet engines for military and civil aircraft, freight and passenger locomotives, motorized systems for mining trucks and drills, and gas turbines for marine and industrial applications.

Leading with PORTFOLIO TRANSFORMATION

CASH GENERATORS

Consumer and Industrial
GE Consumer and Industrial serves customers in more that 100 countries with appliances, lighting products and integrated industrial equipment, systems and services sold under the Monogram®, Profile™, GE®, Hotpoint®, SmartWater™, and Reveal® consumer brands, and the Entellisys™ industrial brand.

Equipment Services
GE Equipment Services helps medium- and large-sized businesses around the world manage, finance and operate a wide variety of business equipment. Products and services include operating leases, loans, sales and transportation asset management services.

Insurance
GE Insurance offers a wide range of insurance and investment products. For businesses, GE Insurance provides insurance and reinsurance products to insurance companies, Fortune 1000 companies, self-insurers and healthcare providers. It helps consumers create and preserve personal wealth, protect assets and enhance their lifestyles.

Advanced Materials
GE Advanced Materials is a world leader in providing customers in a wide range of industries with materials solutions through engineering thermoplastics, silicon-based products and technology platforms, and fused quartz and ceramics.

As of January 1, 2004, GE has reorganized its 13 businesses into 11 focused on markets and customers—seven Growth Engines, which generate about 85% of earnings and are market leaders with strengths in technology, cost, services, global distribution and capital efficiency; and four Cash Generators, which consistently generate strong cash flow and grow earnings in an expanding economy.

This chart reflects the most significant changes: the combination of Aircraft Engines and Rail into GE Transportation; the combination of Industrial Systems and Consumer Products into Consumer & Industrial, with portions of Industrial Systems moving to other businesses; and the formation of Infrastructure from portions of Industrial Systems and Specialty Materials. Results for 2003 in this annual report are reported on the 13-business basis in effect in 2003.

Source: GE 2003 Annual Report, p. 6.

ex-salesman, Immelt had always directed attention toward the customer, and one of his priorities was to redirect GE's somewhat internal focus—an unintended by-product of Welch's obsession with operating efficiency and cost-cutting—toward the external environment. "In a deflationary world, you could get margin by working productivity," he said. "Now you need marketing to get a price."[19]

In 2001, among his first appointments had been Beth Comstock, named as GE's first chief marketing officer. Next, to drive the change deeper, he redeployed most of GE's extensive business development staff into marketing roles, then asked each of GE's businesses to appoint a VP-level marketing head, many of whom had to be recruited from the outside. "We hired literally thousands of marketers," he said. "For the best, we created the Experienced Commercial Leadership Program, the kind of intensive course we've long offered in finance. That's 200 people a year, every year."[20]

In 2003, with strong marketing capabilities now embedded in the businesses, he formed a Commercial Council to bring GE's best sales and marketing leaders together in a forum that could transfer best practice, drive initiatives rapidly through the organization, and develop a world-class commercial culture. Chaired by Immelt personally, the council's agenda included developing world-class marketing capabilities, taking Six Sigma to customers, and driving sales force effectiveness. As always, metrics were attached. Using a tool called Net Promoter Score (NPS), the company began to track changes in customer attitudes and loyalty, tying compensation to improvements in NPS scores. "If we can create a sales and marketing function that's as good as finance at GE, I'll change this company," he said. "But it will take ten years to drive these changes."[21]

Immelt also believed GE could significantly strengthen its customer relationships by becoming more of a services provider. In 2002, $23 billion of the company's $132 billion revenue came from services, but with its massive installed base of more than 100,000 long-lived jet engines, locomotives, power generators, and medical devices in the field, the CEO saw the potential service annuity stream. As someone who had increased GE Medical Systems' share of service business from 25% to 42% in the three and a half years he headed that operation, Immelt was convinced that services could grow much faster than hardware and at much higher profit levels. To underscore his belief, whenever businesses developed important service

contracts—GE Transportation's sale of its IT-based dispatch system to railroad customers to increase locomotive utilization, for example—he celebrated them very publicly.

Yet despite all these efforts, the reality was that just as many of GE's products were becoming commodities, its service contracts were increasingly going to the lowest bidder and not providing the barriers to entry they once did. GE's solution was to make itself indispensable by building enduring relationships based not only on offering its products and services but also its expertise.

One initiative, dubbed "At the Customer, For the Customer" (ACFC, as it soon became known), was designed to bring GE's most effective internal tools and practices to bear on its customers' challenges. Immelt used health care as an example of what GE could offer. With cost control being a major concern as health-care expenditures headed toward 20% of GDP, Immelt felt that GE could help its customers, only 50% of which were profitable. "Through our health care services agreements, we are the hospitals' productivity partner," he said. "We completed more than 6,000 Six Sigma projects with health care providers in 2002 and these projects are improving the quality of patient care and lowering costs."[22] In addition, the company began bundling its services and linking its products to clinical information technology. It also added a health-care financial services business to the GE Health Care organization to provide it with specialized financing support. "The phrase 'solutions provider' is so overused it makes us all snore," said Immelt. "I want GE to be essential to those whom we serve, a critical part of the profit equation, a long-term partner, a friend."[23]

Driving for Growth: New Platforms, New Processes

Beginning in 2002, Immelt had challenged his business leaders to identify growth business platforms with the potential to generate $1 billion in operating profit within the next few years. In response, six opportunities had emerged: health-care information systems, security and sensors, water technology and services, oil and gas technology, Hispanic broadcasting, and consumer finance. By the end of 2002, these businesses represented $9 billion in revenue and $2 billion in operating profit. But, as Immelt pointed out, at a 15% annual organic growth rate, they were on track to become a much larger portion of GE's future business portfolio.

With 2003's major acquisitions such as Amersham and VUE, the company added new growth platforms such as biosciences and film/DVD to its list. Through other acquisitions, renewable energy (wind, solar, biomass), coal gasification, and supply chain financing became elements of GE's new growth platform. And the emphasis on services built a series of businesses in environmental services, nondestructive testing, and asset optimization that were also seen as having high growth potential.

In defining and then building these growth platforms, GE followed its normal disciplined approach. First, management segmented the broad markets and identified the high-growth segments where they believed they could add value. Then, they typically launched their initiative with a small acquisition in that growth platform. After integrating it into GE, the objective was to transform the acquisition's business model by applying GE growth initiatives (services and globalization, for example) that could leverage its existing resources and capabilities. As a final step, the company applied its financial muscle to the new business, allowing it to invest in organic growth or further acquisitions. The objective was to grow it rapidly while simultaneously generating solid returns.

GE's expansion into Hispanic broadcasting provides an example of the process. After identifying this as a fast-growth segment in its broadcast business, the company acquired Telemundo, the number two player in the Hispanic entertainment segment. Believing that the Hispanic demographic would drive growth, management felt that it would be able to apply GE's capabilities to fix Telemundo's struggling business model. Through 2002 and 2003, NBC offered its management and programming expertise, helping Telemundo to evolve from purchasing 80% of its content to producing two-thirds of its own broadcast material. In the second half of 2003, Telemundo grew its ratings by 50% over the first half and captured 25% of the Hispanic advertising market. The company expected revenues to grow more than 20% in 2004. *Success*

As Immelt summarized, "A key GE strength is our ability to conceptualize the future, to identify unstoppable trends, and to develop new ways to grow. The growth platforms we have identified are markets that have above average growth rates and can uniquely benefit from GE's capabilities. . . . Growth is *the* initiative, *the* core competency that we are building in GE."[24]

Aligning Management: New People Profiles

The biggest challenge Immelt saw in implementing his agenda was to make growth the personal mission of every one of the company's 310,000 employees worldwide. "If I want people to take more risks, solve bigger problems, and grow the business in a way that's never been done before, I have to make it personal," he said. "So I tell people, 'Start your career tomorrow. If you had a bad year, learn from it and do better. If you had a good year, I've already forgotten about it.'"[25]

As the company began to implement its new growth strategy, the CEO worried that some of his current management team might not have the skills or abilities to succeed in the more entrepreneurial risk-taking environment he was trying to create. Realizing that this implied a massive challenge to develop a new generation of what he termed "growth leaders," he said:

> Historically, we have been known as a company that developed professional managers . . . broad problem solvers with experience in multiple businesses and functions. However, I wanted to raise a generation of *growth leaders*—people with market depth, customer touch, and technical understanding. This change emphasizes depth. We are expecting people to spend more time in a business or a job. We think this will help leaders develop "market instincts" so important for growth, and the confidence to grow global businesses.[26]

Beyond changes in career path development that emphasized more in-depth experience and fewer job rotations, GE's HR professionals wanted to identify the new personal competencies that growth leaders would need to exhibit. Benchmarking GE against best practice, they researched the leadership profiles at 15 large global companies—Toyota and Dell among them—that had grown for more than a decade at three times GDP rates or better. In late 2004, they arrived at a list of five action-oriented leadership traits they would require: an *external focus* that defines success in market terms; an ability to *think clearly* to simplify strategy into specific actions, make decisions, and communicate priorities; the *imagination and courage* to take risks on people and ideas; an ability to energize teams through *inclusiveness and connection with people*, building both loyalty and commitment; and an *expertise* in a function or domain, using depth as a source of confidence to drive change.

To help develop these characteristics, each business created 20 to 30 "pillar jobs": customer-facing, change-oriented assignments in which growth leaders could be developed in assignments of at least four to five years. The new leadership competencies also became the criteria for all internal training programs and were integrated into the evaluation processes used in all management feedback.

Immelt was also quite involved personally in developing growth leaders on his team. In response to a question about his time utilization, he said, "I'm probably spending 20% of my time with customers, 30% of my time on people, teaching and coaching . . . [and] 10% of my time on governance, working with the board, and meeting with investors. The rest would be time spent on the plumbing of the company, working on operating reviews and strategy sessions."[27] But, as he regularly pointed out, the time he spent on the "plumbing" in operating reviews and strategy sessions—"touch points," he called them—was primarily about people development. He was committed to make "every moment a learning opportunity, every activity a source of evaluation."[28]

Funding the Growth: Operating Excellence

While driving growth, Immelt never forgot that he inherited a great operating company. He did not want long-term growth to distract managers from current performance. "I've always worried about a jailbreak," he said. "How do we make sure people don't say 'Jeff doesn't care about productivity'?"[29] So he insisted that innovation be "funded with an intent to lead, but paid for by increasing productivity."[30] During 2003, for example, about one-third of the Six Sigma specialists were focused on a new initiative called "cash entitlement." The target was for GE to be twice as good as competitors on a number of benchmarks such as accounts receivable or inventory turnover. At full potential, Immelt told his team, it would free up an additional $7 billion in cash.

By 2004, while the drives for cash generation and cost reduction were still in place, Immelt added a new initiative called Lean Six Sigma, which borrowed the classic tools of lean manufacturing and set them to new applications. In its industrial businesses, the focus was on reducing working capital and improving return on equity, while in its commercial finance business it was on margin expansion, risk management, and cost reduction. Through these efforts, in 2003–2004, the company achieved $2.7 billion in improvement in working capital and expected that kind of progress to continue.

Yet another operating initiative called "simplification" aimed at reducing overhead from 11% of revenue to 8%. Targeting reductions in the number of legal entities, headquarters, "rooftops," computer systems, and other overhead-type costs not directly linked to growth, the company set a goal of removing $3 billion of such costs over three years. In the first year, the commercial finance business consolidated into three customer service/operations centers and expected to save $300 million over three years. In another simplification move, the consumer and industrial business brought its three existing headquarters into one, saving more than $100 million in structural costs. And the transportation and energy businesses began sharing some IT and operational assets that also reduced structural costs by some $300 million annually.

Preparing for Liftoff: Innovation and Internationalization

As 2004 progressed, the worldwide economy gradually started to turn around, and GE began showing signs of more robust growth. By year's end, nine of its 11 businesses had grown their earnings by double digits. For the first time, Immelt sounded confident that the company was finally moving beyond the disappointing results of the previous three years and onto the growth trajectory for which he had been preparing it. In his annual letter to stakeholders in February 2005, he recalled his time as a college football player to draw a sports analogy to GE's recent performance:

> GE has "played hurt" for the last few years. . . . So we went to the "training room." These difficult years triggered a critical review of our capabilities, and as a result, we initiated an exciting transformation. We invested more than $60 billion to create a faster-growing company. We committed to divest $15 billion of slow-growth assets. We built new capabilities, launched new products, expanded globally and invested in the GE brand. Now the company has begun an era of strong performance. . . . We're back at full strength. This is our time.[31]

To underscore the point, he predicted that GE's "growth engines"—businesses whose earnings growth since 1999 had averaged 15% annually—would generate 90% of the company's earnings in 2005, compared with only 67% in 2000. (See Exhibit 5 for a representation of the shift.) Due to this transformation of the

EXHIBIT 5

GE's Representation of Its Portfolio Transformation, 2000–2005

Portfolio Transformation	New Growth Capabilities
GE has added more than a dozen new capabilities to its seven Growth Engines, which should generate approximately 90% of GE's earnings in 2005, substantially more than five years ago. The Growth Engines— Transportation, Energy, Healthcare, NBC Universal, Infrastructure, Commercial Finance and Consumer Finance— are robust, capital-effective businesses with leadership positions for sustained double-digit earnings and cash flow growth.	**Biosciences** Film + DVD / Healthcare information technology / Renewable energy (wind, solar, biomass) / Coal gasification / Water / Security / Hispanic television / Oil and gas exploration technology / Services (asset optimization, environmental services, non-destructive testing) / "Vertical" financing / Full supply-chain financing / Real estate operations / Global mortgage

EARNINGS (in billions)

$18.6-19.5

$12.7

Growth Engines: 2000 = 67%, 2005 = 90%

Cash Generators: 2000 = 33%, 2005 = 10%

Source: GE 2004 Annual Report, p. 4.

business portfolio and also the addition of more than a dozen new capabilities from biosciences to renewable energy, Immelt claimed that for the first time in 20 years, GE was positioned to grow its industrial earnings faster than its financial services earnings.

Imagination Breakthroughs

To drive his earlier growth platform challenge deep into the organization, the CEO launched a process he called "imagination breakthroughs," quickly abbreviated to IBs. These were projects—technological innovations, market expansion opportunities, product commercialization proposals, or ideas to create value for customers—that had the potential to generate, over a three-year horizon, at least $100 million in incremental earnings. The process required each business leader to submit at least three breakthrough proposals a year for review by the Commercial Council. "Imagination Breakthroughs are a protected class of ideas—safe from budget slashers because I've

blessed each one," said Immelt. "What we're trying to do is take risks, using my point of view. I have the biggest risk profile and broadest time horizon in the company . . . so I can bring to bear the right risk-taking and time horizon tradeoffs."[32]

A year into the program, 80 IB initiatives had been identified and qualified—half technically based programs and half commercial innovations. Immelt had assigned the company's best people to drive them and had committed $5 billion over the next three years to fully fund them. In that time, they were expected to deliver $25 billion of additional revenue growth. By 2005, 25 IBs were generating revenue. "The big difference is that the business leaders have no choices here," Immelt explained. "Nobody is allowed not to play. Nobody can say, 'I'm going to sit this one out.' That's the way you drive change."[33]

Believing that the businesses could initiate 200 such projects over the next year or two, Immelt said, "Our employees want to live their dreams. It is up to me to give them that platform. I can help them take smart risks that will win over time. . . . We aim to be the best in the world at turning small ideas into huge businesses."[34]

Of Town Halls and Dreaming

To stimulate ideas that would drive the imagination breakthroughs, Immelt continued to push his leaders to get out in the field and in touch with the market. Setting the example himself by spending at least five days a month with customers, he began creating forums he called "town hall meetings." Here, several hundred customers would gather together to hear where GE's CEO wanted to take his company, to provide input on that direction, and to suggest how GE could be more helpful to them.

As an outgrowth of these meetings, Immelt decided to create another forum that he described as "dreaming sessions." In these sessions, he engaged in intensive conversations with a group of senior executives drawn from key customers in a particular industry to try to identify major industry trends, their likely implications for them, and how GE might be able to help them. Immelt understood the importance of his own role in these meetings. "If I show up, we'll get six CEOs to show up," he said. "So you don't have to cut through anything else if we all do it together. We can make some high-level tradeoffs that way."[35]

For example, in one meeting with the CEOs and key operating managers of companies in the railroad industry, Immelt spent an afternoon listening to their view of their industry situation, the key trends, and its five- to 10-year outlook. GE's CEO then asked them to think through a number of scenarios including higher fuel prices, a growth in east-west rail shipments due to increasing Chinese imports, and so on. He then challenged them to think through how they would spend $200 million to $400 million on R&D at GE. The ensuing debate highlighted, for example, the relative importance of spending on fuel efficiency versus information technology to optimize rail movement planning. But Immelt was careful to note that while the company listened carefully to the input, GE always made its own choices on these investments. "I love customers. I get great insight from them, but I would never let them set our strategy for us," he said. "But by talking to them, I can put it in my own language. Customers always pay our bills, but they will never pick our people or set our strategies."[36]

Infrastructure for Developing Countries: A New Growth Market

In 2004, Immelt's push for globalization also began bearing fruit with revenues from outside the U.S. growing 18% to $72 billion. Of this, the developing world accounted for $21 billion, an even more impressive 37% increase on the previous year, leading Immelt to predict that over the next decade, 60% of GE's international growth would come from developing countries. China represented the most visible growth opportunity, but he also planned to expand aggressively into India, Russia, Eastern Europe, Southeast Asia, the Middle East, and South America.

Through the imagination breakthrough program, proposals for improving GE's ways of doing business in the developing world began bubbling up. For example, one plan that would quickly generate $100 million in sales involved shipping unassembled locomotives to Russia, India, and China, where they would be assembled in local factories and workshops.

Furthermore, through an initiative known as "one GE," the company began creating vertical teams to deliver what it called enterprise selling. For example, companywide enterprise teams had targeted the Olympics in Beijing, Vancouver, and London and were aiming to deliver additional sales of $1 billion in energy, security, lighting, and health-care products to those venues. And increasingly GE was adopting "company-to-country relationships" in selling infrastructure projects. It was an approach that had helped it book $8 billion in Middle East orders in 2005, twice the level of 2003.

Reorganizing for Efficiency—and Growth

Driven by such developments, in July 2005, Immelt announced a major reorganization that consolidated GE's 11 businesses into six large units, one of which was GE Infrastructure. Integrating aircraft engines, rail products, water energy, oil and gas, and some financial services, the unit was headed by GE veteran David Calhoun, who aimed to offer one-stop shopping for all infrastructure products and services. Immelt's expectation was that by focusing on the needs of an underserved customer group—the governments of developing countries—GE could tap into investments in developing country infrastructure predicted to be $3 trillion over the next 10 years.

While one objective of the reorganization was to create savings (expected to be $400 million in administrative costs alone), Immelt emphasized that a more important goal was to better align the businesses with customer and market needs. But he also made clear that he wanted to create an organization that gave more opportunity for younger growth leaders to drive their businesses. The six new macrobusiness groups—GE Industrial, GE Commercial Financial Services, NBC Universal, GE Health Care, GE Consumer Finance, and GE Infrastructure—would each be led by one of GE's most experienced top executives. But these individuals would be forced to step back more from operations and spend most of their time coaching, developing, and supporting the younger managers who were to be pulled up into the 50-odd profit-responsible units directly under them. It was all part of the company's

commitment to developing its growth leaders and the businesses they ran.

Going Forward: Immelt's Challenges

In 2006, Immelt felt that GE was well placed on the growth path he had laid out over four years earlier. Between 2002 and 2005, he had put $30 billion of divestitures on the block, completed $65 billion in acquisitions, and made major investments in new capabilities in technology, marketing, and innovation. He now represented GE's growth engine as a linked six-part process (see Exhibit 6). While the components varied little from his original 2001 list

---

EXHIBIT 6

GE Growth Strategy: Core Elements, 2005 Version

Growth Is the GE Initiative. After growing historically at an average of 5% revenue growth, in 2004, we launched this initiative to achieve 8% organic growth per year. This is about twice the rate of our industrial and financial peers. We want to make organic growth a process that is predictable and reliable.

Source: GE 2005 Annual Report.

of growth elements, he explained the difference: "You've got to have a process. Investors have to see it is repeatable. . . . It took time, though, to understand growth as a process. If I had worked out that wheel-shaped diagram in 2001, I would have started with it. But in reality, you get these things by wallowing in them awhile."[37]

His main challenge now as he saw it was to maintain the growth in this $150 billion global giant. But to those who felt GE was too big to grow so fast, he had a clear response:

> The corporate landscape is littered with companies that allowed themselves to be trapped by size. But GE thrives because we use our size to help us grow. Our depth allows us to lead in big markets by providing unmatched solutions for our customers; our breadth allows us to spread concepts across the company, leveraging one small idea to create big financial gains; and our strength allows us to take the risks required to grow. . . . Our goal is not just to be big, but to use our size to be great.[38]

All he had to do now was convince the financial markets that the changes he had initiated would enable this global giant to deliver on his promise of continued double-digit growth.

ENDNOTES

1. GE Annual Report, pp. 4, 12.
2. "Solving GE's Biggest Problems," *The Economist*, October 26, 2002, p. 55.
3. Jeffery R. Immelt, "Growth as a Process," *Harvard Business Review*, June 2006, p. 62.
4. GE 2001 Annual Report.
5. Rachel Silverman, "GE Goes Back to the Future," *The Wall Street Journal*, May 7, 2002, p. B1.
6. Holman W. Jenkins, Jr., "Why GE Should/Shouldn't Go Into the Hospital Business," *The Wall Street Journal*, November 20, 2002, p. A21.
7. "Solving GE's Biggest Problems," *The Economist*, October 26, 2002, p. 55.
8. "GE Goes Back to the Future—R&D Grows in Importance," *The Wall Street Journal*, May 7, 2002, p. B1.
9. Ibid.
10. Robert Buderi, "GE Finds Its Inner Edison," *Technology Review*, October 2003, pp. 46–50.
11. Amy Stone, "GE Investors Saying 'Jack Who?'" BusinessWeek On-Line, May 9, 2003.
12. Ibid.
13. "Business: The Hard Way; General Electric," *The Economist*, October 18, 2003, p. 60.
14. Diane Brady, "Welcome to the Frying Pan, Jeff," *BusinessWeek*, October 8, 2001, p. 82.
15. Mark Gunther, "Money and Morals at GE," *Fortune*, November 15, 2004, pp. 176–182.
16. GE 2002 Annual Report, p. 5.
17. John A. Byrne, "The Fast Company Interview: Jeff Immelt," *Fast Company*, July 2005, pp. 60–65.
18. Diane Brady, "Why GE Went For a Little Glitz," *BusinessWeek*, September 15, 2003, p. 44.
19. Jeffery R. Immelt, "Growth as a Process," *Harvard Business Review*, June 2006, p. 64.
20. Ibid.
21. Ibid.
22. Ibid.
23. GE 2002 Annual Report, p. 13.
24. GE 2003 Annual Report, p. 9.
25. Jeffery R. Immelt, "Growth as a Process," *Harvard Business Review*, June 2006, p. 70.
26. Ibid.
27. John A. Byrne, "The Fast Company Interview: Jeff Immelt," *Fast Company*, July 2005, pp. 60–65.
28. GE 2005 Annual Report, p. 11.
29. Jeffery R. Immelt, "Growth as a Process," *Harvard Business Review*, June 2006, p. 64.
30. GE 2005 Annual Report, p. 7.
31. GE 2002 Annual Report, p. 4.
32. Jeffery R. Immelt, "Growth as a Process," *Harvard Business Review*, June 2006, p. 69.
33. John A. Byrne, "The Fast Company Interview: Jeff Immelt," *Fast Company*, July 2005, pp. 60–65.
34. GE 2005 Annual Report, p. 10.
35. Ibid.
36. Ibid.
37. Jeffery R. Immelt, "Growth as a Process," *Harvard Business Review*, June 2006, pp. 63–64.
38. GE 2005 Annual Report, p. 4.

This case was prepared by Gareth R. Jones, Texas A&M University.

CBS Broadcasting established Viacom as an independent company in 1970 to comply with regulations set forth by the U.S. Federal Communications Commission (FCC) barring television networks from owning cable TV systems or from syndicating their own programs in the United States. The increasing spread of cable television and the continuing possibility of conflicts of interest between television networks and cable television companies made the spinoff necessary, and Viacom separated formally from CBS in 1971 when CBS distributed Viacom's stock to its shareholders at the rate of one share for every seven shares of CBS stock.

Viacom quickly became one of the largest cable operators in the United States, with over 90,000 cable subscribers. It also owned the syndication rights to a large number of popular, previously run CBS television series that it made available for syndication to cable TV stations. Revenue from these rights accounted for a sizable percentage of Viacom's income. In 1976, to take advantage of Viacom's experience in syndicating programming to cable TV stations, its managers decided to establish the Showtime movie network to compete directly with HBO, the leading outlet for films on cable television. In 1977, Viacom earned $5.5 million on sales of $58.5 million. Most of its earnings represented revenues from the syndication of its television series, but they also reflected

growth of its own cable TV systems, which at this time had about 350,000 subscribers. Recognizing that both producing and syndicating television programming could earn greater profits, Viacom's managers decided to produce their own television programs in the late 1970s and early 1980s. Their efforts produced only mixed results, however, no hit series resulted from their work, and the Big Three television networks of ABC, NBC, and CBS continued to dominate the airwaves.

During the early 1980s, the push to expand the cable television side of its business became Viacom's managers' major priority. Cable television is a highly capital-intensive business, and Viacom made a large investment to build its cable infrastructure; for example, it spent $65 million on extending its customer base in 1981 alone. By 1982, Viacom had added 450,000 subscribers to the 90,000 it inherited from CBS, making it the ninth largest cable operator in the United States. Also, by 1982 Viacom sales had grown to $210 million, with about half its revenues coming from program syndication and about half from its cable operations.

Viacom's managers, however, continued to feel that its cable operations were not a strong enough engine for future growth. One reason was that cable TV prices were regulated at this time, and cable companies were limited in how much they could charge customers. Its managers continued to believe that real growth in earnings would come not from providing cable television service but providing the *content* of cable programming—television programs. Given their previous failure in making their own programs, Viacom's managers sought to make acquisitions in the content side of the business—in companies that made entertainment programs. In 1981,

Viacom started in a small way by buying a minority stake in Cable Health Network, a new advertiser-supported television network. Then, in September 1985, in a stroke of fortune, it made the acquisition that would totally change the company's future. Viacom purchased the MTV Networks from Warner Bros., a company that desperately needed cash because Warner's own cable TV system needed a lot of capital to keep it viable.

The MTV Networks included MTV, a new popular music video channel geared toward the fourteen-to-twenty-four-age group; Nickelodeon, a channel geared toward children; and VH-1, a music video channel geared toward an older twenty-five-to-forty-four-age audience. MTV was the most popular property in the MTV Network. Its quick pace and flashy graphics were popular among young television viewers, and its young audience was a major target of large advertisers. The popularity of a station's programming determines how many advertisers it will attract and how much it can charge them. While MTV was performing well, Nickelodeon had been less successful and had not achieved any notable following among young viewers, which limited the revenues it could earn from advertisers. Viacom moved quickly to revamp Nickelodeon, giving it the slick, flashy look of MTV and developing unique programming that appealed to children, programming that was very different from that offered by competitors like the Disney Channel. In the next few years, Nickelodeon went from being the least popular channel on basic cable among children to being the most popular, and Viacom's managers were confident that they had in place the beginning of a new programming strategy to complement Viacom's cable TV interests and to guide the company to long-term profitability.

Enter Sumner Redstone

Viacom's hopes were shattered when its Showtime channel lost about 300,000 customers between March 1985 and March 1986 because of intense competition from HBO. HBO, under its then CEO Frank Biondi, was making itself the dominant pay movie channel by producing its own innovative programming and by forming exclusive agreements with major movie studios like Paramount to offer their movies to HBO first. As a result of the loss of customers, Viacom's cash flow dropped dramatically,

and the company lost $9.9 million on sales of $919.2 million in 1986. Further weakened by the $2 billion debt load it had incurred to fund its cable expansion program and make its programming acquisitions, Viacom became a takeover target.

After a competitive six-month battle to acquire the company, Sumner M. Redstone bought Viacom for $3.4 billion in March 1986. Redstone was the owner of a closely held corporation, National Amusements Inc. (NAI), that owned and operated 675 movie screens in fourteen states in the United States and the United Kingdom. Redstone became chairman of Viacom's board and moved quickly to take control of the company. He had built NAI from fifty drive-in movie theaters to a modern theater chain. He is credited with pioneering the development of the multiplex movie theater concept, which offers moviegoers a choice of a dozen or more screens to choose from. However, running a chain of movie theaters was very different from running a debt-laden media conglomerate as complicated as Viacom.

Many analysts felt that Redstone had overpaid for Viacom, but he saw a great potential for growth. Besides its cable television systems and syndication rights, which now included the popular TV series *The Cosby Show*, Redstone recognized the potential of its MTV and Nickelodeon channels. Moreover, over the years Viacom had acquired five television and eight radio stations in major markets, which he saw as valuable investments. Redstone moved quickly to solve Viacom's problems, and with the "hands-on" directive management style for which he is well known, he fired Viacom's top managers and began the search for capable managers who would be loyal and obedient to him. To turn Showtime around, he immediately hired Frank Biondi, the chief executive who had made HBO the dominant movie channel, as CEO of Viacom.

Frank Biondi was just a few days away from moving to Hollywood to run Columbia Pictures when Redstone called and asked him to take over as CEO of Viacom. The forty-nine-year-old Biondi was known for his strong financial, deal-making, and strategic skills and a knack for managing a diverse group of young executives and building them into a cooperative unit. Unlike Redstone, who likes to be directly involved in the day-to-day operations of a business, however, Biondi felt that his job was to set challenging goals, find the resources—both capital and people—to achieve them, and then get out of the way to let his managers achieve them. His approach was to decentralize control to his managers and to let them get the job done. Analysts felt the combination of Redstone's hands-on approach and Biondi's future thinking style made them a very effective team to head the growing entertainment conglomerate.

Viacom Speeds Up

Redstone's takeover of Viacom was fueled by his belief that cable television programming would become the dominant means of providing consumers with their entertainment content in the future. With the acquisition of Viacom, Redstone now owned 76% of MTV and Nickelodeon, which together gave Viacom access to millions of viewers aged two to twenty-four. Redstone believed Viacom's cable networks were its "crown jewels" because they provided half the company's revenues and profits, which came both from subscribers (the cable companies that bought the programming) and from advertisers (who advertised on these channels). To strengthen the cable channel franchise and build its brand name, Redstone restructured MTV and installed a more aggressive advertising and sales staff. Against the expectations of many industry analysts, MTV and Nickelodeon experienced continued growth and profitability. In 1989, for example, the MTV Networks won 15% of all dollars spent on cable advertising. MTV was expanding throughout the world, broadcasting to Western Europe, Japan, Australia, and large portions of Latin America.

Despite the success of the MTV channels, Redstone still faced the problem of paying off the debt that he had incurred to acquire Viacom—debt that amounted to $450 million in interest in the first two years following the takeover. Several fortuitous events aided him. First, shortly after the buyout, Viacom began to earn millions of dollars from television stations wanting to show reruns of the blockbuster *Cosby Show.* Second, in 1987 Congress deregulated cable television and allowed cable television companies to charge what they liked for their programming. The result was that the prices charged for cable television service soared, and so did the price of cable television franchises. Redstone took full advantage of this situation to sell off some of Viacom's cable assets to help reduce debt. In February 1989, Viacom's Long Island and suburban Cleveland cable systems were sold to Cablevision Systems Corp. for $545 million,

or about twenty times their annual cash flow. Cablevision also bought a 5% stake in Showtime for $25 million, giving it an interest in promoting the channel to Cablevision's customers and helping Showtime get back in competition with HBO. These events enabled Redstone to significantly cut Viacom's debt and negotiate more favorable terms on its loans. However, it was rough going, and Viacom lost $154.4 million in 1987, even though its sales increased to almost $1 billion.

With Viacom's finances on a firmer footing and Showtime showing some renewed vigor, Redstone and Biondi began to plan how to make Viacom a leader in the production of creative entertainment. In a strategic alliance with the Hearst Corp. and Capital Cities/ABC Inc., Viacom introduced Lifetime, a channel geared toward women. Viacom Pictures was started in 1989 so that the company could make its own movies. Viacom Pictures produced ten feature films in its first year at a cost of about $4 million a film—a very low cost compared to the money the major studios like Paramount and Universal spent. Under Biondi, Viacom's television production operations, which had always achieved mixed results, started to achieve great success with programs like *Matlock* for NBC and *Jake and the Fatman* for CBS. To increase subscribers to the important Showtime channel, Redstone sold 50% of Showtime to TCI, a major cable systems operator, for $225 million in 1989. In November of 1989, Viacom bought five more radio stations for $121 million to add to the nine it already owned.

Together with the five television stations and the fourteen cable systems it owned, Viacom's many different properties and assets earned revenues of $1.4 billion in 1989 and generated profits of $131 million. In 1990 and 1991, however, while Viacom's sales continued to increase, Viacom experienced losses of $89 million and $49 million on sales of $1.6 billion and $1.7 billion, respectively, because of increased costs associated with developing new programming and the lackluster performance of its Showtime network.

Viacom in the Early 1990s

The problem facing Redstone and Biondi was how to position Viacom for profitable growth in the 1990s. Both executives felt that developing and expanding Viacom's strengths in content programming—often referred to as entertainment software—were the key to its future success, despite how costly such programming was. They believed that the message or content that is sent is what really matters, not the medium or distribution channels that carry it. As Biondi put it, "In the end, a pipe is just a pipe. The customer doesn't care how the information is obtained; all that matters is the message."

To build its content programming strengths, Biondi worked hard to build and expand on the success of Viacom's MTV channels. His goal was to promote the MTV networks as global brands that were perceived as having something unique to offer. Since MTV's viewers dominate the record-buying audience, Biondi sought to negotiate exclusive contracts that give MTV the first crack at playing most major record companies' music videos—thus making it unique. At the same time, under Redstone and Biondi's control MTV went from being a purely music video channel to a channel that championed new kinds of programming to appeal to a young audience. The result was innovative programming such as *Beavis and Butthead, Road Stories,* and other kinds of youth-oriented programming interspersed with music videos.

In developing its programming strategy, however, Viacom's interest was not in promoting certain specific programs or stars—all of which may have short-lived popularity of fame—but in building its networks as unique brands. For example, on the MTV channel, the goal was to attract viewers because of what the channel as a whole personifies—an appeal to youth. Its success is based not on any particular person but on what MTV stands for. Under its new management, MTV prospered and its franchise was extended into Europe, Asia, and Latin America. Soon, MTV reached 250 million households in seventy-four countries. Viacom began to perform much better: in 1992 it made profits of $48 million on sales of $1.86 billion, and in 1993 it made profits of $70 million on sales of $2 billion.

While the development of innovative new programming was one reason for Viacom's return to profitability, a second, very important reason was Redstone's emphasis on keeping costs under control. Redstone is well known for his frugal way of doing business. He runs Viacom in a cost-conscious manner, and this trend is evident throughout the organization, from the top executives to the lower levels of management. For example, Redstone has his office not in a prestigious Park Avenue, New York, location like the large networks, but in a small unimposing building a couple of blocks from New York's "red light" district. Despite his huge personal net worth, he was walking to work every morning.

Redstone tried to instill his cost-conscious attitude down through the organization and across its many properties into specific business projects. For example, in the last decade costs soared in many Hollywood studios and television networks because the producers were at the mercy of talent agencies that demanded high prices for their stars, writers, and production companies. Not so with Viacom. Redstone insisted that its own programming be produced by its own employees using low-cost, homegrown talent. An example of this is the production of its MTV shows. All of its hosts are virtually unknown and are paid little relative to well-known network hosts who are paid millions of dollars a year.

Changes in the Media and Entertainment Industry

In their efforts to build their companies' programming strengths, Redstone and Biondi realized that the environment around them was rapidly changing and that it was not at all clear how programming would be delivered to customers in the future. First, by the mid-1990s the U.S. cable television industry was in a state of flux. Emerging technologies such as wireless satellite TV and then Internet broadband threatened to bypass traditional cable systems, rendering Viacom's investment in wired cable much less valuable. Second, pressures were building to deregulate the telecommunications industry, and eventually companies in different industries, for example, cable companies, telephone companies, and Internet service providers (ISPs), were allowed to enter each other's markets. These changes reinforced Redstone and Biondi's belief that during the coming decade the most successful companies would not be those that offered customers a channel into the home by cable, telephone wire, or wireless transmission.

Instead, they believed that to prosper in this fast-changing environment an entertainment company should be the provider of the entertainment to all these channels. In other words, the most successful companies would be those that could offer the programming to go on the channels—*the software providers,* not the hardware providers who provided the infrastructure to bring the entertainment into peoples' homes. With its MTV, Nickelodeon, Showtime, and Cinemax channels, as well as its syndicated programming, and its ability to make its own programming, Viacom was in a good position to form alliances with the companies that provided the channels into peoples' homes. It would provide the software (the programming) to the companies that provided the hardware (the wired and wireless cable companies and telephone companies). Viacom's revenues would come both from the fees it charged to the hardware providers for its entertainment channels and, most importantly, from the advertising revenues it would obtain from selling spots on its many channels—revenues that are determined by the extent of the viewing audience. However, Redstone and Biondi had discovered how expensive it is to develop innovative programming and how devastating the effects of a flop of several movies or programs can be for profitability. The question was how to obtain high-quality programming at the right price, especially in an entertainment and media industry in which the value of companies was rocketing as stock prices increased.

The Paramount and Blockbuster Mergers

Viacom now had a new mission: it should become a software-driven company with a goal of driving its entertainment software through every distribution system, to every multimedia application, and to every region on earth. To achieve Viacom's mission, Redstone began to search for a company that possessed the software strengths that could produce the programming content for worldwide distribution. In particular, he went looking for an entertainment company that had an already established film studio that would round out Viacom's programming portfolio by supplying feature films and TV shows to its television channels. Paramount Pictures provided Redstone with his opportunity.

Paramount's many businesses include both entertainment and publishing. Its entertainment businesses include the production, financing, and distribution of motion pictures, television programming, and prerecorded videocassettes; and the operation of motion picture theaters, independent television stations, regional theme parks, and Madison Square Garden. Paramount also owned a large library of movies. Its publishing interests included Simon & Schuster, which publishes and distributes hardcover and paperback books for the general public and textbooks for elementary schools, high schools, and colleges; it also provides information services for businesses and professions.

Redstone and Biondi began to picture the extensive synergies that a merger with Paramount would provide Viacom in the future. As Redstone told reporters, "This merger is not about two plus two equaling four, but six, or eight, or ten." Redstone believed that together Viacom and Paramount would be a much more efficient and profitable organization. He had a vision, for example, of Paramount making films that featured MTV characters like Beavis and Butthead and new cable TV channels supported by Paramount's library of 1,800 films and 6,100 television programs. Both Redstone and Biondi believed that Paramount was a priceless asset for an entertainment company hoping to provide a broad range of programming content for future distribution to global customers. With its strengths not just in visual programming but also in publishing books and magazines, Viacom would become a multimedia entertainment powerhouse that could redraw the competitive map in the entertainment industry.

On September 12, 1993, after behind-the-scene talks between Redstone and Paramount executives, Paramount announced an $8.2 billion merger with Viacom. Soon, however, a bidding war for Paramount started. Barry Diller, the CEO of QVC Network Inc., another large entertainment company and the owner of the home shopping network, recognized the logic behind Viacom's strategy and announced a hostile bid for Paramount. On September 20, 1993, QVC announced an $80 per share or $9.5 billion bid for Paramount, and the battle between Viacom and QVC for ownership of Paramount Communications Inc. was on.

This unwelcome bid from QVC presented a significant problem for Redstone: Viacom still had substantial debt because of his original 1987 acquisition of Viacom and the rapid development of its own television programming. Redstone could not afford to counter QVC's bid unless he obtained other sources of financing, and he had to search around for partners to support his bid. After a career of financing deals with his own pocketbook, including the 1987 Viacom takeover, the seventy-year-old tycoon was forced to turn to other companies to rescue the Paramount deal. Redstone found two potential partners in Nynex and Blockbuster.

Nynex, one of the Baby Bell companies, anticipated that deregulation would allow it to enter the cable television market and wanted an alliance with a company that could supply it with programming content. Blockbuster, under its own energetic CEO Wayne Huizinga, had grown to become the largest chain of video stores in the nation. Blockbuster was cash rich as a result of its recent rapid growth. Huizinga, recognizing the threat that the growth in electronic movie mediums (such as video pay-per-view, wireless cable, and videos through fiber-optic phone lines) could pose to the sale and rental of videocassettes, was on the lookout for a way to reduce this risk. He agreed to support Redstone's bid for Paramount as a way to diversify Blockbuster's interests.

Redstone was not anxious to forge alliances with these companies, commenting that alliances are tricky: "No one who is not a hypocrite or a liar can guarantee how a relationship will look in the future." Moreover, Redstone also saw that Blockbuster's future was in doubt as a result of the growth in electronic means of providing home movie videos. However, his need for cash to outbid QVC for ownership of Paramount was stronger than his worries about forming the alliances. On October 21, 1993, after having aligned himself with these partners, Redstone obtained $600 million cash from Blockbuster and a $1.2 billion commitment from Nynex Corp. He then used this money to match QVC's offer of $80 per share for 51% of Paramount stock with the rest in Viacom stock. Furthermore, anticipating a higher offer by QVC, Viacom raised its bid to $85 a share for 51% of the stock. Many analysts argued that this bidding war had become a personal battle between Redstone and QVC chairman Barry Diller and that whoever was the winner was doomed to pay much too much for Paramount—so much for low-cost programming.

On December 20, QVC raised its offer to $92 a share in cash for 50.1%, topping Viacom, which asked for more time to raise cash. On December 22, Paramount signed a merger agreement with QVC, but the bidding could continue, with a deadline for final bids on February 1, 1994. Redstone, desperate for more cash, went to Blockbuster CEO Wayne Huizinga for more money. Huizinga, increasingly convinced that it was in Blockbuster's shareholders' best interests to merge with Viacom, suggested that Viacom should take over Blockbuster for a hefty stock price. Redstone, recognizing the value of Blockbuster's cash reserves and huge cash flow from current operations, agreed.

On January 7, 1994, Viacom announced an $8.4 billion merger with Blockbuster; it also announced a new bid for Paramount for $105 a share in cash. After the bruising battle with QVC, Viacom gained full ownership of Paramount on July 7, 1994. Redstone hailed the new Viacom as an "entertainment colossus" and "a massive global media company."

Explosive Growth

In a few short years, Redstone had gone from controlling several hundred movie theaters to controlling the properties and franchises of three *Fortune 500* companies; Viacom, Blockbuster, and Paramount. By engineering the three-way merger of Viacom, Paramount, and Blockbuster Entertainment, Redstone created one of the three largest media empires in the United States (the others being the Disney/Capital Cities ABC, and AOL Time Warner), with annual revenues in excess of $10 billion. This was a large jump from the $2 billion revenue that Viacom had just before these mergers. However, Redstone and Biondi faced several major challenges in managing Viacom's new entertainment empire.

Engineering Synergies

To justify the expensive purchase of Paramount and Blockbuster, it became essential that Redstone and Biondi engineer synergies between Viacom's different entertainment properties, each of which was organized as a separate business division. Several efforts were immediately begun. Paramount executives were instructed to evaluate the potential of new shows developed by MTV for sale to television networks and TV stations. Viacom launched its new channel, the United Paramount Network (UPN), in January 1995 to take advantage of all the programming resources across its entertainment divisions. For example, MTV executives were instructed to quickly begin developing programming for the new network channel, which in 1996 was on the air only a few hours a day but today is on the air five days a week and through its TV broadcasting affiliates can reach almost all U.S. television households.

In another attempt to create synergies, Paramount executives were instructed to make their moviemaking skills available to the MTV Network and to help it make inexpensive movies that could be distributed through Paramount. One result of this was a Beavis and Butthead movie produced by Paramount and scheduled for late 1996. This was a first step in Redstone's strategy to boost the output of movies at the Paramount studio without having to finance a big increase in the studio's own movie budget and to find ways of making low-budget movies. Redstone and Biondi also searched for synergies between Blockbuster and Viacom's other divisions. They hoped that Blockbuster could link its retail stores with Viacom's cable networks and Paramount's extensive film library. Perhaps Blockbuster could sell copies of Paramount's vast library of movies to encourage people to create their own video collections. Also, the release of a new Paramount movie on video could be timed to coincide with a major advertising campaign in Blockbuster stores to promote the launch. In addition, Viacom's publishing division, Simon & Schuster, would be able to release paperback books to coincide with the release, and perhaps even a multimedia CD-ROM product could be introduced to boost sales. Finally, the launch of new movies could be timed to coincide with a major advertising blitz on the MTV channel—something that happened when Paramount released *Mission Impossible,* in the summer of 1996. As Redstone said, "Viacom through its new combination of assets is poised to participate in, and in many ways define, the entertainment and information explosion about to engulf the globe." As things turned out, however, there was little potential for synergies to emerge between Viacom's various divisions.

Structure and Management Challenges

Sumner Redstone has always enjoyed hands-on control of the day-to-day running of the company and is constantly involved in managing the problems facing the various divisions. To jump-start the process of leveraging competencies across divisions and reducing costs, he moved quickly to develop a hand-picked team of executives across Viacom's new divisions to install his cost-conscious frugal values in divisional managers. Before being acquired, Paramount was run by an all-powerful boss, Martin S. Davis, and a group of executives who flew corporate jets and spent company funds lavishly. Redstone sold Paramount's two corporate jets and installed his own cost-conscious managers to change Paramount's free-spending habits. Also in 1994 Viacom dismissed Richard E. Snyder, the chairman of Simon & Schuster, who was known for his free-spending ways.

Media and Entertainment Industry Challenges

The fast-changing entertainment and media industry also created many new challenges for Redstone and Biondi. The major Hollywood players were changing rapidly. In the old Hollywood, seven major studios dominated film and the three Big Three networks—ABC, CBS, and NBC—delivered TV programming to mass audiences. Now, the number of distribution channels was exploding. Government regulations preventing broadcast networks from owning TV programming companies were phased out, and the competitive dynamics of the industry changed. Viacom's strategy to develop a full line of entertainment programming fitted well with the changes occurring in the industry. The media and entertainment industry was also experiencing rapid globalization as U.S. movies, news, and TV shows spread around the world. A major challenge facing Viacom was to obtain access to the global marketplace—with a potential market of 900 million viewers in India and a billion-plus in China. As an example of Viacom's global push, in March 1995 Viacom won a cable television license to launch its Nickelodeon and VH-1 channels in Germany, Europe's biggest and potentially most lucrative media market, to complement the MTV pop music network, which has operated in Europe since 1987.

Technology challenges also confronted the media industry. Advances in digital and information technology, including streaming audio and video, began to offer viable new ways to distribute software content to customers. Just as the dominance of the Big Three networks—ABC, NBC, and CBS—has been eroded by the growth of companies like Viacom with its assorted networks, so now many new avenues for distributing content to consumers were emerging with the growth of the Internet and advances in broadband technology. Digital piracy was also becoming evident, as websites were springing up to exchange digital files, and companies like Napster were just a few years away.

Finally, the growing strength of Viacom spurred the consolidation of the entertainment industry. In 1995, Time Warner announced that it would merge with Turner Broadcasting, and Disney announced that it would merge with Capital Cities/ABC. As a result, the industry was now composed of four major players: Disney, Viacom, AOL Time Warner, and News Corp., which owns the Fox channel.

Problems for Viacom

Soon after Redstone's expensive decision to buy Paramount, the Paramount movie *Forrest Gump* became a surprise hit, generating over $250 million for Viacom and silencing those Redstone critics who had argued that he had spent too much to buy the movie company. Viacom's managers began to feel like Forrest Gump, with his philosophy that "life is like a box of chocolates: You never know what you're going to get." It seemed that Redstone and Viacom had been in the right place at the right time and had made a profitable acquisition. Just as Redstone had sensed the potential of MTV, so too had he sensed the potential of Paramount and Blockbuster.

By summer 1995, however, the selection of chocolates in Viacom's box did not seem as good as in 1994. Many of the hoped-for synergies had not been obtained. For example, before the merger Redstone claimed that Blockbuster would be valuable to Viacom as a distributor of its creative programming; however, few benefits of this kind had been achieved. Similarly, analysts argued that Paramount had to cooperate much more closely with Viacom's cable TV channels and with Blockbuster Video if synergies were to be forthcoming. Moreover, the performance of both the Paramount and Blockbuster divisions had been disappointing. The Gump smash hit had been followed by a string of expensive failures. Redstone and Biondi had begun to realize that making movies is a very risky business and that past successes are no indication of future success. Paramount's share of the box office dropped from 14% in 1994 to 10% in 1995. Moreover, Redstone was annoyed about the high marketing and production costs of the movies that Paramount was making, and after a string of failures, he wanted to know what the studio was doing. Hit movies are vital to a movie studio because they provide the cash flow that pays for the flops and bankrolls the future. Paramount's poor performance was hurting Viacom's cash flow and ability to service its debt. Moreover, box-office hits are crucial because they drive the rest of a movie studio's profits from international markets to home video and television.

To compound the Paramount problem, the Blockbuster division was also not doing well. Viacom had bought Blockbuster at the peak of its success—when its revenues were doubling every year and its free cash flow was a valuable asset. After the acquisition Blockbuster began to run into intense competition from two sources. First, a number of new rival video chains such as Hollywood Video had recently sprung up that were giving it intense competition and creating a price war in some markets. Second,

pay-per-view on demand television was spreading rapidly in large urban markets. Blockbuster's revenues were flat, and the hoped-for growth in cash flow to help service Viacom's debts had not occurred.

To make matters worse, Redstone had a falling-out with the top management teams of Paramount and Blockbuster whom he thought were doing a poor job. He forced the resignations of many key executives and went in search of new leadership talent. Then, in January 1996 he stunned the entertainment world when he announced that he was firing his second-in-command Frank Biondi, who was well respected throughout Hollywood, because he believed Biondi did not have the "hands-on skills" needed to manage the kinds of problems that Viacom was facing. Redstone felt that Biondi's decentralized management style was out of place in a company actively searching for synergies and cost reductions. In place of Biondi he promoted his two lieutenants, Phillipe Dauman and Tom Dooley, to orchestrate Viacom's strategy, even though they had little direct experience with the entertainment business.

Viacom's New Moves

In March 1996, Redstone hired William Fields, a senior Wal-Mart manager who had extensive experience in running efficient retail operations through advanced IT, to be the CEO of Blockbuster. Redstone hoped he could find a way to transform the Blockbuster Video stores into broader based entertainment-software stores, given that it currently seemed likely that the video rental business would be swept away by the new wireless cable and direct broadcasting technologies.

Redstone himself became more involved in the day-to-day running of Paramount, spending more time with its marketing and production executives to understand the workings of the business. Many analysts wondered how good a job the seventy-year-old Redstone would do without the aid of a seasoned entertainment executive. Analysts also pointed to Viacom's lack of a strong global presence or any executives who had experience globally. They noted that Redstone did not have any personal international experience.

In the spring of 1996 Viacom's stock price plunged from a high of $54.50 to $35 as investors fled the stock because of problems at Blockbuster and Paramount. In the summer of 1996, after a string of flops (with the exception of *Mission Impossible*), Redstone announced plans to cut back the number of movies Paramount would make and to reduce its production costs as he searched for a new strategy. Chief among Viacom's problems was its huge debt, which had to be pruned by more asset sales. In addition, Redstone and his managers had to find ways to reduce rising operating costs and overheads as well as to find new ways of leveraging resources and competences across divisions to increase revenues and build cash flow.

On the cost side, flat revenues and soon-to-be losses at Blockbuster and Paramount were pulling down the performance of the whole corporation. Blockbuster was now a growing liability, and Field's efforts were not bearing quick results. In fact, Blockbuster's revenues were falling. In 1997, Fields left and Redstone brought in a new CEO, John Antioco. In 1998 they streamlined Blockbuster's operations and sold off its new music store business for $115 million in cash. (Case 13 on Blockbuster provides detailed information on Blockbuster's new strategy.) They also introduced the radical idea of video-rental revenue sharing with the movie studios, and within a few years Blockbuster's revenues were increasing again. Also, in 1998 Redstone sold off all the rest of Paramount Studios' publishing interests, except for its lucrative consumer publishing group, to Pearson for $4.6 billion and used this money to reduce debt.

On the revenue side, there were signs that some potential synergies were emerging. For example, an alliance between MTV and Simon & Schuster resulted in a successful line of "Beavis and Butthead" titles, and Paramount did produce a successful Beavis and Butthead movie. Also, Viacom's global presence was widening as Redstone formed alliances overseas and as its television studios were developing new channels, including a second MTV channel to be called MTV2, which would focus exclusively on music videos, since the regular MTV channel had become more involved in regular programming. In 1997, growing demand for its entertainment content led Viacom to offer to buy the rest of Spelling entertainment with its Star Trek franchise and Big Ticket Television Unit. Its content was perfect for Viacom's growing UPN network, although that network had yet to make a profit. Redstone integrated Spelling into Paramount's television operations to obtain economies of scale and scope in the production of new television programming. He was clearly focused on

reaping the long-term benefits from his entertainment empire, although the poor performance of Viacom's stock was a big personal embarrassment to him as his acquisitions were continually being criticized.

By 1999, Blockbuster's recovering revenues and cash flow allowed Redstone to announce an initial offering of Blockbuster stock so that the performance of that division could be separated from the rest of the company. Redstone believed it was impossible to assess Viacom's true value until a real market value was put on this unit. About 18% of Blockbuster's stock was sold at $16 to $18 a share, and the over $250 million raised was used to pay off its debt.

Also in 1999, Redstone hired the experienced media and entertainment manager and former head of CBS, Mel Karmazin, as Viacom's chief operating officer to help solve its ongoing problems. Karmazin was well known for his ability to select and manage hit programming and for his hands-on ability to find ways to leverage resources to improve operational effectiveness. He set to work restructuring Viacom's businesses to engineer cross-divisional synergies, create new programming content, and enhance its revenue and earnings stream.

Both Redstone and Karmazin also understood that one of the most important reasons to build an entertainment empire was to achieve economies of scale that arise from being able to offer potential advertisers the opportunity to advertise their products across multiple channels that attract different kinds of viewers. In other words, a potential advertiser could produce one or more themed commercials to run across all of Viacom's different TV networks as well as with its movies or in its books, theme parks, and so on. Redstone had also watched Disney merge with the ABC networks to provide it with a major new distribution channel for its Disney franchise, a move that also had made DisneyABC the biggest entertainment and media company in the world.

Since the majority of Viacom's future revenue stream would come from advertising, Redstone established a new unit, Viacom Plus, to provide a centralized advertising service that deals directly with large advertisers and handles advertising for *all* of Viacom's divisions. For example, in 2001 Procter & Gamble and Viacom Plus negotiated a groundbreaking cross-platform deal whereby P&G would pay $300 million for advertising spread across nine of Viacom's major divisions; the success of this deal led it to pay $350 million in 2002 for advertising spread across fourteen of Viacom's divisions. P&G obtained a better deal than if it had negotiated with each Viacom property individually, and Viacom Plus reduced the costs associated with managing the vital advertising process. In 2002, Monster.com, the online job site, signed a $15 million deal with Viacom Plus to put all its "scatter money"—the money a company has to scatter across different channels and demographic groups—into the Viacom platform.

The CBS Acquisition

A new opportunity arose in 1999. CBS networks were in trouble because CBS ratings were dropping, and the company was interested in a merger in the consolidating entertainment industry. Redstone realized that with CBS's assets Viacom would reach the greatest number of viewers and listeners (CBS-owned Infinity Radio Broadcasting) of any media enterprise, spanning all ages and demographics from "cradle to cane." As such, it would become a premier outlet for advertisers around the world because it could now offer them the opportunity to achieve huge economies of scale and scope in their advertising efforts. Advertising content could be driven and promoted across virtually all media segments, including broadcast and cable television, radio, and outdoor advertising and new digital media. Also, channels such as MTV, MTV2, VH-1, and CMT could now be broadcast over Trinity's radio stations and over the Internet, and CBS's high-quality content, such as its news and sports programming, could be broadcast over all Viacom's properties. The huge scale would also give the combined company bargaining power with programming suppliers and allow it to maximize the effectiveness of its sales force across all its divisions—a major source of potential extra revenue and cost savings. Perhaps a part of Viacom's problems was that it was simply not big enough?

In September 1999, Viacom and CBS Corp. announced that they would merge the two companies in the largest media transaction to that date. All operations of the company would report to Mel Karmazin. The range of Viacom's properties was now staggering in its scope, especially because at the time of the merger CBS was in the process of taking control of radio station owner Infinity Broadcasting and King World productions, which syndicated such shows as *Jeopardy* and the *Oprah Winfrey Show*. Moreover, the merger was achieved through a stock swap so that no debt needed to be incurred to fund it, something

Viacom could not afford because its revenues and performance were still slowly increasing.

Karmazin now gave his full attention to structuring and managing Viacom's assets to realize the gains from sharing and leveraging the competencies of its division across all its operations. It began to seem that with the CBS acquisition Viacom had achieved the critical mass that made such gains realizable. In May 2000, Karmazin announced the integration of the company's theme parks, Paramount Parks, into the Viacom Entertainment Group. This move would grow the parks faster by linking them to Viacom's other properties, such as its Nickelodeon and MTV cast of characters. In 2000, Karmazin integrated Paramount's and CBS's television groups, and the new division consisted of thirty-five television stations reaching eighteen of the top twenty television markets in the United States. The hope was that this would lead to major operational and sales efficiencies, especially because all advertising and promotion could be linked to the company's Infinity radio stations and outdoor advertising operations, creating the "advertising bundle" mentioned above. CBS would now function as a local as well as a national broadcaster and it could leverage its news, sports, and other programming across many more markets. In 2000, Viacom's television studios also formed a unit called MTV Films to produce movies for Paramount. Some of its low-budget movies, which generally cost around $30 million to make, half the normal Hollywood budget, made a profit, including the Rugrats and *Beavis and Butthead Do America*.

In 2001, in yet another move to make it the number 1 advertising platform in the world for advertisers with programming that appealed to every demographic category, Viacom acquired Black Entertainment Television (BET) for $3 billion. The BET network reaches 63.4 million U.S. households, and its other channels, like BET on Jazz and BET International, reach thirty countries in Europe and thirty-six in Africa. The BET acquisition was just one part of Viacom's push to become the dominant global media company. Continuing its strategy of leveraging value from its properties, BET is seeking more ways to integrate its activities with other Viacom properties, both by customizing various Viacom TV programming for BET's channels and vice versa, not only popular shows but also news and sports.

All of Viacom's networks were also instructed to follow MTV's lead and develop a global strategy to produce content locally in each country in which they were broadcast to increase the company's global viewing audience. MTV, for example, has a presence in most of the world's major markets; it reaches 125 million households and is a major revenue generator for Viacom. And, while it broadcasts its U.S. programming in countries abroad, it had also produced successful shows in countries abroad that are customized to local tastes; these have proved so popular that they have been transferred successfully to the United States and other countries. In 2001, Redstone met China's president Jaing in Beijing to affirm Viacom's commitment to China, and in May 2001 channels such as MTV and Nickelodeon started to be broadcast in China, also with extensive programming customized to the Chinese market.

Viacom's stock climbed in the spring of 2002, despite the huge fall in advertising revenues caused by the recession in 2000 and the following September 11 tragedy—a fall that caused the earnings of its broadcast networks to drop by 20%. The over 10% fall in advertising revenues affected all entertainment and media companies and caused a plunge in the stock price of companies like Yahoo and AOL Time Warner. Indeed, the latter's stock price fell so far that Viacom became the number 2 global media company in 2002. Analysts felt that Viacom was the best-positioned media company to benefit from the upswing in advertising that was expected in the latter half of 2002 because of its combination of large-scale operations, leading brands, and diverse revenue streams. While the broadcast groups' earnings fell by 20%, for example, the earnings of the cable network division rose by 12%, largely because of greater broadcasting in the United States and abroad. Redstone claimed in the summer of 2002 that the worst was over.

Still reeling from the downturn in advertising, Redstone and Karmazin continued to seek ways to counter future threats to the Viacom empire, particularly because now the threat from digital and broadband technology was hurting its Blockbuster unit and might in the future threaten Viacom's distribution channels as TVs and computers merged as broadband connections to the Internet increased. Indeed, there have been many reports since the hiring of Mel Karmazin that he and Redstone have locked heads on many occasions about major strategic issues. Karmazin was especially critical of Redstone's expensive acquisitions, which increased debt but had no clear future benefits, and he also made strong suggestions that

Viacom should increase its online presence. However, in June 2002 with the positive results from the CBS merger and BET acquisition suggesting the value of Redstone's growth-by-acquisition strategy, Karmazin was joking that their management styles were complementary and that he was in no rush to assume leadership of Viacom, especially since the seventy-nine-year-old Redstone was "good for another thirty to forty years—at least!" Redstone, however, joked that when Karmazin's contract expired in 2003, Karmazin "might want to retire." Karmazin's response? "Never, never, never."

New Problems for Viacom: The Growing Use of the Internet

Viacom made no significant acquisitions in 2002 or 2003. Redstone felt his company has all the right pieces of entertainment property in place and that the main issue for Karmazin was to manage them to realize the stream of advertising revenues and profits locked up in its entertainment assets. Operating revenues from its entertainment division, which included Paramount Pictures and theme parks, rose by 46% during 2003 and its operating income was up 15% to $66 million as a result of higher movie ticket sales and—paradoxically—much stronger sales of DVDs. Its Viacom Plus unit continued to aggressively market its "one-stop-shopping approach across all marketing channels," and, as the economy picked up in 2003, advertising revenues at the national level rebounded. In the spring of 2004, Viacom was happy to announce that the company's overall revenues were up 11% and that 46% of its 2003 revenues came from advertising.

While national advertising revenues on Viacom's many cable channels rebounded, however, local advertising revenues from its TV stations, including the CBS network, and from its radio stations were now lagging behind and hurting the company's performance—Viacom only just met analysts' earnings expectations. The reason local advertising revenues were not keeping pace with national advertising was that fewer and fewer people were watching or listening to local channels, preferring to watch their favorite cable channels or to surf the Web. Slowly but steadily the growing use of the Internet and new online digital media properties were cutting into available advertising revenues. Redstone and Karmazin were slow to pick up on the dangers the Internet posed, not just as a competitor for advertising revenues but also as an important emerging media asset that could complement its existing businesses. And major online companies such as Yahoo were now expensive, and these too were suffering from new competition from upstart websites that began to offer specialist services, such as www.rottentomatoes, the movie review website, and soon Flickr and YouTube, which offered photograph and video content now made possible by the rapidly expanding use of broadband Internet connections. Karmazin and Redstone preferred to regard falling revenues as a temporary phenomenon and announced that they expected revenue increases in 2004 of 5 to 7% and operating profits to increase by 12 to 14%.

At the same time, however, Viacom has always been alert to the threat downloading movies through the Internet or by pay-per-view cable posed for its Blockbuster unit, so Redstone and Karmazin also announced that despite Blockbuster's considerable contributions to its revenues and free cash flow, they believed the business models of both companies had drifted so far apart that the lack of fit between them would hurt Viacom's future profitability. Viacom's business model is based on growing the value of its properties and the advertising revenues they generate. Blockbuster's business model is to increase its presence in the movie DVD rental and retail sales market. The was especially true by 2004 when the prospect of increasing competition from movie downloads through broadband channels started to increase, and so in the future falling revenues from DVD rentals might offset any increase in advertising revenues that Viacom might enjoy. However, divesting Blockbuster and losing its revenues would make Viacom even more dependent on advertising revenues.

Another problem by 2004 was that Viacom's acquisition of CBS was now causing major problems because the anticipated synergies were not forthcoming—buying more media properties also results in a company facing more sets of competitive threats. Investors were becoming increasingly wary of Viacom's stock because they found it more and more difficult to evaluate the real value of each of its many media properties and its cash flow. Spinning off Blockbuster would help eliminate the uncertainty this unit's future performance was having on its stock price. So in January 2004, when Blockbusters stock was trading at a high of $20, Viacom announced that it would divest its remaining shareholding in Blockbuster by allowing holders of Viacom shares to swap them for shares in Blockbuster. New Blockbuster shareholders would also receive a substantial once-and-for all dividend for swapping their Viacom stock for Blockbuster's. This made the deal attractive, and enough Viacom shareholders took advantage of the offer for Redstone to finally spin off the unit into a fully independent company controlled by its current CEO, John Antioco.

The Big Split

At the same time Viacom was failing to build strong Internet and online media assets, it was now also encountering many other problems with its empire of media assets. First, even after the Blockbuster spinoff, the company's erratic performance failed to reassure investors about the value of Viacom's remaining assets. Five years after Redstone bought the CBS television network in 2000, adding its television stations and Infinity Broadcasting radio stations to his movie studio, theme parks, and Blockbuster video stores, it was clear that bigger is not always better. Redstone had learnt the hard way that the different units of a company grow at different rates, and the performance of the weakest unit pulled down the performance of the whole company—and Viacom's growth was slowing fast. Its theme parks, radio stations, and CBS assets had not met Viacom's aggressive growth goals, and Redstone was frustrated that Viacom's slowest growing units were dragging down its stock price, which by 2004 was almost half its 2000 high of nearly $70 per share. Karmazin had warned Redstone about this, and the personal relationship between Redstone and Karmazin continued to deteriorate. Although in 2003 it was announced that Karmazin's contract would be renewed for two more years, Redstone now had other plans for his company, and in 2004 Karmazin was fired (he is now the CEO of Sirius Satellite Radio).

In March 2005 Redstone announced that Viacom would split the steadier, slow-growth units, the CBS side, from the faster-growth side, MTV and the film studio. The $60 billion conglomerate would be split into two smaller, separately traded companies, one running CBS and the stations and the other the movie studio and cable channels, such as MTV and Comedy Central. He also announced the company was looking to sell its slow-growth, expensive Paramount theme parks and buy growing Internet and videogame companies, and that it might also divest its 856 movie screens in Canada—the original Redstone media property.

The split was approved by Viacom's board June 14, 2005, took effect December 31, 2005, and effectively undid the Viacom/CBS merger. The existing Viacom was renamed CBS Corp. and was headed by Les Moonves, its long-time CEO. It now includes Viacom's "slow-growth businesses," namely CBS, the CW network (formerly UPN), CBS Radio, Simon & Schuster, CBS Outdoor (formerly Viacom Outdoor), Showtime, and most television production assets. In addition, CBS Corp. was given Paramount Parks, which it later sold to amusement park operator Cedar Fair, L.P., on June 30, 2006.

Then, a new spin-off company was created called Viacom, which was headed by Tom Freston, the long-time head of MTV networks. It comprises MTV Networks, BET Networks, Paramount's movie studio, and Paramount Pictures' home entertainment operations. Redstone still controls 71% of the voting stock of both companies and is the chairman of both companies—he still earns $27 million a year as its chairman, and he and his family members are a major drain on its cash flow.

Do Media Empires Create Value and Profit?

After a decade of growth by acquisition, media conglomerates such as Viacom, Sony, and Time Warner all began to reconfigure their business models, pushed by new Internet technologies and changing customer viewing habits that had altered the mix of advertising revenues on which media content companies depend. The 1990s cookie-cutter model of a media giant where one could just add different media properties, such as a television network, to others, such as a movie studio, theme parks, music company, or pro sports team, had been shown to be a failure—at least in terms of generating consistent increases in a company's stock price. Nevertheless, in December 2005, Viacom's Paramount Pictures sealed a deal to buy movie studio DreamWorks for $1.6 billion, thwarting rival NBC-Universal's five-month-long attempt to acquire the independent movie studio. "The acquisition of DreamWorks is an enormous step forward in our ongoing work to unlock the full potential of Viacom's brands and businesses," said Redstone. But how the acquisition would actually do this was left unsaid.

Redstone's focus on fixing the ongoing problems with his media empire also made him very late to recognize the growing importance of the Internet and the World Wide Web and the threat of competition from digital video downloading and streaming media. In 2005, Viacom moved to acquire some small Internet media properties; for example, in June 2005 it acquired Neopets, a virtual pet website, and in 2006 it acquired Xfire, iFilm, Quizilla.com and Harmonix Music Systems, and Atom Entertainment. These companies serve niche markets, such as virtual pets, or make music gaming titles. However, these acquisitions had nothing like the reach of a MySpace or YouTube, and despite this progress Viacom was much slower to react to the changes in Internet technology taking place than its rivals, and its stock price suffered.

New threats were also emerging; Disney, which had always had a strong interest in developing media websites, was rebuilding a strong Disney Internet property and announced it was pioneering movie downloading through the Internet. In 2005 it claimed it had a proprietary new technology for delivering movies over the Internet, and in 2006 it formed a close alliance with Apple to download its movies and TV programs over the Internet to iPods. Similarly, after its disastrous start with AOL, Time Warner was also developing a new business model, based on free user access, to build its AOL channel into a major Internet property and so share in the billions of dollars of advertising revenues that were up for grabs. But the company that showed the best developed strategy was News Corp., whose CEO, Rupert Murdock, had pushed early for a strong Internet strategy, and the result was early important strategic Internet acquisitions. The most important of these acquisitions was MySpace.com in 2004, one of the fastest-growing social networking websites ever. It also bought several other specialist websites such as RottenTomatoes.com, a movie review website, and it developed these into major websites to increase advertising revenues and also to advertise its other media assets, such as the movies it made through its Fox Studios.

More Changes at the Top

As the names of its Internet acquisitions suggest, Viacom was failing in its attempt to develop a strong, coherent Internet strategy. In particular, it had lost the battle with News Corp. to acquire MySpace.com, and now this strategic failure too began to hurt its stock price. Its stock, which had been around $45 after the 2005 split, plunged to $35 by the summer of 2006, and Redstone, as usual, responded by firing Viacom's CEO, Freston, blaming him for the company's poor performance. Redstone named Philippe Dauman as the new head of Viacom. Dauman has been a Viacom board member since 1987 and, as mentioned earlier, had been a top Viacom executive from 1994 to 2000.

In his first public announcement, Dauman claimed he had free reign to run things and develop a new business model, and that he wasn't simply a pawn for Redstone to use. Redstone himself had been getting negative attention from analysts who believed he had undermined Freston's authority and was grooming his own children to take over the company when he decides to retire (he turns eighty-four in May 2007). If Redstone attempts to micromanage or meddle in operational issues, Dauman said, "I can push back," but he also indicated he would work to continue Freston's legacy, "creative excellence," while focusing on strategic Internet acquisitions—an area that led to Freston's downfall. However, given the frugal Redstone, he optimistically said that he does not anticipate any acquisition as big as News Corp.'s $580 million MySpace purchase. He will look for companies under $100 million that have the potential to become the next MySpace—companies that will not be easy to find in today's competitive digital environment.

At the same time, Dauman said the company has untapped organic growth, meaning that it could achieve more innovation and product development internally so that the company could make better use of its media resources. He cited BET and Comedy Central as lynchpins with huge future potential and said that even with established brands, such as MTV and Nickelodeon, Viacom could bring in more advertising revenues by offering advertisers opportunities to reach both targeted and mass audiences. Once again, a corporate group focused on selling the aggregated reach of Viacom's cable network assets is being formed, something similar to Viacom's former centralized marketing unit that was disbanded after the split. If advertising revenues don't increase in the next few years, it seems that more divestitures may be likely.

In November 2006, the first financial reporting period under Dauman's leadership, Viacom reported a 16% fall in third-quarter profit, as weakness at the box office from unprofitable movies offset strength in cable and higher advertising revenues. Viacom's share price, which had been recovering, closed down 3.3% at $38.37. As usual, Redstone fired someone, this time Viacom's chief financial officer, and Redstone once again announced that his company would "move rapidly to the forefront of emerging digital markets, keeping us on the path to outstanding long-term financial performance and free cash flow generation" and backed its full-year target to deliver double-digit growth in revenue and operating income. Clearly, even managing a smaller, more focused media company to achieve profitable growth is a difficult task—especially when its units each face complex problems and agile competitors. Only time will tell if the new Viacom will succeed or if, once again, the company may be split apart to realize the value in its assets. Clearly its top executives face difficult choices in figuring out the best corporate and business strategies to pursue to create a highly profitable business model. Having an eighty-three-year-old owner in charge may not be the best thing for its shareholders, apart from Redstone himself, of course.

REFERENCES

Frank Biondi, "A Media Tycoon's Take on the 21st Century," *Business Week,* 21st Century Capitalism, November 18, 1994, p. 190.

Shirley Brady, "BET Seeks More Ways to Work with Viacom Family," *Cable World,* June 10, 2002, p. 24.

"Deals Give Viacom Even More Muscle," *Wall Street Journal,* September 30, 1994, p. B1.

"The Ending of Paramount's Script May Not Be Written Yet," *Business Week,* September 27, 1993, pp. 38–39.

Wayne Friedman, "Viacom Snares Monster TV Deal," *Advertising Age,* April 29, 2002, p. 1.

"Gump Happens—and Viacom Is Thanking Its Lucky Stars," *Business Week,* August 8, 1994, p. 29.

Marc Gunther, "MTV Films: It's a Sleeper," *Fortune,* April 29, 2002, pp. 24–28.

Nancy Hass, "The Message Is the Medium," *Financial World,* June 8, 1993, pp. 24–25.

"Hollywood Scuffle," *Business Week,* December 12, 1994, p. 38.

"IBM Thrusts into Entertainment via Viacom," *Communications Today,* May 8, 2002, p. 1.

International Directory of Company Histories, vol. 7 (St. James Press, 1994,) pp. 560–562.

Dyan Machan, "Redstone Rising," *Forbes,* May 13, 2002, pp. 46–48.

Steve McClellan, "Viacom: Flat and Happy," *Broadcasting & Cable,* February 18, 2002, p. 8.

"The MTV Tycoon—Sumner Redstone Is Turning Viacom into the Hottest Global TV Network," *Business Week,* September 21, 1992, pp. 56–62.

Jack Neff and Wayne Friedman, "P&G Broadens Deal with Viacom Plus," *Advertising Age,* June 17, 2002, p. 3.

"Paramount: Do I Hear $11 Billion?" *Business Week,* November 8, 1993, p. 36.

"The Paramount Takeover: The Drama Ended, Two Stars Get New Scripts; Viacom's Biondi Has to Stretch to Fill Big Role," *Wall Street Journal*, February 16, 1994, p. B1.

"The Paramount Takeover: Wall Street's Final Analysis: Might Made Right," *Wall Street Journal*, February 16, 1994, p. B1.

Martin Peers, "Viacom Passes AOL in Market Value—CBS Acquisition Has Brought Shareholder Value to Media Company," *Wall Street Journal*, June 6, 2002, p. B3.

Martin Peers, "Viacom Posts $1.11 Billion Loss Largely Due to Goodwill Charge," *Wall Street Journal*, April 26, 2002, p. B4.

"Redstone in Motion," *Financial World*, December 6, 1994, pp. 36–38.

"Remaindered at Simon & Schuster," *Business Week*, June 27, 1994, p. 32.

Matthew Schifrin, "I Can't Even Remember the Old Stars' Names," *Forbes*, March 16, 1992, pp. 44–45.

"Sumner at the Summit," *Business Week*, February 28, 1994, p. 32.

"Sumner Redstone Gets a Little Help from His Friends," *Business Week*, October 11, 1993, p. 36.

Viacom, http://www.viacom.com, 1991–2007.

Viacom Annual Reports and 10Ks, 1991–2001.

"Viacom Firms Up Plans for Movies Produced by MTV," *Wall Street Journal*, Jun 14, 1994, p. B8.

"Viacom Inc.: Paramount Gets 'First Look' at MTV Unit's TV Shows," *Wall Street Journal*, November 11, 1994.

"Viacom Inc. Wins German License for Nickelodeon," *Wall Street Journal*, March 1, 1995, p. B10.

"Viacom Now Is a Full Owner of Paramount After Vote," *Wall Street Journal*, July 8, 1994, p. B9.

"Viacom Unit Continues Sell-off of Businesses That Don't Fit Strategy," *Wall Street Journal*, November 22, 1994, p. B4.

Karissa S. Wang, "Mel Sez: CBS 'Pretty Darn Good,'" *Electronic Media*, June 3, 2002, p. 37.

This case was prepared by Gareth R. Jones, Texas A&M University.

In February 2007, Antonio Perez, the chief executive officer (CEO) of the Eastman Kodak Co., was reflecting on Kodak's current situation since he took over almost two years ago. After eight quarters of losses, his revamped digital strategy seemed to be finally starting to pay off. His efforts to cut costs while investing heavily to develop new digital products resulted in a slender profit of $16 million on sales of $3.8 billion and were expected to rise further in 2007.

Following several billion dollars of losses and tens of thousands of job cuts, the news gave Kodak shares a boost. But could Kodak maintain its momentum in the face of its digital rivals that were all introducing new and improved products? Had Kodak finally achieved a distinctive competence in digital imaging? Was its new digital business model—based on strategies to counter the threats posed to Kodak's traditional silver halide-based technology by the convergence of imaging and digital information technology—really working? Did the company have the digital products in place to rebuild its profitability and fulfill its "You press the button, we do the rest" promise? Or, after ten years of declining sales and profits, was the company just on the verge of another downward slope in the face of intense global competition on all product fronts?

Kodak's History

Eastman Kodak Co. was incorporated in New Jersey on October 24, 1901, as successor to the Eastman Dry Plate Co., the business originally established by George Eastman in September 1880. The Dry Plate Co. had been formed to develop a dry photographic plate that was more portable and easier to use than other plates in the rapidly developing photography field. To mass-produce the dry plates uniformly, Eastman patented a plate-coating machine and began to manufacture the plates commercially. Eastman's continuing interest in the infant photographic industry led to his development in 1884 of silver halide paper-based photographic roll film. Eastman capped this invention with his introduction of the first portable camera in 1888. This camera used his own patented film, which was developed using his own proprietary method. Thus Eastman had gained control of all the stages of the photographic process. His breakthroughs made possible the development of photography as a mass leisure activity. The popularity of the "recorded images" business was immediate, and sales boomed. Eastman's inventions revolutionized the photographic industry, and his company was uniquely placed to lead the world in the development of photographic technology.

From the beginning, Kodak focused on four primary objectives to guide the growth of its business: (1) mass production to lower production costs, (2) maintaining the lead in technological developments, (3) extensive product advertising, and (4) the development of a multinational business to exploit the world market. Although common now, those goals were revolutionary at the time. In due course, Kodak's yellow boxes could be found in every country in the world.

Preeminent in world markets, Kodak operated research, manufacturing, and distribution networks throughout Europe and the rest of the world. Kodak's leadership in the development of advanced color film for simple, easy-to-use cameras and in quality film processing was maintained by constant research and development in its many research laboratories. Its huge volume of production allowed it to obtain economies of scale. Kodak was also its own supplier of the plastics and chemicals needed to produce film, and it made most of the component parts for its cameras.

Kodak became one of the most profitable American corporations, and its return on shareholders' equity averaged 18% for many years. To maintain its competitive advantage, it continued to invest heavily in research and development in silver halide photography, remaining principally in the photographic business. In this business, as the company used its resources to expand sales and become a global business, the name *Kodak* became a household word signifying unmatched quality. By 1990, approximately 40% of Kodak's revenues came from sales outside the United States.

Starting in the early 1970s, however, and especially in the 1980s, Kodak ran into major problems, reflected in the drop in return on equity. Its preeminence was being increasingly threatened as the photographic industry and industry competition changed. Major innovations were taking place within the photography business, and new methods of recording images and memories beyond silver halide technology, most noticeably digital imaging, were emerging.

The New Industry Environment

In the 1970s, Kodak began to face an uncertain environment in all its product markets. First, the color film and paper market from which Kodak made 75% of its profits experienced growing competition from Japanese companies, led by Fuji Photo Film Co. Fuji invested in huge, low-cost manufacturing plants, using the latest technology to mass-produce film in large volume. Fuji's low production costs and aggressive, competitive price cutting squeezed Kodak's profit margin. Finding no apparent differences in quality and obtaining more vivid colors with the Japanese product, consumers began to switch to the cheaper Japanese film, and this shift drastically reduced Kodak's market share.

Besides greater industry competition, another liability for Kodak was that it had done little internally to improve productivity to counteract rising costs. Supremacy in the marketplace had made Kodak complacent, and it had been slow to introduce productivity and quality improvements. Furthermore, Kodak (unlike Fuji in Japan) produced film in many different countries in the world rather than in a single country, and this also gave Kodak a cost disadvantage. Thus the combination of Fuji's efficient production and Kodak's own management style allowed the Japanese to become the cost leaders—to charge lower prices and still maintain profit margins.

Kodak was also facing competition on other product fronts. Its cameras had an advantage because of their ease of use as compared with complex 35-mm single-lens reflex models. They were also inexpensive. However, the quality of their prints could not compare with those of 35-mm cameras. In 1970 Kodak had toyed with the idea of producing a simple-to-use 35-mm camera but had abandoned it. In the late 1970s, however, the Japanese did develop an easy-to-use 35-mm pocket camera featuring such innovations as auto flash, focus, and rewind. The quality of the prints produced by these cameras was far superior to the grainy prints produced by the smaller Instamatic and disk cameras, and consumers began to switch to these products in large numbers. This shift led to the need for new kinds of film, which Kodak was slow to introduce, thus adding to its product problems.

Shrinking market share due to increased competition from the Japanese was not Kodak's only problem. In the early 1980s, it introduced several less-than-successful products. In 1982, it introduced a new disk camera as a replacement for the pocket Instamatic. The disk camera used a negative even smaller than the negative of the Instamatic and was smaller and easier to use. Four and a half million units were shipped to the domestic market by Christmas, but almost a million of the units still remained on retailers' shelves in the new year. The disk cameras had been outsold by pocket 35-mm cameras, which produced higher-quality pictures. The disk camera also sold poorly in the European and Japanese markets. Yet Kodak's research showed that 90% of disk camera users were satisfied with the camera and especially liked its high "yield rate" of 93% printable pictures, compared with 75% for the pocket Instamatic.

A final blow on the camera front came when Kodak lost its patent suit with Polaroid Corp. Kodak had forgone the instant photography business in the 1940s when it turned down Edwin Land's offer to develop his instant photography process. Polaroid developed it, and instant photography was wildly successful, capturing a significant share of the photographic market. In response, Kodak set out in the 1960s to develop its own instant camera to compete with Polaroid's. According to testimony in the patent trial, Kodak spent $94 million perfecting its system, only to scrub it when Polaroid introduced the new SX-70 camera in 1972. Kodak then rushed to produce a competing instant camera, hoping to capitalize on the $6.5 billon in sales of instant cameras. However, on January 9, 1986, a federal judge ordered Kodak out of the instant photography business for violating seven of Polaroid's patents in its rush to produce an instant camera. The cost to Kodak for closing its instant photography operation and exchanging the 16.5 million cameras sold to consumers was over $800 million. In 1985 Kodak reported that it had exited the industry at a cost of $494 million. However, the total costs of this misadventure were finally realized on July 15, 1991, when Kodak agreed to pay Polaroid a sum of $925 million to settle out of court a suit that Polaroid had brought against Kodak for patent infringement.

On its third product front, photographic processing, Kodak also experienced problems. It faced stiff competition from foreign manufacturers of photographic paper and from new competitors in the film-processing market. Increasingly, film processors were turning to cheaper sources of paper to reduce the costs of film processing. Once again the Japanese had developed cheaper sources of paper and were eroding Kodak's market share. At the same time, many new independent film-processing companies had emerged and were printing film at far lower rates than Kodak's own official developers. These independent laboratories had opened to serve the needs of drugstores and supermarkets, and many of them offered twenty-four-hour service. They used the less expensive paper to maintain their cost advantage and were willing to accept lower profit margins in return for a higher volume of sales. As a result, Kodak lost markets for its chemical and paper products—products that had contributed significantly to its revenues and profits.

The photographic industry surrounding Kodak had changed dramatically. Competition had increased in all product areas, and Kodak, while still the largest producer, faced increasing threats to its profitability as it was forced to reduce prices to match the competition. To cap the problem, by 1980 the market was all but saturated: 95% of all U.S. households owned at least one camera. Facing increased competition in a mature market was not an enviable position for a company used to high profitability and growth.

The second major problem that Kodak had to confront was due not to increased competition in existing product markets but to the emergence of new industries that provided alternative means of producing and recording images. The introduction of videotape recorders, and later video cameras, gave consumers an alternative way to use their dollars to produce images, particularly moving images. Video basically destroyed the old, film-based home movie business on which Kodak had a virtual monopoly. After Sony's introduction of the Betamax machine in 1975, a video industry grew into a multibillion-dollar business. VCRs and 16-mm video cameras became increasingly hot-selling items as their prices fell with the growth in demand and the standardization of technology. The development of compact 8-mm video cameras that were much smaller than the 16-mm version, and then the later introduction of laser disks, compact disks, and, in the 1990s, DVDs were also significant developments. The vast amount of data that can be recorded on these disks gave them a great advantage in reproducing images through electronic means. It was increasingly apparent that the whole nature of the imaging and recording process was changing from chemical methods of reproduction to electronic, digital methods. Kodak's managers should have perceived this transformation to digital-based methods as a disruptive technology because its technical preeminence was based on silver halide photography. However, as is always the case with such technologies, the real threat lies in the future.

These changes in the competitive environment caused enormous difficulties for Kodak. Between 1972 and 1982, profit margins from sales declined from 15.7 to 10.7%. Kodak's glossy image lost its luster. It was in this declining situation that Colby Chandler took over as chairman in July 1983.

Kodak's New Strategy

Chandler saw the need for dramatic changes in Kodak's businesses and quickly pioneered four changes in strategy: (1) he strove to increase Kodak's control of its existing chemical-based imaging businesses; (2) he aimed to make Kodak the leader in electronic imaging; (3) he spearheaded attempts by Kodak to diversify into new businesses to increase profitability; and (4) he began on major efforts to reduce costs and improve productivity. To achieve the first three objectives, he began a huge program of acquisitions, realizing that Kodak did not have the time to venture new activities internally. Because Kodak was cash rich and had low debt, financing these acquisitions was easy.

For the next six years, Chandler acquired businesses in four main areas, and by 1989 Kodak had been restructured into four main operating groups: imaging, information systems, health, and chemicals. In a statement to shareholders at the annual meeting in 1988, Chandler announced that with the recent acquisition of Sterling Drug for $5 billion the company had achieved its objective: "With a sharp focus on these four sectors, we are serving diversified markets from a unified base of science and manufacturing technology. The logical synergy of the Kodak growth strategy means that we are neither diversified as a conglomerate nor a company with a one-product family."

The way these operating groups developed under Chandler's leadership is described in the following text.

The Imaging Group

Imaging comprised Kodak's original businesses, including consumer products, motion picture and audiovisual products, photo finishing, and consumer electronics. The unit was charged with strengthening Kodak's position in its existing businesses. Kodak's strategy in its photographic imaging business has been to fill gaps in its product line by introducing new products either made by Kodak or bought from Japanese manufacturers and sold under the Kodak name. For example, in attempting to maintain market share in the camera business, Kodak introduced a new line of disk cameras to replace the Instamatic lines. However, in addition, Kodak bought a minority stake and entered into a joint venture with Chinon of Japan to produce a range of 35-mm automatic cameras that would be sold under the Kodak name. This arrangement would capitalize on Kodak's strong brand image and give Kodak a presence in this market to maintain its camera and film sales. That venture succeeded; Kodak sold 500,000 cameras and

gained 15% of the market. In addition, Kodak invested heavily in developing new and advanced film. It introduced a whole new range of "DX" coded film to match the new 35-mm camera market film that possesses the vivid color qualities of Fuji film. Kodak had not developed vivid film color earlier because of its belief that consumers wanted "realistic" color.

Kodak also made major moves to solidify its hold on the film-processing market. It attempted to stem the inflow of foreign low-cost photographic paper by gaining control over the processing market. In 1986 it acquired Texas-based Fox Photo Inc. for $96 million and became the largest national wholesale photograph finisher. In 1987, it acquired the laboratories of American Photographic Group. In 1989, it solidified its hold on the photo-finishing market by forming a joint venture between its operations and the photo-finishing operations of Fuqua industries. The new company, Qualex Inc., had ninety-four laboratories nationwide. These acquisitions provided Kodak with a large, captive customer for its chemical and paper products as well as control over the photo-finishing market. Also, in 1986 Kodak introduced new improved one-hour film-processing labs to compete with other photographic developers. To accompany the new labs, Kodak popularized the Kodak "Color Watch" system that requires these labs to use only Kodak paper and chemicals. Kodak hoped that this would stem the flow of business to one-hour minilabs and also establish the industry standard for quality processing.

New and improved film products, including Kodak Gold Label film and Ektachrome film, were announced during 1988, as were new types of 35-mm cameras. Kodak also formed a battery venture with Matsushita to produce a range of alkaline batteries for Kodak. A gold-topped battery was introduced to compete with Duracell's copper-top battery. Moreover, Kodak internally ventured a new lithium battery that lasted six times as long as conventional batteries. As a result of these moves, Kodak regained control over the processing end of the market and made inroads into the camera, film, and battery ends as well. In 1988, Kodak earnings were helped by the decline in value of the dollar, which forced Fuji Photo, its main competitor, to raise its prices. Consequently, Kodak was able to increase its prices. All these measures increased Kodak's visibility in the market; Kodak was protecting its mission of "You push the button, we do the rest."

Kodak also engaged in a massive internal cost-cutting effort to improve the efficiency of the photographic products group. Beginning in 1984 it introduced more and more stringent efficiency targets aimed at reducing waste while increasing productivity. In 1986, it established a baseline for measuring the total cost of waste incurred in the manufacture of film and paper throughout its worldwide operations. By 1987 it had cut that waste by 15%, and by 1989 it announced total cost savings worth $500 million annually.

Despite these strategic moves, the net earnings of Kodak's photographic business dropped dramatically in 1989. Although Kodak's volume and sales of its products were up, profit margins were down. Polaroid with its new One Film product was advertising aggressively to capture market share. Fuji, realizing the strong threat posed by Kodak's price cutting, responded in kind, and a price war ensued. Both Fuji and Kodak were spending massive amounts to advertise their products in order to increase market share. In 1989, Kodak had 80% of the $7 billion film market while Fuji had 11%, but Fuji increased its advertising budget by 65% in 1989 to increase its market share and simultaneously offered discount coupons on its film products. Moreover, Fuji announced plans for a major new filmmaking plant in Europe—a plant the size of its Japanese plant, which by itself can produce enough film for one-quarter of the world market. The result was a huge amount of excess capacity in global film production as Fuji, the cost leader, went all out to build global market share through aggressive pricing.

Kodak's losses mounted as it was forced to reduce prices to counter Fuji's attempts to build market share and to give multipack discounts on its products. Also to fight back, Kodak announced a fifteen-year agreement with the Walt Disney Co. to use Disney characters in its advertising. However, these moves were very expensive for Kodak and slashed profits. They also offset most of the benefits from Kodak's cost-cutting effort, and the slow growth in Kodak's core photographic imaging business meant that there was little prospect of increasing profitability.

It was because of this slow industry growth that Chandler saw the need for diversification. Because sales increased only 5% a year and Kodak already had 80% of the market, it was tied to the fortunes of one industry. While this made Kodak cash-rich when competition was weak, it made Kodak poor when competition increased. This fact, plus the increasing use and growing applications of digital imaging techniques, led to Chandler's second strategic thrust: an immediate policy of acquisition and diversification into the electronic imaging business with the stated goal of being "first in both industries"—imaging and digital.

The Information Systems Group

In 1988, when Sony introduced an electronic camera that could take still pictures and then transmit them back to a television screen, it became increasingly obvious that the threat to Kodak from new electronic imaging techniques would continue to increase. Although pictures taken with video film could not match the quality achieved with chemical reproduction, the advent of compact disks offered the prospect of an imaging medium that could meet such standards in the future. For the company to survive and prosper in the imaging business, Kodak's managers began to realize that it required expertise in a broad range of technologies to satisfy customers' recording and imaging needs—they began to see the threat posed by the disruptive technology. Kodak's managers saw that a large number of different types of electronic markets were emerging. Electronic imaging had become important in the medical sciences and in all business, technical, and research activities, driven by the advent of powerful personal computers. However, Kodak's managers did not choose to focus on imaging products and markets close to "photographs." They began to target any kind of imaging applications in communications, computer science, and various hard-copy-output technologies that they believed might be important in the imaging markets of the future. Since Kodak had no expertise in digital imaging, it began to buy companies its managers perceived did have these skills, and then pursued its strategy of marketing the products of these companies under its own famous brand name—for instance, an electronic publishing system for corporate documents and an automated microfilm-imaging system.

Kodak thus began a strategy of acquisitions and joint ventures to invest its excess cash in new imaging technologies that it hoped, somehow, would lead to increased future profitability. In the new information systems group, several acquisitions were made, including Atex Inc., Eikonix Corp., and Disconix Inc. Atex, acquired in 1981, made newspaper and magazine electronic publishing and text-editing systems to newspapers and magazines worldwide as well as to government agencies and law firms. Eikonix Corp. was a leader in the design, development, and production of precision digital imaging systems. Further growth within the information systems group came with the development of the Ektaprint line of copier-duplicators. The copiers achieved good sales growth and reached new standards for quality, reliability, and productivity in the very competitive high-volume segment of the copier marketplace. In 1988, Kodak announced another major move into the copier service business. It purchased IBM's copier service business and copier sales agreements in the United States. Kodak also announced that it would market copiers manufactured by IBM while continuing to market its own Ektaprint copiers. This service agreement was eventually extended to sixteen countries outside the United States.

Kodak also announced two new image management packages: the Kodak Ektaprint Electronic Publishing System (KEEPS) and the Kodak Imaging Management System (KIMS). KIMS electronically scans, digitizes, and stores film images and transmits image information electronically. The system enables users with large, active databases to view and manipulate information stored on microfilm and magnetic or optical disks. KEEPS was a high-quality electronic publishing package that had the ability to edit, print, and update text and graphics for publications. However, the KEEPS package included a computer made by Sun Microsystems, software produced by Interleaf Inc. and just enhanced by Kodak, and a printer manufactured by Canon. In 1988, Kodak announced that it would begin marketing a "VY-P1" printer developed in a joint venture with Hitachi to make high-quality still images from VCRs and camcorders. Although Kodak had begun to spend more and more of its R&D budget on digital imaging, it still had not internally ventured any important new products.

Moreover, these new markets did not overlap much with its core photography business. With these moves, Kodak extended its activities into the electronic areas of artificial intelligence, computer systems, consumer electronics, peripherals, telecommunications, and test and measuring equipment. Kodak was hoping to gain a strong foothold in these new businesses to make up for losses in its traditional business—not to strengthen its core business.

Soon, Kodak's managers began to purchase imaging companies that made products as diverse as computer workstations and floppy disks. It aggressively acquired companies to fill in its product lines and obtain technical expertise in information systems. After taking more than a decade to make its first four acquisitions, Kodak completed seven acquisitions in 1985 and more than ten in 1986. Among the 1985 acquisitions—for $175 million—was Verbatim Corp., a major producer of floppy disks. This acquisition made Kodak one of the three big producers in the floppy disk industry.

Entry into the information systems market, like the expansion in its core photographic products business, produced new competitive problems for Kodak. In entering office information systems, Kodak entered areas where it faced strong competition from established companies such as IBM, Apple, and Sun. The Verbatim acquisition brought Kodak into direct competition with 3M. Entering the copier market brought Kodak into direct competition with Japanese firms such as Canon that competitively marketed their own lines of advanced, low-cost products. Kodak was entering new businesses where it had little expertise, where it was unfamiliar with the competitive problems, and where there was already strong competition.

Thus Kodak was forced to retreat from some of these markets. In 1990, it announced that it would sell Verbatim to Mitsubishi. (Mitsubishi was immediately criticized by Japanese investors for buying a company with an old, outdated product line.) Kodak was soon forced to withdraw from many other areas of business by selling assets or closing operations and taking a write-off. For example, to reduce costs it sold Sayett Technology, Kodak Video programs and videocassettes, and Aquidneck Data Corp. The decline in the performance of the information systems group, attributed to increased competition, a flat office systems market, and delays in bringing out new products, reduced earnings from operations from a profit of $311 million in 1988 to a loss of $360 million in 1989.

The Health Group

Kodak's interest in health products emerged from its involvement in the design and production of film for medical and dental x-rays. The growth of imaging in medical sciences offered Kodak an opportunity to apply its skills in new areas, and it began to develop such products as Kodak Ektachem—clinical blood analyzers. It developed other products—Ektascan laser imaging films, printers, and accessories—for improving the display, storage, processing, and retrieval of diagnostic images.

However, Kodak did not confine its interests in medical and health matters to imaging-based products. In 1984, it established within the health group a life sciences division to develop and commercialize new products deriving from Kodak's distinctive competencies in chemistry and biotechnology. One of the division's objectives was to focus on product opportunities in markets with relatively few competitors and high profit potential—products such as nutritional supplements that can be delivered orally or intravenously, as well as nutrition products for sale over the counter to consumers. Another objective was to develop innovative ways to control the absorption of pharmaceutical drugs into the body so that a drug would remain therapeutically effective for the optimum amount of time. A third objective involved developing new applications for existing products and processes. Kodak had in its files about 500,000 chemical formulations on which it could base new products.

Within life sciences was the bioproducts division, which engaged in joint research with biotechnology companies such as Cetus Corp., Amgen, and Immunex. Bioproducts pursued an aggressive strategy to scale up and commercialize products based on biotechnology derived from in-house as well as outside contract research. Ventures entered into by the bioproducts division included an agreement with Advanced Genetic Sciences for the commercial production of SNOW-MAX, a product useful in making artificial snow for ski areas.

Kodak began to enter into joint ventures in the biotechnical industry, both to build its business and to enter new businesses. In April 1985 Kodak and ICN Pharmaceuticals jointly announced the formation of a research institute that would explore new biomedical compounds aimed at stopping the spread of viral infections and slowing the aging process. Kodak and ICN were to invest $45 million over six years to form and operate the Nucleic Acid Research Institute, a joint venture located at ICN's Costa Mesa, California, facility. The institute would dedicate much of its research exclusively to preclinical studies of new antiviral and anti-aging substances.

However, these advances into biotechnology proved expensive, and the uncertainty of the industry caused Kodak to question the wisdom of entering this highly volatile area. In 1988, to reduce the costs of operating the bioproducts division, a joint venture incorporating bioproducts was formed between Kodak and Cultor Ltd. of Finland, and Kodak essentially left the market. The remaining parts of the life sciences division were then folded into the health group in 1988, when Chandler completed Kodak's biggest acquisition, the purchase of Sterling Drug for more than $5 billion.

The Sterling acquisition once again totally altered Kodak's strategy for the health group. Sterling Drug is a worldwide manufacturer and marketer of prescription drugs, over-the-counter medicine, and consumer products. It has such familiar brand names as Bayer aspirin, Phillips' milk of magnesia, and Panadol. Chandler thought this merger would provide Kodak with the marketing infrastructure and international drug registration that it needed to become a major player in the pharmaceuticals industry. With this acquisition, Kodak's health group became pharmaceutically oriented, its mission being to develop a full pipeline of major prescription drugs and a world-class portfolio of over-the-counter medicine.

Analysts, however, questioned the acquisition. Once again Chandler was taking Kodak into an industry where competition was intense and the industry itself was consolidating because of the massive cost of drug development. Kodak had no expertise in this area, despite its forays into biotechnology, and the acquisition was unrelated to the other activities of the health group. Some analysts claimed that the acquisition was aimed at deterring a possible takeover of Kodak and that it was too expensive.

The acquisition of Sterling dramatically increased the sales of the health group but dampened Kodak's earnings and helped lead to a reversal in profits in 1989. Moreover, by purchasing Sterling, Kodak had obtained Sterling's Lehn & Fink products division, which produced products as diverse as Lysol and Minwax wood-care products. Far from wishing to sell this division, Kodak believed that this acquisition would lead to long-term profits. Analysts asked whether this was growth without profitability.

The Chemicals Group

Established more than sixty-five years ago as a supplier of raw materials for Kodak's film and processing businesses, the Eastman Chemical Co. has been responsible for developing many of the chemicals and plastics that have made Kodak the leader in the photographic industry. The company has also been a major supplier of chemicals, fibers, and plastics to thousands of customers worldwide. Kodak has been enjoying increased growth in its plastic material and resins unit because of outstanding performance and enthusiastic customer acceptance of Kodak PET (polyethylene terephthalate), a polymer used in soft-drink bottles and other food and beverage containers. The growth in popularity of 16-ounce PET bottles spurred a record year for both revenue and volume in 1985. Kodak announced the opening of a major new PET facility in England in 1988. In 1986, three new businesses were established within the chemicals group: specialty printing inks, performance plastics, and animal nutrition supplements. They all had the common objective of enabling the chemicals group to move quickly into profitable new market segments where there is the potential for growth.

In its chemical business, too, Kodak ran into the same kinds of problems experienced by its other operating groups. There is intense competition in the plastics industry, not only from U.S. firms like DuPont but also from large Japanese and European firms like Imperial Chemical Industries PLC and Hoech, which compete directly with Kodak for sales. In specialty plastics and PET, for example, volume increased but Kodak was forced to reduce prices by 5% to compete with other firms in the industry. This squeeze in profit margins also contributed to the reversal in earnings in 1989.

Logical Synergies?

With the huge profit reversal in 1989 after all the years of acquisition and internal development, analysts were questioning the existence of the "logical synergy" that Chandler claimed for Kodak's businesses. Certainly, the relative contributions of the various operating groups to Kodak's total sales differed from the past, and Kodak was somewhat less dependent on the photographic industry. But was Kodak positioned to compete successfully in the 1990s? What was the rationale for Kodak's entry into different businesses? What were the synergies that Chandler was talking about? Wasn't the improvement on profits in 1990 due to corporate restructuring to reduce costs?

Corporate Restructuring and Cost Reduction

As Chandler tackled changes in strategy, he also directed his efforts at reshaping Kodak's management style and organizational structure to (1) reduce costs and (2) make the organization more flexible and attuned to the competitive environment. Because of its dominance in the industry, in the past, Kodak had not worried about outside competition. As a result, the organizational culture at Kodak emphasized

traditional, conservative values rather than entrepreneurial values. Kodak was often described as a conservative, plodding monolith because all decision making had been centralized at the top of the organization among a clique of senior managers. Furthermore, the company had been operating along functional lines. Research, production, and sales and marketing had operated separately in different units at corporate headquarters and dispersed to many different global locations. Kodak's different product groups also operated separately. The result of these factors was a lack of communication and slow, inflexible decision making that led to delays in making new product decisions. When the company attempted to transfer resources between product groups, conflict often resulted, and the separate functional operations also led to poor product group relations, for managers protected their own turf at the expense of corporate goals. Moreover, there was a lack of attention to the bottom line, and management failed to institute measures to control waste.

Another factor encouraging Kodak's conservative orientation was its promotion policy. Seniority and loyalty to "mother Kodak" counted nearly as much as ability when it came to promotions. Only twelve presidents had led the company since its beginnings in the 1880s. Long after George Eastman's suicide in 1932, the company followed his cautious ways: "If George didn't do it, his successors didn't either."

Kodak's technical orientation also contributed to its problems. Traditionally, its engineers and scientists had dominated decision making, and marketing had been neglected. The engineers and scientists were perfectionists who spent enormous amounts of time developing, analyzing, testing, assessing, and retesting new products. Little time, however, was spent determining whether the products satisfied consumer needs. As a result of this technical orientation, management passed up the invention of xerography, leaving the new technology to be developed by a small Rochester, New York, firm named Haloid Co. (later Xerox). Similarly, Kodak had passed up the instant camera business. Kodak's lack of a marketing orientation allowed competitors to overtake it in several areas that were natural extensions of the photography business, such as 35-mm cameras and video recorders.

Kodak's early management style, while profitable throughout the 1960s because of the company's privileged competitive position, was thus creating difficulties. With its monopoly in the photographic film and paper industry gone, Kodak was in trouble. Chandler had to alter Kodak's management orientation. He began with some radical changes in the company's culture and structure.

Firmly committed to cost cutting, Chandler orchestrated a massive downsizing of the work force to eliminate the fat that had accumulated during Kodak's prosperous past. Traditionally, Kodak had prided itself on being one of the most "Japanese" of all U.S. companies, hiring college graduates and giving them a permanent career. Now it had to go against one of its founding principles and reduce its work force. Kodak's policy of lifetime employment was swept out the door when declining profitability led to a large employee layoff. Chandler instituted a special early retirement program, froze pay raises, and ordered the company's first layoffs in more than a decade. By 1985, the "yellow box factory" had dropped 12,600 of its 136,000 employees. To further reduce costs in 1986, divisions were required to cut employment by an additional 10% and to cut budgetary expenditures by 5%. These measures helped, but because of Kodak's deteriorating performance, new rounds of cost cutting came in 1988 and 1989. Additional 5% reductions in employment aimed at saving $1 billion. The effect of these huge cuts was seen in 1990 when profits rebounded; however, it was not clear whether their effect on earnings would be short run or long run.

Although these measures had an effect on Kodak's culture, Chandler still needed to reshape Kodak's structure. In 1985 he began by shedding the old, stratified corporate structure for what he called an "entrepreneurial" approach. The first step was to reorganize the imaging group into seventeen operating units. Each of the seventeen lines of business contained all the functions necessary for success, including marketing, financial, planning, product development, and manufacturing. Each unit was treated as an independent profit center and was managed by a young executive with authority over everything from design to production. All units had the common goal of improving quality and efficiency and eliminating problems in the transfer of resources and technology among operating groups. The purpose behind this change was to eliminate the old divisional orientation, which had led to competition and reduced integration within the company. Chandler hoped the changes in organizational control and structure would promote innovation, speed reaction time, and establish clear profit goals. With this restructuring,

Chandler also reduced Kodak's top-heavy management to decentralize decision making to lower levels in the hierarchy. This reorganization was a sign that the company was at last shedding its paternalistic approach to management.

With its new risk-taking attitude, Kodak also attempted to create a structure and culture to encourage internal venturing. It formed a "venture board" to help underwrite small projects and make conventional venture capital investments. In addition, the company created an "office of submitted ideas" to screen outside projects. Kodak received more than three thousand proposals, but only thirty survived the screening process. This aggressive research program led to a breakthrough in tubular silver halide grains, which improve the light-gathering capability of film. The discovery resulted in the new line of 35-mm products. However, Kodak's attempts at new venturing were generally unsuccessful. Of the fourteen ventures that Kodak created, six were shut down, three were sold, and four were merged into other divisions. One reason was Kodak's management style, which also affected its new businesses. Kodak's top managers never gave operating executives real authority or abandoned the centralized, conservative approach of the past. One example is Kodak's managing of Atex Inc., the manufacturer of desktop publishing systems that Kodak bought in 1981. Because of Kodak's overbearing management style, the top executives and employees of Atex resigned, creating serious management problems for Kodak. The Atex executives claimed that Kodak executives were hardworking but bureaucratic and did not understand the competitive nature of computer technology. Kodak managers should have been reacting to the computer marketplace weekly. They did not, and Atex executives could not handle Kodak's slow pace.

Another reason for the failure at managing new ventures and acquisitions was that Kodak did not give managers an equity stake in the new ventures, so they felt that they had no stake in the ventures' success. Having learned its lesson, Kodak announced that throughout the company pay would be more closely related to performance. For example, in 1990 up to 40% of a manager's annual compensation was to be based on corporate performance. Even at the middle-manager level, 15% of compensation was to be linked to company results. Kodak hoped by these measures to make the company more entrepreneurial and to move it along the cost reduction path.

Kodak also reorganized its worldwide facilities to reduce costs. International divisions were turning out identical products at higher cost than their counterparts in the United States. In a plan to coordinate worldwide production to increase productivity and lower costs, Kodak streamlined European production by closing duplicate manufacturing facilities and centralizing production and marketing operations, and it also brought some foreign manufacturing home. As a result, Kodak gained $55 million in productivity savings. However, Fuji's new European facility posed a severe challenge. Starting from scratch and employing production techniques learned from low-cost Japanese operations, Fuji remained the clear cost leader with the ability to start a price war to increase market share.

George Fisher Changes Kodak

Chandler retired as CEO in 1989 and was replaced by his chief operating officer, Kay Whitmore, another Kodak veteran. Whitmore immediately was forced to confront the problem of dealing with the poor performance of Chandler's misguided acquisitions. As Kodak's performance continued to plunge under his leadership, however, he came under intense scrutiny from analysts, who began to question the whole logic behind Kodak's aggressive diversification efforts. Whitmore responded by hiring managers from outside Kodak to help him restructure the company, but when they proposed selling off most of Kodak's new acquisitions and laying off many more thousands of employees to reduce costs, Whitmore resisted. He, too, was entrenched in the old Kodak culture and was unwilling to take such drastic steps. Finally, after continued criticism from analysts, Kodak's board of directors ousted Whitmore as CEO, and in 1993 George Fisher, the first outsider to lead Kodak in 117 years, became the new CEO. Fisher left his job as CEO of Motorola to join Kodak. At Motorola, he had been credited with leading that company into the digital age, and it was his expertise in the digital sector that led to his appointment. Fisher was given 2 million Kodak stock options at around $90 a share, Kodak's then stock price, to reward him for what many felt would be a fast turnaround in Kodak's fortunes.

Fisher's strategy was to reverse Chandler's diversification into any industry in the digital sector. Kodak's principal thrust, Fisher decided, should be to strengthen its competencies in the digital photography industry. However, given that Kodak had spent so much money on making its acquisitions, the question was what to do about its other businesses, especially as the company was now burdened with increasing debt from its acquisitions and falling profits. Fisher's solution was dramatic.

Looking at Kodak's four business groups, he decided that the over-the-counter drugs component of the health products group was doing nothing to add value to Kodak's profitability, and he decided to divest Sterling Drugs and use the cash to pay off debt. Soon, all that was left of this group was the health imaging business. Fisher also decided that the chemicals group, despite its expertise in the invention and manufacture of chemicals, no longer fitted with his new digital strategy. Henceforth Kodak would buy its chemicals in the open market, and in 1995 he spun this group off and gave each Kodak shareholder a share in the new company, Eastman Chemicals, whose stock price soon increased rapidly. The information systems group with its diverse businesses was a more difficult challenge; the issue was which components would help promote Kodak's new digital strategy and which were superfluous and could be sold off. In the end, Fisher decided that Kodak would focus on building its presence in the document imaging industry with a focus on photocopiers, commercial inkjet printers, and commercial digital imaging and either sold or closed down the various other parts of the business that did not fit this theme. However, he also decided to outsource the sales and service end of the business, and in 1995 Kodak announced an agreement with Danka Business Systems for it to sell and service Kodak's high-volume copiers throughout the United States and Canada.

With these actions, within two years Fisher had pared down Kodak's debt by $7 billion, dumped chemicals and health, and boosted Kodak's stock price—all this signaled good times ahead. However, Fisher still had to confront the problems inside Kodak's core photographic imaging group, and here the solution was neither easy nor quick. Kodak was still plagued by high operating costs that were still 27% of annual revenue, and Fisher knew he needed to get these costs down to about 15 to 20% to compete effectively in the digital world. Kodak's work force had shrunk to 95,000 by 1993, and he wanted to avoid further layoffs, which would demoralize an already shaken work force. But with Kodak's current revenue in 1995 of $16 billion, this would mean finding ways to squeeze another couple of billion out of operating costs.

At the same time, Fisher also knew that Kodak had to invest more and more of its R&D budget into digital imaging. Kodak had no particular competency in making either digital cameras or the software necessary to allow them to operate efficiently. Soon Kodak was spending over $400 million a year on digital projects. However, new digital products were slow to come on line. Also, consumers were slow to embrace digital photography, the cameras were expensive and bulky, the software was complicated to use, and printing digital photographs was both expensive and difficult at this time. Neither Kodak nor its customers had ramped up the digital photography learning curve, and by 1997 its digital business was still losing over $100 million a year.

To compound matters, in 1995 Fuji Film decided to open up a state-of-the-art filmmaking operation in the United States to further attack the $6 billion film market with "home-grown" products. Fuji also snatched the biggest photo-finishing contract in the United States, the Wal-Mart account, away from Kodak in 1995, and soon after sales of Fuji film in Wal-Mart started to rocket. Through 1995–1997 Fuji also lowered its prices and started a price war, and by 1997 Kodak's share of the U.S. film market had fallen to 78%, down a further 4% from 1996, while Fuji's had risen to 14%. This loss of four points cost Kodak about $125 million in lost sales, and sales of private-label film were beginning to increase, putting more pressures on revenues and costs.

To speed product development, Fisher reorganized Kodak's product groups into fourteen autonomous business units based on serving the needs of distinct groups of customers, such as those for its health products or commercial products. The idea was to decentralize decision making, thus putting managers closer to their major customers and escaping from Kodak's suffocating centralized style of decision making. Fisher also changed the top managers in charge of the film and camera units; however, he did not bring in many outsiders to spearhead the new digital efforts. This new emphasis on customer groups also meant that overhead costs rose because each unit had its own complement of functions; thus sales forces and so on were duplicated.

Fisher had been performing the roles of Kodak's chairman, CEO, president, *and* COO—something that analysts now started to complain about bitterly.

How could Kodak get rid of its centralized decision-making style when its new leader apparently wanted to centralize all important decision making in his own hands? The reorganization into fourteen autonomous business units had not decentralized control to business unit leaders, and Fisher and his top management team were still overseeing all important strategy decisions. This explained the slow pace of change at Kodak. Thus while Fisher had brought Kodak's focus back to its core photography business, he had not put in place the infrastructure that would allow its managers to achieve its new digital mission.

In 1996, Fisher finally realized his dilemma, and with pressure from the board, Daniel A. Carp was named Kodak's president and COO, the appointment to COO meaning that he was Fisher's heir apparent as Kodak's CEO. Carp was a Kodak veteran who had spearheaded the global consolidation of its operations and its entry into major new international markets such as China. He was widely credited with having had a major impact on Kodak's attempts to fight Fuji on a global level and help it to maintain its market share. Henceforth, Kodak's digital and applied imaging, business imaging, and equipment manufacturing—almost all its major operating groups—would now report to Carp. Carp also retained control of the Greater China region, where potential future film sales were seen as crucial to Kodak's future in its battle with arch-rival Fuji.

However, Kodak's revenues and profits continued to decline during the mid to late 1990s. It was slowly but steadily losing market share in its core film business to Fuji, but now generic film brands were also attracting customers and putting squeezes on profit margins. By 2000 analysts estimated it had only 66% of the U.S. market. Although the major price war with Fuji was over, sales of private-label film were still rising, and Kodak was periodically forced to use tactics such as multipack price discounts and rebates to prevent even further erosions to its market share, even at the cost of profits. Fisher knew that Kodak must preserve its market share to protect its future profitability and to give time both for it to develop its own digital competencies and for customers to develop an understanding and appetite for digital cameras. Meanwhile, the quality of the pictures taken by digital cameras was advancing rapidly as more and more pixels were being crammed into them. Also, at the low end, the price of a basic digital camera was falling rapidly because of economies of scale in production. Perhaps, finally, the digital photography market was taking off, but would Kodak be able to meet the challenge?

Despite early enthusiasm from analysts, Kodak's slow progress on all fronts and Fisher's leadership had become a major disappointment. When in July 1997 Fisher announced poor second-quarter results, analysts and shareholders who had bought into his new strategy for Kodak began to bail out. Its share price soon tumbled to below $70 from $90, and Fisher's stock options that had been granted at $90 were now valueless at this price. Many analysts wondered if Kodak's board had been right in February 1997 to extend Fisher's contract for three more years to December 31, 2000.

Carp's Growing Influence

With Carp now in control of both Kodak's digital and global operations, the pace of change started to quicken. In 1997, Kodak announced it would open an office of the COO in Hong Kong to capitalize on trends in emerging markets, especially because of China's low-cost manufacturing advantages. Also in 1997, Kodak increased its stake in the Japanese camera manufacturer Chinon to 50.1%, effectively taking control of the company that now was making its advanced digital cameras and scanners. In 1998, Kodak announced its lowest-priced-yet digital camera with "megapixel" (million pixels per inch) image quality. This camera looked and operated like a conventional point-and-shoot camera. Kodak also bought Picturevision Inc., whose digital Photonet online network products, combined with Kodak's brand name, would attract more customers who could now scan their pictures into its digital network, transmit the images and share them with others, and also receive outputs ranging from reprints to enlargements. Photo retailers also named Kodak's digital picturemaker kiosks the "top product of the year." Customers could take their ordinary photographs and use the kiosks to remove red eye, do quick and easy color corrections, and zoom or crop to select and print the best part of a photo. Essentially, Kodak was using these kiosks to help customers learn about the advantages of digital photography and to help develop the market. Kodak and Intel also formed an agreement to use Intel digital scanning equipment in Kodak's Qualex photo-finishing labs to make it easy for customers to put photos onto CD-ROM for use in home computers. In 1998, AOL and Kodak announced a strategic alliance to offer AOL members an exclusive online service, "You've Got Pictures," whereby AOL members could have their regular processed pictures delivered in digital format to their AOL mailboxes. Customers were becoming increasingly familiar with how the new digital products worked, and Kodak was in the forefront of online efforts to capture customers and promote the Internet for transmission of digital images.

Thus Kodak was beginning to make steady progress in its digital mission; its digital cameras were growing in popularity, in large part because of its developing competencies in making easy-to-use camera-printer software. Also, its digital kiosks and photo-finishing operations were being increasingly visited by customers, and their number was increasing rapidly both in the United States and globally. In recognition of his progress, in June 1999 Kodak's board named Carp as new CEO of Kodak, and he was to keep his other roles of president and COO. Fisher was to remain chairman until January 2001.

In the next few years, Kodak's developing digital skills led to new products in all its major businesses. In 1999, its health imaging group announced the then fastest digital image management system for echocardiography labs. It also entered the digital radiography market with three state-of-the-art digital systems for capturing x-ray images. Its document imaging group announced several new electronic document management systems. It also teamed up with inkjet maker Lexmark to introduce the stand-alone Kodak Personal Picture Maker by Lexmark, which could print color photos from both compact flash cards and Smart Media. Its commercial and government systems group announced advanced new high-powered digital cameras for uses such as in space and in the military.

With these developments, Kodak's net earnings shot up between 1998 and 2000, and its stock price recovered somewhat. However, one reason for the increase in net revenues was that the devastating price war with Fuji that had raged from 1979 to 1999 had ended as both companies saw that continuing to offer price discounts simply reduced both companies' profits. Kodak also was still not getting quickly to the market the range of new digital imaging products it needed to drive its future profitability, since there was intense competition in the core film businesses, which had traditionally given it 30 to 40% of its profits. Here, as in film products, Kodak's high operating costs overwhelmed the benefits it obtained from its new product introductions and hurt its bottom line—its profits were not increasing.

Kodak in the Early 2000s

New digital product developments and changing industry conditions in most of its markets began to punish Kodak afresh as it entered the 2000s. In the consumer imaging group, for example, Kodak launched a new camera, the EasyShare, in 2001. Over 4 million digital cameras were sold in 2000 and over 6 million in 2001, and over a half-million of the easy-to-use new Kodak camera were sold in 2001. However, given the huge development costs and intense competition from Japanese companies like Sony and Canon, which also make advanced cameras and "digicams," Kodak has not yet made any money from its digital cameras—profit margins are razor thin because of intense competition. Moreover, every time it sells a digital camera, it reduces demand for its high-margin film; so Kodak is cannibalizing a profitable product for an unprofitable one—with no choice in the matter. As a result, its profitability has plunged.

Kodak argued that it would make more money in the future from sales of the paper necessary to print these images and from its photo-finishing operations. However, it is becoming increasingly obvious that consumers are not printing out many of the photographs they take, preferring to save many in disk form and only selecting and printing out the few best ones to send to relatives and friends. With chemical films, one could not pick and choose; the whole roll had to be developed. So revenues are not increasing on this front. Moreover, it is the ink sellers such as Hewlett-Packard and Lexmark that have been charging monopoly prices for ink cartridges, which have been making the money in printing images, and Kodak has failed to use its strengths in chemicals to get into the printer ink business.

On the photo-finishing end, Kodak's future revenues and profits depend on it maximizing the number of its in-store kiosks or the number of photo-finishing contracts with large chain stores. After Kodak lost the Wal-Mart contract to Fuji, it signed new agreements with Walgreens (the second largest U.S. film processor, with over 3,000 stores) and with Kmart. It also operated its own Fox and Qualex photo-finishing labs. However, in 2001, Kmart declared Chapter 11 bankruptcy, and the Fox photo store chain, which was primarily finishing traditional roll film, went bankrupt, causing a large loss to Kodak. To compound matters, in June 2002 it was reported that Walgreens was testing Fuji's new photo-finishing laboratory system in thirty of its stores and that it might award this important contract to Fuji when it came up for renewal sometime in 2002. In June 2002, recognizing that Fuji was gaining a competitive edge in the vital photo-finishing systems market, Kodak announced that it was buying key components of its new digital system from Agfa, a European imaging firm, since it did not have the time to develop them itself. This suggests that Kodak's technology was no better than that of competitors, and it might be even behind that of competitors like Fuji. Thus it was not clear that Kodak had a lead in all the activities—cameras, software, paper, and photo finishing—necessary to dominate the photography market as it had in the past. It did have its powerful brand name going for it, however, which is why it has been so concerned to protect its market share at any cost to its profits.

At the industry level, the emergence of powerful buyers in many markets also seriously hurt Kodak's performance. In photo finishing, large store chains like Wal-Mart and Walgreens are in strong bargaining positions and can threaten Kodak's profitability (it has been estimated that 10% of Kodak's photo-finishing operations are with Walgreens). This same situation occurred in the health imaging industry. Here, Kodak's state-of-the-art imaging products were widely expected to generate large revenues and boost its profitability. However, after a good start, in 2000 Kodak faced the problem of bargaining over prices with Novation Group Purchasing organization, a major buyer of health equipment and therefore a powerful buyer as well. Kodak was forced to slash its prices to win the contract against agile competitors, and this experience was repeated with many other large health care providers. So intense was competition in this segment that in 2001 sales of laser printers and health-related imagining products, which make up Kodak's second biggest business, fell 7% while profit in the segment fell 30%, causing a large drop in Kodak's share price. In 2000, after its profits fell drastically, it announced another 2,000 job cuts, and in 2001 it announced another 5,000, for a total of 7,000, bringing Kodak's work force down to about 78,000.

Also, in 2001 Carp announced another major reorganization of Kodak's businesses. To give it a sharper focus on its products and customers, Kodak announced that it was moving from a structure based on customer groups to one based on strategic product lines, and it created four distinct product groups: the film group, which now contained all its silver halide activities; consumer digital imaging; health imaging group; and growing commercial imaging group, which continued to develop its business imaging and printing applications. Nevertheless, revenues plunged from $19 billion in 2001 to only $13 billion by 2002, its profits almost disappeared, and analysts now wondered if Kodak under Carp was really faring any better than Kodak under Fisher. There was no real change taking place, and Carp was avoiding the massive downsizing that still needed to take place to make Kodak a viable company. Analysts attributed this to Kodak's entrenched, inbred, and unresponsive top management that persisted in doing everything possible to frustrate real efforts to reduce costs and streamline operations. For despite all the advances in its digital skills, Kodak was still burdened with high operating costs, well out of proportion with its declining revenues. Would the layoffs or reorganization be enough to turn Kodak's performance around?

Amazingly, despite its problems, Kodak still paid its shareholders one of the top ten dividends of all companies in the *Fortune 500*. Analysts argue that it should be run for profit now, not in the future. But Kodak's managers replied that the economic recession and events of 2000–2002 were to blame for a large part of its problems and that it had all the pieces in place for a sustained recovery and for dominance in the digital arena using its powerful brand name once the market recovered. Investors didn't believe this story. Kodak's stock price plunged in 2002 and was selling in the $30s by June—a far cry from the $90s when Fisher took over and a continuing sign of the fall of this once economic powerhouse.

The year 2002 proved to be a turning point in the photographic imaging business as sales of digital cameras and other products soared. The result for Kodak's film business was disastrous because not only did sales of Kodak film start to fall sharply, but what analysts had expected was true—photographers printed only a fraction of the pictures they took, so demand for Kodak's paper also fell. In 2003, this trend accelerated as digital cameras became the camera of choice of photographers worldwide and Kodak's film and paper revenues continued to fall. This was very serious for Kodak because sales of film and paper are its most profitable product and generate most of its cash. Kodak's fourth-quarter net income was only $19 million in 2003, compared with a net income of $113 in 2002. This huge fall in Kodak's profitability was somewhat ironic given that Kodak's line of EasyShare digital cameras were the best-selling cameras in the United States by 2003. Sales rose by 87% in 2003, and Kodak now was the number 2 global seller with about 18% of the market. However, rising sales of digital products were not enough to offset losses in film since profit margins remained tight in digital products because of intense competition from companies such as Canon, Olympus, and Nikon.

In the fall of 2003, CEO Daniel Carp announced Kodak's cash-cow yellow box business was in "irreversible decline" and that it was withdrawing from the Advanced Photo Systems camera business and stopping sales of reloadable film cameras, the old silver halide kind. However, Carp also announced a major change of strategy; Kodak would stop investing in its traditional business and pour all its resources into developing new digital products, such as cameras and accessories, to improve its competitive position and margins. It bought the remaining 44% of Chinon, its Japanese unit that designed and made its digital cameras, to protect its competency in digital imaging and ensure the long-term flow of profits from this unit. Kodak began a major push to develop new camera models and also to develop skills in inkjet printing to create digital photo printing systems so its users could directly print from its cameras. Also, Carp announced Kodak would try to grow its digital health imaging business, which was enjoying increased success, and announced a new initiative to make inroads in the digital commercial printing business.

However, analysts and investors reacted to this news badly. Xerox had tried to enter the digital printer business years before with no success against HP, the market leader. Moreover, they wondered how new revenues from digital products could ever make up for the loss of Kodak's film and paper revenues. Carp also announced that to fund this new strategy, Kodak would reduce its hefty dividend by 72% from $1.80 to 50 cents a share, which would raise $1.3 billion for investment in digital products. Investors had no faith in Carp's new plan, and Kodak's stock, which had been around $27, plunged to $22, its lowest price in decades. Analysts argued that Kodak should have funded its new strategy by reducing operating costs to increase business efficiency, pointing out that a 5%

increase in efficiency would have raised the $1.3 billion. Kodak's top management came under intense criticism for not reducing its cost structure, and Kodak's stock price continued to fall as it became clearer that its new strategy would do little to raise its falling revenues.

Finally, in the spring of 2004, Carp announced another change of strategy for Kodak—a strategy that it should have implemented at least a decade ago and probably two decades ago, when competition from Fuji in its film business began to bite into its profits. Announcing that it "was smart business in a business that's shrinking," Carp said Kodak would cut its work force by 21% by the end of 2006 and take charges of $1.5 billion against revenues to cover the cost of this new round of huge layoffs. This would mean that another 12,000 to 15,000 Kodak employees would lose their jobs, but that operating costs would drop by about $1 billion a year. Jobs would be lost in film manufacturing, at the support and corporate levels, and from global downsizing as Kodak reduced its total facilities worldwide by one-third and continued to shutter photo-finishing labs that served retailers.

This news sent Kodak's share price up by 20% in 2004 as investors finally hoped Kodak would be able to take the profits from its new streamlined film business and invest them successfully in new digital imaging technology ventures. However, Kodak was late building the distinctive competences that might give it a competitive advantage in many digital imaging research areas. With so many agile competitors, and a fast-changing digital technology, there were many challenges still facing the company—could it do it?

A New Kodak CEO Takes Control

By 2003 it had become clear that Carp was not the right person to take on the hard job of radically restructuring Kodak's operations. He was too politically involved in the present status quo, and he would never make the changes necessary. So Kodak's board of directors hired Antonio Perez, a former HP executive, as its new president and COO, to take charge of the reorganization effort. Perez was the person who made the hard choices about which divisions Kodak would close and orchestrated the termination of thousands of Kodak's managers and employees. In 2004, Carp realized he had lost the support of the board, and Perez's success at restructuring the company led to his appointment as Kodak's new CEO. He

was now in charge of implementing the downsized, streamlined company's new digital imaging strategy. Perez announced a major three-year restructuring plan in 2004 to continue to 2007 to transform the company into a leader in digital imaging.

Lowering the Cost Structure

On the cost side, Perez announced that Kodak needed "to install a new, lower-cost business model consistent with the realities of a digital business. The reality of digital businesses is thinner margins—we must continue to move to the business model appropriate for that reality." His main objectives were to reduce operating facilities by 33%, divest redundant operations, and reduce its labor force by 20%, and to achieve this Kodak made many strategic changes. In January 2004, it stopped all its traditional camera and film activities except for the Advanced Photo System and 35-mm film. Also in 2004, Kodak implemented SAP's ERP system to link all segments of its value chain activities together and to its suppliers in order to reduce costs. Kodak had benchmarked its competitors and found it had a much larger cost of goods sold than them; using SAP, its goal was to reduce cost of goods sold from 19% to 14% by 2007 and so significantly boost profit margins.

Since 2004 Kodak has steadily laid off more than 25,000 employees, shut down and sold units, and moved to a more centralized structure with all four heads of Kodak's main operating groups reporting directly to Perez. In September 2006, Kodak announced the closing of its synthetic chemicals operation, which seemed to signal one of the last steps in its current drive to lower costs and move from its traditional operations to focus on the digital side of its business. Also, in 2006, Kodak signed deal with Flextronics, a Singapore-based company, to outsource its camera manufacturing and so trim excess capacity and focus on developing new digital core competences.

The costs of this transformation have been huge. It created losses of $900 million in 2004, $1.1 billion in 2005, and around $1 billion in 2006. Because of this transformation, its ROIC was a negative 20% compared to its main digital rival, Canon, which enjoys a positive 14% ROIC.

Building Differentiated Products

Kodak was still organized into four main business units; now the push was on to develop innovative new products in three of these imaging units—consumer, business graphics, and health, while reducing costs in the fourth, film products. The main problem facing Kodak continued to be that profit margins were by far the highest in the declining film unit; digital products result in profit margins 50 to 70% lower than film products, so increasing profit margins in digital sales was vital. Kodak had to increase profit margins in all its consumer, commercial graphics, and health imaging units, and Perez's new goal was to eliminate any digital business in which Kodak was not number 1 or 2 in terms of market share.

In the consumer unit, Perez put the focus on developing new improved digital cameras and bringing out new products several times a year—and to increase profit margins at the expense of increasing market share. It already was the market leader in the United States. Now its goal was to keep its prices and profits high in consumer imaging. So it needed differentiated products, and in 2004, Kodak announced it had developed the world's smallest ultrawide-angle optical zoom digital camera, the Kodak EasyShare V705, and other innovations. But competition from manufacturers like Canon and Nikon came quickly, and in 2005, Kodak brought out a new line of more powerful EasyShare cameras to fight back. However, Kodak gained the number 1 spot in digital camera sales in the United States in the second quarter of 2005, and digital imaging product sales and revenues increased sharply, which seemed to be a boon to the company. As an example, Kodak said sales of its EasyShare line of digital cameras rose 87% compared with the previous year.

At the same time, however, growing consumer acceptance of digital cameras accelerated the decline of Kodak's traditional film business. And, in 2006, the company's prospects deteriorated further as growth in its consumer digital cameras and photo printers came to a standstill because of increased competition and a mature market. This resulted in intensified price pressure in consumer digital products, which forced it to lower prices and so its revenues and profit margins. At the same time, this led to a major decline in its film business, which was still Kodak's major profit maker. Nevertheless, in 2006, the company brought out new products such as its dual-lens cameras and cameras with WiFi that could connect wirelessly to PCs to download and print photographs, and it used these innovations to once again raise prices.

Improving its other consumer digital imaging products and services was also a continuing part of Kodak's new strategy. Perez was determined to make Kodak the leader in digital processing and printing in the United States and even globally. Kodak's EasyShare Internet service that allows customers to download their images to its website and receive back both printed photographs and the images on a CD soared in popularity, for example. EasyShare revenues increased by 55% from 2003 to 2004, and it reached a customer base of 30 million by 2006. However, profit margins were still slim since this is an expensive business.

In another major move to attract and reach customers, Kodak put all its efforts into developing and extending its empire of digital processing kiosks, installing them into stores, pharmacies, and other outlets as fast as possible because it sensed the importance of establishing its brand name in this arena. It configured these kiosks to give customers total control over which pictures to develop at what quantity, quality, and size. Kodak discovered that putting two kiosks in one store reduced customer waiting time significantly and that customers often shopped in stores while waiting for their images to be processed. This led to increased store sales—something that led to more demand for kiosks. In 2005, for example, Kodak and Wal-Mart signed an alliance to put 2,000 kiosks into 1,000 Wal-Mart store. By 2006, Kodak had over 65,000 kiosks worldwide and was the global leader in this business—far ahead of its nearest competitor. Retailers increasingly discovered how Kodak kiosks offer an attractive digital processing alternative at a much lower cost than managing their own onsite digital mini-labs. Kodak, of course, also receives a larger percentage of the photo printing revenues when it controls in-store kiosks, and in 2005 revenues grew by 60% and printing volume by 400%—this looked good for the future.

Kodak also has made major attempts to penetrate the mobile imaging market because of the huge growth in the use of camera phones in the 2000s. Around 600 million camera phones were sold globally in 2006 alone. The Kodak Mobile Imaging Service offers camera phone users several options to view, order, and share prints of all the digital photos on their phones. Users can upload and store pictures from their cameras in their personal EasyShare accounts; then after editing, they can send their favorite photos back to their mobile phones or to anybody else's, and they can be used as photo wallpaper or caller ID. Launching this service required many partnerships and collaborations with wireless providers like Verizon and Cingular and also handset manufacturers such as Nokia, Motorola, and many others that have integrated imaging capability into mobile devices. Kodak benefits from the revenues it receives when camera users take advantage of its processing and printing services as users upload, share, and enjoy pictures via mobile phone capability. In January 2006, Kodak and Motorola announced a ten-year global product cross-licensing and marketing agreement. By combining Motorola's expertise in mobile devise technology and Kodak's experience in digital imaging, the two companies plan to improve the digital capturing feature of the phone.

As a result of its substantial investment in R&D, Kodak is now number 1 in sales of digital cameras and snapshot printing systems in the United States, and second or third globally, and number 1 in online services and in physical digital kiosks in stores. This rosy picture is hampered by the fact that the digital imaging market has intense competition and thin profit margins, however, and Perez decided to keep prices high and sacrifice market share for higher margins. Thus R&D seemed especially important given the progress being made by all digital competitors in improving technology. The costs of research and marketing and selling the new, improved products that need to be continually introduced are high, and all competitors needed to protect their margins. Nevertheless, even though Kodak was now competitive in the consumer digital market segment, it still was not able to make enough profit to offset the losses it incurred from the rapid decline of its cash-cow film business. All its efforts in consumer digital products staved off bankruptcy but contributed little or nothing to increasing its profitability.

Graphic Communications Group

In fact, although its consumer digital business is its most visible unit, Kodak has been putting forth major efforts to increase its strengths and distinctive competencies in its graphic communications group (GCG)—this seemed to be the best bet for increasing its future profitability because profit margins are much higher. In 2005, for example, sales of the graphic communications group more than doubled, and the profit margins of products sold by this unit are three times as high as in its consumer unit because the primary users of these products are companies with large budgets. In this segment, Kodak has also been able to increase sales and profits by keeping its prices high and refusing to lower prices—even during price wars with aggressive competitors like Xerox, Canon, and HP—because of the innovative features of its new imaging products.

The six main customers groups served by the GCG are commercial printers, in-plant printers, data centers, digital service providers, packaging companies, and newspapers. Within each of these segments, Kodak has developed digital products that offer customers a single solution to deliver the products and services they need to compete in their business. Kodak solutions extend from up-front workflow and professional services, to digital pre-press, to print—in other words, all the way from initial composition to final product printing. Kodak was able to develop this end-to-end solution because of its acquisition in the 2000s of specialist digital printing companies such as KPG, CREO, Versamark, and Express. By 2006, it had successfully integrated all these new companies and their employees into the GCG.

From each acquisition Kodak gained access to more products and more customers along with more services and solutions to offer them. No single solution will work for every customer because each business customer uses some combination of traditional offset printing and new digital printing, which is why GCG assembled the broadest product portfolio in the industry. Kodak claims that no other competitor can offer the same breadth of products and solutions that it offers. Kodak's product line includes image scanners and document management systems, the industry's leading portfolio of digital proofing solutions. It also includes offset, flexo, digital plates and CTP award-winning wide-format inkjet printing, including the most robust toner-based platforms for four-color and monochrome printing. Kodak also claims to have the leading continuous inkjet technology for high-speed, high-volume printing, as well as imprinting capabilities that can be combined with traditional offset printing for those customers still in the process of making the transition to digital printing.

The Medical Imaging Group

By 2006 the costs of research and marketing digital products in its consumer and commercial units was putting intense pressure on the company's resources—and Kodak still had to invest large amounts of capital to develop a lasting competitive advantage in its medical imaging unit. Here too in the 2000s, Kodak had made many strategic acquisitions to strengthen its competitive advantage in several areas of the medical imaging segment, such as digital mammography and advanced x-rays. It had developed one of the top five medical imaging groups in the world. However, in May 2006 Kodak put its medical imaging unit up for sale. It realized that this unit required too much future investment in its own right if it was to succeed—and its consumer and commercial groups were not providing the revenue enough for this investment. In addition, Kodak could realize capital from the sale of this unit to reduce its long-term debt and provide some capital to pursue new initiatives in its two remaining digital units. Also, although the medical unit accounted for nearly one-fifth of Kodak's overall sales in 2005, its operating profit had plunged 21% as profit margins fell because of increased competition from major rivals such as GE.

Each of Kodak's digital business units was encountering its own set of competitive threats, and Kodak still lacked a secure "core" digital group on which to base its future success, although now all bets seemed to be on its commercial imaging unit—given its high profit margins. At the same time, profits from its old profitable film unit were declining sharply; Kodak needed more cash, so something had to be done to find a buyer for its medical unit.

In January 2007, Kodak announced that its medical imaging unit had been sold to the Onex Corp., Canada's biggest buyout firm, which owned a small but profitable medical imaging unit in its portfolio, for $2.35 billion. In addition, if the acquisition resulted in substantial synergies that met certain profit targets, Kodak would get another $200 million. Kodak plans to use the proceeds to repay about $1.15 billion of debt and to fund its digital research program. All 8,000 health group employees, who make x-ray film, medical printers, and information management software and storage systems, will now be employed by Onex. Perez said, "We now plan to focus our attention on the significant digital growth opportunities within our businesses in consumer and professional imaging and graphic communications."

In 2007, Kodak entered the fourth year of its digital makeover under Perez. It has accumulated $2 billion in net losses over the last eight quarters and piled up $2.6 billion in restructuring charges since January 2004. However, its losses narrowed to $37 million in the July-to-September quarter as digital profits surged above $100 million. Just a year ago, the film group's gross profit exceeded the consumer digital unit's by $86 million, but now the consumer unit earned a gross profit of $323 million, a 31% increase from the fourth quarter of 2005, versus a $243 million profit for the film unit, a 27% decrease. Also, by disposing of its health imaging unit, trimming manufacturing operations, and cutting 27,000 more jobs, Kodak's global work force is now under 50,000 from a peak of 145,300 in 1988.

After the sale, industry analysts wondered if Kodak was hoping to find a buyer for the rest of its assets because it will be even more exposed to fluctuations in sales without health imaging, previously its second largest revenue earner. But because its competitive position is so uncertain, it is not clear that private equity bidders or even industry buyers would be interested in the company. Another scenario would be for Kodak to use the money it raises from the sale of its medical imaging group to make a takeover attempt of the newly reborn Xerox Corp., which is one of its major competitors in the commercial digital graphic business, a merger that might be welcomed by the stockholders of both companies. Certainly Kodak's stockholders have taken an optimistic view of its future, either as an independent company, as a takeover target, or as an acquirer of another major digital company—its share price rose by 30% in the second half of 2006.

It rose again on February when Kodak announced that it was introducing a revolutionary new line of color digital printers using an advanced Kodak ink that would provide brighter pictures that would keep their clarity for decades. Apparently Perez, who had been in charge of HP's printer business before he left Kodak, had made developing the line a major part of his turnaround strategy, and he and a research team had been working on the new project codenamed "Goya." The new printers will arrive in stores in March priced at $149 to $299, and Kodak is targeting consumers who print loads of photos and are willing to pay full price for high-quality printers. However, Perez's printer strategy is based upon charging a higher price for the printer than competitors like HP and Lexmark, but then charging a much lower price for the ink cartridge to attract a bigger market share. Black ink cartridges will cost $9.99 and color $14.99, which will be about 10 cents a print, far lower than the current 20 to 25 cents per print. Kodak's strategy is that consumers will be willing to buy the printers and then print more pictures, which will give it a share of the market that will make this a multibillion revenues generator in the years ahead. Perez expects inkjet printing to produce Kodak's best profit—in double digits after a three-year investment phase.

At the same time, in a clear sign the U.S. market has matured, shipments of digital cameras fell 3% in the fourth quarter to 12.1 million units from 12.4 million units a year ago, a sharp contrast from double-digit gains in previous years, when the attraction of filmless cameras swelled as consumers replaced their traditional film devices; now much demand is in the direction of upgrading to better digital cameras. As noted earlier, Perez kept prices high to protect profit margins and so for years Canon had a 20% market share, followed by Sony with 17% and Kodak with 16%. But Perez's strategy seems to be the correct one because also in February Panasonic announced a totally new line of advanced digital cameras that will further cut profit margins unless companies drop price competition. So with its paper, kiosk, Internet, and now printer business growing, Kodak might be able to generate profits in the consumer unit too, so that combined with the profits from its commercial graphics unit, it will indeed have turned the corner and will emerge as a digital leader in the coming decade.

REFERENCES

"Agfa to Supply Kodak with Lab Equipment," Yahoo.com, Friday, June 7, 2002.

James Bandler, "Kodak Advances in Market Share of Digital Cameras," *Wall Street Journal*, December 21, 2001, p. B2.

James Bandler, "Kodak Net Plummets 77% on Weak Sales," *Wall Street Journal*, October 25, 2001, p. B9.

James Bandler, "Kodak, Sanyo Agree to Make New Type of Screen Display," *Wall Street Journal*, December 4, 2001, p. B7.

James Bandler, "Kodak Slashes Earnings Forecast, Citing Weak Sales," *Wall Street Journal*, September 20, 2001, p. B4.

James Bandler, "Kodak's Net Fell 93% in Second Quarter on Weakness in Film, Medical Divisions," *Wall Street Journal*, July 18, 2001, p. B4.

James Bandler, "Kodak Stock Falls on Credit Downgrade, Signs Film Market Share Is Decreasing," *Wall Street Journal*, November 1, 2001, p. B8.

James Bandler, "Kodak Will Acquire Ofoto in a Move to Expand Services," *Wall Street Journal*, May 1, 2001, p. B9.

James Bandler, "Kodak Will Offer Its Staff a Chance to Upgrade Options," *Wall Street Journal*, November 30, 2001, p. B7.

James Bandler and Joann Lublin, "Russo's Departure Is a Blow to Kodak as It Seeks to Move into the Digital Age," *Wall Street Journal*, January 8, 2002, p. B4.

Barbara Buell, "A Gust of Fresh Air for the Stodgy Giant of Rochester," *Business Week*, June 10, 1985, p. 93.

Barbara Buell, "Kodak Is Trying to Break Out of Its Shell," *Business Week*, June 10, 1985, pp. 92–95.

Barbara Buell, "Kodak Scrambles to Fill the Gap," *Business Week*, February 8, 1986, p. 30.

"Business Brief—Eastman Kodak Co.: Photo Concern Is Shutting Its Picture Vision Operation," *Wall Street Journal*, November 20, 2001.

"Business Brief—Eastman Kodak Co.: Suit Is Filed Charging Sun with Infringement of Patents," *Wall Street Journal*, February 15, 2002, p. B8.

"Business Brief—Kmart Corp.: Retailer Teams with Kodak in an Online Photo," *Wall Street Journal*, May 9, 2001.

Adrienne Carter, "Kodak's Promising Developments," *Money*, February 2002, p. 39.

"Citigroup Moves to Stress Global Products," Yahoo.com, Tuesday, June 11, 2002.

"Eastman Kodak Rating May Fall a Rung Lower," *Wall Street Journal*, July 24, 2001.

"Eastman Kodak to Acquire Encad," *Daily Deal*, November 16, 2001.

Daniel Eisenburg, "Kodak's Photo Op," *Time*, April 30, 2001, p. 46.

John Greenwald, "Aiming for a Brighter Picture," *Time*, January 9, 1984, p. 49.

John Hechinger, "Kodak to Reorganize Its Business Again," *Wall Street Journal*, November 15, 2001, p. B12.

Laura Heller, "PMA Highlights Print Kiosks, but Digital Imaging Steals Show," *DSN Retailing Today*, March 11, 2002, p. 6.

James S. Hirsch, "Kodak Effort at 'Intrapreneurship' Fails," *Wall Street Journal*, August 17, 1990, p. 32.

Kodak, http://www.Kodak.com, 2002, 2003, 2004, 2005, 2006, 2007.

Kodak Annual Reports, 1980–2007.

"Kodak's New Image: Electronic Imaging," *Electron Business*, January 1986, pp. 38–43.

"Kodak's New Lean and Hungry Look," *Business Week*, May 30, 1983, p. 33.

"Kodak, Walt Disney Sign Multiyear Alliance Agreement," Yahoo.com, Tuesday, May 28, 2002.

"Moody's Downgrades Kodak's Debt Rating on Digital Concerns," *Wall Street Journal*, March 20, 2002, p. B5.

Thomas Moore, "Embattled Kodak Enters the Electronic Age," *Fortune*, August 22, 1983, pp. 120–128.

Fauziah Muhtar, "Kodak Zooms In with New Digital Cameras," *Computimes Malaysia*, May 2, 2002, p. 1.

Emily Nelson and Joseph B. White, "Blurred Image: Kodak Moment Came Early for CEO Fisher, Who Takes a Stumble—Bet on Digital Photography Has Been a Money Loser; Fuji Is Gaining Ground—Dennis Rodman's Film Flop," *Wall Street Journal*, July 25, 1997, p. A1.

Doug Olenick, "Kodak, Sanyo Plan to Produce OEL Flat-Panel Displays," *Twice*, December 17, 2001, p. 90.

Daniel P. Palumbo, "Kodak Embraces Disruptive Technology," *Journal of Business Strategy*, July–August 2001, p. 11.

Franklin Paul, "Kodak Digital Camera, Software Sims to Ease Printing," Yahoo.com, Tuesday, May 21, 2002.

Franklin Paul, "Sony to Muscle into Kodak's Digital Printing Arena," Yahoo.com, Wednesday, June 5, 2002.

Charles K. Ryan, Eastman Kodak, Company Outline, Merrill Lynch, Pierce, Framer & Smith Incorporated, May 7, 1986.

Andy Serwer, "Kodak: In the Noose," *Fortune*, February 4, 2002, pp. 147–148.

Geoffrey Smith and Faith Keenan, "Kodak Is the Picture of Digital Success," *Business Week*, January 14, 2002, p. 39.

"Yellow at the Edges," *Economist*, December 7, 1984, p. 90.

Philips versus Matsushita: A New Century, a New Round

This case was prepared by Christopher A. Bartlett, Harvard Business School.

Throughout their long histories, N.V. Philips (Netherlands) and Matsushita Electric (Japan) had followed very different strategies and emerged with very different organizational capabilities. Philips built its success on a worldwide portfolio of responsive national organizations while Matsushita based its global competitiveness on its centralized, highly efficient operations in Japan.

During the 1990s, both companies experienced major challenges to their historic competitive positions and organizational models, and at the end of the decade, both companies were struggling to reestablish their competitiveness. At the start of the new millennium, new CEOs at both companies were implementing yet another round of strategic initiatives and organizational restructurings. Observers wondered how the changes would affect their long-running competitive battle.

Philips: Background

In 1892, Gerard Philips and his father opened a small light-bulb factory in Eindhoven, Holland. When their venture almost failed, they recruited Gerard's brother, Anton, an excellent salesman and manager. By 1900, Philips was the third largest light-bulb producer in Europe.

From its founding, Philips developed a tradition of caring for workers. In Eindhoven it built company houses, bolstered education, and paid its employees so well that other local employers complained. When Philips incorporated in 1912, it set aside 10% of profits for employees.

Technological Competence and Geographic Expansion

While larger electrical products companies were racing to diversify, Philips made only light-bulbs. This one-product focus and Gerard's technological prowess enabled the company to create significant innovations. Company policy was to scrap old plants and use new machines or factories whenever advances were made in new production technology. Anton wrote down assets rapidly and set aside substantial reserves for replacing outdated equipment. Philips also became a leader in industrial research, creating physics and chemistry labs to address production problems as well as more abstract scientific ones. The labs developed a tungsten metal filament bulb that was a great commercial success and gave Philips the financial strength to compete against its giant rivals.

This case derives from an earlier case, "Philips versus Matsushita: Preparing for a New Round," HBS No. 399-102, prepared by Professor Christopher A. Bartlett, which was an updated version of an earlier case by Professor Bartlett and Research Associate Robert W. Lightfoot, "Philips and Matsushita: A Portrait of Two Evolving Companies," HBS Case No. 392-156. The section on Matsushita summarizes "Matsushita Electric Industrial (MEI) in 1987," HBS Case No. 388-144, by Sumantra Ghoshal (INSEAD) and Christopher A. Bartlett. Some early history on Philips draws from "Philips Group—1987," HBS Case No. 388-050, by Professors Frank Aguilar and Michael Y. Yoshino. This version was also prepared by Professor Bartlett. HBS cases are developed solely as the basis for class discussion. Cases are not intended to serve as endorsements, sources of primary data, or illustrations of effective or ineffective management.

Holland's small size soon forced Philips to look beyond its Dutch borders for enough volume to mass produce. In 1899, Anton hired the company's first export manager, and soon the company was selling into such diverse markets as Japan, Australia, Canada, Brazil, and Russia. In 1912, as the electric lamp industry began to show signs of overcapacity, Philips started building sales organizations in the United States, Canada, and France. All other functions remained highly centralized in Eindhoven. In many foreign countries Philips created local joint ventures to gain market acceptance.

In 1919, Philips entered into the Principal Agreement with General Electric, giving each company the use of the other's patents. The agreement also divided the world into "three spheres of influence": General Electric would control North America; Philips would control Holland; but both companies agreed to compete freely in the rest of the world. (General Electric also took a 20% stake in Philips.) After this time, Philips began evolving from a highly centralized company, whose sales were conducted through third parties, to a decentralized sales organization with autonomous marketing companies in 14 European countries, China, Brazil, and Australia.

During this period, the company also broadened its product line significantly. In 1918, it began producing electronic vacuum tubes; eight years later its first radios appeared, capturing a 20% world market share within a decade; and during the 1930s, Philips began producing X-ray tubes. The Great Depression brought with it trade barriers and high tariffs, and Philips was forced to build local production facilities to protect its foreign sales of these products.

Philips: Organizational Development

One of the earliest traditions at Philips was a shared but competitive leadership by the commercial and technical functions. Gerard, an engineer, and Anton, a businessman, began a subtle competition where Gerard would try to produce more than Anton could sell and vice versa. Nevertheless, the two agreed that strong research was vital to Philips' survival.

During the late 1930s, in anticipation of the impending war, Philips transferred its overseas assets to two trusts, British Philips and the North American Philips Corporation; it also moved most of its vital research laboratories to Redhill in Surrey, England, and its top management to the United States. Supported by the assets and resources transferred abroad, and isolated from their parent, the individual country organizations became more independent during the war.

Because waves of Allied and German bombing had pummeled most of Philips' industrial plants in the Netherlands, the management board decided to build the postwar organization on the strengths of the national organizations (NOs). Their greatly increased self-sufficiency during the war had allowed most to become adept at responding to country-specific market conditions—a capability that became a valuable asset in the postwar era. For example, when international wrangling precluded any agreement on three competing television transmission standards (PAL, SECAM, and NTSC), each nation decided which to adopt. Furthermore, consumer preferences and economic conditions varied: in some countries, rich, furniture-encased TV sets were the norm; in others, sleek, contemporary models dominated the market. In the United Kingdom, the only way to penetrate the market was to establish a rental business; in richer countries, a major marketing challenge was overcoming elitist prejudice against television. In this environment, the independent NOs had a great advantage in being able to sense and respond to the differences.

Eventually, responsiveness extended beyond adaptive marketing. As NOs built their own technical capabilities, product development often became a function of local market conditions. For example, Philips of Canada created the company's first color TV; Philips of Australia created the first stereo TV; and Philips of the United Kingdom created the first TVs with teletext.

While NOs took major responsibility for financial, legal, and administrative matters, fourteen product divisions (PDs), located in Eindhoven, were formally responsible for development, production, and global distribution. (In reality, the NOs' control of assets and the PDs' distance from the operations often undercut this formal role.) The research function remained independent and, with continued strong funding, set up eight separate laboratories in Europe and the United States.

While the formal corporate-level structure was represented as a type of geographic/product matrix, it was clear that NOs had the real power. NOs reported directly to the management board, which Philips enlarged from 4 members to 10 to ensure that top management remained in contact with and control of the highly autonomous NOs. Each NO also regularly sent envoys to Eindhoven to represent its interests. Top management, most of whom had careers that included multiple foreign tours of duty, made frequent overseas visits to the NOs. In 1954, the board established the International Concern Council to formalize regular meetings with the heads of all major NOs.

Within the NOs, the management structure mimicked the legendary joint technical and commercial leadership of the two Philips brothers. Most were led by a technical manager and a commercial manager. In some locations, a finance manager filled out the top management triad that typically reached key decisions collectively. This cross-functional coordination capability was reflected down through the NOs in front-line product teams, product-group-level management teams, and at the senior management committee of the NOs' top commercial, technical, and financial managers.

The overwhelming importance of foreign operations to Philips, the commensurate status of the NOs within the corporate hierarchy, and even the cosmopolitan appeal of many of the offshore subsidiaries' locations encouraged many Philips managers to take extended foreign tours of duty, working in a series of two- or three-year posts. This elite group of expatriate managers identified strongly with each other and with the NOs as a group and had no difficulty representing their strong, country-oriented views to corporate management.

Philips: Attempts at Reorganization

In the late 1960s, the creation of the Common Market eroded trade barriers within Europe and diluted the rationale for maintaining independent, country-level subsidiaries. New transistor- and printed circuit-based technologies demanded larger production runs than most national plants could justify, and many of Philips' competitors were moving production of electronics to new facilities in low-wage areas in East Asia and Central and South America. Despite its many technological innovations, Philips' ability to bring products to market began to falter. In the 1960s, the company invented the audiocassette and the microwave oven but let its Japanese competitors capture the mass market for both products. A decade later, its R&D group developed the V2000 videocassette format—superior technically to Sony's Beta or Matsushita's VHS—but was forced to abandon it when North American Philips decided to outsource, brand, and sell a VHS product which it manufactured under license from Matsushita.

In the following pages, we will see how over three decades, seven chairmen experimented with reorganizing the company to deal with its growing problems. Yet, entering the new millennium, Philips' financial performance remained poor and its global competitiveness was still in question. (See Exhibits 1 and 2.)

Van Reimsdijk and Rodenburg Reorganizations, 1970s

Concerned about what one magazine described as "continued profitless progress," newly appointed CEO Hendrick van Riemsdijk created an organization committee to prepare a policy paper on the division of responsibilities between the PDs and the NOs. Their report, dubbed the "Yellow Booklet," outlined the disadvantages of Philips' matrix organization in 1971: "Without an agreement [defining the relationship between national organizations and product divisions], it is impossible to determine in any given situation which of the two parties is responsible. . . . As operations become increasingly complex, an organizational form of this type will only lower the speed of reaction of an enterprise."

On the basis of this report, van Reimsdijk proposed rebalancing the managerial relationships between PDs and NOs—"tilting the matrix towards the PDs" in his words—to allow Philips to decrease the number of products marketed, build scale by concentrating production, and increase the flow of goods among national organizations. He proposed closing the least efficient local plants and converting the best into International Production Centers (IPCs), each supplying many NOs. In so doing, van Reimsdijk hoped that PD managers would gain control over manufacturing operations. Due to the political and organizational difficulty of closing local plants, however, implementation was slow.

In the late 1970s, his successor CEO, Dr. Rodenburg, continued this thrust. Several IPCs were established, but the NOs seemed as powerful and independent as ever. He furthered matrix simplification by replacing the dual commercial and technical leadership with single management at both the corporate and national organizational levels. Yet the power struggles continued.

EXHIBIT 1

Philips Group—Summary Financial Data, 1970–2000 (millions of guilders, unless otherwise stated)

	2000	1995	1990	1985	1980	1975	1970
Net sales	F83,437	F64,462	F55,764	F60,045	F36,536	F27,115	F15,070
Income from operations (excluding restructuring)	NA	4,090	2,260	3,075	1,577	1,201	1,280
Income from operations (including restructuring)	9,434	4,044	−2,389	N/A	N/A	N/A	N/A
As a percentage of net sales	11.3%	6.3%	−4.3%	5.1%	4.3%	4.5%	8.5%
Income after taxes	12,559	2,889	F−4,447	F1,025	F532	F341	F446
Net income from normal business operations	NA	2,684	−4,526	n/a	328	347	435
Stockholders' equity (common)	49,473	14,055	11,165	16,151	12,996	10,047	6,324
Return on stockholders' equity	42.8%	20.2%	−30.2%	5.6%	2.7%	3.6%	7.3%
Distribution per common share, par value F10 (in guilders)	F2.64	F1.60	F0.0	F2.00	F1.80	F1.40	F1.70
Total assets	86,114	54,683	51,595	52,883	39,647	30,040	19,088
Inventories as a percentage of net sales	13.9%	18.2%	20.7%	23.2%	32.8%	32.9%	35.2%
Outstanding trade receivables in month's sales	1.5	1.6	1.6	2.0	3.0	3.0	2.8
Current ratio	1.2	1.6	1.4	1.6	1.7	1.8	1.7
Employees at year-end (in thousands)	219	265	273	346	373	397	359
Wages, salaries and other related costs	NA	NA	F17,582	F21,491	F15,339	F11,212	F5,890
Exchange rate (period end; guilder/$)	2.34	1.60	1.69	2.75	2.15	2.69	3.62
Selected data in millions of dollars:							
Sales	$35,253	$40,039	$33,018	$21,802	$16,993	$10,098	$4,163
Operating profit	3,986	2,512	1,247	988	734	464	NA
Pretax income	5,837	2,083	−2,380	658	364	256	NA
Net income	5,306	1,667	−2,510	334	153	95	120
Total assets	35,885	32,651	30,549	19,202	18,440	11,186	5,273
Shareholders' equity (common)	20,238	8,784	6,611	5,864	6,044	3,741	1,747

Source: Annual reports; Standard & Poors' *Compustat;* Moody's Industrial and International Manuals.

Note: Exchange rate 12/31/00 was Euro/US$: 1.074

EXHIBIT 2

Philips Group—Sales by Product and Geographic Segment, 1985–2000 (millions of guilders)

	2000		1995		1990		1985	
Net sales by product segment:								
Lighting	F11,133	13%	F 8,353	13%	F 7,026	13%	F 7,976	12%
Consumer electronics	32,357	39	22,027	34	25,400	46	16,906	26
Domestic appliances	4,643	6	—				6,644	10
Professional products/Systems	—		11,562	18	13,059	23	17,850	28
Components/Semiconductors	23,009	28	10,714	17	8,161	15	11,620	18
Software/Services	—		9,425	15	—		—	
Medical systems	6,679	8	—		—		—	
Origin	1,580	2	—		—		—	
Miscellaneous	4,035	5	2,381	4	2,118	4	3,272	5
Total	83,437	100%	64,462	100%	F55,764	100%	F 64,266	100%
Operating income by sector:								
Lighting	1,472	16%	983	24%	419	18%	F910	30%
Consumer electronics	824	9	167	4	1,499	66	34	1
Domestic appliances	632	7	—		—		397	13
Professional products/Systems	—		157	4	189	8	1,484	48
Components/Semiconductors	4,220	45	2,233	55	–43	–2	44	1
Software/Services	—		886	22	—		—	
Medical systems	372	4	—		—		—	
Origin	2,343	25	—		—		—	
Miscellaneous	–249	–3	423	10	218	10	200	7
Increase not attributable to a sector	–181	–2	(805)	(20)	–22	–1	6	0
Total	9,434	100%	4,044	100%	2,260	100%	F3,075	100%

Source: Annual reports.

Notes:

Conversion rate (12/31/00): 1 Euro: 2.20371 Dutch Guilders

Totals may not add due to rounding.

Product sector sales after 1988 are external sales only; therefore, no eliminations are made. Sector sales before 1988 include sales to other sectors; therefore, eliminations are made.

Data are not comparable to consolidated financial summary due to restating.

Wisse Dekker Reorganization, 1982

Unsatisfied with the company's slow response and concerned by its slumping financial performance, upon becoming CEO in 1982, Wisse Dekker outlined a new initiative. Aware of the cost advantage of Philips' Japanese counterparts, he closed inefficient operations—particularly in Europe where 40 of the company's more than 200 plants were shut. He focused on core operations by selling some businesses (for example, welding, energy cables, and furniture) while acquiring an interest in Grundig and Westinghouse's North American lamp activities. Dekker also supported technology-sharing agreements and entered alliances in offshore manufacturing.

To deal with the slow-moving bureaucracy, he continued his predecessor's initiative to replace dual leadership with single general managers. He also continued to "tilt the matrix" by giving PDs formal product management responsibility, but leaving NOs responsible for local profits. And, he energized the management board by reducing its size, bringing on directors with strong operating experience, and creating subcommittees to deal with difficult issues. Finally, Dekker redefined the product planning process, incorporating input from the NOs, but giving global PDs the final decision on long-range direction. Still sales declined and profits stagnated.

Van der Klugt Reorganization, 1987

When Cor van der Klugt succeeded Dekker as chairman in 1987, Philips had lost its long-held consumer electronics leadership position to Matsushita, and was one of only two non-Japanese companies in the world's top ten. Its net profit margins of 1% to 2% not only lagged behind General Electric's 9%, but even its highly aggressive Japanese competitors' slim 4%. Van der Klugt set a profit objective of 3% to 4% and made beating the Japanese companies a top priority.

As van der Klugt reviewed Philips' strategy, he designated various businesses as core (those that shared related technologies, had strategic importance, or were technical leaders) and non-core (standalone businesses that were not targets for world leadership and could eventually be sold if required). Of the four businesses defined as core, three were strategically linked: components, consumer electronics, and telecommunications and data systems. The fourth, lighting, was regarded as strategically vital because its cash flow funded development.

The non-core businesses included domestic appliances and medical systems which van der Klugt spun off into joint ventures with Whirlpool and GE, respectively.

In continuing efforts to strengthen the PDs relative to the NOs, van der Klugt restructured Philips around the four core global divisions rather than the former 14 PDs. This allowed him to trim the management board, appointing the displaced board members to a new policy-making Group Management Committee. Consisting primarily of PD heads and functional chiefs, this body replaced the old NO-dominated International Concern Council. Finally, he sharply reduced the 3,000-strong headquarters staff, reallocating many of them to the PDs.

To link PDs more directly to markets, van der Klugt dispatched many experienced product-line managers to Philips' most competitive markets. For example, management of the digital audio tape and electric-shaver product lines were relocated to Japan, while the medical technology and domestic appliances lines were moved to the United States.

Such moves, along with continued efforts at globalizing product development and production efforts, required that the parent company gain firmer control over NOs, especially the giant North American Philips Corp. (NAPC). Although Philips had obtained a majority equity interest after World War II, it was not always able to make the U.S. company respond to directives from the center, as the V2000 VCR incident showed. To prevent replays of such experiences, in 1987 van der Klugt repurchased publicly owned NAPC shares for $700 million.

Reflecting the growing sentiment among some managers that R&D was not market oriented enough, van der Klugt halved spending on basic research to about 10% of total R&D. To manage what he described as "R&D's tendency to ponder the fundamental laws of nature," he made the R&D budget the direct responsibility of the businesses being supported by the research. This required that each research lab become focused on specific business areas (see Exhibit 3).

Finally, van der Klugt continued the effort to build efficient, specialized, multi-market production facilities by closing 75 of the company's 420 remaining plants worldwide. He also eliminated 38,000 of its 344,000 employees—21,000 through divesting businesses, shaking up the myth of lifetime employment at the company. He anticipated that all these

EXHIBIT 3

Philips Research Labs by Location and Specialty, 1987

Location	Size (Staff)	Specialty
Eindhoven, The Netherlands	2,000	Basic research, electronics, manufacturing technology
Redhill, Surrey, England	450	Microelectronics, television, defense
Hamburg, Germany	350	Communications, office equipment, medical imaging
Aachen, W. Germany	250	Fiber optics, X-ray systems
Paris, France	350	Microprocessors, chip materials, design
Brussels	50	Artificial intelligence
Briarcliff Manor, New York	35	Optical systems, television, superconductivity, defense
Sunnyvale, California	150	Integrated circuits

Source: Philips, in *Business Week*, March 21, 1988, p. 156.

restructurings would lead to a financial recovery by 1990. Unanticipated losses for that year, however—more than 4.5 billion Dutch guilders ($2.5 billion)—provoked a class-action law suit by angry American investors, who alleged that positive projections by the company had been misleading. In a surprise move, on May 14, 1990, van der Klugt and half of the management board were replaced.

Timmer Reorganization, 1990

The new president, Jan Timmer, had spent most of his 35-year Philips career turning around unprofitable businesses. With rumors of a takeover or a government bailout swirling, he met with his top 100 managers and distributed a hypothetical—but fact-based—press release announcing that Philips was bankrupt. "So what action can you take this weekend?" he challenged them.

Under "Operation Centurion," headcount was reduced by 68,000 or 22% over the next 18 months, earning Timmer the nickname "The Butcher of Eindhoven." Because European laws required substantial compensation for layoffs—Eindhoven workers received 15 months' pay, for example—the first round of 10,000 layoffs alone cost Philips $700 million. To spread the burden around the globe and to speed the process, Timmer asked his PD managers to negotiate cuts with NO managers. According to one report, however, country managers were "digging in their heels to save local jobs." But the cuts came—many

from overseas operations. In addition to the job cuts, Timmer vowed to "change the way we work." He established new performance rules and asked hundreds of top managers to sign contracts that committed them to specific financial goals. Those who broke those contracts were replaced—often with outsiders.

To focus resources further, Timmer sold off various businesses including integrated circuits to Matsushita, minicomputers to Digital, defense electronics to Thomson and the remaining 53% of appliances to Whirlpool. Yet profitability was still well below the modest 4% on sales he promised. In particular, consumer electronics lagged with slow growth in a price-competitive market. The core problem was identified by a 1994 McKinsey study that estimated that value added per hour in Japanese consumer electronic factories was still 68% above that of European plants. In this environment, most NO managers kept their heads down, using their distance from Eindhoven as their defense against the ongoing rationalization.

After three years of cost-cutting, in early 1994 Timmer finally presented a new growth strategy to the board. His plan was to expand software, services, and multimedia to become 40% of revenues by 2000. He was betting on Philips' legendary innovative capability to restart the growth engines. Earlier, he had recruited Frank Carrubba, Hewlett-Packard's director of research, and encouraged him to focus on developing 15 core technologies. The list, which included interactive compact disc (CD-i), digital compact cassettes (DCC), high definition television (HDTV), and multimedia software, was soon dubbed "the president's projects." Over the next few years, Philips invested over $2.5 billion in these technologies. But Timmer's earlier divestment of some of the company's truly high-tech businesses and a 37% cut in R&D personnel left it with few who understood the technology of the new priority businesses.

By 1996, it was clear that Philips' analog HDTV technology would not become industry standard, that its DCC gamble had lost out to Sony's Minidisc, and that CD-i was a marketing failure. And while costs in Philips were lower, so too was morale, particularly among middle management. Critics claimed that the company's drive for cost-cutting and standardization had led it to ignore new worldwide market demands for more segmented products and higher consumer service.

Boonstra Reorganization, 1996

When Timmer stepped down in October 1996, the board replaced him with a radical choice for Philips—an outsider whose expertise was in marketing and Asia rather than technology and Europe. Cor Boonstra was a 58-year-old Dutchman whose years as CEO of Sara Lee, the U.S. consumer products firm, had earned him a reputation as a hard-driving marketing genius. Joining Philips in 1994, he headed the Asia Pacific region and the lighting division before being tapped as CEO.

Unencumbered by tradition, he immediately announced strategic sweeping changes designed to reach his target of increasing return on net assets from 17% to 24% by 1999. "There are no taboos, no sacred cows," he said. "The bleeders must be turned around, sold, or closed." Within three years, he had sold off 40 of Philips' 120 major businesses—including such well known units as Polygram and Grundig. He also initiated a major worldwide restructuring, promising to transform a structure he described as "a plate of spaghetti" into "a neat row of asparagus." He said:

> How can we compete with the Koreans? They don't have 350 companies all over the world. Their factory in Ireland covers Europe and their manufacturing facility in Mexico serves North America. We need a more structured and simpler manufacturing and marketing organization to achieve a cost pattern in line with those who do not have our heritage. This is still one of the biggest issues facing Philips.

Within a year, 3,100 jobs were eliminated in North America and 3,000 employees were added in Asia Pacific, emphasizing Boonstra's determination to shift production to low-wage countries and his broader commitment to Asia. And after three years, he had closed 100 of the company's 356 factories worldwide. At the same time, he replaced the company's 21 PDs with 7 divisions, but shifted day-to-day operating responsibility to 100 business units, each responsible for its profits worldwide. It was a move designed to finally eliminate the old PD/NO matrix. Finally, in a move that shocked most employees, he announced that the 100-year-old Eindhoven headquarters would be relocated to Amsterdam with only 400 of the 3,000 corporate positions remaining.

By early 1998, he was ready to announce his new strategy. Despite early speculation that he might abandon consumer electronics, he proclaimed it as the center of Philips' future. Betting on the "digital revolution," he planned to focus on established technologies such as cellular phones (through a joint venture with Lucent), digital TV, digital videodisc, and web TV. Furthermore, he committed major resources to marketing, including a 40% increase in advertising to raise awareness and image of the Philips brand and de-emphasize most of the 150 other brands it supported worldwide—from Magnavox TVs to Norelco shavers to Marantz stereos.

While not everything succeeded (the Lucent cell phone JV collapsed after nine months, for example), overall performance improved significantly in the late 1990s. By 2000, Boonstra was able to announce that he had achieved his objective of a 24% return on net assets.

Kleisterlee Reorganization, 2001

In May 2001, Boonstra passed the CEO's mantle to Gerard Kleisterlee, a 54-year-old engineer (and career Philips man) whose turnaround of the components business had earned him a board seat only a year earlier. Believing that Philips had finally turned around, the board challenged Kleisterlee to grow sales by 10% annually and earnings 15%, while increasing return on assets to 30%.

Despite its stock trading at a steep discount to its breakup value, Philips governance structure and Dutch legislation made a hostile raid all but impossible. Nonetheless, Kleisterlee described the difference as "a management discount" and vowed to eliminate it. "Our fragmented organization makes us carry costs that are too high," he said. "In some production activities where we cannot add value, we will outsource and let others do it for us."

The first sign of restructuring came within weeks, when mobile phone production was outsourced to CEC of China. Then, in August, Kleisterlee announced an agreement with Japan's Funai Electric to take over production of its VCRs, resulting in the immediate closure of the European production center in Austria and the loss of 1,000 jobs. The CEO acknowledged that he was seeking partners to take over the manufacturing of some of its other mass-produced items such as television sets.

But by 2001, a slowing economy resulted in the company's first quarterly loss since 1996, and by year's end the loss had grown to 2.6 billion euros compared to the previous year's 9.6 billion profit. Many felt that these growing financial pressures—and shareholders' growing impatience—were finally leading Philips to recognize that its best hope of survival was to outsource even more of its basic manufacturing and become a technology developer and global marketer. It believed it was time to recognize that its 30-year quest to build efficiency into its global operations had failed.

Matsushita: Background

In 1918, Konosuke Matsushita (or "KM" as he was affectionately known), a 23-year-old inspector with the Osaka Electric Light Company, invested ¥100 to start production of double-ended sockets in his modest home. The company grew rapidly, expanding into battery-powered lamps, electric irons, and radios. On May 5, 1932, Matsushita's 14th anniversary, KM announced to his 162 employees a 250-year corporate plan broken into 25-year sections, each to be carried out by successive generations. His plan was codified in a company creed and in the "Seven Spirits of Matsushita" (see Exhibit 4), which, along with the company song, continued to be woven into morning assemblies worldwide and provided the basis of the "cultural and spiritual training" all new employees received during their first seven months with the company.

In the postwar boom, Matsushita introduced a flood of new products: TV sets in 1952; transistor

---

EXHIBIT 4

Matsushita Creed and Philosophy (excerpts)

Creed Through our industrial activities, we strive to foster progress, to promote the general welfare of society, and to devote ourselves to furthering the development of world culture.

Seven Spirits of Matsushita

Service through Industry

Fairness

Harmony and Cooperation

Struggle for Progress

Courtesy and Humility

Adjustment and Assimilation

Gratitude

KM's Business Philosophy (Selected Quotations)

"The purpose of an enterprise is to contribute to society by supplying goods of high quality at low prices in ample quantity."

"Profit comes in compensation for contribution to society. . . . [It] is a result rather than a goal."

"The responsibility of the manufacturer cannot be relieved until its product is disposed of by the end user."

"Unsuccessful business employs a wrong management. You should not find its causes in bad fortune, unfavorable surroundings or wrong timing."

"Business appetite has no self-restraining mechanism. . . . When you notice you have gone too far, you must have the courage to come back."

Source: "Matsushita Electric Industrial (MEI) in 1987," Harvard Business School Case No. 388-144.

radios in 1958; color TVs, dishwashers, and electric ovens in 1960. Capitalizing on its broad line of 5,000 products (Sony produced 80), the company opened 25,000 domestic retail outlets. With more than six times the outlets of rival Sony, the ubiquitous "National Shops" represented 40% of appliance stores in Japan in the late 1960s. These not only provided assured sales volume, but also gave the company direct access to market trends and consumer reaction. When postwar growth slowed, however, Matsushita had to look beyond its expanding product line and excellent distribution system for growth. After trying many tactics to boost sales—even sending assembly line workers out as door-to-door salesmen—the company eventually focused on export markets.

The Organization's Foundation: Divisional Structure

Plagued by ill health, KM wished to delegate more authority than was typical in Japanese companies. In 1933, Matsushita became the first Japanese company to adopt the divisional structure, giving each division clearly defined profit responsibility for its product. In addition to creating a "small business" environment, the product division structure generated internal competition that spurred each business to drive growth by leveraging its technology to develop new products. After the innovating division had earned substantial profits on its new product, however, company policy was to spin it off as a new division to maintain the "hungry spirit."

Under the "one-product-one-division" system, corporate management provided each largely self-sufficient division with initial funds to establish its own development, production, and marketing capabilities. Corporate treasury operated like a commercial bank, reviewing divisions' loan requests for which it charged slightly higher-than-market interest, and accepting interest-bearing deposits on their excess funds. Divisional profitability was determined after deductions for central services such as corporate R&D and interest on internal borrowings. Each division paid 60% of earnings to headquarters and financed all additional working capital and fixed asset requirements from the retained 40%. Transfer prices were based on the market and settled through the treasury on normal commercial terms. KM expected uniform performance across the company's 36 divisions, and division managers whose operating profits fell below 4% of sales for two successive years were replaced.

While basic technology was developed in a central research laboratory (CRL), product development and engineering occurred in each of the product divisions. Matsushita intentionally under-funded the CRL, forcing it to compete for additional funding from the divisions. Annually, the CRL publicized its major research projects to the product divisions, which then provided funding in exchange for technology for marketable applications. While it was rarely the innovator, Matsushita was usually very fast to market—earning it the nickname "Manishita," or copycat.

Matsushita: Internationalization

Although the establishment of overseas markets was a major thrust of the second 25 years in the 250-year plan, in an overseas trip in 1951 KM had been unable to find any American company willing to collaborate with Matsushita. The best he could do was a technology exchange and licensing agreement with Philips. Nonetheless, the push to internationalize continued.

Expanding Through Color TV

In the 1950s and 1960s, trade liberalization and lower shipping rates made possible a healthy export business built on black and white TV sets. In 1953, the company opened its first overseas branch office—the Matsushita Electric Corporation of America (MECA). With neither a distribution network nor a strong brand, the company could not access traditional retailers, and had to resort to selling its products through mass merchandisers and discounters under their private brands.

During the 1960s, pressure from national governments in developing countries led Matsushita to open plants in several countries in Southeast Asia and Central and South America. As manufacturing costs in Japan rose, Matsushita shifted more basic production to these low-wage countries, but almost all high-value components and subassemblies were still made in its scale-intensive Japanese plants. By the 1970s, an East-West trade war mentality forced the company to establish assembly operations in the Americas and Europe. In 1972, it opened a plant in Canada; in 1974, it bought Motorola's TV business and started manufacturing its Quasar brand in the United States; and in 1976, it built a plant in Cardiff, Wales, to supply the Common Market.

Building Global Leadership Through VCRs

The birth of the videocassette recorder (VCR) propelled Matsushita into first place in the consumer electronics industry during the 1980s. Recognizing the potential mass-market appeal of the VCR—developed by Californian broadcasting company, Ampex, in 1956—engineers at Matsushita began developing VCR technology. After six years of development work, Matsushita launched its commercial broadcast video recorder in 1964, and introduced a consumer version two years later.

In 1975, Sony introduced the technically superior "Betamax" format, and the next year JVC launched a competing "VHS" format. Under pressure from MITI, the government's industrial planning ministry, Matsushita agreed to give up its own format and adopt the established VHS standard. During Matsushita's 20 years of VCR product development, various members of the VCR research team spent most of their careers working together, moving from central labs to the product division's development labs and eventually to the plant producing VCRs.

The company quickly built production to meet its own needs as well as those of OEM customers like GE, RCA, Philips, and Zenith, who decided to forego self-manufacture and outsource to the low-cost Japanese. Between 1977 and 1985, capacity increased 33-fold to 6.8 million units. Increased volume enabled Matsushita to slash prices 50% within five years of product launch, while simultaneously improving quality. In parallel, the company aggressively licensed the VHS format to other manufacturers, including Hitachi, Sharp, Mitsubishi and, eventually, Philips. By the mid-1980s, VCRs accounted for 30% of total sales—over 40% of overseas revenues—and provided 45% of profits.

Changing Systems and Controls

In the mid-1980s, Matsushita's growing number of overseas companies reported to the parent in one of two ways: wholly owned, single-product global plants reported directly to the appropriate product division, while overseas sales and marketing subsidiaries and overseas companies producing a broad product line for local markets reported to Matsushita Electric Trading Company (METC), a separate legal entity. (See Exhibit 5 for METC's organization.)

Throughout the 1970s, the central product divisions maintained strong operating control over their offshore production units. Overseas operations used plant and equipment designed by the parent company, followed manufacturing procedures dictated by the center, and used materials from Matsushita's domestic plants. By the 1980s, growing trends toward local sourcing gradually weakened the divisions' direct control so instead of controlling inputs, they began to monitor measures of output (for example, quality, productivity, inventory levels).

About the same time, product divisions began receiving the globally consolidated return on sales reports that had previously been consolidated in METC statements. By the mid-1980s, as worldwide planning was introduced for the first time, corporate management required all its product divisions to prepare global product strategies.

Headquarters-Subsidiary Relations

Although METC and the product divisions set detailed sales and profits targets for their overseas subsidiaries, local managers were told they had autonomy on how to achieve the targets. "Mike" Matsuoko, president of the company's largest European production subsidiary in Cardiff, Wales, however, emphasized that failure to meet targets forfeited freedom: "Losses show bad health and invite many doctors from Japan, who provide advice and support."

In the mid-1980s, Matsushita had over 700 expatriate Japanese managers and technicians on foreign assignment for four to eight years, but defended that high number by describing their pivotal role. "This vital communication role," said one manager, "almost always requires a manager from the parent company. Even if a local manager speaks Japanese, he would not have the long experience that is needed to build relationships and understand our management processes."

Expatriate managers were located throughout foreign subsidiaries, but there were a few positions that were almost always reserved for them. The most visible were subsidiary general managers whose main role was to translate Matsushita philosophy abroad. Expatriate accounting managers were expected to "mercilessly expose the truth" to corporate headquarters; and Japanese technical managers were sent to transfer product and process technologies and provide headquarters with local market information. These expatriates maintained relationships with senior colleagues in their divisions, who acted as career mentors, evaluated performance (with some input

EXHIBIT 5

Organization of METC, 1985

Source: Harvard Business School Case No. 388-144.

Note: ( ) = number of people.

from local managers), and provided expatriates with information about parent company developments.

General managers of foreign subsidiaries visited Osaka headquarters at least two or three times each year—some as often as every month. Corporate managers reciprocated these visits, and on average, major operations hosted at least one headquarters manager each day of the year. Face-to-face meetings were considered vital: "Figures are important," said

one manager, "but the meetings are necessary to develop judgment." Daily faxes and nightly phone calls between headquarters and expatriate colleagues were a vital management link.

Yamashita's Operation Localization

Although international sales kept rising, as early as 1982 growing host country pressures caused concern about the company's highly centralized operations.

In that year, newly appointed company President Toshihiko Yamashita launched "Operation Localization" to boost offshore production from less than 10% of value-added to 25%, or half of overseas sales, by 1990. To support the target, he set out a program of four localizations—personnel, technology, material, and capital.

Over the next few years, Matsushita increased the number of local nationals in key positions. In the United States, for example, U.S. nationals became the presidents of three of the six local companies, while in Taiwan the majority of production divisions were replaced by Chinese managers. In each case, however, local national managers were still supported by senior Japanese advisors, who maintained a direct link with the parent company. To localize technology and materials, the company developed its national subsidiaries' expertise to source equipment locally, modify designs to meet local requirements, incorporate local components, and adapt corporate processes and technologies to accommodate these changes. And by the mid-1980s, offshore production subsidiaries were free to buy minor parts from local vendors as long as quality could be assured, but still had to buy key components from internal sources.

One of the most successful innovations was to give overseas sales subsidiaries more choice over the products they sold. Each year the company held a two-week internal merchandising show and product planning meeting where product divisions exhibited the new lines. Here, overseas sales subsidiary managers described their local market needs and negotiated for change in features, quantities, and even prices of the products they wanted to buy. Product division managers, however, could overrule the sales subsidiary if they thought introduction of a particular product was of strategic importance.

President Yamashita's hope was that Operation Localization would help Matsushita's overseas companies develop the innovative capability and entrepreneurial initiatives that he had long admired in the national organizations of rival Philips. (Past efforts to develop such capabilities abroad had failed. For example, when Matsushita acquired Motorola's TV business in the United States, the U.S. company's highly innovative technology group atrophied as American engineers resigned in response to what they felt to be excessive control from Japan's highly centralized R&D operations.) Yet despite his four localizations, overseas companies continued to act primarily as the implementation arms of central product divisions. In an unusual act for a Japanese CEO, Yamashita publicly expressed his unhappiness with the lack of initiative at the TV plant in Cardiff. Despite the transfer of substantial resources and the delegation of many responsibilities, he felt that the plant remained too dependent on the center.

Tanii's Integration and Expansion

Yamashita's successor, Akio Tanii, expanded on his predecessor's initiatives. In 1986, feeling that Matsushita's product divisions were not giving sufficient attention to international development—in part because they received only 3% royalties for foreign production against at least 10% return on sales for exports from Japan—he brought all foreign subsidiaries under the control of METC. Tanii then merged METC into the parent company in an effort to fully integrate domestic and overseas operations. Then, to shift operational control nearer to local markets, he relocated major regional headquarters functions from Japan to North America, Europe, and Southeast Asia. Yet still he was frustrated that the overseas subsidiary companies acted as little more than the implementing agents of the Osaka-based product divisions.

Through all these changes, however, Matsushita's worldwide growth continued generating huge reserves. With $17.5 billion in liquid financial assets at the end of 1989, the company was referred to as the "Matsushita Bank," and several top executives began proposing that if they could not develop innovative overseas companies, they should buy them. Flush with cash and international success, in early 1991 the company acquired MCA, the U.S. entertainment giant, for $6.1 billion with the objective of obtaining a media software source for its hardware. Within a year, however, Japan's bubble economy had burst, plunging the economy into recession. Almost overnight, Tanii had to shift the company's focus from expansion to cost containment. Despite his best efforts to cut costs, the problems ran too deep. With 1992 profits less than half their 1991 level, the board took the unusual move of forcing Tanii to resign in February 1993.

Morishita's Challenge and Response

At 56, Yoichi Morishita was the most junior of the company's executive vice presidents when he was tapped as the new president. Under the slogan "simple, small, speedy and strategic," he committed to

EXHIBIT 6

Matsushita—Summary Financial Data, 1970–2000[a]

	2000	1995	1990	1985	1980	1975	1970
In billions of yen and percent:							
Sales	¥7,299	¥6,948	¥6,003	¥5,291	¥2,916	¥1,385	¥932
Income before tax	219	232	572	723	324	83	147
As % of sales	3.0%	3.3%	9.5%	13.7%	11.1%	6.0%	15.8%
Net income	¥100	¥90	¥236	¥216	¥125	¥32	¥70
As % of sales	1.4%	1.3%	3.9%	4.1%	4.3%	2.3%	7.6%
Cash dividends (per share)	¥14.00	¥13.50	¥10.00	¥9.52	¥7.51	¥6.82	¥6.21
Total assets	7,955	8,202	7,851	5,076	2,479	1,274	735
Stockholders' equity	3,684	3,255	3,201	2,084	1,092	573	324
Capital investment	355	316	355	288	NA	NA	NA
Depreciation	343	296	238	227	65	28	23
R&D	526	378	346	248	102	51	NA
Employees (units)	290,448	265,397	198,299	175,828	107,057	82,869	78,924
Overseas employees	143,773	112,314	59,216	38,380	NA	NA	NA
As % of total employees	50%	42%	30%	22%	NA	NA	NA
Exchange rate (fiscal period end; ¥/$)	103	89	159	213	213	303	360
In millions of dollars:							
Sales	$68,862	$78,069	$37,753	$24,890	$13,690	$4,572	$2,588
Operating income before depreciation	4,944	6,250	4,343	3,682	1,606	317	NA
Operating income after depreciation	1,501	2,609	2,847	2,764	1,301	224	NA
Pretax income	2,224	2,678	3,667	3,396	1,520	273	408
Net income	941	1,017	1,482	1,214	584	105	195
Total assets	77,233	92,159	49,379	21,499	11,636	4,206	2,042
Total equity	35,767	36,575	20,131	10,153	5,129	1,890	900

Source: Annual reports; Standard & Poors' *Compustat*; Moody's Industrial and International Manuals.

[a]Data prior to 1987 are for the fiscal year ending November 20; data 1988 and after are for the fiscal year ending March 31.

cutting headquarters staff and decentralizing responsibility. Over the next 18 months, he moved 6,000 staff to operating jobs. In a major strategic reversal, he also sold 80% of MCI to Seagram, booking a $1.2 billion loss on the transaction.

Yet the company continued to struggle. Japan's domestic market for consumer electronics collapsed—from $42 billion in 1989 to $21 billion in 1999. Excess capacity drove down prices and profits evaporated. And although offshore markets were growing, the rise of new competition—first from Korea, then China—created a global glut of consumer electronics, and prices collapsed.

With a strong yen making exports from Japan uncompetitive, Matsushita's product divisions rapidly shifted production offshore during the 1990s, mostly to low-cost Asian countries like China and Malaysia. By the end of the decade, its 160 factories outside Japan employed 140,000 people—about the same number of employees as in its 133 plants in Japan. Yet, despite the excess capacity and strong yen, management seemed unwilling to radically restructure its increasingly inefficient portfolio of production facilities or even lay off staff due to strongly-held commitments to lifetime employment. Despite Morishita's promises, resistance within the organization prevented his implementation of much of the promised radical change.

In the closing years of the decade, Morishita began emphasizing the need to develop more of its technology and innovation offshore. Concerned that only 250 of the company's 3,000 R&D scientists and engineers were located outside Japan, he began investing in R&D partnerships and technical exchanges, particularly in fast emerging fields. For example, in 1998 he signed a joint R&D agreement with the Chinese Academy of Sciences, China's leading research organization. Later that year, he announced the establishment of the Panasonic Digital Concepts Center in California. Its mission was to act as a venture fund and an incubation center for the new ideas and technologies emerging in Silicon Valley. To some it was an indication that Matsushita had given up trying to generate new technology and business initiatives from its own overseas companies.

Nakamura's Initiatives

In April 2000, Morishita became chairman and Kunio Nakamura replaced him as president. Profitability was at 2.2% of sales, with consumer electronics at only 0.4%, including losses generated by one-time cash cows, the TV and VCR divisions. (Exhibit 6 provides the financial history for Matsushita and key product lines.) The new CEO vowed to raise this to 5% by 2004. Key to his plan was to move Matsushita beyond its roots as a "super manufacturer of products" and begin "to meet customer needs through systems and services." He planned to flatten the hierarchy and empower employees to respond to customer needs, and as part of the implementation, all key headquarters functions relating to international operations were transferred to overseas regional offices.

But the biggest shock came in November, when Nakamura announced a program of "destruction and creation," in which he disbanded the product division structure that KM had created as Matsushita's basic organizational building block 67 years earlier. Plants, previously controlled by individual product divisions, would now be integrated into multi-product production centers. In Japan alone 30 of the 133 factories were to be consolidated or closed. And marketing would shift to two corporate marketing entities, one for Panasonic brands (consumer electronics, information and communications products) and one for National branded products (mostly home appliances).

In February, 2001, just three months after raising his earnings estimate for the financial year ending March 2001, Nakamuta was embarrassed to readjust his estimate sharply downward. As Matsushita's first losses in 30 years accelerated, the new CEO announced a round of emergency measures designed to cut costs. When coupled with the earlier structural changes, these were radical moves, but in a company that even in Japan was being talked about as a takeover target, observers wondered if they were sufficient to restore Matsushita's tattered global competitiveness.

Merck, the FDA, and the Vioxx Recall

This case was prepared by Anne T. Lawrence, San Jose State University.

In 2006, the pharmaceutical giant Merck faced major challenges. Vioxx, the company's once best-selling prescription painkiller, had been pulled off the market in September 2004 after Merck learned it increased the risk of heart attacks and strokes. When news of the recall broke, the company's stock price had plunged thirty percent to $33 a share, its lowest point in eight years, where it had hovered since. Standard & Poor's had downgraded the company's outlook from "stable" to "negative." In late 2004, the Justice Department had opened a criminal investigation into whether the company had "caused federal health programs to pay for the prescription drug when its use was not warranted."[1] The Securities and Exchange Commission was inquiring into whether Merck had misled investors. By late 2005, more than 6,000 lawsuits had been filed, alleging that Vioxx had caused death or disability. From many quarters, the company faced troubling questions about the development and marketing of Vioxx, new calls for regulatory reform, and concerns about its political influence on Capitol Hill. In the words of Senator Charles Grassley, chairman of a Congressional committee investigating the Vioxx case, "a blockbuster drug [had become] a blockbuster disaster."[2]

Merck, Inc.[3]

Merck, the company in the eye of this storm, was one of the world's leading pharmaceutical firms. As shown in Exhibit 1, in 2005 the company ranked fourth in sales, after Pfizer, Johnson & Johnson, and

GlaxoSmithKline. In assets and market value, it ranked fifth. However, Merck ranked first in profits, earning $7.33 billion on $30.78 billion in sales (24 percent).

Merck had long enjoyed a reputation as one of the most ethical and socially responsible of the major drug companies. For an unprecedented seven consecutive years (1987 to 1993), *Fortune* magazine had named Merck its "most admired" company. In 1987, Merck appeared on the cover of *Time* under the headline, "The Miracle Company." It had consistently appeared on lists of best companies to work for and in the portfolios of social investment funds. The company's philanthropy was legendary. In the 1940s, Merck had given its patent for streptomycin, a powerful antibiotic, to a university foundation. Merck was especially admired for its donation of Mectizan. Merck's scientists had originally developed this drug for veterinary use, but later discovered that it was an effective cure for river blindness, a debilitating parasitic disease afflicting some of the world's poorest people. When the company realized that the victims of river blindness could not afford the drug, it decided to give it away for free, in perpetuity.[4]

In 1950, George W. Merck, the company's longtime CEO, stated in a speech: "We try never to forget that medicine is for the people. It is not for the profits. The profits follow, and if we have remembered that, they never fail to appear. The better we have remembered that, the larger they have been."[5] This statement was often repeated in subsequent years as a touchstone of the company's core values.

Merck was renowned for its research labs, which had a decades-long record of achievement, turning out one innovation after another, including drugs

EXHIBIT 1

The World's Top Pharmaceutical Companies, 2005

Company	Sales ($bil)	Profits ($bil)	Assets ($bil)	Market Value ($bil)
Pfizer	40.36	6.20	120.06	285.27
Johnson & Johnson	40.01	6.74	46.66	160.96
Merck	**30.78**	**7.33**	**42.59**	**108.76**
Novartis	26.77	5.40	46.92	116.43
Roche Group	25.18	2.48	45.77	95.38
GlaxoSmithKline	34.16	6.34	29.19	124.79
Aventis	21.66	2.29	31.06	62.98
Bristol-Myers Squibb	19.89	2.90	26.53	56.05
AstraZeneca	20.46	3.29	23.57	83.03
Abbott Labs	18.99	2.44	26.15	69.27

Source: Forbes 2000, available online at www.forbes.com. Listed in order of overall ranking in the Forbes 2000.

for tuberculosis, cholesterol, hypertension, and AIDS. In the early 2000s, Merck spent around $3 billion annually on research. Some felt that the company's culture had been shaped by its research agenda. Commented the author of a history of Merck, the company was "intense, driven, loyal, scientifically brilliant, collegial, and arrogant."[6] In 2006, although Merck had several medicines in the pipeline—including vaccines for rotavirus and cervical cancer, and drugs for insomnia, lymphoma, and the effects of stroke—some analysts worried that the pace of research had slowed significantly.

Estimating the company's financial liability from the Vioxx lawsuits was difficult. Some 84 million people had taken the drug worldwide over a five-year period from 1999 to 2004. In testimony before Congress, Dr. David Graham, a staff scientist at the Food and Drug Administration, estimated that as many as 139,000 people in the United States had had heart attacks or strokes as a result of taking Vioxx, and about 55,000 of these had died.[7] Merrill Lynch estimated the company's liability for compensatory damages alone in the range of $4 to $18 billion.[8] However, heart attacks and strokes were common, and they had multiple causes, including genetic predisposition, smoking, obesity, and a sedentary lifestyle. Determining the specific contribution of Vioxx to a particular cardiovascular event would be very difficult.

The company vigorously maintained that it had done nothing wrong and vowed to defend every single case in court. By early 2006, only three cases had gone to trial, and the results had been a virtual draw—one decision for the plaintiff, one for Merck, and one hung jury.

3-decisions

Government Regulation of Prescription Drugs

In the United States, prescription medicines—like Vioxx—were regulated by the Food and Drug Administration (FDA).[9] Before a new drug could be sold to the public, its manufacturer had to carry out clinical trials to demonstrate both safety and effectiveness. Advisory panels of outside medical experts reviewed the results of these trials and recommended to the FDA's Office of Drug Safety whether or not to approve a new drug.[10] After a drug was on the market, the agency's Office of New Drugs continued to monitor it for safety, in a process known as postmarket surveillance. These two offices both reported to the same boss, the FDA's director of the Center for Drug Evaluation and Research.

Once the FDA had approved a drug, physicians could prescribe it for any purpose, but the manufacturer could market it only for uses for which it had been approved. Therefore, companies had an incentive to continue to study approved drugs to provide data that they were safe and effective for the treatment of other conditions.

In the 1980s, the drug industry and some patient advocates had criticized the FDA for being too slow to approve new medicines. Patients were concerned that they were not getting new medicines fast enough, and drug companies were concerned that they were losing sales revenue. Each month an average drug spent under review represented $41.7 million in lost revenue, according to one study.[11]

In 1992, Congress passed the Prescription Drug User Fee Act (PDUFA). This law, which was supported by the industry, required pharmaceutical companies to pay "user fees" to the FDA to review proposed new medicines. Between 1993 and 2001, the FDA received around $825 million in such fees from drug makers seeking approval. (During this period, it also received $1.3 billion appropriated by Congress.) This infusion of new revenue enabled the agency to hire 1,000 new employees and to shorten the approval time for new drugs from 27 months in 1993 to 14 months in 2001.[12]

Despite the benefits of PDUFA, some felt that industry-paid fees were a bad idea. In an editorial published in December 2004, the *Journal of the American Medical Association (JAMA)* concluded: "It is unreasonable to expect that the same agency that was responsible for approval of drug licensing and labeling would also be committed to actively seek evidence to prove itself wrong (i.e., that the decision to approve the product was subsequently shown to be incorrect)." *JAMA* went on to recommend establishment of a separate agency to monitor drug safety.[13] Dr. David Kessler, a former FDA Commissioner, rejected this idea, responding that "strengthening post-marketing surveillance is certainly in order, but you don't want competing agencies."[14]

Some evidence suggested that the morale of FDA staff charged with evaluating the safety of new medicines had been hurt by relentless pressure to bring drugs to market quickly. In 2002, a survey of agency scientists found that only 13 percent were "completely confident" that the FDA's "final decisions adequately assess the safety of a drug." Thirty-one percent were "somewhat confident" and 5 percent lacked "any confidence." Two-thirds of those surveyed lacked confidence that the agency "adequately monitors the safety of prescription jobs once they are on the market." And nearly one in five said they had "been pressured to approve or recommend approval" for a drug "despite reservations about [its] safety, efficacy or quality."[15]

After the FDA shortened the approval time, the percentage of drugs recalled following approval increased from 1.56% for 1993–1996 to 5.35% for 1997–2001.[16] Vioxx was the ninth drug taken off the market in seven years.

Influence at the Top

The pharmaceutical industry's success in accelerating the approval of new drugs reflected its strong presence in Washington. The major drug companies, their trade association PhRMA (Pharmaceutical Research and Manufacturers of America), and their executives consistently donated large sums of money to both political parties and, through their political action committees, to various candidates. The industry's political contributions are shown in Exhibit 2.

Following the Congressional ban on soft money contributions in 2003, the industry shifted much of its contributions to so-called stealth PACs, nonprofit organizations which were permitted by law to take unlimited donations without revealing their source. These organizations could, in turn, make "substantial" political expenditures, providing political activity was not their primary purpose.[17]

In addition, the industry maintained a large corps of lobbyists active in the nation's capital. In 2003, for example, drug companies and their trade association spent $108 million on lobbying and hired 824 individual lobbyists, according to a report by Public Citizen.[18] Merck spent $40.7 million on lobbying between 1998 and 2004.[19] One of the industry's most effective techniques was to hire former elected officials or members of their staffs. For example, Billy Tauzin, formerly a Republican member of Congress from Louisiana and head of the powerful Committee on Energy and Commerce, which oversaw the drug industry, became president of PhRMA at a reported annual salary of $2 million in 2004.[20]

Over the years, the industry's representatives in Washington had established a highly successful record of promoting its political agenda on a range of issues. In addition to faster drug approvals, these had more recently included a Medicare prescription drug benefit, patent protections, and restrictions on drug imports from Canada.

EXHIBIT 2

Pharmaceutical/Health Products Industry: Political Contributions, 1990–2006

Election Cycle	Total Contributions	Contributions from Individuals	Contributions from PACs	Soft Money Contributions	Percentage to Republicans
2006	$5,187,393	$1,753,159	$3,434,234	N/A	70%
2004	$18,181,045	$8,445,485	$9,735,560	N/A	66%
2002	$29,441,951	$3,332,040	$6,957,382	$19,152,529	74%
2000	$26,688,292	$5,660,457	$5,649,913	$15,377,922	69%
1998	$13,169,694	$2,673,845	$4,107,068	$6,388,781	64%
1996	$13,754,796	$3,413,516	$3,584,217	$6,757,063	66%
1994	$7,706,303	$1,935,150	$3,477,146	$2,294,007	56%
1992	$7,924,262	$2,389,370	$3,205,014	$2,329,878	56%
1990	$3,237,592	$771,621	$2,465,971	N/A	54%
Total	$125,291,328	$30,374,643	$42,616,505	$52,300,180	67%

Source: Center for Responsive Politics, online at www.opensecrets.org.

The Blockbuster Model

In the 1990s, 80 percent of growth for the big pharmaceutical firms came from so-called "blockbuster" drugs.[21] Blockbusters have been defined by *Fortune* magazine as "medicines that serve vast swaths of the population and garner billions of dollars in annual revenue."[22] The ideal blockbuster, from the companies' view, was a medicine that could control chronic but usually non-fatal conditions that afflicted large numbers of people with health insurance. These might include, for example, daily maintenance drugs for high blood pressure or cholesterol, allergies, arthritis pain, or heartburn. Drugs that could actually cure a condition—and thus would not need to be taken for long periods—or were intended to treat diseases, like malaria or tuberculosis, that affected mainly the world's poor, were often less profitable.

Historically, drug companies focused most of their marketing efforts on prescribing physicians. The industry hired tens of thousands of sales representatives—often, attractive young men and women—to make the rounds of doctors' offices to talk about new products and give out free samples.[23] Drug companies also offered doctors gifts—from free meals to tickets to sporting events—to cultivate their good will. They also routinely sponsored continuing education events for physicians, often featuring reports on their own medicines, and supported doctors financially with opportunities to consult and to conduct clinical

trials.[24] In 2003 Merck spent $422 million to market Vioxx to doctors and hospitals.[25]

During the early 2000s, when Vioxx and Pfizer's Celebrex were competing head-to-head, sales representatives for the two firms were hard at work promoting their brand to doctors. Commented one rheumatologist of the competition between Merck and Pfizer at the time: "We were all aware that there was a great deal of marketing. Like a Coke-Pepsi war."[26] An internal Merck training manual for sales representatives, reported in *The Wall Street Journal*, was titled "Dodge Ball Vioxx." It explained how to "dodge" doctors' questions, such as "I am concerned about the cardiovascular effects of Vioxx." Merck later said that this document had been taken out of context and that sales representatives "were not trained to avoid physician's questions."[27]

Direct-to-Consumer Advertising

Although marketing to doctors and hospitals continued to be important, in the late 1990s the focus shifted somewhat. In 1997, the FDA for the first time allowed drug companies to advertise directly to consumers. The industry immediately seized this opportunity, placing numerous ads for drugs—from Viagra to Nexium—on television and in magazines and newspapers. In 2004, the industry spent over $4 billion on such direct-to-consumer, or DTC, advertising. For example, in one ad for Vioxx, Olympic figure skating champion Dorothy Hamill glided gracefully across an outdoor ice rink to the tune of "It's a Beautiful Morning" by the sixties pop group The Rascals, telling viewers that she would "not let arthritis stop me." In all, Merck spent more than $500 million advertising Vioxx.[28]

The industry's media blitz for Vioxx and other drugs was highly effective. According to research by the Harvard School of Public Heath, each dollar spent on DTC advertising yielded $4.25 in sales.

The drug companies defended DTC ads, saying they informed consumers of newly available therapies and encouraged people to seek medical treatment. In the age of the Internet, commented David Jones, an advertising executive whose firm included several major drug companies, "consumers are becoming much more empowered to make their own health care decisions."[29]

However, others criticized DTC advertising, saying that it put pressure on doctors to prescribe drugs that might not be best for the patient. "When a patient comes in and wants something, there is a desire to serve them," said David Wofsy, president of the American College of Rheumatology. "There is a desire on the part of physicians, as there is on anyone else who provides service, to keep the customer happy."[30] Even some industry executives expressed reservations. Said Hank McKinnell, CEO of Pfizer, "I'm beginning to think that direct-to-consumer ads are part of the problem. By having them on television without a very strong message that the doctor needs to determine safety, we've left this impression that all drugs are safe. In fact, no drug is safe."[31]

The Rise of Vioxx

Vioxx, the drug at the center of Merck's legal woes, was known as "a selective COX-2 inhibitor." Scientists had long understood that an enzyme called cyclooxygenase, or COX for short, was associated with pain and inflammation. In the early 1990s, researchers learned that there were really two kinds of COX enzyme. COX-1, it was found, performed several beneficial functions, including protecting the stomach lining. COX-2, on the other hand, contributed to pain and inflammation. Existing anti-inflammatory drugs suppressed both forms of the enzyme, which is why drugs like ibuprofen (Advil) relieved pain, but also caused stomach irritation in some users.

A number of drug companies, including Merck, were intrigued by the possibility of developing a medicine that would block just the COX-2, leaving the stomach-protective COX-1 intact. Such a drug would offer distinctive benefits to some patients, such as arthritis sufferers who were at risk for ulcers (bleeding sores in the intestinal tract).[32] As many as 16,500 people died each year in the United States from this condition.[33]

In May 1999, after several years of research and testing by Merck scientists, the FDA approved Vioxx for the treatment of osteoarthritis, acute pain in adults, and menstrual symptoms. The drug was later approved for rheumatoid arthritis. Although Merck, like other drug companies, never revealed what it spent to develop specific new medicines, estimates of the cost to develop a major new drug ran as high as $800 million.[34]

Vioxx quickly became exactly what Merck had hoped: a blockbuster. At its peak in 2001, Vioxx generated $2.1 billion in sales in the United States alone, contributing almost 10 percent of Merck's total sales revenue worldwide, as shown in Exhibit 3.

EXHIBIT 3

Vioxx Sales in the United States, 1999–2004

	U.S. Prescriptions Dispensed	U.S. Sales	U.S. Sales of Vioxx as % of Total Merck Sales
1999	4,845,000	$372,697,000	2.2%
2000	20,630,000	$1,526,382,000	7.6%
2001	25,406,000	$2,084,736,000	9.8%
2002	22,044,000	$1,837,680,000	8.6%
2003	19,959,000	$1,813,391,000	8.1%
2004*	13,994,000	$1,342,236,000	5.9%

*Withdrawn from the market in September 2004.

Sources: Columns 1 and 2: IMS Health (www.imshealth.com); Column 3: Merck Annual Reports (www.merck.com).

The retail price of Vioxx was around $3.00 per pill, compared with pennies per pill for older anti-inflammatory drugs like aspirin and Advil. Of course, Vioxx was often covered, at least partially, under a user's health insurance, while over-the-counter drugs were not.

Safety Warnings

Even before the drug was approved, some evidence cast doubt on the safety of Vioxx. These clues were later confirmed in other studies.

Merck Research

Internal company emails suggested that Merck scientists might have been worried about the cardiovascular risks of Vioxx as early as its development phase. In a 1997 email, reported in *The Wall Street Journal*, Dr. Alise Reicin, a Merck scientist, stated that "the possibility of CV (cardiovascular) events is of great concern." She added, apparently sarcastically, "I just can't wait to be the one to present those results to senior management!" A lawyer representing Merck said this email had been taken out of context.[35]

VIGOR

A study code-named VIGOR, completed in 2000 after the drug was already on the market, compared rheumatoid arthritis patients taking Vioxx with another group taking naproxen (Aleve). Merck financed the research, which was designed to study gastrointestinal side effects. The study found—as the company had expected—that Vioxx was easier on the stomach than naproxen. But it also found that the Vioxx group had nearly five times as many heart attacks (7.3 per thousand person-years) as the naproxen group (1.7 per thousand person-years).[36] Publicly, Merck hypothesized that these findings were due to the heart-protective effect of naproxen, rather than to any defect inherent in Vioxx. Privately, however, the company seemed worried. In an internal email dated March 9, 2000, under the subject line "Vigor," the company's research director, Dr. Edward Scolnick, said that cardiovascular events were "clearly there" and called them "a shame." But, he added, "there is always a hazard."[37] At that time, the company considered reformulating Vioxx by adding an agent to prevent blood clots (and reduce CV risk), but then dropped the project.

The FDA was sufficiently concerned by the VIGOR results that it required Merck to add additional warning language to its label. These changes appeared in April 2002, after lengthy negotiations between the agency and the company over their wording.[38]

Kaiser/Permanente

In August 2004, Dr. David Graham, a scientist at the FDA, reported the results of a study of the records of 1.4 million patients enrolled in the Kaiser health maintenance organization in California. He found that patients on high doses of Vioxx had three times the rate of heart attacks as patients on Celebrex, a competing COX-2 inhibitor made by Pfizer. Merck discounted this finding, saying that studies of patient records were less reliable than double blind clinical studies.[39] Dr. Graham later charged that his superiors at the FDA had "ostracized" him and subjected him to "veiled threats" if he did not qualify his criticism of Vioxx. The FDA called these charges "baloney."[40]

APPROVe

In order to examine the possibility that Vioxx posed a cardiovascular risk, Merck decided to monitor patients enrolled in a clinical trial called APPROVe to see if they those taking Vioxx had more heart attacks and strokes than those who were taking a placebo (sugar pill). This study had been designed to determine if Vioxx reduced the risk of recurrent colon polyps (a precursor to colon cancer); Merck hoped it would lead to FDA approval of the drug for this condition. The APPROVe study was planned before the VIGOR results were known.

Merck Recalls the Drug

On the evening of Thursday, September 23, 2004, Dr. Peter S. Kim, president of Merck Research Labs, received a phone call from scientists monitoring the colon polyp study. Researchers had found, the scientists told him, that after 18 months of continuous use individuals taking Vioxx were more than twice as likely to have a heart attack or stroke than those taking a placebo. The scientists recommended that the study be halted because of "unacceptable" risk.[41]

Dr. Kim later described to a reporter for *The New York Times* the urgent decision-making process that unfolded over the next hours and days as the company responded to this news.

On Friday, I looked at the data with my team. The first thing you do is review the data. We did that. Second is you double-check the data, go through it and make sure that everything is O.K. [At that point] I knew that barring some big mistake in the analysis, we had an issue here. Around noon, I called [CEO] Ray Gilmartin and told him what was up. He said, "Figure out what was the best thing for patient safety." We then spent Friday and the rest of the weekend going over the data and analyzing it in different ways and calling up medical experts to set up meetings where we would discuss the data and their interpretations and what to do.[42]

According to later interviews with some of the doctors consulted that weekend by Merck, the group was of mixed opinion. Some experts argued that Vioxx should stay on the market, with a strong warning label so that doctors and patients could judge the risk for themselves. But others thought the drug should be withdrawn because no one knew why the drug was apparently causing heart attacks. One expert commented that "Merck prides itself on its ethical approach. I couldn't see Merck saying we're going to market a drug with a safety problem."[43]

On Monday, Dr. Kim recommended to Gilmartin that Vioxx be withdrawn from the market. The CEO agreed. The following day, Gilmartin notified the board, and the company contacted the FDA. On Thursday, September 30, Merck issued a press release, which stated in part:

> Merck & Co., Inc. announced today a voluntary withdrawal of VIOXX®. This decision is based on new data from a three-year clinical study. In this study, there was an increased risk for cardiovascular (CV) events, such as heart attack and stroke, in patients taking VIOXX 25 mg compared to those taking placebo (sugar pill). While the incidence of CV events was low, there was an increased risk beginning after 18 months of treatment. The cause of the clinical study result is uncertain, but our commitment to our patients is clear. . . . Merck is notifying physicians and pharmacists and has informed the Food and Drug Administration of this decision. We are taking this action because we believe it best serves the interests of patients. That is why we undertook this clinical trial to better understand the safety profile of VIOXX. And it's why we instituted this voluntary withdrawal upon learning about these data. Be assured that Merck will continue to do everything we can to maintain the safety of our medicines.

ENDNOTES

1. "Justice Dept. and SEC Investigating Merck Drug," *New York Times*, November 9, 2004.
2. "Opening Statement of U.S. Senator Chuck Grassley of Iowa," U.S. Senate Committee on Finance, Hearing—FDA, Merck, and Vioxx: Putting Patient Safety First?" November 18, 2004, online at http://finance.senate.gov.
3. A history of Merck may be found in Fran Hawthorne, *The Merck Druggernaut: The Inside Story of a Pharmaceutical Giant* (Hoboken, NJ: John Wiley & Sons, 2003).
4. Merck received the 1991 Business Enterprise Trust Award for this action. See Stephanie Weiss and Kirk O. Hanson, "Merck and Co., Inc.: Addressing Third World Needs" (Business Enterprise Trust, 1991).
5. Hawthorne, op. cit., pp. 17–18.
6. Hawthorne, op. cit., p. 38.
7. "FDA Failing in Drug Safety, Official Asserts," *New York Times*, November 19, 2004. The full transcript of the hearing of the U.S. Senate Committee on Finance, "FDA, Merck, and Vioxx: Putting Patient Safety First?" is available online at http://finance.senate.gov.
8. "Despite Warnings, Drug Giant Took Long Path to Vioxx Recall," *New York Times*, November 14, 2004.
9. A history of the FDA and of its relationship to business may be found in Philip J. Hilts, *Protecting America's Health: The FDA, Business, and One Hundred Years of Regulation* (New York: Alfred A. Knopf, 2003).
10. Marcia Angell, *The Trust About the Drug Companies* (New York: Random House, 2004), Ch. 2.
11. Merrill Lynch data reported in "A World of Hurt," *Fortune*, January 10, 2005, p. 18.
12. U.S. General Accounting Office, *Food and Drug Administration: Effect of User Fees on Drug Approval Times, Withdrawals, and Other Agency Activities*, September 2002.
13. "Postmarketing Surveillance—Lack of Vigilance, Lack of Trust," *Journal of the American Medical Association* 92(21), December 1, 2004, p. 2649.
14. "FDA Lax in Drug Safety, Journal Warns," *www.sfgate.com*, November 23, 2004.
15. 2002 Survey of 846 FDA scientists conducted by the Office of the Inspector General of the Department of Health and Human Services, online at www.peer.org/FDAscientistsurvey.
16. "Postmarketing Surveillance," op. cit.
17. "Big PhRMA's Stealth PACs: How the Drug Industry Uses 501(c) Non-Profit Groups to Influence Elections," *Congress Watch*, September 2004.
18. "Drug Industry and HMOs Deployed an Army of Nearly 1,000 Lobbyists to Push Medicare Bill, Report Finds," June 23, 2004, www.citizen.org.
19. Data available online at www.publicintegrity.org.
20. "Rep. Billy Tauzin Demonstrates that Washington's Revolving Door Is Spinning Out of Control," *Public Citizen*, December 15, 2004, press release.
21. "The Waning of the Blockbuster," *Business Week*, October 18, 2004.
22. "A World of Hurt," *Fortune*, January 10, 2005, p. 20.
23. In 2005, 90,000 sales representatives were employed by the pharmaceutical industry, about one for every eight doctors. The *New York Times* revealed in an investigative article ("Give Me an Rx! Cheerleaders Pep Up Drug Sales," November 28, 2005) that many companies made a point of hiring former college cheerleaders for this role.
24. The influence of the drug industry on the medical professional is documented in Katharine Greider, *The Big Fix: How the*

Pharmaceutical Industry Rips Off American Consumers (New York: Public Affairs, 2003).

25. "Drug Pullout," *Modern Healthcare,* October 18, 2004.

26. "Marketing of Vioxx: How Merck Played Game of Catch-Up," *New York Times,* February 11, 2005.

27. "E-Mails Suggest Merck Knew Vioxx's Dangers at Early Stage," *Wall Street Journal,* November 1, 2004.

28. IMS Health estimate reported in "Will Merck Survive Vioxx?" *Fortune,* November 1, 2004.

29. "With or Without Vioxx, Drug Ads Proliferate," *New York Times,* December 6, 2004.

30. "A 'Smart' Drug Fails the Safety Test," *Washington Post,* October 3, 2004.

31. "A World of Hurt," *Fortune,* January 10, 2005, p. 18.

32. "Medicine Fueled by Marketing Intensified Troubles for Pain Pills," *New York Times,* December 19, 2004.

33. "New Scrutiny of Drugs in Vioxx's Family," *New York Times,* October 4, 2004.

34. This estimate was hotly debated. See, for example, "How Much Does the Pharmaceutical Industry Really Spend on R&D?" Ch. 3 in Marcia Angell, op. cit., and Merrill Goozner, *The $800 Million Pill: The Truth Behind the Cost of New Drugs* (Berkeley: University of California Press, 2004).

35. "E-Mails Suggest Merck Knew Vioxx's Dangers at Early Stage," *Wall Street Journal,* November 1, 2004.

36. "Comparison of Upper Gastrointestinal Toxicity of Rofecoxib and Naproxen in Patients with Rheumatoid Arthritis," *New England Journal of Medicine,* 2000: 323.

37. "E-Mails Suggest Merck Knew Vioxx's Dangers at Early Stage," *Wall Street Journal,* November 1, 2004.

38. At one of the early Vioxx trials, the plaintiff introduced a Merck internal memo that calculated that the company would make $229 million more in profits if it delayed changes to warning language on the label by four months (*New York Times,* August 20, 2005). The FDA did not have the authority to dictate label language; any changes had to be negotiated with the manufacturer.

39. "Study of Painkiller Suggests Heart Risk," *New York Times,* August 26, 2004.

40. "FDA Official Alleges Pressure to Suppress Vioxx Findings," *Washington Post,* October 8, 2004.

41. "Painful Withdrawal for Makers of Vioxx," *Washington Post,* October 18, 2004. Detailed data reported the following day in the *New York Times* showed that 30 of the 1287 patients taking Vioxx had suffered a heart attack, compared with 11 of 1299 taking a placebo; 15 on Vioxx had had a stroke or transient ischemic attack (minor stroke), compared with 7 taking a placebo.

42. "A Widely Used Arthritis Drug Is Withdrawn," *New York Times,* October 1, 2004.

43. "Painful Withdrawal for Makers of Vioxx," *Washington Post,* October 18, 2004.

Mired in Corruption—Kellogg, Brown and Root in Nigeria

This case was prepared by Charles W. L. Hill, the University of Washington.

In 1998, the large Texas-based oil and gas service firm, Halliburton, acquired Dresser Industries. Among other businesses, Dresser owned M. W. Kellogg, one of the world's largest general contractors for construction projects in distant parts of the globe. After the acquisition, Kellogg was combined with an existing Halliburton business and renamed Kellogg, Brown and Root, or KBR for short. At the time, it looked like a good deal for Halliburton. Among other things, Kellogg was involved in a four-firm consortium that was building a series of liquefied natural gas (LNG) plants in Nigeria. By early 2004, the total value of the contracts associated with these plants had exceeded $8 billion.

In early 2005, however, Halliburton put KBR up for sale. The sale was seen as an attempt by Halliburton to distance itself from several scandals that had engulfed KBR. One of these concerned allegations that KBR had systematically overcharged the Pentagon for services it provided to the U.S. military in Iraq. Another scandal centered on the Nigerian LNG plants and involved KBR employees, several former officials of the Nigeria government, and a mysterious British lawyer named Jeffrey Tesler.

The roots of the Nigerian scandal date back to 1994 when Kellogg and its consortium partners were trying to win an initial contract from the Nigerian government to build two LNG plants. The

contract was valued at around $2 billion. Each of the four firms held a 25% stake in the consortium, and each had veto power over its decisions. Kellogg employees held many of the top positions at the consortium, and two of the other members, Technip of France and JGC of Japan, have claimed that Kellogg managed the consortium (the fourth member, ENI of Italy, has not made any statement regarding management).

The KBR consortium was one of two to submit a bid on the initial contract, and its bid was the lower of the two. By early 1995, the KBR consortium was deep in final negotiations on the contract. It was at this point that Nigeria's oil minister had a falling out with the country's military dictator, General Abacha, and was replaced by Dan Etete. Etete proved to be far less accommodating to the KBR consortium, and suddenly the entire deal looked to be in jeopardy. According to some observers, Etete was a tough customer who immediately began to use his influence over the LNG project for personal gain. Whether this is true or not, what is known is that the KBR consortium quickly entered into a contract with Tesler. The contract, signed by a Kellogg executive, called on Tesler to obtain government permits for the LGN project, maintain good relations with government officials, and provide advice on sales strategy. Tesler's fee for these services was $60 million.

Tesler, it turned out, had long-standing relations with some twenty to thirty senior Nigerian government and military officials. In his capacity as a lawyer, for years Tesler had handled their London affairs, helping them to purchase real estate and set up financial accounts. Kellogg had a relationship with Tesler that dated back to the mid-1980s, when it had employed him to broker the sale of Kellogg's minority interest in a Nigerian fertilizer plant to the Nigerian government.

What happened next is currently the subject of government investigations in France, Nigeria, and the United States. The suspicion is that Tesler promised to funnel big sums to Nigerian government officials if the deal was done. Investigators base these suspicions on a number of factors, including the known corruption of General Abacha's government; the size of the payment to Tesler, which seemed out of all proportion to the services he was contracted to provide; and a series of notes turned up by internal investigators at Halliburton. The handwritten notes, taken by Wojciech Chodan, a Kellogg executive, document a meeting between Chodan and Tesler in which they discussed the possibility of channeling $40 million of Tesler's $60 million payment to General Abacha.

It is not known whether a bribe was actually paid. What is known is that in December 1995, Nigeria awarded the $2 billion contract to the KBR consortium. The LNG plant soon became a success. Nigeria contracted to build a second plant in 1999, two more in 2002, and a sixth in July 2004. KBR rehired Tesler in 1999 and again in 2001 to help secure the new contracts, all of which it won. In total, Tesler was paid some $132.3 million from 1994 through to early 2004 by the KBR consortium.

Tesler's involvement in the project might have remained unknown were it not for an unrelated event. Georges Krammer, an employee of the French company Technip, which along with KBR was a member of the consortium, was charged by the French government for embezzlement. When Technip refused to defend Krammer, he turned around and aired what he perceived to be Technip's dirty linen. This included the payments to Tesler to secure the Nigeria LNG contracts.

This turn of events led French and Swiss officials to investigate Tesler's Swiss bank accounts. They discovered that Tesler was "kicking back" some of the funds he received to executives in the consortium and to sub-contractors. One of the alleged kickbacks was a transfer of $5 million from Tesler's account to that of Albert J. "Jack" Stanley, who was head of M. W. Kellogg

and then Halliburton's KBR unit. Tesler also transferred some $2.5 million into Swiss bank accounts held under a false name by the Nigerian oil minister, Dan Etete. Other payments include a $1 million transfer into an account controlled by Wojciech Chodan, the former Kellogg executive whose extensive handwritten notes suggest the payment of a bribe to General Abacha, and $5 million to a German subcontractor on the LNG project in exchange for "information and advice."

After this all came out in June 2004, Halliburton promptly fired Jack Stanley and severed its long-standing relationship with Jeffrey Tesler, asking its three partners in the Nigeria consortium to do the same. The U.S. Justice Department took things further, establishing a grand jury investigation to determine if Halliburton, through its KBR subsidiary, had been in violation of the Foreign Corrupt Practices Act. In November 2004, the Justice Department widened its investigation to include payments in connection with the Nigerian fertilizer plant that Kellogg had been involved with during the 1980s under the leadership of Jack Stanley. In March 2005, the Justice Department also stated that it was looking at whether Jack Stanley had tried to coordinate bidding with rivals and fix prices on certain foreign construction projects. As of late 2006, the investigation was still ongoing. As for Halliburton's plans to sell KBR, these too had come to naught. In April 2006, Halliburton announced that it would spin off KBR to investors, but a lack of interest in the offering resulted in a delay, and it was not clear when Halliburton would be able to complete the planned transaction.

REFERENCES

R. Gold, "Halliburton to Put KBR Unit of Auction Block," *New York Times*, January 31, 2005, page A2.

R. Gold and C. Flemming, "Out of Africa: In Halliburton Nigeria Inquiry, a Search for Bribes to a Dictator," *Wall Street Journal*, September 29, 2004, page A1.

Halliburton 10K and 10Q documents for 2005 and 2006, filed with the Securities and Exchange Commission.

D. Ivanovich, "Halliburton: Contracts Investigated," *Houston Chronicle*, March 2, 2005, page 1.

T. Sawyer, "Citing Violations, Halliburton Cuts Off Former KBR Chairman," *ENR*, June 28, 2004, page 16.